The American Counties

Origins of names, dates of creation
and organization, area, population,
historical data, and published sources

Third Edition

by

JOSEPH NATHAN KANE

The Scarecrow Press, Inc.
Metuchen, N.J. 1972

Library of Congress Cataloging in Publication Data

Kane, Joseph Nathan, 1899-
The American counties.

1. United States--History, Local. I. Title.
E180.K3 1972 917.3'03 70-186010
ISBN 0-8108-0502-2

CONTENTS

PREFACE

The need for a book about the origin of county names is apparent to those who have had to wade through hundreds of obscure references in annuals, manuals, blue books, state guides, histories and encyclopedias to obtain needed information. In most instances, it is impossible to find data about one county or state in a single satisfactory source.

This book is divided into nine parts. The first, Part I, is an introduction with a brief description of the origins of names of the counties, and tabular data on them as a whole. Part II (the heart of the work) alphabetically lists each American county, the state it is in, the date when the county was created (and the effective date of the statute, if different), the square area, the 1970 population (and the 1960 and the 1950), the county seat, and the nickname of the county, in those cases where applicable. Then, the source of the county name is given, with appropriate descriptive matter (e.g., a capsule biography in the case of a person). Next, the author, title, publisher and year and number of pages are given for a book (or books) suggested to those readers who wish to pursue their interest in a certain county further. (More about these suggested sources at the end of the Preface.)

Part III is a listing alphabetized by state, giving name of county, county seat, date of (legislative) creation, and statute number when known, in a tabular form (with footnotes remarking county name changes). Part IV is an index by year, beginning in 1634, showing each American county that was formed in any year, and the legislative session, or act number, which formed it.

Part V is a listing of counties whose names have changed, alphabetized by present name (with appropriate date and statute of creation) and giving former name (with date and statute). Part VI is an alphabetical list of all county seats in the U. S., with state and county given. Part VII is a list of persons for whom counties have been named (including altered or attributive forms of their names). Part VIII lists independent cities not included within counties, nearly all of which are Virginia cities. And Part IX gives data on Alaskan census divisions and the derivations of their names.

As some counties cannot determine the actual origin of their names, in Part II alternate claims are listed without prejudice. And as the time of early colonial legislation was not reckoned by dates, but by session, the date of the first meeting of the session is given as the date of the enactment of the legislation. Obviously, the law would then have actually been enacted at a later date.

A study of generally accepted dates of the formation of counties reveals many discrepancies. In addition to typographical and natural human errors as a result of annual transcription--and they are plentiful--there are many others due to misconceptions in terminology. Dates often listed as referring to the same event refer to similar but actually different happenings. Research reveals that little, if any, distinction has been made in the various compilations between (1) the date the statute creating a county was passed by the legislature, (2) the date when it was approved by the governor or by a popular election or referendum, or (3) the date when the act took effect. Furthermore, some books list the date when the county complied with all legal requirements for its organization, and some give the particular date specified for the coming into being of the county.

Even in the 1970's some counties are functioning which have never actually met the qualifications necessary for organization and as a consequence they are under the jurisdiction of other counties for judicial purposes.

Original legislation was often inexact and controversial with respect to county boundaries and accordingly new acts were passed to clarify them. As a result, some sources give the date of the original legislation and others, the dates of the amending legislation. Still others may give the dates when areas were taken away from or added to the county. Some counties, whose names have undergone a change, are listed according to the date when the original county was created, while others are listed by the date when the change of name was made or became effective.

In an endeavor to clarify this confusing condition, I have personally checked session laws of forty-eight* state

*Of the other two states: Alaska has never had counties or county-type governments. The state has, however, 29 census

legislatures, governors' proclamations, and extant colonial legislation. The dates used are either of the enactment of the statutes providing for the creation or those when the county was actually created or organized by gubernatorial proclamations. As noted, Part II of the book gives not only the date of the creation, but also the dates when the acts became effective or when organization took place when these dates differ or can be established.

To facilitate research work the number of each act or chapter is given, if such a number exists. To the inexperienced this may not seem important but since many of the early session laws did not contain an index, this will obviate a page-by-page check. Some of the session laws contain a table of contents and record acts according to the date when they were enacted or according to their position in the book. In many session laws, the laws were published without any scheme or reason without regard to order of any kind. Some states list acts chronologically, others group together similar types of legislation, and still others indulge in entirely haphazard arrangements.

Even when there is an index to a state's session laws, one may have difficulty in finding information under present standard headings. Counties are not listed under "counties" or under the specific county names but under such headings as "new counties," "boundaries," etc. In some cases the index contains no reference whatsoever to new counties. If a county were created by separation from another, the only certain way of finding the date of its creation is to know the county from which it was formed and then look for a statute such as "an act for the division of Montgomery County." In some instances a county is created by a "rider" to another, irrelevant piece of legislation. Consequently, it is often necessary to read all the laws of a certain period during which it is believed the county was created in order to ascertain the correct date.

---

divisions, called boroughs or reservations. Historical and population data on these 29 entities appear in an addendum to this book, Part IX. Hawaii, with four counties formed of islands or island groups, is treated as any other state in this work except for dates and effective statutes for county formations: there are no such data for Hawaii except in pre-literate antiquity.

In many instances, the system of numbering acts or chapters was not always carried out for the entire legislative session. Where numbers exist, it should not be presumed that the act with the lowest number was passed earliest. The numbers may refer to the position of the act in the session laws, not to the sequence of its passage. Some states separate general laws from private laws or special laws, and may assign the same number to both a general law and a special law. The numbers are frequently not consecutive and it is necessary to know whether the legislation was through a public or general law or a private or special law. States have often changed their classifications of entries from time to time. As there is no standard procedure, patience and perseverance are sometimes greater virtues than knowledge and experience.

Even if one knows the title of an act, the date it was passed or its chapter number, and whether the act was a general or special one, the desired information may still be difficult to obtain. Legislative sessions do not always begin on the first day of the year and they often carry over from year to year. Thus, it is frequently necessary to consult several years. For example, legislation enacted on May 15, 1815 may be found in the laws of 1814-1815, or in the laws of 1815, or in the laws of 1815-16. To further complicate matters, the date on the spine or cover of the book often bears no true relationship to its actual content. A volume marked "1814" for example may contain the laws of 1813, 1814 or 1815 and in subsequent volumes the method of titling may be changed.

The exact date of the passage of much of the legislation in colonial days is not given and the only date which can be found is when the legislative assembly met or adjourned. In some instances, legislation although earlier passed did not become effective until the conclusion of the session, when all the laws were finally approved. In other cases, colonial laws did not become effective until they were signed by the king.

The dates given in local and state histories have generally been inaccurate and no reliance has been placed upon them. Dates have been checked with prime sources but even here one notices typographical or orthographical errors. In many instances, in the same law the name of the county is variously spelled. Errors in name have sometimes been changed by later legislation but generally corrections have been made by usage, common acceptance, geographic boards or nomenclature groups. Where this situation exists, the present generally accepted spelling is used.

Very few laws specifically mention the derivation of the county name or refer to the person whom the county is intended to honor. Many counties were formed before the states of which they are now a part. County records were not always carefully kept and many deteriorated through ageing or were destroyed by fire and flood. Some reliance in this respect has necessarily been placed on secondary sources such as state histories, county histories, biographies, etc.

The population figures used are based upon the most recent federal census, 1970, compiled by the Bureau of the Census, United States Department of Commerce. (1960 and 1950 populations are given as well.) The area figures are generally correct despite the fact that authorities disagree frequently.

Unfortunately, it is not possible to thank individually the hundreds of county clerks, secretaries of state, historical societies and libraries that have been of much help in this compilation. I would be remiss, however, if I did not single out the New York Public Library, the law library of Columbia University, and the Library of Congress for the privilege of examining their extensive collections of state and colonial laws.

Students desiring more information about counties than that contained in previous editions of this book have encountered much difficulty. To assist researchers, suggested bibliographical sources have been added in this third edition. Here, again, difficulties arose. Many counties have never had their histories recorded in a separate book. Some county histories are so rare that they command premium prices prohibitive for many libraries. Even reprints are often equally high priced. In some instances, a county history is contained in a book about its principal city. These books are often difficult to locate in libraries lacking thorough cross indexing as they are generally listed by titles rather than contents. In some cases, a county history appears in printed versions of speeches which have been delivered at various functions.

The county histories listed herein do not form a complete bibliography. As a rule, only books and pamphlets published after 1900 have been included. Occasionally an earlier book has been listed where its existence should not be overlooked. Where numerous histories of the same county have been published, only a few have been selected to avoid duplication of material. The listing does not necessarily imply approval of the contents or appraisal of worth. In some cases, both useful and less important books have been mentioned as they aid in further research. Sometimes there is only one history with the result that there is no possibility of selection.

It does not axiomatically follow that the dates and facts in this book agree with the bibliographies quoted; data given wrong in other sources may have here been corrected and new material may have been uncovered. As is typical in books about the same subject, the method of presentation differs. Some books are factual, others include anecdotes and reminiscences, and others are rehashed versions of previously printed material. Because a statement is reprinted in one or more books, it does not necessarily assume authenticity. Often it illustrates lack of original research and an author's acceptance of statements without verification. Variances in dates and statements may be due to the author's and printer's diligence and research--or lack of it.

Many county histories are not scholarly. Many contain reminiscences obtained from elderly people whose memory was confused and unreliable. Some histories have been compiled at random, intertwining fact, fiction and imagination. No attempt to assess their veracity or point out obvious errors has been made. Because of unorthodox methods of preparation, trivia have often been magnified while important material may have been omitted. Many histories do not contain indexes. As a result, the researcher is obliged to skim through each page to find an item--if it does appear. In some works, biographies of individuals are contained in the text; in others, a separate biographical section exists.

Publication of a county history was seldom an altruistic enterprise. They were often the brainchild of someone eager for quick profits. Some histories were known as vanity publications or mug books and rendered an aura of glamor for the subscriber. Their contents generally included biographies of the Presidents of the United States followed by biographies of state governors and senators continuing with national and state officials. Interspersed or in the addenda were vanity listings, space being allocated corresponding to the financial contribution made by the subject to the publisher. Adding insult to injury, for an additional sum the subject had this picture included, the size proportionate to the amount of the contribution. Space was allotted also according to the number of copies purchased. Local merchants bought copies to distribute to their customers or sources of supply. Some such "puff books" were so designed that it was possible to tip in a subject's biography in certain copies or substitute others in its place. This is particularly noticeable in cases where histories have been reprinted or revised.

Previously, sophisticates discounted the importance of these puff books, but in many cases they are the only source of the past and today they are considered to serve some purpose. Despite their many shortcomings, it is really too bad that more works of this kind were not undertaken for they are useful if one is able to distinguish the wheat from the chaff. While vanity publications were not always obvious, some were distinguished by the fact that they contained advertising sections. Some publishers produced numerous county histories. Instead of giving the full names of these works, abbreviated versions will suffice. Titles of some books are often long and varied and occupy several lines of type.

Researchers desiring further facts about specific counties should first consult local libraries as many have good local history collections. State libraries and state historical societies should be consulted next. Possibly the greatest sources for a larger and broader look are the New York Public Library, the Library of Congress, the Newberry Library (Chicago), the American Antiquarian Society Library (Worcester), and other large libraries.

The author hopes that this book is free from error. As has been pointed out, however, the inadequacies and conflicts of the primary sources are such that a few mistakes may inevitably have crept in. If any of the facts herein are provably in error, the author will appreciate being apprised of them so that corrections may be made in future editions.

Joseph Nathan Kane

Part I

INTRODUCTION

Much confusion exists about the derivation of the names of counties. There are 17 counties named Lincoln. The supposition is that they were named for President Lincoln. But as some of these counties were named before Abraham Lincoln was born, even the most patriotic, when confronted with the evidence, are obliged to admit that perhaps another Lincoln was intended. The Lincoln for whom many of these counties were named was Benjamin Lincoln, a major general in the Continental Army who was distinguished for his bravery. Twenty-three counties were named Franklin to honor Benjamin Franklin, but Franklin County in Idaho is named for Franklin R. Richards while Franklin County in Texas is named for Benjamin Cromwell Franklin.

So, it is fallacious to assume that a county was named for the most famous bearer of a name. Logan County, Arkansas, for example, was named for James Logan; Logan counties in Colorado, Kansas, Nebraska, North Dakota and Oklahoma were named for John Alexander Logan. Logan, Illinois, was named for Dr. John Logan, while Logan, West Virginia, was named for John Logan, an Indian.

Of the 3, 067 counties, 2, 136 have been named for individuals. This figure includes the 203 counties named for 25 Presidents. The President for whom the greatest number of counties was named was George Washington who leads the list with 31, followed by Thomas Jefferson with 26. Jackson has 21 counties named for him, excluding Hickory County, Missouri, which perpetuates his nickname "Old Hickory." There are 20 counties named for Madison, 17 for Monroe, 17 for Lincoln, 12 for Grant and 11 for Polk. Other Presidents for whom counties have been named are John Adams, eight; Garfield, six; Van Buren, William Henry Harrison, Taylor and Pierce, four each; Fillmore and Buchanan, three each; John Quincy Adams, Cleveland

and Theodore Roosevelt, two each; and Tyler, Hayes, Arthur, Benjamin Harrison, McKinley and Harding, one each.

Only one President had both his first and last name used as the name of a county. Millard Fillmore had Millard County named for him in Utah as well as Fillmore County in Minnesota and Nebraska. Eleven Presidents have not had counties named for them: Andrew Johnson, Taft, Wilson, Coolidge, Hoover, F. D. Roosevelt, Truman, Eisenhower, Kennedy, Lyndon Johnson and Nixon.

Nebraska with an even dozen leads with the greatest number of counties named for Presidents. Other high-ranking states are Iowa 11, Arkansas ten, and Mississippi and Wisconsin, both eight. Eight states, Florida, Georgia, Indiana, Kentucky, Missouri, Ohio, Oklahoma and Tennessee, contain seven such counties. Five states, Illinois, Louisiana, Oregon, Texas and Washington, contain six presidential counties; seven states, Alabama, Colorado, Idaho, Kansas, Minnesota, New Mexico and West Virginia, contain five such counties; three states, Montana, New York and Pennsylvania, contain four; four states, Michigan, North Carolina, Utah and Virginia, contain three; South Dakota contains two Presidents' counties; and seven states, Maine, Maryland, Nevada, North Dakota, Rhode Island, Vermont and Wyoming, contain one such county each. Hickory, Missouri, since it is not directly named is not included in the above statistics. Eight of the 49 states (Alaska is not included in this Introduction)--Arizona, California, Connecticut, Delaware, Hawaii, Massachusetts, New Hampshire, New Jersey and South Carolina--have not named any counties for Presidents.

There were 243 governors of colonies, territories and states for whom 431 counties were named. The state with the greatest number of counties named for governors is Georgia with 40, followed by Kentucky, 24; Tennessee, 22; Missouri, 21; Texas, 20; Illinois and Iowa, 18; Indiana and West Virginia, 17; Arkansas, Mississippi and Nebraska, 16; and Ohio, 13; Alabama, Kansas and Virginia, 12. Other states had fewer. The states with the greatest number of counties named for their own governors are Georgia, 29; Kentucky, 14; Virginia, ten; Mississippi, Nebraska and Texas nine; and Arkansas, North Carolina and Tennessee, eight.

The state which honored the greatest number of governors of other states is West Virginia, with 17 such counties. West Virginia was once a part of Virginia and so honored governors of Virginia. Iowa follows with 16; Illinois, Missouri and Tennessee, 14; Indiana, 13; Georgia and Texas, 11; Kentucky and Ohio, 10; and Alabama and Kansas, 9.

Greater in popularity than a governor was Benjamin Franklin of Pennsylvania for whom 23 counties were named. Of the colonial and state governors, the most honored governor was Patrick Henry of Virginia for whom ten counties were named, nine named Henry and one named Patrick. Excluding those Presidents of the United States who served also as governors, the governors for whom the greatest number of counties were named were Isaac Shelby of Kentucky, nine; Lewis Cass of Michigan and De Witt Clinton of New York, both eight; Meriwether Lewis of Louisiana, six; and John Floyd of Virginia and John Sullivan of New Hampshire, both four.

All of the states except Arizona, California, Connecticut, Delaware, Hawaii, Nevada and Rhode Island have honored governors. Maryland, New Hampshire and South Carolina honored their own governors but did not honor governors of other states. Maine, Massachusetts and West Virginia did not honor their own governors but named counties for governors of other states. Oklahoma honored its governor William Henry "Alfalfa" Murray by naming two counties for him, Murray and Alfalfa.

A breakdown of the 243 governors so honored shows that 30 who had 59 counties named for them had served also in the capacity of both United States Senator and Representative. In this list are included four counties named for William Henry Harrison, 21 named for Andrew Jackson, and one named for John Tyler, all of whom were also Presidents of the United States. There were 37 governors, for whom 80 counties are named, who served also in the United States Senate but not in the house of Representatives. Included in this group are 17 counties named for James Monroe and four counties named for Martin Van Buren, both of whom served also as Presidents. There were 141 other governors for whom 243 counties were named. In this figure are included the 30 counties named for Thomas Jefferson, Grover Cleveland and Theodore Roosevelt.

There are 574 counties named for the 288 men who served in the U. S. Congress. Of these, there were 175 counties named for 66 men who served as both Senator and Representative including the 30 listed in the governor group who served as senator, governor, and representative for whom 59 counties are named. There are 218 counties named for the 128 men who served as Representatives (including the 35 listed in the governor group who served as governor and representative for whom 49 counties are named). There are 181 counties named for the 93 men who served as senators including the 37 senators listed in the governor group who served as governor and senator, for whom 80 counties are named.

Excluding Presidents and governors, the persons for whom the greatest number of counties were named are Benjamin Franklin 23, and Francis Marion, Nathanael Greene and the Marquis de Lafayette, 17 each. Fourteen counties are named Greene County, two are named Green County without the final letter "e" and one is named Greensville; 11 counties are named Fayette County and six counties are named Lafayette County.

Others for whom more than a dozen counties have been named are Richard Montgomery, 16; Henry Clay and Anthony Wayne, 15; Joseph Warren, 14; and Charles Carroll and Stephen Arnold Douglas, 12 each. Eleven counties are named for John Caldwell Calhoun, and ten counties each have been named for John Hancock, James Lawrence, Oliver Hazard Perry and Zebulon Pike. Nine have each been named for Henry Knox, Daniel Morgan, and Israel Putnam. Eight each bear the names of Thomas Hart Benton, Alexander Hamilton, William Jasper, Robert Edwin Lee, John Marshall and Daniel Webster. Those for whom seven counties have been named are Daniel Boone, Robert Fulton and Casimir Pulaski. Six counties have been named for each of the following: George Rogers Clark, George A. Custer, Johann De Kalb, Benjamin Lincoln, Meriwether Lewis, Nathanael Macon and Hugh Mercer.

Many counties have been named for an individual and immediate members of his family. For example, some of the counties named for King George II and his family are: Amelia, Augusta, Caroline, Frederick, Louisa, Lunenberg, Orange, Prince Edward, Prince William. Some of the many counties named for the Calvert family are: Anne Arundel, Baltimore, Calvert, Caroline, Cecil, Charles, Harford, and Talbot.

The family in counties with the greatest span of years is the Harrison family. The progenitor of the family was Benjamin Harrison (1726-1791) for whom Harrison County, West Virginia, was named. His son, William Henry Harrison, the ninth President of the United States, was honored by counties in Indiana, Iowa, Mississippi and Ohio. His great grandson, the grandson of William Henry Harrison, is immortalized by Harrison County Kentucky, named for Benjamin Harrison, the 23rd President of the United States. Many fathers and sons have been honored by having counties named for them, the most prominent being the Adams family. Adams County in Idaho, Iowa, Mississippi, Nebraska, Ohio, Pennsylvania, Washington and Wisconsin have been named for John Adams, the second President of the United States, while the counties in Illinois, Indiana and North Dakota were named for his son, John Quincy Adams, the sixth President of the United States.

Dodge County in Minnesota and Wisconsin is named for Henry Dodge while Dodge County, Nebraska, is named for his son, Augustus Caesar Dodge. Robertson County, Tennessee, is named for James Robertson while Robertson County, Kentucky, is named for his son, George Robertson. Tazewell county, Virginia is named for Henry Tazewell while Tazewell County, Illinois, is named for his son, Littleton Waller Tazewell. Many counties have been named for brothers, and in several instances individual brothers have had individual counties named for them.

Some counties with different names may trace the origin of their names to the same person. For example, King James II was the person honored by James City County, Virginia. In like manner, he was honored when New York and Wyoming used Albany, one of his titles, as the name of a county. He was similarly honored by Maine, Nebraska, Pennsylvania, South Carolina and Virginia when York, another of his titles, was used. New York, N. Y. was also named for him, and Massachusetts named Dukes County to honor him.

In some instances, counties have been named for both a person's first and last names, such as Charles Mix County, South Dakota; Kit Carson County, Colorado; Roger Mills County, Oklahoma; Ben Hill County, Georgia; and Jo Daviess County, Illinois. This practice is most prevalent in Texas where counties have been named for Jim Wells, Jim Hogg, Tom Green, Deaf Smith and Jeff Davis. There is a Jeff

TABLE ONE

Alphabetical List of 49 States with Number of Counties

No.	State	No.	State	No.	State
67	Alabama	16	Maine	88	Ohio
14	Arizona	23	Maryland	77	Oklahoma
75	Arkansas	14	Massachusetts	36	Oregon
58	California	83	Michigan	67	Pennsylvania
63	Colorado	87	Minnesota	5	Rhode Island
8	Connecticut	82	Mississippi	46	South Carolina
3	Delaware	114	Missouri	67	South Dakota
67	Florida	56	Montana	95	Tennessee
159	Georgia	93	Nebraska	254	Texas
4	Hawaii	16	Nevada	29	Utah
44	Idaho	10	New Hampshire	96	Virginia
102	Illinois	21	New Jersey	39	Washington
91	Indiana	32	New Mexico	55	West Virginia
99	Iowa	62	New York	71	Wisconsin
105	Kansas	100	North Carolina	23	Wyoming
120	Kentucky	53	North Dakota	14	Vermont
64	Louisiana				
				3,067	Counties
				29	Alaska (boroughs)
				3,096	Counties

List of 49 States According to Number of Counties

No.	State	No.	State	No.	State
3	Delaware	44	Idaho	82	Mississippi
4	Hawaii	46	South Carolina	83	Michigan
5	Rhode Island	53	North Dakota	87	Minnesota
8	Connecticut	55	West Virginia	88	Ohio
10	New Hampshire	56	Montana	91	Indiana
14	Arizona	58	California	93	Nebraska
14	Massachusetts	62	New York	95	Tennessee
14	Vermont	63	Colorado	96	Virginia
16	Maine	64	Louisiana	99	Iowa
16	Nevada	67	Alabama	100	North Carolina
21	New Jersey	67	Florida	102	Illinois
23	Maryland	67	Pennsylvania	105	Kansas
23	Wyoming	67	South Dakota	114	Missouri
29	Utah	71	Wisconsin	120	Kentucky
32	New Mexico	75	Arkansas	159	Georgia
36	Oregon	77	Oklahoma	254	Texas
39	Washington				
				3,067	Counties
				29	Alaska (boroughs)
				3,096	Counties

Davis County in Georgia and Texas and a Jefferson Davis County in both Louisiana and Mississippi.

American history is indelibly written in the names of counties. Sixteen counties have been named for signers of the Declaration of Independence, six of whom came from Virginia. They were Carter Braxton, Benjamin Harrison, Thomas Jefferson, Richard Henry Lee, Thomas Nelson, Jr., and George Wythe. The three signers so honored from Georgia were Button Gwinnett, Lyman Hall and George Walton. The two signers from Pennsylvania, Benjamin Franklin and Benjamin Rush, also had counties named for them. Other signers and the colonies they represented were Samuel Huntington of Connecticut, Thomas McKean of Delaware, Charles Carrol of Maryland, Lewis Morris of New York and John Adams of Massachusetts Bay.

Nine Vice Presidents of the United States have had 28 counties named for them, the most favored one being John Caldwell Calhoun for whom 11 counties were named. Counties are named for Calhoun in Alabama, Arkansas, Florida, Georgia, Illinois, Iowa, Michigan, Mississippi, South Carolina, Texas and West Virginia. Richard Mentor Johnson had five counties named for him: in Illinois, Kentucky, Missouri and Nebraska. Counties in Arkansas, Iowa, Missouri and Texas have been named for George Mifflin Dallas. Counties have been named for George Clinton in New York and Ohio; for Schuyler Colfax in Nebraska and New Mexico. States having one county named for a Vice President are New York (Daniel D. Tompkins); South Dakota (Hannibal Hamlin) and Washington (William R. King.)

County names have honored also many distinguished foreigners: Lafayette, Simon Bolivar, Edmund Burke, Thaddeus Kosciusko, Lajos Kossuth, Friedrich von Humboldt, Baron von Steuben, Joseph Addison, Isaac Newton, Giacomo Beltrami, Robert Emmet, Arthur Onslow, etc. Texas remembered the slogan "Remember the Alamo" when it named its counties. Twelve heroic defenders who lost their lives on March 6, 1836 were honored by having counties named for them. The counties named for them were Bailey, Bowie, Cochran, Cottle, Crockett, Dickens, Floyd, Kent, Kimble, King, Lynn and Travis. Crockett, Tennessee, was also named for one of these Alamo defenders.

Many counties have derived their names from descriptive words; 228 counties have been named for 141 descriptive words. The most commonly used word is "union" which is used 18 times by Arkansas, Florida, Georgia, Illinois, Indiana, Iowa, Kentucky, Louisiana, Mississippi, New Jersey, New Mexico, North Carolina, Ohio, Oregon, Pennsylvania, South Carolina, South Dakota, and Tennessee. The next most popular word is "lake" used 12 times for counties in California, Colorado, Florida, Illinois, Indiana, Michigan, Minnesota, Montana, Ohio, Oregon, South Dakota, and Tennessee.

Richland has been used five times (Louisiana, Montana, Ohio, South Carolina, and Wisconsin) and so has Saline (Arkansas, Illinois, Kansas, Missouri and Nebraska) The words carbon, iron, liberty, and mineral have each been used four times. Counties named "Carbon" are in Montana, Pennsylvania, Utah and Wyoming; "Iron," in Michigan, Missouri, Utah and Wisconsin; "Liberty," in Florida, Georgia, Montana and Texas, and "Mineral," in Colorado, Montana, Nevada and West Virginia.

Each of the following descriptive words has been used three times as county names: Beaver, Buffalo, Cedar, Delta, Fairfield, Orange, Park, Rock, Summit and Valley. Two counties have been named for each of the following words: Bath, Bay, Big Horn, Butte, Clearwater, Elk, Forest, Golden Valley, Grand, Highland, Limestone, Midland, Portage, Prairie, Red River, Trinity and Vermilion.

Montana leads with descriptive county names having 27 counties, followed by Minnesota with 13, Florida, 12; Idaho and Texas, with 11 each, Nebraska, ten; Colorado, nine; Ohio, Pennsylvania and Wisconsin, eight each; Arkansas, Louisiana, Michigan, South Carolina and Utah, seven each; and Wyoming, six. States having five counties named for descriptive words are California, Illinois, Kentucky and South Dakota; Georgia and North Dakota have four each; Hawaii, Indiana, Mississippi, Missouri, Oklahoma and Virginia, three each; Connecticut, Iowa, Kansas, Nevada, New Jersey, Oregon, Rhode Island, Tennessee and West Virginia, two each; and Alabama, New Mexico, New York, North Carolina, Vermont and Washington, one each.

French words account for the names of 43 counties located in 22 states. The only French word used more than once as the name of a county is Platte, used by Missouri, Nebraska, and Wyoming. The state having the largest number of counties named for French words is Louisiana which has seven parishes with the following names: East Baton Rouge, West Baton Rouge, Lafource, Pointe Coupee, Rapides, Sabine and Terrebonne. Wisconsin has the next largest number of counties with French names. Its five French-named counties are Eau Clair, Fond du lac, La Crosse, Racine and Trempealeau.

There are four counties with French names in Minnesota: Lac Qui Parle, Mille Lacs, Roseau and Traverse; and four counties in Missouri; Maniteau, Maries, Ozark and Platte. The three French-named counties in Nebraska are Box Butte, Loup and Platte. Ohio has two counties with French names, Belmont and Champaign; California has Butte and Siskiyou, and Oregon has Deschutes and Malheur. Other French words used as the names of counties are: Amite, Boise, Bon Homme, Cache, Chicot, Clarion, Des Moines, La Porte, Lamoille, Labette, Pend Oreille, Platte, Presque Isle and Washita.

Spanish has a prominent place in county names. There are 69 counties whose names have been derived from 65 Spanish words. Most of these counties are located in California and Texas. Spanish words used by more than one county are Sierra (California and New Mexico), El Paso (Colorado and Texas), Escambia (Alabama and Florida), and Santa Cruz (California and Arizona). In California, we find 18 counties with the following Spanish names: Alameda, Calaveras, Contra Costa, Del Norte, El Dorado, Fresno, Los Angeles, Madera, Mariposa, Merced, Nevada, Placer, Plumas, Sacramento, Santa Cruz, Sierra, Ventura and Yuba.

Texas has 23 counties named for Spanish words as follows: Angelina, Atascosa, Bandera, Blanco, Bosque, Brazoria, Brazos, Colorado, Comal, Concho, El Paso, Frio, Lampasas, Lavaca, Llano, Matagorda, Nueces, Palo Pinto, Presidio, Refugio, Sabine, San Saba and Val Verde. In Colorado, counties with Spanish names are: Alamosa, Conejos, Costilla, Dolores, El Paso, Huerfano, La Plata, Las Animos, Mesa, Pueblo, Rio Blanco and Rio Grande. There are 16 other counties in seven states named for Spanish words.

There are 161 counties whose names have been derived from Indian words such as Alachua, Alamance, Allegan, Anoka, Appomattox, Aroostoo, Ashtabula, Asotin, Auglaize, Autauga, etc. (Three Hawaiian counties are named for Polynesian descriptive words and one for a Polynesian demi-god.) Michigan, with 20 counties named for Indian words leads the states, followed by New York with 12, and Mississippi and Ohio with 11. Minnesota and Wisconsin have 10 counties each named for Indian words.

The other states with Indian-named counties follow: Washington, eight; Alabama, Florida and Pennsylvania, six each; Maine and Oklahoma, five each; Georgia, and Virginia, four each; California, Idaho, Illinois, Indiana, and Missouri, three each; and Arizona, North Carolina, South Carolina, Tennessee, Utah and West Virginia, two each. The states with only one county with an Indian name are: Arkansas, Colorado, Kansas, Kentucky, Louisiana, Maryland, Massachusetts, Montana, Nebraska, Nevada, New Hampshire, New Jersey, North Dakota, Oregon, South Dakota and Texas.

Sixty-one Indians have had their names immortalized by counties. There may also be other counties named for persons with Anglicized names who have Indian ancestry. The spelling of their names occasionally differs from that often found in histories and biographies. Among the Indian names are the names of seven Indian women whose names designate counties in eight states. They are Attala (Mississippi), Leelanau (Michigan), Marinette (Wisconsin), Sonoma (California), Tippah (Mississippi), Winona (Minnesota), and Pocahontas, whose name has been used by Iowa and West Virginia. The only Indian besides Pocahontas whose name is used more than once is Osceola for whom counties are named in Florida, Iowa and Michigan.

The greatest use of Indian names is made by Oklahoma and Iowa. The 14 Indian-named Oklahoma counties are Adair, Atoka, Carter, Craig, Garvin, Johnston, Le Flore, Love, Mc Curtain, Mc Intosh, Mayes, Pontotoc, Pushmataha and Sequoyah; the ten counties in Iowa are Appanoose, Black Hawk, Keokuk, Mahaska, Osceola, Pocahontas, Poweshiek, Tama, Wapello and Winneshiek. Six counties in Michigan bear Indian names: Leelanau, Mecosta, Missaukee, Newaygo, Osceola and Sanilac. There are also six counties in Mississippi with Indian names: Attala, Itawamba, Leflore, Pontotoc, Tippah and Tishomingo. California has four Indian-named counties: Marin, Solano, Sonoma and Stanislaus. Six states have two Indian-named counties and 11 others have one county each.

In addition to naming counties for Indians and Indian

words, 41 states have named 181 counties for Indian tribes. All states have honored an Indian tribe by naming a county for them except Delaware, Kentucky, Massachusetts, New Jersey, Rhode Island, Tennessee and Vermont. Both Kansas and Oklahoma have 13 counties named for Indian tribes: North Carolina and Oregon have nine; Iowa, New York, Ohio and Wisconsin have eight; and Arizona, California, Louisiana and Washington have seven counties each. The most favored Indian tribe is the Cherokee for whom eight counties have been named. The Delaware and the Ottawa tribes have each had four counties named for them. Sixteen tribes have had three counties named for them; 15 tribes have had two counties named for them.

Another source for the name of counties is words especially coined. In this group there are 28 counties in 18 states. The state which leads in creating names for counties is Michigan which named counties: Alcona, Alpena, Arenac, Benzie, Hillsdale, Oceana, Oscoda and Tuscola.

Eight states have named counties Columbia. They are Arkansas, Florida, Georgia, New York, Oregon, Pennsylvania, Washington and Wisconsin. Arkansas adapted the word from Columbia, the goddess of Liberty; Washington from the "Columbia" the first ship to carry the flag of the United States around the world, while the others named their counties Columbia in honor of Columbus. Other created names for counties are Columbiana, Ohio; Glades, Florida; Itasca, Minnesota, Kay, Oklahoma; Lonoke, Arkansas, Owyhee, Idaho; Pittsylvania, Virginia; Pondera, Montana; and Transylvania, Virginia. Eureka, Nevada, is derived from the Greek; Salem, New Jersey, from the Hebrew; and Schuylkill, Pennsylvania, from the Dutch.

Other sources of names for counties are those persons who have been designated saints. There are 41 counties named for 33 saints. Their names are preceded by the proper forms such as St., Ste., San and Santa. The most popular name is San Juan for whom four counties have been named, and St. Charles, St. Francis, St. Joseph, St. Louis and San Miguel for whom two counties have been named. The states having the most number of counties named for saints are California, nine; Louisiana, nine; Missouri, four; Florida, three; Texas, three; Colorado, two; New Mexico, two; and one each for Arkansas, Indiana, Maryland, Michigan, Minnesota, New Mexico, Utah, Washington and Wisconsin.

There are 45 counties named for women in 24 states; Among the women so honored are seven Indian women and four women who have been sainted. The only woman whose name has been used for more than one county is Pocahontas for whom counties have been named in Iowa and West Virginia. Two counties were named Mecklenburg (in North Carolina and Virginia) for Charlotte Sophia, Princess of Mecklenburg; and two counties named Guadalupe for Our Lady of Guadalupe. Two counties were named Caroline, each for a different person, and two counties were similarly named Florence.

The state most partial to the names of women for counties is Virginia which has nine counties named for women as follows: Amelia, Augusta, Carolina, Charlotte, Elizabeth City, Fluvanna, Louisa, Mecklenburg and Princess Anne. Five counties in Maryland have also been named for women: Anne Arundel, Caroline, Queen Anne's, Somerset and Talbot. Pennsylvania named three counties for women; Huntingdon, Luzerne and Montour. North Carolina also has named three counties for women: Dare, Mecklenburg and Wake, as did Iowa; Bremer, Louisa and Monona. Idaho, New Mexico, New York and Texas named two counties for women, while 14 other states named one county.

Another source of county names is geography. There are 219 counties named for geographical locations. Since many mountains, valleys, rivers and creeks bear the same name, it is not always possible to determine whether the county was named for the river, the mountain, the valley or all of them.

It is not always possible to determine whether the counties have been named for certain areas or for the people who ruled them or those for whom the areas were named. For example, eight counties bear the name Cumberland. Disregarding whether these counties were named for the river, town, city, village, or other feature, one may claim that the counties named Cumberland were named for Cumberland, England. At the same time, it may be claimed that the counties were named for William Augustus, the Duke of Cumberland, while others may insist they were named for subsequent dukes.

In a similar vein, there is an Essex County in Massachusetts, New Jersey, New York, Vermont and Virginia. One may contend that these counties were named for Robert

Devereux, the Earl of Essex, but some may maintain that the counties were named for Essex, England, which area was ruled by Robert Devereux while he was Earl. Only rarely is the distinction made between the site and the ruler as in the case of Norborne Berkeley, the Baron of Botetourt. The county of Berkeley, West Virginia, is named for him, and the county of Botetourt, Virginia, is named for the site. In this book, where the name of a county is the same as that of an individual and a geographical location, the source will be considered as the former.

Quite frequently counties have used different names to honor the same person. The most conspicuous example of this is Fayette County (11 counties) and Lafayette County (six counties) both of whom are named for Lafayette. Nine counties are named Henry for Patrick Henry and one county is named Patrick for him. Two counties are named Dodge for Henry Dodge, and one county is named Henry in his honor. Three counties are named De Soto for Hernando de Soto and one county is named Hernando. Eight of the counties are named Clinton for De Witt Clinton and one county is named De Witt. Two counties are named Fillmore and one county named Millard to honor President Millard Fillmore.

Joseph Hamilton Daviess is honored by three counties named Daviess, and one named Jo Daviess; Jefferson Davis was honored by two counties named Jefferson Davis and two named Jeff Davis. John Middleton Clayton was honored by Clayton, Iowa, and Clay, Arkansas. George Rogers Clark is honored by five counties named Clark and one named Clarke (with an "e"). Three counties are named for William Clark and five for Meriwether Lewis, and one county is named for both of them, Lewis and Clark County. William Pitt leads with the greatest number of deviations. There is a Pitt County in North Carolina, a Chatham County in both Georgia and North Carolina, and a Pittsylvania County in Virginia. [cont. p. 29]

Counties named for the same person are:

Jackson (21 counties)	and	Old Hickory
Botetourt	and	Berkeley
Murray	and	Alfalfa [Wm. H. Murray]
Kittson	and	Norman
Hyde	and	Clarendon
Campbell	and	Loudon and Loudoun

Analysis of County Names by Origin

TABLE TWO

	Counties	Biographic (see p. 30)	Words	French words	Spanish words	Indian (aboriginal) words	Coined words	Assorted	Descriptive	Geography	Indian Tribes
Alabama	67	54	13	-	1	6	-	-	1	2	3
Arizona	14	3	11	-	2	2	-	-	-	-	7
Arkansas	75	61	14	1	-	1	2	-	7	1	2
California	58	20	38	2	18	3	-	1	5	2	7
Colorado	63	36	27	-	12	1	-	1	9	-	4
Connecticut	8	-	8	-	-	-	-	-	2	6	-
Delaware	3	-	3	-	-	-	-	-	-	3	-
Florida	67	41	26	-	2	6	2	-	12	2	2
Georgia	159	143	16	-	-	4	1	-	4	4	3
Hawaii	4	1	-	-	-	3	-	-	-	-	-
Idaho	44	21	23	1	-	3	1	1	11	-	6
Illinois	102	78	24	-	-	3	-	-	5	12	4
Indiana	91	78	13	1	-	3	-	-	3	3	3
Iowa	99	82	17	1	-	-	-	-	2	6	8
Kansas	105	85	20	1	-	1	-	-	2	3	13
Kentucky	120	113	7	-	-	1	-	-	5	1	-
Louisiana (parishes)	64	35	29	7	2	1	-	-	7	5	7
Maine	16	6	10	-	-	5	-	-	-	4	1
Maryland	23	18	5	-	-	1	-	-	-	3	1

Massachusetts	14	3	11	-	-	1	-	-	-	10	-
Michigan	83	38	45	1	-	20	8	-	7	5	4
Minnesota	87	56	31	4	-	10	1	-	13	-	3
Mississippi	82	64	18	1	-	11	-	-	3	1	2
Missouri	114	96	18	4	-	3	-	-	3	7	1
Montana	56	25	31	-	-	1	1	-	27	-	2
Nebraska	93	71	22	3	-	1	-	-	10	2	6
Nevada	16	10	6	-	1	1	1	-	2	-	1
New Hampshire	10	3	7	-	-	1	-	-	-	5	1
New Jersey	21	6	15	-	-	1	1	-	2	11	-
New Mexico	32	22	10	-	6	-	-	-	1	2	1
New York	62	29	33	-	-	12	1	-	1	11	8
North Carolina	100	70	30	-	-	2	1	-	1	17	9
North Dakota	53	47	6	-	-	1	-	-	4	-	1
Ohio	88	50	38	2	-	11	1	-	8	8	8
Oklahoma	77	50	27	1	2	5	1	-	3	2	13
Oregon	36	21	15	2	-	1	1	-	2	-	9
Pennsylvania	67	30	37	1	-	6	2	-	8	15	5

	Counties	Biographic	Words	French words	Spanish words	Indian words	Coined words	Assorted	Descriptive	Geography	Indian Tribes
Rhode Island	5	1	4	-	-	-	-	-	2	2	-
South Carolina	46	25	21	-	-	2	-	-	7	11	1
South Dakota	67	56	11	1	-	1	-	-	5	2	2
Tennessee	95	89	6	-	-	2	-	-	2	2	-
Texas	254	210	44	-	23	1	-	1	11	3	5
Utah	29	15	14	1	-	2	-	-	7	1	3
Vermont	14	5	9	1	-	-	-	-	1	7	-
Virginia	96	54	43	-	-	4	1	-	3	30	4
Washington	39	21	18	-	-	8	1	-	1	1	7
West Virginia	55	47	8	-	-	2	-	-	2	1	3
Wisconsin	71	36	35	5	-	10	1	-	8	3	8
Wyoming	23	11	12	1	-	-	-	-	6	2	3
	3067	2137	929	42	69	160	28	4	225	218	181

Note: It is often possible to list a county under a different classification.

States also have provided names for counties: they are Delaware County, Iowa; Nevada, Arkansas; Oregon, Missouri; Texas, Missouri; and Texas, Oklahoma. Indiana, Pennsylvania, was named for Indiana Territory; Republic, Kansas, for the Pawnee Republic, and Jersey, Illinois, for New Jersey.

Cities in the United States also have provided names for counties such as Dorchester, South Carolina; Lexington, South Carolina; Pittsburgh, Oklahoma; Plymouth, Iowa, and Rutland, Vermont. And famous estates and residences also have been commemorated such as Ashland, Ohio and Ashland, Wisconsin, both named for Henry Clay's estate; Vernon, Louisiana, and Vernon, Wisconsin, for George Washington's home at Mount Vernon; La Grange, Indiana, for Lafayette's home near Paris, and Arlington, Virginia, for John Custis' home.

Forts and military posts have lent their names to counties such as Duchesne, Utah, for Fort Duchesne, Pennsylvania; Fort Bend, Texas, for Fort Bend (Texas); Defiance, Ohio for Fort Defiance (Ohio); and Massac, Illinois, for Fort Massac (Illinois).

Many counties have derived their names from other counties. Illinois named five of its counties for counties in Kentucky: Christian, Hardin, Mason, Scott and Woodford. Illinois named Champaign and Richland counties for counties of the same name in Ohio. Williamson, Illinois, was named for Williamson, Tennessee. Jones County and Walworth County in South Dakota were named for counties in Iowa and Wisconsin. Albany County and Chautauqua County, New York, have given their names to counties in Wyoming and Kansas respectively. Orange County, Indiana, received its name from Orange County, North Carolina.

Although the preponderance of counties named for cities have derived their names from locations in England, there are many that have resorted to Old World cities. Some of the counties thus named are Geneva, Grenada (for Granada), Lorain, Medina, Athens, Goshen, and Marathon.

The New World was not neglected in naming counties. For example, Iowa named three of its counties Buena Vista, Cerro Gordo and Palo Alto for battlegrounds in Mexico. Other names are Acadia, Louisiana; Hidalgo, New Mexico; Nassau, Florida, and Val Verde, Texas.

Analysis of Biographical Names of Counties

TABLE THREE

	Total no. biog. names	Indians	Saints	Women	Pres.	Gov.	Sen.	Rep.	Others
Alabama	54	2	-	1	5	4	13	4	25
Arizona	3	1	-	-	-	-	-	-	2
Arkansas	61	-	1	-	10	6	14	4	26
California	20	4	9	-	-	-	-	-	7
Colorado	36	2	2	-	5	5	5	-	17
Connecticut	-	-	-	-	-	-	-	-	-
Delaware	-	-	-	-	-	-	-	-	-
Florida	41	1	3	-	7	5	5	-	20
Georgia	143	1	-	1	7	26	31	17	60
Hawaii	1	-	-	-	-	-	-	-	1
Idaho	21	1	-	2	5	1	3	1	8
Illinois	78	1	-	-	6	10	17	5	39
Indiana	78	-	1	-	7	8	10	6	47
Iowa	82	9	-	4	11	5	19	5	29
Kansas	85	1	-	1	5	4	15	3	56
Kentucky	113	-	-	1	7	20	7	13	65
Louisiana	35	1	9	1	6	2	4	1	11
Maine	6	-	-	-	1	1	-	-	4
Maryland	18	-	1	5	1	-	2	-	9
Massachusetts	3	-	-	-	-	-	-	-	3
Michigan	38	6	1	1	3	3	9	2	13
Minnesota	56	2	1	-	5	4	9	1	34
Mississippi	64	6	-	-	8	7	12	7	24
Missouri	96	-	4	-	7	12	21	4	48
Montana	25	-	-	1	4	2	2	1	15
Nebraska	71	-	-	1	12	8	13	5	32
Nevada	10	-	-	-	1	-	3	-	1
New Hampshire	3	-	-	-	-	1	1	-	1
New Jersey	6	-	-	-	-	2	-	-	4
New Mexico	22	-	2	2	5	3	2	1	7
New York	29	-	1	2	4	5	1	2	14
North Carolina	70	-	-	3	3	8	4	5	47
North Dakota	47	-	-	-	1	-	5	1	40
Ohio	50	-	-	-	7	6	4	2	31
Oklahoma	50	14	-	1	7	4	5	2	17
Oregon	21	-	-	1	6	1	5	-	8
Pennsylvania	30	-	-	3	4	4	3	1	15

	Total no. biog. names	Indians	Saints	Women	Pres.	Gov.	Sen.	Rep.	Others
Rhode Island	1	-	-	-	1	-	-	-	-
South Carolina	25	-	-	1	-	1	2	2	19
South Dakota	56	-	-	1	2	5	4	3	41
Tennessee	89	-	-	1	7	12	13	8	48
Texas	210	1	3	2	6	12	12	9	165
Utah	15	2	1	-	3	2	-	-	7
Vermont	5	-	-	-	1	2	-	-	2
Virginia	54	1	-	7	3	10	4	2	27
Washington	21	2	1	-	6	4	3	1	4
West Virginia	47	2	-	-	4	14	5	6	16
Wisconsin	36	1	1	1	8	4	4	2	15
Wyoming	11	1	-	-	1	1	1	-	7
	2137	62	41	44	202	234	292	126	1137

Although several counties have the same name, there are variations in spelling. There is an Allegany County in Maryland and New York, but North Carolina and Virginia have an Alleghany County, and Pennsylvania has an Allegheny County. There is a Pottawatomie County in Kansas and Oklahoma, but the county in Iowa is Pottawattamie County. Ohio has its Wyandot County whereas Kansas has a Wyandotte County. Cheboygan County is in Michigan and Sheboygan County is in Wisconsin.

This dissimilarity is true not only of Indian names but of English names. Loudon County in Tennessee and Loudoun County in Virginia are both named for the same man, John Campbell, the fourth Earl of Loudoun. In Ohio, there is a Clark County named for George Rogers Clark, but the county named for him in Virginia is Clarke County.

Some counties have the same sound but are spelled differently because they are named for different people, such as Kearney County, Nebraska, and Kearny County, Kansas. Linn County, Iowa, and Lynn County, Texas are similarly named for different people. There is a great diversity in the orthography of common names such as Smith and Smyth, Stanley and Stanly, Stark and Starke, Stephens and Stevens, Storey and Story, etc.

More than one-third of the counties are located in seven states. Texas has the greatest number of counties, with 254. The six other states having 100 or more are Georgia, 159; Kentucky, 120; Missouri, 114; Kansas, 105; Illinois, 102; and North Carolina, 100. The state with the smallest number of counties is Delaware with only three counties. Texas has more counties than the total number of counties in 15 states. Louisiana is subdivided into 64 parishes, the equivalent of counties.

The Smallest and Largest County in Area

There is no uniformity and there is a great difference in sizes of counties. The largest county in area is San Bernardino, California, which has an area of 20,131 square miles, almost 17 times that of the state of Rhode Island. The smallest is New York County, with 22 square miles. Incidentally, it is the fifth most populated county, exceeded only by Cook County (Chicago), Los Angeles County, Wayne County (Detroit), and Philadelphia County. In the following list, each state's smallest and largest counties are given, with areas in square miles.

Alabama: Limestone 545, Baldwin 1,613
Arizona: Santa Cruz 1,246; Coconino 18,573
Arkansas: Sebastian 529, Union 1,052
California: San Francisco 45, San Bernardino 20,131
Colorado: Denver 58, Moffat 4,754
Connecticut: Middlesex 374, Hartford 741
Delaware: New Castle 437, Sussex 946
Florida: Pinellas 264; Dade 2,054
Georgia: Clarke 125; Warren 912
Hawaii: Honolulu 621; Hawaii 4,039
Idaho: Payette 403, Idaho 8,515
Illinois: Putnam 166, McLean 1,173
Indiana: Ohio 87, Allen 671
Iowa: Dickinson 382, Kossuth 979
Kansas: Wyandotte 151, Butler 1,445
Kentucky: Robertson 101, Christian 726
Louisiana: Orleans 199, Cameron 1,444
Maine: Sagadahoc 257, Aroostook 6,805
Maryland: Calvert 219, Garrett 668
Massachusetts: Nantucket 46, Worcester 1,532

Michigan: Benzie 316, Marquette 1,841
Minnesota: Ramsey 160, Saint Louis 6,182
Mississippi: Walthall 403 (Montgomery 403), Yazoo 938
Missouri: (St. Louis City 61), Worth 267, Texas 1,183
Montana: Deer Lodge 738, Petroleum 1,083
Nebraska: Sarpy 230, Cherry 5,982
Nevada: Storey 262, Nye 18,064
New Hampshire: Strafford 377, Coos 1,825
New Jersey: Hudson 45, Burlington 819
New Mexico: Bernalillo 1,163, Socorro 7,772
New York: New York 22, St. Lawrence 2,772
North Carolina: Chowan 180, Sampson 963
North Dakota: Eddy 643, McKenzie 2,819
Ohio: Lake 232, Ashtabula 706
Oklahoma: Marshall 414, Texas 2,056
Oregon: Multnomah 424, Harney 10,132
Pennsylvania: Philadelphia 135, Lycoming 1,215
Rhode Island: Kent 25, Providence 422
South Carolina: Calhoun 389, Berkeley 1,214
South Dakota: Clay 403, Meade 3,466
Tennessee: Trousdale 116, Shelby 751
Texas: Rockwall 147, Brewster 6,208
Utah: Davis 268, San Juan 7,884
Vermont: Grand Isle 77, Windsor 965
Virginia: Arlington 24, Pittsylvania 1,022
Washington: San Juan 172, Okanogan 5,295
West Virginia: Hancock 88, Randolph 1,046
Wisconsin: Ozaukee 235, Marathon 1,592
Wyoming: Hot Springs 2,022, Sweetwater 10,492

Biographical Portion of Main County List (Part II)

The amount of space accorded to biographies of namesakes in Part II should not be used to evaluate a person's importance. Individuals like Washington, Lincoln, Jefferson, Jackson, Franklin, Lafayette, etc., whose fame is worldwide, have been accorded less space than that to which they are entitled because information about them is readily available. Many unknowns have inversely been granted much more recognition than they deserve. This partiality is deliberate, one of the prime factors being the availability or inaccessibility of biographical material. The purpose is to make inaccessible data readily available for libraries where facilities are limited rather than to determine a scale of importance or greatness.

The biographies are not intended to be complete and to cover every facet and every deed in the subjects' lives, but to supply clues and leads for further study. In some instances, biographies are shorter than may be desired due to the paucity of records. In some instances conflicting claims and statements are so contradictory that the data have been omitted. This is particularly true in the case of the early settlers and Indians for whom little authentic and documented data are available.

In the interest of accuracy and as a warning to the uninitiated, great care should be exercised in the matter of dates. Most biographies unintentionally create confusion. This book should be considered no exception. As an example, let us look at a hypothetical case. Mr. XYZ was sworn in as a Senator on December 10, 1958 and resigned January 5, 1959. The biographical entry would read "Mr. XYZ; Senator 1958-59." This is absolutely correct and standard operating procedure in most books, yet the entry is misleading as the novice might assume that Mr. XYZ served two years, whereas in reality he served less than a month. It is suggested that researchers endeavor to consult original sources and documents to obtain exact dates by days, rather than dates by years.

Part II

COUNTIES LISTED BY COUNTY

Abbeville, S. C. (est. Mar. 12, 1785; 509 sq. mi.; 1970 pop.: 21,112; 1960: 21,417; 1950: 22,456) (Abbeville). Abbeville, France.

Acadia, La. (est. Apr. 10, 1805; 647 sq. mi.; 1970 pop.: 52,109; 1960: 49,931; 1950: 47,050) (Crowley). Original name of Nova Scotia, province of Canada.

Accomack, Va. (est. 1663; 470 sq. mi.; 1970 pop.: 29,004; 1960: 30,635; 1950: 33,832) (Accomac). Accomack Indian tribe; Indian word for "land on the other side." -- Whitelaw, Ralph T., Virginia's Eastern Shore, a history of Northampton and Accomack counties, Richmond: Virginia Historical Society, 1951; 1511 p.

Ada, Idaho (est. Dec. 22, 1864; 1,140 sq. mi.: 1970 pop.: 112,230; 1960: 93,460; 1950: 70,649) (Boise) ("The Center of Idaho's Industry, Agriculture, Mining, Government and Playgrounds"). Ada Riggs (1863-). Daughter of H. C. Riggs, one of the original incorporators of Boise who erected the first building in Boise; member second territorial legislature of Idaho 1864. His daughter was the first white child born in Boise.

Adair, Iowa (est. Jan. 15, 1851; 569 sq. mi.; 1970 pop.: 9,487; 1960: 10,893; 1950: 12,292) (Greenfield). John Adair (1757-1840). Eighth Governor of Kentucky. Served in Revolutionary War; major of volunteers in expedition against the Indians 1791-92; Ky., house of representatives 1793-95, 1798 and 1800-03; Senator from Ky., 1805-06; aide to Governor Shelby at battle of the Thames 1813; commanded Ky., rifle brigade under General Jackson 1814-15; Ky., house of representatives 1817; adjutant general with rank of brigadier general governor of Ky., 1820-24; Representative from Ky., 1831-33. -- Kilburn, Lucian Moody, History of Adair County, Chicago: Pioneer Pub. Co., 1915; 2 vol.

Adair, Ky. (est. Dec. 11, 1801; eff. Apr. 1, 1802; 393 sq. mi.; 1970 pop.: 13,037; 1960: 14,699; 1950: 17,603) (Columbia). John Adair*.

---

*Asterisk refers to preceding entry where fuller data are given.

Adair, Mo. (est. Jan. 29, 1841; 574 sq. mi.; 1970 pop.: 22,472; 1960: 20,105; 1950: 19,689) (Kirksville). John Adair*. -- Violette, Eugene Morrow, History of Adair County, Kirksville, Mo.: Denslow Historical Co., 1911; 1188 p.

Adair, Okla. (est. July 16, 1907; 569 sq. mi.; 1970 pop.: 15,141; 1960: 13,112; 1950: 14,918) (Stilwell). John Lynch Adair (1828-1896). One of the editors of the Indian Chieftain.

Adams, Colo. (est. Apr. 15, 1901; 1,247 sq. mi.; 1970 pop.: 185,789; 1960: 120,296; 1950: 40,234) (Brighton). Alva Adams (1850-1922). Fifth, tenth and fourteenth Governor of Colorado. Colo., leg. 1876; governor of Colo., 1887-89, 1897-99 and 1905; president of Pueblo Savings Bank.

Adams, Idaho. (est. Mar. 3, 1911; 1,377 sq. mi.; 1970 pop.: 2,877; 1960: 2,978; 1950: 3,347) (Council). John Adams (1735-1826). Second President of the United States. Continental Congress 1774-78; signer of Declaration of Independence 1776; commissioner to France 1777-78; negotiated peace treaty with Great Britain 1783; Minister to Great Britain 1785-88; vice president of the U.S. 1789-97 under George Washington; President of the U.S., 1797-1801.

Adams, Ill. (est. Jan. 13, 1825; 866 sq. mi.; 1970 pop.: 70,861; 1960: 68,467; 1950: 64,690)(Quincy). John Quincy Adams (1767-1848). Sixth President of the United States. Son of John Adams; Mass. senate 1802; Senator from Mass., 1803-08; U.S. Minister to Russia 1809-14; negotiated Treaty of Ghent 1815; U.S. Minister to Gt. Britain 1815-17; U.S. Secretary of State in cabinet of Pres. Monroe 1817-25; President of the U.S., 1825-29; Representative from Mass., 1831-48. -- Wilcox, David F., Quincy and Adams County, Chicago: Lewis Pub. Co., 1919; 2 vol.

Adams, Ind. (est. Feb. 7, 1835; org. Jan. 23, 1836 eff. Mar. 1, 1836; 345 sq. mi.; 1970 pop.: 26,871; 1960: 24,643; 1950: 22,392) (Decatur). John Quincy Adams*. -- Quinn, French, A short, short story of Adams County, [Adams Co., Ind.]: Economy Print Concern, 1936; 142 p.

Adams, Iowa. (est. Jan. 15, 1851, org. Jan. 12, 1853, eff. Mar. 7, 1853; 426 sq. mi.; 1970 pop.: 6,322; 1960: 7,468; 1950: 8,753) (Corning). John Adams*.

Adams, Miss. (est. Apr. 2, 1799; 426 sq. mi.; 1970 pop.: 37,293; 1960: 37,730; 1950: 32,256) (Natchez). John Adams*.

Adams, Neb. (est. Feb. 16, 1867, org. Jan. 2, 1872; 562 sq. mi.; 1970 pop.: 30,553; 1960: 28,944; 1950: 28,855)

(Hastings). John Adams*. -- Burton, William R., Past and present of Adams County, Nebraska, Chicago: S. J. Clarke Pub. Co., 1916; 2 vol.

Adams, N. D. (est. Mar 13, 1885, org. Apr. 17, 1907; 990 sq. mi.; 1970 pop.: 3,832; 1960: 4,449; 1950: 4,910) (Hettinger). John Quincy Adams (1848-). General land and townsite agent for the Chicago, Milwaukee, St. Paul and Pacific Railway when the county was formed in 1907.

Adams, Ohio. (est. July 10, 1797; 588 sq. mi.; 1970 pop.: 18,957; 1960: 19,982; 1950: 20,499) (West Union). John Adams*. -- Evans, Nelson Wiley, A history of Adams County, West Union, Ohio: E. B. Stivers, 1900; 946 p.

Adams, Pa. (est. Jan. 22, 1800; 526 sq. mi.; 1970 pop.: 56,937; 1960: 51,906; 1950: 44,197) (Gettysburg). ("The County Where the Apple Is King"). John Adams*. -- McPherson, Edward, The story of the creation of Adams County, Lancaster, Pa.: Inquirer Printing Co., 1889; 50 p.

Adams, Wash. (est. Nov. 28, 1883; 1,895 sq. mi.; 1970 pop.: 12,014; 1960: 9,929; 1950: 6,584) (Ritzville). John Adams*.

Adams, Wis. (est. Mar. 11, 1848; 677 sq. mi.; 1970 pop.: 9,234; 1960: 7,566; 1950: 7,906) (Friendship). John Adams*.

Addison, Vt. (est. Oct. 18, 1785; 785 sq. mi.; 1970 pop.: 24,266; 1960: 20,076; 1950: 19,442) (Middlebury). Joseph Addison (1672-1719). English Under-Secretary of State 1706; Member of Parliament 1708-19; editor of the Spectator 1711-12 and 1714; wrote tragedy "Cato" 1713; political newspaper the "Freeholder" 1715-16; buried in Westminster Abbey. -- Smith, H. Perry, History of Addison County, Vermont, Syracuse, N. Y.: D. Mason and Co., 1886; 774 p.

Aiken, S. C. (est. Mar. 10, 1871; 1,097 sq. mi.; 1970 pop.: 91,023; 1960: 81,039; 1950: 53,137) (Aiken). William Aiken (1806-1887). Thirty-sixth governor of South Carolina. S. C. legislature 1838; governor of S. C. 1844-46; president of S. C. Railroad Co.

Aitkin, Minn. (est. May 23, 1857; 1,824 sq. mi.; 1970 pop.: 11,403; 1960: 12,162; 1950: 14,327) (Aitkin). William Alexander Aitkin (c. 1787-1851). Fur trader, worked for the Fond du Lac department of the American Fur Company under John Jacob Astor.

Alachua, Fla. (est. Dec. 29, 1824; 892 sq. mi.; 1970 pop.: 104,764; 1960: 74,074; 1950: 57,026) (Gainesville). Creek Indian word for "grassy" or "jug."

Alamance, N. C. (est. Jan. 29, 1849; 434 sq. mi.; 1970 pop.: 96, 362; 1960: 85, 674; 1950: 71, 220) (Graham). Indian word for "blue clay." -- Magness, Sallie Walker (Stockard), History of Alamance, Raleigh, N. C.: Capital Printing Co., 1900; 166 p. -- Whitaker, Walter, Centennial history of Alamance County, 1849-1949, Burlington, Chamber of Commerce, Burlington, N. C., 1949; 258 p.

Alameda, Calif. (est. Mar. 25, 1853; 733 sq. mi.; 1970 pop.: 1, 073, 184; 1960: 905, 670; 1950: 740, 315) (Oakland). ("The Garden Spot of California") Spanish literal translation of "a tree-lined road." Freeman, Leslie H., Alameda County, Past and Present, San Leandro, Calif.: Press of the San Leandro Reporter, 1946; 159 p. -- Merritt, Frank Clinton, History of Alameda County, Chicago: S. J. Clarke Pub. Co., 1928; 2 vol.

Alamosa, Colo. (est. Mar. 8, 1913; 720 sq. mi.; 1970 pop.: 11, 422; 1960: 10, 000; 1950: 10, 531) (Alamosa). Spanish for "cottonwood grove."

Albany, N. Y. (est. Nov. 1, 1683; 531 sq. mi.; 1970 pop.: 285, 618; 1960: 272, 926; 1950: 239, 386) (Albany). Duke of York and Albany, James II (1633-1701) King of England, Scotland and Ireland. Upon death of his brother Charles II succeeded to the throne 1685; escaped to France 1688. (See also James City, Va., and York County, Me.) -- Parker, Amasa J., Landmarks of Albany County, Syracuse, N. Y.: D. Mason & Co., 1897; 457 p.

Albany, Wyo. (est. Dec. 16, 1868; 4, 400 sq. mi.; 1970 pop.: 26, 431; 1960: 21, 290; 1950: 19, 055) (Laramie). Albany, N. Y. *. -- Homsher, Lola M., History of Albany County, Wyoming, Lusk, Wyo., 1965; 110 p.

Albemarle, Va. (est. May 6, 1744; session; 739 sq. mi.; 1970 pop.: 37, 780; 1960: 30, 969; 1950: 26, 662) (Charlottesville). William Anne Keppel (1702-1754), Earl of Albemarle. Aide-de-camp to King George I, 1727; governor of Virginia Sept. 26, 1737-1754 but never came to Virginia; brigadier general 1739; major general 1742; lieutenant general 1743; privy councillor 1751. -- Rawlings, Mary, The Albemarle of other days, Charlottesville, Va.: Michie Company, 1925; 146 p. -- St. Claire, Emily (Entwisle), Beautiful and historic Albemarle, Richmond: Appeals Press, 1932; 110 p.

Alcona, Mich. (est. Apr. 1, 1840; 677 sq. mi.; 1970 pop.: 7, 113; 1960: 6, 352; 1950: 5, 856) (Harrisville). Coined word for "the beautiful plains." (originally Neewaygo County; name changed to Alcona on Mar. 8, 1843, Act 67.)

Alcorn, Miss. (est. Apr. 15, 1870; 386 sq. mi.; 1970 pop.: 27, 179; 1960: 25, 282; 1950: 27, 158) (Corinth). James

Lusk Alcorn (1816-1894). Twenty-eighth governor of Mississippi. Deputy sheriff Livingston County, Ky., 1839-44; Kentucky house of representatives 1843; Mississippi house of representatives 1846, 1856-57; Miss. senate 1848-54; in Confederate Army 1864-65; ; Senator-elect from Miss., but not permitted to take seat 1865; governor of Miss., 1870-71; Senator from Miss., 1871-77.

Alexander, Ill. (est. Mar. 4, 1819; 226 sq. mi.; 1970 pop.: 12,015; 1960: 16,061; 1950: 20,316) (Cairo). William M. Alexander. Early Illinois settler; member third Illinois legislature 1822. Speaker Illinois house of representatives. -- Perrin, William Henry, History of Alexander, Union and Pulaski Counties, Chicago: O. L. Baskin & Co., 1883; 588 p.

Alexander, N.C. (est. Jan. 15, 1847; 255 sq. mi.; 1970 pop.: 19,466; 1960: 15,625; 1950: 14,554) (Taylorsville). William Julius Alexander. Member N.C. legislature.

Alfalfa, Okla. (est. July 16, 1907; 884 sq. mi.; 1970 pop.: 7,224; 1960: 8,445; 1950: 10,699) (Cherokee). William Henry "Alfalfa Bill" Murray (1869-1956). Ninth governor of Oklahoma. President of Oklahoma constitutional convention 1906; Oklahoma house of representatives 1907-09; Representative from Okla., 1913-17; governor of Okla., 1931-35.

Alger, Mich. (est. Mar. 17, 1885; org. 1885; 913 sq. mi.; 1970 pop.: 8,568; 1960: 9,250; 1950: 10,007) (Munising). Russell Alexander Alger (1836-1907). Twenty-sixth governor of Michigan. From private to captain Michigan volunteers 1861; major and lt. col. 1862; col. and bvt. brig. gen. 1863; bvt. maj. gen. U.S. volunteers 1864; governor of Michigan 1885-87; U.S. Secretary of War in cabinet of Pres. McKinley 1897-99; Senator from Mich. 1902-07.

Allamakee, Iowa. (est. Feb. 20, 1847; org. Jan. 15, 1849; 639 sq. mi.; 1970 pop.: 14,968; 1960: 15,982; 1950: 16,351) (Waukon). Allan Makee. Indian trader. -- Hancock, Ellery M., Past and present of Allamakee County, Chicago: S.J. Clarke Pub. Co., 1913; 2 vol.

Allegan, Mich. (est. Mar. 2, 1831; org. 1835; 829 sq. mi.; 1970 pop.: 66,575; 1960: 57,729; 1950: 47,493) (Allegan). Indian word. -- Thomas, Henry F., A twentieth century history of Allegan County, Chicago: Lewis Pub. Co., 1907; 655 p.

Allegany, Md. (est. Dec. 25, 1789; 426 sq. mi.; 1970 pop.: 84,044; 1960: 84,169; 1950: 89,556) (Cumberland). Allegewi Indian tribe. Indian word Oolikhanna meaning "beautiful stream." -- Scharf, John Thomas, History of Western Maryland; being a history of Frederick, Montgomery, Carroll, Washington, Allegheny, and Garrett Counties, Philadelphia: L. H. Everts, 1882; 2 vol.

Allegany, N. Y. (est. Apr. 7, 1806; 1,046 sq. mi.; 1970 pop.: 46,458; 1960: 43,978; 1950: 43,784) (Belmont). Allegewi Indian tribe*. -- Minard, John S., Allegany County and its people, Alfred, N. Y.: W. A. Fergusson & Co., 1896; 941 p.

Alleghany, N. C. (est. 1859; 230 sq. mi.; 1970 pop.: 8,134; 1960: 7,734; 1950: 8,155) (Sparta). Allegewi Indian tribe*.

Alleghany, Va. (est. Jan. 5, 1822; 451 sq. mi.; 1970 pop.: 12,461; 1960: 12,128; 1950: 23,139) (Covington). Allegewi Indian tribe*. -- Morton, Oren Frederic, A centennial history of Alleghany County, J. K. Ruebush Co., 1923; 226 p.

Allegheny, Pa. (est. Sept. 24, 1788; 730 sq. mi.; 1970 pop.: 1,605,016; 1960: 1,628,587; 1950: 1,515,237) (Pittsburgh). Allegewi Indian tribe*. -- Kelly, George E., Allegheny County, Pittsburgh, Pa.: Allegheny County Sesqui-centennial Committee, 1938; 364 p.

Allen, Ind. (est. Dec. 17, 1823; eff. Apr. 1, 1824; 671 sq. mi.; 1970 pop.: 280,455; 1960: 232,196; 1950: 182,722) (Fort Wayne). John Allen (-1813). Col., killed in the Battle of the River Basin, 1813.

Allen, Kans. (est. Aug. 30, 1855; 505 sq. mi.; 1970 pop.: 15,043; 1960: 16,369; 1950: 18,187) (Iola). William Allen (1803-1879). Thirty-first governor of Ohio. Representative from Ohio 1833-35; Senator from Ohio 1837-49; declined Democratic presidential nomination 1849; governor of Ohio 1874-76. -- Duncan, Lew Wallace and Scott, Charles F., History of Allen and Woodson Counties, Iola, Kan.: Iola Register, 1901; 896 p.

Allen, Ky. (est. Jan. 11, 1815; 364 sq. mi.; 1970 pop.: 12,598; 1960: 12,269; 1950: 13,787) (Scottsville). John Allen*.

Allen, La. (est. June 12, 1912; 663 sq. mi.; 1970 pop.: 20,794; 1960: 19,867; 1950: 18.835) (Oberlin). Henry Watkins Allen (1820-1866). Nineteenth governor of Louisiana. Texas volunteer 1842; Texas house of representatives 1853; lt. col. 4th La. regiment; brig. gen. in Confederate Army 1863; wounded in cheek at Shiloh 1862; wounded in both cheeks at Baton Rouge 1862; governor of Louisiana 1864-65.

Allen, Ohio. (est. Feb. 12, 1820; 410 sq. mi.; 1970 pop.: 111,144; 1960: 103,691; 1950: 88,183) (Lima). Ethan

Allen (1738-1789). Served in French and Indian war; leader of the Green Mountain Boys captured Ft. Ticonderoga May 10, 1775; captured at Montreal 1775; exchanged 1778; col. 1778. -- Rusler, William, Standard history of Allen County, Chicago: American Historical Society, 1921; 2 vol. -- Miller, Charles Christian & Baxter, S. A., History of Allen County, Chicago: Richmond & Arnold, 1906; 872 p.

Allendale, S. C. (est. Feb. 6, 1919; 418 sq. mi.; 1970 pop.: 9, 692; 1960: 11, 362; 1950: 11, 773) (Allendale) Paul H. Allen. Postmaster of Allendale, S. C.

Alpena, Mich. (est. Apr. 1, 1840; org. 1857; 568 sq. mi.; 1970 pop.: 30, 708; 1960: 28, 556; 1950: 22, 187) (Alpena). Coined word for "the partridge country." (Originally Anamickee County, name changed to Alpena County on Mar. 8, 1843, Act 67). --Oliver, David D., Centennial history of Alpena County, Alpena, Mich.: Argus Printing House, 1903; 186 p.

Alpine, Calif. (est. Mar. 16, 1864; 723 sq. mi.; 1970 pop.: 484; 1960: 397; 1950: 241) (Markleeville). ("The Sportsman's Paradise"). Descriptive of Sierra Nevada mountain territory.

Amador, Calif. (est. May 11, 1854; 594 sq. mi.; 1970 pop.: 11, 821; 1960: 9, 990; 1950: 9, 151) (Jackson). "The County in the Heart of the Mother Lode"; "The Cradle of California"; "The Heart of the Mother Lode"). Jose Maria Amador. Early settler and miner. History of Amador County, Oakland, Calif.: Thompson & West, 1881; 344 p.

Amelia, Va. (est. Feb. 1, 1734; session, eff. Mar. 25, 1734; 366 sq. mi.; 1970 pop.: 7, 592; 1960: 7, 815; 1950: 7, 908) (Amelia). Amelia [Sophia](1711-1786). Second daughter of King George II. -- Jefferson, Mary Armstrong, Old homes and buildings in Amelia County, Amelia, Va., M. A. Jefferson, 1964; 160 p.

Amherst, Va. (est. (1761) seventh session, Sept. 14, 1758; 467 sq. mi.; 1970 pop.: 26, 072; 1960: 22, 953; 1950: 20, 332) (Amherst). Jeffrey Amherst (1717-1797). Col. 15th Regiment of Foot 1756-68; commissioned maj. gen. in America by William Pitt 1758; commander-in-chief of expedition to America; captain gen. and governor of Virginia 1759-68; created Baron Amherst 1776; commander-in-chief British Army 1793-95; Field Marshal 1796. -- Percy, Alfred, The Amherst County story, Madison Heights, Va.: Percy Press, 1961; 126 p.

Amite, Miss. (est. Feb. 24, 1809; 714 sq. mi.; 1970 pop.: 13, 763; 1960: 15, 573; 1950: 19, 261) (Liberty). French word "amité" meaning "friendship."

Anderson, Kans. (est. Aug. 30, 1855; 577 sq. mi.; 1970 pop.: 8,501; 1960: 9,035; 1950: 10,267) (Garnett). Joseph C. Anderson. First Kans. territorial legislature. -- Johnson, Harry, A history of Anderson County, Kansas, Garnett, Kan.: Garnett Review Co., 1936; 383 p.

Anderson, Ky. (est. Jan. 16, 1827; 206 sq. mi.; 1970 pop.: 9,358; 1960: 8,618; 1950: 8,984) (Lawrenceburg). Richard Clough Anderson (1788-1826). Kentucky house of representatives 1815; Representative from Ky., 1817-21; Ky., house of representatives 1821-22 serving as speaker the latter year; U.S. Minister to Colombia 1823; Envoy Extraordinary and Minister Plenipotentiary to the Panama Congress of Nations but died en route 1826.

Anderson, S.C. (est. Dec. 20, 1826; 776 sq. mi.; 1970 pop.: 105,474; 1960: 98,478; 1950: 90,664) (Anderson). Robert Anderson (-1813). Capt. 3rd South Carolina Rangers 1775-79; maj. and lt. col. 1781; adjt. gen. S.C. militia. -- Vandiver, Louise Ayer, Traditions and history of Anderson County, Atlanta, Ga.: Ruralist Press, 1928; 318 p.

Anderson, Tenn. (est. Nov. 6, 1801; 338 sq. mi.; 1970 pop.: 60,300; 1960: 60,032; 1950: 59,407) (Clinton). Joseph Anderson (1757-1837). Bvt. maj., U.S. judge territory south of the River Ohio 1791; Senator from Tenn. 1797-1815; First comptroller of U.S. Treasury 1815-36.

Anderson, Tex. (est. Mar. 24, 1846; 1,068 sq. mi.; 1970 pop.: 27,789; 1960: 28,162; 1950: 31,875) (Palestine). Kenneth Lewis Anderson (1805-1845). Collector of customs San Antonio 1840; Tex. house of representatives 1841-42; district attorney for 5th district 1843; vice president of Republic of Tex. 1844. -- Hohes, Pauline (Buck), A centennial history of Anderson County, Texas, San Antonio, Texas: Naylor Co., 1936; 565 p.

Andrew, Mo. (est. Jan. 29, 1841; 430 sq. mi.; 1970 pop.: 11,913; 1960: 11,062; 1950: 11.727) (Savannah). Andrew Jackson Davis of St. Louis.

Andrews, Tex . (est. Aug. 21, 1876; 1,504 sq. mi.; 1970 pop.: 10,372; 1960: 13,450; 1950: 5,002) (Andrews). Richard Andrews (1814-1835). Known as "Big Dick" wounded at battle of Gonzales Oct. 2, 1835; killed at battle of Concepcion Oct. 28, 1835; first Tex. soldier killed in Tex. revolution.

Androscoggin, Me. (est. Mar. 18, 1854; eff. Mar. 31, 1854; 478 sq. mi.; 1970 pop.: 91,279; 1960: 86,312; 1950: 83,594) (Auburn). Androscoggin Indian tribe,

Indian word for "spear fishing." -- Merrill, Georgia Drew, History of Androscoggin County, Boston: W.A. Fergusson & Co., 1891; 879 p.

Angelina, Tex. (est. Apr. 22, 1846; 857 sq. mi.; 1970 pop.: 49,349; 1960: 39,814; 1950: 36,032) (Lufkin). Spanish word for "little angel."

Anne Arundel, Md. (est. 1650; 417 sq. mi.; 1970 pop.: 297,539; 1960: 206,634; 1950: 117,392) (Annapolis). Anne (Howard) Arundel. Daughter of Thomas, Lord Arundel of Wardour; wife of Cecilius Calvert, the second Lord Baltimore. -- Riley, Elihu Samuel, A history of Anne Arundel County, Annapolis, Md.: C.G. Feldmeyer, 1905; 169 p.

Anoka, Minn. (est. May 23, 1857; 425 sq. mi.; 1970 pop.: 154,556; 1960: 85,916; 1950: 35,579) (Anoka). Dakota or Sioux Indian word for "on both sides of the river." -- Goodrich, Albert Moses, History of Anoka County, Minneapolis, Minn.: Hennepin Pub. Co., 1905; 320 p.

Anson, N.C. (est. session Mar. 17, 1749; 533 sq. mi.; 1970 pop.: 23,488; 1960: 24,962; 1950: 26,781) (Wadesboro). George Lord Anson (1697-1762). English admiral circumnavigated the world 1744; First Lord of the Admiralty 1751-56 and 1757-62.

Antelope, Neb. (est. Mar. 1, 1871; org. Oct. 1872; 853 sq. mi.; 1970 pop.: 9,047; 1960: 10,176; 1950: 11,624) (Neligh). Descriptive. -- Leach, A. J., History of Antelope County, Neb., Chicago: Lakeside Press, 1967; 262 p.

Antrim, Mich. (est. Apr. 1, 1840; org. 1863; 477 sq. mi.; 1970 pop.: 12,612; 1960: 10,373; 1950: 10,721) (Bellaire). Antrim County, Ireland. Originally Meegisee County, name changed to Antrim County on March 8, 1843. Act 67.

Apache, Ariz. (est. Feb. 14, 1879; 11,174 sq. mi.; 1970 pop.: 32,298; 1960: 30,438; 1509: 27,767) (St. Johns). ("The Land of Pine and Painted Desert"). Apache Indian tribe meaning "enemy."

Appanoose, Iowa. (est. Feb. 17, 1843; org. Jan. 3, 1846, eff. Aug. 3, 1846; 523 sq. mi.; 1970 pop.: 15,007; 1960: 16,015; 1950: 19,683) (Centerville). Appanoose. Indian chief of the Sacs and Foxes Indian tribes. -- Taylor, Lewis L., Past and present of Appanoose County, Chicago: S.J. Clarke Pub. Co., 1913; 2 vol.

Appling, Ga. (est. Dec. 15, 1818; 454 sq. mi.; 1970 pop.: 12,726; 1960: 13,246; 1950: 14,003) (Baxley). Daniel Appling (1787-1818). Lt. col. U.S. Army 1805; fought in War of 1812; bvt. lt. col. at Battle of Sandy Creek 1814; awarded sword by legislature of Georgia but died before presentation.

Appomattox, Va. (est. Feb. 8, 1845; 343 sq. mi.; 1970 pop.: 9, 784; 1960: 9, 148; 1950: 8, 764) (Appomattox). Algonquin Indian word meaning "a sinuous tidal estuary." -- Stanley, Vara (Smith), A history of Appomattox County, 1845-1965, Appomattox, Va.: Times-Virginian, 1965; 92 p.

Aransas, Tex. (est. Sept. 18, 1871; 276 sq. mi.; 1970 pop.: 8, 902; 1960: 7, 006; 1950: 4, 252) (Rockport). Rio Nuestra Señora de Aranzazu, a river named for a Spanish palace.

Arapahoe, Colo. (est. Nov. 1, 1861; 827 sq. mi.; 1970 pop.: 162, 142; 1960: 113, 426; 1950: 52, 125) (Littleton). Arapaho Indian tribe.

Archer, Tex. (est. Jan. 22, 1858; 917 sq. mi.; 1970 pop.: 5, 759; 1960: 6, 110; 1950: 6, 816) (Archer City). Dr. Branch Tanner Archer (1790-1856). One of the three commissioners sent by Tex. to Washington, D.C., to solicit U.S. aid 1835; speaker Tex. house of representatives 1836; Tex. legislature 1836; Tex. Secretary of War 1836-42.

Archuleta, Colo. (est. Apr. 14, 1885; 1, 364 sq. mi.; 1970 pop.: 2, 733; 1960: 2, 629; 1950: 3, 030) (Pagosa Springs). Antonio D. Archuleta. Colorado state senator 1885.

Arenac, Mich. (est. Mar. 2, 1831, org. 1883; 368 sq. mi.; 1970 pop.: 11, 149; 1960: 9, 860; 1950: 9, 644) (Standish). Coined word meaning "sandy place" from "arena" with a terminal meaning "place of."

Arkansas, Ark. (est. Dec. 31, 1813; 1, 035 sq. mi.; 1970 pop.: 23, 347; 1960: 23, 355; 1950: 23, 665) (De Witt and Stuttgart). Arkansas Indians*.

Arlington, Va. (est. Mar. 13, 1847; 24 sq. mi.; 1970 pop.: 174, 284; (1960: 163, 401; 1950: 135, 449) (Arlington). Named for old home of George Washington Parke Custis who named his estate to honor the earl of Arlington. (Formerly Alexandria County, named changed to Arlington County, Mar. 16, 1920). -- Templeman, Eleanor Lee (Reading), Arlington heritage: vignettes of a Virginia county, Arlington, Va., 1959; 200 p.

Armstrong, Pa. (est. Mar. 12, 1800; 660 sq. mi.; 1970 pop.: 75, 590; 1960: 79, 524; 1950: 80, 842) (Kittanning). John Armstrong (1758-1843). On staffs of Gen. Gates and Mercer in Revolutionary War; as aide carried Gen. Mercer from Princeton battlefield; Continental Congress 1778-80 and 1787-88; secretary of state of Pa. 1783-87; Senator from N.Y., 1800-02 and 1803-04; U.S. Minister to France 1804-10 also U.S. Minister to Spain 1806; brig. gen. 1812; U.S. Secretary of War in cabinet of President Madison 1813-14. -- Smith, Robert Walter, History of Armstrong County, Chicago: Waterman, Watkins & Co., 1883; 624 p.

Armstrong, S. D. (est. Jan. 8, 1873; (Part of Dewey County) 1970 pop.: 5,170; 1960: 5,257) Moses Kimball Armstrong (1832-1906). Surveyor; Dakota territorial legislature 1861-63; editor "Dakota Union" 1864; clerk Dakota supreme court 1865; treasurer Dakota territory 1865-68; Dakota territorial council 1866-67 and 1870-71; Delegate from Dakota Territory 1871-75. Armstrong County consolidated with Dewey County (see page 126).

Armstrong, Tex. (est. Aug. 21, 1876; org. Feb. 10, 1890; 909 sq. mi.; 1970 pop.: 1,895; 1960: 1,966; 1950: 2,215) (Claude). Armstrong family, pioneers. -- A collection of memories, a history of Armstrong County 1876-1965, Hereford, Texas: Armstrong County Historical Assn., 1965; 567 p.

Aroostook, Me. (est. Mar. 16, 1839, eff. May 1, 1839; 6,805 sq. mi.; 1970 pop.: 92,463; 1960: 106,064; 1950: 96,039) (Houlton). ("The Potato Empire of the Nation"; "The Second Richest Agricultural County in the United States"). Indian word for "clear river." -- Hamlin, Helen, Pine, potatoes and people, New York: W. W. Norton, 1948; 238 p.

Arthur, Neb. (est. Mar. 31, 1887; 706 sq. mi.; 1970 pop.: 606; 1960: 680; 1950: 803) (Arthur). Chester Alan Arthur (1830-1886). Twenty-first President of the U. S. Brig. gen. and Q. M. gen. 1860-62; collector of port of New York 1871-78; Vice President of the U. S., 1881; became President on death of President Garfield.

Ascension, La. (est. Mar. 31, 1807; 291 sq. mi.; 1970 pop.: 37,086; 1960: 27,927; 1950: 22,387) (Donaldsonville). The Ascension of Jesus. -- Marchand, Sidney Albert, Story of Ascension Parish, La., Baton Rouge, La.: J. E. Ortlieb Printing Co., 1931; 194 p.

Ashe, N. C. (est. session Nov. 18, 1799; 427 sq. mi.; 1970 pop.: 19,571; 1960: 19,768; 1950: 21,878) (Jefferson). Samuel Ashe (1725-1813). Ninth governor of N. C. One of the N. C. Council of Thirteen before the const. and served as its president 1776; Halifax convention 1776; state constitutional convention 1776; chief justice of N. C., 1777-95; governor of N. C., 1795-98. -- Fletcher, Arthur L., Ashe County, a history, Jefferson, N. C.: Ashe County Research Assn., 1963; 403 p.

Ashland, Ohio. (est. Feb. 24, 1846; 426 sq. mi.; 1970 pop.: 43,303; 1960: 38,771; 1950: 33,040) (Ashland). "Ashland" the name of Henry Clay's estate near Lexington, Ky. -- Baughman, Abraham J., History of Ashland

County, Chicago: S. J. Clarke Pub. Co., 1909; 864 p. -- Hill, George William, History of Ashland County, Cleveland, Ohio: Williams Bros., 1880; 408 p.

Ashland, Wis. (est. Mar. 27, 1860; 1,037 sq. mi.; 1970 pop.: 16,743; 1960: 17,375; 1950: 19,461) (Ashland). "Ashland."*

Ashley, Ark. (est. Nov. 30, 1848, eff. Jan. 1, 1849; 933 sq. mi.; 1970 pop.: 24,976; 1960: 24,220; 1950: 25,660) (Hamburg). Chester Ashley (1790-1848). Moved to Ark., 1820; Senator from Ark., 1844-48. -- Etheridge, Y. W., History of Ashley County, Arkansas, Van Buren, Ark.: Press-Argus, 1959; 173 p.

Ashtabula, Ohio. (est. Feb. 10, 1807, eff. June 7, 1807; 706 sq. mi.; 1970 pop.: 98,237; 1960: 93,067; 1950: 78,695) (Jefferson). Indian word meaning "fish river."

Asotin, Wash. (est. Oct. 27, 1883; 627 sq. mi.; 1970 pop.: 13,799; 1960: 12,909; 1950: 10,878) (Asotin). Indian word meaning "eel creek."

Assumption, La. (est. Mar. 31, 1807; 484 sq. mi.; 1970 pop.: 19,654; 1960: 17,991; 1950: 17,278) (Napoleonville). The Assumption; festival of the assumption of the blessed virgin Mary, the departure from life of the blessed virgin Mary and her transition into the kingdom of her son [Aug. 15].

Atascosa, Tex. (est. Jan. 25, 1856; 1,206 sq. mi.; 1970 pop.: 18,696; 1960: 18,828; 1950: 20,048) (Jourdanton). Spanish word for "boggy."

Atchison, Kans. (est. Aug. 30, 1855; 421 sq. mi.; 1970 pop.: 19,165; 1960: 20,898; 1950: 21,496) (Atchison). David Rice Atchison (1807-1886). Missouri house of representatives 1834 and 1838; judge Platte County circuit court 1841; Senator from Mo., 1843-55; several times elected president pro tempore of the Senate. -- Ingalls, Sheffield, History of Atchison County, Kans., Lawrence, Kan.: Standard Pub. Co., 1916; 887 p.

Atchison, Mo. (est. Feb. 23, 1843, unnumbered; 549 sq. mi.; 1970 pop.: 9,240; 1960: 9,213; 1950: 11,127) (Rockport). David Rice Atchison.* (Formerly Allen County, name changed Feb. 14, 1845) -- Atchison County Mail, Biographical history, Atchison County, Missouri, Rock Port, Mo.: Atchison County Mail, 1905; 797 p.

Athens, Ohio. (est. Feb. 20, 1805; eff. Mar. 1, 1805; 504 sq. mi.; 1970 pop.: 54,889; 1960: 46,998; 1950: 45,839) (Athens). Athens, capital of Greece. -- Martzolff, Clement Luther, A brief history of Athens County, Athens, Ohio: Clement L. Martzolff, 1916; 40 p. -- Walker, Charles Manning, History of Athens County, Cincinnati, Ohio: R. Clarke & Co., 1869; 600 p.

Atkinson, Ga. (est. Aug. 15, 1917; 330 sq. mi.; 1970 pop.: 5,879; 1960: 6,188; 1950: 7,362) (Pearson). William Yates Atkinson (1854-1899). Fifty-third governor of Ga. Elected Ga. assembly 1886; governor of Ga., 1894-99.

Atlantic, N.J. (est. Feb. 7, 1837; 575 sq. mi.; 1970 pop.: 175,043; 1960: 160,880; 1950: 132,399) (Mays Landing). ("The County on the Move"; "The Fishing Paradise of the World"). Atlantic Ocean -- Atlantic County's Historical Society, Early history of Atlantic County, N. J., Kutztown, Pa., The Press of the Kutztown Pub. Co., 1915.

Atoka, Okla. (est. July 16, 1907; 992 sq. mi.; 1970 pop.: 10,972; 1960: 10,352; 1950: 14,269) (Atoka). Atoka, Choctaw sub-chief. Capt. Atoka, famous ball player.

Attala, Miss. (est. Dec. 23, 1833; 715 sq. mi.; 1970 pop.: 19,570; 1960: 21,335; 1950: 26,652) (Kosciusko). Attala. Indian heroine.

Audrain, Mo. (est. Jan. 12, 1831, org. Dec. 17, 1836; 692 sq. mi.; 1970 pop.: 25,362; 1960: 26,079; 1950: 23,829) (Mexico). James H. Audrain (1782-1831). Missouri legislature. -- Schooley, Herschel, Centennial history of Audrain County, Mexico, Mo.: McIntyre Pub. Co., 1937; 304 p.

Audubon, Iowa. (est. Jan. 15, 1851; 448 sq. mi.; 1970 pop.: 9,595; 1960: 10,919; 1950: 11,579) (Audubon). John James Audubon (1785-1851). Naturalist and ornithologist; ninth volume "Birds of America" completed 1839. -- Andrews, Henry Franklin, ed., History of Audubon County, Indianapolis, 1915; 876 p.

Auglaize, Ohio. (est. Feb. 14, 1848; 400 sq. mi.; 1970 pop.: 38,602; 1960: 36,147; 1950: 30,637) (Wapakoneta). Indian word meaning "fallen timbers." -- McMurray, William James, History of Auglaize County, Indianapolis: Historical Pub. Co., 1923; 2 vol. -- Simkins, Joshua Dean, Early history of Auglaize County, St. Marys, Ohio: Argus Printing Co., 1901; 119 p.

Augusta, Va. (est. Aug. 1, 1738 sess.; 999 sq. mi.; 1970 pop.: 44,220; 1960: 37,363; 1950: 34,154) (Staunton). Augusta (1719-1772), princess of Saxe-Coburg-Gotha, daughter of King George II, wife of Frederick, prince of Wales, mother of King George III of England. - Peyton, John Lewis, History of Augusta County, Bridgewater, Va., 1953; 428 p. -- Waddell, Joseph Addison, Annals of Augusta County, Va., from 1726 to 1871; Bridgewater, Va., C. J. Carrier Co., 1958; (reprint) 545 p.

Aurora, S. D. (est. Feb. 22, 1879; 711 sq. mi.; 1970 pop.: 4,183; 1960: 4,749; 1950: 5,020) (Plankinton). Aurora, wife of Titan Astraeus, Roman goddess of the dawn.

Austin, Tex. (est. Mar. 17, 1836; 662 sq. mi.; 1970 pop.: 13,831; 1960: 13,777; 1950: 14,663) (Belleville). Stephen Fuller Austin (1793-1836). Mo. territorial legislature 1814-20; judge first judicial district of Ark. 1820; surveyed and explored Tex. area for colonization 1822; candidate for the presidency of the Republic of Tex. 1836; defeated by Sam Houston 1836; appointed Secretary of State by Houston 1836.

Autauga, Ala. (est. Nov. 21, 1818; 599 sq. mi.; 1970 pop.: 24,460; 1960: 18,739; 1950: 18,186) (Prattville). Indian word meaning "land of plenty."

Avery, N.C. (est. Feb. 23, 1911; 247 sq. mi.; 1970 pop.: 12,655; 1960: 12,009; 1950: 13,352) (Newland). Waightstill Avery (1745-1821). Mecklenburg convention 1775; N.C. legislature 1776; attorney gen. of N.C., 1777-79; Revolutionary War col. of militia Jones Co. 1779; N.C. house of commons 1782-83 and 1793; N.C. senate 1796. Challenged to duel by Andrew Jackson. -- Cooper, Horton, History of Avery County, Asheville, N.C.: Biltmore Press, 1964; 100 p.

Avoyelles, La. (est. Mar. 31, 1807; 847 sq. mi.; 1970 pop.: 37,751; 1960: 37,606; 1950: 38,031) (Marksville). Avoyelles Indian tribe. -- Saucier, Corinne L., History of Avoyelles Parish, La., New Orleans, La.: Pelican Pub. Co., 1943; 542 p.

B

Baca, Colo. (est. Apr. 16, 1889; 2,565 sq. mi.; 1970 pop.: 5,674; 1960: 6,310; 1950: 7,964) (Springfield). Baca family of Trinidad, Colo., one of whom was the first settler on Two Buttes Creek.

Bacon, Ga. (est. July 27, 1914; 271 sq. mi.; 1970 pop.: 8,233; 1960: 8,359; 1950: 8,940) (Alma). Augustus Octavius Bacon (1839-1914). Adj. Ninth Ga. Regiment 1861-62; capt. Confederate army, Ga., house of representatives 1871-86 serving 2 years as speaker pro tempore and 8 years as speaker; Senator from Ga., 1895-1914.

Bailey, Tex. (est. Aug. 21, 1876; 832 sq. mi.; 1970 pop.: 8,487; 1960: 9,090; 1950: 7,592) (Muleshoe). Peter James Bailey (1812-1836). Private of Springfield, Ky., killed in the defense of the Alamo 1836.

Baker, Fla. (est. Feb. 8, 1861; 585 sq. mi.; 1970 pop.: 9,242; 1960: 7,363; 1950: 6,313) (Macclenny). ("Opportunities Unlimited"; "The Nursery Capital of the State

(10,000,000 ornamental plants, fruit trees and shade trees of 1,000 acres)"). James McNair Baker (1821-1892). Solicitor of eastern circuit 1853-59; judge of eastern circuit 1859-62; Fla. senate 1862-64; Fla. supreme court associate justice 1866; judge 4th judicial circuit 1881.

Baker, Ga. (est. Dec. 12, 1825; org. Dec. 24, 1825; 357 sq. mi.; 1970 pop.: 3,875; 1960: 4,543; 1950: 5,952) (Newton). John Baker, Col.

Baker, Ore. (est. Sept. 22, 1862; 3,084 sq. mi.; 1970 pop.: 14,919; 1960: 17,295; 1950: 16,175) (Baker). Edward Dickinson Baker (1811-1861). Illinois house of representatives 1837; Ill., senate 1840-44; col. Fourth Ill., Volunteer Infantry 1846; Representative from Ill., 1845-47 and 1849-51; Senator from Ore. 1860-61; col. of 71st regiment Pa. Volunteer Infantry 1861; maj. gen. of volunteers 1861; killed at battle of Balls Bluff, Oct. 21, 1861. -- An illustrated history of Baker, Malheur and Harney counties, Spokane, Wash.: Western Hist. Pub. Co., 1902; 788 p.

Baldwin, Ala. (est. Dec. 21, 1809; 1,613 sq. mi.; 1970 pop.: 59,382; 1960: 49,088; 1950: 40,977) (Bay Minette). Abraham Baldwin (1754-1807). Tutor at Yale 1775-79; chaplain Second Continental brigade 1777-83; Ga. house of representatives 1785; president of Univ. of Ga. 1786-1801; Continental Congress 1785-88; federal constitutional convention 1787; Representative from Ga., 1789-99; Senator from Ga., 1799-1807.

Baldwin, Ga. (est. May 11, 1803; org. 1805; 307 sq. mi.; 1970 pop.: 34,240; 1960: 34,064; 1950: 29,706) (Milledgeville). Abraham Baldwin*. Cook, Anna Maria, (Green), History of Baldwin County, Ga., Anderson, S. C.: Keys-Hearn Printing Co., 1925; 484 p.

Ballard, Ky. (est. Feb. 15, 1842; 259 sq. mi.; 1970 pop.: 8,276; 1960: 8,291; 1950: 8,543) (Wickliffe). Bland W. Ballard (1761-1853). Accompanied George Rogers Clark on Piqua expedition, guided gens. Scot and Wilkinson; capt. and maj. in War of 1812; wounded and captured at Battle of the River Raisin.

Baltimore, Md. (est. 1659; the Proprietary's Irish Barony; 610 sq. mi.; 1970 pop.: 621,077; 1960: 492,428; 1950: 270,273) (Towson). Cecilius (or Cecil) Calvert (1605-1675). Second baron of Baltimore; son of George Calvert; never visited Maryland tract but managed it from England.

Bamberg, S. C. (est. Feb. 25, 1897; 395 sq. mi.; 1970 pop.: 15,950; 1960: 16,274; 1950: 17,533) (Bamberg). Bamberg family.

Bandera, Tex. (est. Jan. 26, 1856; 765 sq. mi.; 1970 pop.: 4,747; 1960: 3,892; 1950: 4,410) (Bandera). Spanish word for "flag." (Bandera Mts.) -- Hunter, John Marvin, Pioneer History of Bandera County, Bandera, Texas: Hunter's Printing House, 1922: 287 p.

Banks, Ga. (est. Dec. 11, 1858; 222 sq. mi.; 1970 pop.: 6,833; 1960: 6,497; 1950: 6,935) (Homer). Richard Banks. Physician.

Banner, Neb. (738 sq. mi.; 1970 pop.: 1,034; 1960: 1,269; 1950: 1,325) Descriptive for "the banner state."

Bannock, Idaho. (est. Mar. 6, 1893; 1,820 sq. mi.; 1970 pop.: 52,200; 1960: 49,342; 1950: 41,745) (Pocatello). Bannock Indians. Scotch word meaning "a thick cake of oatmeal baked over a fire." -- Saunders, Arthur C., The History of Bannock County, Pocatello, Idaho: The Tribune Co., 1915; 143 p.

Baraga, Mich. (est. Feb. 19, 1875; org. 1875; 904 sq. mi.; 1970 pop.: 7,789; 1960: 7,151; 1950: 8,037) (L'Anse). Frederic Baraga (1797-1868). Austrian born; ordained priest 1823; came to U.S. in 1830; wrote Chippewa grammar 1850 and Chippewa dictionary 1853; consecrated bishop 1853; established schools in Ohio, Mich., for Chippewa, Ottawa Indians 1830-68. (904 sq. mi.).

Barber, Kan. (est. Feb. 26, 1867; 1146 sq. mi.; 1970 pop.: 7,016; 1960: 8,713; 1950: 8,521) (Medicine Lodge). Thomas W. Barber (- 1855). Free state martyr, murdered near Lawrence, Kan., Dec. 6, 1855. Originally spelled Barbour, changed Mar. 1, 1883).

Barbour, Ala. (est. Dec. 18, 1832; 899 sq. mi.; 1970 pop.: 22,543; 1960: 24,700; 1950: 28,892) (Clayton and Eufaula). James Barbour (1775-1842). Nineteenth gov. of Va. (commonwealth). Va. house of delegates 1796-1812; speaker house of delegates 1809-1812; governor of Va., 1812-14; Senator from Va., 1815-25; U.S. Secretary of War in cabinet of Pres. J.Q. Adams 1825-28; U.S. Minister to England 1828-29. -- Thompson, Mattie Crocker, History of Barbour County, Ala., Eufaula, Ala., 1939; 574 p.

Barbour, W. Va. (est. Mar. 3, 1843; 345 sq. mi.; 1970 pop.: 14,030; 1960: 15,474; 1950: 19,745) (Philippi). Philip Pendleton Barbour (1783-1841). Va. house of delegates 1812-14; Representative from Va., 1814-25; Speaker of the House 1821-22; judge of Va., general court 1826-27; Representative from Va., 1827-30; judge of the U.S. Circuit Court for the Eastern District of Va., Associate Justice U.S. Supreme Court 1836-41. -- Maxwell, Hu., History of Barbour County, West Virginia,

Morgantown, W. Va.: Acme Pub. Co., 1899; 517 p.

Barnes, N. D. (est. Jan. 14, 1875; 1,486 sq. mi.; 1970 pop.: 14,669; 1960: 16,719; 1950: 16,884) (Valley City). A. H. Barnes. Judge of federal district court.

Barnstable, Mass. (est. June 2, 1685; 399 sq. mi.; 1970 pop.: 96,656; 1960: 70,286; 1950: 46,805) (Barnstable). Named for Barnstable, England. -- Kittredge, Henry Crocker, Barnstable, 1639-1939, Barnstable: Barnstable Tercentenary Committee, 1939; 39 p. -- Deyo, S. L., History of Barnstable County, New York: H. W. Blake & Co., 1890; 1010 p.

Barnwell, S. C. (est. 1798; 553 sq. mi.; 1970 pop.: 17,176; 1960: 17,659; 1950: 17,266) (Barnwell). Barnwell family.

Barren, Ky. (est. Dec. 20, 1798, eff. May 10, 1799; 486 sq. mi.; 1970 pop.: 28,677; 1960: 28,303; 1950: 28,461) (Glasgow). Descriptive of the treeless prairie. -- Gorin, Franklin, The times of long ago, Barren County, Kentucky, Louisville, Ky.: J. P. Morton & Co., Inc., 1929; 131 p.

Barron, Wis. (est. Mar. 19, 1859; 866 sq. mi.; 1970 pop.: 33,955; 1960: 34,270; 1950: 34,703) (Barron). Henry D. Barron. Judge of the Circuit Court. (Formerly Dallas Co. name changed to Barron County, Mar. 4, 1869), Chap. 75.

Barrow, Ga. (est. July 7, 1914; 168 sq. mi.; 1970 pop.: 16,859; 1960: 14,485; 1950: 13,115) (Winder). David Crenshaw Barrow (1852-1929). Adjunct professor of mathematics Univ. of Ga. 1878; professor of engineering 1883; professor of mathematics 1889; chancellor of the Univ. of Ga. 1907-1925.

Barry, Mich. (est. Oct. 29, 1829, org. 1839; 549 sq. mi.; 1970 pop.: 38,166; 1960: 31,738; 1950: 26,183) (Hastings). William Taylor Barry (1784-1835). Ky. house of representatives 1807; a Representative from Ky., 1810-11; War of 1812 aide de camp to gen. Shelby; at Battle of the Thames, Oct. 5, 1813; speaker Ky., house of representatives 1814; Senator from Ky., 1814-16; judge of circuit court for the 11th district of Ky., 1816-17; Ky. state senate 1817-21; elected lt. gov. of Ky. 1820; Ky. secretary of state 1824; chief justice Ky., court of appeals 1825; Postmaster gen. of the U. S. 1829-35; appointed Envoy Extraordinary and Minister Plenipotentiary to Spain and died en route. -- History of Allegan and Barry counties, Philadelphia: D. W. Ensign & Co., 1880; 521 p.

Barry, Mo. (est. Jan. 5, 1835; 800 sq. mi.; 1970 pop.: 19,597; 1960: 18,921; 1950: 21,755) (Cassville). William Taylor Barry*. -- Matthews, Addah Longley, Early Barry County, Monett, Mo., Barry County Hist. Soci., 1965; 334 p.

Bartholomew, Ind. (est. Jan. 8, 1821, eff. Feb. 12, 1821; org. Jan. 9, 1821; 402 sq. mi.; 1970 pop.: 57,022; 1960: 48,198; 1950: 36,108) (Columbus). Joseph Bartholomew.

Barton, Kan. (est. Feb. 26, 1867; 892 sq. mi.; 1970 pop.: 30,663; 1960: 32,368; 1950: 29,909) (Great Bend). Clara Barton (1821-1912). Volunteer nurse in Civil War, organizer and first president of American Red Cross 1881. -- Great Bend Tribune, Biographical history of Barton County, Kansas, Great Bend, Kan.: Great Bend Tribune, 1912; 318 p.

Barton, Mo. (est. Dec. 12, 1855; 594 sq. mi.; 1970 pop.: 10,431; 1960: 11,113; 1950: 12,678) (Lamar). David Barton (1788-1837). Attorney gen. of Mo., 1813; first circuit judge of Howard county 1815 and presiding judge 1816; territorial house of representatives 1818; president of Mo. constitutional convention 1820; Senator from Mo., 1821-31; Mo. state senate 1834; circuit judge at Boonville 1835.

Bartow, Ga. (est. Dec. 3, 1832; 471 sq. mi.; 1970 pop.: 32,663; 1960: 28,267; 1950: 27,370) (Cartersville). Francis S. Bartow (-1861). Gen. fell at Manassas Plains, July 21, 1861. (Formerly Cass County, name changed to Bartow County, Dec. 6, 1861) Act 97. -- Cunyus, Lucy Josephine, History of Bartow County, formerly Cass, Cartersville, Ga.: Tribune Pub. Co., 1933; 343 p.

Bastrop, Tex. (est. Mar. 17, 1836; 885 sq. mi.; 1970 pop.: 17,297; 1960: 16,925; 1950: 19,622) (Bastrop). Felipe Enrique Neri, Baron de Bastrop (-1828). Est. colony of Germans 1823, later abandoned because of Indian troubles; first commissioner of Austin's colony. -- Bastrop Historical Society, In the shadow of the lost pines, a history of Bastrop County and her people, Bastrop, Texas: Bastrop Advertiser, 1955; 44 p.

Bates, Mo. (est. Jan. 29, 1841; 841 sq. mi.; 1970 pop.: 15,468; 1960: 15,905; 1950: 17,534) (Butler). Frederick Bates (1777-1825). Second governor of Mo. Judge of Mich. territory 1805; secretary of Louisiana territory 1806; sixth governor of Mo. territory; eighth governor Mo. terr. 1809-10; tenth governor Mo. terr. 1812-13; Mo. constitutional convention 1820; second governor of Mo., 1824-25. -- Tathwell, S.L., Old settler's history of Bates County, Missouri, Amsterdam, Mo.: Tathwell & Maxey, 1900; 212 p.

Bath, Ky. (est. Jan. 15, 1811; 287 sq. mi.; 1970 pop.: 9,235; 1960: 9,114; 1950: 10,410) (Owingsville). Descriptive word. -- Richards, John Adair, A history of Bath County, Yuma, Ariz.: Southwest Printers, 1961; 592 p.

Bath, Va. (est. Dec. 14, 1790; 540 sq. mi.; 1970 pop.: 5,192; 1960: 5,335; 1950: 6,296) (Warm Springs). ("An Exciting Year 'Round Playground in the Heart of Virginia's Alleghenies"; "Historic Past, Active Present, Progressive Future"; "Nature's Gift to Everyone"; "The County Where You Enjoy Life As It Was Meant To Be"; "Year 'Round Playground"). Descriptive word for warm sulphur springs. -- Morton, Oren Frederic, Annals of Bath County, Staunton, Va.: McClure Co., 1917; 208 p.

Baxter, Ark. (est. Mar. 24, 1873; 571 sq. mi.; 1970 pop.: 15,319; 1960: 9,943; 1950: 11,683) (Mountain Home). Elisha Baxter (1827-1899). Eleventh governor of Ark. Ark. legislature 1854 and 1858; raised Fourth Ark., mounted infantry; chief justice of Ark., 1864; register in bankruptcy for the U.S., and circuit judge 1868-72; governor of Ark., 1872-74.

Bay, Fla. (est. Apr. 24, 1913; 753 sq. mi.; 1970 pop.: 75,283; 1960: 67,131; 1950: 42,689) (Panama City). Descriptive (St. Andrew's Bay).

Bay, Mich. (est. Feb. 17, 1857, eff. Apr. 20, 1857; 446 sq. mi.; 1970 pop.: 117,339; 1960: 107,042; 1950: 88,461) (Bay City). Descriptive. -- Butterfield, George Ernest, Bay County, Past and Present, Bay City, Mich.: Bay City Public Schools, 1957; 242 p. -- Gansser, Augustus H., History of Bay County, Chicago: Richmond & Arnold, 1905; 726 p.

Bayfield, Wis. (est. Feb. 19, 1845; 1,474 sq. mi.; 1970 pop.: 11,683; 1960: 11,910; 1950: 13,760) (Washburn). Henry W. Bayfield. Admiral of Royal Navy of England. (Formerly LaPointe County) Chap. 146. Name changed Apr. 12, 1866.

Baylor, Tex. (est. Feb. 1, 1858; 857 sq. mi.; 1970 pop.: 5,221; 1960: 5,893; 1950: 6,875) (Seymour). Henry Weidner Baylor (1818-1853). In Comanche campaign 1840; surgeon in John C. Hay's Tex. Rangers in Mexican War.

Beadle, S.D. (est. Feb. 22, 1879; 1,261 sq. mi.; 1970 pop.: 20,877; 1960: 21,682; 1950: 21,082) (Huron). William Henry Harrison Beadle (1838-1915). In Civil War, private, first lt., capt. Co. A. 31st Indiana Volunteer Infantry, lt. col. Mich. sharpshooters, bvt. col. of volunteers, bvt. brig. gen.; provost marshal at Utica 1865; mustered out 1866; surveyor gen. of Dakota Terr. 1869-73; government surveyor in Dakota 1873-79; Dakota territorial house of representatives 1877; private secretary to Gov. Howard 1878; supt. of public instruction 1879-86; director of an Indian school near Salem, Ore.,

1888-89; president of S. D. State Normal School 1889-1905; prof. emeritus of history 1905-11. -- Jones, Mildred (McEwen), Early Beadle County, 1879 to 1900, Huron? S. D., 1961; 104 p.

Bear Lake, Idaho (est. Jan. 5, 1875; 988 sq. mi.; 1970 pop.: 5,801; 1960: 7,148; 1950: 6,834) (Paris). Descriptive.

Beaufort, N. C. (est. Dec. 3, 1705; 831 sq. mi.; 1970 pop.: 35,980; 1960: 36,014; 1950: 37,134) (Washington). Henry Somerset IV, (1684-1714), Duke of Beaufort. Bought share of Duke of Albemarle and became one of the Lord Proprietors of S. C. 1709. (First named Archdale for Gov. John Archdale, (name changed to Beaufort about 1712). -- Reed, C. Wingate, Beaufort County; two centuries of history, Raleigh? N. C., 1962, 244 p.

Beaufort, S. C. (est. Mar. 12, 1785; 672 sq. mi.; 1970 pop.: 51,136; 1960: 44,187; 1950: 26,993) (Beaufort). Beaufort, France; Duke of Beaufort.

Beauregard, La. (est. June 12, 1912; 1,172 sq. mi.; 1970 pop.: 22,888; 1960: 19,191; 1950: 17,766) (De Ridder). Pierre Gustave Toutant Beauregard (1818-1893). Graduated U. S. Military Academy 1838; served in engineering dept. Army 1840-45; wounded twice in Mexican War 1846; bvt. maj; capt. of engineers 1853; supt. U. S. Military Academy 1861; resigned; joined Confederate Army; defended Charleston, S. C. and directed bombardment of Ft. Sumter, Apr. 12, 1861; at Battle of Bull Run; promoted to gen. 1862; president of New Orleans, Jackson and Mississippi Railroad Co., adjt. gen. of La.; manager of La. state lottery.

Beaver, Okla. (est. July 16, 1907; 1,793 sq. mi.; 1970 pop.: 6,282; 1960: 6,965; 1950: 7,411) (Beaver). Descriptive; English translation of Spanish word "nutria."

Beaver, Pa. (est. Mar. 12, 1800; 441 sq. mi.; 1970 pop.: 208,418; 1960: 206,948; 1950: 175,197) (Beaver). Descriptive. -- Bausman, Joseph Henderson, History of Beaver County, New York: Knickerbocker Press, 1904; 2 vol.

Beaver, Utah. (est. Jan. 5, 1856; 2,587 sq. mi.; 1970 pop.: 3,800; 1960: 4,331; 1950: 4,856) (Beaver). Descriptive.

Beaverhead, Mont. (est. Feb. 2, 1865; 5,556 sq. mi.; 1970 pop.: 8,187; 1960: 7,194; 1950: 6,671) (Dillon). Descriptive of a rock resembling a beaver head in Beaverhead River.

Becker, Minn. (est. Mar. 18, 1858; 1,315 sq. mi.; 1970 pop.: 24,372; 1960: 23,959; 1950: 24,836) (Detroit Lakes). George Loomis Becker (1829-1904). Brig. gen. 1858;

Mayor of St. Paul 1856; land commissioner of St. Paul and Pacific RR Co., 1862; Minn. legislature 1868-71; Minn., railroad and warehouse commission 1885-1901.

Beckham, Okla. (est. July 16, 1907; 898 sq. mi.; 1970 pop.: 15, 754; 1960: 17, 782; 1950: 21, 627) (Sayre). John Crepps Wickliffe Beckham (1869-1940). Thirty-fifth gov. of Ky. Ky. house of representatives 1899; gov. of Ky., 1900-07; Senator from Ky., 1915-21.

Bedford, Pa. (est. Mar. 9, 1771; 1, 018 sq. mi.; 1970 pop.: 42, 353; 1960: 42, 451; 1950: 40, 775) (Bedford), Bedford, England; named for John Russell II (1710-1771) Duke of Bedford. First Lord of the Admiralty 1744; Privy councillor 1744; maj. gen. 1755; lord lt. of Ireland 1756-61; chancellor of Univ. of Dublin 1765. -- Blackburn, E. Howard and Welfley, W. H., History of Bedford and Somerset Counties, New York: Lewis Pub. Co., 1906, 3 vol.

Bedford, Tenn. (est. Dec. 3, 1807; 482 sq. mi.; 1970 pop.: 25, 039; 1960: 23, 150; 1950: 23, 627) (Shelbyville). Thomas Bedford. Capt. lt. col.

Bedford, Va. (est. Feb. 27, 1752 sess, 774 sq. mi.; 1970 pop.: 26, 728; 1960: 31, 028; 1950: 29, 627) (Bedford). John Russell*. -- Parker, Lula Eastman (Jeter), The History of Bedford County, Bedford, Va.: Bedford Democrat, c. 1954; 135 p.

Bee, Tex. (est. Dec. 8, 1857; 842 sq. mi.; 1970 pop.: 22, 737; 1960: 23, 755; 1950: 18, 174) (Beeville). Barnard E. Bee (1787-1853). Joined Tex. army under Thomas J. Rusk; secretary of treasury and state under David G. Burnet in ad interim govt. secretary of war under Sam Houston; Secretary of State under Mirabeau; Minister from Tex. to the U. S., 1838-41; opposed annexation of Tex.; returned to S. C. 1846. -- Madray, I. C., A History of Bee County, Beeville, Tex.: Beeville Pub. Co., 1939; 133 p. -- Rountree, Joseph Gustave, History of Bee County, Texas, Beeville, Texas, 1960; 56 p.

Belknap, N. H. (est. Dec. 22, 1840; 401 sq. mi.; 1970 pop.: 32, 367; 1960: 28, 912; 1950: 26, 632) (Laconia). Jeremy Belknap (1744-1798). Pastor, Dover, N. H., 1767-86; pastor, Federal St. Church, Boston, Mass., 1787-98; founded Mass. Historical Soc. 1792; wrote the "History of New Hampshire" and other books. -- Hurd, D. Hamilton, History of Merrimack and Belknap counties, Philadelphia: J. W. Lewis & Co., 1885; 915 p.

Bell, Ky. (est. Feb. 28, 1867; 370 sq. mi.; 1970 pop.: 31, 087; 1960: 35, 336; 1950: 47, 602) (Pineville). Joshua Fry Bell (1811-1870). Representative from Ky. 1845-47;

Ky., secretary of state 1849; declined Union Democrats nomination for governor 1863; Ky., house of representatives 1862-67. -- Fuson, Henry Harvey, History of Bell County, Kentucky, New York: Hobson Book Press, 1947; 2 vol.

Bell, Tex. (est. Jan. 22, 1850; 1,079 sq. mi.; 1970 pop.: 124,483; 1960: 94,097; 1950: 73,824) (Belton). Peter Hansborough Bell (1812-1898). Third governor of Tex. Battle of San Jacinto 1836; Tex. asst. adjt. gen. 1837; Tex. inspector gen. 1839; capt. Tex. Volunteer Rangers 1845-46; lt. col. mounted volunteers 1846; col. 1848-49; governor of Tex. 1849-53; Representative from Tex. 1853-57; col. N. C. regiment 1861. -- Bell County History, a pictorial history of Bell county, Fort Worth, Texas: Temple Junior Chamber of Commerce, 1958; 220 p. -- Tyler, George W., History of Bell County, San Antonio, Texas: Naylor Co., 1936; 425 p.

Belmont, Ohio. (est. Sept. 7, 1801; 539 sq. mi.; 1970 pop.: 80,917; 1960: 83,864; 1950: 87,740) (St. Clairsville). French for "beautiful mountain."

Beltrami, Minn. (est. Feb. 28, 1866; 2,517 sq. mi.; 1970 pop.: 26,373; 1960: 23,425; 1950: 24,962) (Bemidji). Giacomo Constantino Beltrami (1779-1855) Explorer, exiled from Italy and emigrated to the U. S. 1821; ascended the Miss. River and discovered one of its principal sources.

Benewah, Idaho. (est. Jan. 23, 1915; 791 sq. mi.; 1970 pop.: 6,230; 1960: 6,036; 1950: 6,173) (St. Maries). Benewah. Coeur d'Alene Indian chief.

Ben Hill, Ga. (est. July 31, 1906; 256 sq. mi.; 1970 pop.: 13,171; 1960: 13,633; 1950: 14,879) (Fitzgerald). Benjamin Harvey Hill (1823-1882). Ga. house of representatives 1851; Ga., senate 1859-60; delegate Confederate Provisional Congress 1861; Senator confederate congress 1861-65; Representative from Ga., 1875-77; Senator from Ga., 1877-82.

Bennett, S. D. (est. Mar. 9, 1909; 1,187 sq. mi.; 1970 pop.: 3,088; 1960: 3,053; 1950: 3,396) (Martin). John E. Bennett, judge S. D. supreme court 1889-94. Granville G. Bennett (1833-1910). Civil War 1861-65; Ill. legislature 1865-71; associate judge Dakota terr.

Bennington, Vt. (est. Feb. 11, 1779 session; 672 sq. mi.; 1970 pop.: 29,282; 1960: 25,088; 1950: 24,115) (Bennington and Manchester). Benning Wentworth (1696-1770) Eighteenth Provincial governor of N. H. Governor of province of N. H., 1741-66; gave 500 acres to Dartmouth College, 1768.

Benson, N. D. (est. Mar. 9, 1883, org. June 9, 1883; 1,412 sq. mi.; 1970 pop.: 8,245; 1960: 9,435; 1950: 10,675) (Minnewaukan). B. W. Benson. Dakota territorial legislature 1883.

Bent, Colo. (est. Feb. 11, 1870; 1,533 sq. mi.; 1970 pop.: 6,493; 1960: 7,419; 1950: 8,775) (Las Animas). William Bent (1809-1869). Fur trader, first permanent white settler in Colo.; govt. agent for Cheyenne, Arapaho, Comanche and Kiowa tribes 1859-60; built adobe fortress in 1828 between La Junta and Las Animas used as trading center.

Benton, Ark. (est. Sept. 30, 1836; 886 sq. mi.; 1970 pop.: 50,476; 1960: 36,272; 1950: 38,076) (Bentonville). Thomas Hart Benton (1782-1858). Mo. senate 1809-11; col. Tenn. volunteers 1812-13; col. U. S. Infantry 1813-15; Senator from Mo. 1821-1851; Representative from Mo., 1853-55. -- History of Benton, Washington, Carroll, Madison, Crawford, Franklin and Sebastian Counties, Chicago: Goodspeed Pub. Co., 1889; 1382 p.

Benton, Ind. (est. Feb. 18, 1840; 409 sq. mi.; 1970 pop.: 11,262; 1960: 11,912; 1950: 11,462) (Fowler). Thomas Hart Benton*. -- Barce, Elmore, History of Benton County, Indiana, Fowler, Ind: Benton Review Shop, 1930-31; 2 vol. -- Birch, Jesse Setlington, History of Benton County and historic Oxford, Oxford, Ind.: Craw & Craw, Inc., 1942; 386 p.

Benton, Iowa. (est. Dec. 21, 1837, org. Jan. 17, 1845, eff. Mar. 1, 1845; 718 sq. mi.; 1970 pop.: 22,885; 1960: 23,422; 1950: 22,656) (Vinton). Thomas Hart Benton*. -- Ransom, James Harley, Pioneer recollections... Benton County, Vinton, Iowa: Historical Pub. Co., 1941; 392 p.

Benton, Minn. (est. Oct. 27, 1849, org. Mar. 31, 1851, eff. Sept. 1, 1851; 404 sq. mi.; 1970 pop.: 20,841; 1960: 17,287; 1950: 15,911) (Foley). Thomas Hart Benton*.

Benton, Miss. (est. July 21, 1870; 396 sq. mi.; 1970 pop.: 7,505; 1960: 7,723; 1950: 8,793) (Ashland). Samuel Benton.

Benton, Mo. (est. Jan. 3, 1835; 742 sq. mi.; 1970 pop.: 9,695; 1960: 8,737; 1950: 9.080) (Warsaw). Thomas Hart Benton*.

Benton, Ore. (est. Dec. 23, 1847; 647 sq. mi.; 1970 pop.: 53,776; 1960: 39,165; 1950: 31,570) (Corvallis). Thomas Hart Benton*. History of Benton County. Portland, Ore., David D. Fagan, 1885.

Benton, Tenn. (est. Dec. 19, 1835; eff. Jan. 1, 1836, org. Feb. 7, 1836; 430 sq. mi.; 1970 pop.: 12,126; 1960: 10,662; 1950: 11,475) (Camden) David Benton*.

Benton, Wash. (est. Mar. 8, 1905; 1,738 sq. mi.; 1970 pop.: 67,540; 1960: 62,070; 1950: 51,370) (Prosser). Thomas Hart Benton*.

Benzie, Mich. (est. Feb. 27, 1863, org. 1867; 316 sq. mi.; 1970 pop.: 8,593; 1960: 7,834; 1950: 8,306) (Beulah). Coined word, a corruption of Benzonia from the Hebrew meaning "sons of light."

Bergen, N.J. (est. Mar. 1, 1683; 233 sq. mi.; 1970 pop.: 898,012; 1960: 780,255; 1950: 539,139) (Hackensack). ("Bergen County's Many Faces Make It a Gem of a Location"; "Bergen Has the Best of Everything"). Named for Bergen-op-zoom, Holland. -- Ransom, J.M., Bergen County, a bibliography of historical books, Hackensack, N.J.: Bergen County Historical Society, 1960; 28 p. -- Westervelt, Frances A., History of Bergen County, N.J., 1630-1923, New York: Lewis historical pub. co., Inc., 1923; 3 vol.

Berkeley, S.C. (est. Jan. 31, 1882; 1,214 sq. mi.; 1970 pop.: 56,199; 1960: 38,196; 1950: 30,251) (Monck's Corner). Sir William Berkeley (1610-1677). Governor of Va. (except for the brief Cromwell regime) 1642-77; suppressed Bacon's uprising 1676. John Berkeley (1607-1678), his brother, one of the eight original proprietors of So. Carolina. Obtained proprietary interest in New Jersey and So. Carolina from Charles II.

Berkeley, W. Va. (est. session Feb. 10, 1772; 324 sq. mi.; 1970 pop.: 36,356; 1960: 33,791; 1950: 30,359) (Martinsburg). Norborne Berkeley (1718-1770), Lord Botetcourt, col. governor of Va. Col. of militia 1761; member of Parliament 1741-63; created peer 1764; governor of Va., 1768-70; favored colonists but dissolved the legislature 1769. -- Evans, Willis Fryatt, History of Berkeley County, West Virginia, Wheeling?, 1928; 347 p. -- Gardiner, Mabel Henshaw, Chronicles of old Berkeley, a narrative history of a Virginia county from its beginnings to 1926, Durham, N.C.: Seeman Press, 1938; 323 p.

Berks, Pa. (est. session Oct. 14, 1751; Mar. 11, 1752; 864 sq. mi.; 1970 pop.: 296,382; 1960: 275,414; 1950: 255,740) (Reading). Named for Berkshire County, England. -- Balthaser, Francis Wilhauer, Story of Berks County, Reading, Pa.: Reading Eagle Press, 1925; 373 p.

Berkshire, Mass. (est. session May 28, 1760, eff. June 30, 1761; 942 sq. mi.; 1970 pop.: 149,402; 1960: 142,135; 1950: 132,966) (Pittsfield). Berkshire County, England. -- Birdsall, Richard Davenport, Berkshire County: a cultural history, New Haven: Yale University Press, 1959;

401 p. -- Tague, William H., ed., Berkshire, two hundred years in pictures 1761-1961, Pittsfield, Mass.: Berkshire Eagle, 1961; 113 p.

Bernalillo, N. M. (est. Jan. 9, 1852; 1,163 sq. mi.; 1970 pop.: 315,774; 1960: 262,199; 1950: 145,673) (Albuquerque). Bernal Diaz de Castillo. With Cortez at conquest of Mexico.

Berrien, Ga. (est. Feb. 25, 1856; 455 sq. mi.; 1970 pop.: 11,556; 1960: 12,038; 1950: 13,966) (Nashville). John Macpherson Berrien (1781-1856). Solicitor gen. eastern circuit Ga., 1809; judge eastern judicial circuit 1810-21; col. of cavalry 1810; Ga., senate 1822-23; Senator from Ga., 1825-29; U. S. Attorney General in cabinet of Pres. Jackson 1829-31; Senator from Ga., 1841-45, 1845-47 and 1847-52.

Berrien, Mich. (est. Oct. 29, 1829, org. Mar. 4, 1831; 580 sq. mi.; 1970 pop.: 163,875; 1960: 149,865; 1950: 115,702) (St. Joseph). John Macpherson Berrien*. -- Coolidge, Orville William, A Twentieth Century History of Berrien County, Chicago: Lewis Pub. Co., 1906; 1007 p.

Bertie, N. C. (est. sess. 1722; 693 sq. mi.; 1970 pop.: 20,528; 1960: 24,350; 1950: 26,439) (Windsor). James and Henry Bertie, Lord Proprietors, who owned one-eighth of Carolina.

Bexar, Tex. (est. Mar. 17, 1836; 1,247 sq. mi.; 1970 pop.: 830,460; 1960: 687,151; 1950: 500,460) (San Antonio). San Antonio de Bexar Presidio named for viceroy Balthasar Manuel de Zuñiga y Guzman Sotomayor y Sarmiento, second son of the Duke of Bexar.

Bibb, Ala. (est. Feb. 7, 1818; 625 sq. mi.; 1970 pop.: 13,812; 1960: 14,357; 1950: 17,987) (Centerville). William Wyatt Bibb (1781-1820) First territorial and first state governor of Ala. Graduated as a physician 1801; Ga., house of representatives 1803-05; Representative from Ga., 1807-13; Senator from Ga., 1813-16; territorial governor of Ala. 1817-19; first governor of Ala., 1819-20. (Originally Cahaba County, changed to present name Dec. 4, 1820) Act 24.

Bibb, Ga. (est. Dec. 9, 1822; 277 sq. mi.; 1970 pop.: 143,418; 1960: 141,249; 1950: 114,079) (Macon). William Wyatt Bibb*.

Bienville, La. (est. Mar. 14, 1848; 848 sq. mi.; 1970 pop.: 16,024; 1960: 16,726; 1950: 19,105) (Arcadia). Jean Baptiste Le Moyne, Sieur de Bienville (1680-1765). French governor of Louisiana. Wounded in French navy; expedition to mouth of Mississippi River 1699; est. New

Orleans 1718; removed from office 1724; reinstated 1733; removed from office 1740; returned to France 1743.

Big Horn, Mont. (est. Jan. 13, 1913; petition and election; 5, 033 sq. mi. ; 1970 pop. : 10, 057; 1960: 10, 007; 1950: 9, 824) (Hardin). Descriptive, for big-horn Rocky Mountain sheep.

Big Horn, Wyo. (est. Mar. 12, 1890; 3, 176 sq. mi. ; 1970 pop. : 10, 202; 1960: 11, 898; 1950: 13, 176) (Basin). Descriptive*. --Mercer, Asa Shinn, Big Horn County, Wyoming, the gem of the Rockies, Hyattville: A.S. Mercer, 1906; 115 p.

Big Stone, Minn. (est. Feb. 20, 1862; 510 sq. mi. ; 1970 pop. : 7, 941; 1960: 8, 954; 1950: 9, 607) (Ortonville). Descriptive. -- Wulff, Lydia Sorenson, Big Stone County History, Ortonville, Minn. : L. A. Kaercher, 1959; 122 p.

Billings, N. D. (est. Feb. 10, 1879, org. Apr. 1886; 1, 139 sq. mi. ; 1970 pop. : 1, 198; 1960: 1, 513; 1950: 1, 777) (Medora). Frederick Billings (1823-1890). Director Northern Pacific RR 1870; proposed reorganization plan 1875; elected pres. 1879; resigned 1881.

Bingham, Idaho. (est. Jan. 13, 1885; 2, 072 sq. mi. ; 1970 pop. : 29, 167; 1960: 28, 218; 1950: 23, 271) (Blackfoot). Henry Harrison Bingham (1841-1912). First lt. Pa. Volunteer Infantry 1862; capt. 1862; bvt. maj. 1864; bvt. lt. col. , col. and brig. gen. 1865; awarded Congressional medal 1864; Philadelphia postmaster 1867-72; Representative from Pa. , 1879-1912.

Blackford, Ind. (est. Feb. 15, 1838, eff. Apr. 2, 1838; org. Jan. 29, 1839; 167 sq. mi. ; 1970 pop. : 15, 888; 1960: 14, 792; 1950: 13, 026) (Hartford City). Isaac Newton Blackford (1786-1859). Moved to Ind. 1812; first clerk and recorder Washington county 1813; clerk of Ind. territorial legislature 1814; judge of 1st district court 1814; speaker Ind. legislature 1816; judge of supreme court of Ind. 1817-52; judge of U. S. Court of Claims 1855-59.

Black Hawk, Iowa. (est. Feb. 17, 1843; 567 sq. mi. ; 1970 pop. : 132, 916; 1960: 122, 482; 1950: 100, 448) (Waterloo). Black Hawk (1767-1838). Chief of the Sauk and Fox Indian tribes; warrior at age of 17, 1784; leader in Black Hawk war, captured at battle of Bad Axe River 1832. -- Hartman, John C. , History of Black Hawk County, Chicago: S. J. Clarke Pub. Co. , 1915; 2 vol.

Bladen, N. C. (est. sess. 1734; 879 sq. mi. ; 1970 pop. : 26, 477; 1960: 28, 881; 1950: 29, 703) (Elizabethtown). Martin Bladen (1680-1746). Comptroller of the Mint 1714; commissioner of trade and plantations 1717-46.

Blaine, Idaho. (est. Mar. 5, 1895; 2, 649 sq. mi. ; 1970 pop. : 5, 749; 1960: 4, 598; 1950: 5, 384) (Hailey). James

Gillespie Blaine (1830-1893). Maine house of representatives 1859-62; Maine speaker of the house 1861-62; Representative from Maine 1863-76; Speaker of the House 1869-75; Senator from Me., 1876-81; U. S. Secretary of State in cabinet of President Garfield 1881; unsuccessful Republican candidate for the presidency 1884; U. S. Secretary of State in cabinet of President Harrison 1889-92.

Blaine, Mont. (est. Feb. 29, 1912; petition and election; 4, 267 sq. mi. ; 1970 pop. : 6, 727; 1960: 8, 091; 1950: 8, 516) (Chinook). James Gillespie Blaine*. -- Allison, Janet S., Trial and triumph; 101 years in north central Montana, Chinook, Mont. : North Central Montana Cow Belles, 1968; 211 p. -- Noyes, Alva Joseph, In the land of the Chinook: or, the story of Blaine County, Helena, Mont. : State Pub. Co., 1917; 152 p.

Blaine, Neb. (est. Mar. 5, 1885, org. June 24, 1886; 711 sq. mi. ; 1970 pop. : 847; 1960: 1, 016; 1950: 1, 203) (Brewster). James Gillespie Blaine*.

Blaine, Okla. (est. July 16, 1907; 925 sq. mi. ; 1970 pop. : 11, 794; 1960: 12, 077; 1950: 15, 049) (Watonga). James Gillespie Blaine*.

Blair, Pa. (est. Feb. 26, 1846; 530 sq. mi. ; 1970 pop. : 135, 356; 1960: 137, 270; 1950: 139, 514) (Hollidaysburg). John Blair. Pa. legislature. -- Wolf, George A., ed., Blair County's first hundred years, 1846-1946, Altoona, Pa. : Mirror Press, 1945; 526 p. -- Davis, Tarring S., ed., A History of Blair County, Harrisburg, Pa. : National Historical Association, 1931; 2 vol.

Blanco, Tex. (est. Feb. 12, 1858; 719 sq. mi. ; 1970 pop. : 3, 567; 1960: 3, 657; 1950: 3, 780) (Johnson City). ("The Heartland of a Great American (home of President Lyndon Baines Johnson)"). Spanish word for "white." -- Speer, John W., History of Blanco County, Austin, Texas: Pemberton Press, 1965; 73 p.

Bland, Va. (est. Mar. 30, 1861; 369 sq. mi. ; 1970 pop. : 5, 423; 1960: 5, 982; 1950: 6, 436) (Bland). Richard Bland (1710-1776). Virginia house of burgesses 1745-75; Continental Congress 1774-75; known as the "Virginia Antiquary." -- Bland County Centennial Corporation, History of Bland County, Radford, Va., 1961; 464 p.

Bleckley, Ga. (est. July 30, 1912; 205 sq. mi. ; 1970 pop. : 10, 291; 1960: 9, 642; 1950: 9, 218) (Cochran). Logan Edwin Bleckley (1827-1907). Solicitor gen. of Atlanta, Ga., 1852-56; private in Civil War 1861; supreme court reporter 1864-67; associate justice S. C. supreme court 1875-80; chief justice of supreme court 1887-94. Secretary to governor.

Bledsoe, Tenn. (est. Nov. 30, 1807; 404 sq. mi.; 1970 pop.: 7,643; 1960: 7,811; 1950: 8,561) (Pikeville) Abraham Bledsoe. Revolutionary army maj. also claimed for Anthony Bledsoe, soldier Creek War, War of 1812.

Blount, Ala. (est. Feb. 6, 1818; 640 sq. mi.; 1970 pop.: 26,853; 1960: 25,449; 1950: 28,975) (Oneonta). William Blount (1749-1800). First territorial governor of Ohio. Paymaster 3rd N. C. regiment 1778; N. C. house of commons 1780-89; delegate to Continental Congress 1782-83, 1786 and 1787; N. C. constitutional convention 1787; N. C. senate 1788-90; governor of the terr. South of the River Ohio (Tenn.) 1790-96; Supt. of Indian Affairs 1790-96; Tenn. state constitutional convention 1796; Senator from Tenn., 1796; expelled 1797; Tenn. state senate president 1797.

Blount, Tenn. (est. July 11, 1795; 584 sq. mi.; 1970 pop.: 63,744; 1960: 57,525; 1950: 54,691) (Maryville). ("Most Scenic Entrance to the Great Smoky Mountains"). William Blount*. -- Burns, Inez E., History of Blount County, Tenn., from war trail to landing strip, 1795-1955, Maryville, Tenn., 1957; 375 p.

Blue Earth, Minn. (est. Mar. 5, 1853; 740 sq. mi.; 1970 pop.: 52,322; 1960: 44,385; 1950: 38,327) (Mankato). Descriptive. Bluish green earth used as a pigment. -- Hughes, Thomas, History of Blue Earth County, Chicago: Middle West Pub. Co., 1909; 622 p.

Boise, Idaho. (est. Feb. 4, 1864; 1,913 sq. mi.; 1970 pop.: 1,763; 1960: 1,646; 1950: 1,776) (Idaho City) Corruption of French words "les bois" for "the woods."

Bolivar, Miss. (est. Feb. 9, 1836; 879 sq. mi.; 1970 pop.: 49,409; 1960: 54,464; 1950: 63,004) (Rosedale and Cleveland) Simon Bolivar y Ponte (1783-1830). Known as "the Liberator." Defeated Spaniards in So. America establishing freedom for the colonies. Referred to as "The George Washington of South America." -- Daughters of the American Revolution, Mississippi Delta Chapter, History of Bolivar County, Jackson, Miss.: Hederman Bros., 1948; 634 p.

Bollinger, Mo. (est. Mar. 1, 1851; 621 sq. mi.; 1970 pop.: 8,820; 1960: 9,167; 1950: 11,019) (Marble Hill). George F. Bollinger. Major, early settler.

Bond, Ill. (est. Jan. 4, 1817; 388 sq. mi.; 1970 pop.: 14,012; 1960: 14,060; 1950: 14,157) (Greenville). Shadrach Bond (1773-1832). First governor of Ill. Legislative council of Ind. Territory 1805-08; a delegate from Ill. Terr. 1812-15; receiver of public moneys in land office 1814-18; first governor of Ill. 1818-22; register of land office for Kaskaskia 1823-32. -- Perrin, William Henry, History of Bond and Montgomery Counties, Chicago: O. L. Baskin & Co., 1882; 419 p.

Bon Homme, S. D. (est. Apr. 5, 1862; 580 sq. mi.; 1970 pop.: 8,577; 1960: 9,229; 1950: 9,438) (Tyndall). From the French, "bon homme Jacques," meaning "good man Jack," or "good fellow" literally, the French "Uncle Sam."

Bonner, Idaho. (est. Feb. 21, 1907; eff. Mar. 18, 1907; 1.736 sq. mi.; 1970 pop.: 15,560; 1960: 15,587; 1950: 14,853) (Sandpoint). ("Idaho's Year Round Recreational Wonderland"). Edwin L. Bonner who built a ferry on the Kootenai River in 1864.

Bonneville, Idaho. (est. Feb. 7, 1911; 1,846 sq. mi.; 1970 pop.: 51,250; 1960: 46,906; 1950: 30,210) (Idaho Falls). Benjamin Louis Eulalie de Bonneville (1796-1878). Graduated U. S. Military Academy 1815; capt. of infantry 1825; explored Calif. and Rocky Mts. region 1831-36; returned to Army and saw active service in the Mexican War 1836-45; maj. 1845; lt. col. in 1849 and col. in 1855; retired; bvt. brig. gen. in 1865 for 50 years service. -- Lovell, Edith Haroldsen, Captain Bonneville's county, Idaho Falls, Idaho: Eastern Idaho Farmer, 1963; 275 p.

Boone, Ark. (est. Apr. 9, 1869; 602 sq. mi.; 1970 pop.: 19,073; 1960: 16,116; 1950: 16,260) (Harrison). Daniel Boone (1735-1820). Explorer and Indian fighter. Aided colonists in Revolutionary war; became a col. -- Rea, Ralph R., Boone County and Its People, Van Buren, Ark.: Press Argus, 1955; 224 p.

Boone, Ill. (est. Mar. 4, 1837; 293 sq. mi.; 1970 pop.: 25,440; 1960: 20,326; 1950: 17,070) (Belvidere). Daniel Boone*. -- The Past and Present of Boone County, Chicago: H. F. Kett & Co., 1877; 414 p.

Boone, Ind. (est. Jan. 29, 1830; eff. Apr. 1, 1830; 427 sq. mi.; 1970 pop.: 30,870; 1960: 27,543; 1950: 23,993) (Lebanon). Daniel Boone*.

Boone, Iowa. (est. Jan. 13, 1846; 573 sq. mi.; 1970 pop.: 26,470; 1960: 28,037; 1950: 28,139) (Boone). Nathan Boone. (1782-1863) Dragoon capt. -- Goldthwait, Nathan Edward, History of Boone County, Chicago: Pioneer Pub. Co., 1914; 2 vol.

Boone, Ky. (est. Dec. 13, 1798, eff. June 1, 1799; 252 sq. mi.; 1970 pop.: 32,812; 1960: 21,940; 1950: 13,015) (Burlington). Daniel Boone*.

Boone, Mo. (est. Nov. 16, 1820, eff. Jan. 1, 1821; 683 sq. mi.; 1970 pop.: 80,911; 1960: 55,202; 1950: 48,432) (Columbia).

Daniel Boone*. -- History of Boone County, St. Louis: Western Historical Co., 1882; 1143 p.

Boone, Neb. (est. Mar. 1, 1871, org. Mar. 28, 1871; 683 sq. mi.; 1970 pop.: 8,190; 1960: 9,134; 1950: 10,721) (Albion). Daniel Boone*.

Boone, W. Va. (est. Mar. 11, 1847; 506 sq. mi.; 1970 pop.: 25,118; 1960: 28,764; 1950: 33,173) (Madison). Daniel Boone*.

Borden, Tex. (est. Aug. 21, 1876, org. 1890; 914 sq. mi.; 1970 pop.: 888; 1960: 1,076; 1950: 1,106) (Gail). Gail Borden, Jr., (1801-1874). Surveyor of Stephen F. Austin's colony 1830; publisher of "Telegraph" and "Texas Register" 1835; collector of port of Galveston 1837-38 and 1841-43; invented meat biscuit; condensed milk.

Bosque, Tex. (est. Feb. 4, 1854; 1,003 sq. mi.; 1970 pop.: 10,966; 1960: 10,809; 1950: 11,836) (Meridian). Avvoya Bosque Spanish word for "woody."

Bossier, La. (est. Feb. 24, 1843; 863 sq. mi.; 1970 pop.: 64,519; 1960: 57,622; 1950: 40,139) (Benton). Pierre Evariste John Baptiste Bossier (1797-1844). La. senate 1833-43; Representative from La. 1843-44.

Botetourt, Va. (est. session Nov. 7, 1769; 549 sq. mi.; 1970 pop.: 18,193; 1960: 16,715; 1950: 15,766) (Fincastle). Lord Botetourt, Norborne Berkeley (1718-1770). Col. governor of Va. 1768-70.

Bottineau, N. D. (est. Jan. 4, 1873, org. July 22, 1884; 1,699 sq. mi.; 1970 pop.: 9,496; 1960: 11,315; 1950: 12,140) (Bottineau). Pierre Bottineau. French-Canadian traveler. -- Bottineau County diamond jubilee, 1884-1959, 1959; 50 p.

Boulder, Colo. (est. Nov. 1, 1861; 753 sq. mi.; 1970 pop.: 131,889; 1960: 74,254; 1950: 48,296) (Boulder). Descriptive term.

Boundary, Idaho. (est. Jan. 23, 1915; 1,275 sq. mi.; 1970 pop.: 6,371; 1960: 5,809; 1950: 5,908) (Bonners Ferry). Descriptive, boundary line with Canada.

Bourbon, Kans. (est. Aug. 30, 1855; 639 sq. mi.; 1970 pop.: 15,215; 1960: 16,090; 1950: 19,153) (Fort Scott). Bourbon County, Ky., name for the Bourbons of France.

Bourbon, Ky. (est. sess. Oct. 17, 1785, eff. May 1, 1786; 300 sq. mi.; 1970 pop.: 18,476; 1960: 18,178; 1950: 17,752) (Paris). The Bourbons of France. Louis XIV placed his grandson Philippe, Duke of Anjou, on the Spanish throne who as Philippe V founded the Bourbon dynasty in Spain.

Bowie, Tex. (est. Dec. 17, 1840; 921 sq. mi.; 1970 pop.: 67,813; 1960: 59,971; 1950: 61,966) (Boston). James

Bowie (1795-1836). Resident of San Antonio, col. of Tex. volunteers, inventor of the Bowie knife, killed at the battle of the Alamo, Mar. 6, 1836.

Bowman, N. D. (est. Mar. 8, 1883; org. July 5, 1907; 1, 170 sq. mi. ; 1970 pop. : 3, 901; 1960: 4, 154; 1950: 4, 001) (Bowman) E. M. Bowman. Member of Dakota Terr. Assembly 1883.

Box Butte, Neb. (est. Nov. 2, 1886; org. Apr. 23, 1887; 1, 066 sq. mi. ; 1970 pop. : 10, 094; 1960: 11, 688; 1950: 12, 279) (Alliance). French word for "mound." -- Phillips, Anna (Nerud), History of Box Butte County, Nebraska, Alliance, 1939; 230 p.

Box Elder, Utah. (est. Jan. 5, 1856; 5, 594 sq. mi. ; 1970 pop. : 28, 129; 1960: 25, 061; 1950: 19, 734) (Brigham City). Descriptive, box elder trees. -- Forsgren, Lydia Walker, History of Box Elder County, Salt Lake City, Utah, 1937; 390 p. -- Sons of Utah Pioneers. Box Elder Chapter, Box Elder lore of the nineteenth century, Brigham City, Utah, 1951; 169 p.

Boyd, Ky. (est. Feb. 16, 1860; 159 sq. mi. ; 1970 pop. : 52, 376; 1960: 52, 163; 1950: 49, 949) (Catlettsburg). Linn Boyd (1800-1859). Ky. legislature 1827-30 and 1831-32; Representative from Ky., 1835-37 and 1839-55; speaker of the house 1852-55; elected lt. governor of Ky., but was too ill to serve 1859.

Boyd, Neb. (est. Mar. 20, 1891; org. Aug. 29, 1891; 538 sq. mi. ; 1970 pop. : 3, 752; 1960: 4, 513; 1950: 4, 911) (Butte). James E. Boyd (1834-1906). Seventh and ninth governor of Neb. Manager of City Gas Works of Omaha 1868-69; pres. Omaha Board of Trade 1881-83; clerk of Douglas County, Neb. 1857; clerk of Buffalo County, Neb. ; Neb. legislature 1866; Neb. state constitutional convention 1871 and 1875; Mayor of Omaha 1881-82 and 1885-87; governor of Neb., 1891 removed because of citizenship claim; declared citizen 1892; gov. of Neb. 1892-3.

Boyle, Ky. (est. Feb. 15, 1842; 181 sq. mi. ; 1970 pop. : 21, 090; 1960: 21, 257; 1950: 20, 532) (Danville). John Boyle (1774-1835). Ky. house of representatives 1800; Representative from Ky., 1803-09; declined appointment governor of Ill. Terr. 1809; judge Ky., court of appeals 1809-10; chief justice Ky., court of appeals 1810-26; U. S. judge for district of Ky., 1826-34. -- Daviess, Marion (Thompson), History of Mercer and Boyle Counties, Harrodsburg, Ky. : Harrodsburg-Herald, 1924; 176 p.

Bracken, Ky. (est. Dec. 14, 1796, eff. June 1, 1797; 206 sq. mi. ; 1970 pop. : 7, 227; 1960: 7, 422; 1950: 8, 424)

(Brooksville). William Bracken. Pioneer settler of Ky.

Bradford, Fla. (est. Dec. 21, 1858; 293 sq. mi.; 1970 pop.: 14,625; 1960: 12,446; 1950: 11,457) (Starke). ("Florida's 'Four-Season' County"; "Florida's Winter Strawberry Market"; "The Heart of Florida's Crown"; "The Berry Capital of the World"; "The County of Planned Progress"). Richard Bradford (1839?-1861). First Fla. officer killed in the Civil War, at battle of Santa Rosa Island, Oct. 9, 1861. (Originally New River County, name changed to Bradford County, Dec. 6, 1861, chap. 1300.)

Bradford, Pa. (est. Feb. 21, 1810; 1,147 sq. mi.; 1970 pop.: 57,962; 1960: 54,925; 1950: 51,722) (Towanda). William Bradford (1755-1795). private 1776; capt., col. 1777; resigned 1779; attorney gen. of Pa. 1780-91; assoc. justice supreme court of Pa., 1791. Attorney gen. of the U. S. during Washington's second term 1794-95. (Formerly Ontario County, Mar. 24, 1812, Chap. 109). Heverly, Clement Ferdinand, History and geography of Bradford County, Towanda, Pa.: Bradford County Historical Society, 1926; 594 p.

Bradley, Ark. (est. Dec. 18, 1840; 649 sq. mi.; 1970 pop.: 12,778; 1960: 14,029; 1950: 15,987) (Warren). William L. Bradley.

Bradley, Tenn. (est. Feb. 10, 1836; 338 sq. mi.; 1970 pop.: 50,686; 1960: 38,324; 1950: 32,338) (Cleveland). Edward Bradley (-1829). Lt. col. 1st regiment Tenn. Volunteers 1812-15; Creek War wounded at Talluschatches, Ala., Nov. 2, 1813. -- Wooten, John Morgan, History of Bradley County, Cleveland, Tenn., 1949; 323 p.

Branch, Mich. (est. Oct. 29, 1829, org. 1833; 506 sq. mi.; 1970 pop.: 37,906; 1960: 34,903; 1950: 30,202) (Coldwater). John Branch (1782-1863). Nineteenth governor of N. C. 7th governor of Fla. terr. N. C. state senate 1811-17 and 1822; speaker 1815-17; governor of N. C. 1817-20; Senator from N. C., 1823-29; U. S. Secretary of the Navy in cabinet of Pres. Jackson 1829-31; Representative from N. C., 1831-33; governor of Fla. Terr. 1844-45. -- Johnson, Crisfield, History of Branch County, Philadelphia: Everts & Abbott, 1879; 347 p.

Brantley, Ga. (est. Aug. 14, 1920; 434 sq. mi.; 1970 pop.: 5,940; 1960: 5,891; 1950: 6,387) (Nahunta). Benjamin D. Brantley.

Braxton, W. Va. (est. Jan. 15, 1836; 519 sq. mi.; 1970 pop.: 12,666; 1960: 15,152; 1950: 18,082) (Sutton). Carter Braxton (1736-1797). Va. house of burgesses 1761-71 and 1775; Continental Congress 1775-76, 1777-83 and

1785; signer Declaration of Independence 1776; Va., council of state 1786-91 and 1794-97. -- Sutton, John Davison, History of Braxton County and central West Virginia, Parsons, W. Va.: McClain Printing Co., 1967; 458 p.

Brazoria, Tex. (est. Mar. 17, 1836; 1,441 sq. mi.; 1970 pop.: 108,312; 1960: 76,204; 1950: 46,549) (Angleton). Derived from Spanish word "brazos" meaning "arms" or "forks."

Brazos, Tex. (est. Jan. 30, 1841; 583 sq. mi.; 1970 pop.: 57,978; 1960: 44,895; 1950: 38,390) (Bryan). Spanish for "arms" or "forks." (Formerly Navasoto County, name changed to Brazos County Jan. 28, 1842).

Breathitt, Ky. (est. Feb. 8, 1839; 486 sq. mi.; 1970 pop.: 14,221; 1960: 15,490; 1950: 19,964) (Jackson). John Breathitt (1786-1834). 11th governor of Ky. Emigrated to Ky., 1810; Ky., state legislature 1811; lt. gov. 1828-32; gov. 1832-34; died in office 1834.

Breckinridge, Ky. (est. Dec. 9, 1799, eff. Jan. 1, 1800; 566 sq. mi.; 1970 pop.: 14,789; 1960: 14,734; 1950: 15,528) (Hardinsburg). John Breckinridge (1760-1806). Ky. house of burgesses 1780 but denied seat because of age; Va. militia; Attorney gen. of Ky., 1795-97; Ky., house of representatives 1798-1800; speaker 1799-1800; Senator from Ky., 1801-05; U. S. Attorney General in the cabinet of Pres. Jefferson 1805-06.

Bremer, Iowa. (est. Apr. 29, 1851; 439 sq. mi.; 1970 pop.: 22,737; 1960: 21,108; 1950: 18,884) (Waverly). Frederika Bremer (1801-1865). Swedish traveler and author; philanthropic work, emancipation of women, first book published 1828. -- Lucas, William Vincent, Pioneer days of Bremer County, Waverly, Iowa; Waverly Democrat, 1918; 176 p.

Brevard, Fla. (est. Mar. 14, 1844; 1,032 sq. mi.: 1970 pop.: 230,006; 1960: 111,435; 1950: 23,653) (Titusville). ("Brevard Has Pulling Power"; "The Fastest Growing County in the Nation"; "The Home of the Kennedy Space Center and Air Force Station"; "The Home of the Sunken Treasure Museum"; "The Southern Entry to the Cape Kennedy Area"). Dr. Brevard, author of the Mecklenburg Declaration of Independence, Mecklenburg County, N. C. Theodore Washington Brevard (1804-1877) Florida comptroller. (Originally St. Lucie County (no number) changed to Brevard County Jan. 6, 1855, chapter 651.)

Brewster, Tex. (est. Feb. 2, 1887; 6,208 sq. mi.; 1970 pop.: 7,780; 1960: 6,434; 1950: 7,309) (Alpine). Henry Percy Brewster (1816-1884). Private in Texas army; private at San Jacinto and private secretary to gen.

Houston 1836; Secretary of War under David G. Burnet 1836; district attorney second judicial district 1840-43; attorney gen. of Tex. 1847-49; adj. gen. and chief of staff under gen. Albert Johnston; Tex. Commissioner of Insurance, Statistics and History 1883.

Briscoe, Tex. (est. Aug. 21, 1876; 887 sq. mi.; 1970 pop.: 2,794; 1960: 3,577; 1950: 3,528) (Silverton). Andrew Briscoe (1810-1849). Capt. of Liberty volunteers at battle of Concepcion 1835; signer Tex. declaration of Independence 1836; capt. of infantry regulars at battle of San Jacinto 1836; chief justice of Harrisburg, Tex., 1836-39; railroad builder and promoter 1840-41.

Bristol, Mass. (est. June 2, 1685; 556 sq. mi.: 1970 pop.: 444,301; 1960: 398,488; 1950: 381,569) (Fall River and New Bedford). ("The Gateway to Cape Cod"). Bristol, England. -- Hutt, Frank Walcott, A History of Bristol County, Chicago: Lewis Historical Pub. Co., 1924; 3 vol. -- Our Country and Its People, Boston: Boston History Co., 1899; 799 p.

Bristol, R.I. (est. Feb. 17, 1746-47; 24 sq. mi.; 1970 pop.: 45,937; 1960: 37,146; 1950: 29,079) (Bristol). Bristol, England. -- Howe, Mark Antony De Wolfe, Bristol, R.I., Cambridge, Mass.: Harvard University Press, 1930; 172 p. -- Munro, Wilfred Harold, The History of Bristol, Providence: J.A. and R.A. Reid, 1880; 396 p.

Broadwater, Mont. (est. Feb. 9, 1897; 1,243 sq. mi.; 1970 pop.: 2,526; 1960: 2,804; 1950: 2,922) (Townsend). Descriptive. Col. C. A. Broadwater of Helena.

Bronx, N.Y. (est. Apr. 19, 1912, eff. Jan. 1, 1914; 41 sq. mi.; 1970 pop.: 1,472,216; 1960: 1,424,815; 1950: 1,451,277) (Bronx, New York City). Jonas Bronck. First settler of the region north of the Harlem. -- Wells, James Lee, ed., The Bronx and Its People, New York: Lewis Historical Pub. Co., 1927; 4 vol. -- Jenkins, Stephen, The Story of the Bronx, New York: G. P. Putnam's Sons, 1912; 451 p.

Brooke, W. Va. (est. Nov. 30, 1796; 92 sq. mi.; 1970 pop.: 29,685; 1960: 28,940; 1950: 26,904) (Wellsburg). Robert Brooke (1751-1799), 10th governor of Va. (Commonwealth). Served in Revolutionary War, captured twice; governor of Va. 1794-96; attorney gen. of Va., 1798; Grand Master of the Grand Lodge of Masons of Va. 1795-97.

Brookings, S.D. (est. Apr. 5, 1862; 801 sq. mi.; 1970 pop.: 22,158; 1960: 20,046; 1950: 17,851) (Brookings). Wilmot W. Brookings (1833-18 ?). Pioneer Dakota settler; fell in Split Rock River and lost both legs to gangrene 1858; Dakota council 1862-63; speaker of the house 1864-65; supt. in charge of building road from Minn. line to Crow Creek Agency 1865-68; associate justice Dakota supreme court 1869-73; constitutional convention 1883 and 1885.

Brooks, Ga. (est. Dec. 11, 1858; 514 sq. mi.; 1970 pop.: 13,739; 1960: 15,292; 1950: 18,169) (Quitman). Preston Smith Brooks. -- Huxford, Falks, History of Brooks County 1858-1948, Quitman, Ga.: Daughters of the American Revolution, 1949; 607 p.

Brooks, Tex. (est. Mar. 11, 1911; 908 sq. mi.; 1970 pop.: 8,005; 1960: 8,609; 1950: 9,195) (Falfurrias). James Abijah Brooks (1855-1944). Cattle business 1876-80; Tex. Ranger 1882, capt. 1889; resigned 1906; house of representatives 1909-11; county judge Brooks county 1911-39.

Broome, N.Y. (est. Mar. 28, 1806; 710 sq. mi.; 1970 pop.: 221,815; 1960: 212,661; 1950: 184,698) (Binghamton). John Broome (1738-1810) Committee of safety; N.Y. constitutional convention 1777; 9th pres. of New York City Chamber of Commerce to 1794; lt. gov. of New York 1804-11. -- Smith, H. Perry, ed., History of Broome County, Syracuse, N.Y.: Mason and Co., 1885; 630 p.

Broward, Fla. (est. Apr. 30, 1915; 1,218 sq. mi.; 1970 pop.: 620,100; 1960: 333,946; 1950: 83,933) (Fort Lauderdale). ("The County Where It's Always Sun and Fun Time"). Napoleon Bonaparte Broward (1857-1910). 18th gov. of Fla. Sheriff of Duval County 1887-1900; Fla. legislature 1900; Fla. Board of health 1900-04; gov. 1905-09.

Brown, Ill. (est. Feb. 1, 1839; 297 sq. mi.; 1970 pop.: 5,586; 1960: 6,210; 1950: 7,132) (Mount Sterling). Jacob Brown (1775-1828). Brig. gen. N.Y. volunteers 1813; brig. gen. U.S. Army 1813; maj. gen. 1814; commander-in-chief of army 1815-1828; Received thanks of Congress and a gold medal for action at Chippewa, Niagara and Erie.

Brown, Ind. (est. Feb. 4, 1836, eff. Apr. 1, 1836; 324 sq. mi.; 1970 pop.: 9,057; 1960: 7,024; 1950: 6,209) (Nashville). ("The County in the Hills of Scenic Southern Indiana"). Jacob Brown*.

Brown, Kans. (est. Aug. 30, 1855; 578 sq. mi.; 1970 pop.: 11,685; 1960: 13,229; 1950: 14,651) (Hiawatha). Albert Gallatin Brown (1813-1880). 14th gov. of Miss. Miss. house of representatives 1835-39; Representative from Miss., 1839-41 and 1847-53; judge of the circuit superior court 1842-43; gov. of Miss. 1844-48; Senator from Miss. 1854-61; capt. Miss. Infantry; Confederate senate 1862; brig. gen. Miss. militia. -- Harrington, Grant W., Annals of Brown County, Kansas, Hiawatha, Kan.: Harrington Printing Co., 1903; 564 p. -- Ruley, A. N., A. N. Ruley's History of Brown County, Hiawatha (?), Kan., 1930; 416 p.

Brown, Minn. (est. Feb. 20, 1855, org. Feb. 11, 1856; 613 sq. mi.; 1970 pop.: 28,887; 1960: 27,676; 1950: 25,895) (New Ulm). Joseph Renshaw Brown (1805-1870). Secretary Minn. territorial council 1849-51; Sioux Indian trader; Minn. territorial printer 1853-54; chief clerk Minn. house of representatives 1853; published Minn. "Pioneer" 1852-54 and Henderson "Democrat" 1857-61; Minn. council 1854-55; Minn. house of representatives 1857.

Brown, Neb. (est. Feb. 19, 1883, org. Apr. 5, 1883; 1,218 sq. mi.; 1970 pop.: 4,021; 1960: 4,436; 1950: 5,164) (Ainsworth). Five members of the Neb. legislature named Brown.

Brown, Ohio. (est. Dec. 27, 1817; eff. Mar. 1, 1818, 491 sq. mi.; 1970 pop.: 26,635; 1960: 25,178; 1950: 22,221) (Georgetown). Jacob Brown*. -- Brown County Historical Society, History of Brown County, Georgetown, Ohio, 1968; 80 p. -- History of Brown County, Chicago: W. H. Beers & Co., 1883; 703 p.

Brown, S. D. (est. Feb. 22, 1879; 1,677 sq. mi.; 1970 pop.: 36,920; 1960: 34,106; 1950: 32,617) (Aberdeen). Alfred Brown (1836-). Canadian born; went to Dakota terr. 1874; S. D. territorial legislature 1879; known as "Consolidation Brown." -- Brown County (S. D.) Territorial Pioneers Association, Early History of Brown County, South Dakota, Aberdeen, S. D., 1965; 208 p.

Brown, Tex. (est. Aug. 27, 1856; 949 sq. mi.; 1970 pop.: 25,877; 1960: 24,728; 1950: 28,607) (Brownwood). Henry Stevenson Brown (1793-1834). Trader; battle of Fort Clark, Ill., operated keel boats to New Orleans 1814-24; moved to Tex. 1824; trader with Indians and Mexicans 1824-32; fought Waco Indians 1825; captured Mexican fort at Velasco 1832; delegate to Tex. convention 1832-33. -- Havins, T. R., Something about Brown, Brownwood, Texas: Banner Print. Co., 1958; 208 p.

Brown, Wis. (est. Oct. 26, 1818; 525 sq. mi.; 1970 pop.: 158,244; 1960: 125,082; 1950: 98,314) (Green Bay). Jacob Brown*. -- Martin, Deborah Beaumont, History of Brown County, Chicago: S. J. Clarke Pub. Co., 1913; 2 vol.

Brule, S. D. (est. Jan. 14, 1875; 829 sq. mi.; 1970 pop.: 5, 870; 1960: 6, 319; 1950: 6, 076) (Chamberlain). Brule band of Sioux Indians. The Pawnees set the prairies afire burning Sioux raiding party who were derisively named "sicangu" meaning "burned thighs" later translated by French to "brule" (burned).

Brunswick, N. C. (est. sess. 1764; 873 sq. mi.; 1970 pop.: 24, 223; 1960: 20, 278; 1950: 19, 238) (Southport). ("The South Eastern North Carolina's Land of Enjoyment"). House of Brunswick of which George I, II, III and IV were members. See also Lunenburg, page 173.

Brunswick, Va. (est. Nov. 2, 1720; 579 sq. mi.; 1970 pop.: 16, 172; 1960: 17, 779; 1950: 20, 136) (Lawrenceville). House of Brunswick*. -- Smithey, Marvin, Brunswick County, Virginia, Richmond: Williams Printing Co., 1907; 48 p.

Bryan, Ga. (est. Dec. 19, 1793; 431 sq. mi.; 1970 pop.: 6, 539; 1960: 6, 226; 1950: 5, 965) (Pembroke). Jonathan Bryan.

Bryan, Okla. (est. July 16, 1907; 913 sq. mi.; 1970 pop.: 25, 552; 1960: 24, 252; 1950: 28, 999) (Durant). William Jennings Bryan (1860-1925). Representative from Neb. 1891-95; defeated presidential candidate 1896, 1900 and 1908; U. S. Secretary of State in cabinet of Pres. Wilson 1913-15.

Buchanan, Iowa. (est. Dec. 21, 1837; 569 sq. mi.; 1970 pop.: 21, 746; 1960: 22, 293; 1950: 21, 927) (Independence). James Buchanan (1791-1868). 15th pres. of the United States. At defense of Baltimore, Md., in War of 1812; Pa. house of representatives 1814-15; Representative from Pa., 1821-31; U. S. Minister to Russia 1832-34; Senator from Pa., 1845-49; U. S. Secretary of State in cabinet of Pres. Polk 1845-49; U. S. Minister to Great Britain 1853-56; Pres. of the U. S., 1857-61. -- Chappell, Harry Church, History of Buchanan County, Chicago: S. J. Clarke Pub. Co., 1914; 2 vol.

Buchanan, Mo. (est. Dec. 31, 1838; 411 sq. mi.; 1970 pop.: 86, 915; 1960: 90, 581; 1950: 96, 826) (St. Joseph). James Buchanan*.

Buchanan, Va. (est. Feb. 13, 1858; 508 sq. mi.; 1970 pop.: 32, 071; 1960: 36, 724; 1950: 35, 748) (Grundy). ("Nature's Wonderland"; "The Gateway to the Breaks Interstate Park"; "The Home of the Grand Canyon of the South on the Virginia and Kentucky state line"; "Through Industry We Thrive"). James Buchanan*.

Buckingham, Va. (est. 1761, 7th term of Sept. 14, 1758 session; 576 sq. mi.; 1970 pop.: 10, 597; 1960: 10, 877;

1950: 12, 288) (Buckingham.) Duke of Buckingham.

Bucks, Pa. (est. Mar. 10, 1682; 617 sq. mi. ; 1970 pop. : 415, 056; 1960: 308, 567; 1950: 144, 620) (Doylestown). ("The Founder's County (William Penn, the founder of Pennsylvania established his capital at Pennsbury Manor at the bend of the Delaware River in Bucks County)"; "The Key County of the Keystone State"). Buckinghamshire, England, the old home of the Penn family of Pa. -- Battle, J. H., ed., History of Bucks County, Chicago: A. Warner & Co., 1887; 1176 p.

Buena Vista, Iowa. (est. Jan. 15, 1851; 573 sq. mi. ; 1970 pop. : 20, 693; 1960: 21, 189; 1950: 21, 113) (Storm Lake). Buena Vista, Mexico, site of Gen. Zachary Taylor's victory. -- Wegerslev, C. H., Past and present of Buena Vista County, Chicago: S. J. Clarke Pub. Co., 1909; 659 p.

Buffalo, Neb. (est. Mar. 14, 1855; org. Feb. 12, 1866; 952 sq. mi. ; 1970 pop. : 31, 222; 1960: 26, 236; 1950: 25, 134) (Kearney). Descriptive. -- Bassett County, Nebraska, Buffalo County, Nebraska, and its people, Chicago: S. J. Clarke Pub. Co., 1916; 2 vol.

Buffalo, S. D. (est. Jan. 8, 1873; 494 sq. mi. ; 1970 pop. : 1, 739; 1960: 1, 547; 1950: 1, 615) (Gann Valley). Descriptive.

Buffalo, Wis. (est. July 6, 1853; 712 sq. mi. ; 1970 pop. : 13, 743; 1960: 14, 202; 1950: 14, 719) (Alma). Descriptive. -- Kessinger, Lawrence, History of Buffalo County, Alma, Wis. : L. Kessinger, 1888; 656 p.

Bullitt, Ky. (est. Dec. 13, 1796, eff. Jan. 1, 1797; 300 sq. mi. ; 1970 pop. : 26, 090; 1960: 15, 726; 1950: 11, 349) (Shepherdsville). Alexander Scott Bullitt (1761-1816). Ky. constitutional convention 1792; Ky. senate 1792-1804; Ky. constitutional convention 1799; lt. gov. of Ky., 1800-08.

Bulloch, Ga. (est. Feb. 8, 1796; 688 sq. mi. ; 1970 pop. : 31, 585; 1960: 24, 263; 1950: 24, 740) (Statesboro). ("The County Where Nature Smiles and Progress Has the Right-of-Way"). Archibald Bulloch (1730-1777). First gov. of Ga. (under American rule) Lt. in So. Carolina regiment 1757; speaker Ga. Royal Assembly 1775-76; pres. Ga. Provincial Congress 1775-76; Continental Congress 1775-76; commander-in-chief Ga. forces 1776-77; gov. of Ga. 1776-77.

Bullock, Ala. (est. Dec. 5, 1866; 615 sq. mi. ; 1970 pop. : 11, 824; 1960: 13, 462; 1950: 16, 054) (Union Springs). E. C. Bullock.

Buncombe, N. C. (est. session Dec. 5, 1791; 646 sq. mi.; 1970 pop.: 145,056; 1960: 130,074; 1950: 124,403) (Asheville). Edward Buncombe (1732 or 1742-1778). Col. of N. C. militia 1771; clerk of county court 1774-77; col. N. C. Minute Men 1775; battle of Brandywine 1777; wounded at battle of Germantown Oct. 4, 1777 and died at Philadelphia a prisoner of the British 1778. -- Sandley, Foster Alexander, History of Buncombe County, North Carolina, Asheville, N. C.: Advocate Printing Co., 1930; 2 vol.

Bureau, Ill. (est. Feb. 28, 1837; 881 sq. mi.; 1970 pop.: 38,541; 1960: 37,594; 1950: 37,711) (Princeton). Pierre de Buero. French trader with the Indians. -- Bradsby, Henry C., History of Bureau County, Chicago: World Pub. Co., 1885; 710 p.

Burke, Ga. (est. Feb. 5, 1777; 956 sq. mi.; 1970 pop.: 18,255; 1960: 20,596; 1950: 23,458) (Waynesboro). Edmund Burke (1729-1797). Elected to English Parliament 1765; urged repeal of the Stamp Act and advised conciliation with its American colonies.

Burke, N. C. (est. Apr. 8, 1777; 506 sq. mi.; 1970 pop.: 60,364; 1960: 52,701; 1950: 45,518) (Morganton) Thomas Burke (1747?-1783). 3rd governor of N. C. Physician, lawyer, volunteer at Battle of Brandywine, N. C. member of Continental Congress 1776-81; governor of N. C. 1781-82. British prisoner for four months, escaped Jan. 16, 1782.

Burke, N. D. (est. July 6, 1910; (supreme court decision upheld) 1,121 sq. mi.; 1970 pop.: 4,739; 1960: 5,886; 1950: 6,621) (Bowbells). John Burke (1859-1937). 10th governor of N. D. N. D. house of representatives 1891-92; N. D. state senator 1893-95; governor of N. D., 1907-13; Treasurer of the U. S., 1913.

Burleigh, N. D. (est. Jan. 4, 1873; org. Sept. 25, 1873; 1,648 sq. mi.; 1970 pop.: 40,714; 1960: 34,016; 1950: 25,673) (Bismarck) Walter A. Burleigh. Indian agent and trader, railroad contractor.

Burleson, Tex. (est. Jan. 15, 1842; org. Mar. 24, 1846; 679 sq. mi.; 1970 pop.: 9,999; 1960: 11,177; 1950: 13,000) (Caldwell). Edward Burleson (1798-1852). War of 1812 with Jackson at battle of Horse Shoe Bend, Ala., and Battle of New Orleans; Mexican war, commander of Texas forces, maj. 1835; senator in first Tex. congress 1836; Vice Pres. of Tex. Republic 1841; brig. gen. in command of Tex. troops 1838-41; Tex. state senate 1848; pres. of state senate when he died in 1852.

Burlington, N. J. (est. May 17, 1694; 819 sq. mi. ; 1970 pop. : 323, 132; 1960: 224, 499; 1950: 135, 910) (Mount Holly). ("The New Look For Industry"). Burlington, England, name corrupted from New Beverly, to Bridlington, to Burlington. -- Woodward, E. M., History of Burlington and Mercer counties, Philadelphia, Pa. : Everts & Peck, 1883; 888 p.

Burnet, Tex. (est. Feb. 5, 1852; 1, 003 sq. mi. ; 1970 pop.: 11, 420; 1960: 9, 265; 1950: 10, 356) (Burnet). David Gouverneur Burnet (1788-1870). First Pres. of the Republic of Tex. Lt. in forces seeking liberation of Venezuela 1806; one of three Tex. district judges 1834-36; pres. ad interim colonial govt. Tex. 1836; Tex. vice pres. 1838-41.

Burnett, Wis. (est. Mar. 31, 1856; 840 sq. mi. ; 1970 pop.: 9, 276; 1960: 9, 214; 1950: 10, 236) (Grantsburg). Thomas P. Burnett. Wisconsin legislature.

Burt, Neb. (est. Nov. 23, 1854; procl. ; 474 sq. mi. ; 1970 pop. : 9, 247; 1960: 10, 192; 1950: 11, 536) (Tekamah). Francis Burt (1807-1854). First terr. gov. Neb. Member S. C. nullification convention 1832; S. C. legislature 1832-44; S. C. treasurer 1844; editor Pendleton "Messenger" 1847-51; S. C. constitutional convention 1852; third auditor U. S. Treasury 1853; first territorial gov., Neb., served two days before his death. -- History of Burt County, Nebraska, Wahoo, Neb. : Ludi Printing Co., [n. d.]; 282 p.

Butler, Ala. (est. Dec. 13, 1819; 773 sq. mi. ; 1970 pop. : 22, 007; 1960: 24, 560; 1950: 29, 228) (Greenville). William Butler (-1818). Georgia legislature; Ga., militia, killed by Indians at Butler Springs, Mar. 20, 1818. -- Little, John Buckner, History of Butler County, Alabama, from 1815 to 1885, Cincinnati, Ohio: Elm Street Printing Co., 1885; 256 p.

Butler, Iowa. (est. Jan. 15, 1851; 582 sq. mi. ; 1970 pop. : 16, 953; 1960: 17, 467; 1950: 17, 394) (Allison). William Orlando Butler (1791-1880). Private Kentucky Volunteers 1812; wounded at the battle of the Thames Oct. 6, 1813; imprisoned at Canada; returned as capt. ; bvt. maj. at battle of New Orleans 1815; aide to gen. Jackson 1816-17; Ky., house of representatives 1817-18; Representative from Ky., 1839-43; maj. gen. Ky., volunteers 1846; received thanks of Congress and a sword for gallantry at Monterey, Mex. ; unsuccessful Democratic candidate for Vice President 1848; declined appointment as gov. of Neb. Terr. 1855; delegate to peace conference 1861. -- Hart, Irving H., History of Butler County, Chicago:

S. J. Clarke Pub. Co., 1914; 2 vol.

Butler, Kan. (est. Aug. 30, 1855, org. Feb. 11, 1859; 1,445 sq. mi.; 1970 pop.: 38,658; 1960: 38,395; 1950: 31,001) (El Dorado). Andrew Pickens Butler (1796-1857). S. C. legislature 1824; S. C. senate 1824-33; judge of S. C. session court 1833; judge of S. C. court of common pleas 1835-46; Senator from S. C., 1846-57. -- Mooney, Volney P., History of Butler County, Kansas, Lawrence, Kan.: Standard Pub. Co., 1916; 869 p.

Butler, Ky. (est. Jan. 18, 1810; 443 sq. mi.; 1970 pop.: 9,723; 1960: 9,586; 1950: 11,309) (Morgantown). Richard Butler (1743-1791). Fought under gen. Arthur St. Clair against Indian tribes in the Northwest territory; killed Nov. 3, 1791.

Butler, Mo. (est. Feb. 27, 1849; 716 sq. mi.; 1970 pop.: 33,529; 1960: 34,656; 1950: 37,707) (Poplar Bluff). William Orlando Butler*.

Butler, Neb. (est. Jan. 26, 1856, org. Oct. 21, 1868; 582 sq. mi.; 1970 pop.: 9,461; 1960: 10,312; 1950: 11,432) (David City). David Butler (1829-1891). First gov. of Neb. Neb., territorial legislature 1861; Neb., terr. senate 1863; gov. of Neb., 1867-71; impeached Mar. 1871; verdict rescinded and charge expunged from the record 1877; Neb. senate 1877. -- Brown, George L., Centennial History of Butler County, Nebraska, Lincoln, Neb.: Journal Co., 1876; 34 p.

Butler, Ohio. (est. Mar. 24, 1803; 471 sq. mi.; 1970 pop.: 226,207; 1960: 199,076; 1950: 147,203) (Hamilton). Richard Butler (1743-1791). Maj. 1776; lt. col. 1777; col. 9th Pa. regiment fought at Stony Point 1779; commissioner to negotiate treaty with Iroquois Indians 1783; supt. Indian affairs northern district; justice court of common pleas Allegheny County 1788; Pa. senate 1790; maj. gen. under gen. Arthur St. Clair's expedition against the northwest Indian tribes; killed Nov. 4, 1791. -- Centennial History of Butler County, Hamilton, Ohio: B. F. Bowen & Co., 1905; 989 p.

Butler, Pa. (est. Mar. 12, 1800; 794 sq. mi.; 1970 pop.: 127,941; 1960: 114,639; 1950: 97,320) (Butler). Richard Butler*. -- Brandon, James Campbell, A concise history of Butler County, Butler, Pa.: Butler County Historical Society, 1962; 176 p. -- Sipe, Chester Hale, History of Butler County, Topeka, Kans.: Historical Pub. Co., 1927; 2 vol.

Butte, Calif. (est. Feb. 18, 1850; 1,665 sq. mi.; 1970 pop.: 101,969; 1960: 82,030; 1950: 64,930) (Oroville). Sutter Buttes, a feature of the North Sacramento Valley; French word for "hill." -- McGie, Joseph F., A History of Butte County, Oroville, Calif.: Butte County Office of Education, 1960; 333 p.

Butte, Idaho. (est. Feb. 6, 1917; 2,240 sq. mi.; 1970 pop.: 2,925; 1960: 3,498; 1950: 2,722) (Arco). French word for "hill."

Butte, S. D. (est. Mar. 2, 1883; 2,251 sq. mi.; 1970 pop.: 7,825; 1960: 8,592; 1950: 8,161) (Belle Fourche). French word for "hill."

Butts, Ga. (est. Dec. 24, 1825; 203 sq. mi.; 1970 pop.: 10,560; 1960: 8,976; 1950: 9,079) (Jackson). Sam Butts (1777-1814). Private in Ga. regiment 1812; elected capt., killed at battle of Chillabee, Jan. 27, 1814.

C

Cabarrus, N. C. (est. session Nov. 15, 1792; 360 sq. mi.; 1970 pop.: 74,629; 1960: 68,137; 1950: 63,783) (Concord). Stephen Cabarrus (1754-1808). Speaker North Carolina house of representatives; first board of trustees Univ. of N. C.

Cabell, W. Va. (est. Jan. 2, 1809; 286 sq. mi.; 1970 pop.: 106,918; 1960: 108,202; 1950: 108,035) (Huntington). William H. Cabell (1772-1853). Fourteenth gov. of Va. (Commonwealth). Va. assembly 1795 and 1798; gov. of Va., 1805-08; judge of general court 1808; judge of circuit court of appeals 1811; judge of court of appeals 1830. -- Wallace, George Selden, Cabell County Annals and families, Richmond, Va.: Garret & Massie, 1935; 589 p.

Cache, Utah. (est. Jan. 5, 1856; 1,175 sq. mi.; 1970 pop.: 42,331; 1960: 35,788; 1950: 33,536) (Logan). French for "to hide." -- Ricks, Joel Edward, History of a valley: Cache Valley, Utah, Idaho, Logan, Utah: Cache Valley Centennial Commission, 1956; 504 p.

Caddo, La. (est. Jan. 18, 1838; 880 sq. mi.; 1970 pop.: 230,184; 1960: 223,859; 1950: 176,547) (Shreveport). Caddo Indian tribe.

Caddo, Okla. (est. July 16, 1907; 1,275 sq. mi.; 1970 pop.: 28,931; 1960: 28,621; 1950: 34,913) (Anadarko). Caddo Indian tribe*.

Calaveras, Calif. (est. Feb. 18, 1850; 1,028 sq. mi.; 1970 pop.: 13,585; 1960: 10,289; 1950: 9,902) (San Andreas). ("The Jumping Frog and Big Tree County"). Spanish word for "skull." -- Wood, Richard Coke, Calaveras, the Land of Skulls, Sonora, Calif.: Mother Lode Press, 1955; 158 p.

Calcasieu, La. (est. Mar. 24, 1840; 1,086 sq. mi.; 1970 pop.: 145,415; 1960: 145,745; 1950: 89,635) (Lake Charles). Indian chief Crying Eagle (Attakapas) who gave eagle's cry.

Caldwell, Ky. (est. Jan. 31, 1809; 357 sq. mi.; 1970 pop.: 13,179; 1960: 13,073; 1950: 13,199) (Princeton). John Caldwell (17 ? -1804). Maj. gen. Ky. conventions 1787-88-89; Ky., senate 1792-93; died while presiding over senate at Frankfort, Ky., 1804. -- Baker, Clauscine R., First history of Caldwell County, Kentucky, Madisonville, Ky.: Commercial Printers, 1936; 219 p.

Caldwell, La. (est. Mar. 6, 1838; 531 sq. mi.; 1970 pop.: 9,354; 1960: 9,004; 1950: 10,293) (Columbia). Matthew Caldwell. N.C. frontiersman.

Caldwell, Mo. (est. Dec. 29, 1836; 430 sq. mi.; 1970 pop.: 8,351; 1960: 8,830; 1950: 9,929) (Kingston). John Caldwell. -- Johnston, Carrie (Polk), History of Clinton and Caldwell Counties, Topeka: Historical Pub. Co., 1923; 836 p.

Caldwell, N.C. (est. Jan. 11, 1841; 476 sq. mi.; 1970 pop.: 56,689; 1960: 49,552; 1950: 43,352) (Lenoir). Joseph Caldwell (1773-1835). Prof. of mathematics; first president of the Univ. of N.C. 1804-35 excepting 1812-17. -- Alexander, Nancy, Here Will I dwell: the story of Caldwell County, Salisbury, N.C.: Rowan Printing Co., 1956; 230 p.

Caldwell, Tex. (est. Mar. 6, 1848; 544 sq. mi.; 1970 pop.: 21,178; 1960: 17,222; 1950: 19,350) (Lockhart). Mathew Caldwell (1798-1842). Commanded Tex. Rangers 1838-39; one of the commanders at Plum Creek against the Comanches 1840; Sante Fe expedition 1841; battle of San Jacinto 1836. Signer Tex. declaration of independence 1836; known as "Old Paint."

Caledonia, Vt. (est. Nov. 5, 1792; 614 sq. mi.; 1970 pop.: 22,789; 1960: 22,786; 1950: 24,049) (St. Johnsbury). Old name for Scotland.

Calhoun, Ala. (est. Dec. 18, 1832; 610 sq. mi.; 1970 pop.: 103,092; 1960: 95,878; 1950: 79,539) (Anniston). John Caldwell Calhoun (1782-1850). S.C. house of representatives 1808-09; Representative from S.C., 1811-17; U.S. Secretary of War in cabinet of Pres. Monroe 1817-25; Vice President of the U.S. under Presidents J.Q. Adams and Jackson 1825-32; Senator from S.C., 1832-43; U.S. Secretary of State in cabinet of Pres. Tyler 1844-45; Senator from S.C., 1845-50. (Originally Benton

County, name changed to Calhoun County Jan. 29, 1858, chap. 306).

Calhoun, Ark. (est. Dec. 6, 1850; 628 sq. mi.; 1970 pop.: 5, 573; 1960: 5, 991; 1950: 7, 132) (Hampton). John Caldwell Calhoun*.

Calhoun, Fla. (est. Jan. 26, 1838; 557 sq. mi.; 1970 pop.: 7, 624; 1960: 7, 422; 1950: 7, 922) (Blountstown). ("The Land of Opportunity"; "The Paradise For All"). John Caldwell Calhoun*.

Calhoun, Ga. (est. Feb. 20, 1854; 284 sq. mi.; 1970 pop.: 6, 606; 1960: 7, 341; 1950: 8, 578) (Morgan). John Caldwell Calhoun*.

Calhoun, Ill. (est. Jan. 10, 1825; 256 sq. mi.; 1970 pop.: 5, 675; 1960: 5, 933; 1950: 6, 898) (Hardin). John Caldwell Calhoun*.

Calhoun, Iowa. (est. Jan. 15, 1851; 572 sq. mi.; 1970 pop.: 14, 287; 1960: 15, 923; 1950: 16, 925) (Rockwell City). John Caldwell Calhoun*. (Originally Fox County, name changed to Calhoun County, Jan. 12, 1853) Chap. 12. -- Storebraker, Beaumont E., Past and present of Calhoun County, Chicago: Pioneer Pub. Co., 1915; 2 vol.

Calhoun, Mich. (est. Oct. 29, 1829; org. 1833; 709 sq. mi.; 1970 pop.: 141, 963; 1960: 138, 858; 1950: 120, 813) (Marshall). John Caldwell Calhoun*. -- Gardner, Washington, History of Calhoun County, Chicago: Lewis Pub. Co., 1913; 2 vol.

Calhoun, Miss. (est. Mar. 8, 1852; 579 sq. mi.; 1970 pop.: 14, 623; 1960: 15, 941; 1950: 18, 369) (Pittsboro). John Caldwell Calhoun*.

Calhoun, S. C. (est. Feb. 14, 1908; 389 sq. mi.; 1970 pop.: 10, 780; 1960: 12, 256; 1950: 14, 753) (St. Matthews). John Caldwell Calhoun*.

Calhoun, Tex. (est. Apr. 4, 1846; 537 sq. mi.; 1970 pop.: 17, 831; 1960: 16, 592; 1950: 9, 222) (Port Lavaca). John Caldwell Calhoun*.

Calhoun, W. Va. (est. Mar. 5, 1856; 280 sq. mi.; 1970 pop.: 7, 046; 1960: 7, 948; 1950: 10, 259) (Grantsville). John Caldwell Calhoun*.

Callahan, Tex. (est. Feb. 1, 1858; 857 sq. mi.; 1970 pop.: 8, 205; 1960: 7, 929; 1950: 9, 087) (Baird). James Hughes Callahan (1814-1856). Tex. volunteer, prisoner of war captured with Fannin's men at Goliad, Tex. 1836; escaped massacre, capt. Tex. Rangers led three companies against Indians 1855; killed 1856.

Callaway, Mo. (est. Nov. 25, 1820; eff. Jan. 1, 1821; 835 sq. mi.; 1970 pop.: 25, 850; 1960: 23, 858; 1950: 23, 316) (Fulton). James Callaway (-1815). Second lt. Rangers

1813; Capt. July 1814; killed in battle with Indians Mar. 7, 1815.

Calloway, Ky. (est. Dec. 19, 1821; 407 sq. mi.; 1970 pop.: 27, 692; 1960: 20, 972; 20, 147) (Murray). Richard Calloway. Col.

Calumet, Wis. (est. Dec. 7, 1836; repealed Aug. 13, 1840, recreated Feb. 18, 1842, eff. Apr. 4, 1842, 315 sq. mi.; 1970 pop.: 27, 604; 1960: 22, 268; 1950: 18, 840) (Chilton), Indian word for "pipe."

Calvert, Md. (est. 1654; 219 sq. mi.; 1970 pop.: 20, 682; 1960: 15, 826; 1950: 12, 100) (Prince Frederick). George Calvert, baron of Baltimore (c. 1580-1632). Knighted 1617; Sec. of State under James I, 1619; resigned 1624; raised to Irish peerage as Baron of Baltimore 1625; died before charter was signed for Maryland tract. (Originally Patuxent County). -- Scharf, John Thomas, History of Baltimore City and county, Philadelphia: L. H. Everts, 1881; 947 p. -- Stein, Charles Francis, History of Calvert County Baltimore, 1960; 404 p.

Camas, Idaho. (est. Feb. 6, 1917; 1, 057 sq. mi.; 1970 pop.: 728; 1960: 917; 1950: 1, 079) (Fairfield). Descriptive. Camas root used as food by Indians, Chinook word meaning "sweet."

Cambria, Pa. (est. Mar. 26, 1804; 695 sq. mi.; 1970 pop.: 186, 785; 1960: 203, 283; 1950: 209, 541) (Ebensburg). Old name for Wales. -- Storey, Henry Wilson, History of Cambria County, New York: Lewis Pub. Co., 1907; 3 vol.

Camden, Ga. (est. Feb. 5, 1777; 711 sq. mi.; 1970 pop.: 11, 334; 1960: 9, 975; 1950: 7, 322) (Woodbine). Charles Pratt, Earl of Camden (1714-1794). English attorney general 1757; chief justice court of common pleas 1761-66; House of Lords 1766; opposed Stamp Act and tax of American colonies as unconstitutional; Lord Chancellor 1766-70; lord pres. of council 1782, 1784-94.

Camden, Mo. (est. Jan. 29, 1841; 655 sq. mi.; 1970 pop.: 13, 315; 1960: 9, 116; 1950: 7, 861) (Camdenton). Earl of Camden*. (Formerly Kinderhook County, name changed Feb. 23, 1843).

Camden, N. J. (est. Mar. 13, 1844; 221 sq. mi.; 1970 pop.: 456, 291; 1960: 392, 035; 1950: 300, 743) (Camden). Earl of Camden*. -- Cranston, Paul F., Camden County, 1681-1931, Camden, N. J.: Camden County Chamber of Commerce, 1931; 193 p.

Camden, N. C. (est. Apr. 8, 1777; 239 sq. mi.; 1970 pop.: 5, 453; 1960: 5, 598; 1950: 5, 223) (Camden). Earl of Camden*.

Cameron, La. (est. Mar. 15, 1870; 1,501 sq. mi.; 1970 pop.: 8,194; 1960: 6,909; 1950: 6,244) (Cameron). Simon Cameron (1799-1889). Senator from Pa. 1845-49, 1857-61 and 1867-77; U. S. Secretary of War in Pres. Lincoln's cabinet 1861-62; organized Union forces 1862; U. S. Minister to Russia 1862.

Cameron, Pa. (est. Mar. 29, 1860; 401 sq. mi.; 1970 pop.: 7,096; 1960: 7,586; 1950: 7,023) (Emporium). Simon Cameron*.

Cameron, Tex. (est. Feb. 12, 1848; 883 sq. mi.; 1970 pop.: 140,368; 1960: 151,098; 1950: 125,170) (Brownsville). Ewin Cameron (-1843). Ky. volunteer in Tex. revolution; leader in Mier Expedition 1842 captured 1842; led prison break but recaptured 1843; shot by order of Santa Anna April 25, 1843.

Camp, Tex. (est. Apr. 6, 1874; 190 sq. mi.; 1970 pop.: 8,005; 1960: 7,849; 1950: 8,740) (Pittsburg). John Lafayette Camp (1828-1891). Capt. Upshur County militia 1861; col. 14th Tex. Regulars Confederate Army 1861; twice wounded and captured; elected Representative from Tex. but was refused a seat, Tex. senate 1874; district judge 1878.

Campbell, Ky. (est. Dec. 17, 1794, eff. May 10, 1795; 151 sq. mi.; 1970 pop.: 88,501; 1960: 86,803; 1950: 76,196) (Alexandria and Newport). John Campbell. -- Jones, Mary K., History of Campbell County, Newport, Ky., 1876; 16 p.

Campbell, S. D. (est. Jan. 8, 1873; 763 sq. mi.; 1970 pop.: 2,866; 1960: 3,531; 1950: 4,046) (Mound City). Norman B. Campbell. Dakota Terr. legislature 1872-73.

Campbell, Tenn. (est. Sept. 11, 1806; 447 sq. mi.; 1970 pop.: 26,045; 1960: 27,936; 1950: 34,369) (Jacksboro). George Washington Campbell (1769-1848). Representative from Tenn. 1803-09; judge Tenn., supreme court of errors and appeals 1809-11; Senator from Tenn., 1811-14; U. S. Secretary of the Treasury in Pres. Madison's cabinet 1814; Senator from Tenn., 1815-18; U. S. Minister to Russia 1818-21. Also claimed for Arthur Campbell negotiated treaty with the Indians 1781.

Campbell, Va. (est. Nov. 5, 1781 session, eff. Feb. 1, 1782; 530 sq. mi.; 1970 pop.: 43,319; 1960: 32,958; 1950: 28,877) (Rustberg). William Campbell (1745-1781). Capt. 1st Va. reg. 1775; resigned 1776; col. Va., militia 1777-80; battle of Kings Mt. Oct. 7, 1780 and Guilford Court House; brig. gen. Va., militia 1780; siege of Yorktown 1781. -- Early, Ruth Hairston, Campbell chronicles and family sketches, embracing the history of

Campbell County, Lynchburg, Va.: J. P. Bell Co., 1927; 554 p.

Campbell, Wyo. (est. Feb. 13, 1911; 4,755 sq. mi.; 1970 pop.: 12,957; 1960: 5,861; 1950: 4,839) (Gillette). Robert Campbell. Fought on Gen. Wm. H. Ashley's expedition up the Mo. River 1822. John Allen Campbell (1835-1880). Second lt. volunteers 1861; maj. 1862; asst. adj. gen. 1862; bvt. col. volunteers 1865; bvt. brig. gen. 1865 for Shiloh, Murfreesboro; mustered out 1866; second lt. regular army 1867; bvt. first lt. 1867; Shiloh 1867; Stone River, Tenn., 1867; capt., maj., lt. col. Resaca, Ga. and Franklin, Tenn., asst. on staff of Gen. Schofield; asst. Secretary of War, resigned 1869; first gov. of Wyo. 1869-75; third asst. U. S. Secretary of State 1875.

Canadian, Okla. (est. July 16, 1907; 885 sq. mi.; 1970 pop.: 32,245; 1960: 24,727; 1950: 25,644) (El Reno). Canadian River, named for Canada, Spanish diminuitive of canyon.

Candler, Ga. (est. July 17, 1914; 228 sq. mi.; 1970 pop.: 6,412; 1960: 6,672; 1950: 8,063) (Metter). Allen Daniel Candler (1834-1910). Fifty-fourth gov. of Ga. In Civil War; private Co. H., 34th Ga. regiment 1861; capt. 1863; lt. col. 4th Ga. reserves 1864; col. 1864; wounded at Kennesaw Mt.; lost eye at Jonesboro; vice pres. Monroe Female College 1865-66; principal Clayton High School 1867-69; pres. of Bailey Institute 1870-71; mayor of Jonesboro, Tenn. 1866; mayor of Gainesville, Ga., 1872; Ga. house of representatives 1873-77; Ga. senate 1878-79; Representative from Ga., 1883-91; Ga. secretary of state 1894-98; gov. of Ga. 1899-1902.

Cannon, Tenn. (est. Jan. 31, 1836; 270 sq. mi.; 1970 pop.: 8,467; 1960: 8,537; 1950: 9,174) (Woodbury). Newton Cannon (1781-1842). Tenth gov. of Tenn.; Representative in Tenn. legislature 1811; private in Creek War, advanced to capt. and col. of Tenn. mounted rifles 1813; Representative from Tenn., 1814-17; commissioner to negotiate a treaty with Chickasaw Indians 1819; Representative from Tenn. 1819-23; gov. of Tenn. 1836-39. -- Brown, Sterling Spurlick, History of Woodbury and Cannon County, Tennessee, Manchester, Tenn.: Dock Printing Co., 1836; 235 p.

Canyon, Idaho. (est. Mar. 7, 1891; 580 sq. mi.; 1970 pop.: 61,288; 1960: 57,662; 1950: 53,597) (Caldwell). Descriptive word.

Cape Girardeau, Mo. (est. Oct. 1, 1812, procl.; 576 sq. mi.; 1970 pop.: 49,350; 1960: 42,020; 1950: 38,397) (Jackson). Sieur de Girardot.

Cape May, N. J. (est. Nov. 12, 1692; 267 sq. mi.; 1970 pop.: 59,554; 1960: 48,555; 1950: 37,131) (Cape May Court House). ("The Heart of New Jersey's Vacationland"). Cornelius Jacobsen May. Capt. director gen of Dutch W. I. Co's New Netherlands. -- Stevens, Lewis Townsend, History of Cape May County, Cape May City, N. J.: L. T. Stevens, 1897; 479 p. -- Hand, Albert, A Book of Cape May, Cape May, N. J.: Albert Hand Co., 1937, 48 p.

Carbon, Mont. (est. Mar. 4, 1895; 2,070 sq. mi.; 1970 pop.: 7,080; 1960: 8,317; 1950: 10,241) (Red Lodge). Descriptive term.

Carbon, Pa. (est. Mar. 13, 1843; 405 sq. mi.; 1970 pop.: 50,573; 1960: 52,889; 1950: 57,558) (Mauch Chunk). Descriptive. -- Brenckman, Fred, History of Carbon County, Harrisburg, Pa.: J. J. Nungesser, 1913; 626 p.

Carbon, Utah. (est. Mar. 8, 1894; 1,474 sq. mi.; 1970 pop.: 15,647; 1960: 21,135; 1950: 24,901) (Price). Descriptive.

Carbon, Wyo. (est. Dec. 16, 1868; 7,965 sq. mi.; 1970 pop.: 13,354; 1960: 14,937; 1950: 15,742) (Rawlins). Descriptive.

Caribou, Idaho. (est. Feb. 11, 1919; 1,175 sq. mi.; 1970 pop.: 6,534; 1960: 5,976; 1950: 5,576) (Soda Springs). Caribou Fairchild. Early settler who was named for Caribou, British Columbia.

Carlisle, Ky. (est. Apr. 3, 1886; eff. May 3, 1886; 196 sq. mi.; 1970 pop.: 5,354; 1960: 5,608; 1950: 6,206) (Bardwell). John Griffin Carlisle (1835-1910). Ky. house of representatives 1859-61; Ky., senate 1866-71; Ky., lt. gov. 1871-75; representative from Ky., 1877-90; Speaker 1883-89; Senator from Ky., 1890-93; U. S. Secretary of the Treasury in cabinet of Pres. Cleveland 1893-97.

Carlton, Minn. (est. May 23, 1857; 860 sq. mi.; 1970 pop.: 28,072; 1960: 27,932; 1950: 24,584) (Carlton). Reuben B. Carlton (1812-1863). Blacksmith 1847; Minn. senate 1858.

Caroline, Md. (est. June 15, 1773 session, eff. Mar. 1774; 320 sq. mi.; 1970 pop.: 19,781; 1960: 19,462; 1950: 18,324) (Denton). Caroline Calvert. Lady Calvert, sister of the last Lord Baltimore. -- History of Caroline County, Federalsburg, Md.: J. W. Stowell Printing Co., 1920; 348 p.

Caroline, Va. (est. Feb. 1, 1727; sess.; 544 sq. mi.; 1970 pop.: 13,925; 1960: 12,725; 1950: 12,471) (Bowling Green). Princess Wilhelmina Carolina of Anspach

(1683-1737). Queen of England 1727-1737; daughter of John Frederick, Margrave of Brandenburg-Anspach and second wife; married King George II, Aug. 22, 1705 o. s. -- Wingfield, Marshall, A History of Caroline County, Richmond: Trevret Christian and Co., Inc., 1924; 528 p.

Carroll, Ark. (est. Nov. 1, 1833; eff. Dec. 25, 1833; 634 sq. mi.; 1970 pop.: 12,301; 1960: 11,284; 1950: 13,244) (Berryville and Eureka Springs). Charles Carroll (1737-1832). Continental commissioner to Canada 1776; Continental Congress 1776-8; Md. senate 1777-1800; signer of Declaration of Independence 1776; Senator from Md. 1789-1792; last surviving signer of the Declaration of Independence. -- Braswell, O. Klute, History of Carroll County, Arkansas, Berryville, Ark.: Braswell Printing Co., 196-?; 1079 p. -- Call, Cora Pinkley, Pioneer tales of Eureka Springs and Carroll County, Eureka Springs, Ark., 1930; 116 p.

Carroll, Ga. (est. Dec. 11, 1826; 492 sq. mi.; 1970 pop.: 45,404; 1960: 36,451; 1950: 34,112) (Carrollton). Charles Carroll*.

Carroll, Ill. (est. Feb. 22, 1839; 453 sq. mi.; 1970 pop.: 19,276; 1960: 19,507; 1950: 18,976) (Mount Carroll). Charles Carroll*. -- History of Carroll County, Chicago: H. F. Kett & Co., 1878; 501 p.

Carroll, Ind. (est. Jan. 7, 1828, eff. May 1, 1828; 374 sq. mi.; 1970 pop.: 17,734; 1960: 16,934; 1950: 16,010) (Delphi). Charles Carroll*.

Carroll, Iowa. (est. Jan. 15, 1851; 574 sq. mi.; 1970 pop.: 22,912; 1960: 23,431; 1950: 23,065) (Carroll). Charles Carroll*. -- Maclean, Paul, History of Carroll County, Chicago: S. J. Clarke Pub. Co., 1912; 2 vol.

Carroll, Ky. (est. Feb. 9, 1838; 131 sq. mi.; 1970 pop.: 8,523; 1960: 7,978; 1950: 8,517) (Carrollton). Charles Carroll*.

Carroll, Md. (est. Jan. 19, 1837; 456 sq. mi.; 1970 pop.: 69,006; 1960: 52,785; 1950: 44,907) (Westminster). Charles Carroll*.

Carroll, Miss. (est. Dec. 23, 1833; 624 sq. mi.; 1970 pop.: 9,397; 1960: 11,177; 1950: 15,499) (Carrollton and Vaiden). Charles Carroll*.

Carroll, Mo. (est. Jan. 2, 1833; 694 sq. mi.; 1970 pop.: 12,565; 1960: 13,847; 1950: 15,589) (Carrollton). Charles Carroll*.

Carroll, N. H. (est. Dec. 22, 1840; 938 sq. mi.; 1970 pop.: 18,548; 1960: 15,829; 1950: 15,868) (Ossipee). Charles Carroll*. -- Merrill, Georgia Drew, ed., History of Carroll County, Boston, Mass.: W. A. Fergusson & Co.,

1889; 987 p.

Carroll, Ohio (est. Dec. 25, 1832; 396 sq. mi.; 1970 pop.: 21,579; 1960: 20,857; 1950: 19,039) (Carrollton). Charles Carroll*. -- Echley, Harvey J., History of Carroll and Harrison counties, Chicago: Lewis Pub. Co., 1921; 2 vol.

Carroll, Tenn. (est. Nov. 7, 1821; 596 sq. mi.; 1970 pop.: 25,741; 1960: 23,476; 1950: 26,553) (Huntingdon). William Carroll. Sixth and ninth gov. of Tenn. Gen. under Andrew Jackson at battle of New Orleans 1815; gov. of Tenn. 1821-27 and 1829-35.

Carroll, Va. (est. Jan. 17, 1842; 496 sq. mi.; 1970 pop.: 23,092; 1960: 23,178; 1950: 26,695) (Hillsville). Charles Carroll*.

Carson, Tex. (est. Aug. 21, 1876; 899 sq. mi.; 1970 pop.: 6,358; 1960: 7,781; 1950: 6,852) (Panhandle). Samuel Price Carson (1798-1838). N.C. senate 1822-24; representative from N.C., 1825-33; N.C. senate 1834; N.C. constitutional convention 1835; Tex. constitutional convention 1836; Tex. secretary of state 1836-38; signer Tex. declaration of independence 1836; commissioner to Washington, D.C., to intercede for Tex. -- Carson County Historical Survey Committee, A time to purpose, a chronicle of Carson County, Pioneer Publishers, 1966; 2 vol.

Carter, Ky. (est. Feb. 9, 1838; 402 sq. mi.; 1970 pop.: 19,850; 1960: 20,817; 1950: 22,559) (Grayson). William G. Carter. Col.

Carter, Mo. (est. Mar. 10, 1859; 506 sq. mi.; 1970 pop.: 3,878; 1960: 3,973; 1950: 4,777) (Van Buren). Zimri A. Carter. Pioneer.

Carter, Mont. (est. Feb. 22, 1917; 3,313 sq. mi.; 1970 pop.: 1,956; 1960: 2,493; 1950: 2,798) (Ekalaka). Thomas Henry Carter (1854-1911). Moved from Iowa to Mont. 1882; delegate from Mont. 1889; representative from Mont. 1889-1891; Commissioner of General Land Office 1891-93, senator from Mont., 1895-1901 and 1905-11. Claude Carter. Buffalo hunter and bartender.

Carter, Okla. (est. July 16, 1907; 825 sq. mi.; 1970 pop.: 37,349; 1960: 39,044; 1950: 36,455) (Ardmore). Benjamin Wisnor Carter. Cherokee Indian, supt. of Chickasaw Male Academy. capt. in Confederate Army. Okla. terr. judge. -- History of Carter County, Fort Worth, Texas: University Supply & Equipment Co., 1957; (unpaged).

Carter, Tenn. (est. Apr. 9, 1796; 355 sq. mi.; 1970 pop.: 42,575; 1960: 41,578; 1950: 42,432) (Elizabethton). Landon Carter. Active in Watauga settlement and Revolutionary War, advocate of the state of Franklin. --

Merritt, Frank, Early History of Carter County, 1760-1861, Knoxville, Tenn.: East Tennessee Historical Society, 1950; 213 p.

Carteret, N. C. (est. 1722; 532 sq. mi.; 1970 pop.: 31, 603, 1960: 30, 940; 1950: 23, 059) (Beaufort). ("Ocean Gateway to the Phosphate, Chemicals, Industrial Phosphate Field, Chemical Complex"; "The Gateway to Action"). John Carteret (1690-1763). House of Lords 1711; English ambassador to Sweden 1719; sec. of state 1721-24; lord lt. of Ireland 1724-30; opposed Sir Robert Walpole in the House of Lords; refused to sell his share to the king 1728; became Earl Granville 1744; lord president of council 1751-63. Knight-baronet-vice chancellor of our household. (see also Granville, N. C. p. 161)

Carver, Minn. (est. Feb. 20, 1855, org. Mar. 3, 1855; 358 sq. mi.; 1970 pop.: 28, 310; 1960: 21, 358; 1950: 18, 155). (Chaska). Jonathan Carver (1732-1780). Military leader, capt. in French Indian war 1755; spent winter at Minn. 1766, signed Indian treaty 1767.

Cascade, Mont. (est. Sept. 12, 1887; 2, 658 sq. mi.; 1970 pop.: 81, 804; 1960: 73, 418; 1950: 53, 027) (Great Falls). Descriptive.

Casey, Ky. (est. Nov. 14, 1806, eff. May 4, 1807; 435 sq. mi.; 1970 pop.: 12, 930; 1960: 14, 327; 1950: 17, 446) (Liberty). William Casey. Col. -- Watkins, Willie Moss, The men, women, events, institutions and lore of Casey County, Ky., Louisville, Ky.: Standard Printing Co., 1939; 223 p.

Cass, Ill. (est. Mar. 3, 1837; 371 sq. mi.; 1970 pop.: 14, 219; 1960: 14, 539; 1950: 15, 097) (Virginia). Lewis Cass (1782-1866). Fourth to ninth gov. of Mich. terr. Ohio house of representatives 1806; U. S. marshall Ohio district 1807-12; col. 27th Regiment U. S. Infantry 1813; brig. gen. 1813; military and civil gov. Mich. terr. embracing period 1813-30; U. S. secretary of war in cabinet of Pres. Jackson 1831-36; U. S. Minister to France 1836-42; Senator from Mich., 1845-48; unsuccessful Democratic candidate for the presidency 1848; Senator from Mich., 1849-57; U. S. Secretary of State in cabinet of Pres. Buchanan 1857-60. -- Perrin, William Henry, History of Cass County, Chicago: O. L. Baskin & Co., 1882; 357 p.

Cass, Ind. (est. Dec. 18, 1828, eff. Apr. 14, 1829; 415 sq. mi.; 1970 pop.: 40, 456; 1960: 40, 931; 1950: 38, 793) (Logansport). Lewis Cass*. -- Powell, Jehu Z. (ed.), History of Cass County, Indiana, N. Y.: Lewis Pub. Co., 1913; 2 vol.

Cass, Iowa. (est. Jan. 15, 1851, org. Jan. 12, 1853; 559 sq. mi.; 1970 pop.: 17,007; 1960: 17,919; 1950: 18,532) (Atlantic). Lewis Cass*.

Cass, Mich. (est. Oct. 29, 1829; 488 sq. mi.; 1970 pop.: 43,312; 1960: 36,932; 1950: 28,185) (Cassopolis). Lewis Cass*. -- Rogers, Howard S., History of Cass County, from 1823 to 1875, Cassopolis, Mich., Vigilant Book and Job Printing, 1875.

Cass, Minn. (est. Mar. 31, 1851; 2,053 sq. mi.; 1970 pop.: 17,323; 1960: 16,720; 1950: 19,468) (Walker). Lewis Cass*.

Cass, Mo. (est. Mar. 3, 1835, 698 sq. mi.; 1970 pop.: 39,448; 1960: 29,702; 1950: 19,325) (Harrisonville). Lewis Cass*. (Formerly Van Buren, changed Feb. 19, 1849 (unnumb.) -- Webber, A. L., History and directory of Cass County, Mo., Harrisonville, Mo.: Cass County Leader, 1908; 408 p.

Cass, Neb. (est. Nov. 3, 1854, procl. org. Jan. 5, 1857; 552 sq. mi.; 1970 pop.: 18,076; 1960: 17,821; 1950: 16,361) (Plattsmouth). Lewis Cass. *

Cass, N. D. (est. Jan. 4, 1873, org. Oct. 27, 1873; 1,749 sq. mi.; 1970 pop.: 73,653; 1960: 66,947; 1950: 58,877) (Fargo). George W. Cass. Pres. No. Pacific RR Co.

Cass, Tex. (est. Apr. 25, 1846; 965 sq. mi.; 1970 pop.: 24,133; 1960: 23,496; 1950: 26,732) (Linden). Lewis Cass*. (Originally Cass County, name changed to Davis County, Dec. 17, 1861; changed to Cass County, May 16, 1871, Chap. 95).

Cassia, Idaho (est. Feb. 20, 1879; 2,544 sq. mi.; 1970 pop.: 17,017; 1960: 16,121; 1950: 14,629) (Burley). Descriptive; cassia plant.

Castro, Tex. (est. Aug. 21, 1876; 876 sq. mi.; 1970 pop.: 10,394; 1960: 8,923; 1950: 5,417) (Dimmitt). Henri Castro (1786-1865). Established Tex. settlement known as Castro's colony 1842; first of twenty-seven ships brought over 5,000 immigrants 1842; consul gen. of Tex. to France 1842.

Caswell, N. C. (est. Apr. 8, 1777; 435 sq. mi.; 1970 pop.: 19,055; 1960: 19,912; 1950: 20,870) (Yanceyville). Richard Caswell (1729-1789). First and fifth gov. of N. C. N. C. assembly 1754-1771; speaker N. C. assembly 1769-71; delegate Continental Congress 1774-76; brig. gen. 1776; Halifax, N. C., convention 1776; gov. of N. C., 1775-79 and 1784-87; battle of Camden 1780; N. C. senate 1788.

Catahoula, La. (est. Mar. 23, 1808; 718 sq. mi.; 1970 pop.: 11,769; 1960: 11,421; 1950: 11,834) (Harrisonburg). Catahoula Indian tribe, name derived from Indian words "cata cola" meaning "big clear lake."

Catawba, N. C. (est. Dec. 12, 1842; 406 sq. mi.; 1970 pop.: 90, 873; 1960: 73, 191; 1950: 61, 794) (Newton). Catawba Indian tribe. -- Catawba County Historical Association, A history of Catawba County, Salisbury, N. C.: Rowan Printing Co., 1954; 526 p.

Catoosa, Ga. (est. Dec. 5, 1853; 169 sq. mi.; 1970 pop.: 28, 271; 1960: 21, 101; 1950: 15, 146) (Ringgold). Catoosa, Indian chief. -- McDaniel, Susie Blaylock, Official History of Catoosa County, 1853-1953, Ringgold, Ga., 1953; 231 p.

Catron, N. M. (est. Feb. 25, 1921; 6, 898 sq. mi.; 1970 pop.: 2, 198; 1960: 2, 773; 1950: 3, 533) (Reserve). Thomas Benton Catron (1840-1921) In Confederate Army 1860-64; district attorney third district N. M. 1866-68; attorney gen. of N. M. 1869; U. S. attorney 1870; terr. council 1884, 1888, 1890, 1899, 1905 and 1909; delegate from N. M., 1895-97; senator from N. M., 1912-17.

Cattaraugus, N. Y. (est. Mar. 11, 1808, 1335 sq. mi.; 1970 pop.: 81, 666; 1960: 80, 187; 1950: 27, 901) (Little Valley). Seneca Indian word meaning "bad smelling banks." -- History of Cattaraugus County, Philadelphia: L. H. Everts, 1879; 512 p. -- Adams, William, Historical gazeteer and biographical memorial of Cattaraugus County, Syracuse, N. Y.: Lyman Horton, 1893; 1164 p.

Cavalier, N. D. (est. Jan. 4, 1873, org. July 8, 1885; 1, 513 sq. mi.; 1970 pop.: 8, 213; 1960: 10, 064; 1950: 11, 840) (Langdon) Charles Cavalier. Early settler in the Dakotas.

Cayuga, N. Y. (est. Mar. 8, 1799; 699 sq. mi.; 1970 pop.: 77, 439; 1960: 73, 942; 1950: 70, 136) (Auburn). Cayuga Indian tribe in the Iroquois League. -- Stroke, Elliot G. and Smith, J. H., History of Cayuga County, Syracuse, N. Y.: D. Mason & Co., 1879; 518 p. -- History of Cayuga County, Auburn, N. Y., 1908; 598 p.

Cecil, Md. (est. 1674; 352 sq. mi.; 1970 pop.: 53, 291; 1960: 48, 408; 1950: 33, 356) (Elkton). Cecilius (or Cecil) Calvert (1605-1675). Second baron of Baltimore; son of George Calvert; never visited Maryland tract but managed it from England. -- Johnston, George, History of Cecil County, Elkton, Md.: G. Johnston, 1881; 548 p.

Cedar, Iowa. (est. Dec. 21, 1837; 585 sq. mi.; 1970 pop.: 17, 655; 1960: 17, 791; 1950: 16, 910) (Tipton). Descriptive word. -- Aurner, Clarence Ray, A topical history of Cedar County, Chicago: S. J. Clarke Pub. Co., 1910; 2 vol.

Cedar, Mo. (est. Feb. 14, 1845; 496 sq. mi.; 1970 pop.: 9, 424; 1960: 9, 185; 1950: 10, 663) (Stockton). Descriptive word. -- Abbott, Clayton, Historical sketches of Cedar County, Missouri, Stockton, Mo., 1967; 276 p.

Cedar, Neb. (est. Feb. 12, 1857; 743 sq. mi.; 1970 pop.: 12,192; 1960: 13,368; 1950: 13,843) (Hartington). Descriptive word.

Centre, Pa. (est. Feb. 13, 1800; 1,115 sq. mi.; 1970 pop.: 99,267; 1960: 78,580; 1950: 65,922) (Bellefonte). Descriptive; the geographical center of the state. -- Lee, J. Marvin, Centre County, State College, Pa., 1965; 234 p.

Cerro Gordo, Iowa (est. Jan. 15, 1851; 576 sq. mi.; 1970 pop.: 49,335; 1960: 49,894; 1950: 46,053) (Mason City). Cerro Gordo, Mexico, site of the battle of Apr. 18, 1847 in the Mexican War. -- History of Franklin and Cerro Gordo counties, Springfield, Ill.: Union Pub. Co., 1883; 1005 p.

Chaffee, Colo. (est. Nov. 1, 1861; 1,039 sq. mi.; 1970 pop.: 10,162; 1960: 8,298; 1950: 7,168) (Salida). Jerome Bunty Chaffee (1825-1886). Moved to Colo. Terr. 1860; one of the founders of Denver, Colo.; Colo. terr. house of representatives 1861-63; Colo. terr. house of representatives, speaker of the house 1863; pres. First National Bank of Denver 1865-80; delegate from Colo. 1871-75; senator from Colo. 1876-79. (Originally Lake County Nov. 1, 1861; name changed to Chaffee County on Feb. 10, 1879, unnumbered).

Chambers, Ala. (est. Dec. 18, 1832; 598 sq. mi.; 1970 pop.: 36,356; 1960: 37,828; 1950: 39,528) (Lafayette). Henry Chambers (1790-1826). Physician, surgeon on staff of Gen. Andrew Jackson; Ala. constitutional convention 1819; Ala. house of representatives 1820; senator from Ala., 1825-26.

Chambers, Tex. (est. Feb. 12, 1858; 618 sq. mi.; 1970 pop.: 12,187; 1960: 10,379; 1950: 7,871) (Anahuac). Thomas Jefferson Chambers (1802-1865). Surveyor gen. of Tex. 1829; Tex. attorney 1834; maj. gen. of reserves 1836; secession convention 1861; assassinated Mar. 15, 1865.

Champaign, Ill. (est. Feb. 20, 1833; 1,043 sq. mi.; 1970 pop.: 163,281; 1960: 132,436; 1950: 106,100) (Urbana). Champaign County, Ohio. -- Biographical Record of Champaign County, Chicago: S. J. Clarke Pub. Co., 1900; 655 p.

Champaign, Ohio (est. Feb. 20, 1805; 433 sq. mi.; 1970 pop.: 30,491; 1960: 29,714; 1950: 26,793) (eff. Mar. 1, 1805) (Urbana). Derived from French meaning "a plain." -- Middleton, Evan Perry, ed., History of Champaign

County, Indianapolis, Ind.: B. F. Bowen & Co., Inc., 1917; 2 vol.

Chariton, Mo. (est. Nov. 16, 1820; 759 sq. mi.; 1970 pop.: 11,084; 1960: 12,720; 1950: 14,944) (Keytesville). Joseph (or John) Chorette. (Chariton) French fur trader. -- Gehrig, Pearl Sims and Smith, T. Berry, History of Chariton and Howard Counties, Topeka, Kan.: Historical Pub. Co., 1923; 856 p.

Charles, Md. (est. 1658; 458 sq. mi.; 1970 pop.: 47,678; 1960: 32,572; 1950: 23,415) (La Plata). ("Charles County, God Bless You!"). Charles Calvert (1637?-1715), the third Lord Baltimore, son of Cecilius Calvert, the second Lord Baltimore; commissioned gov. of Maryland 1661 (to 1675); and the second proprietary 1675-1715. -- Klapthor, Margaret (Brown), The History of Charles County, Md., La Plata, Md.: Charles County Tercentenary Inc., 1958; 204 p.

Charles City, Va. (est. 1634; 184 sq. mi.; 1970 pop.: 6,158; 1960: 5,492; 1950: 4,676) (Charles City). King Charles the First of England (1600-1649). Second son of James VI of Scotland (James I of England); created duke of Albany 1600; duke of York 1605; prince of Wales on death of older brother 1616; king of England 1625-49; crowned Feb. 2, 1626 - married May 11, 1625 to Henrietta Maria, daughter of Henry IV; condemned and beheaded 1649.

Charles Mix, S. D. (est. May 8, 1862; 1,131 sq. mi.; 1970 pop.: 9,994; 1960: 11,785; 1950: 15,558) (Lake Andes) Charles E. Mix. U. S. Commissioner of Indian Affairs in 1858. Also claimed for Charles H. Mix, volunteer and govt. scout. -- Peterson, E. Frank and Peterson E. F., History of Charles Mix County, South Dakota, Geddes, S. D.: H. C. Tucker & Sons, 1907; 184 p.

Charleston, S. C. (est. Mar. 12, 1785; 945 sq. mi.: 1970 pop.: 247,650; 1960: 216,382; 1950: 164,856) (Charleston). King Charles the Second of England (1630-1685). Son of King Charles I; title of prince of Wales from birth 1630; known as "the merry monarch." king of England 1660-85. Crowned Apr. 23, 1661, married May 21, 1662 to Katherine of Braganza, Infanta of Portugal. -- Lesesne, Thomas Petigru, History of Charleston County, Charleston, S. C.: W. H. Cawston, 1931; 369 p.

Charlevoix, Mich. (est. Apr. 1, 1840; org. 1869; 414 sq. mi.; 1970 pop.: 16,541; 1960: 13,421; 1950: 13,475) (Charlevoix) Pierre Francois Xavier de Charlevoix (1682-1761) Jesuit historian and explorer who traveled through the Great Lakes down the Ill. and Miss. rivers to New Orleans in 1720-22. (Originally Reshkauko County; name changed to Charlevoix County on Mar. 8, 1843, Act 67.)

Charlton, Ga. (est. Feb. 18, 1854; 792 sq. mi.; 1970 pop.: 5, 680; 1960: 5, 313; 1950: 4, 821) (Folkston). Robert Milledge Charlton (1807-1854). Ga. legislature 1829; U. S. District Attorney 1830; judge of the superior court for eastern district of Ga., 1832; senator from Ga., 1852-53; mayor of Savannah, Ga. -- McQueen, Alexander Stephens, History of Charlton Co., Atlanta, Ga.: Stein Printing Co., 1932; 269 p.

Charlotte, Fla. (est. Apr. 23, 1921; 705 sq. mi.; 1970 pop.: 27, 559; 1960: 12, 594; 1950: 4, 286) (Punta Gorda). ("It's Fashionable to Visit, Enjoy and Stay In"; "The County Where You're Bound To Enjoy a New World of Entertainment"; "The County Where Your Vacation Land Suddenly Becomes Your New Home"; "The Gem of the Sun Coast"; "The Home of the Fighting Silver King Tarpon"; "The Hub of Pleasure"; "The Pleasure Paradise"; "This Is the Place to Vacation"). Corruption of Spanish and French "Carlos" name used to denote the Calusa Indian tribe living in the section for whom Charlotte Harbor was named.

Charlotte, Va. (est. May 26, 1764 session, eff. Mar. 1, 1765; 468 sq. mi.; 1970 pop.: 11, 551; 1960: 13, 368; 1950: 14, 057) (Charlotte Court). Charlotte Sophia (1774-1818), princess of Mecklenburg-Strelitz; married king George III of England 1761. -- Gaines, R., Handbook of Charlotte County, Richmond: E. Waddey, 1889; 78 p. (see also Mecklenburg, N.C.)

Chase, Kan. (est. Feb. 11, 1859; 774 sq. mi.; 1970 pop.: 3, 408; 1960: 3, 921; 1950: 4, 831) (Cottonwood Falls). Salmon Portland Chase (1808-1873). Twenty-third gov. of Ohio. Cincinnati, Ohio council 1840; Senator from Ohio 1849-53; gov. of Ohio 1855-59; Senator from Ohio for two days 1861; U. S. Secretary of the Treasury in Pres. Lincoln's cabinet 1861-64; chief justice U. S. Supreme Court 1864-73; presided over trial of Pres. Johnson 1868.

Chase, Neb. (est. Feb. 27, 1873, org. Apr. 24, 1886; 894 sq. mi.; 1970 pop.: 4, 129; 1960: 4, 317; 1950: 5, 176) (Imperial). Champion S. Chase. Mayor of Omaha, Neb.

Chatham, Ga. (est. Feb. 5, 1777; 370 sq. mi.; 1970 pop.: 187, 767; 1960: 188, 299; 1950: 151, 481) (Savannah). William Pitt, Earl of Chatham. (see also Pitt, N. C., p. 291)

Chatham, N. C. (est. session Dec. 5, 1770; 707 sq. mi.; 1970 pop.: 29, 554; 1960: 26, 785; 1950: 25, 392) (Pittsboro). William Pitt, Earl of Chatham*.

Chattahoochee, Ga. (est. Feb. 13, 1854; 218 sq. mi.; 1970 pop.: 25, 813; 1960: 13, 011; 1950: 12, 149) (Cusseta). Indian word for "painted stone." -- Rogers, Norma Kate, History of Chattahoochee County, Ga., Columbus, Ga.: Columbus Office Supply Co., 1933; 397 p.

Chattooga, Ga. (est. Dec. 28, 1838; 328 sq. mi.; 1970 pop.: 20, 541; 1960: 19, 954; 1950: 21, 197) (Summerville). Chattooga River.

Chautauqua, Kan. (est. Mar. 3, 1875, eff. June 1, 1875; 647 sq. mi.; 1970 pop.: 4, 642; 1960: 5, 956; 1950: 7, 376) (Sedan). Chautauqua County, N.Y.

Chautauqua, N.Y. (est. Mar. 11, 1808; 1, 080 sq. mi.; 1970 pop.: 147, 305; 1960: 145, 377; 1950: 135, 189) (Mayville). ("The Beautiful Interesting Vacationland"). Contraction of Seneca Indian word meaning "where the fish was taken out." -- Downs, John Phillips, History of Chautauqua County, New York: American Historical Society, Inc., 1921; 3 vol. -- McMahon, Helen Grace, Chautauqua County, Buffalo, N.Y.: H. Stewart, 1958; 339 p.

Chaves, N.M. (est. Feb. 25, 1889; 6, 094 sq. mi.; 1970 pop.: 43, 335; 1960: 57, 649; 1950: 40, 605) (Roswell). Mariano Chaves.

Cheatham, Tenn. (est. Feb. 28, 1856; 305 sq. mi.; 1970 pop.: 13, 199; 1960: 9, 428; 1950: 9, 167) (Ashland City). Edwin S. Cheatham. Speaker of Tenn. Senate when county was formed. Also claimed for Benjamin F. Cheatham and Nathaniel Cheatham.

Cheboygan, Mich. (est. Apr. 1, 1840; org. 1853; 725 sq. mi.; 1970 pop.: 16, 573; 1960: 14, 550; 1950: 13, 731) (Cheboygan). Indian word for "the river that comes out of the ground," "place of ore" or "great pipe."

Chelan, Wash. (est. Mar. 13, 1899; 2, 931 sq. mi.; 1970 pop.: 41, 355; 1960: 40, 744; 1950: 39, 301) (Wenatchee), Indian word for "deep water."

Chemung, N.Y. (est. Mar. 29, 1836; 412 sq. mi.; 1970 pop.: 101, 537; 1960: 98, 706; 1950: 86, 827) (Elimira). Delaware Indian village and word for "big horn." -- Chemung County Historical Society, Chemung County: its history, Elmira, N.Y., 1961; 108 p. -- Towner, Ausburn, A brief history of Chemung County, New York: A. S. Barnes & Co., 1907; 103 p.

Chenango, N.Y. (est. Mar. 15, 1798; 908 sq. mi.; 1970 pop.: 46, 368; 1960: 43, 243; 1950: 39, 138) (Norwich). Onondaga Indian word for "large bull-thistle." -- Smith, James Hadden, History of Chenango and Madison counties, Syracuse, N.Y.: D. Mason & Co., 1880; 760 p. -- Gallinger, Roy, Oxcarts along the Chenango, Sherburne, N.Y.: Heritage Press, 1965; 160 p.

Cherokee, Ala. (est. Jan. 9, 1836; 600 sq. mi.; 1970 pop.: 15, 606; 1960: 16, 303; 1950: 17, 634) (Centre). Cherokee Indian tribe; chickasaw word "chiluk-ki" for "cave people." -- Stewart, Mrs. Frank Ross, Cherokee County History, 1836-1956, 1958-59; 2 vol.

Cherokee, Ga. (est. Dec. 26, 1831; 429 sq. mi.; 1970 pop.: 31, 059; 1960: 23, 001; 1950: 20, 750) (Canton). Cherokee Indian tribe*. -- Marlin, Lloyd Garrison, History of Cherokee County, Atlanta, Ga.: Walter W. Brown Pub., Co., 1932; 289 p.

Cherokee, Iowa. (est. Jan. 15, 1851; 573 sq. mi.; 1970 pop.: 17, 269; 1960: 18, 598; 1950: 19, 052) (Cherokee). Cherokee Indian tribe*.

Cherokee, Kan. (est. Aug. 30, 1855; org. Feb. 18, 1860; 587 sq. mi.; 1970 pop.: 21, 549; 1960: 22, 279; 1950: 25, 144) (Columbus). Cherokee Indian tribe*. (Formerly McGee County, changed Feb. 18, 1860, chap. 30) -- Allison, Nathaniel Thompson, History of Cherokee County, Kansas, Chicago: Biographical Pub. Co., 1904; 630 p.

Cherokee, N. C. (est. Jan. 4, 1839; 467 sq. mi.; 1970 pop.: 16, 330; 1960: 16, 335; 1950: 18, 294) (Murphy). Cherokee Indian tribe*. -- Freel, Margaret (Walker), Our heritage; the people of Cherokee County, North Carolina, 1540-1955, Asheville, N. C.: Miller Printing Co., 1956; 407 p.

Cherokee, Okla. (est. July 16, 1907; 782 sq. mi.; 1970 pop.: 23, 174; 1960: 17, 762; 1950: 18, 989) (Tahlequah). Cherokee Indian tribe*.

Cherokee, S. C. (est. Feb. 25, 1897; 394 sq. mi.; 1970 pop.: 36, 791; 1960: 35, 205; 1950: 34, 992) (Gaffney). Cherokee Indian tribe*.

Cherokee, Tex. (est. Apr. 11, 1846; 1, 054 sq. mi.; 1970 pop.: 32, 008; 1960: 33, 120; 1950: 38, 694) (Rusk). Cherokee Indian tribe*. -- Roach, Hattie Joplin, History of Cherokee County, Texas, Dallas, Texas: Southwest Press, 1934; 178 p.

Cherry, Neb. (est. Feb. 23, 1883, org. Apr. 4, 1883; 5, 982 sq. mi.; 1970 pop.: 6, 846; 1960: 8, 218; 1950: 8, 397) (Valentine) Samuel A. Cherry (-1881). lt. fifth cavalry, killed near Rock Creek, Dakota terr. May 11, 1881. -- Reece, Charles S., History of Cherry County, Nebraska, Simeon, Neb., 1945; 173 p.

Cheshire, N. H. (est. Apr. 29, 1769; 117 sq. mi.; 1970 pop.: 52, 364; 1960: 43, 342; 1950: 28, 811) (Keene). Cheshire County, England. -- Hurd, D., History of Cheshire and Sullivan Counties, Philadelphia: J. W. Lewis & Co., 1886; 585 p.

Chester, Pa. (est. 1682; 760 sq. mi.; 1970 pop.: 278, 311; 1960: 210, 608; 1950: 159, 141) (West Chester). Adapted from Cheshire, England. -- Heathcote, Charles William, A history of Chester County, Harrisburg, Pa.: National Historical Association, 1932; 479 p. -- Futhey, John Smith, History of Chester County, Philadelphia: L. H.

Everts, 1881; 782 p.

Chester, S. C. (est. Mar. 12, 1785; 585 sq. mi.; 1970 pop.: 29, 811; 1960: 30, 888; 1950: 32, 597) (Chester). Adapted from Cheshire, England.

Chester, Tenn. (est. Mar. 4, 1879; 285 sq. mi.; 1970 pop.: 9, 927; 1960: 9, 569; 1950: 11, 149) (Henderson). Robert I. Chester. Postmaster at Jackson, Tenn.; U. S. Marshal; quartermaster Fourth Tennessee Regiment War of 1812.

Chesterfield, S. C. (est. Mar. 12, 1785; 793 sq. mi.; 1970 pop.: 33, 667; 1960: 33, 717; 1950: 36, 236) (Chesterfield). Philip Dormer Stanhope, fourth earl of Chesterfield (1694-1773). Member of Parliament 1816-26; ambassador to the Hague 1728-32 and 1744; lord lt. of Ireland 1745-46; wrote "Letters To His Son" published after his death in 1774.

Chesterfield, Va. (est. May 1, 1749, eff. May 25, 1749; 475 sq. mi.; 1970 pop.: 76, 855; 1960: 71, 197; 1950: 40, 400) (Chesterfield) ("The Ruhr Valley of the South"). Philip Dormer Stanhope, Earl of Chesterfield*. -- Lutz, Earle, Chesterfield, an old Virginia county, Richmond: W. Byrd Press, 1954; 385 p.

Cheyenne, Colo. (est. Mar. 25, 1889; 1, 772 sq. mi.; 1970 pop.: 2, 396; 1960: 2, 789; 1950: 3, 453) (Cheyenne Wells). Cheyenne Indian tribe.

Cheyenne, Kan. (est. Mar. 6, 1873, org. Apr. 1, 1886; 1, 027 sq. mi.; 1970 pop.: 4, 256; 1960: 4, 708; 1950: 5, 668) (St. Francis). Cheyenne Indian tribe*.

Cheyenne, Neb. (est. June 22, 1867, org. Dec. 17, 1870; 1, 186 sq. mi.; 1970 pop.: 10, 778; 1960: 14, 848; 1950: 12, 081) (Sidney). Cheyenne Indian tribe*.

Chickasaw, Iowa. (est. Jan. 15, 1851; 505 sq. mi.; 1970 pop.: 14, 969; 1960: 15, 034; 1950: 15, 226) (New Hampton). Chickasaw Indian tribe. -- Fairbairn, Robert Herd, History of Chickasaw and Howard Counties, Chicago: S. J. Clarke, 1919; 2 vol.

Chickasaw, Miss. (est. Feb. 9, 1836; 501 sq. mi.; 1970 pop.: 16, 805; 1960: 16, 891; 1950: 18, 951) (Houston and Okolona). Chickasaw Indian tribe*.

Chicot, Ark. (est. Oct. 25, 1823; 647 sq. mi.; 1970 pop.: 18, 164; 1960: 18, 990; 1950: 22, 306) (Lake Village). French word for "a stub."

Childress, Tex. (est. Aug. 21, 1876; 701 sq. mi.; 1970 pop.: 6, 605; 1960: 8, 421; 1950: 12, 123) (Childress). George Campbell Childress (1804-1841). One of the five commissioners who drafted the Texas declaration of independence 1836; constitutional convention 1836; suicide at

Galveston 1841.

Chilton, Ala. (est. Dec. 30, 1868; 699 sq. mi.; 1970 pop.: 25,180; 1960: 25,693; 1950: 26,922) (Clanton). William Parish Chilton (1810-1871). Alabama legislature 1839; supreme court of Ala., 1847; chief justice of supreme court of Ala., 1852-56; Ala., senate 1859; provisional Congress of the Confederacy 1860; Confederate Congress 1861-65. (Originally Baker County, Dec. 30, 1868, Act 142, name changed Dec. 17, 1874, Act 72.) -- Wyatt, Thomas Eugene, Chilton County and Her People, Clanton, Ala.: Union Banner, 1960; 168 p.

Chippewa, Mich. (est. Dec. 22, 1826; eff. Feb. 1, 1827; org. 1843; 1,580 sq. mi.; 1970 pop.: 32,412; 1960: 32,655; 1950: 29,206) (Sault Ste. Marie). Chippewa Indian tribe.

Chippewa, Minn. (est. Feb. 20, 1862; 582 sq. mi.; 1970 pop.: 15,109; 1960: 16,320; 1950: 16,739) (Montevideo). Chippewa Indian tribe*.

Chippewa, Wis. (est. Feb. 3, 1845; 1,025 sq. mi.; 1970 pop.: 47,717; 1960: 45,096; 1950: 42,839) (Chippewa Falls). Chippewa Indian tribe*. -- Chippewa County, Wisconsin, past and present, Chicago: S.J. Clarke Pub. Co., 1913; 2 vol.

Chisago, Minn. (est. Mar. 31, 1851; eff. Sept. 1, 1851, org. Jan. 1, 1852; 419 sq. mi.; 1970 pop.: 17,492; 1960: 13,419; 1950: 12,669) (Center City). Indian word "kichi" for large and "saga" for fair. The first syllable was dropped.

Chittenden, Vt. (est. Oct. 22, 1787; 532 sq. mi.; 1970 pop.: 99,131; 1960: 74,425; 1950: 62,570) (Burlington). Thomas Chittenden (1730-1797). First and third terr. gov. of Vt. First gov. Conn. colonial assembly; col. of Conn., military regiment; first pres. of Committee of Safety; terr. gov. of Vt., 1778-79 and 1790-91; gov. 1791-97. -- Rann, W. S., History of Chittenden County, Vermont, Syracuse, N.Y.: D. Mason and Co., 1886; 867 p.

Choctaw, Ala. (est. Dec. 29, 1847; 918 sq. mi.; 1970 pop.: 16,589; 1960: 17,870; 1950: 19,152) (Butler). Choctaw Indian tribe.

Choctaw, Miss. (est. Dec. 23, 1833; 414 sq. mi.; 1970 pop.: 8,440; 1960: 8,423; 1950: 11,009) (Ackerman). Choctaw Indian tribe*.

Choctaw, Okla. (est. July 16, 1907; 784 sq. mi.; 1970 pop.: 15,141; 1960: 16,637; 1950: 20,405) (Hugo). Choctaw Indian tribe*.

Chouteau, Mont. (est. Feb. 2, 1865; 3,920 sq. mi.; 1970 pop.: 6,473; 1960: 7,348; 1950: 6,974) (Fort Benton). Charles P. Chouteau. Fort Benton fur trader.

Chowan, N. C. (est. 1760; 180 sq. mi.; 1970 pop.: 10,764; 1960: 11,729; 1950: 12,540) (Edenton). Chowan Indian tribe, name meaning "they of the south."

Christian, Ill. (est. Feb. 15, 1839; 700 sq. mi.; 1970 pop.: 35,948; 1960: 37,207; 1950: 38,816) (Taylorville). Christian County, Ky. (Name changed from Dane County to Christian County Feb. 1, 1840). -- McBride, J. C., Past and Present of Christian County, Chicago: S. J. Clarke Pub. Co., 1904; 582 p.

Christian, Ky. (est. Dec. 13, 1796, eff. Mar. 1, 1797; 726 sq. mi.; 1970 pop.: 56,224; 1960: 56,904; 1950: 42,359) (Hopkinsville). William Christian. Col. -- Meacham, Charles Mayfield (ed.), A history of Christian County, Kentucky, Nashville, Tenn.: Marshall & Bruce, 1930; 695 p.

Christian, Mo. (est. Mar. 8, 1859; 567 sq. mi.; 1970 pop.: 15,124; 1960: 12,359; 1950: 12,412) (Ozark). William Christian*. -- Christian County Centennial, Inc., Christian County, its first 100 years, Ozark, Mo., 1959; 212 p.

Churchill, Nev. (est. Nov. 25, 1861; 4,907 sq. mi.; 1970 pop.: 10,513; 1960: 8,452; 1950: 6,161) (Fallon). Charles C. Churchill. Capt.

Cimarron, Okla. (est. July 16, 1907; 1,832 sq. mi.; 1970 pop.: 4,145; 1960: 4,496; 1950: 4,589) (Boise City). Spanish for "unruly."

Citrus, Fla. (est. June 2, 1887; 570 sq. mi.; 1970 pop.: 19,196; 1960: 9,268; 1950: 6,111) (Inverness). ("The All-In-One Vacationland"; "The County With Rural Charm and Modern Living"). Descriptive.

Clackamas, Ore. (est. July 5, 1843; 1,890 sq. mi.; 1970 pop.: 166,088; 1960: 113,038; 1950: 86,716) (Oregon City). ("Cool Green Oregon Vacationland"). Clackamas Indian tribe.

Claiborne, La. (est. Mar. 13, 1828; 778 sq. mi.; 1970 pop.: 17,024; 1960: 19,407; 1950: 25,063) (Homer). William Charles Coles Claiborne (1775-1817) First gov. of La. Terr. and first gov. of La. and second gov. of Miss. Terr. Tenn. state constitutional convention 1796; judge of superior court 1796; Representative from Tenn., 1797-1801; gov. of Miss. Terr. 1801-05; commissioner to accept transfer of La. from France 1803; gov. of Orleans terr. 1804-12; gov. of La. 1812-16; Senator from La. 1817. -- Harris, D. W., Hulse, B. M., History of Claiborne Parish, La., New Orleans, La.: Press of W. B. Stansbury, 1886; 263 p.

Claiborne, Miss. (est. Jan. 27, 1802; 489 sq. mi.; 1970 pop.: 10,086; 1960: 10,845; 1950: 11,944) (Port Gibson).

William Charles Coles Claiborne*.

Claiborne, Tenn. (est. Oct. 29, 1801; 445 sq. mi.; 1970 pop.: 19,420; 1960: 19,067; 1950: 24,788) (Tazewell). William Charles Coles Claiborne*.

Clallam, Wash. (est. Apr. 26, 1854; 1,753 sq. mi.; 1970 pop.: 34,770; 1960: 30,022; 1950: 26,396) (Port Angeles) Indian word for "brave people."

Clare, Mich. (est. Apr. 1, 1840; org. 1871; 572 sq. mi.; 1970 pop.: 16,695; 1960: 11,647; 1950: 10,253) (Harrison). Clare County, Ireland. (Originally Kaykakee County, name changed to Clare County, Mar. 8, 1843, Act 67.)

Clarendon, S. C. (est. Mar. 12, 1785; 694 sq. mi.; 1970 pop.: 25,604; 1960: 29,490; 1950: 32,215) (Mamming). Edward Hyde II, (1661-1724) third earl of Clarendon. Col. Royal Regiment of Dragoons 1685-88; capt.-gen. and gov.-in-chief of N. Y. and N. J. 1701-08; commander-in-chief of the militia and forces of Conn., E. and W. Jersey 1701; Vice Admiral of N. Y. and E. and W. Jersey 1701-08; privy councillor 1711; envoy extraordinary to Hanover 1714. (see also Hyde, N. C., p. 190)

Clarion, Pa. (est. Mar. 11, 1839; 599 sq. mi.; 1970 pop.: 38,414; 1960: 37,408; 1950: 38,344) (Clarion). French for "clear." -- Davis, Aaron J., ed., History of Clarion County, Rimersburg, Pa.: Record Press, 1887 (reprint 1968); 664 p.

Clark, Ark. (est. Dec. 15, 1818; eff. Mar. 1, 1819; 878 sq. mi.; 1970 pop.: 21,537; 1960: 20,950; 1950: 22,998) (Arkadelphia). William Clark (1770-1838). Eleventh terr. gov. of Mo. Frontier service against Indians 1791-96; resigned from army 1807; appointed brig. gen. of militia for La. terr. and Supt. of Indian Affairs at St. Louis 1807; gov. of Mo. terr. 1813-20; surveyor gen. for Ill., Mo. and Ark.

Clark, Idaho. (est. Feb. 1, 1919; 1,751 sq. mi.; 1970 pop.: 741; 1960: 915; 1950: 918) (Dubois). Sam Clark. Pioneer cattleman.

Clark, Ill. (est. Mar. 22, 1819; 493 sq. mi.; 1970 pop.: 16,216; 1960: 16,546; 1950: 17,362) (Marshall) George Rogers Clark (1752-1818). Frontier leader; surveyor; volunteer under gov. Dunmore against Shawnees; maj. of militia 1776; lt. col. 1777; attacked British garrison at Vincennes 1779; brig. gen. of Continental Army 1781. -- Perrin, William Henry, History of Crawford and Clark Counties, Chicago: O. L. Baskin & Co., 1883; 374 p.

Clark, Ind. (est. Feb. 3, 1801; 384 sq. mi.; 1970 pop.: 75,876; 1960: 62,795; 1950: 48,330) (Jeffersonville) George Rogers Clark*. -- Baird, Lewis C., Baird's history of Clark County, Indiana, Indianapolis, Ind.: B. F. Bowen & Co., 1909; 919 p.

Clark, Kan. (est. Feb. 16, 1867, abolished 1883, re-created Mar. 7, 1885, org. May 5, 1885; 984 sq. mi.; 1970 pop.: 2,896; 1960: 3,396; 1950: 3,946) (Ashland) Charles F. Clarke (18 -1862). Capt. sixth Kan. cavalry, died at Memphis Dec. 10, 1862.

Clark, Ky, (est. Dec. 6, 1792, eff. Feb. 1, 1793; 259 sq. mi.; 1970 pop.: 24,090; 1960: 21,075; 1950: 18,898) (Winchester) George Rogers Clark*.

Clark, Mo. (est. Dec. 16, 1836; 509 sq. mi.; 1970 pop.: 8,260; 1960: 8,725; 1950: 9,003) (Kahoka) William Clark*.

Clark, Nev. (est. Feb. 5, 1909; eff. July 1, 1909; 7,927 sq. mi.; 1970 pop.: 273,288; 1960: 127,016; 1950: 48,289) (Las Vegas) ("Chance, Sunshine and Choice (Las Vegas"). William Andrews Clark (1839-1925). Went to Montana 1863; placer mining 1863-65; maj. of battalion that pursued Chief Joseph 1877; pres. of Montana constitutional convention 1884 and 1889; Senator from Mont. 1899-1900; vacated his seat 1900; appointed to fill his own vacancy caused by his resignation, but did not qualify; Senator from Mont. 1901-07.

Clark, Ohio. (est. Dec. 26, 1817, eff. Mar. 1, 1818; 402 sq. mi.; 1970 pop.: 157,115; 1960: 131,440; 1950: 111,661) (Springfield). George Rogers Clark*. -- Steele, Alden P., History of Clark County, Chicago: W. H. Beers & Co., 1881; 1077 p.

Clark, S. D. (est. Jan. 8, 1873; 976 sq. mi.; 1970 pop.: 5,515; 1960: 7,134; 1950: 8,369) (Clark). Newton Clark. Taught school in Sioux Falls; Dakota terr. legislature 1872-73.

Clark, Wash. (est. June 27, 1844; 633 sq. mi.; 1970 pop.: 128,454; 1960: 93,809; 1950: 85,307) (Vancouver). William Clark*. (Formerly Vancouver County, name changed to Clark County, Sept. 3, 1849).

Clark, Wis. (est. July 6, 1853; 1,222 sq. mi.; 1970 pop.: 30,361; 1960: 31,527; 1950: 32,459) (Neillsville) George Rogers Clark*. -- Clark County Centennial, The book of the years, 1953; 96 p.

Clarke, Ala. (est. Dec. 10, 1812; 1,241 sq. mi.; 1970 pop.: 26,724; 1960: 25,738; 1950: 26,548) (Grove Hill) John Clarke. Indian fighter. gen. -- Graham, John Simpson, History of Clarke County, Birmingham, Ala.: Birmingham Printing Co., 1924??; 345 p. -- Ball, Timothy Horton, A glance into the great south-east, or Clarke County, Alabama, Tuscaloosa, Ala., Willo Pub. Co., 1962; 770 p.

Clarke, Ga. (est. Dec. 5, 1801; 114 sq. mi.; 1970 pop.: 65,177; 1960: 45,363; 1950: 36,550) (Athens). Elijah Clarke (17 ?-1805). Capt. Ga. militia 1776; col.; wounded at Alligator Creek 1778; battles of Wofford's Iron Works 1780; Musgrove's Mill 1780, Augusta 1780, wounded at battle of Long Cane, S. C. 1780; brig. gen. Ga. militia 1781-83. -- Rowe, H. J., History of Athens and Clarke County, 1923; 180 p. -- Strahan, Charles Morton, Clarke County Ga., Athens, Ga., 1893; 88 p.

Clarke, Iowa. (est. Jan. 13, 1846; org. Dec. 27, 1848; 429 sq. mi.; 1970 pop.: 7,581; 1960: 8,222; 1950: 9,369) (Osceola) James Clarke (1811-1850). Third terr. gov. Iowa terr. 1845-46; gov. Iowa 1845-46; terr. printer first Wis. legislature 1836; est. Burlington, Iowa "Gazette" 1837; secretary Iowa terr; last terr. gov. Iowa 1845-46.

Clarke, Miss. (est. Dec. 10, 1812; 675 sq. mi.; 1970 pop.: 15,049; 1960: 16,493; 1950: 19,362) (Quitman). Joshua G. Clarke. First chancellor of Miss.

Clarke, Va. (est. Mar. 8, 1836; 174 sq. mi.; 1970 pop.: 8,102; 1960: 7,942; 1950: 7,074) (Berryville) ("Virginia's Gateway to the Shenandoah Valley"). George Rogers Clarke*. -- Gold, Thomas Daniel, History of Clarke County, Berryville, Va.: reprint Chesapeake Book Co., 1962; 337 p.

Clatsop, Ore. (est. June 22, 1844; 820 sq. mi.; 1970 pop.: 28,473; 1960: 27,380; 1950: 30,776) (Astoria). Clatsop Indian tribe. -- Miller, Emma Gene, Clatsop County, Portland, Ore.: Binfords & Mort, 1958; 291 p.

Clay, Ala. (est. Dec. 7, 1866; 603 sq. mi.; 1970 pop.: 12,636; 1960: 12,400; 1950: 13,929) (Ashland). Henry Clay (1777-1852). Ky. house of representatives 1803; Senator from Ky., 1806-07; Ky., house of representatives 1808-09; Senator from Ky., 1810-11; Representative from Ky., 1811-14 and 1815-21 and 1823-25; U. S. Secretary of State in cabinet of Pres. J. Q. Adams 1825-29; Senator from Ky., 1831-42 and 1849-52; unsuccessful candidate on the Whig ticket for the presidency, 1824, 1832 and 1844.

Clay, Ark. (est. Mar. 24, 1873; 650 sq. mi.; 1970 pop.: 18,771; 1960: 21,258; 1950: 26,674) (Piggott and Corning). John Middleton Clayton (1796-1856) Del. house of representatives 1824; Del. secretary of state 1826-28; Senator from Del., 1829-36; chief justice of Del., 1837-39; Senator from Del., 1845-49; Secretary of State in Pres. Taylor's cabinet 1849-50; Senator from Del., 1853-56. (Formerly Clayton County, name changed to

Clay County, Dec. 6, 1875, Act 42.)

Clay, Fla. (est. Dec. 31, 1858; 598 sq. mi.; 1970 pop.: 32,059; 1960: 19,535; 1950: 14,323) (Green Cove Springs) ("Invitation to Unlimited Potential"). Henry Clay*.

Clay, Ga. (est. Feb. 16, 1854; 203 sq. mi.; 1970 pop.: 3,636; 1960: 4,551; 1950: 5,844) (Fort Gaines). Henry Clay*.

Clay, Ill. (est. Dec. 23, 1824; 462 sq. mi.; 1970 pop.: 14,735; 1960: 15,815; 1950: 17,445) (Louisville). Henry Clay*.

Clay, Ind. (est. Feb. 12, 1825, eff. Apr. 1, 1825; 364 sq. mi.; 1970 pop.: 23,933; 1960: 24,207; 1950: 23,918) (Brazil). Henry Clay*.

Clay, Iowa. (est. Jan. 15, 1851; 571 sq. mi.; 1970 pop.: 18,464; 1960: 18,504; 1950: 18,103) (Spencer). Henry Clay Jr. (1807-1847). Graduated U.S. Military Academy 1831; bvt. second lt. 1831; resigned 1831; lt. col. 2nd Ky. volunteers 1846; killed at the battle of Buena Vista Feb. 23, 1847. -- Gillespie, Samuel, History of Clay County, Chicago: S.J. Clarke Pub. Co., 1909; 682 p.

Clay, Kan. (est. Feb. 27, 1857, org. Feb. 21, 1860, eff. Apr. 10, 1860; 658 sq. mi.; 1970 pop.: 9,890; 1960: 10,675; 1950: 11,697) (Clay Center). Henry Clay*.

Clay, Ky. (est. Dec. 2, 1806, eff. Apr. 1, 1807; 475 sq. mi.; 1970 pop.: 18,481; 1960: 20,748; 1950: 23,116) (Manchester). Green Clay (1757-1826). Surveyor in Ky. 1777; Va. legislature 1788-89; Ky. legislature 1793-94; Ky., constitutional convention 1799; Ky. senate 1795-98 and 1807; led 3,000 volunteers to aid at Ft. Meigs 1813; left in command of Ft. Meigs 1813; maj. gen. Ky. militia.

Clay, Minn. (est. Mar. 18, 1858; 1,050 sq. mi.; 1970 pop.: 46,585; 1960: 39,080; 1950: 30,363) (Moorhead). Henry Clay*. (Originally Breckinridge County, name changed to Clay County, Mar. 6, 1862, chap. 33.) -- Turner, John, History of Clay and Norman Counties, Indianapolis, Ind.: B. F. Bowen & Co., 1918; 2 vol.

Clay, Miss. (est. May 12, 1871; 408 sq. mi.; 1970 pop.: 18,840; 1960: 18,933; 1950: 17,757) (West Point). Henry Clay*. (Originally Colfax County, name changed to Clay County, Apr. 10, 1876, Chapter 103.)

Clay, Mo. (est. Jan. 2, 1822; 413 sq. mi.; 1970 pop.: 123,322; 1960: 87,474; 1950: 45,221) (Liberty). Henry Clay*.

Clay, Neb. (est. Mar. 7, 1855, org. Feb. 16, 1867; 570 sq. mi.; 1970 pop.: 8,266; 1960: 8,717; 1950: 8,700) (Clay Center). Henry Clay*. -- Stough, Dale, P. (compiler), History of Hamilton and Clay Counties, Nebraska, Chicago:

S. J. Clarke Pub. Co., 1921; 2 vol.

Clay, N. C. (est. Feb. 20, 1861; 219 sq. mi.; 1970 pop.: 5, 180; 1960: 5, 526; 1950: 6, 006) (Hayesville). Henry Clay*.

Clay, S. D. (est. Apr. 10, 1862; org. Jan. 3, 1863; 403 sq. mi.; 1970 pop.: 12, 923; 1960: 10, 810; 1950: 10, 993) (Vermillion). Henry Clay*.

Clay, Tenn. (est. June 24, 1870; 264 sq. mi.; 1970 pop.: 6, 624; 1960: 7, 289; 1950: 8, 701) (Celina). Henry Clay*.

Clay, Tex. (est. Dec. 24, 1857; 1, 101 sq. mi.; 1970 pop.: 8, 079; 1960: 8, 351; 1950: 9, 896) (Henrietta). Henry Clay*. -- Douthitt, Katherine Christian, Romance and dim trails, a history of Clay County, Dallas, Texas: W. T. Tardy, 1938; 280 p.

Clay, W. Va. (est. Mar. 29, 1858; 346 sq. mi.; 1970 pop.: 9, 330; 1960: 11, 942; 1950: 14, 961) (Clay). Henry Clay*.

Clayton, Ga. (est. Nov. 30, 1858; 142 sq. mi.; 1970 pop.: 98, 043; 1960: 46, 365; 1950: 22, 872) (Jonesboro). Augustin Smith Clayton (1783-1839). Ga. legislature 1810-12; clerk Ga., house of representatives 1813-15; Ga. senate 1826-27; judge of Ga., superior court 1819-25 and 1825-31; Representative from Ga., 1832-35.

Clayton, Iowa. (est. Dec. 21, 1837; 778 sq. mi.; 1970 pop.: 20, 606; 1960: 21, 962; 1950: 22, 522) (Elkader). John Middleton Clayton*. -- Price, Realto Exzeque, History of Clayton County, Chicago: R. O. Law Co., 1916; 2 vol.

Clear Creek, Colo. (est. Nov. 1, 1861; 394 sq. mi.; 1970 pop.: 4, 819; 1960: 2, 793; 1950: 3, 289) (Georgetown). Descriptive.

Clearfield, Pa. (est. Mar. 26, 1804; 1, 144 sq. mi.; 1970 pop.: 74, 619; 1960: 81, 534; 1950: 85, 957) (Clearfield). Descriptive. -- Aldrich, Lewis Cass, History of Clearfield County, Syracuse, N. Y.: D. Mason & Co., 1887; 731 p. -- Swoope, Roland Davis, Twentieth century history of Clearfield County, Chicago: Richmond-Arnold Pub. Co., 1911; 481 p.

Clearwater, Idaho (est. Feb. 27, 1911; 2, 522 sq. mi.; 1970 pop.: 10, 871; 1960: 8, 548; 1950: 8, 217) (Orofino). Descriptive.

Clearwater, Minn. (est. Dec. 20, 1902; 1, 005 sq. mi.; 1970 pop.: 8, 013; 1960: 8, 864; 1950: 10, 204) (Bagley). Descriptive.

Cleburne, Ala. (est. Dec. 6, 1866; 574 sq. mi.; 1970 pop.: 10, 996; 1960: 10, 911; 1950: 11, 904) (Heflin). Patrick Ronayne Cleburne (1828-1864). Went to New Orleans from Ireland 1849; druggist; capt. and col. 15th Ark. Infantry; brig. gen. and maj. gen. 1862; battle of Shiloh Apr. 6-7,

1862; wounded at battle of Richmond Aug. 30, 1862; battle of Missionary Ridge, Ringgold Gap, Resaca, New Hope Church; killed battle of Franklin, Tenn., Nov. 30, 1864.

Cleburne, Ark. (est. Feb. 20, 1883; 595 sq. mi.; 1970 pop.: 10,349; 1960: 9,059; 1950: 11,487) (Heber Springs). Patrick Ronayne Cleburne*.

Clermont, Ohio (est. Dec. 6, 1800; 458 sq. mi.; 1970 pop.: 95,725; 1960: 80,530; 1950: 42,182) (Batavia). Clermont, France; descriptive French for "clear mountain." -- Rockey, J. L., History of Clermont County, Philadelphia: L. H. Everts, 1880; 557 p.

Cleveland, Ark. (est. Apr. 17, 1873; 601 sq. mi.; 1970 pop.: 6,605; 1960: 6,944; 1950: 8,956) (Rison). Grover Cleveland (1837-1908). Twenty-second and twenty-fourth Pres. of the U. S.; thirty-first gov. of N. Y. (Formerly Dorsey County, name changed to Cleveland County, Mar. 5, 1885) Act 38.

Cleveland, N. C. (est. Jan. 11, 1841; 466 sq. mi.; 1970 pop.: 72,556; 1960: 66,048; 1950: 64,357) (Shelby). Benjamin Cleveland (1738-1806) Ensign Second N. C. Regiment 1775; lt. 1776; capt. 1776; retired 1778; col. N. C. militia 1778; hero battle of King's Mountain 1780. -- Weathers, Lee B., The living past of Cleveland County, a history, Shelby, N. C.: Star Pub. Co., 1956; 269 p.

Cleveland, Okla. (est. July 16, 1907; 547 sq. mi.; 1970 pop.: 81,839; 1960: 47,600; 1950: 41,443) (Norman). Grover Cleveland*.

Clinch, Ga. (est. Feb. 14, 1850; 747 sq. mi.; 1970 pop.: 6,405; 1960: 6,545; 1950: 6,007) (Homerville). Duncan Lamont Clinch (1787-1849). First lt. Third Infantry U. S. Army 1808; capt. Dec. 31, 1810; lt. col. 1813; col. 1819; bvt. brig. gen. for ten years service 1829; fought in first and second Seminole War 1835; resigned 1836; Representative from Ga., 1844-45. -- Huxford, Folks, History of Clinch County, Georgia, Macon, Ga.: J. W. Burke, 1916; 309 p.

Clinton, Ill. (est. Dec. 27, 1824; 483 sq. mi.; 1970 pop.: 28,315; 1960: 24,029; 1950: 22,594) (Carlyle). De Witt Clinton (1769-1828). Seventh and ninth gov. of N. Y. Secretary to gov. George Clinton; N. Y. assembly 1798; N. Y. senate 1798-1802 and 1806-11; Senator from N. Y., 1802-03; Mayor of New York City 1803-07, 1810-11, 1813-15; gov. of N. Y., 1817-21 and 1825-28. -- Portrait and Biographical Record of Clinton, Washington, Marion and Jefferson Counties, Chicago: Chapman Pub. Co., 1894; 584 p.

Clinton, Ind. (est. Jan. 29, 1830, eff. Mar. 1, 1830; 407 sq. mi.; 1970 pop.: 30,547; 1960: 30,765; 1950: 29,734) (Frankfort). De Witt Clinton*. -- Claybaugh, Joseph, History of Clinton County, Indiana, Indianapolis: A. W. Bowen & Co., 1913.

Clinton, Iowa (est. Dec. 21, 1837, org. Jan. 11, 1840; 695 sq. mi.; 1970 pop.: 56,749; 1960: 55,060; 1950: 49,664) (Clinton). De Witt Clinton*. -- Le Prevost, Estelle, Clinton County History, Clinton, Iowa: Allen Printing Co., 1930; 128 p. -- Wolfe, Patrick B., Wolfe's history of Clinton County, Indianapolis, Ind.: B. F. Bowen & Co., 1911; 2 vol.

Clinton, Ky. (est. Feb. 20, 1836; 206 sq. mi.; 1970 pop.: 8,174; 1960: 8,886; 1950: 10,605) (Albany). De Witt Clinton*.

Clinton, Mich. (est. Mar. 2, 1831, org. 1839; 571 sq. mi.; 1970 pop.: 48,492; 1960: 37,969; 1950: 31,195) (St. Johns). De Witt Clinton*. -- Daboll, Sherman B., Past and Present of Clinton County, Chicago: S. J. Clarke Pub. Co., 1906; 575 p.

Clinton, Mo. (est. Jan. 2, 1833; 420 sq. mi.; 1970 pop.: 12,462; 1960: 11,588; 1950: 11,726) (Plattsburg). De Witt Clinton*. -- Johnston, Carrie (Polk), History of Clinton and Caldwell Counties, Missouri, Topeka: Historical Pub. Co., 1923; 836 p.

Clinton, N. Y. (est. Mar. 7, 1788; 1,059 sq. mi.; 1970 pop.: 72,934; 1960: 72,722; 1950: 53,622) (Plattsburg). ("New York's Loveliest Vacation Area"; "The Famous Popular Vacation Area"; "The Gateway to the Adirondack Mountains"; "The Heart of the Big Lake County"). George Clinton (1739-1812). First and third gov. of N. Y. Clerk of the court of common pleas of N. Y. 1759; district attorney 1765; N. Y. assembly 1768; Continental Congress 1775-76; brig. gen. 1777; gov. of N. Y. 1777-95 and 1801-04; Vice Pres. of the U. S. 1805-12. -- Hurd, Duane Hamilton, History of Clinton and Franklin counties, Philadelphia: J. W. Lewis & Co., 1880; 508 p. -- Kellogg, David Sherwood, Recollections of Clinton County, Plattsburgh, N. Y.: Clinton County Historical Association, 1964; 75 p.

Clinton, Ohio (est. Feb. 19, 1810; 412 sq. mi.; 1970 pop.: 31,464; 1960: 30,004; 1950: 25,572) (Wilmington). George Clinton*. -- Brown, Albert J., History of Clinton County, Indianapolis: B. F. Bowen, 1915; 967 p. -- History of Clinton County, Chicago: W. H. Beers & Co., 1882; 1180 p.

Clinton, Pa. (est. June 21, 1839; 902 sq. mi.; 1970 pop.: 37,721; 1960: 37,619; 1950: 36,532) (Lock Haven). De Witt Clinton*. -- A picture of Clinton County, Harrisburg, Pa.: Commissioners of Clinton County, 1942; 195 p.

Cloud, Kan. (est. Feb. 27, 1860; 711 sq. mi.; 1970 pop.: 13,466; 1960: 14,407; 1950: 16,104) (Concordia). William F. Cloud. Col. Second Kan. regiment. (Name changed from Shirley County to Cloud County, Chap. 40, Feb. 26, 1867). -- Hollibaugh, E. F., Biographical history of Cloud County, Kansas, Chicago:, 1903; 919 p.

Coahoma, Miss. (est. Feb. 9, 1836; 530 sq. mi.; 1970 pop.: 40,447; 1960: 46,212; 1950: 49,361) (Clarksdale). Choctaw Indian word for "red panther."

Coal, Okla. (est. July 16, 1907; 526 sq. mi.; 1970 pop.: 5,525; 1960: 5,546; 1950: 8,056) (Coalgate). Descriptive.

Cobb, Ga. (est. Dec. 3, 1832; 353 sq. mi.; 1970 pop.: 196,793; 1960: 114,174; 1950: 61,830) (Marietta). Thomas Willis Cobb (1784-1830). Representative from Ga., 1817-21 and 1823-24; Senator from Ga., 1824-28; judge of superior court of Ga., 1828. -- Temple, (Gober) Sarah Blackwell, The First Hundred Years, A Short History of Cobb County, Atlanta: Walter W. Brown Pub. Co., 1935; 901 p.

Cochise, Ariz. (est. Feb. 1, 1881; 6,256 sq. mi.; 1970 pop.: 61,910; 1960: 55,039; 1950: 31,488) (Bisbee). ("Arizona's Wonderland of Rocks"). Cochise, Chiricahua Apache Indian chief, led raids in Arizona, surrendered 1871.

Cochran, Tex. (est. Aug. 21, 1876; 782 sq. mi.; 1970 pop.: 5,326; 1960: 6,417; 1950: 5,928) (Morton). Robert Cochran (-1836). Settled in Tex. 1835; private; killed at the Alamo Mar. 6, 1836.

Cocke, Tenn. (est. Oct. 9, 1797; 434 sq. mi.; 1970 pop.: 25,283; 1960: 23,390; 1950: 22,991) (Newport). William Cocke (1747-1828). Explored eastern and western Tenn. with Daniel Boone; led Virginians against Indians 1776; Va., house of burgesses; moved to Tenn., 1776; Tenn. constitutional convention 1796; Senator from Tenn., 1796-97 and 1799-1805; judge of first circuit 1809; Miss. legislature 1813; served under Gen. Jackson, War of 1812; Indian agent Chickasaw Nation 1814. -- O'Dell, Ruth Webb, Over the Misty Blue Hills; the story of Cocke County, Tenn., 1950; 369 p.

Coconino, Ariz. (est. Feb. 19, 1891; 18,573 sq. mi.; 1970 pop.: 48,326; 1960: 41,857; 1950: 23,910) (Flagstaff). ("Arizona's Land of Superlatives"; "The County In Which There Is Room to Have Fun"; "Rooms To Live in";

"The Scenic Empire"). Havasupai Indian word for "little water."

Codington, S. D. (est. 1877, org. Aug. 7, 1878; 691 sq. mi.; 1970 pop.: 19,140; 1960: 20,220; 1950: 18,944) (Watertown). G. S. S. Codington. Congregational clergyman, Dakota terr. legislature 1877.

Coffee, Ala. (est. Dec. 29, 1841; 677 sq. mi.; 1970 pop.: 34,872; 1960: 30,583; 1950: 30,720) (Elba and Enterprise). John Coffee (1772-1833). Surveyor; col. Tenn. volunteers 1812-13; brig. gen. Tenn. mounted 1813; wounded in battle with Creek Indians 1814; led Tennesseans at battle of New Orleans 1815; U. S. surveyor of public lands 1817. -- Watson, Fred Shelton, Piney Wood echoes; a history of Dale and Coffee Counties, Elba, Ala. Elba Clipper, 1949; 200 p.

Coffee, Ga. (est. Feb. 9, 1854; 632 sq. mi.; 1970 pop.: 22,828; 1960: 21,953; 1950: 23,961) (Douglas). ("The Heart of the South Georgia Empire"). John Coffee (1782-1836). Gen. of Ga. militia Creek war 1814; Ga., senate 1819-27; Representative from Ga., 1833-36, a cousin of John Coffee listed above. -- Ward, Warren P., Ward's History of Coffee County, Atlanta: Press of Foote & Davies Co., 1930; 354 p.

Coffee, Tenn. (est. Jan. 8, 1836; 435 sq. mi.; 1970 pop.: 32,572; 1960: 28,603; 1950: 23,049) (Manchester). John Coffee (1772-1833). See biography 2 above.

Coffey, Kan. (est. Aug. 30, 1855, org. Feb. 17, 1857; 656 sq. mi.; 1970 pop.: 7,397; 1960: 8,403; 1950: 10,408) (Burlington). A. M. Coffey. Kan. terr. legislature.

Coke, Tex. (est. Mar. 13, 1889; 915 sq. mi.; 1970 pop.: 3,087; 1960: 3,589; 1950: 4,045) (Robert Lee). Richard Coke (1829-1897). Fourteenth gov. of Tex. Private, Confederate Army, advanced to capt. 1861-65; district court judge at Waco 1865; judge of Tex. supreme court 1866; removed in 1867; gov. of Tex. 1874-76; Senator from Tex. 1877-85.

Colbert, Ala. (est. Feb. 6, 1867; 616 sq. mi.; 1970 pop.: 49,632; 1960: 46,506; 1950: 39,561) (Tuscumbia). George Colbert and Levi Colbert, Chickasaw Indians. -- Leftwich, Nina, Two hundred years at Muscle Shoals, being an authentic history of Colbert County 1700-1900, Tuscumbia, Ala., 1935; 279 p.

Cole, Mo. (est. Nov. 16, 1820; 385 sq. mi.; 1970 pop.: 46,228; 1960: 40,761; 1950: 35,464) (Jefferson City). Stephen Cole. Indian fighter.

Coleman, Tex. (est. Feb. 1, 1858; 1,282 sq. mi.; 1970 pop.: 10,288; 1960: 12,458; 1950: 15,503) (Coleman).

Robert M. Coleman (1799-1837). Aide-de-camp of Gen. Houston at battle of San Jacinto 1836; signer Tex. declaration of independence 1836; Tex. Ranger 1836-37; drowned in Brazos River 1837. -- Gay, Beatrice Grady, Into the Setting Sun, a history of Coleman County, Santa Anna, Texas, 1936; 193 p.

Coles, Ill. (est. Dec. 25, 1830; 525 sq. mi.; 1970 pop.: 47, 815; 1960: 42, 860; 1950: 40, 328) (Charleston). Edward Coles (1786-1868). Second gov. of Ill. Private secretary to Pres. Madison 1809-15; on mission to Moscow 1816; settled in Ill. 1818; gov. 1822-26. Freed his slaves and gave each 160 acres of land. -- History of Coles County, Evansville, Ind.: Le Baron, W., 1879; 699 p.

Colfax, Neb. (est. Feb. 15, 1869; 405 sq. mi.; 1970 pop.: 9, 498; 1960: 9, 595; 1950: 10, 010) (Schuyler). Schuyler Colfax (1823-1885). Vice pres. of the U. S. Editor and proprietor "Valley Register," St. Joseph, Ind., 1845; Ind. constitutional convention 1850; Representative from Ind., 1855-69; vice pres. 1869-73; unsuccessful candidate for renomination in 1872.

Colfax, N. M. (est. Jan. 25, 1869; 3, 765 sq. mi.; 1970 pop.: 12, 170; 1960: 13, 806; 1950: 16, 761) (Raton). Schuyler Colfax*.

Colleton, S. C. (est. Mar. 12, 1783; 1, 048 sq. mi.; 1970 pop.: 27, 622; 1960: 27, 816; 1950: 28, 242) (Walterboro). John Colleton, one of eight proprietors of S. C.

Collier, Fla. (est. May 8, 1923; 2, 032 sq. mi.; 1970 pop.: 38, 040; 1960: 15, 753; 1950: 6, 488) (Everglades). ("Florida's Fifth Fastest Growing County"). Barron Gift Collier (1873-1939). Industrialist; held advertising concession in cars; owned Fla. real estate and hotels; reclaimed sections of the Everglades, etc. -- Tebeau, Charlton W., Florida's last Frontier, the history of Collier County, Coral Gables, Fla.: University of Miami Press, 1966; 278 p.

Collin, Tex. (est. Apr. 3, 1846; 886 sq. mi.; 1970 pop.: 66, 920; 1960: 41, 247; 1950: 41, 692) (McKinney). Collin McKinney (1766-1861). Tex constitutional convention 1836; signer Tex. declaration of independence 1836; first, second and fourth Tex. legislature. -- Stambaugh, Jacob Lee, History of Collin County, Texas, Texas State Historical Association, 1958; 303 p.

Collingsworth, Tex. (est. Aug. 21, 1876; 899 sq. mi.; 1970 pop.: 4, 755; 1960: 6, 276; 1950: 9, 139) (Wellington). James T. Collinsworth (1806-1838). Tex. constitutional convention 1836; maj. and aide-de-camp to Gen. Houston

1836; Tex. senate 1836; first chief justice Tex. Republic 1837; accidental death by drowning 1838. (An error in spelling named the county Collingsworth instead of Collinsworth). -- Wellington Leader, History of Collingsworth County, Wellington, Texas: Wellington Leader, 1925; 107 p.

Colorado, Tex. (est. Mar. 17, 1836; 950 sq. mi. ; 1970 pop. : 17, 638; 1960: 18, 463; 1950: 17, 576) (Columbus). Spanish word for "colored."

Colquitt, Ga. (est. Feb. 25, 1856; 529 sq. mi. ; 1970 pop. : 32, 200; 1960: 34, 048; 1950: 33, 999) (Moultrie), Walter Terry Colquitt (1799-1855). Judge of the Chattahoochie circuit 1826; Methodist preacher 1827; Ga. senate 1834 and 1837; Representative from Ga., 1839-40 and 1842-43; Senator from Ga., 1843-48. -- Covington, W. A., History of Colquitt County, Atlanta, Ga. : Foote and Davies Co., 1937; 365 p.

Columbia, Ark. (est. Dec. 17, 1852; 768 sq. mi. ; 1970 pop. : 25, 952; 1960: 26, 400; 1950: 28, 770) (Magnolia). Columbia, the Goddess of Liberty. -- Killgore, Nettie Hicks, History of Columbia County, Magnolia, Ark., 1947; 231 p.

Columbia, Fla. (est. Feb. 4, 1832; 786 sq. mi. ; 1970 pop.: 25, 250; 1960: 20, 077; 1950: 18, 216) (Lake City). Christopher Columbus (1451-1506). Italian navigator, sailed from Palos, Spain Aug. 3, 1492; discovered San Salvador Oct. 12, 1492.

Columbia, Ga. (est. Dec. 10, 1790; 350 sq. mi. ; 1970 pop.: 22, 327; 1960: 13, 423; 1950: 9, 525) (Appling). Christopher Columbus*.

Columbia, N. Y. (est. Apr. 4, 1786; 643 sq. mi. ; 1970 pop.: 51, 519; 1960: 47, 322; 1950: 43, 182) (Hudson). Christopher Columbus*. -- Columbia County at the end of a century, Hudson, N. Y. : Record Printing & Pub. Co., 1900; 2 vol. -- Ellis, Franklin, History of Columbus County, Philadelphia: Everts & Ensign, 1878; 447 p.

Columbia, Ore. (est. Jan. 16, 1854; 646 sq. mi. ; 1970 pop. : 28, 790; 1960: 22, 379; 1950: 22, 967) (Saint Helens). Named for Columbia River which was named for the ship in which Capt. Gray sailed up the river.

Columbia, Pa. (est. Mar. 22, 1813; 484 sq. mi. ; 1970 pop. : 55, 114; 1960: 53, 489; 1950: 53, 460) (Bloomsburg). Christopher Columbus*. -- Barton, Edwin Michelet, History of Columbia County, Bloomsburg, Pa. : Columbia County Historical Society, 1958.

Columbia, Wash. (est. Nov. 11, 1875; 860 sq. mi. ; 1970 pop. : 4, 439; 1960: 4, 569; 1950: 4, 860) (Dayton). Columbia River *.

Columbia, Wis. (est. Feb. 3, 1846; 778 sq. mi.; 1970 pop.: 40, 150; 1960: 36, 708; 1950: 34, 023) (Portage). Christopher Columbus*. -- Jones, James Edwin, A history of Columbia County, Chicago: Lewis Pub. Co., 1914; 2 vol.

Columbiana, Ohio (est. Mar. 25, 1803; 535 sq. mi.; 1970 pop.: 108, 310; 1960: 107, 004; 1950: 98, 920) (Lisbon). Christopher Columbus and Anna. -- Barth, Harold Bradshaw, History of Columbiana County, Topeka, Kan.: Historical Pub. Co., 1926; 2 vol. -- McCord, William B., History of Columbiana County, Chicago: Biographical Pub. Co., 1905; 848 p.

Columbus, N. C. (est. Dec. 15, 1808; 939 sq. mi.; 1970 pop.: 46, 937; 1960: 48, 973; 1950: 50, 621) (Whiteville). Christopher Columbus*.

Colusa, Calif. (est. Feb. 18, 1850; 1, 153 sq. mi.; 1970 pop.: 12, 430; 1960: 12, 175; 1950: 11, 651) (Colusa). Colus Indian tribe. -- Green, William Semple, The History of Colusa County, Sacramento: Sacramento Lithograph Co., 1950; 196 p.

Comal, Tex. (est. Mar. 24, 1846; 567 sq. mi.; 1970 pop.: 24, 165; 1960: 19, 844; 1950: 16, 357) (New Braunfels). Spanish word for "basin" or "pan for cooking maize cakes" or "griddle." -- Haas, Oscar, History of New Braunfels and Comal County, Austin, Texas: Steck Co., 1968; 338 p.

Comanche, Kan. (est. Feb. 26, 1867, org. Feb. 27, 1885; 800 sq. mi.; 1970 pop.: 2, 702; 1960: 3, 271; 1950: 3, 888) (Coldwater). Comanche Indian tribe.

Comanche, Okla. (est. July 16, 1907; 1, 088 sq. mi.; 1970 pop.: 108, 144; 1960: 90, 803; 1950: 55, 165) (Lawton). Comanche Indian tribe*.

Comanche, Tex. (est. Jan. 25, 1856; 972 sq. mi.; 1970 pop.: 11, 898; 1960: 11, 865; 1950: 15, 516) (Comanche). Comanche Indian tribe. -- Wells, Eulalia Nabers, Blazing the way; tales of Comanche County, Blanket, Texas, c. 1942; 168 p.

Concho, Tex. (est. Feb. 1, 1858; 1, 004 sq. mi.; 1970 pop.: 2, 937; 1960: 3, 672; 1950: 5, 078) (Paint Rock). Concho River, Spanish word for "shell." -- Walter, Hazie Davis, Concho County history, 1858-1958, Eden, Texas, 1959; 2 vol.

Concordia, La. (est. Apr. 10, 1805; 714 sq. mi.; 1970 pop.: 22, 578; 1960: 20, 467; 1950: 14, 398) (Vidalia). Descriptive of concord. In 1798, Don Jose Vidal petitioned de Lemos, gov. gen. of New Orleans.

Conecuh, Ala. (est. Feb. 13, 1818; 850 sq. mi.; 1970 pop.: 15,645; 1960: 17,762; 1950: 21,776) (Evergreen). Indian word for "crooked." -- Riley, Benjamin Franklin, History of Conecuh County, Ala., Weekly Packet, 1964 (reprint of 1881 edition), 246 p.

Conejos, Col. (est. Nov. 1, 1861; 1,272 sq. mi.; 1970 pop.: 7,846; 1960: 8,428; 1950: 10,171) (Conejos). Spanish word for "rabbits." (Formerly Guadalupe County, name changed to Conejos County, Nov. 7, 1861).

Contra Costa, Cal. (est. Feb. 18, 1850; 734 sq. mi.; 1970 pop.: 558,389; 1960: 409,030; 1950: 298,984) (Martinez). ("The Largest Industrial County in California"). Spanish for "opposite coast." -- Purcell, Mae Fisher, History of Contra Costa County, Berkeley, Calif.: Gillick Press, 1940; 742 p. -- History of Contra Costa County, Los Angeles, Calif.: Historic Record Co., 1926; 1102 p.

Converse, Wyo. (est. Mar. 9, 1888; 4,167 sq. mi.; 1970 pop.: 5,938; 1960: 6,366; 1950: 5,933) (Douglas). A. H. Converse. Stockman and banker.

Conway, Ark. (est. Oct. 20, 1825, eff. Jan. 1, 1826; 560 sq. mi.; 1970 pop.: 16,805; 1960: 15,430; 1950: 18,137) (Morrilton). Henry Wharton Conway (1793-1827). Ensign and lt. 1813; clerk U. S. Treasury 1817; moved to Ark. terr. 1820; Delegate from Ark. terr. 1823-27.

Cook, Ga. (est. July 30, 1918; 241 sq. mi.; 1970 pop.: 12,129; 1960: 11,822; 1950: 12,201) (Adel). Philip Cook (1817-1894). Ga. senate 1859, 1860, 1863 and 1864; private Confederate army 1861; brig. gen. 1863; Representative from Ga., 1873-83; Ga., secretary of state 1890-94. Parrish, J.J., History of Cook County, 134 p.

Cook, Ill. (est. Jan. 15 1831; 933 sq. mi.; 1970 pop.: 5,492,369; 1960: 5,129,725; 1950: 4,508,792) (Chicago). Daniel Pope Cook (1794-1827). First attorney gen., Ill. Mar. 5 to Mar. 15, 1819; Representative from Ill., 1819-27. -- Goodspeed, Weston Arthur, History of Cook County, Chicago: Goodspeed Historical Assn., 1911(?); 2 vol.

Cook, Minn. (est. Mar. 9, 1874; 1,403 sq. mi.; 1970 pop.: 3,423; 1960: 3,377; 1950: 2,900) (Grand Marais). Michael Cook (1828-1864). Minn. terr. and state senator 1857-1862; maj. Tenth Minn. regiment 1864; died from wounds received at battle of Nashville, Dec. 16, 1864. Also claimed for John Cook. Killed by Ojibway Indians.

Cooke, Tex. (est. Mar. 20, 1848; 909 sq. mi.; 1970 pop.: 23,471; 1960: 22,560; 1950: 22,146) (Gainesville). William G. Cooke (1808-1847). Capt. of the New Orleans Grays in the Tex. Revolution at Bexar Dec. 5, 1835; in service to Sept. 1837; Q. M. gen. in army Aug. 1839. -- Smith, Alex Morton, First 100 years in Cooke County, San Antonio, Texas: Naylor Co., 1955; 249 p.

Cooper, Mo. (est. Dec. 17, 1818; 563 sq. mi.; 1970 pop.: 14,732; 1960: 15,448; 1950: 16,608) (Boonville). Sarshel Cooper. Pioneer. -- Johnson, William Foreman, History of Cooper County, Missouri, Topeka: Historical Pub. Co., 1919; 1167 p. -- Melton, Elston Joseph, Melton's History of Cooper County, Missouri, Columbia, Mo.: E. W. Stephens Pub. Co., 1937; 584 p.

Coos, N. H. (est. Dec. 24, 1803; eff. Mar. 1, 1805; 1,825 sq. mi.; 1970 pop.: 34,291; 1960: 37,140; 1950: 35,932) (Lancaster). Indian word "cohos"("pines"). -- Merrill, G. D., ed., History of Coos County, Syracuse, N. Y.: W. A. Fergusson & Co., 1888; 956 p.

Coos, Ore. (est. Dec. 22, 1853; 1,611 sq. mi.; 1970 pop.: 56,515; 1960: 54,955; 1950: 42,265) (Coquille). Coos Indian tribe*. -- Dodge, Orvil, Pioneer history of Coos and Curry counties, Salem, Ore.: Capital Printing Co., 1898; 468 p.

Coosa, Ala. (est. Dec. 18, 1832; 648 sq. mi.; 1970 pop.: 10,662; 1960: 10,726; 1950: 11,766) (Rockford). Indian tribe, Indian word for "rippling."

Copiah, Miss. (est. Jan. 21, 1823; 769 sq. mi.; 1970 pop.: 24,749; 1960: 27,051; 1950: 30,493) (Hazlehurst). Indian word for "calling panther."

Corson, S. D. (est. Mar. 2, 1909; 2,525 sq. mi.; 1970 pop.: 4,994; 1960: 5,798; 1950: 6,168) (McIntosh). Dighton Corson (1827-1915). Wis. legislature 1857-58; Wis. attorney; Nev. District Attorney and State Attorney. Nev. constitutional convention 1885 and 1889; first judge supreme court of S. D. 1889-1913.

Cortland, N. Y. (est. Apr. 8, 1808; 502 sq. mi.; 1970 pop.: 45,894; 1960: 41,113; 1950: 37,158) (Cortland). Pierre Van Cortlandt, Jr. (1762-1848). N. Y. assembly 1811-12; Representative from N. Y., 1811-13; pres. Westchester County Bank 1835-48. -- Smith, H. Perry, ed., History of Cortland County, Syracuse, N. Y.: D. Mason & Co., 1885; 552 p. -- Souvenir Book, Cortland county sesquicentennial celebration, Cortland, N. Y., 1958; 192 p.

Coryell, Tex. (est. Feb. 4, 1854; 1,043 sq. mi.; 1970 pop.: 35,311; 1960: 23,961; 1950: 16,284) (Gatesville). James Coryell (1801-1837). Settled in Tex. 1829; Tex. Ranger 1836; killed by Indians while exploring silver mine May 27, 1837. -- Mears, Mildred, Coryell county scrapbook, Waco, Texas, 1963; 253 p. -- Scott, Zelma, History of Coryell County, Texas, Austin, Texas: Texas

State Historical Assn., 1965; 278 p.

Coshocton, Ohio (est. Jan. 31, 1810; 562 sq. mi.; 1970 pop.: 33,486; 1960: 32,224; 1950: 31,141) (Coshocton). Delaware Indian name meaning "union of waters" or "black bear town." -- Bahmer, William J., Centennial history of Coshocton County, Chicago: S. J. Clarke Pub. Co., 1909; 2 vol. -- Hill, Norman Newell, History of Coshocton County, Newark, Ohio: A. A. Graham & Co., 1881; 833 p.

Costilla, Colo. (est. Nov. 1, 1861; 1,215 sq. mi.; 1970 pop.: 3,091; 1960: 4,219; 1950: 6,067) (San Luis). Spanish for "rib" and "furring timber."

Cottle, Tex. (est. Aug. 21, 1876; 901 sq. mi.; 1970 pop.: 3,204; 1960: 4,207; 1950: 6,099) (Paducah). George Washington Cottle (1798-1836). Private, resident of Gonzalez, Tex.; killed in defense of Alamo Mar. 6, 1836.

Cotton, Okla. (est. by election Aug. 22, 1912, gov. procl. Aug. 27, 1912; 629 sq. mi.; 1970 pop.: 6,832; 1960: 8,031; 1950: 10,180) (Walters). Descriptive.

Cottonwood, Minn. (est. May 23, 1857, org. Mar. 3, 1870; 640 sq. mi.; 1970 pop.: 14,887; 1960: 16,166; 1950: 15,763) (Windom). Cottonwood River, descriptive. -- Brown, John A., History of Cottonwood and Watonwan Counties, Indianapolis: B. F. Bowen & Co., 1916; 2 vol.

Covington, Ala. (est. Dec. 7, 1821; 1,034 sq. mi.; 1970 pop.: 34,079; 1960: 35,631; 1950: 40,373) (Andalusia). Leonard Wailes Covington (1768-1813). U. S. Army 1792; lt. of Dragoons 1793; resigned 1795; Maryland house of delegates; Representative from Md., 1805-07; lt. col. and col. of light Dragoons 1809; brig. gen. 1813; mortally wounded at battle of Crystler's Field 1813. (Name changed to Jones County Aug. 6, 1868; name changed to original and present name Oct. 10, 1868. Act 39.)

Covington, Miss. (est. Feb. 5, 1819; 410 sq. mi.; 1970 pop.: 14,002; 1960: 13,637; 1950: 16,036) (Collins). Leonard Covington*.

Coweta, Ga. (est. Dec. 11, 1826; 443 sq. mi.; 1970 pop.: 32,310; 1960: 28,893; 1950: 27,786) (Newnan) Indian chief. -- Jones, Mary, (Gibson), Coweta County chronicles, Atlanta: Stein Printing Co., 1928; 869 p.

Cowley, Kan. (est. Feb. 26, 1867, 1,136 sq. mi.; 1970 pop.: 35,012; 1960: 37,861; 1950: 36,905) (Winfield). Matthew Cowley (-1864). First lt. Co. I, Ninth Kan. died at Little Rock, Ark., Oct. 7, 1864.

Cowlitz, Wash. (est. Apr. 21, 1854; 1,146 sq. mi.; 1970 pop.: 68,616; 1960: 57,801; 1950: 53,369) (Kelso). Cowlitz Indian tribe.

Craig, Okla. (est. July 16, 1907; 764 sq. mi.; 1970 pop.: 14, 722; 1960: 16, 303; 1950: 18, 263) (Vinita). Granville Craig. A Cherokee.

Craig, Va. (est. Mar. 21, 1851; 336 sq. mi.; 1970 pop.: 3, 524; 1960: 3, 356; 1950: 3, 452) (New Castle). Robert Craig (1792-1852). Virginia house of delegates 1817-18 and 1825-29 and 1850-52; Va. board of public works 1820-23; Representative from Va., 1829-33 and 1835-41.

Craighead, Ark. (est. Feb. 19, 1859; 717 sq. mi.; 1970 pop.: 52, 078; 1960: 47, 303; 1950: 50, 613) (Jonesboro and Lake City). Thomas B. Craighead (1800-) Miss. senate. -- Stuck, Charles Albert, The story of Craighead County, Jonesboro, Ark., 1960; 335 p. -- Williams, Harry Lee, History of Craighead County, Arkansas, Little Rock, Ark.: Parke-Harper Co., 1930; 648 p.

Crane, Tex. (est. Feb. 26, 1887; 796 sq. mi.; 1970 pop.: 4, 172; 1960: 4, 699; 1950: 3, 965) (Crane). William Carey Crane (1816-1885). Ordained Baptist minister 1838; pres. of Miss. Female College 1851-57; pres. of Baylor Univ. 1863-85.

Craven, N. C. (est. Dec. 3, 1705; 725 sq. mi.; 1970 pop.: 62, 554; 1960: 58, 773; 1950: 48, 823) (New Bern). William Craven, Second Earl of Craven (1668-1711), one of the eight proprietors of Carolina. Second Baron Craven of Hamsted-Marshall 1697; Lord Palatine of the Province of Carolina. (Originally Archdale County, name changed to Craven County, 1712.)

Crawford, Ark. (est. Oct. 18, 1820, eff. Jan. 1, 1821; 598 sq. mi.; 1970 pop.: 25, 677; 1960: 21, 318; 1950: 22, 727) (Van Buren). William Harris Crawford (1772-1834). Ga. house of representatives 1803-07; Senator from Ga., 1807-13; pres. pro tempore of the Senate 1812; U. S. Minister to France 1813-15; U. S. Secretary of War in Cabinet of Pres. Madison 1815-16; U. S. Secretary of the Treasury in cabinet of Pres. Madison 1816-25; Ga. Circuit judge 1827-34. -- Eno, Clara B., History of Crawford County, Arkansas, Van Buren, Ark.: Press-Argus, (n. d.); 499 p.

Crawford, Ga. (est. Dec. 9, 1822; 319 sq. mi.; 1970 pop.: 5, 748; 1960: 5, 816; 1950: 6, 080) (Knoxville). William Harris Crawford*.

Crawford, Ill. (est. Dec. 31, 1816; 453 sq. mi.; 1970 pop.: 19, 824; 1960: 20, 751; 1950: 21, 137) (Robinson). William Harris Crawford*. -- Perrin, William Henry, History of Crawford and Clark Counties, Chicago: O. L. Baskin & Co., 1883; 374 p.

Crawford, Ind. (est. Jan. 29, 1818, eff. Feb. 15, 1818, org. Dec. 31, 1821; 312 sq. mi.; 1970 pop.: 8,033; 1960: 8,379; 1950: 9,289) (English). William Harris Crawford * or see below William Crawford*. -- Pleasant, Hazen Hayes, History of Crawford County, Indiana, Greenfield, Ind.: Wm. Mitchell Printing Co., 1926; 644 p.

Crawford, Iowa (Denison). (est. Jan. 15, 1851; 716 sq. mi.; 1970 pop.: 18,780; 1960: 18,569; 1950: 19,741) William Harris Crawford*. -- Meyers, F. W., History of Crawford County, Chicago: S. J. Clarke Pub. Co., 1911; 2 vol.

Crawford, Kan. (est. Feb. 13, 1867, org. Mar. 3, 1868; 598 sq. mi.; 1970 pop.: 37,850; 1960: 37,032; 1950: 40,231) (Girard). Samuel J. Crawford (1835-1913). Third gov. of Kan.; Kan. legislature 1861; resigned and organized a company of volunteers, chosen capt., promoted to col. bvt. brig. gen. 1864; gov. 1865-68; resigned to command 19th Kan. cavalry against the Indians, 1868.

Crawford, Mich. (est. Apr. 1, 1840, org. 1879; 563 sq. mi.; 1970 pop.: 6,482; 1960: 4,971; 1950: 4,151) (Grayling). William Crawford (1732-1782). Surveyor, served under Gen. Braddock; capt. 1761; Pontiac War 1763-64; in Revolutionary war fought at battles of Long Island, Trenton, Princeton; resigned as col. 1781; fought Wyandot and Del. Indians on Sandusky River, captured, tortured and burned to death at the stake, June, 1782. Originally Shawaho County, name changed to Crawford County on Mar. 8, 1843.

Crawford, Mo. (est. Jan. 23, 1829; 760 sq. mi.; 1970 pop.: 14,826; 1960: 12,647; 1950: 11,615) (Steelville). William Harris Crawford*.

Crawford, Ohio (est. Feb. 12, 1820; 404 sq. mi.; 1970 pop.: 50,364; 1960: 46,775; 1950: 38,738) (Bucyrus). William Crawford*. -- Hopley, John Edward, History of Crawford County, Chicago: Richmond-Arnold Pub. Co., 1912; 1254 p. -- Perrin, W. H., History of Crawford County, Chicago: Baskin & Battey, 1881; 1047 p.

Crawford, Pa. (est. Mar. 12, 1800; 1,016 sq. mi.; 1970 pop.: 81,342; 1960: 77,956; 1950: 78,948) (Meadville). William Crawford*. -- Bates, Samuel Penniman, Our country and its people, Meadville, Pa.: W. A. Ferguson & Co., 1899; 972 p.

Crawford, Wis. (est. Oct. 26, 1818; 586 sq. mi.; 1970 pop.: 15,252; 1960: 16,351; 1950: 17,652) (Prairie du Chien). William Harris Crawford*. -- Gregory, John Goodby, ed., Southwestern Wisconsin: a history of old

Crawford County, Chicago: S. J. Clarke Pub. Co., 1932; 4 vol.

Creek, Okla. (est. July 16, 1907; 972 sq. mi.; 1970 pop.: 45, 532; 1960: 40, 495; 1950: 43, 143) (Sapulpa). Creek Indian tribe.

Crenshaw, Ala. (est. Nov. 24, 1866; 611 sq. mi.; 1970 pop.: 13, 188; 1960: 14, 909; 1950: 18, 981) (Luverne). Anderson Crenshaw.

Crisp, Ga. (est. Aug. 17, 1905; 277 sq. mi.; 1970 pop.: 18, 087; 1960: 17, 768; 1950: 17, 663) (Cordele). Charles Frederick Crisp (1845-1896). Served in Confederate Army 1861-64; lt. when a prisoner of war in 1864; released 1865; solicitor gen. of southwestern judicial circuit 1872-77; judge of superior court 1877-82; Representative from Ga., 1883-1896. -- Daughers of American Revolution, History of Crisp County, Cordele, Ga.: Daughters of American Revolution, 1916; 29 p.

Crittenden, Ark. (est. Oct. 22, 1825, eff. Jan. 1, 1826; 623 sq. mi.; 1970 pop.: 48, 106; 1960: 47, 564; 1950: 47, 184) (Marion). Robert Crittenden. Soldier in War of 1812. Secretary of Ark. terr. Mortally wounded Congressman Henry Wharton Conway in a duel in 1827.

Crittenden, Ky. (est. Jan. 26, 1842; 365 sq. mi.; 1970 pop.: 8, 493; 1960: 8, 648; 1950: 10, 818) (Marion). John Jordan Crittenden (1787-1863). Seventeenth gov. of Ky. Attorney gen. of Ill. Terr. 1809-10; in War of 1812 on staff of Gen. Shelby at battle of the Thames 1813; Ky. state legislature 1811-17; speaker Ky. state legislature 1817; Senator from Ky., 1817-19; Ky. house of representatives 1825 and 1829-32; U. S. district attorney 1827-29; nominated to U. S. Supreme Court by Pres. J. Q. Adams but not confirmed 1828; Senator from Ky., 1835-41; Attorney gen. of the U. S., 1841; Senator from Ky., 1842-48; gov. of Ky., 1848-50; Attorney gen. of the U. S., 1850-53; Senator from Ky., 1855-61; Representative from Ky., 1861-63.

Crockett, Tenn. (est. Dec. 20, 1845, eff. Mar. 14, 1846; 269 sq. mi.; 1970 pop.: 14, 402; 1960: 14, 594; 1950: 16, 624) (Alamo). David Crockett (1786-1836). Creek Indian campaign 1813-14; Tenn., house of representatives 1821-25; Representative from Tenn., 1827-31 and 1833-35; aided Tex. independence and was killed in the defense of the Alamo, Mar. 6, 1836.

Crockett, Tex. (est. Jan. 22, 1875; 2, 794 sq. mi.; 1970 pop.: 3, 885; 1960: 4, 209; 1950: 3, 981) (Ozona). David Crockett*.

Crook, Ore. (est. Oct. 24, 1882; 2,980 sq. mi.; 1970 pop.: 9,985; 1960: 9,430; 1950: 8,991) (Prineville). George Crook (1829-1890). Graduated U. S. Military Academy 1852; lt. in Oregon terr. 1852-60; maj. gen. 1860; commander of districts of Idaho and Ariz. 1866-72.

Crook, Wyo. (est. Dec. 8, 1875, org. Dec. 15, 1877; 2,897 sq. mi.; 1970 pop. 4,535; 1960: 4,691; 1950: 4,738) (Sundance). George Crook.*

Crosby, Tex. (est. Aug. 21, 1876; 911 sq. mi.; 1970 pop.: 9,085; 1960: 10,347; 1950: 9,582) (Crosbyton). Stephen Crosby (1808-1869). Chief clerk in land office Tex. 1853-57 and 1859-67. -- Spikes, Nellie, Through the years, a history of Crosby County, Texas, San Antonio, Texas: Naylor Co., 1952; 493 p.

Cross, Ark. (est. Nov. 15, 1862; 626 sq. mi.; 1970 pop.: 19,783; 1960: 19,551; 1950: 24,757) (Wynne). Edward Cross (1798-1887). U. S. judge for Ark. Terr. 1830; U. S. surveyor gen. for Ark., 1836-38; Representative from Ark., 1839-45; Ark. supreme court judge 1845-55; attorney gen. of Ark., 1874.

Crow Wing, Minn. (est. May 23, 1857; 999 sq. mi.; 1970 pop.: 34,826; 1960: 32,134; 1950: 30,875) (Brainerd). Descriptive, from Chippewa Indian word "kayaugeweguan" meaning "crow's wing" or "crow's feather."

Crowley, Colo. (est. May 29, 1911; 803 sq. mi.; 1970 pop.: 3,086; 1960: 3,978; 1950: 5,222) (Ordway). John H. Crowley. Colo. senator.

Culberson, Tex. (est. Mar. 10, 1911; 3,848 sq. mi.; 1970 pop.: 3,429; 1960: 2,794; 1950: 1,825) (Van Horn). David Browning Culberson (1830-1903). Tex. legislature 1859; entered Confederate Army as a private, col. 18th Tex. Infantry, adjt. gen. of Tex. with rank of col.; Tex. house of representatives 1864; Tex. senate 1873-75; Representative from Tex. 1875-97; commissioner to codify U. S. laws 1897-1900.

Cullman, Ala. (est. Jan. 24, 1877; 743 sq. mi.; 1970 pop.: 52,445; 1960: 45,572; 1950: 49,046) (Cullman). John G. Cullman. Settler in German colony about 1873.

Culpeper, Va. (est. Mar. 23, 1748; 389 sq. mi.; 1970 pop.: 18,218; 1960: 15,088; 1950: 13,242) (Culpeper). Thomas Lord Culpeper (1635-1689). Second (Royal Province) gov. of Va. Received 31 year grant from King Charles II for entire Va. colony 1673; purchased rights of Earl of Arlington 1675; proclaimed gov. of Va. for life 1675; went to Va. and was sworn in 1680; commission declared forfeited 1683; served 1677-1683. -- Green, Raleigh Travers, Genealogical and historical notes on

Culpeper County, Baltimore: Regional Pub. Co., 1964; 160 p.

Cumberland, Ill. (est. Mar. 2, 1843; 353 sq. mi.; 1970 pop.: 9,772; 1960: 9,936; 1950: 10,496) (Toledo) Cumberland Rd., first national thoroughfare opened in 1818 from Cumberland, Md., to Wheeling, Va. (now W. Va.). Named for William Augustus, Duke of Cumberland, (1721-1765), Second son of King George II and Queen Caroline; commanded the English troops at the battle of Culloden in Scotland in 1745 defeating the Scotch Highlanders. The Cumberland Road, the Cumberland River, the Cumberland Mountains and a county in England were all named for him. Privy Councillor 1742; maj. gen. 1742; lt. gen. 1743; capt. gen. of the army 1745-57. -- Counties of Cumberland, Jasper & Richland, Chicago: Historical Society Publishers, 1968; 839 p.

Cumberland, Ky. (est. Dec. 14, 1798, eff. July 1, 1799; 313 sq. mi.; 1970 pop.: 6,850; 1960: 7,835; 1950: 9,309) (Burkesville). Duke of Cumberland*. -- Wells, Joseph William, History of Cumberland County, Louisville, Ky.: Standard Printing Co., 1947; 480 p.

Cumberland, Me. (est. sess. May 28, 1760, eff. Nov. 1, 1760, 881 sq. mi.; 1970 pop.: 192,528; 1960: 182,751; 1950: 169,201) (Portland). ("The Gateway to Vacationland"; "The Scenic Wonderland"). Duke of Cumberland*. -- Clayton, W. Woodford, History of Cumberland County, Philadelphia, Pa.: Everts & Peck, 1880; 456 p.

Cumberland, N.J. (est. Jan. 19, 1748; 503 sq. mi.; 1970 pop.: 121,374; 1960: 106,850; 1950: 88,597) (Bridgeton). Duke of Cumberland*. -- Elmer, Lucius Quintius Cincinnatus, History of the early settlement and progress of Cumberland County, Bridgeton, N.J.: G. F. Nixon, 1869; 142 p. -- Mulford, William C., Historical tales of Cumberland County, Bridgeton, N.J.: Evening News Co., 1941; 197 p.

Cumberland, N.C. (est. session Feb. 19, 1754; 661 sq. mi.; 1970 pop.: 212,042; 1960: 148,418; 1950: 96,006) Fayetteville). Duke of Cumberland*.

Cumberland, Pa. (est. Jan. 27, 1750; 555 sq. mi.; 1970 pop.: 158,177; 1960: 124,816; 1950: 94,457) (Carlisle). Duke of Cumberland*. -- Biographical annals of Cumberland County, Chicago: Genealogical Pub. Co., 1905; 850 p.

Cumberland, Tenn. (est. Nov. 16, 1855; 679 sq. mi.; 1970 pop.: 20,733; 1960: 19,135; 1950: 18,877) (Crossville). Duke of Cumberland*. -- Krechniak, Helen Bullard and Krechniak, Joseph Marshall, Cumberland County's First Hundred Years, Crossville, Tenn.: Centennial Committee, 1956; 377 p.

Cumberland, Va. (est. Mar. 23, 1855, org. Oct. 12, 1858; 288 sq. mi.; 1970 pop.: 6,179; 1960: 6,360; 1950: 7,252) (Cumberland). Duke of Cumberland*.

Cuming, Neb. (est. Mar. 16, 1855; 571 sq. mi.; 1970 pop.: 12,034; 1960: 12,435; 1950: 12,994) (Westpoint). Thomas B. Cuming (-1858). Acting gov. of Neb. Terr. 1854-55 and 1857-58; Secretary Neb. Terr. 1854-1858.

Currituck, N. C. (est. 1670; 273 sq. mi.; 1970 pop.: 6,976; 1960: 6,601; 1950: 6,201) (Currituck). Currituck Indian tribe.

Curry, N.M. (est. Feb. 25, 1909; 1,403 sq. mi.; 1970 pop.: 39,517; 1960: 32,691; 1950: 23,351) (Clovis), George Curry (1863-1947). Eighteenth terr. gov. of N.M. terr. Deputy treasurer Lincoln County, N.M., 1886-87; county clerk 1888; lt. and capt. in Roosevelt's Rough Riders in Spanish American War 1898; sheriff Otero County 1899; provost marshal and provost judge and gov. of provinces in the Philippine Islands 1899-1907; gov. of N.M. Terr. 1907-11; Representative from N.M., 1912-13; state historian of N.M. 1945-47.

Curry, Ore. (est. Dec. 18, 1855; 1,622 sq. mi.; 1970 pop.: 13,006; 1960: 13,983; 1950: 6,048) (Gold Beach). George Law Curry (1820-1878). Fifth, seventh and eighth terr. gov. of Ore. Emigrated to Ore. 1846; Ore. legislature 1848-49 and 1851; acting secretary of Ore. legislature 1849; third editor of Ore. "Spectator," the first newspaper west of the Rockies 1846; terr. gov. of Ore. 1853, 1854 and 1854-59. -- Peterson, Emil R., A century of Coos and Curry, Binfords & Mort, 1952; 599 p.

Custer, Colo. (est. Mar. 9, 1877; 737 sq. mi.; 1970 pop.; 1,120; 1960: 1,305; 1950: 1,573) (Westcliffe). George Armstrong Custer (1839-1876). Graduated U. S. Military Academy 1861; second lt. at battle of Bull Run; bvt. lt. col. for Yellow Tavern 1864; bvt. col. for Winchester, 1864; bvt. brig. gen. 1865; led campaign against Cheyennes 1868; sent to Dakota terr. 1873; killed with his entire command at Little Big Horn, June 25, 1876.

Custer, Idaho (est. Jan. 8, 1881, eff. Apr. 1, 1882; 4,983 sq. mi.; 1970 pop.: 2,967; 1960: 2,996; 1950: 3,318) (Challis). George Armstrong Custer*. -- Yarber, Esther, Land of the Yankee Fork, Denver: Sage Books, 1963; 207 p.

Custer, Mont. (est. Feb. 2, 1865; 3,765 sq. mi.; 1970 pop.: 12,174; 1960: 13,227; 1950: 12,661) (Miles City). George Armstrong Custer*. (Originally Big Horn County, name changed Feb. 16, 1877.

Custer, Neb. (est. Feb. 17, 1877, org. June 27, 1877; 2,362 sq. mi.; 1970 pop.: 14,092; 1960: 16,517; 1950: 19,170) (Broken Bow). George Armstrong Custer*. -- Butcher, Solomon Devore, Pioneer history of Custer County, Nebraska, Denver: Sage Books, 1965; 410 p. -- Gaston, William Levi, History of Custer County, Nebraska, Lincoln, Neb.: Western Pub. & Engraving Co., 1919; 1175 p.

Custer, Okla. (est. July 16, 1907; 999 sq. mi.; 1970 pop.: 22,665; 1960: 21,040; 1950: 21,097) (Arapaho). George Armstrong Custer*.

Custer, S. D. (est. Jan. 11, 1875; 1,552 sq. mi.; 1970 pop.: 4,698; 1960: 4,906; 1950: 5,517) (Custer). George Armstrong Custer*.

Cuyahoga, Ohio (est. Feb. 10, 1807, eff. Feb. 10, 1808; 456 sq. mi.; 1970 pop.: 1,721,300; 1960: 1,647,895; 1950: 1,389,532) (Cleveland). Indian word meaning "crooked." -- Coates, William R., A history of Cuyahoga County, Chicago: American Historical Society, 1924; 3 vol.

D

Dade, Fla. (est. Feb. 4, 1836; 2,054 sq. mi.; 1970 pop.: 1,267,792; 1960: 935,047; 1950: 495,084) (Miami). Francis Langhorne Dade (1793-1835). Third lt. in U. S. Infantry 1813; first lt. 1816; capt. 1818; bvt. maj. 1828; killed in ambush by Seminole chiefs Micanope and Jumper Dec. 28, 1835. -- Hollingsworth, Tracy, History of Dade County, Miami, Fla.: Miami Post, 1936; 151 p.

Dade, Ga. (est. Dec. 25, 1837; 186 sq. mi.; 1970 pop.: 9,910; 1960: 8,666; 1950: 7,364) (Trenton). Francis Langhorne Dade*.

Dade, Mo. (est. Jan. 29, 1841; 504 sq. mi.; 1970 pop.: 6,850; 1960: 7,577; 1950: 9,324) (Greenfield). Francis Langhorne Dade*.

Daggett, Utah. (est. procl. Nov. 17, 1917, eff. Jan. 7, 1918, org. Mar. 4, 1919; 764 sq. mi.; 1970 pop.: 666; 1960: 1,164; 1950: 364) (Manila). Ellsworth Daggett. Surveyor of canal system for Daggett section of Utah.

Dakota, Minn. (est. Oct. 27, 1849; 571 sq. mi.; 1970 pop.: 139,808; 1960: 78,303; 1950: 49,019) (Hastings). Dakota Indian tribe. -- Neill, Edward D., History of Dakota County, North Star Pub. Co., 1881; 551 p.

Dakota, Neb. (est. Mar. 7, 1855, org. Jan. 5, 1857; 255 sq. mi.; 1970 pop.: 13,137; 1960: 12,168; 1950: 10,401)

(Dakota City). Dakota Indian tribe. -- Warner, Moses M., Warner's history of Dakota County, Nebraska, Dakota City, Neb., Lyons Mirror Job Office, 1893; 387 p.

Dale, Ala. (est. Dec. 22, 1824, eff. Oct. 1825; 560 sq. mi.; 1970 pop.: 52,938; 1960: 31,066; 1950: 20,828) (Ozark). Sam Dale (1772-1841). Indian scout 1793; maj. against Creek Indians 1794; col. of militia; brig. gen.; Ala. legislature 1819-20 and 1824-28; Miss. legislature 1836. -- Watson, Fred Shelton, Forgotten Trails, History of Dale County, Ala., 1824-1966, Birmingham, Ala.: Banner Press, 1968; 288 p. -- Watson, Fred Shelton, Piney Wood echoes; a history of Dale and Coffee Counties, Elba Clipper, Elba, Ala., 1949; 200 p.

Dallam, Tex. (est. Aug. 21, 1876; 1,494 sq. mi.; 1970 pop.: 6,012; 1960: 6,302; 1950: 7,640) (Dalhart). James Wilmer Dallam (1818-1847). Compiler of "A Digest of the Laws of Texas, Opinions of the Supreme Court of Texas from 1840-44." Died at New Orleans while on a trip to establish a newspaper at Indianola, Tex. -- Hunter, Lillie Mae, Book of Years; a history of Dallam and Hartley counties, Hereford, Texas: Pioneer Book Publishers, 1969; 206 p.

Dallas, Ala. (est. Feb. 9, 1818; 976 sq. mi.; 1970 pop.: 55,296; 1960: 56,667; 1950: 56,270) (Selma). Alexander James Dallas (1759-1817). U. S. District Attorney in Pa. 1810-14; U. S. Secretary of the Treasury (1814-16) and U. S. Secretary of War ad interim 1815 in cabinet of Pres. Madison.

Dallas, Ark. (est. Jan. 1, 1845; 672 sq. mi.; 1970 pop.: 10,022; 1960: 10,522; 1950: 12,416) (Fordyce). George Mifflin Dallas (1792-1864). Solicitor of U. S. Bank 1815-17; deputy attorney gen. 1817; mayor of Philadelphia 1829; U. S. district attorney for eastern district of Pa., 1829-31; Senator from Pa., 1831-33; Attorney gen. of Pa., 1833-35; U. S. Minister to Russia 1837-39; Vice Pres. of the U. S., under Polk 1845-49; U. S. Minister to Great Britain 1856-61. -- Smith, Jonathan Kennon, Romance of Tulip Ridge, Baltimore, Md.: Deford, 1966; 100 p.

Dallas, Iowa (est. Jan. 13, 1846, org. Feb. 16, 1847, eff. Mar. 1, 1847; 597 sq. mi.; 1970 pop.: 26,085; 1960: 24,123; 1950: 23,661) (Adel). George Mifflin Dallas*. -- Wood, Robert F., Past and present of Dallas County, Chicago: S. J. Clarke Pub. Co., 1907; 795 p.

Dallas, Mo. (est. Jan. 29, 1841; 537 sq. mi.; 1970 pop.: 10,054; 1960: 9,314; 1950: 10,394) (Buffalo). George Mifflin

Dallas*. (Formerly Niangua County. Changed Dec. 16, 1844.)-- Hemphill, Elva Murrell, Early days in Dallas County, 1954.

Dallas, Tex. (est. Mar. 30, 1846; 893 sq. mi. ; 1970 pop. : 1, 327, 321; 1960: 951, 527; 1950: 614, 799) (Dallas). George Mifflin Dallas*. -- Cochran, John H., Dallas County, a record of its pioneers and progress, Dallas, Tex. : Service Pub. Co., 1928; 296 p.

Dane, Wis. (est. Dec. 7, 1836; 1, 197 sq. mi. ; 1970 pop. : 290, 272; 1960: 222, 095; 1950: 169, 357) (Madison). Nathan Dane (1752-1835). Mass. house of representatives 1782-85; Continental Congress 1785-88; Mass. senate 1790-91 and 1794-97; Essex County judge of court of common pleas 1794; commissioner to codify laws of Mass., 1795; author of "Abridgment and Digest of American Law." -- History of Dane County, Chicago: Western Historical Co., 1880; 1289 p.

Daniels, Mont. (est. Aug. 30, 1920, petition and election; 1, 443 sq. mi. ; 1970 pop. : 3, 083; 1960: 3, 755; 1950: 3, 946) (Scobey). Mansfield A. Daniels. Pioneer rancher.

Dare, N. C. (est. Feb. 3, 1870; 388 sq. mi. ; 1970 pop. : 6, 995; 1960: 5, 935; 1950: 5, 405) (Manteo). Virginia Dare (1587-16). First English child born in America; granddaughter of John White, gov. of the Va. Colony sent out by Sir Walter Raleigh in 1587.

Darke, Ohio (est. Jan. 3, 1809; 605 sq. mi. ; 1970 pop. : 49, 141; 1960: 45, 612; 1950: 41, 799) (Greenville). William Darke (1736-1801). Served under gen. Braddock at Ft. Duquesne 1755; Indian fighter 1755-70; Continental Army 1775; capt. 8th Va., 1776; maj. 1777; wounded and captured at Germantown, Pa., 1777; exchanged 1780; lt. col. 4th Va., 1781; lt. col., militia 1781; retired 1783; brig. gen. ; federal constitutional convention 1788, lt. col. Ky. militia at St. Clair's defeat 1791. -- Wilson, Frazer Ellis, History of Darke County, Milford, Ohio: Hobart Pub. Co., 1914; 2 vol. -- History of Darke County, Chicago: W. H. Beers & Co., 1880; 772 p.

Darlington, S. C. (est. Mar. 12, 1785; 545 sq. mi. ; 1970 pop. : 53, 442; 1960: 52, 928; 1950: 50, 016) (Darlington). Darlington, England. -- Ervin, Eliza Cowan, ed., Darlingtoniana, Columbia, S. C. : R. L. Bryan, 1964; 502 p.

Dauphin, Pa. (est. Mar. 4, 1785; 520 sq. mi. ; 1970 pop. : 223, 834; 1960: 220, 255; 1950: 197, 784) (Harrisburg). Hereditary title of eldest son of King of France. Humbert II yielded province of Dauphiné, southeast France to Philip VI (1293-1350) of France (House of Valois) in 1349 on condition that the title "Dauphin" be always borne by the king's eldest son. -- Kelker, Luther Reily, History of Dauphin County, New York: Lewis Pub. Co., 1907; 3 vol.

Davidson, N. C. (est. 1822; 548 sq. mi.; 1970 pop.: 95,627; 1960: 79,493; 1950: 62,244) (Lexington). William Lee Davidson (1746-1781). Maj. 4th N. C. 1776; lt. col. 1777; brig. gen. N. C., militia; battle of Camden 1780; killed at battle of Cowan's Pass, Jan. 17, 1781. -- Leonard, Jacob Calvin, Centennial History of Davidson County, North Carolina, Raleigh, N. C.: Edward & Broughton Co., 1927; 523 p.

Davidson, Tenn. (est. sess. Apr. 18, 1783; 532 sq. mi.; 1970 pop.: 447,877; 1960: 399,743; 1950: 321,758) (Nashville). William Lee Davidson*. -- Bell, Lily Cartwright, History of the Dickinson Road, Nashville (?), 1937; 40 p.

Davie, N. C. (est. Dec. 20, 1836; 264 sq. mi.; 1970 pop.: 18,855; 1960: 16,728; 1950: 15,420) (Mocksville). William Richardson Davie (1756-1820). Capt. in Pulaski's legion 1779; col. N. C. cavalry 1780; federal convention 1787; brig. gen. U. S. army 1798; gov. N. C., Dec. 7, 1798 to Nov. 23, 1799.

Daviess, Ind. (est. Dec. 24, 1816, eff. Feb. 15, 1817; 433 sq. mi.; 1970 pop.: 26,602; 1960: 26,636; 1950: 26,762) (Washington). Joseph Hamilton Daviess (1774-1811). Prosecuted Aaron Burr for treason 1807. Killed at battle of Tippecanoe 1811.

Daviess, Ky. (est. Jan. 14, 1815; 466 sq. mi.; 1970 pop.: 79,486; 1960: 70,588; 1950: 57,241) (Owensboro). Joseph Hamilton Daviess*. -- History of Daviess County, Chicago: Inter-State Pub. Co., 1883; 870 p.

Daviess, Mo. (est. Dec. 29, 1836; 563 sq. mi.; 1970 pop.: 8,420; 1960: 9,502; 1950: 11,180) (Gallatin). Joseph Hamilton Daviess*. -- Leopard, John C., History of Daviess and Gentry Counties, Missouri, Topeka: Historical Pub. Co., 1922; 1039 p.

Davis, Iowa (est. Feb. 17, 1843, org. Feb. 15, 1844, eff. Mar. 1, 1844; 509 sq. mi.; 1970 pop.: 8,207; 1960: 9,199; 1950: 9,959) (Bloomfield). Garrett Davis (1801-1872). Ky. house of representatives 1833-35; Representative from Ky., 1839-47; Senator from Ky., 1861-72. -- Evans, Harry Carroll, The pioneers and politics of Davis County, Bloomfield, Iowa: Bloomfield Democrat, 1929; 57 p.

Davis, Utah (est. Mar. 3, 1852; 268 sq. mi.; 1970 pop.: 99,028; 1960: 64,760; 1950: 30,867) (Farmington). Daniel C. Davis. Capt. Mormon battalion.

Davison, S. D. (est. Jan. 8, 1873; 432 sq. mi.; 1970 pop.: 17,319; 1960: 16,681; 1950: 16,522) (Mitchell). Henry C. Davison. Early settler 1869; filed claim at Riverside,

S. D., 1872.

Dawes, Neb. (est. Feb. 19, 1885; 1, 389 sq. mi.; 1970 pop.: 9, 693; 1960: 9, 536; 1950: 9, 708) (Chadron). James William Dawes (1845-1887). Fifth gov. of Neb. Neb. constitutional convention 1875; Neb. senate 1876; Neb. gov. 1883-87.

Dawson, Ga. (est. Dec. 3, 1857; 216 sq. mi.; 1970 pop.: 3, 639; 1960: 3, 590; 1950: 3, 712) (Dawsonville). William Crosby Dawson (1798-1856) Clerk American Fur Co., clerk, Ga. house of representatives, compiler, laws of Ga., 1820-30; capt. vol. co. Creek war 1836; Representative from Ga., 1836-41; judge of superior court of Ocmulgee circuit court 1845; Senator from Ga., 1849-55.

Dawson, Mont. (est. Jan. 15, 1869; 2, 358 sq. mi.; 1970 pop.: 11, 269; 1960: 12, 314; 1950: 9, 092) (Glendive) Andrew Dawson.

Dawson, Neb. (est. Jan. 11, 1860, org. Sept. 2, 1871; 983 sq. mi.; 1970 pop.: 19, 467; 1960: 19, 405; 1950: 19, 393) (Lexington). ("The County in the Heart of the Platte Valley"). Jacob Dawson. Postmaster of Lancaster (now Lincoln).

Dawson, Tex. (est. Feb. 1, 1858; 899 sq. mi.; 1970 pop.: 16, 604; 1960: 19, 185; 1950: 19, 113) (Lamesa). Nicholas Mosby Dawson (1808-1842). Second lt. at battle of San Jacinto 1836; lt. in Co. C, 1837; capt. of vol. co. 1842; killed (Dawson massacre) Sept. 18, 1842.

Day, S. D. (est. Feb. 22, 1879; 1, 060 sq. mi.; 1970 pop.: 8, 713; 1960: 10, 516; 1950: 12, 294) (Webster). Merritt H. Day (1844-1900). Pioneer, Civil war. Dakota terr. legislature 1879-89; commander S. D. state militia in Messiah War of 1890.

Deaf Smith, Tex. (est. Aug. 21, 1876; 1, 507 sq. mi.; 1970 pop.: 18, 999; 1960: 13, 187; 1950: 9, 111) (Hereford). Erastus Smith (1787-1837). Settled in Tex. 1821; scout for Sam Houston; battle of Concepcion 1835; destroyed Vince's Bridge before battle of San Jacinto 1836; capt. of co. of rangers 1837. -- Patterson, Bessie Chambers, History of Deaf Smith County, Hereford, Texas: Pioneer Publishers, 1964; 167 p.

Dearborn, Ind. (est. Mar. 7, 1803; 306 sq. mi.; 1970 pop.: 29, 430; 1960: 28, 674; 1950: 25, 141) (Lawrenceburg). Henry Dearborn (1751-1829). Capt. in Stark's Regiment 1775; fought at battle of Bunker Hill 1775; at storming of Quebec 1775; taken prisoner, released on parole 1776; fought at battles of Stillwater 1777; Saratoga 1777; Monmouth 1778; and Newton 1779; deputy quartermaster with rank of col. on Gen. Washington's staff 1781; brig. gen.

of militia 1787; maj. gen. 1789; U. S. marshal for district of Me. 1789; Representative from Mass. 1793-97; U. S. Secretary of War in cabinet of Pres. Jefferson 1801-09; collector of the port of Boston 1809-12; senior maj. gen. U. S. Army 1812; U. S. Minister to Portugal 1822-24.

DeBaca, N. M. (est. Feb. 28, 1917; 2, 358 sq. mi. ; 1970 pop. : 2, 547; 1960: 2, 991; 1950: 3, 464) (Fort Sumner) Ezequiel Cabeza de Baca (1864-1917). Second gov. of N. M. Publisher and business manager of Spanish newspaper; lt. gov. of N. M. 1911-16; gov. of N. M. 1917, died six weeks later.

Decatur, Ga. (est. Dec. 8, 1823; org. Dec. 19, 1823; 583 sq. mi. ; 1970 pop. : 22, 310; 1960: 25, 203; 1950: 23, 620) (Bainbridge) Stephen Decatur (1779-1820). Commanded schooner Enterprise in Tripolitan War and United States in War of 1812. Forced Barbary pirates to submit to terms. Killed in a duel Mar. 22, 1820 by Commodore James Barron 1821.

Decatur, Ind. (est. Dec. 31, 1821, eff. Mar. 4, 1822; 370 sq. mi. ; 1970 pop. : 22, 738; 1960: 20, 019; 1950: 18, 218) (Greensburg). Stephen Decatur*.

Decatur, Iowa (est. Jan. 13, 1846, org. Apr. 1, 1850; 530 sq. mi. ; 1970 pop. : 9, 737; 1960: 10, 539; 1950: 12, 601) (Leon). Stephen Decatur*. -- Howell, J. M. and Smith, H. C., History of Decatur County, Chicago: S. J. Clarke Pub. Co., 1915; 2 vol.

Decatur, Kan. (est. Mar. 6, 1873; 899 sq. mi. ; 1970 pop. : 4, 988; 1960: 5, 778; 1950: 6, 185) (Oberlin). Stephen Decatur*.

Decatur, Tenn. (est. Nov. 1845; 346 sq. mi. ; 1970 pop. : 9, 457; 1960: 8, 324; 1950: 9, 442) (Decaturville). Stephen Decatur*.

Deer Lodge, Mont. (est. Feb. 2, 1865; 738 sq. mi. ; 1970 pop. : 15, 652; 1960: 18, 640; 1950: 16, 553) (Anaconda). ("Magicland Headquarters"). Descriptive, a site where deer were frequently seen near a hotel.

Defiance, Ohio (est. Mar. 4, 1845; 410 sq. mi. ; 1970 pop.: 36, 949; 1960: 31, 508; 1950: 25, 925) (Defiance) Ft. Defiance, at Defiance, Ohio built in 1794 by Gen. Anthony Wayne.

DeKalb, Ala. (est. Jan. 9, 1836; 778 sq. mi. ; 1970 pop. : 41, 981; 1960: 41, 417; 1950: 45, 048) (Ft. Payne). ("Alabama's Natural Wonderland"; "The Land of Natural Beauty"; "The Land of Natural Wonders"). Johann De Kalb (1721-1780). Brig. in French Army 1764; aided American colonists, commissioned maj. gen. in Continental

Army 1777, wounded at battle of Camden, N.J., Aug. 16, 1780 and died three days later.

DeKalb, Ga. (est. Dec. 9, 1822; 272 sq. mi.; 1970 pop.: 415,387; 1960: 256,782; 1950: 136,395) (Decatur). Johann De Kalb*.

De Kalb, Ill., (est. Mar. 4, 1837; 638 sq. mi.; 1970 pop.: 71,654; 1960: 51,714; 1950: 40,781) (Sycamore). Johann De Kalb*. -- Davy, Harriet (Wilson), From Oxen to Jets, a History of DeKalb County, Dixon, Ill.: DeKalb County Board of Supervisors, 1963; 272 p.

DeKalb, Ind. (est. Feb. 7, 1835, org. Jan. 14, 1837, eff. May 1, 1837; 365 sq. mi.; 1970 pop.: 30,837; 1960: 28,271; 1950: 26,023) (Auburn). Johann De Kalb*.

DeKalb, Mo. (est. Feb. 25, 1845; 423 sq. mi.; 1970 pop.: 7,305; 1960: 7,226; 1950: 8,047) (Maysville). Johann De Kalb*.

DeKalb, Tenn. (est. Dec. 11, 1837, org. Mar. 5, 1838; 317 sq. mi.; 1970 pop.: 11,151; 1960: 10,774; 1950: 11,680) (Smithville). Johann De Kalb*. -- Hale, William Thomas, History of DeKalb County, Tenn., Nashville, Tenn.: P. Hunter, 1915; 254 p.

Delaware, Ind. (est. Jan. 26, 1827, eff. Apr. 1, 1827; 400 sq. mi.; 1970 pop.: 129,219; 1960: 110,938; 1950: 90,252) (Muncie). Del. Indian tribe. -- Haimbaugh, Frank D. (ed.), History of Delaware County, Indiana, Indianapolis, Ind.: Historical Pub. Co., 1924; 2 vol. -- Kemper, General William Harrison, A Twentieth Century history of Delaware County, Indiana, Chicago: Lewis Pub. Co., 1908; 2 vol.

Delaware, Iowa (est. Dec. 21, 1837, org. Dec. 20, 1839; 573 sq. mi.; 1970 pop.: 18,770; 1960: 18,483; 1950: 17,734) (Manchester). The state of Delaware. Named in appreciation of the services of Senator John Middleton Clayton of Del. 1829-36, 1845-49 and 1853-56. -- Merry, John F., ed., History of Delaware County, Chicago: S. J. Clarke Pub. Co., 1914; 2 vol.

Delaware, N.Y (est. Mar. 10, 1797; 1,470 sq. mi.; 1970 pop.: 44,718; 1960: 43,540; 1950: 44,420) (Delhi). ("The Newest Four Season Vacationland"). Thomas West, third baron of Del. or De La Warr (1577-1618). Succeeded to the peerage 1602; appointed first col. gov. of Va. and capt.-gen. for life 1609; resident in Va. June 1610 to March 1611; returned to England 1611; made second voyage to Va. and died en route 1618. -- Monroe, John Duncan, Chapters in the history of Delaware County, Margaretville, N.Y.: Delaware County Historical Association, 1949; 132 p. -- Murray, D., Delaware County history of the century, Delhi, N. Y.: W. Clark, 1898; 604 p.

Delaware, Ohio (est. Feb. 10, 1808; 459 sq. mi.; 1970 pop.: 42,908; 1960: 36,107; 1950: 30,278) (Delaware). Delaware Indian tribe. -- Pabst, Anna C. Smith, ed., Berlin township & Delaware County, Delaware, Ohio, 1955-58; 4 vol. -- Lytle, James Robert, Twentieth Century History of Delaware County, Chicago: Biographical Pub. Co., 1908; 896 p.

Delaware, Okla. (est. July 16, 1907; 778 sq. mi.; 1970 pop.: 17,767; 1960: 13,198; 1950: 14,734) (Jay). Delaware Indian tribe.

Delaware, Pa. (est. Sept. 26, 1789; 185 sq. mi.; 1970 pop.: 600,035; 1960: 553,154; 1950: 414,234) (Media). Delaware Indian tribe. -- Ashmead, Henry Graham, History of Delaware County, Philadelphia: L. H. Everts & Co., 1884; 767 p. -- Palmer, Charles, ed., A history of Delaware County, Harrisburg: National Historical Association, 1932; 2 vol.

Del Norte, Calif. (est. Mar. 2, 1857; 1,003 sq. mi.; 1970 pop.: 14,580; 1960: 17,771; 1950: 8,078) (Crescent City). Spanish for "of the north." -- Smith, Esther Ruth, History of Del Norte County, Oakland, Calif.: Holmes Book Co., 1953; 224 p.

Delta, Colo. (est. Feb. 11, 1883; 1,157 sq. mi.; 1970 pop.: 15,286; 1960: 15,602; 1950: 17,365) (Delta). Descriptive. Located on the delta of the Uncompahgre River.

Delta, Mich. (est. Mar. 9, 1843; org. 1861; 1,180 sq. mi.; 1970 pop.: 35,924; 1960: 34,298; 1950: 32,913) (Escanaba). Descriptive. For the Greek letter "D" the shape of the county.

Delta, Tex. (est. July 29, 1870; 276 sq. mi.; 1970 pop.: 4,927; 1960: 5,860; 1950: 8,964) (Cooper). Descriptive. For the Greek letter "D" the shape of the county.

Dent, Mo. (est. Feb. 10, 1851; 756 sq. mi.; 1970 pop.: 11,457; 1960: 10,445; 1950: 10,936) (Salem). Lewis Dent. Settler 1835, congressman.

Denton, Tex. (est. Apr. 11, 1846; 942 sq. mi.; 1970 pop.: 75,633; 1960: 47,432; 1950: 41,365) (Denton). John B. Denton (1806-1841). Itinerant minister; lawyer; missionary; capt. and aide to Col. Edward H. Tarrant; killed near Ft. Worth, Tex., in attack against Indians May 22, 1841. -- Bates, Edmond Franklin, History and reminiscences of Denton County, McNitzky Printing Co., 1918; 412 p.

Denver, Colo. (est. Mar. 18, 1901; 58 sq. mi.; 1970 pop.: 514,678; 1960: 493,887; 1950: 415,786) (Denver). James

William Denver (1817-1892). Fifth gov. of Kan. Terr. Capt. under gen. Scott 1847-48; moved to Calif., 1850; Calif. Senate 1851; secretary of state Calif., 1852; Representative from Calif., 1855-57; Commissioner of Indian Affairs 1857; gov. Kan. Terr. 1857-58; Commissioner of Indian Affairs 1858-59; brig. gen. 1861; resigned 1863; suggested as Democratic candidate for the presidency 1884.

Deschutes, Ore. (est. Dec. 13, 1916; 3,041 sq. mi.; 1970 pop.: 30,442; 1960: 23,100; 1950: 21,812) (Bend), French derivation "riviere des chutes" for "river of the falls."

Desha, Ark. (est. Dec. 12, 1838, eff. Mar. 1, 1839; 776 sq. mi.; 1970 pop.: 18,761; 1960: 20,770; 1950: 25,155) (Arkansas City). Benjamin Desha (-1835).

Des Moines, Iowa (est. Sept. 6, 1834, eff. Oct. 1, 1834; org. Dec. 7, 1836; 409 sq. mi.; 1970 pop.: 46,982; 1960: 44,605; 1950: 42,056) (Burlington). French "river of monks." -- Antrobus, Augustine M., History of Des Moines County, Chicago: S. J. Clarke Pub. Co., 1915; 2 vol.

De Soto, Fla. (est. May 19, 1887; 648 sq. mi.; 1970 pop.: 13,060; 1960: 11,683; 1950: 9,242) (Arcadia). Hernando De Soto (1496-1542). Spanish conqueror and explorer, served under Pizarro in Panama and Peru; received title gov. of Fla. and Cuba from Charles I; explored Miss. region, contracted fever and died, buried in Miss. River.

De Soto, La. (est. Apr. 1, 1843; 872 sq. mi.; 1970 pop.: 22,764; 1960: 24,248; 1950: 24,398) (Mansfield). Hernando De Soto. -- Slawson, J. A. H., De Soto Parish History and Cemetary Records, Center, Texas: J. B. Sanders, 1967; 114 p.

DeSoto, Miss. (est. Feb. 9, 1836; 475 sq. mi.; 1970 pop.: 35,885; 1960: 23,891; 1950: 24,599) (Hernando). Hernando De Soto*.

Deuel, Neb. (est. 1888, org. Jan. 21, 1889; 435 sq. mi.; 1970 pop.: 2,717; 1960: 3,125; 1950: 3,300) (Chappell). Henry Porter Deuell (1836-). Agent K. C., St. J and C. B. R. R. now Burlington System to 1888; Omaha city passenger agent 1888-96; agent Burlington station Omaha 1896; auditor Douglas County 1899-1901.

Deuel, S. D. (est. Apr. 5, 1862; 636 sq. mi.; 1970 pop.: 5,686; 1960: 6,782; 1950: 7,689) (Clear Lake). Jacob S. Deuel (1830-). First and second Dakota terr. legislature 1862-63; owned small store and sawmill; moved to Neb. 1863.

Dewey, Okla. (est. July 16, 1907; 990 sq. mi.; 1970 pop.: 5,656; 1960: 6,051; 1950: 8,789) (Taloga). George

Dewey (1837-1917). Graduated U. S. Naval Academy 1858; served under Admiral Farragut in Civil War 1861; commanded Asiatic squadron Spanish War 1897; won battle of Manila Bay, May 1, 1898; appointed first "admiral of the navy" 1899.

Dewey, S. D. (est. Jan. 8, 1873, org. Dec. 3, 1910; 1, 893 sq. mi. ; 1970 pop. : 5, 170; 1960: 5, 257; 1950: 4, 916) (Timber Lake). William Pitt Dewey (-1900) pioneer; terr. surveyor gen. of Dakotas 1873-77. (Formerly Rusk County, name changed to Dewey County, Mar. 9, 1883, chap. 17).

DeWitt, Ill. (est. Mar. 1, 1839; 415 sq. mi. ; 1970 pop. : 16, 975; 1960: 17, 253; 1950: 16, 894) (Clinton). De Witt Clinton (see biographical description under Clinton). -- Biographical Record of De Witt County, Chicago: S. J. Clarke Pub. Co., 1901; 478 p.

De Witt, Tex. (est. Mar. 24, 1846; 910 sq. mi. ; 1970 pop.: 18, 660; 1960: 20, 683; 1950: 22, 973) (Cuero). Green C. De Witt (1787-1835). Established small colony in Mexico 1825; represented Gonzalez in convention 1833.

Dickens, Tex. (est. Aug. 21, 1876; 930 sq. mi. ; 1970 pop. : 3, 737; 1960: 4, 963; 1950: 7, 177) (Dickens). J. Dickens (18 -1836). In Mexican War, killed at the Alamo 1836.

Dickenson, Va. (est. Mar. 3, 1880; 335 sq. mi. ; 1970 pop.: 16, 077; 1960: 20, 211; 1950: 23, 393) (Clintwood). William J. Dickenson.

Dickey, N. D. (est. Mar. 5, 1881; 1, 144 sq. mi. ; 1970 pop.: 6, 976; 1960: 8, 147; 1950: 9, 121) (Ellendale). Alfred M. Dickey. Lt. gov. of N. D. 1889-90. -- Dickey County Historical Society, History of Dickey County, North Dakota, Ellendale, N. D. : Dickey County Historical Society, 1930; 333 p.

Dickinson, Iowa. (est. Jan. 15, 1851; 332 sq. mi. ; 1970 pop. : 12, 565; 1960: 12, 574; 1950: 12, 756) (Spirit Lake). Daniel Stevens Dickinson (1800-1866). Postmaster of Guilford, N. Y., 1827-32; N. Y. assembly 1837-40; lt. gov. of N. Y., 1842-44; Senator from N. Y., 1844-51; attorney gen. of N. Y., 1861; U. S. attorney for southern district of N. Y., 1865-66. -- Smith, Rodney A., A history of Dickinson County, Des Moines: Kenyon Printing and Mfg. Co., 1902; 598 p.

Dickinson, Kan. (est. Feb. 20, 1857; org. Feb. 27, 1860; 855 sq. mi. ; 1970 pop. : 19, 993; 1960: 21, 572; 1950: 21, 190) (Abilene). Daniel Stevens Dickinson*.

Dickinson, Mich. (est. May 21, 1891; 757 sq. mi. ; 1970 pop. : 23, 753; 1960: 23, 917; 1950: 24, 844) (Iron Mountain). Donald McDonald Dickinson (1846-1917). Postmaster gen. of the U. S. 1887-89 in Pres. Cleveland's administration.

Dickson, Tenn. (est. Oct. 25, 1803; 486 sq. mi.; 1970 pop.: 21, 977; 1960: 18, 839; 1950: 18, 805) (Charlotte). William Dickson (1770-1816). Physician; Tenn. house of representatives 1799-1803; Representative from Tenn., 1801-07; trustee of Univ. of Nashville 1806-16. -- Corlew, Robert Ewing, History of Dickson County, Tenn., Nashville, Tenn.: Tennessee Historical Commission and Dickson County Historical Society, 1956; 243 p.

Dillon, S. C. (est. Feb. 5, 1910; 407 sq. mi.; 1970 pop.: 28, 838; 1960: 30, 584; 1950: 30, 930) (Dillon). J. W. Dillon.

Dimmit, Tex. (est. Feb. 1, 1858; 1, 341 sq. mi.; 1970 pop.: 9, 039; 1960: 10, 095; 1950: 10, 654) (Carrizo Springs). Philip Dimmit (1801-1841). Capt. of troops at Goliad after its capture. Took poison July 1841 rather than go to Mexican prison, at seige of Bexar.

Dinwiddie, Va. (est. Session Feb. 27, 1752; 507 sq. mi.; 1970 pop.: 25, 046; 1960: 22, 183; 1950: 18, 839) (Dinwiddie). Robert Dinwiddie (1693-1770). Lt. gov. of Va., (Royal Province) 1751-1756 and 1756-58; fought French; dispatched Braddock; returned to England 1758. (provisioned May 1, 1752). -- U. S. Works Progress Administration, Virginia, Dinwiddie County, Richmond, Va.: Whittet & Shepperson, 1942; 302 p.

Divide, N. D. (est. Dec. 9, 1910 by election Nov. 8, 1910, 1, 303 sq. mi.; 1970 pop.: 4, 564; 1960: 5, 566; 1950: 5, 967) (Crosby). Descriptive term, for the mountains which divide the county.

Dixie, Fla. (est. Apr. 25, 1921; 688 sq. mi.; 1970 pop.: 5, 480; 1960: 4, 479; 1950: 3, 928) (Cross City). Popular term applied to the south.

Dixon, Neb. (est. Jan. 26, 1856, org. Nov. 1, 1858; 480 sq. mi.; 1970 pop.: 7, 453; 1960: 8, 106; 1950: 9, 129) (Ponca). Dixon. -- Huse, William, History of Dixon County, Nebraska, Norfolk, Neb.: Press of the Daily News, 1896; 372 p.

Doddridge, W. Va. (est. Feb. 4, 1845; 321 sq. mi.; 1970 pop.: 6, 389; 1960: 6, 970; 1950: 9, 026) (West Union). Philip Doddridge (1773-1832). House of delegates of Va., 1815, 1816, 1822, 1823, 1828 and 1829; Va., constitutional convention 1829; Representative from Va., 1829-32.

Dodge, Ga. (est. Oct. 26, 1870; 431 sq. mi.; 1970 pop.: 15, 658; 1960: 16, 483; 1950: 17, 865) (Eastman). William Earle Dodge (1805-1883). Mercantile pursuits 1818-66; delegate to peace convention to prevent the Civil War

1861; a Representative from N. Y., 1866-67; mercantile pursuits 1867-83. -- Cobb, Addie (Davis) and Cobb, Wilton Philip, History of Dodge County, Atlanta, Ga.: Foote & Davis Co., 1932; 256 p.

Dodge, Minn. (est. Feb. 20, 1855; 435 sq. mi.; 1970 pop.: 13,037; 1960: 13,259; 1950: 12,624) (Mantorville). Henry Dodge (1782-1867). First and fourth gov. of Wis. terr. Served in War of 1812; in Black Hawk War 1832 and other Indian wars; maj. U. S. Rangers 1832; resigned from Army with rank of col. 1836; gov. of Wis. terr. 1836-41 and 1845-48; Delegate from Wis. terr. 1841-45; Senator from Wis., 1848-57; declined appt. as gov. of Washington Terr. (Augustus Caesar Dodge, also claim)

Dodge, Neb. (est. procl. Nov. 23, 1854, org. Jan. 6, 1857; 529 sq. mi.; 1970 pop.: 34,782; 1960: 32,471; 1950: 26,265) (Fremont). Augustus Caesar Dodge (1812-1883). In Black Hawk wars; register of land offices at Burlington, Iowa 1838-40; Delegate from Iowa 1840-46; Senator from Iowa 1848-55; U. S. Minister to Spain 1855-59; mayor of Burlington, Iowa 1874-75. -- Buss, William Henry, History of Dodge and Washington Counties, Nebraska, Chicago: American Historical Society, 1921; 2 vol.

Dodge, Wis. (est. Dec. 7, 1836; 892 sq. mi.; 1970 pop.: 69,004; 1960: 63,170; 1950: 57,611) (Juneau). Henry Dodge*. -- Hubbell, Homer Bishop, Dodge County, Chicago: S. J. Clarke Pub. Co., 1913; 2 vol.

Dolores, Colo. (est. Feb. 19, 1881; 1,028 sq. mi.; 1970 pop.: 1,641; 1960: 2,196; 1950: 1,966) (Rico). Spanish word. Dolores River; Rio de Nuestra Senora de los Dolores, River of Our Lady of Sorrows.

Dona Ana, N. M. (est. Jan. 9, 1852; 3,804 sq. mi.; 1970 pop.: 69,773; 1960: 59,948; 1950: 39,557) (Las Cruces). Ana (18??-18??). Daughter of col. Ana captured by the Apache Indians.

Doniphan, Kan. (est. Aug. 30, 1855; 391 sq. mi.; 1970 pop.: 9,107; 1960: 9,574; 1950: 10,499) (Troy). Alexander William Doniphan (1808-1887) Mo. legislature 1836, 1840 and 1854; brig. gen. of militia of Mo., to drive Mormons out of the state 1838; in Mexican War col. of First regiment of Mo., mounted vol. 1846; captured Chihuahua, Saltillo, etc. 1847. -- Gray, Patrick Leonard, Gray's Doniphan County history, Bendena, Kan.: Roycroft Press, 1905; 166 p.

Donley, Tex. (est. Aug. 21, 1876; 909 sq. mi.; 1970 pop.: 3,641; 1960: 4,449; 1950: 6,216) (Clarendon). Stockton P. Donley (1821-1871). District attorney sixth judicial district, Tex. 1852; Confederate army 1861; Supreme Court of Tex. 1866; removed 1867.

Dooly, Ga. (est. May 15, 1821; 397 sq. mi.; 1970 pop.: 10,404; 1960: 11,474; 1950: 14,159) (Vienna). John Dooly (-1780). Capt. first Ga. 1775; resigned 1776; col. Ga., militia; he and his family were murdered by Tories Aug. 1780.

Door, Wis. (est. Feb. 11, 1851; 491 sq. mi.; 1970 pop.: 20,106; 1960: 20,685; 1950: 20,870) (Sturgeon Bay). ("The County Where Nature Smiles For Miles and Miles"; "The Vacation Paradise"; "Wisconsin's Air-Conditioned Peninsula Playground"; "Wisconsin's Peninsula Playground"). Descriptive, entrance to Green Bay. -- Holand, Hjalmar Rued, History of Door County, Chicago: S. J. Clarke Pub. Co., 1917; 2 vol.

Dorchester, Md. (est. 1668; 580 sq. mi.; 1970 pop.: 29,405; 1960: 29,666; 1950: 27,815) (Cambridge). ("God's Country"; "The Sportsman's Paradise"). Richard Sackville II, the earl of Dorset (1622-1677). A friend of the Calverts, succeeded as the fifth earl of Dorset, July 17, 1652. -- Jones, Elias, Revised history of Dorchester County, Baltimore, Md.: Read-Taylor Press, 1925; 603 p.

Dorchester, S. C. (est. Feb. 25, 1897; 564 sq. mi.; 1970 pop.: 32,276; 1960: 24,383; 1950: 22,601) (St. George). Named for Dorchester, Mass.

Dougherty, Ga. (est. Dec. 15, 1853; 342 sq. mi.; 1970 pop.: 89,639; 1960: 75,680; 1950: 43,617) (Albany). Charles Dougherty (1801-1853). Judge of the western circuit. -- Daughters of the American Revolution, History and Reminiscences of Dougherty, Albany, Ga.: Daughters of American Revolution, 1924; 411 p.

Douglas, Colo. (est. Nov. 1, 1861; 843 sq. mi.; 1970 pop.: 8,407; 1960: 4,816; 1950: 3,507) (Castle Rock). Stephen Arnold Douglas (1813-1861). Ill. house of representatives 1836-37; register land office Springfield, Ill., 1837; Ill. secretary of state 1840-41; Representative from Ill., 1843-47; Senator from Ill., 1847-61; Democratic nominee for the presidency, defeated by Pres. Lincoln 1860.

Douglas, Ga. (est. Oct. 17, 1870; 208 sq. mi.; 1970 pop.: 28,659; 1960: 16,741; 1950: 12,173) (Douglasville). Stephen Arnold Douglas*.

Douglas, Ill. (est. Feb. 8, 1859; 417 sq. mi.; 1970 pop.: 18,997; 1960: 19,243; 1950: 16,706) (Tuscola). Stephen Arnold Douglas*. -- Gresham, John M., Historical and Biographical Record of Douglas County, Logansport, Ind: Press of Wilson, Humphreys & Co., 1900; 299 p.

Douglas, Kan. (est. Aug. 30, 1855; 468 sq. mi.; 1970 pop.: 57,932; 1960: 43,720; 1950: 34,086) (Lawrence). Stephen Arnold Douglas*.

Douglas, Minn. (est. Mar. 8, 1858; 637 sq. mi.; 1970 pop.: 22,892; 1960: 21,313; 1950: 21,304) (Alexandria). Stephen Arnold Douglas*.

Douglas, Mo. (est. Oct. 29, 1857; 809 sq. mi.; 1970 pop.: 9,268; 1960: 9,653; 1950: 12,638) (Ava). Stephen Arnold Douglas*.

Douglas, Neb. (est. Nov. 23, 1854, procl., 335 sq. mi.; 1970 pop.: 389,455; 1960: 343,490; 1950: 281,020) (Omaha). Stephen Arnold Douglas*. -- Wakeley, Arthur Cooper, Omaha, the gate city, and Douglas County, Neb., Chicago: S. J. Clarke Pub. Co., 1917; 2 vol.

Douglas, Nev. (est. Nov. 25, 1861; 724 sq. mi.; 1970 pop.: 6,882; 1960: 3,481; 1950: 2,029) (Minden). Stephen Arnold Douglas*.

Douglas, Ore. (est. Jan. 7, 1852; 5,062 sq. mi.; 1970 pop.: 71,743; 1960: 68,458; 1950: 54,549) (Roseburg). ("The County To Stay and Play"). Stephen Arnold Douglas*.

Douglas, S. D. (est. Jan. 8, 1873; 435 sq. mi.; 1970 pop.: 4,569; 1960: 5,113; 1950: 5,636) (Armour). Stephen Arnold Douglas*.

Douglas, Wash. (est. Nov. 28, 1883; 1,841 sq. mi.; 1970 pop.: 16,787; 1960: 14,890; 1950: 10,817) (Waterville). Stephen Arnold Douglas*.

Douglas, Wis. (est. Feb. 9, 1854; 1,310 sq. mi.; 1970 pop.: 44,657; 1960: 45,008; 1950: 46,715) (Superior). Stephen Arnold Douglas*.

Drew, Ark. (est. Nov. 26, 1846; 836 sq. mi.; 1970 pop.: 15,157; 1960: 15,213; 1950: 17,959) (Monticello). Thomas Stevenson Drew (1802-1879). Third gov. of Ark. In mercantile pursuits, taught school; clerk of county 1823-25; gov. of Ark., 1844-49.

DuBois, Ind. (est. Dec. 20, 1817, eff. Feb. 1, 1818; 433 sq. mi.; 1970 pop.: 30,934; 1960: 27,463; 1950: 23,785) (Jasper). Toussaint Dubois. Emigrated from France.

Dubuque, Iowa (est. Sept. 6, 1834, eff. Oct. 1, 1834, orig. Dec. 21, 1837; 608 sq. mi.; 1970 pop.: 90,609; 1960: 80,048; 1950: 71,337) (Dubuque). Julien Dubuque (1764-1810). First white settler in Iowa; received option from the Indians to work the lead mines which product he sold at St. Louis, Mo. -- Goodspeed, Weston Arthur, History of Dubuque County, Chicago: Goodspeed Historical Association, 1911; 943 p.

Duchesne, Utah. (est. procl. Aug. 13, 1914; 3,260 sq. mi.; 1970 pop.: 7,299; 1960: 7,179; 1950: 8,134) (Duchesne)

Duchesne River, named for Ft. Duchesne, Pa., built 1754.

Dukes, Mass. (est. June 22, 1695; 106 sq. mi.; 1970 pop.: 6,117; 1960: 5,829; 1950: 5,633) (Edgartown). Duke of York. See biographical material York.

Dundy, Neb. (est. Feb. 27, 1873, org. June 12, 1884; 921 sq. mi.; 1970 pop.: 2,926; 1960: 3,570; 1950: 4,354) (Benkelman). Elmer S. Dundy. Neb. terr. legislature 1858-61; U. S. Circuit Court.

Dunklin, Mo. (est. Feb. 14, 1845; 543 sq. mi.; 1970 pop.: 33,742; 1960: 39,139; 1950: 45,329) (Kennett). Daniel Dunklin (1790-1844). Fifth gov. of Mo.; Sheriff, Washington County; Mo., constitutional convention 1820; lt. gov. Mo., 1828; gov. of Mo., 1833-36; surveyor-gen. Mo., Ill., and Ark., appointed by Pres. Jackson 1836.

Dunn, N. D. (est. Mar. 9, 1883; org. Jan. 17, 1908; 2,068 sq. mi.; 1970 pop.: 4,895; 1960: 6,350; 1950: 7,212) (Manning). John P. Dunn. Mayor of Bismarck, N. D.

Dunn, Wis. (est. Feb. 3, 1854; 858 sq. mi.; 1970 pop.: 29,154; 1960: 26,156; 1950: 27,341) (Menomonie) Charles Dunn. First Chief Justice of Wis. Terr.

Du Page, Ill. (est. Feb. 9, 1839; 345 sq. mi.; 1970 pop.: 491,882; 1960: 313,459; 1950: 154,599) (Wheaton) Du Page (De Page). Indian who lived on the banks of the Du Page River about 1800. -- Knoblauch, Marion, Du Page County, (American Guide Series), 1948 (re-edited); 253 p.

Duplin, N. C. (est. session Mar. 17, 1749; 822 sq. mi.; 1970 pop.: 38,015; 1960: 40,270; 1950: 41,074) (Kenansville). George Henry Hay, Lord Duplin. English nobleman, created Viscount Duplin and Lord Hay of Kinfauns May 4, 1627.

Durham, N. C. (est. Feb. 28, 1881; 299 sq. mi.; 1970 pop.: 132,681; 1960: 111,995; 1950: 101,639) (Durham). Dr. Bartholomew Durham.

Dutchess, N. Y. (est. Nov. 1, 1683; 816 sq. mi.; 1970 pop.: 222,295; 1960: 176,008; 1950: 136,781) (Poughkeepsie) Duchess of York, Anne, elder daughter of Sir Edward Hyde (1659-1671). Wife of James Stuart who succeeded to the Crown as King James II on Feb. 6, 1685; "the lady of a duke." -- Hasbrouck, Frank, ed., The history of Dutchess County, Poughkeepsie, N. Y.: S. A. Matthieu, 1909; 791 p. -- MacCracken, Henry Noble, Old Dutchess Forever! The story of an American county, New York: Hastings House, 1956; 503 p.

Duval, Fla. (est. Aug. 12, 1822; 777 sq. mi.; 1970 pop.: 528,865; 1960: 455,411; 1950: 304,029) (Jacksonville). William Pope DuVal (1784-1854). Second terr. gov. of Fla. Capt. of mounted rangers in Ky., 1812; Representative from Ky., 1813-15; U.S. judge east Fla. district 1821; gov. of the terr. of Fla. 1822-34; law agent in Fla. 1841. -- Gold, Pleasant Daniel, History of Duval County, St. Augustine, Fla.: The Record Co., 1928; 693 p.

Duval, Tex. (est. Feb. 1, 1858; 1,814 sq. mi.; 1970 pop.: 11,722; 1960: 13,398; 1950: 15,643) (San Diego). Burr H. Duval (1809-1836). Capt. of Ky. Mustangs who joined Fannin and was massacred at Goliad, Tex., Mar. 27, 1836.

Dyer, Tenn. (est. Oct. 16, 1823; 527 sq. mi.; 1970 pop.: 30,427; 1960: 29,537; 1950: 33,473) (Dyersburg). Robert Henry Dyer. Served on Natchez expedition, Creek War, battle of New Orleans, Seminole campaign of 1818.

E

Eagle, Colo. (est. Feb. 11, 1883; 1,685 sq. mi.; 1970 pop.: 7,498; 1960: 4,677; 1950: 4,488) (Eagle). Descriptive.

Early, Ga. (est. Dec. 15, 1818; org. Dec. 24, 1825; 524 sq. mi.; 1970 pop.: 12,682; 1960: 13,151; 1950: 17,413) Blakely). Peter Early (1773-1817) Twenty-fifth gov. of Ga. Representative from Ga., 1803-07; first judge of the superior court of the Ocmulgee circuit 1807-13; gov. of Ga., 1813-15; Ga. senate 1815-17.

East Baton Rouge, La. (est. 1810; 455 sq. mi.; 1970 pop.: 285,167; 1960: 230,058; 1950: 158,236) (Baton Rouge). "Baton Rouge" French words for "red stick." -- Jennings, Virginia (Lobdell), The Plains and the People: a history of upper East Baton Rouge Parish, New Orleans: Pelican Pub. Co., 1962; 396 p.

East Carroll, La. (est. Mar. 28, 1877; 420 sq. mi.; 1970 pop.: 12,884; 1960: 14,433; 1950: 16,302) (Lake Providence). Charles Carroll (1737-1832). See Carroll, Ark.

East Feliciana, La. (est. Feb. 17, 1824; 464 sq. mi.; 1970 pop.: 17,657; 1960: 20,198; 1950: 19,133) (Clinton). "Feliciana" Spanish word for "happiness." -- Reeves, Miriam G., The Felicianas of Louisiana, Baton Rouge, La.: Claitor's Book Store, 1967; 126 p.

Eastland, Tex. (est. Feb. 1, 1858; 955 sq. mi.; 1970 pop.: 18,092; 1960: 19,526; 1950: 23,942) (Eastland). William Mosby Eastland (1806-1843). First lt. fought Waco Indians 1835; at battle of San Jacinto 1836; capt. 1836-38; shot by Santa Anna's order Mar. 25, 1843. -- Cox, Edwin T., History of Eastland County, Texas, San Antonio, Texas: Naylor, 1950; 95 p. -- Ghormley, Pearl (Foreman), Eastland County, Texas, Austin, Texas: Rupegy Pub. Co., 1969; 397 p. -- Langston, Carolyne Lavinia, History of Eastland County, Texas, Dallas, Texas: A. D. Aldridge & Co., 1904; 220 p.

Eaton, Mich. (est. Oct. 29, 1829, org. 1837; 567 sq. mi.; 1970 pop.: 68,892; 1960: 49,684; 1950: 40,023) (Charlotte) John Henry Eaton (1790-1856). Third terr. gov. of Fla. Tenn. house of representatives 1815-16; Senator from Tenn., 1818-29; Secretary of War in cabinet of Pres. Jackson 1829-31; gov. of the terr. of Fla. 1834-36; Envoy Extraordinary and Minister Plenipotentiary to Spain 1836-40. -- Durant, Samuel W., History of Ingham and Eaton Counties, Philadelphia: D. W. Ensign & Co., 1880; 586 p.

Eau Clair, Wis. (est. Oct. 6, 1856; 649 sq. mi.; 1970 pop.: 67,219; 1960: 58,300; 1950: 54,187) (Fairchild). French for "clear water."

Echols, Ga. (est. Dec. 13, 1858; 362 sq. mi.; 1970 pop.: 1,924; 1960: 1,876; 1950: 2,494) (Statenville). Robert M. Echols (1800?-1847). Ga. assembly; col. infantry 13th U. S. Regiment 1847; bvt. brig. gen. 1847; killed at Natural Bridge, Mexico, Dec. 3, 1847.

Ector, Tex. (est. Feb. 26, 1887; 907 sq. mi.; 1970 pop.: 91,805; 1960: 90,995; 1950: 42,102) (Odessa). Matthew Duncan Ector (1822-1879). Tex. legislature; 3rd Tex. Cavalry; brig. gen. in the Army of Cumberland; district judge 1866; judge of sixth district court of Texas 1874; judge of court of appeals 1876-1879.

Eddy, N. M. (est. Feb. 25, 1889; 4,163 sq. mi.; 1970 pop.: 41,119; 1960: 50,783; 1950: 40,640) (Carlsbad). Charles B. Eddy. Carlsbad irrigation project. -- Griffin, Marcus These are my neighbors, Carlsbad, N. M., 1945.

Eddy, N. D. (est. Mar. 9, 1885, org. Apr. 27, 1885; 643 sq. mi.; 1970 pop.: 4,103; 1960: 4,936; 1950: 5,732) (New Rockford). E. B. Eddy. Founder of First National Bank, Fargo, N. D.

Edgar, Ill. (est. Jan. 3, 1823; 621 sq. mi.; 1970 pop.: 21,591; 1960: 22,550; 1950: 23,407) (Paris). John Edgar. Pioneer merchant and politician. -- History of Edgar County, Chicago: Wm. Le Baron & Co., 1879; 798 p.

Edgecombe, N. C. (est. Apr. 4, 1741; 511 sq. mi.; 1970 pop.: 52,341; 1960: 54,226; 1950: 51,634) (Tarboro). Richard Edgecombe (1680-1758). Baron Edgecombe (Edgecumbe) lord of English treasury 1716; vice treasurer, treasurer of war and paymaster gen. of His Majesty's services in Ireland, maj. gen. 1755. -- Turner, Joseph Kelly, History of Edgecombe County, North

Carolina, Raleigh, N. C.: Edward & Broughton Printing Co., 1920; 486 p.

Edgefield, S. C. (est. Mar. 12, 1785; 481 sq. mi.; 1970 pop.: 15,692; 1960: 15,735; 1950: 16,591) (Edgefield). Descriptive. -- Chapman, John A., History of Edgefield County, Newberry, S. C.: E. H. Aull, 1897; 521 p.

Edmonson, Ky. (est. Jan. 12, 1825; 304 sq. mi.: 1970 pop.: 8,751; 1960: 8,085; 1950: 9,376) (Brownsville). John Edmonson. Raised company of vol. riflemen commissioned col. 1812; killed at Frenchtown battle on the River Raisin, Mich., Jan. 18, 1813.

Edmunds, S. D. (est. Jan. 8, 1873; 1,163 sq. mi.; 1970 pop.: 5,548; 1960: 6,079; 1950: 7,275) (Ipswich). Newton Edmunds (1819-1908). Second terr. gov. of Dakota 1863-66. Chief clerk in surveyor's office 1861; desired peace with Indians, terr. gov. of Dakota terr. 1863-66; banking business.

Edwards, Ill. (est. Nov. 28, 1814; 238 sq. mi.: 1970 pop.: 7,090; 1960: 7,940; 1950: 9,056) (Albion). Ninian Edwards (1775-1833). First terr. gov. and third gov. of Ill. Ky. house of representatives 1796-97; judge of Ky. gen. court 1803; judge of Ky. circuit court; judge of court of appeals 1806; chief justice of Ky. 1808; gov. of Ill. terr. 1809-18; Senator from Ill., 1818-24; gov. of Ill. 1826-30. -- McDonough, J., Combined history of Edwards, Lawrence & Wabash Counties, Philadelphia: J. L. McDonough & Co., 1883; 377 p.

Edwards, Kan. (est. Mar. 7, 1874; 614 sq. mi.; 1970 pop.: 4,581; 1960: 5,118; 1950: 5,936) (Kinsley). W. C. Edwards.

Edwards, Tex. (est. Feb. 1, 1858; 2,075 sq. mi.; 1970 pop.: 2,107; 1960: 2,317; 1950: 2,908) (Rocksprings). Hayden Edwards (1771-1849). Founded colony at Nacogdoches, Tex. 1825. (org. 1883)

Effingham, Ga. (est. Feb. 5, 1777; 448 sq. mi.; 1970 pop.: 13,632; 1960: 10,144; 1950: 9,133) (Springfield). Thomas Howard (1746-1791), ninth baron Howard, third earl of Effingham 1763; lt. and capt. First Regiment of Foot Guards 1766; capt. 22nd Regiment 1772, deputy earl marshal of England 1777-82; lt. col. British army 1782; favored colonists in struggle for independence.

Effingham, Ill. (est. Feb. 15, 1831; 511 sq. mi.; 1970 pop.: 24,608; 1960: 23,107; 1950: 21,675) (Effingham). Feldhake, Hilda Engbring, Effingham Co., Ill. — Past and Present, Effingham, Ill.: Effingham Regional Historical Society, 1968; 418 p.

El Dorado, Calif. (est. Feb. 18, 1850; 1,725 sq. mi.; 1970 pop.: 43,833; 1960: 29,390; 1950: 16,207) (Placerville). ("The County in the Fabulous Mother Lode of California"; "The Gold Discovery County"). Spanish for "the gilded one." -- Jerrett, Herman Daniel, Hills of Gold, Sacramento, Calif.: Cal-Central Press, 1963; 100 p.

Elbert, Colo. (est. Feb. 2, 1874; 1,864 sq. mi.; 1970 pop.: 3,903; 1960: 3,708; 1950: 4,477) (Kiowa). Samuel Hitt Elbert (1833-1907). Sixth terr. gov. of Colo. Secretary of terr. of Colo., 1862; Colo. terr. legislature 1869; Colo. terr. gov. 1873-74; justice of Colo. supreme court 1876-1880; chief justice of Colo. Supreme Court 1880-83.

Elbert, Ga. (est. Dec. 10, 1790; 361 sq. mi.; 1970 pop.: 17,262; 1960: 17,835; 1950: 18,585) (Elberton) Samuel Elbert (1743-1782) Capt. of a grenadier company 1774; member of Ga. council of safety 1775; lt. col. and col. 1776; expedition against English in east Florida 1777; defended Savannah; wounded and taken prisoner Briar Creek 1779; bvt brig. gen. 1783; gov. of Ga. 1785; maj. gen. of militia. -- McIntosch, John Hawes, Official History of Elbert County, 1790-1935, Elberton, Ga.: Daughters of American Revolution, 1940; 554 p.

Elizabeth City County, Va., consolidated with Hampton City. Incorporated as Hampton City on July 1, 1952.

Elk, Kan. (est. Mar. 3, 1875; eff. June 1, 1875; 647 sq. mi.; 1970 pop.: 3,858; 1960: 5,048; 1950: 6,679) (Howard). Descriptive.

Elk, Pa. (est. Apr. 18, 1843; 809 sq. mi.; 1970 pop.: 37,770; 1960: 37,328; 1950: 34,503) (Ridgway). Descriptive.

Elkhart, Ind. (est. Jan. 29, 1830, eff. Apr. 1, 1830; 468 sq. mi.; 1970 pop.: 126,529; 1960: 106,790; 1950: 84,512) (Goshen). Elkhart Indian tribe. -- Deahl, Anthony, A twentieth century history and biographical record of Elkhart County, Ind., Chicago: The Lewis Pub. Co., 1905; 793 p. -- Weaver, Abraham E. (ed.), Standard history of Elkhart County, Indiana, Chicago: American Historical Society, 1916; 2 vol.

Elko, Nev. (est. Mar. 5, 1869; 17,140 sq. mi.; 1970 pop.: 13,958; 1960: 12,011; 1950: 11,654) (Elko). ("The Cattle County"). Indian word for "first white woman."

Elliott, Ky. (est. Jan. 26, 1869; 240 sq. mi.; 1970 pop.: 5,933; 1960: 6,330; 1950: 7,085) (Sandy Hook). John Milton Elliott (1820-1879). Ky. house of representatives 1847 and 1861; Representative from Ky., 1853-59; first and second Confederate congress circuit judge 1868-74; judge of court of appeals 1876-79; assassinated at Frankfort, Ky., 1879.

Ellis, Kan. (est. Feb. 26, 1867; 900 sq. mi.; 1970 pop.: 24,730; 1960: 21,270; 1950: 19,043) (Hays). George Ellis (18 -1864). First lt., col., Twelfth Kan. killed at Jenkins Ferry, Ark., Apr. 30, 1864.

Ellis, Okla. (est. July 16, 1907; 1,222 sq. mi.; 1970 pop.: 5,129; 1960: 5,457; 1950: 7,326) (Arnett). Albert H. Ellis. Second vice pres. and delegate Okla. constitutional convention 1907.

Ellis, Tex. (est. Dec. 20, 1849; 953 sq. mi.; 1970 pop.: 46,638; 1960: 43,395; 1950: 45,645) (Waxahachie). Richard Ellis (1781-1846). Ala. constitutional convention 1819; supreme court of Ala. 1819-25; pres. of convention of 1836; 4 terms in Senate.

Ellsworth, Kan. (est. Feb. 26, 1867; 723 sq. mi.; 1970 pop.: 6,146; 1960: 7,677; 1950: 8,465) (Ellsworth). Allen Ellsworth. Second lt. co. H, seventh Iowa cavalry.

Elmore, Ala. (est. Feb. 15, 1866; 628 sq. mi.; 1970 pop.: 33,535; 1960: 30,524; 1950: 31,649) (Wetumpka). John Archer Elmore. Early settler, gen.

Elmore, Idaho (est. Feb. 7, 1889; 2,968 sq. mi.; 1970 pop.: 17,479; 1960: 16,719; 1950: 6,687) (Mountain Home). Ida Elmore, whose name was given to a quartz mine discovered in 1863. -- Groefsema, Olive De Ette (Jenson), Elmore County, its historical gleanings, Idaho: Mountain Home, 1949; 453 p.

El Paso, Colo. (est. Nov. 1, 1861; 2,158 sq. mi.; 1970 pop.: 235,972; 1960: 143,742; 1950: 74,523) (Colorado Springs). Spanish for "the pass."

El Paso, Tex. (est. Jan. 3, 1850; 1,054 sq. mi.; 1970 pop.: 359,291; 1960: 314,070; 1950: 194,968) (El Paso). Spanish for "the pass."

Emanuel, Ga. (est. Dec. 10, 1812; 764 sq. mi.; 1970 pop.: 18,189; 1960: 17,815; 1950: 19,789) (Swainsboro). David Emanuel (1742-1808). Twentieth gov. of Ga. Revolutionary war, Ga. legislature; pres. Ga. senate, gov. of Ga. 1801.

Emery, Utah (est. Feb. 12, 1880; 4,442 sq. mi.; 1970 pop.: 5,137; 1960: 5,546; 1950: 6,304) (Castle Dale). George W. Emery. Terr. gov. of Utah 1875-80. -- Daughters of Utah Pioneers, Castle Valley, a history of Emery County, Salt Lake City, Utah: Daughters of Utah Pioneers, 1949; 343 p.

Emmet, Iowa (est. Jan. 15, 1851; 395 sq. mi.; 1970 pop.: 14,009; 1960: 14,871; 1950: 14,102) (Estherville). Robert Emmet (1778-1803). Irish patriot and fighter; captured and executed Sept. 20, 1803 for his activity in the Irish rebellion. -- History of Emmet County and Dickinson

County, Chicago: Pioneer Pub. Co., 1917; 2 vol.

Emmet, Mich. (est. Apr. 1, 1840, org. 1853; 461 sq. mi.; 1970 pop.: 18,331; 1960: 15,904; 1950: 16,534) (Petoskey). Robert Emmet*. Originally Tonedagana County, name changed to Emmet on Mar. 8, 1843. (act 67)

Emmons, N. D. (est. Feb. 10, 1879, org. Nov. 9, 1883; 1,546 sq. mi.; 1970 pop.: 7,200; 1960: 8,462; 1950: 9,715) (Linton). James A. Emmons. Pioneer.

Erath, Tex. (est. Jan. 25, 1856; 1,085 sq. mi.; 1970 pop.: 18,141; 1960: 16,236; 1950: 18,434) (Stephenville). George Bernard Erath (1813-1891). Moved to Tex. 1833; Moore's expedition against Indians 1835; battle of San Jacinto 1836; capt. Tex. Rangers 1839; Indian fighter 1839-41; Somervell expedition 1842; Tex. legislature 1843-45; first state legislature 1846; Tex. senate 1857-61; Tex. regiment 1861-64; Tex. senate 1874. -- Stephen, Homer, Fragments of History; Erath County, Stephenville, Texas: H. Stephen, 1966; 137 p.

Erie, N. Y. (est. Apr. 2, 1821; 1,054 sq. mi.; 1970 pop.: 1,113,491; 1960: 1,064,688; 1950: 899,238) (Buffalo). Erie Indians, Indian tribe in western N. Y. state defeated by the Five Nations in 1655, from an Indian word meaning "cat." -- Johnson, Crisfield, Centennial history of Erie County, Buffalo: Printing house of Matthews & Warren, 1876; 512 p. -- White, Truman C., Our County and Its People, Boston: Boston History Co., 1898; 2 vol.

Erie, Ohio (est. Mar. 15, 1838; 264 sq. mi.; 1970 pop.: 75,909; 1960: 68,000; 1950: 52,565) (Sandusky). Erie Indians*. -- Peeke, Hewson Lindsley, Centennial history of Erie County, Cleveland: Penton Press Co., 1925; 2 vol. -- Aldrich, Lewis Cass, History of Erie County, Syracuse, N. Y.: D. Mason & Co., 1889; 653 p.

Erie, Pa. (est. Mar. 12, 1800; 812 sq. mi.; 1970 pop.: 263,654; 1960: 250,682; 1950: 219,388) (Erie). Erie Indians*. -- Spencer, Herbert Reynolds, Erie, a history, Erie, Pa.: H. R. Spencer, 1962; 275 p. -- History of Erie County, Chicago: Warner, Beers & Co., 1884; 1006 p.

Escambia, Ala. (est. Dec. 10, 1868; 962 sq. mi.; 1970 pop.: 34,906; 1960: 33,511; 1950: 31,443) (Brewton). From Spanish "cambiar" meaning "to exchange."

Escambia, Fla. (est. Aug. 12, 1822; 663 sq. mi.; 1970 pop.: 205,334; 1960: 173,829; 1950: 112,706) (Pensacola). From Spanish "cambiar" meaning "to exchange." -- Armstrong, Henry Clay, History of Escambia County, St. Augustine, Fla.: The Record Co., 1930; 482 p.

Esmeralda, Nev. (est. Nov. 25, 1861; 3, 570 sq. mi. ; 1970 pop. : 629; 1960: 619; 1950: 614) (Goldfield). Spanish word for "emerald."

Essex, Mass. (est. May 10, 1643; 500 sq. mi. ; 1970 pop. : 637, 887; 1960: 568, 831; 1950: 522, 384) (Lawrence, Newburyport and Salem). ("The Heart of Heritage Land, U. S. A."). Essex County, England, named for Robert Devereux (1567-1601) the earl of Essex, who was lord lt. of Ireland in 1599 and condemned to death and executed in 1601. -- Hurd, D. Hamilton, History of Essex County, Philadelphia: J. W. Lewis & Co., 1888; 2 vol. -- Fuess, Claude Moore, The Story of Essex County, New York: American Historical Society, Inc., 1935; 4 vol.

Essex, N. J. (est. Mar. 1, 1683; 128 sq. mi. ; 1970 pop. : 929, 986; 1960: 923, 545; 1950: 905, 949) (Newark). Essex County, England*. -- Arny, Mary (Travis), Red lion rampant, an informal history of Essex County, Montclair, N. J., 1965; 160 p.

Essex, N. Y. (est. Mar. 1, 1799; 1, 826 sq. mi. ; 1970 pop.: 34, 631; 1960: 35, 300; 1950: 35, 036) (Elizabethtown). Essex County, England*. -- Smith, H. Perry, ed., History of Essex County, Syracuse, N. Y. : D. Mason & Co., 1885; 754 p.

Essex, Vt. (est. Nov. 5, 1792; 664 sq. mi. ; 1970 pop. : 5, 416; 1960: 6, 083; 1950: 6, 257) (Guildhall). Essex County, England*.

Essex, Va. (est. Apr. 16, 1692 sess. ; 250 sq. mi. ; 1970 pop. : 7, 099; 1960: 6, 690; 1950: 6, 530) (Tappahannock). Essex County, England*.

Estill, Ky. (est. Jan. 27, 1808, eff. Apr. 1, 1808; 262 sq. mi. ; 1970 pop. : 12, 752; 1960: 12, 466; 1950: 14, 677) (Irvine). James Estill. Capt.

Etowah, Ala. (est. Dec. 7, 1866; 555 sq. mi. ; 1970 pop. : 94, 144; 1960: 96, 980; 1950: 93, 892) (Gadsden). Indian word for "pine tree." (Originally Baine County (Act 92), abolished by constitutional convention Dec. 3, 1867 (Act 27), act repealed and county reestablished with present name Dec. 1, 1868 (Act 20).

Eureka, Nev. (est. Mar. 1, 1873; eff. Mar. 20, 1873; 4, 182 sq. mi. ; 1970 pop. : 948; 1960: 767; 1950: 896) (Eureka). Derived from Greek "I have found it."

Evangeline, La. (est. June 15, 1910; 681 sq. mi. ; 1970 pop.: 31, 932; 1960: 31, 639; 1950: 31, 629) (Ville Platte). Evangeline, heroine of Longfellow's poem.

Evans, Ga. (est. Aug. 11, 1914; 287 sq. mi. ; 1970 pop. : 7, 290; 1960: 6, 952; 1950: 6, 653) (Claxton). Clement Anselm Evans (1833-1911). Judge of Stewart County court

1854; Ga. senate 1859; private Co. 31st Ga., maj. 1861; col. 1862; brig. gen. 1863; wounded at Gettysburg 1863; Monocacy 1864; battle of the Wilderness 1864; Methodist minister 1866. -- Hodges, Lucile, A History of Our Locale, Macon, Ga.: Southern Press, 1965; 322 p.

F

Fairfax, Va. (est. May 6, 1742; session; 416 sq. mi.; 1970 pop.: 455,021; 1960: 275,002; 1950: 98,557) (Fairfax). Lord Thomas Fairfax (1612-1671). Oliver Cromwell's first parliament 1653; aided Charles II's return to the crown. In Council of State 1649-51 and 1659-60; constable of the Tower of London 1647-50. -- Fairfax County (Va.) Supervisors, Board of, Industrial and historical sketch of Fairfax County, Fairfax, Va.: Newell Printing Co., 1907; 95 p.

Fairfield, Conn. (est. May 10, 1666 session; 633 sq. mi.; 1970 pop.: 792,814; 1960: 653,589; 1950: 504,342) (No county seat). ("The Bedroom Community for Manhattan Executives"; "The Research Community"). Descriptive. -- Wilson, Lynn Winfield, History of Fairfield County, Chicago: S. J. Clarke Pub. Co., 1929; 3 vol. -- Hurd, Duane Hamilton, History of Fairfield County, Philadelphia: J. W. Lewis & Co., 1881; 878 p.

Fairfield, Ohio (est. Dec. 9, 1800; 505 sq. mi.; 1970 pop.: 73,301; 1960: 63,912; 1950: 52,130) (Lancaster). Descriptive. -- Graham, A. A., History of Fairfield & Perry Counties, Chicago: W. H. Beers & Co., 1883; 1186 p. -- Scott, Hervey, A complete history of Fairfield County, Columbus, Ohio: Siebert & Lilley, 1877; 304 p.

Fairfield, S. C. (est. Mar. 12, 1785; 699 sq. mi.; 1970 pop.: 19,999; 1960: 20,713; 1950: 21,780) (Winnsboro). Descriptive. -- Ederington, William, History of Fairfield County, Tuscaloosa, Ala.: Wills Pub. Co., 196?; 95 p.

Fall River, S. D. (est. Mar. 6, 1883; 1,748 sq. mi.; 1970 pop.: 7,505; 1960: 10,688; 1950: 10,439) (Hot Springs). Descriptive; literal translation of Indian name.

Fallon, Mont. (est. Dec. 9, 1913; petition and election; 1,633 sq. mi.; 1970 pop.: 4,050; 1960: 3,997; 1950: 3,660) (Baker). Benjamin O. Fallon. Indian agent, army officer.

Falls, Tex. (est. Jan. 28, 1850; 761 sq. mi.; 1970 pop.: 17,300; 1960: 21,263; 1950: 26,724) (Marlin). Descriptive; falls of the Brazos River. -- Old Settlers and Veterans Association of Falls County, History of Falls County, Texas, Marlin, Texas, 1947; 312 p.

Fannin, Ga. (est. Jan. 21, 1854; 401 sq. mi.; 1970 pop.: 13,357; 1960: 13,620; 1950: 15,192) (Blue Ridge). James Walker Fannin (1805-1836). The hero of Concepción 1835; defeated at Goliad, killed Mar. 27, 1836.

Fannin, Tex. (est. Dec. 14, 1837; 906 sq. mi.; 1970 pop.: 22,705; 1960: 23,880; 1950: 31,253) (Bonham). James Walker Fannin*. -- Hodge, Floy Crandall, History of Fannin County, Pioneer Publishers, 1966; 267 p.

Faribault, Minn. (est. Feb. 20, 1855, org. Feb. 23, 1856; 713 sq. mi.; 1970 pop.: 20,896; 1960: 23,685; 1950: 23,879) (Blue Earth). Jean Baptiste Faribault (1774-1860). French-Canadian fur trader. Agent in the northwest for the American Fur Co., 1796-1806; in business for himself; taught agriculture to the Indians. -- Kiester, J. A., History of Faribault County, Minneapolis: Harrison & Smith, 1896; 687 p.

Faulk, S. D. (est. Jan. 8, 1873; 997 sq. mi.; 1970 pop.: 3,893; 1960: 4,397; 1950: 4,752) (Faulkton). Andrew Jackson Faulk (1814-1898). Third terr. gov. of Dakota. Post trader to Yankton Indians 1861; oil business at Oil City, Pa., 1864-66; third gov. of Dakota terr. and supt. of Indian Affairs 1866-69; mayor of Yankton; clerk of federal and terr. courts. -- Ellis, Caleb Holt, History of Faulk County, South Dakota, Faulkton, S. D.: Record Print, 1909; 508 p.

Faulkner, Ark. (est. Apr. 12, 1873; 656 sq. mi.; 1970 pop.: 31,572; 1960: 24,303; 1950: 25,289) (Conway). Sanford C. Faulkner. Composer of "The Arkansas Traveler." -- Gatewood, Robert L., Faulkner County, Arkansas, 1778-1964, Conway, Ark., 1964; 188 p.

Fauquier, Va. (est. Sept. 14, 1758 session, eff. May 1, 1759; 660 sq. mi.; 1970 pop.: 26,375; 1960: 24,066; 1950: 21,248) (Warrenton). Francis Fauquier (1704-1768). Lt. gov. of Va., 1758-68; opposed colonial attempts of government and self-expression. -- Fauquier County Bicentennial Committee, Fauquier County, Virginia, 1759-1959, Warrenton, Va., 1959; 335 p.

Fayette, Ala. (est. Dec. 20, 1824; 627 sq. mi.; 1970 pop.: 16,252; 1960: 16,148; 1950: 19,388) (Fayette). Marie Jean Paul Roch Yves Gilbert Motier, Marquis de Lafayette (1757-1834). Resigned from French military service to aid American cause of independence; commissioned maj. gen. in Continental Army 1777; returned to Paris 1781; became commander-in-chief of the National Guard

1789; captured by Austrians 1792; revisited U. S. in 1784 and 1824-25. -- Newell, Herbert Moses, History of Fayette County, Ala., Fayette, Ala.: Newell Offset Print, 1960; 460 p.

Fayette, Ga. (est. May 15, 1821; 234 sq. mi.; 1970 pop.: 11,364; 1960: 8,199; 1950: 7,978) (Fayetteville). Marquis de Lafayette*.

Fayette, Ill. (est. Feb. 14, 1821; 729 sq. mi.; 1970 pop.: 20,752; 1960: 21,946; 1950: 24,582) (Vandalia). Marquis de Lafayette*.

Fayette, Ind. (est. Dec. 28, 1818; eff. Jan. 1, 1819; 215 sq. mi.; 1970 pop.: 26,216; 1960: 24,454; 1950: 23,391) (Connersville). Marquis de Lafayette*.

Fayette, Iowa (est. Dec. 21, 1837, org. Feb. 3, 1847; 728 sq. mi.; 1970 pop.: 26,898; 1960: 28,581; 1950: 28,294) (West Union). Marquis de Lafayette*. -- History of Fayette County, Chicago: Western Hist. Co., 1878; 758 p.

Fayette, Ky. (est. May 1, 1780 sess.; eff. Nov. 1, 1780; 280 sq. mi.; 1970 pop.: 174,323; 1960: 131,906; 1950: 100,746) (Lexington). Marquis de Lafayette*. -- Perrin, William Henry (ed.), History of Fayette County, Kentucky, Chicago: O. L. Baskin & Co., 1882; 905 p.

Fayette, Ohio (est. Feb. 19, 1810; 406 sq. mi.; 1970 pop.: 25,461; 1960: 24,775; 1950: 22,554) (Washington Court House). Marquis de Lafayette*. -- Allen, Frank M. ed., History of Fayette County, Indianapolis: B. F. Bowen & Co., 1914; 756 p. -- Putnam, Rufus, Pioneer record and reminiscences, Cincinnati, Ohio: Applegate, Pounsford & Co. Print., 1872; 120 p.

Fayette, Pa. (est. Sept. 26, 1783; 800 sq. mi.; 1970 pop.: 154,667; 1960: 169,340; 1950: 189,899) (Uniontown). Marquis de Lafayette*. -- Ellis, Franklin, History of Fayette County, Philadelphia: L. H. Everts & Co., 1882; 841 p. -- Jordan, John Woolf & J. Hadden, Genealogical and personal history of Fayette and Greene Counties, New York: Lewis Historical Pub. Co., 1912; 3 vol.

Fayette, Tenn. (est. Sept. 29, 1824; 704 sq. mi.; 1970 pop.: 22,692; 1960: 24,577; 1950: 27,535) (Somerville). Marquis de Lafayette*.

Fayette, Tex. (est. Dec. 14, 1837; 936 sq. mi.; 1970 pop.: 17,650; 1960: 20,384; 1950: 24,176) (La Grange). Marquis de Lafayette*. -- Lotto, F., Fayette County, her history and her people, Schulenburg, Texas: Lotto, 1902; 424 p. -- Weyand, Leonie (Rummel), An early history of Fayette County, LaGrange, Texas: LaGrange, 1936; 383 p.

Fayette, W. Va. (est. Feb. 28, 1831; 666 sq. mi.; 1970 pop.: 49,332; 1960: 61,731; 1950: 82,443) (Fayetteville). Marquis de Lafayette*. -- Donnelly, Clarence Shirley, Historical notes on Fayette County, W. Va., Oak Hill, W. Va., 1958; 178 p. -- Peters, J. T. and Carden, H. B., History of Fayette County, West Virginia, Charleston, W. Va., Jarrett Printing Co., 1926; 772 p.

Fentress, Tenn. (est. Nov. 28, 1823; 499 sq. mi.; 1970 pop.: 12,593; 1960: 13,288; 1950: 14,917) (Jamestown). James Fentress. Speaker Tenn. House of Representatives 1814-23. -- Hogue, Albert R., History of Fentress County, Tenn., the old home of Mark Twain's Ancestors, Nashville, Tenn.: Williams Printing Co., 1916; 165 p.

Fergus, Mont. (est. Mar. 12, 1885; 4,250 sq. mi.; 1970 pop.: 12,611; 1960: 14,018; 1950: 14,015) (Lewistown). John Fergus. Stock grower.

Ferry, Wash. (est. Feb. 18, 1899; 2,241 sq. mi.; 1970 pop.: 3,655; 1960: 3,889; 1950: 4,096) (Republic). Elisha Peyre Ferry (1825-1895). Eleventh terr. and first gov. of Washington. Ill. constitutional convention 1861; bank commissioner 1861-63; surveyor-gen. of Washington terr. 1869; gov. of Wash. terr. 1872-80; gov. of Wash. 1889-93.

Fillmore, Minn. (est. Mar. 5, 1853; 859 sq. mi.; 1970 pop.: 21,916; 1960: 23,768; 1950: 24,465) (Preston). Millard Fillmore (1800-1874). N. Y. assembly 1829-31; Representative from N. Y., 1833-35 and 1837-1843; N. Y. comptroller 1847-49; Vice Pres. of the U. S. 1849-50; became Pres. upon death of Pres. Taylor 1850-53; unsuccessful candidate for presidency Whig party 1852. -- Neill, Edward D., History of Fillmore County, Minneapolis: Minnesota Historical Co., 1882; 626 p.

Fillmore, Neb. (est. Jan. 26, 1856; org. Apr. 21, 1871; 577 sq. mi.; 1970 pop.: 8,137; 1960: 9,425; 1950: 9,610) (Geneva). Millard Fillmore*. -- Gaffney, Wilbur G., The Fillmore County Story, Geneva, Neb.: Geneva Community Grange No. 403, 1968; 398 p.

Finney, Kan. (est. Mar. 6, 1873; 1,302 sq. mi.; 1970 pop.: 18,947; 1960: 16,093; 1950: 15,092) (Garden City.) David W. Finney. Lt. gov. of Kan. 1861-65. (Originally Sequoyah County, name changed to Finney County Feb. 21, 1883).

Fisher, Tex. (est. Aug. 21, 1876; 906 sq. mi.; 1970 pop.: 6,344; 1960: 7,865; 1950: 11,023) (Roby). Samuel Rhoads Fisher (1794-1839). Tex. constitutional convention 1836; signer Tex. declaration of independence 1836;

secretary of Tex. navy.

Flagler, Fla. (est. Apr. 28, 1917; 483 sq. mi.; 1970 pop.: 4,454; 1960: 4,566; 1950: 3,367) (Bunnell). Henry Morrison Flagler (1830-1913). Capitalist and industrialist, made fortune in oil industry, built railroads and hotels.

Flathead, Mont. (est. Feb. 6, 1893; 5,177 sq. mi.; 1970 pop.: 39,460; 1960: 32,965; 1950: 31,495) (Kalispell). Flathead Indian tribe.

Fleming, Ky. (est. Feb. 10, 1798, eff. Mar. 1, 1798; 350 sq. mi.; 1970 pop.: 11,366; 1960: 10,890; 1950: 11,962) (Flemingsburg) John Fleming.

Florence, S. C. (est. Dec. 22, 1888; 805 sq. mi.; 1970 pop.: 89,636; 1960: 84,438; 1950: 79,710) (Florence) Florence Hardlee, daughter of Gen. W. W. Hardlee.

Florence, Wis. (est. Mar. 18, 1882; 489 sq. mi.; 1970 pop.: 3,298; 1960: 3,437; 1950: 3,756) (Florence). Florence Hulst, wife of Dr. N. P. Hulst for whom a mine and town were named.

Floyd, Ga. (est. Dec. 3, 1832; 502 sq. mi.; 1970 pop.: 73,742; 1960: 69,130; 1950: 62,899) (Rome). John Floyd (1769-1839). Brig. gen. Ga., militia 1813-14 and 1814-15; fought Creek and Choctaw Indians; Ga. house of representatives 1820-27; Representative from Ga. 1827-29. -- Battey, George Magruder, History of Rome and Floyd County, Atlanta, Ga.: Webb & Vary Co., 1922; 639 p.

Floyd, Ind. (est. Jan. 2, 1819; eff. Feb. 1, 1819; 149 sq. mi.; 1970 pop.: 55,622; 1960: 51,397; 1950: 43,955) (New Albany). John Floyd (1783-1837). Twenty-sixth gov. of Va. (Commonwealth). Justice of the peace Montgomery County, Va., 1807; maj. Va. militia 1807-12; Va. house of delegates 1814-15; brig. gen. of militia 1813; Representative from Va., 1817-29; gov. of Va. 1830-34.

Floyd, Iowa (est. Jan. 15, 1851; 503 sq. mi.; 1970 pop.: 19,860; 1960: 21,102; 1950: 21,505) (Charles City). Charles Floyd (-1804) Sgt. in expedition of Lewis and Clark; first white man buried in Iowa. -- History of Floyd County, Chicago: Inter-state Pub. Co., 1882; 1142 p.

Floyd, Ky. (est. Dec. 13, 1799, eff. June 1, 1800; 402 sq. mi.; 1970 pop.: 35,889; 1960: 41,642; 1950: 53,500) (Prestonsburg) John Floyd*.

Floyd, Tex. (est. Aug. 21, 1876; 993 sq. mi.; 1970 pop.: 11,044; 1960: 12,369; 1950: 10,535) (Floydada). Dolfin Ward Floyd (1807-1836). Resident of Gonzalez, Tex., killed at the battle of the Alamo, Mar. 6, 1836.

Floyd, Va. (est. Jan. 15, 1831; 383 sq. mi.; 1970 pop.: 9,775; 1960: 10,462; 1950: 11,351) (Floyd). John Floyd*.

Fluvanna, Va. (est. session May 5, 1777, eff. July 1, 1777; 282 sq. mi.; 1970 pop.: 7,621; 1960: 7,227; 1950: 7,121) (Palmyra). Fluvanna River; named for Queen Anne of England (1665-1714); second daughter of James II; married George, Prince of Denmark, crowned Apr. 23, 1702.

Foard, Tex. (est. Mar. 3, 1891; 676 sq. mi.; 1970 pop.: 2,211; 1960: 3,125; 1950: 4,216) (Crowell). Robert J. Foard (1831-1898). Attorney; maj. Confederate Army.

Fond du Lac, Wis. (est. Dec. 7, 1836; 724 sq. mi.; 1970 pop.: 84,567; 1960: 75,085; 1950: 67,829) (Fond Du Lac). French words for "end of the lake." -- McKenna, Maurice, Fond du Lac County, Chicago: S. J. Clarke Pub. Co., 1912; 2 vol.

Ford, Ill. (est. Feb. 17, 1859; 488 sq. mi.; 1970 pop.: 16,382; 1960: 16,606; 1950: 15,901) (Paxton). Thomas Ford (1800-1850). Eighth gov. of Ill. Newspaper work St. Louis, Mo., 1824; Ill. state attorney 1829-33; judge of sixth circuit 1836; judge municipal court Chicago, Ill., 1837; Ill. Supreme Court 1840; gov. of Ill., 1842-46. -- Portrait and Biographical Record of Ford County, Chicago: Lake City Pub. Co., 1892; 812 p.

Ford, Kan. (est. Feb. 26, 1867, org. Mar. 6, 1873; 1,083 sq. mi.; 1970 pop.: 22,587; 1960: 20,938; 1950: 19,670) (Dodge City). James Hobart Ford (-1867). Capt. Colo. infantry 1861; maj. Colo. infantry 1862; col. 1863; bvt. brig. gen. vol. 1864; honorable discharge 1865. -- Rath, Ida Ellen, Early Ford County, North Newton, Kan.: Mennonite Press, 1964; 267 p.

Forest, Pa. (est. resolution Apr. 11, 1848; 420 sq. mi.; 1970 pop.: 4,926; 1960: 4,485; 1950: 4,944) (Tionesta). Descriptive word.

Forest, Wis. (est. Apr. 11, 1885; 1,010 sq. mi.; 1970 pop.: 7,691; 1960: 7,542; 1950: 9,437) (Crandon). Descriptive word.

Forrest, Miss. (est. Apr. 19, 1906, election May 1907, org. Jan. 6, 1908; 462 sq. mi.; 1970 pop.: 57,849; 1960: 52,722; 1950: 45,055) (Hattiesburg). Nathan Bedford Forrest (1821-1877). Enlisted in mounted rifle company 1861; lt. col. with vol. company 1861; battle of Sacramento Dec. 26, 1861; battle of Ft. Donelson Feb. 11, 1862; captured Murfreesboro 1862; brig. gen. 1862; 29 horses were shot under him in his numerous engagements.

Forsyth, Ga. (est. Dec. 3, 1832; 247 sq. mi.; 1970 pop.: 16,928; 1960: 12,170; 1950: 11,005) (Cumming). John Forsyth (1780-1841). Thirty-first gov. of Ga. Attorney gen. of Ga., 1808; Representative from Ga., 1813-18 and

1823-27; Senator from Ga., 1818-1819 and 1829-34; U. S. Minister to Spain 1819-23; gov. of Ga. 1827-29; U. S. Secretary of State under Pres. Jackson and Van Buren 1834-41.

Forsyth, N. C. (est. Jan. 16, 1849; 424 sq. mi.; 1970 pop.: 214, 348; 1960: 189, 428; 1950: 146, 135) (Winston-Salem). Benjamin Forsyth (17 -1814). Second lt. N. C. Infantry 1800; capt. of riflemen 1808; N. C. legislature 1807-08; commanded assault at Gananoque Upper Canada 1812; bvt. lt. col. at Elizabethtown; killed near Odelltown (or Oldtown), N. Y. June 28, 1814. -- Fries, Adelaide Lisetta, Forsyth, A County on the March, Chapel Hill, N. C.: University of North Carolina, 1949; 248 p.

Fort Bend, Tex. (est. Dec. 29, 1837; 867 sq. mi.; 1970 pop.: 52, 314; 1960: 40, 527; 1950: 31, 056) (Richmond). Fort Bend, built at bend of the Brazos River 1821. -- Sowell, Andrew Jackson, History of Fort Bend County, Waco, Texas: W. M. Morrison, 1964; 373 p. -- Wharton, Clarence Ray, Wharton's History of Fort Bend County, San Antonio, Texas: Naylor Co., 1939; 250 p.

Foster, N. D. (est. Jan. 4, 1873, org. Oct. 11, 1883; 648 sq. mi.; 1970 pop.: 4, 832; 1960: 5, 361; 1950: 5, 337) (Carrington). James S. Foster. Commissioner of Immigration.

Fountain, Ind. (est. Dec. 20, 1825, eff. Apr. 1, 1826; 397 sq. mi.; 1970 pop.: 18, 257; 1960: 18, 706; 1950: 17, 836) (Covington). James Fontaine. Maj. -- Clifton, Thomas A. (ed.), Past and present of Fountain and Warren Counties, Ind., Indianapolis, Ind.: B. F. Bowen & Co., 1913; 989 p.

Franklin, Ala. (est. Feb. 6, 1818, eff. June 1, 1818; 644 sq. mi.; 1970 pop.: 23, 933; 1960: 21, 988; 1950: 25, 705) (Russellville). Benjamin Franklin (1706-1790). Printer. Founded Pa. "Gazette" 1728; clerk Pa. gen. assembly 1736-50; postmaster of Philadelphia 1737; provincial assembly 1744-45; deputy postmaster gen. of the British No. American Colonies 1753-1774; Continental Congress 1775-76; signed the Declaration of Independence 1776; Pa. constitutional convention 1776; commissioner and minister to France 1776-85; gov. of Pa. 1785-88; federal constitutional convention 1787.

Franklin, Ark. (est. Dec. 19, 1837; 615 sq. mi.; 1970 pop.: 11, 301; 1960: 10, 213; 1950: 12, 358) (Charleston and Ozark). Benjamin Franklin*.

Franklin, Fla. (est. Feb. 8, 1832; 544 sq. mi.; 1970 pop.: 7, 065; 1960: 6, 576; 1950: 5, 814) (Apalachicola). Benjamin Franklin*.

Franklin, Ga. (est. Feb. 25, 1784; 279 sq. mi.; 1970 pop.: 12, 784; 1960: 13, 274; 1950: 14, 446) (Carnesville). Benjamin Franklin*.

Franklin, Idaho (est. Jan. 20, 1913; 541 sq. mi.; 1970 pop.: 7, 373; 1960: 8, 457; 1950: 9, 867) (Preston). Franklin Dewey Richards (1821-1899). High priest Church of Latter Day Saints 1844; led group of settlers to Salt Lake Valley 1848; ordained one of twelve apostles Feb. 12, 1849; Utah legislature 1849; pres. Utah legislature 1856; regent Univ. of Deseret brig. gen. Nauvoo Legion 1859; judge of probate and county court Weber County 1869-83; historian Mormon Church 1889-99.

Franklin, Ill. (est. Jan. 2, 1818; 445 sq. mi.; 1970 pop.: 38, 329; 1960: 39, 281; 1950: 48, 685) (Benton). Benjamin Franklin*.

Franklin, Ind. (est. Nov. 27, 1810, eff. Jan. 1, 1811; 394 sq. mi.; 1970 pop.: 16, 943; 1960: 17, 015; 1950: 16, 034) (Brookville). Benjamin Franklin*.

Franklin, Iowa (est. Jan. 15, 1851; 586 sq. mi.; 1970 pop.: 13, 255; 1960: 15, 472; 1950: 16, 268) (Hampton). Benjamin Franklin*. -- History of Franklin and Cerro Gordo Counties, Springfield, Ill.: Union Pub. Co., 1883; 1005 p. -- History of Franklin County, Chicago: S. J. Clarke Pub. Co., 1914; 2 vol.

Franklin, Kan. (est. Aug. 30, 1855, org. Feb. 23, 1857; 577 sq. mi.; 1970 pop.: 20, 007; 1960: 19, 548; 1950: 19, 928) (Ottawa). Benjamin Franklin*.

Franklin, Ky. (est. Dec. 7, 1794, eff. May 10, 1795; 211 sq. mi.; 1970 pop.: 34, 481; 1960: 29, 421; 1950: 25, 933) (Frankfort). Benjamin Franklin*. -- Jillson, Willard Rouse, Early Frankfort and Franklin County, Kentucky, Louisville, Ky.: Standard Printing Co., 1936; 182 p. -- Johnson, Lewis Franklin, History of Franklin County, Kentucky, Frankfort, Ky.: Roberts Printing Co., 1912; 286 p.

Franklin, La. (est. Mar. 1, 1843; 630 sq. mi.; 1970 pop.: 23, 946; 1960: 26, 088; 1950: 29, 376) (Winnsboro). Benjamin Franklin*.

Franklin, Me. (est. Mar. 20, 1838, eff. May 9, 1838; 1, 717 sq. mi.; 1970 pop.: 22, 444; 1960: 20, 069; 1950: 20, 682) (Farmington). Benjamin Franklin*.

Franklin, Mass. (est. June 24, 1811, eff. Dec. 2, 1811; 722 sq. mi.; 1970 pop.: 59, 210; 1960: 54, 864; 1950: 52, 747) (Greenfield). Benjamin Franklin*. -- Biographical Review, Boston: Biographical Review Pub. Co., 1895; 668 p.

Franklin, Miss. (est. Dec. 21, 1809; 547 sq. mi.; 1970

pop.: 8,011; 1960: 9,286; 1950: 10,929) (Meadville). Benjamin Franklin*.

Franklin, Mo. (est. Dec. 11, 1818; 932 sq. mi.; 1970 pop.: 55,116; 1960: 44,566; 1950: 36,046) (Union). Benjamin Franklin*.

Franklin, Neb. (est. Feb. 16, 1867, org. June 21, 1871; 578 sq. mi.; 1970 pop.: 4,566; 1960: 5,449; 1950: 7,096) (Franklin). Benjamin Franklin*.

Franklin, N.Y. (est. Mar. 11, 1808; 1,685 sq. mi.; 1970 pop.: 43,931; 1960: 44,742; 1950: 44,830) (Malone). ("Northern New York's Year-Around Adirondack Vacationland"). Benjamin Franklin*. -- Seaver, Frederick J., _Historical sketches of Franklin County_, Albany, N.Y.: J.B. Lyon Co., 1918; 819 p.

Franklin, N.C. (est. sess. Apr. 14, 1778; 497 sq. mi.; 1970 pop.: 26,820; 1960: 28,755; 1950: 31,341) (Louisburg). Benjamin Franklin*.

Franklin, Ohio (est. Mar. 30, 1803; 538 sq. mi.; 1970 pop.: 833,249; 1960: 682,962; 1950: 503,410) (Columbus). Benjamin Franklin*. -- Moore, Opha, _History of Franklin County_, Topeka, Kan.: Historical Pub. Co., 1930; 1424 p.

Franklin, Pa. (est. Sept. 9, 1784; 754 sq. mi.; 1970 pop.: 100,833; 1960: 88,172; 1950: 75,927) (Chambersburg). Benjamin Franklin*. -- McCauley, I.H., _Historical Sketch of Franklin County_, Chambersburg, Pa.: D. F. Pursel, 1878; 322 p.

Franklin, Tenn. (est. Dec. 3, 1807; 561 sq. mi.; 1970 pop.: 27,244; 1960: 25,528; 1950: 25,431) (Winchester). Benjamin Franklin*.

Franklin, Tex. (est. Mar. 6, 1875; 293 sq. mi.; 1970 pop.: 5,291; 1960: 5,101; 1950: 6,257) (Mount Vernon). Benjamin Cromwell Franklin (1805-1873). District judge Republic of Tex. 1836; 1835 expedition vs. Indians - 1836 comm. capt. in Tex. Army; at battle of San Jacinto Apr. 1836; judge Brazoria judicial district, 1837-39.

Franklin, Vt. (est. Nov. 5, 1792; 659 sq. mi.; 1970 pop.: 31,282; 1960: 29,474; 1950: 29,894) (St. Albans). Benjamin Franklin*. -- Aldrich, Lewis Cass, _History of Franklin and Grand Isle Counties_, Syracuse, N.Y.: D. Mason and Co., 1891; 821 p.

Franklin, Va. (est. Oct. 17, 1785 sess.; 718 sq. mi.; 1970 pop.: 26,858; 1960: 25,925; 1950: 24,560) (Rockymount). Benjamin Franklin*. -- Wingfield, Marshall, _Franklin County, Virginia, a history_, Berryville, Va.: Chesapeake Book Co., 1964; 309 p.

Franklin, Wash. (est. Nov. 28, 1883; 1,262 sq. mi.; 1970

25, 816; 1960: 23, 342; 1950: 13, 563) (Pasco). Benjamin Franklin*.

Frederick, Md. (est. June 10, 1748; 664 sq. mi.; 1970 pop.: 84, 927; 1960: 71, 930; 1950: 62, 287) (Frederick). Frederick Calvert (1731-1771). Sixth Baron of Baltimore, fifth palatine of Md., son of Lord Charles Calvert, created baron of Baltimore 1751; married Lady Egerton, daughter of duke of Bridgewater 1753; last Lord Baltimore tried to give title to Henry Harford, his illegitimate son by Hester Wheland of Ireland. (or Frederick the Great, or Frederick Louis). -- Williams, Thomas John Chew, History of Frederick County, Md., Baltimore, Md.: Regional Pub. Co., 1967; 2 vol.

Frederick, Va. (est. Aug. 1, 1738 sess.; 432 sq. mi.; 1970 pop.: 28, 893; 1960: 21, 941; 1950: 17, 537) (Winchester). Frederick Louis (1707-1751). Prince of Wales, eldest son of George II and Queen Caroline; married Princess Augusta of Saxe-Gotha 1736; father of George III.

Freeborn, Minn. (est. Feb. 20, 1855, org. Mar. 6, 1857; 702 sq. mi.; 1970 pop.: 38, 064; 1960: 37, 891; 1950: 34, 517) (Albert Lea). William Freeborn (1816-18). Minn. terr. legislature 1854-57; emigrated to Mont. 1864; to Calif. in 1868.

Freestone, Tex. (est. Sept. 6, 1850; 862 sq. mi.; 1970 pop.: 11, 116; 1960: 12, 525; 1950: 15, 696) (Fairfield). Descriptive term (as opposed to limestone).

Fremont, Colo. (est. Nov. 1, 1861; 1, 562 sq. mi.; 1970 pop.: 21, 942; 1960: 20, 196; 1950: 18, 366) (Canon City). John Charles Fremont (1813-1890). Third provisional gov. of Calif. and fifth terr. gov. of Ariz. Numerous overland trail expeditions; maj. Calif. vol. 1846; lt. col. U. S. Mounted Rifles 1846; ordered to act as gov. of Calif.; tried by court martial, found guilty, pardoned by Pres. Polk, resigned from army 1848; Senator from Calif., 1850-51; unsuccessful Republican candidate for the presidency 1856; maj. gen. U. S. Army 1861 commanded western district 1861; gov. of Ariz. Terr. 1878-81; appointed a maj. gen. U. S. Army on the retired list 1890.

Fremont, Idaho (est. Mar. 4, 1893; 1, 819 sq. mi.; 1970 pop.: 8, 710; 1960: 8, 679; 1950: 9, 351) (St. Anthony). John Charles Fremont*.

Fremont, Iowa (est. Feb. 24, 1847; 512 sq. mi.; 1970 pop.: 9, 282; 1960: 10, 282; 1950: 12, 323) (Sidney). John Charles Fremont*.

Fremont, Wyo. (est. Mar. 5, 1884; 9, 244 sq. mi.; 1970 pop.: 28, 352; 1960: 26, 168; 1950: 19, 580) (Lander). John Charles Fremont*.

Fresno, Calif. (est. Apr. 19, 1856; 5, 985 sq. mi. ; 1970 pop. : 413, 053; 1960: 365, 945; 1950: 276, 515) (Fresno). ("The Agricultural and Recreational Center of California"; "The Agricultural and Scientific Hub of the Golden State"; "The Land of Sunshine, Fruits and Flowers"; "The Richest Agricultural County in the World"). Spanish word for "ash." -- Walker, Ben Randal, The Fresno County Blue Book, Fresno, Calif. : A. H. Cawston, 1941; 555p. -- Winchell, Lilbourne Alsip, History of Fresno County, Fresno, Calif. : A. H. Cawston, 1933; 323 p.

Frio, Tex. (est. Feb. 1, 1858; 1, 116 sq. mi. ; 1970 pop. : 11, 159; 1960: 10, 112; 1950: 10, 357) (Pearsall). Spanish word for "cold."

Frontier, Neb. (est. Jan. 17, 1872, org. Feb. 5, 1872; 966 sq. mi. ; 1970 pop. : 3, 982; 1960: 4, 311; 1950: 5, 282) (Stockville). Descriptive.

Fulton, Ark. (est. Dec. 21, 1842, eff. Jan. 1, 1843; 611 sq. mi. ; 1970 pop. : 7, 669; 1960: 6, 657; 1950: 9, 187) (Salem). William Savin Fulton (1795-1844). Fourth terr. gov. of Ark. On staff of col. Armistead in defense of Ft. McHenry 1814; private secretary to gen. Andrew Jackson in the Seminole War 1818; ed. of Florence, Ala., "Gazette" 1821; judge of county court 1822; secretary of Ark. terr. 1829-35; terr. gov. of Ark. 1835-36; Senator from Ark. 1836-44.

Fulton, Ga. (est. Dec. 20, 1853; 193 sq. mi. ; 1970 pop. : 607, 592; 1960: 556, 326; 1950: 473, 572) (Atlanta). ("The County With the Largest Industrial Area in the South East States"). Robert Fulton (1765-1815). Inventor, experimented with a submarine boat in France 1801; built the Clermont, a steamboat, which sailed up the Hudson River 1807. (Also claimed for Hamilton Fulton, engineer.) -- Cooper, Walter Gerald, Official History of Fulton County, Atlanta: Walter W. Brown Pub. Co., 1934; 912 p. -- Knight, Lucian Lamar, History of Fulton County, Georgia, Atlanta, Ga. : A. H. Cawston, 1930; 514 p.

Fulton, Ill. (est. Jan. 28, 1823; 884 sq. mi. ; 1970 pop. : 41, 890; 1960: 41, 954; 1950: 43, 716) (Lewistown). Robert Fulton*. -- Drury, John, This Is Fulton County, Chicago: Loree Co., 1954; 478 p.

Fulton, Ind. (est. Feb. 7, 1835, org. Jan. 23, 1836, eff. Apr. 1, 1836; 367 sq. mi. ; 1970 pop. : 16, 984; 1960: 16, 957; 1950: 16, 565) (Rochester). Robert Fulton*.

Fulton, Ky. (est. Jan. 15, 1845; 205 sq. mi. ; 1970 pop. : 10, 183; 1960: 11, 256; 1950: 13, 668) (Hickman). Robert Fulton*.

Fulton, N. Y. (est. Apr. 18, 1838; 497 sq. mi. ; 1970 pop. :

52, 637; 1960: 51, 304; 1950: 51, 021) (Johnstown). ("Letherland, U. S. A. (leather apparel manufacturing)"; "The Adirondack Wonderland"; "The County of Forty-Four Lakes"; "The Unspoiled Adirondack Vacation Land"). Robert Fulton*. -- Frothingham, Washington, History of Fulton County, Syracuse, N. Y. : D. Mason & Co., 1892; 800 p.

Fulton, Ohio (est. Feb. 28, 1850; 407 sq. mi.; 1970 pop.: 33, 071; 1960: 29, 301; 1950: 25, 580) (Wauseon). Robert Fulton*. -- Reighard, Frank H., A standard history of Fulton County, Chicago: Lewis Pub. Co., 1920; 2 vol.

Fulton, Pa. (est. Apr. 19, 1850; 435 sq. mi.; 1970 pop.: 10, 776; 1960: 10, 597; 1950: 10, 387) (McConnellsburg). Robert Fulton*.

Furnas, Neb. (est. Feb. 27, 1873; org. June 7, 1873; 722 sq. mi.; 1970 pop.: 6, 897; 1960: 7, 711; 1950: 9, 385) (Beaver City). Robert Wilkinson Furnas (1824-1905). Second gov. of Neb. Editor Troy, Ohio "Times" 1826-31; ed. Neb. "Advertiser" 1855-61; Neb. legislative assembly 1856-60; organized and commanded three regiment of Indians 1861; col. 2nd Neb. cavalry 1861; col. U. S. Army 1862; Neb. legislature, gov. of Neb. 1873-75; regent Univ. of Neb. 1875-81; author of numerous agricultural and horticultural reports. -- Merwin, F. N., Pioneer stories of Furnas County, Nebraska, University Place, Neb.: Claflin Printing Co., 1914; 212 p.

G

Gadsden, Fla. (est. June 24, 1823; 508 sq. mi.; 1970 pop.: 39, 184; 1960: 41, 989; 1950: 36, 457) (Quincy). James Gadsden (1788-1858). Served in War of 1812 aide-de-camp to Gen. Jackson 1818; in charge of removal of Seminoles to Fla. 1820; U. S. Minister to Mexico 1853; negotiated Gadsden Purchase from Mexico 1854.

Gage, Neb. (est. Mar. 16, 1855, org. Mar. 13, 1858; 858 sq. mi.; 1970 pop.: 25, 719; 1960: 26, 818; 1950: 28, 052) (Beatrice). William D. Gage (1803-1885). Methodist clergyman; chaplain both houses Neb. terr. legislature; treas. Otoe County 1855-56; county commissioner Cass County 1857. -- Dobbs, Hugh Jackson, History of Gage County, Nebraska, Lincoln, Neb.: Western Pub. & Engraving Co., 1918; 1100 p.

Gaines, Tex. (est. Aug. 21, 1876; 1, 479 sq. mi.; 1970 pop.: 11, 593; 1960: 12, 267; 1950: 8, 909) (Seminole).

James Gaines (1776-1850). Served in Mexican Army 1813; first judge of municipality of Sabine, signer Tex. declaration of independence 1836; Tex. senate 1838-42; joined Calif. gold rush 1849.

Gallatin, Ill. (est. Sept. 14, 1812; 338 sq. mi.; 1970 pop.: 7,418; 1960: 7,638; 1950: 9,818) (Shawneetown). Abraham Alfonse Albert Gallatin (1761-1849). Pa. constitutional convention 1789; Pa. house of representatives 1790-92; elected as Senator from Pa., which was declared void 1794; Representative from Pa., 1795-1801; U. S. Secretary of the Treas. in the cabinets of Pres. Jefferson and Madison 1802-14; U. S. Minister to France 1815-23; U. S. Minister to Gt. Britain 1826-27.

Gallatin, Ky. (est. Dec. 14, 1798; eff. May 13, 1799; 100 sq. mi.; 1970 pop.: 4,134; 1960: 3,867; 1950: 3,969) (Warsaw) Abraham Alfonse Albert Gallatin*.

Gallatin, Mont. (est. Feb. 2, 1865; 2,517 sq. mi.; 1970 pop.: 32,505; 1960: 26,045; 1950: 21,902) (Bozeman). Abraham Alfonse Albert Gallatin*.

Gallia, Ohio (est. Mar. 25, 1803; 471 sq. mi.; 1970 pop.: 25,239; 1960: 26,120; 1950: 24,910) (Gallipolis). Gaul, the Latin name for France.

Galveston, Tex. (est. May 15, 1838; 430 sq. mi.; 1970 pop.: 169,812; 1960: 140,364; 1950: 113,066) (Galveston). Bernardo de Galvez (1746-1786). Fourth gov. of La. under Spanish rule. Served in army at Portugal 1762; in New Spain (Mexico) against the Apaches, and in Algiers; gov. of La. province 1776; entered upon duties Feb. 1, 1777; fought British to 1783; capt. at Baton Rouge, Mobile 1780 and Pensacola 1781; viceroy of New Spain 1785.

Garden, Neb. (est. by election, Nov. 2, 1909; 1,685 sq. mi.; 1970 pop.: 2,929; 1960: 3,472; 1950: 4,114) (Oshkosh). Descriptive.

Garfield, Colo. (est. Feb. 10, 1883; 2,994 sq. mi.; 1970 pop.: 14,821; 1960: 12,017; 1950: 11,625) (Glenwood Springs). James Abram Garfield (1831-1881). Pres. Hiram College 1857-61; Ohio senate 1859; lt. col. and col. Forty-Second Regiment Ohio Vol. Infantry 1861; brig. gen. of vol. 1862; maj. gen. 1863; Representative from Ohio 1863-1880; Pres. of the U. S. 1881; shot by assassin 1881.

Garfield, Mont. (est. Feb. 7, 1919; 4,793 sq. mi.; 1970 pop.: 1,796; 1960: 1,981; 1950: 2,172) (Jordan). James Abram Garfield*. -- Highland, Geneva, Big dry country, Billings, Mont.: Billings Printing Co., 1960; 176 p.

Garfield, Neb. (est. Nov. 8, 1884 procl. 570 sq. mi.; 1970

pop.: 2,411; 1960: 2,699; 1950: 2,912) (Burwell). James Abram Garfield*.

Garfield, Okla. (est. July 16, 1907; 1,054 sq. mi.; 1970 pop.: 55,365; 1960: 52,975; 1950: 52,820) (Enid). James Abram Garfield*.

Garfield, Utah (est. Mar. 9, 1882; 5,217 sq. mi.; 1970 pop.: 3,157; 1960: 3,577; 1950: 4,151) (Panguitch). James Abram Garfield*. -- Daughters of Utah Pioneers, Golden nuggets of pioneer days; a history of Garfield County, Panguitch, Utah: Garfield County News, 1949; 374 p.

Garfield, Wash. (est. Nov. 29, 1881; 714 sq. mi.; 1970 pop.: 2,911; 1960: 2,976; 1950: 3,204) (Pomeroy). James Abram Garfield*.

Garland, Ark. (est. Apr. 5, 1873; 721 sq. mi.; 1970 pop.: 54,131; 1960: 46,697; 1950: 47,102) (Hot Springs). Augustus Hill Garland, twelfth gov. of Ark. (1832-1899). Confederate States provisional congress 1861; Confederate States House of Representatives and Senate; Senator from Ark., 1867 but denied seat; gov. of Ark. 1874-76; Senator from Ark., 1877-85; U.S. Attorney Gen. in cabinet of Pres. Cleveland 1885-89.

Garrard, Ky. (est. Dec. 17, 1796, eff. June 1, 1797; 234 sq. mi.; 1970 pop.: 9,457; 1960: 9,747; 1950: 11,029) (Lancaster). James Garrard (1749-1822). Second gov. of Ky. Capt. of militia 1776-77; Va. legislature 1779; Ky. constitutional convention 1792; gov. of Ky. 1796-1804. -- Calico, Forrest, History of Garrard County, Kentucky, New York: Hobson Book Press, 1947; 518 p.

Garrett, Md. (est. Apr. 1, 1872; 668 sq. mi.; 1970 pop.: 21,476; 1960: 20,420; 1950: 21,259) (Oakland). ("Western Maryland's Mountain Top Playground"). John Work Garrett (1820-1884). Industrialist and financier; director of Baltimore and Ohio RR Co. 1855; Pres. of Baltimore and Ohio RR Co. 1858-84; interested in mercantile endeavors, steamship lines, telegraph cables, etc.

Garvin, Okla. (est. July 16, 1907; 814 sq. mi.; 1970 pop.: 24,874; 1960: 28,290; 1950: 29,500) (Pauls Valley). Samuel Garvin.

Garza, Tex. (est. Aug. 21, 1876; 914 sq. mi.; 1970 pop.: 5,289; 1960: 6,611; 1950: 6,281) (Post). Gerónimo Garza, one of first thirteen families from Canary Islands, founded San Antonio.

Gasconade, Mo. (est. Nov. 25, 1820, eff. Jan. 1, 1821; 520 sq. mi.; 1970 pop.: 14,878; 1960: 12,195; 1950: 12,342) (Hermann) Derived from Gascon, inhabitant of Gascony.

Gaston, N.C. (est. Dec. 21, 1846; 358 sq. mi.; 1970 pop.:

148,415; 1960: 127,074; 1950: 110,836) (Gastonia). William Gaston (1778-1844). N. C. senate 1800; N. C. house of representatives 1807-09; N. C. senate 1812, 1818-19; Representative from N. C., 1813-17; N. C. house of representatives 1824, 1827-29 and 1831; judge of Supreme Court of N. C. 1833-44; wrote the state song "The Old North State." -- Cope, Robert F., The County of Gaston; two centuries of a North Carolina region, Gastonia, N. C.: Gaston County Historical Society, 1961; 274 p. -- Puett, Minnie Stowe, History of Gaston County, Charlotte, N.C.: Observer Printing House, 1939; 218 p.

Gates, N. C. (est. sess. Apr. 14, 1778; 348 sq. mi.; 1970 pop.: 8,524; 1960: 9,254; 1950: 9,555) (Gatesville). Horatio Gates (1728-1806). Under gen. Edward Cornwallis in Nova Scotia 1749-50; wounded under gen. Braddock at Ft. Duquesne 1755; conquest of Martinique 1761; returned and lived in England 1762-72; adj. gen. and brig. gen. Continental Army 1775; maj. gen. 1776; defeated Burgoyne at battle of Saratoga 1777 and awarded congressional medal for surrender of British Army 1777; battle of Camden 1780; N. Y. legislature 1800-01.

Geary, Kan. (est. Aug. 30, 1855; 399 sq. mi.; 1970 pop.: 28,111; 1960: 28,779; 1950: 21,671) (Junction City). John White Geary (1819-1873). Fourth gov. of Kan. Terr. Fifteenth gov. of Pa. In Pa. Infantry in Mexican War, wounded at Chapultepec, adv. to col. 1846; Postmaster of San Francisco and gen. mail agt 1849; first mayor of San Francisco 1850; gov. of Kan. terr. 1856-57; brig. gen. of vol. 1862; military gov. of Savannah 1864; gov. of Pa. 1867-73. (Formerly Davis County, changed Feb. 28, 1889, chap. 132).

Geauga, Ohio (est. Dec. 31, 1805; eff. Mar. 1, 1806; 407 sq. mi.; 1970 pop.: 62,977; 1960: 47,573; 1950: 26,646) (Chardon). Indian word for "raccoon." -- Geauga County Historical and Memorial Society, Columbus, Ohio: Pioneer and general history of Geauga County, 1953; 783 p.

Gem, Idaho (est. Mar. 19, 1915; 555 sq. mi.; 1970 pop.: 9,387; 1960: 9,127; 1950: 8,730) (Emmett). Descriptive, gem of the mountain.

Genesee, Mich. (est. Mar. 28, 1835, org. Mar. 8, 1836; 644 sq. mi.; 1970 pop.: 444,341; 1960: 374,313; 1950: 270,963) (Flint). Indian word for "beautiful valley." -- Ellis, Franklin, History of Genesee County, Philadelphia: Everts & Abbott, 1879; 446 p.

Genesee, N. Y. (est. Mar. 30, 1802; 501 sq. mi.; 1970 pop.: 58,722; 1960: 53,994; 1950: 47,584) (Batavia). ("The Mother of Counties"; "The Promised Land"). Indian word for "beautiful valley." -- Hungerford, Edward, The Genesee Country, New York: Gallery Press, 1946; 22 p. -- Kennedy, John, The Genesee Country, Batavia, N.Y.: Calkins & Lenti, 1895; 230 p.

Geneva, Ala. (est. Dec. 26, 1868; 578 sq. mi.; 1970 pop.: 21, 924; 1960: 22, 310; 1950: 25, 899) (Geneva). Geneva, Switzerland.

Gentry, Mo. (est. Feb. 12, 1841; 488 sq. mi.; 1970 pop.: 8, 060; 1960: 8, 793; 1950: 11, 036) (Albany). Richard Gentry (1788-1837). Capt. in militia, Mo. senate 1826 and 1828; maj. gen. 1832; commander of Mo. troops Black Hawk War; postmaster Columbia Mo.; killed fighting Seminoles at Okeechobee, Fla., Dec. 25, 1837. -- Leopold, John C., History of Davies and Gentry Counties, Missouri, Topeka: Historical Pub. Co., 1922; 1039 p.

George, Miss. (est. Mar. 16, 1910; 475 sq. mi.; 1970 pop.: 12, 459; 1960: 11, 098; 1950: 10, 012) (Lucedale). James Zachariah George (1826-1897). In Mexican War 1846; Miss. Supreme Court reporter 1854; capt., col. and brig. gen. Confederate Army; Miss. Supreme Court 1879; Senator from Miss., 1881-97.

Georgetown, S. C. (813 sq. mi.; 1970 pop.: 33, 500; 1960: 34, 798; 1950: 31, 762) (Georgetown). George II (1683-1760). George Augustus married Caroline of Anspach 1705; elected prince of Hanover; fought under Marlborough; created Prince of Wales, succeeded to the throne of England 1727; battle of Dettingen 1743.

Gibson, Ind. (est. Mar. 9, 1813, eff. Apr. 1, 1813; 499 sq. mi.; 1970 pop.: 30, 444; 1960: 29, 949; 1950: 30, 720) (Princeton). John Gibson (1740-1822). Soldier in French and Indian wars 1758; Revolutionary war, col. 1777, gen.; judge court of common pleas; secretary of Indian terr. -- Stormont, Gilbert R., History of Gibson County, Ind., Indianapolis, Ind.: B. F. Bowen & Co., 1914; 1076 p.

Gibson, Tenn. (est. Oct. 21, 1823, org. Jan. 5, 1824; 607 sq. mi.; 1970:47, 871; 1960:44, 699; 1950:48, 132) (Trenton and Humboldt). John Gibson. Maj. in Gen. Jackson's Natchez expedition 1812-13. -- Culp, Frederick M., Gibson County, Past and Present, the first general history of one of west Tennessee's pivotal counties, Trenton, Tenn.: Gibson County Historical Society, 1961; 583 p.

Gila, Ariz. (est. Feb. 8, 1881; 4, 750 sq. mi.; 1970 pop.: 24, 255; 1960: 25, 745; 1950: 24, 158) (Globe). ("The Land of the Famed Apaches"). Gila monster.

Gilchrist, Fla. (est. Dec. 4, 1925; 339 sq. mi.; 1970 pop.: 3, 551; 1960: 2, 868; 1950: 3, 499) (Trenton). ("Florida's Land of Opportunity"; "The County Way Down Upon the

Suwannee River"; "The No-Better-Place-To-Live County"; "The Sportsman's Paradise"). Albert Waller Gilchrist 1858-1926). Nineteenth gov. of Fla. Fla. Southern RR Co., 1885-87; brig. gen. Fla. militia 1898; enlisted as private in Co. C 3rd U. S. Vol. Infantry 1898; served at Santiago, Cuba 1898; capt. 1899; Fla., house of representatives 1893-1903; gov. of Fla. 1909-13.

Giles, Tenn. (est. Nov. 14, 1809; 619 sq. mi.; 1970 pop.: 22, 138; 1960: 22, 410; 1950: 26, 961) (Pulaski). McCallum, James, Brief History of the Settlement and Early History of Giles County, Tenn., Pulaski, Tenn.: Pulaski Citizen, 1928; 125 p. (See next entry.)

Giles, Va. (est. Jan. 16, 1806, eff. May 1, 1806; 356 sq. mi.; 1970 pop.: 16, 741; 1960: 17, 219; 1950: 18, 956) (Pearlsburg). William Branch Giles (1762-1830).

Gillespie, Tex. (est. Feb. 23, 1848; 1, 055 sq. mi.; 1970 pop.: 10, 553; 1960: 10, 048; 1950: 10, 520) (Fredericksburg). Robert Addison Gillespie (-1846). Somervell expedition 1842; Tex. ranger, wounded 1844; killed leading men in charge at Bishop's Palace, Monterey, Mexico, Sept. 21, 1846. -- Gillespie County Historical Society, Pioneers in God's hills; a history of Fredericksburg and Gillespie County, Austin, Texas: Von Boeckmann-Jones, 1960; 305 p.

Gilliam, Ore. (est. Feb. 25, 1885; 1, 211 sq. mi.; 1970 pop.: 2, 342; 1960: 3, 069; 1950: 2, 817) (Condon). Cornelius Gilliam (1798-1848). Sheriff Clay County, Mo., Black Hawk War; capt. Seminole War 1837; commander of forces of provisional govt.; Cayuse war, accidentally shot Mar. 24, 1848.

Gilmer, Ga. (est. Dec. 3, 1832; 440 sq. mi.; 1970 pop.: 8, 956; 1960: 8, 922; 1950: 9, 963) (Ellijay). George Rockingham Gilmer (1790-1859). Thirty-second and thirty-fourth gov. of Ga. First lt. in campaign against Creek Indians 1813-15; Ga. house of representatives 1818, 1819 and 1824; Representative from Ga., 1821-23; trustee Univ. of Ga., 1826-27; Representative from Ga., 1827-29; Gov. of Ga. 1829-31; Representative from Ga. 1833-35; gov. of Ga. 1837-39. -- Ward, George Gordon, Annals of Upper Georgia centered in Gilmer Co., Thomasson Print. & Office Equipment Co., 1965; 692 p.

Gilmer, W. Va. (est. Feb. 3, 1845; 342 sq. mi.; 1970 pop.: 7, 782; 1960: 8, 050; 1950: 9, 746) (Glenville). Thomas Walker Gilmer (1802-1844). Thirtieth gov. of Va. (Commonwealth). Va. house of delegates 1829-36; speaker of the house 1834-36; Va. house of delegates 1839-40; gov. of Va. 1840-41; Representative from Va., 1841-44; Secretary of the Navy 1844; killed in an explosion on U. S. S. "Princeton."

Gilpin, Colo. (est. Nov. 1, 1861; 149 sq. mi.; 1970 pop.: 1,272; 1960: 685; 1950: 850) (Central City). William Gilpin (1822-1894). First terr. gov. of Colo. Graduated U. S. Military Academy 1836; second lt. 2nd Dragoons 1836; first lt. 1836; in Seminole War 1838; resigned 1838; maj. First Mo. Vol. in Mexican War 1846. -- Kemp, Donald Campbell, Colorado's Little Kingdom, Golden, Colo.: Sage Books, 1949; 153 p.

Glacier, Mont. (est. Feb. 17, 1919; 2,974 sq. mi.; 1970 pop.: 10,783; 1960: 11,565; 1950: 9,645) (Cut Bank). Descriptive.

Glades, Fla. (est. Apr. 23, 1921; 746 sq. mi.; 1970 pop.: 3,669; 1960: 2,950; 1950: 2,199) (Moore Haven). Last syllable of "everglades."

Gladwin, Mich. (est. Mar. 2, 1831, org. 1875; 503 sq.mi.; 1970 pop.: 13,471; 1960: 10,769; 1950: 9,451) (Gladwin). ("The Year Around Vacationland"). Henry Gladwin. Maj. saved Detroit 1763.

Glascock, Ga. (est. Dec. 19, 1857; 170 sq. mi.; 1970 pop.: 2,280; 1960: 2,672; 1950: 3,579) (Gibson). Thomas Glascock (1790-1841). Ga. constitutional convention 1798; capt. of vol. War of 1812; brig. gen. Seminole War 1817; Ga. house of representatives 1821, 1823, 1831, 1834 and 1839; Representative from Ga., 1835-39.

Glasscock, Tex. (est. Apr. 4, 1887; 864 sq. mi.; 1970 pop.: 1,155; 1960: 1,118; 1950: 1,089) (Garden City). George Washington Glasscock (1810-1879). Partner of Abraham Lincoln on the Sangamon River; built flour mill at Austin, Tex., 10th and 11th Tex. legislature.

Glenn, Calif. (est. Mar. 11, 1891; 1,317 sq. mi.; 1970 pop.: 17,521; 1960: 17,245; 1950: 15,448) (Willows). Hugh J. Glenn. Physician known as "the wheat king."

Gloucester, N. J. (est. May 28, 1686; 329 sq. mi.; 1970 pop.: 172,681; 1960: 134,840; 1950: 91,727) (Woodbury). Gloucester, England, named for the Duke of Gloucester, Henry (1640-1660), third son of King Charles I and Henrietta Maria. Vol. with Spanish Army 1657; Knight 1658; Privy councillor 1658; Earl of Cambridge and Duke of Gloucester, 1660. -- Simpson, Hazel B., ed., Under four flags: Old Gloucester County, 1686-1964, (Woodbury, N. J.): Board of Chosen Freeholders, 1965; 125 p. -- Stewart, Frank H., Notes on old Gloucester County, Camden, N. J.: S. Chew, 1917-64; 4 vol.

Gloucester, Va. (est. 1651; 225 sq. mi.; 1970 pop.: 14,059; 1960: 11,919; 1950: 10,343) (Gloucester). ("America's

Daffodil Capital"; "The Land of Life Worth Living"). Henry, Duke of Gloucester*. -- Gray, Mary Wiatt, Gloucester County, Richmond: Cottrell & Cooke, Inc., 1936; 243 p.

Glynn, Ga. (est. Feb. 5, 1777; 439 sq. mi.; 1970 pop.: 50,528; 1960: 41,954; 1950: 29,046) (Brunswick). John Glynn.

Gogebic, Mich. (est. Feb. 7, 1887; 1,112 sq. mi.; 1970 pop.: 20,676; 1960: 24,370; 1950: 27,053) (Bessemer). Indian word for "rock."

Golden Valley, Mont. (est. Oct. 4, 1920; petition and election; 1,178 sq. mi.; 1970 pop.: 931; 1960: 1,203; 1950: 1,337) (Ryegate). Descriptive.

Golden Valley, N.D. (est. Nov. 19, 1912, election Nov. 1910; 1,014 sq. mi.; 1970 pop.: 2,611; 1960: 3,100; 1950: 3,499) (Beach). Descriptive.

Goliad, Tex. (est. Mar. 17, 1836; 871 sq. mi.; 1970 pop.: 4,869; 1960: 5,429; 1950: 6,219) (Goliad). Derived from Goliath of Gath, an anagram of (H)idalgo, the first promoter of Mexican independence.

Gonzales, Tex. (est. Mar. 17, 1836; 1,058 sq. mi.; 1970 pop.: 16,375; 1960: 17,845; 1950: 21,164) (Gonzales). Rafael Gonzales (1789-1857). Second lt. 1814; first lt. 1815; capt. 1818; lt. col. 1821. Gov. of Coahuila and Tex. 1824-26.

Goochland, Va. (est. Feb. 1, 1727 sess.; 289 sq. mi.; 1970 pop.: 10,069; 1960: 9,206; 1950: 8,934) (Goochland). William Gooch (1681-1751). Lt. col.; gov. of Va. (Royal Province) Va. col. gov. 1727-1737 and 1737-1740; assumed command of forces to attack Carthagena, New Granada because of death of Gen. Alexander Spotswood; wounded and contracted fever, returned to Va. and governed colony 1741-49; promoted to maj. gen. 1747; created a baronet 1748. -- Agee, Helène (Barret), Facets of Goochland County's History, Richmond, Va.: Dietz Press, 1962; 227 p. -- Wight, Richard C., The Story of Goochland, Richmond, Va.: Richmond Press, 1943; 76 p.

Goodhue, Minn. (est. Mar. 5, 1853; 758 sq. mi.; 1970 pop.: 34,763; 1960: 33,035; 1950: 32,118) (Red Wing). James Madison Goodhue (1810-1852). Owned Wisconsin "Herald" 1845-49; Minn. "Pioneer," first newspaper in Minn. 1849. -- Curtiss-Wedge, Franklin, ed., History of Goodhue County, Chicago: H. C. Cooper, Jr. & Co., 1909; 1074 p. -- Rasmussen, Christian A., A history of Goodhue County, Red Wing, Minn.: Red Wing Printing Co., 1935; 336 p.

Gooding, Idaho (est. Jan. 28, 1913; 722 sq. mi.; 1970 pop.:

8, 645; 1960: 9, 544; 1950: 11, 101) (Gooding). Frank Robert Gooding (1859-1928). Seventh gov. of Idaho. Idaho senate 1898-1902; gov. of Idaho 1905-09; Senator from Idaho 1921-28.

Gordon, Ga. (est. Feb. 13, 1850; 358 sq. mi.; 1970 pop.: 23, 570; 1960: 19, 228; 1950: 18, 922) (Calhoun). William Washington Gordon (1796-1842). Grad. West Point, 1814; 3rd lt. 1815; aide to Gen. Gaines, resigned 1815; first Pres. of Ga. Central RR. -- Pitts, Lulie, History of Gordon County, Calhoun, Ga.: Calhoun Times, 1933; 480 p.

Goshen, Wyo. (est. Feb. 9, 1911; 2, 230 sq. mi.; 1970 pop.: 10, 885; 1960: 11, 941; 1950: 12, 634) (Torrington). Goshen, biblical Land of Goshen.

Gosper, Neb. (est. Nov. 26, 1873; 466 sq. mi.; 1970 pop.: 2, 178; 1960: 2, 489; 1950: 2, 734) (Elwood) John J. Gosper. Neb. Secretary of State 1873-75.

Gove, Kan. (est. Mar. 2, 1868; org. Sept. 2, 1886; 1, 070 sq. mi.; 1970 pop.: 3, 940; 1960: 4, 107; 1950: 4, 447) (Gove). Grenville L. Gove (-1864). Private in Co. F Sixth Kan. cavalry; raised Co. G 11th Kan. cavalry and commissioned first lt. 1862; promoted to capt. 1864, died Nov. 7, 1864. -- Harrington, W. P., History of Gove County, Kansas, Gove City, Kan.: Republican-Gazette Off. 1930; 37 p.

Grady, Ga. (est. Aug. 17, 1905, eff. Jan. 1, 1906; 467 sq. mi.; 1970 pop.: 17, 826; 1960: 18, 015; 1950: 18, 928) (Cairo). Henry Woodfin Grady (1850-1889). Ga. representative of N. Y. "Herald" 1871; ed. and part owner of Atlanta "Constitution" 1880.

Grady, Okla. (est. July 16, 1907; 1, 092 sq. mi.; 1970 pop.: 29, 354; 1960: 29, 590; 1950: 34, 872) (Chickasha). Henry Woodfin Grady*.

Grafton, N. H. (est. Apr. 29, 1769; 1, 717 sq. mi.; 1970 pop.: 54, 914; 1960: 48, 857; 1950: 47, 923) (Woodsville). Augustus Henry Fitzroy (1735-1811), third duke of Grafton. England's secretary of state for northern dep. 1765-66; privy seal 1771-75 and 1782-83.

Graham, Ariz. (est. Mar. 10, 1881; 4, 610 sq. mi.; 1970 pop.: 16, 578; 1960: 14, 045; 1950: 12, 985) (Safford) ("The Land of the Storied Gila"). Name origin in doubt.

Graham, Kan. (est. Feb. 26, 1867; 891 sq. mi.; 1970 pop.: 4, 751; 1960: 5, 586; 1950: 5, 020) (Hill City). John L. Graham (-1863). Capt. Co. D of the 8th Kan. regiment, killed in action at Chickamauga, before being mustered, on Sept. 19, 1863.

Graham, N. C. (est. Jan. 30, 1872; 295 sq. mi.; 1970 pop.:

6, 562; 1960: 6, 432; 1950: 6, 886) (Robbinsville). William Alexander Graham (1804-1875). Thirtieth gov. of N. C. N. C. house of commons 1836, 1838, 1840 and speaker 1838, 1840; Senator from N. C. 1840-43; gov. of N. C. 1845-49; Secretary of the Navy 1850-52; unsuccessful vice pres. candidate 1852; N. C. senate 1854, 1862 and 1865; elected Confederate Senate 1863; elected to U. S. Senate but credentials were not presented 1866; arbiter dispute Va. -Md., boundary 1873-75.

Grainger, Tenn. (est. Apr. 22, 1796; 310 sq. mi.; 1970 pop.: 13, 948; 1960: 12, 506; 1950: 13, 086) (Rutledge). Mary Grainger. Daughter of col. Caleb Grainger of Wilmington, N. C., who married gov. William Blount on Feb. 12, 1778.

Grand, Colo. (est. Feb. 2, 1874; 1, 867 sq. mi.; 1970 pop.: 4, 107; 1960: 3, 557; 1950: 3, 963) (Hot Sulphur Springs). Descriptive.

Grand, Utah. (est. Mar. 13, 1890; 3, 692 sq. mi.; 1970 pop.: 6, 688; 1960: 6, 345; 1950: 1, 903) (Moab). Descriptive, Grand River (now Colo. River).

Grand Forks, N. D. (est. Jan. 4, 1873, org. Mar. 2, 1875; 1, 438 sq. mi.; 1970 pop.: 61, 102; 1960: 48, 677; 1950: 39, 443) (Grand Forks). Descriptive.

Grand Isle, Vt. (est. Nov. 9, 1802, org. Nov. 2, 1805; eff. Dec. 1, 1805; 77 sq. mi.; 1970 pop.: 3, 574; 1960: 2, 927; 1950: 3, 406) (North Hero). Descriptive. -- Aldrich, Lewis Cass, <u>History of Franklin and Grand Isle Counties,</u> Syracuse, N. Y.: D. Mason and Co., 1891; 821 p.

Grand Traverse, Mich. (est. Apr. 1, 1840; 464 sq. mi.; 1970 pop.: 39, 175; 1960: 33, 490; 1950: 28, 598) (Traverse City). Descriptive. (Originally Omeena County, name changed to Grand Traverse Apr. 17, 1851). -- Sprague, Elvin Lyons, <u>Sprague's History of Grand Traverse and Leelanau Counties,</u> Indianapolis: B. F. Bowen, 1903; 806 p.

Granite, Mont. (est. Mar. 2, 1893; 1, 717 sq. mi.; 1970 pop.: 2, 737; 1960: 3, 014; 1950: 2, 773) (Philipsburg). Descriptive.

Grant, Ark. (est. Feb. 4, 1869; 631 sq. mi.; 1970 pop.: 9, 711; 1960: 8, 294; 1950: 9, 024) (Sheridan). Ulysses Simpson Grant (1822-1885). Eighteenth pres. of the U. S. Grad. of U. S. Military Academy. Served in Mexican War. Enlisted as col. in Civil War, June 17, 1861. Advanced to brig. gen. and maj. gen. Received Gen. Lee's surrender Apr. 9, 1865 at Appomattox Court House. Appointed first gen. of the U. S. on July 25, 1866. Eighteenth pres. of the U. S. 1869-77.

Grant, Ind. (est. Feb. 10, 1831, eff. Apr. 1, 1831; 421 sq. mi.; 1970 pop.: 63, 955; 1960: 75, 741; 1950: 62, 156) (Marion). Samuel Grant (-1790) and Moses Grant (-1790) who were killed in Indian battles in the southern part of Indiana.

Grant, Kan. (est. Mar. 6, 1873; 568 sq. mi.; 1970 pop.: 5, 961; 1960: 5, 269; 1950: 4, 638) (Ulysses). Ulysses Simpson Grant*. -- Wilson, Robert R., History of Grant County, Kansas, Wichita, Kan., 1950; 278 p.

Grant, Ky. (est. Feb. 12, 1820; 250 sq. mi.; 1970 pop.: 9, 999; 1960: 9, 489; 1950: 9, 809) (Williamstown). Samuel Grant.

Grant, La. (est. Mar. 4, 1869; 683 sq. mi.; 1970 pop.: 13, 671; 1960: 13, 330; 1950: 14, 263) (Colfax). Ulysses Simpson Grant*.

Grant, Minn. (est. Mar. 6, 1868; 557 sq. mi.; 1970 pop.: 7, 462; 1960: 8, 870; 1950: 9, 542) (Elbow Lake). Ulysses Simpson Grant*.

Grant, Neb. (est. Mar. 31, 1887, org. May 13, 1888; 762 sq. mi.; 1970 pop.: 1, 019; 1960: 1, 009; 1950: 1, 057) (Hyannis). Ulysses Simpson Grant*.

Grant, N. M. (est. Jan. 30, 1868; 3, 970 sq. mi.; 1970 pop.: 22, 030; 1960: 18, 700; 1950: 21, 649) (Silver City). Ulysses Simpson Grant*.

Grant, N. D. (est. Nov. 25, 1916, election Nov. 7, 1916), 1, 672 sq. mi.; 1970 pop.: 5, 009; 1960: 6, 248; 1950: 7, 114) (Carson). Ulysses Simpson Grant*.

Grant, Okla. (est. July 16, 1907; 999 sq. mi.; 1970 pop.: 7, 117; 1960: 8, 140; 1950: 10, 461) (Medford). Ulysses Simpson Grant *.

Grant, Ore. (est. Oct. 14, 1864; 4, 532 sq. mi.; 1970 pop.: 6, 996; 1960: 7, 726; 1950: 8, 329) (Canyon City). Ulysses Simpson Grant*.

Grant, S. D. (est. Jan. 8, 1873; org. June 12, 1878; 684 sq. mi.; 1970 pop.: 9, 005; 1960: 9, 913; 1950: 10, 233) (Milbank). Ulysses Simpson Grant*.

Grant, Wash. (est. Feb. 24, 1909; 2, 777 sq. mi.; 1970 pop.: 41, 881; 1960: 46, 477; 1950: 24, 346) (Ephrata). Ulysses Simpson Grant*.

Grant, W. Va. (est. Feb. 14, 1866; 478 sq. mi.; 1970 pop.: 8, 607; 1960: 8, 304; 1950: 8, 756) (Petersburg). Ulysses Simpson Grant*. -- Judy, Elvin Lycurgus, History of Grant and Hardy Counties, West Virginia, Charleston, W. Va.: Charleston Printing Co., 1951; 466 p.

Grant, Wis. (est. Dec. 8, 1836; 1, 168 sq. mi.; 1970 pop.: 48, 398; 1960: 44, 419; 1950: 41, 460) (Lancaster). (eff. Mar. 4, 1837) Grant, a fur trapper. -- Western

Historical Company, History of Grant County, Chicago: Western Historical Co., 1881; 1046 p.

Granville, N. C. (est. sess., June 28, 1746; 543 sq. mi.; 1970 pop.: 32, 762; 1960: 33, 110; 1950: 31, 793) (Oxford). John Carteret (1690-1763), the earl of Granville. House of Lords 1711; English ambassador to Sweden 1719; secretary of state 1721-24; lord lt. of Ireland 1724-30; one of the lord proprietors of Carolina, refused to sell his share to the king 1728; became Earl Granville 1744; lord pres. of council 1751-63.

Gratiot, Mich. (est. Mar. 2, 1831, org. 1855; 566 sq. mi.; 1970 pop.: 39, 246; 1960: 37, 012; 1950: 33, 429) (Ithaca). Charles Gratiot (1786-1855). Grad. U. S. Military Academy 1806; chief engineer in army 1812; bvt. col. 1814; participated in attack on Ft. Meigs 1813, at Ft. Mackinac 1814; chief engineer U. S. Army 1828-38; bvt. brig. gen. 1828. -- Tucker, William Davis, Gratiot County, Saginaw: Seemann & Peters, 1913; 1353 p.

Graves, Ky. (est. Dec. 19, 1821; 560 sq. mi.; 1970 pop.: 30, 939; 1960: 30, 021; 1950: 31, 364) (Mayfield). Benjamin Graves (-1813). Maj. in regiment of Col. Lewis 1812; col. 1812; killed at battle of the River Raisin 1813.

Gray, Kan. (est. Mar. 5, 1887, org. July 20, 1887; 869 sq. mi.; 1970 pop.: 4, 516; 1960: 4, 380; 1950: 4, 894) (Cimarron). Alfred Gray. Secretary of Kan. State Board of Agriculture 1873-80. (Gray County abolished in 1883 was re-established in 1887.

Gray, Tex. (est. Aug. 21, 1876; 937 sq. mi.; 1970 pop.: 26, 949; 1960: 31, 535; 1950: 24, 728) (Pampa). Peter W. Gray (1819-1874). Capt. Second Brigade Tex. Army 1840; district attorney 1841; alderman Houston, Tex., 1841; first Tex. congress, fourth Tex. senate; district judge 1861-64; Confederate congress 1861-63; justice Tex. Supreme Court 1874.

Grays Harbor, Wash. (est. Apr. 14, 1854; 1905 sq. mi.; 1970 pop.: 59, 553; 1960: 54, 465; 1950: 53, 644) (Montesano). Robert Gray (1755-1806). Discoverer. Returned to Boston, Mass. in the sloop "Washington" the first ship to carry the flag of the U. S. around the world 1790. (Originally Chehalis County, name changed to Grays Harbor County, Mar. 15, 1915).

Grayson, Ky. (est. Jan. 25, 1810, eff. Apr. 1, 1810; 514 sq. mi.; 1970 pop.: 16, 445; 1960: 15, 834; 1950: 17, 063) (Leitchfield). William Grayson (1740-1790). Capt. of independent co. of cadets Prince William County, Va., 1774; aide de camp to Gen. George Washington 1776; organized Grayson's Additional Continental Regiment 1777;

col. 1777; fought at battle of Monmouth; Continental Congress 1784-87; Va. constitutional convention 1788; Senator from Va. 1789-90.

Grayson, Tex. (est. Mar. 17, 1846; 984 sq. mi.; 1970 pop.: 83, 225; 1960: 73, 043; 1950: 70, 467) (Sherman). Peter William Grayson (1788-1838). Aide de camp to Austin 1835; attorney gen. of Republic of Tex. under Pres. Burnett 1836; mediator at Washington, D. C., between Tex. and Mexico 1836; attorney gen. of Tex. 1837; committed suicide 1838. -- Landrum, Graham, Grayson County, Fort Worth, Texas: Historical Publishers, 1967; 195 p. -- Lucas, Mattie Davis, History of Grayson County, Texas, Sherman, Texas: Scruggs Printing Co., 1936; 209 p.

Grayson, Va. (est. Nov. 7, 1792; 451 sq. mi.; 1970 pop.: 15, 439; 1960: 17, 390; 1950: 21, 379) (Independence). ("The Rooftop of Virginia"). William Grayson*.

Greeley, Kan. (est. Mar. 6, 1873; org. July 9, 1888; 783 sq. mi.; 1970 pop.: 1, 819; 1960: 2, 087; 1950: 2, 010) (Tribune). Horace Greeley (1811-1872). Founded N. Y. "Tribune" 1841; Representative from N. Y., 1848-49; comm. to the Paris exposition 1855; constitutional convention 1867; defeated for the presidency 1872.

Greeley, Neb. (est. Mar. 1, 1871; org. Jan. 20, 1873; 570 sq. mi.; 1970 pop.: 4, 000; 1960: 4, 595; 1950: 5, 575) (Greeley). Horace Greeley*. -- McDermott, Edith (Swain), Pioneer History of Greeley County, Nebraska, Greeley, Neb.: Citizen Printing Co., 1939; 174 p.

Green, Ky. (est. Dec. 20, 1792, eff. Jan. 1, 1793; 282 sq. mi.; 1970 pop.: 10, 350; 1960: 11, 249; 1950: 11, 261) (Greensburg). Nathanael Greene (1742-1786). Brig. gen. R. I. troops, 1775; brig. gen. Continental Army 1775; maj. gen. 1776; Q. M. gen. 1778-80; commanded Army of the South 1780; pres. of the court of inquiry for Maj. Andre. (Name misspelled); served until Nov. 3, 1783.

Green, Wis. (est. Dec. 8, 1836; 586 sq. mi.; 1970 pop.: 26, 714; 1960: 25, 851; 1950: 24, 172) (Monroe). ("America's Little Switzerland"). Nathanael Greene*. (Name misspelled). -- Bingham, Helen Maria, History of Green County, Milwaukee: Burdick & Armitage, 1877; 310 p. -- History of Green County, Springfield, Ill.: Union Pub. Co., 1884; 1158 p.

Green Lake, Wis. (est. Mar. 5, 1858; 355 sq. mi.; 1970 pop.: 16, 878; 1960: 15, 418; 1950: 17, 749) (Green Lake). Descriptive.

Greenbriar, W. Va. (est. Oct. 20, 1777; eff. Mar. 1, 1778; 1, 022 sq. mi.; 1970 pop.: 32, 090; 1960: 34, 446; 1950:

39, 295) (Lewisburg). Descriptive. -- Dayton, Ruth (Woods), Greenbrier pioneers and their homes, Charleston, W. Va.: West Virginia Pub. Co., 1942; 383 p.

Greene, Ala. (est. Dec. 13, 1819; 645 sq. mi.; 1970 pop.: 10, 650; 1960: 13, 600; 1950: 16, 482) (Eutaw) Nathanael Greene*.

Greene, Ark. (est. Nov. 5, 1833, est. Nov. 1, 1834; 579 sq. mi.; 1970 pop.: 24, 765; 1960: 25, 198; 1950: 29, 149) (Paragould). Nathanael Greene*. -- Hansbrough, Vivian (Mayo), History of Greene County, Arkansas, Little Rock, Ark.: Democrat Printing & Lithographing Co., 1946; 201 p.

Greene, Ga. (est. Feb. 3, 1786; 416 sq. mi.; 1970 pop.: 10, 212; 1960: 11, 193; 1950: 12, 843) (Greensboro). Nathanael Greene*. -- Rice, Thaddeus Brockett, History of Greene County 1786-1886, Macon, Ga.: J. W. Burke Co., 1961; 648 p.

Greene, Ill. (est. Jan. 20, 1821; 515 sq. mi.; 1970 pop.: 17, 014; 1960: 17, 460; 1950: 18, 852) (Carrollton). Nathanael Greene*. -- Miner, Ed., Past and Present of Greene County, Chicago: S. J. Clarke Pub. Co., 1905; 645 p.

Greene, Ind. (est. Jan. 5, 1821, eff. Feb. 5, 1821; 549 sq. mi.; 1970 pop.: 26, 894; 1960: 26, 327; 1950: 27, 886) (Bloomfield). Nathanael Greene*. -- Baber, Jack, Early history of Greene County, Indiana, Worthington, Ind.: N. B. Milleson, 1875; 96 p.

Greene, Iowa (est. Jan. 15, 1851; 569 sq. mi.; 1970 pop.: 12, 716; 1960: 14, 379; 1950: 15, 544) (Jefferson). Nathanael Greene*.

Greene, Miss. (est. Dec. 9, 1811; 710 sq. mi.; 1970 pop.: 8, 545; 1960: 8, 366; 1950: 8, 215) (Leakesville). Nathanael Greene*.

Greene, Mo. (est. Jan. 2, 1833; 677 sq. mi.; 1970 pop.: 152, 929; 1960: 126, 276; 1950: 104, 823) (Springfield). Nathanael Greene*. -- Fairbanks, Jonathan, Past and present of Greene County, Missouri, Indianapolis, Ind.: A. W. Bowen, 1915; 2 vol.

Greene, N. Y. (est. Mar. 25, 1800; 653 sq. mi.; 1970 pop.: 33, 136; 1960: 31, 372; 1950: 28, 745) (Catskill). ("The Land of Rip Van Winkle"; "The Mountains Vacationland"). Nathanael Greene*. -- Vedder, Jessie V. V., Official History of Greene County, N. Y., Greene County Board of Supervisors, Catskill, N. Y., 1927. 207 p. --Smith, Mabel Parker, Greene County, E. and G. Press, Catskill, N. Y.: 1968; 21 p.

Greene, N. C. (est. sess. Nov. 18, 1799; 269 sq. mi.; 1970 pop.: 14, 967; 1960: 16, 741; 1950: 18, 024) (Snow Hill).

Nathanael Greene*.

Greene, Ohio (est. Mar. 24, 1803; eff. May 1, 1803; 416 sq. mi.; 1970 pop.: 125,057; 1960: 94,642; 1950: 58,892) (Xenia). Nathanael Greene*. -- Greene County Sesquicentennial Organization, Out of the wilderness, Ann Arbor, Mich.: Edward Bros., 1953; 306 p. -- Broadstone, Michael A., ed., History of Greene County, Ohio, Indianapolis: B. F. Bowen, 1918; 2 vol.

Greene, Pa. (est. Feb. 9, 1796; 577 sq. mi.; 1970 pop.: 36,090; 1960: 39,424; 1950: 45,394) (Waynesburg). Nathanael Greene*. -- Bates, Samuel Penniman, History of Greene County, Chicago: Nelson, Rishforth & Co., 1888; 898 p. -- Hanna, William, History of Greene County, Pa., W. Hanna, n. p., 1882; 350 p.

Greene, Tenn. (est. sess. Apr. 18, 1783; 617 sq. mi.; 1970 pop.: 47,630: 1960: 42,163; 1950: 41,048) (Greeneville). Nathanael Greene*.

Greene, Va. (est. Jan. 24, 1838; 153 sq. mi.; 1970 pop.: 5,248; 1960: 4,715; 1950: 4,745) (Standardsville). Nathanael Greene*.

Greenlee, Ariz. (est. Mar. 10, 1909, org. Jan. 1, 1911; 1,874 sq. mi.; 1970 pop.: 10,330; 1960: 11,509; 1950: 12,805) (Clifton). ("The Place Where Coronado Walked"). Marc Greenlee. Prospector.

Greensville, Va. (est. Oct. 16, 1780 sess. eff. Feb. 1, 1781; 301 sq. mi.; 1970 pop.: 9,604; 1960: 16,155; 1950: 16,319) (Emporia). Nathanael Greene*. -- Brown, Douglas Summers (ed.), Sketches of Greensville County, Emporta, Va., 1968; 439 p.

Greenup, Ky. (est. Dec. 12, 1803; 350 sq. mi.; 1970 pop.: 33,192; 1960: 29,238; 1950: 24,887) (Greenup). Christopher Greenup (1750-1818). Third gov. of Ky. Promoted to col. in Revolutionary War; later in Indian wars; admitted to the bar 1783; clerk of district court at Harrodsburg, Ky., 1785-92; Va. house of delegates 1785; Representative from Ky., 1792-97; Ky. house of representatives 1798; clerk of Ky. senate 1799-1802; judge of circuit court 1802; gov. of Ky. 1804-08; Ky. house of representatives 1809; Franklin County justice of the peace 1812. -- Biggs, Nina Mitchell, History of Greenup County, Kentucky, Louisville, Ky., 1951; 345 p.

Greenville, S. C. (est. Mar. 22, 1786; 789 sq. mi.; 1970 pop.: 240,546; 1960: 209,776; 1950: 168,152) (Greenville). Descriptive, or Isaac Green who ran a mill in Reedy River around which the town grew. -- Richardson, James McDowell, History of Greenville County, Atlanta, Ga.: A. H. Cawston, 1930; 342 p.

Greenwood, Kan. (est. Aug. 30, 1855, org. Feb. 27, 1860; 1, 150 sq. mi. ; 1970 pop. : 9, 141; 1960: 11, 253; 1950: 13, 574) (Eureka). Alfred Burton Greenwood (1811-1889). Ark. house of representatives 1842-45; Ark. prosecuting attorney 1845-51; Ark. circuit judge 1851-53; Representative from Ark. 1853-59; Commissioner of Indian Affairs 1859-61; Confederate States house of representatives 1862-65.

Greenwood, S. C. (est. Mar. 2, 1897; 458 sq. mi. ; 1970 pop. : 49, 686; 1960: 44, 346; 1950: 41, 628) (Greenwood). Descriptive.

Greer, Okla. (est. July 16, 1907; 637 sq. mi. ; 1970 pop. : 7, 979; 1960: 8, 877; 1950: 11, 749) (Mangum). John A. Greer. Lt. gov. of Okla.

Gregg, Tex. (est. Apr. 12, 1873; 284 sq. mi. ; 1970 pop. : 75, 929; 1960: 69, 436; 1950: 61, 258) (Longview). John Gregg (1828-1864). Went to Tex. 1854; Judge of the 13th district 1856-60; delegate provisional congress of the confederacy 1860; organized Seventh Regiment Tex. Vol. 1861; captured at Ft. Donelson; brig. gen. 1862; killed near Ft. Harrison Oct. 7, 1864.

Gregory, S. D. (est. May 8, 1862; 1, 023 sq. mi. ; 1970 pop.: 6, 710; 1960: 7, 399; 1950: 8, 556) (Burke). John Shaw Gregory (1831-). Grad. U. S. Naval Academy; S. D. terr. legislature 1862-64; U. S. Indian agent for the Ponca tribe.

Grenada, Miss. (est. May 9, 1870; 442 sq. mi. ; 1970 pop.: 19, 854; 1960: 18, 409; 1950: 18, 830) (Grenada). Granada, Spain.

Griggs, N. D. (est. Feb. 18, 1881, org. June 16, 1882; 714 sq. mi. ; 1970 pop. : 4, 184; 1960: 5, 023; 1950: 5, 460) (Cooperstown). Alexander Griggs.

Grimes, Tex. (est. Apr. 6, 1846; 801 sq. mi. ; 1970 pop. : 11, 855; 1960: 12, 709; 1950: 15, 135) (Anderson). Jesse Grimes (1788-1866) Elected first lt. of First Co. 1829; Gen. Council 1835; signer Tex. declaration of Independence 1836; enrolled co. of vol. for three months service 1836; Tex. senate 1836-37; Tex. legislature 1841-45. -- Blair, Eric Lee, Early History of Grimes County, Austin, Texas, 1930; 253 p.

Grundy, Ill. (est. Feb. 17, 1841, org. May 24, 1841; 432 sq. mi. ; 70: 26, 535; 1960: 22, 350; 1950: 19, 217) (Morris). Felix Grundy (1777-1840). Ky. house of representatives 1800-05; Ky. Supreme Court judge 1806; Ky. Supreme Court chief justice 1807; Representative from Tenn., 1811-14; Tenn. house of representatives 1815-19; Senator from Tenn., 1829-38; Attorney gen. of the U. S. in cabinet of

Pres. Van Buren 1838-39, Senator from Tenn., 1839-40. -- History of Grundy County, Chicago: O. L. Baskin & Co., 1882.

Grundy, Iowa (est. Jan. 15, 1851; 501 sq. mi.; 1970 pop.: 14, 119; 1960: 14, 132; 1950: 13, 722) (Grundy Center). Felix Grundy*.

Grundy, Mo. (est. Jan. 29, 1841; 435 sq. mi.; 1970 pop.: 11, 819; 60: 12, 220; 1950: 13, 220) (Trenton). Felix Grundy*. -- Denslow, William Ray, Centennial history of Grundy County, Missouri, 1839-1939, Trenton, Mo.: W. R. Denslow, 1939; 402 p. -- Ford, James Everett, A history of Grundy County, Trenton, Mo.: News Pub. Co., 1908; 875 p.

Grundy, Tenn. (est. Jan. 29, 1844; 358 sq. mi.; 1970 pop.: 10, 631; 1960: 11, 512; 1950: 12, 558) (Altamont). Felix Grundy*.

Guadalupe, N. M. (est. Feb. 26, 1891; 2, 998 sq. mi.; 1970 pop.: 4, 969; 1960: 5, 610; 1950: 6, 772) (Santa Rosa). Guadalupe River, Guadalupe Hidalgo, city and federal district in Mexico. About two and a half miles northeast of Mexico City is the church, Our Lady of Guadalupe, the patron saint of Mexico.

Guadalupe, Tex. (est. Mar. 30, 1846; 715 sq. mi.; 1970 pop.: 33, 554; 1960: 29, 017; 1950: 25, 392) (Seguin). ("The Gateway to South Texas"). Our Lady of Guadalupe*. -- Weinert, Willie Mae, An authentic history of Guadalupe County, Sequin, Texas: Sequin Enterprise, 1951; 92 p.

Guernsey, Ohio (est. Jan. 31, 1810; 529 sq. mi.; 1970 pop.: 37, 665; 1960: 38, 579; 1950: 38, 452) (Cambridge). Isle of Guernsey, Great Britain. -- Sarchet, Cyrus Parkinson Beatty, History of Guernsey County, Indianapolis: B. F. Bowen & Co., 1911; 2 vol. -- Wolfe, William G., Stories of Guernsey County, Cambridge, Ohio: W. G. Wolfe, 1943; 1093 p.

Guilford, N. C. (est. sess., Dec. 5, 1770; 651 sq. mi.; 1970 pop.: 288, 590; 1960: 246, 520; 1950: 191, 057) (Greensboro). Francis North (1637-1685), the first earl of Guilford. Knighted 1671; Attorney gen. of England 1675-82; created Baron Guilford 1683. -- Magness, Sallie Walker (Stockard), The history of Guilford County, North Carolina, Knoxville, Tenn.: Gaut-Ogden Co., 1902; 197 p.

Gulf, Fla. (est. June 6, 1925; 557 sq. mi.; 1970 pop.: 10, 096; 1960: 9, 937; 1950: 7, 460) (Wewahitchka). Descriptive.

Gunnison, Colo. (est. Mar. 9, 1877; 3, 242 sq. mi.; 1970 pop.: 7, 578; 1960: 5, 477; 1950: 5, 716) (Gunnison). John

William Gunnison (1812-1853). Grad. U. S. Military Academy 1837; appointed second lt. Second Cavalry 1837; Cherokee War, Fla., 1837-38; in Seminole campaign 1839; advanced to first lt. in 1846 and capt. in 1853; killed by Indians near Sevier Lake, Utah on Oct. 26, 1853 while on surveying expedition to establish a railroad from the Miss. River to the Pacific Coast. -- Wallace, Betty (Steele), Gunnison Country, Denver: Sage Books, 1960; 208 p.

Guthrie, Iowa (est. Jan. 15, 1851; 596 sq. mi.; 1970 pop.: 12, 243; 1960: 13, 607; 1950: 15, 197) (Guthrie Center). Edwin Guthrie (-1847). Capt. of Iowa vol. in Mexican War 1847; died of wounds received in action at La Hoya, Mex., on June 20, 1847. -- Past and present of Guthrie County, Chicago: S. J. Clarke Pub. Co., 1907; 879 p.

Gwinnett, Ga. (est. Dec. 15, 1818; 440 sq. mi.; 1970 pop.: 72, 349; 1960: 43, 541; 1950: 32, 320) (Lawrenceville). Button Gwinnett (1732-1777). Second pres. Ga. Provisional Council; Continental Congress 1776-77; signer Declaration of Independence 1776; Ga., constitutional convention 1777; Acting Pres. and commander-in-chief of Ga., 1777; killed in a duel with Gen. Lachlan McIntosh. -- Flanigan, James C., History of Gwinnett County, Hapeville, Ga.: Tyler & Co., 1943 vol. 1 - 1959 vol. 2.

H

Haakon, S. D. (est. Nov. 1914; 1, 815 sq. mi.; 1970 pop.: 2, 802; 1960: 3, 303; 1950: 3, 167) (Philip) King Haakon VII (1872-1957). Second son of Frederick VIII of Denmark, married Princess Maud, youngest daughter of Edward VII of England 1896, crowned King of Norway June 22, 1906.

Habersham, Ga. (est. Dec. 15, 1818; 290 sq. mi.; 1970 pop.: 20, 691; 1960: 18, 116; 1950: 16, 553) (Clarkesville). Joseph Habersham (1751-1815). Maj., lt. col., col. First Ga. Regiment 1776; resigned 1778; Continental Congress 1785-86; Postmaster gen. 1795-1801. -- Church, Mary L., The Hills of Habersham, Clarksville, Ga., 1962; 165 p.

Hale, Ala. (est. Jan. 30, 1867; 663 sq. mi.; 1970 pop.: 15, 888; 1960: 19, 537; 1950: 20, 832) (Greensboro). Stephen F. Hale (1816-1878), graduated from law school 1839, Mexican War 1846-48; Lt. Col. 11th Ala. Inf. Reg.

Hale, Tex. (est. Aug. 21, 1876; 979 sq. mi.; 1970 pop.: 34, 137; 1960: 36, 798; 1950: 28, 211) (Plainview). John C.

Hale (-1836). Went to Tex. in 1831; lt. in Capt. Bryant's co., killed at battle of San Jacinto 1836. -- Cox, Mary L., History of Hale County, Texas, Plainview, Texas, 1937; 230 p.

Halifax, N. C. (est. sess.; Dec. 12, 1754; 722 sq. mi.; 1970 pop.: 53, 884; 1960: 58, 956; 1950: 58, 377) (Halifax). George Montagu Dunk, Earl of Halifax (1716-1771). Second earl of Halifax; pres. of Board of Trade 1748-61; lord lt. of Ireland 1761-63, first lord of admiralty, 1762; secretary of state 1762, lord privy seal 1770. -- Allen, William Cicero, History of Halifax County, Boston, Mass.: Cornhill Co., 1918; 235 p.

Halifax, Va. (est. sess., Feb. 27, 1752; eff. May 10, 1752; 808 sq. mi.; 1970 pop.: 30, 076; 1960: 33, 637; 1950: 41, 442) (Halifax). George Montagu Dunk, Earl of Halifax*. -- Carrington, Wirt Johnson, A history of Halifax County, Richmond: Appeals Press, Inc., 1924; 525 p. -- Barbour, William Breckenridge, "Halifacts," Danville, Va.: J. T. Townes Printing Co., Inc., 1941; 281 p.

Hall, Ga. (est. Dec. 15, 1818; 437 sq. mi.; 1970 pop.: 59, 405; 1960: 49, 739; 1950: 40, 113) (Gainesville). Lyman Hall 1731-1790). Ninth gov. of Ga. Provisional council of Ga., 1774-75; Continental Congress 1774-80; signer of Declaration of Independence 1776; physician; gov. of Ga. 1783. -- McRay, Sybil Wood, Hall County, Georgia 1819-1839, Gainesville, Ga., 1968; 67 p. -- Powell, Margaret, Hall through the years, Gainesville, Ga.: W. O. Sexton Printing Service, 1968; 150 p.

Hall, Neb. (est. Nov. 4, 1858, org. Jan. 7, 1867; 540 sq. mi.; 1970 pop.: 42, 851; 1960: 35, 757; 1950: 32, 186) (Grand Island). Augustus Hall (1814-1861). Assistant U. S. marshal in Ohio 1839; prosecuting attorney Union County 1840-42; Representative from Iowa 1855-57; chief justice Neb. Terr. 1858-61. -- Buechler, August F., History of Hall County, Nebraska, Lincoln, Neb.: Western Pub. & Engraving Co., 1920; 965 p.

Hall, Tex. (est. Aug. 21, 1876; 896 sq. mi.; 1970 pop.: 6, 015; 1960: 7, 322; 1950: 10, 930) (Memphis). Warren D. C. Hall (1788-1867). Mexican Army, Committee of Safety 1835; Adj. gen. Republic of Tex. 1835; Secretary of War, Tex. Republic. -- Baker, Inez, Yesterday in Hall County, Texas, Memphis, Tenn., 1940; 219 p.

Hamblen, Tenn. (est. June 8, 1870; 174 sq. mi.; 1970 pop.: 38, 696; 1960: 33, 092; 1950: 23, 976) (Morristown). Hezekiah Hamblen, of Hawkins County.

Hamilton, Fla. (est. Dec. 26, 1827; 514 sq. mi.; 1970 pop.: 7, 787; 1960: 7, 705; 1950: 8, 981) (Jasper). ("The

Florida Crown"). Alexander Hamilton (1757-1804). Capt. of artillery Continental Army 1776; aide de camp to Gen. Washington 1777-81; Continental Congress 1782-83 and 1787-88; N. Y. assembly 1787; Pa. constitutional convention 1788; U. S. Secretary of the Treas. in the cabinet of Pres. Washington 1789-95; mortally wounded in duel with Aaron Burr.

Hamilton, Ill. (est. Feb. 8, 1821; 455 sq. mi.; 1970 pop.: 8,665; 1960: 10,010; 1950: 12,256) (McLeansboro). Alexander Hamilton*.

Hamilton, Ind. (est. Jan. 8, 1823, eff. Apr. 7, 1823; 403 sq. mi.; 1970 pop.: 54,532; 1960: 40,132; 1950: 28,491) (Noblesville). Alexander Hamilton*. -- Shirts, Augustus Finch, History of the formation and development of Hamilton County, Indiana, 1901; 370 p.

Hamilton, Iowa (est. Dec. 22, 1856; 577 sq. mi.; 1970 pop.: 18,383; 1960: 20,032; 1950: 19,660) (Webster City). William H. Hamilton, pres. of Iowa senate 1856-57. -- Lee, Jesse W., History of Hamilton County, Chicago: S. J. Clarke Pub. Co., 1912; 2 vol.

Hamilton, Kan. (est. Mar. 6, 1873, org. Jan. 29, 1886; 992 sq. mi.; 1970 pop.: 2,747; 1960: 3,144; 1950: 3,696) (Syracuse). Alexander Hamilton*.

Hamilton, Neb. (est. Feb. 16, 1867, org. Oct. 1870; 541 sq. mi.; 1970 pop.: 8,867; 1960: 8,714; 1950: 8,778) (Aurora). ("The Deep Well Irrigation Center of the Nation"). Alexander Hamilton*. -- Bremer, Bertha G., Centennial History of Hamilton County, Aurora, Neb.: Hamilton County Centennial Association, 1967; 263 p. -- Stough, Dale P. (compiler), History of Hamilton and Clay Counties, Chicago: S. J. Clarke Pub. Co., 1921; 2 vol.

Hamilton, N. Y. (est. Apr. 12, 1816; 1,747 sq. mi.; 1970 pop.: 4,714; 1960: 4,267; 1950: 4,105) (Lake Pleasant). Alexander Hamilton*. -- Aber, Ted, The History of Hamilton County, Lake Pleasant, N. Y., 1965; 1209 p.

Hamilton, Ohio (est. Jan. 2, 1790; 414 sq. mi.; 1970 pop.: 924,018; 1960: 864,121; 1950: 723,952) (Cincinnati). Alexander Hamilton*. -- Ford, Henry A. and Ford, K. B., History of Hamilton County, Cleveland: L. A. Williams & Co., 1881; 432 p.

Hamilton, Tenn. (est. Oct. 25, 1819; 576 sq. mi.; 1970 pop.: 254,236; 1960: 237,905; 1950: 208,255) (Chattanooga). Alexander Hamilton*. -- Armstrong, Zella, History of Hamilton County and Chattanooga, Tenn., Chattanooga, Tenn.: Lookout Pub. Co., 1931-1940; 2 vol.

Hamilton, Tex. (est. Feb. 2, 1842; 844 sq. mi.; 1970 pop.: 7,198; 1960: 8,488; 1950: 10,660) (Hamilton). James

Hamilton, Jr. (1786-1857). Twenty-eighth gov. of S. C. Maj. in War of 1812; mayor of Charleston 1822-24; Representative from S. C. 1822-29; gov. of S. C. 1830-32; brig. gen. of S. C. troops 1833; drowned in Gulf of Mexico 1857.

Hamlin, S. D. (est. Jan. 8, 1873; 520 sq. mi.; 1970 pop.: 5, 172; 1960: 6, 303; 1950: 7, 058) (Hayti). Hannibal Hamlin (1809-1891). Gov. of Me. Me. house of representatives 1836-40 and 1847; Representative from Me., 1843-47; Senator from Me., 1848-57; gov. of Me. 1857; Senator from Me., 1857-61; Vice Pres. of the U. S., 1861-65; enlisted in Me. state guards for period of sixty days as a private 1864; collector of the port of Boston 1865-66; Senator from Me., 1869-81; U. S. Minister to Spain 1881-82.

Hampden, Mass. (est. Feb. 25, 1812, eff. Aug. 1, 1812; 621 sq. mi.; 1970 pop.: 459, 050; 1960: 429, 353; 1950: 367, 971) (Springfield). John Hampden (1594-1643). English patriot, resisted attempt of king to force loans and raise taxes. Was arrested and involved in famous suit against the king. In 1642 was impeached by attorney gen. Served in Short Parliament in 1640. Mortally wounded in action in 1643. -- Johnson, Clifton, Hampden County, 1636-1936, New York: American Historical Society, Inc., 1936; 3 vol. -- Copeland, Alfred Minott, Our Country and Its People, Boston: Century Memorial Pub. Co., 1902; 3 vol.

Hampshire, Mass. (est. May 7, 1662; 537 sq. mi.; 1970 pop.: 123, 981; 1960: 103, 229; 1950: 87, 594) (Northampton). Hampshire County, England. -- Hampshire Gazette, The Hampshire History, Northampton, Mass.: Hampshire County Commissioners, 1964; 364 p. -- Johnson, Clifton, Historic Hampshire, Springfield, Mass.: Milton Bradley Co., 1932; 406 p.

Hampshire, W. Va. (est. Feb. 27, 1752 sess, eff. Dec. 13, 1753; 641 sq. mi.; 1970 pop.: 11, 710; 1960: 11, 705; 1950: 12, 257) (Romney). Hampshire County, England. -- Maxwell, Hu, History of Hampshire County, West Virginia, Morgantown, W. Va.: A. B. Boughner, 1897; 744 p.

Hampton, S. C. (est. Feb. 18, 1878; 562 sq. mi.; 1970 pop.: 15, 878; 1960: 17, 425; 1950: 18, 027) (Hampton). Wade Hampton (1818-1902) Gov. of S. C.

Hancock, Ga. (est. Dec. 17, 1793; 530 sq. mi.; 1970 pop.: 9, 019; 1960: 9, 979; 1950: 11, 052) (Sparta). John Hancock (1737-1793). First gov. of Mass. (Commonwealth). Mass. provincial legislature 1766-72; Continental Congress 1775-80, 1785-86; pres. Continental Congress 1775-77;

first signer of the Declaration of Independence 1776; maj. gen. of Mass. Militia; Mass. constitutional convention 1780; gov. of Mass. 1780-85 and 1787-93.

Hancock, Ill. (est. Jan. 13, 1825; 780 sq. mi.; 1970 pop.: 23,645; 1960: 24,574; 1950: 25,790) (Carthage). John Hancock*. -- Drury, John, This Is Hancock County, Chicago: Loree Co., 1955; 570 p.

Hancock, Ind. (est. Jan. 26, 1827, org. Dec. 24, 1807, eff. Mar. 1, 1828, 305 sq. mi.; 1970 pop.: 35,096; 1960: 26,665; 1950: 20,332) (Greenfield). John Hancock*. -- Binford, John H., History of Hancock County, Indiana, Greenfield, Ind.: King & Binford, 1882; 536 p. -- Richman, George J., History of Hancock County, Indiana, Indianapolis, Ind.: Federal Pub. Co., 1916; 1155 p.

Hancock, Iowa (est. Jan. 15, 1851; 570 sq. mi.; 1970 pop.: 13,227; 1960: 14,604; 1950: 15,077) (Garner). John Hancock*. -- History of Kossuth, Hancock and Winnebago Counties, Springfield, Ill.: Union Pub. Co., 1884; 933 p. -- History of Winnebago County and Hancock County, Chicago: Pioneer Pub. Co., 1917; 2 vol.

Hancock, Ky. (est. Jan. 3, 1829; 187 sq. mi.; 1970: 7,080; 1960: 5,330; 1950: 6,009) (Hawesville). John Hancock*.

Hancock, Me. (est. June 25, 1789, eff. May 1, 1790; 1,542 sq. mi.; 1970 pop.: 34,590; 1960: 32,293; 1950: 32,105) (Ellsworth). John Hancock*. -- Wasson, Samuel, A survey of Hancock County, Augusta, Me.: Sprague, Owen and Nash, 1878; 91 p.

Hancock, Miss. (est. Dec. 18, 1812; 469 sq. mi.; 1970 pop.: 17,387; 1960: 14,039; 1950: 11,891) (Bay St. Louis). John Hancock*.

Hancock, Ohio (est. Feb. 12, 1820; 532 sq. mi.; 1970 pop.: 61,217; 1960: 53,686; 1950: 44,280) (Findlay). John Hancock*. -- Heminger, R. L., Across the years in Findlay and Hancock County, Findlay, Ohio: Republican-Courier, 1963; 205 p. -- Spaythe, Jacob A., History of Hancock County, Toledo, Ohio: B. F. Wade Printing Co., 1903; 312 p.

Hancock, Tenn. (est. Jan. 7, 1844; 231 sq. mi.; 1970 pop.: 6,719; 1960: 7,757; 1950: 9,116) (Sneedville). John Hancock*.

Hancock, W. Va. (est. Jan. 15, 1848; 88 sq. mi.; 1970 pop.: 39,749; 1960: 39,615; 1950: 34,388) (New Cumberland). John Hancock*. -- Welch, Jack, History of Hancock County; Virginia and West Virginia, Wheeling, W. Va.: Wheeling News Printing & Lithographing Co., 1963; 202 p.

Hand, S. D. (est. Jan. 8, 1873; 1,436 sq. mi.; 1970 pop.: 5,883; 1960: 6,712; 1950: 7,149) (Miller). George H.

Hand (1837-1891). In Civil War U. S. Attorney for Dakota terr. 1866-69; seventh secretary of Dakota terr. 1874-83.

Hanover, Va. (est. Nov. 2, 1720 sess.; 466 sq. mi.; 1970 pop.: 37,479; 1960: 27,550; 1950: 21,985) (Hanover). George I, (1660-1727), Duke of Hanover. First king of house of Hanover, married Sophia Dorothea Nov. 21, 1682; crowned king of Great Britain and Ireland Oct. 20, 1714. -- Page, Rosewell, Hanover County: its history and legends, Richmond, 1926; 153 p.

Hansford, Tex. (est. Aug. 21, 1876; 907 sq. mi.; 1970 pop.: 6,351; 1960: 6,208; 1950: 4,202) (Spearman). John M. Hansford (-1844) Went to Tex. 1837; judge of seventh judicial district 1840-42; attorney gen. of Tex.; killed by Regulators 1844.

Hanson, S. D. (est. Jan. 13, 1871; 431 sq. mi.; 1970 pop.: 3,781; 1960: 4,584; 1950: 4,896) (Alexandria). Joseph R. Hanson (1837-1917). Secretary of first terr. legislature of Dakota terr; territorial auditor; second legislature; judge advocate; Sioux Indian agent 1865-70.

Haralson, Ga. (est. Jan. 26, 1856; 284 sq. mi.; 1970 pop.: 15,927; 1960: 14,543; 1950: 14,663) (Buchanan). Hugh Anderson Haralson (1805- 1854). Ga. house of representatives 1831-32; Ga. senate 1837-38; maj. gen. Ga., militia 1838-50; Representative from Ga. 1843-51.

Hardee, Fla. (est. Apr. 23, 1921; 630 sq. mi.; 1970 pop.: 14,889; 1960: 12,370; 1950: 10,073) (Wauchula). ("The Cucumber Capital of the World"; "The Fertile Grove Land"; "The Perfect Area for Lush-Bearing Citrus Groves"). Cary Augustus Hardee (1876-1957). Gov. of Fla. Fla. attorney third judicial circuit 1905-13; speaker house of representatives 1915-17; gov. of Fla. 1921-25.

Hardeman, Tenn. (est. Oct. 16, 1823; 655 sq. mi.; 1970 pop.: 22,435; 1960: 21,517; 1950: 23,311) (Bolivar). Thomas Jones Hardeman (1788-1854). Col. Tenn. militia war of 1812; brigade quartermaster in the Natchez expedition 1812-13; member of Congress of Tex. Republic; assoc. justice Bastrop county 1843; chief justice Bastrop county 1845; Most Worshipful Grand Master of Tex. Free and Accepted Masons 1850.

Hardeman, Tex. (est. Feb. 1, 1858; 685 sq. mi.; 1970 pop.: 6,795; 1960: 8,275; 1950: 10,212) (Quanah). Bailey Hardeman (1795-1836). West Tenn. Vol. War of 1812; first lt. 1813; signer Tex. declaration of Independence 1836; secretary of treasury ad interim Tex. Republic 1836. Brother of Thomas Jones Hardeman*. -- Neal, W. O., The last frontier, the story of Hardeman County, Quanah,

Texas: Quanah Tribune-Chief, 1966; 276 p.

Hardin, Ill. (est. Mar. 2, 1839; 185 sq. mi.; 1970 pop.: 4,914; 1960: 5,879; 1950: 7,530) (Elizabethtown). Hardin County, Ky.

Hardin, Iowa (est. Jan. 15, 1851; 574 sq. mi.; 1970 pop.: 22,248; 1960: 22,533; 1950: 22,218) (Eldora). John J. Hardin. Killed in Mexican War.

Hardin, Ky. (est. Dec. 15, 1792, eff. Feb. 20, 1793; 616 sq. mi.; 1970 pop.: 78,421; 1960: 67,789; 1950: 50,312) (Elizabethtown). John Hardin (1753-1792). In gov. Dunmore's expedition; second lt. in Eighth Pa. Continental Army 1777; resigned as first lt. Dec. 1779; Indian fighter; commissioned brig. gen. Ky. militia 1792, murdered by Indians while on a peace mission.

Hardin, Ohio (est. Feb. 12, 1820; 467 sq. mi.; 1970 pop.: 30,813; 1960: 29,933; 1950: 28,673) (Kenton). John Hardin*. -- Blue, Herbert Tenney Orren, Centennial History of Hardin County, Canton, Ohio: Rogers-Miller Co., 1933; 180 p. -- Kohler, Minnie Ichler, A twentieth century history of Hardin County, Chicago: Lewis Pub. Co., 1910; 2 vol.

Hardin, Tenn. (est. Nov. 13, 1819; 595 sq. mi.; 1970 pop.: 18,212; 1960: 17,397; 1950: 16,908) (Savannah). Joseph Hardin. Served in Continental Army; speaker in second terr. assembly Tenn. house of representatives. -- Brazelton, B. G., History of Hardin County, Tenn., Nashville, Tenn.: Cumberland Presbyterian Pub. House, 1885; 135 p.

Hardin, Tex. (est. Jan. 22, 1858; 895 sq. mi.; 1970 pop.: 29,996; 1960: 24,629; 1950: 19,535) (Kountze). William Hardin (1801-1839). Went to Tex. 1825; primary judge of Liberty 1834. -- Abernethy, Francis Edward, Tales from the big thicket, Austin, Texas: University of Texas, 1966; 244 p.

Harding, N. M. (est. Mar. 4, 1921; 2,136 sq. mi.; 1970 pop.: 1,348; 1960: 1,874; 1950: 3,013) (Mosquero). Warren Gamaliel Harding (1865-1923). Twenty-ninth Pres. of the U. S. Editor Marion, Ohio, "Star" 1884; Ohio senate 1899-1903; lt. gov. of Ohio 1904-05; Senator from Ohio 1915-21; Pres. of the U. S. 1921-23.

Harding, S. D. (est. Feb. 26, 1909; 2,683 sq. mi.; 1970 pop.: 1,855; 1960: 2,371; 1950: 2,289) (Buffalo). J. A. Harding. Speaker of the house, 14th S. D. terr. legislature 1881.

Hardy, W. Va. (est. Oct. 17, 1785 sess.; 575 sq. mi.; 1970 pop.: 8,855; 1960: 9,308; 1950: 10,032) (Moorefield). Samuel Hardy (1758-1785). Va. house of delegates 1780;

member of executive council 1781; member of Continental Congress from Va. 1783-85. -- Judy, Elvin Lycurgus, History of Grant and Hardy Counties, West Virginia, Charleston, W. Va.: Charleston Printing Co., 1951; 466 p. -- Moore, Alvin Edward, History of Hardy County of the borderland, Parsons, W. Va.: McClain Printing Co., 1963; 303 p.

Harford, Md. (est. Mar. 2, 1774; 448 sq. mi.; 1970 pop.: 115, 378; 60: 76, 722; 1950: 51, 782) (Bel Air). Henry Harford. Last proprietary; son of Frederick, sixth Lord Baltimore; did not inherit title because of his illegitimate birth. -- Mason, Samuel, Historical sketches of Harford County, Darlington, Md.: Little Pines Farm, 1955; 177 p. -- Wright, C. Milton, Our Harford Heritage, n. p., 1967; 460 p.

Harlan, Ky. (est. Jan. 28, 1819; 469 sq. mi.; 1970 pop.: 37, 370; 1960: 51, 107; 1950: 71, 751) (Harlan). Silas Harlan. Maj. -- Condon, Mabel Green, A history of Harlan County, Nashville, Tenn.: Parthenon Press, 1962; 216 p. -- Spelman, John Adams, At home in the hills, glimpses of Harlan County, Pine Mountain, Ky.: Pine Mountain Print Shop, 1939; 87 p.

Harlan, Neb. (est. June 3, 1871, org. July 29, 1872; 575 sq. mi.; 1970 pop.: 4, 357; 1960: 5, 081; 1950: 7, 189) (Alma). Thomas Harlan. Pioneer.

Harmon, Okla. (est. elec. May 22, 1909, gov. procl. June 2, 1909; 532 sq. mi.; 1970 pop.: 5, 136; 1960: 5, 852; 1950: 8, 079) (Hollis). Judson Harmon (1846-1927). Forty-fifth gov. of Ohio. Judge of common pleas court Ohio 1876; judge of superior court of Cincinnati 1878-87; Attorney gen. of the U. S. 1895-97; gov. of Ohio 1909-13.

Harnett, N. C. (est. Feb. 7, 1855; 606 sq. mi.; 1970 pop.: 49, 667; 1960: 48, 236; 1950: 47, 605) (Lillington). Cornelius Harnett (1723-1781). N. C. legislature 1770-71; Wilmington Committee of Safety 1774; Continental Congress 1777-80; author of the Halifax Resolves of Apr. 12, 1776; died of disease contracted while prisoner of the British. -- Fowler, Malcolm, They Passed this way, a personnel narrative of Harnett County history, Harnett County Centennial (n. p.), 1955; 167 p.

Harney, Ore. (est. Feb. 25, 1889; 10, 132 sq. mi.; 1970 pop.: 7, 215; 1960: 6, 744; 1950: 6, 113) (Burns). William Selby Harney (1800-1889). Soldier, second lt. 1818; first lt. 1819; capt. 1825; maj. and paymaster 1833; lt. col. 1836; served in Black Hawk War; in Seminole War; in Mexican War 1847; bvt. brig. gen. 1847; col. 1848; brig. gen. 1858; assigned to command department of Ore.; bvt.

maj. gen. for long and faithful services 1865. -- Brimlow, George Francis, Harney County, Portland, Ore.: Binfords & Mort., 1951; 316 p.

Harper, Kan. (est. Feb. 26, 1867; 801 sq. mi.; 1970 pop.: 7,871; 1960: 9,541; 1950: 10,263) (Anthony). Marion Harper (-1863). First sgt. Co. E Second Kan., died from wounds Dec. 30, 1863.

Harper, Okla. (est. July 16, 1907; 1,034 sq. mi.; 1970 pop.: 5,151; 1960: 5,956; 1950: 5,977) (Buffalo). O. G. Harper. Clerk, Okla. constitutional convention 1907.

Harris, Ga. (est. Dec. 24, 1827; 501 sq. mi.; 1970 pop.: 11,520; 1960: 11,167; 1950: 11,265) (Hamilton). Charles Harris (1772-1827). Lawyer, alderman or mayor of Savannah, Ga., for about 30 years; offered many judicial posts but declined them. -- Barfield, Louise (Calhoun), History of Harris County, Georgia, Columbus, Ga., 1961; 766 p.

Harris, Tex. (est. Mar. 17, 1836; 1,747 sq. mi.; 1970 pop.: 1,741,912; 1960: 1,243,158; 1950: 806,701) (Houston). John Richardson Harris (1790-1829). Emigrated to Tex. 1824; established trading post; operated boats between Tex. and New Orleans; died of yellow fever at New Orleans 1829. (Originally Harrisburg County, name changed to Harris County Dec. 28, 1839 by joint resolution). -- Jones, C. Anson, Early History of Harris County, Texas, Houston, 1928; 15 p.

Harrison, Ind. (est. Oct. 11, 1808, eff. Dec. 1, 1808; 479 sq. mi.; 1970 pop.: 20,423; 1960: 19,207; 1950: 17,858) (Corydon). William Henry Harrison (1773-1841). Ninth Pres. of the U.S. First terr. gov. of Ind. In Indian Wars capt. commanding Ft. Washington 1797; secretary of Northwest terr. 1798-99; delegate from Northwest terr. 1799-1800; terr. gov. of Ind. 1800-1811; Indian commissioner 1801-13; defeated Indians at Tippecanoe 1811 and at the Thames 1813 for which he was awarded a Congressional medal; maj. gen. U.S. Army 1813; Representative from Ohio 1816-19; Ohio senate 1819-21; Senator from Ohio 1825-28; U.S. Minister to Colombia 1828-29; Pres. of the U.S., March 4 - Apr. 4, 1841. -- Roose, William H., Indiana's birthplace; a history of Harrison County, Indiana, Chicago: Adams Press, 1966; 92 p.

Harrison, Iowa (est. Jan. 15, 1851, org. Jan. 12, 1853; 693 sq. mi.; 1970 pop.: 16,240; 1960: 17,600; 1950: 19,560) (Logan). William Henry Harrison*. (org. eff. Mar. 7, 1853). -- Smith, Joe H., History of Harrison County, Des Moines: Iowa Printing Co., 1888; 491 p.

Harrison, Ky. (est. Dec. 21, 1793, eff. Feb. 1, 1794;

308 sq. mi.; 1970 pop.: 14,158; 1960: 13,704; 1950: 13,736) (Cynthiana). Benjamin Harrison (1833-1901). Twenty-third Pres. of the U. S. Second lt. to col. Indiana Vol. Infantry 1862-65; bvt. brig. gen. 1865; reporter Ind. supreme court 1865-69; Senator from Ind., 1881-87; Pres. of the U. S. 1889-93; attorney for Venezuela in dispute with Great Britain arbitrated at Paris in 1900.

Harrison, Miss. (est. Feb. 5, 1841; 570 sq. mi.; 1970 pop.: 134,582; 1960: 119,489; 1950: 84,073) (Gulfport). William Henry Harrison*. -- Lang, John H., History of Harrison County, Gulfport, Miss.: Dixie Press, 1936; 303 p.

Harrison, Mo. (est. Feb. 14, 1845; 720 sq. mi.; 1970 pop.: 10,257; 1960: 11,603; 1950: 14,107) (Bethany). Albert Galliton Harrison (1800-1839). Board of Visitors at U. S. Military Academy 1828; comm. to adjust land titles of Spanish grants 1829-35; Representative from Mo., 1835-39. -- Wanamaker, George W., History of Harrison County, Mo., Topeka: Historical Pub. Co., 1921; 855 p.

Harrison, Ohio (est. Jan. 2, 1813; 411 sq. mi.; 1970 pop.: 17,013; 1960: 17,995; 1950: 19,054) (Cadiz). William Henry Harrison*. -- Hanna, Charles Augustus, Historical collections of Harrison County, C. A. Hanna, 1900; 636 p.

Harrison, Tex. (est. Jan. 28, 1839; 892 sq. mi.; 1970 pop.: 44,841; 1960: 45,594; 1950: 47,745) (Marshall). Jonas Harrison (1777-1837). Lawyer; U. S. coll. of customs at Niagara Falls; master of chancery N. Y. State; moved to Tex. in 1820.

Harrison, W. Va. (est. May 3, 1784, sess.; eff. July 20, 1784; 417 sq. mi.; 1970 pop.: 73,028; 1960: 77,856; 1950: 85,296) (Clarksburg). Benjamin Harrison (1726-1791). Fifth gov. of Va. (Commonwealth). Father of William Henry Harrison and great grandfather of Benjamin Harrison. Va. house of burgesses 1749-75; Continental Congress 1774-77; signer Declaration of Independence 1776; speaker, Va. house of delegates 1778-81 and 1785; Va. constitutional convention 1788; gov. of Va. 1781-84. -- Haymond, Henry, History of Harrison County, Morgantown, W. Va., Acme Pub. Co., 1910; 451 p.

Hart, Ga. (est. Dec. 7, 1853; 261 sq. mi.; 1970 pop.: 15,814; 1960: 15,229; 1950: 14,495) (Hartwell). Nancy Morgan Hart (1750?-). Married Benjamin Hart of Ky., moved to Elbert County, Ga., mother of six sons and two daughters; a sharpshooter and patriot reported to have routed and captured many Tories. -- Baker, John William, History of Hart County, 1933; Atlanta, Ga.: Foote & Davies Co., 1933; 426 p.

Hart, Ky. (est. Jan. 28, 1819; 425 sq. mi.; 1970 pop.: 13,980; 1960: 14,119; 1950: 15,321) (Munfordville). Nathaniel Hart (-1813). Captured at battle of River Raisin, Jan. 18, 1813 killed by Indians.

Hartford, Conn. (est. May 10, 1666 sess.; 741 sq. mi.; 1970 pop.: 816,737; 1960: 689,555; 1950: 539,661) (no county seat). Hertford in Hertfordshire, England. -- Burpee, Charles Winslow, History of Hartford County, Chicago: S. J. Clarke Pub. Co., 1928; 3 vol.

Hartley, Tex. (est. Aug. 21, 1876; 1,489 sq. mi.; 1970 pop.: 2,782; 1960: 2,171; 1950: 1,913) (Channing). Oliver Cromwell Hartley (1823-1859). Went to Tex. 1846; compiler of "A Digest of Laws of Texas" 1848-49; Tex. legislature 1851-52; reporter of decisions of Tex. supreme court 1859; in Mexican War. (Brother, Rufus K. Hartley, both lawyers.) -- Hunter, Lillie Mae, Book of years; a history of Dallam and Hartley Counties, Hereford, Texas: Pioneer Book Publishers, 1969; 206 p.

Harvey, Kan. (est. Feb. 29, 1872; 540 sq. mi.; 1970 pop.: 27,236; 1960: 25,865; 1950: 21,698) (Newton). James Madison Harvey (1833-1894). Fourth gov. of Kan. Enlisted in Civil War 1861; mustered out of Kan. Vol. Infantry as capt. 1864; member Kan. house of representatives 1865-66; served in Kan. senate 1867-68; gov. of Kan. 1869-73; Senator from Kan. 1874-77; govt. surveyor in Nev., N. M., Okla. and Utah.

Haskell, Kan. (est. Mar. 5, 1887; 579 sq. mi.; 1970 pop.: 3,672; 1960: 2,990; 1950: 2,606) (Sublette). Dudley Chase Haskell (1842-1883). Owned silver mine in Colo. 1859; quartermaster dept. Army 1861-62; Kan. house of representatives 1872, 1875-76; speaker Kan. house of representatives 1876; declined Prohibition Party nomination for the presidency 1874; Representative from Kan. 1877-83. Haskell Institute, Indian school at Lawrence, Kan., named for him.

Haskell, Okla. (est. July 16, 1907; 614 sq. mi.; 1970 pop.: 9,578; 1960: 9,121; 1950: 13,313) (Stigler). Charles Nathaniel Haskell (1860-1933). First gov. of Okla. Okla. constitutional convention 1906; gov. of Okla. 1907-11.

Haskell, Tex. (est. Feb. 1, 1858; 888 sq. mi.; 1970 pop.: 8,512; 1960: 11,174; 1950: 13,736) (Haskell). Charles Ready Haskell (1817-1836). Left school in Tenn. enlisted under Fannin, at battle of Coleto killed in Goliad massacre Mar. 27, 1836.

Hawaii, Hawaii (4,039 sq. mi.; 1970 pop.: 63,468; 1960: 61,332) (Hilo) ("The Bastion of the Pacific"; "The Big Island"; "The Orchid Island"). From Polynesian word for "beyond the doors of death." -- Kuykendall, R. S. and Day, A. G., Hawaii, a history - Englewood Cliffs, N. J., Prentice-Hall, 1961; 331 p.

Hawkins, Tenn. (est. sess. of Nov. 18, 1786; 494 sq. mi.; 1970 pop.: 33,726; 1960: 30,468; 1950: 30,494) (Rogersville). Benjamin Hawkins (1754-1816). French interpreter for Gen. Washington in Revolutionary War; N. C. house of commons 1778, 1779 and 1784; Continental Congress 1781-84, and 1786-87; Senator from N. C., 1789-95; Indian agent for all tribes south of the Ohio River 1796-1816.

Hayes, Neb. (est. Feb. 19, 1877; 711 sq. mi.; 1970 pop.: 1,530; 1960: 1,919; 1950: 2,404) (Hayes Center). Rutherford Birchard Hayes (1822-1893). Nineteenth Pres. of the U. S. Cincinnati, Ohio, city solicitor 1857-59; maj. and lt. col. Ohio vol. infantry 1861; col. 1862; brig. gen. 1864; bvt. maj. gen. 1865; resigned 1865; Representative from Ohio 1865-67; twenty-ninth gov. of Ohio 1868-72 and thirty-second gov. 1876-77; Pres. of the U. S. 1877-81.

Hays, Tex. (est. Mar. 1, 1848; 670 sq. mi.; 1970 pop.: 27,642; 1960: 19,934; 1950: 17,840) (San Marcos). John Coffee Hays (1817-1883). Surveyor, went to Tex. 1837; capt. in Tex. Rangers; col. in command of First Regiment Mounted Troops in Gen. Taylor's army; battles of Monterey and Mexico City 1846; resigned 1848; sheriff of San Francisco County, Calif., 1849-53; surveyor gen. of Calif., 1859.

Haywood, N. C. (est. Dec. 15, 1808; 543 sq. mi.; 1970 pop.: 41,710; 1960: 39,711; 1950: 37,631) (Waynesville). John Haywood. State treas. of N. C. -- Allen, William Cicero, Annals of Haywood County, North Carolina, 1935; 628 p.

Haywood, Tenn. (est. Nov. 3, 1823; 519 sq. mi.; 1970 pop.: 19,596; 1960: 23,393; 1950: 26,212) (Brownsville). John Haywood (1753-1826). Attorney gen. of N. C. 1791-94; judge of superior court of N. C., 1794-1800; settled in Tenn. 1810; supreme court judge of Tenn. 1816-26.

Heard, Ga. (est. Dec. 22, 1830; 285 sq. mi.; 1970 pop.: 5,354; 1960: 5,333; 1950: 6,975) (Franklin). Stephen Heard (-1815). Sixth gov. of Ga. Battle of Kettle Creek 1781; pres. of Ga., council gov. de facto Jan. 1871-Aug. 1871; pres. of Ga. council 1782; chief justice Ga. inferior court.

Hemphill, Tex. (est. Aug. 21, 1876; 909 sq. mi.; 1970 pop.: 3,084; 1960: 3,185; 1950: 4,123) (Canadian). John Hemphill (1803-1862). Second lt. fought Seminole Indians 1836; emigrated to Tex. 1838; judge of fourth judicial district of Tex. 1840-42; adj. gen. Mier expedition 1842; chief justice supreme court Tex. 1846-58; Senator from Tex. 1859-61 when expelled; provisional congress Confederate states 1861.

Hempstead, Ark. (est. Dec. 15, 1818 eff. Mar. 1, 1819; 735 sq. mi.; 1970 pop.: 19,308; 1960: 19,661; 1950: 25,080) (Hope). Edward Hempstead.

Henderson, Ill. (est. Jan. 20, 1841; 381 sq. mi.; 1970 pop.: 8,451; 1960: 8,237; 1950: 8,416) (Oquawka). Richard Henderson. Henderson River. -- History of Mercer and Henderson Counties, Chicago: H. H. Hill & Co., 1882; 1414 p.

Henderson, Ky. (est. Dec. 21, 1798; eff. May 15, 1799; 440 sq. mi.; 1970 pop.: 36,031; 1960: 33,519; 1950: 30,715) (Henderson). Henderson River; Richard Henderson*. -- Starling, Edmund L., History of Henderson County, Henderson, Ky., 1887; 832 p.

Henderson, N. C. (est. Dec. 15, 1838; 382 sq. mi.; 1970 pop.: 42,804; 1960: 36,163; 1950: 30,921) (Hendersonville). Leonard Henderson (1772-1833). Judge N. C. appellate court 1808-18; N. C. supreme court 1818-29; chief justice, N. C. supreme court 1829. -- Patton, Sadie Smathers, Story of Henderson County, Asheville, N. C., Miller Printing Co., 1947; 290 p.

Henderson, Tenn. (est. Nov. 7, 1821; 515 sq. mi.; 1970 pop.: 17,291; 1960: 16,115; 1950: 17,173) (Lexington). James Henderson. Col. Tenn. militia; quartermaster on staff of Gen. Andrew Jackson in the Natchez expedition 1812-13. -- Powers, Auburn, History of Henderson County, Auburn Powers, 1930; 169 p.

Henderson, Tex. (est. Apr. 27, 1846; 940 sq. mi.: 1970 pop.: 26,466; 1960: 21,786; 1950: 23,405) (Athens). James Pinckney Henderson (1808-1858). Gov. of Tex. Tex. Army brig. gen. 1836; Attorney gen. Republic of Tex. 1836; Secretary of State 1837; Tex. representative in Europe 1838; Minister to the U. S. 1844; Tex. constitutional convention 1845; Gov. of Tex. 1846-47; in Mexican War as maj. gen. U. S. Army and voted a sword by Congress for bravery at Monterey; Senator from Tex. 1857-58. -- Faulk, J. J., History of Henderson County, Texas, Athens, Texas: Athens Review Printing Co., 1929; 322 p.

Hendricks, Ind. (est. Dec. 20, 1823, eff. Apr. 1, 1824; 417 sq. mi.; 1970 pop.: 53,974; 1960: 40,896; 1950: 24,594) (Danville). William Hendricks (1782-1850). Third gov. of Ind. Printer in Ind. Terr. 1812; Secretary, Ind. gen. assembly 1814-15; secretary, Ind. constitutional convention 1816; Representative from Ind., 1816-22; gov. of Ind. 1822-25; Senator from Ind. 1825-37; trustee of Ind. Univ. 1829-40.

Hendry, Fla. (est. May 11, 1923; 1,187 sq. mi.; 1970 pop.: 11,859; 1960: 8,119; 1950: 6,051) (La Belle). ("America's Winter Market Basket"). Francis Asbury Hendry.

Hennepin, Minn. (est. Mar. 6, 1852; 565 sq. mi.; 1970 pop.: 960,080; 1960: 842,854; 1950: 676,579) (Minneapolis). Louis Hennepin (1640?-1701). Roman Catholic friar who with La Salle explored Great Lakes 1679; explored Upper Miss. region 1680. -- Public Information Office, _Hennepin today_, Public Information Office, 1968; 77 p.

Henrico, Va. (est. 1634; 241 sq. mi.; 1970 pop.: 154,364; 1960: 117,339; 1950: 57,340) (Richmond). Prince Henry; Henry Frederick, prince of Wales (1594-1612), eldest son of James VI of Scotland, (James I of England) by his queen Anne, second daughter of Frederick II; created Earl of Chester and Prince of Wales 1610.

Henry, Ala. (est. Dec. 13, 1819; 565 sq. mi.; 1970 pop.: 13,254; 1960: 15,286; 1950: 18,674) (Abbeville). Patrick Henry (1736-1799). First and sixth gov. of Va. (Commonwealth). Va. house of burgesses 1765; Continental Congress 1774-76; gov. of Va. 1776-79 and 1784-86; Va. constitutional convention 1788; elected to Va. senate but did not take his seat 1799.

Henry, Ga. (est. May 15, 1821; 324 sq. mi.; 1970 pop.: 23,724; 1960: 17,619; 1950: 15,857) (McDonough). Patrick Henry*.

Henry, Ill. (est. Jan. 13, 1825; 826 sq. mi.; 1970 pop.: 53,217; 1960: 49,317; 1950: 46,492) (Cambridge). Patrick Henry*. -- Drury, John, _This Is Henry County_, Chicago: Loree Co., 1955; 610 p. -- Polson, Terry Ellen, _Corn, Commerce and Country Living, a History of Henry County_, Moline, Ill.: Desaulniers & Co., 1968; 360 p.

Henry, Ind. (est. Dec. 31, 1821, eff. June 1, 1822; 400 sq. mi.; 1970 pop.: 52,603; 1960: 48,899; 1950: 45,505) (Newcastle). Patrick Henry*. -- Hazzard, George, _Hazzard's history of Henry County, Indiana 1822-1906_, New Castle, Ind.: G. Hazzard, 1906; 2 vol. -- Pleas, Elwood, _Henry County, past and present_, Knightstown, Ind.: Eastern Indiana Pub. Co., 1967; 154 p.

Henry, Iowa (est. Dec. 7, 1836; 440 sq. mi.; 1970 pop.: 18,114; 1960: 18,187; 1950: 18,708) (Mount Pleasant). Henry Dodge (1782-1867). Gov. of Wis. Terr. Served in Black Hawk and other Indian wars, maj. U.S. Rangers 1832; resigned from the Army with rank of col. 1836; gov. of Wis. Terr. 1836-41 and 1845-48; Delegate from

Wis. Terr. 1841-45; Senator from Wis. 1848-57; declined appointment as gov. of Washington Terr. -- History of Henry County, Chicago: Western Hist. Co., 1879; 668 p.

Henry, Ky. (est. Dec. 14, 1798, eff. June 1, 1799; 289 sq. mi.; 1970 pop.: 10,910; 1960: 10,987; 1950: 11,394) (New Castle). Patrick Henry*. -- Drane, Maude (Johnston), History of Henry County, Kentucky, Eminence?, Ky., 1948; 274 p.

Henry, Mo. (est. Dec. 13, 1834; 737 sq. mi.; 1970 pop.: 18,451; 1960: 19,226; 1950: 20,043) (Clinton). Patrick Henry*. (Form. Rives, name changed Feb. 15, 1841). History Henry/St. Clair C'ties, St. Jo., Mo.: 1883, 1224 p.

Henry, Ohio (est. Feb. 12, 1820; 416 sq. mi.; 1970 pop.: 27,058; 1960: 25,392; 1950: 22,423) (Napoleon). Patrick Henry*. -- Aldrich, Lewis Cass, History of Henry and Fulton Counties, Syracuse, N.Y.: D. Mason & Co., 1888; 713 p.

Henry, Tenn. (est. Nov. 7, 1821; 599 sq. mi.; 1970 pop.: 23,749; 1960: 22,275; 1950: 23,828) (Paris). Patrick Henry*.

Henry, Va. (est. Oct. 7, 1776 sess., 392 sq. mi.; 1970 pop.: 50,901; 1960: 40,335; 1950: 31,219) (Martinsville). Patrick Henry*. -- Hill, Judith Parks American, A History of Henry County, Martinsville, Va., 1925; 332 p. -- Pedigo, Virginia G. and Pedego, L. G., History of Patrick and Henry Counties, Roanoke, Va.: Stone Printing and Mfg. Co., 1933; 400 p.

Herkimer, N.Y. (est. Feb. 16, 1791; 1,442 sq. mi.; 1970 pop.: 67,440; 1960: 66,370; 1950: 61,407) (Herkimer). Nicholas Herkimer (1728-1777). Brig. gen. N.Y. militia 1775; wounded at Oriskany, N.Y. Aug. 6, 1777; died Aug. 17, 1777. -- Hardin, George A., History of Herkimer County, Syracuse, N.Y.: D. Mason & Co., 1893; 826 p.

Hernando, Fla. (est. Feb. 24, 1843; 488 sq. mi.; 1970 pop.: 17,004; 1960: 11,205; 1950: 6,693) (Brooksville). Hernando de Soto (1496-1542). Spanish conqueror and explorer; served under Pizarro in Panama and Peru; received title gov. of Fla. and Cuba from Charles I.; explored Miss. region; contracted fever and died; buried in Miss. River. (Name changed to Benton County, March 6, 1844 and back to Hernando County Dec. 24, 1850, chap. 415.)

Hertford, N.C. (est. Dec. 12, 1754 sess.; 356 sq. mi.; 1970 pop.: 23,529; 1960: 22,718; 1950: 21,453) (Winton). Hertford, England. Francis Seymour Conway, Marquis of Hertford (1719-1794). Privy Councillor of Ireland 1749;

Ambassador extraordinary and plenipotentiary to Paris 1763-65; lord lt. of Ireland 1765-66; lord Chamberlain of the Household 1766-82. -- Winborne, Benjamin Brodie, The colonial and state political history of Hertford, Murfreesboro, N. C.: Edward & Broughton, 1906; 348 p.

Hettinger, N. D. (est. Mar. 9, 1883, org. Apr. 17, 1907; 1, 135 sq. mi.; 1970 pop.: 5, 075; 1960: 6, 317; 1950: 7, 100) (Mott). Hettinger. N. D. terr. legislature; father-in-law of Erastis A. Williams.

Hickman, Ky. (est. Dec. 19, 1821; 248 sq. mi.; 1970 pop.: 6, 264; 1960: 6, 747; 1950: 7, 778) (Clinton). Paschal Hickman. Capt.

Hickman, Tenn. (est. Dec. 3, 1807; 613 sq. mi.; 1970 pop.: 12, 096; 1960: 11, 862; 1950: 13, 353) (Centerville). Edwin Hickman (-1791). American explorer killed by Indians while exploring Duck River. -- Spence, W. Jerome and Spence, David L., A history of Hickman County, Tennessee, Nashville, Tenn.: Gospel Advocate Pub. Co., 1900; 509 p.

Hickory, Mo. (est. Feb. 14, 1845; 410 sq. mi.; 1970 pop.: 4, 481; 1960: 4, 516; 1950: 5, 387) (Hermitage). "Old Hickory" nickname of Andrew Jackson. (See biography under Jackson). -- Butts, Opal Stewart, Tales of old Hickory County, Dallas, Texas: Royal Pub. Co., 1966; 83 p.

Hidalgo, N. M. (est. Feb. 25, 1919; 3, 447 sq. mi.; 1970 pop.: 4, 734; 1960: 4, 961; 1950: 5, 095) (Lordsburg). Guadalupe Hidalgo, Mexico.

Hidalgo, Tex. (est. Jan. 24, 1852; 1, 641 sq. mi.; 1970 pop.: 181, 535; 1960: 180, 900; 1950: 160, 446) (Edinburg). Miguel Hidalgo y Costilla (1753-1811). Mexican, ordained priest 1779; served thirty years; with his parishioners seized prison at Dolores 1810; decisively beaten at Aculo (1810) and Calderon 1811; shot as a rebel Aug. 1, 1811.

Highland, Ohio (est. Feb. 18, 1805, eff. May 1, 1805; 554 sq. mi.; 1970 pop.: 28, 996; 1960: 29, 716; 1950: 28, 188) (Hillsboro). Descriptive. -- Klise, J. W., ed., The County of Highland, Madison, Wis.: Northwestern Historical Association, 1902; 535 p. -- Morgan, Violet, Folklore of Highland County, Greenfield, Ohio: Greenfield Printing & Pub. Co., 1946; 240 p.

Highland, Va. (est. Mar. 19, 1847; 416 sq. mi.; 1970 pop.: 2, 529; 1960: 3, 221; 1950: 4, 069) (Monterey). Descriptive. -- Morton, Oren Frederic, A History of Highland County, Monterey, Va.: O. F. Morton, 1911; 419 p.

Highlands, Fla. (est. Apr. 23, 1921; 1, 041 sq. mi.; 1970

pop.: 29,507; 1960: 21,338; 1950: 13,636) (Sebring). Descriptive.

Hill, Mont. (est. Feb. 28, 1912 petition and election; 2,944 sq. mi.; 1970 pop.: 17,358; 1960: 18,653; 1950: 14,285) (Havre). James Jerome Hill (1838-1916). RR builder; vice pres. of re-organized St. Paul, Minn. and Manitoba Railway Co. 1882; pres. 1883.

Hill, Tex. (est. Feb. 7, 1853; org. May 14, 1853; 1,028 sq. mi.; 1970 pop.: 22,596; 1960: 23,650; 1950: 31,282) (Hillsboro). George Washington Hill (1814-1860). Surg. at Ft. Houston 1836-37; Tex. congress; secretary of war and navy under Tex. presidents Houston and Jones. 1847, returned to practicing medicine. -- Bailey, Ellis, History of Hill County, Texas, Waco, Texas: Texas Press, 1966; 269 p.

Hillsborough, Fla. (est. Jan. 25, 1834; 1,040 sq. mi.; 1970 pop.: 490,265; 1960: 397,788; 1950: 249,894) (Tampa). Wills Hill, Earl of Hillsborough (1718-1793). Privy councillor of Ireland 1746; English secretary of state for the colonies 1768-72; councillor of King George III. -- Robinson, Ernest Lauren, History of Hillsborough County, St. Augustine, Fla.: The Record Co., 1928; 424 p.

Hillsborough, N.H. (est. Apr. 29, 1769; 890 sq. mi.; 1970 pop.: 223,941; 1960: 178,161; 1950: 156,987) (Nashua and Manchester). Wills Hill, Earl of Hillsborough*. -- Hurd, D. Hamilton, History of Hillsborough County, Philadelphia, Pa.: J.W. Lewis & Co., 1885; 748 p.

Hillsdale, Mich. (est. Oct. 29, 1829, org. 1835; 601 sq. mi.; 1970 pop.: 37,171; 1960: 34,742; 1950: 31,916) (Hillsdale). Descriptive of hill and dale. -- History of Hillsdale County, Philadelphia: Everts & Abbott, 1879; 334 p.

Hinds, Miss. (est. Feb. 12, 1821; 858 sq. mi.; 1970 pop.: 214,973; 1960: 187,045; 1950: 142,164) (Raymond and Jackson). Thomas Hinds (1780-1840). War of 1812, bvt. for gallantry at New Orleans; representative of Miss. in negotiations with Choctaw tribe. Representative from Miss. 1828-31.

Hinsdale, Colo. (est. Feb. 10, 1874; 1,057 sq. mi.; 1970 pop.: 202; 1960: 208; 1950: 263) (Lake City). George A. Hinsdale. Lt. gov. of Colo.

Hitchcock, Neb. (est. Feb. 27, 1873; org. Aug. 30, 1873; 722 sq. mi.; 1970 pop.: 4,051; 1960: 4,829; 1950: 5,867). (Trenton). Phineas Warrener Hitchcock (1831-1881). U.S. marshal 1861-64; delegate from Neb. 1865-67; surveyor gen. of Neb., and Iowa 1867-69; Senator from Neb. 1871-77.

Hocking, Ohio (est. Jan. 3, 1818; 421 sq. mi.; 1970 pop.: 20,322; 1960: 20,168; 1950: 19,520) (Logan). Hocking River named for a Delaware Indian word "hockhock" for "gourd" or "bottle" and "ing" meaning "place" so-called because the river at that point assumed a bottle-like appearance.

Hockley, Tex. (est. Aug. 21, 1876; 903 sq. mi.; 1970 pop.: 20,396; 1960: 22,340; 1950: 20,407) (Levelland). George Washington Hockley (1802-1854). Chief of staff under Sam Houston 1835; battle of San Jacinto 1836; col. of ordinance 1836; Tex. secretary of war 1838 and 1841.

Hodgeman, Kan. (est. Mar. 6, 1873; 860 sq. mi.; 1970 pop.: 2,662; 1960: 3,115; 1950: 3,312) (Jetmore). Amos Hodgeman (18 -1863). Capt. Co. H. Seventh Kan.; died of wounds Oct. 16, 1863.

Hoke, N. C. (est. Feb. 17, 1911; 414 sq. mi.; 1970 pop.: 16,436; 1960: 16,356; 1950: 15,756) (Raeford). Robert Frederick Hoke (1837-1906). Private First N. C. Vol. in Confederate Army 1861; maj., lt. col. 33rd N. C. infantry; col. eleventh N. C. regiment; brig. gen. 1863; maj. gen. 1864; surrendered at Durham Sta., N. C., 1865; pres. Georgia, Carolina and Northern Railway Co., of Seaboard Air Line.

Holmes, Fla. (est. Jan. 8, 1848; 483 sq. mi.; 1970 pop.: 10,720; 1960: 10,844; 1950: 13,988) (Bonifay). ("The County That Can Offer You More"; "The Hub of the Florida Panhandle"). Thomas J. Holmes. Went from N. C. to Fla. 1830. (Indian chief named Holmes.)

Holmes, Miss. (est. Feb. 19, 1833; 751 sq. mi.; 1970 pop.: 23,120; 1960: 27,096; 1950: 33,301) (Lexington). David Holmes (1769-1832). Fourth terr. gov. of Miss., first and fifth gov. of Miss. Representative from Va. 1797-1809; Miss. terr. gov. 1809-17; gov. of Miss. 1817-20 and 1826; Senator from Miss. 1820-25.

Holmes, Ohio (est. Jan. 20, 1824; 424 sq. mi.; 1970 pop.: 23,024; 1960: 21,591; 1950: 18,760) (Millersburg). Andrew Hunter Holmes (-1814). Capt. 24th Infantry Miss. 1812; maj. 1813; bvt. maj. 1814; killed at Ft. Mackinac, Mich., Aug. 4, 1814.

Holt, Mo. (est. Jan. 29, 1841; 456 sq. mi.; 1970 pop.: 6,654; 1960: 7,885; 1950: 9,833) (Oregon). David Rice Holt (1803-1840). Mo. legislature; renounced ministry and entered Va. gen. assembly Nov. 16, 1840. (Formerly Nodaway County, name changed to Holt County, Feb. 15, 1841).

Holt, Neb. (est. Jan. 13, 1860, org. July 13, 1876; 2,408 sq. mi.; 1970 pop.: 12,933; 1960: 13,722; 1950: 14,859)

(O'Neill). Joseph Holt (1807-1894). U. S. Commissioner of Patents 1857; U. S. Postmaster gen. 1859-61; U. S. Secretary of War 1861; judge adv. gen. U. S. Army 1862-75. (Formerly West County, name changed to Holt County, Jan. 9, 1862).

Honolulu, Hawaii (621 sq. mi.; 1970 pop.: 629,176; 1960: 500,409) (Honolulu). ("The Crossroads of the Pacific"). From two Polynesian words, "hono" (fair haven) and "lulu" (calm or quiet). Discovered in 1792 by Capt. William Brown who entered the harbor, although seen by Capt. James Cook in 1778. -- Gessler, C., Tropic Landfall, G'dn City, N. Y., Doubleday, Doran, 1942; 331 p.

Hood, Tex. (est. Nov. 3, 1865; 426 sq. mi.; 1970 pop.: 6,368; 1950: 5,443; 1950: 5,287) (Granbury). John Bell Hood (1831-1879). Graduated U. S. Military Academy 1853; third lt. 1855; first lt. 1858; resigned 1861; commanded 4th Tex. Infantry 1861; brig. gen. and maj. gen. 1862; lt. gen. 1864; lost right leg at Chicamauga 1863; succeeded Gen. Albert Sidney Johnston in command of Confederate Army of Tenn. 1864; defeated at Nashville, relieved of command 1865; died in New Orleans of yellow fever 1879.

Hood River, Ore. (est. June 23, 1908; 529 sq. mi.; 1970 pop.: 13,187; 1960: 13,395; 1950: 12,740) (Hood River). Arthur William Acland Hood (1824-1901). English Navy lt. 1846; commander 1854; at capture of China 1857; director of naval ordnance 1869-74; rear admiral 1876; commander in chief channel fleet 1879-82; First Sea Lord of the Admiralty 1885-89; admiral 1886; elevated to the peerage 1892.

Hooker, Neb. (est. Mar. 29, 1889, org. Apr. 13, 1889; 722 sq. mi.; 1970 pop.: 939; 1960: 1,130; 1950: 1,061) (Mullen). Joseph Hooker (1814-1879). Graduated U. S. Military Academy 1837; first lt. 1838; bvt. capt. 1846; capt. 1848; maj. 1847; lt. col. 1847; resigned 1853; brig. gen. of vol. 1861; maj. gen. vol. 1862; brig. gen. U. S. Army 1862; voted thanks of Congress 1864; bvt. maj. gen. 1865; retired 1868.

Hopkins, Ky. (est. Dec. 9, 1806, eff. May 1, 1807; 555 sq. mi.; 1970 pop.: 38,167; 1960: 38,458; 1950: 38,815) (Madisonville). Samuel Hopkins (1756?-1819) Capt. 6th Va. Regiment 1776; maj. 1777; wounded at Germantown 1777; lt. col. 1778; taken prisoner at Charleston 1780; exchanged 1781.

Hopkins, Tex. (est. Mar. 25, 1846; 793 sq. mi.; 1970 pop.: 20,710; 1960: 18,594; 1950: 23,490) (Sulphur Springs). Hopkins family. -- St. Clair, Gladys Annelle, History of

Hopkins County, Texas, Austin?, Texas, 1965; 90 p.

Horry, S. C. (est. Dec. 19, 1801; 1, 152 sq. mi. ; 1970 pop.: 69, 992; 1960: 68, 247; 1950: 59, 820) (Conway). Peter Horry. Capt. 2nd South Carolina Regiment 1775; maj. 1776; col. S. C. militia 1779-81; brig. gen. ; wounded Eutaw Springs 1781; served to close of war.

Hot Spring, Ark. (est. Nov. 2, 1829; 621 sq. mi. ; 1970 pop. : 21, 963; 1960: 21, 893; 1950: 22, 181) Descriptive. (Malvern).

Hot Springs, Wyo. (est. Feb. 9, 1911; 2, 022 sq. mi. ; 1970 pop. : 4, 952; 1960: 6, 365; 1950: 5, 250) (Thermopolis). Descriptive.

Houghton, Mich. (est. Mar. 19, 1845, org. May 18, 1846; 1, 030 sq. mi. ; 1970 pop. : 34, 652; 1960: 35, 654; 1950: 39, 771) (Houghton). Douglas Houghton (1809-1845). Prof. of chemistry and natural history Rensselaer Polytechnic Institute 1828-30; first state geologist Mich. 1838-41; sank salt well at Salt Creek 1845; drowned in Lake Superior 1845.

Houston, Ala. (est. Feb. 9, 1903; 578 sq. mi. ; 1970 pop. : 56, 574; 1960: 50, 718; 1950: 46, 522) (Dothan). George Smith Houston (1808-1879). Twenty-fifth gov. of Ala. Ala. house of representatives 1832; Ala. state attorney 1836; Representative from Ala. 1841-49 and 1851-61; withdrew 1861; elected but not permitted to take seat 1866; gov. of Ala., 1874-78; Senator from Ala. 1879.

Houston, Ga. (est. May 15, 1821; 443 sq. mi. ; 1970 pop. : 62, 924; 1960: 39, 154; 1950: 20, 964) (Perry). John Houston (1744-1796). Second and tenth gov. of Ga. Chairman Ga. Sons of Liberty 1774; Continental Congress 1775-76; Ga. executive council 1777; gov. of Ga. 1778 and 1784.

Houston, Minn. (est. Feb. 23, 1854; 565 sq. mi. ; 1970 pop. : 17, 556; 1960: 16, 588; 1950: 14, 435) (Caledonia) Samuel Houston (1793-1863). Second and fourth pres. of Tex. Republic, sixth gov. of Tex. Served under Gen. Jackson as sergeant in Creek War, lt. in May 1814, Tenn. adj. gen. 1820, maj. gen. 1821; Representative from Tenn. 1823-27; gov. of Tenn. 1827-29; member of Tex. constitutional convention 1835; commander in chief of the Tex. Army, routed Santa Anna Apr. 21, 1836 battle of San Jacinto, Pres. of Republic of Tex. 1836-38 and 1841-44; Senator from Tex. 1846-59; gov. of Tex. 1859-61. Refused to take oath of allegiance to the Confederate States and was deposed Mar. 18, 1861. Signed Tex. declaration of independence 1836.

Houston, Tenn. (est. Jan. 23, 1871; 207 sq. mi. ; 1970 pop.:

5, 845; 1960: 4, 794; 1950: 5, 318) (Erin). Sam Houston*. -- McClain, Iris Hopkins, History of Houston County, Columbia?, Tenn., 1966; 241 p.

Houston, Tex. (est. June 12, 1837; 1, 232 sq. mi.; 1970 pop.: 17, 855; 1960: 19, 376; 1950: 22, 825) (Crockett). ("The Largest Cattle County in East Texas"). Sam Houston*. -- Aldrich, Armistead Albert, History of Houston County, Texas, San Antonio, Texas: Naylor Co., 1943; 225 p.

Howard, Ark. (est. Apr. 17, 1873; 600 sq. mi.; 1970 pop.: 11, 412; 1960: 10, 878; 1950: 13, 342) (Nashville). James Howard.

Howard, Ind. (est. Jan. 15, 1844, org. Jan. 15, 1844, eff. May 1, 1844; 293 sq. mi.; 1970 pop.: 83, 198; 1960: 69, 509; 1950: 54, 498) (Kokomo). Tilghman Ashurst Howard (1797-1844). Tenn. state senate 1824; district attorney for Ind. 1833-37; Representative from Ind. 1839-40; charge d'affaires to Republic of Tex. 1844. (Formerly Richardville County, name changed to Howard County Dec. 28, 1846). (chap. 168) -- Morrow, Jackson, History of Howard County, Indiana, Indianapolis, Ind.: D. F. Bowen & Co., 1909; 2 vol.

Howard, Iowa (est. Jan. 15, 1851; 471 sq. mi.; 1970 pop.: 11, 442; 1960: 12, 734; 1950: 13, 105) (Cresco). Tilghman Ashurst Howard*. -- Fairbairn, Robert Herd, History of Chickasaw and Howard Counties, Chicago: S. J. Clarke, 1919; 2 vol.

Howard, Md. (est. Maryland Constitution May 13, 1851, art. 8, sec. 1; 251 sq. mi.; 1970 pop.: 61, 911; 1960: 36, 152; 1950: 23, 119) (Ellicott City). John Eager Howard (1752-1827) Fifth gov. of Md. Commanded co. at battle of White Plains 1776; capt. 1776; maj. 1777; lt. col. and col. 1778; received thanks and a medal from Congress for gallantry at Cowpens 1781; wounded Eutaw Springs 1781; retired 1783; Continental Congress 1784-88; gov. of Md., 1788-91; Md. senate 1791-95; Senator from Md. 1796-1803.

Howard, Mo. (est. Jan. 13, 1816; 469 sq. mi.; 1970 pop.: 10, 561; 1960: 10, 859; 1950: 11, 857) (Fayette). ("The Mother of Counties (of Missouri)"). Benjamin Howard (1760-1814). Ky. house of representatives 1800; Representative from Ky., 1807-10; gov. of La. Terr. 1810-12; brig. gen. U. S. Army 1813; commanded the Eighth Military department, terr. west of the Miss. River. -- History of Chariton and Howard Counties, Topeka: Historical Pub. Co., 1923; 856 p. -- History of Howard and Cooper Counties, St. Louis: National Historical Co., 1883; 1167 p.

Howard, Neb. (est. Mar. 1, 1871, org. Mar. 9, 1871; 566 sq. mi.; 1970 pop.: 6,807; 1960: 6,541; 1950: 7,226) (St. Paul). Oliver Otis Howard (1830-1909). Grad. U. S. Military Academy 1854; served in Seminole War, col. of Me. vol. regiment in Civil War, made brig. gen. of vol., served at Bull Run, and lost his right arm at battle of Fair Oaks. Commanded Army of the Cumberland and later Army of the Tenn. Brig. gen. in regular army 1864. Commissioner of the Freedmen's Bureau 1865; pres. of Howard Univ. 1869-73. Supt. at West Point 1881, commanded various departments, promoted to maj. gen. 1886, retired 1894.

Howard, Tex. (est. Aug. 21, 1876; 912 sq. mi.; 1970 pop.: 37,796; 1960: 40,139; 1950: 26,722) (Big Spring). Volney Erskine Howard (1809-1889). Miss. house of representatives 1836; moved to Tex. 1847; state constitutional convention 1845; Representative from Tex. 1849-53; district attorney Los Angeles 1861-70; judge of superior court in Los Angeles 1878-79. Injured in duel with Hiram G. Runnels.

Howell, Mo. (est. Mar. 2, 1857; 920 sq. mi.; 1970 pop.: 23,521; 1960: 22,027; 1950: 22,725) (West Plains). James Howell.

Hubbard, Minn. (est. Feb. 26, 1883; 932 sq. mi.; 1970 pop.: 10,583; 1960: 9,962; 1950: 11,085) (Park Rapids). Lucius Frederick Hubbard (1836-1913). Ninth gov. of Minn. Est. Red Wing, Minn., "Republican" 1857; private 5th Minn. infantry 1861; capt., lt. col. and col. 1862; wounded at Corinth, Miss., 1862; wounded at Nashville, Tenn., bvt. brig. gen. 1864; railroad operations 1868; Minn. senate 1872-76; gov. of Minn. 1882-87; appointed brig. gen. by Pres. McKinley and served in Spanish American War.

Hudson, N.J. (est. Feb. 22, 1840; 45 sq. mi.; 1970 pop.: 609,266; 1960: 610,734; 1950: 647,437) (Jersey City). Henry Hudson (c1569-1611). English navigator; sailed from Amsterdam in "Half Moon" to New York Bay 1609; sailed up North River to Albany, N.Y., set adrift by his crew on the "Discoverie" 1611. -- Stinson, Robert R., comp., Hudson County today, Union, N.J.: Hudson Dispatch, 1915; 162 p. -- Winfield, Charles Hardenbergh, History of the county of Hudson, New York: Kennard & Hay, 1874; 568 p.

Hudspeth, Tex. (est. Feb. 16, 1917; 4,533 sq. mi.; 1970 pop.: 2,392; 1960: 3,343; 1950: 4,298) (Sierra Blanca). Claude Benton Hudspeth (1877-1941). Tex. house of representatives 1902-06; Tex. senate 1906-18; Representative from Texas 1919-31.

Huerfano, Colo. (est. Nov. 1, 1861; 1, 578 sq. mi.; 1970 pop.: 6, 590; 1960: 7, 867; 1950: 10, 549) (Waisenburg). Spanish word for "orphan" referring to Huerfano Butte, an isolated cone-shaped butte in the Huerfano River.

Hughes, Okla. (est. July 16, 1907; 810 sq. mi.; 1970 pop.: 13, 228; 1960: 15, 144; 1950: 20, 664) (Holdenville). William C. Hughes. Okla. constitutional convention 1907.

Hughes, S. D. (est. Jan. 8, 1873; 762 sq. mi.; 1970 pop.: 11, 632; 1960: 12, 725; 1950: 8, 111) (Pierre). Alexander Hughes, of Elk Point; pres. of tenth council in Dakota Terr. legislature 1872-73. -- Hughes County, S. D., office of Superintendent of Schools, Hughes County history, Pierre, S. D., 1937; 205 p.

Humboldt, Calif. (est. May 12, 1853; 3, 573 sq. mi.; 1970 pop.: 99, 692; 1960: 104, 892; 1950: 69, 241) (Eureka). ("The Heart of the Redwood Region"). Friedrich Heinrich Alexander von Humboldt (1769-1859). German naturalist, explorer and statesman. -- Irvine, Leigh Hadley, History of Humboldt County, Los Angeles, Calif.: Historic Record Co., 1915; 1290 p. -- Thornbury, Delmar L., California's Redwood Wonderland, San Francisco, Calif.: Sunset Press, 1923; 167 p.

Humboldt, Iowa (est. Jan. 15, 1851; 435 sq. mi.; 1970 pop.: 12, 519; 1960: 13, 156; 1950: 13, 117) (Dakota City). Friedrich Heinrich Alexander von Humboldt. *. (re-created Jan. 28, 1857)

Humboldt, Nev. (est. Nov. 25, 1861; 9, 702 sq. mi.; 1970 pop.: 6, 375; 1960: 5, 708; 1950: 4, 838) (Winnemucca). Friedrich Heinrich Alexander von Humboldt*.

Humphreys, Miss. (est. Mar. 28, 1918; 408 sq. mi.; 1970 pop.: 14, 601; 1960: 19, 093; 1950: 23, 115) (Belzoni). Benjamin Grubb Humphreys (1808-1882). Twenty-sixth gov. of Miss. Attended U. S. Military Academy 1825-28; Miss. legislature 1837; Miss. senate 1839; capt. Miss. and promoted to col. 21st Miss. regiment; promoted brig. gen. for gallantry 1863; wounded 1864; gov. of Miss. 1865-66.

Humphreys, Tenn. (est. Oct. 19, 1809; 555 sq. mi.; 1970 pop.: 13, 560; 1960: 11, 511; 1950: 11, 030) (Waverly). Parry Wayne Humphreys (1780?-1839). Judge Tenn. superior court 1807-09; judge Tenn. judicial circuit 1809-13 and 1818-36; Representative from Tenn. 1813-15. -- Garrett, Jill Knight, History of Humphreys County, Tenn., Columbia?, Tenn.: J. K. Garrett, 1963; 376 p.

Hunt, Tex. (est. Apr. 11, 1846; 910 sq. mi.; 1970 pop.: 47, 948; 1960: 39, 399; 1950: 42, 736) (Greenville). Memucan Hunt (1807-1856). Maj. gen. Tex. army 1836; brig.

gen. 1836; Minister of the Tex. Republic to the U. S. to secure Tex. recognition 1836; Secretary of the Navy, Tex. Republic 1838-39; boundary commissioner 1839; adj. gen. Somervell expedition 1842.

Hunterdon, N. J. (est. Mar. 13, 1714; 435 sq. mi.; 1970 pop.: 69, 718; 1960: 54, 107; 1950: 42, 736) (Flemington). Robert Hunter (-1734). Appointed gov. of Va. (Royal Province). Maj. gen. English army appointed gov. Va. colony 1707; captured by French at sea, never reached Va.; appointed gov. of New York and of East and West Jersey 1710; resigned 1719; gov. of Jamaica 1727-34. -- Snell, James P. and Ellis, Franklin, History of Hunterdon and Somerset Counties, Philadelphia, Pa.: Everts & Peck, 1881; 864 p.

Huntingdon, Pa. (est. Sept. 20, 1787; 895 sq. mi.; 1970 pop.: 39, 108; 1960: 39, 457; 1950: 40, 872) (Huntingdon). Selina Shirley Hastings (1707-1791), countess of Huntingdon, second of three daughters and co-heiresses of Washington Shirley, second Earl Ferrers, wife of Theophilus Hastings II, ninth Earl of Huntingdon; interested in religion and missionary work. -- Lytle, Milton Scott, History of Huntingdon County, Lancaster, Pa.: W. R. Roy, 1876; 361 p.

Huntington, Ind. (est. Feb. 2, 1832, eff. Apr. 1, 1832, org. Feb. 1, 1834; 390 sq. mi.; 1970 pop.: 34, 970; 1960: 33, 814; 1950: 31, 400) (Huntington). Samuel Huntington (1731-1796). Third gov. of Conn. Continental Congress 1776; pres. Continental Congress 1779-81; chief justice Conn., superior court 1784; lt. gov. of Conn., 1785; gov. of Conn. 1786-96.

Huron, Mich. (est. Apr. 1, 1840, org. 1859; 822 sq. mi.; 1970 pop.: 34, 083; 1960: 34, 006; 1950: 33, 149) (Bad Axe). Huron Indians.

Huron, Ohio (est. Feb. 7, 1809; 497 sq. mi.; 1970 pop.: 49, 587; 1960: 47, 326; 1950: 39, 353) (Norwalk). Huron Indians. -- Baughman, Abraham J., History of Huron County, Chicago: S. J. Clarke Pub. Co., 1909; 2 vol.

Hutchinson, S. D. (est. May 8, 1862; 814 sq. mi.; 1970 pop.: 10, 379; 1960: 11, 085; 1950: 11, 423) (Olivet). John Hutchinson. Acting gov. Dakota terr. 1861-63; secretary of Dakota terr. 1861-65.

Hutchinson, Tex. (est. Aug. 21, 1876; 884 sq. mi.; 1970 pop.: 24, 443; 1960: 34, 419; 1950: 31, 580) (Stinnett). Anderson Hutchinson (1798-1853). District judge 1841 Republic of Tex.; while presiding at court was taken prisoner when San Antonio was captured 1842.

Hyde, N. C. (est. Dec. 3, 1705; 634 sq. mi.; 1970 pop.:

5, 571; 1960: 5, 765; 1950: 6, 479) (Swan Quarter). Edward Hyde, Earl of Clarendon (1661-1723). Deputy gov. of N. C. Appointed by William of Orange as gov. of N. Y. and N. J. 1701; dissolved colonial assemblies; replaced by Lord Lovelace 1708; returned to England; imprisoned for debts; paid debts and released. (Formerly Wickham County, name changed to Hyde County 1712).

Hyde, S. D. (est. Jan. 8, 1873; 869 sq. mi.; 1970 pop.: 2, 515; 1960: 2, 602; 1950: 2, 811) (Highmore). James Hyde (1842-1902). Co. B, second Battalion 16th U. S. Infantry 1862; honorable discharge 1865; confined three months in Libby prison and eleven months at Andersonville; Dakota terr. legislature 1872. -- Perkins, John B., History of Hyde County, South Dakota, [Highmore], 1908; 300 p.

I

Iberia, La. (est. Oct. 30, 1868; 589 sq. mi.; 1970 pop.: 57, 397; 1960: 51, 657; 1950: 40, 059) (New Iberia). Original name for Spain.

Iberville, La. (est. Apr. 10, 1805; 584 sq. mi.; 1970 pop.: 30, 746; 1960: 29, 939; 1950: 26, 750) (Plaquemine). Pierre le Moyne Iberville (1661-1706). In French navy, assisted in capture of English forts at Hudson Bay in 1686; captured Ft. Severns and Albany 1689; other important victories 1689-97; built Ft. Biloxi at Biloxi Bay 1699; captured island of Nevis 1706. -- Grace, Albert L., The Heart of the Sugar Bowl, Plaquemine, La., 1946; 249 p.

Ida, Iowa (est. Jan. 15, 1851; 431 sq. mi.; 1970 pop.: 9, 190; 1960: 10, 269; 1950: 10, 697) (Ida Grove). Ida Mountain, Crete, named at the suggestion of Eliphalet Price.

Idaho, Idaho (est. Feb. 4, 1864; 8, 515 sq. mi.; 1970 pop.: 12, 891; 1960: 13, 542; 1950: 11, 423) (Grangeville). Indian word, contraction of Shoshoni "Ee-da-how," meaning "It's sunrise" or "It's morning." -- Elsensohn, Alfreda, Pioneer Days In Idaho County, Caldwell, Idaho: Caxton Printers, 1951; 2 vol.

Imperial, Calif. (est. election Aug. 6, 1907, org. Aug. 26, 1907; 4, 284 sq. mi.; 1970 pop.: 74, 492; 1960: 72, 105; 1950: 69, 241) (El Centro). ("The Winter Vegetable Garden"). Named for Imperial Land Co. which sold property in the Colo. desert. -- Farr, Finis C., History of Imperial County, Berkeley, Calif.: Elms and Frank, 1918; 516 p.

Independence, Ark. (est. Oct. 23, 1820; 755 sq. mi. ; 1970 pop. : 22, 723; 1960: 20, 048; 1950: 23, 488) (Batesville). The Declaration of Independence.

Indian River, Fla. (est. May 30, 1925; 511 sq. mi. ; 1970 pop. : 35, 992; 1960: 25, 309; 1950: 11, 872) (Vero Beach). Descriptive.

Indiana, Pa. (est. Mar. 30, 1803; 831 sq. mi. ; 1970 pop. : 79, 451; 1960: 75, 366; 1950: 77, 106) (Indiana). ("The Christmas Tree County (cutting approximately 750, 000 trees annually)"; "The Christmas Tree Capital of the World"; "The Coal Capital of Central Pennsylvania (in the heart of the bituminous coal region)"). Indiana terr. -- Stewart, Joshua Thompson, comp., Indiana County, Chicago: J. H. Beers & Co., 1913; 2 vol.

Ingham, Mich. (est. Oct. 29, 1829, org. 1838; 559 sq. mi.; 1970 pop. : 261, 039; 1960: 211, 296; 1950: 172, 941) (Mason). Samuel Delucenna Ingham (1779-1860). Pa. house of representatives 1806-08; Representative from Pa., 1813-18 and 1822-29; prothonotary of the courts of Buck County 1818-19; Secretary of Pa., 1819-20; Secretary of the Treas. in the cabinet of Pres. Jackson 1829-31. -- Durant, Samuel W., History of Ingham and Eaton Counties, Philadelphia: D. W. Ensign & Co., 1880; 586 p.

Inyo, Calif. (est. Mar. 22, 1866; 10, 091 sq. mi. ; 1970 pop.: 15, 571; 1960: 11, 684; 1950: 11, 658) (Independence). ("The Photographers Playground"; "The Picture County"; "The Vacation and Recreation Land"). Indian word for "dwelling place of a great spirit." -- Chalfont, Willie Arthur, The Story of Inyo, Los Angeles, Calif., 1933; 430 p. -- Inyo, 1866-1966; Bishop, Calif.: Chalfant Press, 1966; 95 p.

Ionia, Mich. (est. Mar. 2, 1831, org. Mar. 18, 1837, eff. Apr. 7, 1837; 575 sq. mi. ; 1970 pop. : 45, 848; 1960: 43, 132; 1950: 38, 158) (Ionia). Ionia, Greece. -- Branch, Elam Edgar, History of Ionia County, Indianapolis: B. F. Bowen & Co., Inc., 1916; 2 vol.

Iosco, Mich. (est. Apr. 1, 1840, org. 1857; 547 sq. mi. ; 1970 pop. : 24, 905; 1960: 16, 505; 1950: 10, 906) (Tawas City). Indian word for "shining water." (Originally Kanotin County, name changed to Iosco County on March 8, 1843).

Iowa, Iowa (est. Feb. 17, 1843, org. June 10, 1845, eff. July 1, 1845; 584 sq. mi. ; 1970 pop. : 15, 419; 1960: 16, 396; 1950: 15, 835) (Marengo). Iowa Indian tribe whose name means "sleepy ones," or "drowsy ones." -- History of Iowa County, Des Moines: Union Historical Co., 1881; 774 p.

Iowa, Wis. (est. Oct. 9, 1829; 761 sq. mi.; 1970 pop.: 19,306; 1960: 19,631; 1950: 19,610) (Dodgeville). Iowa Indian tribe*. -- History of Iowa County, Chicago: Western Historical Co., 1881; 970 p.

Iredell, N. C. (est. sess. Nov. 3, 1788; 591 sq. mi.; 1970 pop.: 72,197; 1960: 62,526; 1950: 56,303) (Statesville). ("The Dairyland County in North Carolina"; "The Dairyland of the Southeastern United States"). James Iredell (1788-1853). Twenty-third gov. of N. C. Capt. of vol. company in War of 1812; N. C. house of commons 1813 and 1816-28; speaker 1817-22; N. C. superior court judge 1819; gov. of N. C. 1827-28; Senator from N. C., 1828-31; reporter of N. C. supreme court 1840-52.

Irion, Tex. (est. Mar. 7, 1889; 1,073 sq. mi.; 1970 pop.: 1,070; 1960: 1,183; 1950: 1,590) (Mertzon). Robert Anderson Irion (1802-1861). Physician; senator in first Tex. congress 1836-37; secretary of state in Houston's cabinet of Republic of Tex. 1837-38. -- Crawford, Leta, History of Irion County, Waco, Tex., Texian Press, 1966; 152 p.

Iron, Mich. (est. Apr. 3, 1885; 1,197 sq. mi.; 1970 pop.: 13,813; 1960: 17,184; 1950: 17,692) (Crystal Falls). Descriptive. -- Hill, Jack, A History of Iron County, Iron River, Mich., 1955; 129 p.

Iron, Mo. (est. Feb. 17, 1857; 554 sq. mi.; 1970 pop.: 9,529; 1960: 8,041; 1950: 9,458) (Ironton). Descriptive.

Iron, Utah (est. Mar. 3, 1852; 3,300 sq. mi.; 1970 pop.: 12,177; 1960: 10,795; 1950: 9,642) (Parowan). Descriptive. (Form. Little Salt Lake County, name ch. Dec. 3, 1850.)

Iron, Wis. (est. Mar. 1, 1893; 748 sq. mi.; 1970 pop.: 6,533; 1960: 7,830; 1950: 8,714) (Hurley). Descriptive.

Iroquois, Ill. (est. Feb. 26, 1833; 1,121 sq. mi.; 1970 pop.: 33,532; 1960: 33,562; 1950: 32,348) (Watseka). Iroquois Indian tribe. -- Beckwith, H. W., History of Iroquois County, Chicago: H. H. Hill & Co., 1880; 671 p.

Irwin, Ga. (est. Dec. 15, 1818; 378 sq. mi.; 1970 pop.: 8,036; 1960: 9,211; 1950: 11,973) (Ocilla). Jared Irwin (1750-1818). Eighteenth and twenty-third gov. of Ga. Brig. gen. of Ga., militia; Ga. constitutional convention 1789; Ga. legislature 1790; gov. of Ga. 1796-98 and 1806-09; permanent constitutional convention 1798. -- Clements, James Bagley, History of Irwin County, Atlanta, Foote & Davies Co., 1932; 539 p.

Isabella, Mich. (est. Mar. 2, 1831, org. 1859; 572 sq.mi.; 1970 pop.: 44,594; 1960: 35,348; 1950: 28,864) (Mount Pleasant). Isabella of Castille (1451-1504) Queen of Spain, married Ferdinand V, King of Aragon; financed Columbus' expedition.

Isanti, Minn. (est. Feb. 13, 1857; 442 sq. mi.; 1970 pop.: 16, 560; 1960: 13, 530; 1950: 12, 123) (Cambridge). Izatys Indians (now Santees).

Island, Wash. (est. Jan. 6, 1853; 206 sq. mi.; 1970 pop.: 27, 011; 1960: 19, 638; 1950: 11, 079) (Coupeville). Descriptive.

Isle of Wight, Va. (est. 1634; 321 sq. mi.; 1970 pop.: 18, 285; 1960: 17, 164; 1950: 14, 906) (Isle of Wight). Isle of Wight, England. (Form. Warrosquyoake until 1637.)

Issaquena, Miss. (est. Jan. 23, 1844; 406 sq. mi.; 1970 pop.: 2, 737; 1960: 3, 576; 1950: 4, 966) (Mayersville). Indian name for "deer river."

Itasca, Minn. (est. Oct. 27, 1849, org. Mar. 6, 1857; 2, 663 sq. mi.; 1970 pop.: 35, 530; 1960: 38, 006; 1950: 33, 321) (Grand Rapids). Coined word; last two syllables of Latin "veritas" (truth) with first syllable of "caput" (head or source).

Itawamba, Miss. (est. Feb. 9, 1836; 529 sq. mi.; 1970 pop.: 16, 847; 1960: 15, 080; 1950: 17, 216) (Fulton). Itawamba. Indian chief. -- Reed, Forrest Francis, Itawamba, a History of a County in Northeast Miss., Nashville, Tenn.: Reed & Co., 1966; 186 p.

Izard, Ark. (est. Oct. 27, 1825, eff. Jan. 1, 1826; 574 sq. mi.; 1970 pop.: 7, 381; 1960: 6, 766; 1950: 9, 953) (Melbourne). George Izard (1777-1828). Second terr. gov. of Ark. Lt. of artillery 1794; in charge of Charleston harbor fortifications 1798; on staff of maj. gen. Alexander Hamilton 1799; resigned as capt. of artillery 1803; col. of U. S. artillery in War of 1812; brig. gen. 1813; maj. gen. 1814; terr. gov. of Ark. 1825-29; died in office. -- Shannon, Karr, History of Izard County, Little Rock, Ark.: Democrat Printing & Lithographing Co., 1947; 158 p.

J

Jack, Tex. (est. Aug. 27, 1856; 944 sq. mi.; 1970 pop.: 6, 711; 1960: 7, 418; 1950: 7, 755) (Jacksboro). William Houston Jack (1806-1844). Ga. legislature 1829; battle of San Jacinto 1836; Tex. Secretary of State under David G. Burnet, Apr. 2 - Oct. 22, 1836; Tex. house of representatives; Tex. senate. His brother Patrick Churchill Jack (1808-1844). Delegate to conventions of 1822 and 1823, Tex. house of representatives 1837-38; district attorney first judicial district 1840 and sixth judicial district 1841; died of yellow fever. -- Huckabay, Ida (Lasater), Ninety-four years in Jack County 1854-1948, Jacksboro?, Texas, 1949; 513 p.

Jackson, Ala. (est. Dec. 13, 1819; 1,124 sq. mi.; 1970 pop.: 39,202; 1960: 36,681; 1950: 38,998) (Scottsboro). Andrew Jackson (1767-1845). Seventh Pres. of the U.S.; first terr. gov. of Fla. Tenn. constitutional convention 1788; Representative from Tenn., 1796-97; Senator from Tenn. 1797-98; judge Tenn. supreme court 1798-1804; maj. gen. of vol. 1812-14; fought Creek War 1813; brig. gen. U.S. Army and maj. gen. 1814; defeated British at battle of New Orleans 1815; received gold medal and thanks of Congress 1815; captured Fla. 1817; military gov. of Fla. 1821-22; Senator from Tenn. 1823-25; Pres. of the U.S. 1829-37. -- Kennamer, John Robert, History of Jackson County, Winchester, Tenn.: Press of Southern Printing & Pub. Co., 1935; 210 p.

Jackson, Ark. (est. Nov. 5, 1829, eff. Dec. 25, 1829; 637 sq. mi.; 1970 pop.: 20,452; 1960: 22,843; 1950: 25,912) (Newport). Andrew Jackson*.

Jackson, Colo. (est. May 5, 1909; 1,623 sq. mi.; 1970 pop.: 1,811; 1960: 1,758; 1950: 1,976) (Walden). Andrew Jackson*.

Jackson, Fla. (est. Aug. 12, 1822; 942 sq. mi.; 1970 pop.: 34,434; 1960: 36,208; 1950: 34,645) (Marianna). ("North Florida's Greatest Agricultural County"; "Northwest Florida's Key Agricultural County"; "The Peanut Center (world's largest peanut mill at Graceville)"). Andrew Jackson*. -- Stanley, J. Randall, History of Jackson County, Marianna?, Fla.: Jackson County Historical Society, 1950; 281 p.

Jackson, Ga. (est. Feb. 11, 1796; 355 sq. mi.; 1970 pop.: 21,093; 1960: 18,499; 1950: 18,997) (Jefferson). James Jackson (1757-1806). Nineteenth gov. of Ga. In Revolutionary War, lt., wounded at Midway, Ga., brig. gen. 1778; Representative from Ga., 1789-91; Senator from Ga., 1793-95; gov. of Ga. 1798-1801; Senator from Ga., 1801-06. -- Elrod, Frary, Historical Notes on Jackson County, Jefferson, Ga., 1967; 234 p. -- Wilson, Gustavus James Nash, Early History of Jackson County, Atlanta, Ga.: Foote & Davies Co., 1914; 343 p.

Jackson, Ill. (est. Jan. 10, 1816; 588 sq. mi.; 1970 pop.: 55,008; 1960: 42,151; 1950: 38,124) (Murphysboro). Andrew Jackson*. -- Portrait and Biographical Record of Randolph, Jackson, Perry and Monroe Counties, Chicago: Biographical Pub. Co., 1894; 882 p.

Jackson, Ind. (est. Dec. 18, 1835, eff. Jan. 1, 1816; 520 sq. mi.; 1970 pop.: 33,187; 1960: 30,556; 1950: 28,237)

(Brownstown). Andrew Jackson*.

Jackson, Iowa (est. Dec. 21, 1837; 644 sq. mi.; 1970 pop.: 20,839; 1960: 20,754; 1950: 18,622) (Maquoketa). Andrew Jackson*. -- Ellis, James Whitcomb, History of Jackson County, Chicago: S. J. Clarke Pub. Co., 1910; 2 vol.

Jackson, Kan. (est. Aug. 30, 1855; 656 sq. mi.; 1970 pop.: 10,342; 1960: 10,309; 1950: 11,098) (Holton). Andrew Jackson*. (Originally Calhoun County, name changed to Jackson County, Feb. 11, 1859).

Jackson, Ky. (est. Feb. 2, 1858; 337 sq. mi.; 1970 pop.: 10,005; 1960: 10,677; 1950: 13,101) (McKee). Andrew Jackson*.

Jackson, La. (est. Feb. 27, 1845; 578 sq. mi.; 1970 pop.: 15,963; 1960: 15,828; 1950: 15,434) (Jonesboro). Andrew Jackson*.

Jackson, Mich. (est. Oct. 29, 1829, org. June 26, 1832, eff. Aug. 1, 1832; 705 sq. mi.; 1970 pop.: 143,274; 1960: 131,994; 1950: 107,925) (Jackson). Andrew Jackson*. -- History of Jackson County, Chicago: Inter-State Pub. Co., 1881; 1156 p.

Jackson, Minn. (est. May 23, 1857; 698 sq. mi.; 1970 pop.: 14,352; 1960: 15,501; 1950: 16,306) (Jackson). Henry Jackson. One of the first merchants in St. Paul, Minn., 1842; first justice of the peace 1843; first postmaster 1846-49; first terr. legislature. -- Rose, Arthur P., An illustrated history of Jackson County, Jackson, Minn.: Northern History Pub. Co., 1910; 586 p.

Jackson, Miss. (est. Dec. 18, 1812; 710 sq. mi.; 1970 pop.: 87,975; 1960: 55,522; 1950: 31,401) (Pascagoula). ("Mississippi's Number One Port and Industrial County"). Andrew Jackson*. -- McCain, William David, The story of Jackson, Jackson, Miss.: J. F. Hyer Pub. Co., 1953; 2 vol.

Jackson, Mo. (est. Dec. 15, 1826; 603 sq. mi.; 1970 pop.: 654,558; 1960: 622,732; 1950: 541,035) (Independence). Andrew Jackson*. -- Hickman, W. Z., History of Jackson County, Missouri, Topeka: Historical Pub. Co., 1920; 832 p.

Jackson, N. C. (est. Jan. 29, 1851; 499 sq. mi.; 1970 pop.: 21,593; 1960: 17,780; 1950: 19,261) (Sylva). Andrew Jackson*.

Jackson, Ohio (est. Jan. 12, 1816; 420 sq. mi.; 1970 pop.: 27,174; 1960: 29,372; 1950: 27,767) (Jackson). Andrew Jackson*. -- Williams, Daniel Webster, A history of Jackson County, Jackson, Ohio, 1900.

Jackson, Okla. (est. July 16, 1907; 780 sq. mi.; 1970 pop.: 30,902; 1960: 29,736; 1950: 20,082) (Altus). Andrew Jackson*.

Jackson, Ore. (est. Jan. 12, 1852; 2,817 sq. mi.; 1970 pop.: 94,533; 1960: 73,962; 1950: 58,510) (Medford). Andrew Jackson*.

Jackson, S. D. (est. Nov. 1914, org. Feb. 9, 1915; 809 sq. mi.; 1970 pop.: 1,531; 1960: 1,985; 1950: 1,768) (Kadoka). John R. Jackson of Valley Springs, speaker of the house 13th sess. 1879. Councilman fifteenth Dakota terr. legislature 1883. -- Jackson-Washabaugh County Historical Society, Jackson-Washabaugh Counties, Kadoka, S. D. ?, 1966; 345 p.

Jackson, Tenn. (est. Nov. 6, 1801; 327 sq. mi.; 1970 pop.: 8,141; 1960: 9,233; 1950: 12,348) (Gainesboro). Andrew Jackson*.

Jackson, Tex. (est. Mar. 17, 1836; 854 sq. mi.; 1970 pop.: 12,975; 1960: 14,040; 1950: 12,916) (Edna). Andrew Jackson*. -- Taylor, Ira Thomas, The cavalcade of Jackson County, San Antonio, Texas: Naylor Co., 1938; 471 p.

Jackson, W. Va. (est. Mar. 1, 1831; 472 sq. mi.; 1970 pop.: 20,903; 1960: 18,541; 1950: 15,299) (Ripley). Andrew Jackson*.

Jackson, Wis. (est. Feb. 11, 1853; 1,000 sq. mi.; 1970 pop.: 15,325; 1960: 15,151; 1950: 16,073) (Black River Falls). Andrew Jackson*.

James City, Va. (est. 1634; 150 sq. mi.; 1970 pop.: 17,853; 1960: 11,539; 1950: 6,317) (Williamsburg). See James I, 1603-1625. James II (1633-1701), King of England, Scotland and Ireland 1685-88. Became king upon death of his brother, Charles II, 1685; escaped to France after William of Orange landed in England 1688; landed in Ireland 1689 and decisively beaten at the battle of the Boyne 1690.

Jasper, Ga. (est. Dec. 10, 1807; 321 sq. mi.; 1970 pop.: 5,760; 1960: 6,135; 1950: 7,473) (Monticello). William Jasper (1750-1779). Private and sergeant in Col. William Moultrie's Second S. C. Infantry 1775; distinguished himself during attack on Ft. Moultrie June 28, 1776; killed while planting S. C. flag at battle of Savannah Oct. 9, 1779. (Originally Randolph County, name changed on Dec. 10, 1812.)

Jasper, Ill. (est. Feb. 15, 1831; 495 sq. mi.; 1970 pop.: 10,741; 1960: 11,346; 1950: 12,266) (Newton). William Jasper*.

Jasper, Ind. (est. Feb. 7, 1835, org. Feb. 17, 1838, eff. Mar. 15, 1838; 562 sq. mi.; 1970 pop.: 20,429; 1960: 18,842; 1950: 17,031) (Rensselaer). William Jasper*.

Jasper, Iowa (est. Jan. 13, 1846; 736 sq. mi.; 1970 pop.: 35,425; 1960: 35,282; 1950: 32,305) (Newton). William Jasper*.

Jasper, Miss. (est. Dec. 23, 1833; 667 sq. mi.; 1970 pop.: 15,994; 1960: 16,909; 1950: 18,912) (Bay Springs and Paulding). William Jasper*.

Jasper, Mo. (est. Jan. 29, 1841; 642 sq. mi.; 1970 pop.: 79,852; 1960: 78,863; 1950: 79,106) (Carthage). William Jasper*. -- Livingston, Joel Thomas, A history of Jasper County, Missouri, Chicago: Lewis Pub. Co., 1912; 2 vol.

Jasper, S.C. (est. Jan. 30, 1912; 578 sq. mi.; 1970 pop.: 11,885; 1960: 12,237; 1950: 10,995) (Ridgeland). William Jasper*. -- Perry, Grace (Fox), Moving finger of Jasper, Ridgeland, S.C.: Jasper County Centennial Commission, 1962; 218 p.

Jasper, Tex. (est. Mar. 17, 1836; 969 sq. mi.; 1970 pop.: 24,692; 1960: 22,100; 1950: 20,049) (Jasper). William Jasper*.

Jay, Ind. (est. Feb. 7, 1835, org. Jan. 30, 1836, eff. Mar. 1, 1836; 386 sq. mi.; 1970 pop.: 23,575; 1960: 22,572; 1950: 23,157) (Portland). John Jay (1745-1829). Second gov. of N.Y. Continental Congress 1774-77, 1778 and 1779; chief justice N.Y. supreme court 1777-78; pres. of Continental Congress 1778-79; U.S. Minister to Spain 1779; minister to negotiate peace treaty with Great Britain 1781; Secretary of Foreign Affairs 1784-89; first Chief Justice of U.S. Supreme Court 1789-95; U.S. Minister to Great Britain 1794-95; gov. of N.Y. 1795-1801; retired.

Jeff Davis, Ga. (est. Aug. 18, 1905, eff. Jan. 1, 1906; 300 sq. mi.; 1970: 9,425; 1960: 8,914; 1950: 9,299) (Hazlehurst). Jefferson Davis (1808-1889). Graduated U.S. Military Academy 1828; Black Hawk War 1830-31; Representative from Miss. 1845-46; commanded Miss Riflemen 1846; with Gen. Taylor in Mexico 1846; declined appointment as brig. gen. 1847; Senator from Miss., 1847-51; U.S. Secretary of War in cabinet of Pres. Pierce 1853-57; Senator from Miss. 1857-61; resigned from U.S. Senate 1861; maj. gen. of Miss. militia 1861; pres. of provisional Confederate congress 1861; president of the Confederacy 1862; captured 1865; indicted for treason 1866; paroled 1867.

Jeff Davis, Tex. (est. Mar. 15, 1887; 2,258 sq. mi.; 1970 pop.: 1,527; 1960: 1,582; 1950: 2,090) (Fort Davis). Jefferson Davis*.

Jefferson, Ala. (est. Dec. 13, 1819; 1,117 sq. mi.; 1970 pop.: 644,991; 1960: 634,864; 1950: 558,928) (Birmingham). Thomas Jefferson (1743-1826). Third Pres. of the U.S. Second gov. of Va. (Commonwealth). Va. house of burgesses 1769-74; Continental Congress 1775-76;

signer of Declaration of Independence 1776; gov. of Va., 1779-81; Va. house of delegates 1782; Continental Congress 1783-85; U. S. Minister to France 1784-87; U. S. Secretary of State in cabinet of Pres. Washington 1790-93; vice pres. of the U. S. 1797-1801; Pres. of the U. S. 1801-09. -- DuBose, John Witherspoon, Jefferson County and Birmingham, Ala., Birmingham, Ala.: Temple & Smith, 1887; 595 p.

Jefferson, Ark. (est. Nov. 2, 1829, eff. Jan. 1, 1820; 890 sq. mi.; 1970 pop.: 85,329; 1960: 81,373; 1950: 76,075) (Pine Bluff). Thomas Jefferson*.

Jefferson, Colo. (est. Nov. 1, 1861; 786 sq. mi.; 1970 pop.: 233,031; 1960: 127,520; 1950: 55,687) (Golden). Thomas Jefferson*.

Jefferson, Fla. (est. Jan. 6, 1827; 598 sq. mi.; 1970 pop.: 8,778; 1960: 9,543; 1950: 10,413) (Monticello). ("The County of Charm, Culture, Tradition"; "The Crossroads of Florida"). Thomas Jefferson*.

Jefferson, Ga. (est. Feb. 20, 1796; 646 sq. mi.; 1970 pop.: 17,174; 1960: 17,468; 1950: 18,855) (Louisville). Thomas Jefferson*. -- Thomas, Z. V., History of Jefferson County, J. W. Burke Co., 1927; 144 p.

Jefferson, Idaho (est. Feb. 18, 1913; 1,089 sq. mi.; 1970 pop.: 11,619; 1960: 11,672; 1950: 10,495) (Rigby). Thomas Jefferson*.

Jefferson, Ill. (est. Mar. 26, 1819; 603 sq. mi.; 1970 pop.: 31,446; 1960: 32,315; 1950: 35,892) (Mount Vernon). Thomas Jefferson*. -- Perrin, William Henry, History of Jefferson County, Chicago: Globe Pub. Co., 1883; 419 p.

Jefferson, Ind. (est. Nov. 23, 1810, eff. Feb. 1, 1811; 366 sq. mi.; 1970 pop.: 27,006; 1960: 24,061; 1950: 21,613) (Madison). Thomas Jefferson*.

Jefferson, Iowa (est. Jan. 21, 1839; 436 sq. mi.; 1970 pop.: 15,774; 1960: 15,818; 1950: 15,696) (Fairfield). Thomas Jefferson*. -- Weaver, James Baird, Past and present of Jasper County, Indianapolis: B. F. Bowen & Co., 1912; 2 vol. -- Fulton, Charles J., History of Jefferson County, Chicago: S. J. Clarke Pub. Co., 1914; 2 vol.

Jefferson, Kan. (est. Aug. 30, 1855; 549 sq. mi.; 1970 pop.: 11,945; 1960: 11,252; 1950: 11,084) (Oskaloosa). Thomas Jefferson*. -- First One Hundred Years of Jefferson County, 1855-1955.

Jefferson, Ky. (est. May 1, 1780, sess. eff. Nov. 1, 1780; 375 sq. mi.; 1970 pop.: 695,055; 1960: 610,947; 1950: 484,615) (Louisville). Thomas Jefferson*.

Jefferson, La. (est. Feb. 11, 1825; 426 sq. mi.; 1970 pop.: 357,568; 1960: 208,769; 1950: 103,873) (Gretna). Thomas Jefferson*.

Jefferson, Miss. (est. Apr. 2, 1799 procl., Jan. 11, 1802; 507 sq. mi.; 1970 pop.: 9,295; 1960: 10,142; 1950: 11,306) (Fayette). Thomas Jefferson*. (Formerly Pickering County, name changed to Jefferson County, Jan. 11, 1802).

Jefferson, Mo. (est. Dec. 8, 1818; 667 sq. mi.; 1970 pop.: 105,248; 1960: 66,377; 1950: 38,007) (Hillsboro). Thomas Jefferson*. -- Boyer, Mary Joan, Jefferson County, Missouri, in story and pictures, Imperial, Mo., 1958; 179 p.

Jefferson, Mont. (est. Feb. 2, 1865; 1,651 sq. mi.; 1970 pop.: 5,238; 1960: 4,297; 1950: 4,014) (Boulder). Thomas Jefferson*.

Jefferson, Neb. (est. Jan. 26, 1856, org. Oct. 23, 1865; 577 sq. mi.; 1970 pop.: 10,436; 1960: 11,620; 1950: 13,623) (Fairbury). Thomas Jefferson*. (Form. Jones City, name changed to Jefferson Oct. 23, 1865).

Jefferson, N.Y. (est. Mar. 28, 1805; 1,293 sq. mi.; 1970 pop.: 88,508; 1960: 87,835; 1950: 85,521) (Watertown). Thomas Jefferson*. -- Durant, Samuel W. and Peirce, Henry B., History of Jefferson County, Philadelphia: L. H. Evarts & Co., 1878; 593 p. -- Emerson, Edgar C., Our County and its people, Boston: Boston History Co., 1254 p.

Jefferson, Ohio (est. July 27, 1797; 411 sq. mi.; 1970 pop.: 96,193; 1960: 99,201; 1950: 96,495) (Steubenville). Thomas Jefferson*. -- Sinclair, Mary (Donaldson), Pioneer days, Steubenville, Ohio, 1962; 172 p.

Jefferson, Okla. (est. July 16, 1907; 755 sq. mi.; 1970 pop.: 7,125; 1960: 8,192; 1950: 11,122) (Waurika). Thomas Jefferson*.

Jefferson, Ore. (est. Dec. 12, 1914; 1,794 sq. mi.; 1970 pop.: 8,548; 1960: 7,130; 1950: 5,536) (Madras). Thomas Jefferson*. -- Jefferson County Library Association, Jefferson County Reminiscences, Portland, Ore.: Binfords & Mort., 1957; 384 p.

Jefferson, Pa. (est. Mar. 26, 1804; 652 sq. mi.; 1970 pop.: 43,695; 1960: 46,792; 1950: 49,147) (Brookville). Thomas Jefferson*. -- McKnight, William James, Jefferson County, Chicago: J.H. Beers & Co., 1917; 2 vol.

Jefferson, Tenn. (est. June 11, 1792; 318 sq. mi.; 1970 pop.: 24,940; 1960: 21,493; 1950: 19,667) (Dandridge). Thomas Jefferson*.

Jefferson, Tex. (est. Mar. 17, 1836; 945 sq. mi.; 1970 pop.: 244,773; 1960: 245,659; 1950: 195,083) (Beaumont). Thomas Jefferson*. -- East, Lorecia, History and progress of Jefferson County, Dallas, Texas: Royal Pub. Co., 1961; 168 p.

Jefferson, Wash. (est. Dec. 22, 1852; 1,812 sq. mi.; 1970

pop.: 10,661; 1960: 9,639; 1950: 11,618) (Port Townsend). Thomas Jefferson*. -- Jefferson County Historical Society, With pride in heritage, history of Jefferson County, Port Townsend, Wash.: Jefferson County Historical Society, 1966; 422 p.

Jefferson, W. Va. (est. Jan. 8, 1801; 212 sq. mi.; 1970 pop.: 21,280; 1960: 18,665; 1950: 17,184) (Charles Town). Thomas Jefferson*. -- Bushong, Millard Kessler, A history of Jefferson County, Charles Town, W. Va.: Jefferson Pub. Co., 1941.

Jefferson, Wis. (est. Dec. 7, 1836, 564 sq. mi.; 1970 pop.: 60,060; 1960: 50,094; 1950: 43,069) (Jefferson). Thomas Jefferson*. -- Ott, John Henry, Jefferson County; Chicago: S. J. Clarke Pub. Co., 1917; 2 vol.

Jefferson Davis, La. (est. June 12, 1912; 729 sq. mi.; 1970 pop.: 29,554; 1960: 29,825; 1950: 26,298) (Jennings). Jefferson Davis*.

Jefferson Davis, Miss. (est. Mar. 31, 1906; 404 sq. mi.; 1970 pop.: 12,936; 1960: 13,540; 1950: 15,500) (Prentiss). Jefferson Davis*.

Jenkins, Ga. (est. Aug. 17, 1905; 342 sq. mi.; 1970 pop.: 8,332; 1960: 9,148; 1950: 10,264) (Millen). Charles Jones Jenkins (1805-1883). Forty-third gov. of Ga. Ga. legislature 1830; Ga. attorney gen. 1831; solicitor gen. of Ga. middle circuit 1831; elected ten times to Ga. leg. 1836-49; speaker of the house 1840, 1843 and 1845; Ga. senate 1856; Ga. supreme court 1860; gov. of Ga. 1865-67; pres. Ga. constitutional convention 1877.

Jennings, Ind. (est. Dec. 27, 1816, eff. Feb. 1, 1817; 377 sq. mi.; 1970 pop.: 19,454; 1960: 17,267; 1950: 15,250) (Vernon). Jonathan Jennings (1784-1834). First gov. of Ind. Clerk in Ind. Terr. legislature 1807; Representative from Ind. 1809-16 and 1822-31; Ind. constitutional convention 1816; gov. of Indiana 1816-22; one of commission of three appointed by Pres. Jackson to settle Indian claims 1833.

Jerauld, S. D. (est. Mar. 9, 1883; 528 sq. mi.; 1970 pop.: 3,310; 1960: 4,048; 1950: 4,476) (Wessington Springs). H. A. Jerauld. Dakota terr. legislature 1883. -- Dunham, Niles J., History of Jerauld County, South Dakota, from the earliest settlement to Jan. 1, 1909, Washington Springs, S. D., 1910; 441 p. -- Dunham, Fred N., History of Jerauld County South Dakota from Jan. 1, 1909 to Dec. 31, 1961, Washington Springs, S. D., 1963; 552 p.

Jerome, Idaho (est. Feb. 8, 1919; 593 sq. mi.; 1970 pop.: 10,253; 1960: 11,712; 1950: 12,030) (Jerome). Jerome Hill.

Jersey, Ill. (est. Feb. 28, 1839; 367 sq. mi.; 1970 pop.: 18,492; 1960: 17,023; 1950: 15,264) (Jerseyville). New Jersey. -- Hamilton, Oscar Brown, History of Jersey County, Chicago: Munsell Pub. Co., 1919; 664 p.

Jessamine, Ky. (est. Dec. 19, 1798, eff. Feb. 1, 1799; 177 sq. mi.; 1970 pop.: 17,430; 1960: 13,625; 1950: 12,458) (Nicholasville). Douglas Jessamine. -- Young, Bennett Henderson, A history of Jessamine County, Kentuckey, Courier Journal Job Printing Co., 1898; 286 p.

Jewell, Kan. (est. Feb. 26, 1867; 915 sq. mi.; 1970 pop.: 6,099; 1960: 7,217; 1950: 9,698) (Mankato). Lewis R. Jewell. Lt. col. Sixth Kan. cavalry; died of wounds (action at Cone Hill, Ark.) Nov. 30, 1862.

Jim Hogg, Tex. (est. Mar. 31, 1913; 1,139 sq. mi.; 1970 pop.: 4,654; 1960: 5,022; 1950: 5,389) (Hebbronville). James S. Hogg, 20th gov. Va. (1851-1906). Established Longview, Tex. "News" 1871; printed it at Quitman, Tex., 1872-75; attorney Wood County 1878-80; district attorney seventh judicial district 1880-84; attorney gen. of Tex. 1886-90; gov. of Tex. 1891-95.

Jim Wells, Tex. (est. Mar. 25, 1911; 846 sq. mi.; 1970 pop.: 33,032; 1960: 34,548; 1950: 27,991) (Alice). James B. Wells. Judge.

Jo Daviess, Ill. (est. Feb. 17, 1827; 623 sq. mi.; 1970 pop.: 21,766; 1960: 21,821; 1950: 21,459) (Galena). Joseph Hamilton Daviess. U.S. District Attorney for Ky.; prosecuted Aaron Burr for treason 1807; killed at battle of Tippecanoe Nov. 7, 1811. -- History of Jo Daviess County, Chicago: H. F. Kett & Co., 1878; 845 p.

Johnson, Ark. (est. Nov. 16, 1833, eff. Dec. 25, 1833; 676 sq. mi.; 1970 pop.: 13,630; 1960: 12,421; 1950: 16,138) (Clarksville). Benjamin Johnson. Judge supreme court Ark. terr. -- Langford, Ella Molloy, Johnson County, Arkansas, the first hundred years, Clarksville, Ark.: Ella M. Langford, 1921; 210 p.

Johnson, Ga. (est. Dec. 11, 1858; 292 sq. mi.; 1970 pop.: 7,727; 1960: 8,048; 1950: 9,893) (Wrightsville). Herschel Vespasian Johnson (1812-1880). Fortieth gov. of Ga. Senator from Ga., 1848-49; judge of the superior court of Ocmulgee circuit 1849-53; gov. of Ga., 1853-57; senator from Ga., in Second Confederate Congress 1862-65; pres. of Ga. constitutional convention 1865; elected Senator but not permitted to qualify 1866; judge of the middle circuit of Ga., 1873-80.

Johnson, Ill. (est. Sept. 14, 1812; 348 sq. mi.; 1970 pop.: 7,550; 1960: 6,928; 1950: 8,729) (Vienna). ("The Land of George Rogers Clark"). Richard Mentor Johnson

(1781-1850). Ky. house of representatives 1804-07 and 1819; Representative from Ky., 1807-19; during congressional term served as col. of Ky., vol. in engagements in lower Canada 1813; fought at battle of the Thames 1813; presented sword by Congress for his heroism; Senator from Ky., 1819-29; Representative from Ky., 1829-37; Vice Pres. of the U. S., 1837-41; Ky. house of representatives 1841-42. -- Chapman, Leorah May, A History of Johnson County, Herrin, Ill.: Press of the Herrin News, 1925; 502 p.

Johnson, Ind. (est. Dec. 31, 1822, eff. May 5, 1823; 315 sq. mi.; 1970 pop.: 61,138; 1960: 43,704; 1950: 26,183) (Franklin). John Johnson. Judge Ind. Supreme court. -- Branigin, Elba L., History of Johnson County, Indiana, Indianapolis, Ind.: B. F. Bowen & Co., Inc., 1913; 863 p.

Johnson, Iowa (est. Dec. 21, 1837; 620 sq. mi.; 1970 pop.: 72,127; 1960: 53,663; 1950: 45,766) (Iowa City). Richard Mentor Johnson. -- Aurner, Clarence Ray, Leading events in Johnson County history, Cedar Rapids, Iowa: Western Historical Press, 1912; 2 vol.

Johnson, Kan. (est. Aug. 30, 1855; 476 sq. mi.; 1970 pop.: 217,662; 1960: 143,792; 1950: 62,783) (Olathe). Rev. Thomas Johnson (1802-1865). Shawnee Manual Training School 1838; missionary to the Shawnee Indians 1829-58; first terr. legislature Kan. 1855; robbed and murdered 1865. -- Blair, Ed., History of Johnson County, Kansas, Lawrence, Kan.: Standard Pub. Co., 1915; 469 p.

Johnson, Ky. (est. Feb. 24, 1843; 264 sq. mi.; 1970 pop.: 17,539; 1960: 19,748; 1950: 23,846) (Paintsville). Richard Mentor Johnson*. -- Hall, Mitchel, Johnson County, Kentucky, Louisville, Ky.: Standard Press, 1928; 2 vol.

Johnson, Mo. (est. Dec. 13, 1834; 826 sq. mi.; 1970 pop.: 34,172; 1960: 28,981; 1950: 20,716) (Warrensburg). Richard Mentor Johnson*. -- Cockrell, Ewing, History of Johnson County, Missouri, Topeka: Historical Pub. Co., 1918; 1144 p.

Johnson, Neb. (est. Mar. 2, 1855; 377 sq. mi.; 1970 pop.: 5,743; 1960: 6,281; 1950: 7,251) (Tecumseh). Richard Mentor Johnson*.

Johnson, Tenn. (est. Jan. 2, 1836; 299 sq. mi.; 1970 pop.: 11,569; 1960: 10,765; 1950: 12,278) (Mountain City). Cave Johnson (1793-1866). Prosecuting attorney Montgomery County, Tenn., 1817; Representative from Tenn., 1829-37 and 1839-45; Postmaster Gen. of the U. S. in the cabinet of Pres. Polk 1845-49; judge of seventh judicial circuit 1850-51; president of the bank of Tenn. 1854-60.

Johnson, Tex. (est. Feb. 13, 1854; 740 sq. mi.; 1970 pop.: 45, 769; 1960: 34, 720; 1950: 31, 390) (Cledburne). Middleton Tate Johnson (1810-1866). Ala. legislature 1844; battle of Monterey under Gen. Zachary Taylor; commanded Tex. Rangers 1848-50; surveyed So. Pacific RR west of Ft. Worth 1851; Tex. senate; represented Tex. at Washington, D. C., Tex. legislature 1866.

Johnson, Wyo. (est. Dec. 8, 1875, org. Dec. 15, 1877; 4, 175 sq. mi.; 1970 pop.: 5, 587; 1960: 5, 475; 1950: 4, 707) (Buffalo). E. P. Johnson. Cheyenne attorney. (Formerly Pease County, name changed to Johnson County Dec. 13, 1879). -- Walker, William, The longest rope, Caldwell, Idaho: Caxton Printers, Ltd.: 1940; 320 p.

Johnston, N. C. (est. sess. June 28, 1746; 795 sq. mi.; 1970 pop.: 61, 737; 1960: 62, 936; 1950: 65, 906) (Smithfield). Gabriel Johnston (1699-1752). Third gov. of N.C. (under the crown). Emigrated to N. C. from England 1734; gov. of N. C., 1734-52.

Johnston, Okla. (est. July 16, 1907; 657 sq. mi.; 1970 pop.: 7, 870; 1960: 8, 517; 1950: 10, 608) (Tishomingo). Douglas H. Johnston. Gov. of the Chickasaw nation.

Jones, Ga. (est. Dec. 10, 1807; 377 sq. mi.; 1970 pop.: 12, 218; 1960: 8, 468; 1950: 7, 538) (Gray). James Jones (17 -1801). First lt. Ga. militia 1790; Ga. house of representatives 1796-98; Ga. constitutional convention 1798; Representative from Ga. 1799-1801. -- Williams, Carolyn White, History of Jones County, Georgia, Macon, Ga.: J. W. Burke Co., 1957; 1103 p.

Jones, Iowa (est. Dec. 21, 1837, org. Jan. 24, 1839, eff. June 1, 1839; 585 sq. mi.; 1970 pop.: 19, 868; 1960: 20, 693; 1950: 19, 401) (Anamosa). George Wallace Jones (1804-1896). Clerk of U. S. courts in Mo. 1860; Delegate from Michigan terr. and Wisconsin terr. 1835-39; appointed surveyor of public lands for the territories of Wis. and Iowa 1840; Senator from Iowa 1848-59. -- Corbit, Robert McClain, History of Jones County, Chicago: S. J. Clarke Pub. Co., 1910; 2 vol.

Jones, Miss. (est. Jan. 24, 1826; 696 sq. mi.; 1970 pop.: 56, 357; 1960: 59, 542; 1950: 57, 235) (Ellisville and Laurel). John Paul Jones (1747-1792). Added last name of Jones to his name, 1773; Third mate of ship in slave trade. Returning to Scotland as a passenger the capt. died and he brought ship to port and was appointed its master 1766-70; first lt. in Continental Navy on "Alfred" June 1775; capt. of "Bon Homme Richard" which captured the "Serapis" 1779; admiral in Russian navy 1788.

Jones, N. C. (est. sess. Apr. 14, 1778; 467 sq. mi.; 1970

pop.: 9,779; 1960: 11,005; 1950: 11,004) (Trenton). Willie Jones. Pres. of Council of Safety.

Jones, S. D. (est. 1916, org. Jan. 16, 1917; 973 sq. mi.; 1970 pop.: 1,882; 1960: 2,066; 1950: 2,281) (Murdo). Jones County, Iowa. -- Proving Up-Jones County History, Murdo, S. D.: Book and Thimble Club, 1969.

Jones, Tex. (est. Feb. 1, 1858; 959 sq. mi.; 1970 pop.: 16,106; 1960: 19,299; 1950: 22,147) (Anson). Anson Jones (1798-1858). Surgeon at San Jacinto 1836; apothecary gen. of Tex. army; Tex. congress 1837-38; Secretary of State Tex. Republic 1841-44; fifth pres. Tex. Republic 1844-46.

Josephine, Ore. (est. Jan. 22, 1856; 1,625 sq. mi.; 1970 pop.: 35,746; 1960: 29,917; 1950: 26,542) (Grants Pass). Josephine Rollins. Josephine Creek; named for the daughter of a miner.

Juab, Utah (est. Mar. 3, 1852; 3,412 sq. mi.; 1970 pop.: 4,574; 1960: 4,597; 1950: 5,981) (Nephi). Indian word "yoab" meaning "thirsty plain." -- McCune, Alice Paxman, History of Juab County, Nephi?, Utah, 1947; 301 p.

Judith Basin, Mont. (est. Dec. 10, 1920 pet. and election; 1,880 sq. mi.; 1970 pop.: 2,667; 1960: 3,085; 1950: 3,200) (Stanford). Judith Hancock. (-1820). Judith River, Mont., named for Julia Hancock of Fincastle, Va., maiden name of wife of lt. William Clark.

Juneau, Wis. (est. Oct. 13, 1856; 795 sq. mi.; 1970 pop.: 18,455; 1960: 17,490; 1950: 18,930) (Mauston). [Laurent] Solomon Juneau (1793-1856). Agent of Northwest Fur Co., agent of American Fur Co., first mayor of Milwaukee.

Juniata, Pa. (est. Mar. 2, 1831; 387 sq. mi.; 1970 pop.: 16,712; 1960: 15,874; 1950: 15,243) (Mifflintown). Indian word for "they stay long" or "beyond the great bend."

K

Kalamazoo, Mich. (est. Oct. 29, 1829, org. July 30, 1830; 567 sq. mi.; 1970 pop.: 201,550; 1960: 169,712; 1950: 126,707) (Kalamazoo). Indian word claimed to mean "beautiful water," "otter tail," "bright sparkling water," "stones like otters," etc.

Kalkaska, Mich. (est. Apr. 1, 1840, org. 1871; 564 sq. mi.; 1970 pop.: 5,272; 1960: 4,382; 1950: 4,597) (Kalkaska). Chippewa word for "burned over." (Formerly Wabassee County, name changed to Kalkaska, Mar. 8, 1843).

Kanabec, Minn. (est. Mar. 13, 1858; 525 sq. mi.; 1970 pop.: 9, 775; 1960: 9, 007; 1950: 9, 192) (Mora). Ojibway Indian word for "snake."

Kanawha, W. Va. (est. Nov. 14, 1788; 913 sq. mi.; 1970 pop.: 229, 515; 1960: 252, 925; 1950: 239, 629) (Charleston). (Kanawha Indian tribe. -- Laidley, William Sydney, History of Charleston and Kanawha County, West Virginia, Chicago: Richmond-Arnold Pub. Co., 1911; 1021 p.

Kandiyohi, Minn. (est. Mar. 20, 1858; 824 sq. mi.; 1970 pop.: 30, 548; 1960: 29, 987; 1950: 28, 644) (Willmar). Sioux Indian word for "where the buffalo-fish come." -- Thurn, Karl, Round robin of Kandiyohi County, Wilmar, Minn.: Karl and Helen Thurn, 1958; 253 p.

Kane, Ill. (est. Jan. 16, 1836; 527 sq. mi.; 1970 pop.: 251, 005; 1960: 208, 246; 1950: 150, 388) (Geneva). Elisha Kent Kane (1796-1835). Judge of Ill. Terr. 1816; Ill. constitutional convention 1818; Ill. secretary of state 1818-22; Ill. house of representatives 1824; Senator from Ill. 1825-35. -- Joslyn, Rodolphus Waite, History of Kane County, Chicago: Pioneer Pub. Co., 1908; 2 vol.

Kane, Utah (est. Jan. 16, 1864; 4, 105 sq. mi.; 1970 pop.: 2, 421; 1960: 2, 667; 1950: 2, 299) (Kanab). Thomas Leiper Kane (1822-1883). Col., asked by Brigham Young to act as his intermediary in his dispute with Gov. Alfred Cummings referred to as the Mormon War 1858; Lt. col. 13th Pa. 1861; wounded at Dranesville 1861; and Harrisonburg 1862; brig. gen. vol. 1862; bvt. maj. gen. for service at battle of Gettysburg, 1863. -- Carroll, Elsie Chamberlain, History of Kane County, Salt Lake City, Utah: Daughters of Utah pioneers, 1960; 472 p.

Kankakee, Ill. (est. Feb. 11, 1853; 668 sq. mi.; 1970 pop.: 97, 250; 1960: 92, 063; 1950: 73, 524) (Kankakee). Kankakee Indian tribe. -- Portrait and Biographical Record of Kankakee County, Chicago: Lake City Pub. Co., 1893; 736 p.

Karnes, Tex. (est. Feb. 4, 1854; 758 sq. mi.; 1970 pop.: 13, 462; 1960: 14, 995; 1950: 17, 139) (Karnes City). Henry Wax Karnes (1812-1840). Left Tenn. for Tex. 1831; Tex. scout and ranger, commanded scouts for gen. Houston; at battle of San Antonio Dec. 5-9, 1835; capt. of cavalry at San Jacinto; Indian battles 1836-40. Died yellow fever 1840. -- Didear, Hedwig Krell, History of Karnes County, Austin, Texas: San Felipe Press, 1969; 124 p.

Kauai, Hawaii (623 sq. mi.; 1970 pop.: 29, 761; 1960: 28, 176) ("The Garden Island"). Polynesian word meaning "drying place."

Kaufman, Tex. (est. Feb. 26, 1848; 816 sq. mi.; 1970 pop.: 32, 392; 1960: 29, 931; 1950: 31, 170) (Kaufman). David

Spangler Kaufman (1813-1851). Tex. house of representatives 1839-43; Tex. senate 1843-45; Charge d'Affaires of Tex. to the U. S., 1845; Representative from Tex. 1846-51.

Kay, Okla. (est. July 16, 1907; 944 sq. mi.; 1970 pop.: 48,791; 1960: 51,042; 1950: 48,892) (Newkirk). The initial "K" spelled out. -- Kay County Gas Company, Kay County, Okla., Ponca City, Okla.: Kay County Gas Co., 1919; 75 p.

Kearney, Neb. (est. Jan. 10, 1860, org. June 17, 1872; 512 sq. mi.; 1970 pop.: 6,707; 1960: 6,580; 1950: 6,409) (Minden). Stephen Watts Kearney (1794-1848). Fourth provisional gov. of Calif. First lt. 1812; fought at battle of Queenstown Heights 1812; remained in army advanced to lt. col. of dragoons 1833; col. 1836; brig. gen. 1846; wounded twice at San Pasqual 1846; bvt. maj. gen. 1846; proclaimed himself gov. of Calif. from March-June 1847; military and civil gov. of Vera Cruz 1848.

Kearny, Kan. (est. Mar. 6, 1873, org. Mar. 5, 1887; 853 sq. mi.; 1970 pop.: 3,047; 1960: 3,108; 1950: 3,492) (Lakin). Philip Kearny (1815-1862). Lt. of First Dragoons 1837 and 1841-46; Second lt. First Dragoons 1837; first lt. 1839; resigned 1848; reinstated as capt. 1846; bvt. maj. 1847 for gallantry at battles of Contreras and Churubusco, Mex., resigned 1851; brig. gen. commanding first N. J. brigade in Army of the Potomac 1861; maj. gen. of vol. 1862; killed at battle of Chantilly, Va., Sept. 1862. (Act of Feb. 25, 1889 changed name from Kearney County to Kearny County Chap. 167).

Keith, Neb. (est. Feb. 27, 1873, org. June 9, 1873; 1,072 sq. mi.; 1970 pop.: 8,487; 1960: 7,958; 1950: 7,449) (Ogallala). M. C. Keith. Ranchman.

Kemper, Miss. (est. Dec. 23, 1833; 752 sq. mi.; 1970 pop.: 10,233; 1960: 12,277; 1950: 15,893) (De Kalb). Reuben Kemper.

Kendall, Ill. (est. Feb. 19, 1841; 324 sq. mi.; 1970 pop.: 26,374; 1960: 17,540; 1950: 12,115) (Yorkville). Amos Kendall (1789-1869). Fourth auditor U. S. Treas.; Postmaster gen. of the U. S. in cabinet of Pres. Jackson and Van Buren, 1835-40; first pres. of Columbia Institution for the Deaf and Dumb; publisher of Washington "Evening Star." -- Hicks, E. W., History of Kendall County, Aurora, Ill.: Knickerbocker & Hodder, 1877; 438 p.

Kendall, Tex. (est. Jan. 10, 1862; 670 sq. mi.; 1970 pop.: 6,964; 1960: 5,889; 1950: 5,423) (Boerne). George Wilkins Kendall (1809-1867). Journalist; one of the founders and news correspondent New Orleans "Picayune"; capt. on

Sante Fe expedition 1841; captured and imprisoned 1841-43; wrote "The War Between The States and Mexico" 1851.

Kenedy, Tex. (est. Apr. 2, 1921; 1,407 sq. mi.; 1970 pop.: 678; 1960: 884; 1950: 632) (Sarita). Mifflin Kenedy (1818-1895). Sailed to Orient 1834-36; steamship clerk and capt. 1836-42; on "Champion" 1842-46; on U. S. S. "Corvette" on the Rio Grande; shipping business 1850-74; half interest in King ranch 1860-68; acquired Laurelos ranch 1868; sold both ranches 1882; acquired 600 sq. mi. of pastureland; owned part of Tex. narrow gauge railroad 1876-81.

Kennebec, Me. (est. Feb. 20, 1799, eff. Apr. 1, 1799; 865 sq. mi.; 1970 pop.: 95,247; 1960: 89,150; 1950: 83,881) (Augusta). ("The County of Vacations"; "The Heart of the Nation's Vacationland"). Indian word for "long lake." -- Kingsbury, Henry D., ed., Illustrated history of Kennebec County, New York: H. W. Blake & Co., 1892; 1273 p.

Kenosha, Wis. (est. Jan. 30, 1850; 273 sq. mi.; 1970 pop.: 117,917; 1960: 100,615; 1950: 75,238) (Kenosha). Indian word meaning "pickeral."

Kent, Del. (est. 1680; 806 sq. mi.; 1970 pop.: 81,892; 1960: 65,651; 1950: 37,870) (Dover). Kent County, England from Welsh "caint" for "plain open country." (Formerly St. Jones County). -- Works Progress Administration, Delaware, a guide to the first state, New York City: Viking Press, 1938; 549 p.

Kent, Md. (est. Dec. 16, 1642; 284 sq. mi.; 1970 pop.: 16,146; 1960: 15,481; 1950: 13,677) (Chestertown). Kent County, England*. -- Usilton, Frederick G., History of Kent County, Md., n. p., 1916; 250 p.

Kent, Mich. (est. Mar. 2, 1831, org. Mar. 24, 1836; 862 sq. mi.; 1970 pop.: 411,044; 1960: 363,187; 1950: 288,292) (Grand Rapids). James Kent (1763-1847). New York legislature 1796; N. Y. City recorder 1797; N. Y. supreme court judge 1798-1804; N. Y. supreme court chief justice 1804-14; chancellor 1814-23. -- History of Kent County, Chicago: Chas. C. Chapman & Co., 1881; 1426 p.

Kent, R. I. (est. June 11, 1750; 174 sq. mi.; 1970 pop.: 142,382; 1960: 112,619; 1950: 77,763) (East Greenwich). Kent County, England*. -- Cole, J. R., History of Washington and Kent Counties, New York: W. W. Preston & Co., 1889; 1334 p.

Kent, Tex. (est. Aug. 21, 1876; 901 sq. mi.; 1970 pop.: 1,434; 1960: 1,727; 1950: 2,249) (Clairemont). Andrew Kent (1798-1836). Private; resident of Gonzalez, Tex., killed at the Alamo, Mar. 6, 1836.

Kenton, Ky. (est. Jan. 29, 1840; 166 sq. mi.; 1970 pop.:

129, 440; 1960: 120, 700; 1950: 104, 254) (Covington and Independence). Simon Kenton (1755-1836). Pioneer scout, served with Daniel Boone; Indian fighter, fought with Kentucky troops at the battle of the Thames 1813.

Keokuk, Iowa (est. Dec. 21, 1837, org. Feb. 5, 1844, eff. Mar. 1, 1844; 579 sq. mi.; 1970 pop.: 13, 943; 1960: 15, 492; 1950: 15, 797) (Sigourney) Keokuk (1780-1848). Chief of the Sac and Fox tribes; opposed aiding Black Hawk war; claimed Iowa by conquest at Washington conference.

Kern, Calif. (est. Apr. 2, 1866; 8, 170 sq. mi.; 1970 pop.: 329, 162; 1960: 291, 984; 1950: 228, 309) (Bakersfield). ("California's Golden Empire"; "The Golden Empire of Kern"; "The Land of Magic"). Edward Kern. Topographer served with Fremont. -- Kern County Centennial Almanac, Bakersfield, Calif.: Kern County Centennial Observance Committee, 1966; 127 p. -- Miller, Thelma (Bernard), History of Kern County, Chicago: S. J. Clarke Pub. Co., 1929; 2 vol.

Kerr, Tex. (est. Jan. 26, 1856; 1, 101 sq. mi.; 1970 pop.: 19, 454; 1960: 16, 800; 1950: 14, 022) (Kerrville). James Kerr. (1790-1850). Tex. const. conv.; Tex. congress. -- Bennett, Bob, Kerr County, Texas, San Antonio, Texas: Naylor, 1956; 332 p.

Kershaw, S. C. (786 sq. mi.; 1970 pop.: 34, 727; 1960: 33, 585; 1950: 32, 287) (Camden). Joseph Kershaw. Col., S. C. militia 1776-80; taken prisoner at Charleston, May 12, 1780.

Kewaunee, Wis. (est. Apr. 16, 1852; 331 sq. mi.; 1970 pop.: 18, 961; 1960: 18, 282; 1950: 17, 366) (Kewaunee). ("The County of Opportunity"). Chippewa Indian word for "prairie hen" "wild duck" or "to go around."

Keweenaw, Mich. (est. Mar. 11, 1861; 544 sq. mi.; 1970 pop.: 2, 264; 1960: 2, 417; 1950: 2, 918) (Eagle River). ("The Copper Country"). Keweenaw Indian word for "canoe carried back" "carrying place," for a place of portage. -- Moyer, Claire Inch, Ke-wee-naw (the crossing place), Denver, Colo.: Big Mountain Press, 1966; 237 p.

Keya Paha, Neb. (est. 1884, org. Feb. 9, 1885; 769 sq. mi.; 1970 pop.: 1, 340; 1960: 1, 672; 1950: 2, 160) (Springview). Indian word for "turtle" and "hill."

Kidder, N. D. (est. Jan. 4, 1873, org. Mar. 22, 1881; 1, 377 sq. mi.; 1970 pop.: 4, 362; 1960: 5, 386; 1950: 6, 168) (Steele). Jefferson Parish Kidder (1815-1883). Vermont constitutional convention 1843; state's attorney 1843-47; Vt. senate 1847-48; lt. gov. of Vt. 1853-54; Minn. house of representatives 1863-64; associate justice supreme court Dakota Terr. 1865-75 and 1879-83; Delegate from Dakota Terr. 1875-79.

Kimball, Neb. (est. 1888, org. Jan. 22, 1889; 953 sq. mi.; 1970 pop.: 6, 009; 1960: 7, 975; 1950: 4, 283) (Kimball). Thomas Lord Kimball (1831-1899). In jewelry business in Me., worked for Pennsylvania RR Co., 1857-61; gen. ticket and passenger agent Union Pacific RR 1871.

Kimble, Tex. (est. Jan. 22, 1858; 1, 274 sq. mi.; 1970 pop.: 3, 904; 1960: 3, 943; 1950: 4, 619) (Junction). George C. Kimble (1810-1836). Resident of Gonzalez, Tex., lt.; died at the Alamo Mar. 6, 1836. (Name variously spelled as Kimball, Kimbell, Kimble). -- Fisher, Ovie Clark, It occurred in Kimble, Houston, Texas: Anson Jones Press, 1937; 237 p.

King, Tex. (est. Aug. 21, 1876; 944 sq. mi.; 1970 pop.: 464; 1960: 640; 1950: 870) (Guthrie). William King (1812-1836). Resident of Gonzalez, Tex., private, died at the Alamo Mar. 6, 1836.

King, Wash. (est. Dec. 22, 1852; 2, 136 sq. mi.; 1970 pop.: 1, 156, 633; 1960: 935, 014; 1950: 732, 992) (Seattle). William Rufus de Vane King (1786-1853). North Carolina house of commons 1807-09; Wilmington, N. C. city solicitor 1810; Representative from N. C., 1811-16; secretary of U. S. legations at Naples and St. Petersburg 1817-18; Senator from Ala., 1819-44; U. S. Minister to France 1844-46; Senator from Ala., 1848-52; Vice Pres. of the U. S. sworn in at Havana, Cuba, Mar. 4, 1853; died Apr. 18, 1853. -- Bagley, Clarence Booth, History of King County, Wash., Chicago: S. J. Clarke Pub. Co., 1929; 4 vol.

King and Queen, Va. (est. Apr. 16, 1691 sess.; 318 sq. mi.; 1970 pop.: 5, 491; 1960: 5, 889; 1950: 6, 299) (King and Queen Courthouse). King William of Orange (1650-1702) and Queen Mary II (1662-1694). William ruled jointly with Mary 1689-94 and alone from 1694-1702. -- Bagby, Alfred, King and Queen County, New York: Neale Pub. Co., 1908; 402 p.

King George, Va. (est. Nov. 2, 1720; 178 sq. mi.; 1970 pop.: 8, 039; 1960: 7, 243; 1950: 6, 710) (King George). King George I (1660-1727). First king of House of Hanover; King of Great Britain and Ireland 1714-27; crowned at Westminster 1714.

King William, Va. (est. Dec. 5, 1700 sess.; 278 sq. mi.; 1970 pop.: 7, 497; 1960: 7, 563; 1950: 7, 589) (King William). King William of Orange*. -- Ryland, Elizabeth Hawes, King William County, Richmond: Dietz Press, 1955; 137 p.

Kingfisher, Okla. (est. July 16, 1907; 894 sq. mi.; 1970 pop.: 12, 857; 1960: 10, 635; 1950: 12, 860) (Kingfisher). Kingfisher Creek; descriptive of the bird; King Fisher; a settler who operated a stage coach on the Chisholm trail.

Kingman, Kan. (est. Feb. 29, 1872; org. Feb. 27, 1874; 865 sq. mi.; 1970 pop.: 8, 886; 1960: 9, 958; 1950: 10, 324) (Kingman). Samuel Austin Kingman (1822-18). County clerk 1842; county attorney 1844; Ky. legislature 1849-50 and 1851; moved to Kan. 1857; Kan., constitutional convention 1859; associate justice S. C. supreme court 1861-65; chief justice S. C. supreme court 1866-77.

Kings, Calif. (est. Mar. 22, 1893; 1, 395 sq. mi.; 1970 pop.: 64, 610; 1960: 49, 954; 1950: 46, 768) (Hanford). Kings River; River of the Holy Kings from the Spanish "rio de los Santas Reyes." -- Brown, Robert R., History of Kings County, Hanford, Calif.: A. H. Cawston, 1940; 385 p.

Kings, N. Y. (est. Nov. 1, 1683; 71 sq. mi.; 1970 pop.: 2, 601, 852; 1960: 2, 627, 319; 1950: 2, 738, 175) (Brooklyn, N. Y.) King Charles II (1630-1685), king of England 1660-85; son of Charles I and Henrietta Maria.

Kingsbury, S. D. (est. Jan. 8, 1873; 819 sq. mi.; 1970 pop.: 7, 657; 1960: 9, 227; 1950: 9, 962) (De Smet). George Washington Kingsbury (1837-1925). Dakota terr. legislature 1863-67 and 1872-73; one of the founders of the Yankton "Press and Dakotan" 1861; S. D. Board of Charities and Corrections 1897-1901; wrote "History of Dakota Territory."

Kinney, Tex. (est. Jan. 28, 1850; 1, 391 sq. mi.; 1970 pop.: 2, 006; 1960: 2, 452; 1950: 2, 668) (Brackettville). H. L. Kinney. Tex. legislature.

Kiowa, Colo. (est. Apr. 11, 1889; 1, 792 sq. mi.; 1970 pop.: 2, 029; 1960: 2, 425; 1950: 3, 003) (Eads). Kiowa Indian tribe, corrupted from Indian "ka-i-gwu" meaning "principal people" or "prominent people."

Kiowa, Kan. (est. Feb. 26, 1867, abolished 1875, recreated Feb. 10, 1886, org. Mar. 23, 1886) 720 sq. mi.; 1970 pop.: 4, 088; 1960/50: 4, 700) Kiowa Indian tribe.

Kiowa, Okla. (est. July 16, 1907; 1, 032 sq. mi.; 1970 pop.: 12, 532; 1960: 14, 825; 1950: 18, 926) (Hobart). Kiowa Indian tribe. *

Kit Carson, Colo. (est. Apr. 11, 1889; 2, 171 sq. mi.; 1970 pop.: 7, 530; 1960: 6, 957; 1950: 8, 600) (Burlington). Kit (Christopher) Carson (1809-1868). Guide on Fremont's expeditions 1842-43 and 1845; Indian agent 1853-61; served in southwest against Indians in Civil War and bvt. brig. gen. 1865.

Kitsap, Wash. (est. Jan. 16, 1857; 402 sq. mi.; 1970 pop.: 101,732; 1960: 84,176; 1950: 75,724) (Port Orchard). Kitsap, Indian chief whose warning saved the settlers in Puyallup Valley from massacre; Indian word for "brave." (Originally Slaughter County, name changed to Kitsap County, July 13, 1857 by popular vote)

Kittitas, Wash. (est. Nov. 24, 1883; 2,315 sq. mi.; 1970 pop.: 25,039; 1960: 20,467; 1950: 22,235) (Ellensburg). Indian word for "gray gravel bank."

Kittson, Minn. (est. Apr. 24, 1862, org. Feb. 25, 1879; 1,124 sq. mi.; 1970 pop.: 6,853; 1960: 8,343; 1950: 9,649) (Hallock). Norman Wolfred Kittson (1814-1888). Fur trader, manager American Fur Co., Minn. terr. legislature 1851-55; mayor, St. Paul, Minn., 1858; interested in steamboat, barge and steamship lines. (Originally Pembina County, changed to Kittson County, Mar. 9, 1878, chap. 59).

Klamath, Ore. (est. Oct. 17, 1882; 5,973 sq. mi.; 1970 pop.: 50,021; 1960: 47,475; 1950: 42,150) (Klamath Falls). ("The Center of the Great Western Market in Southern Oregon's Finest Recreationland"). Klamath Indians.

Kleberg, Tex. (est. Feb. 27, 1913; 851 sq. mi.; 1970 pop.: 33,166; 1960: 30,052; 1950: 21,991) (Kingsville). Robert Kleberg. German immigrant, fought at battle of San Jacinto. Chief justice Austin and De Witt counties.

Klickitat, Wash. (est. Dec. 20, 1859; 1,912 sq. mi.; 1970 pop.: 12,138; 1960: 13,455; 1950: 12,049) (Goldendale). Indian tribe, Indian word for "robber." -- Ballou, Robert, Early Klickitat valley days, Goldendale, Wash.: Goldendale Sentinel, 1938; 496 p.

Knott, Ky. (est. May 5, 1884; 356 sq. mi.; 1970 pop.: 14,698; 1960: 17,362; 1950: 20,320) (Hindman). James Proctor Knott (1830-1911). Twentyninth gov. of Ky. Mo. house of representatives 1857-59; Mo. attorney gen. 1859-60; Representative from Ky. 1867-71 and 1875-83; gov. of Ky. 1883-87; Ky. constitutional convention 1891; professor of civics and economics Centre College 1892-94; dean of law school 1894-1901.

Knox, Ill. (est. Jan. 13, 1825; 711 sq. mi.; 1970 pop.: 61,280; 1960: 61,280; 1950: 54,366) (Galesburg). Henry Knox (1750-1806). brig. gen. and maj. gen. Continental Army; Bunker Hill 1775; col. continental regiment of artillery 1775; brig. gen. and chief of artillery 1776; maj. gen. 1782; commander-in-chief of army 1783-84; commanded U.S. Military Academy 1782; U.S. Secretary of

War in cabinet of Pres. Washington 1789-95. -- Drury, John, This Is Knox County, Chicago: Loree County, 1955; 522 p.

Knox, Ind. (est. June 20, 1790; 517 sq. mi.; 1970 pop.: 41,546; 1960: 41,591; 1950: 43,415) (Vincennes). Henry Knox*. -- Greene, George E., History of old Vincennes and Knox County, Indiana, Chicago: S. J. Clarke Pub. Co., 1911; 2 vol.

Knox, Ky. (est. Dec. 19, 1799, eff. June 2, 1800; 373 sq. mi.; 1970 pop.: 23,689; 1960: 25,258; 1950: 30,409) (Barbourville). Henry Knox*.

Knox, Me. (est. Mar. 9, 1860, eff. Apr. 1, 1860; 362 sq. mi.; 1970 pop.: 29,013; 1960: 28,575; 1950: 28,121) (Rockland). ("Maine's Maritime Scenic Wonderland"). Henry Knox*.

Knox, Mo. (est. Feb. 14, 1845; 512 sq. mi.; 1970: 5,692; 1960: 6,558; 1950: 7,617) (Edina). Henry Knox*.

Knox, Neb. (est. Feb. 10, 1857; org. Feb. 21, 1873; 1,124 sq. mi.; 1970 pop.: 11,723; 1960: 13,300; 1950: 14,820) (Originally L'eau Qui Court, Neb. name changed to Emmett County Feb. 18, 1867, changed to Knox County, Feb. 21, 1873, eff. Apr. 1, 1873) (Center). Henry Knox*. -- Draper, Solomon, An historical sketch of Knox County, Nebraska, Niobrara, Neb.: Pioneer Pub. House, 1876; 15 p.

Knox, Ohio (est. Jan. 30, 1808; 532 sq. mi.; 1970 pop.: 41,795; 1960: 38,808; 1950: 35,287) (Mount Vernon). Henry Knox*. -- Williams, Albert B., Past and present of Knox County, Indianapolis: B. F. Bowen & Co., 1912; 2 vol. -- Hill, Norman Newell, comp., History of Knox County, Mt. Vernon, Ohio: A. A. Graham & Co., 1881; 854 p.

Knox, Tenn. (est. June 11, 1792; 517 sq. mi.; 1970 pop.: 276,293; 1960: 250,523; 1950: 223,007) (Knoxville). Henry Knox*. -- Hicks, Nannie Lee, Historic treasure spots of Knox County, Tenn., Knoxville, Tenn.: D. A. R., 1964; 82 p.

Knox, Tex. (est. Feb. 1, 1858; 854 sq. mi.; 1970 pop.: 5,972; 1960: 7,857; 1950: 10,082) (Benjamin). Henry Knox*. -- Gray, Jewel Bernice (Nutt), Early days in Knox County, New York: Carlton Press, 1963; 260 p.

Koochiching, Minn. (est. Dec. 19, 1906; 3,129 sq. mi.; 1970 pop.: 17,131; 1960: 18,190; 1950: 16,910) (International Falls). Cree Indian word for "rainy river."

Kootenai, Idaho (est. Dec. 22, 1864; 1,256 sq. mi.; 1970 pop.: 35,332; 1960: 29,556; 1950: 24,947) (Coeur d'Alene). Kutenai Indian tribe, name means "water people."

Kosciusko, Ind. (est. Feb. 7, 1835, org. Feb. 4, 1836, eff. June 1, 1836; 538 sq. mi.; 1970 pop.: 48,127; 1960: 40,373; 1950: 33,002) (Warsaw) ("Indiana's Favorite Vacationland"; "Indiana's Popular Lake Area"). Thaddeus Kosciusko (1746-1817). Polish patriot emigrated to American 1776; col. engineers 1776; served in Revolutionary war, bvt. brig. gen. 1783; returned to Poland 1786, appointed maj. gen. and later commander-in-chief of the Polish insurgent army.

Kossuth, Iowa (est. Jan. 15, 1851; 979 sq. mi.; 1970 pop.: 22,937; 1960: 25,314; 1950: 26,241) (Algona). Lajos Kossuth (1802-1894). Minister of Finance Hungarian govt. 1848; appointed gov. or dictator of Hungary, sought refuge in Turkey 1849. -- History of Kossuth, Hancock and Winnebago Counties, Springfield, Ill.: Union Pub. Co., 1884; 933 p.

L

Labette, Kan. (est. Feb. 7, 1867; 654 sq. mi.; 1970 pop.: 25,775; 1960: 26,805; 1950: 29,285) (Oswego). French for "the best." -- Case, Nelson, History of Labette County, Kansas, Chicago: Biographical Pub. Co., 1901; 825 p.

Lackawanna, Pa. (est. election Aug. 13, 1878, procl. Aug. 21, 1878; 454 sq. mi.; 1970 pop.: 234,107; 1960: 234,531; 1950: 257,396) (Scranton). Lechauhanne, Delaware Indian word for the "stream that forks." -- McKune, Robert H., Memorial of the erection of Lackawanna County, Scranton, Pa.: M.R. Walton, 1882; 115 p.

Laclede, Mo. (est. Feb. 24, 1849; 770 sq. mi.; 1970 pop.: 19,944; 1960: 18,991; 1950: 19,010) (Lebanon). Pierre Laclède Liguest (1724-1778). French fur trader in Missouri River Valley who established site of St. Louis in Dec. 1763.

Lac Qui Parle, Minn. (est. Mar. 6, 1871; 773 sq. mi.; 1970 pop.: 11,164; 1960: 13,330; 1950: 14,545) (Madison). French for "the lake which talks" evidently referring to an echo.

La Crosse, Wis. (est. Mar. 1, 1851, org. May 1851; 469 sq. mi.; 1970 pop.: 80,468; 1960: 72,465; 1950: 67,587) (La Crosse). ("The Community of Opportunity Rich in Economic, Social and Natural Resources"; "The Gateway to the Wisconsin Coulee Region"). French name of Indian game. -- History of La Crosse County, Chicago:

Western Historical Co., 1881; 862 p.

Lafayette, Ark. (est. Oct. 15, 1827, eff. Feb. 1, 1828; 537 sq. mi.; 1970 pop.: 10,018; 1960: 11,030; 1950: 13,203) (Lewisville). Marie Joseph Paul Yves Roch Gilbert du Motier (1767-1834) Marquis de Lafayette. French military service 1771-76; resigned to aid American cause of independence; commissioned maj. gen. in Continental Army 1777; returned to France 1781; captured by Austrians 1792; revisited U. S. in 1784 and 1824-25.

Lafayette, Fla. (est. Dec. 23, 1856; 543 sq. mi.; 1970 pop.: 2,892; 1960: 2,889; 1950: 3,440) (Mayo). Marquis de Lafayette*.

Lafayette, La. (est. Jan. 17, 1823; 279 sq. mi.; 1970 pop.: 109,716; 1960: 84,656; 1950: 57,743) (Lafayette). Marquis de Lafayette*. -- Griffin, Harry Lewis, <u>The Attakapas Country, a History of Lafayette Parish, La.</u>, New Orleans, La.: Pelican Pub. Co., 1959; 263 p.

Lafayette, Miss. (est. Feb. 9, 1836; 664 sq. mi.; 1970 pop.: 24,181; 1960: 21,355; 1950: 22,798) (Oxford). ("The Reforestation Capitol of the World (great numbers of individual reforestation of pine tree farms)"). Marquis de Lafayette*.

Lafayette, Mo. (est. Nov. 16, 1820; 634 sq. mi.; 1970 pop.: 26,626; 1960: 25,274; 1950: 25,272) (Lexington). Marquis de Lafayette*. (Formerly Lillard County, name changed to Lafayette County Feb. 16, 1825). (chap. 1).

Lafayette, Wis. (est. Jan. 31, 1846; 643 sq. mi.; 1970 pop.: 17,456; 1960: 18,142; 1950: 18,137) (Darlington). Marquis de Lafayette*. -- <u>History of La Fayette County,</u> Chicago: Western Historical Co., 1881; 799 p.

Lafourche, La. (est. Apr. 10, 1805; 991 sq. mi.; 1970 pop.: 68,941; 1960: 55,381; 1950: 42,209) (Thibodaux). French word for "the fork."

La Grange, Ind. (est. Feb. 2, 1832, eff. Apr. 1, 1832; 379 sq. mi.; 1970 pop.: 20,890; 1960: 17,380; 1950: 15,347) (La Grange). Name of Lafayette's home near Paris.

Lake, Calif. (est. May 20, 1861; 1,256 sq. mi.; 1970 pop.: 19,548; 1960: 13,786; 1950: 11,481) (Lakeport). ("The Year Round Fun County"). Descriptive word. -- Mauldin, Henry K., <u>History of Lake County</u>, San Francisco: East Wind Printers, 1960; 64 p.

Lake, Colo. (est. Nov. 1, 1861; 380 sq. mi.; 1970 pop.: 8,282; 1960: 7,101; 1950: 6,150) (Leadville). Descriptive word. (Formerly Carbonate County, name changed to Lake Feb. 10, 1879)

Lake, Fla. (est. May 27, 1887; 996 sq. mi.; 1970 pop.:

69,305; 1960: 57,383; 1950: 36,340) (Tavares). ("America's Finest County"; "The Natural Advantages for Health and Recreation County"). Descriptive word. -- Kennedy, William Thomas, History of Lake County, Saint Augustine, Fla.: The Record Co., 1929; 311 p.

Lake, Ill. (est. Mar. 1, 1839; 455 sq. mi.; 1970 pop.: 382,638; 1960: 293,656; 1950: 179,097) (Waukegan). Descriptive word. -- Halsey, John Julius, History of Lake County, Philadelphia: R. S. Bates, 1912; 872 p.

Lake, Ind. (est. Jan. 28, 1836, eff. Feb. 1, 1836; org. Jan. 18, 1837, eff. Feb. 15, 1837; 514 sq. mi.; 1970 pop.: 546,253; 1960: 513,269; 1950: 368,152) (Crown Point). Descriptive word. -- Woods, Sam B., The first hundred years of Lake County, Indiana, Crown Point?, Ind.: 1938; 418 p.

Lake, Mich. (est. Apr. 1, 1840, org. 1871; 572 sq. mi.; 1970 pop.: 5,661; 1960: 5,338; 1950: 5,257) (Baldwin). Descriptive word. (Originally Aishcum County, name changed to Lake County on Mar. 8, 1843) -- Judkins, La Verne, M., "Going Farther," a treatise on Lake County, Ludington, Mich., 1962; 45 p.

Lake, Minn. (est. Mar. 1, 1856; 2,132 sq. mi.; 1970 pop.: 13,351; 1960: 13,702; 1950: 7,781) (Two Harbors). Descriptive word.

Lake, Mont. (est. May 11, 1923; 1,500 sq. mi.; 1970 pop.: 14,445; 1960: 13,104; 1950: 13,835) (Polson). Descriptive word.

Lake, Ohio (est. Mar. 6, 1840; 232 sq. mi.; 1970 pop.: 197,200; 1960: 148,700; 1950: 75,979) (Painesville). Descriptive word. -- Lake County Historical Society, Here is Lake County, Cleveland: H. Allen, 1964; 134 p.

Lake, Ore. (est. Oct. 24, 1874; 8,270 sq. mi.; 1970 pop.: 6,343; 1960: 7,158; 1950: 6,649) (Lakeview). Descriptive word.

Lake, S. D. (est. Jan. 8, 1873; 571 sq. mi.; 1970 pop.: 11,456; 1960: 11,764; 1950: 11,792) (Madison). Descriptive word.

Lake, Tenn. (est. June 24, 1870; 164 sq. mi.; 1970 pop.: 7,896; 1960: 9,572; 1950: 11,655) (Tiptonville). Descriptive word.

Lake of the Woods, Minn. (est. Nov. 28, 1922; 1,308 sq. mi.; 1970 pop.: 3,987; 1960: 4,304; 1950: 4,955) (Baudette). Descriptive word.

Lamar, Ala. (est. Feb. 4, 1867; 605 sq. mi.; 1970 pop.: 14,335; 1960: 14,271; 1950: 16,441) (Vernon). Lucius Quintus Cincinnatus Lamar (1825-1893) Ga. house of representatives 1853; Representative from Miss. 1857-60 and 1873-77; lt. col. and col. 18th Miss. regiment; diplomatic mission to Russia, France and England for the Confederate States 1863; prof. of political economy Univ. of Miss., 1866; prof. of law 1867; Senator from Miss., 1877-85; Secretary of the Interior in Pres. Cleveland's cabinet 1885-88; U. S. Supreme Court Justice 1888-93. (Originally Jones County Feb. 4, 1867, chap. 298, abolished Nov. 13, 1867 by Constitutional Convention; re-established as Sanford County Oct. 8, 1868, act 13, name changed to Lamar County Feb. 8, 1877, act. 205.)

Lamar, Ga. (est. Aug. 17, 1920; 184 sq. mi.; 1970 pop.: 10,688; 1960: 10,240; 1950: 10,242) (Barnesville). L. Q. C. Lamar*. -- Lambdin, Augusta (Riviere), (ed.), History of Lamar County, Barnesville, Ga.: Barnesville News-Gazette, 1932; 516 p.

Lamar, Miss. (est. Feb. 19, 1904; 495 sq. mi.; 1970 pop.: 15,209; 1960: 13,675; 1950: 13,225) (Purvis). L. Q. C. Lamar*.

Lamar, Tex. (est. Dec. 17, 1840; 906 sq. mi.; 1970 pop.: 36,062; 1960: 34,234; 1950: 43,033) (Paris). Mirabeau Buonaparte Lamar (1798-1859). Editor Columbus, Ga., "Enquirer" 1826; commanded cavalry, at battle of San Jacinto 1836; Republic of Tex. attorney gen.; Secretary of War; Vice Pres. 1836-38; Pres. 1838-41. -- Neville, Alexander White, History of Lamar County, Paris, Texas, North Texas Pub. Co., c 1937 246 p.

Lamb, Tex. (est. Aug. 21, 1876; 1,022 sq. mi.; 1970 pop.: 17,770; 1960: 21,896; 1950: 20,015) (Olton). George A. Lamb (1814-1836). Lt. killed at the battle of San Jacinto Apr. 21, 1836.

Lamoille, Vt. (est. Oct. 26, 1835; 475 sq. mi.; 1970 pop.: 13,309; 1960: 11,027; 1950: 11,388) (Hyde Park). ("The Heart of Recreational Vermont"). Corruption of La Mouette, the name given to the river by Champlain.

La Moure, N. D. (est. Jan. 4, 1873, org. Oct. 22, 1881; 1,137 sq. mi.; 1970 pop.: 7,117; 1960: 8,705; 1950: 9,498) (La Moure). Judson La Moure (1839-1918). Commissioner of Dakota terr. 1890.

Lampasas, Tex. (est. Feb. 1, 1856; 726 sq. mi.; 1970 pop.: 9,323; 1960: 9,418; 1950: 9,929) (Lampasas). Spanish word for "water lily." -- Elzner, Jonnie (Ross), Lamplights of Lampasas County, Texas, Austin, Texas: Firm Foundation Pub. House, c. 1951; 219 p.

Lancaster, Neb. (est. Mar. 6, 1855; 845 sq. mi.; 1970 pop.: 167,972; 1960: 155,272; 1950: 119,741) (Lincoln). Lancaster, England. -- Sawyer, Andrew J., Lincoln, the capital city, and Lancaster County, Nebraska, Chicago:

S. J. Clarke Pub. Co., 1916; 2 vol.

Lancaster, Pa. (est. sess. Oct. 14, 1728; 945 sq. mi.; 1970 pop.: 319,693; 1960: 278,359; 1950: 234,717) (Lancaster). ("The County of Contrasts"; "The Garden Spot of America"; "The Garden Spot of the World"; "The Heart of the Pennsylvania Dutch Country"; "The Home of the Pennsylvania Dutch"). Lancaster, England. -- Ellis, Franklin and S. Evans, History of Lancaster County, Philadelphia: Everts & Peck, 1883; 1101 p. -- Klein, Frederick Shriver, Lancaster County since 1841, Lancaster, Pa.: Lancaster County National Bank, 1955; 239 p.

Lancaster, S. C. (est. Mar. 12, 1785; 504 sq. mi.; 1970 pop.: 43,328; 1960: 39,352; 1950: 37,071) (Lancaster). Lancaster, England.

Lancaster, Va. (est. 1652; 142 sq. mi.; 1970 pop.: 9,126; 1960: 9,174; 1950: 8,640) (Lancaster). Lancaster, England.

Lander, Nev. (est. Dec. 19, 1862; 5,621 sq. mi.; 1970 pop.: 2,666; 1960: 1,566; 1950: 1,850) (Austin). Frederick William Lander (1822-1862). Railroad surveyor to chief engineer of No. Pacific comissioned brig. gen. 1861; built wagon roads across Nev.

Lane, Kan. (est. Mar. 6, 1873, org. June 3, 1886; 720 sq. mi.; 1970 pop.: 2,707; 1960: 3,060; 1950: 2,808) (Dighton). James Henry Lane (1814-1866). Col. in Mexican war 1846-47; Third Ind. vol. 1846-47; Fifth Ind. Infantry 1847-48; lt. gov. of Ind. 1849; Representative from Ind. 1853-55; Senator from Kan. 1861-66; brig. gen. of vol. 1861-62.

Lane, Ore. (est. Jan. 28, 1851; 4,594 sq. mi.; 1970 pop.: 213,358; 1960: 162,890; 1950: 125,776) (Eugene). Joseph Lane 1801-1881). First and fourth terr. gov. of Ore. Ind. house of representatives 1822-23, 1831-33, 1838-39; Ind. Senate 1844-46; col. and brig. gen. Ind. vol. regiment 1846; bvt. maj. gen. 1847; honorable discharge 1848; gov. of Ore. terr. 1849-50 and 1853; Delegate from Ore., 1851-59; served as Senator from Ore., Feb. 14, 1859 to Mar. 3, 1961; Democratic vice presidential nominee in 1860. -- Harpham, Josephine Evans, Doorways into history, Eugene?, Ore., 1966; 55 p.

Langlade, Wis. (est. Feb. 27, 1879; 858 sq. mi.; 1970 pop.: 19,220; 1960: 19,916; 1950: 21,975) (Antigo). Charles Langlade (1724-). Fought in French and Indian war; early settler at Green Bay, Wis. (Augustin De Langlade (1695-1771) married Indian girl.) (Formerly New County, name changed to Langlade County Feb. 19, 1880).

Lanier, Ga. (est. Aug. 11, 1919; 191 sq. mi.; 1970 pop.:

5, 031; 1960: 5, 097; 1950: 5, 151) (Lakeland). Sidney Lanier (1842-1881). Tutor Oglethorpe College, Ga., 1860-61; private in Macon volunteers 1861; wrote "Tiger Lilies" and many poems; practiced law at Macon, Ga. 1868-72; lecturer in English literature at Johns Hopkins Univ.

Lapeer, Mich. (est. Sept. 10, 1822, org. 1835; 659 sq. mi. ; 1970 pop. : 52, 317; 1960: 41, 926; 1950: 35, 794) (Lapeer). Indian word for flint translated into French as "la pierre" contracted into "lapeer."

LaPlata, Colo. (est. Feb. 10, 1874; 1, 689 sq. mi. ; 1970 pop. : 19, 199; 1960: 19, 225; 1950: 14, 880) (Durango). Spanish word for "silver."

LaPorte, Ind. (est. Jan. 9, 1832; eff. Apr. 1, 1832; 608 sq. mi. ; 1970 pop. : 105, 342; 1960: 95, 111; 1950: 76, 808) (La Porte.) French word for "the door" or "port."

Laramie, Wyo. (est. Jan. 9, 1867; 2, 703 sq. mi. ; 1970 pop. : 56, 360; 1960: 60, 149; 1950: 47, 662) (Cheyenne) Jacques La Ramie (-1820). French-Canadian trapper killed by Indians about 1820.

Larimer, Colo. (est. Nov. 1, 1861; 2, 619 sq. mi. ; 1970 pop. : 89, 900; 1960: 53, 343; 1950: 43, 554) (Ft. Collins). William Larimer. Pioneer. -- Watrous, Ansel, History of Larimer County, Fort Collins: Courier Printing & Pub. Co., 1911; 513 p.

Larue, Ky. (est. Mar. 4, 1843; 260 sq. mi. ; 1970 pop. : 10, 672; 1960: 10, 346; 1950: 9, 956) (Hodgenville). John Larue. Pioneer; emigrated from Va.

La Salle, Ill. (est. Jan. 15, 1831; 1, 146 sq. mi. ; 1970 pop.: 111, 409; 1960: 110, 800; 1950: 100, 610) (Ottawa). Robert Cavalier de la Salle. (1643-1687). French explorer, sailed down the Miss. River to Gulf of Mexico claiming the terr. for France which he named Louisiana for Louis XIV, 1682; attempting to colonize the area on a second expedition, he was killed by his men in 1687. -- Hoffman, Urias John, History of La Salle County, Chicago: S. J. Clarke Pub. Co., 1906; 1177 p.

La Salle, La. (est. July 3, 1908; 640 sq. mi. ; 1970 pop. : 13, 295; 1960: 13, 011; 1950: 12, 717) (Jena). Robert Cavalier de la Salle*.

La Salle, Tex. (est. Feb. 1, 1858; 1, 501 sq. mi. ; 1970 pop. : 5, 014; 1960: 5, 972; 1950: 7, 485) (Cotulla). Robert Cavalier de la Salle*.

Las Animos, Colo. (est. Feb. 9, 1866, eff. Nov. 1, 1866; 4, 794 sq. mi. ; 1970 pop. : 15, 744; 1960: 19, 983; 1950: 25, 902) (Trinidad). Spanish for "the souls" named for "El Rio de las Animas Perdidas en Purgatoria," the

River of the Souls Lost in Purgatory.

Lassen, Calif. (est. Apr. 1, 1864; 4,548 sq. mi.; 1970 pop.: 14,960; 1960: 13,597; 1950: 18,474) (Susanville). Peter Lassen (1793-1859). Danish pioneer led immigrant band to Sacramento Valley in 1848; killed by Indians Apr. 26, 1859. -- Fairfield, Asa Merrill, Fairfield's Pioneer History of Lassen County, San Francisco, Calif.: H. S. Crocker Co., 1916; 506 p.

Latah, Idaho. (est. Dec. 22, 1864; 1,090 sq. mi.; 1970 pop.: 24,891; 1960: 21,170; 1950: 20,971) (Moscow). Coined word; first syllables of Nez Percé Indian words "la-kah" for "pine trees" and "tahol" for "pestles" used to pound and smash roots, forming "latah" meaning "pine and pestle place."

Latimer, Okla. (est. July 16, 1907; 737 sq. mi.; 1970 pop.: 8,601; 1960: 7,738; 1950: 9,690) (Wilburton). J. S. Latimer. Member of Okla. Constitutional Convention 1907.

Lauderdale, Ala. (est. Feb. 6, 1818; eff. June 1, 1818; 688 sq. mi.; 1970 pop.: 68,111; 1960: 61,622; 1950: 54,179) (Florence). James Lauderdale (-1814). Col. killed in action Dec. 23, 1814 at New Orleans. -- Garrett, Jill Knight, History of Lauderdale County, Ala., Columbia, Tenn., 1964; 264 p.

Lauderdale, Miss. (est. Dec. 23, 1833; 700 sq. mi.; 1970 pop.: 67,087; 1960: 67,119; 1950: 64,171) (Meridian). James Lauderdale*.

Lauderdale, Tenn. (est. Nov. 24, 1835; 487 sq. mi.; 1970 pop.: 20,271; 1960: 21,844; 1950: 25,047) (Ripley). James Lauderdale*.

Laurel, Ky. (est. Dec. 12, 1825; 448 sq. mi.; 1970 pop.: 27,386; 1960: 24,901; 1950: 25,797) (London). Descriptive. -- Sentinel-Echo Laurel County, Ky., London, Ky.: Sentinel-Echo, 1954; 292 p.

Laurens, Ga. (est. Dec. 10, 1807; 806 sq. mi.; 1970 pop.: 32,738; 1960: 32,313; 1950: 33,123) (Dublin). John Laurens (1753-1782). Served in Revolutionary War under Gen. George Washington; wounded at battle of Germantown, Oct. 4, 1777; captured one of the redoubts at Yorktown, Va.; received Cornwallis' sword. Killed in skirmish, Combahee River, S. C., Aug. 27, 1782. -- Hart, Bertha Sheppard, Official history of Laurens County, Georgia, 1807-1941, Dublin, Ga.: Daughters of the American Revolution, 1941; 546 p.

Laurens, S. C. (est. Mar. 12, 1785; 713 sq. mi.; 1970 pop.: 49,713; 1960: 47,609; 1950: 46,974) (Laurens). Henry Laurens (1724-1792). Favored American independence and advised English Parliament against port bill; pres.

of Continental Congress 1777-78; appointed minister to Holland in 1779 but his ship was captured by the English and he was imprisoned; exchanged for Lord Cornwallis; one of the signers of the preliminary treaties of peace with Great Britain.

Lavaca, Tex. (est. Apr. 6, 1846; 975 sq. mi.; 1970 pop.: 17, 903; 1960: 20, 174; 1950: 22, 159) (Hallettsville). Spanish word "la vaca" meaning "the cow." -- Boethel, Paul C., History of Lavaca County, Austin, Texas: Von Boeckmann-Jones, 1959; 172 p.

Lawrence, Ala. (est. Feb. 6, 1818, eff. June 1, 1818; 686 sq. mi.; 1970 pop.: 27, 281; 1960: 24, 501; 1950: 27, 128) (Moulton). James Lawrence (1781-1813). American naval commander served in war with Tripoli 1804; promoted to capt. 1812; commanded "Chesapeake" and was mortally wounded in engagement with British frigate "Shannon" June 1, 1813. Issued the famous order "Don't give up the ship."

Lawrence, Ark. (est. Jan. 15, 1815, eff. Mar. 1, 1815; 592 sq. mi.; 1970 pop.: 16, 320; 1960: 17, 267; 1950: 21, 303) (Powhatan and Walnut Ridge). James Lawrence*.

Lawrence, Ill. (est. Jan. 16, 1821; 258 sq. mi.; 1970 pop.: 17, 522; 1960: 18, 540; 1950: 20, 539) (Lawrenceville). James Lawrence*. -- McDonough, J., Combined History of Edwards, Lawrence & Wabash Counties, Philadelphia: J. L. McDonough & Co., 1883; 377 p.

Lawrence, Ind. (est. Jan. 7, 1818, eff. Mar. 16, 1818; 459 sq. mi.; 1970 pop.: 38, 038) (Bedford). James Lawrence*. -- History of Lawrence and Monroe Counties, Indiana, Indianapolis, Ind.: B. F. Bowen & Co., Inc., 1914; 764 p.

Lawrence, Ky. (est. Dec. 14, 1821; 425 sq. mi.; 1970 pop.: 10, 726; 1960: 12, 134; 1950: 14, 418) (Louisa). James Lawrence*.

Lawrence, Miss. (est. Dec. 22, 1814; 418 sq. mi.; 1970 pop.: 11, 137; 1960: 10, 215; 1950: 12, 639) (Monticello). James Lawrence*.

Lawrence, Mo. (est. Feb. 14, 1845; 619 sq. mi.; 1970 pop.: 24, 585; 1960: 23, 260; 1950: 23, 420) (Mt. Vernon). James Lawrence*.

Lawrence, Ohio (est. Dec. 21, 1815; 456 sq. mi.; 1970 pop.: 56, 868; 1960: 55, 438; 1950: 49, 115) (Ironton). James Lawrence*.

Lawrence, Pa. (est. Mar. 20, 1849; 367 sq. mi.; 1970 pop.: 107, 374; 1960: 112, 965; 1950: 105, 120) (New Castle).

Lawrence, S. D. (est. Jan. 11, 1875; 800 sq. mi.; 1970 pop.: 17, 453; 1960: 17, 075; 1950: 16, 648) (Deadwood).

John Lawrence. Councilman eleventh Dakota terr. legislature 1874-75. Supt. of Sioux City and Ft. Randall Wagon Road. -- Lawrence County Centennial Committee, Lawrence County for the Dakota territory centennial, S. D.: Lawrence County Centennial Committee Lead, 1960; 186 p.

Lawrence, Tenn. (est. Oct. 21, 1817; 634 sq. mi.; 1970 pop.: 29,097; 1960: 28,049; 1950: 28,818) (Lawrenceburg). James Lawrence*.

Lea, N. M. (est. Mar. 7, 1917; 4,393 sq. mi.; 1970 pop.: 49,554; 1960: 53,429; 1950: 30,717) (Lovington). Joseph C. Lea. Pioneer of Chaves County, N. M.

Leake, Miss. (est. Dec. 23, 1833; 576 sq. mi.; 1970 pop.: 17,085; 1960: 18,660; 1950: 21,610) (Carthage). Walter Leake (1762-1825). Third gov. of Miss.; Va. legislature 1805; judge of Miss. terr. 1807; Senator from Miss., 1817-20; U. S. marshal for Miss. district 1820; gov. of Miss. 1822-25.

Leavenworth, Kan. (est. Aug. 30, 1855; 465 sq. mi.; 1970 pop.: 53,340; 1960: 48,524; 1950: 42,361) (Leavenworth). Henry Leavenworth (1783-1834). Capt. 25th Inf., 1812; maj. 1813; lt. col. 1818; col. 1825; bvt. lt. col. for distinguished service at battle of Chippewa, Upper Canada 1814; bvt. col. for distinguished service at Niagara Falls, Upper Canada, 1814, and brig. gen. for ten years service, 1824; defeated Aricara tribe, Aug. 10, 1823.

Lebanon, Pa. (est. Feb. 16, 1813; 363 sq. mi.; 1970 pop.: 99,665; 1960: 90,853; 1950: 81,683) (Lebanon). ("The Valley of Planned Progress"). Mount Lebanon in Israel; name suggested by cedar trees. -- Croll, Philip Columbus, Lebanon County Imprints, Harrisburg, Pa., 1909; 42 p.

Lee, Ala. (est. Dec. 5, 1866; 612 sq. mi.; 1970 pop.: 61,268; 1960: 49,754; 1950: 45,073) (Opelika). Robert Edward Lee (1807-1870). Graduated from U. S. Military Academy 1829; Mexican war wounded at Chapultepec; resigned as col. U. S. Army 1861; commander-in-chief of Confederate Army 1865; surrendered at Appomattox Court House 1865; pres. of Washington College.

Lee, Ark. (est. Apr. 17, 1873; 620 sq. mi.; 1970 pop.: 18,884; 1960: 21,001; 1950: 24,322) (Marianna). Robert Edward Lee*.

Lee, Fla. (est. May 13, 1887; 786 sq. mi.; 1970 pop.: 105,216; 1960: 54,539; 1950: 23,404) (Fort Myers). ("The Gladiola Capital of the World"). Robert Edward Lee*.

Lee, Ga. (est. Dec. 11, 1826; 326 sq. mi.; 1970 pop.: 7,044; 1960: 6,204; 1950: 6,674) (Leesburg). Richard Henry Lee (1732-1794). Justice of the peace Westmoreland County, Va., 1757; Va. house of burgesses 1758-1775; Continental Congress 1774-80; signer of the Declaration of Independence 1776; Va. house of delegates 1777, 1780 and 1785; Continental Congress 1784-87; Senator from Va., 1789-92.

Lee, Ill. (est. Feb. 27, 1839; 742 sq. mi.; 1970 pop.: 37,947; 1960: 38,749; 1950: 36,451) (Dixon). Richard Henry Lee. -- Stevens, Frank Everett, History of Lee County, Chicago: S. J. Clarke Pub. Co., 1914; 2 vol.

Lee, Iowa (est. Dec. 7, 1836; 522 sq. mi.; 1970 pop.: 42,996; 1960: 44,207; 1950: 43,102) (Ft. Madison and Keokuk). Lee of Marsh, Delevan and Lee of Albany, N. Y., and of the New York Land Company. -- Roberts, Nelson Commins, Story of Lee County, Iowa, Chicago: S. J. Clarke Pub. Co., 1914; 2 vol.

Lee, Ky. (est. Jan. 29, 1870; 210 sq. mi.; 1970 pop.: 6,587; 1960: 7,420; 1950: 8,739) (Beattyville). Robert Edward Lee*. -- Caudill, Bernice Calmes, Remembering Lee County, Danville, Ky.: Bluegrass Printing Co., 1968?; 65 p.

Lee, Miss. (est. Oct. 26, 1866; 443 sq. mi.; 1970 pop.: 46,148; 1960: 40,589; 1950: 38,237) (Tupelo). ("The Capital of the Great Chickasaw Nation"). Robert Edward Lee*.

Lee, N. C. (est. Mar. 6, 1907; 255 sq. mi.; 1970 pop.: 30,467; 1960: 26,561; 1950: 23,522) (Sanford). Robert Edward Lee*.

Lee, S. C. (est. Feb. 25, 1902; 409 sq. mi.; 1970 pop.: 18,323; 1960: 21,832; 1950: 23,173) (Bishopville). Robert Edward Lee*.

Lee, Tex. (est. Apr. 14, 1874; 644 sq. mi.; 1970 pop.: 8,048; 1960: 8,949; 1950: 10,174) (Giddings). Robert Edward Lee*.

Lee, Va. (est. Oct. 25, 1792 sess.; 434 sq. mi.; 1970 pop.: 20,321; 1960: 25,824; 1950: 36,106) (Jonesville). Henry Lee (1756-1818). Ninth gov. of Va. (Commonwealth). Capt. Va. Dragoons 1776; voted thanks of Congress and gold medal 1779; lt. col. 1780; known as "Lighthorse Harry," maj. gen. U. S. Army 1798-1800; Continental Congress 1785-88; gov. of Va. 1791-94; commanded troops Whisky Insurrection 1794; Representative from Va. 1799-1801; wrote famous Washington funeral oration "first in war, first in peace, etc."

Leelanau, Mich. (est. Apr. 1, 1840, org. Feb. 27, 1863; 349 sq. mi.; 1970 pop.: 10,872; 1960: 9,321; 1950: 8,647) (Leland). Leelanau, Chippewa Indian maiden. -- Sprague, Elvin Lyons, Sprague's History of Grand Traverse and Leelanau Counties, Indianapolis: B. F. Bowen, 1903; 806 p. -- Littell, Edmund M., 100 Years in Leelanau, Leland, Mich.: The Print Shop, 1965; 80 p.

Leflore, Miss. (est. Mar. 15, 1871; 572 sq. mi.; 1970 pop.: 42,111; 1960: 47,142; 1950: 51,813) (Greenwood). Greenwood Leflore (1800-1865). Choctaw chieftain; large cotton plantation; Miss. senate 1841-44; opposed secession.

Le Flore, Okla. (est. July 16, 1907; 1,575 sq. mi.; 1970 pop.: 32,137; 1960: 29,106; 1950: 35,276) (Poteau). Le Flore, Choctaw Indian chief. -- Peck, Henry L., Proud Heritage of Le Flore County, a History of an Oklahoma County, Van Buren, Ark.: Press Argus, 1963; 402 p.

Lehigh, Pa. (est. Mar. 6, 1812; 347 sq. mi.; 1970 pop.: 255,304; 1960: 227,536; 1950: 198,207) (Allentown). Indian word "lechauwekink" shortened to "Lecha." -- Roberts, Charles Rhoads, History of Lehigh County, Pa., Allentown, Pa.: Lehigh Valley Pub. Co., Ltd., 1914; 3 vol.

Lemhi, Idaho (est. Jan. 9, 1869; 4,585 sq. mi.; 1970 pop.: 5,566; 1960: 5,816; 1950: 6,278) (Salmon). Limhi, a character in the Book of Mormon for whom Ft. Lemhi was named.

Lenawee, Mich. (est. Sept. 10, 1822, org. Nov. 20, 1826; 754 sq. mi.; 1970 pop.: 81,609; 1960: 77,789; 1950: 64,629) (Adrian). Indian word for "man." -- Bonner, Richard Illenden, Memoirs of Lenawee County, Madison, Wis.: Western Historical Association, 1909; 2 vol.

Lenoir, N. C. (sess. Dec. 5, 1791; 391 sq. mi.; 1970 pop.: 55,204; 1960: 55,276; 1950: 45,953) (Kinston). William Lenoir (1751-1839). Capt. in Col. Cleaveland's regiment at battle of King's mountain, wounded in arm and side; served N. C. militia from sgt. to maj. gen.; first pres. of board of Univ. of N. C. -- Johnson, Talmage Casey, Story of Kinston & Lenoir County, Raleigh, N. C.: Edwards & Broughton, 1954; 413 p.

Leon, Fla. (est. Dec. 29, 1824; 685 sq. mi.; 1970 pop.: 103,047; 1960: 74,225; 1950: 51,590) (Tallahassee) Ponce de Leon (1460?-1521). Discoverer of Fla.; gov. of Porto Rico 1510; set sail for "fountain of youth" located on Bimini 1513; discovered Fla. 1513; second expedition to Fla. 1521; wounded and returned to Cuba where he died. -- Paisley, Clifton, From cotton to quail, an agricultural chronicle of Leon County, Gainesville, Fla.: University of Florida Press, 1968; 162 p.

Leon, Tex. (est. Mar. 17, 1846; 1,099 sq. mi.; 1970 pop.: 8,738; 1960: 9,951; 1950: 12,024) (Centerville) Martin de Leon; also claimed for Leon Prairie where a Spanish lion ("leon") was killed. -- Gates, J. Y. and Fox, H. B., A History of Leon County, Centerville, Texas: Leon County News, 1936; 34 p.

Leslie, Ky. (est. Mar. 29, 1878, eff. Apr. 15, 1878; 412 sq. mi.; 1970 pop.: 11,623; 1960: 10,941; 1950: 15,537) (Hyden). Preston Hopkins Leslie (1819-1907). Twenty-sixth gov. of Ky. Ninth terr. gov. of Mont. County attorney Monroe County 1842-44; Ky. house of representatives 1844 and 1850; Ky. senate 1851 and 1867; gov. of Ky. 1871-75; circuit judge 1881; terr. gov. of Mont. 1887-89; U. S. District Attorney for Mont. 1894-98.

Le Sueur, Minn. (est. Mar. 5, 1853; 441 sq. mi.; 1970 pop.: 21,332; 1960: 19,906; 1950: 19,088) (Le Center). ("The home of the Jolly Green Giant"). Pierre Charles Le Sueur (1657-1702). Trader, miner, fur trader, built fort on Prairie Island, near Red Wing, Minn. in 1695, ascended Miss. to Mankato where he built a fort in 1700, explored valley of Miss. River. -- Gresham, William G., History of Nicollet and Le Sueur Counties, Indianapolis: B. F. Bowen & Co., 1916; 2 vol.

Letcher, Ky. (est. Mar. 3, 1842; 339 sq. mi.; 1970 pop.: 23,165; 1960: 30,102; 1950: 39,522) (Whitesburg). Robert Perkins Letcher (1788-1861). Fifteenth gov. of Ky. Ky. house of representatives 1813-15, 1817, 1836-38, Representative from Ky. 1823-33 and 1834-35; gov. of Ky. 1840-44; U. S. Minister to Mexico 1849-52.

Levy, Fla. (est. Mar. 10, 1845; 1,103 sq. mi.; 1970 pop.: 12,756; 1960: 10,364; 1950: 10,637) (Bronson). David Levy (Yulee) (1810-1886). Delegate from Fla. 1841-45; Fla. constitutional convention 1845; Senator from Fla. 1845-51 and 1855-61; served in Confederate Congress 1861-65.

Lewis, Idaho (est. Mar. 3, 1911; 478 sq. mi.; 1970 pop.: 3,867; 1960: 4,423; 1950: 4,208) (Nezperce). Meriwether Lewis (1774-1809). Served in army against Whiskey Rebellion 1794, lt. in U. S. Army 1795, capt. 1797; private secretary to Thomas Jefferson 1801-03; commanded expedition with capt. William Clark in 1803 and reached headwaters of Columbia River, returned to Washington 1807, gov. of La. Terr. 1807-09.

Lewis, Ky. (est. Dec. 2, 1806, eff. Apr. 1, 1807; 485 sq. mi.; 1970 pop.: 12,355; 1960: 13,115; 1950: 13,520) (Vanceburg). Meriwether Lewis*.

Lewis, Mo. (est. Jan. 2, 1833; 505 sq. mi.; 1970 pop.: 10,993; 1960: 10,984; 1950: 10,733) (Monticello). Meriwether Lewis*.

Lewis, N. Y. (est. Mar. 28, 1805; 1,293 sq. mi.; 1970

pop.: 23,644; 1960: 23,249; 1950: 22,521) (Lowville). Morgan Lewis (1754-1844). Fourth gov. of N.Y. Served in Continental Army 1774, became col. and chief of staff to gen. Gates and Q.M. gen. of northern army, member N.Y. state legislature; attorney gen. of N.Y.; gov. of N.Y. 1804-07; maj. gen. in War of 1812. -- Hough, Franklin Benjamin, History of Lewis County, Syracuse, N.Y.: D. Mason & Co., 1883; 606 p.

Lewis, Tenn. (est. Dec. 21, 1843; 285 sq. mi.; 1970 pop.: 6,761; 1960: 6,269; 1950: 6,078) (Hohenwald). Meriwether Lewis*.

Lewis, Wash. (est. Dec. 21, 1845; 2,447 sq. mi.; 1970 pop.: 45,467; 1960: 41,858; 1950: 43,755) (Chehalis). Meriwether Lewis*.

Lewis, W. Va. (est. Dec. 18, 1816; 391 sq. mi.; 1970 pop.: 17,847; 1960: 19,711; 1950: 21,074) (Weston). Charles Lewis (-1774). Served in Revolutionary war, killed at battle of Point Pleasant, Oct. 10, 1774. -- Smith, Edward Conrad, A history of Lewis County, Weston, W. Va.: E.C. Smith, 1920; 427 p.

Lewis and Clark, Mont. (est. Feb. 2, 1865; 3,478 sq. mi.; 1970 pop.: 33,281; 1960: 28,006; 1950: 24,540) Meriwether Lewis* (see above) and William Clark (1770-1838). U.S. Army lt. 1792; served in wars against Indians 1791-96, with Meriwether Lewis commanded exploring expedition to Columbia River 1803-07; gov. of Mo. Terr. 1813-21. (Formerly Edgerton County, name changed to Lewis and Clark County, Dec. 20, 1867, eff. Mar. 1, 1868, unnumbered).

Lexington, S.C. (est. Mar. 12, 1785; 716 sq. mi.; 1970 pop.: 89,012; 1960: 60,726; 1950: 44,279) (Lexington). Lexington, Mass., commemorating battle in the Revolutionary War.

Liberty, Fla. (est. Dec. 15, 1855; 838 sq. mi.; 1970 pop.: 3,379; 1960: 3,138; 1950: 3,182) (Bristol). Descriptive.

Liberty, Ga. (est. Feb. 5, 1777; 503 sq. mi.; 1970 pop.: 17,569; 1960: 14,487; 1950: 8,444) (Hinesville). Descriptive.

Liberty, Mont. (est. Feb. 11, 1920 petition and election; 1,459 sq. mi.; 1970 pop.: 2,359; 1960: 2,624; 1950: 2,180) (Chester). Descriptive.

Liberty, Tex. (est. Mar. 17, 1836; 1,173 sq. mi.; 1970 pop.: 33,014; 1960: 31,595; 1950: 26,729) (Liberty). Descriptive. -- Pickett, Arlene, Historic Liberty County, Dallas, Texas: Tardy Pub. Co., 1936; 117 p.

Licking, Ohio (est. Jan. 30, 1808; 686 sq. mi.; 1970 pop.: 107,799; 1960: 90,242; 1950: 70,645) (Newark). Descriptive, salt lick area. -- Brister, Edwin M. P., Centennial History of Newark & Licking County, Chicago: S. J. Clarke Pub. Co., 1909; 2 vol. -- Hill, Norman Newell, History of Licking County, Newark, Ohio: A. A. Graham & Co., 1881; 822 p.

Limestone, Ala. (est. Feb. 6, 1818; 545 sq. mi.; 1970 pop.: 41,699; 1960: 36,513; 1950: 35,766) (Athens). Descriptive.

Limestone, Tex. (est. Apr. 11, 1846; 932 sq. mi.; 1970 pop.: 18,100; 1960: 20,413; 1950: 25,251) (Groesbeck). Descriptive.

Lincoln, Ark. (est. Mar. 28, 1871; 565 sq. mi.; 1970 pop.: 12,913; 1960: 14,447; 1950: 17,079) (Star City). Abraham Lincoln (1809-1865). Sixteenth Pres. of the U. S. Capt. with Sangamon County Rifles in Black Hawk War 1832; postmaster New Salem, Ill. 1833-36; deputy county surveyor 1834-36; Ill. house of representatives 1834, 1836, 1838 and 1840; Representative from Ill., 1847-49; Pres. of the U. S., 1861-65; assassinated 1865.

Lincoln, Colo. (est. Apr. 11, 1889; 2,593 sq. mi.; 1970 pop.: 4,836; 1960: 5,310; 1950: 5,909) (Hugo). Abraham Lincoln*.

Lincoln, Ga. (est. Feb. 20, 1796; 291 sq. mi.; 1970 pop.: 5,895; 1960: 5,906; 1950: 6,462) (Lincolnton). Benjamin Lincoln (1733-1810). Maj. gen. in Continental Army 1776; at siege of Yorktown, received sword of Cornwallis 1781; Secretary of War 1781-83; stopped Shay's Rebellion 1787; lt. gov. of Mass. 1788; Collector of the Port, Boston, Mass. 1789-1808.

Lincoln, Idaho (est. Mar. 18, 1895; 1,203 sq. mi.; 1970 pop.: 3,057; 1960: 3,686; 1950: 4,256) (Shoshone). Abraham Lincoln*.

Lincoln, Kan. (est. Feb. 26, 1867; 726 sq. mi.; 1970 pop.: 4,582; 1960: 5,556; 1950: 6,643) (Lincoln). Abraham Lincoln*.

Lincoln, Ky. (est. May 1, 1780 sess., eff. Nov. 1, 1780; 340 sq. mi.; 1970 pop.: 16,663; 1960: 16,503; 1950: 18,668) (Stanford). Benjamin Lincoln*.

Lincoln, La. (est. Feb. 27, 1873; 472 sq. mi.; 1970 pop.: 33,800; 1960: 28,535; 1950: 25,782) (Ruston). Abraham Lincoln*.

Lincoln, Me. (est. sess. May 28, 1760, eff. Nov. 1, 1760; 457 sq. mi.; 1970 pop.: 20,537; 1960: 18,497; 1950: 18,004) (Wiscasset). Benjamin Lincoln*.

Lincoln, Minn. (est. Mar. 1, 1866; 540 sq. mi.; 1970 pop.: 8,143; 1960: 9,651; 1950: 10,150) (Ivanhoe). Abraham Lincoln*.

Lincoln, Miss. (est. Apr. 7, 1870; 576 sq. mi.; 1970 pop.: 26,198; 1960: 26,759; 1950: 27,899) (Brookhaven). Abraham Lincoln*.

Lincoln, Mo. (est. Dec. 14, 1818; 629 sq. mi.; 1970 pop.: 18,041; 1960: 14,783; 1950: 13,748) (Troy). Benjamin Lincoln*.

Lincoln, Mont. (est. Mar. 9, 1909, eff. July 1, 1909; 3,715 sq. mi.; 1970 pop.: 18,063; 1960: 12,537; 1950: 8,693) (Libby). Abraham Lincoln*.

Lincoln, Neb. (est. Jan. 7, 1860, org. Oct. 1, 1866; 2,525 sq. mi.; 1970 pop.: 29,538; 1960: 28,491; 1950: 27,380) (North Platte). Abraham Lincoln*. (Formerly Shorter County, name changed Dec. 11, 1861.) -- Bare, Ira L. and McDonald, W. H., An illustrated history of Lincoln County, Nebraska, Chicago, Ill.: American Historical Society, 1920; 2 vol.

Lincoln, Nev. (est. Feb. 26, 1866; 10,649 sq. mi.; 1970 pop.: 2,557; 1960: 2,431; 1950: 3,837) (Pioche). ("The Home of the State Parks"). Abraham Lincoln*.

Lincoln, N. M. (est. Jan. 16, 1869; 4,859 sq. mi.; 1970 pop.: 7,560; 1960: 7,744; 1950: 7,409) (Carrizozo). Abraham Lincoln*.

Lincoln, N. C. (est. sess. Apr. 14, 1778; 308 sq. mi.; 1970 pop.: 32,682; 1960: 28,814; 1950: 27,459) (Lincolnton). Benjamin Lincoln*. -- Sherrill, William Lander, Annals of Lincoln County, North Carolina, Baltimore, Md.: Regional Pub. Co., 1967; 536 p.

Lincoln, Okla. (est. July 16, 1907; 973 sq. mi.; 1970 pop.: 19,482; 1960: 18,783; 1950: 22,102) (Chandler). Abraham Lincoln*.

Lincoln, Ore. (est. Feb. 20, 1893; 1,006 sq. mi.; 1970 pop.: 25,755; 1960: 24,635; 1950: 21,308) (Toledo). ("America's Finest Vacationland"). Abraham Lincoln*.

Lincoln, S. D. (est. Apr. 5, 1862, org. Dec. 30, 1867; 576 sq. mi.; 1970 pop.: 11,761; 1960: 12,371; 1950: 12,767) (Canton). Abraham Lincoln*.

Lincoln, Tenn. (est. Nov. 14, 1809; 581 sq. mi.; 1970 pop.: 24,318; 1960: 23,829; 1950: 25,624) (Fayetteville). Benjamin Lincoln*.

Lincoln, Wash. (est. Nov. 24, 1883; 2,317 sq. mi.; 1970 pop.: 9,572; 1960: 10,919; 1950: 10,970) (Davenport). Abraham Lincoln*.

Lincoln, W. Va. (est. Feb. 23, 1867; 437 sq. mi.; 1970 pop.: 18,912; 1960: 20,267; 1950: 22,466) (Hamlin). Abraham Lincoln*.

Lincoln, Wis. (est. Mar. 4, 1874; 900 sq. mi.; 1970 pop.: 23,499; 1960: 22,338; 1950: 22,235) (Merrill). Abraham

Lincoln*.

Lincoln, Wyo. (est. Feb. 20, 1911; 4,101 sq. mi.; 1970 pop.: 8,640; 1960: 9,018; 1950: 9,023) (Kemmerer). Abraham Lincoln*.

Linn, Iowa (est. Dec. 21, 1837, org. Jan. 15, 1839, eff. June 1, 1839; 713 sq. mi.; 1970 pop.: 163,213; 1960: 136,899; 1950: 104,272) (Cedar Rapids) Lewis Fields Linn (1795-1843) Surgeon in Col. Henry Dodge's mounted riflemen in War of 1812; graduated as a doctor 1815; authority on Asiatic cholera 1817; Mo. senate 1820; French Land Claims Commission in Mo. in 1832; Senator from Mo. 1833-43. -- Brewer, Luther A. and Wick, B. L., History of Linn County, Iowa, Chicago: Pioneer Pub. Co., 1911; 2 vol.

Linn, Kan. (est. Aug. 30, 1855; 607 sq. mi.; 1970 pop.: 7,770; 1960: 8,274; 1950: 10,053) (Mound City). Lewis Field Linn*. -- Mitchell, William Ansel, Linn County, Kansas, Kansas City, Mo., 1928; 404 p.

Linn, Mo. (est. Jan. 6, 1837; 624 sq. mi.; 1970 pop.: 15,125; 1960: 16,815; 1950: 18,865) (Linneus). Lewis Field Linn*.

Linn, Ore. (est. Dec. 28, 1847; 2,294 sq. mi.; 1970 pop.: 71,914; 1960: 58,867; 1950: 54,317) (Albany). Lewis Field Linn*.

Lipscomb, Tex. (est. Aug. 21, 1876; 934 sq. mi.; 1970 pop.: 3,486; 1960: 3,406; 1950: 3,658) (Lipscomb). Abner S. Lipscomb (1789-1858) Ala. terr. legislature 1818; justice Ala. Supreme court 1820; chief justice 1824; chief justice under Ala. constitution 1830; to Tex. 1838; Secretary of State under Pres. Lamar 1839-40; Tex. constitutional convention 1845; associate justice Tex. supreme court 1846-58.

Litchfield, Conn. (est. sess. Oct. 14, 1751; 938 sq. mi.; 1970 pop.: 144,091; 1960: 119,856; 1950: 98,872) (no county seat). Litchfield, England. -- History of Litchfield County, Philadelphia: J. W. Lewis & Co., 1881; 730 p.

Little River, Ark. (est. Mar. 5, 1867; 544 sq. mi.; 1970 pop.: 11,194; 1960: 9,211; 1950: 11,690) (Ashdown). Descriptive.

Live Oak, Tex. (est. Feb. 2, 1856; 1,072 sq. mi.; 1970 pop.: 6,697; 1960: 7,846; 1950: 9,054) (George West). Descriptive.

Livingston, Ill. (est. Feb. 27, 1837; 1,043 sq. mi.; 1970 pop.: 40,690; 1960: 40,341; 1950: 37,809) (Pontiac). Edward Livingston (1764-1836). Representative from N. Y. 1795-1801; U. S. District Attorney 1801-03; mayor of N. Y.

City 1801-03; on staff of Gen. Jackson at battle of New Orleans 1815; La. house of representative 1820; Representative from La. 1823-29; Senator from La. 1829-31; U. S. Secretary of State in cabinet of Pres. Jackson 1829-31; U. S. Minister to France 1833-35. -- Drury, John, This Is Livingston County, Chicago: Loree Co., 1955; 722 p.

Livingston, Ky. (est. Dec. 13, 1798; eff. May 1799; 318 sq. mi.; 1970 pop.: 7, 596; 1960: 7, 029; 1950: 7, 184) (Smithland). Robert R. Livingston (1746-1813). City of N. Y. Recorder 1773-75; provincial convention 1775; Continental Congress 1775-77 and 1779-81; N. Y. constitutional convention 1777; Secretary of Foreign Affairs 1781-83; chancellor of N. Y. state 1777-1801; administered oath of office to Pres. Washington Apr. 30, 1789; U. S. Minister to France 1801-04.

Livingston, La. (est. Feb. 10, 1832; 662 sq. mi.; 1970 pop.: 36, 511; 1960: 26, 974; 1950: 20, 054) (Livingston). Robert R. Livingston*.

Livingston, Mich. (est. Mar. 21, 1833, org. Mar. 24, 1836; 571 sq. mi.; 1970 pop.: 58, 967; 1960: 38, 233; 1950: 26, 725) (Howell). Edward Livingston*. -- History of Livingston County, Philadelphia: Everts & Abbott, 1880; 462 p.

Livingston, Mo. (est. Jan. 6, 1837; 533 sq. mi.; 1970 pop.: 15, 368; 1960: 15, 771; 1950: 16, 532) (Chillicothe). Edward Livingston*.

Livingston, N. Y. (est. Feb. 23, 1821; 638 sq. mi.; 1970 pop.: 54, 041; 1960: 44, 053; 1950: 40, 257) (Geneseo). Robert R. Livingston*. -- Doty, Lockwood Lyon, A history of Livingston County, Geneseo, N. Y.: E. E. Doty, 1876; 685 p.

Llano, Tex. (est. Feb. 1, 1856; 947 sq. mi.; 1970 pop.: 6, 979; 1960: 5, 240; 1950: 5, 377) (Llano). El Rio de los Llanos, The River of the Prairies; Spanish for "plain."

Logan, Ark. (est. Mar. 22, 1871; 727 sq. mi.; 1970 pop.: 16, 789; 1960: 15, 957; 1950: 20, 260) (Booneville and Paris). James Logan. (Originally Sarber County, act 25, name changed to Logan County, Dec. 14, 1875, act 62).

Logan, Colo. (est. Feb. 25, 1887; 1, 827 sq. mi.; 1970 pop.: 18, 852; 1960: 20, 302; 1950: 17, 187) (Sterling). John Alexander Logan (1826-1886). Mexican War second lt. First Ill. Inf. 1847; clerk of Jackson County Court, Ill., 1849; Ill. house of representatives 1852, 1853, 1856 and 1857; prosecuting attorney for third judicial district of Ill. 1853-57; Representative from Ill. 1859-62; col.

31st. Ill. Inf. 1861; brig. gen. of vol. 1862; maj. gen. of vol. 1862-65; Representative from Ill. 1867-71; Senator from Ill., 1871-77 and 1879-86; Republican nominee for vice pres. 1884. -- Conklin, Emma Burke, A Brief history of Logan County, Sterling, Colo.: Daughters of the American Revolution, 1928; 354 p.

Logan, Ill. (est. Feb. 15, 1839; 617 sq. mi.; 1970 pop.: 33,538; 1960: 33,656; 1950: 30,671) (Lincoln). John Logan. Physician, father of Gen. John Alexander Logan; emigrated from Ireland 1823; Ill. legislature. -- Biographical Record of Logan County, Chicago: S. J. Clarke Pub. Co., 1901; 654 p.

Logan, Kan. (est. Mar. 4, 1881, org. Sept. 17, 1887; 1,073 sq. mi.; 1970 pop.: 3,814; 1960: 4,036; 1950: 4,206) Russell Springs). John Alexander Logan*. (Formerly St. John County, name changed Feb. 24, 1887, chap. 173).

Logan, Ky. (est. June 28, 1792, eff. Sept. 1, 1792; 563 sq. mi.; 1970 pop.: 21,793; 1960: 20,896; 1950: 22,335) (Russellville). Benjamin Logan (1752-1802). Indian fighter, built fort at Stanford, Ky., 1776; second in command against Indians at Chillicothe, Ohio; Ky. constitutional committee; Ky. state legislature. -- Coffman, Edward, The story of Logan County, Russellville, Ky.: E. Coffman, 1962; 303 p. -- Finley, Alexander C., The history of Russellville and Logan County, Russellville, Ky.: O. C. Rhea, 1878; 2 vol.

Logan, Neb. (est. Feb. 24, 1885; 570 sq. mi.; 1970 pop.: 991; 1960: 1,108; 1950: 1,357) (Stapleton). John Alexander Logan*.

Logan, N. D. (est. Jan. 4, 1873, org. Sept. 1, 1884; 1,003 sq. mi.; 1970 pop.: 4,245; 1960: 5,369; 1950: 6,357) (Napoleon). John Alexander Logan*.

Logan, Ohio (est. Dec. 30, 1817, 461 sq. mi.; 1970 pop.: 35,072; 1960: 34,803; 1950: 31,329) (Bellefontaine). Benjamin Logan*. -- Kennedy, Robert Patterson, Historical review of Logan County, Chicago: S. J. Clarke Pub. Co., 1903; 823 p. -- Perrin, William Henry and Battle, J. H., History of Logan County, Chicago: O. L. Baskin and Co., 1880; 840 p.

Logan, Okla. (est. July 16, 1907; 747 sq. mi.; 1970 pop.: 19,645; 1960: 18,662; 1950: 22,170) (Guthrie). John Alexander Logan*.

Logan, W. Va. (est. Jan. 12, 1824; 455 sq. mi.; 1970 pop.: 46,269; 1960: 61,570; 1950: 77,391) (Logan). John Logan (1725-1780), Cayuga Indian chief named Tah-gah-jute, friendly to whites. Was educated by James Logan of Pa. His family was massacred in 1774 which instituted war against settlers of the west; was killed by one of his own tribe in self defense. -- Ragland, Henry Clay, History of Logan County, Logan, W. Va., 1949; 122 p.

Long, Ga. (est. Aug. 14, 1920; 393 sq. mi.; 1970 pop.: 3,746; 1960: 3,874; 1950: 3,598) (Ludowici). Crawford Williamson Long (1815-1878). Physician; used sul-ether in surgical operation at Jefferson, Ga. 1841.

Lonoke, Ark. (est. Apr. 16, 1873; 800 sq. mi.; 1970 pop.: 26,249; 1960: 24,551; 1950: 27,278) (Lonoke). Contraction of "lone oak."

Lorain, Ohio (est. Dec. 26, 1822, eff. Jan. 21, 1824; 495 sq. mi.; 1970 pop.: 256,843; 1960: 217,500; 1950: 148,162) (Elyria). Lorraine, French province. -- Wright, George Frederick, A standard history of Lorain County, Chicago: Lewis Pub. Co., 1916; 2 vol.

Los Alamos, N. M. (est. Mar. 16, 1949; 108 sq. mi.; 1970 pop.: 15,198; 1960: 13,037; 1950: 10,746) (Los Alamos). Spanish for "the trees."

Los Angeles, Calif. (est. Feb. 18, 1850; 4,071 sq. mi.; 1970 pop.: 7,032,075; 1960: 6,038,771; 1950: 4,151,687) (Los Angeles). Spanish for "the angels." -- The Historical volume and reference works, Los Angeles, Calif.: Historical Publishers, 1962-63; 2 vol. -- McGroarty, John Steven, History of Los Angeles County, Chicago: American Historical Society, 1923; 3 vol.

Loudon, Tenn. (est. June 2, 1870; 240 sq. mi.; 1970 pop.: 24,266; 1960: 23,757; 1950: 23,182) (Loudon). John Campbell, the fourth Earl of Loudoun (1705-1782). In British army 1726; commander-in-chief of British forces in America 1756; in French and Indian War lost forts Oswego and William Henry; failed at invasion of Canada; recalled 1757; acting commander British troops in Portugal 1762-63; gen. 1770. (Formerly Christiana County, name changed to Loudoun County on July 7, 1870).

Loudoun, Va. (est. sess. Mar. 25, 1757; 517 sq. mi.; 1970 pop.: 37,150; 1960: 24,549; 1950: 21,147) (Leesburg). ("A Good Place to Live to Play to Work"; "I Byde My Time"; "The Gateway to the World"; "Virginia's Garden County"; "The History of Centrally Located Loudoun is Surpassed Only by its Beauty"). John Campbell, the fourth earl of Loudoun*. -- Head, James William, History and Comprehensive Description of Loudoun County, Washington, D. C.: Park View Press, c. 1908; 186 p.

Louisa, Iowa (est. Dec. 7, 1836; 403 sq. mi.; 1970 pop.: 10,682; 1960: 10,290; 1950: 11,101) (Wapello). Louisa Massey. Pioneer heroine who shot and wounded her brother's murderer. -- Springer, Arthur, History of

Louisa County, Chicago: S. J. Clarke Pub. Co., 1912; 2 vol.

Louisa, Va. (est. May 6, 1742 sess.; 514 sq. mi.; 1970 pop.: 14,004; 1960: 12,959; 1950: 12,826) (Louisa). Queen Louisa of Denmark (1724-1751) eighth child and youngest daughter of King George II of England (1683-1760), married in 1744 to Frederick V of Denmark (1723-1766) who ruled from 1746-66. -- Harris, Malcolm Hart, History of Louisa County, Richmond: Dietz Press, 1936; 525 p.

Loup, Neb. (est. Mar. 6, 1855, org. Feb. 23, 1883; 574 sq. mi.; 1970 pop.: 854; 1960: 1,097; 1950: 1,348) (Taylor). French translation of Pawnee word "skidi" meaning "wolf."

Love, Okla. (est. July 16, 1907; 503 sq. mi.; 1970 pop.: 5,637; 1960: 5,862; 1950: 7,721) (Marietta). Chickasaw family.

Loving, Tex. (est. Feb. 26, 1887; 647 sq. mi.; 1970 pop.: 164; 1960: 226; 1950: 227) (Mentone). Oliver Loving. Rancher, drove large herds of cattle to Ill. Pioneer, killed by Indians.

Lowndes, Ala. (est. Jan. 20, 1830; 716 sq. mi.; 1970 pop.: 12,897; 1960: 15,417; 1950: 18,018) (Hayneville). William Jones Lowndes (1782-1822). S. C. house of representatives 1806-10; capt. of militia 1807; Representative from S. C., 1811-22; died at sea 1822.

Lowndes, Ga. (est. Dec. 23, 1825, org. Dec. 24, 1825; 483 sq. mi.; 1970 pop.: 55,112; 1960: 49,270; 1950: 35,211) (Valdosta). William Jones Lowndes*. -- History of Lowndes County, Georgia, 1825-1941, Valdosta, Ga.: Daughters of the American Revolution, 1942?; 400 p.

Lowndes, Miss. (est. Jan. 30, 1830; 499 sq. mi.; 1970 pop.: 49,700; 1960: 46,639; 1950: 37,852) (Columbus). William Jones Lowndes*.

Lubbock, Tex. (est. Aug. 21, 1876; 892 sq. mi.; 1970 pop.: 179,295; 1960: 156,271; 1950: 101,048) (Lubbock). Thomas S. Lubbock. Col. in Terry's Tex. rangers.

Lucas, Iowa (est. Jan. 13, 1846, org. Jan. 15, 1849, eff. July 4, 1849; 434 sq. mi.; 1970 pop.: 10,163; 1960: 10,923; 1950: 12,069) (Charlton). Robert Lucas (1781-1853). First terr. gov. of Iowa; Twelfth gov. of Ohio. Surveyor Scioto County 1804; justice of the peace for Union township 1806; maj. gen. Ohio militia; capt. in U.S. Army 1812; advanced to col.; Ohio legislature 1816-32; gov. of Ohio 1832-36; first gov. of Iowa terr. 1838-41. -- Stuart, Theodore M., Past and present of Lucas and Wayne Counties, Chicago: S. J. Clarke Pub. Co., 1913; 2 vol.

Lucas, Ohio (est. June 20, 1835; 343 sq. mi.; 1970 pop.: 484, 370; 1960: 456, 931; 1950: 395, 551) (Toledo). Robert Lucas*. -- Scribner, Harvey, Memoirs of Lucas County, Madison, Wisc.: Western Historical Association, 1910; 2 vol.

Luce, Mich. (est. Mar. 1, 1887; 914 sq. mi.; 1970 pop.: 6, 789; 1960: 7, 827; 1950: 8, 147) (Newberry). Cyrus Gray Luce (1824-1905). Twentyseventh gov. of Mich. Supervisor Gilead township 1842-54; Mich. legislature 1854; county treas. 1858-60; Mich. senate 1865 and 1876; Mich. constitutional convention 1867; gov. 1887-96.

Lumpkin, Ga. (est. Dec. 3, 1832; 280 sq. mi.; 1970 pop.: 8, 728; 1960: 7, 241; 1950: 6, 574) (Dahlonega). Wilson Lumpkin (1783-1870). Thirty-third gov. of Ga. Ga. house of representatives 1808-12; Ga. senate 1812-15; Representative from Ga., 1815-17 and 1827-31; gov. of Ga. 1831-35; Senator from Ga. 1837-41. -- Cain, Andrew W., History of Lumpkin County for the first hundred years, 1832-1932, Atlanta, Ga.: Stein Printing Co., 1932; 506 p.

Luna, N. M. (est. Mar. 16, 1901; 2, 957 sq. mi.; 1970 pop.: 11, 706; 1960: 9, 839; 1950: 8, 753) (Deming). Solomon Luna. Sheep rancher.

Lunenburg, Va. (est. May 6, 1745 sess.; 443 sq. mi.; 1970 pop.: 11, 687; 1960: 12, 523; 1950: 14, 116) (Lunenburg). Karl Wilhelm Ferdinand, (1735-1806), Duke of Brunswick-Lunenburg, a title of King George II. -- Pulley, Mary Croft, History of Lunenburg County in World War II, Richmond: Dietz Press, 1949; 122 p. -- Bell, Landon Covington, The Old Free State, Richmond: William Byrd Press, Inc., 1927; 2 vol. (See also Brunswick, N. C.)

Luzerne, Pa. (est. Sept. 25, 1786; 891 sq. mi.; 1970 pop.: 342, 301; 1960: 346, 972; 1950: 392, 241) (Wilkes-Barre). Anna Cesar, Chevalier de la Luzerne. (See also Brunswick) -- Pearce, Stewart, Annals of Luzerne County, Philadelphia: J. B. Lippincott, 1866; 564 p.

Lycoming, Pa. (est. Apr. 13, 1795; 1, 215 sq. mi.; 1970 pop.: 113, 296; 1960: 109, 367; 1950: 101, 249) (Williamsport). Delaware Indian word for "sandy [or gravel-bed] creek." -- Lloyd, Thomas W., History of Lycoming County, Indianapolis: Historical Pub. Co., 1929; 2 vol. -- Meginness, John Franklin, Lycoming County, Williamsport, Pa.: Gazette & Bulletin Printing House, 1895; 82 p.

Lyman, S. D. (est. Jan. 8, 1873; 1, 685; sq. mi.; 1970 pop.: 4, 060; 1960: 4, 428; 1950: 4, 572) (Kennebec). W. P. Lyman. Early settler; maj.; Dakota terr. legislature 1872-73).

Lynn, Tex. (est. Aug. 21, 1876; 915 sq. mi.; 1970 pop.: 9,107; 1960: 10,914; 1950: 11,030) (Tahoka). W. Lynn (-1836). Killed at the Alamo, 1836.

Lyon, Iowa (est. Jan. 15, 1851; 588 sq. mi.; 1970 pop.: 13,340; 1960: 14,468; 1950: 14,697) (Rock Rapids). Nathaniel Lyon (1818-1861). Graduated U. S. Military Academy 1841; Seminole War 1841-42; Mexican War 1846-47; capt. 1851; commanded U. S. arsenal at St. Louis, Mo., killed leading First Iowa Inf. at battle of Wilson's Creek, Mo. Aug. 10, 1861. (Formerly Buncombe County, name changed to Lyon County, Sept. 11, 1862.) (chap. 23)

Lyon, Kan. (est. Feb. 17, 1857; 852 sq. mi.; 1970 pop.: 32,071; 1960: 26,928; 1950: 26,576) (Emporia). Nathaniel Lyon*. (Formerly Breckenridge County, name changed to Lyon County, Feb. 5, 1862). -- French, Laura Margaret, History of Emporia and Lyon County, Emporia, Kan.: Emporia Gazette Print., 1929; 292 p.

Lyon, Ky. (est. Jan. 14, 1854; 262 sq. mi.; 1970 pop.: 5,562; 1960: 5,924; 1950: 6,853) (Eddyville). Chittenden Lyon (1787-1842). Ky. house of representatives 1822-24; Ky. senate 1827-35; Representative from Ky., 1827-35.

Lyon, Minn. (est. Mar. 6, 1868; 713 sq. mi.; 1970 pop.: 24,273; 1960: 22,655; 1950: 22,253) (Marshall). Nathaniel Lyon*. -- Rose, Arthur P., An illustrated history of Lyon County, Marshall, Minn.: Northern History Pub. Co., 1912; 616 p.

Lyon, Nev. (est. Nov. 25, 1861; 2,012 sq. mi.; 1970 pop.: 8,221; 1960: 6,143; 1950: 3,679) (Yerington). Nathaniel Lyon*.

M

Mackinac, Mich. (est. Oct. 26, 1818, org. 1849; 1,014 sq. mi.; 1970 pop.: 9,660; 1960: 10,853; 1950: 9,287) (St. Ignace). ("The Historic Mackinac"). Indian word "michilimackinac" meaning "the island of the great turtle." (Orig. Michilimackinac, changed Mar. 9, 1843, Act 89.)

Macomb, Mich. (est. Jan. 15, 1818, org. 1822; 481 sq.mi.; 1970 pop.: 625,309; 1960: 405,804; 1950: 184,961) (Mount Clemens) ("The County Heading Towards a Brighter Industrial Future"; "The Hot House Rhubarb Capital of the World"). Alexander Macomb (1782-1841). Enlisted U. S. Army in 1799, appointed brig. gen. in 1814, commanded northern frontier on Lake Champlain sector, defeating British squadron. Received thanks of Congress and a gold medal for victory at Plattsburgh, N. Y. 1814; Commander-in-chief of the army 1835-41. -- History of Macomb County, Chicago: M. A. Leeson & Co., 1882; 924 p.

Macon, Ala. (est. Dec. 18, 1832; 616 sq. mi.; 1970 pop.: 24, 841; 1960: 26, 717; 1950: 30, 561) (Tuskegee). Nathaniel Macon (1757-1837). Revolutionary War; N. C. senate 1780-82, 1784 and 1785; Representative from N. C. 1791-1815; Speaker House of Representatives 1801-07; Senator from N. C. 1815-28; pres. N. C. constitutional convention 1835.

Macon, Ga. (est. Dec. 14, 1837; 332 sq. mi.; 1970 pop.: 12, 933; 1960: 13, 170; 1950: 14, 213) (Oglethorpe). Nathaniel Macon*. -- Hays, Louise (Frederick), History of Macon County, Georgia, Atlanta, Ga.: Stein Printing Co., 1933; 803 p.

Macon, Ill. (est. Jan. 19, 1829; 585 sq. mi.; 1970 pop.: 125, 010; 1960: 118, 257; 1950: 98, 853) (Decatur). Nathaniel Macon*.

Macon, Mo. (est. Jan. 6, 1837; 814 sq. mi.; 1970 pop.: 15, 432; 1960: 16, 473; 1950: 18, 332) (Macon). Nathaniel Macon*.

Macon, N. C. (est. 1828; 520 sq. mi.; 1970 pop.: 15, 788; 1960: 14, 935; 1950: 16, 174) (Franklin). Nathaniel Macon*. -- Smith, C. D., Brief History of Macon County, North Carolina, Franklin, N. C.: Franklin Press Printing, 1891; 15 p.

Macon, Tenn. (est. Jan. 18, 1842; 304 sq. mi.; 1970 pop.: 12, 315; 1960: 12, 197; 1950: 13, 599) (LaFayette). Nathaniel Macon*.

Macoupin, Ill. (est. Jan. 17, 1829; 860 sq. mi.; 1970 pop.: 44, 557; 1960: 43, 524; 1950: 44, 210) (Carlinville) Indian name for "white potato." -- Biographical Record, Chicago: Richmond & Arnold, 1904; 558 p.

Madera, Calif. (est. Mar. 11, 1893; 2, 148 sq. mi.; 1970 pop.: 41, 519; 1960: 40, 468; 1950: 36, 964) (Madera). Spanish for "wood" or "timber." -- Clough, Charles W., Madera, Madera(?), Calif.: Charles W. Clough, 1968; 96 p.

Madison, Ala. (est. Dec. 13, 1808, procl. of gov. of Miss. terr.; 803 sq. mi.; 1970 pop.: 186, 540; 1960: 117, 348; 1950: 72, 803) (Huntsville). ("The Rocket County (the rocket research of the free world started here)"). James Madison (1751-1836). Fourth pres. of the U. S. First gen. assembly of Va. 1776; Continental Congress 1780-83 and 1786-88; federal constitutional convention 1787; Representative from Va., 1789-97; U. S. Secretary of State in cabinet of Pres. Jefferson 1801-09; Pres. of the U. S.

1809-17.

Madison, Ark. (est. Sept. 30, 1836; 832 sq. mi.; 1970 pop.: 9,453; 1960: 9,068; 1950: 11,734) (Huntsville). James Madison*.

Madison, Fla. (est. Dec. 26, 1827; 702 sq. mi.; 1970 pop.: 13,481; 1960: 14,154; 1950: 14,197) (Madison). James Madison*.

Madison, Ga. (est. Dec. 5, 1811; 284 sq. mi.; 1970 pop.: 13,517; 1960: 11,246; 1950: 12,238) (Danielsville). James Madison*.

Madison, Idaho (est. Feb. 18, 1913; 473 sq. mi.; 1970 pop.: 13,452; 1960: 9,417; 1950: 9,156) (Rexburg). James Madison*.

Madison, Ill. (est. Sept. 14, 1812; 737 sq. mi.; 1970 pop.: 250,934; 1960: 224,689; 1950: 182,307) (Edwardsville). James Madison*. -- History of Madison County, Edwardsville, Ill.: W. R. Brink & Co., 1882; 603 p.

Madison, Ind. (est. Jan. 4, 1823, eff. July 1, 1823; 453 sq. mi.; 1970 pop.: 138,451; 1960: 125,819; 1950: 103,911) (Anderson). James Madison*. -- Netterville, James J., Centennial History of Madison County, Indiana, Historian's Associates, 1925; 2 vol.

Madison, Iowa (est. Feb. 15, 1844, org. Jan. 13, 1846; 565 sq. mi.; 1970 pop.: 11,558; 1960: 12,295; 1950: 13,131) (Winterset). James Madison*. -- Mueller, Herman A., History of Madison County, Chicago: S. J. Clarke Pub. Co., 1915; 2 vol.

Madison, Ky. (est. sess. Oct. 17, 1785, eff. Aug. 1, 1786; 446 sq. mi.; 1970 pop.: 42,730; 1960: 33,482; 1950: 31,179) (Richmond). James Madison*. -- Dorris, Jonathan Truman, Glimpses of Historic Madison County, Nashville, Tenn.: Williams Printing Co., 1955; 334 p. -- Todd, Russell I., This Is Boone Country, Louisville, Ky.: Gateway Press, 1968; 128 p.

Madison, La. (est. Jan. 19, 1838; 650 sq. mi.; 1970 pop.: 15,065; 1960: 16,444; 1950: 17,451) (Tallulah). James Madison*.

Madison, Miss. (est. Jan. 29, 1828; 725 sq. mi.; 1970 pop.: 29,737; 1960: 32,904; 1950: 33,860) (Canton). ("The Banner County"). James Madison*.

Madison, Mo. (est. Dec. 14, 1818; 496 sq. mi.; 1970 pop.: 8,641; 1960: 9,366; 1950: 10,380) (Fredericktown). James Madison*.

Madison, Mont. (est. Feb. 2, 1865; 3,530 sq. mi.; 1970 pop.: 5,014; 1960: 5,211; 1950: 5,998) (Virginia City). James Madison*.

Madison, Neb. (est. Jan. 26, 1856, org. Apr. 6, 1868;

572 sq. mi.; 1970 pop. 27, 402; 1960: 25, 145; 1950: 24, 338) (Madison). James Madison*.

Madison, N. Y. (est. Mar. 21, 1806; 661 sq. mi.; 1970 pop.: 62, 864; 1960: 54, 635; 1950: 46, 214) (Wampsville). James Madison*. -- Lehman, Karl H., ed., Madison County Today, N. Y., 1943; 214 p. -- Smith, John E., Our county and its people, Boston: Boston Hist. Co., 1899; 649 p.

Madison, N. C. (est. Jan. 27, 1851; 456 sq. mi.; 1970 pop.: 16, 003; 1960: 17, 217; 1950: 20, 522) (Marshall). James Madison*.

Madison, Ohio (est. Feb. 16, 1810; 464 sq. mi.; 1970 pop.: 28, 318; 1960: 26, 454; 1950: 22, 300) (London). James Madison*. -- History of Madison County, Chicago: W. H. Beers & Co., 1883; 1165 p.

Madison, Tenn. (est. Nov. 7, 1821; 561 sq. mi.; 1970 pop.: 65, 727; 1960: 60, 655; 1950: 60, 128) (Jackson). James Madison*. -- Williams, Emma Inman, Historic Madison, the story of Jackson and Madison County, Tennessee, Jackson, Tenn.: Madison County Historical Society, 1946; 553 p.

Madison, Tex. (est. Feb. 2, 1842; 478 sq. mi.; 1970 pop.: 7, 693; 1960: 6, 749; 1950: 7, 996) (Madisonville). James Madison*.

Madison, Va. (est. Dec. 4, 1792 sess., eff. May 1, 1793; 327 sq. mi.; 1970 pop.: 8, 638; 1960: 8, 187; 1950: 8, 273) (Madison). James Madison*. -- Yowell, Claude Lindsay, A History of Madison County, Strasburg, Va.: Shenandoah Pub. House, 1926; 203 p.

Magoffin, Ky. (est. Feb. 22, 1860; 303 sq. mi.; 1970 pop.: 10, 443; 1960: 11, 156; 1950: 13, 839) (Salyersville). Beriah Magoffin (1815-1885). Twenty-first gov. of Ky. Ky. senate 1850; gov. of Ky. 1859-62; Ky. house of representatives 1867.

Mahaska, Iowa (est. Feb. 17, 1843, org. Feb. 5, 1844, eff. Mar. 1, 1844; 572 sq. mi.; 1970 pop.: 22, 177; 1960: 23, 602; 1950: 24, 672) (Oskaloosa). Mahaska (1784-1834). Chief of the Iowa Indian tribe; name means "white cloud." Killed by a disgruntled Indian who wanted war declared. -- Hoffman, Phil, Roustabout's history of Mahaska County, Oskaloosa?, Iowa, 1916; 102 p. -- Phillips, Semira Ann, Proud Mahaska, Oskaloosa, Iowa: Herald Print, 1900; 383 p.

Mahnomen, Minn. (est. Dec. 27, 1906 procl.; 574 sq. mi.; 1970 pop.: 5, 638; 1960: 6, 341; 1950: 7, 059) (Mahnomen). Ojibway Indian word for "wild rice."

Mahoning, Ohio (est. Feb. 16, 1846; 419 sq. mi.; 1970 pop.:

303,424; 1960: 300,480; 1950: 257,629) (Youngstown). Indian word for "at the licks."

Major, Okla. (est. July 16, 1907; 945 sq. mi.; 1970 pop.: 7,529; 1960: 7,808; 1950: 10,279) (Fairview). John C. Major. Delegate to Okla. Constitutional Convention 1907.

Malheur, Ore. (est. Feb. 17, 1887; 9,870 sq. mi.; 1970 pop.: 23,169; 1960: 22,764; 1950: 23,223) (Vale). French word for "evil hour" or "misfortune." -- Gregg, Jacob Ray, Pioneer days in Malheur County, Los Angeles, Calif.: L. L. Morrison, 1950; 442 p.

Manatee, Fla. (est. Jan. 9, 1855; 701 sq. mi.; 1970 pop.: 97,115; 1960: 69,168; 1950: 34,704) (Bradenton). ("The Keystone of the Florida Suncoast"). Descriptive, sea cow or manatee. -- McDuffee, Lillie (Brown), The Lure of Manatee, Nashville: Marshall & Bruce Co., 1933; 322 p.

Manistee, Mich. (est. Apr. 1, 1840, org. 1855; 558 sq. mi.; 1970 pop.: 20,094; 1960: 19,042; 1950: 18,524) (Manistee). Indian word for "lost river, vermillion river" or "island in the river."

Manitowoc, Wis. (est. Dec. 7, 1836; 589 sq. mi.; 1970 pop.: 82,294; 1960: 75,215; 1950: 61,607) (Manitowoc). Indian word for "spirit land." -- Plumb, Ralph Gordon, A history of Manitowoc County, Manitowac, Wisc.: Brandt Printing & Binding Co., 1904; 316 p.

Marathon, Wis. (est. Feb. 9, 1850; 1,592 sq. mi.; 1970 pop.: 97,457; 1960: 88,874; 1950: 80,337) (Wausau). Marathon, Greece.

Marengo, Ala. (est. Feb. 6, 1818; 743 sq. mi.; 1970 pop.: 23,819; 1960: 27,098; 1950: 29,494) (Linden). Marengo, Italy, where Napoleon defeated the Austrians, June 14, 1800.

Maricopa, Ariz. (est. Feb. 14, 1871; 9,231 sq. mi.; 1970 pop.: 967,522; 1960: 663,510; 1950: 331,770) (Phoenix). ("Arizona's Valley of the Sun"). Maricopa Indian tribe, named by Spaniards "mariposa" meaning "butterfly."

Maries, Mo. (est. Mar. 2, 1855; 526 sq. mi.; 1970 pop.: 6,851; 1960: 7,282; 1950: 7,423) (Vienna). Maries River, named for "marais" French word for "marsh" or "swamp." -- King, Everett Marshall, History of Maries County, Girardeau, Mo.: Ramfre Press, 1963; 829 p.

Marin, Calif. (est. Feb. 18, 1850; 521 sq. mi.; 1970 pop.: 206,038; 1960: 146,820; 1950: 85,619) (San Rafael). ("The Pleasure Boating Center of the Bay Area"). Marin. Chief of the Licatiut Indians who was baptized "El Marinero" meaning "the mariner." -- Munro-Fraser, J. P., History of Marin County, San Francisco: Alley, Bowen & Co., 1880; 516 p.

Marinette, Wis. (est. Feb. 27, 1879; 1, 388 sq. mi. ; 1970 pop. : 35, 810; 1960: 34, 660; 1950: 35, 748) (Marinette) Marinette Chevalier. French-Chippewa half-breed, wife of John B. Jacobs and later wife of William Farnsworth.

Marion, Ala. (est. Feb. 13, 1818; 743 sq. mi. ; 1970 pop. : 23, 788; 1960: 21, 837; 1950: 27, 264) (Hamilton). Francis Marion (1732-1795). Brig. gen. , commander of Marion's brigade, known as "the Swamp Fox;" harrassed English troops in the Revolutionary War; won battle of Eutaw Springs; served in S. C. state senate 1782-90.

Marion, Ark. (est. Nov. 3, 1835, eff. Dec. 25, 1835; 628 sq. mi. ; 1970 pop. : 7, 000; 1960: 6, 041; 1950: 8, 609) (Yellville). Francis Marion*. (Formerly Searcy County, name changed to Marion County, Sept. 29, 1836, unnumbered).

Marion, Fla. (est. Mar. 14, 1844; 1, 617 sq. mi. ; 1970 pop. : 69, 030; 1960: 51, 616; 1950: 38, 187) (Ocala). ("Marion County Is Horse Country"; "The Kingdom of the Sun"). Francis Marion*.

Marion, Ga. (est. Dec. 24, 1827; 360 sq. mi. ; 1970 pop. : 5, 099; 1960: 5, 477; 1950: 6, 521) (Buena Vista). Francis Marion*. -- Powell, Nettie, History of Marion County, Georgia, Columbus, Ga. , Historical Pub. Co. , 1931; 178 p.

Marion, Ill. (est. Jan. 24, 1823; 569 sq. mi. ; 1970 pop. : 38, 986; 1960: 39, 349; 1950: 41, 700) (Salem). Francis Marion*. -- Brinkerhoff, J. , Brinkerhoff's History of Marion County, Indianapolis: J. H. G. Brinkerhoff, 1909; 862 p.

Marion, Ind. (est. Dec. 31, 1821, eff. Apr. 1, 1822; 402 sq. mi.; 70: 792, 299; 1960: 697, 567; 1950: 551, 777)(Indianapolis). Francis Marion*. dissolved Jan. 1, 1970 (merged with Indianapolis).

Marion, Iowa (est. June 10, 1845; 568 sq. mi. ; 1970 pop. : 26, 352; 1960: 25, 886; 1950: 25, 930) (Knoxville). Francis Marion*. -- Wright, John W. , History of Marion County, Chicago: S. J. Clarke Pub. Co. , 1915; 2 vol.

Marion, Kan. (est. 1855, org. Feb. 17, 1860; 959 sq. mi. ; 1970 pop. : 13, 935; 1960: 15, 143; 1950: 16, 307) (Marion). Francis Marion*.

Marion, Ky. (est. Jan. 25, 1834; 343 sq. mi. ; 1970 pop. : 16, 714; 1960: 16, 887; 1950: 17, 212) (Lebanon). Francis Marion*.

Marion, Miss. (est. Dec. 9, 1811; 535 sq. mi. ; 1970 pop. : 22, 871; 1960: 23, 293; 1950: 23, 967) (Columbia). Francis Marion*.

Marion, Mo. (est. Dec. 14, 1822, org. Dec. 23, 1826; 440 sq. mi. ; 1970 pop. : 28, 121; 1960: 29, 522; 1950: 29, 765)

(Palmyra). Francis Marion*.

Marion, Ohio (est. Feb. 12, 1820; 405 sq. mi.; 1970 pop.: 64, 724; 1960: 60, 221; 1950: 49, 959) (Marion). Francis Marion*. -- Jacoby, John Wilbur, History of Marion County, Chicago: Biographical Pub. Co., 1907; 834 p.

Marion, Ore. (est. July 5, 1843; 1, 173 sq. mi.; 1970 pop.: 151, 309; 1960: 120, 888; 1950: 101, 401) (Salem). Francis Marion*. (Formerly Champoick). -- Steeves, Sarah (Hunt), Book of remembrance of Marion County Oregon, pioneers, Portland, Ore.: Berncliff Press, 1927; 348 p.

Marion, S. C. (est. Mar. 12, 1785; 480 sq. mi.; 1970 pop.: 30, 270; 1960: 32, 014; 1950: 33, 110) (Marion). Francis Marion*. -- Sellers, William W., A history of Marion County, R. L. Bryan Co., 1902; 647 p.

Marion, Tenn. (est. Nov. 20, 1817; 507 sq. mi.; 1970 pop.: 20, 577; 1960: 21, 036; 1950: 20, 520) (Jasper). Francis Marion*.

Marion, Tex. (est. Feb. 8, 1860; 400 sq. mi.; 1970 pop.: 8, 517; 1960: 8, 049; 1950: 10, 172) (Jefferson). Francis Marion*. -- Bullard, Lucille Blackburn, Marion County, Texas 1860-1870, Jefferson, Texas, 1965; 115 p.

Marion, W. Va. (est. Jan. 14, 1842; 313 sq. mi.; 1970 pop.: 61, 356; 1960: 63, 717; 1950: 71, 521) (Fairmont). Francis Marion*. -- Dunnington, George A., History and progress of the county of Marion, Fairmont, W. Va.: G. A. Dunnington, 1880; 162 p. -- Lough, Glenn D., Now and long ago, Fairmont, W. Va.: Marion County Historical Society, 1969; 698 p.

Mariposa, Calif. (est. Feb. 18, 1850; 1, 455 sq. mi.; 1970 pop.: 6, 015; 1960: 5, 064; 1950: 5, 145) (Mariposa). ("The Southern Gateway to the Mother Lode"). Spanish for "butterfly." -- Wood, Raymond F., California's Agua Fria, the early history of Mariposa County, Fresno: Academy Library Guild, 1954; 112 p.

Marlboro, S. C. (est. Mar. 12, 1785; 482 sq. mi.; 1970 pop.: 27, 151; 1960: 28, 529; 1950: 31, 766) (Bennettsville). John Churchill (1650-1722) duke of Marlborough; col. in English army 1678; commanded English forces in Ireland 1689; won victory at Blenheim 1704; Ramillies 1706 and Malplaquet 1709. -- Thomas, J. A., A history of Marlboro County, Atlanta, Ga.: Foote & Davies Co., 1897; 292 p.

Marquette, Mich. (est. Mar. 9, 1843, org. May 18, 1846, re-org. 1848; 1, 841 sq. mi.; 1970 pop.: 64, 686; 1960: 56, 154; 1950: 47, 654) (Marquette). ("The Rockhound's Paradise"). Jacques Marquette (1637-1675). Explorer and Jesuit missionary who, accompanied by Joliet, explored Wis. and Miss. rivers.

Marquette, Wis. (est. Dec. 7, 1836; 457 sq. mi.; 1970 pop.: 8,865; 1960: 8,516; 1950: 8,839) (Montello). Jacques Marquette*.

Marshall, Ala. (est. Jan. 9, 1836; 571 sq. mi.; 1970 pop.: 54,211; 1960: 48,018; 1950: 45,090) (Guntersville). John Marshall (1755-1835). Lt. and capt. Va. militia 1777; served until 1781; Va. house of burgesses 1780 and 1782-88; federal constitutional convention 1788; U.S. Commissioner to France 1797-98; Representative from Va., 1799-1800; U.S. Secretary of State under Pres. Adams 1800; Chief Justice U.S. Supreme Court 1801-35. -- Duncan, K. M. and Smith, L. J., History of Marshall County, Albertville, Ala., Thompson Printing, 1969.

Marshall, Ill. (est. Jan. 19, 1839; 396 sq. mi.; 1970 pop.: 13,302; 1960: 13,334; 1950: 13,025) (Lacon). John Marshall*.

Marshall, Ind. (est. Feb. 7, 1835, org. Feb. 4, 1836, eff. Apr. 1, 1836; 444 sq. mi.; 1970 pop.: 34,986; 1960: 32,443; 1950: 29,468) (Plymouth). John Marshall*. -- Swindell, Minnie Harris, The story of Marshall County, Plymouth, Ind., 1923; 87 p.

Marshall, Iowa (est. Jan. 13, 1846; 574 sq. mi.; 1970 pop.: 41,076; 1960: 37,984; 1950: 35,611) (Marshalltown). John Marshall*.

Marshall, Kan. (est. Aug. 30, 1855; 911 sq. mi.; 1970 pop.: 13,139; 1960: 15,598; 1950: 17,926) (Marysville). Francis J. Marshall. Kan. first terr. legislature. -- Forter, Emma Elizabeth (Calderhead), History of Marshall County, Kansas, Indianapolis, Ind.: B. F. Bowen & Co., 1917; 1041 p.

Marshall, Ky. (est. Feb. 12, 1842; 336 sq. mi.; 1970 pop.: 20,381; 1960: 16,736; 1950: 13,387) (Benton). John Marshall*.

Marshall, Minn. (est. Feb. 25, 1879; 1,800 sq. mi.; 1970 pop.: 13,060; 1960: 14,262; 1950: 16,125) (Warren). William Rainey Marshall (1825-1896). Fifth gov. of Minn. Surveyor of Wis. lands 1847; Wis. legislature 1848; banking business 1855-57; established newspaper St. Paul 1861; lt. col. Seventh Minn. inf. 1862; won battle of Wood Lake 1862; col. 1863; Sioux outbreak 1863; bvt. brig. gen. 1865; gov. of Minn. 1866-70.

Marshall, Miss. (est. Feb. 9, 1836; 689 sq. mi.; 1970 pop.: 24,027; 1960: 24,503; 1950: 25,106) (Holly Springs). John Marshall*.

Marshall, Okla. (est. July 16, 1907; 414 sq. mi.; 1970 pop.: 7,682; 1960: 7,263; 1950: 8,177) (Madill). Marshall.

Maiden name of the mother of George A. Henshaw, delegate to Okla. Constitutional convention 1907.

Marshall, S. D. (est. Mar. 10, 1885; 875 sq. mi.; 1970 pop.: 5, 965; 1960: 6, 663; 1950: 7, 835) (Britton). William Rainey Marshall*. (also claimed for Marshall Vincent, operator of flour and feed store, first county commissioner when county was created.)

Marshall, Tenn. (est. Feb. 20, 1836; 377 sq. mi.; 1970 pop.: 17, 319; 1960: 16, 859; 1950: 17, 768) (Lewisburg). John Marshall*.

Marshall, W. Va. (est. Mar. 12, 1835; 315 sq. mi.; 1970 pop.: 37, 598; 1960: 38, 041; 1950: 36, 893) (Moundsville). John Marshall*. -- Powell, Scott, History of Marshall County from forest to field, Moundsville, W. Va., 1925; 334 p.

Martin, Fla. (est. May 30, 1925; 559 sq. mi.; 1970 pop.: 28, 035; 1960: 16, 932; 1950: 7, 807) (Stuart). ("Martin County Has More," "Sailfish Capital of the World"). John Wellborn Martin (1884-1958). Twenty-third gov. of Fla. Mayor of Jacksonville, Fla. 1917-23; gov. of Fla. 1925-29.

Martin, Ind. (est. Jan. 17, 1820; eff. Feb. 1, 1820; 345 sq. mi.; 1970 pop.: 10, 969; 1960: 10, 608; 1950: 10, 678) (Shoals). John P. Martin. Col. -- Holt, Harry Q., History of Martin County, Indiana, Paoli, Ind.: Stout's Print Shop, 1953-66; 2 vol.

Martin, Ky. (est. Mar. 10, 1870; 231 sq. mi.; 1970 pop.: 9, 377; 1960: 10, 201; 1950: 11, 677) (Inez). John Preston Martin (1811-1862). Ky. house of representatives 1841-43; Representative from Ky., 1845-47; Ky. senate 1855-59.

Martin, Minn. (est. May 23, 1857, org. Dec. 16, 1857; 707 sq. mi.; 1970 pop.: 24, 316; 1960: 26, 986; 1950: 25, 655) (Fairmont). Henry Martin (1832-1908). Settler 1856-57. -- Nelson, Arthur Magnus, Know Your Own County, a history of Martin County, Fairmont, Minn.: Martin County Historical Society, 1947; 65 p.

Martin, N. C. (est. Mar. 2, 1774; 481 sq. mi.; 1970 pop.: 24, 730; 1960: 27, 139; 1950: 27, 988) (Williamston). Josiah Martin (1737-1786). Ninth gov. of N. C. (under the Crown). Royal gov. of N. C. 1771-75; dissolved the assembly 1775.

Martin, Tex. (est. Aug. 21, 1876; 911 sq. mi.; 1970 pop.: 4, 774; 1960: 5, 068; 1950: 5, 541) (Stanton). Wyly Martin. Pres. of the consultation.

Mason, Ill. (est. Jan. 20, 1841; 555 sq. mi.; 1970 pop.: 16, 161; 1960: 15, 193; 1950: 15, 326) (Havana). Mason

County, Ky. -- Cochrane, Joseph, Centennial History of Mason County, Springfield, Ill.: Rokker's Steam Printing House, 1876; 352 p.

Mason, Ky. (est. Nov. 5, 1788, org. May 1, 1789; 239 sq. mi.; 1970 pop.: 17,273; 1960: 18,454; 1950: 18,486) (Maysville). George Mason (1725-1792). Member Va. house of burgesses 1759; member of Va. Convention of 1775, author of Va. Declaration of Rights adopted June 12, 1776; member of Va. Assembly 1776-80 and 1786-88; member of the Constitutional Convention of 1787. -- Clift, Garrett Glenn, History of Maysville and Mason County, Lexington, Ky.: Transylvania Printing Co., Inc., 1936; 461 p.

Mason, Mich. (est. Apr. 1, 1840, org. 1855; 493 sq. mi.; 1970 pop.: 22,612; 1960: 21,929; 1950: 20,474) (Ludington). Stevens Thomson Mason (1811-1843). First and second gov. of Mich. Secretary and acting gov. of Mich. Terr. 1831-35; gov. of Mich. 1835-38. (Originally Notipekago County, name changed to Mason County on Mar. 8, 1843, Act 67.)

Mason, Tex. (est. Jan. 22, 1858; 935 sq. mi.; 1970 pop.: 3,356; 1960: 3,780; 1950: 4,945) (Mason). G. T. Mason. Lt. killed in Mexican War. -- Polk, Stella Gipson, Mason and Mason County, a history, Austin, Texas: Pemberton Press, 1966; 119 p.

Mason, Wash. (est. Mar. 13, 1854; 967 sq. mi.; 1970 pop.: 20,918; 1960: 16,251; 1950: 15,022) (Shelton). Charles H. Mason. First secretary of the Washington Terr. (Formerly Sawamish County, name changed to Mason County, Jan. 8, 1864).

Mason, W. Va. (est. Jan. 2, 1804; 445 sq. mi.; 1970 pop.: 24,306; 1960: 24,459; 1950: 23,537) (Point Pleasant). George Mason*.

Massac, Ill. (est. Feb. 8, 1843; 240 sq. mi.; 1970 pop.: 13,889; 1960: 14,341; 1950: 13,594) (Metropolis). Fort Massac, fortified by the French in 1757, originally Ft. Ascension. It was renamed in honor of Massiac, French minister of Marine. -- May, George W., History of Massac County, Galesburg, Ill.: Wagoner Print Co., 1955; 232 p.

Matagorda, Tex. (est. Mar. 17, 1836, org. 1837; 1,141 sq. mi.; 70: pop.: 27,913; 1960: 25,744; 1950: 21,559) (Bay City). Spanish words "mata" for "small bush" and "gorda" for "fat, coarse."

Mathews, Va. (est. Dec. 16, 1790, 87 sq. mi.; 1970 pop.: 7,168; 1960: 7,121; 1950: 7,148) (Mathews) "An Abundance of Everything for Which One Could Wish"; "The

County That Captures the Heart of the Sports-Loving Vacationist"; "The Midway Garden Spot of the Atlantic Coast"). Thomas Mathews. Gen.

Maui, Hawaii (1, 173 sq. mi. ; 1970 pop. : 46, 156 incl. Maui; 1960: 42, 576 not incl. Kalawao 279) (Wailuku) ("The Valley Island"). A demi-god of Polynesian mythology.

Maury, Tenn. (est. Nov. 16, 1807; 614 sq. mi. ; 1970 pop. : 43, 376; 1960: 41, 699; 1950: 40, 368) (Columbia). Abram Maury. -- Smith, Frank Harrison, History of Maury County, Tenn., Columbia, Tenn. : Maury County Historical Society, 1969; 391 p.

Maverick, Tex. (est. Feb. 2, 1856; 1, 279 sq. mi. ; 1970 pop. : 18, 093; 1960: 14, 508; 1950: 12, 292) (Eagle Pass). Samuel Augustus Maverick (1803-1870). Tex. independence convention 1836; mayor San Antonio, Tex., 1839; Tex. legislature 1845.

Mayes, Okla. (est. July 16, 1907; 680 sq. mi. ; 1970 pop. : 23, 302; 1960: 20, 073; 1950: 19, 743) (Pryor). Samuel Houston Mayes. Cherokee Indian chief.

McClain, Okla. (est. July 16, 1907; 559 sq. mi. ; 1970 pop.: 14, 157; 1960: 12, 740; 1950: 14, 681) (Purcell). Charles M. McClain. Okla. Constitutional convention 1907.

McCone, Mont. (est. Feb. 20, 1919; 2, 638 sq. mi. ; 1970 pop. : 2, 875; 1960: 3, 321; 1950: 3, 258) (Circle). George McCone. Mont. senator active in establishing the county.

McCook, S. D. (est. Jan. 8, 1873; 577 sq. mi. ; 1970 pop. : 7, 246; 1960: 8, 268; 1950: 8, 828) (Salem). Edwin S. McCook (1837-1873). Gen. ; fifth secretary of Dakota terr. 1872-73; assassinated at Yankton, S. D. by a political rival Sept. 1873.

McCormick, S. C. (est. Feb. 19, 1916; 403 sq. mi. ; 1970 pop. : 7, 955; 1960: 8, 629; 1950: 9, 577) (McCormick). Cyrus Hall McCormick (1809-1884). Inventor of a successful reaper, patented 1834.

McCracken, Ky. (est. Dec. 17, 1824; 251 sq. mi. ; 1970 pop. : 58, 281; 1960: 57, 306; 1950: 49, 137) (Paducah). Virgil McCracken. Capt. in col. John Allen's regiment, killed at battle of the River Raisin, Jan. 19, 1813.

McCreary, Ky. (est. Mar. 12, 1912; 421 sq. mi. ; 1970 pop. : 12, 548; 1960: 12, 463; 1950: 16, 660) (Whitley City). Twenty-seventh and thirty-seventh gov. of Ky. Enlisted in Confederate Army as private 1862; lt. col. 1863; Ky. house of representatives 1869-73; speaker in 1871 and 1873; gov. of Ky. 1875-79; Representative from Ky., 1885-97; Senator from Ky., 1903-09; gov. of Ky., 1911-15.

McCulloch, Tex. (est. Aug. 27, 1856; 1, 066 sq. mi. ; 1970

pop.: 8,571; 1960: 8,815; 1950: 11,701) (Brady). Benjamin McCulloch (1811-1862). Battle of San Jacinto 1836; Tex. congress 1839; battles of Monterey, Buena Vista and Mexico City; U. S. marshal in Tex. 1853; brig. gen. Confederate Army; killed at Pea Ridge, Ark.

McCurtain, Okla. (est. July 16, 1907; 1,854 sq. mi.; 1970 pop.: 28,642; 1960: 25,851; 1950: 31,588) (Idabel). Green McCurtain. Choctaw Indian chief. -- Carter, W. A., McCurtain County and Southeast Oklahoma, Idabel, Okla.: Tribune Pub. Co., 1923; 381 p.

McDonald, Mo. (est. Mar. 3, 1849; 540 sq. mi.; 1970 pop.: 12,357; 1960: 11,798; 1950: 14,144) (Pineville). Alexander McDonald. Revolutionary War.

McDonough, Ill. (est. Jan. 25, 1826; 588 sq. mi.; 1970 pop.: 36,653; 1960: 28,928; 1950: 28,199) (Macomb). Thomas McDonough (1783-1825). Fought Tripoli pirates; capt. in War of 1812, highest rank in the navy; received gold medal from Congress, and estate from Vermont legislature; cruised to Mediterranean on the "Constitution" in 1824. Midshipman 1800; served on "Constellation" and "Philadelphia" first lt. on "Enterprise" won naval battle of Plattsburg, Sept. 11, 1814 causing English to retreat to Canada. -- Clarke, S. J., History of McDonough County, Springfield, Ill.: D. W. Lusk, 1878; 692 p.

McDowell, N. C. (est. Dec. 19, 1842; 442 sq. mi.; 1970 pop.: 30,648; 1960: 26,742; 1950: 25,720) (Marion). Joseph McDowell (1756-1801). Fought Cherokees 1776; maj. N. C. militia in command at battle of King's Mountain Oct. 7, 1780; N. C. house of commons 1785-88; N.C. senate 1791-95; federal constitutional convention 1788-89; Representative from N. C. 1797-99.

McDowell, W. Va. (est. Feb. 20, 1858; 538 sq. mi.; 1970 pop.: 50,666; 1960: 71,359; 1950: 98,887) (Welch). James McDowell (1796-1851). Thirty-fourth gov. of Va. (Commonwealth). Va. house of delegates 1830-35 and 1838; gov. of Va. 1842-46; Representative from Va. 1846-51. -- Daughters of the American Revolution, McDowell County History, Fort Worth: University Supply and Equipment Co., 1959; 132 p.

McDuffie, Ga. (est. Oct. 18, 1870; 287 sq. mi.; 1970 pop.: 15,276; 1960: 12,627; 1950: 11,443) (Thomson). George McDuffie (1790-1851). Thirtieth gov. of S. C., S. C. house of representatives 1818-20; Representative from S. C., 1821-34; gov. of S. C., 1834-36; Senator from S. C. 1842-46.

McHenry, Ill. (est. Jan. 16, 1836; 620 sq. mi.; 1970 pop.: 111,555; 1960: 84,210; 1950: 50,656) (Woodstock). William

McHenry. War of 1812, 3rd lt. rangers 1813; maj. Ill. mounted vol. 1832; Black Hawk war 1832. -- History of McHenry County, Chicago: Inter-state Pub. Co., 1885; 941 p.

McHenry, N. D. (est. Jan. 4, 1873; org. Feb. 19, 1885; 1, 890 sq. mi.; 1970 pop.: 8, 977; 1960: 11, 099; 1950: 12, 556) (Towner). James McHenry.

McIntosh, Ga. (est. Dec. 19, 1793; 470 sq. mi.; 1970 pop.: 7, 371; 1960: 6, 364; 1950: 6, 008) (Darien). William McIntosh (1775-1825). Creek Indian chief, leader of Lower Creeks served in Seminole War 1817-18; brig. gen. U. S. Army, killed by his tribesmen who considered him a traitor.

McIntosh, N. D. (est. Mar. 9, 1883, org. Oct. 4, 1884; 993 sq. mi.; 1970 pop.: 5, 545; 1960: 6, 702; 1950: 7, 590) (Ashley). E. H. McIntosh. Dakota terr. legislature. -- Wishek, Nina (Farley), Along the trails of yesterday, a story of McIntosh county, Ashley, N. D.: Ashley Tribune, 1941; 437 p.

McIntosh, Okla. (est. July 16, 1907; 715 sq. mi.; 1970 pop.: 12, 472; 1960: 12, 371; 1950: 17, 829) (Eufaula). D. N. McIntosh. Creek Indian.

McKean, Pa. (est. Mar. 26, 1804; 997 sq. mi.; 1970 pop.: 51, 915; 1960: 54, 517; 1950: 56, 607) (Smethport). Thomas McKean (1734-1817). Second gov. of Pa. Del. assembly 1752-59; opposed Stamp Act 1765; Continental Congress 1774-83, signer Declaration of Independence (1776) and Articles of Confederation 1778; chairman Pa. Committee of Safety, Pa. chief justice 1777-79; Pa. gov. 1799-1808. -- Stone, Rufus Barrett, McKean, the governor's county, New York: Lewis Historical Pub. Co., Inc., 1926; 315 p.

McKenzie, N. D. (est. Mar. 9, 1883; 2, 810 sq. mi.; 1970 pop.: 6, 127; 1960: 7, 296; 1950: 6, 849) (Watford City). Alexander McKenzie (1856-1922). Sheriff Burleigh County.

McKinley, N. M. (est. Feb. 23, 1899; 5, 450 sq. mi.; 1970 pop.: 43, 208; 1960: 37, 209; 1950: 27, 451) (Gallup). William McKinley (1843-1901). Enlisted as private; bvt. maj. 1865; prosecuting attorney Stark County, Ohio 1869-71; Representative from Ohio 1877-84 and 1885-91; gov. of Ohio 1892-96; Pres. of the U. S. 1897-1901; assassinated 1901.

McLean, Ill. (est. Dec. 25, 1830; 1, 191 sq. mi.; 1970 pop.: 104, 389; 1960: 83, 877; 1950: 76, 577) (Bloomington). John McLean (1791-1830). Representative from Ill. 1818-19; Ill. legislature 1820, 1826 and 1828; Senator from Ill., 1824-25 and 1829-30. -- Duis, E., The Good Old Times in McLean County, Bloomington?, Ill.: McKnight and

McKnight Pub. Co., 1968; 865 p.

McLean, Ky. (est. Feb. 6, 1854; 257 sq. mi.; 1970 pop.: 9,062; 1960: 9,355; 1950: 10,021) (Calhoun). Alney McLean (1779-1841). Ky. house of representatives 1812-13; capt. War of 1812; Representative from Ky. 1815-17 and 1819-21; judge of fourteenth district Ky. 1821-41.

McLean, N. D. (est. Mar. 8, 1883, org. Nov. 1, 1883; 2,289 sq. mi.; 1970 pop.: 11,251; 1960: 14,030; 1950: 18,824) (Washburn). John A. McLean. -- Williams, Mary A. Barnes, Fifty pioneer mothers of McLean County, North Dakota, Washburn, N. D.: Washburn Leader, 1932; 200 p.

McLennan, Tex. (est. Jan. 22, 1850; 1,035 sq. mi.; 1970 pop.: 147,553; 1960: 150,091; 1950: 130,194) (Waco). Neil McLennan (1777-1867). Emigrated from Scotland; in Fla. 1816-34; to Tex. 1834; surveyor; Indians attacked his home 1835.

McLeod, Minn. (est. Mar. 1, 1856; 498 sq. mi.; 1970 pop.: 27,662; 1960: 24,401; 1950: 22,198) (Glencoe) Martin McLeod (1813-1860). Fur trader; Minn. terr. legislature 1849-53; pres. of Minn. terr. legislature council 1853.

McMinn, Tenn. (est. Nov. 13, 1819; 435 sq. mi.; 1970 pop.: 35,462; 1960: 33,662; 1950: 32,024) (Athens). Joseph McMinn. (1758-1824). Fifth gov. of Tenn. Revolutionary War 1776; Tenn. constitutional convention 1796; Tenn. senate 1796, 1798 and 1812; speaker Tenn. senate 1805, 1807 and 1809; gov. of Tenn. 1815-21. Known as "the Quaker governor."

McMullen, Tex. (est. Feb. 1, 1858; 1,159 sq. mi.; 1970 pop.: 1,095; 1960: 1,116; 1950: 1,187) (Tilden). John McMullen.

McNairy, Tenn. (est. Oct. 8, 1823; 569 sq. mi.; 1970 pop.: 18,369; 1960: 18,085; 1950: 20,390) (Selmer). John McNairy. Judge superior court Western District 1788; judge U. S. District Court for Tenn. 1797.

McPherson, Kan. (est. Feb. 26, 1867; 895 sq. mi.; 1970 pop.: 24,778; 1960: 24,285; 1950: 23,670) (McPherson). James Birdseye McPherson (1828-1864). Graduated U. S. Military Academy 1849; second lt. engineers 1853; first lt. 1858; capt. 1861; lt. col. 1861; brig. gen. vol. Tenn. 1862; maj. gen. vol. 1862; brig. gen. 1863; killed in action Atlanta, Ga., July 22, 1864. -- Nyquist, Edna, Pioneer life and lore of McPherson County, Kansas, McPherson, Kan.: Democrat-Opinion Press, 1932; 184 p.

McPherson, Neb. (est. Mar. 31, 1887; 855 sq. mi.; 1970 pop.: 623; 1960: 733; 1950: 825) (Tryon). James Birdseye McPherson*.

McPherson, S. D. (est. Jan. 8, 1873; 1, 151 sq. mi. ; 1970 pop. : 5, 022; 1960: 5, 821; 1950: 7, 071) (Leola). James Birdseye McPherson*.

Meade, Kan. (est. Mar. 6, 1873, dissolved 1883, re-established Mar. 7, 1885, org. Nov. 4, 1885; 976 sq. mi. ; 1970 pop. : 4, 912; 1960: 5, 505; 1950: 5, 710) (Meade). George Gordon Meade (1815-1872). Graduated U. S. Military Academy 1835; Seminole war 1836; Mexican War 1842; Mexican War, battles of Resaca, Palo Alto and Monterey 1846; capt. 1856; brig. gen. vol. 1861; maj. gen. vol. 1862; wounded at Glendale 1862; commanded Army of the Potomac, victorious at Gettysburg 1863; brig. gen. 1863.

Meade, Ky. (est. Dec. 17, 1823; 308 sq. mi. ; 1970 pop. : 18, 796; 1960: 18, 938; 1950: 9, 422) (Brandenburg). James Meade (-1813). Col., killed at battle of the River Raisin, Mich., Jan. 19, 1813.

Meade, S. D. (est. Feb. 7, 1889; 3, 466 sq. mi. ; 1970 pop. : 16, 618; 1960: 12, 044; 1950: 11, 516) (Sturgis). Ft. Meade, named for George Gordon Meade*. -- Stoneville Steadies Extension Club, Central Meade County, Stoneville, S. D., 1964; 416 p.

Meagher, Mont. (est. Nov. 16, 1867; 2, 354 sq. mi. ; 1970 pop. : 2, 122; 1960: 2, 616; 1950: 2, 079) (White Sulphur Springs). Thomas Francis Meagher (1823-1867). Civil War brig. gen. 1862; secretary Mont. Terr. 1865; Mont. acting gov. 1865-66; drowned at Ft. Benton, Mont.

Mecklenburg, N. C. (est. sess. Nov. 3, 1762; 542 sq. mi. ; 1970 pop. : 354, 656; 1960: 272, 111; 1950: 197, 052) (Charlotte). Charlotte Sophia (1774-1818), princess of Mecklenburg-Strelitz; married King George III of England 1761. -- Alexander, John Brevard, The history of Mecklenburg County from 1740 to 1900, Charlotte, N. C. : Observer Printing House, 1902; 431 p. -- Tompkins, Daniel Augustus, History of Mecklenburg County and the City of Charlotte, 1740 to 1903, Charlotte, N. C. : Observer Printing House, 1903; 2 vol.

Mecklenburg, Va. (est. May 26, 1764 sess., eff. Mar. 1, 1765; 665 sq. mi. ; 1970 pop. : 29, 426; 1960: 31, 428; 1950: 33, 497) (Boydton). Charlotte Sophia*.

Mecosta, Mich. (est. Apr. 1, 1840, org. 1859; 563 sq. mi. ; 1970 pop. : 27, 992; 1960: 21, 051; 1950: 18, 968) (Big Rapids). Mecosta. Indian chief, signer of treaty 1836.

Medina, Ohio (est. Feb. 18, 1812; 424 sq. mi. ; 1970 pop. : 82, 717; 1960: 65, 315; 1950: 40, 417) (Medina). Medina, Arabia, refuge of Mohammed who fled from Mecca in 622. The name of the county seat was originally Mecca but was later changed to Medina. -- Medina County Historical Society, History of Medina County, Fostoria, Ohio: Gray Printing Co., 1948; 419 p. -- Northrup, Nira B., Pioneer history of Medina County, Medina, Ohio: O. G. Redway, 1861; 224 p.

Medina, Tex. (est. Feb. 12, 1848; 1,353 sq. mi.; 1970 pop.: 20,249; 1960: 18,904; 1950: 17,013) (Hondo). Medina. Sgt. maj. of De Leon's expedition into Tex.

Meeker, Minn. (est. Feb. 23, 1856; 620 sq. mi.; 1970 pop.: 18,810; 1960: 18,887; 1950: 18,966) (Litchfield). Bradley B. Meeker. Associate justice Minn. supreme court 1849-53. -- Lamson, Frank Bailey, Condensed history of Meeker County, Litchfield, Minn.: Brown Printing Co., 1939; 240 p.

Meigs, Ohio (est. Jan. 21, 1819; 434 sq. mi.; 1970 pop.: 19,799; 1960: 22,159; 1950: 23,227) (Pomeroy). Return Jonathan Meigs (1764-1824). Fourth gov. of Ohio. Indian fighter, Ohio terr. judge 1802-3; chief justice Ohio supreme court 1803-04; pvt. U. S. Army col., commanded St. Charles district, La., 1804-06; judge La. supreme court 1805-06; judge U. S. District Court for Mich. Terr. 1807-08; Senator from Ohio 1808-10; gov. of Ohio 1810-14; Postmaster gen. in cabinets of pres. Madison and Monroe 1814-23. -- Ervin, Edgar, Pioneer history of Meigs County, Meigs County Pioneer Society [n. p.], 1949; 514 p. -- Larkin, Stillman Carter, Pioneer history of Meigs County, Columbus, Ohio: Berlin Printing Co., 1908; 208 p.

Meigs, Tenn. (est. Jan. 20, 1836; 213 sq. mi.; 1970 pop.: 5,219; 1960: 5,160; 1950: 6,080) (Decatur). Return Jonathan Meigs*.

Mellette, S. D. (est. Mar. 9, 1909, org. May 25, 1911; 1,306 sq.mi.; 1970: 2,420; 1960: 2,664; 1950: 3,046) (White River). Arthur C. Mellette (1842-1896). Tenth terr. gov. of Dakota Terr. and first gov. of S. D. Private Co. M, 9th Ind. Inf.; prosecuting attorney Muncie 1868; Ind. house of representatives 1871; editor Muncie, Ind. "Times"; register of the general land office S. D. 1878; provisional gov. but did not take office as state was not admitted 1885; tenth terr. gov. Dakota terr. 1889; first gov. of S. D. 1889-93. -- Reutter, Winifred, Mellette County Memories, South Dakota, 1911-1961, White River, S. D.: Mellette County Centennial Committee, 1961; 318 p.

Menard, Ill. (est. Feb. 15, 1839; 312 sq. mi.; 1970 pop.: 9,685; 1960: 9,248; 1950: 9,639) (Petersburg). Pierre Menard (1766-1844). Maj. Randolph County, Ill. militia 1795-1800; judge of county court common pleas 1801;

Ind. legislature 1803-09; lt. col. county militia 1806; first presiding officer Ill. terr. legislature 1812; first lt. gov. of Ill. 1818-22. -- Drury, John, This Is Menard County, Chicago: Loree Co., 1955; 202 p.

Menard, Tex. (est. Jan. 22, 1858; 914 sq. mi.; 1970 pop.: 2,646; 1960: 2,964; 1950: 4,175) (Menard). Michael Branaman Menard (1803-1856). Came to Tex. 1833; trader; signer Tex. declaration of independence Mar. 2, 1836; Tex. legislature 1840-42; founded Galveston, Tex., nephew of Pierre Menard, above. -- Pierce, Norval Harvey, The free state of Menard, a history of the county, Menard News Press, 1946; 213 p.

Mendocino, Calif. (est. Feb. 18, 1850; 3,510 sq. mi.; 1970 pop.: 51,101; 1960: 51,059; 1950: 40,854) (Ukiah). Cape Mendocino, named for Antonio de Mendoza (c1485-1552). Spanish col. gov. First viceroy New Spain (Mexico) 1535-49; viceroy of Peru 1551-52; sent out expeditions under Coronado which explored what is now Colo. and N.M. -- Gibson, Lilburn I., Some reminiscences...., Elk, Calif.: L. Gibson, 1967; 203 p. -- History of Mendocino County, San Francisco: Alley, Bowen & Co., 1880; 676 p.

Menifee, Ky. (est. Mar. 10, 1869; 210 sq. mi.; 1970 pop.: 4,050; 1960: 4,276; 1950: 4,798) (Frenchburg). Richard Hickman Menefee (1809-1841). Ky. commonwealth attorney 1832; Ky. house of representatives 1836-37; Representative from Ky. 1837-39.

Menominee, Mich. (est. Mar. 19, 1863; 1,032 sq. mi.; 1970 pop.: 24,587; 1960: 24,685; 1950: 25,299) (Menominee). Menominee Indian tribe, Indian name for "wild rice eaters." (Formerly Bleeker County, name changed to Menominee County, Mar. 19, 1863, act 163)

Menominee, Wis. (est. July 30, 1959; eff. May 1, 1961; 365 sq. mi.; 1970 pop.: 2,607) (Keshena) Indian tribe. *

Merced, Calif. (est. Apr. 19, 1855; 1,983 sq. mi.; 1970 pop.: 104,629; 1960: 90,446; 1950: 69,780) (Merced). ("The Land of Opportunity"). Merced River (El Rio de Nuestra Senora de la Merced) River of Our Lady of Mercy; Spanish word for mercy. -- Radcliffe, Corwin, History of Merced County, Merced, Calif., A.H. Cawston, 1940; 414 p.

Mercer, Ill. (est. Jan. 13, 1825; 556 sq. mi.; 1970 pop.: 17,294; 1960: 17,149; 1950: 17,374) (Aledo). Hugh Mercer (1726-1777). Physician, capt. in Braddock's expedition at Ft. Duquesne 1756; col. 3rd battalion 1759; col. Va. militia 1775-76; col. 3rd Va. regiment 1776; brig. gen. 1776; mortally wounded battle of Princeton Jan. 3, 1777, died Jan. 12, 1777. -- History of Mercer & Henderson Counties, Chicago: H. H. Hill & Co., 1882; 1414 p.

Mercer, Ky. (est. sess. Oct. 17, 1785, eff. Aug. 1, 1786; 256 sq. mi.; 1970 pop.: 15,960; 1960: 14,596; 1950: 14,643) (Harrodsburg). Hugh Mercer*. -- Daviess, Maria (Thompson), History of Mercer & Boyle Counties, Harrodsburg, Ky.: Harrodsburg Herald, 1924; 176 p.

Mercer, Mo. (est. Feb. 14, 1845; 456 sq. mi.; 1970 pop.: 4,910; 1960: 5,750; 1950: 7,235) (Princeton). John Francis Mercer (1759-1821). Twelfth gov. of Md. Revolutionary War, wounded at battle of Brandywine; lt. col. Va. cavalry; Continental Congress 1782-85; Md. House of delegates 1788, 1789, 1791 and 1792; Representative from Del., 1792-94; Md. house of delegates 1800, 1803-06; gov. of Md. 1801-13.

Mercer, N.J. (est. Feb. 22, 1838; 228 sq. mi.; 1970 pop.: 303,968; 1960: 266,392; 1950: 229,781) (Trenton). ("The County That Leads in Research"; "The Major Center of Research"). Hugh Mercer*. -- Woodward, E. M., History of Burlington & Mercer Counties, Philadelphia: Everts & Peck, 1883; 888 p.

Mercer, N.D. (est. Jan. 14, 1875, org. Aug. 22, 1884; 1,092 sq. mi.; 1970 pop.: 6,175; 1960: 6,805; 1950: 8,686) (Stanton). William H. Mercer.

Mercer, Ohio (est. Feb. 12, 1820; 454 sq. mi.; 1970 pop.: 35,265; 1960: 32,559; 1950: 28,311) (Celina). Hugh Mercer*. -- Scranton, S. S., History of Mercer County, Ohio, Chicago: Biographical Pub. Co., 1907; 751 p.

Mercer, Pa. (est. Mar. 12, 1800; 681 sq. mi.; 1970 pop.: 127,175; 1960: 127,519; 1950: 111,954) (Mercer). Hugh Mercer*. -- History of Mercer County, Chicago: Brown, Runk & Co., 1888; 1210 p. -- White, John G., A twentieth century history of Mercer County, Chicago: Lewis Pub. Co., 1909; 2 vol.

Mercer, W. Va. (est. Mar. 17, 1837; 423 sq. mi.; 1970 pop.: 63,206; 1960: 68,206; 1950: 75,013) (Princeton). Hugh Mercer*.

Meriwether, Ga. (est. Dec. 24, 1827; 496 sq. mi.; 1970 pop.: 19,461; 1960: 19,756; 1950: 21,055) (Greenville). David Meriwether (1800-1893). Elected thirteen times to Ky. legislature 1832-83; Ky. constitutional convention 1849; Ky. secretary of state 1851; Senator from Ky. 1852; gov. of N. M. terr. 1853-55; Ky. house of representatives 1858-85; speaker Ky. house of representatives 1859.

Merrick, Neb. (est. Nov. 4, 1858; org. Oct. 12, 1859; 467 sq. mi.; 1970 pop.: 8,751; 1960: 8,363; 1950: 8,812) (Central City). Mrs. Elvira Merrick De Puy.

Merrimack, N.H. (est. July 1, 1823; eff. Aug. 1, 1823;

931 sq. mi.; 1970 pop.: 80, 925; 1960: 67, 785; 1950: 63, 022) (Concord). Indian word for "sturgeon" or "swift water." -- Hurd, D. Hamilton, History of Merrimack and Belknap Counties, Philadelphia: J. W. Lewis & Co., 1885; 915 p.

Mesa, Colo. (est. Feb. 14, 1883; 3, 313 sq. mi.; 1970 pop.: 54, 374; 1960: 50, 715; 1950: 38, 974) (Grand Junction). Spanish for "table."

Metcalfe, Ky. (est. Feb. 1, 1860; 296 sq. mi.; 1970 pop.: 8, 177; 1960: 8, 367; 1950: 9, 851) (Edmonton). Thomas Metcalfe (1780-1855). Tenth gov. of Ky. Capt. in War of 1812; Ky. house of representatives 1812-16; Representative from Ky., 1819-28; gov. of Ky. 1828-32; Ky. senate 1834, Senator from Ky. 1848-49.

Miami, Ind. (est. Feb. 2, 1832, eff. Apr. 1, 1832, org. Jan. 2, 1834, eff. Mar. 1, 1834; 380 sq. mi.; 1970 pop.: 39, 246; 1960: 38, 000; 1950: 28, 201) (Peru). Miami Indian tribe, Indian word for "mother." -- Bodurtha, Arthur Lawrence, History of Miami County, Indiana, Chicago: Lewis Pub. Co., 1914; 2 vol.

Miami, Kan. (est. Aug. 30, 1855; 592 sq. mi.; 1970 pop.: 19, 254; 1960: 19, 884; 1950: 19, 693) (Paola). Miami Indian tribe*. (Formerly Lykins County, name changed June 3, 1861, chap. 18).

Miami, Ohio (est. Jan. 16, 1807; 407 sq. mi.; 1970 pop.: 84, 372; 1960: 72, 901; 1950: 61, 309) (Troy). Miami Indian tribe*. -- Hill, Leonard U., ed., A history of Miami County, Piqua, Ohio: Miami County Sesquicentennial historical committee, c1953; 403 p. -- Kinder, William Rusk, Historic notes of Miami County, Troy, Ohio: Troy Foundation, 1953; 213 p.

Middlesex, Conn. (est. May 2, 1785 sess.; 374 sq. mi.; 1970 pop.: 114, 816; 1960: 88, 865; 1950: 67, 332) (no county seat). ("The Maritime County"). Middlesex, England, tribal name of the Middle Saxons. -- History of Middlesex County, New York: J. B. Beers & Co., 1884; 579 p.

Middlesex, Mass. (est. May 10, 1643; 829 sq. mi.; 1970 pop.: 1, 397, 268; 1960: 1, 238, 742; 1950: 1, 064, 569) (Cambridge and Lowell). Middlesex England*. -- Conklin, Edwin P., Middlesex County and Its People, New York: Lewis Historical Pub. Co., 1927; 4 vol. -- Drake, Samuel Adams, History of Middlesex County, Boston: Estes & Lauriat, 1880; 2 vol.

Middlesex, N. J. (est. Mar. 1, 1683; 312 sq. mi.; 1970 pop.: 583, 813; 1960: 433, 856; 1950: 264, 872) (New Brunswick). Middlesex, England.* -- Wall, John Patrick and

Pickersgill, Harold E., History of Middlesex County, New York: Lewis Historical Pub. Co., 1921; 3 vol. -- Miers, Earl Schenk, Where the Raritan flows, New Brunswick, N. J.: Rutgers University Press, 1964; 174 p.

Middlesex, Va. (est. Sept. 21, 1674 sess.; 132 sq. mi.; 1970 pop.: 6,295; 1960: 6,319; 1950: 6,715) (Saluda). Middlesex, England*.

Midland, Mich. (est. Mar. 2, 1831, org. 1850; 520 sq.mi.; 1970 pop.: 63,769; 1960: 51,450; 1950: 35,662) (Midland). Descriptive, near Mich. geographic center.

Midland, Tex. (est. Mar. 4, 1885; 938 sq. mi.; 1970 pop.: 65,371; 1960: 67,717; 1950: 25,785) (Midland). Descriptive; midland between Ft. Worth and El Paso on the Tex. and Pacific Railway.

Mifflin, Pa. (est. Sept. 19, 1789; 431 sq. mi.; 1970 pop.: 45,268; 1960: 44,348; 1950: 43,691) (Lewistown). Thomas Mifflin (1744-1800). First gov. of Pa. Continental Congress 1774-76 and 1782-84, pres. in 1783; served in Continental Army advancing to maj. gen. in 1779; speaker Pa. house of representatives 1785-88; federal constitutional convention 1787; pres. of the supreme executive council of Pa. 1788-90; gov. of Pa., 1790-99. -- Cochran, Joseph, History of Mifflin County, Harrisburg, Pa.: Patriot Pub. Co., 1879.

Milam, Tex. (est. Mar. 17, 1836; 1,027 sq. mi.; 1970 pop.: 20,028; 1960: 22,263; 1950: 23,585) (Cameron). Benjamin Rush Milam (-1836). Col., killed at capture of San Antonio, Dec. 7, 1836.

Millard, Utah (est. Oct. 4, 1851; 6,648 sq. mi.; 1970 pop.: 6,988; 1960: 7,866; 1950: 9,387) (Fillmore). Millard Fillmore (1800-1874). Thirteenth Pres. of the U. S. N. Y. assembly 1829-31; Representative from N. Y., 1833-35 and 1837-43; Comptroller of N. Y. 1847-49; vice pres. of the U. S., inaugurated Mar. 4, 1849; became Pres. upon the death of Pres. Taylor and served from July 9, 1850 to Mar. 3, 1853.

Mille Lacs, Minn. (est. May 23, 1857; 568 sq. mi.; 1970 pop.: 15,703; 1960: 14,560; 1950: 15,165) (Milaca). French words, descriptive for "a thousand lakes."

Miller, Ark. (est. Apr. 1, 1820; 627 sq. mi.; 1970 pop.: 33,385; 1960: 31,686; 1950: 32,614) (Texarkana). James Miller (1776-1851). First terr. gov. of Ark. U. S. Army bvt. col. 1812 and brig. gen. 1819; terr. gov. of Ark., 1819-25; collector of the port, Salem, Mass., 1825-49.

Miller, Ga. (est. Feb. 26, 1856; 253 sq. mi.; 1970 pop.: 6,397; 1960: 6,908; 1950: 9,023) (Colquitt). Andrew Jackson Miller (1806-1856). Ga. house of representatives

1836; Ga. senate 1838-56; judge Ga. superior court.

Miller, Mo. (est. Feb. 6, 1837; 603 sq. mi.; 1970 pop.: 15,025; 1960: 13,800; 1950: 13,734) (Tuscumbia). John Miller (1781-1846). Fourth gov. of Mo. In War of 1812; lt. col. Seventeenth U. S. Inf.; col.; resigned 1818; register of land office Franklin, Mo. 1820-25; gov. of Mo., 1825-32; Representative from Mo. 1837-43.

Mills, Iowa (est. Jan. 15, 1851; 431 sq. mi.; 1970 pop.: 11,606; 1960: 13,050; 1950: 14,064) (Glenwood). Frederick D. Mills (-1847). Maj., inf. 1845; attack on San Antonio Garita, Mexico; killed Aug. 20, 1847.

Mills, Tex. (est. Mar. 15, 1887; 734 sq. mi.; 1970 pop.: 4,212; 1960: 4,467; 1950: 5,999) (Goldthwaite). John T. Mills. District judge Republic of Tex. -- Bowles, Flora (Gatlin), A no man's land becomes a county, Austin?, Texas, 1958; 332 p.

Milwaukee, Wis. (est. Sept. 6, 1834, org. Aug. 25, 1835; 239 sq. mi.; 1970 pop.: 1,054,063; 1960: 1,036,041; 1950: 871,047) (Milwaukee). ("The Fun Center of the Midwest"; "The Great Place to Live, to Work and to Play"). Indian word "Mahn-a-waukee Seepe" for "gathering place by the river." -- Watrous, Jerome Anthony, Memoirs of Milwaukee County, Western Historical Association, 1909; 2 vol.

Miner, S. D. (est. Jan. 8, 1873; 571 sq. mi.; 1970 pop.: 4,454; 1960: 5,398; 1950: 6,268) (Howard). Nelson Miner (1827-1879) organized and capt. of a company of one hundred men, Co. A. Dakota cavalry, registrar of Dakota land office four years; terr. legislature 1869-1879. Ephraim Miner (1833-) member of tenth terr. legislature 1872-73 and recorder of deeds when the county was created.

Mineral, Colo. (est. Mar. 27, 1893; 921 sq. mi.; 1970 pop.: 786; 1960: 424; 1950: 698) (Creede). Descriptive.

Mineral, Mont. (est. Aug. 7, 1914, petition and election; 1,223 sq. mi.; 1970 pop.: 2,958; 1960: 3,037; 1950: 2,081) (Superior). Descriptive.

Mineral, Nev. (est. Feb. 10, 1911; 3,734 sq. mi.; 1970 pop.: 7,051; 1960: 6,329; 1950: 5,560) (Hawthorne). Descriptive.

Mineral, W. Va. (est. Feb. 1, 1866; 330 sq. mi.; 1970 pop.: 23,109; 1960: 22,354; 1950: 22,333) (Keyser). Descriptive.

Mingo, W. Va. (est. Jan. 30, 1895; 423 sq. mi.; 1970 pop.: 32,780; 1960: 39,742; 1950: 47,409) (Williamson). Mingo Indian tribe.

Minidoka, Idaho (est. Jan. 28, 1913, 750 sq. mi.; 1970

15,731; 1960: 14,394; 1950: 9,785) (Rupert). Shoshoni Indian word for "broad expanse."

Minnehaha, S.D. (est. Apr. 5, 1862, org. Jan. 4, 1868; 815 sq. mi.; 1970 pop.: 95,209; 1960: 86,575; 1950: 70,910) (Sioux Falls). Sioux Indian word for "waterfall where the water laughs." -- Bailey, Dana R., History of Minnehaha County, South Dakota, Sioux Falls, S.D.: Brown and Saenger, 1899; 1091 p.

Missaukee, Mich. (est. Apr. 1, 1840, org. 1871; 565 sq. mi.; 1970 pop.: 7,126; 1960: 6,784; 1950: 7,458) (Lake City). Missaukee. Ottawa Indian chief, signed treaties of 1831 and 1833.

Mississippi, Ark. (est. Nov. 1, 1833, eff. Jan. 1, 1834; 919 sq. mi.; 1970 pop.: 62,060; 1960: 70,174; 1950: 82,375) (Blytheville and Osceola). Miss. River; Algonquin Indian words "missi" meaning "great" and "seepee" meaning "water." -- Edrington, Mabel (Flannigan), History of Mississippi County, Ocala, Fla., 1962; 428 p.

Mississippi, Mo. (est. Feb. 14, 1845; 411 sq. mi.; 1970 pop.: 16,647; 1960: 20,695; 1950: 22,551) (Charleston). Mississippi River*.

Missoula, Mont. (est. Feb. 2, 1865; 2,629 sq. mi.; 1970 pop.: 58,263; 1960: 44,663; 1950: 35,493) (Missoula). Indian word "in-mis-sou-let-ka" meaning "the river of awe" or "by the chilling water;" or Flathead Indian word for "at the stream" or "water of surprise" or "ambush."

Mitchell, Ga. (est. Dec. 21, 1857; 548 sq. mi.; 1970 pop.: 18,956; 1960: 19,652; 1950: 22,528) (Camilla). Henry Mitchell. Gen.

Mitchell, Iowa (est. Jan. 15, 1851; 467 sq. mi.; 1970 pop.: 13,108; 1960: 14,043; 1950: 13,945) (Osage). John Mitchell. -- Clyde, Jefferson F. and Dwelle, H. A., History of Mitchell and Worth Counties, Chicago: S. J. Clarke Pub. Co., 1918; 2 vol.

Mitchell, Kan. (est. Feb. 26, 1867; 716 sq. mi.; 1970 pop.: 8,010; 1960: 8,866; 1950: 10,320) (Beloit). William D. Mitchell (-1865). Private Co. B, Second Kan.; capt. cavalry; killed Mar. 10, 1865.

Mitchell, N.C. (est. Feb. 16, 1861; 220 sq. mi.; 1970 pop.: 13,447; 1960: 13,906; 1950: 15,143) (Bakersville). Elisha Mitchell (1793-1857). Prof. Univ. of N.C.; discovered the highest peak east of the Rocky Mountains in N.C.; killed by a fall and buried on the mountain 1857.

Mitchell, Tex. (est. Aug. 21, 1876; 922 sq. mi.; 1970 pop.: 9,073; 1960: 11,255; 1950: 14,357) (Colorado City). Asa Mitchell (1795-1865) and Eli Mitchell, members of Austin's colony. Asa fought at battle of San Jacinto, Apr. 21, 1836.

Mobile, Ala. (est. Aug. 1, 1812; 1,248 sq. mi.; 1970 pop.: 317,308; 1960: 314,301; 1950: 231,105) (Mobile). Maubila or Mauvila Indian name of the Spanish; Mobile of the French.

Modoc, Calif. (est. Feb. 17, 1874; 4,094 sq. mi.; 1970 pop.: 7,469; 1960: 8,308; 1950: 9,678) (Alturas). Modoc Indian tribe. -- Brown, William Samuel, California Northeast; the bloody ground, Oakland, Calif.: Biobooks, 1951; 207 p.

Moffat, Colo. (est. Feb. 27, 1911; 4,754 sq. mi.; 1970 pop.: 6,525; 1960: 7,061; 1950: 5,946) (Craig). David Halliday Moffat (1839-1911). Cashier First National Bank of Denver; pres. of the Rio Grande RR 1884-91.

Mohave, Ariz. (est. Dec. 21, 1864; 13,260 sq. mi.; 1970 pop.: 25,857; 1960: 7,736; 1950: 8,510) (Kingman). ("The Land of Blue Lakes"). Mohave Indian tribe; Indian word for "three mountains."

Moniteau, Mo. (est. Feb. 14, 1845; 418 sq. mi.; 1970 pop.: 10,742; 1960: 10,500; 1950: 10,840) (California). French translation of "spirit of God." -- Ford, James Everett, A history of Moniteau County, Missouri, California, Mo.: M. H. Crawford, 1936; 528 p.

Monmouth, N.J. (est. Mar. 1, 1683; 477 sq. mi.; 1970 pop.: 459,379; 1960: 334,401; 1950: 225,327) (Freehold). ("New Jersey's Front Window"). Monmouth County, Eng., named for James Scott, (1649-1685) Duke of Monmouth, the son of Charles II. -- Ellis, Franklin, History of Monmouth County, Philadelphia: R. T. Peck, 1885; 902 p. -- Hornor, William Stockton, This old Monmouth of ours, Freehold, N.J.: Moreau Brothers, 1932; 444 p.

Mono, Calif. (est. Apr. 24, 1861; 3,045 sq. mi.; 1970 pop.: 4,016; 1960: 2,213; 1950: 2,115) (Bridgeport). ("The Fisherman's Paradise"). Indian tribe of the Shoshonean Indians, named for Spanish word for "monkey." -- Cain, Ella M. (Cody), The Story of Early Mono County, Fearon, San Francisco, 1961; 166 p.

Monona, Iowa (est. Jan. 15, 1851; 689 sq. mi.; 1970 pop.: 12,069; 1960: 13,916; 1950: 16,303) (Onawa). Monona. Indian maiden who jumped from a high cliff into the Miss. River committing suicide in the belief that her tribesmen killed her white lover. -- History of Monona County, Chicago: National Pub. Co., 1890; 661 p.

Monongalia, W. Va. (est. Oct. 7, 1776; 368 sq. mi.; 1970 pop.: 63,714; 1960: 55,617; 1950: 60,797) (Morgantown). Variant spelling of Monongahela, Indian word for "falling in river bank." -- Wiley, Samuel T., History of Monongalia County, Kingwood, W. Va.: Preston Pub. Co., 1883; 776 p.

Monroe, Ala. (est. June 29, 1815; 1,035 sq. mi.; 1970 pop.: 20,883; 1960: 22,372; 1950: 25,732) (Monroeville). James Monroe (1758-1831). Fifth Pres. of the U.S. Twelfth and sixteenth gov. Va. (Commonwealth). Revolutionary War; Va. legislature; Continental Congress 1783-86; Senator from Va., 1790-94; U.S. Secretary of State under Pres. James Madison; Pres. of the U.S., 1817-25.

Monroe, Ark. (est. Nov. 2, 1829, eff. Jan. 1, 1830; 617 sq. mi.; 1970 pop.: 15,657; 1960: 17,327; 1950: 19,540) (Clarendon). James Monroe*.

Monroe, Fla. (est. July 3, 1823, eff. Dec. 29, 1824; 994 sq. mi.; 1970 pop.: 52,586; 1960: 47,921; 1950: 29,957) (Key West). James Monroe*.

Monroe, Ga. (est. May 15, 1821; 470 sq. mi.; 1970 pop.: 10,991; 1960: 10,495; 1950: 10,523) (Forsyth). James Monroe*.

Monroe, Ill. (est. Jan. 6, 1816; 389 sq. mi.; 1970 pop.: 18,831; 1960: 15,507; 1950: 13,282) (Waterloo). James Monroe*. -- Klein, Helen (Ragland), Arrowheads to Aerojets, Valmeyer, Ill.: Myron Roever Associates, 1967; 959 p.

Monroe, Ind. (est. Jan. 14, 1818; eff. Apr. 10, 1819; 412 sq. mi.; 1970 pop.: 84,849; 1960: 59,225; 1950: 50,080) (Bloomington) James Monroe*. -- History of Lawrence and Monroe Counties, Ind., Indianapolis, Ind.: B. F. Bowen & Co., Inc., 1914; 764 p.

Monroe, Iowa (est. Feb. 17, 1843, org. June 11, 1845, eff. July 1, 1845; 435 sq. mi.; 1970 pop.: 9,357; 1960: 10,463; 1950: 11,314) (Albia). James Monroe*. (Originally Kishkekosh County, name changed to Monroe County, Jan. 19, 1846, chap. 21 -- History of Monroe County, Chicago: Western Historical Co., 1878; 508 p.

Monroe, Ky. (est. Jan. 19, 1820; 334 sq. mi.; 1970 pop.: 11,642; 1960: 11,799; 1950: 13,770) (Tompkinsville). James Monroe*.

Monroe, Mich. (est. July 14, 1817, org. 1822; 562 sq. mi.; 1970 pop.: 118,479; 1960: 101,120; 1950: 75,666) (Monroe). James Monroe*. -- Wing, Talcott, E., History of Monroe County, New York: Munsell & Co., 1890; 53 p.

Monroe, Miss. (est. Feb. 9, 1821; 770 sq. mi.; 1970 pop.: 34,043; 1960: 33,953; 1950: 36,543) (Aberdeen). James Monroe*.

Monroe, Mo. (est. Jan. 6, 1831; 669 sq. mi.; 1970 pop.: 9,542; 1960: 10,688; 1950: 11,314) (Paris). James Monroe*.

Monroe, N.Y. (est. Feb. 23, 1821; 673 sq. mi.; 1970 pop.: 711,917; 1960: 586,387; 1950: 487,632) (Rochester).

James Monroe*.

Monroe, Ohio (est. Jan. 29, 1813; 455 sq. mi.; 1970 pop.: 15, 739; 1960: 15, 268; 1950: 15, 362) (Woodsfield). James Monroe*.

Monroe, Pa. (est. Apr. 1, 1836; 611 sq. mi.; 1970 pop.: 45, 422; 1960: 39, 567; 1950: 33, 373) (Stroudsburg). ("Pennsylvania's Picturesque Playground"). James Monroe*. -- Keller, Robert Brown, History of Monroe County, Stroudsburg, Pa.: Monroe Pub. Co., 1927; 500 p.

Monroe, Tenn. (est. Nov. 13, 1819; 665 sq. mi.; 1970 pop.: 23, 475; 1960: 23, 316; 1950: 24, 513) (Madisonville). James Monroe*.

Monroe, W. Va. (est. Jan. 14, 1799, eff. May 1, 1799; 473 sq. mi.; 1970 pop.: 11, 272; 1960: 11, 584; 1950: 13, 123) (Union). James Monroe*. -- Morton, Oren Frederic, A history of Monroe County, Dayton, Va.: Ruebush-Elkins Co., 1916; 509 p.

Monroe, Wis. (est. Mar. 21, 1854; 915 sq. mi.; 1970 pop.: 31, 610; 1960: 31, 241; 1950: 31, 378) (Sparta). James Monroe*.

Montague, Tex. (est. Dec. 24, 1857; 937 sq. mi.; 1970 pop.: 15, 326; 1960: 14, 893; 1950: 17, 070) (Montague). Daniel Montague. -- Potter, Fannie Cora (Bellows), History of Montague County, Austin, Texas: E. I. Stech, 1912; 191 p.

Montcalm, Mich. (est. Mar. 2, 1831, org. 1835; 712 sq. mi.; 1970 pop.: 39, 660; 1960: 35, 795; 1950: 31, 013) (Stanton). Louis Joseph de Saint Veran Montcalm (1712-1759). Brig. gen. in command of French troops in Canada, captured Ft. Ontario, Ft. William Henry; mortally wounded at Heights of Abraham, Sept. 14, 1759.

Monterey, Calif. (est. Feb. 18, 1850; 3, 324 sq. mi.; 1970 pop.: 250, 071; 1960: 198, 351; 1950: 130, 498) (Salinas) ("The Premier County of California"). (Gaspar de Zuniga y Azevedo, Count of Monterey (1540?-1606). Spanish colonial administrator, viceroy of Mexico 1595-1603; sent out exploring expeditions. Named by Sebastian Vizcaino who landed in 1603. -- Watkins, Rolin G., History of Monterey and Santa Cruz Counties, Chicago: S. J. Clarke Pub. Co., 1925; 2 vol.

Montezuma, Colo. (est. Apr. 16, 1889; 2, 095 sq. mi.; 1970 pop.: 12, 952; 1960: 14, 024; 1950: 9, 991) (Cortez). Montezuma (1479-1520). Aztec chief conquered by Cortez and killed June 30, 1520. -- Freeman, Ira S., A History of Montezuma County, Boulder, Colo.: Johnson Pub. Co., 1958; 323 p.

Montgomery, Ala. (est. Dec. 6, 1816; 790 sq. mi.; 1970 pop.: 167, 790; 1960: 169, 210; 1950: 138, 965) (Montgomery).

Lemuel Purnell Montgomery (-1814). Maj. under gen. Jackson killed in battle with Creek Indians at Horseshoe Bend, Mar. 29, 1814.

Montgomery, Ark. (est. Dec. 9, 1842; 801 sq. mi.; 1970 pop.: 5, 821; 1960: 5, 370; 1950: 6, 680) (Mount Ida). Richard Montgomery (1738-1775). Provincial Congress 1775; brig. gen. Continental Army; Captured Montreal, Canada. Killed leading assault against Quebec on Dec. 31, 1775.

Montgomery, Ga. (est. Dec. 19, 1793; 190 sq. mi.; 1970 pop.: 6, 099; 1960: 6, 284; 1950: 7, 901) (Mount Vernon). Richard Montgomery*.

Montgomery, Ill. (est. Feb. 12, 1821; 689 sq. mi.; 1970 pop.: 30, 260; 1960: 31, 244; 1950: 32, 460) (Hillsboro). Richard Montgomery*. -- Perrin, William Henry, History of Bond and Montgomery Counties, Chicago: O. L. Baskin & Co., 1882; 419 p.

Montgomery, Ind. (est. Dec. 21, 1822, eff. Mar. 1, 1823; 507 sq. mi.; 1970 pop.: 33, 930; 1960: 32, 089; 1950: 29, 122) (Crawfordsville). Richard Montgomery*. -- Gronert, Theodore Gregory, Sugar Creek saga; a history and development of Montgomery County, Indiana, Crawford, Ind.: 1958; 496 p. -- History of Montgomery County, Indiana, Indianapolis, Ind.: A. W. Bowen & Co., 1914; 2 vol.

Montgomery, Iowa (est. Jan. 15, 1851; 422 sq. mi.; 70: 12, 781; 60: 14, 467; 1950: 15, 685) (Red Oak). Richard Montgomery*. -- Merritt, W. W., A History of the County of Montgomery, Red Oak, Iowa: Express Pub. Co., 1906; 343 p.

Montgomery, Kan. (est. Feb. 26, 1867, org. June 3, 1869; 649 sq. mi.; 1970 pop.: 39, 949; 1960: 45, 007; 1950: 46, 487) (Independence). Richard Montgomery*. -- History of Montgomery County, Kansas, by its own people, Iola, Kan.: Iola Register, 1903; 852 p.

Montgomery, Ky. (est. Dec. 14, 1796, eff. Mar. 1, 1797; 204 sq. mi.; 1970 pop.: 15, 364; 1960: 13, 461; 1950: 13, 025) (Mount Sterling). Richard Montgomery*.

Montgomery, Md. (est. Resolve of convention Sept. 6, 1776, org. Oct. 1, 1776; 494 sq. mi.; 1970 pop.: 522, 809; 1960: 340, 928; 1950: 164, 401) (Rockville). ("The Historic County"; "The Science Center, U. S. A."). Richard Montgomery*. -- Boyd, Thomas Hulings Stockton, The History of Montgomery County, Md., Baltimore, Md.: Regional Pub. Co., 1968 [reprint of 1879 ed.]; 187 p. -- Farquhar, Roger Brooke, Historic Montgomery County, Silver Spring, Md.: 1952; 373 p.

Montgomery, Miss. (est. May 13, 1871; 398 sq. mi.; 1970

pop.: 12,918; 1960: 13,320; 1950: 14,470) (Winona). Richard Montgomery*.

Montgomery, Mo. (est. Dec. 14, 1818; 533 sq. mi.; 1970 pop.: 11,000; 1960: 11,097; 1950: 11,555) (Montgomery City). Richard Montgomery*.

Montgomery, N.Y. (est. Mar. 12, 1772; 409 sq. mi.; 1970 pop.: 55,883; 1960: 57,240; 1950: 59,594) (Fonda). Richard Montgomery*. (Formerly Tryon County, name changed to Montgomery County, Apr. 2, 1784). -- Frothingham, Washington, ed., History of Montgomery County, Syracuse, N.Y.: D. Mason & Co., 1892; 450 p.

Montgomery, N.C. (est. sess., Apr. 14, 1778; 488 sq. mi.; 1970 pop.: 19,267; 1960: 18,408; 1950: 17,260) (Troy). Richard Montgomery*.

Montgomery, Ohio (est. Mar. 24, 1803; 465 sq. mi.; 1970 pop.: 606,148; 1960: 527,080; 1950: 398,441) (Dayton). Richard Montgomery*. -- The History of Montgomery County, Chicago: W.H. Beers & Co., 1882; 760 p. -- Kjellenberg, Marion S., Ole Montgomery the village of lovely homes and friendly people, history and directory, Montgomery, Ohio, 1960; 160 p.

Montgomery, Pa. (est. Sept. 10, 1784; 484 sq. mi.; 1970 pop.: 623,799; 1960: 516,682; 1950: 353,068) (Norristown). ("The Key to the Keystone State"). Richard Montgomery*. -- Alderfer, Everett Gordon, The Montgomery County Story, Norristown, Pa.: Commissioners of Montgomery County, 1951; 301 p. -- Kriebel, Howard Wiegner, A brief history of Montgomery County, Norristown, Pa., 1923; 216 p.

Montgomery, Tenn. (est. Apr. 9, 1796; 543 sq. mi.; 1970 pop.: 62,721; 1960: 55,645; 1950: 44,186) (Clarksville). John Montgomery (-1794). Explored Cumberland County 1771; campaign against Indian chief Dragging Canoe; commanded terr. troops Nickajack expedition 1794; killed by Indians 1794. -- Beach, Ursula (Smith), Along the Warioto, a History of Montgomery County, Tenn., Clarksville, Tenn., 1964; 390 p.

Montgomery, Tex. (est. Dec. 14, 1837; 1,090 sq. mi.; 1970 pop.: 49,479; 1960: 26,836; 1950: 24,504) (Conroe). Richard Montgomery*.

Montgomery, Va. (est. sess. Oct. 7, 1776; 395 sq. mi.; 1970 pop.: 47,157; 1960: 32,923; 1950: 29,780) (Christiansburg). Richard Montgomery*. -- Crush, Charles W., ed., The Montgomery County Story 1776-1957, Christiansburg, Va., 1957; 167 p.

Montmorency, Mich. (est. Apr. 1, 1840, org. May 21, 1881; 555 sq. mi.; 1970 pop.: 5,247; 1960: 4,424; 1950:

4, 125) (Atlanta). Lord Raymond de Montmorency (1806-1889). French soldier, officer 10th Hussars; indicted for libel and sentenced to twelve months imprisonment, Dec. 1852. (Originally Chenoquet County name changed to Montmorency County on Mar. 8, 1843.)

Montour, Pa. (est. May 3, 1850; 130 sq. mi.; 1970 pop.: 16, 508; 1960: 16, 730; 1950: 16, 001) (Danville). Madame Montour. Indian interpreter, celebrated French half-breed for whose son, Andrew, the town of Montoursville, Pa., was named; and for whose daughter, Margaret, the Indian village French Margaret's Town (now Williamsport, Pa.) was named.

Montrose, Colo. (est. Feb. 11, 1883; 2, 239 sq. mi.; 1970 pop.: 18, 366; 1960: 18, 286; 1950: 15, 220) (Montrose). Named for Sir Walter Scott's novel "The Legend of Montrose" (1819) because it resembled the land described in the book.

Moody, S. D. (est. Jan. 8, 1873; 523 sq. mi.; 1970 pop.: 7, 622; 1960: 8, 810; 1950: 9, 252) (Flandreau). Gideon Curtis Moody (1832-1904). Prosecuting attorney Floyd County, Ind., 1854; Ind. house of representatives 1861; capt., lt. col. and col. in Civil War; Delegate from Dakota terr. 1867-69 and 1874-75; associate justice supreme court Dakota terr. 1878-83; Senator from S. D., 1889-91.

Moore, N. C. (est. sess. Apr. 18, 1784; 672 sq. mi.; 1970 pop.: 39, 048; 1960: 36, 733; 1950: 33, 129) (Carthage). Alfred Moore (1755-1810). Capt. in Revolutionary War; attorney gen. of N. C. 1782; Associate Justice of the U. S. Supreme Court 1799-1804. -- Robinson, Blackwell P., History of Moore County, North Carolina, 1747-1847, Southern Pines, N. C.: Moore County Historical Association, 1956; 270 p. -- Wellman, Manly Wade, The County of Moore 1847-1947, a North Carolina region's second hundred years, County Hist. Assoc., 1962.

Moore, Tenn. (est. Dec. 14, 1871; 122 sq. mi.; 1970 pop.: 3, 568; 1960: 3, 454; 1950: 3, 948) (Lynchburg). William Moore. Commanded company under gen. Jackson in Creek War; maj. gen. in War of 1812; Tenn. house of representatives 1825-27.

Moore, Tex. (est. Aug. 21, 1876; 912 sq. mi.; 1970 pop.: 14, 060; 1960: 14, 773; 1950: 13, 349) (Dumas). Edwin Ward Moore. Served in the navy of the Republic of Tex. -- Thomas, Myrna Tryon, The windswept land, a history of Moore County, Texas, Dumas, Texas, 1967; 145 p.

Mora, N. M. (est. Feb. 1, 1860; 1, 942 sq. mi.; 1970 pop.: 4, 673; 1960: 6, 028; 1950: 8, 720) (Mora). Spanish for "raspberries."

Morehouse, La. (est. Mar. 25, 1844; 831 sq. mi.; 1970 pop.: 32,463; 1960: 33,709; 1950: 32,038) (Bastrop). Abraham Morehouse.

Morgan, Ala. (est. Feb. 6, 1818; 574 sq. mi.; 1970 pop.: 77,306; 1960: 60,454; 1950: 52,924) (Decatur). Daniel Morgan (1736-1802). Teamster under Gen. Braddock 1755; lt. in Pontiac's War 1764; capt. in Dunmore's War 1774; capt. Va. riflemen 1775; captured at Quebec Dec. 31, 1775; col. of Va. regiment 1776; at battle of Saratoga brig. gen. 1780; defeated Gen. Tarleton at battle of Cowpens 1781; commanding Va. militia suppressed Whiskey Insurrection in Pa. 1794; Representative from Va., 1797-99. (Originally Cotaco County, changed to present name June 14, 1821.)

Morgan, Colo. (est. Feb. 19, 1889; 1,282 sq. mi.; 1970 pop.: 20,105; 1960: 21,192; 1950: 18,074) (Fort Morgan). Christopher A. Morgan.

Morgan, Ga. (est. Dec. 10, 1807; 390 sq. mi.; 1970 pop.: 9,904; 1960: 10,280; 1950: 11,899) (Madison). Daniel Morgan*.

Morgan, Ill. (est. Jan. 31, 1823; 576 sq. mi.; 1970 pop.: 36,174; 1960: 36,571; 1950: 35,568) (Jacksonville). Daniel Morgan*. -- Eames, Charles M., Historic Morgan and Classic Jacksonville, Jacksonville, Ill.: Daily Journal St. Job Pr. Office, 1885; 336 p.

Morgan, Ind. (est. Dec. 31, 1821, eff. Feb. 15, 1822; 406 sq. mi.; 1970 pop.: 44,176; 1960: 33,875; 1950: 23,726) (Martinsville). Daniel Morgan*.

Morgan, Ky. (est. Dec. 7, 1822; 369 sq. mi.; 1970 pop.: 10,019; 1960: 11,056; 1950: 13,624) (West Liberty). Daniel Morgan*.

Morgan, Mo. (est. Jan. 5, 1833; 596 sq. mi.; 1970 pop.: 10,068; 1960: 9,476; 1950: 10,207) (Versailles). Daniel Morgan*.

Morgan, Ohio (est. Dec. 29, 1817; 418 sq. mi.; 1970 pop.: 12,375; 1960: 12,747; 1950: 12,836) (McConnelsville). Daniel Morgan*.

Morgan, Tenn. (est. Oct. 15, 1817; 539 sq. mi.; 1970 pop.: 13,619; 1960: 14,304; 1950: 15,727) (Wartburg). Daniel Morgan*.

Morgan, Utah (est. Jan. 17, 1862; 610 sq. mi.; 1970 pop.: 3,983; 1960: 2,837; 1960: 2,519) (Morgan). Jedediah Morgan Grant (-1856). Legislator, churchman, public official. Counselor to Brigham Young; father of Heber J. Grant, pres. of the Latter-day Saints church 1940. -- Fine Arts Study Group, Mountains conquered; the story of Morgan, Morgan, Utah, 1959; 355 p.

Morgan, W. Va. (est. Feb. 9, 1820; 231 sq. mi.; 1970 pop.: 8,547; 1960: 8,376; 1950: 8,276) (Berkeley Springs). Daniel Morgan*.

Morrill, Neb. (est. 1908; 1,403 sq. mi.; 1970 pop.: 5,813; 1960: 7,057; 1950: 8,263) (Bridgeport). Charles Henry Morrill.

Morris, Kan. (est. Aug. 30, 1855; 707 sq. mi.; 1970 pop.: 6,432; 1960: 7,392; 1950: 8,485) (Council Grove). Thomas Morris (1776-1844). Fought Indians 1793; Ohio house of representatives 1806-08, 1810, 1820-21; Ohio senate 1813-15, 1821-23, 1825-29 and 1831-33; Senator from Ohio 1833-39; nominated for the vice presidency on the Liberty ticket 1844. (Originally Wise County, name changed to Morris County, Feb. 11, 1859). chap. 60

Morris, N. J. (est. Mar. 15, 1739; 468 sq. mi.; 1970 pop.: 383,454; 1960: 261,620; 1950: 164,371) (Morristown). ("The County With a History and a Future"). Lewis Morris (1671-1746). First gov. of N. J. Judge of the Superior Court of N. Y. and N. J. 1692; chief justice of N. Y. and N. J. 1710-38; acting gov. of N. J. 1731; gov. of N. J. 1738-46. -- Pitney, H. C., ed., History of Morris County, New York: Lewis Historical Pub. Co., 1914; 2 vol.

Morris, Tex. (est. Mar. 6, 1875; 263 sq. mi.; 1970 pop.: 12,310; 1960: 12,576; 1950: 9,433) (Daingerfield). W. W. Morris.

Morrison, Minn. (est. Feb. 25, 1856; 1,136 sq. mi.; 1970 pop.: 26,949; 1960: 26,641; 1950: 25,832) (Little Falls). Allan Morrison (-1878). Fur trader, Minn. terr. legislature. Brother, William Morrison, fur trader. -- Fuller, Clara K., History of Morrison and Todd Counties, Indianapolis, Ind.: B. F. Bowen and Co., 1915; 2 vol.

Morrow, Ohio (est. Feb. 24, 1848; 404 sq. mi.; 1970 pop.: 21,348; 1960: 19,405; 1950: 17,168) (Mount Gilead). Jeremiah Morrow (1771-1852). Ninth gov. of Ohio. Ohio terr. house of representatives 1801-02; Ohio Senate 1803; Representative from Ohio 1803-13; Senator from Ohio 1813-19; gov. of Ohio 1822-26; Ohio senate 1827; Ohio house of representatives 1829 and 1835; Representative from Ohio 1840-43. -- Baughman, Abraham J., History of Morrow County, Chicago: Lewis Pub. Co., 1911; 2 vol. -- History of Morrow County and Ohio, Chicago: O. L. Baskin & Co., 1880; 838 p.

Morrow, Ore. (est. Feb. 16, 1885; 2,059 sq. mi.; 1970 pop.: 4,465; 1960: 4,871; 1950: 4,783) (Heppner). Jackson L. Morrow. Legislator from Umatilla 1853. -- Parsons, William and Shiach, W. S., An illustrated history of Umatilla County and of Morrow County, W. H. Lever, [n. p.], 1902; 581 p.

Morton, Kan. (est. Feb. 18, 1886, org. Nov. 18, 1886; 725 sq. mi.; 1970 pop.: 3,576; 1960: 3,354; 1950: 2,610) (Richfield). Oliver Hazard Perry Throck Morton (1823-1877). Fourteenth gov. of Ind. Judge sixth judicial circuit Ind. 1852; gov. of Ind. 1861-67; Senator from Ind., 1867-77.

Morton, N. D. (est. Jan. 8, 1873, org. Feb. 28, 1881; 1,933 sq. mi.; 1970 pop.: 20,310; 1960: 20,992; 1950: 19,295) (Mandan). Oliver Hazard Perry Throck Morton*.

Motley, Tex. (est. Aug. 21, 1876; 1,011 sq. mi.; 1970 pop.: 2,178; 1960: 2,870; 1950: 3,963) (Matador). Dr. Junius William Mottley (1812- 1836). Graduated as physician 1834, settled in Tex. 1835; signer Tex. declaration of independence 1836; aide to Gen. Rush at battle of San Jacinto where he was killed Apr. 21, 1836. An error in the spelling of his name resulted in the name Motley, instead of Mottley. -- Campbell, Harry H., The early history of Motley County, San Antonio, Texas: Naylor Co., 1958; 74 p.

Moultrie, Ill. (est. Feb. 16, 1843; 338 sq. mi.; 1970 pop.: 13,263; 1960: 13,635; 1950: 13,171) (Sullivan). William Moultrie (1731-1805). Sixth and ninth gov. of S. C.; fought Cherokee Indians 1761; col. in Revolutionary Army advanced to maj. gen.; gov. of S. C. 1785-87 and 1792-94.

Mountrail, N. D. (est. Jan. 4, 1873; 1,900 sq. mi.; 1970 pop.: 8,437; 1960: 10,077; 1950: 9,418) (Stanley). "Savage" Joseph Mountraille, who carried the mail. -- Breeling, Lutie (Taylor), When the trail was new in Mountraille, Ross?, N. D., 1956; 115 p.

Mower, Minn. (est. Feb. 20, 1855, org. Mar. 1, 1856; 703 sq. mi.; 1970 pop.: 43,783; 1960: 48,498; 1950: 42,277) (Austin.) John E. Mower. Minn. terr. legislature 1854-55; Minn. house of representatives 1874-75.

Muhlenberg, Ky. (est. Dec. 14, 1798, eff. May 15, 1799; 482 sq. mi.; 1970 pop.: 27,537; 1960: 27,791; 1950: 32,501) (Greenville). John Peter Gabriel Muhlenberg (1746-1807) Member Va. house of burgesses 1774, col. in Continental Army, brig. gen. in 1777 and maj. gen. in 1783; vice pres. of Pa. Supreme executive council 1785-87; Representative from Pa. 1789-91, 1793-95, 1799-1801, collector of port of Philadelphia 1803-07. -- Rothert, Otto A., A history of Muhlenberg County, Louisville, Ky.: J. P. Morton & Co., 1913; 496 p.

Multnomah, Ore. (est. Dec. 22, 1854; 424 sq. mi.; 1970

pop.: 556, 667; 1960: 522, 813; 1950: 471, 537) (Portland). ("The Land of Adventure and Opportunity"). Multnomah Indian tribe.

Murray, Ga. (est. Dec. 3, 1832; 342 sq. mi.; 1970 pop.: 12, 986; 1960: 10, 447; 1950: 10, 676) (Chatsworth). Thomas W. Murray (1790-1832). 1818 Ga. leg.; speaker of the house; nominated for U. S. congress but died before election. -- Shriner, Charles H., History of Murray County, (n. p.), 1911; 48 p.

Murray, Minn. (est. May 23, 1857; 708 sq. mi.; 1970 pop.: 12, 508; 1960: 14, 743; 1950: 14, 801) (Slayton). William Pitt Murray. Minn. terr. legislature 1852-53 and 1857; member of the council 1854-55; Minn. house of representatives 1863 and 1868; Minn. state senator 1866-67 and 1875-76.

Murray, Okla. (est. July 16, 1907; 428 sq. mi.; 1970 pop.: 10, 669; 1960: 10, 622; 1950: 10, 775) (Sulphur). William Henry "Alfalfa Bill" Murray (1869-1956). Ninth gov. of Okla. Pres. of Okla. constitutional convention 1906; Okla. house of representatives 1907-09; Representative from Okla. 1913-17; gov. of Okla. 1931-35.

Muscatine, Iowa (est. Dec. 7, 1836; 439 sq. mi.; 1970 pop.: 37, 181; 1960: 33, 840; 1950: 32, 148) (Muscatine). Mascoutin Indian tribe. -- Richman, Irving Berdine, History of Muscatine County, Chicago: S. J. Clarke Pub. Co., 1911; 2 vol.

Muscogee, Ga. (est. Dec. 11, 1826, org. Dec. 24, 1827; 235 sq. mi.; 1970 pop.: 167, 377; 1960: 158, 673; 1950: 118, 028) (Columbus). Muscogee Indian tribe.

Muskegon, Mich. (est. Jan. 7, 1859; 504 sq. mi.; 1970 pop.: 157, 426; 1960: 149, 943; 1950: 121, 545) (Muskegon). Chippewa Indian word for "river with marshes."

Muskingum, Ohio (est. Jan. 7, 1804, eff. Mar. 1, 1804; 667 sq. mi.; 1970 pop.: 77, 826; 1960: 79, 159; 1950: 74,535) (Zanesville). Indian word for "by the rivers' side." -- Everhart, J. F., History of Muskingum County, Columbus, Ohio: J. F. Everhart, 1882; 480 p.

Muskogee, Okla. (est. July 16, 1907; 822 sq. mi.; 1970 pop.: 59, 542; 1960: 61, 866; 1950: 65, 573) (Muskogee). Muscogee Indian tribe*.

Musselshell, Mont. (est. Feb. 11, 1911; 1, 886 sq. mi.; 1970 pop.: 3, 734; 1960: 4, 888; 1950: 5, 408) (Roundup). Descriptive, Musselshell River, (mussel shells found along its banks).

N

Nacogdoches, Tex. (est. Mar. 17, 1836; 963 sq. mi.; 1970 pop.: 36,362; 1960: 28,046; 1950: 30,326) (Nacogdoches). Nacogdoches Indian tribe.

Nance, Neb. (est. Feb. 13, 1879, org. June 21, 1879; 438 sq. mi.; 1970 pop.: 5,142; 1960: 5,635; 1950: 6,512) (Fullerton). Albinus Nance (1848-1911). Fourth gov. of Neb. Private in Illinois cavalry 1864; Neb. legislature 1874-78; speaker Neb. house of representatives 1877; gov. of Neb. 1879-83.

Nansemond, Va. (est. Mar. 1645 sess.; 402 sq. mi.; 1970 pop.: 35,166; 1960: 31,366; 1950: 25,238) (Suffolk). ("The World's Largest Peanut Market"). Indian word for "fishing point." -- Dunn, Joseph B., The History of Nansemond County, Suffolk, Va., 1907; 71 p.

Nantucket, Mass. (est. June 22, 1695; 46 sq. mi.; 1970 pop.: 3,774; 1960: 3,559; 1950: 3,484) (Nantucket). Indian word "nantican" meaning "at the promontory" or "nanticut" meaning "far away land" or "nantuck" meaning "sandy, sterile soil tempted no one" -- Starbuck, Alexander, The History of Nantucket; county, island and town, Boston, Mass.: C. E. Goodspeed and Co., 1924; 871 p. -- Douglas-Lithgow, Robert Alexander, Nantucket, a History, New York: G. P. Putnam's Sons, 1914; 389 p.

Napa, Calif. (est. Feb. 18, 1850; 780 sq. mi.; 1970 pop.: 79,140; 1960: 65,890; 1950: 46,603) (Napa). Indian word for "fish harpoon" or "abundant." -- Palmer, Lyman L., History of Napa and Lake Counties, San Francisco: Slocum, Bowen & Co., 1881; 291 p.

Nash, N.C. (est. sess. Nov. 15, 1777; 552 sq. mi.; 1970 pop.: 59,122; 1960: 61,002; 1950: 59,919) (Nashville). Francis Nash (1742-1777). Justice of the peace 1763; N.C. house of commons 1764; assembly 1771, 1773-75; provincial council 1775; lt. col. 1775; brig. gen. 1777; mortally wounded at battle of Germantown.

Nassau, Fla. (est. Dec. 29, 1824; 650 sq. mi.; 1970 pop.: 20,626; 1960: 17,189; 1950: 12,811) (Fernandina). Nassau, Duchy of Nassau in Germany.

Nassau, N.Y. (est. Apr. 27, 1898; 300 sq. mi.; 1970 pop.: 1,422,905; 1960: 1,300,171; 1950: 672,765) (Mineola). ("Happiness County, U.S.A."; "The County Where Happiness Is Happening"; "The Gateway to New York City"). William of Nassau. -- Mepham, Wellington C., Exploring Nassau County, New York: Noble & Noble, Inc., 1938; 275 p.

Natchitoches, La. (est. Apr. 10, 1805; 1,289 sq. mi.; 1970 pop.: 35,219; 1960: 35,653; 1950; 38,144) (Natchitoches). Natchitoches Indian tribe.

Natrona, Wyo. (est. Mar. 9, 1888; 5,342 sq. mi.; 1970 pop.: 51,264; 1960: 49,623; 1950: 31,437) (Casper). Descriptive, for the natron or soda deposits in the county. -- Mokler, Alfred James, History of Natrona County, Wyoming, Argonaut Press, 1923; 477 p.

Navajo, Ariz. (est. Mar. 21, 1895; 9,911 sq. mi.; 1970 pop.: 47,715; 1960: 37,994; 1950: 29,446) (Holbrook). ("The Land of Sand and Slick Rock"). Navajo Indian tribe whose name means "enemies hiding hole."

Navarro, Tex. (est. Apr. 25, 1846; 1,084 sq. mi.; 1970 pop.: 31,150; 1960: 34,423; 1950: 39,916) (Corsicana). Juan Jose Antonio Navarro (1795-1870). Mexican patriot; land commissioner for De Witt's colony 1831; for the district of Bexar 1834-35; signer Tex. declaration of Independence 1836; Tex. constitution 1836; one of the commissioners to Santa Fe 1840; captured by Mexicans while on Santa Fe expedition and imprisoned 1840-45; Tex. constitutional convention 1845. -- Love, Annie (Carpenter), History of Navarro County, Dallas, Texas: Southwest Press, 1933; 278 p.

Nelson, Ky. (est. sess. Oct. 18, 1784; eff. Jan. 1, 1785 sess.; 438 sq. mi.; 1970 pop.: 23,477; 1960: 22,168; 1950: 19,521) (Bardstown). Thomas Nelson (1738-1789); Va. house of burgesses 1761, 1774-75; Continental Congress 1775-77; signer Declaration of Independence 1776; Va. assembly 1779-80; gov. of Va. 1781; brig. gen. and commander-in-chief of Va. Militia 1779-80.

Nelson, N.D. (est. Mar. 9, 1883, org. June 9, 1883; 997 sq. mi.; 1970 pop.: 5,776; 1960: 7,034; 1950: 8,090) (Lakota). N. E. Nelson. N. D. legislature.

Nelson, Va. (est. sess. Dec. 25, 1807; 468 sq. mi.; 1970 pop.: 11,702; 1960: 12,752; 1950: 14,042) (Lovingston). Thomas Nelson*.

Nemaha, Kan. (est. Aug. 30, 1855; 709 sq. mi.; 1970 pop.: 11,825; 1960: 12,897; 1950: 14,341) (Seneca). Nemaha Indian tribe, Indian word for "muddy water." -- Tennal, Ralph, History of Nemaha County, Kansas, Lawrence, Kan.: Standard Pub. Co., 1916; 816 p.

Nemaha, Neb. (est. Nov. 23, 1854; 399 sq. mi.; 1970 pop.: 8,976; 1960: 9,099; 1950: 10,973) (Auburn). Nemaha Indian tribe*. (Formerly Forney County, name changed to Nemaha County). -- Dundas, John H., Nemaha County, Auburn, Neb., 1902; 220 p.

Neosho, Kan. (est. Aug. 30, 1855; 587 sq. mi.; 1970 pop.:

18,812; 1960: 19,455; 1950: 20,348) (Erie). Indian word "clear, cold water." (Originally Dorn County, name changed to Neosho County, June 3, 1861). chap. 18

Neshoba, Miss. (est. Dec. 23, 1833; 561 sq. mi.; 1970 pop.: 20,802; 1960: 20,927; 1950: 25,730) (Philadelphia). Indian word for "grey wolf."

Ness, Kan. (est. Feb. 26, 1867; 1,081 sq. mi.; 1970 pop.: 4,791; 1960: 5,470; 1950: 6,322) (Ness City). Noah V. Ness (-1864). Corporal Co. G., 7th Kan. Cavalry; died Aug. 22, 1864 of wounds received in action Aug. 19, 1864. -- Millbrook, Minnie (Dubbs), Ness, western county, Kansas, Detroit: Millbrook Printing Co., 1955; 319 p.

Nevada, Ark. (est. Mar. 20, 1871; 616 sq. mi.; 1970 pop.: 10,111; 1960: 10,700; 1950: 14,781) (Prescott). Nev., the state; Spanish for "snow-covered."

Nevada, Calif. (est. Apr. 25, 1851, org. May 28, 1851; 979 sq. mi.; 1970 pop.: 26,346; 1960: 20,911; 1950: 19,888) (Nevada City). Nevada*.

New Castle, Del. (est. 1664?; 493 sq. mi.; 1970 pop.: 385,318; 1960: 307,446; 1950: 218,879) (Wilmington). New Castle, England; named for the Duke of Newcastle, William Cavendish (1592-1676), created duke 1665; or Newcastle-on-Tyne in England. In Oct. 1664 name changed from New Amstel to New Castle. -- Stillman, Charles A., A time to remember, 1920-1960, Wilmington, Del., 1962; 160 p.

New Hanover, N. C. (est. Nov. 27, 1729; 194 sq. mi.; 1970 pop.: 82,996; 1960: 71,742; 1950: 63,272) (Wilmington). Hanover, Germany (in honor of King George I of England who came from Hanover.) -- Waddell, Alfred Moore, A history of New Hanover County, Wilmington, N. C., 1909.

New Haven, Conn. (est. May 10, 1666 sess.; 609 sq. mi.; 1970 pop.: 744,948; 1960: 660,315; 1950: 545,784) (no county seat). Descriptive. -- Mitchell, Mary (Hewitt), History of New Haven County, Chicago: Pioneer Historical Pub. Co., 1930; 3 vol.

New Kent, Va. (est. Nov. 20, 1654 sess.; 212 sq. mi.; 1970 pop.: 5,300; 1960: 4,504; 1950: 3,995) (New Kent). Kent, England.

New London, Conn. (est. May 10, 1666 sess.; 672 sq. mi.; 1970 pop.: 230,348; 1960: 185,745; 1950: 144,821) (no county seat). London, England. -- Hurd, Duane Hamilton, History of New London County, Philadelphia: J. W. Lewis & Co., 1882; 768 p. -- Marshall, Benjamin Tinkham, A Modern History of New London County, New York City: Lewis Historical Pub. Co., 1922; 3 vol.

New Madrid, Mo. (est. Oct. 1, 1812, procl.; 679 sq. mi.; 1970 pop.: 23,420; 1960: 31,350; 1950: 39,444) (New Madrid). Madrid, Spain.

New York, N. Y. (est. Nov. 1, 1683; 22 sq. mi.; 1970 pop.: 1,524,541; 1960: 1,698,281; 1950: 1,960,101) (New York City). Duke of York.

Newaygo, Mich. (est. Apr. 1, 1840, org. 1851; 857 sq. mi.; 1970 pop.: 27,992; 1960: 24,160; 1950: 21,567) (White Cloud). Newaygo. Indian chief, signer of Saginaw Treaty 1819.

Newberry, S. C. (est. Mar. 12, 1785; 630 sq. mi.; 1970 pop.: 29,273; 1960: 29,416; 1950: 31,771) (Newberry). Captain, Sumter's state troops. -- Summer, George Leland, Newberry County, Newberry, S. C., 1950; 469 p.

Newport, R. I. (est. June 22, 1703; 114 sq. mi.; 1970 pop.: 94,559; 1960: 81,891; 1950: 61,539) (Newport). Descriptive. Originally incorporated as Rhode Island County; incorporated as Newport County June 16, 1729.

Newton, Ark. (est. Dec. 14, 1842; 822 sq. mi.; 1970 pop.: 5,844; 1960: 5,963; 1950: 8,685) (Jasper). Thomas Willoughby Newton (1804-1853). Ark. senate 1844-48; Representative from Ark., Feb. 6-Mar. 3, 1847. -- Lackey, Walter Fowler, History of Newton County, Arkansas, Independence, Mo.: Zion's Printing and Pub. Co., 1950; 432 p.

Newton, Ga. (est. Dec. 24, 1821; 262 sq. mi.; 1970 pop.: 26,282; 1960: 20,999; 1950: 20,185) (Covington). John Newton. Sgt. who with William Jasper captured ten British soldiers who were taking colonial prisoners to Savannah to be hanged. -- Burge, Dolly Sumner (Lunt), Diary, University of Georgia Press, Athens, Ga., 1962; 141 p.

Newton, Ind. (est. Feb. 7, 1859; 413 sq. mi.; 1970 pop.: 11,606; 1960: 11,502; 1950: 11,006) (Kentland). John Newton*. (Originally created Feb. 7, 1835, consolidated with Jasper, Jan. 29, 1839).

Newton, Miss. (est. Feb. 25, 1836; 568 sq. mi.; 1970 pop.: 18,983; 1960: 19,517; 1950: 22,681) (Decatur). Isaac Newton (1642-1727). English mathematician and natural philosopher; prof. at Cambridge 1669; fellow Royal Society 1671; knighted by Queen Anne 1705; announced law of gravitation. -- Brown, A. J., History of Newton County, Miss., from 1834 to 1894, Jackson, Miss.: Clarion Ledger, 1894; 472 p.

Newton, Mo. (est. Dec. 30, 1838; 629 sq. mi.; 1970 pop.: 32,901; 1960: 30,090; 1950: 28,240) (Neosho). John Newton*.

Newton, Tex. (est. Apr. 22, 1846; 941 sq. mi.; 1970 pop.: 11,657; 1960: 10,372; 1950: 10,832) (Newton). John Newton*.

Nez Perce, Idaho (est. Feb. 4, 1864; 847 sq. mi.; 1970 pop.: 30,376; 1960: 27,066; 1950: 22,658) (Lewiston). Nez Perce Indian tribe, French words for "pierced nose."

Niagara, N.Y. (est. Mar. 11, 1808; 533 sq. mi.; 1970 pop.: 235,720; 1960: 242,269; 1950: 189,992) (Lockport). ("The Hub of the World's Richest Market"). Indian word for "bisected bottom lands." -- Aiken, John, Outpost of empires, Phoenix, N.Y.: F.E. Richards, 1961; 152 p. -- Williams, Edward Theodore, Niagara County, Chicago: J.H. Beers & Co., 1921; 2 vol.

Nicholas, Ky. (est. Dec. 18, 1799, eff. June 1, 1800; 204 sq. mi.; 1970 pop.: 6,508; 1960: 6,677; 1950: 7,532) (Carlisle). George Nicholas (1754-1799). Capt.; col.; Va. house of delegates 1781; Va. constitutional convention 1788; Ky. constitutional convention 1792; first attorney gen. of Ky.

Nicholas, W. Va. (est. Jan. 30, 1818; 656 sq. mi.; 1970 pop.: 22,552; 1960: 25,417; 1950: 27,696) (Summersville). Wilson Cary Nicholas (1761-1820). Twentieth gov. of Va. (Commonwealth). Commanded Washington's Life Guard 1783; Va. house of delegates 1784-88, 1789, and 1794-1800; Senator from Va. 1799-1804; collector of the port of Norfolk 1804-07; Representative from Va. 1807-09; gov. of Va., 1814-16. -- Brown, William Griffee, History of Nicholas County, Dietz Press, 1954; 425 p.

Nicollet, Minn. (est. Mar. 5, 1853; 459 sq. mi.; 1970 pop.: 24,518; 1960: 23,196; 1950: 20,929) (St. Peter). Joseph Nicolas Nicollet (1786-1843). French mathematician; emigrated to New Orleans 1832; geographer and explorer; led govt. exploring and surveying trips; made canoe trip from Ft. Snelling to Lake Itasca, source of the Miss. River. -- Gresham, William G., History of Nicollet and Le Sueur Counties, Indianapolis: B.F. Bowen & Co., 1916; 2 vol.

Niobrara, Wyo. (est. Feb. 14, 1911; 2,613 sq. mi.; 1970 pop.: 2,924; 1960: 3,750; 1950: 4,701) (Lusk). Niobrara Indian tribe.

Noble, Ind. (est. Feb. 7, 1835, eff. June 1, 1835; org. Feb. 6, 1836, eff. Mar. 1, 1836; 410 sq. mi.; 1970 pop.: 31,382; 1960: 28,162; 1950: 25,075) (Albion). James Noble (1785-1831). Ind. constitutional committee 1816; Ind. house of representatives; Senator from Ind. 1816-31-

Noble, Ohio (est. Mar. 11, 1851; 404 sq. mi.; 1970 pop.: 10,428; 1960: 10,982; 1950: 11,750) (Caldwell). James

Noble, Warren P. Noble. -- History of Noble County, Ohio, Chicago: L. H. Watkins & Co., 1887; 597 p.

Noble, Okla. (est. July 16, 1907; 744 sq. mi.; 1970 pop.: 10,043; 1960: 10,376; 1950: 12,156) (Perry). John Willock Noble (1831-1912). Third Iowa Cavalry 1861; bvt. brig. gen. 1865; U. S. district attorney for eastern district of Mo. 1867; declined position of solicitor gen. 1872; U. S. Secretary of the Interior in cabinet of Pres. Harrison 1889-93.

Nobles, Minn. (est. May 23, 1857; 712 sq. mi.; 1970 pop.: 23,208; 1960: 23,365; 1950: 22,435) (Worthington). William H. Nobles (1816-1876) Minn. terr. legislature 1854 and 1856; appointed to lay out wagon road to the Pacific; discovered Nobles Pass through Rocky Mountains; served in Civil War. -- Rose, Arthur, An illustrated history of Nobles County, Worthington, Minn.: Northern History Pub. Co., 1908; 637 p.

Nodaway, Mo. (est. Jan. 29, 1841; 877 sq. mi.; 1970 pop.: 22,467; 1960: 22,215; 1950: 24,033) (Maryville). Potawatomi Indian word for "placid."

Nolan, Tex. (est. Aug. 21, 1876; 921 sq. mi.; 1970 pop.: 16,220; 1960: 18,963; 1950: 19,808) (Sweetwater). Philip Nolan (1771-1801). Horse trader 1791; American filibuster; built fort near Nacogdoches 1800; killed by Spanish force sent to capture him Mar. 4, 1801. -- Wade, Lelia Jeanette, Our community, organization and development of Nolan County, Sweetwater?, Texas, 1960; 87 p.

Norfolk, Mass. (est. Mar. 26, 1793, eff. June 20, 1793; 403 sq. mi.; 1970 pop.: 605,051; 1960: 510,256; 1950: 392,308) (Dedham). Norfolk County, England. -- Cook, Louis Atwood, History of Norfolk County, Chicago: S. J. Clarke Pub. Co., 1918; 2 vol. -- Hurd, Duane Hamilton, History of Nolfolk County, Philadelphia: J. W. Lewis & Co., 1884; 1001 p.

Norfolk, Va. (est. 1636; 364 sq. mi.; 1970 pop.: unlisted; 1960: 51,612; 1950: 99,937) (Portsmouth). Norfolk County, England. -- Norfolk County and South Norfolk County were incorporated as Chesapeake on Jan. 1, 1963.

Norman, Minn. (est. Feb. 17, 1881; 885 sq. mi.; 1970 pop.: 10,008; 1960: 11,253; 1950: 12,909) (Ada) Norman Wolfred Kittson. Minn. terr. legislature 1851-55; mayor of St. Paul 1858. Also claimed for Norsemen. -- Turner, John, History of Clay and Norman Counties, Indianapolis: B. F. Bowen & Co., 1918; 2 vol.

Northampton, N. C. (est. sess. 1741; 540 sq. mi.; 1970 pop.: 24,009; 1960: 26,811; 1950: 28,432) (Jackson).

Northampton, England; George, earl of Northampton.

Northampton, Pa. (est. sess. Oct. 14, 1751, Mar. 11, 1752; 374 sq. mi.; 1970 pop.: 214,368; 1960: 201,412; 1950: 185,243) (Easton). Northampton, England*. -- Alderfer, Everett Gordon, Northampton Heritage, Easton, Pa.: Northampton County Historical and Genealogical Society, 1953; 328 p. -- Heller, William Jacob, History of Northampton County, Boston: American Historical Society, 1920; 3 vol.

Northampton, Va. (est. 1634; 226 sq. mi.; 1970 pop.: 14,442; 1960: 16,966; 1950: 17,300) (Eastville). Northampton, England*.

Northumberland, Pa. (est. Mar. 21, 1772; 454 sq. mi.; 1970 pop.: 99,190; 1960: 104,138; 1950: 117,115) (Sunbury). Northumberland County, England. -- Bell, Herbert Charles, ed., History of Northumberland County, Chicago: Brown, Runk & Co., 1891; 1266 p.

Northumberland, Va. (est. Oct. 12, 1648 sess.; 200 sq. mi.; 1970 pop.: 9,239; 1960: 10,185; 1950: 10,012) (Heathsville). Northumberland County, England.

Norton, Kan. (est. Feb. 26, 1867; 880 sq. mi.; 1970 pop.: 7,279; 1960: 8,035; 1950: 8,808) (Norton). Orloff Norton (-1864). Capt. Co. L 15th Kan., killed at Cone Hill, Ark., Nov. 11, 1864. (Name changed to Billings County, Mar. 6, 1873, and changed back to Norton County, Feb. 19, 1874). -- Bowers, Darius N., Seventy years in Norton County, Kansas, 1872-1942, Norton, Kan.: Norton County Champion, 1942; 238 p.

Nottoway, Va. (est. Dec. 22, 1788; 308 sq. mi.; 1970 pop.: 14,260; 1960: 15,141; 1950: 15,479) (Nottoway). Nottoway Indian tribe.

Nowata, Okla. (est. July 16, 1907; 577 sq. mi.; 1970 pop.: 9,773; 1960: 10,848; 1950: 12,734) (Nowata). Delaware Indian word for "welcome."

Noxubee, Miss. (est. Dec. 23, 1833; 682 sq. mi.; 1970 pop.: 14,288; 1960: 16,826; 1950: 20,022) (Macon). Indian word for "stinking water."

Nueces, Tex. (est. Apr. 18, 1846; 838 sq. mi.; 1970 pop.: 237,544; 1960: 221,573; 1950: 165,471) (Corpus Christi). Spanish for "pecans." -- Taylor, Paul Schuster, An American-Mexican frontier, Nueces County, Texas, Chapel Hill, No. Car.: University of North Carolina Press, 1934; 337 p.

Nuckolls, Neb. (est. Jan. 13, 1860, org. June 27, 1871; 579 sq. mi.; 1970 pop.: 7,404; 1960: 8,217; 1950: 9,609) (Nelson). Stephen Friel Nuckolls (1825-1879). Neb. terr. legislature 1859; Representative from Wyo. 1869-71.

-- <u>From 'hoppers to 'copters; stories of Nuckolls County for 100 years,</u> [n. p.], 1967; 136 p.

Nye, Nev. (est. Feb. 16, 1864; 18, 064 sq. mi. ; 1970 pop. : 5, 599; 1960: 4, 374; 1950: 3, 101) (Tonopah). ("The County That Makes Silver Booms to Atom Bombs"). James Warren Nye (1814-1876). District attorney Madison County N. Y. 1839; surrogate 1844-47; judge of county court 1847-51; pres. Metropolitan Board of Police N. Y. City 1857-60; gov. of Washoe (Nev.) Terr. 1861-64; Senator from Nev., 1864-73.

O

Oakland, Mich. (est. Jan. 12, 1819, org. 1820; 877 sq. mi. ; 1970 pop. : 907, 871; 1960: 690, 259; 1950: 396, 001) (Pontiac). Descriptive. -- Seeley, Thaddeus De Witt, ed., <u>History of Oakland County</u>, Chicago: Lewis Pub. Co., 1912; 2 vol.

Obion, Tenn. (est. Oct. 24, 1823; 550 sq. mi. ; 1970 pop. : 29, 936; 1960: 26, 957; 1950: 29, 056) (Union City). Indian word for "many prongs. " Obion River; Obion, French lt.

O'Brien, Iowa (est. Jan. 15, 1851; 575 sq. mi. ; 1970 pop. : 17, 522; 1960: 18, 840; 1950: 18, 970) (Primghar). William Smith O'Brien (1803-1864) England's House of Commons 1826-39; leader of Irish Independence movement 1848; arrested, sentenced to death 1848; sentence commuted to life imprisonment 1849; transported to Tasmania 1849; fully pardoned 1856. -- Peck, John Licinius Everett, <u>Past and present of O'Brien and Osceola Counties</u>, Indianapolis: B. F. Bowen & Co., Inc., 1914; 2 vol.

Ocean, N. J. (est. Feb. 15, 1850; 639 sq. mi. ; 1970 pop. : 208, 470; 1960: 108, 241; 1950: 56, 622) (Toms River). ("New Jersey's Sparkling County"; "The County Where Parkway Meets Atlantic Ocean"; "The County Where Progress Is a Habit"; "The County Where Progress Is Planned for Tomorrow"; "The County Where the Tang of the Sea Meets the Scent of Pine"; "The County With The Habit of Always Being First in New Jersey"; "The Fastest Growing County in the State"; "The Land and Sea of Romance, Sportsmanship and Opportunity"; "The Sun Sea of New Jersey"). Descriptive, Atlantic Ocean. -- Salter, Edwin, <u>Old times in Ocean County</u>, Forked River, 1876; 84 p.

Oceana, Mich. (est. Mar. 2, 1831, org. 1851; re-org. 1855; 536 sq. mi. ; 1970 pop. : 17, 984; 1960: 16, 547; 1950:

16, 105) (Hart). Descriptive; fresh water ocean of Great Lakes. -- Hartwick, L. M. and Tuller, W. H., Oceana County Pioneers, Pentwater, Mich.: Pentwater New Steam Print., 1890; 432 p.

Ochiltree, Tex. (est. Aug. 21, 1876; 905 sq. mi.; 1970 pop.: 9, 704; 1960: 9, 380; 1950: 6, 024) (Perryton). William Beck Ochiltree (1811-1867). Emigrated to Tex. 1840; judge fifth judicial district court Tex. 1842; secretary of the Treas. Republic of Tex. 1844; attorney gen. 1845; Tex. legislature 1855; Tex. constitutional convention 1861; provisional congress of Confederated states 1861; col. inf. regiment 1861.

Oconee, Ga. (est. Feb. 25, 1875; 172 sq. mi.; 1970 pop.: 7, 915; 1960: 6, 304; 1950: 7, 009) (Watkinsville). Indian word for "the place of springs" or "the water eyes of the hills."

Oconee, S. C. (est. Jan. 29, 1768; 670 sq. mi.; 1970 pop.: 40, 728; 1960: 40, 204; 1950: 39, 050) (Walhalla). Indian word for "the place of springs."*

Oconto, Wis. (est. Feb. 6, 1851; 1, 106 sq. mi.; 1970 pop.: 25, 553; 1960: 25, 110; 1950: 26, 238) (Oconto). Indian word for "red river" or "place of the pickerel."

Ogemaw, Mich. (est. Apr. 1, 1840, org. 1873, re-org. 1875; 574 sq. mi.; 1970 pop.: 11, 903; 1960: 9, 680; 1950: 9, 345) (West Branch). Chippewa Indian word for "chief."

Ogle, Ill. (est. Jan. 16, 1836; 756 sq. mi.; 1970 pop.: 42, 867; 1960: 38, 106; 1950: 33, 429) (Oregon). Joseph Ogle. Ill. militia. -- History of Ogle County, Chicago: H. F. Kett & Co., 1878; 858 p.

Oglethorpe, Ga. (est. Dec. 19, 1793; 504 sq. mi.; 1970 pop.: 7, 598; 1960: 7, 926; 1950: 9, 958) (Lexington). First gov. of Ga. under the trustees. Colonizer of Georgia; landed at Charleston 1733; returned to England 1734; second trip to Ga. 1736; advocated religious freedom; returned to England 1743; surrendered charter of Ga., 1752; gen. commander of English forces 1765.

Ohio, Ind. (est. Jan. 4, 1844, eff. May 1, 1844; 87 sq. mi.; 1970 pop.: 4, 289; 1960: 4, 165; 1950: 4, 233) (Rising Sun). Indian for "beautiful river." (also claimed for Ohio, the state)

Ohio, Ky. (est. Dec. 17, 1798, eff. July 1, 1799; 596 sq. mi.; 1970 pop.: 18, 790; 1960: 17, 725; 1950: 20, 840) (Hartford). Indian for "beautiful river." -- Taylor, Harrison D., Ohio County, Kentucky, in the olden days, Louisville, Ky.: J. P. Morton & Co., 1926; 204 p.

Ohio, W. Va. (est. Oct. 7, 1776; 109 sq. mi.; 1970 pop.: 64, 197; 1960: 68, 437; 1950: 71, 672) (Wheeling). Indian for "beautiful river."

Okaloosa, Fla. (est. June 3, 1915; 938 sq. mi.; 1970 pop.: 88,187; 1960: 61,175; 1950: 27,533) (Crestview). Indian for "pleasant place" or "blackwater."

Okanogan, Wash. (est. Feb. 2, 1888; 5,295 sq. mi.; 1970 pop.: 25,867; 1960: 25,520; 1950: 29,131) (Okanogan). Indian for "rendezvous."

Okeechobee, Fla. (est. May 8, 1917; 780 sq. mi.; 1970 pop.: 11,233; 1960: 6,424; 1950: 3,454) (Okeechobee). Indian for "large water."

Okfuskee, Okla. (est. July 16, 1907; 638 sq. mi.; 1970 pop.: 10,683; 1960: 11,706; 1950: 16,948) (Okemah). Indian name of a Creek town on the Talahoosa River in Ala.

Oklahoma, Okla. (est. July 16, 1907; 709 sq. mi.; 1970 pop.: 526,805; 1960: 439,506; 1950: 325,352) (Oklahoma City). Combined and corrupted Indian word "okla" meaning "people" and "humma" meaning "red."

Okmulgee, Okla. (est. July 16, 1907; 700 sq. mi.; 1970 pop.: 35,358; 1960: 36,945; 1950: 44,561) (Okmulgee). Indian for "boiling water."

Oktibbeha, Miss. (est. Dec. 23, 1833; 457 sq. mi.; 1970 pop.: 28,752; 1960: 26,175; 1950: 24,569) (Starkville). ("The Nation's Birthplace of the Jersey Cow Industry"). Indian for "bloody water" or "ice there in creek." -- Carroll, Thomas Battle, Historical Sketches of Oktibbeha County, Miss., Gulfport, Miss., 1931; 263 p.

Oldham, Ky. (est. Dec. 15, 1823; 184 sq. mi.; 1970 pop.: 14,687; 1960: 13,388; 1950: 11,018) (La Grange). William Oldham (-1791). First lt. of Nelson's Independent Rifle Co., 1776; capt. 1776; transferred to Fifth Pa. Regiment 1777; resigned 1779; killed at Gen. St. Clair's defeat by the Indians 1791.

Oldham, Tex. (est. Aug. 21, 1876; org. Dec. 8, 1880, 1,466 sq. mi.; 1970 pop.: 2,258; 1960: 1,928; 1950: 1,672) (Vega). Williamson Simpson Oldham (1813-1868). Ark. gen. assembly 1838-42; speaker of the Ark. gen. assembly 1842; associate justice of supreme court of Ark. 1844; moved to Tex. 1849; assoc. editor "State Gazette" 1854; Tex. secession convention 1861; appointed commission to Ark. to induce them to secede. Member Provisional Confederate Congress; Senator from Tex. to Confederate Congress.

Oliver, N. D. (est. Mar. 12, 1885, org. May 18, 1885; 720 sq. mi.; 1970 pop.: 2,322; 1960: 2,610; 1950: 3,091) (Center). Harry S. Oliver. Member of Dakota Terr. legislature 1885 (16th sess.)

Olmsted, Minn. (est. Feb. 20, 1855; 655 sq. mi.; 1970

pop.: 84,104; 1960: 65,532; 1950: 48,228) (Rochester). David Olmsted (1822-1861). Pres. first terr. legislature of Minn. 1849-50; proprietor of "Minnesota Democrat" 1853; first mayor of St. Paul Minn. 1854.

Oneida, Idaho. (est. Jan. 22, 1864; 1,191 sq. mi.; 1970 pop.: 2,864; 1960: 3,603; 1950: 4,387) (Malad City). Oneida, N.Y., named for Oneida Indians.

Oneida, N.Y. (est. Mar. 15, 1798; 1,227 sq. mi.; 1970 pop.: 273,037; 1960: 264,401; 1950: 222,855) (Utica and Rome). ("The Keystone County for Industrial Progress in New York State"). Oneida Indian tribe. -- Wager, Daniel E., Our county and its people, Boston: Boston History Co., 1896.

Oneida, Wis. (est. Apr. 11, 1885; 1,114 sq. mi.; 1970 pop.: 24,427; 1960: 22,112; 1950: 20,648) (Rhinelander). ("The County in the Heart of Wisconsin's 'Lake Rich' Region"; "The County Where Nature Lingered Longer"; "The World's Most Concentrated Lake Region"; "Wisconsin's Leisure-land"). Oneida Indian tribe*.

Onondaga, N.Y. (est. Mar. 5, 1794; 792 sq. mi.; 1970 pop.: 472,185; 1960: 423,028; 1950: 341,719) (Syracuse). Onondaga Indian tribe. -- Clayton, W. Woodford, History of Onondaga County, Syracuse, N.Y.: D. Mason & Co., 1878; 430 p. -- Sneller, Anne Gertrude, A vanished world, Syracuse, N.Y.: Syracuse University Press, 1964; 365 p.

Onslow, N.C. (est. sess. 1734; 756 sq. mi.; 1970 pop.: 103,126; 1960: 82,706; 1950: 42,047) (Jacksonville). Arthur Onslow (1691-1768). Unanimously elected English House of Commons 1728; Chancellor to Queen Caroline 1729; treasurer of the navy 1734-42; re-elected to house of commons 1735, 1741, 1747 and 1754; speaker house of commons 1728-61; the third member of his family who had been speaker. -- Brown, Joseph Parsons, The commonwealth of Onslow, a history, O.G. Dunn, 1960; 434 p.

Ontario, N.Y. (est. Jan. 27, 1789; 649 sq. mi.; 1970 pop.: 78,849; 1960: 68,070; 1950: 60,172) (Canandaigua). Iroquois Indian word corruption meaning "beautiful lake." -- Aldrich, Lewis Cass, comp., History of Ontario County, Syracuse, N.Y.: D. Mason & Co., 1893; 518 p. -- Milliken, Charles F., A history of Ontario County, New York, N.Y.: Lewis Historical Pub. Co., 1911; 2 vol.

Ontonagon, Mich. (est. Mar. 9, 1843, org. May 18, 1846; re-org. 1848, legalized by the legislature 1853; 1,321 sq. mi.; 1970 pop.: 10,548; 1960: 10,584; 1950: 10,282) (Ontonagon). Indian word for "fishing place," "hunting river" or "lost dish." -- Jamison, James K., This Ontonagon Country, Ontonagon, Mich.: Ontonagon Herald Co., 1939; 269 p.

Orange, Calif. (est. Mar. 11, 1889; 782 sq. mi.; 1970 pop.: 1, 420, 386; 1960: 703, 925; 1950: 216, 224) (Santa Ana). Descriptive. -- Pleasants, Adalina (Brown), History of Orange County, Los Angeles, J. R. Finnell & Sons Pub. Co., 1931; 3 vol. -- Friis, Leo J., Orange County Through Four Centuries, Santa Ana, Calif.: Pioneer Press, 1965; 225 p.

Orange, Fla. (est. Dec. 29, 1824; 916 sq. mi.; 1970 pop.: 344, 311; 1960: 263, 540; 1950: 114, 950) (Orlando). ("The County for Your Outdoor Recreation and Relaxation"). Descriptive. (Originally Mosquito county name changed to present name Jan. 30, 1845.) -- Blackman, William Fremont, History of Orange County, De Land, Fla.: E. O. Painter Printing Co., 1927; 232 p.

Orange, Ind. (est. Dec. 26, 1815, eff. Feb. 1, 1816; 405 sq. mi.; 1970 pop.: 16, 968; 1960: 16, 877; 1950: 16, 879) (Paoli). Orange County, N. C.

Orange, N. Y. (est. Nov. 1, 1683; 829 sq. mi.; 1970 pop.: 220, 558; 1960: 183, 734; 1950: 152, 255) (Goshen). Prince William IV of Orange (1738-1820) who became King George III of England. Son of John William Friso, first prince of Orange 1713. -- Akers, Dwight, Outposts of history in Orange County, Washingtonville, N. Y.: Blooming Grove Chapter D. A. R., 1937; 114 p. -- Moffat, Almet S., comp., Orange County, N. Y., Washingtonville, N. Y., 1928; 87 p.

Orange, N. C. (est. sess. Mar. 31, 1752; 398 sq. mi.; 1970 pop.: 57, 707; 1960: 42, 970; 1950: 34, 435) (Hillsboro). Prince William IV of Orange*. -- Lefler, Hugh Talmage and Wager, Paul, Orange County, 1752-1952, Chapel Hill, N. C., Orange Printshop, 1953; 389 p.

Orange, Tex. (est. Feb. 5, 1852; 356 sq. mi.; 1970 pop.: 71, 170; 1960: 60, 357; 1950: 40, 567) (Orange). Descriptive.

Orange, Vt. (est. Feb. 22, 1781; 690 sq. mi.; 1970 pop.: 17, 676; 1960: 16, 014; 1950: 17, 027) (Chelsea). Prince William IV of Orange*.

Orange, Va. (est. sess. Feb. 1, 1734; 354 sq. mi.; 1970 pop.: 13, 792; 1960: 12, 900; 1950: 12, 755) (Orange). Prince William IV of Orange*. -- Scott, William Wallace, A History of Orange County, Berryville, Va.: reprint Chesapeake Book Company, 1962; 292 p.

Orangeburg, S. C. (est. Mar. 12, 1785; 1, 120 sq. mi.; 1970 pop.: 69, 789; 1960: 68, 559; 1950: 68, 726) (Orangeburg). Prince William IV of Orange. * -- Salley, Alexander Samuel, Jr., The history of Orangeburg County, Orangeburg, S. C.: R. L. Berry, 1898; 572 p.

Oregon, Mo. (est. Feb. 14, 1845; 784 sq. mi.; 1970 pop.: 9,180; 1960: 9,845; 1950: 11,978) (Alton). Oreg. Terr., from name used in 1778 by Jonathan Carver, taken from writings of Robert Rogers, English army officer.

Orleans, La. (est. Apr. 10, 1805, org. Mar. 31, 1807; 196 sq. mi.; 1970 pop.: 593,471; 1960: 627,525; 1950: 570,445) (New Orleans). Orleans, France.

Orleans, N. Y. (est. Nov. 12, 1824; 396 sq. mi.; 1970 pop.: 37,305; 1960: 34,159; 1950: 29,832) (Albion). Orleans, France.* -- Thomas, Arad, Pioneer history of Orleans County, Albion, N. Y.: H. A. Bruner, 1871; 463 p. -- Signor, Isaac Smith, ed., Landmarks of Orleans County, Syracuse, N. Y.: D. Mason & Co., 1894; 242 p.

Orleans, Vt. (est. Nov. 5, 1792; 715 sq. mi.; 1970 pop.: 20,153; 1960: 20,143; 1950: 21,190) (Newport City).

Ormsby, Nev. (est. Nov. 25, 1861; 141 sq. mi.; 1970 pop.: 15,468; 1960: 5,163; 1950: 4,172) (Carson City). William M. Ormsby (-1860) Maj. killed in battle with Indians, Pyramid Lake, 1860. -- Ormsby County became Carson City, an independent city.

Osage, Kan. (org. Aug. 30, 1855; 721 sq. mi.; 1970 pop.: 13,352; 1960: 12,886; 1950: 12,811) (Lyndon). Osage Indians; French corruption of "wazhazhe" Indian word for "people." (Originally Weller County, name changed to Osage County, Feb. 11, 1859) (chap. 100).

Osage, Mo. (est. Jan. 29, 1841; 601 sq. mi.; 1970 pop.: 10,994; 1960: 10,867; 1950: 11,301) (Linn). Osage Indians.*

Osage, Okla. (est. July 16, 1907; 2,293 sq. mi.; 1970 pop.: 29,750; 1960: 32,441; 1950: 33,071) (Pawhuska). Osage Indians*.

Osborne, Kan. (est. Feb. 26, 1867, 898 sq. mi.; 1970 pop.: 6,416; 1960: 7,506; 1950: 8,558) (Osborne). Vincent B. Osborn (-1865). Private Co. A. 2nd Kan.; wounded Jan. 17, 1865.

Osceola, Fla. (est. May 12, 1887; 1,325 sq. mi.; 1970 pop.: 25,267; 1960: 19,029; 1950: 11,406) (Kissimmee). Osceola (1804-1838). Indian chief, opposed cession of Seminole lands; seized Oct. 1837 under flag of truce; imprisoned at St. Augustine, Fla. and later at Ft. Moultrie, S. C., where he died Jan. 30, 1838.

Osceola, Iowa (est. Jan. 15, 1851; 398 sq. mi.; 1970 pop.: 8,555; 1960: 10,064; 1950: 10,181) (Sibley). Osceola*. -- Peck, John Licinius Everett, Past and present of O'Brien and Osceola Counties, Indianapolis: B. F. Bowen & Co., 1914; 2 vol.

Osceola, Mich. (est. Apr. 1, 1840, org. 1869; 581 sq. mi.;

1970 pop.: 14,838; 1960: 13,595; 1950: 13,797) (Reed City). Osceola*. (Originally Unwattin County, name changed to Osceola County on Mar. 8, 1843) -- Portrait and biographical album of Osceola County, Chicago: Chapman Brothers, 1884; 422 p.

Oscoda, Mich. (est. Apr. 1, 1840, org. Mar. 10, 1881; 565 sq. mi.; 1970 pop.: 4,726; 1960: 3,447; 1950: 3,134) (Mio). Coined word, "ossin" for "stone and pebbles" and "muskoda" for "prairie;" combined as "oscoda" meaning "pebbly prairie."

Oswego, N.Y. (est. Mar. 1, 1816; 968 sq. mi.; 1970 pop.: 100,897; 1960: 86,118; 1950: 77,181) (Oswego). Iroquois word meaning "the outpouring;" specifically "the Oswego river mouth." -- Johnson, Crisfield, History of Oswego County, Philadelphia: L.H. Everts & Co., 1877; 449 p. -- Snyder, Charles McCool, Oswego, from buckskin to bustles, Port Washington, N.Y.: I.J. Friedman, 1968; 286 p.

Otero, Colo. (est. Mar. 25, 1889; 1,267 sq. mi.; 1970 pop.: 23,523; 1960: 24,128; 1950: 25,275) (La Junta). Miguel Otero.

Otero, N.M. (est. Jan. 30, 1899; 6,638 sq. mi.; 1970 pop.: 41,097; 1960: 36,976; 1950: 14,000) (Alamogordo). Miguel Antonio Otero (1859-1944). Gov. of N.M., treas. of Las Vegas 1883-84; clerk San Miguel county 1889-90; clerk U.S. District Court 1890-93; gov. of N.M. 1897-1906; treas. of N.M., 1909-11.

Otoe, Neb. (est. Nov. 24, 1854, org. Dec. 1, 1856; 613 sq. mi.; 1970 pop.: 15,576; 1960: 16,503; 1950: 17,056) (Nebraska City). Otoe Indian tribe. (Formerly Pierce County, name changed to Otoe.)

Otsego, Mich. (est. Apr. 1, 1840, org. 1875; 530 sq. mi.; 1970 pop.: 10,422; 1960: 7,545; 1950: 6,435) ("A Great Place to Live, Work, Play, Retire"). (Gaylord). Indian word for "place of the rock." (Originally Okkuddo County, name changed to Otsego on Mar. 8, 1843).

Otsego, N.Y. (est. Feb. 16, 1791; 1,013 sq. mi.; 1970 pop.: 56,181; 1960: 51,942; 1950: 50,763) (Cooperstown). Indian word for "place of the rock." -- Bacon, Edwin Faxon, Otsego County, Oneonta, N.Y.: The Oneonta Herald, 1902; 85 p. -- Jones, Louis Clark, Growing up in the Cooper Country, Syracuse, N.Y.: Syracuse University Press, 1965; 198 p.

Ottawa, Kan. (est. Feb. 27, 1860; 723 sq. mi.; 1970 pop.: 6,183; 1960: 6,779; 1950: 7,265) (Minneapolis). Ottawa Indian tribe; "adawe" meaning "to trade" or "trader."

Ottawa, Mich. (est. Mar. 2, 1831, org. 1837; 564 sq.mi.;

1970 pop. : 128, 181; 1960: 98, 719; 1950: 73, 751) (Grand Haven). Ottawa Indian tribe*.

Ottawa, Ohio (est. Mar. 6, 1840; 263 sq. mi. ; 1970 pop. : 37, 099; 1960: 35, 323; 1950: 29, 469) (Port Clinton). Ottawa Indian tribe*.

Ottawa, Okla. (est. July 16, 1907; 483 sq. mi. ; 1970 pop. : 29, 800; 1960: 28, 301; 1950: 32, 218) (Miami). Ottawa Indian tribe*.

Otter Tail, Minn. (est. Mar. 18, 1858; 2, 000 sq. mi. ; 1970 pop. : 46, 097; 1960: 48, 960; 1950: 51, 320) (Fergus Falls). Descriptive, formation of land. (org. Mar. 16, 1868)

Ouachita, Ark. (est. Nov. 29, 1842; 738 sq. mi. ; 1970 pop.: 30, 896; 1960: 31, 641; 1950: 74, 713) (Camden). Ouachita Indian tribe*. Anglicized as Washita from Indian words meaning "people of the clear sparkling waters" or "good hunting grounds."

Ouachita, La. (est. Apr. 10, 1805; org. Mar. 31, 1807; 642 sq. mi. ; 1970 pop. : 115, 387; 1960: 101, 663; 1950: 74, 713) (Monroe). Ouachita Indian tribe*.

Ouray, Colo. (est. Jan. 18, 1877; 540 sq. mi. ; 1970 pop. : 1, 546; 1960: 1, 601; 1950: 2, 103) (Ouray). Ouray (1820-1880). Indian chief, friendly to the whites; frequent visitor to Washington, D. C., in behalf of his tribe. (Originally Uncompahgre County, name changed to Ouray, Mar. 2, 1883).

Outagamie, Wis. (est. Feb. 17, 1851; 634 sq. mi. ; 1970 pop. : 119, 356; 1960: 101, 794; 1950: 81, 722) (Appleton). Chippewa Indian name for the Fox Indian tribe. -- Outagamie County Pioneer Association, The pioneers of Outgamie County, Appleton, Wis. : Post Pub. Co., 1895; 303 p.

Overton, Tenn. (est. Sept. 11, 1806; 442 sq. mi. ; 1970 pop.: 14, 866; 1960: 14, 661; 1950: 17, 566) (Livingston). John Overton (1766-1833). Purchased Rice tract, founded Memphis 1794; Tenn. superior court 1804-10; Tenn. supreme court 1811-16.

Owen, Ind. (est. Dec. 21, 1818, eff. Jan. 1, 1819; 391 sq. mi. ; 1970 pop. : 12, 163; 1960: 11, 400; 1950: 11, 763) (Spencer). Abraham Owen (17 -1811). Col. under William Henry Harrison, killed at battle of Tippecanoe Nov. 7, 1811.

Owen, Ky. (est. Feb. 6, 1819; 351 sq. mi. ; 1970 pop. : 7, 470; 1960: 8, 237; 1950: 11, 763) (Owenton). Abraham Owen*.

Owsley, Ky. (est. Jan. 23, 1843; 197 sq. mi. ; 1970 pop. : 5, 023; 1960: 5, 369; 1950: 7, 324) (Booneville). William Owsley. Judge.

Owyhee, Idaho (est. Dec. 31, 1863; 7,648 sq. mi.; 1970 pop.: 6,422; 1960: 6,375; 1950: 6,307) (Murphy). Corruption of Hawaii. -- A Historical Descriptive and Commercial Directory of Owyhee County, Silver City, Idaho: The Owyhee Avalanche, 1898; 140 p.

Oxford, Me. (est. Mar. 4, 1805; 2,085 sq. mi.; 1970 pop.: 43,457; 1960: 44,345; 1950: 44,221) (South Paris). Oxford University, England, fully equipped 12th century. Earl of Oxford.

Ozark, Mo. (est. Jan. 29, 1841; 756 sq. mi.; 1970 pop.: 6,226; 1960: 6,744; 1950: 8,856) (Gainesville). Ozark Mountains; anglicized version of French abbreviation "aux arcs" for "aux Arkansas" meaning "in the country of the Arkansas." (Name changed to Decatur County, Feb. 22, 1843 unnumbered, changed to Ozark County, Mar. 24, 1845 unnumbered)

Ozaukee, Wis. (est. Mar. 7, 1853; 235 sq. mi.; 1970 pop.: 54,421; 1960: 38,441; 1950: 23,361) (Port Washington). Chippewa form of the tribal name of the Sauk Indians.

P

Pacific, Wash. (est. Feb. 4, 1851; 925 sq. mi.; 1970 pop.: 15,796; 1960: 14,674; 1950: 16,558) (South Bend). Descriptive, Pacific Ocean. -- Williams, Lewis R., Our Pacific County, Raymond, Wash.: Raymond Herald, 1930; 104 p.

Page, Iowa (est. Feb. 24, 1847; 535 sq. mi.; 1970 pop.: 18,507; 1960: 21,023; 1950: 23,921) (Clarinda). John Page (-1846). Second lt. 1818; first lt. 1819; capt. 1831; died of wounds received at battle of Palo Alto May 8, 1846. -- Kershaw, W. L., History of Page County, Chicago: S. J. Clarke Pub. Co., 1909; 2 vol. -- U. S. W. P. A., Page County History, Clarinda, Iowa, 1942; 99 p. typescript.

Page, Va. (est. Mar. 30, 1831; 316 sq. mi.; 1970 pop.: 16,581; 1960: 15,572; 1950: 15,152) (Luray). John Page (1743-1808). Thirteenth gov. of Va. (Commonwealth). Served under Washington in French and Indian war 1755; Va. constitutional convention 1776; lt. gov. of Va. under Patrick Henry 1776-79; col.; Va. house of delegates 1781-83 and 1785-88; Representative from Va., 1789-97; Va. house of delegates 1797, 1798, 1800-01; gov. of Va., 1802-05; U. S. commissioner of loans for Va. 1805-08. -- Strickler, Harry Miller, A short history of Page

County, Richmond, Va.: Dietz Press, 1952; 442 p.

Palm Beach, Fla. (est. Apr. 30, 1909; 1, 978 sq. mi.; 1970 pop.: 348, 753; 1960: 228, 106; 1950: 114, 688) (West Palm Beach). Descriptive. -- Hannau, Hans W., Palm Beach, Munich, Germany: W. Andermann, 1968; 60 p.

Palo Alto, Iowa (est. Jan. 15, 1851; 561 sq. mi.; 1970 pop.: 13, 289; 1960: 14, 736; 1950: 15, 891) (Emmetsburg). Palo Alto, Tex., site of the battle of May 8, 1846. -- McCarty, Dwight G., History of Palo Alto County, Cedar Rapids, Iowa: Torch Press, 1910; 201 p.

Palo Pinto, Tex. (est. Aug. 27, 1856; 982 sq. mi.; 1970 pop.: 28, 962; 1960: 20, 516; 1950: 17, 154) (Palo Pinto). Spanish for "painted trees" or "stained timber."

Pamlico, N. C. (est. Feb. 8, 1872; 341 sq. mi.; 1970 pop.: 9, 467; 1960: 9, 850; 1950: 9, 993) (Bayboro). Pamlico Indian tribe.

Panola, Miss. (est. Feb. 9, 1836; 696 sq. mi.; 1970 pop.: 26, 829; 1960: 28, 791; 1950: 31, 271) (Batesville and Sardis). Indian word "ponolo" meaning cotton.

Panola, Tex. (est. Mar. 30, 1846; 880 sq. mi.; 1970 pop.: 15, 894; 1960: 16, 870; 1950: 19, 250) (Carthage). Indian word for cotton.

Park, Colo. (est. Nov. 1, 1861; 2, 166 sq. mi.; 1970 pop.: 2, 185; 1960: 1, 822; 1950: 1, 870) (Fairplay). Descriptive, South Park.

Park, Mont. (est. Feb. 23, 1887; eff. May 1, 1887; 2, 627 sq. mi.; 1970 pop.: 11, 197; 1960: 13, 168; 1950: 11, 999) (Livingston). Descriptive, Yellowstone National Park.

Park, Wyo. (est. Feb. 15, 1909; 5, 217 sq. mi.; 1970 pop.: 17, 752; 1960: 16, 874; 1950: 15, 182) (Cody). Descriptive. Yellowstone National Park.

Parke, Ind. (est. Jan. 9, 1821, eff. Apr. 2, 1821; 451 sq. mi.; 1970 pop.: 14, 600; 1960: 14, 804; 1950: 15, 674) (Rockville). ("The Covered Bridge Capital of the World"; "The Covered Bridge County of the United States of America"). Benjamin Parke (1777-1835). Attorney gen. Ind. Terr. 1804-08; Ind. Terr. house of representatives 1805; delegate from Ind. Terr. 1805-08; Ind. Terr. judge 1808-17; judge of U. S. District Court of Ind. 1817-35.

Parker, Tex. (est. Dec. 12, 1855; 904 sq. mi.; 1970 pop.: 33, 880; 1960: 22, 880; 1950: 21, 528) (Weatherford). Isaac Parker (1793-1883). Emigrated to Tex. 1833; Tex. revolution; Tex. house of representatives, Tex. senate. -- Smythe, Henry, Historical sketch of Parker County and Weatherford, L. C. Lavat, 1877; 476 p.

Parmer, Tex. (est. Aug. 21, 1876; 859 sq. mi.; 1970 pop.: 10, 509; 1960: 9, 583; 1950: 5, 787) (Farwell). Martin

Parmer (1778-1850). Emigrated to Tex. 1825; Fredonia revolt 1827; Tex. legislature; Tex. constitutional convention 1836; signer Tex. declaration of independence 1836; chief justice Jasper County 1839-40.

Pasco, Fla. (est. June 2, 1887; 751 sq. mi.; 1970 pop.: 75,955; 1960: 36,785; 1950: 20,529) (Dade City). Samuel Pasco (1834-1917). Private, Confederate Army 1861; wounded and captured at Missionary Ridge, imprisoned until paroled 1865; clerk of circuit court Jefferson County, Fla. 1866-68; pres. Fla. constitutional convention 1885; Fla. house of representatives 1886-87; Senator from Fla. 1887-99.

Pasquotank, N. C. (est. 1670; 2,229 sq. mi.; 1970 pop.: 26,824; 1960: 25,630; 1950: 24,347) (Elizabeth City). Pasquotank Indian tribe whose name means "divided tidal river."

Passaic, N. J. (est. Feb. 7, 1837; 194 sq. mi.; 1970 pop.: 460,782; 1960: 406,618; 1950: 337,093) (Paterson). Indian word for "peace" or "valley." -- Nelson, William, Historical sketch of the County of Passaic, Paterson, N. J.: Chiswell & Wurts, 1877; 39 p.

Patrick, Va. (est. Nov. 26, 1790; 469 sq. mi.; 1970 pop.: 15,282; 1960: 15,282; 1950: 15,642) (Stuart). Patrick Henry (1736-1799). Va. house of burgesses 1765; Continental Congress 1774-76; gov. of Va. 1776-79 and 1784-86; Va. constitutional convention 1788. -- Pedigo, Virginia G. and Pedigo, L. G., History of Patrick and Henry Counties, Roanoke, Va.: Stone Printing and Mfg. Co., 1933; 400 p.

Paulding, Ga. (est. Dec. 3, 1832; 324 sq. mi.; 1970 pop.: 17,520; 1960: 13,101; 1950: 11,752) (Dallas). John Paulding (1758-1818). One of the captors of maj. John Andre Sept. 23, 1780; received silver medal from Congress and pension of $200.

Paulding, Ohio (est. Feb. 12, 1820; 416 sq. mi.; 1970 pop.: 19,329; 1960: 16,792; 1950: 15,047) (Paulding). John Paulding*.

Pawnee, Kan. (est. Feb. 26, 1867; 749 sq. mi.; 1970 pop.: 8,484; 1960: 10,254; 1950: 11,041) (Larned). Pawnee Indian tribe.

Pawnee, Neb. (est. Mar. 6, 1855, org. Nov. 4, 1856; 433 sq. mi.; 1970 pop.: 4,473; 1960: 5,356; 1950: 6,744) (Pawnee City). Pawnee Indian tribe*. -- Edwards, Joseph L., Centennial history of Pawnee County, Neb., Pawnee City, Neb.: A. E. Hassler, 1876; 50 p.

Pawnee, Okla. (est. July 16, 1907; 591 sq. mi.; 1970 pop.: 11,338; 1960: 10,884; 1950: 13,616) (Pawnee). Pawnee

Indian tribe*.

Payette, Idaho (est. Feb. 28, 1917; 403 sq. mi.; 1970 pop.: 12,401; 1960: 12,363; 1950: 11,921) (Payette). Francis Payette. Hudson Bay trapper.

Payne, Okla. (est. July 16, 1907; 697 sq. mi.; 1970 pop.: 50,654; 1960: 44,231; 1950: 46,436) (Stillwater). David L. Payne (1836-1884). Private; Ind. legislature 1864; leader of the "boomers" led eight invasions into Okla. Terr., was arrested and removed as an intruder.

Peach, Ga. (est. July 18, 1924; 179 sq. mi.; 1970 pop.: 15,990; 1960: 13,846; 1950: 11,705) (Fort Valley). Descriptive, Georgia peach.

Pearl River, Miss. (est. Feb. 22, 1890; 797 sq. mi.; 1970 pop.: 27,802; 1960: 22,411; 1950: 20,641) (Poplarville). Descriptive.

Pecos, Tex. (est. May 3, 1871; 4,736 sq. mi.; 1970 pop.: 13,748; 1960: 11,957; 1950: 9,939) (Fort Stockton). ("The Highest Cotton Producing County in the World"). Pecos Indian tribe; Pecos River.

Pembina, N.D. (est. Jan. 9, 1867, org. Aug. 12, 1867; 1,124 sq. mi.; 1970 pop.: 10,728; 1960: 12,946; 1950: 13,990) (Cavalier). Chippewa word for "high cranberry bush."

Pemiscot, Mo. (est. Feb. 19, 1851; 488 sq. mi.; 1970 pop.: 26,373; 1960: 38,095; 1950: 45,624) (Caruthersville). Indian word for "liquid mud."

Pend Oreille, Wash. (est. Mar. 1, 1911; 1,406 sq. mi.; 1970 pop.: 6,025; 1960: 6,914; 1950: 7,413) (Newport). Pend Oreille Indian tribe; French word for "ear bob."

Pender, N.C. (est. Feb. 16, 1875; 857 sq. mi.; 1970 pop.: 18,149; 1960: 18,508; 1950: 18,423) (Burgaw). William Dorsey Pender (1834-1863). Graduated U.S. Military Academy; capt. Confederate Army 1861; maj. gen. 1863; killed at battle of Gettysburg, July 18, 1863.

Pendleton, Ky. (est. Dec. 4, 1787; org. May 10, 1799, eff. May 10, 1799; 279 sq. mi.; 1970 pop.: 9,949; 1960: 9,968; 1950: 9,610) (Falmouth). Edmund Pendleton (1721-1803). Va. house of burgesses 1752-54; Continental Congress 1774-75; pres. Committee of Safety 1775; pres. of Va. conventions 1775 and 1776; Va. house of delegates 1776-77; presiding judge Va. court of appeals 1779; pres. Va. Constitutional convention 1788.

Pendleton, W. Va. (est. Dec. 4, 1787; eff. May 1, 1788; 696 sq. mi.; 1970 pop.: 7,031; 1960: 8,093; 1950: 9,313) (Franklin). Edmund Pendleton*. -- Morton, Oren Frederic, A history of Pendleton County, Franklin, W. Va.: O. F. Morton, 1910; 493 p.

Pennington, Minn. (est. Nov. 23, 1910; 622 sq. mi.; 1970 pop.: 13,266; 1960: 12,468; 1950: 12,965) (Thief River Falls.) Edmund Pennington (1848-1926). Supt. Minn., St. Paul and Sault Ste. Marie RR Co., 1888-89; gen. manager 1899-1905; pres. 1909.

Pennington, S. D. (est. Jan. 11, 1875; 2,776 sq. mi.; 1970 pop.: 59,349; 1960: 58,195; 1950: 34,053) (Rapid City). John L. Pennington. Fifth terr. gov. of Dakota terr. 1874-78; collector of internal revenue of Dakota territory.

Penobscot, Me. (est. Feb. 15, 1816, eff. Apr. 1, 1816; 3,408 sq. mi.; 1970 pop.: 125,393; 1960: 126,346; 1950: 108,198) (Bangor). Indian word for "rocky place" or "river of rocks." -- History of Penobscot County, Cleveland: Williams, Chase & Co., 1882; 922 p.

Peoria, Ill. (est. Jan. 13, 1825; 636 sq. mi.; 1970 pop.: 195,308; 1960: 189,044; 1950: 174,347) (Peoria). Peoria Indian tribe. -- Drury, John, This is Peoria County, Chicago: Loree Company, 1955; 482 p. -- May, George W., Students' history of Peoria County, Galesburg, Ill.: Wagoner Printing Co., 1968; 321 p.

Pepin, Wis. (est. Feb. 25, 1858; 237 sq. mi.; 1970 pop.: 7,319; 1960: 7,332; 1950: 7,462) (Durand). Pepin le Bref.

Perkins, Neb. (est. 1887; 885 sq. mi.; 1970 pop.: 3,423; 1960: 4,189; 1950: 4,809) (Grant). Charles Elliott Perkins (1840-1907). Assistant treas. Burlington and Mo. RR Co.; pres. Chicago, Burlington and Quincy RR Co. 1881-1901.

Perkins, S. D. (est. Feb. 26, 1909; 2,866 sq. mi.; 1970 pop.: 4,769; 1960: 5,977; 1950: 6,776) (Bison). Henry E. Perkins. S. D. senate 1903, 1907 and 1911.

Perquimans, N. C. (est. 1672; 261 sq. mi.; 1970 pop.: 8,351; 1960: 9,178; 1950: 9,602) (Hertford). Perquiman Indian tribe. -- Winslow, Ellen Goode (Rawlings), History of Perquimans County, Raleigh, N. C.: Edwards & Broughton, 1931; 118 p.

Perry, Ala. (est. Dec. 13, 1819; 734 sq. mi.; 1970 pop.: 15,388; 1960: 17,358; 1950: 20,439) (Marion). Oliver Hazard Perry (1785-1819). Midshipman 1799; lt. 1807; commanded schooner 1809; commanded division of gunboats 1812; superintended equipment and construction of a fleet of nine vessels 1813; fought battle of Lake Erie 1813; his flagship "Lawrence" was damaged and he went to the "Niagara;" sent message to Gen. Harrison "We have met the enemy and they are ours." Appointed a commodore in 1819; died of yellow fever on mission to Venezuela.

Perry, Ark. (est. Dec. 18, 1840; 556 sq. mi.; 1970 pop.:

5, 634; 1960: 4, 927; 1950: 5, 978) (Perryville). Oliver Hazard Perry*.

Perry, Ill. (est. Jan. 29, 1827; 443 sq. mi. ; 1970 pop. : 19, 757; 1960: 19, 184; 1950: 21, 684) (Pinckneyville). Oliver Hazard Perry*. -- Portrait and Biographical Record of Randolph, Jackson, Perry and Monroe Counties, Chicago: Biographical Pub. Co., 1894; 882 p.

Perry, Ind. (est. Sept. 7, 1814, eff. Nov. 1, 1814; 384 sq. mi. ; 1970 pop. : 19, 075; 1960: 17, 232; 1950: 17, 367) (Cannelton). Oliver Hazard Perry*. -- De la Hunt, Thomas James, Perry County, [Ind.] a history, Indianapolis, Ind. : W. K. Stewart Co. 1916, 1916; 359 p.

Perry, Ky. (est. Nov. 2, 1820; 343 sq. mi. ; 1970 pop. : 25, 714; 1960: 34, 961; 1950: 46, 566) (Hazard). Oliver Hazard Perry*. -- Daughters of the American Revolution, History of Perry County, Ky., Hazard, Ky., 1953; 286 p.

Perry, Miss. (est. Feb. 3, 1820; 644 sq. mi. ; 1970 pop. : 9, 065; 1960: 8, 745; 1950: 9, 108) (New Augusta). Oliver Hazard Perry*.

Perry, Mo. (est. Nov. 16, 1820; 476 sq. mi. ; 1970 pop. : 14, 393; 1960: 14, 642; 1950: 14, 890) (Perryville). Oliver Hazard Perry*.

Perry, Ohio (est. Dec. 26, 1817; 409 sq. mi. ; 1970 pop. : 27, 434; 1960: 27, 864; 1950: 28, 999) (New Lexington). Oliver Hazard Perry*. -- Martzolff, Clement L., History of Perry County, New Lexington, Ohio: Ward & Weiland, 1902; 195 p.

Perry, Pa. (est. Mar. 22, 1820; 550 sq. mi. ; 1970 pop. : 28, 615; 1960: 26, 582; 1950: 24, 782) (New Bloomfield). Oliver Hazard Perry*. -- Hain, Harry Harrison, History of Perry County, Harrisburg, Pa. : Hain-Moore Co., 1922; 1088 p.

Perry, Tenn. (est. Nov. 14, 1821; 419 sq. mi. ; 1970 pop. : 5, 238; 1960: 5, 273; 1950: 6, 462) (Linden). Oliver Hazard Perry*.

Pershing, Nev. (est. Mar. 18, 1919; 5, 993 sq. mi. ; 1970 pop. : 2, 670; 1960: 3, 199; 1950: 3, 103) (Lovelock). ("Nevada's Nile Valley"). John Joseph Pershing (1860-1948). Graduated U. S. Military Academy 1886; fought in Apache campaign 1886-87; Sioux campaign 1890-91; Cree campaign 1896; Cuba campaign 1898; Philippine campaign 1899; punitive expedition against Francisco Villa 1915; commanded American Expeditionary Force in Europe 1917; full rank of gen. Oct. 6, 1917; Chief of Staff 1921.

Person, N. C. (est. sess. Dec. 5, 1791; 400 sq. mi. ; 1970 pop. : 25, 914; 1960: 26, 394; 1950: 24, 361) (Roxboro). Thomas Person (1733-1800). Justice of the peace 1756;

sheriff 1762; N. C. assembly 1764; N. C. provincial council 1775; council of safety 1776; justice of the peace 1776; N. C. house of commons 1777-86, 1788-91, 1793-95 and 1797; N. C. senate 1787 and 1791.

Petroleum, Mont. (est. Nov. 24, 1924; 1, 664 sq. mi. ; 1970 pop. : 675; 1960: 894; 1950: 1, 026) (Winnett). Descriptive.

Pettis, Mo. (est. Jan. 26, 1833; 679 sq. mi. ; 1970 pop. : 34, 137; 1960: 35, 120; 1950: 31, 577) (Sedalia). Spencer Pettis. (1802-1831) Mo. House of Rep. -- McGruder, Mark Austin, History of Pettis County, Mo., Topeka: Historical Pub. Co., 1919; 835 p.

Phelps, Mo. (est. Nov. 13, 1857; 677 sq. mi. ; 1970 pop. : 29, 481; 1960: 25, 396; 1950: 21, 504) (Rolla). John Smith Phelps (1814-1886). Twenty-third gov. of Mo. Mo. house of representatives 1840; Representative from Mo. 1845-63; lt. col. and col. 1861; military gov. of Ark. 1862; brig. gen. 1862; gov. of Mo., 1876-80.

Phelps, Neb. (est. Feb. 11, 1873; 545 sq. mi. ; 1970 pop. : 9, 553; 1960: 9, 800; 1950: 9, 048) (Holdrege). William Phelps. Miss. steamboat capt.

Philadelphia, Pa. (est. Mar. 10, 1682; 135 sq.mi.; 1970 pop.: 1, 948, 609; 1960: 2, 002, 512; 1950: 2, 071, 605) (Philadelphia). Philadelphia, Asia Minor; from the Greek "philadelphos" meaning "loving one's brother." -- Scharf, John Thomas, History of Philadelphia, 1609-1884, Philadelphia: L. H. Everts & Co., 1884; 3 vol.

Phillips, Ark. (est. May 1, 1820, eff. June 1, 1820; 704 sq. mi. ; 1970 pop. : 40, 046; 1960: 43, 997; 1950: 46, 254) (Helena) Sylvanus Phillips (1766-1830). Explored Ark. River 1798.

Phillips, Colo. (est. Mar. 27, 1889; 680 sq. mi. ; 1970 pop. : 4, 131; 1960: 4, 440; 1950: 4, 924) (Holyoke). R. O. Phillips. Secretary of Lincoln Land Co.

Phillips, Kan. (est. Feb. 26, 1867; 806 sq. mi. ; 1970 pop.: 7, 888; 1960: 8, 709; 1950: 9, 273) (Phillipsburg). William Phillips (-1856). Free state martyr, murdered at Leavenworth, Kan., Sept. 1, 1856.

Phillips, Mont. (est. Feb. 5, 1915; petition and election; 5, 264 sq. mi. ; 1970 pop. : 5, 386; 1960: 6, 027; 1950: 6, 334) (Malta). Benjamin D. Phillips. Rancher; pioneer livestock man.

Piatt, Ill. (est. Jan. 27, 1841; 437 sq. mi. ; 1970 pop. : 15, 509; 1960: 14, 960; 1950: 13, 970) (Monticello). Benjamin Piatt. Attorney gen. Ill. Terr. 1810-13. -- Morgan, Jessie Borror, The good life in Piatt County, Moline, Ill. : Piatt County Board of Supervisors, 1968; 287 p.

Pickaway, Ohio (est. Jan. 12, 1810; 507 sq. mi.; 1970 pop.: 40,071; 1960: 35,855; 1950: 29,352) (Circleville). Piqua Indian tribe, Indian word "piqua" for "ashes." -- Van Cleaf, Aaron R., History of Pickaway County, Chicago: Biographical Pub. Co., 1906; 882 p.

Pickens, Ala. (est. Dec. 19, 1820; 887 sq. mi.; 1970 pop.: 20,326; 1960: 21,882; 1950: 24,349) (Carrollton). Andrew Pickens (1739-1817). Fought Cherokee Indians 1760; capt. to brig. gen. Revolutionary War 1779-81; awarded sword by Congress for victory at Cowpens 1781; fought Cherokee Indians 1782; S.C. house of representatives 1781-94; S.C. constitutional convention 1790; Representative from S.C., 1793-95; maj. gen. of militia 1795; S.C. house of representatives 1800-12. -- Clanahan, James F., History of Pickens County, Ala., 1546-1920, Carrollton, Ala.: Clanahan Publication, 1964; 422 p.

Pickens, Ga. (est. Dec. 5, 1853; 231 sq. mi.; 1970 pop.: 9,620; 1960: 8,903; 1950: 8,855) (Jasper). Andrew Pickens*. -- Tate, Lucius Eugene, History of Pickens County, Atlanta, Ga.: W. W. Brown Pub. Co., 1935; 322p.

Pickens, S. C. (est. Dec. 20, 1826; 501 sq. mi.; 1970 pop.: 58,956; 1960: 46,030; 1950: 40,058) (Pickens). Andrew Pickens*. -- McFall, Pearl Smith, It happened in Pickens County, Pickens, S. C.: Sentinel Press, 1959; 216 p.

Pickett, Tenn. (est. Feb. 27, 1879; 174 sq. mi.; 1970 pop.: 3,774; 1960: 4,431; 1950: 5,093) (Byrdstown). H. L. Pickett. Representative from Wilson County who aided the act establishing Pickett County.

Pierce, Ga. (est. Dec. 18, 1857; 345 sq. mi.; 1970 pop.: 9,281; 1960: 9,678; 1950: 11,112) (Blackshear). Franklin Pierce (1804-1869). Pres. of the U. S. New Hampshire house of representatives 1829-33; Representative from N. H. 1833-37; Senator from N. H. 1837-42; col. in Mexican war; brig. gen. 1847; N. H. constitutional convention 1850; Pres. of the U. S. 1853-57.

Pierce, Neb. (est. Jan. 26, 1856, org. Sept. 21, 1870; 573 sq. mi.; 1970 pop.: 8,493; 1960: 8,722; 1950: 9,405) (Pierce). Franklin Pierce*. (Formerly Otoe County)

Pierce, N. D. (est. Mar. 11, 1887, org. Apr. 11, 1889; 1,053 sq. mi.; 1970 pop.: 6,323; 1960: 7,394; 1950: 8,326) (Rugby). Gilbert Ashville Pierce (1839-1901). Second lt. Ninth Regiment Ind., Vol. Inf., capt., lt. col. and chief quartermaster 1864; col. 1865; bvt. maj. and lt. col. 1865; Ind. house of representatives 1868; assistant financial clerk U. S. Senate 1869-71; gov. of Dakota Terr. 1884-87; Senator from N. D. 1889-91; U. S. Minister to Portugal for four months, 1893.

Pierce, Wash. (est. Dec. 22, 1852; 1,680 sq. mi.; 1970 pop.: 411,027; 1960: 321,590; 1950: 275,876) (Tacoma). Franklin Pierce*. -- Bonney, William Pierce, History of Pierce County, Washington, Chicago: Pioneer Historical Pub. Co., 1927; 3 vol.

Pierce, Wis. (est. Mar. 14, 1853; 591 sq. mi.; 1970 pop.: 26,652; 1960: 22,503; 1950: 21,448) (Ellsworth). Franklin Pierce*.

Pike, Ala. (est. Dec. 17, 1821; 673 sq. mi.; 1970 pop.: 25,038; 1960: 25,987; 1950: 30,608) (Troy). Zebulon Montgomery Pike (1779-1813). -- Farmer, Margaret Pace, History of Pike County, Ala., Troy, Ala., 1952; 144 p.

Pike, Ark. (est. Nov. 1, 1833, eff. Dec. 1, 1833; 615 sq. mi.; 1970 pop.: 8,711; 1960: 7,864; 1950: 10,032) (Murfreesboro). Zebulon Montgomery Pike*.

Pike, Ga. (est. Dec. 9, 1822, org. Dec. 20, 1824; 237 sq. mi.; 1970 pop.: 7,316; 1960: 7,138; 1950: 8,459) (Zebulon). Zebulon Montgomery Pike*.

Pike, Ill. (est. Jan. 31, 1821; 786 sq. mi.; 1970 pop.: 19,185; 1960: 20,552; 1950: 22,155) (Pittsfield). ("The County Beautiful by Nature"; "The County Progressive by Choice"; "The County Steeped in History"). Zebulon Montgomery Pike*. -- Drury, John, This Is Pike County, Chicago: Loree Co., 1955; 522 p.

Pike, Ind. (est. Dec. 21, 1816, eff. Feb. 1, 1817; 335 sq. mi.; 1970 pop.: 12,281; 1960: 12,797; 1950: 14,995) (Petersburg). Zebulon Montgomery Pike*.

Pike, Ky. (est. Dec. 19, 1821; 786 sq. mi.; 1970 pop.: 61,059; 1960: 68,264; 1950: 81,154) (Pikeville). Zebulon Montgomery Pike*.

Pike, Miss. (est. Dec. 9, 1815; 407 sq. mi.; 1970 pop.: 31,756; 1960: 35,063; 1950: 35,137) (Magnolia). Zebulon Montgomery Pike*. -- Conerly, Luke Ward, Pike County, Miss., 1798-1876, Nashville, Tenn.: Brandon Printing Co., 1909; 368 p.

Pike, Mo. (est. Dec. 14, 1818; 681 sq. mi.; 1970 pop.: 16,928; 1960: 16,706; 1950: 16,844) (Bowling Green). Zebulon Montgomery Pike*.

Pike, Ohio (est. Jan. 4, 1815; 443 sq. mi.; 1970 pop.: 19,114; 1960: 19,380; 1950: 14,607) (Waverly). Zebulon Montgomery Pike*. -- McCormick, Mrs. Harold, History of Pike County, [Waverly, Ohio] Commissioners of Pike County, 1958; 42 p.

Pike, Pa. (est. Mar. 26, 1814; 545 sq. mi.; 1970 pop.: 11,818; 1960: 9,158; 1950: 8,425) (Milford). Zebulon Montgomery Pike*.

Pima, Ariz. (est. Dec. 15, 1864; 9,241 sq. mi.; 1970 pop.: 351,667; 1960: 265,660; 1950: 141,216) (Tucson). ("The County in the Heart of the Sun Country"). Pima Indians, from Indian word "pia" meaning "I don't know."

Pinal, Ariz. (est. Feb. 1, 1875; 5,378 sq. mi.; 1970 pop.: 67,916; 1960: 62,673; 1950: 43,191) (Florence). ("The County in the Shadow of the Superstitious"). Indian word for "deer."

Pine, Minn. (est. Mar. 1, 1856, org. Feb. 13, 1857; 1,412 sq. mi.; 1970 pop.: 16,821; 1960: 17,004; 1950: 18,223) (Pine City). Descriptive.

Pinellas, Fla. (est. May 23, 1911; 264 sq. mi.; 1970 pop.: 522,329; 1960: 374,665; 1950: 159,249) (Clearwater). ("The County Near the Blue Waters of the Gulf of Mexico"). Spanish derivation; from "pinta pinal" for "point of the pines." -- Straub, William L., History of Pinellas County, Saint Augustine, Fla.: The Record Co., 1929; 507 p.

Pipestone, Minn. (est. May 23, 1857, org. Jan. 27, 1879; 464 sq. mi.; 1970 pop.: 12,791; 1960: 13,605; 1950: 14,003) (Pipestone). Descriptive of pipestone or catlinite. -- Rose, Arthur P., An illustrated history of the counties of Rock and Pipestone, Luverne, Minn.: Northern History Pub. Co., 1911; 802 p.

Piscataquis, Me. (est. Mar. 23, 1838, eff. Apr. 30, 1838; 3,948 sq. mi.; 1970 pop.: 16,285; 1960: 17,379; 1950: 18,617) (Dover-Foxcroft). ("The County of Lakes"). Indian word for "divided tidal river." -- Loring, Amasa, History of Piscataquis County, Portland: Hoyt, Fogg & Donham, 1880; 304 p.

Pitkin, Colo. (est. Feb. 23, 1881; 974 sq. mi.; 1970 pop.: 6,185; 1960: 2,381; 1950: 1,646) (Aspen). Frederick Walker Pitkin (1837-1886). Second gov. of Colo. Went to Colo. for his health 1874; gov. of Colo. 1879-83.

Pitt, N.C. (est. sess. Apr. 24, 1760; 656 sq. mi.; 1970 pop.: 73,900; 1960: 69,942; 1950: 63,789) (Greenville). William Pitt (1708-1778). English statesman, entered Parliament 1735; Secretary of State and leader of the House of Commons 1756; Earl of Chatham. -- King, Henry Thomas, Sketches of Pitt County, a brief history of the county 1704-1910, Raleigh, N.C.: Edwards & Broughton Printing Co., 1911; 263 p.

Pittsburg, Okla. (est. July 16, 1907; 1,359 sq. mi.; 1970 pop.: 37,521; 1960: 34,360; 1950: 41,031) (McAlester). Pittsburgh, Pa., named for William Pitt. The final letter "h" was omitted.

Pittsylvania, Va. (est. sess. Nov. 6, 1766; 1,022 sq. mi.;

1970 pop.: 58, 789; 1960: 58, 296; 1950: 66, 096) (Chatham). William Pitt*. -- Clement, Maud Carter, The history of Pittsylvania County, Lynchburg, Va.: J. P. Bell Co., Inc., 1929; 340 p. -- Swetnam, George, Pittsylvania County.

Piute, Utah (est. Jan. 16, 1865; 753 sq. mi.; 1970 pop.: 1, 164; 1960: 1, 436; 1950: 1, 911) (Junction). Paiute Indian tribe, from Indian words "pai" meaning "water" and "ute" name of Indian tribe.

Placer, Calif. (est. Apr. 25, 1851, org. May 28, 1851; 1, 431 sq. mi.; 1970 pop.: 77, 306; 1960: 56, 998; 1950: 41, 649) (Auburn). ("The Continent Within a County"; "The Northern Gateway to the Mother Lode"). Spanish for "surface mining for gold." -- Lewis, Harriet Jane, Stories of Placer County (for juveniles), Sacramento, Calif.: Chas. N. Fleming Co., Inc., 1932; 61 p. -- History of Placer County, Oakland, Calif.: Thompson & West., 1882; 416 p.

Plaquemines, La. (est. Mar. 31, 1807; 1, 007 sq. mi.; 1970 pop.: 25, 225; 1960: 22, 545; 1950: 14, 239) (Pointe-a-la-Hache). Indian word for "persimmons."

Platte, Mo. (est. Dec. 31, 1838; 414 sq. mi.; 1970 pop.: 32, 081; 1960: 23, 350; 1950: 14, 973) (Platte City). French word for "flat" or "shallow."

Platte, Neb. (est. Jan. 26, 1856; 672 sq. mi.; 1970 pop.: 26, 508; 1960: 23, 992; 1950: 19, 910) (Columbus). French word for "flat." -- Phillips, George Walter, Past and present of Platte County, Nebraska, Chicago: S. J. Clarke Pub. Co., 1915; 2 vol.

Platte, Wyo. (est. Feb. 9, 1911; 2, 114 sq. mi.; 1970 pop.: 6, 486; 1960: 7, 195; 1950: 7, 925) (Wheatland). French word for "flat."

Pleasants, W. Va. (est. Mar. 29, 1851; 130 sq. mi.; 1970 pop.: 7, 274; 1960: 7, 124; 1950: 6, 369) (St. Marys). James Pleasants (1769-1836). Twenty-third gov. of Va. (Commonwealth). Va. house of delegates 1797-1802; Rep. from Va. 1811-19; Senator from Va., 1819-22; gov. of Va. 1822-25. -- Pemberton, Robert Landon, A history of Pleasants County, St. Mary's, W. Va.: Oracle Press, 1929; 272 p.

Plumas, Calif. (est. Mar. 18, 1854; 2, 570 sq. mi.; 1970 pop.: 11, 707; 1960: 11, 620; 1950: 13, 519) (Quincy). El Rio de Las Plumas, Spanish for "the river of the feathers" or "Feather River." -- Illustrated History of Plumas, Lassen & Sierra Counties, San Francisco: Fariss & Smith, 1882; 507 p.

Plymouth, Iowa (est. Jan. 15, 1851; 863 sq.mi.; 1970: 24, 312; 1960: 23, 906; 1950: 23, 252) (Le Mars). Plymouth, Mass., the landing place of the Pilgrims. -- History of the counties of Woodbury and Plymouth, Chicago: A. Warner & Co., 1890-91; 1022 p.

Plymouth, Mass. (est. June 2, 1685; 664 sq. mi.; 1970 pop.: 333, 314; 1960: 248, 449; 1950: 189, 468) (Plymouth). Plymouth, England, the seaport from which the "Mayflower" sailed. -- Thompson, Elroy Sherman, History of Plymouth, Norfolk and Barnstable Counties, New York: Lewis Historical Pub. Co., 1928; 3 vol. -- Hurd, Duane Hamilton, History of Plymouth County, Philadelphia: J. W. Lewis & Co., 1884; 1199 p.

Pocahontas, Iowa (est. Jan. 15, 1851;580 sq.mi.; 70: 12, 729; 60: 14, 234; 1950: 15, 496) (Pocahontas). Pocahontas (1595-1617). Daughter of Powhatan, Indian chief, married colonist John Rolfe 1614; interceded with her father to save life of Capt. John Smith. -- Fleckinger, Robert E., The pioneer history of Pocahontas County, Fonda, Iowa: G. Sanborn, 1904; 910 p.

Pocahontas, W. Va. (est. Dec. 21, 1821; 942 sq. mi.; 1970 pop.: 8, 870; 1960: 10, 136; 1950: 12, 480) (Marlinton). Pocahontas*. -- Price, William Thomas, Historical sketches of Pocahontas County, Parsons, W. Va.: reprinted by McClain Printing Co., 1963; 622 p.

Poinsett, Ark. (est. Feb. 28, 1838; 762 sq. mi.; 1970 pop.: 26, 822; 1960: 30, 834; 1950: 39, 311) (Harrisburg). Joel Roberts Poinsett (1779-1851). S. C. house of representatives 1816-20; Representative from S. C., 1821-25; U. S. Minister to Mexico 1825-29; U. S. Secretary of War in cabinet of Pres. Van Buren 1837-41.

Pointe Coupee, La. (est. Apr. 10, 1805; 576 sq. mi.; 1970 pop.: 22, 002; 1960: 22, 488; 1950: 21, 841) (New Roads). French word for "cut-off point."

Polk, Ark. (est. Nov. 30, 1844; 860 sq. mi.; 1970 pop.: 13, 297; 1960: 11, 981; 1950: 14, 182) (Mena). James Knox Polk (1795-1849). Eleventh pres. of the U. S. Chief clerk Tenn. senate 1821-23; Tenn. house of representatives 1823-25; Representative from Tenn., 1825-39; gov. of Tenn., 1839-41; Pres. of the U. S. 1845-49.

Polk, Fla. (est. Feb. 8, 1861; 1, 861 sq. mi.; 1970 pop.: 227, 222; 1960: 195, 139; 1950: 123, 997) (Bartow). ("The County of Progress and Opportunity"; "The Heartland of Florida"; "The Land of Flowers"). James Knox Polk*. -- Hetherington, M. F., History of Polk County, Saint Augustine, Fla.: The Record Co., 1928; 379 p.

Polk, Ga. (est. Dec. 20, 1851; 317 sq. mi.; 1970 pop.: 29, 656; 1960: 28, 015; 1950: 30, 976) (Cedartown). James Knox Polk*.

Polk, Iowa (est. Jan. 17, 1846, org. Apr. 6, 1846; 594 sq. mi.; 1970 pop.: 286,101; 1960: 266,315; 1950: 226,010) (Des Moines). James Knox Polk*. -- Dixon, J.M., Centennial history of Polk County, Des Moines, Iowa: State Register, 1876; 339 p. -- History of Polk County, Des Moines, Iowa: Union Historical Co., 1880; 1037 p.

Polk, Minn. (est. July 20, 1858; 2,012 sq. mi.; 1970 pop.: 34,435; 1960: 36,182; 1950: 35,900) (Crookston). James Knox Polk*.

Polk, Mo. (est. Jan. 5, 1835; 642 sq. mi.; 1970 pop.: 15,415; 1960: 13,753; 1950: 16,062) (Bolivar). James Knox Polk*.

Polk, Neb. (est. Jan. 26, 1856, org. Aug. 6, 1870; 433 sq. mi.; 1970 pop.: 6,468; 1960: 7,210; 1950: 8,044) (Osceola). James Knox Polk*. -- Flodman, Mildred Newman, Early days in Polk County, Lincoln, Neb.: Union College Press, 1966; 453 p.

Polk, N.C. (est. Jan. 18, 1847; 234 sq. mi.; 1970 pop.: 11,735; 1960: 11,395; 1950: 11,627) (Columbus). William Polk (1758-1834). Served in Revolution at Germantown, Brandywine, Eutaw Springs; maj. 9th Regiment N.C. 1776; at Valley Forge; N.C. house of Commons 1785-88 and 1790; supervisor of internal revenue for N.C., 1791-1808. -- Patton, Sadie Smathers, Sketches of Polk County history, Hendersonville, N.C., 1950; 161 p.

Polk, Ore. (est. Dec. 22, 1845; 739 sq. mi.; 1970 pop.: 35,349; 1960: 26,523; 1950: 26,317) (Dallas). James Knox Polk*.

Polk, Tenn. (est. Nov. 28, 1839; 436 sq. mi.; 1970 pop.: 11,669; 1960: 12,160; 1950: 14,074) (Benton). James Knox Polk*.

Polk, Tex. (est. Mar. 30, 1846; 1,094 sq. mi.; 1970 pop.: 14,457; 1960: 13,861; 1950: 16,194) (Livingston). James Knox Polk*. -- Haynes, Emma R., History of Polk County, Livingston, Texas, 1937; 160 p.

Polk, Wis. (est. Mar. 14, 1853; 934 sq. mi.; 1970 pop.: 26,666; 1960: 24,968; 1950: 24,944) (Balsam Lake). James Knox Polk*.

Pondera, Mont. (est. Feb. 17, 1919; 1,643 sq. mi.; 1970 pop.: 6,611; 1960: 7,653; 1950: 6,392) (Conrad). Phonetic spelling for Pend d'Oreille (ear pendant) to avoid confusion with lake and town in Idaho.

Pontotoc, Miss. (est. Feb. 9, 1836; 494 sq. mi.; 1970 pop.: 17,363; 1960: 17,232; 1950: 19,994) (Pontotoc). Pontotoc. Chickasaw Indian chief, name means "weed prairie." -- Winston, E.T., Story of Pontotoc, Pontotoc, Miss.: Pontotoc Progress Print, 1931; 319 p.

Pontotoc, Okla. (est. July 16, 1907; 719 sq. mi.; 1970 pop.: 27,867; 1960: 28,089; 1950: 30,875) (Ada). Pontotoc*. -- Winston, E. T., Story of Pontotoc, Pontotoc Progress Print, 1931; 319 p.

Pope, Ark. (est. Nov. 2, 1829, eff. Dec. 25, 1829; 816 sq. mi.; 1970 pop.: 28,607; 1960: 21,177; 1950: 23,291) (Russellville). John Pope (1770-1845). Third terr. gov. of Ark. Ky. house of representatives 1802, 1806 and 1807; Senator from Ky., 1807-13; Ky. senate 1825-29; terr. gov. of Ark. 1829-35; Representative from Ky., 1837-43.

Pope, Ill. (est. Jan. 10, 1816; 385 sq. mi.; 1970 pop.: 3,857; 1960: 4,061; 1950: 5,779) (Golconda). Nathaniel Pope (1784-1850). First terr. Secretary of Ill. Terr. 1809-16; Delegate from Ill. Terr. 1816-18; registrar of the land office at Edwardsville, Ill., 1818-19; U. S. judge for the district of Ill. 1819-1850.

Pope, Minn. (est. Feb. 20, 1862; 681 sq. mi.; 1970 pop.: 11,107; 1960: 11,914; 1950: 12,862) (Glenwood). John Pope (1823-1892). Graduated U. S. Military Academy 1842; Second lt.; in Mexican War under gen. Zachary Taylor; bvt. first lt. 1846; bvt. capt. battle of Buena Vista 1847; exploring expedition up Red River 1849; topographical engineer N. M. 1849-53; explored Rocky Mts. 1854-59; in Civil War, brig. gen. 1861; captured New Madrid and Island No. 10, maj. gen. of vol. and brig. gen. in regular army 1862; fought at second battle of Bull Run; maj. gen. in regular army 1882; retired 1886. -- Armstrong, Hart R., ed., A hundred years of greatness, Pope County Historical Society, n. p., 1966; 32 p.

Portage, Ohio (est. Feb. 10, 1807, eff. June 7, 1807; 509 sq. mi.; 1970 pop.: 125,868; 1960: 91,798; 1950: 63,954) (Ravenna). Descriptive; old Indian portage or carrying path between the Cuyahoga and Mahoning rivers. -- James B. Holm, ed., Portage Heritage, [Kent, Ohio]: Portage County Historical Society, 1957; 824 p. -- A history of Portage County, Chicago: Warner, Beers & Co., 1885; 927 p.

Portage, Wis. (est. Dec. 7, 1836, org. Feb. 18, 1841, eff. Mar. 1841; 810 sq. mi.; 1970 pop.: 47,541; 1960: 36,964; 1950: 34,858) (Stevens Point). Descriptive for the Fox-Wisconsin portage. -- Rosholt, Malcolm Leviatt, Our county, our story, Stevens Point, Wis.: Portage County Board of Supervisors, 1959; 600 p.

Porter, Ind. (est. Feb. 7, 1835, org. Jan. 28, 1836, eff. Feb. 1, 1836; 425 sq. mi.; 1970 pop.: 87,114; 1960: 60,279; 1950: 40,076) (Valparaiso). David Porter (1780-

1843). Commanded the "Essex" in the War of 1812; commanded squadron in the West Indies against the pirates 1823-25; U. S. consul general to Algiers 1830; U. S. Minister to Turkey 1839. -- Drury, John, This is Porter County, Indiana, Chicago: Inland Photo Co., 1956; 355 p.

Posey, Ind. (est. Sept. 7, 1814, eff. Nov. 1, 1814; 414 sq. mi.; 1970 pop.: 21,740; 1960: 19,214; 1950: 19,818) (Mount Vernon). Thomas Posey (1750-1818). Third gov. Ind. Terr. Revolutionary war capt. of Va. regiment 1776-78; maj. 1778; col. 1789; at surrender of Yorktown 1781; brig. gen. 1793; presiding officer La. senate 1805-06; lt. gov. of Ky.; Senator from La., 1812-13; gov. of Ind. Terr. 1813-16; Indian agent 1816-18. -- Leffel, John C., History of Posey County, Indiana, Standard Pub. Co., 1913; 401 p.

Pottawatomie, Kan. (est. Feb. 20, 1857; 850 sq. mi.; 1970 pop.: 11,755; 1960: 11,957; 1950: 12,344) (Westmoreland). Pottawattomie Indian tribe, from Algonquin "Pottawatomink" meaning "people of the place of fire." -- Crevecoeur, Ferdinand Francis, Old Settlers' tales, Onaga, Kan., 1902; 162 p.

Pottawatomie, Okla. (est. July 16, 1907; 799 sq. mi.; 1970 pop.: 43,134; 1960: 41,486; 1950: 43,517) (Shawnee). Pottawattamie Indian tribe*. -- Forston, John L., Pott County and What Has Come of It, (a history of Pottawatomie County), Shawnee, Okla.: Pottawatomie County Historical Society, 1936; 90 p.

Pottawattamie, Iowa (est. Jan. 15, 1851, 946 sq. mi.; 1970 pop.: 86,991; 1960: 83,102; 1950: 69,682) (Council Bluffs). Pottawattamie Indian tribe*. -- Field, Homer H[oward] and Reed, J. R., History of Pottawattamie County, Chicago: S. J. Clarke Pub. Co., 1907; 2 vol.

Potter, Pa. (est. Mar. 26, 1804; 1,092 sq. mi.; 1970 pop.: 16,395; 1960: 16,483; 1950: 16,810) (Coudersport). ("The Big Game Country of Pennsylvania"). James Potter (1729-1789). Col. Pa. militia 1776-77; wounded at Princeton, N. J., 1777; brig. gen. 1777; maj. gen. 1782; served to end of war. -- Beebe, Victor Llewellyn, History of Potter County, Coudersport, Pa.: Potter County Historical Society, 1934; 280 p.

Potter, S. D. (est. Jan. 14, 1875; 887 sq. mi.; 1970 pop.: 4,449; 1960: 4,926; 1950: 4,688) (Gettysburg). Joel A. Potter. Physician, steward of the S. D. State Hospital.

Potter, Tex. (est. Aug. 21, 1876, org. 1887; 901 sq. mi.; 1970 pop.: 90,511; 1960: 115,580; 1950: 73,366) (Amarillo). Robert Potter (1800-1842). U. S. Navy 1815-21; N. C. house of commons 1826 and 1828; Representative from N. C., 1829-

31; N. C. house 1834-35; signer Tex. declaration of Independence 1836; secretary of the navy in cabinet of provisional pres. David Gouverneur Burnet of the Republic of Tex. 1836; enrolled in Nacogdoches vol. 1835; commission in Tex. Navy 1835; fought at battle of San Jacinto; Tex. congress 1837-41; killed in Regulator-Moderator War, Mar. 2, 1842. -- Key, Della Tyler, In the cattle country, history of Potter County, Amarillo, Texas: Tyler-Berkley Co., 1961; 367 p.

Powder River, Mont. (est. Mar. 7, 1919; effective Apr. 1, 1919; 3, 285 sq. mi.; 1970 pop.: 2, 862; 1960: 2, 485; 1950: 2, 693) (Broadus). Powder River, descriptive, fine black sand resembling gunpowder found along the river's banks. -- Echoing Footsteps, Butte, Mont.: Ashton Printing & Engraving Co., 1967; 719 p.

Powell, Ky. (est. Jan. 7, 1852; 173 sq. mi.; 1970 pop.: 7, 704; 1960: 6, 674; 1950: 6, 812) (Stanton). Lazarus Whitehead Powell (1812-1866). Nineteenth gov. of Ky. Ky. house of representatives 1836; gov. of Ky., 1851-55; U. S. commissioner to Utah 1858; Senator from Ky. 1859-65.

Powell, Mont. (est. Jan. 31, 1901; 2, 337 sq. mi.; 1970 pop.: 6, 660; 1960: 7, 002; 1950: 6, 301) (Deer Lodge). John Wesley Powell (1834-1902). Private in Civil War, lost arm 20th Ill. vol.; battle of Shiloh 1862; promoted to major and lt. col. of vol.; geologist and explorer of Grand Canyon of the Colo. 1870; U. S. Geological Survey 1875; director 1881-94; Bureau of Ethnology of Smithsonian Institution 1879-1902; published many scientific reports.

Power, Idaho (est. Jan. 30, 1913; 1, 411 sq. mi.; 1970 pop.: 4, 864; 1960: 4, 111; 1950: 3, 988) (American Falls). Descriptive. American Falls where the Snake River is 1, 000 feet wide and drops about 40 feet.

Poweshiek, Iowa (est. Feb. 17, 1843, org. Jan. 24, 1848, eff. Apr. 3, 1848; 589 sq. mi.; 1970 pop.: 18, 803; 1960: 19, 300; 1950: 19, 344) (Montezuma). Poweshiek. Chief of the Sacs. -- Parker, L. Fletcher, History of Poweshiek County, Chicago: S. J. Clarke Pub. Co., 1911; 2 vol.

Powhatan, Va. (est. sess. May 5, 1777, eff. July 1, 1777; 268 sq. mi.; 1970 pop.: 7, 696; 1960: 6, 747; 1950: 5, 556) (Powhatan). Powhatan (1550-1618). Indian chief of the Powhatan Indian tribe. His Indian name was Wahunsonacook and he commanded about 8, 000 Indians in about 30 tribes; father of the Indian maiden Pocahontas who married John Rolfe; Indian name for "falls in a current of water."

Prairie, Ark. (est. Nov. 25, 1846; 674 sq. mi.; 1970 pop.: 10, 249; 1960: 10, 515; 1950: 13, 768) (Des Arc and De Valls Bluff). Descriptive.

Prairie, Mont. (est. Feb. 5, 1915, petition and election; 1, 727 sq. mi. ; 1970 pop. : 1, 752; 1960: 2, 318; 1950: 2, 377) (Terry). Descriptive.

Pratt, Kan. (est. Feb. 26, 1867; 729 sq. mi. ; 1970 pop. : 10, 056; 1960: 12, 122; 1950: 12, 156) (Pratt). Caleb Pratt (-1861). Second lt. Co. D, 2nd Kan., killed at Wilson Creek, Mo., Aug. 10, 1861.

Preble, Ohio (est. Feb. 15, 1808, eff. Mar. 1, 1808; 428 sq. mi. ; 1970 pop. : 34, 719; 1960: 32, 498; 1950: 27, 081) (Eaton). Edward Preble (1761-1807). Served in Mass. Navy, commissioned lt. in U. S. Navy in 1798, and commanded the "Essex" in 1799, commanded the "Constitution" in 1803, bombarded Tripoli 1804; forced renewal of treaty with the Sultan of Morocco. -- Runyon, Grace Carroll, Historical facts on Preble County, Eaton, Ohio, 1945; 122 p. -- A biographical history of Preble County, Chicago: Lewis Pub. Co., 1900; 573 p.

Prentiss, Miss. (est. Apr. 15, 1870; 409 sq. mi. ; 1970 pop. : 20, 133; 1960: 17, 949; 1950: 19, 810) (Booneville). Sergeant Smith Prentiss (1808-1950). Miss. house of representatives 1835; Representative from Miss., 1838-39.

Presidio, Tex. (est. Jan. 3, 1850; 3, 877 sq. mi. ; 1970 pop. : 4, 842; 1960: 5, 460; 1950: 7, 354) (Maria). Spanish for "a fortress garrisoned by soldiers."

Presque Isle, Mich. (est. Apr. 1, 1840, org. 1871; 654 sq. mi. ; 1970 pop. : 12, 836; 1960: 13, 117; 1950: 11, 996) (Rogers City). French for "almost an island."

Preston, W. Va. (est. Jan. 19, 1818; 653 sq. mi. ; 1970 pop. : 25, 455; 1960: 27, 233; 1950: 31, 399) (Kingwood). James Patton Preston (1774-1843). Twenty-first gov. of Va. (Commonwealth). Organized artillery company; Va. senate 1802; lt. col. of inf. 1812; promoted to col. 1813; wounded at battle of Chrysler's Farm, Canada, Nov. 11, 1813; gov. of Va. 1816-19; postmaster at Richmond, Va. -- Morton, Oren Frederic, A history of Preston County, Kingwood, W. Va. : Journal Pub. Co., 1914; 2 vol. -- Wiley, Samuel T., History of Preston County, Kingwood, W. Va. : Journal Printing House, 1882; 529 p.

Price, Wis. (est. Feb. 26, 1879; 1, 268 sq. mi. ; 1970 pop.: 14, 520; 1960: 14, 370; 1950: 16, 344) (Phillips). William Thompson Price (1824-1886). Judge of Jackson County 1854 and 1859; Crawford County treasurer 1856-57; Wis. senate 1857, 1870 and 1878-81; collector of internal revenue 1863-65; deputy sheriff Crawford County 1849; Wis. legislature 1851 and 1882; Representative from Wis. 1883-86.

Prince Edward, Va. (est. Feb. 27, 1752 sess. ; 357 sq.

mi. ; 1970 pop. : 14, 379; 1960: 14, 121; 1950: 15, 398) (Farmville). Prince Edward (1733-1761) Edward Augustus, second son of Frederick, second Prince of Wales. -- Bradshaw, Herbert Clarence, History of Prince Edward County, Richmond: Dietz Press, 1955; 934 p. -- Burrell, Charles Edward, A History of Prince Edward County, Richmond: Williams Printing Co., 1922; 408 p.

Prince George, Va. (est. Dec. 5, 1700 sess. ; 286 sq. mi.; 1970 pop. : 29, 092; 1960: 20, 270; 1950: 19, 679) (Prince George). Prince George (1653-1708) prince of Denmark, son of King Frederick II (1609-1670) king of Denmark and Norway; married Queen Anne of England, 1683; became naturalized British subject, duke of Cumberland 1689; lord high admiral of England 1702.

Prince George's, Md. (est. May 20, 1695, eff. Apr. 23, 1696; 485 sq.mi.; 70: 660, 567; 60: 357, 395; 50: 194, 182) (Upper Marlboro). Prince George*.

Prince William, Va. (est. Feb. 1, 1727 sess. ; 347 sq. mi. ; 1970 pop. : 111, 102; 1960: 50, 164; 1950: 22, 612) (Manassas). Prince William (1721-1765); William Augustus, duke of Cumberland, third son of George II and Queen Caroline, stopped Jacobite uprising with such severity that he was known as "the butcher." -- Harrison, Fairfax, Landmarks of Old Prince William, Berryville, Va. : Chesapeake Book Co., 1964; 724 p.

Princess Anne, Va. (est. Apr. 16, 1691 sess. ; 267 sq. mi. ; 1960 pop. : 76, 124; 1950: 42, 277) (Princess Anne). Princess Anne (1665-1714). Second daughter of James II and Anne Hyde; married Prince George of Denmark 1683; Queen Anne of Great Britain and Ireland 1702-14. -- (Princess Anne County was consolidated with Virginia Beach and is now the city of Virginia Beach)

Providence, R. I. (est. June 22, 1703; 430 sq. mi. ; 1970 pop. : 580, 261; 1960: 568, 778; 1950: 574, 973) (Providence). Descriptive, for God's merciful providence. Incorporated as the County of Providence Plantations, name changed to Providence County, June 16, 1729.

Prowers, Colo. (est. Apr. 11, 1889; 1, 626 sq. mi. ; 1970 pop. : 13, 258; 1960: 13, 296; 1950: 14, 836) (Lamar). John W. Prowers. Pioneer.

Pueblo, Colo. (est. Nov. 1, 1861; 2, 401 sq. mi. ; 1970 pop.: 118, 238; 1960: 118, 707; 1950: 90, 188) (Pueblo). Spanish for "town" or "village."

Pulaski, Ark. (est. Dec. 15, 1818, eff. Mar. 1, 1819; 781 sq. mi. ; 1970 pop. : 287, 189; 1960: 242, 980; 1950: 196, 685) (Little Rock). Casimir Pulaski (1748-1779). Polish nobleman who came to America in 1777 to aid

American independence; fought at Brandywine and Germantown; mortally wounded at siege of Savannah, Ga., Oct. 9, 1779.

Pulaski, Ga. (est. Dec. 13, 1808; 258 sq. mi.; 1970 pop.: 8,066; 1960: 8,204; 1950: 8,808) (Hawkinsville). Casimir Pulaski*. -- Daughters of the American Revolution, History of Pulaski County, Georgia, Atlanta, Ga.: W. W. Brown, 1935; 599 p.

Pulaski, Ill. (est. Mar. 3, 1843; 190 sq. mi.; 1970 pop.: 8,741; 1960: 10,490; 1950: 13,639) (Mound City). Casimir, Pulaski*. -- Perrin, William Henry, History of Alexander, Union & Pulaski Counties, Chicago: O. L. Baskin & Co., 1883; 588 p.

Pulaski, Ind. (est. Feb. 7, 1835; org. Feb. 18, 1839; eff. May 6, 1839; 433 sq. mi.; 1970 pop.: 12,534; 1960: 12,837; 1950: 12,493) (Winamac). Casimir Pulaski*.

Pulaski, Ky. (est. Dec. 10, 1798; eff. June 1, 1799; 676 sq. mi.; 1970 pop.: 35,234; 1960: 34,403; 1950: 38,455) (Somerset). Casimir Pulaski*. -- Owens, Alma Tibbals, A history of Pulaski County: Kentucky, Bagdad, Ky.: G. O. Moore, 1952; 272 p.

Pulaski, Mo. (est. Jan. 19, 1833; 551 sq. mi.; 1970 pop.: 53,781; 1960: 46,567; 1950: 10,392) (Waynesville). Casimir Pulaski*. -- Mottaz, Mabel (Manes), Lest we forget; a history of Pulaski County, Missouri, Springfield,? Mo., 1960; 81 p.

Pulaski, Va. (est. Mar. 30, 1839; 333 sq. mi.; 1970 pop.: 29,564; 1960: 27,258; 1950: 27,758) (Pulaski). Casimir Pulaski*.

Pushmataha, Okla. (est. July 16, 1907; 1,423 sq. mi.; 1970 pop.: 9,385; 1960: 9,088; 1950: 12,001) (Antlers). Choctaw Indian chief Apushmatacha whose name means "the sapling is ready (or finished) for him." Died on visit to Washington, D.C., and buried in Congressional Cemetery, 1824.

Putnam, Fla. (est. Jan. 13, 1849; 803 sq. mi.; 1970 pop.: 36,290; 1960: 32,212; 1950: 23,615) (Palatka). ("The Bass Capital of the World"). Israel Putnam (1718-1790). Served in French and Indian War 1754-63; Pontiac's War 1764; maj. gen. Continental Army 1775-79; commanded at N.Y. and Philadelphia. (Benjamin A. Putnam, second Seminole war.)

Putnam, Ga. (est. Dec. 10, 1807; 361 sq. mi.; 1970 pop.: 8,394; 1960: 7,798; 1950: 7,731) (Eatonton). Israel Putnam*.

Putnam, Ill. (est. Jan. 13, 1825; 173 sq. mi.; 1970 pop.: 5,007; 1960: 4,570; 1950: 4,746) (Hennepin). Israel Putnam*. -- Ellsworth, Spencer, Records of the Olden Time, Lacon, Ill.: Home Journal Steam Printing Establishment, 1880; 772 p.

Putnam, Ind. (est. Dec. 31, 1821, eff. Apr. 1, 1822; 490 sq. mi.; 1970 pop.: 26,932; 1960: 24,927; 1950: 22,950) (Greencastle). Israel Putnam*. -- Weik, Jesse William, Weik's history of Putnam County, Ind., Indianapolis, Ind.: B. F. Bowen & Co., 1910; 785 p.

Putnam, Mo. (est. Feb. 22, 1843; 518 sq. mi.; 1970 pop.: 5,916; 1960: 6,999; 1950: 9,166) (Unionville). Israel Putnam*.

Putnam, N.Y. (est. June 12, 1812; 235 sq. mi.; 1970 pop.: 56,696; 1960: 31,722; 1950: 20,307) (Carmel). Israel Putnam*. -- Blake, William J., The history of Putnam County, New York: Baker & Scribner, 1849; 368 p. -- Pelletreau, William Smith, History of Putnam County, Philadelphia: W. W. Preston & Co., 1886; 771 p.

Putnam, Ohio (est. Feb. 12, 1820; 486 sq. mi.; 1970 pop.: 31,134; 1960: 28,331; 1950: 25,248) (Ottawa). Israel Putnam*.

Putnam, Tenn. (est. Feb. 2, 1842; 408 sq. mi.; 1970 pop.: 35,487; 1960: 29,236; 1950: 29,869) (Cookeville). Israel Putnam*. -- McClain, Walter Stephen, History of Putnam County, Tenn., Cookeville, Tenn.: Q. Ayer & Co., 1925; 152 p.

Putnam, W. Va. (est. Mar. 11, 1848; 350 sq. mi.; 1970 pop.: 27,625; 1960: 23,561; 1950: 21,021) (Winfield). Israel Putnam*.

Q

Quay, N.M. (est. Feb. 28, 1903; 2,883 sq. mi.; 1970 pop.: 10,903; 1960: 12,279; 1950: 13,971) (Tucumcari). Matthew Stanley Quay (1833-1904). Lt. Tenth Pa. Reserves, 134th Pa. Inf.; won Congressional Medal of Honor for bravery at Fredericksburg, Va. 1862; col. 1862; lt. col.; military secretary to gov. 1863-65; Pa. house of representatives 1865-67; secretary of the Commonwealth 1872-78 and 1879-82; Pa. treasurer 1885-87; Senator from Pa. 1887-99 and 1901-04.

Queen Anne's, Md. (373 sq. mi.; 1970 pop.: 18,422; 1960: 16,569; 1950: 14,579) (Centreville). Queen Anne of Great Britain and Ireland (1665-1714). Second daughter of King James II and Anne Hyde, married George, Prince of Denmark 1683; signed Treaty of Utrecht 1713. (est. Apr. 18,

1706). -- Emory, Frederic, Queen Anne's County, Baltimore, Md.: Maryland Historical Society, 1950; 629 p.

Queens, N.Y. (est. Nov. 1, 1683; 108 sq. mi.; 1970 pop.: 1,973,708; 1960: 1,809,578; 1950: 1,550,849) (Jamaica). ("The Biggest Borough in the Biggest City in the World"; "The Borough of Magnificent Opportunities"; "The Fastest Growing County of New York City"). Queen Catherine of Braganza (1638-1705). Daughter of John IV, Duke of Braganza, who became King of Portugal in 1640; married Charles II of England 1662; retired to Lisbon 1693; regent of Portugal for her brother Peter II (1704-05) gaining successes over Spain. -- Skal, Georg von, Illustrated history of the Borough of Queens, New York City, 1908; 169 p.

Quitman, Ga. (est. Dec. 10, 1858; 144 sq. mi.; 1970 pop.: 2,180; 1960: 2,432; 1950: 3,015) (Georgetown). John Anthony Quitman (1799-1858). Tenth and sixteenth gov. of Miss. Miss. house of representatives 1826-27; chancellor of Miss., 1828-35; pres. Miss. senate 1835-36; acting gov. Miss. 1835-36; judge high court of errors and appeals 1838; brig. gen. vol. 1846; maj. gen. regular army 1847; gov. of Miss., 1850-51; Representative from Miss., 1855-58.

Quitman, Miss. (est. Feb. 1, 1877; 395 sq. mi.; 1970 pop.: 15,888; 1960: 21,019; 1950: 25,885) (Marks). John Anthony Quitman*.

R

Rabun, Ga. (est. Dec. 21, 1819; 377 sq. mi.; 1970 pop.: 8,327; 1960: 7,456; 1950: 7,424) (Clayton). William Rabun (1771-1819). Twenty-seventh gov. of Ga. Ga. assembly; pres. of Ga. senate; gov. of Ga. 1817-19; died in office, Oct. 24, 1819. -- Ritchie, Andrew Jackson, Sketches of Rabun County history, 1818-1948, Clayton?, Ga., 1948; 503 p.

Racine, Wis. (est. Dec. 7, 1836; 337 sq. mi.; 1970 pop.: 170,838; 1960: 141,781; 1950: 109,585) (Racine). French word for "root." -- The history of Racine and Kenosha counties, Chicago: Western Historical Co., 1879; 282 p.

Rains, Tex. (est. June 9, 1870; 235 sq. mi.; 1970 pop.: 3,752; 1960: 2,993; 1950: 4,266) (Emory). Emory Rains (1800-1878). Emigrated to Tex. 1826; Tex. legislature 1837; helped survey county named for him 1869.

Raleigh, W. Va. (est. Jan. 23, 1850; 610 sq. mi.; 1970 pop.: 70,080; 1960: 77,826; 1950: 96,273) (Beckley). Sir

Walter Raleigh (1552-1618). First Lord Proprietor of Va. 1584-1603. Favorite of Queen Elizabeth, organized expeditions to colonize America; secret marriage with Elizabeth Throckmorton caused him to be banished from England 1592; confined in Tower of London 1603-1616; released and headed unsuccessful expedition and was beheaded 1618.

Ralls, Mo. (est. Nov. 16, 1820; 478 sq. mi.; 1970 pop.: 7,764; 1960: 8,078; 1950: 8,686) (New London). Daniel Ralls (1785-1820), Mo. assembly.

Ramsey, Minn. (est. Oct. 27, 1849, org. Mar. 31, 1851, eff. Sept. 1, 1851) 160 sq. mi.; 1970 pop.: 476,255; 1960: 422,525; 1950: 355,332) (St. Paul). Alexander Ramsey (1815-1903). First terr. gov. of Minn. and second gov. of Minn. Clerk, Pa. house of representatives 1841; Representative from Pa. 1843-47; first terr. gov. of Minn. 1860-63; Senator from Minn. 1863-75; U. S. Secretary of War in cabinet of Pres. Hayes 1879-81. -- Warner, George E. and Foote, C. M., History of Ramsey County, Minneapolis: North Star Pub. Co., 1881; 650 p.

Ramsey, N. D. (est. Jan. 4, 1873, org. Jan. 25, 1885; 1,214 sq. mi.; 1970 pop.: 12,915; 1960: 13,443; 1950: 14,373) (Devils Lake). Alexander Ramsey*.

Randall, Tex. (Aug. 21, 1876; 916 sq. mi.; 1970 pop.: 53,885; 1960: 33,913; 1950: 13,774) (Canyon). Horace Randal (1833-1864). Graduated U. S. Military Academy 1854; resigned at outbreak of war 1861; col. second brigade; 28th Cavalry regiment; commissioned brig. gen. 1864; killed in action at Saline, Ark. Apr. 30, 1864. -- Warwick, Grace (Winkelman), The Randall County Story from 1541 to 1910, Hereford, Texas: Pioneer Book Publishers, 1969; 360 p.

Randolph, Ala. (est. Dec. 18, 1832; 581 sq. mi.; 1970 pop.: 18,331; 1960: 19,477; 1950: 22,513) (Wedowee). John Randolph (1773-1833). Representative from Va. 1799-1813, 1815-17, 1819-25, 1827-29 and 1833; Senator from Va., 1825-27; Va., constitutional convention 1829; U. S. Minister to Russia 1830-31; fought duel with Henry Clay Apr. 8, 1826.

Randolph, Ark. (est. Oct. 29, 1835; 637 sq. mi.; 1970 pop.: 12,645; 1960: 12,520; 1950: 15,982) (Pocahontas). John Randolph*. -- Dalton, Lawrence, History of Randolph County, Arkansas, Little Rock, Ark.: Democrat Printing & Lithographic Co., 1946; 359 p.

Randolph, Ga. (est. Dec. 20, 1828; 436 sq. mi.; 1970 pop.: 8,734; 1960: 11,078; 1950: 13,804) (Cuthbert). John Randolph*.

Randolph, Ill. (est. Oct. 5, 1795; procl.; 587 sq. mi.; 1970 pop.: 31,379; 1960: 29,988; 1950: 31,673) (Chester). Edmund Jennings Randolph (1753-1813). Gov. of Va. Aide-de-camp to Gen. Washington 1775; Va. attorney gen. 1776; Continental Congress 1779-82; gov. of Va. 1786-88; U.S. constitutional convention 1788-89; first Attorney Gen. of the U.S., 1789; Secretary of State in the cabinet of Pres. Washington 1794-95. -- Portrait and biographical record of Randolph, Jackson, Perry and Monroe Counties, Chicago: Biographical Pub. Co., 1894; 882 p.

Randolph, Ind. (est. Jan. 10, 1818, eff. Aug. 10, 1818; 457 sq. mi.; 1970 pop.: 28,915; 1960: 28,434; 1950: 27,141) (Winchester). Randolph County, N.C.; Thomas Randolph.

Randolph, Mo. (est. Jan. 22, 1829; 484 sq. mi.; 1970 pop.: 22,434; 1960: 22,014; 1950: 22,918) (Huntsville). John Randolph*. -- Waller, Alexander H., History of Randolph County, Missouri, Topeka: Historical Pub. Co., 1920; 852 p.

Randolph, N.C. (est. sess. Apr. 14, 1778; 801 sq. mi.; 1970 pop.: 76,358; 1960: 61,497; 1950: 50,804) (Asheboro). Peyton Randolph (1721-1775). King's Attorney for Va. 1748; Va. House of burgesses 1764-74 and speaker 1766; chairman of committee of correspondence 1773; pres. of Va. convention 1774 and 1775; Continental Congress 1774-75.

Randolph, W. Va. (est. sess. Oct. 16, 1786, eff. May 5, 1787; 1,046 sq. mi.; 1970 pop.: 24,596; 1960: 26,349; 1950: 30,558) (Elkins). Edmund Jennings Randolph*. -- Bosworth, Albert S., A history of Randolph County, Elkins?, W. Va., 1916; 448 p.

Rankin, Miss. (est. Feb. 4, 1828; 791 sq. mi.; 1970 pop.: 43,933; 1960: 34,322; 1950: 28,881) (Brandon). Christopher Rankin (1788-1826). Miss. terr. legislature 1813; Miss. constitutional convention 1817; Representative from Miss. 1819-26.

Ransom, N.D. (est. Jan. 4, 1873, org. Apr. 4, 1881; 863 sq. mi.; 1970 pop.: 7,102; 1960: 8,078; 1950: 8,876) (Lisbon). Fort Ransom built 1867, named for Gen. Thomas Edward Greenfield Ransom (1834-1864). Fought at Ft. Donelson, Shiloh, Atlanta, etc.; bvt. maj. gen. of vol. 1864.

Rapides, La. (est. Apr. 10, 1805; 1,370 sq. mi.; 1970 pop.: 118,078; 1960: 111,351; 1950: 90,648) (Alexandria). French for "rapids." -- Whittington, George Parnell, Rapides Parish, La., a History, repr. 1964?; 192 p.

Rappahannock, Va. (est. Feb. 8, 1833; 267 sq. mi.; 1970

5, 199; 1960: 5, 368; 1950: 6, 112) (Washington). Rappahannock Indian tribe.

Ravalli, Mont. (est. Feb. 16, 1893; 2, 384 sq. mi. ; 1970 pop. : 14, 409; 1960: 12, 341; 1950: 13, 101) (Hamilton). Father Anthony Ravalli (1812-1884). Studied medicine; entered Society of Jesuits 1827; landed at British Columbia with Father De Smet 1844; missionary to the Flathead Indians, Mont. 1845-50; superior at mission in Idaho 1850; returned to Mont. 1863.

Rawlins, Kan. (est. Mar. 6, 1873, org. Mar. 11, 1881; 1, 078 sq. mi. ; 1970 pop. : 4, 393; 1960: 5, 279; 1950: 5, 728) (Atwood). John Aaron Rawlins (1831-1869). Attorney for Galena, Mo. 1857; maj. 45th Ill., adj. gen. to gen. Grant; lt. col. 1862; brig. gen. 1863; bvt. maj. gen. 1865; Secretary of War in cabinet of Pres. Grant 1869.

Ray, Mo. (est. Nov. 16, 1820; 574 sq. mi. ; 1970 pop. : 17, 599; 1960: 16, 075; 1950: 15, 932) (Richmond). John Ray. Mo. constitutional convention.

Reagan, Tex. (est. Mar. 7, 1903; 1, 133 sq. mi. ; 1970 pop.: 3, 239; 1960: 3, 782; 1950: 3, 127) (Big Lake). John Henninger Reagan (1818-1905). Fought Cherokee Indians 1839; surveyor 1839-42; justice of the peace 1842; lt. col. of militia 1846; Tex. house of representatives 1847-49; judge of the district court 1852-57; Representative from Tex. 1857-61; deputy Provisional Congress of the Confederacy; postmaster gen. of the Confederacy 1861-64; acting Secretary of the treasury of the Confederacy; Representative from Tex. 1875-87; Senator from Tex. 1887-91; headed Railroad Commission.

Real, Tex. (est. Apr. 3, 1913; 625 sq. mi. ; 1970 pop. : 2, 013; 1960: 2, 079; 1950: 2, 479) (Leakey). Julius Real (1860-1944). County judge and school supt. 1902-09; Tex. senate 1910-14 and 1924-28.

Red Lake, Minn. (est. Dec. 24, 1896; 432 sq. mi. ; 1970 pop. : 5, 388; 1960: 5, 830; 1950: 6, 806) (Red Lake Falls). Descriptive.

Red River, La. (est. Mar. 16, 1848; 400 sq. mi. ; 1970 pop. : 9, 226; 1960: 9, 978; 1950: 12, 113) (Coushatta). Descriptive.

Red River, Tex. (est. Mar. 17, 1836; 1, 033 sq. mi. ; 1970 pop. : 14, 298; 1960: 15, 682; 1950: 21, 851) (Clarksville). Descriptive.

Red Willow, Neb. (est. Feb. 27, 1873, org. May 27, 1873; 716 sq. mi. ; 1970 pop. : 12, 191; 1960: 12, 940; 1950: 12, 977) (McCook). Descriptive.

Redwood, Minn. (est. Feb. 6, 1862; 874 sq. mi. ; 1970 pop.: 20, 024; 1960: 21, 718; 1950: 22, 127) (Redwood Falls).

Descriptive. -- Webb, Wayne, Redwood, the story of a county, Redwood Falls, Minn.: Redwood County Board of Commissioners, 1964; 537 p.

Reeves, Tex. (est. Apr. 14, 1883; 2,600 sq. mi.; 1970 pop.: 16,526; 1960: 17,644; 1950: 11,745) (Pecos). George R. Reeves (1826-1882). Emigrated to Tex. 1846; tax collector Grayson County 1848-50; sheriff Grayson County 1850-54; house of representatives 1855-61; Confederate Army 1861; col. 1863; Tex. house of representatives 1873; speaker of the house 1881-82.

Refugio, Tex. (est. Mar. 17, 1836; 771 sq. mi.; 1970 pop.: 9,494; 1960: 10,975; 1950: 10,113) (Refugio). Spanish for "refuge" named for the mission "Our Lady of Refuge" in honor of the Virgin Mary. -- Huson, Hobart, Refugio, a comprehensive history of Refugio County, Woodsboro, Texas: Rocke Foundation, 1953-55; 2 vol.

Reno, Kan. (est. Feb. 26, 1867; 1,255 sq. mi.; 1970 pop.: 67,665; 1960: 59,055; 1950: 54,058) (Hutchinson). Jesse Lee Reno (1823-1862). Graduated U. S. Military Academy 1846; bvt. second lt. 1846; second lt. 1847; first lt. 1853; bvt. for gallantry at Cerro Gordo; made capt. for action at Chapultepec 1860; commanded arsenal at Mt. Vernon, Ala., 1859-61; brig. gen. vol. 1861; maj. gen. 1862; killed at battle of So. Mountain, Md., Sept. 14, 1862. -- Ploughe, Sheridan, History of Reno County, Kansas, Indianapolis, Ind.: B. F. Bowen & Co., 1917; 2 vol.

Rensselaer, N. Y. (est. Feb. 7, 1791; 665 sq. mi.; 1970 pop.: 152,510; 1960: 142,585; 1950: 132,607) (Troy). Kiliaen Van Rensselaer (1595-1644). Dutch merchant and patroon; organizer of the Dutch West India Co.; purchased large tracts of land in N. Y. -- Anderson, George Baker, Landmarks of Rensselaer County, Syracuse, N. Y.: D. Mason & Co., 1897; 460 p. -- Sylvester, Nathaniel Bartlett, History of Rensselaer County, Philadelphia: Everts & Peck, 1880; 564 p.

Renville, Minn. (est. Feb. 20, 1855; 980 sq. mi.; 1970 pop.: 21,139; 1960: 23,249; 1950: 23,954) (Olivia). Joseph Renville (1779-1846). His father was a French trader, his mother a Sioux; interpreter Lt. Pike's conference with the Sioux 1805-06; led Sioux warriors against U. S. frontiers; capt. in British army 1812; aided in translating Bible in Siouan language. -- Curtiss-Wedge, Franklyn, ed., The history of Renville County, Chicago: H. C. Cooper, Jr. and Co., 1916; 2 vol.

Renville, N. D. (est. Jan. 4, 1873, org. July 20, 1910; 901 sq. mi.; 1970 pop.: 3,828; 1960: 4,698; 1950: 5,405) (Mohall). Gabriel Renville.

Republic, Kan. (est. Feb. 27, 1860; 719 sq. mi.; 1970 pop.: 8,498; 1960: 9,768; 1950: 11,478) (Belleville). Pawnee Republic, one of the principal divisions of the Pawnee Indians. -- Savage, Isaac O., A history of Republic County, Kansas, Beloit, Kan.: Jones & Chubbic, 1901; 321 p.

Reynolds, Mo. (est. Feb. 25, 1845; 822 sq. mi.; 1970 pop.: 6,106; 1960: 5,161; 1950: 6,918) (Centerville). Thomas Reynolds (1796-1844). Seventh gov. of Mo. Clerk of Ill. house of representatives; member and speaker Ill. house of representatives; chief justice of supreme court 1822-25; Mo. legislature 1828; speaker Mo. legislature 1832; gov. of Mo. 1840-44.

Rhea, Tenn. (est. Nov. 30, 1807; 335 sq. mi.; 1970 pop.: 17,202; 1960: 15,863; 1950: 16,041) (Dayton). John Rhea (1753-1832). Ensign 7th Va. Regiment 1777; fought at battle of King's Mountain in the Revolutionary War 1780; delegate to convention that ratified the federal constitution in 1789; attorney gen. of Greene County, Tenn., 1796. Tenn. house of representatives 1796-97, Representative 1803-15, and 1817-23. -- Campbell, Thomas Jefferson, Records of Rhea, Dayton, Tenn.: Rhea Pub. Co., 1940; 204 p.

Rice, Kan. (est. Feb. 26, 1867; 721 sq. mi.; 1970 pop.: 12,320; 1960: 13,909; 1950: 15,635) (Lyons). Samuel Allen Rice (1828-1864). County attorney, Oskaloosa, Iowa 1853; county attorney, Iowa 1856; commissioned col. of Iowa vol. 1862; promoted brig. gen. at Helena, Ark., 1862; wounded at Jenkins Ferry, Ark., Apr. 30, 1864; died July 6, 1864. -- Jones, Horace, The story of early Rice County, Wichita, Kan.: Wichita Eagle Press, 1928; 135 p.

Rice, Minn. (est. Mar. 5, 1853; 495 sq. mi.; 1970 pop.: 41,582; 1960: 38,988; 1950: 36,235) (Faribault). Henry Mower Rice (1817-1894). Negotiated treaty with the Indians 1847; delegate from Minn. 1853-57; Senator from Minn. 1858-63; regent of Univ. of Minn., 1851-59; treasurer Ramsey County 1878-84. -- Curtiss-Wedge, Franklyn, History of Rice and Steele Counties, Chicago: H. C. Cooper, Jr., and Co., 1910; 2 vol.

Rich, Utah (est. Jan. 16, 1864; 1,022 sq. mi.; 1970 pop.: 1,615; 1960: 1,685; 1950: 1,673) (Randolph). Charles Coulson Rich. Mormon apostle; on Jan. 29, 1868 name was changed from Richland County to Rich County.

Richardson, Neb. (est. Nov. 23, 1854 procl.; 548 sq. mi.; 1970 pop.: 12,277; 1960: 13,903; 1950: 16,886) (Falls City). William Alexander Richardson (1811-1875). Third terr. gov. of Neb. State attorney Ill. 1834-35; Ill. house of representatives 1836-38 and 1844-46; Ill. speaker 1844; Ill. senate 1838-42; capt. and maj. Mexican War; Representative from Ill. 1847-56 and 1861-63; Senator from Ill., 1863-65; third terr. gov. of Neb. 1858. -- Edwards, Lewis C., History of Richardson County, Nebraska, Indianapolis, Ind.: B. F. Bowen & Co., 1917; 1417 p.

Richland, Ill. (est. Feb. 24, 1841; 357 sq. mi.; 1970 pop.: 16, 829; 1960: 16, 299; 1950: 16, 889) (Olney). Richland County, Ohio. -- Counties of Cumberland, Jasper and Richland, Chicago: Historical Society Publishers, 1968; 839 p.

Richland, La. (est. Mar. 11, 1852; 565 sq. mi.; 1970 pop.: 21, 774; 1960: 23, 824; 1950: 26, 672) (Rayville). Descriptive.

Richland, Mont. (est. May 27, 1914, petition and election; 2, 065 sq. mi.; 1970 pop.: 9, 837; 1960: 10, 504; 1950: 10, 366) (Sidney). Descriptive.

Richland, N. D. (est. Jan. 4, 1873, org. Nov. 25, 1873; 1, 450 sq. mi.; 1970 pop.: 18, 089; 1960: 8, 824; 1950: 19, 865) (Wahpeton). M. T. Rich. Early Dakota settler.

Richland, Ohio (est. Jan. 30, 1808; 499 sq. mi.; 1970 pop.: 129, 997; 1960: 117, 761; 1950: 91, 305) (Mansfield). Descriptive. -- Diriam, H. Kenneth, Bits of history, Mansfield, Ohio: Richland County Historical Society, 1962. -- Baughman, Abraham J., History of Richland County, Chicago: S. J. Clarke Pub. Co., 1908; 2 vol.

Richland, S. C. (est. Mar. 12, 1785; 748 sq. mi.; 1970 pop.: 233, 868; 1960: 200, 102; 1950: 142, 565) (Columbia). Descriptive. -- Green, Edwin Luther, A history of Richland County, Columbia, S. C.: R. L. Bryan Co., 1932.

Richland, Wis. (est. Feb. 18, 1842; 584 sq. mi.; 1970 pop.: 17, 079; 1960: 17, 684; 1950: 19, 245) (Richland Center). Descriptive.

Richmond, Ga. (est. Feb. 5, 1777; 319 sq. mi.; 1970 pop.: 162, 437; 1960: 135, 601; 1950: 108, 876) (Augusta). Charles Lennox, Third Duke of Richmond (1735-1806). Third son of second Duke of Richmond; British Minister Extraordinary in Paris 1765; Secretary of State for Southern Department 1766; resigned 1767; favored American colonies and wanted troops withdrawn 1778. -- Rowland, Arthur Ray, A guide to the study of Augusta and Richmond County, Richmond County Historical Society, 1967; 69 p.

Richmond, N. Y. (est. Nov. 1, 1683; 57 sq. mi.; 1970 pop.: 295, 443; 1960: 221, 991; 1950: 191, 555) (Saint George). Duke of Richmond*. -- Bayles, Richard Mather, History of Richmond County, New York City: L. E. Preston & Co.,

1887; 741 p.

Richmond, N. C. (est. sess. Oct. 18, 1779; 477 sq. mi.; 1970 pop.: 39, 889; 1960: 39, 202; 1950: 39, 597) (Rockingham). Duke of Richmond*.

Richmond, Va. (est. Apr. 16, 1692 sess.; 192 sq. mi.; 1970 pop.: 5, 841; 1960: 6, 375; 1950: 6, 189) (Warsaw). Richmond, Surry County, England.

Riley, Kan. (est. Aug. 30, 1855; 624 sq. mi.; 1970 pop.: 56, 788; 1960: 41, 904; 1950: 33, 405) (Manhattan). Bennett Riley (1787-1853). Seventh provisional gov. of Calif. Ensign of rifles 1813; third lt. 1813; second lt. 1814; first lt. 1817; capt. 1818; Indian War Arickee Indians 1823; bvt. maj. of ten years faithful service in one grade 1828; maj. 1837; lt. col. 1839; bvt. col. for bravery at Charlotte, Fla. against Seminoles 1840; bvt. brig. gen. and maj. gen. 1847; terr. gov. of Calif. 1849; col. of first inf. 1850-53. -- Slagg, Winifred N., Riley County, Kansas, Manhattan, Kan., 1968; 255 p.

Ringgold, Iowa (est. Feb. 24, 1847, org. Jan. 18, 1855; 538 sq. mi.; 1970 pop.: 6, 373; 1960: 7, 910; 1950: 9, 528) (Mount Ayr). Samuel Ringgold. Second lt. 1818; first lt. 1822; capt. 1836; bvt. capt. for ten years faithful service in one grade 1832; bvt. maj. for meritorious service against Florida Indians; died from wounds received at battle of Palo Alto, Mex., 1846. -- Biographical and historical record of Ringgold and Decatur Counties, Chicago: Lewis Pub. Co., 1887; 796 p.

Rio Arriba, N. M. (est. Jan. 9, 1852; 5, 855 sq. mi.; 1970 pop.: 25, 170; 1960: 24, 193; 1950: 24, 997) (Tierra Amarilla). Spanish word for "upper river."

Rio Blanco, Colo. (est. Mar. 25, 1889; 3, 263 sq. mi.; 1970 pop.: 4, 842; 1960: 5, 150; 1950: 4, 719) (Meeker). Spanish word for "white river."

Rio Grande, Colo. (est. Feb. 10, 1874; 916 sq. mi.; 1970 pop.: 10, 494; 1960: 11, 160; 1950: 12, 832) (Del Norte). Spanish for "large river" original name of which was Rio Grande del Norte, Great River of the North.

Ripley, Ind. (est. Dec. 27, 1816, org. Jan. 14, 1818; eff. Apr. 10, 1818; 442 sq. mi.; 1970 pop.: 21, 138; 1960: 20, 641; 1950: 18, 763) (Versailles). Eleazar Wheelock Ripley (1782-1839). Mass. house of representatives 1807 and 1811; Mass. senate 1812; lt. col. 1812; bvt. maj. gen. 1814; served at Chippewa, Niagara and Erie; La. senate 1820; Representative from La., 1835-39.

Ripley, Mo. (est. Jan. 5, 1833; 639 sq. mi.; 1970 pop.: 9, 803; 1960: 9, 096; 1950: 11, 414) (Doniphan). Eleazar Wheelock Ripley*.

Ritchie, W. Va. (est. Feb. 18, 1843; 455 sq. mi.; 1970 pop.: 10, 145; 1960: 10, 877; 1950: 12, 535) (Harrisville). Thomas Ritchie (1778-1854). Purchased Richmond, Va. "Examiner" 1804; edited it 41 years as the "Enquirer;" managed Washington, D. C. "Union" 1845-51. -- Lowther, Minnie Kendall, History of Ritchie County, Wheeling, W. Va.: Wheeling News Lithograph Co., 1911; 681 p.

Riverside, Calif. (est. Mar. 11, 1893; 7, 179 sq. mi.; 1970 pop.: 459, 074; 1960: 306, 191; 1950: 170, 046) (Riverside). ("Agriculture--Industry--Tourism, California's Key County"; "The Key County of Southern California (physical shape resembles a key),"; "The Key to America's Largest Market"). Descriptive. -- Gabbert, John Raymond, History of Riverside, city and county, Phoenix: Record Pub. Co., 1935; 615 p. -- Holmes, Elmer Wallace, History of Riverside, Los Angeles: Historic Record Co., 1912; 783 p.

Roane, Tenn. (est. Nov. 6, 1801; 379 sq. mi.; 1970 pop.: 38, 881; 1960: 39, 133; 1950: 31, 665) (Kingston). ("The County Boosting and Building a Better Life for All"; "The County in the Heart of the Tennessee Valley"). Archibald Roane (1759-1819). Second gov. of Tenn. At surrender of Cornwallis 1781; Tenn. constitutional convention 1796; Tenn. superior court 1796-1801; gov. of Tenn. 1801-03; Tenn. supreme court 1815-19. -- Wells, Emma Helm (Middleton), History of Roane County, Tenn., Chattanooga, Tenn.: Lookout Pub. Co., 1927; 308 p.

Roane, W. Va. (est. Mar. 11, 1856; 379 sq. mi.; 1970 pop.: 14, 111; 1960: 15, 720; 1950: 18, 408) (Spencer). Spencer Roane. Justice Va. supreme court of appeals; married Anne Henry, daughter of Patrick Henry. -- Bishop, William Henry, History of Roane County, Spencer, W. Va.: W. H. Bishop, 1927; 711 p.

Roanoke, Va. (est. Mar. 30, 1838; 292 sq. mi.; 1970 pop.: 67, 339; 1960: 61, 693; 1950: 41, 486) (Salem). Indian word for a shell used for money. -- McCauley, William, History of Roanoke County, Chicago: Biographical Pub. Co., 1902; 560 p.

Roberts, S. D. (est. Mar. 8, 1883; 1, 111 sq. mi.; 1970 pop.: 11, 678; 1960: 13, 190; 1950: 14, 929) (Sisseton). S. G. Roberts. Book publisher, S. D. terr. legislature 1879 and 1883. -- Roberts County History, Sisseton, S. D.: Roberts County Centennial Committee, 1961; 136 p.

Roberts, Tex. (est. Aug. 21, 1876; 892 sq. mi.; 1970 pop.: 967; 1960: 1, 075; 1950: 1, 031) (Miami). John S. Roberts (1796-1871). Joined Gen. Jackson at battle of New Orleans 1815; maj. Fredonian rebellion; battle of Nacogdoches 1832; first lt. Nacogdoches vol. 1835; signer Tex. declaration of independence 1836. Also named for Oran Milo Roberts (1815-1898). Sixteenth gov. of Tex. Ala. legislature 1837; Tex. district judge 1846-51; Tex. supreme court 1857; col. 11th Tex. regiment 1862; chief justice Tex. supreme court 1864; Tex. constitutional convention 1866; prof. of law Gilmer, Tex. 1868-70; chief justice Tex. supreme court 1874; gov. of Tex. 1879-83; prof. of law Univ. of Tex. 1883.

Robertson, Ky. (est. Feb. 11, 1867; 101 sq. mi.; 1970 pop.: 2,163; 1960: 2,443; 1950: 2,881) (Mount Olivet). George Robertson (1790-1874). Representative from Ky., 1817-21; Ky. house of representatives 1822-27; speaker Ky. house of representatives 1824-27; Ky. secretary of state 1828; associate justice Ky. court of appeals 1829; chief justice Ky. court of appeals 1829-34; law professor Transylvania Univ. 1834-57; Ky. house of representatives 1848 and 1851-52 when he was speaker; justice of court of appeals for second district of Ky., 1864-71 and acting chief justice.

Robertson, Tenn. (est. Apr. 9, 1796; 474 sq. mi.; 1970 pop.: 29,102; 1960: 27,335; 1950: 27,024) (Springfield). James Robertson (1742-1814). Indian fighter; capt. 1777; col. of militia 1781; N. C. assembly 1785; resigned as brig. gen. 1794; Tenn. constitutional convention 1796; Tenn. senate 1798; Indian agent to Chickasaws; founded Nashborough later named Nashville.

Robertson, Tex. (est. Dec. 14, 1837; 874 sq. mi.; 1970 pop.: 14,389; 1960: 16,157; 1950: 19,908) (Franklin). Sterling Clark Robertson (1785-1842). Battle of New Orleans, asst. Q. M. gen.; maj. 1812; visited Tex. 1822-23; fought at battle of New Orleans 1815; maj. gen. on staff of Gen. Carroll; colonizer of Tex. 1828-34; elected to convention which declared for Tex. independence; signed Tex. declaration of independence 1836; Tex. senate 1836 and 1840. -- Parker, Richard Denny, Historical recollections of Robertson County, Salado, Texas: A. Jones Press, 1955; 254 p.

Robeson, N. C. (est. sess. Nov. 18, 1786; 944 sq. mi.; 1970 pop.: 84,842; 1960: 89,102; 1950: 87,769) (Lumberton). Thomas Robeson (1740-1785). N. C. provincial convention 1775-76; battle of Moore's Creek 1776; leader in Elizabethtown battle 1781; col.; paid troops out of his own funds, was not reimbursed. -- Lawrence, Robert C., The state of Robeson, N. Y.: J. J. Little & Ives Co., 1939; 279 p.

Rock, Minn. (est. May 23, 1857, org. Mar. 5, 1870; 485

sq. mi.; 1970 pop.: 11,346; 1960: 11,864; 1950: 11,278) (Luverne). Descriptive. -- Rose, Arthur, An illustrated history of the counties of Rock and Pipestone, Luverne, Minn.: Northern History Pub. Co., 1911; 802 p.

Rock, Neb. (est. 1888, org. Jan. 8, 1889; 1,012 sq. mi.; 1970 pop.: 2,231; 1960: 2,554; 1950: 3,026) (Bassett). Descriptive.

Rock, Wis. (est. Dec. 7, 1836; 721 sq. mi.; 1970 pop.: 131,970; 1960: 113,913; 1950: 92,778) (Janesville). Descriptive. -- Brown, William Fiske, Rock County, Chicago: C. F. Cooper & Co., 1908; 2 vol.

Rock Island, Ill. (est. Feb. 9, 1831; 424 sq. mi.; 1970 pop.: 166,734; 1960: 150,991; 1950: 133,558) (Rock Island). Descriptive. -- Past and Present of Rock Island County, Chicago: H. F. Kett & Co., 1877; 474 p.

Rockbridge, Va. (est. Oct. 20, 1777; eff. Mar. 1, 1778; 604 sq. mi.; 1970 pop.: 16,637; 1960: 24,039; 1950: 23,359) (Lexington). Descriptive of natural bridge over Cedar Creek. -- Morton, Oren Frederic, A History of Rockbridge County, Staunton, Va.: The McClure Co. Inc., 1920; 574 p. -- Tompkins, Edmund Pendleton, Rockbridge County, Richmond, Va.: Whittet & Shepperson, 1952; 187 p.

Rockcastle, Ky. (est. Jan. 8, 1810; 312 sq. mi.; 1970 pop.: 12,305; 1960: 12,334; 1950: 13,925) (Mount Vernon). Descriptive.

Rockdale, Ga. (est. Oct. 18, 1870; 119 sq. mi.; 1970 pop.: 18,152; 1960: 10,572; 1950: 8,464) (Conyers). Descriptive.

Rockingham, N. H. (est. Apr. 29, 1769; 691 sq. mi.; 1970 pop.: 138,951; 1960: 99,029; 1950: 70,059) (Exeter). Charles Watson Wentworth (1730-1782). Second marquis of Rockingham; Prime Minister of Great Britain when Stamp Act was repealed 1765-66; favored independence of American colonies; Prime Minister 1782. -- Hurd, Duane Hamilton, History of Rockingham and Strafford Counties, Philadelphia: J. W. Lewis & Co., 1882; 890 p.

Rockingham, N. C. (est. sess. Nov. 19, 1785; 572 sq. mi.; 1970 pop.: 72,402; 1960: 69,629; 1950: 64,816) (Wentworth). Marquis of Rockingham*.

Rockingham, Va. (est. Oct. 20, 1777; eff. Mar. 1, 1778; 869 sq. mi.; 1970 pop.: 47,890; 1960: 40,485; 1950: 35,079) (Harrisonburg). Marquis of Rockingham*. -- Wayland, John W., A History of Rockingham County, Dayton, Va.: Ruebush-Elkins Co., 1912; 466 p.

Rockland, N. Y. (est. Feb. 23, 1798; 178 sq. mi.; 1970 pop.: 229,903; 1960: 136,803; 1950: 89,276) (New City). Descriptive. -- Cole, David, History of Rockland County,

New York: J. B. Beers & Co., 1884; 344 p. -- Bedell, Cornelia F., Now and then and long ago in Rockland County, Tallman, N. Y.: Historical Society of Rockland County, 1968; 399 p.

Rockwall, Tex. (est. Mar. 1, 1873; 147 sq. mi.; 1970 pop.: 7, 046; 1960: 5, 878; 1950: 6, 156) (Rockwall). Descriptive, underground rock walls.

Roger Mills, Okla. (est. July 16, 1907; 1, 124 sq. mi.; 1970 pop.: 4, 452; 1960: 5, 090; 1950: 7, 395) (Cheyenne). Roger Quarles Mills (1832-1911). Tex. house of representatives 1859-60; col. in Tenth Regiment Tex. inf. Confederate Army; wounded at Missionary Ridge and Atlanta; Representative from Tex. 1873-92; Senator from Tex. 1892-99. -- Taylor, Nat Massie, Brief History of Roger Mills County, Cheyenne, Wyo., 194..?, 64 p.

Rogers, Okla. (est. July 16, 1907; 713 sq. mi.; 1970 pop.: 28, 425; 1960: 20, 614; 1950: 19, 532) (Claremore). Clement V. Rogers. Member Okla. Constitutional Convention; father of Will Rogers.

Rolette, N. D. (est. Jan. 4, 1873, org. Oct. 14, 1884; 913 sq. mi.; 1970 pop.: 11, 549; 1960: 10, 641; 1950: 11, 102) (Rolla). Joseph Rolette (1820-1871). Pioneer, fur trader, opened post for American Fur Co. -- Law, Laura Thompson, History of Rolette County, North Dakota, Minneapolis, Minn.: Lund Press, 1953; 276 p.

Rooks, Kan. (est. Feb. 26, 1867; 893 sq. mi.; 1970 pop.: 7, 628; 1960: 9, 734; 1950: 9, 043) (Stockton). John C. Rooks (-1862). Private 11th Kan. Died Dec. 11, 1862 from wounds received at battle of Prairie Grove, Ark.

Roosevelt, Mont. (est. Feb. 18, 1919; 2, 385 sq. mi.; 1970 pop.: 10, 365; 1960: 11, 731; 1950: 9, 580) (Wolf Point). Theodore Roosevelt (1858-1919). Twenty-sixth Pres. of the U. S. and thirty-sixth gov. of N. Y. N. Y. Assembly 1882-84; U. S. Civil Service Commission 1889-95, pres. N. Y. Board of Police Commissioners 1895-96; Asst. Secretary of the Navy 1897-98; Spanish American War becoming Col., gov. of N. Y. 1899-1900; vice pres. of the U. S. 1901, becoming Pres. Sept. 14, 1901 upon death of Pres. McKinley, elected Pres. serving 1905-09.

Roosevelt, N. M. (est. Feb. 28, 1903; 2, 455 sq. mi.; 1970 pop.: 16, 479; 1960: 16, 198; 1950: 16, 409) (Portales). Theodore Roosevelt*.

Roscommon, Mich. (est. Apr. 1, 1840; org. 1875; 521 sq. mi.; 1970 pop.: 9, 892; 1960: 7, 200; 1950: 5, 916) (Roscommon). Roscommon County, Ireland. (Formerly Mikenauk County, name changed to Roscommon County Mar. 8, 1843, Act 67.)

Roseau, Minn. (est. Feb. 28, 1894; 1,676 sq. mi.; 1970 pop.: 11,569; 1960: 12,154; 1950: 14,505) (Roseau). French for "reed" or "rush."

Rosebud, Mont. (est. Feb. 11, 1901; 5,032 sq. mi.; 1970 pop.: 6,032; 1960: 6,187; 1950: 6,570) (Forsyth). Descriptive.

Ross, Ohio (est. Aug. 20, 1798; 687 sq. mi.; 1970 pop.: 61,211; 1960: 61,215; 1950: 54,424) (Chillicothe). James Ross (1762-1847). Pa. constitutional convention 1789-90; Senator from Pa. 1794-1803; unsuccessful candidate for gov. of Pa. 1799, 1801 and 1808. -- Evans, Lyle Sanford, ed., A standard history of Ross County, Chicago: Lewis Pub. Co., 1917; 2 vol. -- Finley, Isaac Jackson & Putnam, Rufus, Pioneer record & reminiscences..., Cincinnati, Ohio: Isaac J. Finley & Rufus Putnam, 1871; 148 p.

Routt, Colo. (est. Jan. 29, 1877; 2,330 sq. mi.; 1970 pop.: 6,592; 1960: 5,900; 1950: 8,940) (Steamboat Springs). John Long Routt (1826-1907). Eighth terr. and first and seventh gov. of Colo. Sheriff of McLean County, Ill., 1860; treasurer McLean County, Ill., 1866-68; U. S. marshal for southern district of Ill., 1869; Second asst. postmaster 1871-75; gov. Colo. terr. 1875-76; mayor of Denver, Colo., 1883; gov. of Colo. 1876-79 and 1891-93.

Rowan, Ky. (est. Mar. 15, 1856; 290 sq. mi.; 1970 pop.: 17,010; 1960: 12,808; 1950: 12,708) (Morehead). John Rowan (1773-1843). Secretary of state Ky. 1804-06; Representative from Ky. 1807-09; Ky. house of representatives 1813-17; 1822 and 1824; judge of the court of appeals 1819-21; Senator from Ky. 1825-31; commissioner for carrying out treaty with Mexico 1839.

Rowan, N. C. (est. sess. Mar. 27, 1753; 517 sq. mi.; 1970 pop.: 90,035; 1960: 82,817; 1950: 75,410) (Salisbury). Matthew Rowan (-1760). N. C. gen. assembly 1729; justice of the peace New Hanover county 1735; justice of the peace Bladen county 1737; surveyor gen. of N. C., 1736; pres. and commander-in-chief of the council 1753-54. -- Brawley, James S., The Rowan story, 1753-1953; a narrative history of Rowan County, North Carolina, Salisbury, N. C.: Rowan Printing Co., 1953; 402 p.

Runnels, Tex. (est. Feb. 1, 1858; 1,060 sq. mi.; 1970 pop.: 12,108; 1960: 15,016; 1950: 16,771) (Ballinger). Hardin Richard Runnels (1820-1873). Fifth gov. of Tex. Tex. legislature 1847-53; speaker Tex. house of representatives 1853-54; only person to defeat Sam Houston in a political election; lt. gov. 1855; gov. of Tex. 1857-59; delegate to Tex. secession convention; delegate to Tex.

constitutional convention 1866.

Rush, Ind. (est. Dec. 31, 1821; 409 sq. mi.; 1970 pop.: 20,352; 1960: 20,393; 1950: 19,799) (Rushville). Benjamin Rush (1745-1813). Physician, Continental Congress 1776 and 1777, signer of the Declaration of Independence 1776; surgeon gen. and physician gen. in Continental Army, founder of the Pennsylvania Hospital, treas. U.S. Mint at Philadelphia 1799-1813. -- Alexander, Mary M., Sketches of Rush County, Ind., Rushville, Ind.: Jacksonville Pub. Co., 1915; 97 p. (Hiram George Runnels??)

Rush, Kan. (est. Feb. 26, 1867; 724 sq. mi.; 1970 pop.: 5,117; 1960: 6,160; 1950: 7,231) (La Crosse). Alexander Rush (-1864). Capt. Co. H, 2nd Kan. colored cavalry, killed at Jenkins Ferry, Ark., Apr. 3, 1864.

Rusk, Tex. (est. Jan. 16, 1843; 944 sq. mi.; 1970 pop.: 34,102; 1960: 36,421; 1950: 42,348) (Henderson). Thomas Jefferson Rusk (1803-1857). Delegate to convention that declared for Independence for Tex. 1836; first Secretary of War of Tex. Republic; commanded troops at battle of San Jacinto; member of the second congress of the Republic of Tex.; chief justice of the supreme court of Tex. 1838-42; appointed brig. gen. of militia of Republic of Tex. 1843; senator from Tex. 1846-57; Pres. pro tempore of the senate 1857; signer Tex. Declaration of Independence 1836. -- Farmer, Garland, R., The realm of Rusk County, Henderson, Texas: Henderson Times, 1951; 223 p. -- Winfrey, Dorman H., History of Rusk County, Texas, Waco, Texas: Texian Press, 1961; 179 p.

Rusk, Wis. (est. May 15, 1901; 910 sq. mi.; 1970 pop.: 14,238; 1960: 14,794; 1950: 16,790) (Ladysmith). Jeremiah McLain Rusk (1830-1893). Fourteenth gov. of Wis.; sheriff of Viroqua, Wis. 1855-57; coroner 1857; Wis. assembly 1862; maj. 25th Regiment Wis. Vol. Inf. 1862; lt. col. 1863; bvt. col. and brig. gen. 1865; bank comptroller of Wis. 1866-69; Representative from Wis. 1871-77; gov. of Wis. 1882-89; U.S. Secretary of Agriculture in cabinet of Pres. Harrison 1889-93. (Formerly Gates County, name changed June 19, 1905, Chap. 463).

Russell, Ala. (est. Dec. 18, 1832; 639 sq. mi.; 1970 pop.: 45,394; 1960: 46,351; 1950: 40,364) (Phenix City). Gilbert Christian Russell. Ensign 1803; second lt. 1804; first lt. 1807; capt. 1808; maj. 1809; lt. col. 1811; col. 1814; honorable discharge 1815. -- Walker, Anne Kendrick, Russell County in Retrospect, Richmond, Va.: Dietz Press, 1950; 423 p.

Russell, Kan. (est. Feb. 26, 1867; 897 sq. mi.; 1970 pop.: 9,428; 1960: 11,348; 1950: 13,406) (Russell). Avra P.

Russell (-1862). Capt. Co. K, 2nd Kan., honorable discharge 1862; died of wounds in battle of Prairie Grove, Ark. Dec. 1, 1862.

Russell, Ky. (est. Dec. 14, 1825; 282 sq. mi.; 1970 pop.: 10,542; 1960: 11,076; 1950: 13,717) (Jamestown). William Russell (1758-1825). In Revolutionary War; lt. at battle of King's Mountain, Oct. 7, 1780; rose to capt. in St. Clair's expedition; lt. col. of Ky. mounted vol. 1793; served under gen. Wayne 1794; col. 7th Inf. 1808; Va. legislature; Ky. legislature; battle of Tippecanoe Nov. 7, 1811.

Russell, Va. (est. Oct. 17, 1785 sess.; eff. May 1, 1786; 483 sq. mi.; 1970 pop.: 24,533; 1960: 26,290; 1950: 26,818) (Lebanon). William Russell*.

Rutherford, N.C. (est. Apr. 14, 1779 sess.; 566 sq. mi.; 1970 pop.: 47,337; 1960: 45,091; 1950: 46,356) (Rutherfordton). Griffith Rutherford (-1794). Legislative council of Terr. So. of the River Ohio 1775; defeated Cherokees 1776; brig. gen. 1776; commanded brigade at battle of Camden, taken prisoner; N.C. senate 1784; pres. Tenn. legislative council 1796. -- Griffin, Clarence W., History of Rutherford County 1937-1951, Asheville, N.C.: Inland Press, 1952; 136 p. -- Griffin, Clarence W., History of Old Tryon and Rutherford Counties, North Carolina, Asheville, N.C.: Miller Printing Co., 1937; 640 p.

Rutherford, Tenn. (est. Oct. 25, 1803; 630 sq. mi.; 1970 pop.: 59,428; 1960: 52,368; 1950: 40,696) (Murfreesboro). Griffith Rutherford*. -- Sims, Carlton C., History of Rutherford County, Tenn., Murfreesboro, Tenn., 1947; 236 p. -- Hughes, Mary B., Hearthstones, the story of historic Rutherford County homes, Murfreesboro, Tenn.: Mid-South Pub. Co. Inc., 1942; 68 p.

Rutland, Vt. (est. Feb. 22, 1781; 929 sq. mi.; 1970 pop.: 52,637; 1960: 46,719; 1950: 45,905) (Rutland City). Rutland, Mass., named for Rutland, England. -- Smith, H. Perry, History of Rutland County, Vermont, Syracuse, N.Y.: D. Mason and Co., 1886; 959 p.

S

Sabine, La. (est. Mar. 7, 1843; 1,020 sq. mi.; 1970 pop.: 18,638; 1960: 18,564; 1950: 20,880) (Many). Spanish (French) for "cyprus." -- Belisle, John G., History of Sabine Parish, La., from the first explorers to the present, Many, La.: Sabine Banner Press, 1912; 319 p.

Sabine, Tex. (est. Mar. 17, 1836; 564 sq. mi.; 1970 pop.: 7,187; 1960: 7,302; 1950: 8,568) (Hemphill). Spanish for "cyprus forests." -- Gomer, Robert Austin, Memories of Sabine County, Texas, Center?, Texas, 1967; 121 p.

Sac, Iowa (est. Jan. 15, 1851; 578 sq. mi.; 1970 pop.: 15,573; 1960: 17,007; 1950: 17,518) (Sac City). Sac Indian tribe. -- Hart, William H., History of Sac County, Indianapolis: B. F. Bowen & Co., Inc., 1914; 918 p.

Sacramento, Calif. (est. Feb. 18, 1850; 985 sq. mi.; 1970 pop.: 631,498; 1960: 502,778; 1950: 277,140) (Sacramento). In honor of the Holy Sacrament. -- Reed, G. Walter, History of Sacramento County, Los Angeles: Historic Record Co., 1923; 1004 p.

Sagadahoc, Me. (est. Apr. 4, 1854; 257 sq. mi.; 1970 pop.: 23,452; 1960: 22,793; 1950: 20,911) (Bath). Indian word for "mouth."

Saginaw, Mich. (est. Sept. 10, 1822, org. Mar. 2, 1831; 812 sq. mi.; 1970 pop.: 219,743; 1960: 190,752; 1950: 153,515) (Saginaw). Ojibway Indian word for "Sauk place." -- Mills, James Cooke, History of Saginaw County, Saginaw, Mich.: Seeman & Peters, 1918; 2 vol.

Saguache, Colo. (est. Dec. 29, 1866; 3,144 sq. mi.; 1970 pop.: 3,827; 1960: 4,573; 1950: 5,664) (Saguache). Form of Ute Indian word meaning "blue earth" or "water at the blue earth."

St. Bernard, La. (est. Mar. 31, 1807; 617 sq. mi.; 1970 pop.: 51,185; 1960: 32,186; 1950: 11,087) (Chalmette). St. Bernard of Clairvaux (1091-1153). Established 68 Cistercian houses; first abbe of Cistercian monastery of Clairvaux. Canonized by Pope Alexander III in 1173.

St. Charles, La. (est. Mar. 31, 1807 procl.; 295 sq. mi.; 1970 pop.: 29,550; 1960: 21,219; 1950: 13,363) (Hahnville). Saint Charles Borromeo (1538-1584). Archbishop and cardinal 1560; archbishop of Milan; nephew of Pope Pius IV; canonized 1610.

St. Charles, Mo. (est. Oct. 1, 1812; 561 sq. mi.; 1970 pop.: 92,954; 1960: 52,970; 1950: 29,834) (St. Charles). Saint Charles Borromeo*.

St. Clair, Ala. (est. Nov. 20, 1818; 641 sq. mi.; 1970 pop.: 27,956; 1960: 25,388; 1950: 26,687) (Pell City). Arthur St. Clair (1734-1818). Served under Gen. Wolfe at Quebec 1758; resigned 1762; col. Pa. militia 1776; brig. gen. Continental Army 1776-83; maj. gen. 1791; Continental Congress 1785-87; first gov. Northwest Terr. 1788-1802.

St. Clair, Ill. (est. Apr. 27, 1790; 663 sq. mi.; 1970 pop.: 285,176; 1960: 262,509; 1950: 205,995) (Belleville).

Arthur St. Clair*. -- Portrait and Biographical Record of St. Clair County, Chicago: Chapman Brothers, 1892; 672 p.

St. Clair, Mich. (est. Mar. 28, 1820, org. 1821; 740 sq. mi.; 1970 pop.: 120, 175; 1960: 107, 201; 1950: 91, 599) (Port Huron). Arthur St. Clair*. -- Jenks, William Lee, St. Clair County, Chicago: Lewis Pub. Co., 1912; 2 vol.

St. Clair, Mo. (est. Jan. 29, 1841; 699 sq. mi.; 1970 pop.: 7, 667; 1960: 8, 421; 1950: 10, 482) (Osceola). Arthur St. Clair*. See Henry County, Mo., for published work.

St. Croix, Wis. (est. Jan. 9, 1840; 736 sq. mi.; 1970 pop.: 34, 354; 1960: 29, 164; 1950: 25, 905) (Hudson). St. Croix River named for St. Croix who was drowned at its mouth.

St. Francis, Ark. (est. Oct. 13, 1827, eff. Dec. 1, 1827; 636 sq. mi.; 1970 pop.: 30, 799; 1960: 33, 303; 1950: 36, 841) (Forrest City). Saint Francis of Assisi (1182-1226). Founder of order, Friars Minor, 1209; sailed for Palestine to evangelize the Mohammedans 1219; canonized by Pope Gregory IX, 1228.

St. Francois, Mo. (est. Dec. 19, 1821; 457 sq. mi.; 1970 pop.: 36, 818; 1960: 36, 516; 1950: 35, 276) (Farmington). Saint Francis*.

St. Helena, La. (est. Oct. 27, 1810; 420 sq. mi.; 1970 pop.: 9, 937; 1960: 9, 162; 1950: 9, 013) (Greensburg). Saint Helen (250-330). Mother of Constantine the Great; wife of Constantine Chlorus; became a Christian 313; helped build churches.

St. James, La. (est. Mar. 31, 1807; 254 sq. mi.; 1970 pop.: 19, 733; 1960: 18, 369; 1950: 15, 334) (Convent). -- Bourgeois, Lillian G., Cabanocey; the history, customs and folklore of St. James Parish, New Orleans: Pelican Pub. Co., 1957; 211 p.

St. John the Baptist, La. (est. Mar. 31, 1807; 231 sq. mi.; 1970 pop.: 23, 813; 1960: 18, 439; 1950: 14, 861) (Edgard). Saint John the Baptist. -- Eyraud, Jean M. (and others), History of St. John the Baptist Parish, Marrero, La.: Hope Haven Press, 1939; 143 p.

St. Johns, Fla. (est. Aug. 12, 1822; 609 sq. mi.; 1970 pop.: 30, 727; 1960: 30, 034; 1950: 24, 998) (St. Augustine). Saint John the Baptist*.

St. Joseph, Ind. (est. Jan. 29, 1830, eff. Apr. 1, 1830; 467 sq. mi.; 1970 pop.: 245, 045; 1960: 238, 614; 1950: 205, 058) (South Bend). Joseph, husband of the Virgin Mary.

St. Joseph, Mich. (est. Oct. 29, 1829, org. 1829; 508 sq. mi.; 1970 pop.: 47, 392; 1960: 42, 332; 1950: 34, 071) (Centerville). Joseph*. -- Silliman, Sue Imogene, St.

Joseph In Homespun, Three Rivers, Mich.: Three Rivers Pub. Co., 1931; 213 p.

St. Landry, La. (est. Mar. 31, 1807; 964 sq. mi.; 1970 pop.: 80, 364; 1960: 81, 493; 1950: 78, 476) (Opelousas). Saint Landri (Landericus). Bishop of Paris 651; governed abbey of Soignies.

St. Lawrence, N. Y. (est. Mar. 3, 1802; 2, 772 sq. mi.; 1970 pop.: 111, 991; 1960: 111, 239; 1950: 98, 897) (Canton). Saint Lawrence River, named for Saint Laurent on whose birthday the river was discovered by the French explorer, Jacques Cartier. -- History of St. Lawrence County, Philadelphia: L. H. Everts & Co., 1878; 521 p.

St. Louis, Minn. (est. Feb. 20, 1855; 6, 281 sq. mi.; 1970 pop.: 220, 693; 1960: 231, 588; 1950: 206, 062) (Duluth). ("America's Finest Fishing Country"; "Minnesota's Arrowhead County, "; "The Fisherman's Paradise"; "The Fishing Area In Our Country"; "The Largest Concentration of Fresh Water Lakes in the United States"; "The Vacation Land Supreme"; "Your Target for Vacation Pleasure"). Saint Louis (1215-1270). Louis IX, 1215-1270). King of France 1226-1270; father of eleven children; defeated King Henry VIII of England at Taillebourg 1242; led two crusades, made prisoner in Egypt at the first; died in the second; canonized 1297. (Originally Superior County, name changed to St. Louis County, Mar. 3, 1855). chap. 22. -- Van Brunt, Walter, Duluth and St. Louis County, Minn., Chicago: American Historical Society, 1921; 3 vol.

St. Louis, Mo. (est. Oct. 1, 1812 procl. 497 sq. mi.; 1970 pop.: 951, 353; 1960: 703, 532; 1950: 406, 349) (Clayton). St. Louis*.

St. Lucie, Fla. (est. May 24, 1905; 588 sq. mi.; 1970 pop.: 50, 836; 1960: 39, 294; 1950: 20, 180) (Fort Pierce). Saint Luke*. (Spanish). Saint Lucie of Syracuse.

St. Martin, La. (est. Mar. 31, 1807; 525 sq. mi.; 1970 pop.: 32, 453; 1960: 29, 063; 1950: 26, 353) (St. Martinville). Saint Martin (316-397). Left cavalry, served St. Hilary, bishop of Poitiers; lived ten years as a recluse; bishop of Tours.

St. Mary, La. (est. Apr. 17, 1811; 632 sq. mi.; 1970 pop.: 60, 752; 1960: 48, 833; 1950: 35, 848) (Franklin). Mary, the mother of Jesus.

St. Mary's, Md. (est. 1637; 367 sq. mi.; 1970 pop.: 47, 388; 1960: 38, 915; 1950: 29, 111) (Leonardtown). The Virgin Mary. The ships "Ark" and "Dove" carrying colonists landed at St. Mary's on the Feast of the Annunciation, Mar. 25, 1634. -- Pogue, Robert E. T., Yesterday in old St. Mary's County, New York: Carlton Press, 1968; 464 p.

St. Tammany, La. (est. Oct. 27, 1810; 906 sq. mi.; 1970 pop.: 63, 585; 1960: 38, 643; 1950: 26, 988) (Covington). Tammany. Chief of the Delaware Indians whose name means "beaver landing."

Ste. Genevieve, Mo. (est. Oct. 1, 1812 procl., 500 sq.mi.; 1970 pop.: 12, 867; 1960: 12, 116; 1950: 11, 237) (Ste. Genevieve). Saint Genevieve (453-512) patroness of Paris. Feast day Jan. 3rd.

Salem, N.J. (est. May 17, 1694; 350 sq. mi.; 1970 pop.: 60, 346; 1960: 58, 711; 1950: 49, 508) (Salem). Descriptive. Hebrew word Shalom which means "peace." -- Chew, William H., ed., Salem County hand book, Salem, N.J.: Salem National Banking Co., 1924; 71 p. -- Salem County Tercentenary Committee, Fenwick's colony; Salem County Pictorial, 1675-1964, Salem, N.J.: Salem County Tercentenary Committee, 1964; 191 p.

Saline, Ark. (est. Nov. 2, 1835; 725 sq. mi.; 1970 pop.: 36, 107; 1960: 28, 956; 1950: 23, 816) (Benton). Descriptive word (containing salt).

Saline, Ill. (est. Feb. 25, 1847; 399 sq. mi.; 1970 pop.: 25, 721; 1960: 26, 227; 1950: 33, 420) (Harrisburg). Descriptive word. -- Saline County, A Century of History, Harrisburg(?), Ill.: Saline County Historical Society, 1947; 330 p.

Saline, Kan. (est. Feb. 15, 1860; 720 sq. mi.; 1970 pop.: 46, 592; 1960: 54, 715; 1950: 33, 409) (Salina). Descriptive word.

Saline, Mo. (est. Nov. 25, 1820; 759 sq. mi.; 1970 pop.: 24, 633; 1960: 25, 148; 1950: 26, 694) (Marshall). Descriptive word. Eff. Jan. 1, 1821.

Saline, Neb. (est. Mar. 6, 1855, org. Feb. 18, 1867; 575 sq. mi.; 1970 pop.: 12, 809; 1960: 12, 542; 1950: 14, 046) (Wilber). Descriptive word. -- Kaura, J. W., Saline County, Nebraska, a history, De Witt, Neb., 1962; 211 p.

Salt Lake, Utah (est. Dec. 1849; 764 sq. mi.; 1970 pop.: 458, 607; 1960: 383, 035; 1950: 274, 895) (Salt Lake City). Descriptive. (Formerly Great Salt Lake County, name changed to Salt Lake County, Jan. 29, 1868)

Saluda, S.C. (est. Feb. 25, 1896; 442 sq. mi.; 1970 pop.: 14, 528; 1960: 14, 554; 1950: 15, 924) (Saluda). Indian word for "corn river."

Sampson, N.C. (est. sess. Apr. 18, 1784; 963 sq. mi.; 1970 pop.: 44, 954; 1960: 48, 013; 1950: 49, 780) (Clinton). John Sampson. Col., N.C. council of Josiah Martin, last royal gov.

San Augustine, Tex. (est. Mar. 17, 1836; 612 sq. mi.; 1970 pop.: 7,858; 1960: 7,722; 1950: 8,837) (San Augustine). Saint Augustine for whom the presidio at San Augustine de Ahumade was named. -- Crocket, George Lewis, Two centuries in East Texas, a history of San Augustine County, Dallas, Texas: Southwest Press, 1932; 372 p.

San Benito, Calif. (est. Feb. 12, 1874; 1,396 sq. mi.; 1970 pop.: 18,226; 1960: 15,396; 1950: 14,370) (Hollister). ("The County With California's Finest Year Round Climate"). Saint Benedict (480-543?) Studied at Rome about 500; retired as a hermit in a cave, founded twelve monasteries of the Benedictine order.

San Bernardino, Calif. (est. Apr. 26, 1853; 20,131 sq. mi.; 1970 pop.: 684,072; 1960: 503,591; 1950: 281,642) (San Bernardino). ("The Greatest County in the U. S. A."; "The Imperial County"). Saint Bernard of Sienna named because the valley was entered on his feast day, May 20 in 1810. -- Robinson, William Wilcox, Story of San Bernardino County, San Bernardino: Pioneer Title Insurance Company, 1958; 79 p. -- Beattie, George William, Heritage of the Valley: San Bernardino's first century, Pasadena, Calif.: San Pasqual Press, 1939, 439 p.

San Diego, Calif. (est. Feb. 18, 1850; 4,258 sq. mi.; 1970 pop.: 1,357,854; 1960: 1,033,011; 1950: 556,808) (San Diego). ("The Lower Lefthand Corner of the U. S. A. (bounded by the Pacific Ocean on one side and Mexico on another)"). Saint Didacus (-1207). Entered order of St. Francis, became a lay brother, went to Canary Islands; recalled to Spain; San Diego Harbor named for him. Feast day celebrated Nov. 14th. -- Stuart, Gordon, San Diego Back Country, Pacific Palisades, Calif., 1966; 241 p.

San Francisco, Calif. (est. Feb. 18, 1850; 45 sq. mi.; 1970 pop.: 715,674; 1960: 742,855; 1950: 775,357) (San Francisco). Saint Francis de Assisi -- Beebe, Lucius Morris, San Francisco's Golden Era, Berkeley, Calif.: Howell-North, 1960; 255 p.

San Jacinto, Tex. (est. Aug. 13, 1870; 619 sq. mi.; 1970 pop.: 6,702; 1960: 6,153; 1950: 7,172) (Coldspring). Saint Hyacinth, site of the battle fought Apr. 21, 1836 named for the ponderance of water hyacinths.

San Joaquin, Calif. (est. Feb. 18, 1850; 1,410 sq. mi.; 1970 pop.: 290,208; 1960: 249,989; 1950: 200,750) (Stockton). Saint Joachim, the father of Our Lady and the husband of St. Anne, feast day Aug. 16th. -- An Illustrated History of San Joaquin County, Chicago: Lewis Pub. Co., 1890; 666 p.

San Juan, Colo. (est. Jan. 31, 1876, eff. May 1, 1876; 392 sq. mi.; 1970 pop.: 831; 1960: 849; 1950: 1,471) (Silverton). Saint John the Baptist, son of Zachary; cast into the fortress of Machaerus; beheaded to satisfy promise made to Salome; feast day June 24th. -- Cornelius, Temple H., Sheepherder's Gold, Denver: Sage Books, 1964; 186 p.

San Juan, N. M. (est. Feb. 24, 1887; 5,515 sq. mi.; 1970 pop.: 52,517; 1960: 53,306; 1950: 18,292) (Aztec). Saint John*.

San Juan, Utah. (est. Feb. 17, 1880; 7,884 sq. mi.; 1970 pop.: 9,606; 1960: 9,040; 1950: 5,315) (Monticello). Saint John*.

San Juan, Wash. (est. Oct. 31, 1873; 172 sq. mi.; 1970 pop.: 3,856; 1960: 2,872; 1950: 3,245) (Friday Harbor). Saint John*.

San Luis Obispo, Calif. (est. Feb. 18, 1850; 3,326 sq. mi.; 1970 pop.: 105,690; 1960: 81,044; 1950: 51,417) (San Luis Obispo). ("California's Newest Vacationland"; "The County Nature Preserved"). Saint Louis, the Bishop of Toulouse. -- History of San Luis Obispo County, Oakland, Calif.: Thompson & West, 1883; 391 p.

San Mateo, Calif. (est. Apr. 19, 1856; 454 sq. mi.; 1970 pop.: 556,234; 1960: 444,387; 1950: 235,659) (Redwood City) Saint Matthew. Apostle, wrote his gospel. Feast day Sept. 21. -- Goodman, Marian, San Mateo County-its story, Redwood City, Calif.: Goodman Pub. Co., 1967; 44 p. -- Cloud, Roy Walter, History of San Mateo County, Chicago: S. J. Clarke Pub. Co., 1928; 2 vol.

San Miguel, Colo. (est. Nov. 1, 1861; 1,283 sq. mi.; 1970 pop.: 1,949; 1960: 2,944; 1950: 2,693) (Telluride). Saint Michael, the archangel who smote the rebel Lucifer. Feast day Sept. 29th.

San Miguel, N. M. (est. Jan. 9, 1852; 4,749 sq. mi.; 1970 pop.: 21,951; 1960: 23,468; 1950: 26,512) (Las Vegas). Saint Michael*.

San Patricio, Tex. (est. Mar. 17, 1836; 689 sq. mi.; 1970 pop.: 47,288; 1960: 45,021; 1950: 35,842) (Sinton). Saint Patrick (389-461) taken captive to Ireland 405; escaped 411; returned to Ireland as missionary bishop 432; established Catholic Church in Ireland; first organizer of the Irish Church with the primatical see at Armagh.

San Saba, Tex. (est. Feb. 1, 1856; 1,122 sq. mi.; 1970 pop.: 5,540; 1960: 6,381; 1950: 8,666) (San Saba). Spanish contraction for San Sabado, Holy Saturday, the day when the San Saba river was discovered. -- Hamrick, Alma (Ward), The call of the San Saba, a history of San Saba County, San Antonio, Texas: Naylor Co., 1941; 331 p.

Sanborn, S. D. (est. Mar. 9, 1883; 571 sq. mi.; 1970 pop.: 3,697; 1960: 4,641; 1950: 5,142) (Woonsocket). George W. Sanborn. Division supt. of the Milwaukee RR in S. D. when the line was being built through the county in 1883. -- Brown, Alice Mitchell, Sanborn County history 1873-1963, [n. p.], 1964?; 232 p.

Sanders, Mont. (est. Feb. 7, 1905; 2,811 sq. mi.; 1970 pop.: 7,093; 1960: 6,880; 1950: 6,983) (Thompson Falls). Wilbur Fisk Sanders (1834-1905). In Civil War recruited a company of infantry and a battery of artillery 1861; commissioned first lt. 64th Regiment Ohio Inf.; asst. adj. gen. on the staff of gen. James W. Forsyth; Mont. terr. house of representatives 1873-79; a Senator from Mont. 1890-93; editor of first newssheet in Mont. 1864.

Sandoval, N. M. (est. Mar. 10, 1903; 3,811 sq. mi.; 1970 pop.: 17,492; 1960: 14,201; 1950: 12,438) (Bernalillo). Sandoval family.

Sandusky, Ohio (est. Feb. 12, 1820; 410 sq. mi.; 1970 pop.: 60,983; 1960: 56,486; 1950: 46,114) (Fremont). Indian word for "cold water." -- Meek, Basil, Twentieth century history of Sandusky County, Chicago: Richmond-Arnold Pub. Co., 1909; 934 p. -- History of Sandusky County, Cleveland: H. Z. Williams & Brother, 1882; 834 p.

Sangamon, Ill. (est. Jan. 30, 1821; 876 sq. mi.; 1970 pop.: 161,335; 1960: 146,539; 131,484) (Springfield) Corruption of Indian name for "good hunting ground." -- History of Sangamon County, Chicago: Interstate Pub. Co., 1881; 1067 p.

Sanilac, Mich. (est. Sept. 10, 1822, org. 1848; 961 sq. mi.; 1970 pop.: 34,889; 1960: 32,314; 1950: 30,837) (Sandusky) Sanilac. Indian chief.

Sanpete, Utah (est. Mar. 3, 1852; 1,597 sq. mi.; 1970 pop.: 10,976; 1960: 7,053; 1950: 13,891) (Manti). San Pitch. Corrupted name of Indian chief.

Santa Barbara, Calif. (est. Feb. 18, 1850; 2,745 sq. mi.; 1970 pop.: 264,324; 1960: 168,962; 1950: 98,220) (Santa Barbara). ("The American Riviera"). Mission Santa Barbara discovered Dec. 4, 1603 by Vizcaino who entered the channel on St. Barbara's day. Barbara, virgin martyr, executed by her father Dec. 4. -- History of Santa Barbara & Ventura Counties, Berkeley, Calif.: Howell-North, 1961; 477 p. -- Phillips, Michael James, History of Santa Barbara County, Chicago: S. J. Clarke Pub. Co., 1927; 2 vol.

Santa Clara, Calif. (est. Feb. 18, 1850; 1,305 sq. mi.;

1970 pop.: 1,064,714; 1960: 642,315; 1950: 290,547) (San Jose). Saint Claire. Abbess, went barefooted; observed perpetual abstinence, constant silence and perfect poverty; founded order outside Assissi. -- Sawyer, Eugene T., History of Santa Clara County, Los Angeles: Historic Record Co., 1922; 1692 p.

Santa Cruz, Ariz. (est. Mar. 15, 1899; 1,246 sq. mi.; 1970 pop.: 13,966; 1960: 10,808; 1950: 9,344) (Nogales). ("Arizona's Gateway to Sonora Mexico"). Spanish for "sainted cross."

Santa Cruz, Calif. (est. Feb. 18, 1850; 439 sq. mi.; 1970 pop.: 123,790; 1960: 84,219; 1950: 66,534) (Santa Cruz). ("The County Where the Redwoods Meet the Sea"). Spanish for "sainted cross." (Originally Branciforte; (chap. 15) changed to Santa Cruz, Apr. 5, 1850, chap. 61). -- Harrison, E. S., History of Santa Cruz County, San Francisco, Calif.: E. S. Harrison, 1892; 379 p.

Santa Fe, N. M. (est. Jan. 9, 1852; 1,943 sq. mi.; 1970 pop.: 53,756; 1960: 44,970; 1950: 38,153) (Santa Fe). Spanish for "holy faith." -- Frost, Max and Walter, Paul A. F., Santa Fe County, Santa Fe: N. M. Bureau of Immigration, 1906; 145 p.

Santa Rosa, Fla. (est. Feb. 18, 1842; 1,024 sq. mi.; 1970 pop.: 37,741; 1960: 29,547; 1950: 18,554) (Milton). Santa Rosa Island named for Saint Rose de Viterbo.

Sarasota, Fla. (est. May 14, 1921; 586 sq. mi.; 1970 pop.: 120,413; 1960: 76,895; 1950: 28,827) (Sarasota). ("Florida's Distinctive Resort Area"). Indian word for "point of rocks." -- Grismer, Karl Hiram, The Story of Sarasota, Sarasota, Fla., 1946; 376 p.

Saratoga, N. Y. (est. Feb. 7, 1791; 814 sq. mi.; 1970 pop.: 121,679; 1960: 89,096; 1950: 74,869) (Ballston Spa). ("The County Where the Past Meets the Future"; "The County With a Practical Step to Profit, Health and Fun"; "The Fun County, U. S. A."; "The Gateway to the Adirondacks"). Corruption of Indian word meaning "the side hill." -- Anderson, George Baker, Our county and its people, Boston, Mass.: The Boston History Co., 1899; 584 p. -- Sylvester, Nathaniel Bartlett, History of Saratoga County, Philadelphia: Everts & Ensign, 1878; 514 p.

Sargent, N. D. (est. Mar. 3, 1883, org. Oct. 8, 1883; 855 sq. mi.; 1970 pop.: 5,937; 1960: 6,856; 1950: 7,616). (Forman). H. E. Sargent. Supt. Northern Pacific RR Co.

Sarpy, Neb. (est. Feb. 7, 1857, org. June 19, 1857; 230 sq. mi.; 1970 pop.: 63,696; 1960: 31,281; 1950: 15,693) (Papillion). Peter A. Sarpy (1805-1865) Settler, had trading post; built ship for John Charles Fremont 1842;

quartermaster Neb. vol. regiment 1855.

Sauk, Wis. (est. Jan. 11, 1840; 840 sq. mi.; 1970 pop.: 39, 057; 1960: 36, 179; 1950: 38, 120) (Baraboo). Sauk Indian tribe. -- Canfield, William Harvey, Outline sketches of Sauk County, Baraboo, Wis.: A. N. Kellogg, 1890; 2 vol.

Saunders, Neb. (est. Jan. 26, 1856; org. Nov. 10, 1866; 756 sq. mi.; 1970 pop.: 17, 018; 1960: 17, 270; 1950: 16, 923) (Wahoo). Alvin Saunders (1817-1899). Fifth gov. of Neb. Terr. Postmaster Mt. Pleasant, Iowa 1836-43; Iowa constitutional convention 1846; Iowa senate 1854-56 and 1858-60; gov. of Neb. Terr.; Senator. (Formerly Calhoun, name changed Jan. 8, 1862). -- Perky, Charles, Past and present of Saunders County, Nebraska, Chicago: S. J. Clarke Pub. Co., 1915; 2 vol.

Sawyer, Wis. (est. Mar. 10, 1883; 1, 273 sq. mi.; 1970 pop.: 9, 670; 1960: 9, 475; 1950: 10, 323) (Hayward). ("The County in the Indianhead Country"). Philetus Sawyer (1861-1900). Wisconsin assembly 1857 and 1861; mayor of Oshkosh, Wis., 1863-64; Representative from Wis., 1865-1875; Senator from Wis., 1881-93.

Schenectady, N. Y. (est. Mar. 7, 1809; 209 sq. mi.; 1970 pop.: 160, 979; 1960: 152, 896; 1950: 142, 497) (Schenectady). Mohawk Indian word for "on the other side of the pine lands." -- Yates, Austin, A., Schenectady County, New York: New York History Co., 1902.

Schleicher, Tex. (est. Apr. 1, 1887; 1, 331 sq. mi.; 1970 pop.: 2, 277; 1960: 2, 791; 1950: 2, 852) (Eldorado). Gustave Schleicher (1823-1879). Founded settlement on the Dano River; went to Tex. 1850; Tex. house of representatives 1853-54; surveyor Bexar County district 1854-59; Tex. senate 1859-61; Capt. Conf. Army 1861; Representative from Tex. 1875-79. -- Holt, R. D., Schleicher County, or eighty years of development in southwest Texas, Eldorado, Texas: Eldorado Success, 1930; 110 p.

Schley, Ga. (est. Dec. 22, 1857; 154 sq. mi.; 1970 pop.: 3, 097; 1960: 3, 256; 1950: 4, 036) (Ellaville). William Schley (1758-1858). Thirty-fourth gov. of Ga. Judge Ga. superior court 1825-28; Ga. house of representatives 1830; Representative from Ga. 1833-35; gov. of Ga. 1835-37.

Schoharie, N. Y. (est. Apr. 6, 1795; 625 sq. mi.; 1970 pop.: 24, 750; 1960: 22, 616; 1950: 22, 702) (Schoharie). ("New York's Undiscovered County"). Mohawk Indian word for "floating driftwood." -- Noyes, Marion F., A history of Schoharie County, Richmondville, N. Y.: Richmondville Phoenix, 1964; 184 p. -- Simms, Jeptha Root, History of Schoharie County, Albany, N.Y.: Munsell & Tanner, 1845; 672 p.

Schoolcraft, Mich. (est. Mar. 9, 1843, org. May 18, 1846; 1,199 sq. mi.; 1970 pop.: 8,226; 1960: 8,953; 1950: 9,148) (Manistique). Henry Rowe Schoolcraft (1793-1864). Exploring trips to Mo. and Ark. 1818-20; to upper Miss. and Lake Superior region 1820-22; Mich. terr. legislature 1828-32; ethnologist and author of numerous books about Indians; Supt. of Indian Affairs for Mich. 1836-41.

Schuyler, Ill. (est. Jan. 13, 1825; 432 sq. mi.; 1970 pop.: 8,135; 1960: 8,746; 1950: 9,613) (Rushville). Philip John Schuyler (1733-1804). Capt. in British Army 1755; chief commissary 1756-57; rejoined Army with rank of maj. 1758; in England settling colonial claims 1758-63; Continental Congress 1775-77 and 1778-81; maj. gen. in Continental Army 1775; resigned 1779; N.Y. senator 1780-84 and 1786-90 and 1792-97; Senator from N.Y. 1789-91 and 1797-98.

Schuyler, Mo. (est. Feb. 14, 1845; 306 sq. mi.; 1970 pop.: 4,665; 1960: 5,052; 1950: 5,760) (Lancaster). Philip John Schuyler*.

Schuyler, N.Y. (est. Apr. 17, 1854; 331 sq. mi.; 1970 pop.: 16,737; 1960: 15,044; 1950: 14,182) (Watkins Glen). Philip John Schuyler*. -- Bell, Barbara, More tales from little Schuyler, Watkins Glen, N.Y.: B. Bell, 1967; 89 p.

Schuylkill, Pa. (est. Mar. 1, 1811; 783 sq. mi.; 1970 pop.: 160,089; 1960: 173,027; 1950: 200,577) (Pottsville). From the Dutch meaning "hidden stream." -- Pottsville, School District, The history of Schuylkill County, Frackville, Pa.: Schuylkill Printing Co., 1950; 107 p. -- Schalck, Adolf W. and D.C. Henning, History of Schuylkill County, Pa., Philadelphia?: 1907; State Historical Association, 2 vol.

Scioto, Ohio (est. Mar. 24, 1803; eff. May 1, 1803; 609 sq. mi.; 1970 pop.: 76,951; 1960: 84,216; 1950: 82,910) (Portsmouth). Wyandot Indian name for "deer." -- Bannon, Henry Towne, Stories old and often told, Baltimore: Waverly Press, Inc., 1927; 275 p. -- Evans, Nelson Wiley, A history of Scioto County, Portsmouth, Ohio: N.W. Evans, 1903; 1322 p.

Scotland, Mo. (est. Jan. 29, 1841; 441 sq. mi.; 1970 pop.: 5,499; 1960: 6,484; 1950: 7,332) (Memphis). Scotland, Great Britain.

Scotland, N.C. (est. Feb. 20, 1899; 317 sq. mi.; 1970 pop.: 26,929; 1960: 25,183; 1950: 26,336) (Laurinburg). Scotland, Great Britain*. -- Henley, Nettie (McCormick), The home place, New York City: Vantage Press, 1955; 182 p.

Scott, Ark. (est. Nov. 5, 1833, eff. Dec. 1, 1833; 898 sq. mi.; 1970 pop.: 8,207; 1960: 7,297; 1950: 10,057) (Waldron). Andrew Scott. Judge superior court of Ark. terr. 1819-21. -- Goodner, Norman, History of Scott County, Arkansas, Siloam Springs, Ark.: Bar D Press, 1941; 89 p. -- McCutchen, Henry Grady, History of Scott County, Arkansas, H. G. Pugh & Co., 1922; 74 p.

Scott, Ill. (est. Feb. 16, 1839; 249 sq. mi.; 1970 pop.: 6,096; 1960: 6,377; 1950: 7,245) (Winchester). Scott County, Ky.

Scott, Ind. (est. Jan. 12, 1820, eff. Feb. 1, 1820; 193 sq. mi.; 1970 pop.: 17,144; 1960: 14,643; 1950: 11,519) (Scottsburg). Charles Scott (1733-1813). Fourth gov. of Ky. French and Indian war; col. 1776; brig. gen. 1777; captured 1780; Indian war guide under gen. St. Clair 1791; under gen. Wayne at battle of Fallen Timbers; gov. of Ky. 1808-12.

Scott, Iowa (est. Dec. 21, 1837; 453 sq. mi.; 1970 pop.: 142,687; 1960: 119,067; 1950: 100,698) (Davenport). Winfield Scott (1786-1866). Capt. Va. light artillery 1808; lt. col. 1812; col. 1813; brig. gen. 1814; bvt. maj. gen. for services at Chippewa and Niagara Falls, Upper Canada, 1814; awarded gold medal by resolutions of Congress 1814; commander-in-chief U. S. Army 1841-61; captured Vera Cruz 1847; occupied Mexico City 1847; presented gold medals by Congress 1848; lt. gen. 1852. -- Downer, Harry E., History of Davenport and Scott County, Chicago: S. J. Clarke Pub. Co., 1910; 2 vol.

Scott, Kan. (est. Mar. 6, 1873, org. Jan. 29, 1886; 723 sq. mi.; 1970 pop.: 5,606; 1960: 5,228; 1950: 4,921) (Scott City). Winfield Scott*.

Scott, Ky. (est. June 22, 1792, eff. Sept. 1, 1792; 284 sq. mi.; 1970 pop.: 17,948; 1960: 15,376; 1950: 15,141) (Georgetown). Charles Scott (1739-1813). French and Indian war; lt. col. and col. 1776; brig. gen. Continental Army 1777; prisoner 1780-83; maj. gen. under St. Clair and Wilkinson 1783; gov. of Ky. 1808-12. -- Gaines, B. O., History of Scott County, Georgetown, Ky.: The Graphic, 1957; 120 p.

Scott, Minn. (est. Mar. 5, 1853; 352 sq. mi.; 1970 pop.: 32,423; 1960: 21,909; 1950: 16,486) (Shakopee). Winfield Scott*.

Scott, Miss. (est. Dec. 23, 1833; 597 sq. mi.; 1970 pop.: 21,369; 1960: 21,187; 1950: 21,681) (Forest). Abram M. Scott (-1833). Seventh gov. of Miss. Fought Creek Indians 1811; Miss. constitutional convention 1817; Miss. legislature; lt. gov. of Miss.; gov. of Miss. 1832-33.

Scott, Mo. (est. Dec. 28, 1821; 418 sq. mi.; 1970 pop.: 33,250; 1960: 32,748; 1950: 32,842) John Scott (1782-1861) (Benton).

Scott, Tenn. (est. Dec. 17, 1849; 549 sq. mi.; 1970 pop.: 14,762; 1960: 15,413; 1950: 17,362) (Huntsville). Winfield Scott*.

Scott, Va. (est. Nov. 24, 1814; 539 sq. mi.; 1970 pop.: 24,376; 1960: 25,813; 1950: 27,640) (Gate City). Winfield Scott*. -- Addington, Robert Milford, History of Scott County, Kingsport, Tenn.: Kingsport Press, 1932; 364 p.

Scotts Bluff, Neb. (est. Nov. 6, 1888, org. Jan. 28, 1889; 726 sq. mi.; 1970 pop.: 36,432; 1960: 33,809; 1950: 33,939) (Gering). Scotts Bluff Mountain, named for a traveler named Scott, a member of capt. Bonneville's expedition of 1832 who was deserted by his companions and perished.

Screven, Ga. (est. Dec. 14, 1793; 794 sq. mi.; 1970 pop.: 12,591; 1960: 14,919; 1950: 18,000) (Sylvania). James Screven (-1778). Gen. Capt. 3rd Ga. Rangers 1776; col. 1776; resigned 1778; brig. gen. Ga. militia; killed at Midway Church, Liberty County, Ga.

Scurry, Tex. (est. Aug. 21, 1876; 909 sq. mi.; 1970 pop.: 15,760; 1960: 20,369; 1950: 22,779) (Snyder). Richardson Scurry (1811-1862). Went to Tex. and joined Tex. army 1836; first sgt. battle of San Jacinto 1836; secretary of Tex. senate 1836; delegate to Tex. independence convention 1836; district attorney of first judicial district 1836-41; house of representatives 1842-44; Representative from Tex. 1851-53; adj. gen. on staff of gen. Albert Sidney Johnston 1861. -- Cotten, Kathryn, Saga of Scurry, San Antonio, Texas: Naylor, 1957; 165 p.

Searcy, Ark. (est. Nov. 3, 1835, eff. Dec. 25, 1835; 664 sq. mi.; 1970 pop.: 7,731; 1960: 8,124; 1950: 10,414) (Marshall) Richard Searcy.

Sebastian, Ark. (est. Jan. 6, 1851; 529 sq. mi.; 1970 pop.: 79,237; 1960: 66,685; 1950: 64,202) (Fort Smith and Greenwood). William King Sebastian (1812-1865). Ark. circuit court judge 1840-43; associate justice Ark. supreme court 1843-45; pres. Ark. senate 1846-47; Senator from Ark. 1848-61.

Sedgwick, Colo. (est. Apr. 9, 1889; 544 sq. mi.; 1970 pop.: 3,405; 1960: 4,242; 1950: 5,095) (Julesburg). John Sedgwick (1813-1864). Graduated U. S. Military Academy 1837; brig. gen. of vol. 1861; maj. gen. 1862; killed at battle of Spotsylvania, May 9, 1864.

Sedgwick, Kan. (est. Feb. 26, 1867; 999 sq. mi.; 1970 pop.:

350, 694; 1960: 343, 231; 1950: 222, 290) (Wichita). John Sedgwick*.

Seminole, Fla. (est. Apr. 25, 1913; 321 sq. mi.; 1970 pop.: 83, 692; 1960: 54, 947; 1950: 26, 883) (Sanford). ("Paradise Living for All the Family"; "The County That Offers a New Adventure in Living"; "The Gateway to Nova"; "The Retirement Haven"; "The Retirement Heaven"). Seminole Indian tribe.

Seminole, Ga. (est. July 8, 1920; 240 sq. mi.; 1970 pop.: 7, 059; 1960: 6, 802; 1950: 7, 904) (Donaldsonville). Seminole Indian tribe*.

Seminole, Okla. (est. July 16, 1907; 629 sq. mi.; 1970 pop.: 25, 144; 1960: 28, 066; 1950: 40, 672) (Wewoka). Seminole Indian tribe*.

Seneca, N. Y. (est. Mar. 24, 1804; 330 sq. mi.; 1970 pop.: 35, 083; 1960: 31, 984; 1950: 29, 253) (Ovid and Waterloo). Seneca Indian tribe.

Seneca, Ohio (est. Feb. 12, 1820; 551 sq. mi.; 1970 pop.: 60, 696; 1960: 59, 326; 1950: 52, 978) (Tiffin). Seneca Indian tribe*. -- Baughman, Abraham J., History of Seneca County, Ohio, Chicago: Lewis Pub. Co., 1911; 2 vol. -- History of Seneca County, Chicago: Warner, Beers & Co., 1886; 1069 p.

Sequatchie, Tenn. (est. Dec. 9, 1857; 273 sq. mi.; 1970 pop.: 6, 331; 1960: 5, 915; 1950: 5, 685) (Dunlap). Indian word for "hog trough."

Sequoyah, Okla. (est. July 16, 1907; 703 sq. mi.; 1970 pop.: 23, 370; 1960: 18, 001; 1950: 19, 773) (Sallisaw). Sequoyah (-1842). Indian chief invented Cherokee alphabet 1821; printed Indian newspaper "The Phoenix."

Sevier, Ark. (est. Oct. 17, 1828, eff. Nov. 1, 1828; 585 sq. mi.; 1970 pop.: 11, 272; 1960: 10, 156; 1950: 12, 293) (De Queen). Ambrose Hundley Sevier (1801-1848). Ark. terr. house of representatives 1823-27; delegate from Ark., 1828-36; Senator from Ark. 1836-48; U. S. Minister to Mexico 1848.

Sevier, Tenn. (est. Sept. 27, 1794; 603 sq. mi.; 1970 pop.: 28, 241; 1960: 24, 251; 1950: 25, 375) (Sevierville). John Sevier (1745-1815). First and third gov. of Tenn. Capt. of colonial militia under Washington in gov. Dunmore's war against the Indians in 1773 and 1774; N. C. county clerk and district judge 1777-80; first and only gov. of the proclaimed state of Franklin 1785-88; a Representative from N. C., 1789-91; brig. gen. of militia for territory south of the Ohio 1791; gov. of Tenn. 1796-1801 and 1803-09; brig. gen. of the provisional army 1798; Representative from Tenn. 1811-15.

Sevier, Utah (est. Jan. 16, 1865; 1,932 sq. mi.; 1970 pop.: 10,103; 1960: 10,565; 1950: 12,072) (Richfield). John Sevier*. Also claimed as a corruption of Rio Sebrero.

Seward, Kan. (est. Aug. 30, 1855; re-created Feb. 18, 1886; 639 sq. mi.; 1970 pop.: 15,744; 1960: 15,930; 1950: 9,972) (Liberal). William Henry Seward (1801-1872). Fourteenth gov. of N. Y. N. Y. Senator 1830-34; gov. of N. Y. 1838-42; senator from N. Y. 1849-61; U. S. Secretary of State in cabinets of Pres. Lincoln and Johnson 1861-69; negotiated treaty with Russia for the purchase of Alaska. (Orig. Godfroy, name ch. June 3, 1861, chap. 18.)

Seward, Neb. (est. Mar. 6, 1855, org. Feb. 9, 1866; 572 sq. mi.; 1970 pop.: 14,460; 1960: 13,581; 1950: 13,155) (Seward). William Henry Seward*. (Formerly Greene County, name changed to Seward County Jan. 3, 1862). -- Waterman, John Henry, General history of Seward County, Nebraska, Beaver Crossing, Neb., 1916; 291 p.

Shackelford, Tex. (est. Feb. 1, 1858; 887 sq. mi.; 1970 pop.: 3,323; 1960: 3,990; 1950: 5,001) (Albany). John Shackelford (1790-1857). Fought in War of 1812; Ala. senate 1822-24; outfitted land army known as Red Rovers and arrived in Tex. 1836; fought in Goliad campaign 1836; captured by Mexicans, but was not executed as he was a physician and attended to the wounded 1836; returned to Ala. where he practiced medicine.

Shannon, Mo. (est. Jan. 29, 1841; 999 sq. mi.; 1970 pop.: 7,196; 1960: 7,087; 1950: 8,377) (Eminence). George Shannon. Served with the Lewis and Clark expedition.

Shannon, S. D. (est. Jan. 11, 1875; 2,100 sq. mi.; 1970 pop.: 8,198; 1960: 6,000; 1950: 5,669) (unorganized -- attached to Fall River County for governmental purposes). Peter C. Shannon. Chief justice Supreme Court Dakota Terr. 1873-82.

Sharkey, Miss. (est. Mar. 29, 1876; 442 sq. mi.; 1970 pop.: 8,937; 1960: 10,738; 1950: 12,903) (Rolling Fork). William Lewis Sharkey (1798-1873). Twenty-fifth gov. of Miss. Moved to Miss. 1816; Miss. house of representatives 1828-29; circuit court judge 1832; trustee Univ. of Miss. 1844-65; provisional gov. of Miss. 1865; elected Senator, but denied seat.

Sharp, Ark. (est. July 18, 1868; 596 sq. mi.; 1970 pop.: 8,233; 1960: 6,319; 1950: 8,999) (Evening Shade and Hardy). Ephraim Sharp (1833-). Lt. in Co. L, Tappen's brigade, in many skirmishes and battle of Prairie Grove.

Shasta, Calif. (est. Feb. 18, 1850; 3,846 sq. mi.; 1970 pop.: 77,640; 1960: 59,468; 1950: 36,413) (Redding).

Shasta Indian tribe from Sasti Shastika Tsasdi meaning "three" referring to a triple-peak mountain. -- Giles, Rosena, Shasta County, Oakland: Biobooks 1949; 301 p.

Shawano, Wis. (est. Feb. 16, 1853; 1, 176 sq. mi.; 1970 pop.: 32, 650; 1960: 34, 351; 1950: 35, 249) (Shawano). Chippewa Indian word for "southern".

Shawnee, Kan. (est. Aug. 30, 1855; 545 sq. mi.; 1970 pop.: 155, 322; 1960: 141, 286; 1950: 105, 418) (Topeka). Indian word, contraction of "shawanogi" meaning "southerners." -- King, James L., History of Shawnee County, Kansas, Chicago: Richmond & Arnold, 1905; 628 p.

Sheboygan, Wis. (est. Dec. 7, 1836; 506 sq. mi.; 1970 pop.: 96, 660; 1960: 86, 484; 1950: 80, 631) (Sheboygan). Indian word for "a noise underground." -- Buchen, Gustave William, Historic Sheboygan County, Sheboygan, Wis., 1944; 347 p.

Shelby, Ala. (est. Feb. 7, 1818; 801 sq. mi.; 1970 pop.: 38, 037; 1960: 32, 132; 1950: 30, 362) (Columbiana). ("The Heart of the Heart of Dixie"). Isaac Shelby (1750-1826). First and fifth gov. of Ky. Served in Revolutionary War; defeated British at King's Mountain, Oct. 7, 1780; N. C. legislature 1781-82; gov. of Ky., 1792-96 and 1812-16; led Ky. vol. in War of 1812.

Shelby, Ill. (est. Jan. 23, 1837; 772 sq. mi.; 1970 pop.: 22, 589; 1960: 23, 404; 1950: 24, 434) (Shelbyville). Isaac Shelby*.

Shelby, Ind. (est. Dec. 31, 1821; eff. Apr. 1, 1822; 409 sq. mi.; 1970 pop.: 37, 797; 1960: 34, 093; 1950: 28, 026) (Shelbyville). Isaac Shelby*.

Shelby, Iowa (est. Jan. 15, 1851, org. Jan. 12, 1853, eff. Mar. 7, 1853; 587 sq. mi.; 1970 pop.: 15, 528; 1960: 15, 825; 1950: 15, 942) (Harlan). Isaac Shelby*.

Shelby, Ky. (est. June 23, 1792, eff. Sept. 1, 1792; 384 sq. mi.; 1970 pop.: 18, 999; 1960: 18, 493; 1950: 17, 912) (Shelbyville). Isaac Shelby*. -- Willis, George Lee, History of Shelby County, Ky., Louisville, Ky.: C. T. Dearing Printing Co., 1929; 268 p.

Shelby, Mo. (est. Jan. 2, 1835; 502 sq. mi.; 1970 pop.: 7, 906; 1960: 9, 063; 1950: 9, 730) (Shelbyville). Isaac Shelby*.

Shelby, Ohio (est. Jan. 7, 1819; 409 sq. mi.; 1970 pop.: 37, 748; 1960: 33, 586; 1950: 28, 488) (Sidney). Isaac Shelby*. -- Hitchcock, Almon Baldwin Carrington, History of Shelby County, Chicago: Richmond-Arnold Pub. Co., 1913; 862 p.

Shelby, Tenn. (est. Nov. 24, 1819; 751 sq. mi.; 1970 pop.:

722, 014; 1960: 627, 019; 1950: 482, 393) (Memphis). Isaac Shelby*.

Shelby, Tex. (est. Mar. 17, 1836; 819 sq. mi.; 1970 pop.: 19, 672; 1960: 20, 479; 1950: 23, 479) (Center). Isaac Shelby*.

Shenandoah, Va. (est. Mar. 1772, eff. May 15, 1772; 507 sq. mi.; 1970 pop.: 22, 852; 1960: 21, 825; 1950: 21, 169) (Woodstock). Indian word for "sprucy stream." (Formerly Dunmore County, name changed to Shenandoah County, Oct. 20, 1777, eff. Feb. 1, 1778 sess.) -- Wayland, John Walter, A History of Shenandoah County, Strasburg, Va.: Shenandoah Pub. House, 1927; 874 p.

Sherburne, Minn. (est. Feb. 25, 1856; 438 sq. mi.; 1970 pop.: 18, 344; 1960: 12, 861; 1950: 10, 661) (Elk River). Moses Sherburne (1808-1868). Associate justice supreme court of Minn. terr. 1853-57.

Sheridan, Kan. (est. Mar. 6, 1873; 893 sq. mi.; 1970 pop.: 3, 859; 1960: 4, 267; 1950: 4, 607) (Hoxie). Philip Henry Sheridan (1831-1888). Graduated U. S. Military Academy 1853; bvt. second lt. inf. 1853; first lt. 1861; capt. 1861; col. second Mich. cavalry 1862; brig. gen. vol. 1862; maj. gen. vol. 1863; brig. gen. U. S. Army 1864; maj. gen. 1864; succeeded Gen. Sherman as commander-in-chief of U. S. Army 1864; lt. gen. 1869; commander-in-chief of army 1883-88.

Sheridan, Mont. (est. Mar. 24, 1913, petition and election; 1, 700 sq. mi.; 1970 pop.: 5, 779; 1960: 6, 458; 1950: 6, 674) (Plentywood). Philip Henry Sheridan*.

Sheridan, Neb. (est. Feb. 25, 1885, org. July 25, 1885; 2, 466 sq. mi.; 1970 pop.: 7, 285; 1960: 9, 049; 1950: 9, 539) (Rushville). Philip Henry Sheridan*.

Sheridan, N. D. (est. Jan. 4, 1873, org. Nov. 1908; 995 sq. mi.; 1970 pop.: 3, 232; 1960: 4, 350; 1950: 5, 253) (McClusky). Philip Henry Sheridan*.

Sheridan, Wyo. (est. Mar. 9, 1888, org. May 11, 1888; 2, 531 sq. mi.; 1970 pop.: 17, 852; 1960: 18, 989; 1950: 20, 185) (Sheridan). Philip Henry Sheridan*.

Sherman, Kan. (est. Mar. 6, 1873, org. Sept. 20, 1886; 1, 055 sq. mi.; 1970 pop.: 7, 792; 1960: 6, 682; 1950: 6, 421) (Goodland). William Tecumseh Sherman (1820-1891). Graduated U. S. Military Academy 1840; second lt. 1840; first lt. 1841; capt. 1850; bvt. capt. for gallant and meritorious service in Calif. during Mexican War 1848; resigned Sept. 1853; col. 1861; brig. gen. vol. 1861; maj. gen. 1862-64; made famous "march to the sea"; succeeded Gen. Grant as commander of the army 1869.

Sherman, Neb. (est. Mar. 1, 1871, org. Apr. 1, 1873;

570 sq. mi.; 1970 pop.: 4,725; 1960: 5,382; 1950: 6,421) (Loup City). William Tecumseh Sherman*.

Sherman, Ore. (est. Feb. 1889; 830 sq. mi.; 1970 pop.: 2,139; 1960: 2,446; 1950: 2,271) (Moro). William Tecumseh Sherman*. -- French, Giles, The Golden land, a history of Sherman County, Portland, Oregon: Oregon Historical Society, 1958; 237 p.

Sherman, Tex. (est. Aug. 21, 1876; 914 sq. mi.; 1970 pop.: 3,657; 1960: 2,605; 1950: 2,443) (Stratford). Sidney Sherman (1805-1873). Raised company of vol. at Cincinnati and Covington and reported to Gen. Houston 1836; elected col.; served at San Jacinto 1836; elected maj. gen. of Tex. Republic 1839; maj. gen. of militia 1843; Tex. legislature 1842 and 1852-53.

Shiawassee, Mich. (est. Sept. 10, 1822, org. Mar. 18, 1837; 540 sq. mi.; 1970 pop.: 63,075; 1960: 53,446; 1950: 45,967) (Corunna). Indian word for "river that twists about."

Shoshone, Idaho (est. Feb. 4, 1864; 2,609 sq. mi.; 1970 pop.: 19,718; 1960: 20,876; 1950: 22,806) (Wallace). Shoshonean Indian tribe.

Sibley, Minn. (est. Mar. 5, 1853, org. Mar. 2, 1854; 581 sq. mi.; 1970 pop.: 15,845; 1960: 16,228; 1950: 15,816) (Gaylord). Henry Hastings Sibley (1811-1891). First gov. of Minn. Delegate from Wis. terr. 1848-49; delegate from Minn. terr. 1849-53; Minn. terr. legislature 1855; gov. of Minn. 1858-60; brig. gen. of vol. 1862-63; bvt. maj. gen. of vol. 1863.

Sierra, Calif. (est. Apr. 16, 1852; 958 sq. mi.; 1970 pop.: 2,365; 1960: 2,247; 1950: 2,410) (Downieville). Spanish for "mountain range."

Sierra, N. M. (est. Apr. 3, 1884; 3,034 sq. mi.; 1970 pop.: 7,189; 1960: 6,409; 1950: 7,186) (Truth or Consequences). Spanish for "mountain range."

Silver Bow, Mont. (est. Feb. 16, 1881, 716 sq. mi.; 1970 pop.: 41,981; 1960: 46,454; 1950: 48,422) (Butte). Descriptive.

Simpson, Ky. (est. Jan. 28, 1819; 239 sq. mi.; 1970 pop.: 13,054; 1960: 11,548; 1950: 11,678) (Franklin). John Simpson. Ky legislature; raised company of riflemen, killed at battle of River Raisin 1812.

Simpson, Miss. (est. Jan. 23, 1824; 575 sq. mi.; 1970 pop.: 19,947; 1960: 20,454; 1950: 21,819) (Mendenhall). Josiah Simpson.

Sioux, Iowa (est. Jan. 13, 1851; 766 sq. mi.; 1970 pop.: 27,996; 1960: 26,375; 1950: 26,381) (Orange City) Sioux Indian tribe. -- Dyke, Charles L., The Story of Sioux

County, Sioux City, Iowa: Verstegen Printing Co., 1942; 567 p.

Sioux, Neb. (est. Feb. 19, 1877, org. Sept. 20, 1886; 2,063 sq. mi.; 1970 pop.: 2,034; 1960: 2,575; 1950: 3,124) (Harrison). Sioux Indian tribe. -- Harrison Ladies Community Club, Sioux County, memoirs of its pioneers, Harrison, Neb.: Harrison Sun-News, 1967; 304 p.

Sioux, N. D. (est. Sept. 3, 1914, procl.; 1,124 sq. mi.; 1970 pop.: 3,632; 1960: 3,662; 1950: 3,696) (Fort Yates). Sioux Indian tribe.

Siskiyou, Calif. (est. Mar. 22, 1852; 6,313 sq. mi.; 1970 pop.: 33,225; 1960: 32,885; 1950: 30,733) (Yreka). ("California's Uncrowded Sportsland"). Chinook word for "bobtailed horse" from Cree language; French translation "six Cailleux" of Indian word for "six stories."

Skagit, Wash. (est. Nov. 28, 1883; 1,735 sq. mi.; 1970 pop.: 52,381; 1960: 51,350; 1950: 43,273) (Mount Vernon). Skagit Indian tribe.

Skamania, Wash. (est. Mar. 9, 1854; 1,676 sq. mi.; 1970 pop.: 5,845; 1960: 5,207; 1950: 4,788) (Stevenson). Indian for "swift river."

Slope, N. D. (est. Jan. 14, 1915, election of Nov. 3, 1914; 1,226 sq. mi.; 1970 pop.: 1,484; 1960: 1,893; 1950: 2,315) (Amidon). Descriptive.

Smith, Kan. (est. Feb. 26, 1867; 893 sq. mi.; 1970 pop.: 6,757; 1960: 7,776; 1950: 8,846) (Smith Center). J. Nelson Smith (-1864). Maj. 2nd Colo. Vol.; killed at battle of Little Blue, Mo. on Oct. 23, 1864.

Smith, Miss. (est. Dec. 23, 1833; 626 sq. mi.; 1970 pop.: 13,561; 1960: 14,303; 1950: 16,740) (Raleigh). David Smith.

Smith, Tenn. (est. Oct. 26, 1799; 325 sq. mi.; 1970 pop.: 12,509; 1960: 12,059; 1950: 14,098) (Carthage). Daniel Smith (1748-1818). Deputy; surveyor of Augusta County, Va. 1773; justice of the peace 1776; fought in Revolutionary War; col.; secretary of the Terr. South of the Ohio River 1790, member of first Tenn. constitutional convention 1796; mapped Tenn.; gen. of state militia; senator 1798-99 and 1805-09.

Smith, Tex. (est. Apr. 11, 1846; 939 sq. mi.; 1970 pop.: 97,096; 1960: 86,350; 1950: 74,701) (Tyler). James Smith (1792-1855). Soldier War of 1812; moved to Tex. 1835; organized cavalry troop 1836; advanced from capt. to col.; brig. gen. in charge of northwest frontier 1841; Regulator-Moderator war 1844; Tex. house of representatives 1846-47. -- Woldert, Albert, A history of Tyler and Smith County, Texas, San Antonio, Texas: Naylor Co.,

1948; 165 p.

Smyth, Va. (est. Feb. 23, 1832; 435 sq. mi.; 1970 pop.: 31, 349; 1960: 31, 066; 1950: 30, 187) (Marion). Alexander Smyth (1765-1830). Va. house of delegates 1792, 1796, 1801, 1802 and 1804-08; Va. Senate 1808-09; col. U. S. Army rifleman regiment 1808-12; inspector gen. with rank of brig. gen. 1812-13; Va. house of delegates 1816, 1817, 1826 and 1827; Representative from Va., 1817-25 and 1827-30. -- Wilson, Goodridge, Smyth County History and Traditions, Kingsport, Tenn.: Kingsport Press, Inc., 1932; 397 p.

Snohomish, Wash. (est. Jan. 14, 1861; 2, 100 sq. mi.; 1970 pop.: 265, 236; 1960: 172, 199; 1950: 111, 580) (Everett). Snohomish Indian tribe, Indian name for "union." -- Johnston, Elmer E., A text book of Snohomish County, Everett, Wash.: Tribune Job Print., 1909; 56 p. -- Whitfield, William, History of Snohomish County, Chicago: Pioneer Historical Pub. Co., 1926; 2 vol.

Snyder, Pa. (est. Mar. 2, 1855; 329 sq. mi.; 1970 pop.: 29, 269; 1960: 25, 922; 1950: 22, 912) (Middleburg). Simon Snyder (1759-1819). Third gov. of Pa. Justice of the peace 1777-89; justice of court of common pleas; Pa. constitutional convention 1789-90; Pa. assembly 1797-1807; speaker of the house 1802-07; gov. of Pa. 1808-17; Pa. senate 1817. -- Dunkelberger, George Franklin, The story of Snyder County, Selinsgrove, Pa.: Snyder County Historical Society, 1948; 982 p.

Socorro, N. M. (est. Jan. 9, 1852; 7, 772 sq. mi.; 1970 pop.: 9, 763; 1960: 10, 168; 1950: 9, 670) (Socorro). Spanish name for "succor" or "relief." Nuestra Senora del Socorro County. -- Stanley, F., pseud, Socorro, the oasis, Denver, Colo., 1950; 221 p.

Solano, Calif. (est. Feb. 18, 1850; 827 sq. mi.; 1970 pop.: 169, 941; 1960: 134, 597; 1950: 104, 833) (Fairfield). Solano. Indian chief who adopted the Christian faith. -- Gregory, Thomas Jefferson, History of Solano and Napa Counties, Los Angeles: Historic Record Co., 1912; 1044 p. -- Hunt, Margarite, History of Solano County, Chicago: S. J. Clarke Pub. Co., 1926; 2 vol.

Somerset, Me. (est. Mar. 1, 1809; 3, 948 sq. mi.; 1970 pop.: 40, 597; 1960: 39, 749; 1950: 39, 785) (Showhegan). Somerset County, England.

Somerset, Md. (est. Aug. 22, 1666; 332 sq. mi.; 1970 pop.: 18, 924; 1960: 19, 623; 1950: 20, 745) (Princess Anne). Mary Somerset. Sister of Cecilius, second Lord Baltimore. -- Torrence, Clayton, Old Somerset on the eastern shore of Maryland, Richmond: Whittel & Shepperson, 1935; 583 p.

Somerset, N. J. (est. May 1688; 307 sq. mi.; 1970 pop.: 198, 372; 1960: 143, 913; 1950: 99, 052) (Somerville). Somersetshire, England. -- Van Horn, James H., Historic Somerset, New Brunswick, N. J.: Historical Societies of Somerset County, N. J., 1965; 223 p.

Somerset, Pa. (est. Apr. 17, 1795; 1, 084 sq. mi.; 1970 pop.: 76, 037; 1960: 77, 450; 1950: 81, 813) (Somerset). ("Pennsylvania's Penthouse"; "The Gateway to Laurel Highlands"; "The 'Roof Garden' County of the Keystone State"; "The Ski Capital of Pennsylvania"; "The Year 'Round Tourist and Vacation Playground"). Somerset County, England.

Somervell, Tex. (est. Mar. 13, 1875; 197 sq. mi.; 1970 pop.: 2, 793; 1960: 2, 577; 1950: 2, 542) (Glen Rose). Alexander Somervell (1796-1854). Moved to Tex. 1832; at storming of San Antonio 1836; lt. col. battle of San Jacinto 1836; acting secretary of war in Burnet's cabinet Tex. Republic 1836; Tex. congress 1836-38; brig. gen. 1839; commanded Somervell expedition 1842; collector of customs 1842-45; accidentally drowned 1854.

Sonoma, Calif. (est. Feb. 18, 1850; 1, 579 sq. mi.; 1970 pop.: 204, 885; 1960: 147, 375; 1950: 103, 405) (Santa Rosa). ("The County of Agriculture, Industry and Agriculture"). Tso-noma, Indian chief, name meaning "valley of the moon." -- Gregory, Thomas Jefferson, History of Sonoma County, Los Angeles: Historic Record Co., 1911; 1112 pages. -- Murphy, Celeste Granice, The people of the Pueblo, or The Story of Sonoma, Sonoma, Calif.: W. L. & C. G. Murphy, 1935; 266 p.

Southampton, Va. (est. Apr. 30, 1749; 607 sq. mi.; 1970 pop.: 18, 582; 1960: 27, 195; 1950: 26, 522) (Courtland). Henry Wriothesley, second earl of Southampton (1573-1624). Second son of Henry I; councillor to the queen 1604; councillor for the colony of Va. May 23, 1609; councillor for the Plantation of New England Nov. 3, 1620.

Spalding, Ga. (est. Dec. 20, 1851; 209 sq. mi.; 1970 pop.: 39, 514; 1960: 35, 404; 1950: 31, 045) (Griffin). Thomas Spalding (1774-1851). Ga. house of representatives 1794; Ga. constitutional convention 1798; Ga. senate 1805-06; commissioner to determine Ga.-Fla. boundary line.

Spartanburg, S. C. (est. Mar. 12, 1785; 830 sq. mi.; 1970 pop.: 173, 724; 1960: 156, 830; 1950: 150, 349) (Spartanburg). Descriptive term for the county which behaved in a Spartan manner during the Revolutionary war. -- Landrum, John Belton O'Neall, History of Spartanburg County, Atlanta, Ga.: Franklin Printing & Pub. Co., 1900 (reprint 1960); 543 p.

Spencer, Ind. (est. Jan. 10, 1818, eff. Feb. 1, 1818; 396 sq. mi.; 1970 pop.: 17,134; 1960: 16,074; 1950: 16,174) (Rockport). ("The Scenic County"). Spear Spencer. Capt.

Spencer, Ky. (est. Jan. 7, 1824; 193 sq. mi.; 1970 pop.: 5,488; 1960: 5,680; 1950: 6,157) (Taylorsville). Spear Spencer.*

Spink, S. D. (est. Jan. 8, 1873; 1,506 sq. mi.; 1970 pop.: 10,595; 1960: 11,706; 1950: 12,204) (Redfield). Solomon Lewis Spink (1831-1881). Ill. house of representatives 1864; second secretary of Dakota terr. 1865-69; del. from Dak. terr. 1869-71. -- Harlow, Dana D., Prairie Echoes, Spink County in the making, Aberdeen?, S. D., 1961; 436 p.

Spokane, Wash. (est. Jan. 29, 1858; 1,763 sq. mi.; 1970 pop.: 287,487; 1960: 278,333; 1950: 221,561) (Spokane). Indian for "chief of the sun" or "child of the sun." -- Durham, Nelson, W., History of the city of Spokane and Spokane country, Chicago: S. J. Clarke Pub. Co., 1912; 3 vol. -- Edwards, Jonathan, An illustrated history of Spokane county, W. H. Lever [n. p.], 1900; 726 p.

Spotsylvania, Va. (est. Nov. 2, 1720; 413 sq. mi.; 1970 pop.: 16,424; 1960: 13,819; 1950: 11,920) (Spotsylvania). Alexander Spotswood (1676-1740). Lt. gov. of Va. 1710-22 under George Hamilton Douglas, earl of Orkney, who never came to America; deputy postmaster gen. of American colonies 1730-39.

Stafford, Kan. (est. Feb. 26, 1867; 794 sq. mi.; 1970 pop.: 5,943; 1960: 7,451; 1950: 8,816) (St. John). Lewis Stafford (-1863). Capt. Co. E 1st Kan.; killed at Young's Point, La., Jan. 31, 1863.

Stafford, Va. (est. June 5, 1666 sess.; 271 sq. mi.; 1970: 24,587; 60: 16,9; 50: 11,9) (Stafford). Stafford County, England.

Stanislaus, Calif. (est. Apr. 1, 1854; 1,506 sq. mi.; 1970 pop.: 194,506; 1960: 157,294; 1950: 127,231) (Modesto). ("The Gateway County of the Great Joaquin Valley"; "The Land of Peaches and Cream"). Corruption of Estanislao, baptismal name of Indian chief. -- Tinkham, George Henry, History of Stanislaus County, Los Angeles: Historic Record Co., 1921; 1495 p.

Stanley, S. D. (est. Jan. 8, 1873; 1,495 sq. mi.; 1970 pop.: 2,457; 1960: 4,065; 1950: 2,055) (Fort Pierre). David Sloane Stanley (1828-1902). Graduated U. S. Military Academy 1852; commandant at Ft. Sully, S. D.; brig. gen. 1884; bvt. maj.-gen. retired 1892; gov. of U. S. Soldiers' Home, Washington, D. C. 1893-98.

Stanly, N. C. (est. Jan. 11, 1841; 399 sq. mi.; 1970 pop.: 42,822; 1960: 40,873; 1950: 37,130) (Albemarle). John

Stanly (1774-1834). N. C. house of commons 1798-99; Representative from N. C., 1801-03 and 1809-11; various terms in N. C., house of commons 1812-26.

Stanton, Kan. (est. Mar. 6, 1873, org. Mar. 5, 1887; 676 sq. mi.; 1970 pop.: 2, 287; 1960: 2, 108; 1950: 2, 263) (Johnson). Edward McMasters Stanton (1814-1869). U. S. Attorney Gen. 1860-61, U. S. Secretary of War under Pres. Lincoln 1862-65 and Pres. Johnson 1865-68, appointed Associate Justice U. S. Supreme Court, but died before taking office.

Stanton, Neb. (est. Mar. 6, 1855, org. Jan. 23, 1867; 431 sq. mi.; 1970 pop.: 5, 758; 1960: 5, 783; 1950: 6, 387) (Stanton). Edward McMasters Stanton*. (Formerly Izard County, name changed to Stanton County)

Stark, Ill. (est. Mar. 2, 1839; 290 sq. mi.; 1970 pop.: 7, 510; 1960: 8, 152; 1950: 8, 721) (Toulon). John Stark (1728-1822). Lt. in French and Indian war 1755; col. N. H. regiment 1775; fought at Bunker Hill, 1775; Bennington 1777; in command battles of Trenton, 1776; Princeton 1777; brig.-gen. 1777; commanded Northern District 1778, served until end of war.

Stark, N. D. (est. Feb. 10, 1879, org. May 25, 1882; 1, 319 sq. mi.; 1970 pop.: 19, 613; 1960: 8, 451; 1950: 16, 137) (Dickinson). George Stark. Gen. manager No. Pacific RR Co.

Stark, Ohio (est. Feb. 13, 1808, eff. Jan. 1, 1809; 580 sq. mi.; 1970 pop.: 372, 210; 1960: 340, 345; 1950: 283, 194) (Canton). John Stark*. -- Heald, Edward Thornton, History of Stark County, Canton, Ohio: Stark County Historical Society, 1963; 183 p. -- Lehman, John H., ed., A standard history of Stark County, Chicago: Lewis Pub. Co., 1916; 3 vol.

Starke, Ind. (est. Feb. 7, 1835, org. Jan. 15, 1850; 311 sq. mi.; 1970 pop.: 19, 280; 1960: 17, 911; 1950: 15, 282) (Knox) John Stark*. -- McCormick, Chester A., McCormick's guide to Starke County, Indianapolis, Ind.: Hoosier bookshop, 1962; 102 p.

Starr, Tex. (est. Feb. 10, 1848; 1, 207 sq. mi.; 1970 pop.: 17, 707; 1960: 17, 137; 1950: 13, 948) (Rio Grande City). James Harper Starr (1809-1890). Physician and surgeon; moved to Tex. 1837; pres. of board of land commissioners 1837; secretary of treasury Republic of Tex. May-Aug., 1839; Confederate agent for postal service west of Miss. River 1863.

Stearns, Minn. (est. Feb. 20, 1855, org. Mar. 3, 1855; 1, 356 sq. mi.; 1970 pop.: 95, 400; 1960: 80, 345; 1950: 70, 681) (St. Cloud). Charles Thomas Stearns (1807-

1898). Minn. terr. legislature 1853-54.

Steele, Minn. (est. Feb. 20, 1855; 425 sq. mi.; 1970 pop.: 26,931; 1960: 25,029; 1950: 21,155) (Owatonna). Franklin Steele. First board of regents, Univ. of Minn. -- Curtiss-Wedge, Franklyn, History of Rice and Steele Counties, Chicago: H. C. Cooper, Jr. and Co., 1910; 2 vol.

Steele, N.D. (est. Mar. 8, 1883, org. June 13, 1883; 710 sq. mi.; 1970 pop.: 3,749; 1960: 4,719; 1950: 5,145) (Finley). Franklin Steele. *

Stephens, Ga. (est. Aug. 18, 1905; 166 sq. mi.; 1970 pop.: 20,331; 1960: 18,391; 1950: 16,647) (Toccoa). Alexander Hamilton Stephens (1812-1883). Forty-ninth gov. of Ga. Ga. house of representatives 1836-41; Ga. senate 1842; Representative from Ga. 1843- 59; vice pres. of Confederate provisional govt. 1861; imprisoned for five months 1865; elected senator by Ga., but did not present his credentials as Ga. was not readmitted to representation 1866; Representative from Ga. 1873-82; gov. of Ga. 1882-83.

Stephens, Okla. (est. July 16, 1907; 393 sq. mi.; 1970 pop.: 35,902; 1960: 37,990; 1950: 34,071) (Duncan). John Hall Stephens (1847-1924). Tex. senate 1886-88; Representative from Tex. 1897-1917.

Stephens, Tex. (est. Jan. 22, 1858[as Buchanon Cy.]; 927 sq.mi.; 70: 8,414; 1960: 8,885; 1950: 10,597) (Breckenridge). Alexander Hamilton Stephens*. (org. Sept. 20, 1860)

Stephenson, Ill. (est. Mar. 4, 1837; 559 sq. mi.; 1970 pop.: 48,861; 1960: 46,207; 1950: 41,595) (Freeport). Benjamin Stephenson (-1822). Sheriff of Randolph County, Ill. 1809; adj. gen. of Ill. Terr. 1813; col. in two campaigns War of 1812; Delegate from Ill. Terr. 1814-1816; receiver of public moneys at land office, Edwardsville, Ill. 1816-22; Ill. constitutional committee 1818; pres. of Edwardsville bank 1819-22. -- Fulwider, Addison L., History of Stephenson County, Chicago: S. J. Clarke Pub. Co., 1910; 2 vol.

Sterling, Tex. (est. Mar. 4, 1891; 914 sq. mi.; 1970 pop.: 1,056; 1960: 1,177; 1950: 1,282) (Sterling City). W. S. Sterling (-1881). Indian fighter, dealer in buffalo hides and skins, rancher; U. S. marshal in Ariz. 1881; ambushed and killed by Apache Indians 1881.

Steuben, Ind. (est. Feb. 7, 1835; org. Jan. 18, 1837, eff. May 1, 1837; 310 sq. mi.; 1970 pop.: 20,159; 1960: 17,184; 1950: 17,087) (Angola) Friedrich Wilhelm Ludolf Gerhard Augustin von Steuben (1730-1794). Served under Frederick the Great 1756-63, came to America and became inspector gen. Continental Army, trained troops until 1784.

Steuben, N. Y. (est. Mar. 18, 1796; 1, 408 sq. mi.; 1970 pop.: 99, 546; 1960: 97, 691; 1950: 91, 439) (Bath). Friedrich Wilhelm Ludolf Gerhard Augustin von Steuben*. -- McMaster, Guy Humphrey, History of the settlement of Steuben County, Bath, N. Y.: R. S. Underhill & Co., 1853; 318 p. -- Near, Irvin W., A history of Steuben County, Chicago: Lewis Pub. Co., 1911; 2 vol.

Stevens, Kan. (est. Mar. 6, 1873, org. Aug. 3, 1886; 729 sq. mi.; 1970 pop.: 4, 198; 1960: 4, 400; 1950: 4, 516) (Hugoton). Thaddeus Stevens (1792-1868). Pa. house of representatives 1833-35, 1837 and 1841; Pa. constitutional convention 1838; Representative from Pa. 1849-53 and 1859-68. -- Thomson, Edith Campbell, History of Stevens County, Kansas, [n. p.], 1967; 165 p.

Stevens, Minn. (est. Feb. 20, 1862; 570 sq. mi.; 1970 pop.: 11, 218; 1960: 11, 262; 1950: 11, 106) (Morris). Isaac Ingalls Stevens (1818-1862). First terr. gov. of Washington. Graduated U. S. Military Academy 1839; on staff of Gen. Scott, Mexican War; organized and commanded survey of railroad route from St. Paul to Puget Sound 1853; gov. of Wash. terr. 1853-57; Delegate from Wash. Terr. 1857-61; brig. gen. and maj. gen. Civil War; killed at battle of Chantilly, Va., Sept. 1, 1862.

Stevens, Wash. (est. Jan. 20, 1863; 2, 521 sq. mi.; 1970 pop.: 17, 405; 1960: 17, 884; 1950: 18, 580) (Colville). Isaac Ingalls Stevens*.

Stewart, Ga. (est. Dec. 23, 1830; 411 sq. mi.; 1970 pop.: 6, 511; 1960: 7, 371; 1950: 9, 194) (Lumpkin). Daniel Stewart (1759-1829). Brig. gen. Continental Army. -- Terrill, Helen Eliza, History of Stewart County, Georgia, Columbus, Ga.: Columbus Office Supply Co., 1958; 735 p.

Stewart, Tenn. (est. Nov. 1, 1803; 484 sq. mi.; 1970 pop.: 7, 319; 1960: 7, 851; 1950: 9, 175) (Dover). Duncan Stewart.

Stillwater, Mont. (est. Mar. 24, 1913 petition and election; 1, 797 sq. mi.; 1970 pop.: 4, 632; 1960: 5, 526; 1950: 5, 416) (Columbus). Stillwater River, descriptive.

Stoddard, Mo. (est. Jan. 2, 1835; 837 sq. mi.; 1970 pop.: 25, 771; 1960: 29, 490; 1950: 33, 463) (Bloomfield). Amos Stoddard (1762-1813). Served in Revolutionary War 1779-83; clerk supreme court of Mass.; capt. of artillery 1798; first civil and military commandant of Upper La. 1804; maj. 1807; deputy quartermaster 1812; wounded at siege of Ft. Meigs, May 1813; died as result of wound 1813.

Stokes, N. C. (est. sess. Nov. 2, 1789; 459 sq. mi.; 1970

pop.: 23,782; 1960: 22,314; 1950: 21,520) (Danbury). John Stokes (1756-1790). Ensign 6th Va., Continental Regiment 1776; second and first lt. 1776; capt. 1778; col. wounded at Waxhaw Massacre 1780; hand amputated; exchanged May 1, 1783; U.S. judge for district N.C. 1783; N.C. senate 1786-87; N.C. house of representatives 1789; U.S. judge for district of N.C. died at Fayetteville (of fever) on way to attend his first court.

Stone, Ark. (est. Apr. 21, 1873; 610 sq. mi.; 1970 pop.: 6,838; 1960: 6,294; 1950: 7,662) (Mountain View). Descriptive.

Stone, Miss. (est. Apr. 3, 1916; 443 sq. mi.; 1970 pop.: 8,101; 1960: 7,013; 1950: 6,264) (Wiggins). John Marshall Stone (1830-1900). Thirty-first and thirty-third gov. of Miss. Capt. of rifles in Miss. inf.; wounded, advanced to col.; Miss. senate 1870-76; acting gov. of Miss. 1876-82; pres. of Miss. Agricultural and Mechanical College; gov. of Miss. 1890-96.

Stone, Mo. (est. Feb. 10, 1851; 509 sq. mi.; 1970 pop.: 9,921; 1960: 8,176; 1950: 9,748) (Galena). William Stone. Judge.

Stonewall, Tex. (est. Aug. 21, 1876; 927 sq. mi.; 1970 pop.: 2,397; 1960: 3,017; 1950: 3,679) (Aspermont). Thomas Jonathan "Stonewall" Jackson (1824-1863). Graduated U.S. Military Academy 1846; bvt. second lt. 1846; second lt., first lt. 1847; with Gen. Scott at Vera Cruz, Chapultepec and Contreras; bvt. capt. and maj. 1847; resigned 1852; prof. of artillery tactics and philosophy Va. Military Inst. 1852-61; col. Va. vol. 1861; brig. gen. and maj. gen. 1861; died as result of wounds at Chancellorsville 1863.

Storey, Nev. (est. Nov. 25, 1861; 262 sq. mi.; 1970 pop.: 695; 1960: 568; 1950: 671) (Virginia City). Edward Faris Storey (-1860). Capt. Killed in battle with Paiute Indians, Pyramid Lake, 1860.

Story, Iowa (est. Jan. 13, 1846; 568 sq. mi.; 1970 pop.: 62,783; 1960: 49,327; 1950: 44,294) (Nevada). Joseph Story (1779-1845). Mass. house of representatives 1805-07; Representative from Mass., 1808-09; associate justice U.S. Supreme Court 1811-45. -- Allen, William Gilmer, comp., A history of Story County, Iowa, Des Moines, Iowa: Iowa Printing Co., 1887; 485 p. -- Payne, William Orson, History of Story County, Chicago: S.J. Clarke Pub. Co., 1911; 2 vol.

Strafford, N.H. (est. Apr. 29, 1769; 377 sq. mi.; 1970 pop.: 70,431; 1960: 59,799; 1950: 51,567) (Dover). Strafford, England, named for Thomas Wentworth, the earl of

Strafford (1593-1641); leader in the House of Commons 1628; lord deputy of Ireland 1633-39; adviser to Charles I; impeached by Long Parliament and beheaded -- Scales, John, History of Strafford County, Chicago: Richmond-Arnold Pub. Co., 1914; 593 p.

Stutsman, N. D. (est. Jan. 4, 1873, org. June 10, 1873; 2, 274 sq. mi.; 1970 pop.: 23, 550; 1960: 25, 137; 1950: 24, 158) (Jamestown). Enos Stutsman. Dakota Council 1862-65; speaker 7th sess. 1867-68; special agent U. S. Treas. Dept.

Sublette, Wyo. (est. Feb. 15, 1921; 4, 876 sq. mi.; 1970 pop.: 3, 755; 1960: 3, 778;1950: 2, 481) (Pinedale). William Lewis Sublette (1799-1845). Organized Rocky Mountain Fur Co., with Gen. William H. Ashley's expedition 1823; organized expeditions for the Rocky Mountains 1828 and 1832; for Sante Fe 1831; built Ft. William on Laramie River 1834.

Suffolk, Mass. (est. May 10, 1643; 50 sq. mi.; 1970 pop.: 735, 190; 1960: 791, 329; 1950: 896, 615) (Boston). Suffolk County, England. -- Davis, William T., Professional and industrial history of Suffolk County, Boston: History Co., 1894; 3 vol.

Suffolk, N. Y. (est. Nov. 1, 1683; 922 sq. mi.; 1970 pop.: 1, 116, 672; 1960: 666, 784; 1950: 276, 129) (Riverhead). ("The Sunrise County (the easternmost part of New York State)"). Suffolk County, England*. -- Howell, Nathaniel R., Know Suffolk, Islip, N. Y.: Buys Bros., 1952; 181 p. -- McDermott, Charles J., Suffolk County, New York: J. H. Heineman, 1965; 86 p.

Sullivan, Ind. (est. Dec. 30, 1816, eff. Jan. 15, 1817; 457 sq. mi.; 1970 pop.: 19, 889; 1960: 21, 721; 1950: 23, 667) (Sullivan). Daniel Sullivan. -- Wolfe, Thomas Jefferson, A history of Sullivan County, Indiana, New York: Lewis Pub. Co., 1909; 2 vol.

Sullivan, Mo. (est. Feb. 14, 1845; 654 sq. mi.; 1970 pop.: 7, 572; 1960: 8, 783; 1950: 11, 299) (Milan). James Sullivan.

Sullivan, N. H. (est. July 5, 1827, eff. Sept. 1827; 537 sq. mi.; 1970 pop.: 30, 949; 1960: 29, 067; 1950: 26, 441) (Newport). John Sullivan (1740-1795). Continental Congress 1774-75; brig. gen. and maj. gen. Revolutionary War 1775-80; Continental Congress 1780-81; attorney gen. of N. H. 1782-86; Pres. of N. H. 1786-88 and 1789-90; federal constitutional convention 1787; speaker N. H. house of representatives; judge of U. S. District Court of N. H., 1789-95. -- History of Sullivan County and Claremont, N. H., [n. p.], 189?; 146 p.

Sullivan, N. Y. (est. Mar. 27, 1809, eff. Sept. 4, 1827; 986 sq. mi.; 1970 pop.: 52, 580; 1960: 45, 272; 1950: 40, 731) (Monticello). ("A Good Place to Visit and You Would Want to Live There"; "First in Second Homes"; "The County of Hunting, Fishing, Touring, Golfing, Camping, Harness-Racing and Skiing"; "The World's Fairest Vacationland"). John Sullivan*. -- Quinlan, James Eldridge, G. M. Beebe and W. T. Morgans, History of Sullivan County, Liberty, N. Y., 1873; 700 p.

Sullivan, Pa. (est. Mar. 15, 1847; 478 sq. mi.; 1970 pop.: 5, 961; 1960: 6, 251; 1950: 6, 745) (Laporte). John Sullivan*. -- Ingham, Thomas J., History of Sullivan County, Chicago: Lewis Pub. Co., 1899; 218 p.

Sullivan, Tenn. (est. sess. of Oct. 18, 1779; 428 sq. mi.; 1970 pop.: 127, 329; 1960: 114, 139; 1950: 95, 063) (Blountville). John Sullivan*. -- Taylor, Oliver, Historic Sullivan, a History of Sullivan County, Tenn., Bristol, Tenn.: King Printing Co., 1909; 330 p.

Sully, S. D. (est. Jan. 8, 1873; 1, 061 sq. mi.; 1970 pop.: 2, 362; 1960: 2, 607; 1950: 2, 713) (Onida). Alfred Sully (1821-1879). Graduated U. S. Military Academy 1841; second lt. 1841; in Sioux wars; in Seminole war; in Mexican war first lt. 1847; capt. 1852; in Civil war maj. 1862; col. Minn. inf. 1862; brig. gen. vol. 1862; bvt. gen. 1865; maj. gen. vol. 1865. -- Onida Watchman, 75 years of Sully County history, 1883-1958, Onida, S. D.: Onida Watchman, 1958; 391 p.

Summers, W. Va. (est. Feb. 27, 1871; 367 sq. mi.; 1970 pop.: 13, 213; 1960: 15, 640; 1950: 19, 183) (Hinton). George William Summers (1804-1868). Va. house of delegates 1830-32 and 1834-36; Representative from Va. 1831-45; Va. constitutional convention 1850; judge of the eighteenth judicial circuit of Va. 1852-58; Washington, D. C. peace conference 1861. -- Miller, James Henry, History of Summers County, Hinton, W. Va.: J. H. Miller, 1908; 838 p.

Summit, Colo. (est. Nov. 1, 1861; 615 sq. mi.; 1970 pop.: 2, 665; 1960: 2, 073; 1950: 1, 135) (Breckenridge). Descriptive.

Summit, Ohio (est. Mar. 3, 1840; 413 sq. mi.; 1970 pop.: 553, 371; 1960: 513, 569; 1950: 410, 032) (Akron). Descriptive. Highest elevation on Ohio canal. -- Doyle, William Barnabas, Centennial history of Summit County, Chicago: Biographical Pub. Co., 1908; 1115 p. -- Perrin, William Henry, History of Summit County, Chicago: Baskin & Battey, 1881; 1050 p.

Summit, Utah (est. Jan. 17, 1854; 1, 860 sq. mi.; 1970 pop.:

5, 879; 1960: 5, 673; 1950: 6, 745) (Coalville). Descriptive; summit of the watershed between Green River Valley (Colo. River drainage) and Salt Lake Valley (Green Basin drainage).

Sumner, Kan. (est. Feb. 26, 1867, orig. Nov. 7, 1871; 1, 183 sq.mi. ; 70: 23, 553; 1960: 25, 316; 1950: 23, 646) (Wellington). ("The Wheat Capital of the World"). Charles Sumner (1811-1874). Lecturer Harvard Law School 1835-37; Senator from Mass. 1851-74; chairman of the committee on foreign affairs 1861-71. -- Sanders, Gwendoline and Sanders, Paul, The Sumner County story, North Newton, Kan. : Mennonite Press, 1966; 190 p.

Sumner, Tenn. (est. sess. Nov. 18, 1786; 552 sq. mi. ; 1970 pop. : 56, 106; 1960: 36, 217; 1950: 33, 533) (Gallatin). Jethro Sumner (1733-1785). In French and Indian War; in Va. militia 1755-61; commanded Ft. Bedford, Va. 1760; justice of the peace N. C. 1768; sheriff 1772-77; col. of Third battalion, N. C. 1776; brig. gen. 1780-83. -- Cisco, Jay Guy, Historic Sumner County, Tenn., Nashville, Tenn. : Folk-Keelin Printing Co., 1909; 319 p. -- Durham, Walter Thomas, The great leap westward, a history of Sumner County, Tennessee, Gallatin, Tenn. : Sumner County Public Library Board, 1969; 225 p.

Sumter, Ala. (est. Dec. 18, 1832; 914 sq. mi. ; 1970 pop. : 16, 974; 1960: 20, 041; 1950: 23, 610) (Livingston). Thomas Sumter (1734-1832). Lt. col. Sixth Continental Regiment; brig. gen. of militia 1780; voted the thanks of Congress 1781; S. C. state senate 1781-82; Representative from S. C. 1789-93 and 1797-1801; Senator from S. C., 1801-10.

Sumter, Fla. (est. Jan. 8, 1853; 561 sq. mi. : 1970 pop. : 4, 839; 1960: 11, 869; 1950: 11, 330) (Bushnell). ("Live Better--Today"; "The County Where Business Is a Pleasure and Pleasure Is a Business"; "The County Where Life Is Easy, Casual and Comfortable"; "The Growing County in a Growing State"; "The Place To Locate"). Thomas Sumter*.

Sumter, Ga. (est. Dec. 26, 1831; 456 sq. mi. ; 1970 pop. : 26, 931; 1960: 24, 652; 1950: 24, 208) (Americus). Thomas Sumter*.

Sumter, S. C. (est. 1785; 689 sq.mi.; 1970: 79, 425; 1960: 74, 941; 1950: 57, 634) (Sumter). Thomas Sumter*. -- Gregorie, Anne King, History of Sumter County, Sumter, S. C. : Library Board of Sumter County, 1954; 553 p.

Sunflower, Miss. (est. Feb. 15, 1844; 674 sq. mi. ; 1970 pop. : 37, 047; 1960: 45, 750; 1950: 56, 031) (Indianola). Sunflower River, descriptive.

Surry, N. C. (est. sess. Dec. 5, 1770; 537 sq. mi. ; 1970

pop.: 51, 415; 1960: 48, 205; 1950: 45, 593) (Dobson). Lord Surry of Whig party, England, who opposed taxation. -- Hollingsworth, Jesse Gentry, History of Surry County, Greensboro, N. C.: W. H. Fisher Co., 1935; 280 p.

Surry, Va. (est. 1652; 280 sq. mi.; 1970 pop.: 5, 882; 1960: 6, 220; 1950: 6, 220) (Surry). Surrey County, England.

Susquehanna, Pa. (est. Feb. 21, 1810; 836 sq. mi.; 1970 pop.: 34, 344; 1960: 33, 137; 1950: 31, 970) (Montrose). Contraction of Indian words "sisku" for "mud" and "hanne" for "river." -- Blackman, Emily C., History of Susquehanna County, Philadelphia, 1873 (reprint 1970); 685 p.

Sussex, Del. (est. 1664; 1, 107 sq. mi.; 1970 pop.: 80, 356; 1960: 73, 195; 1950: 61, 336) (Georgetown). ("Delaware's Waking Giant"). Sussex County, England. Original tribal name of South Saxons. -- Turner, C. H. B., Some Records of Sussex County, 1909; 387 p.

Sussex, N. J. (est. May 16, 1753 sess.; 528 sq. mi.; 1970 pop.: 77, 528; 1960: 49, 255; 1950: 34, 423) (Newton). ("The Highlands of New Jersey"; "The Top of New Jersey"). Sussex county*. -- Cummings, Warren D., Sussex County, Rotary Club of Newton, N. J., 1964; 70 p. -- Snell, James P., ed., History of Sussex and Warren Counties, Philadelphia: Everts & Peck, 1881; 748 p.

Sussex, Va. (est. Feb. 27, 1752 sess.; 496 sq. mi.; 1970 pop.: 11, 464; 1960: 12, 411; 1950: 12, 785) (Sussex). Sussex county*. -- U. S. Works Progress Administration (Virginia), Sussex County, a tale of three centuries, Richmond: Whittet & Shepperson, 1942; 324 p.

Sutter, Calif. (est. Feb. 18, 1850; 607 sq. mi.; 1970 pop.: 41, 935; 1960: 33, 380; 1950: 26, 239) (Yuba City). John Augustus Sutter (1803-1880). German immigrant became Mexican citizen 1841; settled at Sacramento, Calif.; gold was discovered on his property Jan. 24, 1848; squatters seized his property and he became bankrupt; received a pension from Calif.

Sutton, Tex. (est. Apr. 1, 1887; 1, 493 sq. mi.; 1970 pop.: 3, 175; 1960: 3, 738; 1950: 3, 746) (Sonora). John S. Sutton (1821-62). Capt. in Sante Fe Expedition; lt. col. of 7th Tex. cavalry and captured at Val Verde, Tex. Feb. 21, 1862; leg was shattered and he refused amputation, and died as a result.

Suwannee, Fla. (est. Dec. 21, 1858; 677 sq. mi.; 1970 pop.: 15, 559; 1960: 14, 961; 1950: 16, 986) (Live Oak). ("Florida's Largest Tobacco Growing Center"; "The County in the Heart of the Famous Suwannee River Valley"; "The Home of the Florida Sheriffs' Boys Ranch (home for boys)"). Indian word for "sawni" meaning "echo."

Swain, N. C. (est. Feb. 24, 1871; 544 sq. mi. ; 1970 pop. : 7, 861; 1960: 8, 387; 1950: 9, 921) (Bryson City). David Lowrie Swain (1801-1868). Twenty-sixth gov. of N. C. 1832-35; pres. of the Univ. of N. C. 1835-68.

Sweet Grass, Mont. (est. Mar. 5, 1895; 1, 846 sq. mi. ; 1970 pop. : 2, 980; 1960: 3, 290; 1950: 3, 621) (Bigtimber). Descriptive.

Sweetwater, Wyo. (est. Dec. 27, 1867, org. Jan. 3, 1868; 10, 492 sq. mi. ; 1970 pop. : 18, 391; 1960: 17, 920; 1950: 22, 017) (Green River). Descriptive. (Originally Carter County, changed to Sweetwater County, Dec. 13, 1869, chap. 35).

Swift, Minn. (est. Feb. 18, 1870; 747 sq. mi. ; 1970 pop. : 13, 177; 1960: 14, 936; 1950: 15, 837) (Benson). Henry Adoniram Swift (1823-1869). Minn. senate 1862-63 and 1864-65; elected lt. gov. of Minn. served for gov. Alexander Ramsey who resigned 1863-64; Register, U. S. Land Office 1865-69.

Swisher, Tex. (est. Aug. 21, 1876; 888 sq. mi. ; 1970 pop.: 10, 373; 1960: 10, 607; 1950: 8, 249) (Tulia). James Gibson Swisher (1795-1864). Surveyor, private Tenn. militia 1813-14; private U. S. mounted rangers 1814-15; capt. of vol. company at Bexar 1835; resigned from army 1836; in William W. Hill's Ranger Co. 1836; signer Tex. Declaration of Independence 1836.

Switzerland, Ind. (est. Sept. 7, 1814; eff. Oct. 1, 1814; 221 sq. mi. ; 1970 pop. : 6, 307; 1960: 7, 092; 1950: 7, 599) (Vevay). Switzerland. -- Dufour, Perret, Swiss settlement of Switzerland County, Indiana, Indiana Historical Commission, 1925; 446 p.

T

Talbot, Ga. (est. Dec. 14, 1827; 312 sq. mi. ; 1970 pop. : 6, 625; 1960: 7, 127; 1950: 7, 687) (Talbotton). Matthew Talbot (1762-1827). Twenty-eighth gov. of Ga. ; member Ga. constitutional convention 1798; Ga. state senate 1808; pres. Ga. senate 1818-23; ex officio gov. of Ga. 1819.

Talbot, Md. (est. Feb. 18, 1661-2; 279 sq. mi. ; 1970 pop.: 23, 682; 1960: 21, 578; 1950: 19, 428) (Easton). Grace Talbot. Daughter of George, the first Lord Baltimore; sister of Cecilius, the second Lord Baltimore. -- Tilghman, Oswald, comp. , History of Talbot County, Maryland, 1661-1861, Baltimore, Md. : Williams & Wilkins Co. , 1915; 2 vol.

Taliaferro, Ga. (est. Dec. 24, 1825; 212 sq. mi.; 1970 pop.: 2,423; 1960: 3,370; 1950: 4,515) (Crawfordville). Benjamin Taliaferro (1750-1821). In Revolutionary War, lt. in rifle corps of Gen. Morgan; promoted to capt.; captured by the British at Charleston, S. C., 1780; pres. Ga. state senate; delegate Ga. state constitutional convention 1798; Representative from Ga., 1799-1802; judge of the superior court.

Talladega, Ala. (est. Dec. 18, 1832; 750 sq. mi.: 1970 pop.: 65,280; 1960: 65,495; 1950: 63,639) (Talladega). Muscogee Indian words for "hill-town" or "border-town."

Tallahatchie, Miss. (est. Dec. 23, 1833; 629 sq. mi.; 1970 pop.: 19,338; 1960: 24,081; 1950: 30,486) (Charleston and Sumner). Indian word for "rock river."

Tallapoosa, Ala. (est. Dec. 18, 1832; 711 sq. mi.; 1970 pop.: 33,840; 1960: 35,007; 1950: 35,074) (Dadeville). Indian word for "swift current" or "stranger" or "newcomer."

Tama, Iowa (est. Feb. 17, 1843; org. Jan. 22, 1853; 720 sq. mi.; 1970 pop.: 20,147; 1960: 21,413; 1950: 21,688) (Toledo). Taomah, wife of Poweshiek. -- Caldwell, John R., A history of Tama County, Chicago: Lewis Pub. Co., 1910; 2 vol.

Taney, Mo. (est. Jan. 6, 1837; 656 sq. mi.; 1970 pop.: 13,023; 1960: 10,238; 1950: 9,863) (Forsyth). Roger Brooke Taney (1777-1864). U. S. Attorney Gen. 1831-33; U. S. Secretary of the Treas. 1833-34 but not confirmed by the Senate; Chief Justice of the Supreme Court 1836-64.

Tangipahoa, La. (est. Mar. 6, 1869; 790 sq. mi.; 1970 pop.: 65,873; 1960: 59,434; 1950: 53,218) (Amite). Tangipahoa Indian tribe, Indian name meaning "those who gather maize stalks."

Taos, N. M. (est. Jan. 9, 1852; 2,256 sq. mi.; 1970 pop.: 17,516; 1960: 15,934; 1950: 17,146) (Taos). Taos Indian tribe.

Tarrant, Tex. (est. Dec. 20, 1849; 877 sq. mi.; 1970 pop.: 716,317; 1960: 538,495; 1950: 361,253) (Fort Worth). Edward H. Tarrant (1796-1858). Fought Indians, at battle of New Orleans 1815; joined Tex. Rangers 1835; Tex. congress 1837-38; brig. gen. 1841; Tex. constitutional convention 1845; Tex. legislature 1846.

Tate, Miss. (est. Apr. 15, 1873; 400 sq. mi.; 1970 pop.: 18,544; 1960: 18,138; 1950: 18,011) (Senatobia). T. S. Tate.

Tattnall, Ga. (est. Dec. 5, 1801; 466 sq. mi.; 1970 pop.: 16,557; 1960: 15,837; 1950: 15,939) (Reidsville). Josiah

Tattnall (1764-1803). Twenty-first gov. of Ga. In Revolutionary War under Gen. Anthony Wayne 1782; col. of Ga. regiment promoted to brig. gen. 1801; Ga. house of representatives 1795 and 1796; Senator from Ga. 1796-99; gov. of Ga. 1801-02.

Taylor, Fla. (est. Dec. 23, 1856; 1,032 sq. mi.; 1970 pop.: 13,641; 1960: 13,168; 1950: 10,416) (Perry). Zachary Taylor. Twelfth pres. of the U. S. 1849-50. (1784-1850).

Taylor, Ga. (est. Jan. 15, 1852; 340 sq. mi.; 1970 pop.: 7,865; 1960: 8,311; 1950: 9,113) (Butler). Zachary Taylor*.

Taylor, Iowa (est. Feb. 24, 1847; 528 sq. mi.; 1970 pop.: 8,790; 1960: 10,288; 1950: 12,420) (Bedford). Zachary Taylor*.

Taylor, Ky. (est. Jan. 13, 1848; 284 sq. mi.; 1970 pop.: 17,138; 1960: 16,285; 1950: 14,403) (Campbellsville). Zachary Taylor*.

Taylor, Tex. (est. Feb. 1, 1858; 913 sq. mi.; 1970 pop.: 97,853; 1960: 101,078; 1950: 63,370) (Abilene) Edward Taylor. Member of Robertson's colony, settled at Belton.

Taylor, W. Va. (est. Jan. 19, 1844; 177 sq. mi.; 1970 pop.: 13,878; 1960: 15,010; 1950: 18,422) (Grafton). John Taylor (1754-1824). Served in Revolutionary War as maj. and col. member of Va. House of Delegates 1779-85 and 1796-1800; lt. col. in Gen. Alexander Spotswood's Legionary Corps; Senator from Va. 1792-94, 1803 and 1822-24.

Taylor, Wis. (est. Mar. 4, 1875; 979 sq. mi.; 1970 pop.: 16,958; 1960: 17,843; 1950: 18,456) (Medford). William Robert Taylor (1820-1909). Eleventh gov. of Wis. 1874-76.

Tazewell, Ill. (est. Jan. 31, 1827; 647 sq. mi.; 1970 pop.: 118,649; 1960: 99,789; 1950: 76,165) (Pekin). Littleton Waller Tazewell (1774-1860). Twenty-seventh gov. of Va. (Commonwealth). Va. house of delegates 1796-1800 and 1816; Representative from Va., 1800-01; Senator from Va. 1824-32; gov. of Va. 1834-36.

Tazewell, Va. (est. Dec. 17, 1799; 522 sq. mi.; 1970 pop.: 39,816; 1960: 44,791; 1950: 47,512) (Tazewell) Henry Tazewell (1753-1799). Va. house of burgesses 1775, delegate to Va. state constitutional convention 1775-76, judge of the Va. supreme court 1785-93 and chief justice 1785-93, judge of the Va. high court of appeals 1793, Senator 1794-99. -- Harman, John Newton, Annals of Tazewell County, Richmond: W. C. Hill Printing Co., 1922-25; 2 vol. -- Pendleton, William Cecil, History of Tazewell County, Richmond, Va.: Hill Printing Co., 1920; 700 p.

Tehama, Calif. (est. Apr. 9, 1856; 2, 974 sq. mi. ; 1970 pop. : 29, 517; 1960: 25, 305; 1950: 19, 276) (Red Bluff). Tehama Indian tribe.

Telfair, Ga. (est. Dec. 10, 1807; 373 sq. mi. ; 1970 pop. : 11, 381; 1960: 11, 715; 1950: 13, 221) (Mc Rae) Edward Telfair (1735-1791). Twelfth and sixteenth gov. of Ga. Member of Ga. council of safety in 1775 and 1776, delegate to the Provincial Congress at Savannah in 1776; member of the Continental Congress 1777-79 and 1780-83; one of the signers of the Articles of Confederation and delegate to Constitutional convention; gov. of Ga. in 1786 and 1790-93.

Teller, Colo. (est. Mar. 23, 1899; 554 sq. mi. ; 1970 pop.: 3, 316; 1960: 2, 495; 1950: 2, 754) (Cripple Creek). Henry Moore Teller (1830-1914). Maj. gen. Colo. militia 1862-64; Senator from Colo. 1876-82; U. S. Secretary of the Interior in cabinet of Pres. Arthur 1882-85; Senator from Colo., 1885-1909.

Tensas, La. (est. Mar. 17, 1843; 632 sq. mi. ; 1970 pop. : 9, 732; 1960: 11, 796; 1950: 13, 209) (St. Joseph). Tensas Indian tribe.

Terrebonne, La. (est. Mar. 22, 1822; 1, 756 sq. mi. ; 1970 pop. : 76, 049; 1960: 60, 771; 1950: 43, 328) (Houma). French for "good land."

Terrell, Ga. (est. Feb. 16, 1856; 322 sq. mi. ; 1970 pop. : 11, 416; 1960: 12, 742; 1950: 14, 314) (Dawson). William Terrell (1778-1855). Physician, Ga. house of representatives 1810-13; Representative from Ga. 1817-21.

Terrell, Tex. (est. Apr. 8, 1905; 2, 388 sq. mi. ; 1970 pop. : 1, 940; 1960: 1, 600; 1950: 3, 189) (Sanderson). Alexander Watkins Terrell (1827-1912). Moved to Tex. 1852; judge of Second judicial district 1857-62; lt. col. 34th Tex. cavalry 1863; col. ; fought at Mansfield, Pleasant Hill, Jenkin's Ferry; brig. gen. 1865; fled to Mexico 1866; served under Emperor Maximilian; Tex. state legislature 1875-82; U. S. Minister Plenipotentiary to Turkey 1893-97.

Terry, Tex. (est. Aug. 21, 1876; 898 sq. mi. ; 1970 pop. : 14, 118; 1960: 16, 286; 1950: 13, 107) (Brownfield). Benjamin Franklin Terry (1821-1861). Col. 8th Tex. Cavalry; delegate to secession convention 1861; fought at battle of Manassas; killed near Woodsonville, Ky. Dec. 17, 1861. -- Terry County Historical Survey Committee, Early settlers of Terry, a history of Terry County, Hereford, Texas: Pioneer Book Publishers, 1968; 118 p.

Teton, Idaho (est. Jan. 26, 1915; 459 sq. mi. ; 1970 pop. : 2, 351; 1960: 2, 639; 1950: 3, 204) (Driggs). Teton Indian tribe, name meaning "prairie dwellers."

Teton, Mont. (est. Feb. 7, 1893; 2, 294 sq. mi.; 1970 pop.: 6, 116; 1960: 7, 295; 1950: 7, 232) (Choteau). Teton Indian tribe; Indian name "tee win-ot" meaning "three pinnacles" or "three breasts."

Teton, Wyo. (est. Feb. 15, 1921; 2, 815 sq. mi.; 1970 pop.: 4, 823; 1960: 3, 062; 1950: 2, 593) (Jackson). ("The Last of the Old West"). Teton Indian tribe*.

Texas, Mo. (est. Feb. 17, 1843; 1, 183 sq. mi.; 1970 pop.: 18, 320; 1960: 17, 758; 1950: 18, 992) (Houston). Republic of Texas. (Formerly Ashley County, name changed to Texas County, Feb. 14, 1845, unnumbered).

Texas, Okla. (est. July 16, 1907; 2, 056 sq. mi.; 1970 pop.: 16, 352; 1960: 14, 162; 1950: 14, 235) (Guymon). Texas*.

Thayer, Neb. (est. Jan. 26, 1856, org. Dec. 30, 1871; 577 sq. mi.; 1970 pop.: 7, 779; 1960: 9, 118; 1950: 10, 563) (Hebron). John Milton Thayer (1820-1906). Second gov. of Wyo. terr. and sixth and eighth gov. of Neb. Brig. gen. and maj. gen. 1855-61; captured Pawnee Indians 1859; Neb. terr. senate 1860; Neb. constitutional convention 1860; col. First Regiment Neb. vol. inf. 1861; brig. gen. 1862; bvt. maj. gen. of vol. 1865; Neb. constitutional convention 1866; Senator from Neb. 1867-71; gov. of Wyo. terr. 1875-78; gov. of Neb. 1887-91 and 1891-92. (Formerly Jefferson County, name changed to Thayer County, Mar. 1, 1871).

Thomas, Ga. (est. Dec. 23, 1825; 530 sq. mi.; 1970 pop.: 34, 515; 1960: 34, 319; 1950: 33, 932) (Thomasville). Jett Thomas (1776-1817). Capt. of artillery under Gen. John Floyd; maj. gen. Ga. militia; built state capitol at Milledgeville, Ga., 1807. -- MacIntyre, William Irwin, <u>History of Thomas County, Georgia,</u> Thomasville, Ga., 1923.

Thomas, Kan. (est. Mar. 6, 1873, org. Oct. 8, 1885; 1, 070 sq. mi.; 1970 pop.: 7, 501; 1960: 7, 358; 1950: 7, 572) (Colby). George Henry Thomas (1816-1870). Graduated U. S. Military Academy 1840; second lt. 1840; first lt. 1844; capt. 1853; maj. 1855; lt. col. and col. 1861; brig. gen. and maj. gen. of vol. 1861; brig. gen. U. S. Army 1863; maj. gen. U. S. Army 1864; received thanks of Congress on Mar. 3, 1865 for driving Gen. Hood out of Tenn.

Thomas, Neb. (est. Mar. 31, 1887, org. Oct. 7, 1887; 716 sq. mi.; 1970 pop.: 954; 1960: 1, 078; 1950: 1, 206) (Thedford). George Henry Thomas*.

Throckmorton, Tex. (est. Jan. 13, 1858; 913 sq. mi.; 1970 pop.: 2, 205; 1960: 2, 767; 1950: 3, 618) (Throckmorton).

William Edward Throckmorton (1795-1843). Physician, father of gov. James Webb Throckmorton.

Thurston, Neb. (est. Mar. 28, 1889, org. Apr. 1, 1889; 390 sq. mi.; 1970 pop.: 6, 942; 1960: 7, 237; 1950: 8, 590) (Pender). John Mellen Thurston (1847-1916). Omaha, Neb., city council 1872-74; Omaha city attorney 1874-77; Neb. house of representatives 1875-77; Senator from Neb. 1895-1901.

Thurston, Wash. (est. Jan. 12, 1852; 719 sq. mi.; 1970 pop.: 76, 894; 1960: 55, 049; 1950: 44, 884) (Olympia). Samuel Royal Thurston (1816-1851). Delegate from Ore. terr. 1849-51; editor of Iowa "Gazette;" died while at sea en route to his home from Washington, D. C.

Tift, Ga. (est. Aug. 17, 1905; 243 sq. mi.; 1970 pop.: 27, 288; 1960: 23, 487; 1950: 22, 645) (Tifton). Nelson Tift (1810-1877). Founded Augusta, Ga. guards 1835; Baker County inferior court 1840-41 and 1849; col. militia Baker County 1840; Ga. house of representatives 1841, 1847, 1851-52; editor Albany "Patriot" 1845-58; capt. in Confederate Navy 1861; Representative from Ga. 1868-69. -- Williams, Ida Belle (ed.), History of Tift County, Macon, Ga.: J. W. Burke Co., 1948; 503 p.

Tillamook, Ore. (est. Dec. 15, 1853; 1, 115 sq. mi.; 1970 pop.: 17, 930; 1960: 18, 955; 1950: 18, 606) (Tillamook). ("The Land of Trees, Cheese and Ocean Breeze"). Tillamook Indian tribe, originally spelled Killamook.

Tillman, Okla. (est. July 16, 1907; 861 sq. mi.; 1970 pop.: 12, 901; 1960: 14, 654; 1950: 17, 598) (Frederick). Benjamin Ryan Tillman (1847-1918). Sixtieth gov. of S. C. Gov. of S. C. 1890-94; founded Clemson Agricultural and Mechanical College 1893; S. C. constitutional convention 1895; Senator from S. C. 1895-1918.

Tioga, N. Y. (est. Feb. 16, 1791; 525 sq. mi.; 1970 pop.: 46, 513; 1960: 37, 802; 1950: 30, 166) (Owego). Indian tribe, meaning "at the forks." -- Peirce, H. B. and Hurd, D. Hamilton, History of Tioga, Chemung, Tompkins and Schuyler Counties, Philadelphia: Everts & Ensign, 1879; 735 p. -- Kingman, Leroy Wilson, Our county and its people, Elmira, N. Y.: W. A. Fergussen & Co., 1897; 2 vol. in 1.

Tioga, Pa. (est. Mar. 26, 1804; 1, 150 sq. mi.; 1970 pop.: 39, 691; 1960: 36, 614; 1950: 35, 474) (Wellsboro). Indian tribe*. -- Brown, R. C., History of Tioga County, Harrisburg?, Pa.: R. C. Brown & Co., 1897; 1186 p.

Tippah, Miss. (est. Feb. 9, 1836; 446 sq. mi.; 1970 pop.: 15, 852; 1960: 15, 093; 1950: 17, 522) (Ripley). Tippah name meaning "cut-off". Wife of Chickasaw Indian chief.

Tippecanoe, Ind. (est. Jan. 20, 1826, eff. Mar. 1, 1826; 501 sq. mi.; 1970 pop.: 109,378; 1960: 89,122; 1950: 74,473) (Lafayette). Indian word for "at the great clearing" or "buffalo-fish" or "long-lipped pike." -- De Hart, Richard P., Past and present of Tippecanoe County Indianapolis, B. F. Bowen & Co., 1909; 2 vol.

Tipton, Ind. (est. Jan. 15, 1844, org. Jan. 15, 1844, eff. May 1, 1844; 261 sq. mi.; 1970 pop.: 16,650; 1960: 15,856; 1950: 15,566) (Tipton). John Tipton (1786-1839). Served with the "Yellow Jackets" in the Tippecanoe campaign; brig. gen. of militia; sheriff of Harrison County, Ind., 1815-19; Ind. house of representatives 1819-23; Senator from Ind. 1832-39.

Tipton, Tenn. (est. Oct. 29, 1823; 458 sq. mi.; 1970 pop.: 28,001; 1960: 28,564; 1950: 29,782) (Covington). Jacob Tipton (-1791). Served under Gen. Arthur St. Clair; killed in battle with Indians Nov. 4, 1791.

Tishomingo, Miss. (est. Feb. 9, 1836; 428 sq. mi.; 1970 pop.: 14,940; 1960: 13,889; 1950: 15,544) (Iuka). Tishomingo. Chief of Chickasaw Indians, name means "warrior chief."

Titus, Tex. (est. May 11, 1846; 418 sq. mi.; 1970 pop.: 16,702; 1960: 16,785; 1950: 17,302) (Mount Pleasant). Andrew Jackson Titus (1823-1855). Mexican War; Tex. legislature 1851-52. -- Russell, Traylor, History of Titus County, Texas, Waco, Texas: W. M. Morrison, 1965-66; 2 vol.

Todd, Ky. (est. Dec. 30, 1819; 377 sq. mi.; 1970 pop.: 10,823; 1960: 11,364; 1950: 12,890) (Elkton). John Todd. Col.

Todd, Minn. (est. Feb. 20, 1855, org. Mar. 1, 1856; 947 sq. mi.; 1970 pop.: 22,114; 1960: 23,119; 1950: 25,420) (Long Prairie). John Blair Smith Todd (1814-1872). Graduated U. S. Military Academy 1837; capt. 1843; Seminole wars 1837-42; siege of Vera Cruz; battle of Cerro Gordo; commander Ft. Ripley, Minn. 1849-56; Indian trader in Dakota 1856-61; brig. gen. of vol. 1861-62; Delegate from Dakota terr. 1861-63 and 1864-65; Dakota terr. legislature and speaker of the house 1866-67. -- Fuller, Clara K., History of Morrison and Todd counties, Indianapolis: B. F. Bowen & Co., Inc., 1915; 2 vol.

Todd, S. D. (est. Mar. 9, 1909; 1,388 sq. mi.; 1970 pop.: 6,606; 1960: 4,661; 1950: 4,758) (attached to Tripp County for governmental purposes). John Blair Smith Todd*.

Tolland, Conn. (est. Oct. 13, 1785 sess.; 416 sq. mi.; 1970 pop.: 103,440; 1960: 68,737; 1950: 44,709) (no county seat). Tolland, England in Somerset County. -- History of Tolland County, New York City: W.W. Preston & Co., 1888; 992 p.

Tom Green, Tex. (est. Mar. 13, 1874; 1,543 sq. mi.; 1970 pop.: 71,047; 1960: 64,630; 1950: 58,929) (San Angelo). Thomas Green (1814-1864). Emigrated to Tex. 1835; Tex. Army 1836; private, battle of San Jacinto 1836; asst. adj. gen. 1836; capt. Mexican war; brig. gen. Confederate army; killed at battle of Blairs Landing, La., Apr. 12, 1864.

Tompkins, N.Y. (est. Apr. 7, 1817; 491 sq. mi.; 1970 pop.: 76,879; 1960: 66,164; 1950: 59,122) (Ithaca). ("The Gateway to the Finger Lakes"). Daniel D. Tompkins (1774-1825). Fifth gov. of N.Y. N.Y. constitutional convention 1801; associate justice N.Y., supreme court 1804-07; gov. of N.Y. 1807-17; Vice Pres. of the U.S. 1817-25; N.Y. constitutional convention 1821. -- Selkreg, John H., ed., Landmarks of Tompkins County, Syracuse, N.Y.: 1894.

Tooele, Utah (est. Mar. 3, 1852; 6,911 sq. mi.; 1970 pop.: 21,545; 1960: 17,868; 1950: 14,636) (Tooele). Tuilla. Indian chief; also corruption of Spanish word "tule" for "rushes;" also contraction of Mattuglio Valley, Europe; also Indian word "tuilla" for "a species of flower." -- Daughters of Utah Pioneers, History of Tooele County, Salt Lake City, Utah, 1961; 668 p.

Toole, Mont. (est. May 7, 1914, petition and election; 1,965 sq. mi.; 1970 pop.: 5,839; 1960: 7,904; 1950: 6,867) (Shelby). Joseph Kemp Toole (1851-1929). First and fourth gov. of Mont.; district attorney Lewis and Clark Co., 1872-76; Mont. terr. legislature 1879-81; member and pres. Mont. terr. council 1881-83; Mont. constitutional convention 1884 and 1889; Delegate from Mont. 1885-89; gov. of Mont. 1889-93 and 1901-08.

Toombs, Ga. (est. Aug. 18, 1905; 393 sq. mi.; 1970 pop.: 19,151; 1960: 16,837; 1950: 17,382) (Lyons). Robert Toombs (1810-1885). Commanded a company in Creek War serving under Gen. Scott 1836; Ga. house of representatives 1837-40 and 1841-44; Representative from Ga. 1845-53; Senator from Ga. 1853-61; Confederate provisional congress; secretary of state of the Confederate States; brig. gen. Confederate army.

Torrance, N.M. (est. Mar. 16, 1903; 3,340 sq. mi.; 1970 pop.: 5,290; 1960: 6,497; 1950: 8,012) (Estancia). Francis J. Torrance. Promoter N.M. Central RR.

Towner, N.D. (est. Mar. 8, 1883, org. Jan. 24, 1824; 1,044 sq. mi.; 1970 pop.: 4,645; 1960: 5,624; 1950: 6,300)

(Cando). O. M. Towner.

Towns, Ga. (est. Mar. 6, 1856; 181 sq. mi.; 1970 pop.: 4,565; 1960: 4,538; 1950: 4,803) (Hiawassee). George Washington Bonaparte Towns (1801-1854). Thirty-eighth gov. of Ga. Ga. house of representatives 1829-30; Ga. senate 1832-34; Representative from Ga. 1835-36; 1837-39 and 1846-47; gov. of Ga. 1847-51.

Traill, N.D. (est. Jan. 12, 1875, org. Feb. 23, 1875; 861 sq. mi.; 1970 pop.: 9,571; 1960: 10,583; 1950: 11,359) (Hillsboro). Walter Traill.

Transylvania, N.C. (est. Feb. 15, 1861; 379 sq. mi.; 1970 pop.: 19,713; 1960: 16,372; 1950: 15,194) (Brevard). Latin derivation "trans" for "across" and "sylva" for "woods" for "beyond the woods."

Traverse, Minn. (est. Feb. 20, 1862; 572 sq. mi.; 1970 pop.: 6,254; 1960: 7,503; 1950: 8,053) (Wheaton). French translation "lac travers" from Indian words meaning "lake lying crosswise."

Travis, Tex. (est. Jan. 25, 1840; 1,015 sq. mi.; 1970 pop.: 295,516; 1960: 212,136; 1950: 160,980) (Austin). William Barret Travis (1809-1836). Emigrated to Tex. 1830; maj. of artillery 1835; lt. col. of cavalry 1835; led expedition to disarm Mexicans sent by Santa Anna to regarrison fort at Anahuac 1835; when Bowie was stricken at the Alamo, he commanded the regulars and the vol. March 6, 1836. -- Barkley, Mary (Starr), History of Travis County and Austin, Austin?, Texas, 1963; 388 p.

Treasure, Mont. (est. Feb. 7, 1919; 984 sq. mi.; 1970 pop.: 1,069; 1960: 1,345; 1950: 1,402) (Hysham). Descriptive.

Trego, Kan. (est. Feb. 26, 1867; 901 sq. mi.; 1970 pop.: 4,436; 1960: 5,473; 1950: 5,868) (Wakeeney). Edward P. Trego (-1863). Capt. Co. H, 8th Kan., killed at Chickamauga Sept. 19, 1863.

Trempealeau, Wis. (est. Jan. 27, 1854; 739 sq. mi.; 1970 pop.: 23,344; 1960: 23,377; 1950: 23,730) (Whitehall). French translation "la montagne qui trempe a l'eau" meaning "the mountain that is steeped in water."

Treutlen, Ga. (est. Aug. 21, 1917; 262 sq. mi.; 1970 pop.: 5,647; 1960: 5,874; 1950: 6,522) (Soperton). John Adam Treutlen (-1783). First gov. of Ga. under the constitution. Provincial Congress 1775; gov. of Ga. 1777-78.

Trigg, Ky. (est. Jan. 27, 1820; 466 sq. mi.; 1970 pop.: 8,620; 1960: 8,870: 1950: 9,683) (Cadiz). Stephen Trigg (-1782). Emigrated to Ky. from Va. 1779; court of land commissioners 1779-80; col., killed fighting Indians at battle of Blue Licks Aug. 19, 1782.

Trimble, Ky. (est. Feb. 9, 1837; 146 sq. mi.; 1970 pop.:

5, 349; 1960: 5, 102; 1950: 5, 148) (Bedford). Robert Trimble (1777-1828). Member Ky. legislature 1803; judge of Ky. Court of Appeals 1808; chief justice of Ky. 1810; district judge in Ky. 1816-26; assoc. justice U. S. Supreme Court 1826-28.

Trinity, Calif. (est. Feb. 18, 1850; 3, 191 sq. mi.; 1970 pop.: 7, 615; 1960: 9, 706; 1950: 5, 087) (Weaverville). Trinity Sunday, the day it was discovered by the Spaniards.

Trinity, Tex. (est. Feb. 11, 1850; 704 sq. mi.; 1970 pop.: 7, 628; 1960: 7, 539; 1950: 10, 040) (Groveton). The Trinity, the union of three persons, the Father, the Son and the Holy Ghost into one godhead.

Tripp, S. D. (est. Jan. 8, 1873; 1, 620 sq. mi.; 1970 pop.: 8, 171; 1960: 8, 761; 1950: 9, 139) (Winner). Bartlett Tripp (1842-1911). Pres. of the convention that drafted the constitution of S. D. 1883; 6th chief justice of the Dakota terr. 1886-89. U. S. Minister to Austria-Hungary 1893.

Troup, Ga. (est. Dec. 11, 1826, org. Dec. 24, 1827; 435 sq. mi.; 1970 pop.: 44, 466; 1960: 47, 189; 1950: 49, 841) (La Grange). George Michael Troup (1780-1856). Thirtieth gov. of Ga. Ga. house of representatives 1803-05; Representative from Ga. 1807-15; Senator from Ga. 1816-18; Gov. of Ga. 1823-27; Senator from Ga., 1829-33. -- Smith, Clifford Lewis, History of Troup County, Atlanta, Ga.: Foote & Davies Co., 1935; 323 p.

Trousdale, Tenn. (est. June 21, 1870; 116 sq. mi.; 1970 pop.: 5, 155; 1960: 4, 914; 1950: 5, 520) (Hartsville). William Trousdale (1790-1872). Fifteenth gov. of Tenn. Creek war battles of Tallahatchee and Talladega 1813; lt. under Gen. Jackson at Pensacola and New Orleans 1815; Tenn. legislature 1835; maj. gen. of vol. 1836; Seminole War, Fla. 1836; in Mexican War at Contreras, Churubusco, Molino del Rey; wounded twice at Chapultepec, Mexico; bvt. brig. gen. U. S. Regular Army; gov. of Tenn. 1849-51; U. S. Minister to Brazil 1852-57.

Trumbull, Ohio (est. July 10, 1800; 630 sq. mi.; 1970 pop.: 232, 579; 1960: 208, 526; 1950: 158, 915) (Warren). Jonathan Trumbull (1740-1809). Colonial and state gov. of Conn. Conn. legislature; paymaster Continental Army 1776-80; secretary and aide-de-camp to Gen. George Washington 1780-83; Representative from Conn., 1789-95; Senator from Conn., 1795-96; lt. gov. of Conn., 1796-97; colonial gov. of Conn., 1769-76; state gov. 1776-84 and 1798-1809. -- Upton, Harriet Taylor, A twentieth century history of Trumbull county, Chicago: Lewis Pub. Co., 1909; 2 vol. -- History of Trumbull and Mahoning counties, Cleveland, Ohio: H. Z. Williams & Brother, 1882; 2 vol.

Tucker, W. Va. (est. Mar. 7, 1856; 421 sq. mi.; 1970 pop.: 7,447; 1960: 7,750; 1950: 10,600) (Parsons). Henry St. George Tucker (1780-1848). Cavalry capt. 1812; Representative from Va. 1815-19; chancellor of the fourth judicial district of Va., 1824-31; pres. of the court of appeals of Va., 1831-41; prof. of law Univ. of Va., 1841-45; wrote several textbooks. -- Fansler, Homer Floyd, History of Tucker County, Parsons, W. Va.: McClain Printing Co., 1962; 702 p.

Tulare, Calif. (est. Apr. 20, 1852; 4,845 sq. mi.; 1970 pop.: 188,322; 1960: 168,403; 1950: 149,264) (Visalia). ("The County in the Garden of the Sun"). "Los Tules" named by Commandante Fages in 1773 from Aztec "tullin" for "cat-tail" or similar plants with sword-like leaves. -- Menefee, Eugene L. and F. A. Dodge, History of Tulare and Kings counties, Los Angeles: Historic Record Co., 1913; 890 p. -- Small, Kathleen Edwards, History of Tulare County, Chicago: S. J. Clarke Pub. Co., 1926; 2 vol.

Tulsa, Okla. (est. July 16, 1907; 572 sq. mi.; 1970 pop.: 401,603; 1960: 346,038; 1950: 251,686) (Tulsa). "Tulwa" Creek name for "town."

Tunica, Miss. (est. Feb. 9, 1836; 418 sq. mi.; 1970 pop.: 11,854; 1960: 16,826; 1950: 21,664) (Tunica). Tunica Indians.

Tuolumne, Calif. (est. Feb. 18, 1850; 2,275 sq. mi.; 1970 pop.: 22,169; 1960: 14,404; 1950: 12,584) (Sonora). ("The Home of Columbia 'Gem' of the Southern Mines"). Tualamme Indian tribe whose name means "group of stone huts" or "collection of wigwams." -- Stoddard, Thomas Robertson, Annals of Tuolumne County, Sonora, Calif.: Mother Lode Press, 1963; 188 p.

Turner, Ga. (est. Aug. 18, 1905, eff. Jan. 1, 1906; 231 sq.mi.; 1970: 8,790; 1960: 8,439; 1950: 10,479) (Ashburn). Henry Gray Turner (1839-1904). Private Confederate Army 1861; advanced to capt.; wounded battle of Gettysburg; Ga. house of representatives; 1874-76, 1878 and 1879; Representative from Ga., 1881-97; associate justice Ga. supreme court 1903. -- Pate, John Ben, History of Turner county, Atlanta, Ga.: Stein Printing Co., 1933; 198 p.

Turner, S. D. (est. Jan. 13, 1871; 611 sq. mi.; 1970 pop.: 9,872; 1960: 11,159; 1950: 12,100) (Parker). John W. Turner (1800-1883). Pioneer; Mich. gen. assembly 1851; sheriff Saginaw county; Dakota terr. legislature 1865-66 and 1872; supt. of public instruction 1870-71.

Tuscaloosa, Ala. (est. Feb. 6, 1818; 1,340 sq. mi.; 1970 pop.: 116,029; 1960: 109,047; 1950: 94,092) (Tuscaloosa).

Tuscaloosa. Indian chief whose name means "black warrior."

Tuscarawas, Ohio (est. Feb. 13, 1808, eff. Mar. 15, 1808; 571 sq. mi.; 1970 pop.: 77,211; 1960: 76,789; 1950: 70,320) (New Philadelphia). Indian word for "open mouth." -- The history of Tuscarawas County, Chicago: Warner Beers & Co., 1884; 1007 p.

Tuscola, Mich. (est. Apr. 1, 1840, org. 1850; 816 sq. mi.; 1970 pop.: 48,603; 1960: 43,305; 1950: 38,258) (Caro). Coined word for "level place."

Twiggs, Ga. (est. Dec. 14, 1809; 314 sq. mi.; 1970 pop.: 8,222; 1960: 7,935; 1950: 8,308) (Jeffersonville). John Twiggs. Maj. gen. 1781; aide of Gen. Greene; commissioner to negotiate treaty with the Creek Indians 1783. -- Faulk, Lanette (O'Neal), History of Twiggs County, Georgia, Jeffersonville, Ga.: Daughters of the American Revolution, 1960.

Twin Falls, Idaho (est. Feb. 21, 1907; 1,942 sq. mi.; 1970 pop.: 41,807; 1960: 41,842; 1950: 40,979) (Twin Falls). Descriptive; Twin Falls or Little Falls of the Snake River.

Tyler, Tex. (est. Apr. 3, 1846; 927 sq. mi.; 1970 pop.: 12,417; 1960: 10,666; 1950: 11,292) (Woodville). John Tyler (1790-1862). Tenth Pres. of the U.S.; fifteenth gov. of Va. (Commonwealth). Capt. of military company 1813; Va. house of delegates 1811-16; council of states 1816; Representative from Va. 1817-21; Va. house of delegates 1823-25; gov. of Va. 1825-27; Senator from Va. 1827-36; Va. constitutional convention 1829-30; vice pres. of the U.S. 1841; Pres. of the U.S., 1841-45; delegate to peace conference 1861; Confederate provisional congress 1861.

Tyler, W. Va. (est. Dec. 6, 1814; 260 sq. mi.; 1970 pop.: 9,929; 1960: 10,026; 1950: 10,535) (Middlebourne). John Tyler (1747-1813). Fifteenth gov. of Va. Father of Pres. John Tyler; judge Va. general court 1789-1808; gov. of Va. 1808-11.

Tyrrell, N.C. (est. 1729; 399 sq. mi.; 1970 pop.: 3,806; 1960: 4,520; 1950: 5,048) (Columbia). John Tyrrell. Lord Proprietor of Carolina.

U

Uinta, Wyo. (est. Dec. 1, 1869; 2,070 sq. mi.; 1970 pop.: 7,100; 1960: 7,484; 1950: 7,331) (Evanston). ("The Gateway to Wyoming's Parks, Mountains and Great Scenic

Attractions"). Uinta Indian tribe. -- Stone, Elizabeth Arnold, Uinta County, its place in history, Laramie, Wyo.: Laramie Printing Co., 1924; 276 p.

Uintah, Utah (est. Feb. 18, 1880; 4,420 sq. mi.; 1970 pop.: 12,684; 1960: 7,582; 1950: 10,300) (Vernal). Ute Indian tribe known as "Yugwintats."

Ulster, N.Y. (est. Nov. 1, 1683; 1,143 sq. mi.; 1970 pop.: 141,241; 1960: 118,804; 1950: 92,621) (Kingston). ("Utopia, U.S.A."). Ulster, Ireland, named for the Duke of York's earldom in Ireland. -- Sylvester, Nathaniel Bartlett, History of Ulster County, Philadelphia: Everts & Peck, 1880.

Umatilla, Ore. (est. Sept. 27, 1862; 3,231 sq. mi.; 1970 pop.: 44,923; 1960: 44,352; 1950: 41,703) (Pendleton). Umatilla River; Umatilla Indian tribe. -- Parsons, William, An illustrated history of Umatilla County, W.H. Lever, n.p., 1902; 581 p.

Unicoi, Tenn. (est. Mar. 23, 1875; 185 sq. mi.; 1970 pop.: 15,254; 1960: 15,082; 1950: 15,886) (Erwin). Indian word "unaka" for "white."

Union, Ark. (est. Nov. 2, 1829; 1,052 sq. mi.; 1970 pop.: 45,428; 1960: 49,518; 1950: 49,686) (El Dorado). Descriptive.

Union, Fla. (est. May 20, 1921; 240 sq. mi.; 1970 pop.: 8,112; 1960: 6.043; 1950: 8,906) (Lake Butler). Descriptive.

Union, Ga. (est. Dec. 3, 1832; 324 sq. mi.; 1970 pop.: 6,811; 1960: 6,510; 1950: 7,318) (Blairsville). Descriptive.

Union, Ill. (est. Jan. 2, 1818; 403 sq. mi.; 1970 pop.: 16,071; 1960: 17,645; 1950: 20,500) (Jonesboro). Named for union meeting of Dunkards and Baptists. -- Perrin, William Henry, History of Alexander, Union and Pulaski Counties, Chicago: O.L. Baskin & Co., 1883; 588 p.

Union, Ind. (est. Jan. 5, 1821, eff. Feb. 1, 1821; 168 sq. mi.; 1970 pop.: 6,582; 1960: 6,457; 1950: 6,412) (Liberty). Descriptive.

Union, Iowa (est. Jan. 15, 1851; org. Jan. 12, 1853, eff. May 1, 1853; 426 sq. mi.; 1970 pop.: 13,557; 1960: 13,712; 1950: 15,651) (Creston). -- Ide, George A., History of Union County, Chicago: S.J. Clarke Pub. Co., 1908; 836 p.

Union, Ky. (est. Jan. 15, 1811; 343 sq. mi.; 1970 pop.: 15,882; 1960: 14,537; 1950: 14,893) (Morganfield). Descriptive. Motto on state seal. -- Union County, Past and Present, Louisville, Ky.: Schuhmann Printing Co., 1941; 2 vol.

Union, La. (est. Mar. 13, 1839; 918 sq. mi.; 1970 pop.: 18,447; 1960: 17,624; 1950: 19,141) (Farmerville). Descriptive.

Union, Miss. (est. July 7, 1870; 412 sq. mi.; 1970 pop.: 19,096; 1960: 18,904; 1950: 20,262) (New Albany). Descriptive.

Union, N.J. (est. Mar. 19, 1857; 103 sq. mi.; 1970 pop.: 543,116; 1960: 504,255; 1950: 398,138) (Elizabeth). ("The County With One Hundred Years of Progress"). Descriptive. (eff. Apr. 13, 1857) -- Honeyman, Abraham Van Doren, History of Union County, New York: Lewis Historical Pub. Co., 1923; 3 vol. -- Ricord, F.W., History of Union County, Newark, N.J.: East Jersey Historical Co., 1897; 656 p.

Union, N.M. (est. Feb. 23, 1893; 3,817 sq. mi.; 1970 pop.: 4,925; 1960: 6,068; 1950: 7,372) (Clayton). Descriptive.

Union, N.C. (est. Dec. 19, 1842; 643 sq. mi.; 1970 pop.: 54,714; 1960: 44,670; 1950: 42,034) (Monroe). Descriptive. -- Walden, H. Nelson, History of Union County, Monroe, N.C., 1964; 79 p.

Union, Ohio (est. Jan. 10, 1820, eff. Apr. 1, 1820; 434 sq. mi.; 1970 pop.: 23,786; 1960: 22,853; 1950: 20,687) (Marysville). Descriptive. Union of four counties. -- The history of Union County, Chicago: W.H. Beers & Co., 1883; 694 p.

Union, Ore. (est. Oct. 14, 1864; 2,032 sq. mi.; 1970 pop.: 19,377; 1960: 18,180; 1950: 17,962) (La Grande). Descriptive.

Union, Pa. (est. Mar. 22, 1813; 318 sq. mi.; 1970 pop.: 28,603; 1960: 25,646; 1950: 23,150) (Lewisburg). Descriptive. -- Deans, Thomas R., The story of a county, Lewisburg, Pa., 196-?; unpaged.

Union, S.C. (est. Mar. 12, 1785; 515 sq. mi.; 1970 pop.: 29,230; 1960: 30,015; 1950: 31,334) (Union). Descriptive. Union church erected 1765 for various denominations.

Union, S.D. (est. Apr. 10, 1862; 454 sq. mi.; 1970 pop.: 9,643; 1960: 10,197; 1950: 10,792) (Elk Point). Descriptive. (Formerly Cole County, name changed to Union County, 1864).

Union, Tenn. (est. Oct. 9, 1797; 212 sq. mi.; 1970 pop.: 9,072; 1960: 8,498; 1950: 8,670) (Maynardville). Descriptive. (Originally Cocke County, name changed to Union County, Jan. 28, 1846).

Upshur, Tex. (est. Apr. 27, 1846; org. July 13, 1846; 589 sq. mi.; 1970 pop.: 20,976; 1960: 19,793; 1950: 20,822) (Gilmer). Abel Parker Upshur (1791-1844).

Lawyer, Va. legislature 1825; judge Va. courts 1826-41; U. S. Secretary of the Navy 1841-43; U. S. Secretary of State 1843-44 in cabinet of Pres. John Tyler; killed by explosion of gun during test on U. S. S. Princeton, Feb. 28, 1844. -- Loyd, Doyal T., A history of Upshur County, Waco, Texas: Texian Press, 1966; 136 p. -- Baird, G. H., A Brief History of Upshur County, Gilmer Mirror, 1946; 76 p.

Upshur, W. Va. (est. Mar. 26, 1851; 354 sq. mi.; 1970 pop.: 19,092; 1960: 18,292; 1950: 19,242) (Buckhannon). Abel Parker Upshur*.

Upson, Ga. (est. Dec. 15, 1824, org. Dec. 20, 1824; 317 sq. mi.; 1970 pop.: 23,505; 1960: 23,800; 1950: 25,078) (Thomaston). Stephen Upson (1784-1824). Graduated from Yale. -- Nottingham, Carolyn (Walker) and Hannah, E., History of Upson County, Georgia, Macon, Ga.: J. W. Burke Co., 1930; 1122 p.

Upton, Tex. (est. Feb. 26, 1887; 1,312 sq. mi.; 1970 pop.: 4,697; 1960: 6,239; 1950: 5,307) (Rankin). John Cunningham Upton (1823-1862). Raised company 1861 and served under Hood's Tex. Brigade; became lt. col.; killed at Manassas, Va. Aug. 30, 1862.

Utah, Utah (est. Mar. 3, 1852; 1,998 sq. mi.; 1970 pop.: 137,776; 1960: 106,991; 1950: 81,912) (Provo). Ute Indian tribe, part of the Shoshone Indian tribe. The Apaches and Navajo Indians nicknamed them "Utes" meaning "the hill dwellers" or "the upper people." -- Daughters of Utah Pioneers, Memories that live; Utah County centennial history, Provo, 1947; 488 p.

Uvalde, Tex. (est. Feb. 8, 1850; 1,588 sq. mi.; 1970 pop.: 17,348; 1960: 16,814; 1950: 16,015) (Uvalde). Juan de Ugalde. Civil and military gov. of Coahuila and Tex. 1777; four campaigns against Apache Indians 1779-83; removed as gov. in 1783; col. in Mexican Army 1783-86; campaigns against Apaches 1787; campaigns against Mescaleros 1789; won victory at Soledad Creek.

V

Val Verde, Tex. (est. Feb. 20, 1885; 3,242 sq. mi.; 1970 pop.: 27,471; 1960: 24,461; 1950: 16,635) (Del Rio). Spanish for "green valley."

Valencia, N. M. (est. Jan. 9, 1852; 5,637 sq. mi.; 1970 pop.: 40,539; 1960: 39,085; 1950: 22,481) (Los Lunas). Valencia, Spain.

Valley, Idaho (est. Feb. 26, 1917; 3, 719 sq. mi. ; 1970 pop.: 3, 609; 1960: 3, 663; 1950: 4, 270) (Cascade). Descriptive.

Valley, Mont. (est. Feb. 6, 1893; 5, 082 sq. mi. ; 1970 pop. : 11, 471; 1960: 17, 080; 1950: 11, 353) (Glasgow). Descriptive.

Valley, Neb. (est. Mar. 1, 1871; procl., org. June 23, 1873; 570 sq. mi. ; 1970 pop. : 5, 783; 1960: 6, 590; 1950: 7, 252) (Ord). Descriptive, Loup River Valley.

Van Buren, Ark. (est. Nov. 11, 1833; 714 sq. mi. ; 1970 pop. : 8, 275; 1960: 7, 228; 1950: 9, 687) (Clinton). Martin Van Buren (1782-1862). Eighth Pres. of the U. S. Eleventh gov. of N. Y. Surrogate of Columbia County 1808-13; N. Y. senate 1813-20; attorney gen. of N. Y. 1815-19; N. Y. constitutional convention 1821; Senator from N. Y. , 1821-28; gov. of N. Y. 1828-29; U. S. Secretary of State in cabinet of Pres. Jackson 1829-31; Vice Pres. of the U. S. 1833-37; Pres. of the U. S. 1837-41.

Van Buren, Iowa (est. Dec. 7, 1836; 487 sq. mi. ; 1970 pop.: 8, 643; 1960: 9, 778; 1950: 11, 007) (Keosauqua). Martin Van Buren*. -- The History of Van Buren County, Chicago: Western Historical Co. , 1878; 606 p.

Van Buren, Mich. (est. Oct. 29, 1829, org. Mar. 18, 1837, eff. Apr. 7, 1837; 607 sq. mi. ; 1970 pop. : 56, 173; 1960: 48, 395; 1950: 39, 184) (Paw Paw). Martin Van Buren*. -- Rowland, Oran W. , A History of Van Buren County, Chicago: Lewis Pub. Co. , 1912; 2 vol.

Van Buren, Tenn. (est. Jan. 3, 1840; 255 sq. mi. ; 1970 pop. : 3, 758; 1960: 3, 671; 1950: 3, 985) (Spencer). Martin Van Buren*.

Van Wert, Ohio (est. Feb. 12, 1820; 409 sq. mi. ; 1970 pop.: 29, 194; 1960: 28, 840; 1950: 26, 971) (Van Wert). Isaac Van Wert (-1828). One of the captors of Maj. John Andre on Sept. 23, 1780; act of Continental Congress of Nov. 3, 1780 awarded him a silver medal and $200 in specie during life.

Van Zandt, Tex. (est. Mar. 20, 1848; 855 sq. mi. ; 1970 pop. : 22, 155; 1960: 19, 091; 1950: 22, 593) (Canton). Isaac Van Zandt (1813-1847). Charge d'affaires from Tex. to the U. S. 1842; Tex. constitutional convention 1842; died of yellow fever while campaigning for gov. 1847. Texas house of representatives 1840-42. -- Mills, William Samuel, History of Van Zandt County, Canton?, Texas, 1950; 237 p.

Vance, N. C. (est. Mar. 5, 1881; 269 sq. mi. ; 1970 pop. : 32, 691; 1960: 32, 002; 1950: 32, 101) (Henderson). Zebulon Baird Vance (1830-1894). Thirty-seventh and forty-second gov. of N. C. Prosecuting attorney Buncombe County 1852;

N. C. house of commons 1854; Representative from N. C. 1858-61; capt. and col. in Confederate Army 1861; gov. of N. C. 1862-65 and 1877-79; Senator from N. C., 1879-94. -- Peace, Samuel Thomas, Zeb's Black Baby; Vance County, North Carolina, a short history, Henderson, N. C., 1956; 457 p.

Vanderburgh, Ind. (est. Jan. 7, 1818, eff. Feb. 1, 1818; 241 sq. mi.; 1970 pop.: 168,772; 1960: 165,794; 1950: 160,422) (Evansville). Henry Vanderburgh. Judge Ind. Terr.

Venango, Pa. (est. Mar. 12, 1800; 675 sq. mi.; 1970 pop.: 62,353; 1960: 65,295; 1950: 65,328) (Franklin). Indian word for "a figure carved on a tree." -- Babcock, Charles Almanzo, Venango County, Chicago: J. H. Beers & Co., 1919; 2 vol. -- History of Venango County, Chicago: Brown, Runk & Co., 1890; 1164 p.

Ventura, Calif. (est. Mar. 22, 1872; 1,857 sq. mi.; 1970 pop.: 376,430; 1960: 199,138; 1950: 114,647) (Ventura). Spanish word for "fortune" named for Mission San Buenaventura established Mar. 31, 1782; from Spanish "buena" for "good" and "ventura" for "fortune." Named for San Buenaventura, a saint. -- Outland, Charles F., Mines, Murders and Grizzlies, Ventura: Ventura County Historical Society, 1969; 134 p.

Vermilion, Ill. (est. Jan. 18, 1826; 921 sq. mi.; 1970 pop.: 97,047; 1960: 96,176; 1950: 87,079) (Danville). Descriptive of soil. -- Jones, Lottie E., History of Vermilion County, Chicago: Pioneer Pub. Co., 1911; 2 vol.

Vermilion, La. (est. Mar. 25, 1844; 1,213 sq. mi.; 1970 pop.: 43,071; 1960: 38,855; 1950: 36,929) (Abbeville). Descriptive.

Vermillion, Ind. (est. Jan. 2, 1824, eff. Feb. 1, 1824; 263 sq. mi.; 1970 pop.: 16,793; 1960: 17,683; 1950: 19,723) (Newport). Descriptive. (Variant spelling).

Vernon, La. (est. Mar. 30, 1871; 1,367 sq. mi.; 1970 pop.: 53,794; 1960: 18,301; 1950: 18,974) (Leesville). Named for Mount Vernon, the home of George Washington. -- Cupit, John Thomas, Brief History of Vernon Parish, La., Rosepine, La., 1963; 137 p.

Vernon, Mo. (est. Feb. 17, 1851; 838 sq. mi.; 1970 pop.: 19,065; 1960: 20,540; 1950: 22,685) (Nevada). Miles Vernon. Mo. legislator.

Vernon, Wis. (est. Mar. 1. 1851, org. May 1851; 805 sq. mi.; 1970 pop.: 24,557; 1960: 25,663; 1950: 27,906) (Viroqua). Named for Mount Vernon, the home of George Washington. (Formerly Bad Axe County, name changed to Vernon County, Mar. 22, 1862). -- History of Vernon

<u>County</u>, Springfield, Ill.: Union Pub. Co., 1884; 826 p.

Victoria, Tex. (est. Mar. 17, 1836; 893 sq. mi.; 1970 pop.: 53, 766; 1960: 46, 475; 1950: 31, 241) (Victoria). Guadalupe Victoria (-1843). First Pres. of the Republic of Mexico, inaugurated Oct. 10, 1824. (His real name was Juan Fernandez Fernandez). -- Grimes, Roy, <u>Three hundred years in Victoria County</u>, Victoria, Texas: Victoria Advocate Pub. Co., 1968; 646 p. -- Morris, Leopold, <u>Pictorial history of Victoria and Victoria County</u>, San Antonio?, 1953; 92 p.

Vigo, Ind. (est. Jan. 21, 1818, eff. Feb. 15, 1818; 415 sq. mi.; 1970 pop.: 114, 528; 1960: 108, 458; 1950: 105, 160) (Terre Haute). Joseph Maria Francesco Vigo (1740-1836) Fur trader; known as Francis Vigo; assisted George Rogers Clark in exploratory trips, and financial backer; surprised fort at Vincennes 1778; commissioned to trade with the Chickasaw and Choctaws.

Vilas, Wis. (est. Apr. 12, 1893; 867 sq. mi.; 1970 pop.: 10, 958; 1960: 9, 332; 1950: 9, 363) (Eagle River). William Freeman Vilas (1840-1908). Capt., maj. and lt. col. 23rd Regiment Wis. Vol. Inf.; prof. of law Univ. of Wis. 1868-85 and 1889-92; regent of Univ. of Wis. 1880-85 and 1898-1905; U. S. Postmaster Gen. in cabinet of Pres. Cleveland 1885-88; U. S. Secretary of the Interior in cabinet of Pres. Cleveland 1888-89; Senator from Wis. 1891-97.

Vinton, Ohio (est. Mar. 23, 1850; 411 sq. mi.; 1970 pop.: 9, 420; 1960: 10, 274; 1950: 10, 759) (McArthur). ("The Wonderland of Ohio"). Samuel Finley Vinton (1792-1862). Representative from Ohio 1823-37 and 1843-51; president of Cleveland and Toledo RR 1853-54. -- Ogan, Lew, <u>History of Vinton County, Ohio</u>, [McArthur, Ohio], [1954-55]; 329 p.

Volusia, Fla. (est. Dec. 29, 1854; 1, 115 sq. mi.; 1970 pop.: 169, 487; 1960: 125, 319; 1950: 74, 229) (De Land). According to tradition named for a Belgian or Frenchman named Veluche who owned a trading post. His name was pronounced Voolooshay and was anglicized as Volusia. (Originally created as Mosquito County on Dec. 29, 1824; name changed to present name Dec. 29, 1854). -- Gold, Pleasant Daniel, <u>History of Volusia County</u>, De Land, Fla.: E. O. Painter Printing Co., 1927; 525 p.

W

Wabash, Ill. (est. Dec. 27, 1824; 220 sq. mi.; 1970 pop.:

12,841; 1960: 14,047; 1950: 14,651) (Mt. Carmel). Indian word for "white water." -- McDonough, J., Combined History of Edwards, Lawrence & Wabash Counties, Philadelphia: J. L. McDonough & Co., 1883; 377 p.

Wabash, Ind. (est. Feb. 2, 1832, org. Jan. 22, 1835, eff. Mar. 1, 1835; 421 sq. mi.; 1970 pop.: 35,553; 1960: 32,605; 1950: 29,047) (Wabash). Indian word for "white water."

Wabasha, Minn. (est. Oct. 27, 1849; 521 sq. mi.; 1970 pop.: 17,224; 1960: 17,007; 1950: 16,878) (Wabasha). Wabasha, name of three successive generations of Indian chieftains, name meaning "red leaf."

Wabaunsee, Kan. (est. Aug. 30, 1855, org. Feb. 11, 1859; 791 sq. mi.; 1970 pop.: 6,397; 1960: 6,648; 1950: 7,212) (Alma). Wabaunsee. Pottawatomie Indian chief. (Originally Richardson County, name changed to Wabaunsee County Feb. 11, 1859).

Wadena, Minn. (est. June 11, 1858; 536 sq. mi.; 1970 pop.: 12,412; 1960: 12,199; 1950: 12,806) (Wadena). Named for the Wadena trading posts on the old trail from Crow Wing to Otter Tail City and Pembina, an Ojibway Indian word for "a little round hill."

Wagoner, Okla. (est. July 16, 1907; 584 sq. mi.; 1970 pop.: 22,163; 1960: 15,673; 1950: 16,741) (Wagoner). Henry Samuel "Bigfoot" Wagoner of Parsons, Kan., dispatcher for the Missouri, Kansas and Texas RR in 1886.

Wake, N.C. (est. sess. Dec. 5, 1770; 866 sq. mi.; 1970 pop.: 228,453; 1960: 169,082; 1950: 136,450) (Raleigh). Margaret Wake. Maiden name of the wife of Gov. William Tryon (1729-1788) of N.Y. who resigned in 1778 and returned to England. -- Chamberlain, Hope (Summerell), History of Wake County, North Carolina, Edwards & Broughton Printing Co., 1922; 302 p.

Wahkiakum, Wash. (est. Apr. 24, 1854; 269 sq. mi.; 1970 pop.: 3,592; 1960: 3,426; 1950: 3,835) (Cathlamet). Wahkiakum. Indian chief.

Wakulla, Fla. (est. Mar. 11, 1843; 614 sq. mi.; 1970 pop.: 6,308; 1960: 5,257; 1950: 5,258) (Crawfordville). Indian word for "mystery."

Waldo, Me. (est. Feb. 7, 1827, eff. July 3, 1827; 734 sq. mi.; 1970 pop.: 23,328; 1960: 22,632; 1950: 21,687) (Belfast). Samuel Waldo. Proprietor of Waldo patent, imported forty families from Brunswick and Saxony 1740.

Walker, Ala. (est. Dec. 26, 1823; 809 sq. mi.; 1970 pop.: 56,246; 1960: 54,211; 1950: 63,769) (Jasper). John Williams Walker (1783-1823) Ala. terr. house of representatives 1817; Ala. constitutional convention 1819; Senator from Ala. 1819-22. -- Dombhart, John Martin, History of Walker County, Its Towns and Its People, Thornton, Ark.: Cayce Pub. Co., 1937; 382 p.

Walker, Ga. (est. Dec. 18, 1833; 432 sq. mi.; 1970 pop.: 50,691; 1960: 45,264; 1950: 38,198) (Lafayette). Freeman Walker (1780-1827). Ga. house of representatives 1807-11; maj.; mayor of Augusta, Ga. 1818-19; Senator from Ga. 1819-21; mayor of Augusta 1823. -- Sartain, James Alfred, History of Walker County, Georgia, Dalton, Ga.: A. J. Showalter Co., 1932; 519 p.

Walker, Tex. (est. Apr. 6, 1846; 786 sq. mi.; 1970 pop.: 27,680; 1960: 21,475; 1950: 20,163) (Huntsville). Robert James Walker (1801-1869). Fourth terr. gov. of Kan., Senator from Miss. 1835-45; U.S. Secretary of the Treas. in the cabinet of Pres. Polk 1845-49; terr. gov. of Kan. (nine months) 1857, U.S. financial agent to Europe 1863-64; introduced resolution in the Senate for the annexation of Tex.

Samuel Hamilton Walker (1809-1847). Tex. Ranger 1836; captured on Mier Expedition 1842; served in Mexican War under Gen. Zachary Taylor; killed at Huamantla, Mexico, Oct. 9, 1847.

In Dec. 1865, the name of the honoré was changed by state legislature.

Walla Walla, Wash. (est. Apr. 25, 1854; 1,288 sq. mi.; 1970 pop.: 42,176; 1960: 42,195; 1950: 40,135) (Walla Walla). Indian word for "many waters." -- Lyman, W.D., An illustrated history of Walla Walla County, [n.p.], 1901; 510 p.

Wallace, Kan. (est. Mar. 2, 1868, org. Jan. 5, 1889; 911 sq. mi.; 1970 pop.: 2,215; 1960: 2,069; 1950: 2,508) (Sharon Springs). William Harvey Lamb Wallace (-1862). Second lt. Ill. inf. 1846; mustered out 1847; col. Ill. inf. 1861; brig. gen. 1862; died Apr. 10, 1862 from wounds received at Shiloh, Tenn.

Waller, Tex. (est. Apr. 28, 1873; 507 sq. mi.; 1970 pop.: 14,285; 1960: 12,071; 1950: 11,961) (Hempstead). Edwin Waller (1800-1883). Signed Tex. Declaration of Independence; first mayor of Austin, Tex. 1840; postmaster gen. Tex. Republic for 2 days, Dec. 9-11, 1839; chief justice Austin County 1844-56; Secession Convention 1861.

Wallowa, Ore. (est. Feb. 11, 1887; 3,178 sq. mi.; 1970 pop.: 6,247; 1960: 7,102; 1950: 7,264) (Enterprise). Nez Perce Indian word for "tripod of poles used to support fish-nets."

Walsh, N.D. (est. Feb. 18, 1881, org. Aug. 30, 1887; 1,287 sq. mi.; 1970 pop.: 16,251; 1960: 17,997; 1950:

18, 859) (Grafton). George H. Walsh. N. D. legislative council 1881, 1883, 1885 and 1889.

Walthall, Miss. (est. Mar. 16, 1910; 389 sq. mi.; 1970 pop.: 12, 500; 1960: 13, 512; 1950: 15, 563) (Tylertown). Edward Cary Walthall (1831-1898). District attorney for tenth judicial district Miss. 1856 and 1859; lt. 15th Miss. regiment 1861; col. 29th Miss. regiment 1862; brig. gen. 1862; lost one-third of forces at Chickamauga; on defense Lookout Mountain; maj. gen. June 1864; Senator from Miss., 1885-94 and 1895-98.

Walton, Fla. (est. Dec. 29, 1824; 1, 046 sq. mi.; 1970 pop.: 16, 087; 1960: 15, 576; 1950: 14, 725) (De Funiak Springs). George Walton (1740-1804) Col.; Secretary of W. Fla. under Gov. Andrew Jackson, 1821-22. -- McKinnon, John Love, History of Walton County, Atlanta, Ga.: Byrd Printing Co., 1911; 389 p.

Walton, Ga. (est. Dec. 15, 1818; 331 sq. mi.; 1970 pop.: 23, 404; 1960: 20, 481; 1950: 20, 230) (Monroe). George Walton (1750-1804). Fourth gov. of Ga. Secretary Provisional Congress 1774; delegate Continental Congress 1776-81; signer Declaration of Independence 1776; col. of militia captured at battle of Savannah; held prisoner until 1779; gov. of Ga. 1779-80; chief justice of Ga. 1783-86; gov. of Ga. 1789; judge of superior courts of eastern judicial circuit 1790; chief justice of Ga. 1793; Senator from Ga. 1795-96; judge of the middle circuit of Ga. 1799-1804. -- Sams, Anita B., Wayfarers in Walton, a history of Walton County, Georgia, 1818-1967, Monroe, Ga.: General Charitable Foundation of, 1967; 885 p.

Walworth, S. D. (est. Jan. 8, 1873; 737 sq. mi.; 1970 pop.: 7, 842; 1960: 8, 097; 1950: 7, 648) (Selby). ("The Community of Attractive Opportunities"; "The County of Attractive Opportunities"). Walworth County, Wis.

Walworth, Wis. (est. Dec. 7, 1836; 560 sq. mi.; 1970 pop.: 63, 444; 1960: 52, 368; 1950: 41, 584) (Elkhorn). Reuben Hyde Walworth (1788-1867). Master in chancery and circuit judge 1811; aide de camp to Gen. Benj. Mooers and division judge advocate with rank of col. 1812; Representative from N. Y. 1821-23; judge fourth judicial district of N. Y. 1823-28; chancellor of N. Y. 1828-48; nominated Associate Justice of the U. S. Supreme Court in 1844 by Pres. Tyler but nomination was not confirmed. -- Beckwith, Albert Clayton, History of Walworth County, Indianapolis: B. F. Bowen & Co., 1912; 2 vol.

Wapello, Iowa (est. Feb. 17, 1843, org. Feb. 13, 1844, eff. Mar. 1, 1844; 437 sq. mi.; 1970 pop.: 42, 149; 1960: 46, 126; 1950: 47, 397) (Ottumwa). Wapello. Chief of the

Fox Indian tribe. -- Waterman, Harrison Lyman, History of Wapello County, Chicago: S. J. Clarke Pub. Co., 1914; 2 vol.

Ward, N D. (est. Apr. 14, 1885, org. Nov. 23, 1885; 2, 048 sq. mi.; 1970 pop.: 58, 560; 1960: 47, 072; 1950: 34, 782) (Minot). J. P. Ward. N. D. legislature 1885.

Ward, Tex. (est. Feb. 26, 1887; 827 sq. mi.; 1970 pop.: 13, 019; 1960: 14, 917; 1950: 13, 346) (Monahans). Thomas William Ward (1807-1872). Member New Orleans Grays 1835; battle of Bexar 1835; recruited vol. 1841; lost his leg, nicknamed "Peg Leg Ward," lost his arm celebrating; Commissioner General Land Office 1841-48; mayor of Austin, Tex. 1840, 1857 and 1865; U. S. consul to Panama 1840, 1853 and 1865; Collector of Customs at Corpus Christi 1865-69.

Ware, Ga. (est. Dec. 15, 1824, org. Dec. 20, 1824; 771 sq. mi.; 1970 pop.: 33, 525; 1960: 34, 219; 1950: 30, 289) (Waycross). Nicholas Ware. -- Walker, Laura (Singleton), History of Ware County, Georgia, Macon, Ga.: J. W. Burke Co., 1934; 547 p.

Warren, Ga. (est. Dec. 19, 1793; 404 sq. mi.; 1970 pop.: 6, 669; 1960: 7, 360; 1950: 8, 779) (Warrenton). Joseph Warren (1741-1775). Physician; pres. of Provincial Congress 1775; maj. gen. Continental Army 1775; killed at battle of Breed's Hill (Bunker Hill) June 17, 1775.

Warren, Ill. (est. Jan. 13, 1825; 546 sq. mi.; 1970 pop.: 21, 595; 1960: 21, 587; 1950: 21, 981) (Monmouth). Joseph Warren*. -- The Past and Present of Warren County, Chicago: H. F. Kett & Co., 1877; 352 p.

Warren, Ind. (est. Jan. 19, 1827, eff. Mar. 1, 1827; 368 sq. mi.; 1970 pop.: 8, 705; 1960: 8, 545; 1950: 8, 535) (Williamsport). Joseph Warren*.

Warren, Iowa (est. Jan. 13, 1846; org. Feb. 10, 1849; 572 sq. mi.; 1970 pop.: 27, 432; 1960: 20, 829; 1950: 17, 758) (Indianola). Joseph Warren*. -- Schultz, Gerard, History of Warren County, Indianola, Iowa: Record and Tribune Co., 1953; 355 p.

Warren, Ky. (est. Dec. 14, 1796, eff. Mar. 1, 1797; 546 sq. mi.; 1970 pop.: 57, 432; 1960: 45, 491; 1950: 42, 758) (Bowling Green). Joseph Warren*.

Warren, Miss. (est. Dec. 22, 1809; 572 sq. mi.; 1970 pop.: 44, 981; 1960: 42, 206; 1950: 39, 616) (Vicksburg). Joseph Warren*.

Warren, Mo. (est. Jan. 5, 1833; 428 sq. mi.; 1970 pop.: 9, 699; 1960: 8, 750; 1950: 7, 666) (Warrenton). Joseph Warren*.

Warren, N. J. (est. Nov. 20, 1824; 361 sq. mi.; 1970 pop.:

73, 879; 1960: 63, 220; 1950: 54, 374) (Belvidere). Joseph Warren*. -- Cummins, George Wyckoff, History of Warren County, New York: Lewis Historical Pub. Co., 1911; 433 p. -- Shampanore, Frank, History and directory of Warren County, Washington, N. J.: Shampanore & Sons, 1929; 706 p.

Warren, N. Y. (est. Mar. 12, 1813; 883 sq. mi.; 1970 pop.: 49, 402; 1960: 44, 002; 1950: 39, 205) (Lake George). ("The All Season Vacation Paradise"; "The Convention Center"; "The County Close to Home Wherever You Live"; "The County of Historical Interest and Incomparable Beauty"; "The Four Season Playground"; "The Gateway to the Adirondacks"; "The Honeymoon Haven"; "New York State's 'Happiest' Vacationland"; "The Playground of the Adirondacks"; "The Vacation Paradise in Any Season"; "The Vacation Paradise in the Adirondacks"; "The Vacationist's Paradise"; "The Warpath of the Nations"). Joseph Warren*. -- Brown, William H., History of Warren County, New York, Board of Supervisors of Warren County, [n. p.], 1963; 302 p.

Warren, N. C. (est. sess. Apr. 14, 1779; 445 sq. mi.; 1970 pop.: 15, 810; 1960: 19, 652; 1950: 23, 539) (Warrenton). Joseph Warren*. -- Wellman, Manly Wade, The County of Warren, North Carolina, 1586-1917, Chapel Hill, N.C.: University of North Carolina Press, 1959; 282 p.

Warren, Ohio (est. Mar. 24, 1803; 408 sq. mi.; 1970 pop.: 84, 925; 1960: 65, 711; 1950: 38, 505) (Lebanon). Joseph Warren*. -- The history of Warren County, Chicago: W. H. Beers, 1882; 1070 p.

Warren, Pa. (est. Mar. 12, 1800; 910 sq. mi.; 1970 pop.: 47, 682; 1960: 45, 582; 1950: 42, 698) (Warren). Joseph Warren*. -- Schenck, J. S. and Rann, W. S., editors, History of Warren County, Syracuse, N. Y.: D. Mason & Co., 1887; 692 p.

Warren, Tenn. (est. Nov. 26, 1807; 443 sq. mi.; 1970 pop.: 26, 972; 1960: 23, 102; 1950: 22, 271) (McMinnville). Joseph Warren*. -- Hale, William Thomas, Early History of Warren County, McMinnville, Tenn.: Standard Printing Co., 1930; 59 p.

Warren, Va. (est. Mar. 9, 1836; 219 sq. mi.; 1970 pop.: 15, 301; 1960: 14, 655; 1950: 14, 801) (Front Royal). Joseph Warren*.

Warrick, Ind. (est. Mar. 9, 1813, eff. Apr. 1, 1813; 391 sq. mi.; 1970 pop.: 27, 972; 1960: 23, 577; 1950: 21, 527) (Boonville). Jacob Warrick. Capt. War of 1812.

Warwick, Va. (inc. as Warwick City, July 16, 1952). Consolidated with Newport News, July 1958.

Wasatch, Utah (est. Jan. 17, 1862; 1, 194 sq. mi.; 1970 pop.: 5, 863; 1960: 5, 308; 1950: 5, 574) (Heber City). Ute Indian word meaning "mountain pass" or "a low pass over a high range." -- Mortimer, William James, How beautiful upon the mountains, a centennial history of Wasatch County, Daughters of Utah Pioneers, 1963; 1198 p.

Wasco, Ore. (est. Jan. 11, 1854; 2, 387 sq. mi.; 1970 pop.: 20, 133; 1960: 20, 205; 1950: 15, 552) (The Dalles). Wasco Indian tribe named for a cup or small bowl made of horn.

Waseca, Minn. (est. Feb. 27, 1857; 415 sq. mi.; 1970 pop.: 16, 663; 1960: 16, 041; 1950: 14, 957) (Waseca). Dakota or Sioux Indian word for "rich, especially in provisions."

Washabaugh, S. D. (Mar. 9, 1883; 1, 061 sq. mi.; 1970 pop.: 1, 369; 1960: 1, 042; 1950: 1, 551) (Unorganized county, for governmental purposes attached to Jackson County.) Frank J. Washabaugh, S. D. terr. legislatures 1883, 1885, 1887 and 1889; S. D. senator 1889-91; pres. pro tempore S. D. senate 1889-90. -- Jackson-Washabaugh County Historical Society, Jackson-Washabaugh Counties, Kadoka, S. D., 1966; 345 p.

Washakie, Wyo. (est. Feb. 9, 1911; 2, 262 sq. mi.; 1970 pop.: 7, 569; 1960: 8, 883; 1950: 7, 252) (Worland). Washakie (1804-1900). Chief of the Shoshoni tribe for about sixty years. An unsupported assertion is that he killed a Crow chief in personal combat and ate his heart. His name means "rawhide rattle."

Washburn, Wis. (est. Mar. 27, 1883; 816 sq. mi.; 1970 pop.: 10, 601; 1960: 10, 301; 1950: 11, 665) (Shell Lake). Cadwallader Colden Washburn (1818-1882). Tenth gov. of Wis. Surveyor of Rock Island County, Ill., 1840; emigrated to Wis. 1842; Representative from Wis. 1855-61; col. 2nd Regiment Wis. Vol. cavalry 1862; brig. gen. of vol. 1862; maj. gen. 1862-65; Representative from Wis. 1867-71; gov. of Wis. 1872-73; owned and operated flour mills in Minneapolis, Minn.

Washington, Ala. (est. June 4, 1800; 1, 069 sq. mi.; 1970 pop.: 16, 241; 1960: 15, 372; 1950: 15, 612) (Chatom). George Washington (1732-1799). First Pres. of the U. S. 1789-97. Assumed command of all Continental Armies July 3, 1775; successfully conducted Revolutionary War ending with Cornwallis's surrender Oct. 19, 1781; resigned commission Dec. 23, 1783; presided over federal constitutional convention 1787; first Pres. of the U. S. from Apr. 30, 1789 to Mar. 3, 1797; accepted commission on July 3, 1798 as lt. gen. and commander-in-chief of the U. S. Army when war with France threatened, retaining the commission until his death Dec. 14, 1799.

Washington, Ark. (est. Oct. 17, 1828, eff. Nov. 1, 1828; 963 sq. mi.; 1970 pop.: 77, 370; 1960: 55, 797; 1950: 49, 979) (Fayetteville). George Washington*.

Washington, Colo. (est. Feb. 9, 1887; 2, 525 sq. mi.; 1970 pop.: 5, 550; 1960: 6, 625; 1950: 7, 520) (Akron). George Washington*. -- Washington County Museum Association, The Pioneer Book of Washington County, Akron, Colo.: Washington County Museum Association, 1959; 392 p.

Washington, Fla. (est. Dec. 9, 1825; 597 sq. mi.; 1970 pop.: 11, 453; 1960: 11, 249; 1950: 11, 888) (Chipley). George Washington*.

Washington, Ga. (est. Feb. 25, 1784; 699 sq. mi.; 1970 pop.: 17, 480; 1960: 18, 903; 1950: 21, 012) (Sandersville). George Washington*. -- Mitchell, Ella, History of Washington County, Atlanta, Ga.: Byrd Printing Co., 1924; 171 p.

Washington, Idaho (est. Feb. 20, 1879; 1, 475 sq. mi.; 1970 pop.: 7, 633; 1960: 8, 378; 1950: 8, 576) (Weiser). George Washington*.

Washington, Ill. (est. Jan. 2, 1818; 561 sq. mi.; 1970 pop.: 13, 780; 1960: 13, 569; 1950: 14, 460) (Nashville). George Washington*. -- Portrait and Biographical Record of Clinton, Washington, Marion and Jefferson Counties, Chicago: Chapman Pub. Co., 1894; 584 p.

Washington, Ind. (est. Dec. 21, 1813, eff. Jan. 17, 1814; 516 sq. mi.; 1970 pop.: 19, 278; 1960: 17, 819; 1950: 15, 520) (Salem). George Washington*. -- Stevens, Warder W., Centennial history of Washington County, Ind., Indianapolis, Ind.: B. F. Bowen, 1916; 76 p.

Washington, Iowa (est. Jan. 16, 1837; org. Jan. 18, 1838; 568 sq. mi.; 1970 pop.: 18, 967; 1960: 19, 406; 1950: 19, 557) (Washington). George Washington*. (Orginally Slaughter County, name changed to Washington County, Jan. 25, 1839). -- Burrell, Howard A., History of Washington County, Chicago: S. J. Clarke Pub. Co., 1909; 2 vol.

Washington, Kan. (est. 1855; org. Feb. 21, 1860; 891 sq. mi.; 1970 pop.: 9, 249; 1960: 10, 739; 1950: 12, 977) (Washington). George Washington*.

Washington, Ky. (est. June 22, 1792, eff. Sept. 1, 1792; 307 sq. mi.; 1970 pop.: 10, 728; 1960: 11, 168; 1950: 12, 777) (Springfield). George Washington*. -- Baylor, Orval Walker, Early times in Washington County, Cynthiana, Ky.: The Hobson Press, 1942; 154 p.

Washington, La. (est. Mar. 6, 1819; 655 sq. mi.; 1970 pop.: 41, 987; 1960: 44, 015; 1950: 38, 371) (Franklinton). George Washington*.

Washington, Me. (est. June 25, 1789, eff. May 1, 1790;

2,553 sq. mi.; 1970 pop.: 29,859; 1960: 32,908; 1950: 35,187) (Machais). ("The Sunrise County of the U. S. A.") George Washington*.

Washington, Md. (est. Resolve of convention, Sept. 6, 1776; eff. Oct. 1, 1776; 462 sq. mi.; 1970 pop.: 103,829; 1960: 91,219; 1950: 78,886) (Hagerstown). George Washington*. -- Williams, Thomas John Chew, A history of Washington County, Hagerstown, Md.: J. M. Rank and L. R. Titsworth, 1906; 2 vol.

Washington, Minn. (est. Oct. 27, 1849, org. Mar. 31, 1851, eff. Sept. 1, 1851; 390 sq. mi.; 1970 pop.: 82,948; 1960: 52,432; 1950: 34,544) (Stillwater) George Washington*. -- Warner, George E. and Foote, C. M., History of Washington County, Minneapolis: North Star Pub. Co., 1881; 636 p.

Washington, Miss. (est. Jan. 29, 1827; 723 sq. mi.; 1970 pop.: 70,581; 1960: 78,638; 1950: 70,504) (Greenville). George Washington*.

Washington, Mo. (est. Aug. 21, 1813; 760 sq. mi.; 1970 pop.: 15,086; 1960: 14,346; 1950: 14,689) (Potosi). George Washington*.

Washington, Neb. (est. Nov. 23, 1854 procl.; 385 sq. mi.; 1970 pop.: 13,310; 1960: 12,103; 1950: 11,511) (Blair). George Washington*. -- Buss, William Henry, History of Dodge and Washington Counties, Nebraska, Chicago: American Historical Society, 1921; 2 vol. -- Shrader, Forrest B., A History of Washington County, Nebraska, Omaha, Neb., 1937; 350 p.

Washington, N. Y. (est. Mar. 12, 1772; 837 sq. mi.; 1970 pop.: 52,725; 1960: 48,476; 1950: 47,144) (Hudson Falls). George Washington*. (Formerly Charlotte County, name changed to Washington County, Apr. 2, 1784). -- Stone, William Leete, Washington County, New York: New York Historical Co., 1901.

Washington, N. C. (est. sess. Nov. 15, 1777; 336 sq. mi.; 1970 pop.: 14,038; 1960: 13,488; 1950: 13,180) (Plymouth). George Washington*.

Washington, Ohio (est. July 27, 1788; 637 sq. mi.; 1970 pop.: 57,160; 1960: 51,689; 1950: 44,407) (Marietta). George Washington*. -- Andrews, Israel Ward, Washington County, Cincinnati: P. G. Thomson, 1877; 83 p. -- History of Washington County, Cleveland: H. Z. Williams & Brother, 1881; 739 p.

Washington, Okla. (est. July 16, 1907; 425 sq. mi.; 1970 pop.: 42,277; 1960: 42,347; 1950: 32,880) (Bartlesville). George Washington*.

Washington, Ore. (est. July 5, 1843; 716 sq. mi.; 1970 pop.:

157, 920; 1960: 92, 237; 1950: 61, 269) (Hillsboro). George Washington*. (Formerly Twality, name changed Sept. 3, 1849.)

Washington, Pa. (est. Mar. 28, 1781; 857 sq. mi.; 1970 pop.: 210, 876; 1960: 217, 271; 1950: 209, 628) (Washington). George Washington*. -- Forrest, Earle Robert, History of Washington County, Chicago: S. J. Clarke Pub. Co., 1926; 3 vol.

Washington, R.I. (est. June 3, 1729; 325 sq. mi.; 1970 pop.: 83, 586; 1960: 59, 054; 1950: 48, 542) (West Kingston). ("The South County"). George Washington*. Originally called the Narragansett country. Named King's Province March 20, 1654. Boundaries established May 21, 1669. Incorporated June 16, 1729 as King's county. Name changed to Washington County Oct. 29, 1781. -- Cole, J. R., History of Washington and Kent Counties, New York: W. W. Preston & Co., 1889; 1334 p.

Washington, Tenn. (est. sess. of Nov. 15, 1777; 327 sq. mi.; 1970 pop.: 73, 924; 1960: 64, 832; 1950: 59, 971) (Jonesboro and Johnson City). George Washington*.

Washington, Tex. (est. Mar. 17, 1836; 611 sq. mi.; 1970 pop.: 18, 842; 1960: 19, 145; 1950: 20, 542) (Brenham). George Washington*. -- Dietrich, Wilfred O., The blazing story of Washington County, Brenham, Texas: Banner Press, 1960; 122 p. -- Schmidt, Charles Frank, History of Washington County, San Antonio, Texas: Naylor Co., 1949; 146 p.

Washington, Utah (est. Mar. 3, 1852; 2, 425 sq. mi.; 1970 pop.: 13, 669; 1960: 10, 271; 1950: 9, 836) (St. George). George Washington*. -- Daughters of Utah Pioneers, Under Dixie sun: A history of Washington County, Salt Lake City, Utah, 1950; 438 p.

Washington, Vt. (est. Nov. 1, 1810, org. Oct. 16, 1811, eff. Dec. 1, 1811; 708 sq. mi.; 1970 pop.: 47, 659: 1960: 42, 860; 1950: 42, 870) (Montpelier). George Washington*. (Originally Jefferson County, name changed Nov. 8, 1814, chap. 79). -- Hemenway, Abby Maria, History of Washington County, Montpelier, Vt.: Vermont Watchman and State Journal Press, 1882; 932 p.

Washington, Va. (est. sess. Oct. 7, 1776; 581 sq. mi.; 1970 pop.: 40, 835; 1960: 38, 076; 1950: 37, 536) (Abingdon). George Washington*.

Washington, Wis. (est. Dec. 7, 1836, org. Aug. 13, 1840; eff. Sept. 28, 1840, 428 sq. mi.; 1970 pop.: 63, 839; 1960: 46, 119; 1950: 33, 902) (West Bend). George Washington*. -- Quickert, Carl, The story of Washington County, West Bend, Wis.: C. Quickert, 1923; 230 p.

Washita, Okla. (est. July 16, 1907; 1, 009 sq. mi.; 1970

pop.: 12,141; 1960: 18,121; 1950: 17,657) (Cordell). French derivation; "faux Ouachita" for "false Washita" as opposed to the true Ouachita of Ariz.

Washoe, Nev. (est. Nov. 25, 1861; 6,281 sq. mi.; 1970 pop.: 121,068; 1960: 84,743; 1950: 50,205) (Reno). Washoe Indian tribe. Originally spelled Wassau or Wassou, anglicized to Washoe meaning "tall bunchgrass" or "ryegrass."

Washtenaw, Mich. (est. Sept. 10, 1822, org. Nov. 20, 1826 re-org. 1829; 716 sq. mi.; 1970 pop.: 234,103; 1960: 172,440; 1950: 134,606) (Ann Arbor). Chippewa Indian word for "river that is far off." -- Beakes, Samuel Willard, Past and present of Washtenaw County, Chicago: S. J. Clarke Pub. Co., 1906; 823 p.

Watauga, N. C. (est. Jan. 27, 1849; 320 sq. mi.; 1970 pop.: 23,404; 1960: 17,529; 1950: 18,342) (Boone). Watauga Indian tribe. -- Arthur, John Preston, A history of Watauga county, North Carolina, Richmond, Va.: Everett Waddey Co., 1915; 364 p. -- Whitener, Daniel Jay, History of Watauga County, Boone N. C., 1949; 112 p.

Watonwan, Minn. (est. Feb. 25, 1860; 433 sq. mi.; 1970 pop.: 13,298; 1960: 14,460; 1950: 13,881) (St. James). Watonwan River; Dakota or Sioux Indian word for "where fish abound" or "I see." -- Brown, John A., History of Cottonwood and Watonwan Counties, Indianapolis: B. F. Bowen & Co., Inc., 1916; 2 vol.

Waukesha, Wis. (est. Jan. 31, 1846; 556 sq. mi.; 1970 pop.: 231,365; 1960: 158,249; 1950: 85,901) (Waukesha). ("The Fastest Growing County in the State"). Pottawattomi Indian word for "fox." -- The history of Waukesha County, Chicago: Western Historical Co., 1880; 1006 p.

Waupaca, Wis. (est. Feb. 17, 1851; 751 sq. mi.; 1970 pop: 37,780; 1960: 35,340; 1950: 35,056) (Waupaca). Indian word for "white sand bottom." -- Wakefield, Josephus, The history of Waupaca County, Waupaca, Wis.: D. L. Stinchfield, 1890; 219 p.

Waushara, Wis. (est. Feb. 15, 1851; 628 sq. mi.; 1970 pop.: 14,795; 1960: 13,497; 1950: 13,920) (Wautoma). Indian word for "good land river."

Wayne, Ga. (est. May 11, 1803; 615 sq. mi.; 1970 pop.: 17,858; 1960: 17,921; 1950: 14,248) (Jesup). Anthony Wayne (1745-1796). Nicknamed "Mad Anthony;" Pa. house of representatives 1774-75; col. Fourth Regiment Pa. troops; wounded at battle of Three Rivers 1776; brig. gen. 1777; captured Stony Point; awarded thanks of Congress and a gold medal 1779; bvt. maj. gen. 1783; retired from army 1784; Pa. assembly 1784; Representative from Ga. 1791-92; maj. gen. and general-in-chief of Army, defeated Indians at Fallen Timbers 1793.

Wayne, Ill. (est. Mar. 26, 1819; 733 sq. mi.; 1970 pop.: 17,004; 1960: 19,008; 1950: 20,933) (Fairfield). Anthony Wayne*.

Wayne, Ind. (est. Nov. 27, 1810, eff. Feb. 1, 1811; 405 sq. mi.; 1970 pop.: 79,109; 1960: 74,039; 1950: 68,566) (Richmond). Anthony Wayne*.

Wayne, Iowa (est. Jan. 13, 1846; 532 sq. mi.; 1970 pop.: 8,405; 1960: 9,800; 1950: 11,737) (Corydon). Anthony Wayne*. -- Stuart, Theodore M., Past and present of Lucas and Wayne counties, Chicago: S.J. Clarke Pub.Co., 1913; 2 vol.

Wayne, Ky. (est. Dec. 18, 1800; 485 sq. mi.; 1970 pop.: 14,268; 1960: 14,700; 1950: 16,475) (Monticello). Anthony Wayne*. -- Johnson, Augusta (Phillips), A Century of Wayne County, Kentucky, 1800-1900, Louisville, Ky.: Standard Printing Co., Inc., 1939; 281 p.

Wayne, Mich. (est. Nov. 21, 1815, org. 1815; 607 sq. mi.; 1970 pop.: 2,666,751; 1960: 2,666,297; 1950: 2,435,235) (Detroit). Anthony Wayne*. -- Burton, Clarence Monroe, History of Wayne County, Chicago: S.J. Clarke Pub. Co., 1930; 5 vol.

Wayne, Miss. (est. Dec. 21, 1809; 812 sq. mi.; 1970 pop.: 16,650; 1960: 16,258; 1950: 17,010) (Waynesboro). Anthony Wayne*.

Wayne, Mo. (est. Dec. 11, 1818; 777 sq. mi.; 1970 pop.: 8,546; 1960: 8,638; 1950: 10,514) (Greenville). Anthony Wayne*.

Wayne, Neb. (est. Mar. 4, 1871, org. Mar. 4, 1871; 443 sq. mi.; 1970 pop.: 10,400; 1960: 9,959; 1950: 10,129) (Wayne). Anthony Wayne*. -- Nyberg, Dorothy (Huse), History of Wayne County, Neb., Wayne, Neb.: Wayne Herald, 1938; 306 p.

Wayne, N.Y. (est. Apr. 11, 1823; 607 sq. mi.; 1970 pop.: 79,404; 1960: 67,989; 1950: 57,323) (Lyons). Anthony Wayne*. -- Cowles, George Washington, Landmarks of Wayne County, New York: D. Mason and Co., 1895.

Wayne, N.C. (est. sess. Oct. 18, 1779; 555 sq. mi.; 1970 pop.: 85,408; 1960: 82,059; 1950: 64,267) (Goldsboro). Anthony Wayne*. -- Daniels, Frank Arthur, History of Wayne County, 1914; 43 p.

Wayne, Ohio (est. procl. Aug. 15, 1796; 561 sq. mi.; 1970 pop.: 87,123; 1960: 75,497; 1950: 58,716) (Wooster). Anthony Wayne*. -- Douglass, Ben, History of Wayne County, Indianapolis: R. Douglass, 1878; 868 p.

Wayne, Pa. (est. Mar. 21, 1798; 744 sq. mi.; 1970 pop.: 29,581; 1960: 28,237; 1950: 28,478) (Honesdale). Anthony

Wayne*. -- Goodrich, Phineas Grover, History of Wayne County, Honesdale, Pa.: Haines & Beardsley, 1880; 409p.

Wayne, Tenn. (est. Nov. 24, 1817; 741 sq. mi.; 1970 pop.: 12, 365; 1960: 11, 908; 1950: 13, 864) (Waynesboro). Anthony Wayne*.

Wayne, Utah (est. Mar. 10, 1892; 2, 489 sq. mi.; 1970 pop.: 1, 483; 1960: 1, 728; 1950: 2, 205) (Loa). Wayne Robinson. Son of Willis Robinson, Utah legislature.

Wayne, W. Va. (est. Jan. 18, 1842; 517 sq. mi.; 1970 pop.: 37, 581; 1960: 38, 977; 1950: 38, 696) (Wayne). Anthony Wayne*.

Weakley, Tenn. (est. Oct. 21, 1823; 576 sq. mi.; 1970 pop.: 28, 827; 1960: 24, 227; 1950: 27, 962) (Dresden). Robert Weakley (1764-1845). Revolutionary War 1780; N. C. house of representatives 1796; Representative from Tenn. 1809-11; Tenn. senate 1823-24; speaker Tenn. senate; Tenn. constitutional convention 1834.

Webb, Tex. (est. Jan. 28, 1848; 3, 295 sq. mi.; 1970 pop.: 72, 859; 1960: 64, 791; 1950: 56, 141) (Laredo). James Webb (1792-1856). Served in War of 1812; U. S. District Judge at Fla.; Tex. attorney gen. 1839-41; Tex. legislature 1841-44; Tex. Secretary of State 1850-51; constitutional convention 1845; Tex. Secretary of State 1850-51; Judge of 14th Judicial District 1854-56. Tex. supreme court reporter 1846-49.

Weber, Utah (est. Mar. 3, 1852; 549 sq. mi.; 1970 pop.: 126, 278; 1960: 110, 744; 1950: 83, 319) (Ogden). John G. Weber. Trapper under Gen. William H. Ashley 1823.

Webster, Ga. (est. Dec. 16, 1853; 302 sq. mi.; 1970 pop.: 2, 362; 1960: 3, 247; 1950: 4, 081) (Preston). Daniel Webster (1782-1852). Representative from N. H. 1813-17; Mass. constitutional convention 1820; Representative from Mass., 1823-27; Senator from Mass., 1827-41 and 1845-50; U. S. Secretary of State in cabinet of Pres. Tyler 1841-43 and Pres. Fillmore 1850-52. (Formerly Kinchafoonee County, name changed Feb. 21, 1856, act 367.)

Webster, Iowa (est. Jan. 15, 1851; 718 sq. mi.; 1970 pop.: 48, 391; 1960: 47, 810; 1950: 44, 241) (Fort Dodge). Daniel Webster*. (Formerly Risley County, name changed to Webster County, Jan. 12, 1853, eff. Mar. 1, 1853). -- Pratt, Harlow Munson, History of Fort Dodge and Webster County, Chicago: Pioneer Pub. Co., 1913; 2 vol.

Webster, Ky. (est. Feb. 29, 1860; 339 sq. mi.; 1970 pop.: 13, 282; 1960: 14, 244; 1950: 15, 555) (Dixon). Daniel Webster*.

Webster, La. (est. Feb. 27, 1871; 609 sq. mi.; 1970 pop.: 39, 939; 1960: 39, 701; 1950: 35, 704) (Minden). Daniel Webster*.

Webster, Miss. (est. Apr. 6, 1874; 416 sq. mi.; 1970 pop.: 10,047; 1960: 10,580; 1950: 11,607) (Walthall). Daniel Webster*. (Originally Sumner County, name changed to Webster County, Jan. 30, 1882, chap. 132.)

Webster, Mo. (est. Mar. 3, 1855; 590 sq. mi.; 1970 pop.: 15,562; 1960: 13,753; 1950: 15,072) (Marshfield). Daniel Webster*.

Webster, Neb. (est. Feb. 16, 1867, org. July 5, 1871; 575 sq. mi.; 1970 pop.: 6,477; 1960: 6,224; 1950: 7,395) (Red Cloud). Daniel Webster*.

Webster, W. Va. (est. Jan. 10, 1860; 558 sq. mi.; 1970 pop.: 9,809; 1960: 13,719; 1950: 17,888) (Webster Springs). Daniel Webster*. -- Thompson, R. L., _Webster County history-folklore_, Webster Springs, W. Va.: Star Printers, 1942; 200 p.

Weld, Colo. (est. Nov. 1, 1861; 4,004 sq. mi.; 1970 pop.: 89,297; 1960: 72,344; 1950: 67,504) (Greeley). ("The Land of Milk, Honey, Spuds and Sugar"; "The Largest County in the U. S. A."). Lewis Ledyard Weld. First Secretary of Colo. Terr. -- Jeffs, Mary L., _Under ten flags: a history of Weld County_, Greeley, Colo., 1938; 318 p. -- Krakel, Dean Fenton, _South Platte Country: a history of old Weld county,_ Laramie, Wyo.: Powder River, publishers, 1954; 301 p.

Wells, Ind. (est. Feb. 7, 1835, org. Feb. 2, 1837, eff. May 1, 1837; 368 sq. mi.; 1970 pop.: 23,821; 1960: 21,220; 1950: 19,564) (Bluffton). William Wells (- 1812). Adopted by Chief Little Turtle; aided Indians in war victories over Generals Harmar and St. Clair; returned to the whites where he served as Indian agent; aided Gen. Harrison's forces at Tippecanoe 1811; killed at Ft. Dearborn 1812.

Wells, N. D. (est. Jan. 4, 1873; 1,300 sq. mi.; 1970 pop.: 7,847; 1960: 9,237; 1950: 10,417) (Fessenden). Edward P. Wells (1847-18). N. D. terr. legislature 1881; land operator; banker, railroad man. (Formerly Gingras County, name changed to Wells County, Feb. 26, 1881).

West Baton Rouge, La. (est. Mar. 31, 1807; 214 sq. mi.; 1970 pop.: 16,864; 1960: 14,796; 1950: 11,738) (Port Allen). French words "baton rouge" meaning "red stick."

West Carroll, La. (est. Mar. 28, 1877; 366 sq. mi.; 1970 pop.: 13,028; 1960: 14,177; 1950: 17,248) (Oak Grove). Charles Carroll (1737-1832). See biography under Carroll.

West Feliciana, La. (est. Feb. 17, 1824; 352 sq. mi.; 1970 pop.: 11,376; 1960: 12,395; 1950: 10,169) (St. Francisville). Spanish "feliciana" meaning "happiness."

Westchester, N. Y. (est. Nov. 1, 1683; 435 sq. mi.; 1970

pop.: 891,409; 1960: 808,891; 1950: 625,816) (White Plains). Chester, England. -- Scharf, John Thomas, History of Westchester County, Philadelphia: L. E. Preston, 1886; 2 vol. -- Shonnard, Frederic and Spooner, W. W., History of Westchester County, New York: The New York History Co., 1900; 638 p.

Westmoreland, Pa. (est. Feb. 26, 1773; 1,025 sq. mi.; 1970 pop.: 376,935; 1960: 352,629; 1950: 313,179) (Greensburg). Westmoreland County, England. -- Bomberger, Christian Martin Hess, A short history of Westmoreland County, Jeannette, Pa.: Jeannette Pub. Co., 1941; 100 p. -- Boucher, John N., History of Westmoreland County, New York: Lewis Pub. Co., 1906; 3 vol.

Westmoreland, Va. (est. July 5, 1653; 236 sq. mi.; 1970 pop.: 12,142; 1960: 11,042; 1950: 10,148) (Montross). ("The Athens of Virginia (because of its great statesmen)"; "The Land of Worthwhile Living"). Westmoreland County, England. -- Wright, Thomas Roane Barnes, Westmoreland County, Richmond: Whittet & Shepperson, 1912; 153 p.

Weston, Wyo. (est. Mar. 12, 1890; 2,408 sq. mi.; 1970 pop.: 6,307; 1960: 7,929; 1950: 6,733) (Newcastle). J. B. Weston, Physician.

Wetzel, W. Va. (est. Jan. 10, 1846; 360 sq. mi.; 1970 pop.: 20,314; 1960: 19,347; 1950: 20,154) (New Martinsville). Lewis Wetzel (1764-1808). Indian fighter and scout; scalped by Indians. -- McEldowney Jr., John C., History of Wetzel County, 1901; 183 p.

Wexford, Mich. (est. Apr. 1, 1840, org. 1869; 563 sq. mi.; 1970 pop.: 19,717; 1960: 18,466; 1950: 18,618) (Cadillac). Wexford County, Ireland. (Originally laid out as Kautawaubet County, name changed to Wexford County on Mar. 8, 1843), Act 67.

Wharton, Tex. (est. Apr. 3, 1846; 1,079 sq. mi.; 1970 pop.: 36,729; 1960: 38,152; 1950: 36,077) (Wharton). William Harris Wharton (1802-1839). Emigrated to Tex. 1827; Tex. convention which asked for statehood 1832; siege at Bexar; one of three Tex. commissioners sent to U. S., for aid 1835; first Tex. minister to the U. S. 1836; returning from Washington captured and imprisoned by Mexicans 1837; escaped 1837; Tex. senate 1838; killed by pistol charge while dismounting from horse 1839.

Whatcom, Wash. (est. Mar. 9, 1854; 2,151 sq. mi.; 1970 pop.: 81,950; 1960: 70,317; 1950: 66,733) (Bellingham). Indian word "whuks-qua-koos-ta-qua" for "creek with the rumbling noise" or "noisy water." Also claimed for Indian chief Whatcom. -- Roth, Charlotte Tuttle (Roeder),

History of Whatcom County, Chicago: Pioneer Historical Pub. Co., 1926; 2 vol.

Wheatland, Mont. (est. Feb. 22, 1917; 1,425 sq. mi.; 1970 pop.: 2,529; 1960: 3,026; 1950: 3,187) (Harlowton). Descriptive.

Wheeler, Ga. (est. Aug. 14, 1912; 264 sq. mi.; 1970 pop.: 4,596; 1960: 5,342; 1950: 6,712) (Alamo). Joseph Wheller (1836-1906). Graduated U. S. Military Academy 1859; resigned commission entered Confederate Army 1861; commanded Army of the Miss. 1862; lt. gen. 1865; senior cavalry gen. Confederate Armies 1864; Representative from Ala. 1881-82, 1883 and 1885-1900; maj. gen. of vol. and commanded cavalry regiment 1898; commanded at battle of Las Guasimas 1898; senior member of commission which negotiated surrender of Spanish Army in Cuba 1898; fought in Tarlac campaign Philippine Islands 1899-1900; brig. gen. U. S. Regular Army 1900; wrote numerous books.

Wheeler, Neb. (est. Feb. 17, 1877, org. Apr. 11, 1811; 576 sq. mi.; 1970 pop.: 1,054; 1960: 1,297; 1950: 1,526) (Bartlett). Daniel H. Wheeler. Secretary Neb. Board of Administration.

Wheeler, Ore. (est. Feb. 17, 1899; 1,707 sq. mi.; 1970 pop.: 1,849; 1960: 2,722; 1950: 3,313) (Fossil). Henry H. Wheeler (1826-1915). Drove ox cart from Wis. to Calif. 1857; operated stage line between The Dalles and Canyon City, Ore., attacked by Indians; shot through the cheeks Sept. 7, 1866 but escaped, returned later to scene of attack and retrieved most of the loot.

Wheeler, Tex. (est. Aug. 21, 1876; 916 sq. mi.; 1970 pop.: 6,434; 1960: 7,947; 1950: 10,317) (Wheeler). Royal Tyler Wheeler (1810-1864). District attorney Fifth Judicial District Tex. 1842; District Judge 1844; assoc. justice Tex. supreme court 1854; chief justice Tex. supreme court 1857; prof. of law Austin College, 1858.

White, Ark. (est. Oct. 23, 1835, eff. Dec. 1, 1835; 1,042 sq. mi.; 1970 pop.: 39,253; 1960: 32,745; 1950: 38,040) (Searcy). Hugh Lawson White (1773-1840). Fought Cherokees; judge Tenn. supreme court 1801-07; Tenn. senate 1807-09; U. S. District Attorney 1808; judge of the supreme court 1809-15; Tenn. Senate 1817-25; Senator from Tenn., 1825-40; pres. pro tempore U. S. Senate 1832.

White, Ga. (est. Dec. 22, 1857; 245 sq. mi.; 1970 pop.: 7,742; 1960: 6,935; 1950: 5,951) (Cleveland). David T. White.

White, Ill. (est. Dec. 9, 1815; 507 sq. mi.; 1970 pop.: 17,312; 1960: 19,373; 1950: 20,935) (Carmi). Leonard

White. Ill. Constitutional convention 1818.

White, Ind. (est. Feb. 1, 1834, eff. Apr. 1, 1834; 497 sq. mi.; 1970 pop.: 20, 995; 1960: 19, 709; 1950: 18, 042) (Monticello). Isaac White. Col.

White, Tenn. (est. Sept. 11, 1806; 385 sq. mi.; 1970 pop.: 17, 088; 1960: 15, 577; 1950: 16, 204) (Sparta). John White (-1782). Col. 4th Ga. Battalion. He and six men lit fires in the woods at Savannah, Ga. on Oct. 1, 1779 and loudly shouted commands. The French capt. gave up 130 stands of arms and surrendered himself and regulars. -- Seals, Monroe, History of White County, Sparta, Tenn., c1935; 152 p.

White Pine, Nev. (est. Mar. 2, 1869; eff. Apr. 1, 1869; 8, 893 sq. mi.; 1970 pop.: 10, 150; 1960: 9, 808; 1950: 9, 424) (Ely). Descriptive. -- Read, Effie (Oxborrow), White Pine lang syne; a true history of White Pine County, Denver, Colo.: Big Mountain Press, 1965; 318 p.

Whiteside, Ill. (est. Jan. 16, 1836; 679 sq. mi.; 1970 pop.: 62, 877; 1960: 59, 987; 1950: 49, 336) (Morrison). Samuel Whiteside. Capt. mounted rifles 1812; capt. rangers 1813; honorable discharge 1814; brig. gen. Ill. vol. 1832; Black Hawk war; Ill. assembly. -- Bastian, Wayne, A History of Whiteside County, Ill., Morrison, Ill.: Whiteside County Board of Supervisors, 1968; 480 p. -- Davis, William W., History of Whiteside County, Ill., Chicago: Pioneer Pub. Co., 1908; 2 vol.

Whitfield, Ga. (est. Dec. 30, 1851; 283 sq. mi.; 1970 pop.: 55, 108; 1960: 42, 109; 1950: 34, 432) (Dalton). George Whitefield (1714-1770). Church of England clergyman arrived Savannah, Ga., May 7, 1738; constructed orphanage at Savannah 1740; compiled hymnbook 1753. -- Whitfield County History Commission, Official history of Whitfield County, Georgia, Dalton, Ga.: A. J. Showalter Co., 1936; 238 p.

Whitley, Ind. (est. Feb. 7, 1835, org. Feb. 17, 1838, eff. Apr. 1, 1838; 336 sq. mi.; 1970 pop.: 23, 395; 1960: 20, 954; 1950: 18, 828) (Columbia City). William Whitley (1749-1813). Indian fighter; enlisted as private at age of 63 served under Gov. Isaac Shelby in War of 1812; killed at battle of the River Thames 1813. -- Kaler, Samuel P., History of Whitley County, Indiana, Indianapolis: B. F. Bowen & Co., 1907; 861 p.

Whitley, Ky. (est. Jan. 17, 1818; 460 sq. mi.; 1970 pop.: 24, 145; 1960: 25, 815; 1950: 31, 940) (Williamsburg). William Whitley*.

Whitman, Wash. (est. Nov. 29, 1871; 2, 167 sq. mi.; 1970 pop.: 37, 900; 1960: 31, 263; 1950: 32, 469) (Colfax). Marcus

Whitman (1802-1847). Missionary in Ore. region 1835, 1836-42, 1843-47. He, his wife Narcissa Prentiss Whitman, and twelve others were massacred by Indians at the Cayuse outbreak on Nov. 29, 1847.

Wibaux, Mont. (est. Aug. 17, 1914 pet. and election; 889 sq. mi.; 1970 pop.: 1,465; 1960: 1,698; 1950: 1,807) (Wibaux). Pierre Wibaux. Cattleman, emigrated to Mont. 1883; owned 75,000 head of cattle.

Wichita, Kan. (est. Mar. 6, 1873, org. Dec. 24, 1886; 724 sq. mi.; 1970 pop.: 3,274; 1960: 2,765; 1950: 2,640) (Leoti). Wichita Indian tribe, named for Ouichita Indians; Indian for "big arbor" or "men of the north."

Wichita, Tex. (est. Feb. 1, 1858; 612 sq. mi.; 1970 pop.: 121,862; 1960: 123,528; 1950: 98,493) (Wichita Falls). Wichita Indian tribe*.

Wicomico, Md. (est. Constitution Aug. 17, 1867 (Article 13, Section 2-4); 380 sq. mi.; 1970 pop.: 54,236; 1960: 49,050; 1950: 39,641) (Salisbury). Wicomico River; Indian word "wicko-mekee" for "where house are built."

Wilbarger, Tex. (est. Feb. 1, 1858; 954 sq. mi.; 1970 pop.: 15,355; 1960: 17,748; 1950: 20,552) (Vernon). Josiah Pugh Wilbarger (1801-1845). Teacher and surveyor, member of surveying party attacked by Comanche Indians and scalped 1833; died 12 years later. Brother: Mathias Wilbarger (1807-1853). Emigrated to Tex. in 1829 to join his brother. -- Vernon Times, Early-day history of Wilbarger County, Vernon, Texas, 1933; 208 p.

Wilcox, Ala. (est. Dec. 13, 1819; 900 sq. mi.; 1970 pop.: 16,303; 1960: 18,739; 1950: 23,476) (Camden). Lt. Joseph M. Wilcox. Killed by Indians 1814.

Wilcox, Ga. (est. Dec. 22, 1857; 403 sq. mi.; 1970 pop.: 6,998; 1960: 7,905; 1950: 10,167) (Abbeville). John Wilcox. Capt.

Wilkes, Ga. (est. Feb. 5, 1777; 458 sq. mi.; 1970 pop.: 10,184; 1960: 10,961; 1950: 12,388) (Washington). John Wilkes (1727-1797). England's house of commons; favored colonies in American Revolution. -- Bowen, Eliza A., Story of Wilkes County, Georgia, Marietta, Ga.: Continental Book Co., 1950; 192 p.

Wilkes, N.C. (est. sess. Nov. 15, 1777; 765 sq. mi.; 1970 pop.: 49,524; 1960: 45,269; 1950: 45,243) (Wilkesboro). John Wilkes*. -- Hayes, Johnson J., The land of Wilkes, Wilkesboro, N.C.: Wilkes County Historical Society, 1962; 577 p. -- Hickerson, Thomas Felix, Happy Valley, history and genealogy, Chapel Hill, N.C., 1940; 244 p.

Wilkin, Minn. (est. Mar. 18, 1858; 752 sq. mi.; 1970 pop.: 9,389; 1960: 10,650; 1950: 10,567) (Breckenridge).

Alexander Wilkin (-1864). Capt. inf. 1847; resigned 1848; Secretary of Minn. Terr. 1851-53; U. S. Marshal for Minn., capt. 1st Minn. inf. 1861; mustered out 1861; maj. 2nd Minn. inf. 1861; lt. col. and col. 1862; killed battle of Tupelo, Miss. July 14, 1864. (Originally Toombs County, name changed to Andy Johnson County Mar. 18, 1862; name changed from Andy Johnson County to Wilkin County, Mar. 6, 1868, chap. 115)

Wilkinson, Ga. (est. May 11, 1803, org. Dec. 1805; 472 sq. mi.; 1970 pop.: 9,393; 1960: 9,250; 1950: 9,781) (Irwinton). James Wilkinson (1757-1825). Capt. in Continental Army; fought under Arnold, Gates and Washington in Revolutionary War; forced to resign 1781; fought Indians 1791; brig. gen. U. S. Army 1792; represented U.S. in taking over Louisiana Terr.; first gov. of La. terr. 1805-07; commanded troops in attacks against Canadian border War of 1812. -- Davidson, Victor, History of Wilkinson County, Macon, Ga.: J. W. Burke Co., 1930; 645 p.

Wilkinson, Miss. (est. Jan. 30, 1802; 667 sq. mi.; 1970 pop.: 11,099; 1960: 13,235; 1950: 14,116) (Woodville). James Wilkinson*.

Will, Ill. (est. Jan. 12, 1836; 844 sq. mi.; 1970 pop.: 249,498; 1960: 191,617; 1950: 134,336) (Joliet). Conrad Will. Ill. constitutional convention; Ill. general assembly. -- Maue, August, History of Will County, Topeka: Historical Pub. Co., 1928; 2 vol.

Willacy, Tex. (est. Mar. 11, 1911; 595 sq. mi.; 1970 pop.: 15,570; 1960: 20,084; 1950: 20,920) (Raymondville). John G. Willacy (1850-1943). Emigrated to Tex. 1892; Tex. legislature 1899-1914.

Williams, N. D. (est. Jan. 8, 1873; 2,100 sq. mi.; 1970 pop.: 19,301; 1960: 22,051; 1950: 16,442) (Williston). Erastus A. Williams. Emigrated to Dakota Terr. 1872; Dakota terr. legislature; N. D. surveyor general.

Williams, Ohio (est. Feb. 12, 1820; 421 sq. mi.; 1970 pop.: 33,669; 1960: 29,968; 1950: 26,202) (Bryan). David Williams. One of the capturers of John Andre on Sept. 23, 1780. -- Shinn, Williams Henry, The County of Williams, Madison, Wis.: Northwestern Historical Association, 1905; 611 p. -- Whitson, Rolland Lewis, A standard history of Williams County, Chicago: Lewis Pub. Co., 1920; 2 vol.

Williamsburg, S. C. (est. Mar. 12, 1785; 931 sq. mi.; 1970 pop.: 34,243; 1960: 40,932; 1950: 43,807) (Kingstree). William III (1650-1702). Son of William II Prince of Orange and Mary; married his cousin, Mary, 1677; landed at Torbay, Devonshire, with Dutch Army 1688; crowned king with Mary queen 1689; reigned as sole soverign after her death 1694; died from fall off horse 1702. -- Boddie, William Willis, History of Williamsburg, Columbia, S. C. : The State Co., 1923; 611 p.

Williamson, Ill. (est. Feb. 28, 1839; 449 sq. mi. ; 1970 pop. : 49, 021; 1960: 46, 117; 1950: 48, 621) (Marion). Williamson County, Tenn. -- Erwin, Mils, History of Williamson County, Marion, Ill. : Mils Erwin, 1876; 189 p.

Williamson, Tenn. (est. Oct. 26, 1799; 594 sq. mi. ; 1970 pop. : 34, 330; 1960: 25, 267; 1950: 24, 307) (Franklin). Hugh Williamson (1735-1819). Studied theology; licensed to preach 1757; prof. of mathematics, College of Philadelphia; practiced as physician until 1773; surgeon general troops of N. C. 1779-82; N. C. house of commons 1782; Continental Congress 1782-85, 1787 and 1788; Federal Constitutional Convention 1787; Representative from N. C. 1789-93.

Williamson, Tex. (est. Mar. 13, 1848; 1, 126 sq. mi. ; 1970 pop. : 37, 305; 1960: 35, 044; 1950: 38, 853) (Georgetown). Robert McAlpin Williamson (1806-1859) known as "Three Legged Willie" because of his wooden leg. Emigrated to Tex. 1826; edited "The Cotton Plant" 1829-31; maj. Tex. Republic army 1835; battle of San Jacinto 1836; judge third judicial district 1836; Tex. legislature.

Wilson, Kan. (est. Aug. 30, 1855; 574 sq. mi. ; 1970 pop. : 11, 317; 1960: 13, 077; 1950: 14, 815) (Fredonia). Hiero T. Wilson. Early settler and merchant at Ft. Scott, Kan. 1843-54.

Wilson, N. C. (est. Feb. 13, 1855; 373 sq. mi. ; 1970 pop. : 57, 486; 1960: 57, 716; 1950: 54, 506) (Wilson). Louis D. Wilson (1789-1847). Represented Edgecombe County for 19 years in N. C. general assembly; capt. N. C. vol. 1847; col. inf. 1847; died of fever at Vera Cruz.

Wilson, Tenn. (est. Oct. 26, 1799; 580 sq. mi. ; 1970 pop. : 36, 999; 1960: 27, 668; 1950: 26, 318) (Lebanon). David Wilson. Revolutionary War. Tenn. terr. assembly 1794; speaker Tenn. terr. house of representatives 1794. -- History Associates of Wilson County, History of Wilson County, [Lebanon, Tenn., 1961], 453 p.

Wilson, Tex. (est. Feb. 13, 1860; 802 sq. mi. ; 1970 pop. : 13, 041; 1960: 13, 267; 1950: 14, 672) (Floresville). James Charles Wilson (1816-1861). Private Mier expedition 1842; Somervell expedition imprisoned and escaped 1843; Brazoria district clerk 1845; Tex. senate 1851-52.

Windham, Conn. (est. sess. May 12, 1726; 516 sq. mi. ; 1970 pop. : 84, 515; 1960: 68, 572; 1950: 61, 759) (No county seat). Windham, England. -- Lincoln, Allen Bennett, A Modern History of Windham County, Chicago: S. J. Clarke Pub. Co., 1920; 2 vol. -- Larned, Ellen Douglas, History of Windham County, Worcester, Mass., 1880; 2 vol.

Windham, Vt. (est. Feb. 22, 1781; 793 sq. mi.; 1970 pop.: 33, 074; 1960: 29, 776; 1950: 28, 749) (Newfane). Windham, Conn.

Windsor, Vt. (est. Feb. 22, 1781; 965 sq. mi.; 1970 pop.: 44, 082; 1960: 42, 483; 1950: 40, 885) (Woodstock). Windsor, England.

Winkler, Tex. (est. Feb. 26, 1887; 887 sq. mi.; 1970 pop.: 9, 640; 1960: 13, 652; 1950: 10, 064) (Kermit). Clinton McKamy Winkler (1827-1882). Went to Tex., fought Indians 1840; deputy clerk Robertson County 1842-43; Tex. legislature 1848; Confederate Army 1861; wounded at Gettysburg 1863; maj.; lt. col.; judge of Court of Civil Appeals 1876-82.

Winn. La. (est. Feb. 24, 1852; 969 sq. mi.; 1970 pop.: 16, 369; 1960: 16, 034; 1950: 16, 119) (Winnfield). Walter O. Winn. Attorney, Alexandria, La.

Winnebago, Ill. (est. Jan. 16, 1836; 529 sq. mi.; 1970 pop.: 246, 623; 1960: 209, 765; 1950: 152, 385) (Rockford). Winnebago Indian tribe; "people of stinking water." -- Drury, John, This Is Winnebago County, Chicago: Inland Photo Co., 1956; 386 p.

Winnebago, Iowa (est. Feb. 20, 1847, org. Jan. 15, 1851; 402 sq. mi.; 1970 pop.: 12, 990; 1960: 13, 099; 1950: 13, 450) (Forest City). Winnebago Indian tribe*. -- History of Kossuth, Hancock and Winnebago Counties, Springfield, Ill.: Union Pub. Co., 1884; 933 p. -- History of Winnebago County and Hancock County, Chicago: Pioneer Pub. Co., 1917; 2 vol.

Winnebago, Wis. (est. Jan. 6, 1840, org. Feb. 18, 1842, eff. Apr. 4, 1842; 454 sq. mi.; 1970 pop.: 129, 931; 1960: 107, 928; 1950: 91, 103) (Oshkosh). Winnebago Indian tribe*. -- Harney, Richard J., History of Winnebago County, Oshkosh, Wis.: Allen & Hicks, 1880; 348 p.

Winneshiek, Iowa (est. Feb. 20, 1847, org. Jan. 15, 1851, eff. Mar. 1, 1851; 688 sq. mi.; 1970 pop.: 21, 758; 1960: 21, 651; 1950: 21, 639) (Decorah). ("The Scenic Wonderland of Iowa). Winneshiek. Chief of the Winnebago Indian tribe. -- Bailey, Edwin C., Past and present of Winneshiek County, Chicago: S. J. Clarke Pub. Co., 1913; 2 vol.

Winona, Minn. (est. Feb. 23, 1854; 623 sq. mi.; 1970 pop.: 44, 409; 1960: 40, 937; 1950: 39, 841) (Winona). Winona. Dakota Indian woman, cousin of Wabasha, the last chief, who moved the tribe to its present site; diminutive of "wino" meaning "woman."

Winston, Ala. (est. Feb. 12, 1850; 633 sq. mi.; 1970 pop.: 16,654; 1960: 14,858; 1950: 18,250) (Double Springs). John Anthony Winston (1812-1871). Fifteenth gov. of Ala. Cotton commission house, Mobile, Ala., 1844-71; Ala. assembly 1840-45; Ala. senate 1845; col. First Ala. vol. 1846; Ala. senate 1851; Ala. gov. 1853-57; Confederate Army. Ala. senate 1867. (Originally Hancock County; changed to present name Jan. 22, 1858), Act 322.

Winston, Miss. (est. Dec. 23, 1833; 597 sq. mi.; 1970 pop.: 18,406; 1960: 19,246; 1950: 22,231) (Louisville). Louis Winston.

Wirt, W. Va. (est. Jan. 19, 1848; 234 sq. mi.; 1970 pop.: 4,154; 1960: 4,391; 1950: 5,119) (Elizabeth). William Wirt (1774-1838). Prosecuted case against Aaron Burr 1807; Va. house of delegates 1808; capt. of artillery 1812; attorney for district of Richmond 1816; U. S. Attorney Gen. 1817-29; presidential candidate 1832.

Wise, Tex. (est. Jan. 23, 1856; 909 sq. mi.; 1970 pop.: 19,687; 1960: 17,012; 1950: 16,141) (Decatur). Henry Alexander Wise (1806-1876). Thirty-eighth gov. of Va. (Commonwealth). Representative from Va. 1833-44; U.S. Minister to Brazil 1844-47; Va. constitutional convention 1850; gov. of Va. 1856-60; Va. secession convention 1861; brig. gen.; maj. gen. Confederate Army. -- Gates, Cliff Donahue, Pioneer History of Wise County, Decatur, Texas, 1907; 471 p.

Wise, Va. (est. Feb. 16, 1856; 414 sq. mi.; 1970 pop.: 35,947; 1960: 43,579; 1950: 56,336) (Wise). Henry Alexander Wise*. -- Addington, Luther F., The Story of Wise County, Va., 1956; 296 p. -- Johnson, Charles A., A Narrative History of Wise County, Norton, Va.: The Norton Press, Inc., 1938; 416 p.

Wolfe, Ky. (est. Mar. 5, 1860; 227 sq. mi.; 1970 pop.: 5,669; 1960: 6,534; 1950: 7,615) (Campton). Nathaniel Wolfe (1810-1865). Ky. attorney 1839-52; Ky. senate 1853-55; Ky. house of representatives 1859-61 and 1861-63. -- Wolfe County Woman's Club, Early and Modern History of Wolfe County, Compton, Ky., 1958; 340 p.

Wood, Ohio (est. Feb. 12, 1820; 618 sq. mi.; 1970 pop.: 89,722; 1960: 72,596; 1950: 59,605) (Bowling Green). Eleazer Derby Wood (1783-1814). Built Ft. Meigs, Ohio, 1813. -- Evers, Charles W., Many incidents and reminiscences of the early history of Wood County, Bowling Green, Ohio: The Democrat, 1910; 264 p.

Wood, Tex. (est. Feb. 5, 1850; 723 sq. mi.; 1970 pop.:

18,859; 1960: 17,653; 1950: 21,308) (Quitman). ("The Jewel of East Texas"). George Tyler Wood (1795-1856). Second gov. of Tex. Battle of Horseshoe Bend, Creek Indian War 1814; Ga. assembly 1837-38; Tex. constitutional convention 1845; Tex. Mounted Vol. 1846; Tex. senate 1846; gov. of Tex. 1847-49.

Wood, W. Va. (est. Dec. 21, 1798; 377 sq. mi.; 1970 pop.: 86,818; 1960: 78,331; 1950: 66,540) (Parkersburg). James Wood (1741-1813). Tenth gov. of Va. (Commonwealth). Fought Indians 1763; capt. 1764; fought Indians 1774; Va. house of burgesses 1775; col. 8th regiment 1776; battle of Brandywine 1777; supt. of all troops in Va. 1781; brig. gen. Va. troops 1783; Va. executive council 1784; gov. of Va. 1796-99. -- Shaw, Stephen Chester, Sketches of Wood County, Parkersburg, W. Va.: reprinted by W. G. Tetrick, 1932.

Wood, Wis. (est. Mar. 29, 1856; 812 sq. mi.; 1970 pop.: 65,362; 1960: 59,105; 1950: 50,500) (Wisconsin Rapids). Joseph Wood. County judge 1857.

Woodbury, Iowa (est. Jan. 15, 1851, org. Jan. 12, 1853, eff. Mar. 7, 1853; 866 sq. mi.; 1970 pop.: 103,052; 1960: 107,849; 1950: 103,917) (Sioux City). Levi Woodbury (1789-1851). Ninth gov. of N. H. N. H. gov. 1823-24; N. H. house of representatives 1825; Senator from N. H., 1825-31 and 1841-45; U. S. Secretary of the Navy in Pres. Jackson's cabinet 1831-34; U. S. Secretary of the Treas. in the cabinets of Pres. Jackson and Pres. Van Buren 1834-41; Associate Justice U. S. Supreme Court 1845-51. (Formerly Wahkaw County, name changed to Woodbury, County, Jan. 12, 1853, eff. Mar. 7, 1853, Chap. 12). -- History of the counties of Woodburg and Plymouth, Chicago: A. Warner & Co., 1890-91; 1022 p.

Woodford, Ill. (est. Feb. 27, 1841; 528 sq. mi.; 1970 pop.: 28,012; 1960: 24,579; 1950: 21,335) (Eureka). -- Drury, John, This Is Woodford County, Chicago: Loree Co., 1955; 410 p.

Woodford, Ky. (est. Nov. 12, 1788, eff. May 1, 1789; 193 sq. mi.; 1970 pop.: 14,434; 1960: 11,913; 1950: 11,212) (Versailles). William Woodford (1735-1780). French and Indian war 1755; col. second Va. regiment 1775; brig. gen. Continental Army 1777; wounded at Brandywine 1777; prisoner at Charleston, died in captivity 1780. -- Railey, William Edward, History of Woodford County, Frankfort, Ky.: Roberts Printing Co., 1938; 449 p.

Woodruff, Ark. (est. Nov. 26, 1862; 592 sq. mi.; 1970 pop.: 11,566; 1960: 13,954; 1950: 18,957) (Augusta). William E. Woodruff (1795-1885). Journeyman printer 1817; artillery company 1812; established Ark. "Gazette" 1818; Ark. state treas. 1836-38; postmaster, Little Rock, Ark., 1845; Ark. "Gazette" and "Democrat" 1850.

Woods, Okla. (est. July 16, 1907; 1,272 sq. mi.; 1970 pop.: 11,920; 1960: 11,932; 1950: 14,526) (Alva). Samuel N. Wood (-1814). Cy. name misspelled. Grad. U. S. Mil. Aca., 1805; 2nd lt. engineers 1806; 1st lt. 1808; capt. 1812; bvt. maj. 1813 for distinguished services at Ft. Meigs, Ohio; bvt. lt. col. for distinguished service, battle of Niagara, Upper Canada; killed in sortie from Ft. Erie, Upper Canada, Sept. 17, 1814. -- Crissman, George R., History of Woods County, Okla., Alva, Okla., 1930?; 119 p.

Woodson, Kan. (est. Aug. 30, 1855; 504 sq. mi.; 1970 pop.: 4,789; 1960: 5,423; 1950: 6,711) (Yates Center). Daniel Woodson. Secretary of Kan. Terr. 1854-57.

Woodward, Okla. (est. July 16, 1907; 1,235 sq. mi.; 1970 pop.: 15,537; 1960: 13,902; 1950: 14,383) (Woodward). B. W. Woodward. Sante Fe RR Co. director.

Worcester, Md. (est. Oct. 29, 1742; 483 sq. mi.; 1970 pop.: 24,442; 1960: 23,733; 1950: 23,148) (Snow Hill). Worcester, England. Earl of Worcester.

Worcester, Mass. (est. Apr. 5, 1731, eff. July 10, 1731; 1,532 sq. mi.; 1970 pop.: 637,969; 1960: 583,228; 1950: 546,401) (Fitchburg and Worcester). Worcester, England*. -- Crane, Ellery Bicknell, History of Worcester County, Chicago: Lewis Historical Pub. Co., 1924; 3 vol.

Worth, Ga. (est. Dec. 20, 1853; 651 sq. mi.; 1970 pop.: 14,770; 1960: 16,682; 1950: 19,357) (Sylvester). William Jenkins Worth (1794-1849). First lt. U. S. Inf. 1813; capt. 1814; maj. 1832; bvt. capt. for distinguished conduct at Chippewa, Upper Canada 1814; lt. col. for ten years; commandant of cadets at U. S. Military Academy 1820-28; service as maj. 1824; col. 1838; fought Seminole Indians in Fla. 1838; bvt. brig. gen. for heroism against Fla. Indians 1842; bvt. maj. gen. for heroism against Mexicans 1846; awarded sword by Congress 1847. -- Grubbs, Lillie (Martin), History of Worth County, Georgia, Macon, Ga.: J. W. Burke Co., 1934; 594 p.

Worth, Iowa (est. Jan. 15, 1851; 401 sq. mi.; 1970 pop.: 8,968; 1960: 10,259; 1950: 11,068) (Northwood). William Jenkins Worth*. -- Clyde, Jefferson F. and Dwelle, H.A., History of Mitchell and Worth counties, Chicago: S. J. Clarke Pub. Co., 1918; 2 vol.

Worth, Mo. (est. Feb. 8, 1861; 267 sq. mi.; 1970 pop.:

3,359; 1960: 3,936; 1950: 5,120) (Grant City). William Jenkins Worth*.

Wright, Iowa (est. Jan. 15, 1851; 577 sq. mi.; 1970 pop.: 17,294; 1960: 19,447; 1950: 19,652) (Clarion). Joseph Albert Wright (1810-1867). Gov. of Ind.; Ind. house of representatives 1833; Ind. senate 1840; Representative from Ind. 1843-45; gov. of Ind. 1849-57; U.S. Minister to Prussia 1857-61 and 1865-67; Senator from Ind., 1862-1863. Also claimed to have been named for Silas Wright (1795-1847). Sixteenth gov. of N.Y. Surrogate St. Lawrence County, N.Y. 1821-24; N.Y. Senate 1824-27; brig. gen. N.Y. militia 1827; Representative from N.Y. 1827-29; N.Y. State comptroller 1829-33; Senator from N.Y. 1833-45; gov. of N.Y. 1844-46. -- Stevenson, J.H., History and business directory of Wright County, Des Moines: J.H. Stevenson, 1870; 92 p.

Wright, Minn. (est. Feb. 20, 1855, org. Mar. 2, 1855; 671 sq. mi.; 1970 pop.: 38,933; 1960: 29,935; 1950: 27,716) (Buffalo). Silas Wright*. -- French, Clarence A. and Lamson, F.B., Condensed history of Wright County, Delano, Minn.: Eagle Printing Co., 1935; 228 p.

Wright, Mo. (est. Jan. 29, 1841; 684 sq. mi.; 1970 pop.: 13,667; 1960: 14,183; 1950: 15,834) (Hartville). Silas Wright*.

Wyandot, Ohio (est. Feb. 3, 1845; 406 sq. mi.; 1970 pop.: 21,826; 1960: 21,648; 1950: 19,785) (Upper Sandusky). Wyandot Indians, Indian word meaning "around the plains." -- Marsh, Thelma R., Lest we forget, Upper Sandusky, Ohio, 1967; 54 p.

Wyandotte, Kan. (est. Jan. 29, 1859; 151 sq. mi.; 1970 pop.: 186,845; 1960: 185,495; 1950: 165,318) (Kansas City). Wyandotte Indian tribe*.

Wyoming, N.Y. (est. May 19, 1841; 598 sq. mi.; 1970 pop.: 37,688; 1960: 34,793; 1950: 32,822) (Warsaw). Wyoming Indian tribe. Indian word for "broad bottom lands" or "big plains." -- Child, Hamilton, Gazetteer and business directory of Wyoming County, Syracuse, N.Y.: Journal Office, 1870; 237 p.

Wyoming, Pa. (est. Apr. 4, 1842; 396 sq. mi.; 1970 pop.: 19,082; 1960: 16,813; 1950: 16,766) (Tunkhannock). Wyoming Indian tribe*.

Wyoming, W. Va. (est. Jan. 26, 1850; 507 sq. mi.; 1970 pop.: 30,095; 1960: 34,836; 1950: 37,540) (Pineville). Wyoming Indian tribe*. -- Bowman, Mary Keller, Reference book of Wyoming County history Parsons, W. Va.: McClain Printing Co., 1965; 492 p.

Wythe, Va. (est. Dec. 1, 1789, eff. May 1, 1790; 460 sq.

mi.; 1970 pop.: 22,139; 1960: 21,975; 1950: 23,327) (Wytheville). George Wythe (1726-1806). Va. house of burgesses 1758-68; Va. committee of correspondence 1759; clerk Va. house of burgesses 1768-75; Continental Congress 1775-77; signer Declaration of Independence 1776; chancellor of Va., 1778; prof. of law William and Mary College 1779-91; federal constitutional convention 1787.

Y

Yadkin, N. C. (est. Dec. 28, 1850; 335 sq. mi.; 1970 pop.: 24,599; 1960: 22,804; 1950: 22,133) (Yadkinville). Indian word for "reatkin." -- Rutledge, William E., An illustrated history of Yadkin County 1850-1965, Yadkinville, N. C., 1965; 180 p.

Yakima, Wash. (est. Jan. 21, 1865; 4,273; sq. mi.; 1970 pop.: 144,971; 1960: 145, ; 1950: 136,) (Yakima). Yakima Indian tribe, word for "black bear."

Yalobusha, Miss. (est. Dec. 23, 1833; 490 sq. mi.; 1970 pop.: 11,915; 1960: 12,502; 1950: 15,191) (Coffeeville and Water Valley). Indian word for "tadpole place."

Yamhill, Ore. (est. July 5, 1843; 709 sq. mi.; 1970 pop.: 40,213; 1960: 32,478; 1950: 33,484) (McMinnville). Yamhill River; Yamhill [Yamel] Indian tribe.

Yancey, N. C. (est. 1833; 311 sq. mi.; 1970 pop.: 12,629; 1960: 14,008; 1950: 16,306) (Burnsville). Bartlett Yancey (1785-1828). Representative from N. C. 1813-17; N. C. senate 1817-27; declined appointment as U. S. Minister to Peru and to supreme court of N. C.; died while a candidate for the Senate.

Yankton, S. D. (est. Apr. 10, 1862; 524 sq. mi.; 1970 pop.: 19,039; 1960: 17,551; 1950: 16,804) (Yankton). Yankton Indian tribe; corruption of Sioux word "ihanktonwan" meaning "end village."

Yates, N. Y. (est. Feb. 5, 1823; 344 sq. mi.; 1970 pop.: 19,831; 1960: 18,614; 1950: 17,615) (Penn Yan). Joseph Christopher Yates (1768-1837). Eighth gov. of N. Y. First mayor of Schenectady, N. Y. 1798; N. Y. senate 1805; N. Y. supreme court 1808-22; gov. of N. Y. 1823-24. -- Aldrich, Lewis Cass, History of Yates County, Syracuse: D. Mason & Co., 1892; 671 p.

Yavapai, Ariz. (est. Dec. 21, 1864; 8,091 sq. mi.; 1970 pop.: 36,733; 1960: 28,912; 1950: 24,991) (Prescott). ("The County Where the Historic Verde Flows"). Yavapai Indian tribe. "Yava" meaning "the hill" and "pais"

Spanish word for the county. -- Yavapai Cow Belles of Arizona, Echoes of the Past, Prescott, Arizona, 1964; 2 vol.

Yazoo, Miss. (est. Jan. 21, 1823; 905 sq. mi.; 1970 pop.: 27,304; 1960: 31,653; 1950: 35,712) (Yazoo City). ("The Mecca for the Sportsman"). Yazoo tribe, name meaning "to blow on an instrument."

Yell, Ark. (est. Dec. 5, 1840; 942 sq. mi.; 1970 pop.: 14,208; 1960: 11,940; 1950: 14,057) (Danville and Dardanelle). Archibald Yell (1797-1847). Second gov. of Ark. Fought against Creek Indians; fought at battle of New Orleans 1815; judge of Ark. Terr. 1832-35; Representative from Ark. 1836-39 and 1845-46; gov. of Ark., 1840-44; col. First Ark. Vol. Cavalry 1846; killed at battle of Buena Vista, Feb. 22, 1847. -- Banks, Wayne, History of Yell County, Arkansas, Van Buren, Ark.: Press Argus, 1959; 298 p.

Yellow Medicine, Minn. (est. Mar. 6, 1871; 758 sq. mi.; 1970 pop.: 14,418; 1960: 15,523; 1950: 16,279) (Granite Falls). Yellow Medicine River. Translation of Dakota or Sioux name referring to yellow root of the moonseed used as a medicine by the Indians. -- Rose, Arthur P., An illustrated history of Yellow Medicine County, Marshall, Minn.: Northern History Pub. Co., 1914; 562 p.

Yellowstone, Mont. (est. Feb. 26, 1883, eff. May 1, 1883; 2,635 sq. mi.; 1970 pop.: 87,367; 1960: 79,016; 1950: 55,875) (Billings). Descriptive.

Yoakum, Tex. (est. Aug. 21, 1876; 830 sq. mi.; 1970 pop.: 7,344; 1960: 8,032; 1950: 4,339) (Plains). Henderson King Yoakum (1810-1856). Graduated U. S. Military Academy 1832; second lt. 1832; resigned 1833; capt. Tenn. mounted militia 1836; mayor of Murfreesboro, Ark. 1837; col. Tenn. inf. Cherokee war 1838; Tenn. senate 1839; private to first lt. Mexican war 1846; battle of Monterey, Mex., 1846; trustee Austin College 1849-56; wrote "History of Texas" 1855.

Yolo, Calif. (est. Feb. 18, 1850; 1,034 sq. mi.; 1970 pop.: 91,788; 1960: 65,727; 1950: 40,640) (Woodland). ("California's Reserve Fuel Bin"). Yoloy Indian tribe. -- Gregory, Thomas Jefferson, Los Angeles: Historic Record Co., 1913; 889 p.

York, Me. (est. Nov. 20, 1652; 1,000 sq. mi.; 1970 pop.: 111,576; 1960: 99,402; 1950: 93,541) (Alfred). ("Main in a Nutshell"; "The Show Window of Maine"; "The Southern Gateway to Maine"). James II, (1633-1701). Duke of York and Albany; second son of Charles I and Queen Henrietta Maria; created Duke of York and Albany 1643;

succeded to the throne upon death of Charles II and became King of England, Scotland and Ireland 1685; escaped to France 1688; decisively defeated at the battle of the Boyne by William 1690. -- Clayton, W. Woodford, History of York County, Philadelphia: Everts & Peck, 1880; 442 p.

York, Neb. (est. Mar. 13, 1855, org. Jan. 4, 1870; 577 sq. mi.; 1970 pop.: 13,685; 1960: 13,724; 1950: 14,346) (York). Duke of York*. -- Sedgwick, T. E., York County, Nebraska and its people, Chicago: S. J. Clarke Pub. Co., 1921; 2 vol.

York, Pa. (est. sess. Oct. 14, 1748; Aug. 19, 1749; 914 sq. mi.; 1970 pop.: 272,603; 1960: 238,336; 1950: 202,737) (York). Duke of York*. -- Gibson, John, History of York County, Chicago: F. A. Battey Pub. Co., 1886; 772p. -- Prowell, George R., History of York County, Chicago: J. H. Beers & Co., 1907; 2 vol.

York, S. C. (est. Mar. 12, 1785; 685 sq. mi.; 1970 pop.: 85,216; 1960: 78,760; 1950: 71,596) (York). Duke of York*.

York, Va. (est. 1634; 123 sq. mi.; 1970 pop.: 33,203; 1960: 21,583; 1950: 11,750) (Yorktown). Duke of York*.

Young, Tex. (est. Feb. 2, 1856; 899 sq. mi.; 1970 pop.: 15,400; 1960: 17,254; 1950: 16,810) (Graham). William Cocke Young (1812-1862). Sheriff Red River County, Tex. 1837; district attorney Seventh Judicial District Republic of Tex. 1844; Tex. constitutional convention 1845; Mexican War 1846; U. S. marshal at Shawneetown, Ill. 1851; organized and commanded 11th Tex. Regiment, Cavalry, 1861; murdered in Ute uprising Oct. 16, 1862. -- Crouch, Carrie (Johnson), History of Young County, Texas, Austin, Texas: State Historical Assn., 1956; 326 p.

Yuba, Calif. (est. Feb. 18, 1850; 638 sq. mi.; 1970 pop.: 44,736; 1960: 33,859; 1950: 24,420) (Marysville). Spanish word, corruption "uvas" for "grapes." -- Yuba County, Calif., Board of Supervisors Yuba County, Marysville, 1908; 31 p.

Yuma, Ariz. (est. Dec. 21, 1864; 9,985 sq. mi.; 1970 pop.: 60,827; 1960: 46,235; 1950: 28,006) (Yuma). ("The County Where the Sun Is King"). Yuma Indian tribe. -- Woznicki, Robert, The History of Yuma, Calexico?, Calif., 1968; 116 p.

Yuma, Colo. (est. Mar. 15, 1889; 2,383 sq. mi.; 1970 pop.: 8,544; 1960: 8,912; 1950: 10,827) (Wray). Yuma Indian tribe.

Z

Zapata, Tex. (est. Jan. 22, 1858; 1,080 sq. mi.; 1970 pop.: 4,352; 1960: 4,393; 1950: 4,405) (Zapata). Antonio Zapata (-1840). Cattle owner, col. in Mexican army 1838; captured on his own land, head severed and placed on a pole as a warning, Mar. 15, 1840. -- Lott, Virgil N., Kingdom of Zapata, San Antonio, Texas: Naylor, 1953; 254 p.

Zavala, Tex. (est. Feb. 1, 1858; 1,292 sq. mi.; 1970 pop.: 11,370; 1960: 12,696; 1950: 11,281) (Crystal City). Manuel Lorenzo Justiniano de Zavalo (1789-1836). Secretary of Merida (Yucatan, Mexico) City Council 1812-14; practiced medicine 1817; escaped from Spain to London 1820; deputy in Mexican congress 1823-24; presiding officer of Mexican constitutional convention 1824; Senator in first congress under the constitution 1825-26; gov. of state of Mexico 1827-30; Mexican revolution fled to U. S. 1830; Mexican Minister to France 1834; signer Texas declaration of independence 1836; ad interim vice pres. Republic of Tex. 1836.

Ziebach, S. D. (est. Feb. 1, 1911; 1,982 sq. mi.; 1970 pop.: 2,221; 1960: 2,495; 1950: 2,606) (Dupree). Frank M. Ziebach (1830-1929). Editor of "Weekly Dakotan" 1861; capt. of military company 1862; S. D. constitutional convention 1883.

Part III

COUNTIES LISTED BY STATE

ALABAMA (67 counties) 22nd state.
Organized as territory March 3, 1817.
Admitted as state December 14, 1819.

County	County Seat	Created	Statute
Autauga	Prattville	Nov. 21, 1818	Unnumb.
Baldwin	Bay Minette	Dec. 21, 1809	Unnumb.
Barbour	Clayton; Eufaula	Dec. 18, 1832	Act 11
Bibb* 1	Centerville	Feb. 7, 1818	Unnumb.
Blount	Oneonta	Feb. 6, 1818	Unnumb.
Bullock	Union Springs	Dec. 5, 1866	Act 84
Butler	Greenville	Dec. 13, 1819	Unnumb.
Calhoun* 2	Anniston	Dec. 18, 1832	Act 11
Chambers	Lafayette	Dec. 18, 1832	Act 11
Cherokee	Centre	Jan. 9, 1836	Act 179
Chilton* 3	Clanton	Dec. 30, 1868	Act 142
Choctaw	Butler	Dec. 29, 1847	Act 213
Clarke	Grove Hill	Dec. 10, 1812	Act 5
Clay	Ashland	Dec. 7, 1866	Act 110
Cleburne	Heflin	Dec. 6, 1866	Act 89
Coffee	Elba; Enterprise	Dec. 29, 1841	Act 190
Colbert	Tuscumbia	Feb. 6, 1867	Act 321
Conecuh	Evergreen	Feb. 13, 1818	Unnumb.
Coosa	Rockford	Dec. 18, 1832	Act 11
Covington* 4	Andalusia	Dec. 7, 1821	Unnumb.
Crenshaw	Luverne	Nov. 24, 1866	Act 39
Cullman	Cullman	Jan. 24, 1877	Act 56
Dale	Ozark	Dec. 22, 1824	Unnumb.
Dallas	Selma	Feb. 9, 1818	Unnumb.
De Kalb	Fort Payne	Jan. 9, 1836	Act 179
Elmore	Wetumpka	Feb. 15, 1866	Act 312
Escambia	Brewton	Dec. 10, 1868	Act 34
Etowah* 5	Gadsden	Dec. 7, 1866	Act 92
Fayette	Fayette	Dec. 20, 1824	Unnumb.
Franklin	Russellville	Feb. 6, 1818	Unnumb.
Geneva	Geneva	Dec. 26, 1868	Act 110
Greene	Eutaw	Dec. 13, 1819	Unnumb.

County	County Seat	Created	Statute
Hale	Greensboro	Jan. 30, 1867	Act 418
Henry	Abbeville	Dec. 13, 1819	Unnumb.
Houston	Dothan	Feb. 9, 1903	Act 27
Jackson	Scottsboro	Dec. 13, 1819	Unnumb.
Jefferson	Birmingham	Dec. 13, 1819	Unnumb.
Lamar* 6	Vernon	Feb. 4, 1867	Act 298
Lauderdale	Florence	Feb. 6, 1818	Unnumb.
Lawrence	Moulton	Feb. 6, 1818	Unnumb.
Lee	Opelika	Dec. 5, 1866	Act 61
Limestone	Athens	Feb. 6, 1818	Unnumb.
Lowndes	Hayneville	Jan. 20, 1830	Unnumb.
Macon	Tuskegee	Dec. 18, 1832	Act 11
Madison	Huntsville	Dec. 13, 1808	Procl.
Marengo	Linden	Feb. 6, 1818	Unnumb.
Marion	Hamilton	Feb. 13, 1818	Unnumb.
Marshall	Guntersville	Jan. 9, 1836	Act 47
Mobile	Mobile	Aug. 1, 1812	Procl.
Monroe	Monroeville	June 29, 1815	Procl.
Montgomery	Montgomery	Dec. 6, 1816	Act 8
Morgan* 7	Decatur	Feb. 6, 1818	Unnumb.
Perry	Marion	Dec. 13, 1819	Unnumb.
Pickens	Carrollton	Dec. 19, 1820	Act 26
Pike	Troy	Dec. 17, 1821	Act 32
Randolph	Wedowee	Dec. 18, 1832	Act 11
Russell	Phenix City	Dec. 18, 1832	Act 11
Saint Clair	Pell City	Nov. 20, 1818	Unnumb.
Shelby	Columbiana	Feb. 7, 1818	Unnumb.
Sumter	Livingston	Dec. 18, 1832	Act 11
Talladega	Talladega	Dec. 18, 1832	Act 11
Tallapoosa	Dadeville	Dec. 18, 1832	Act 11
Tuscaloosa	Tuscaloosa	Feb. 6, 1818	Unnumb.
Walker	Jasper	Dec. 26, 1823	Unnumb.
Washington	Chatom	June 4, 1800	Procl.
Wilcox	Camden	Dec. 13, 1819	Unnumb.
Winston* 8	Double Springs	Feb. 12, 1850	Act 58

1 Formerly Cahaba County, changed to Bibb County, Dec. 4, 1820, act 24.

2 Formerly Benton County, changed to Calhoun County, Jan. 29, 1858, act 306.

3 Formerly Baker County, changed to Chilton County, Dec. 17, 1874, act 72.

4 Formerly Covington County, changed to Jones County, Aug. 6, 1868, unnumbered; changed back to Covington County, Oct. 10, 1868, act. 39.

5 Formerly Baine County, abolished Dec. 3, 1867, act 27;

act repealed and established as Etowah County, Dec. 1, 1868, act 20.
6 Formerly Jones County, abolished Nov. 13, 1867, act 1; re-established as Sanford County, Oct. 8, 1868, act 13; changed to Lamar County, Feb. 8, 1877, act 205.
7 Formerly Cotaco County, changed to Morgan County, June 14, 1821, unnumbered.
8 Formerly Hancock County, changed to Winston County, Jan. 22, 1858, act 322.

ALASKA (29 census divisions) 49th state.
Admitted as state January 3, 1959.

See special addendum on Alaska, Part IX.

ARIZONA (14 counties) 48th state.
Organized as territory February 24, 1863.
Admitted as state February 14, 1912.

County	County Seat	Created	Statute
Apache	Saint Johns	Feb. 14, 1879	Act 58
Cochise	Bisbee	Feb. 1, 1881	Act 7
Coconino	Flagstaff	Feb. 19, 1891	Act 14
Gila	Globe	Feb. 8, 1881	Act 17
Graham	Safford	Mar. 10, 1881	Act 87
Greenlee	Clifton	Mar. 10, 1909	Act 21
Maricopa	Phoenix	Feb. 14, 1871	Unnumb.
Mohave	Kingman	Dec. 21, 1864	Unnumb.
Navajo	Holbrook	Mar. 21, 1895	Act 60
Pima* 1	Tucson	Dec. 15, 1864	Unnumb.
Pinal	Florence	Feb. 1, 1875	Unnumb.
Santa Cruz	Nogales	Mar. 15, 1899	Act 44
Yavapai	Prescott	Dec. 21, 1864	Unnumb.
Yuma* 2	Yuma	Dec. 21, 1864	Unnumb.

1 Formerly Ewell.
2 Formerly Castle Dome.

ARKANSAS (75 counties) 25th state.
Organized as territory March 2, 1819, eff. July 4, 1819.
Admitted as state June 15, 1836

Arkansas	DeWitt-Stuttgart	Dec. 31, 1813	Unnumb.
Ashley	Hamburg	Nov. 30, 1848	Unnumb.

County	County Seat	Created	Statute
Baxter	Mountain Home	Mar. 24, 1873	Act 26
Benton	Bentonville	Sept. 30, 1836	Unnumb.
Boone	Harrison	Apr. 9, 1869	Act 70
Bradley	Warren	Dec. 18, 1840	Unnumb.
Calhoun	Hampton	Dec. 6, 1850	Unnumb.
Carroll	Berryville-Eureka Springs	Nov. 1, 1833	Unnumb.
Chicot	Lake Village	Oct. 25, 1823	Unnumb.
Clark	Arkadelphia	Dec. 15, 1818	Unnumb.
Clay* 1	Piggott-Corning	Mar. 24, 1873	Act 27
Cleburne	Heber Springs	Feb. 20, 1883	Act 24
Cleveland* 2	Rison	Apr. 17, 1873	Act 58
Columbia	Magnolia	Dec. 17, 1852	Unnumb.
Conway	Morrilton	Oct. 20, 1825	Unnumb.
Craighead	Jonesboro, Lake City	Feb. 19, 1859	Act 171
Crawford	Van Buren	Oct. 18, 1820	Unnumb.
Crittenden	Marion	Oct. 22, 1825	Unnumb.
Cross	Wynne	Nov. 15, 1862	Unnumb.
Dallas	Fordyce	Jan. 1, 1845	Unnumb.
Desha	Arkansas City	Dec. 12, 1838	Unnumb.
Drew	Monticello	Nov. 26, 1846	Unnumb.
Faulkner	Conway	Apr. 12, 1873	Act 44
Franklin	Ozark-Charleston	Dec. 19, 1837	Unnumb.
Fulton	Salem	Dec. 21, 1842	Unnumb.
Garland	Hot Springs	Apr. 5, 1873	Act 34
Grant	Sheridan	Feb. 4, 1869	Act 15
Greene	Paragould	Nov. 5, 1833	Unnumb.
Hempstead	Hope	Dec. 15, 1818	Unnumb.
Hot Spring	Malvern	Nov. 2, 1829	Unnumb.
Howard	Nashville	Apr. 17, 1873	Act 57
Independence	Batesville	Oct. 23, 1820	Unnumb.
Izard	Melbourne	Oct. 27, 1825	Unnumb.
Jackson	Newport	Nov. 5, 1829	Unnumb.
Jefferson	Pine Bluff	Nov. 2, 1829	Unnumb.
Johnson	Clarksville	Nov. 16, 1833	Unnumb.
Lafayette	Lewisville	Oct. 15, 1827	Unnumb.
Lawrence	Powhatan and Walnut Ridge	Jan. 15, 1815	Unnumb.
Lee	Marianna	Apr. 17, 1873	Act 60
Lincoln	Star City	Mar. 28, 1871	Act 68
Little River	Ashdown	Mar. 5, 1867	Act 104
Logan* 3	Booneville and Paris	Mar. 22, 1871	Act 25
Lonoke	Lonoke	Apr. 16, 1873	Act 47
Madison	Huntsville	Sept. 30, 1836	Unnumb.

County	County Seat	Created	Statute
Marion* 4	Yellville	Nov. 3, 1835	Unnumb.
Miller	Texarkana	Apr. 1, 1820	Unnumb.
Mississippi	Blytheville and Osceola	Nov. 1, 1833	Unnumb.
Monroe	Clarendon	Nov. 2, 1829	Unnumb.
Montgomery	Mount Ida	Dec. 9, 1842	Unnumb.
Nevada	Prescott	Mar. 20, 1871	Act 20
Newton	Jasper	Dec. 14, 1842	Unnumb.
Ouachita	Camden	Nov. 29, 1842	Unnumb.
Perry	Perryville	Dec. 18, 1840	Unnumb.
Phillips	Helena	May 1, 1820	Unnumb.
Pike	Murfreesboro	Nov. 1, 1833	Unnumb.
Poinsett	Harrisburg	Feb. 28, 1838	Unnumb.
Polk	Mena	Nov. 30, 1844	Unnumb.
Pope	Russellville	Nov. 2, 1829	Unnumb.
Prairie	Des Arcs and De Valls Bluff	Nov. 25, 1846	Unnumb.
Pulaski	Little Rock	Dec. 15, 1818	Unnumb.
Randolph	Pocahontas	Oct. 29, 1835	Unnumb.
St. Francis	Forrest City	Oct. 13, 1827	Unnumb.
Saline	Benton	Nov. 2, 1835	Unnumb.
Scott	Waldron	Nov. 5, 1833	Unnumb.
Searcy	Marshall	Nov. 3, 1835	Unnumb.
Sebastian	Fort Smith and Greenwood	Jan. 6, 1851	Unnumb.
Sevier	De Queen	Oct. 17, 1828	Unnumb.
Sharp	Evening Shade and Hardy	July 18, 1868	Act 42
Stone	Mountain View	Apr. 21, 1873	Act 74
Union	El Dorado	Nov. 2, 1829	Unnumb.
Van Buren	Clinton	Nov. 11, 1833	Unnumb.
Washington	Fayetteville	Oct. 17, 1828	Unnumb.
White	Searcy	Oct. 23, 1835	Unnumb.
Woodruff	Augusta	Nov. 26, 1862	Unnumb.
Yell	Danville and Dardanelle	Dec. 5, 1840	Unnumb.

1 Formerly Clayton County, changed to Clay County, Dec. 6, 1875, act. 42.

2 Formerly Dorsey County, changed to Cleveland County, March 5, 1885, act 38.

3 Formerly Sarber County, changed to Logan County, Dec. 14, 1875, act 62.

4 Formerly Searcy County, changed to Marion County, Sept. 29, 1836, unnumbered.

CALIFORNIA (58 counties) 31st state.
Admitted as state Sept. 9, 1850.

County	County Seat	Created	Statute
Alameda	Oakland	Mar. 25, 1853	Chap. 41
Alpine	Markleeville	Mar. 16, 1864	Chap. 180
Amador	Jackson	May 11, 1854	Chap. 42
Butte	Oroville	Feb. 18, 1850	Chap. 15
Calaveras	San Andreas	Feb. 18, 1850	Chap. 15
Colusa	Colusa	Feb. 18, 1850	Chap. 15
Contra Costa	Martinez	Feb. 18, 1850	Chap. 15
Del Norte	Crescent City	Mar. 2, 1857	Chap. 52
El Dorado	Placerville	Feb. 18, 1850	Chap. 15
Fresno	Fresno	Apr. 19, 1856	Chap. 127
Glenn	Willows	Mar. 11, 1891	Chap. 94
Humboldt	Eureka	May 12, 1853	Chap. 114
Imperial	El Centro	Aug. 6, 1907	Unnumb.
Inyo	Independence	Mar. 22, 1866	Chap. 316
Kern	Bakersfield	Apr. 2, 1866	Chap. 569
Kings	Hanford	Mar. 22, 1893	Chap. 150
Lake	Lakeport	May 20, 1861	Chap. 498
Lassen	Susanville	Apr. 1, 1864	Chap. 261
Los Angeles	Los Angeles	Feb. 18, 1850	Chap. 15
Madera	Madera	Mar. 11, 1843	Chap. 143
Marin	San Rafael	Feb. 18, 1893	Chap. 15
Mariposa	Mariposa	Feb. 18, 1850	Chap. 15
Mendocino	Ukiah	Feb. 18, 1850	Chap. 15
Merced	Merced	Apr. 19, 1855	Chap. 104
Modoc	Alturas	Feb. 17, 1874	Chap. 107
Mono	Bridgeport	Apr. 24, 1861	Chap. 233
Monterey	Salinas	Feb. 18, 1850	Chap. 15
Napa	Napa	Feb. 18, 1850	Chap. 15
Nevada	Nevada City	Apr. 25, 1851	Chap. 14
Orange	Santa Ana	Mar. 11, 1889	Chap. 110
Placer	Auburn	Apr. 25, 1851	Chap. 14
Plumas	Quincy	Mar. 18, 1854	Chap. 1
Riverside	Riverside	Mar. 11, 1893	Chap. 142
Sacramento	Sacramento	Feb. 18, 1850	Chap. 15
San Benito	Hollister	Feb. 12, 1874	Chap. 87
San Bernardino	San Bernardino	Apr. 26, 1853	Chap. 78
San Diego	San Diego	Feb. 18, 1850	Chap. 15
San Francisco	San Francisco	Feb. 18, 1850	Chap. 15
San Joaquin	Stockton	Feb. 18, 1850	Chap. 15
San Luis Obispo	San Luis Obispo	Feb. 18, 1850	Chap. 15
San Mateo	Redwood City	Apr. 19, 1856	Chap. 125
Santa Barbara	Santa Barbara	Feb. 18, 1850	Chap. 15
Santa Clara	San Jose	Feb. 18, 1850	Chap. 15

County	County Seat	Created	Statute
Santa Cruz* 1	Santa Cruz	Feb. 18, 1850	Chap. 15
Shasta	Redding	Feb. 18, 1850	Chap. 15
Sierra	Downieville	Apr. 16, 1852	Chap. 145
Siskiyou	Yreka	Mar. 22, 1852	Chap. 146
Solano	Fairfield	Feb. 18, 1850	Chap. 15
Sonoma	Santa Rosa	Feb. 18, 1850	Chap. 15
Stanislaus	Modesto	Apr. 1, 1854	Chap. 81
Sutter	Yuba City	Feb. 18, 1850	Chap. 15
Tehama	Red Bluff	Apr. 9, 1856	Chap. 100
Trinity	Weaverville	Feb. 18, 1850	Chap. 15
Tulare	Visalia	Apr. 20, 1852	Chap. 153
Tuolumne	Sonora	Feb. 18, 1850	Chap. 15
Ventura	Ventura	Mar. 22, 1872	Chap. 151
Yolo	Woodland	Feb. 18, 1850	Chap. 15
Yuba	Marysville	Feb. 18, 1850	Chap. 15

1 Formerly Branciforte County, changed to Santa Cruz County, April 5, 1850, chap. 61.

COLORADO (63 counties) 38th state.
Organized as territory February 28, 1861.
Admitted as state August 1, 1876.

County	County Seat	Created	Statute
Adams	Brighton	Apr. 15, 1901	Chap. 57
Alamosa	Alamosa	Mar. 8, 1913	Chap. 6
Arapahoe	Littleton	Nov. 1, 1861	Unnumb.
Archuleta	Pagosa Springs	Apr. 14, 1885	S. B. 144
Baca	Springfield	Apr. 16, 1889	S. B. 37
Bent	Las Animas	Feb. 11, 1870	Unnumb.
Boulder	Boulder	Nov. 1, 1861	Unnumb.
Chaffee* 1	Salida	Nov. 1, 1861	Unnumb.
Cheyenne	Cheyenne Wells	Mar. 25, 1889	S. B. 116
Clear Creek	Georgetown	Nov. 1, 1861	Unnumb.
Conejos* 2	Conejos	Nov. 1, 1861	Unnumb.
Costilla	San Luis	Nov. 1, 1861	Unnumb.
Crowley	Ordway	May 29, 1911	Chap. 111
Custer	Westcliffe	Mar. 9, 1877	Chap. 400
Delta	Delta	Feb. 11, 1883	Unnumb.
Denver	Denver	Mar. 18, 1901	Chap. 46
Dolores	Rico	Feb. 19, 1881	Unnumb.
Douglas	Castle Rock	Nov. 1, 1861	Unnumb.
Eagle	Eagle	Feb. 11, 1883	Unnumb.
Elbert	Kiowa	Feb. 2, 1874	Unnumb.
El Paso	Colorado Springs	Nov. 1, 1861	Unnumb.
Fremont	Canon City	Nov. 1, 1861	Unnumb.

County	County Seat	Created	Statute
Garfield	Glenwood Springs	Feb. 10, 1883	Unnumb.
Gilpin	Central City	Nov. 1, 1861	Unnumb.
Grand	Hot Sulphur Springs	Feb. 2, 1874	Unnumb.
Gunnison	Gunnison	Mar. 9, 1877	Chap. 411
Hinsdale	Lake City	Feb. 10, 1874	Unnumb.
Huerfano	Walsenburg	Nov. 1, 1861	Unnumb.
Jackson	Walden	May 5, 1909	Chap. 179
Jefferson	Golden	Nov. 1, 1861	Unnumb.
Kiowa	Eads	Apr. 11, 1889	H. B. 337
Kit Carson	Burlington	Apr. 11, 1889	S. B. 48
Lake* 3	Leadville	Nov. 1, 1861	Unnumb.
La Plata	Durango	Feb. 10, 1874	Unnumb.
Larimer	Fort Collins	Nov. 1, 1861	Unnumb.
Las Animos	Trinidad	Feb. 9, 1866	Unnumb.
Lincoln	Hugo	Apr. 11, 1889	S. B. 106
Logan	Sterling	Feb. 25, 1887	S. B. 72
Mesa	Grand Junction	Feb. 14, 1883	Unnumb.
Mineral	Creede	Mar. 27, 1893	S. B. 57
Moffat	Craig	Feb. 27, 1911	Chap. 173
Montezuma	Cortez	Apr. 16, 1889	H. B. 230
Montrose	Montrose	Feb. 11, 1883	Unnumb.
Morgan	Fort Morgan	Feb. 19, 1889	S. B. 40
Otero	La Junta	Mar. 25, 1889	S. B. 34
Ouray* 4	Ouray	Jan. 18, 1877	Unnumb.
Park	Fairplay	Nov. 1, 1861	Unnumb.
Phillips	Holyoke	Mar. 27, 1889	H. B. 127
Pitkin	Aspen	Feb. 23, 1881	Unnumb.
Prowers	Lamar	Apr. 11, 1889	S. B. 35
Pueblo	Pueblo	Nov. 1, 1861	Unnumb.
Rio Blanco	Meeker	Mar. 25, 1889	H. B. 107
Rio Grande	Del Norte	Feb. 10, 1874	Unnumb.
Routt	Steamboat Springs	Jan. 29, 1877	Chap. 393
Saguache	Saguache	Dec. 29, 1866	Unnumb.
San Juan	Silverton	Jan. 31, 1876	Unnumb.
San Miguel* 5	Telluride	Nov. 1, 1861	Unnumb.
Sedgwick	Julesburg	Apr. 9, 1889	H. B. 148
Summit	Breckenridge	Nov. 1, 1861	Unnumb.
Teller	Cripple Creek	Mar. 23, 1899	S. B. 52
Washington	Akron	Feb. 9, 1887	H. B. 51
Weld	Greeley	Nov. 1, 1861	Unnumb.
Yuma	Wray	Mar. 15, 1889	H. B. 90

1 Formerly Lake County, changed to Chaffee County, Feb. 10, 1879, unnumbered.

2 Formerly Guadalupe County, changed to Conejos County,

Nov. 7, 1861, unnumbered.

3 Formerly Carbonate County, changed to Lake County, Feb. 10, 1879, unnumbered.

4 Formerly Uncompahgre County, changed to Ouray County, March 2, 1883, unnumbered.

5 Formerly Ouray County, changed to San Miguel County, March 2, 1883, unnumbered.

CONNECTICUT (8 counties) 5th state.
Admitted as state January 9, 1788.

County	No County Seats	Created	Statute
Fairfield		Sess. May 10, 1666	
Hartford		Sess. May 10, 1666	
Litchfield		Sess. Oct. 14, 1751	
Middlesex		Sess. May 2, 1785	
New Haven		Sess. May 10, 1666	
New London		Sess. May 10, 1666	
Tolland		Sess. Oct. 13, 1785	
Windham		Sess. May 12, 1726	

DELAWARE (3 counties) 1st state.
Admitted as state December 7, 1787.
(Exact dates unknown; varies according to periods considered)

Kent* 1	Dover	Dec. 25, 1682
New Castle	Wilmington	1673
Sussex* 2	Georgetown	Dec. 25, 1682

1 Formerly St. Jones County, changed to Kent County, 1683.

2 Formerly Deale County, changed to Sussex County, 1683.

FLORIDA (67 counties) 27th state.
Organized as territory March 30, 1822.
Admitted as state March 3, 1845.

Alachua	Gainesville	Dec. 29, 1824	Unnumb.
Baker	Macclenny	Feb. 8, 1861	Chap. 1, 185
Bay	Panama City	Apr. 24, 1913	Chap. 6, 505
Bradford* 1	Starke	Dec. 21, 1858	Chap. 895
Brevard* 2	Titusville	Mar. 14, 1844	Unnumb.
Broward	Fort Lauderdale	Apr. 30, 1915	Chap. 6, 934

County	County Seat	Created	Statute
Calhoun	Blountstown	Jan. 26, 1838	Chap. 8
Charlotte	Punta Gorda	Apr. 23, 1921	Chap. 8,513
Citrus	Inverness	June 2, 1887	Chap. 3,772
Clay	Green Cove Springs	Dec. 31, 1858	Chap. 866
Collier	Everglades	May 8, 1923	Chap. 9,362
Columbia	Lake City	Feb. 4, 1832	Chap. 25
Dade	Miami	Feb. 4, 1836	Chap. 937
De Soto	Arcadia	May 19, 1887	Chap. 3,770
Dixie	Cross City	Apr. 25, 1921	Chap. 8,514
Duval	Jacksonville	Aug. 12, 1822	Unnumb.
Escambia	Pensacola	Aug. 12, 1822	Unnumb.
Flagler	Bunnell	Apr. 28, 1917	Chap. 7,379
Franklin	Apalachicola	Feb. 8, 1832	Chap. 42
Gadsden	Quincy	June 24, 1823	Unnumb.
Gilchrist	Trenton	Dec. 4, 1925	Chap. 11, 371
Glades	Moore Haven	Apr. 23, 1921	Chap. 8,513
Gulf	Wewahitchka	June 6, 1925	Chap. 10, 132
Hamilton	Jasper	Dec. 26, 1827	Unnumb.
Hardee	Wauchula	Apr. 23, 1921	Chap. 8,513
Hendry	La Belle	May 11, 1923	Chap. 9,360
Hernando* 3	Brooksville	Feb. 24, 1843	Chap. 51
Highlands	Sebring	Apr. 23, 1921	Chap. 8,513
Hillsborough	Tampa	Jan. 25, 1834	Chap. 764
Holmes	Bonifay	Jan. 8, 1848	Chap. 176
Indian River	Vero Beach	May 30, 1925	Chap. 10, 148
Jackson	Marianna	Aug. 12, 1822	Unnumb.
Jefferson	Monticello	Jan. 6, 1827	Unnumb.
Lafayette	Mayo	Dec. 23, 1856	Chap. 806
Lake	Tavares	May 27, 1887	Chap. 3,771
Lee	Fort Myers	May 13, 1887	Chap. 3,769
Leon	Tallahassee	Dec. 29, 1824	Unnumb.
Levy	Bronson	Mar. 10, 1845	Chap. 30
Liberty	Bristol	Dec. 15, 1855	Chap. 771
Madison	Madison	Dec. 26, 1827	Unnumb.
Manatee	Bradenton	Jan. 9, 1855	Chap. 628
Marion	Ocala	Mar. 14, 1844	Unnumb.
Martin	Stuart	May 30, 1925	Chap. 10, 180
Monroe	Key West	July 3, 1823	Unnumb.
Nassau	Fernandina	Dec. 29, 1824	Unnumb.
Okaloosa	Crestview	June 3, 1915	Chap. 6,937
Okeechobee	Okeechobee	May 8, 1917	Chap. 7,401

County	County Seat	Created	Statute
Orange* 4	Orlando	Dec. 29, 1824	Unnumb.
Osceola	Kissimmee	May 12, 1887	Chap. 3, 768
Palm Beach	West Palm Beach	Apr. 30, 1909	Chap. 5, 970
Pasco	Dade City	June 2, 1887	Chap. 3, 772
Pinellas	Clearwater	May 23, 1911	Chap. 6, 247
Polk	Bartow	Feb. 8, 1861	Chap. 1, 201
Putnam	Palatka	Jan. 13, 1849	Chap. 280
St. Johns	St. Augustine	Aug. 12, 1822	Unnumb.
St. Lucie	Fort Pierce	May 24, 1905	Chap. 5, 567
Santa Rosa	Milton	Feb. 18, 1842	Unnumb.
Sarasota	Sarasota	May 14, 1921	Chap. 8, 515
Seminole	Sanford	Apr. 25, 1913	Chap. 6, 511
Sumter	Bushnell	Jan. 8, 1853	Chap. 548
Suwanee	Live Oak	Dec. 21, 1858	Chap. 895
Taylor	Perry	Dec. 23, 1856	Chap. 806
Union	Lake Butler	May 20, 1921	Chap. 8, 516
Volusia	De Land	Dec. 29, 1854	Chap. 624
Wakulla	Crawfordville	Mar. 11, 1843	Chap. 25
Walton	De Funiak Springs	Dec. 29, 1824	Unnumb.
Washington	Chipley	Dec. 9, 1825	Unnumb.

1 Formerly New River County, changed to Bradford County, Dec. 6, 1861, chap. 1300.

2 Formerly St. Lucie County, changed to Brevard County, Jan. 6, 1855, chap. 651.

3 Formerly Hernando County, changed to Benton County, March 6, 1844, unnumbered; changed to Hernando County, December 24, 1850, chap. 415.

4 Formerly Mosquito County, changed to Orange County, January 30, 1845, chap. 31.

GEORGIA (159 counties) 4th state.
Admitted as state Jan. 2, 1788.

County	County Seat	Created	Statute
Appling	Baxley	Dec. 15, 1818	Unnumb.
Atkinson	Pearson	Aug. 15, 1917	Act 180
Bacon	Alma	July 27, 1914	Act 298
Baker	Newton	Dec. 12, 1825	Unnumb.
Baldwin	Milledgeville	May 11, 1803	Unnumb.
Banks	Homer	Dec. 11, 1858	Act 19
Barrow	Winder	July 7, 1914	Act 278
Bartow* 1	Cartersville	Dec. 3, 1832	Unnumb.
Ben Hill	Fitzgerald	July 31, 1906	Act 372
Berrien	Nashville	Feb. 25, 1856	Act 48

County	County Seat	Created	Statute
Bibb	Macon	Dec. 9, 1822	Unnumb.
Bleckley	Cochran	July 30, 1912	Act 355
Brantley	Nahunta	Aug. 14, 1920	Act 626
Brooks	Quitman	Dec. 11, 1858	Act 21
Bryan	Pembroke	Dec. 19, 1793	Unnumb.
Bulloch	Statesboro	Feb. 8, 1796	Unnumb.
Burke	Waynesboro	Feb. 5, 1777	Const.
Butts	Jackson	Dec. 24, 1825	Unnumb.
Calhoun	Morgan	Feb. 20, 1854	Act 217
Camden	Woodbine	Feb. 5, 1777	Const.
Candler	Metter	July 17, 1914	Act 282
Carroll	Carrollton	Dec. 11, 1826	Unnumb.
Catoosa	Ringgold	Dec. 5, 1853	Act 218
Charlton	Folkston	Feb. 18, 1854	Act 220
Chatham	Savannah	Feb. 5, 1777	Const.
Chattahoochie	Cusseta	Feb. 13, 1854	Act 219
Chattooga	Summerville	Dec. 28, 1838	Unnumb.
Cherokee	Canton	Dec. 26, 1831	Unnumb.
Clarke	Athens	Dec. 5, 1801	Unnumb.
Clay	Fort Gaines	Feb. 16, 1854	Act 221
Clayton	Jonesboro	Nov. 30, 1858	Act 17
Clinch	Homerville	Feb. 14, 1850	Unnumb.
Cobb	Marietta	Dec. 3, 1832	Unnumb.
Coffee	Douglas	Feb. 9, 1854	Act 222
Colquitt	Moultrie	Feb. 25, 1856	Act 46
Columbia	Appling	Dec. 10, 1790	Unnumb.
Cook	Adel	July 30, 1918	Act 292
Coweta	Newnan	Dec. 11, 1826	Unnumb.
Crawford	Knoxville	Dec. 9, 1822	Unnumb.
Crisp	Cordele	Aug. 17, 1905	Act 19
Dade	Trenton	Dec. 25, 1837	Unnumb.
Dawson	Dawsonville	Dec. 3, 1857	Act 19
Decatur	Bainbridge	Dec. 8, 1823	Unnumb.
De Kalb	Decatur	Dec. 9, 1822	Unnumb.
Dodge	Eastman	Oct. 26, 1870	Act 7
Dooly	Vienna	May 15, 1821	Unnumb.
Dougherty	Albany	Dec. 15, 1853	Act 223
Douglas	Douglasville	Oct. 17, 1870	Act 5
Early	Blakely	Dec. 15, 1818	Unnumb.
Echols	Statenville	Dec. 13, 1858	Act 22
Effingham	Springfield	Feb. 5, 1777	Const.
Elbert	Elberton	Dec. 10, 1790	Unnumb.
Emanuel	Swainsboro	Dec. 10, 1812	Unnumb.
Evans	Claxton	Aug. 11, 1914	Act 371
Fannin	Blue Ridge	Jan. 21, 1854	Act 224
Fayette	Fayetteville	May 15, 1821	Unnumb.

County	County Seat	Created	Statute
Floyd	Rome	Dec. 3, 1832	Unnumb.
Forsyth	Cumming	Dec. 3, 1832	Unnumb.
Franklin	Carnesville	Feb. 25, 1784	Unnumb.
Fulton	Atlanta	Dec. 20, 1853	Act 225
Gilmer	Ellijay	Dec. 3, 1832	Unnumb.
Glascock	Gibson	Dec. 19, 1857	Act 20
Glynn	Brunswick	Feb. 5, 1777	Const.
Gordon	Calhoun	Feb. 13, 1850	Unnumb.
Grady	Cairo	Aug. 17, 1905	Act 31
Greene	Greensboro	Feb. 3, 1786	Unnumb.
Gwinnett	Lawrenceville	Dec. 15, 1818	Unnumb.
Habersham	Clarkesville	Dec. 15, 1818	Unnumb.
Hall	Gainesville	Dec. 15, 1818	Unnumb.
Hancock	Sparta	Dec. 17, 1793	Unnumb.
Haralson	Buchanan	Jan. 26, 1856	Act 47
Harris	Hamilton	Dec. 24, 1827	Unnumb.
Hart	Hartwell	Dec. 7, 1853	Act 226
Heard	Franklin	Dec. 22, 1830	Unnumb.
Henry	McDonough	May 15, 1821	Unnumb.
Houston	Perry	May 15, 1821	Unnumb.
Irwin	Ocilla	Dec. 15, 1818	Unnumb.
Jackson	Jefferson	Feb. 11, 1796	Unnumb.
Jasper* 2	Monticello	Dec. 10, 1807	Unnumb.
Jeff Davis	Hazlehurst	Aug. 18, 1905	Act 157
Jefferson	Louisville	Feb. 20, 1796	Unnumb.
Jenkins	Millen	Aug. 17, 1905	Act 142
Johnson	Wrightsville	Dec. 11, 1858	Act 20
Jones	Gray	Dec. 10, 1807	Unnumb.
Lamar	Barnesville	Aug. 17, 1920	Act 738
Lanier	Lakeland	Aug. 11, 1919	Act 78
Laurens	Dublin	Dec. 10, 1807	Unnumb.
Lee	Leesburg	Dec. 11, 1826	Unnumb.
Liberty	Hinesville	Feb. 5, 1777	Const.
Lincoln	Lincolnton	Feb. 20, 1796	Unnumb.
Long	Ludowici	Aug. 14, 1920	Act 814
Lowndes	Valdosta	Dec. 23, 1825	Unnumb.
Lumpkin	Dahlonega	Dec. 3, 1832	Unnumb.
Macon	Oglethorpe	Dec. 14, 1837	Unnumb.
Madison	Danielsville	Dec. 5, 1811	Unnumb.
Marion	Buena Vista	Dec. 24, 1827	Unnumb.
McDuffie	Thomson	Oct. 18, 1870	Act 8
McIntosh	Darien	Dec. 19, 1793	Unnumb.
Meriwether	Greenville	Dec. 24, 1827	Unnumb.
Miller	Colquitt	Feb. 26, 1856	Act 49
Mitchell	Camilla	Dec. 21, 1857	Act 22
Monroe	Forsyth	May 15, 1821	Unnumb.

County	County Seat	Created	Statute
Montgomery	Mount Vernon	Dec. 19, 1793	Unnumb.
Morgan	Madison	Dec. 10, 1807	Unnumb.
Murray	Chatsworth	Dec. 3, 1832	Unnumb.
Muscogee	Columbus	Dec. 11, 1826	Unnumb.
Newton	Covington	Dec. 24, 1821	Unnumb.
Oconee	Watkinsville	Feb. 25, 1875	Chap. 123
Oglethorpe	Lexington	Dec. 19, 1793	Unnumb.
Paulding	Dallas	Dec. 3, 1832	Unnumb.
Peach	Fort Valley	July 18, 1924	Act 274
Pickens	Jasper	Dec. 5, 1853	Act 228
Pierce	Blackshear	Dec. 18, 1857	Act 23
Pike	Zebulon	Dec. 9, 1822	Unnumb.
Polk	Cedartown	Dec. 20, 1851	Act 26
Pulaski	Hawkinsville	Dec. 13, 1808	Unnumb.
Putnam	Eatonton	Dec. 10, 1807	Unnumb.
Quitman	Georgetown	Dec. 10, 1858	Act 18
Rabun	Clayton	Dec. 21, 1819	Unnumb.
Randolph	Cuthbert	Dec. 20, 1828	Unnumb.
Richmond	Augusta	Feb. 5, 1777	Const.
Rockdale	Conyers	Oct. 18, 1870	Act 6
Schley	Ellaville	Dec. 22, 1857	Act 24
Screven	Sylvania	Dec. 14, 1793	Unnumb.
Seminole	Donaldsonville	July 8, 1920	Act 319
Spalding	Griffin	Dec. 20, 1851	Act 28
Stephens	Toccoa	Aug. 18, 1905	Act 215
Stewart	Lumpkin	Dec. 23, 1830	Unnumb.
Sumter	Americus	Dec. 26, 1831	Unnumb.
Talbot	Talbotton	Dec. 14, 1827	Unnumb.
Taliaferro	Crawfordville	Dec. 24, 1825	Unnumb.
Tattnall	Reidsville	Dec. 5, 1801	Unnumb.
Taylor	Butler	Jan. 15, 1852	Act 29
Telfair	McRae	Dec. 10, 1807	Unnumb.
Terrell	Dawson	Feb. 16, 1856	Act 50
Thomas	Thomasville	Dec. 23, 1825	Unnumb.
Tift	Tifton	Aug. 17, 1905	Act 3
Toombs	Lyons	Aug. 18, 1905	Act 232
Towns	Hiawassee	Mar. 6, 1856	Act 51
Treutlen	Soperton	Aug. 21, 1917	Act 250
Troup	La Grange	Dec. 11, 1826	Unnumb.
Turner	Ashburn	Aug. 18, 1905	Act 75
Twiggs	Jeffersonville	Dec. 14, 1809	Unnumb.
Union	Blairsville	Dec. 3, 1832	Unnumb.
Upson	Thomaston	Dec. 15, 1824	Unnumb.
Walker	La Fayette	Dec. 18, 1833	Unnumb.
Walton	Monroe	Dec. 15, 1818	Unnumb.
Ware	Waycross	Dec. 15, 1824	Unnumb.

County	County Seat	Created	Statute
Warren	Warrenton	Dec. 19, 1793	Unnumb.
Washington	Sandersville	Feb. 25, 1784	Unnumb.
Wayne	Jesup	May 11, 1803	Unnumb.
Webster* 3	Preston	Dec. 16, 1853	Act 227
Wheeler	Alamo	Aug. 14, 1912	Act 449
White	Cleveland	Dec. 22, 1857	Act 25
Whitfield	Dalton	Dec. 30, 1851	Act 27
Wilcox	Abbeville	Dec. 22, 1857	Act 26
Wilkes	Washington	Feb. 5, 1777	Const.
Wilkinson	Irwinton	May 11, 1803	Unnumb.
Worth	Sylvester	Dec. 20, 1853	Act 229

1 Formerly Cass County, changed to Bartow County, Dec. 6, 1861, act 97.
2 Formerly Randolph County, changed to Jasper County, Dec. 10, 1812, unnumbered.
3 Formerly Kinchafoonee County, changed to Webster County, Feb. 21, 1856, act. 367.

HAWAII (4 counties) 50th state.
Admitted as state August 21, 1959.

County	County Seat	1970 Population
Hawaii	Hilo	63, 468
Honolulu	Honolulu	629, 176
Kauai	Lihue	29, 761
Maui	Wailuku	46, 156

IDAHO (44 counties) 43rd state.
Organized as territory March 3, 1863.
Admitted as state July 3, 1890.

Ada	Boise	Dec. 22, 1864	Chap. 29
Adams	Council	Mar. 3, 1911	Chap. 31
Bannock	Pocatello	Mar. 6, 1893	Unnumb.
Bear Lake	Paris	Jan. 5, 1875	Unnumb.
Benewah	St. Maries	Jan. 23, 1915	Chap. 4
Bingham	Blackfoot	Jan. 13, 1885	Unnumb.
Blaine	Hailey	Mar. 5, 1895	S. B. 31
Boise	Idaho City	Feb. 4, 1864	Unnumb.
Bonner	Sandpoint	Feb. 21, 1907	H. B. 43
Bonneville	Idaho Falls	Feb. 7, 1911	Chap. 5
Boundary	Bonners Ferry	Jan. 23, 1915	Chap. 7
Butte	Arco	Feb. 6, 1917	Chap. 98

County	County Seat	Created	Statute
Camas	Fairfield	Feb. 6, 1917	Chap. 97
Canyon	Caldwell	Mar. 7, 1891	Unnumb.
Caribou	Soda Springs	Feb. 11, 1919	Chap. 5
Cassia	Burley	Feb. 20, 1879	Unnumb.
Clark	Dubois	Feb. 1, 1919	Chap. 3
Clearwater	Orofino	Feb. 27, 1911	Chap. 34
Custer	Challis	Jan. 8, 1881	Unnumb.
Elmore	Mountain Home	Feb. 7, 1889	Unnumb.
Franklin	Preston	Jan. 30, 1913	Chap. 5
Fremont	St. Anthony	Mar. 4, 1893	Unnumb.
Gem	Emmett	Mar. 19, 1915	Chap. 165
Gooding	Gooding	Jan. 28, 1913	Chap. 4
Idaho	Grangeville	Feb. 4, 1864	Unnumb.
Jefferson	Rigby	Feb. 18, 1913	Chap. 25
Jerome	Jerome	Feb. 8, 1919	Chap. 4
Kootenai	Coeur d'Alene	Dec. 22, 1864	Chap. 30
Latah	Moscow	Dec. 22, 1864	Chap. 30
Lemhi	Salmon	Jan. 9, 1869	Chap. 19
Lewis	Nezperce	Mar. 3, 1911	Chap. 37
Lincoln	Shoshone	Mar. 18, 1895	S. B. 83
Madison	Rexburg	Feb. 18, 1913	Chap. 26
Minidoka	Rupert	Jan. 28, 1913	Chap. 3
Nez Perce	Lewiston	Feb. 4, 1864	Unnumb.
Oneida	Malad City	Jan. 22, 1864	Unnumb.
Owyhee	Murphy	Dec. 31, 1863	Unnumb.
Payette	Payette	Feb. 28, 1917	Chap. 11
Power	American Falls	Jan. 30, 1913	Chap. 6
Shoshone	Wallace	Feb. 4, 1864	Unnumb.
Teton	Driggs	Jan. 26, 1915	Chap. 8
Twin Falls	Twin Falls	Feb. 21, 1907	H. B. 48
Valley	Cascade	Feb. 26, 1917	Chap. 99
Washington	Weiser	Feb. 20, 1879	Unnumb.

ILLINOIS (102 counties) 21st state.
Organized as territory Feb. 3, 1809, eff. Mar. 1, 1809.
Admitted as state Dec. 3, 1818.

Adams	Quincy	Jan. 13, 1825	Unnumb.
Alexander	Cairo	Mar. 4, 1819	Unnumb.
Bond	Greenville	Jan. 4, 1817	Unnumb.
Boone	Belvidere	Mar. 4, 1837	Unnumb.
Brown	Mount Sterling	Feb. 1, 1839	Unnumb.
Bureau	Princeton	Feb. 28, 1837	Unnumb.
Calhoun	Hardin	Jan. 10, 1825	Unnumb.
Carroll	Mount Carroll	Feb. 22, 1839	Unnumb.

County	County Seat	Created	Statute
Cass	Virginia	Mar. 3, 1837	Unnumb.
Champaign	Urbana	Feb. 20, 1833	Unnumb.
Christian* 1	Taylorville	Feb. 15, 1839	Unnumb.
Clark	Marshall	Mar. 22, 1819	Unnumb.
Clay	Louisville	Dec. 23, 1824	Unnumb.
Clinton	Carlyle	Dec. 27, 1824	Unnumb.
Coles	Charleston	Dec. 25, 1830	Unnumb.
Cook	Chicago	Jan. 15, 1831	Unnumb.
Crawford	Robinson	Dec. 31, 1816	Unnumb.
Cumberland	Toledo	Mar. 2, 1843	Unnumb.
De Kalb	Sycamore	Mar. 4, 1837	Unnumb.
De Witt	Clinton	Mar. 1, 1839	Unnumb.
Douglas	Tuscola	Feb. 8, 1859	Unnumb.
Du Page	Wheaton	Feb. 9, 1839	Unnumb.
Edgar	Paris	Jan. 3, 1823	Unnumb.
Edwards	Albion	Nov. 28, 1814	Unnumb.
Effingham	Effingham	Feb. 15, 1831	Unnumb.
Fayette	Vandalia	Feb. 14, 1821	Unnumb.
Ford	Paxton	Feb. 17, 1859	Unnumb.
Franklin	Benton	Jan. 2, 1818	Unnumb.
Fulton	Lewistown	Jan. 28, 1823	Unnumb.
Gallatin	Shawneetown	Sept. 14, 1812	Procl.
Greene	Carrollton	Jan. 20, 1821	Unnumb.
Grundy	Morris	Feb. 17, 1841	Unnumb.
Hamilton	McLeansboro	Feb. 8, 1821	Unnumb.
Hancock	Carthage	Jan. 13, 1825	Unnumb.
Hardin	Elizabethtown	Mar. 2, 1839	Unnumb.
Henderson	Oquawka	Jan. 20, 1841	Unnumb.
Henry	Cambridge	Jan. 13, 1825	Unnumb.
Iroquois	Watseka	Feb. 26, 1833	Unnumb.
Jackson	Murphysboro	Jan. 10, 1816	Unnumb.
Jasper	Newton	Feb. 15, 1831	Unnumb.
Jefferson	Mt. Vernon	Mar. 26, 1819	Unnumb.
Jersey	Jerseyville	Feb. 28, 1839	Unnumb.
Jo Daviess	Galena	Feb. 17, 1827	Unnumb.
Johnson	Vienna	Sept. 14, 1822	Procl.
Kane	Geneva	Jan. 16, 1836	Unnumb.
Kankakee	Kankakee	Feb. 11, 1853	Unnumb.
Kendall	Yorkville	Feb. 19, 1841	Unnumb.
Knox	Galesburg	Jan. 13, 1825	Unnumb.
Lake	Waukegan	Mar. 1, 1839	Unnumb.
La Salle	Ottawa	Jan. 15, 1831	Unnumb.
Lawrence	Lawrenceville	Jan. 16, 1821	Unnumb.
Lee	Dixon	Feb. 27, 1839	Unnumb.
Livingston	Pontiac	Feb. 27, 1837	Unnumb.
Logan	Lincoln	Feb. 15, 1839	Unnumb.

County	County Seat	Created	Statute
Macon	Decatur	Jan. 19, 1829	Unnumb.
Macoupin	Carlinville	Jan. 17, 1829	Unnumb.
Madison	Edwardsville	Sept. 14, 1812	Procl.
Marion	Salem	Jan. 24, 1823	Unnumb.
Marshall	Lacon	Jan. 19, 1839	Unnumb.
Mason	Havana	Jan. 20, 1841	Unnumb.
Massac	Metropolis	Feb. 8, 1843	Unnumb.
McDonough	Macomb	Jan. 25, 1826	Unnumb.
McHenry	Woodstock	Jan. 16, 1836	Unnumb.
McLean	Bloomington	Dec. 25, 1830	Unnumb.
Menard	Petersburg	Feb. 15, 1839	Unnumb.
Mercer	Aledo	Jan. 13, 1825	Unnumb.
Monroe	Waterloo	Jan. 6, 1816	Unnumb.
Montgomery	Hillsboro	Feb. 12, 1821	Unnumb.
Morgan	Jacksonville	Jan. 31, 1823	Unnumb.
Moultrie	Sullivan	Feb. 16, 1843	Unnumb.
Ogle	Oregon	Jan. 16, 1836	Unnumb.
Peoria	Peoria	Jan. 13, 1825	Unnumb.
Perry	Pinckneyville	Jan. 29, 1827	Unnumb.
Piatt	Monticello	Jan. 27, 1841	Unnumb.
Pike	Pittsfield	Jan. 31, 1821	Unnumb.
Pope	Golconda	Jan. 10, 1816	Unnumb.
Pulaski	Mound City	Mar. 3, 1843	Unnumb.
Putnam	Hennepin	Jan. 13, 1825	Unnumb.
Randolph	Chester	Oct. 5, 1795	Procl.
Richland	Olney	Feb. 24, 1841	Unnumb.
Rock Island	Rock Island	Feb. 9, 1831	Unnumb.
St. Clair	Belleville	Apr. 27, 1790	Procl.
Saline	Harrisburg	Feb. 25, 1847	Unnumb.
Sangamon	Springfield	Jan. 30, 1821	Unnumb.
Schuyler	Rushville	Jan. 13, 1825	Unnumb.
Scott	Winchester	Feb. 16, 1839	Unnumb.
Shelby	Shelbyville	Jan. 23, 1827	Unnumb.
Stark	Toulon	Mar. 2, 1839	Unnumb.
Stephenson	Freeport	Mar. 4, 1837	Unnumb.
Tazewell	Pekin	Jan. 31, 1827	Unnumb.
Union	Jonesboro	Jan. 2, 1818	Unnumb.
Vermilion	Danville	Jan. 18, 1826	Unnumb.
Wabash	Mt. Carmel	Dec. 27, 1824	Unnumb.
Warren	Monmouth	Jan. 13, 1825	Unnumb.
Washington	Nashville	Jan. 2, 1818	Unnumb.
Wayne	Fairfield	Mar. 26, 1819	Unnumb.
White	Carmi	Dec. 9, 1815	Unnumb.
Whiteside	Morrison	Jan. 16, 1836	Unnumb.
Will	Joliet	Jan. 12, 1836	Unnumb.
Williamson	Marion	Feb. 28, 1839	Unnumb.

County	County Seat	Created	Statute
Winnebago	Rockford	Jan. 16, 1836	Unnumb.
Woodford	Eureka	Feb. 27, 1841	Unnumb.

1 Formerly Dane County, changed to Christian County, Feb. 1, 1840, unnumbered.

INDIANA (91 counties) 19th state.
Organized as territory May 7, 1800, eff. July 4, 1800.
Admitted as state Dec. 11, 1816.

County	County Seat	Created	Statute
Adams	Decatur	Feb. 7, 1835	Chap. 25
Allen	Fort Wayne	Dec. 17, 1823	Chap. 18
Bartholomew	Columbus	Jan. 8, 1821	Chap. 31
Benton	Fowler	Feb. 18, 1840	Chap. 40
Blackford	Hartford City	Feb. 15, 1838	Chap. 97
Boone	Lebanon	Jan. 29, 1830	Chap. 24
Brown	Nashville	Feb. 4, 1836	Chap. 19
Carroll	Delphi	Jan. 7, 1826	Chap. 16
Cass	Logansport	Dec. 18, 1828	Chap. 19
Clark	Jeffersonville	Feb. 3, 1801	Procl.
Clay	Brazil	Feb. 12, 1825	Chap. 15
Clinton	Frankfort	Jan. 29, 1830	Chap. 25
Crawford	English	Jan. 29, 1818	Chap. 11
Daviess	Washington	Dec. 24, 1816	Chap. 63
Dearborn	Lawrenceburg	Mar. 7, 1803	Procl.
Decatur	Greensburg	Dec. 31, 1821	Chap. 33
De Kalb	Auburn	Feb. 7, 1835	Chap. 25
Delaware	Muncie	Jan. 26, 1827	Chap. 10
Du Bois	Jasper	Dec. 20, 1817	Chap. 7
Elkhart	Goshen	Jan. 29, 1830	Chap. 23
Fayette	Connersville	Dec. 28, 1818	Chap. 28
Floyd	New Albany	Jan. 2, 1819	Chap. 27
Fountain	Covington	Dec. 20, 1825	Chap. 9
Franklin	Brockville	Nov. 27, 1810	Chap. 6
Fulton	Brookville	Feb. 7, 1835	Chap. 25
Gibson	Princeton	Mar. 9, 1813	Chap. 23
Grant	Marion	Feb. 10, 1831	Chap. 12
Greene	Bloomfield	Jan. 5, 1821	Chap. 49
Hamilton	Noblesville	Jan. 8, 1823	Chap. 52
Hancock	Greenfield	Jan. 26, 1827	Chap. 91
Harrison	Corydon	Oct. 11, 1808	Chap. 1
Hendricks	Danville	Dec. 20, 1823	Chap. 91
Henry	New Castle	Dec. 31, 1821	Chap. 60
Howard* 1	Kokomo	Jan. 15, 1844	Chap. 3

County	County Seat	Created	Statute
Huntington	Huntington	Feb. 2, 1832	Chap. 119
Jackson	Brownstown	Dec. 18, 1815	Chap. 1
Jasper	Rensselaer	Feb. 7, 1835	Chap. 25
Jay	Portland	Feb. 7, 1835	Chap. 25
Jefferson	Madison	Nov. 23, 1810	Chap. 2
Jennings	Vernon	Dec. 27, 1816	Chap. 45
Johnson	Franklin	Dec. 31, 1822	Chap. 15
Knox	Vincennes	June 20, 1790	Procl.
Kosciusko	Warsaw	Feb. 7, 1835	Chap. 25
La Grange	La Grange	Feb. 2, 1832	Chap. 117
Lake	Crown Point	Jan. 28, 1836	Chap. 18
La Porte	La Porte	Jan. 9, 1832	Chap. 2
Lawrence	Bedford	Jan. 7, 1818	Chap. 5
Madison	Anderson	Jan. 4, 1823	Chap. 50
Marshall	Plymouth	Feb. 7, 1835	Chap. 25
Martin	Shoals	Jan. 17, 1820	Chap. 31
Miami	Peru	Feb. 2, 1832	Chap. 119
Monroe	Bloomington	Jan. 14, 1818	Chap. 6
Montgomery	Crawfordsville	Dec. 21, 1822	Chap. 6
Morgan	Martinsville	Dec. 31, 1821	Chap. 24
Newton	Kentland	Feb. 7, 1835	Chap. 25
Noble	Albion	Feb. 7, 1835	Chap. 24
Ohio	Rising Sun	Jan. 4, 1844	Chap. 2
Orange	Paoli	Dec. 26, 1815	Chap. 12
Owen	Spencer	Dec. 21, 1818	Chap. 26
Parke	Rockville	Jan. 9, 1821	Chap. 24
Perry	Cannelton	Sept. 7, 1814	Chap. 7
Pike	Petersburg	Dec. 21, 1816	Chap. 51
Porter	Valparaiso	Feb. 7, 1835	Chap. 25
Posey	Mt. Vernon	Sept. 7, 1814	Chap. 7
Pulaski	Winamac	Feb. 7, 1835	Chap. 25
Putnam	Greencastle	Dec. 31, 1821	Chap. 36
Randolph	Winchester	Jan. 10, 1818	Chap. 8
Ripley	Versailles	Dec. 27, 1816	Chap. 45
Rush	Rushville	Dec. 31, 1821	Chap. 35
St. Joseph	South Bend	Jan. 29, 1830	Chap. 23
Scott	Scottsburg	Jan. 12, 1820	Chap. 30
Shelby	Shelbyville	Dec. 31, 1821	Chap. 31
Spencer	Rockport	Jan. 10, 1818	Chap. 9
Starke	Knox	Feb. 7, 1835	Chap. 25
Steuben	Angola	Feb. 7, 1835	Chap. 25
Sullivan	Sullivan	Dec. 30, 1816	Chap. 49
Switzerland	Vevay	Sept. 7, 1814	Chap. 9
Tippecanoe	Lafayette	Jan. 20, 1826	Chap. 10
Tipton	Tipton	Jan. 15, 1844	Chap. 3

County	County Seat	Created	Statute
Union	Liberty	Jan. 5, 1821	Chap. 58
Vanderburgh	Evansville	Jan. 7, 1818	Chap. 10
Vermillion	Newport	Jan. 2, 1824	Chap. 20
Vigo	Terre Haute	Jan. 21, 1818	Chap. 14
Wabash	Wabash	Feb. 2, 1832	Chap. 119
Warren	Williamsport	Jan. 19, 1827	Chap. 11
Warrick	Boonville	Mar. 9, 1813	Chap. 23
Washington	Salem	Dec. 21, 1813	Chap. 10
Wayne	Richmond	Nov. 27, 1810	Chap. 6
Wells	Bluffton	Feb. 7, 1835	Chap. 25
White	Monticello	Feb. 1, 1834	Chap. 30
Whitley	Columbia City	Feb. 7, 1835	Chap. 25

1 Formerly Richardville County, changed to Howard County, Dec. 28, 1846, chap. 168.

IOWA (99 counties) 29th state.
Organized as territory June 12, 1838, eff. July 3, 1838.
Admitted as state December 28, 1846.

County	County Seat	Created	Statute
Adair	Greenfield	Jan. 15, 1851	Chap. 9
Adams	Corning	Jan. 15, 1851	Chap. 9
Allamakee	Waukon	Feb. 20, 1847	Chap. 66
Appanoose	Centerville	Feb. 17, 1843	Chap. 34
Audubon	Audubon	Jan. 15, 1851	Chap. 9
Benton	Vinton	Dec. 21, 1837	Chap. 6
Black Hawk	Waterloo	Feb. 17, 1843	Chap. 34
Boone	Boone	Jan. 13, 1846	Chap. 82
Bremer	Waverly	Jan. 15, 1851	Chap. 9
Buchanan	Independence	Dec. 21, 1837	Chap. 6
Buena Vista	Storm Lake	Jan. 15, 1851	Chap. 9
Butler	Allison	Jan. 15, 1851	Chap. 9
Calhoun* 1	Rockwell City	Jan. 15, 1851	Chap. 9
Carroll	Carroll	Jan. 15, 1851	Chap. 9
Cass	Atlantic	Jan. 15, 1851	Chap. 9
Cedar	Tipton	Dec. 21, 1837	Chap. 6
Cerro Gordo	Mason City	Jan. 15, 1851	Chap. 9
Cherokee	Cherokee	Jan. 15, 1851	Chap. 9
Chickasaw	New Hampton	Jan. 15, 1851	Chap. 9
Clarke	Osceola	Jan. 13, 1846	Chap. 82
Clay	Spencer	Jan. 15, 1851	Chap. 9
Clayton	Elkader	Dec. 21, 1837	Chap. 6
Clinton	Clinton	Dec. 21, 1837	Chap. 6
Crawford	Denison	Jan. 15, 1851	Chap. 9
Dallas	Adel	Jan. 13, 1846	Chap. 82

County	County Seat	Created	Statute
Davis	Bloomfield	Feb. 17, 1843	Chap. 34
Decatur	Leon	Jan. 13, 1846	Chap. 82
Delaware	Manchester	Dec. 21, 1837	Chap. 6
Des Moines	Burlington	Sept. 6, 1834	Unnumb.
Dickinson	Spirit Lake	Jan. 15, 1851	Chap. 9
Dubuque	Dubuque	Sept. 6, 1834	Unnumb.
Emmet	Estherville	Jan. 15, 1851	Chap. 9
Fayette	West Union	Dec. 21, 1837	Chap. 6
Floyd	Charles City	Jan. 15, 1851	Chap. 9
Franklin	Hampton	Jan. 15, 1851	Chap. 9
Fremont	Sidney	Feb. 24, 1847	Chap. 83
Greene	Jefferson	Jan. 15, 1851	Chap. 9
Grundy	Grundy Center	Jan. 15, 1851	Chap. 9
Guthrie	Guthrie Center	Jan. 15, 1851	Chap. 9
Hamilton	Webster City	Dec. 22, 1856	Chap. 15
Hancock	Garner	Jan. 15, 1851	Chap. 9
Hardin	Eldora	Jan. 15, 1851	Chap. 9
Harrison	Logan	Jan. 15, 1851	Chap. 9
Henry	Mount Pleasant	Dec. 7, 1836	Chap. 21
Howard	Cresco	Jan. 15, 1851	Chap. 9
Humboldt	Dakota City	Jan. 15, 1851	Chap. 9
Ida	Ida Grove	Jan. 15, 1851	Chap. 9
Iowa	Marengo	Feb. 17, 1843	Chap. 34
Jackson	Maquoketa	Dec. 21, 1837	Chap. 6
Jasper	Newton	Jan. 13, 1846	Chap. 82
Jefferson	Fairfield	Jan. 21, 1839	Unnumb.
Johnson	Iowa City	Dec. 21, 1837	Chap. 6
Jones	Anamosa	Dec. 21, 1837	Chap. 6
Keokuk	Sigourney	Dec. 21, 1837	Chap. 6
Kossuth	Algona	Jan. 15, 1851	Chap. 9
Lee	Fort Madison and Keokuk	Dec. 7, 1836	Chap. 21
Linn	Cedar Rapids	Dec. 21, 1837	Chap. 6
Louisa	Wapello	Dec. 7, 1836	Chap. 21
Lucas	Charlton	Jan. 13, 1846	Chap. 82
Lyon* 2	Rock Rapids	Jan. 15, 1851	Chap. 9
Madison	Winterset	Feb. 15, 1844	Chap. 124
Mahaska	Oskaloosa	Feb. 17, 1843	Chap. 34
Marion	Knoxville	June 10, 1845	Chap. 57
Marshall	Marshalltown	Jan. 13, 1846	Chap. 82
Mills	Glenwood	Jan. 15, 1851	Chap. 9
Mitchell	Osage	Jan. 15, 1851	Chap. 9
Monona	Onawa	Jan. 15, 1851	Chap. 9
Monroe* 3	Albia	Feb. 17, 1843	Chap. 34
Montgomery	Red Oak	Jan. 15, 1851	Chap. 9
Muscatine	Muscatine	Dec. 7, 1836	Chap. 21

County	County Seat	Created	Statute
O'Brien	Primghar	Jan. 15, 1851	Chap. 9
Osceola	Sibley	Jan. 15, 1851	Chap. 9
Page	Clarinda	Feb. 24, 1847	Chap. 83
Palo Alto	Emmetsburg	Jan. 15, 1851	Chap. 9
Plymouth	Le Mars	Jan. 15, 1851	Chap. 9
Pocahontas	Pocahontas	Jan. 15, 1851	Chap. 9
Polk	Des Moines	Jan. 13, 1846	Chap. 82
Pottawattamie	Council Bluffs	Jan. 15, 1851	Chap. 9
Poweshiek	Montezuma	Feb. 17, 1843	Chap. 34
Ringgold	Mount Ayr	Feb. 24, 1847	Chap. 83
Sac	Sac City	Jan. 15, 1851	Chap. 9
Scott	Davenport	Dec. 21, 1837	Chap. 6
Shelby	Harlan	Jan. 15, 1851	Chap. 9
Sioux	Orange City	Jan. 15, 1851	Chap. 9
Story	Nevada	Jan. 13, 1846	Chap. 82
Tama	Toledo	Feb. 17, 1843	Chap. 34
Taylor	Bedford	Feb. 24, 1847	Chap. 83
Union	Creston	Jan. 15, 1851	Chap. 9
Van Buren	Keosauqua	Dec. 7, 1836	Chap. 21
Wapello	Ottumwa	Feb. 17, 1843	Chap. 34
Warren	Indianola	Jan. 13, 1846	Chap. 82
Washington* 4	Washington	Jan. 16, 1837	Chap. 248
Wayne	Corydon	Jan. 13, 1846	Chap. 82
Webster* 5	Fort Dodge	Jan. 15, 1851	Chap. 9
Winnebago	Forest City	Feb. 20, 1847	Chap. 66
Winneshiek	Decorah	Feb. 20, 1847	Chap. 66
Woodbury* 6	Sioux City	Jan. 15, 1851	Chap. 9
Worth	Northwood	Jan. 15, 1851	Chap. 9
Wright	Clarion	Jan. 15, 1851	Chap. 9

1 Formerly Fox County, changed to Calhoun County, Jan. 12, 1853, chap. 12.
2 Formerly Buncombe County, changed to Lyon County, Sept. 11, 1862, chap. 23.
3 Formerly Kishkekosh County, changed to Monroe County, Jan. 19, 1846, chap. 21.
4 Formerly Slaughter County, changed to Washington County, Jan. 25, 1839, unnumbered.
5 Formerly Risley County, changed to Webster County, Jan. 12, 1853, chap. 12.
6 Formerly Wahkaw County, changed to Woodbury County, Jan. 12, 1853, chap. 12.

KANSAS (105 counties) 34th state.
Organized as territory May 30, 1854.

Admitted as state January 29, 1861.

County	County Seat	Created	Statute
Allen	Iola	Aug. 30, 1855	Chap. 30
Anderson	Garnett	Aug. 30, 1855	Chap. 30
Atchison	Atchison	Aug. 30, 1855	Chap. 30
Barber	Medicine Lodge	Feb. 26, 1867	Chap. 33
Barton	Great Bend	Feb. 26, 1867	Chap. 33
Bourbon	Fort Scott	Aug. 30, 1855	Chap. 30
Brown	Hiawatha	Aug. 30, 1855	Chap. 30
Butler	El Dorado	Aug. 30, 1855	Chap. 30
Chase	Cottonwood Falls	Feb. 11, 1859	Chap. 46
Chautauqua	Sedan	Mar. 3, 1875	Chap. 106
Cherokee* 1	Columbus	Aug. 30, 1855	Chap. 30
Cheyenne	St. Francis	Mar. 6, 1873	Chap. 72
Clark	Ashland	Mar. 7, 1885	Chap. 71
Clay	Clay Center	Feb. 20, 1857	Unnumb.
Cloud* 2	Concordia	Feb. 27, 1860	Chap. 43
Coffey	Burlington	Aug. 30, 1855	Chap. 30
Comanche	Coldwater	Feb. 26, 1867	Chap. 33
Cowley	Winfield	Feb. 26, 1867	Chap. 33
Crawford	Girard	Feb. 13, 1867	Chap. 32
Decatur	Oberlin	Mar. 6, 1873	Chap. 72
Dickinson	Abilene	1855	
Doniphan	Troy	Aug. 30, 1855	Chap. 30
Douglas	Lawrence	Aug. 30, 1855	Chap. 30
Edwards	Kinsley	Mar. 7, 1874	Chap. 59
Elk	Howard	Mar. 3, 1875	Chap. 106
Ellis	Hays	Feb. 26, 1867	Chap. 33
Ellsworth	Ellsworth	Feb. 26, 1867	Chap. 33
Finney* 3	Garden City	Feb. 21, 1883	Chap. 70
Ford	Dodge City	Mar. 6, 1873	Chap. 72
Franklin	Ottawa	Aug. 30, 1855	Chap. 30
Geary* 4	Junction City	Aug. 30, 1855	Chap. 30
Gove	Gove	Mar. 2, 1868	Chap. 14
Graham	Hill City	Feb. 26, 1867	Chap. 33
Grant	Ulysses	Mar. 6, 1873	Chap. 72
Gray	Cimarron	Mar. 5, 1887	Chap. 81
Greeley	Tribune	Mar. 6, 1873	Chap. 72
Greenwood	Eureka	Aug. 30, 1855	Chap. 30
Hamilton	Syracuse	Mar. 6, 1873	Chap. 72
Harper	Anthony	Feb. 26, 1867	Chap. 33
Harvey	Newton	Feb. 29, 1872	Chap. 97
Haskell	Sublette	Mar. 5, 1887	Chap. 81
Hodgeman	Jetmore	Mar. 6, 1873	Chap. 72
Jackson* 5	Holton	Aug. 30, 1855	Chap. 30
Jefferson	Oskaloosa	Aug. 30, 1855	Chap. 30

County	County Seat	Created	Statute
Jewell	Mankato	Feb. 26, 1867	Chap. 33
Johnson	Olathe	Aug. 30, 1855	Chap. 30
Kearny	Lakin	Mar. 6, 1873	Chap. 72
Kingman	Kingman	Feb. 10, 1886	Chap. 35
Kiowa	Greensburg	Feb. 10, 1886	Chap. 33
Labette	Oswego	Feb. 7, 1867	Chap. 29
Lane	Dighton	Mar. 6, 1873	Chap. 72
Leavenworth	Leavenworth	Aug. 30, 1855	Chap. 30
Lincoln	Lincoln	Feb. 26, 1867	Chap. 33
Linn	Mound City	Aug. 30, 1855	Chap. 30
Logan* 6	Russell Springs	Mar. 4, 1881	Chap. 48
Lyon* 7	Emporia	Feb. 17, 1857	Unnumb.
Marion	Marion	1855 (no date)	Chap. 33
Marshall	Marysville	Aug. 30, 1855	Chap. 30
McPherson	McPherson	Feb. 26, 1867	Chap. 33
Meade	Meade	Mar. 7, 1885	Chap. 71
Miami* 8	Paola	Aug. 30, 1855	Chap. 30
Mitchell	Beloit	Feb. 26, 1867	Chap. 33
Montgomery	Independence	Feb. 26, 1867	Chap. 33
Morris* 9	Council Grove	Aug. 30, 1855	Chap. 30
Morton	Richfield	Feb. 18, 1886	Chap. 37
Nemaha	Seneca	Aug. 30, 1855	Chap. 30
Neosho* 10	Erie	Aug. 30, 1855	Chap. 30
Ness	Ness City	Feb. 26, 1867	Chap. 33
Norton* 11	Norton	Feb. 26, 1867	Chap. 33
Osage* 12	Lyndon	Aug. 30, 1855	Chap. 30
Osborne	Osborne	Feb. 26, 1867	Chap. 33
Ottawa	Minneapolis	Feb. 27, 1860	Chap. 43
Pawnee	Larned	Feb. 26, 1867	Chap. 33
Phillips	Phillipsburg	Feb. 26, 1867	Chap. 33
Pottawatomie	Westmoreland	Feb. 20, 1857	Unnumb.
Pratt	Pratt	Feb. 26, 1867	Chap. 33
Rawlins	Atwood	Mar. 6, 1873	Chap. 72
Reno	Hutchinson	Feb. 26, 1867	Chap. 33
Republic	Belleville	Feb. 27, 1860	Chap. 43
Rice	Lyons	Feb. 26, 1867	Chap. 33
Riley	Manhattan	Aug. 30, 1855	Chap. 30
Rooks	Stockton	Feb. 26, 1867	Chap. 33
Rush	La Crosse	Feb. 26, 1867	Chap. 33
Russell	Russell	Feb. 26, 1867	Chap. 33
Saline	Salina	Feb. 15, 1860	Chap. 44
Scott	Scott City	Mar. 6, 1873	Chap. 72
Sedgwick	Wichita	Feb. 26, 1867	Chap. 33
Seward* 13	Liberal	Aug. 30, 1855	Chap. 30
Shawnee	Topeka	Aug. 30, 1855	Chap. 30
Sheridan	Hoxie	Mar. 6, 1873	Chap. 72

County	County Seat	Created	Statute
Sherman	Goodland	Mar. 6, 1873	Chap. 72
Smith	Smith Center	Feb. 26, 1867	Chap. 33
Stafford	St. John	Feb. 26, 1867	Chap. 33
Stanton	Johnson	Mar. 6, 1873	Chap. 72
Stevens	Hugoton	Mar. 6, 1873	Chap. 72
Sumner	Wellington	Feb. 26, 1867	Chap. 33
Thomas	Colby	Mar. 6, 1873	Chap. 72
Trego	Wakeeney	Feb. 26, 1867	Chap. 33
Wabaunsee* 14	Alma	Aug. 30, 1855	Chap. 30
Wallace	Sharon Springs	Mar. 2, 1868	Chap. 14
Washington	Washington	1855, (no date)	Chap. 33
Wichita	Leoti	Mar. 6, 1873	Chap. 72
Wilson	Fredonia	Aug. 30, 1855	Chap. 30
Woodson	Yates Center	Aug. 30, 1855	Chap. 30
Wyandotte	Kansas City	Jan. 29, 1859	Chap. 47

1 Formerly McGee County, changed to Cherokee County, Feb. 18, 1860, chap. 30.

2 Formerly Shirley County, changed to Cloud County, Feb. 26, 1867, chap. 40.

3 Formerly Sequoyah County, changed to Finney County, Feb. 21, 1883, chap. 71.

4 Formerly Davis County, changed to Geary County, Feb. 28, 1889, chap. 132.

5 Formerly Calhoun County, changed to Jackson County, Feb. 11, 1859, chap. 99.

6 Formerly St. John County, changed to Logan County, Feb. 24, 1887, chap. 173.

7 Formerly Breckenridge County, changed to Lyon County, Feb. 5, 1862, chap. 61.

8 Formerly Lykins County, changed to Miami County, June 3, 1861, chap. 18.

9 Formerly Wise County, changed to Morris County, Feb. 11, 1859, chap. 60.

10 Formerly Dorn County, changed to Neosho County, June 3, 1861, chap. 18.

11 Formerly Norton County, changed to Billings County, Mar. 6, 1873, chap. 72; changed back to Norton County, Feb. 19, 1874, chap. 55.

12 Formerly Weller County, changed to Osage County, Feb. 11, 1859, chap. 100.

13 Formerly Godfroy County, changed to Seward County, June 3, 1861, chap. 18; restored Feb. 18, 1886, chap. 37.

14 Formerly Richardson County, changed to Wabaunsee County, Feb. 11, 1859, chap. 49.

KENTUCKY (120 counties) 15th state.
Admitted as state June 1, 1792.

County	County Seat	Created	Statute
Adair	Columbia	Dec. 11, 1801	Chap. 43
Allen	Scottsville	Jan. 11, 1815	Chap. 188
Anderson	Lawrenceburg	Jan. 16, 1827	Chap. 35
Ballard	Wickliffe	Feb. 15, 1842	Chap. 188
Barren	Glasgow	Dec. 20, 1798	Chap. 43
Bath	Owingsville	Jan. 15, 1811	Chap. 221
Bell	Pineville	Feb. 28, 1867	Chap. 1,553
Boone	Burlington	Dec. 13, 1798	Chap. 4
Bourbon	Paris	Sess. Oct. 17, 1785	Chap. 37
Boyd	Cattlettsburg	Feb. 16, 1860	Chap. 288
Boyle	Danville	Feb. 15, 1842	Chap. 189
Bracken	Brooksville	Dec. 14, 1796	Unnumb.
Breathitt	Jackson	Feb. 8, 1839	Chap. 1,192
Breckinridge	Hardinsburg	Dec. 9, 1799	Chap. 72
Bullitt	Shepherdsville	Dec. 13, 1796	Unnumb.
Butler	Morgantown	Jan. 18, 1810	Chap. 33
Caldwell	Princeton	Jan. 31, 1809	Chap. 33
Calloway	Murray	Dec. 19, 1821	Chap. 112
Campbell	Alexandria and Newport	Dec. 17, 1794	Chap. 19
Carlisle	Bardwell	Apr. 3, 1886	Chap. 495
Carroll	Carrollton	Feb. 9, 1838	Chap. 773
Carter	Grayson	Feb. 9, 1838	Chap. 760
Casey	Liberty	Nov. 14, 1806	Unnumb.
Christian	Hopkinsville	Dec. 13, 1796	Unnumb.
Clark	Winchester	Dec. 6, 1792	Chap. 16
Clay	Manchester	Dec. 2, 1806	Unnumb.
Clinton	Albany	Feb. 20, 1836	Chap. 245
Crittenden	Marion	Jan. 26, 1842	Chap. 97
Cumberland	Burkesville	Dec. 14, 1798	Chap. 54
Daviess	Owensboro	Jan. 14, 1815	Chap. 190
Edmonson	Brownsville	Jan. 12, 1825	Chap. 204
Elliott	Sandy Hook	Jan. 26, 1869	Chap. 1,297
Estill	Irvine	Jan. 27, 1808	Chap. 38
Fayette	Lexington	Sess. May 1, 1780	Unnumb.
Fleming	Flemingsburg	Feb. 10, 1798	Chap. 32
Floyd	Prestonsburg	Dec. 13, 1799	Chap. 73
Franklin	Frankfort	Dec. 7, 1794	Chap. 13
Fulton	Hickman	Jan. 15, 1845	Chap. 44
Gallatin	Warsaw	Dec. 14, 1798	Chap. 58
Garrard	Lancaster	Dec. 17, 1796	Unnumb.
Grant	Williamstown	Feb. 12, 1820	Chap. 561
Graves	Mayfield	Dec. 19, 1821	Chap. 112

County	County Seat	Created	Statute
Grayson	Leitchfield	Jan. 25, 1810	Chap. 133
Green	Greensburg	Dec. 20, 1792	Chap. 44
Greenup	Greenup	Dec. 12, 1803	Chap. 76
Hancock	Hawesville	Jan. 3, 1829	Chap. 32
Hardin	Elizabethtown	Dec. 15, 1792	Chap. 17
Harlan	Harlan	Jan. 28, 1819	Chap. 341
Harrison	Cynthiana	Dec. 21, 1793	Chap. 24
Hart	Munfordville	Jan. 28, 1819	Chap. 352
Henderson	Henderson	Dec. 21, 1798	Chap. 57
Henry	New Castle	Dec. 14, 1798	Chap. 49
Hickman	Clinton	Dec. 19, 1821	Chap. 112
Hopkins	Madisonville	Dec. 9, 1806	Unnumb.
Jackson	McKee	Feb. 2, 1858	Chap. 167
Jefferson	Louisville	Sess. May 1, 1780	Unnumb.
Jessamine	Nicholasville	Dec. 19, 1798	Chap. 62
Johnson	Paintsville	Feb. 24, 1843	Chap. 167
Kenton	Covington and Independence	Jan. 29, 1840	Chap. 175
Knott	Hindman	May 5, 1884	
Knox	Barbourville	Dec. 19, 1799	Chap. 74
Larue	Hodgenville	Mar. 4, 1843	Chap. 210
Laurel	London	Dec. 12, 1825	Chap. 29
Lawrence	Louisa	Dec. 14, 1821	Chap. 274
Lee	Beattyville	Jan. 29, 1870	Chap. 202
Leslie	Hyden	Mar. 29, 1878	Chap. 666
Letcher	Whitesburg	Mar. 3, 1842	Chap. 394
Lewis	Vanceburg	Dec. 2, 1806	Unnumb.
Lincoln	Stanford	Sess. May 1, 1780	Unnumb.
Livingston	Smithland	Dec. 13, 1798	Chap. 61
Logan	Russellville	June 28, 1792	Chap. 12
Lyon	Eddyville	Jan. 14, 1854	Chap. 32
Madison	Richmond	Sess. Oct. 17, 1785	Chap. 54
Magoffin	Salyersville	Feb. 22, 1860	Chap. 437
Marion	Lebanon	Jan. 25, 1834	Chap. 285
Marshall	Benton	Feb. 12, 1842	Chap. 180
Martin	Inez	Mar. 10, 1870	Chap. 554
Mason	Maysville	Nov. 5, 1788	Chap. 4
McCracken	Paducah	Dec. 17, 1824	Chap. 48
McCreary	Whitley City	Mar. 12, 1912	Chap. 46
McLean	Calhoun	Feb. 6, 1854	Chap. 125
Meade	Brandenburg	Dec. 17, 1823	Chap. 609
Menifee	Frenchburg	Mar. 10, 1869	Chap. 1, 872
Mercer	Harrodsburg	Sess. Oct. 17, 1785	Chap. 44
Metcalfe	Edmonton	Feb. 1, 1860	Chap. 104
Monroe	Tompkinsville	Jan. 19, 1820	Chap. 474
Montgomery	Mount Sterling	Dec. 14, 1796	Unnumb.

County	County Seat	Created	Statute
Morgan	West Liberty	Dec. 7, 1822	Chap. 460
Muhlenberg	Greenville	Dec. 14, 1798	Chap. 65
Nelson	Bardstown Sess.	Oct. 18, 1784	Chap. 62
Nicholas	Carlisle	Dec. 18, 1799	Chap. 11
Ohio	Hartford	Dec. 17, 1798	Chap. 73
Oldham	La Grange	Dec. 15, 1823	Chap. 620
Owen	Owenton	Feb. 6, 1819	Chap. 387
Owsley	Booneville	Jan. 23, 1843	Chap. 43
Pendleton	Falmouth	Dec. 4, 1787	Chap. 94
Perry	Hazard	Nov. 2, 1820	Chap. 9
Pike	Pikeville	Dec. 19, 1821	Chap. 297
Powell	Stanton	Jan. 7, 1852	Chap. 325
Pulaski	Somerset	Dec. 10, 1798	Chap. 1
Robertson	Mount Olivet	Feb. 11, 1867	Chap. 1, 317
Rockcastle	Mount Vernon	Jan. 8, 1810	Chap. 102
Rowan	Morehead	Mar. 15, 1856	
Russell	Jamestown	Dec. 14, 1825	Chap. 39
Scott	Georgetown	June 22, 1792	Chap. 3
Shelby	Shelbyville	June 23, 1792	Chap. 9
Simpson	Franklin	Jan. 28, 1819	Chap. 342
Spencer	Taylorsville	Jan. 7, 1824	Chap. 708
Taylor	Campbellsville	Jan. 13, 1848	Chap. 26
Todd	Elkton	Dec. 30, 1819	Chap. 460
Trigg	Cadiz	Jan. 27, 1820	Chap. 489
Trimble	Bedford	Feb. 9, 1837	Chap. 248
Union	Morganfield	Jan. 15, 1811	Chap. 220
Warren	Bowling Green	Dec. 14, 1796	Unnumb.
Washington	Springfield	June 22, 1792	Chap. 2
Wayne	Monticello	Dec. 18, 1800	Chap. 46
Webster	Dixon	Feb. 29, 1860	Chap. 822
Whitley	Williamsburg	Jan. 17, 1818	Chap. 183
Wolfe	Campton	Mar. 5, 1860	Chap. 1, 326
Woodford	Versailles	Nov. 12, 1788	Chap. 10

LOUISIANA (64 counties) (known as Parishes) 18th state. Organized as territory March 3, 1805, eff. July 4, 1805. Admitted as state April 30, 1812.

Acadia	Crowley	Apr. 10, 1805	Chap. 25
Allen	Oberlin	June 12, 1912	Act 6
Ascension	Donaldsonville	Mar. 31, 1807	Act 1
Assumption	Napoleonville	Mar. 31, 1807	Act 1
Avoyelles	Marksville	Mar. 31, 1807	Act 1
Beauregard	De Ridder	June 12, 1912	Act 8

County	County Seat	Created	Statute
Bienville	Arcadia	Mar. 14, 1848	Act 183
Bossier	Benton	Feb. 24, 1843	Act 33
Caddo	Shreveport	Jan. 18, 1838	Unnumb.
Calcasieu	Lake Charles	Mar. 24, 1840	Act 72
Caldwell	Columbia	Mar. 6, 1838	Act 48
Cameron	Cameron	Mar. 15, 1870	Act 102
Catahoula	Harrisonburg	Mar. 23, 1808	Act 9
Claiborne	Homer	Mar. 13, 1828	Act 42
Concordia	Vidalia	Apr. 10, 1805	Chap. 25
De Soto	Mansfield	Apr. 1, 1843	Act 88
East Baton Rouge	Baton Rouge	Dec. 22, 1810	Dates vary
East Carroll	Lake Providence	Mar. 28, 1877	Act 24
East Feliciana	Clinton	Feb. 17, 1824	Unnumb.
Evangeline	Ville Platte	June 15, 1910	Act 15
Franklin	Winnsboro	Mar. 1, 1843	Act 41
Grant	Colfax	Mar. 4, 1869	Act 82
Iberia	New Iberia	Oct. 30, 1868	Act 208
Iberville	Plaquemine	Apr. 10, 1805	Chap. 25
Jackson	Jonesboro	Feb. 27, 1845	Act 38
Jefferson	Gretna	Feb. 11, 1825	Unnumb.
Jefferson Davis	Jennings	June 12, 1912	Act 7
Lafayette	Lafayette	Jan. 17, 1823	Unnumb.
Lafourche	Thibodaux	Apr. 10, 1805	Chap. 25
La Salle	Jena	July 3, 1908	Act 177
Lincoln	Ruston	Feb. 27, 1873	Act 32
Livingston	Livingston	Feb. 10, 1832	Unnumb.
Madison	Tallulah	Jan. 19, 1838	Unnumb.
Morehouse	Bastrop	Mar. 25, 1844	Act 118
Natchitoches	Natchitoches	Apr. 10, 1805	Chap. 25
Orleans	New Orleans	Apr. 10, 1805	Chap. 25
Ouachita	Monroe	Apr. 10, 1805	Chap. 25
Plaquemines	Pointe-a-la-Hache	Mar. 31, 1807	Act 1
Pointe Coupee	New Roads	Apr. 10, 1805	Chap. 25
Rapides	Alexandria	Apr. 10, 1805	Chap. 25
Red River	Coushatta	Mar. 16, 1848	Act 219
Richland	Rayville	Mar. 11, 1852	Act 149
Sabine	Many	Mar. 7, 1843	Act 46
St. Bernard	Chalmette	Mar. 31, 1807	Act 1
St. Charles	Hahnville	Mar. 31, 1807	Act 1
St. Helena	Greensburg	Oct. 27, 1810	Dates vary
St. James	Convent	Mar. 31, 1807	Act 1
St. John the Baptist	Edgard	Mar. 31, 1807	Act 1
St. Landry	Opelousas	Mar. 31, 1807	
St. Martin	St. Martinville	Mar. 31, 1807	
St. Mary	Franklin	Apr. 17, 1811	Act 24

County	County Seat	Created	Statute
St. Tammany	Covington	Oct. 27, 1810	Dates vary
Tangipahoa	Amite	Mar. 6, 1869	Act 85
Tensas	St. Joseph	Mar. 17, 1843	Act 61
Terrebonne	Houma	Mar. 22, 1822	Unnumb.
Union	Farmerville	Mar. 13, 1839	Act 22
Vermilion	Abbeville	Mar. 25, 1844	Act 81
Vernon	Leesville	Mar. 30, 1871	Act 71
Washington	Franklinton	Mar. 6, 1819	Unnumb.
Webster	Minden	Feb. 27, 1871	Act 26
West Baton Rouge	Port Allen	Mar. 31, 1807	Act 1
West Carroll	Oak Grove	Mar. 28, 1877	Act 24
West Feliciana	St. Francisville	Feb. 17, 1824	Unnumb.
Winn	Winnfield	Feb. 24, 1852	Act 85

MAINE (16 counties) 23rd state.
Admitted as state March 15, 1820.

County	County Seat	Created	Statute
Androscoggin	Auburn	Mar. 18, 1854*	Chap. 60
Aroostook	Houlton	Mar. 16, 1839*	Chap. 395
Cumberland	Portland Sess.	May 28, 1760	Chap. 2
Franklin	Farmington	Mar. 20, 1838	Chap. 328
Hancock	Ellsworth	June 25, 1789	Chap. 25
Kennebec	Augusta	Feb. 20, 1799	Chap. 23
Knox	Rockland	Mar. 9, 1860*	Chap. 146
Lincoln	Wiscasset Sess.	May 28, 1760	Chap. 2
Oxford	South Paris	Mar. 4, 1805	Chap. 24
Penobscot	Bangor	Feb. 15, 1816*	Chap. 121
Piscataquis	Dover-Foxcroft	Mar. 23, 1838*	Chap. 355
Sagadahoc	Bath	Apr. 4, 1854	Chap. 70
Somerset	Skowhegan	Mar. 1, 1809*	Chap. 62
Waldo	Belfast	Feb. 7, 1827*	Chap. 354
Washington	Machais	June 25, 1789	Chap. 25
York	Alfred	Nov. 20, 1652	Unnumb.

*Massachusetts Law

MARYLAND (23 counties) 7th state.
Admitted as state April 28, 1788.

County	County Seat	Created	Statute
Allegany	Cumberland	Dec. 25, 1789	Chap. 29
Anne Arundel	Annapolis Sess.	Apr. 9, 1650	Chap. 8
Baltimore	Towson	1659	
Calvert	Prince Frederick	1654	

County	County Seat	Created	Statute
Caroline	Denton Sess.	June 15, 1773	
		Dec. 5, 1773	Chap. 10
Carroll	Westminster	Jan. 19, 1837	Chap. 19
Cecil	Elkton	1674	
Charles	La Plata	1658	
Dorchester	Cambridge	1668	
Frederick	Frederick	June 10, 1748	Chap. 15
Garrett	Oakland	Apr. 1, 1872	Chap. 212
Harford	Bel Air	Mar. 2, 1774	
Howard	Ellicott City	May 13, 1851	Const. (Art. 8, sect. 1)
Kent	Chestertown	Dec. 16, 1642	
Montgomery	Rockville	Sept. 6, 1776	Resolve
Prince George's	Upper Marlboro	May 20, 1695	Chap. 13
Queen Anne's	Centreville	Apr. 18, 1706	Chap. 3
St. Mary's	Leonardtown	1637	
Somerset	Princess Anne	Aug. 22, 1666	Procl.
Talbot	Easton	Feb. 18, 1661-2	
Washington	Hagerstown	Sept. 6, 1776	Resolve
Wicomico	Salisbury	Aug. 17, 1867	Const.
Worcester	Snow Hill	Oct. 29, 1742	Chap. 19

Formerly Patuxent, name changed in 1658.

MASSACHUSETTS (14 counties) 6th state.
Admitted as state Feb. 6, 1788.

County	County Seat	Created	Statute
Barnstable	Barnstable	June 2, 1685	
Berkshire	Pittsfield Sess.	May 28, 1760	Chap. 4
Bristol	Fall River and New Bedford	June 2, 1685	
Dukes	Edgartown	June 22, 1695	Chap. 7
Essex	Lawrence, Newburyport and Salem	May 10, 1643	
Franklin	Greenfield	June 24, 1811	Chap. 61
Hampden	Springfield	Feb. 25, 1812	Chap. 137
Hampshire	Northampton	May 7, 1662	
Middlesex	Cambridge and Lowell	May 10, 1643	
Nantucket	Nantucket	June 22, 1695	Chap. 7
Norfolk	Dedham	Mar. 26, 1793	Chap. 43
Plymouth	Plymouth	June 2, 1685	
Suffolk	Boston	May 10, 1643	
Worcester	Fitchburg and Worcester	Apr. 5, 1731	Chap. 13

MICHIGAN (83 counties) 26th state.
Organized as territory January 11, 1805, eff. June 30, 1805.
Admitted as state January 26, 1837.

County	County Seat	Created	Statute
Alcona* 1	Harrisville	Apr. 1, 1840	Act 119
Alger	Munising	Mar. 17, 1885	Act 23
Allegan	Allegan	Mar. 2, 1831	Unnumb.
Alpena* 2	Alpena	Apr. 1, 1840	Act 119
Antrim* 3	Bellaire	Apr. 1, 1840	Act 119
Arenac	Standish	Mar. 2, 1831	Unnumb.
Baraga	L'Anse	Feb. 19, 1875	Act 14
Barry	Hastings	Oct. 29, 1829	Unnumb.
Bay	Bay City	Feb. 17, 1857	Act 171
Benzie	Beulah	Feb. 27, 1863	Act 48
Berrien	St. Joseph	Oct. 29, 1829	Unnumb.
Branch	Coldwater	Oct. 29, 1829	Unnumb.
Calhoun	Marshall	Oct. 29, 1829	Unnumb.
Cass	Cassopolis	Oct. 29, 1829	Unnumb.
Charlevoix* 4	Charlevoix	Apr. 1, 1840	Act 119
Cheboygan	Cheboygan	Apr. 1, 1840	Act 119
Chippewa	Sault Ste. Marie	Dec. 22, 1826	Unnumb.
Clare* 5	Harrison	Apr. 1, 1840	Act 119
Clinton	St. Johns	Mar. 2, 1831	Unnumb.
Crawford* 6	Grayling	Apr. 1, 1840	Act 119
Delta	Escanaba	Mar. 9, 1843	Act 89
Dickinson	Iron Mountain	May 21, 1891	Act 89
Eaton	Charlotte	Oct. 29, 1829	Unnumb.
Emmet* 7	Petoskey	Apr. 1, 1840	Act 119
Genesee	Flint	Mar. 28, 1835	Unnumb.
Gladwin	Gladwin	Mar. 2, 1831	Unnumb.
Gogebic	Bessemer	Feb. 7, 1887	Act 337
Grand Traverse	Traverse City	Apr. 1, 1840	Act 119
Gratiot	Ithaca	Mar. 2, 1831	Unnumb.
Hillsdale	Hillsdale	Oct. 29, 1829	Unnumb.
Houghton	Houghton	Mar. 19, 1845	Act 48
Huron	Bad Axe	Apr. 1, 1840	Act 119
Ingham	Mason	Oct. 29, 1829	Unnumb.
Ionia	Ionia	Mar. 2, 1831	Unnumb.
Iosco* 8	Tawas City	Apr. 1, 1840	Act 119
Iron	Crystal Falls	Apr. 3, 1885	Act 35
Isabella	Mt. Pleasant	Mar. 2, 1831	Unnumb.
Jackson	Jackson	Oct. 29, 1829	Unnumb.
Kalamazoo	Kalamazoo	Oct. 29, 1829	Unnumb.
Kalkaska* 9	Kalkaska	Apr. 1, 1840	Unnumb.
Kent	Grand Rapids	Mar. 2, 1831	Unnumb.
Keweenaw	Eagle River	Mar. 11, 1861	Chap. 118

County	County Seat	Created	Statute
Lake* 10	Baldwin	Apr. 1, 1840	Act 119
Lapeer	Lapeer	Sept. 10, 1822	Unnumb.
Leelanau	Leland	Apr. 1, 1840	Act 119
Lenawee	Adrian	Sept. 10, 1822	Unnumb.
Livingston	Howell	Mar. 21, 1833	Unnumb.
Luce	Newberry	Mar. 1, 1887	Act 363
Mackinac* 11	St. Ignace	Oct. 26, 1818	Procl.
Macomb	Mount Clemens	Jan. 15, 1818	Procl.
Manistee	Manistee	Apr. 1, 1840	Act 119
Marquette	Marquette	Mar. 9, 1843	Act 89
Mason* 12	Ludington	Apr. 1, 1840	Act 119
Mecosta	Big Rapids	Apr. 1, 1840	Act 119
Menominee* 13	Menominee	Mar. 15, 1861	Act 213
Midland	Midland	Mar. 2, 1831	Unnumb.
Missaukee	Lake City	Apr. 1, 1840	Act 119
Monroe	Monroe	July 14, 1817	Procl.
Montcalm	Stanton	Mar. 2, 1831	Unnumb.
Montmorency* 14	Atlanta	Apr. 1, 1840	Act 119
Muskegon	Muskegon	Feb. 4, 1859	Act 55
Newaygo	White Cloud	Apr. 1, 1840	Act 119
Oakland	Pontiac	Jan. 12, 1819	Procl.
Oceana	Hart	Mar. 2, 1831	Unnumb.
Ogemaw	West Branch	Apr. 1, 1840	Act 119
Ontonagon	Ontonagon	Mar. 9, 1843	Act 89
Osceola* 15	Reed City	Apr. 1, 1840	Act 119
Oscoda	Mio	Apr. 1, 1840	Act 119
Otsego* 16	Gaylord	Apr. 1, 1840	Act 119
Ottawa	Grand Haven	Mar. 2, 1831	Unnumb.
Presque Isle	Rogers City	Apr. 1, 1840	Act 119
Roscommon* 17	Roscommon	Apr. 1, 1840	Act 119
Saginaw	Saginaw	Sept. 10, 1822	Unnumb.
St. Clair	Port Huron	Mar. 28, 1820	Procl.
St. Joseph	Centerville	Oct. 29, 1829	Unnumb.
Sanilac	Sandusky	Sept. 10, 1822	Unnumb.
Schoolcraft	Manistique	Mar. 9, 1843	Chap. 89
Shiawassee	Corunna	Sept. 10, 1822	Unnumb.
Tuscola	Caro	Apr. 1, 1840	Act 119
Van Buren	Paw Paw	Oct. 29, 1829	Unnumb.
Washtenaw	Ann Arbor	Sept. 10, 1822	Unnumb.
Wayne	Detroit	Nov. 21, 1815	Procl.
Wexford* 18	Cadillac	Apr. 1, 1840	Act 119

1 Formerly Neewago County, changed to Alcona County, Mar. 8, 1843, act 67.

2 Formerly Anamickee County, changed to Alpena County, Mar. 8, 1843, act 67.

3 Formerly Meegisee County, changed to Antrim County, Mar. 8, 1843, act 67.
4 Formerly Reshkauko County, changed to Charlevoix County, Mar. 8, 1843, act. 67.
5 Formerly Kaykakee County, changed to Clare County, Mar. 8, 1843, act 67.
6 Formerly Shawano County, changed to Crawford County, Mar. 8, 1843, act 67.
7 Formerly Tonedagana County, changed to Emmet County, Mar. 8, 1843, act 67.
8 Formerly Kanotin County, changed to Iosco County, Mar. 8, 1843, act 67.
9 Formerly Wabassee County, changed to Kalkaska County, Mar. 8, 1843, act 67.
10 Formerly Aishcum County, changed to Lake County, Mar. 8, 1843, act 67.
11 Formerly Michilimackinac County, changed to Mackinac County, Mar. 9, 1843, act 89.
12 Formerly Notipekago County, changed to Mason County, Mar. 8, 1843, act 67.
13 Formerly Bleeker County, changed to Menominee County, Mar. 19, 1863, act 163.
14 Formerly Cheonoquet County, changed to Montmorency County, Mar. 8, 1843, act 67.
15 Formerly Unwattin County, changed to Osceola County, Mar. 8, 1843, act 67.
16 Formerly Okkuddo County, changed to Otsego County, Mar. 8, 1843, act 67.
17 Formerly Mikenauk County, changed to Roscommon County, Mar. 8, 1843, act 67.
18 Formerly Kautawaubet County, changed to Wexford County, Mar. 8, 1843, act 67.

MINNESOTA (87 counties) 32nd state.
Organized as territory Mar. 3, 1849.
Admitted as state May 11, 1858.

County	County Seat	Created	Statute
Aitkin	Aitkin	May 23, 1857	Chap. 5
Anoka	Anoka	May 23, 1857	Chap. 64
Becker	Detroit Lakes	Mar. 18, 1858	Chap. 34
Beltrami	Bemidji	Feb. 28, 1866	Chap. 46
Benton	Foley	Oct. 27, 1849	Chap. 5
Big Stone	Ortonville	Feb. 20, 1862	Chap. 22
Blue Earth	Mankato	Mar. 5, 1853	Chap. 11

County	County Seat	Created	Statute
Brown	New Ulm	Feb. 20, 1855	Chap. 6
Carlton	Carlton	May 23, 1857	Chap. 5
Carver	Chaska	Feb. 20, 1855	Chap. 6
Cass	Walker	Mar. 31, 1851	Unnumb.
Chippewa	Montevideo	Feb. 20, 1862	Chap. 22
Chisago	Center City	Mar. 31, 1851	Unnumb.
Clay* 1	Moorhead	Mar. 18, 1858	Chap. 34
Clearwater	Bagley	Dec. 20, 1902	Procl.
Cook	Grand Marais	Mar. 9, 1874	Chap. 100
Cottonwood	Windom	May 23, 1857	Chap. 14
Crow Wing	Brainerd	May 23, 1857	Chap. 5
Dakota	Hastings	Oct. 27, 1849	Chap. 5
Dodge	Mantorville	Feb. 20, 1855	Chap. 6
Douglas	Alexandria	Mar. 8, 1858	Chap. 74
Faribault	Blue Earth	Feb. 20, 1855	Chap. 6
Fillmore	Preston	Mar. 5, 1853	Chap. 11
Freeborn	Albert Lea	Feb. 20, 1855	Chap. 6
Goodhue	Red Wing	Mar. 5, 1853	Chap. 11
Grant	Elbow Lake	Mar. 6, 1868	Chap. 109
Hennepin	Minneapolis	Mar. 6, 1852	Chap. 32
Houston	Caledonia	Feb. 23, 1854	Chap. 29
Hubbard	Park Rapids	Feb. 26, 1883	Chap. 78
Isanti	Cambridge	Feb. 13, 1857	Chap. 70
Itasca	Grand Rapids	Oct. 27, 1849	Chap. 5
Jackson	Jackson	May 23, 1857	Chap. 14
Kanabec	Mora	Mar. 13, 1858	Chap. 56
Kandiyohi	Willmar	Mar. 20, 1858	Chap. 65
Kittson* 2	Hallock	Apr. 24, 1862	Chap. 17
Koochiching	International Falls	Dec. 19, 1906	Procl.
Lac Qui Parle	Madison	Mar. 6, 1871	Chap. 100
Lake	Two Harbors	Mar. 1, 1856	Chap. 35
Lake of the Woods	Baudette	Nov. 28, 1922	Procl.
Le Sueur	Le Center	Mar. 5, 1853	Chap. 11
Lincoln	Ivanhoe	Mar. 1, 1866	Chap. 45
Lyon	Marshall	Mar. 6, 1868	Chap. 112
Mahnomen	Mahnomen	Dec. 27, 1906	Procl.
Marshall	Warren	Feb. 25, 1879	Chap. 10
Martin	Fairmont	May 23, 1857	Chap. 14
Mc Leod	Glencoe	Mar. 1, 1856	Chap. 26
Meeker	Litchfield	Feb. 23, 1856	Chap. 68
Mille Lacs	Milaca	May 23, 1857	Chap. 5
Morrison	Little Falls	Feb. 25, 1856	Chap. 38
Mower	Austin	Feb. 20, 1855	Chap. 6
Murray	Slayton	May 23, 1857	Chap. 14
Nicollet	St. Peter	Mar. 5, 1853	Chap. 11

County	County Seat	Created	Statute
Nobles	Worthington	May 23, 1857	Chap. 14
Norman	Ada	Feb. 17, 1881	Chap. 92
Olmstead	Rochester	Feb. 20, 1855	Chap. 6
Otter Tail	Fergus Falls	Mar. 18, 1858	Chap. 34
Pennington	Thief River Falls	Nov. 23, 1910	Procl.
Pine	Pine City	Mar. 1, 1856	Chap. 36
Pipestone	Pipestone	May 23, 1857	Chap. 14
Polk	Crookston	July 20, 1858	Chap. 67
Pope	Glenwood	Feb. 20, 1862	Chap. 22
Ramsey	St. Paul	Oct. 27, 1849	Chap. 5
Red Lake	Red Lake Falls	Dec. 24, 1896	Procl.
Redwood	Redwood Falls	Feb. 6, 1862	Chap. 21
Renville	Olivia	Feb. 20, 1855	Chap. 6
Rice	Faribault	Mar. 5, 1853	Chap. 11
Rock	Luverne	May 23, 1857	Chap. 14
Roseau	Roseau	Feb. 28, 1894	Procl.
St. Louis* 3	Duluth	Feb. 20, 1855	Chap. 6
Scott	Shakopee	Mar. 5, 1853	Chap. 11
Sherburne	Elk River	Feb. 25, 1856	Chap. 38
Sibley	Gaylord	Mar. 5, 1853	Chap. 11
Stearns	St. Cloud	Feb. 20, 1855	Chap. 6
Steele	Owatonna	Feb. 20, 1855	Chap. 6
Stevens	Morris	Feb. 20, 1862	Chap. 22
Swift	Benson	Feb. 18, 1870	Chap. 90
Todd	Long Prairie	Feb. 20, 1855	Chap. 6
Traverse	Wheaton	Feb. 20, 1862	Chap. 22
Wabasha	Wabasha	Oct. 27, 1849	Chap. 5
Wadena	Wadena	June 11, 1858	Chap. 179
Waseca	Waseca	Feb. 27, 1857	Chap. 57
Washington	Stillwater	Oct. 27, 1849	Chap. 5
Watonwan	St. James	Feb. 25, 1860	Chap. 13
Wilkin* 4	Breckenridge	Mar. 18, 1858	Chap. 64
Winona	Winona	Feb. 23, 1854	Chap. 29
Wright	Buffalo	Feb. 20, 1855	Chap. 6
Yellow Medicine	Granite Falls	Mar. 6, 1871	Chap. 98

1 Formerly Breckinridge County, changed to Clay County, Mar. 6, 1862, chap. 33.

2 Formerly Pembina County, changed to Kittson County, Mar. 9, 1878, chap. 59.

3 Formerly Superior County, changed to St. Louis County, Mar. 3, 1855, chap. 22.

4 Formerly Toombs County, changed to Andy Johnson County, Mar. 18, 1858; changed to Wilkin County, Mar. 6, 1868, chap. 115.

MISSISSIPPI (82 counties) 20th state.
Organized as territory April 7, 1798.
Admitted as state December 10, 1817.

County	County Seat	Created	Statute
Adams	Natchez	Apr. 2, 1799	Procl.
Alcorn	Corinth	Apr. 15, 1870	Chap. 51
Amite	Liberty	Feb. 24, 1809	Unnumb.
Attala	Kosciusko	Dec. 23, 1833	Unnumb.
Benton	Ashland	July 21, 1870	Chap. 50
Bolivar	Cleveland, Rosedale	Feb. 9, 1836	Unnumb.
Calhoun	Pittsboro	Mar. 8, 1852	Chap. 15
Carroll	Carrollton, Vaiden	Dec. 23, 1833	Unnumb.
Chickasaw	Houston, Okolona	Feb. 9, 1836	Unnumb.
Choctaw	Ackerman	Dec. 23, 1833	Unnumb.
Claiborne	Port Gibson	Jan. 27, 1802	Unnumb.
Clarke	Quitman	Dec. 10, 1812	Unnumb.
Clay* 1	West Point	May 12, 1871	Chap. 430
Coahoma	Clarksdale	Feb. 9, 1836	Unnumb.
Copiah	Hazlehurst	Jan. 21, 1823	Chap. 49
Covington	Collins	Feb. 5, 1819	Unnumb.
De Soto	Hernando	Feb. 9, 1836	Unnumb.
Forrest	Hattiesburg	Apr. 19, 1906	Chap. 165
Franklin	Meadville	Dec. 21, 1809	Unnumb.
George	Lucedale	Mar. 16, 1910	Chap. 248
Greene	Leakesville	Dec. 9, 1811	Unnumb.
Grenada	Grenada	May 9, 1870	Chap. 240
Hancock	Bay St. Louis	Dec. 18, 1812	Unnumb.
Harrison	Gulfport	Feb. 5, 1841	Chap. 35
Hinds	Raymond, Jackson	Feb. 12, 1821	Chap. 70
Holmes	Lexington	Feb. 19, 1833	Chap. 78
Humphreys	Belzoni	Mar. 28, 1918	Chap. 348
Issaquena	Mayersville	Jan. 23, 1844	Chap. 47
Itawamba	Fulton	Feb. 9, 1836	Unnumb.
Jackson	Pascagoula	Dec. 18, 1812	Unnumb.
Jasper	Bay Springs, Paulding	Dec. 23, 1833	Unnumb.
Jefferson* 2	Fayette	Apr. 2, 1799	Procl.
Jefferson Davis	Prentiss	Mar. 31, 1906	Chap. 166
Jones	Ellisville, Laurel	Jan. 24, 1826	Chap. 47
Kemper	De Kalb	Dec. 23, 1833	Unnumb.
Lafayette	Oxford	Feb. 9, 1836	Unnumb.
Lamar	Purvis	Feb. 19, 1904	Chap. 102
Lauderdale	Meridan	Dec. 23, 1833	Unnumb.

County	County Seat	Created	Statute
Lawrence	Monticello	Dec. 22, 1814	Unnumb.
Leake	Carthage	Dec. 23, 1833	Unnumb.
Lee	Tupelo	Oct. 26, 1866	Chap. 20
Leflore	Greenwood	Mar. 15, 1871	Chap. 238
Lincoln	Brookhaven	Apr. 7, 1870	Chap. 55
Lowndes	Columbus	Jan. 30, 1830	Chap. 14
Madison	Canton	Jan. 29, 1828	Chap. 14
Marion	Columbia	Dec. 9, 1811	Unnumb.
Marshall	Holly Springs	Feb. 9, 1836	Unnumb.
Monroe	Aberdeen	Feb. 9, 1821	Chap. 30
Montgomery	Winona	May 13, 1871	Chap. 241
Neshoba	Philadelphia	Dec. 23, 1833	Unnumb.
Newton	Decatur	Feb. 25, 1836	Unnumb.
Noxubee	Macon	Dec. 23, 1833	Unnumb.
Oktibbeha	Starkville	Dec. 23, 1833	Unnumb.
Panola	Batesville, Sardis	Feb. 9, 1836	Unnumb.
Pearl River	Poplarville	Feb. 22, 1890	Chap. 76
Perry	New Augusta	Feb. 3, 1820	Chap. 18
Pike	Magnolia	Dec. 9, 1815	Unnumb.
Pontotoc	Pontotoc	Feb. 9, 1836	Unnumb.
Prentiss	Booneville	Apr. 15, 1870	Chap. 51
Quitman	Marks	Feb. 1, 1877	Chap. 35
Rankin	Brandon	Feb. 4, 1828	Chap. 93
Scott	Forest	Dec. 23, 1833	Unnumb.
Sharkey	Rolling Fork	Mar. 29, 1876	Chap. 63
Simpson	Mendenhall	Jan. 23, 1824	Unnumb.
Smith	Raleigh	Dec. 23, 1833	Chap. 5
Stone	Wiggins	Apr. 3, 1916	Chap. 527
Sunflower	Indianola	Feb. 15, 1844	Chap. 49
Tallahatchie	Charleston, Sumner	Dec. 23, 1833	Unnumb.
Tate	Senatobia	Apr. 15, 1873	Chap. 1
Tippah	Ripley	Feb. 9, 1836	Unnumb.
Tishomingo	Iuka	Feb. 9, 1836	Unnumb.
Tunica	Tunica	Feb. 9, 1836	Unnumb.
Union	New Albany	July 7, 1870	Chap. 54
Walthall	Tylertown	Mar. 16, 1910	Chap. 321
Warren	Vicksburg	Dec. 22, 1809	Unnumb.
Washington	Greenville	Jan. 29, 1827	Chap. 80
Wayne	Waynesboro	Dec. 21, 1809	Unnumb.
Webster* 3	Walthall	Apr. 6, 1874	Chap. 112
Wilkinson	Woodville	Jan. 30, 1802	Unnumb.
Winston	Louisville	Dec. 23, 1833	Unnumb.
Yalobusha	Coffeeville, Water Valley	Dec. 23, 1833	Unnumb.

County	County Seat	Created	Statute
Yazoo	Yazoo City	Jan. 21, 1823	Chap. 49

1 Formerly Colfax County, changed to Clay County, Apr. 10, 1876, chap. 103.
2 Formerly Pickering County, changed to Jefferson County, Jan. 11, 1802, unnumbered.
3 Formerly Sumner County, changed to Webster County, Jan. 30, 1882, chap. 132.

MISSOURI (114 counties) 24th state.
Organized as territory June 4, 1812, eff. December 7, 1812.
Admitted as state August 10, 1821.

County	County Seat	Created	Statute
Adair	Kirksville	Jan. 29, 1841	Unnumb.
Andrew	Savannah	Jan. 29, 1841	Unnumb.
Atchison* 1	Rockport	Feb. 23, 1843	Unnumb.
Audrain	Mexico	Jan. 12, 1831	Chap. 13
Barry	Cassville	Jan. 5, 1835	Unnumb.
Barton	Lamar	Dec. 12, 1855	Unnumb.
Bates	Butler	Jan. 29, 1841	Unnumb.
Benton	Warsaw	Jan. 3, 1835	Unnumb.
Bollinger	Marble Hill	Mar. 1, 1851	Unnumb.
Boone	Columbia	Nov. 16, 1820	Chap. 14
Buchanan	St. Joseph	Dec. 31, 1838	Unnumb.
Butler	Poplar Bluff	Feb. 27, 1849	Unnumb.
Caldwell	Kingston	Dec. 29, 1836	Unnumb.
Callaway	Fulton	Nov. 25, 1820	Chap. 29
Camden* 2	Camdenton	Jan. 29, 1841	Unnumb.
Cape Girardeau	Jackson	Oct. 1, 1812	Procl.
Carroll	Carrollton	Jan. 2, 1833	Chap. 24
Carter	Van Buren	Mar. 10, 1859	Unnumb.
Cass* 3	Harrisonville	Mar. 3, 1835	Unnumb.
Cedar	Stockton	Feb. 14, 1845	Unnumb.
Chariton	Keytesville	Nov. 16, 1820	Chap. 14
Christian	Ozark	Mar. 8, 1859	Unnumb.
Clark	Kahoka	Dec. 16, 1836	Unnumb.
Clay	Liberty	Jan. 2, 1822	Chap. 39
Clinton	Plattsburg	Jan. 2, 1833	Chap. 25
Cole	Jefferson City	Nov. 16, 1820	Chap. 16
Cooper	Boonville	Dec. 17, 1818	Unnumb.
Crawford	Steelville	Jan. 23, 1829	Chap. 19
Dade	Greenfield	Jan. 29, 1841	Unnumb.
Dallas* 4	Buffalo	Jan. 29, 1841	Unnumb.
Daviess	Gallatin	Dec. 29, 1836	Unnumb.

County	County Seat	Created	Statute
De Kalb	Maysville	Feb. 25, 1845	Unnumb.
Dent	Salem	Feb. 10, 1851	Unnumb.
Douglas	Ava	Oct. 29, 1857	Unnumb.
Dunklin	Kennett	Feb. 14, 1845	Unnumb.
Franklin	Union	Dec. 11, 1818	Unnumb.
Gasconade	Hermann	Nov. 25, 1820	Chap. 28
Gentry	Albany	Feb. 12, 1841	Unnumb.
Greene	Springfield	Jan. 2, 1833	Chap. 26
Grundy	Trenton	Jan. 29, 1841	Unnumb.
Harrison	Bethany	Feb. 14, 1845	Unnumb.
Henry* 5	Clinton	Dec. 13, 1834	Unnumb.
Hickory	Hermitage	Feb. 14, 1845	Unnumb.
Holt* 6	Oregon	Jan. 29, 1841	Unnumb.
Howard	Fayette	Jan. 13, 1816	Unnumb.
Howell	West Plains	Mar. 2, 1857	Unnumb.
Iron	Ironton	Feb. 17, 1857	Unnumb.
Jackson	Independence	Dec. 15, 1826	Chap. 20
Jasper	Carthage	Jan. 29, 1841	Unnumb.
Jefferson	Hillsboro	Dec. 8, 1818	Unnumb.
Johnson	Warrensburg	Dec. 13, 1834	Unnumb.
Knox	Edina	Feb. 14, 1845	Unnumb.
Laclede	Lebanon	Feb. 24, 1849	Unnumb.
Lafayette* 7	Lexington	Nov. 16, 1820	Chap. 10
Lawrence	Mount Vernon	Feb. 14, 1845	Unnumb.
Lewis	Monticello	Jan. 2, 1833	Chap. 28
Lincoln	Troy	Dec. 14, 1818	Unnumb.
Linn	Linneus	Jan. 6, 1837	Unnumb.
Livingston	Chillicothe	Jan. 6, 1837	Unnumb.
Macon	Macon	Jan. 6, 1837	Unnumb.
Madison	Fredericktown	Dec. 14, 1818	Unnumb.
Maries	Vienna	Mar. 2, 1855	Unnumb.
Marion	Palmyra	Dec. 14, 1822	Chap. 38
McDonald	Pineville	Mar. 3, 1849	Unnumb.
Mercer	Princeton	Feb. 14, 1845	Unnumb.
Miller	Tuscumbia	Feb. 6, 1837	Unnumb.
Mississippi	Charleston	Feb. 14, 1845	Unnumb.
Moniteau	California	Feb. 14, 1845	Unnumb.
Monroe	Paris	Jan. 6, 1831	Chap. 15
Montgomery	Montgomery City	Dec. 14, 1818	Unnumb.
Morgan	Versailles	Jan. 5, 1833	Chap. 29
New Madrid	New Madrid	Oct. 1, 1812	Procl.
Newton	Neosho	Dec. 30, 1838	Unnumb.
Nodaway	Maryville	Jan. 29, 1841	Unnumb.
Oregon	Alton	Feb. 14, 1845	Unnumb.
Osage	Linn	Jan. 29, 1841	Unnumb.
Ozark* 8	Gainesville	Jan. 29, 1841	Unnumb.

County	County Seat	Created	Statute
Pemiscot	Caruthersville	Feb. 19, 1851	Unnumb.
Perry	Perryville	Nov. 16, 1820	Chap. 15
Pettis	Sedalia	Jan. 26, 1833	Chap. 30
Phelps	Rolla	Nov. 13, 1857	Unnumb.
Pike	Bowling Green	Dec. 14, 1818	Unnumb.
Platte	Platte City	Dec. 31, 1838	Unnumb.
Polk	Bolivar	Jan. 5, 1835	Unnumb.
Pulaski	Waynesville	Jan. 19, 1833	Chap. 31
Putnam	Unionville	Feb. 22, 1843	Unnumb.
Ralls	New London	Nov. 16, 1820	Chap. 12
Randolph	Huntsville	Jan. 22, 1829	Chap. 29
Ray	Richmond	Nov. 16, 1820	Chap. 14
Reynolds	Centerville	Feb. 25, 1845	Unnumb.
Ripley	Doniphan	Jan. 5, 1833	Chap. 32
St. Charles	St. Charles	Oct. 1, 1812	Procl.
St. Clair	Osceola	Jan. 29, 1841	Unnumb.
St. Francois	Farmington	Dec. 19, 1821	Chap. 26
St. Louis	Clayton	Oct. 1, 1812	Procl.
Ste. Genevieve	Ste. Genevieve	Oct. 1, 1812	Procl.
Saline	Marshall	Nov. 25, 1820	Chap. 27
Schuyler	Lancaster	Feb. 14, 1845	Unnumb.
Scotland	Memphis	Jan. 29, 1841	Unnumb.
Scott	Benton	Dec. 28, 1821	Chap. 28
Shannon	Eminence	Jan. 29, 1841	Unnumb.
Shelby	Shelbyville	Jan. 2, 1835	Unnumb.
Stoddard	Bloomfield	Jan. 2, 1835	Unnumb.
Stone	Galena	Feb. 10, 1851	Unnumb.
Sullivan	Milan	Feb. 17, 1843	Unnumb.
Taney	Forsyth	Jan. 6, 1837	Unnumb.
Texas* 9	Houston	Feb. 14, 1845	Unnumb.
Vernon	Nevada	Feb. 17, 1851	Unnumb.
Warren	Warrenton	Jan. 5, 1833	Chap. 95
Washington	Potosi	Aug. 21, 1813	Unnumb.
Wayne	Greenville	Dec. 11, 1818	Unnumb.
Webster	Marshfield	Mar. 3, 1855	Unnumb.
Worth	Grant City	Feb. 8, 1861	Unnumb.
Wright	Hartville	Jan. 29, 1841	Unnumb.

1 Formerly Allen County, changed to Atchison County, Feb. 14, 1845, unnumbered.

2 Formerly Kinderhook County, changed to Camden County, Feb. 23, 1843, unnumbered.

3 Formerly Van Buren County, changed to Cass County, Feb. 19, 1849, unnumbered.

4 Formerly Niangua County, changed to Dallas County, Dec. 16, 1844, unnumbered.

5 Formerly Rives County, changed to Henry County, Feb. 15, 1841, unnumbered.
6 Formerly Nodaway County, changed to Holt County, Feb. 15, 1841, unnumbered.
7 Formerly Lillard County, changed to Lafayette County, Feb. 16, 1825, chap. 1.
8 Formerly Ozark County, changed to Decatur County, Feb. 22, 1843, unnumbered; changed to Ozark County, Mar. 24, 1845, unnumbered.
9 Formerly Ashley County, changed to Texas County, Feb. 14, 1845, unnumbered.

MONTANA (56 counties) 41st state.
Organized as territory May 26, 1864.
Admitted as state Nov. 8, 1889.

County	County Seat	Created	Statute
Beaverhead	Dillon	Feb. 2, 1865	Unnumb.
Big Horn	Hardin	Jan. 13, 1913	P and E
Blaine	Chinook	Feb. 29, 1912	P and E
Broadwater	Townsend	Feb. 9, 1897	H. B. 24
Carbon	Red Lodge	Mar. 4, 1895	H. B. 9
Carter	Ekalaka	Feb. 22, 1917	Chap. 56
Cascade	Great Falls	Sept. 12, 1887	Unnumb.
Chouteau	Fort Benton	Feb. 2, 1865	Unnumb.
Custer* 1	Miles City	Feb. 2, 1865	Unnumb.
Daniels	Scobey	Aug. 30, 1920	P and E
Dawson	Glendive	Jan. 15, 1869	Unnumb.
Deer Lodge	Anaconda	Feb. 2, 1865	Unnumb.
Fallon	Baker	Dec. 9, 1913	P and E
Fergus	Lewistown	Mar. 12, 1885	Unnumb.
Flathead	Kalispell	Feb. 6, 1893	Unnumb.
Gallatin	Bozeman	Feb. 2, 1865	Unnumb.
Garfield	Jordan	Feb. 7, 1919	Chap. 4
Glacier	Cut Bank	Feb. 17, 1919	Chap. 21
Golden Valley	Ryegate	Oct. 4, 1920	P and E
Granite	Philipsburg	Mar. 2, 1893	Unnumb.
Hill	Havre	Feb. 28, 1912	P and E
Jefferson	Boulder	Feb. 2, 1865	Unnumb.
Judith Basin	Stanford	Dec. 10, 1920	P and E
Lake	Polson	May 11, 1923	Procl.
Lewis and Clark* 2	Helena	Feb. 2, 1865	Unnumb.
Liberty	Chester	Feb. 11, 1920	P and E
Lincoln	Libby	Mar. 9, 1909	Chap. 133
Madison	Virginia City	Feb. 2, 1865	Unnumb.

County	County Seat	Created	Statute
McCone	Circle	Feb. 20, 1919	Chap. 33
Meagher	White Sulphur Springs	Nov. 16, 1867	Unnumb.
Mineral	Superior	Aug. 7, 1914	P and E
Missoula	Missoula	Feb. 2, 1865	Unnumb.
Mussellshell	Roundup	Feb. 11, 1911	Chap. 25
Park	Livingston	Feb. 23, 1887	Unnumb.
Petroleum	Winnett	Nov. 24, 1924	Procl.
Phillips	Malta	Feb. 5, 1915	P and E
Pondera	Conrad	Feb. 17, 1919	Chap. 22
Powder River	Broadus	Mar. 7, 1919	Chap. 141
Powell	Deer Lodge	Jan. 31, 1901	S. B. 3
Prairie	Terry	Feb. 5, 1915	P and E
Ravalli	Hamilton	Feb. 16, 1893	Unnumb.
Richland	Sidney	May 27, 1914	P and E
Roosevelt	Wolf Point	Feb. 18, 1919	Chap. 23
Rosebud	Forsyth	Feb. 11, 1901	S. B. 21
Sanders	Thompson Falls	Feb. 7, 1905	Chap. 9
Sheridan	Plentywood	Mar. 24, 1913	P and E
Silver Bow	Butte	Feb. 16, 1881	Unnumb.
Stillwater	Columbus	Mar. 24, 1913	P and E
Sweet Grass	Bigtimber	Mar. 5, 1895	H. B. 17
Teton	Choteau	Feb. 7, 1893	Unnumb.
Toole	Shelby	May 7, 1914	P and E
Treasure	Hysham	Feb. 7, 1919	Chap. 5
Valley	Glasgow	Feb. 6, 1893	Unnumb.
Wheatland	Harlowton	Feb. 22, 1917	Chap. 55
Wibaux	Wibaux	Aug. 17, 1914	P and E
Yellowstone	Billings	Feb. 26, 1883	Unnumb.

1 Formerly Big Horn County, changed to Custer County, Feb. 16, 1877, unnumbered.

2 Formerly Edgerton County, changed to Lewis and Clark County, Dec. 20, 1867, eff. Mar. 1, 1868, unnumbered.

NEBRASKA (93 counties) 37th state.
Organized as territory May 30, 1854.
Admitted as state March 1, 1867.

Adams	Hastings	Feb. 16, 1867	Unnumb.
Antelope	Neligh	Mar. 1, 1871	Unnumb.
Arthur	Arthur	Mar. 31, 1887	Chap. 21
Banner	Harrisburg	1888	Procl.
Blaine	Brewster	Mar. 5, 1885	Chap. 31
Boone	Albion	Mar. 1, 1871	Unnumb.

County	County Seat	Created	Statute
Box Butte	Alliance	Mar. 23, 1887	Procl.
Boyd	Butte	Mar. 20, 1891	Chap. 20
Brown	Ainsworth	Feb. 19, 1883	Chap. 31
Buffalo	Kearney	Mar. 14, 1855	Unnumb.
Burt	Tekamah	Nov. 23, 1854	Procl.
Butler	David City	Jan. 26, 1856	Unnumb.
Cass	Plattsmouth	Nov. 23, 1854	Procl.
Cedar	Hartington	Feb. 12, 1857	Unnumb.
Chase	Imperial	Feb. 27, 1873	Unnumb.
Cherry	Valentine	Feb. 23, 1883	Chap. 32
Cheyenne	Sidney	June 22, 1867	Unnumb.
Clay	Clay Center	Mar. 7, 1855	Unnumb.
Colfax	Schuyler	Feb. 15, 1869	Unnumb.
Cuming	Westpoint	Mar. 16, 1855	Unnumb.
Custer	Broken Bow	Feb. 17, 1877	Unnumb.
Dakota	Dakota City	Mar. 7, 1855	Unnumb.
Dawes	Chadron	Feb. 19, 1885	Chap. 32
Dawson	Lexington	Jan. 11, 1860	Unnumb.
Deuel	Chappell	1888	
Dixon	Ponca	Jan. 26, 1856	Unnumb.
Dodge	Fremont	Nov. 23, 1854	Procl.
Douglas	Omaha	Nov. 23, 1854	Procl.
Dundy	Benkelman	Feb. 27, 1873	Unnumb.
Fillmore	Geneva	Jan. 26, 1856	Unnumb.
Franklin	Franklin	Feb. 16, 1867	Unnumb.
Frontier	Stockville	Jan. 17, 1872	Unnumb.
Furnas	Beaver City	Feb. 27, 1873	Unnumb.
Gage	Beatrice	Mar. 16, 1855	Unnumb.
Garden	Oshkosh	Nov. 2, 1909	Election
Garfield	Burwell	Nov. 8, 1884	Procl.
Gosper	Elwood	Nov. 26, 1873	Unnumb.
Grant	Hyannis	Mar. 31, 1887	Chap. 22
Greeley	Greeley	Mar. 1, 1871	Unnumb.
Hall	Grand Island	Nov. 4, 1858	Unnumb.
Hamilton	Aurora	Feb. 16, 1867	Unnumb.
Harlan	Alma	June 3, 1871	Unnumb.
Hayes	Hayes Center	Feb. 19, 1877	Unnumb.
Hitchcock	Trenton	Feb. 27, 1873	Unnumb.
Holt* 1	O'Neill	Jan. 13, 1860	Unnumb.
Hooker	Mullen	Mar. 29, 1889	Chap. 1
Howard	St. Paul	Mar. 1, 1871	Unnumb.
Jefferson	Fairbury	Jan. 26, 1856	Unnumb.
Johnson	Tecumseh	Mar. 2, 1855	Unnumb.
Kearney	Minden	Jan. 10, 1860	Unnumb.
Keith	Ogallala	Feb. 27, 1873	Unnumb.
Keya Paha	Springview	1884	Procl.

County	County Seat	Created	Statute
Kimball	Kimball	1888	Procl.
Knox* 2	Center	Feb. 10, 1857	Unnumb.
Lancaster	Lincoln	Mar. 6, 1855	Unnumb.
Lincoln* 3	North Platte	Jan. 7, 1860	Unnumb.
Logan	Stapleton	Feb. 24, 1885	Chap. 33
Loup	Taylor	Mar. 6, 1855	Unnumb.
Madison	Madison	Jan. 26, 1856	Unnumb.
McPherson	Tryon	Mar. 31, 1887	Chap. 23
Merrick	Central City	Nov. 4, 1858	Unnumb.
Morrill	Bridgeport	1908	
Nance	Fullerton	Feb. 13, 1879	Unnumb.
Nemaha* 4	Auburn	Nov. 23, 1854	Procl.
Nuckolls	Nelson	Jan. 13, 1860	Unnumb.
Otoe* 5	Nebraska City	Nov. 23, 1854	Procl.
Pawnee	Pawnee City	Mar. 6, 1855	Unnumb.
Perkins	Grant	1887	Procl.
Phelps	Holdrege	Feb. 11, 1873	Unnumb.
Pierce* 6	Pierce	Jan. 26, 1856	Unnumb.
Platte	Columbus	Jan. 26, 1856	Unnumb.
Polk	Osceola	Jan. 26, 1856	Unnumb.
Red Willow	McCook	Feb. 27, 1873	Unnumb.
Richardson	Falls City	Nov. 23, 1854	Procl.
Rock	Bassett	May 23, 1857	Chap. 14
Saline	Wilber	Mar. 6, 1855	Unnumb.
Sarpy	Papillion	Feb. 7, 1857	Unnumb.
Saunders* 7	Wahoo	Jan. 26, 1856	Unnumb.
Scotts Bluff	Gering	1881	
Seward* 8	Seward	Mar. 6, 1855	Unnumb.
Sheridan	Rushville	Feb. 25, 1885	Chap. 34
Sherman	Loup City	Mar. 1, 1871	Unnumb.
Sioux	Harrison	Feb. 19, 1877	Unnumb.
Stanton* 9	Stanton	Mar. 6, 1855	Unnumb.
Thayer* 10	Hebron	Jan. 26, 1856	Unnumb.
Thomas	Thedford	Mar. 31, 1887	Chap. 24
Thurston	Pender	Mar. 28, 1889	Chap. 3
Valley	Ord	Mar. 1, 1871	Unnumb.
Washington	Blair	Nov. 23, 1854	Procl.
Wayne	Wayne	Mar. 4, 1871	Unnumb.
Webster	Red Cloud	Feb. 16, 1867	Unnumb.
Wheeler	Bartlett	Feb. 17, 1877	Unnumb.
York	York	Mar. 13, 1855	Unnumb.

1 Formerly West County, changed to Holt County, Jan. 9, 1862, unnumbered.

2 Formerly L'eau Qui Court County, changed to Emmet County Feb. 18, 1867, changed to Knox County, Feb. 21, 1873.

3 Formerly Shorter County, changed to Lincoln County, Dec. 11, 1861, unnumbered.
4 Formerly Forney County, changed to Nemaha County.
5 Formerly Pierce County, changed to Otoe County.
6 Formerly Otoe County.
7 Formerly Calhoun County, changed to Saunders County, Jan. 8, 1862, unnumbered.
8 Formerly Greene County, changed to Seward County, Jan. 3, 1862.
9 Formerly Izard County, changed to Stanton County.
10 Formerly Jefferson County, changed to Thayer County, Mar. 1, 1871.

NEVADA (16 counties) 36th state.
Organized as territory March 2, 1861.
Admitted as state October 31, 1864.

County	County Seat	Created	Statute
Churchill	Fallon	Nov. 25, 1861	Chap. 24
Clark	Las Vegas	Feb. 5, 1909	Chap. 11
Douglas	Minden	Nov. 25, 1861	Chap. 24
Elko	Elko	Mar. 5, 1869	Chap. 94
Esmeralda	Goldfield	Nov. 25, 1861	Chap. 24
Eureka	Eureka	Mar. 1. 1873	Chap. 46
Humboldt	Winnemucca	Nov. 25, 1861	Chap. 24
Lander	Austin	Dec. 19, 1862	Chap. 58
Lincoln	Pioche	Feb. 26, 1866	Chap. 48
Lyon	Yerington	Nov. 25, 1861	Chap. 24
Mineral	Hawthorne	Feb. 10, 1911	Chap. 13
Nye	Tonopah	Feb. 16, 1864	Chap. 102
Pershing	Lovelock	Mar. 18, 1919	Chap. 62
Storey	Virginia City	Nov. 25, 1861	Chap. 24
Washoe	Reno	Nov. 25, 1861	Chap. 24
White Pine	Ely	Mar. 2, 1869	Chap. 60

NEW HAMPSHIRE (10 counties) 9th state.
Admitted as state June 21, 1788.

Belknap	Laconia	Dec. 22, 1840	Chap. 539
Carroll	Ossipee	Dec. 22, 1840	Chap. 539
Cheshire	Keene	Apr. 29, 1769**	
Coos	Lancaster	Dec. 24, 1803	Unnumb.
Grafton	Woodsville	Apr. 29, 1769**	
Hillsborough	Nashua and Manchester	Apr. 29, 1769**	

County	County Seat	Created	Statute
Merrimack	Concord	July 1, 1823	Chap. 40
Rockingham	Exeter	Apr. 29, 1769**	
Strafford	Dover	Apr. 29, 1769**	
Sullivan	Newport	July 5, 1827	Chap. 48

** Not confirmed by the king until Mar. 19, 1771.

NEW JERSEY (21 counties) 3rd state.
Admitted as state December 18, 1787.

Atlantic	Mays Landing	Feb. 7, 1837	Unnumb.
Bergen	Hackensack	Mar. 1, 1683	Unnumb.
Burlington	Mount Holly	May 17, 1694	Unnumb.
Camden	Camden	Mar. 13, 1844	Unnumb.
Cape May	Cape May Court House	Nov. 12, 1692	Unnumb.
Cumberland	Bridgeton	Jan. 19, 1748	Chap. 92
Essex	Newark	Mar. 1, 1683	Unnumb.
Gloucester	Woodbury	May 28, 1686	Unnumb.
Hudson	Jersey City	Feb. 22, 1840	Unnumb.
Hunterdon	Flemington	Mar. 13, 1714	Unnumb.
Mercer	Trenton	Feb. 22, 1838	Unnumb.
Middlesex	New Brunswick	Mar. 1, 1683	Unnumb.
Monmouth	Freehold	Mar. 1, 1683	Unnumb.
Morris	Morristown	Mar. 15, 1739	Chap. 63
Ocean	Toms River	Feb. 15, 1850	Unnumb.
Passaic	Paterson	Feb. 7, 1837	Unnumb.
Salem	Salem	May 17, 1694	Unnumb.
Somerset	Somerville	May 1688	Unnumb.
Sussex	Newton	Sess. May 16, 1753	Unnumb.
Union	Elizabeth	Mar. 19, 1857	Chap. 82
Warren	Belvidere	Nov. 20, 1824	Unnumb.

NEW MEXICO (32 counties) 47th state.
Organized as territory September 9, 1850.
Admitted as state January 6, 1912.

Bernalillo	Albuquerque	Jan. 9, 1852	Unnumb.
Catron	Reserve	Feb. 25, 1921	Chap. 28
Chaves	Roswell	Feb. 25, 1889	Chap. 87
Colfax	Raton	Jan. 25, 1869	Chap. 24
Curry	Clovis	Feb. 25, 1909	Chap. 6
De Baca	Fort Sumner	Feb. 28, 1917	Chap. 11
Dona Ana	Las Cruces	Jan. 9, 1852	Unnumb.

County	County Seat	Created	Statute
Eddy	Carlsbad	Feb. 25, 1889	Chap. 87
Grant	Silver City	Jan. 30, 1868	Chap. 20
Guadalupe	Santa Rosa	Feb. 26, 1891	Chap. 88
Harding	Mosquero	Mar. 4, 1921	Chap. 48
Hidalgo	Lordsburg	Feb. 25, 1919	Chap. 11
Lea	Lovington	Mar. 7, 1917	Chap. 23
Lincoln	Carrizozo	Jan. 16, 1869	Chap. 8
Los Alamos	Los Alamos	Mar. 16, 1949	Chap. 134
Luna	Deming	Mar. 16, 1901	Chap. 38
McKinley	Gallup	Feb. 23, 1899	Chap. 19
Mora	Mora	Feb. 1, 1860	Unnumb.
Otero	Alamogordo	Jan. 30, 1899	Chap. 3
Quay	Tucumcari	Feb. 28, 1903	Chap. 8
Rio Arriba	Tierra Amarilla	Jan. 9, 1852	Unnumb.
Roosevelt	Portales	Feb. 28, 1903	Chap. 7
San Juan	Aztec	Feb. 24, 1887	Chap. 13
San Miguel	Las Vegas	Jan. 9, 1852	Unnumb.
Sandoval	Bernalillo	Mar. 10, 1903	Chap. 27
Sante Fe	Santa Fe	Jan. 9, 1852	Unnumb.
Sierra	Truth or Consequences	Apr. 3, 1884	Chap. 59
Socorro	Socorro	Jan. 9, 1852	Unnumb.
Taos	Taos	Jan. 9, 1852	Unnumb.
Torrance	Estancia	Mar. 16, 1903	Chap. 70
Union	Clayton	Feb. 23, 1893	Chap. 49
Valencia	Los Lunas	Jan. 9, 1852	Unnumb.

NEW YORK (62 counties) 11th state.
Admitted as state July 26, 1788.

County	County Seat	Created	Statute
Albany	Albany	Nov. 1, 1683	Chap. 4
Allegany	Belmont	Apr. 7, 1806	Chap. 162
Bronx	Bronx	Apr. 19, 1912	Chap. 548
Broome	Binghamton	Mar. 28, 1806	Chap. 89
Cattaraugus	Little Valley	Mar. 11, 1808	Chap. 60
Cayuga	Auburn	Mar. 8, 1799	Chap. 26
Chautauqua	Mayville	Mar. 11, 1808	Chap. 60
Chemung	Elmira	Mar. 29, 1836	Chap. 77
Chenango	Norwich	Mar. 15, 1798	Chap. 31
Clinton	Plattsburg	Mar. 7, 1788	Chap. 63
Columbia	Hudson	Apr. 4, 1786	Chap. 28
Cortland	Cortland	Apr. 8, 1808	Chap. 194
Delaware	Delhi	Mar. 10, 1797	Chap. 33
Dutchess	Poughkeepsie	Nov. 1, 1683	Chap. 4
Erie	Buffalo	Apr. 2, 1821	Chap. 228

County	County Seat	Created	Statute
Essex	Elizabethtown	Mar. 1, 1799	Chap. 24
Franklin	Malone	Mar. 11, 1808	Chap. 43
Fulton	Johnstown	Apr. 18, 1838	Chap. 332
Genesee	Batavia	Mar. 30, 1802	Chap. 64
Greene	Catskill	Mar. 25, 1800	Chap. 59
Hamilton	Lake Pleasant	Apr. 12, 1816	Chap. 120
Herkimer	Herkimer	Feb. 16, 1791	Chap. 10
Jefferson	Watertown	Mar. 28, 1805	Chap. 51
Kings	Brooklyn	Nov. 1, 1683	Chap. 4
Lewis	Lowville	Mar. 28, 1805	Chap. 51
Livingston	Geneseo	Feb. 23, 1821	Chap. 58
Madison	Wampsville	Mar. 21, 1806	Chap. 70
Monroe	Rochester	Feb. 23, 1821	Chap. 57
Montgomery* 1	Fonda	Mar. 12, 1772	Chap. 613
Nassau	Mineola	Apr. 27, 1898	Chap. 588
New York	Manhattan	Nov. 1, 1683	Chap. 4
Niagara	Lockport	Mar. 11, 1808	Chap. 60
Oneida	Utica and Rome	Mar. 15, 1798	Chap. 31
Onondaga	Syracuse	Mar. 5, 1794	Chap. 18
Ontario	Canandaigua	Jan. 27, 1789	Chap. 11
Orange	Goshen	Nov. 1, 1683	Chap. 4
Orleans	Albion	Nov. 12, 1824	Chap. 266
Oswego	Oswego	Mar. 1, 1816	Chap. 22
Otsego	Cooperstown	Feb. 16, 1791	Chap. 10
Putnam	Carmel	June 12, 1812	Chap. 143
Queens	Jamaica	Nov. 1, 1683	Chap. 4
Rensselaer	Troy	Feb. 7, 1791	Chap. 4
Richmond	St. George	Nov. 1, 1683	Chap. 4
Rockland	New City	Feb. 23, 1798	Chap. 16
St. Lawrence	Canton	Mar. 3, 1802	Chap. 16
Saratoga	Ballston Spa	Feb. 7, 1791	Chap. 4
Schenectady	Schenectady	Mar. 7, 1809	Chap. 65
Schoharie	Schoharie	Apr. 6, 1795	Chap. 42
Schuyler	Watkins Glen	Apr. 17, 1854	Chap. 386
Seneca	Waterloo and Ovid	Mar. 24, 1804	Chap. 331
Steuben	Bath	Mar. 18, 1796	Chap. 29
Suffolk	Riverhead	Nov. 1, 1683	Chap. 4
Sullivan	Monticello	Mar. 27, 1809	Chap. 126
Tioga	Owego	Feb. 16, 1791	Chap. 10
Tompkins	Ithaca	Apr. 7, 1817	Chap. 189
Ulster	Kingston	Nov. 1, 1683	Chap. 4
Warren	Lake George	Mar. 12, 1813	Chap. 50
Washington* 2	Hudson Falls	Mar. 12, 1772	Chap. 613
Wayne	Lyons	Apr. 11, 1823	Chap. 138
Westchester	White Plains	Nov. 1, 1683	Chap. 4
Wyoming	Warsaw	May 19, 1841	Chap. 196

County	County Seat	Created	Statute
Yates	Penn Yan	Feb. 5, 1823	Chap. 30

1 Formerly Tryon County, changed to Montgomery County, Apr. 2, 1784, chap. 17.
2 Formerly Charlotte County, changed to Washington County, Apr. 2, 1784, chap. 17.

NORTH CAROLINA (100 counties) 12th state.
Admitted as state Nov. 21, 1789.

Alamance	Graham	Jan. 29, 1849	Chap. 14
Alexander	Taylorsville	Jan. 15, 1847	Chap. 22
Alleghany	Sparta	1859	Chap. 3
Anson	Wadesboro	Sess. Mar. 17, 1749	Chap. 2
Ashe	Jefferson	Sess. Nov. 18, 1799	Chap. 36
Avery	Newland	Feb. 23, 1911	Chap. 33
Beaufort* 1	Washington	Dec. 3, 1705	
Bertie	Windsor	Sess. Aug. 2, 1722	Chap. 5
Bladen	Elizabethtown	Sess. 1734	Chap. 8
Brunswick	Southport	Sess. Jan. 30, 1764	Chap. 14
Buncombe	Asheville	Sess. Dec. 5, 1791	Chap. 52
Burke	Morgantown	Apr. 8, 1777	Chap. 19
Cabarrus	Concord	Sess. Nov. 15, 1792	Chap. 21
Caldwell	Lenoir	Jan. 11, 1841	Chap. 11
Camden	Camden	Apr. 8, 1777	Chap. 18
Carteret	Beaufort	1722	
Caswell	Yanceyville	Apr. 8, 1777	Chap. 17
Catawba	Newton	Dec. 12, 1842	Chap. 8
Chatham	Pittsboro	Sess. Dec. 5, 1770	Chap. 27
Cherokee	Murphy	Jan. 4, 1839	Chap. 10
Chowan	Edenton	1670	
Clay	Hayesville	Feb. 20, 1861	Chap. 6
Cleveland	Shelby	Jan. 11, 1841	Chap. 9
Columbus	Whiteville	Dec. 15, 1808	Chap. 1
Craven* 2	New Bern	Dec. 3, 1705	
Cumberland	Fayetteville	Sess. Feb. 19, 1754	Chap. 8
Currituck	Currituck	1670	
Dare	Manteo	Feb. 3, 1870	Chap. 36
Davidson	Lexington	Dec. 9, 1822	Chap. 47
Davie	Mocksville	Dec. 20, 1836	Chap. 4
Duplin	Kenansville	Sess. Mar. 17, 1749	Chap. 1
Durham	Durham	Feb. 28, 1881	Chap. 138
Edgecombe	Tarboro	Apr. 4, 1741	Chap. 7
Forsyth	Winston-Salem	Jan. 16, 1849	Chap. 23
Franklin	Louisburg	Sess. Apr. 14, 1778	Chap. 19

County	County Seat		Created	Statute
Gaston	Gastonia		Dec. 21, 1846	Chap. 24
Gates	Gatesville	Sess.	Apr. 14, 1778	Chap. 20
Graham	Robbinsville		Jan. 30, 1872	Chap. 77
Granville	Oxford	Sess.	June 28, 1746	Chap. 3
Greene	Snow Hill	Sess.	Nov. 18, 1799	Chap. 39
Guilford	Greensboro	Sess.	Dec. 5, 1770	Chap. 24
Halifax	Halifax	Sess.	Dec. 12, 1754	Chap. 13
Harnett	Lillington		Feb. 7, 1855	Chap. 8
Haywood	Waynesville		Dec. 15, 1808	Chap. 1
Henderson	Hendersonville		Dec. 15, 1838	Chap. 12
Hertford	Winton	Sess.	Dec. 12, 1754	Chap. 4
Hoke	Raeford		Feb. 17, 1911	Chap. 24
Hyde* 3	Swan Quarter		Dec. 3, 1705	
Iredell	Statesville	Sess.	Nov. 3, 1788	Chap. 36
Jackson	Sylva		Jan. 29, 1851	Chap. 38
Johnston	Smithfield	Sess.	June 28, 1746	Chap. 2
Jones	Trenton	Sess.	Apr. 14, 1778	Chap. 18
Lee	Sanford		Mar. 6, 1907	Chap. 624
Lenoir	Kinston	Sess.	Dec. 5, 1791	Chap. 47
Lincoln	Lincolnton	Sess.	Apr. 14, 1778	Chap. 23
Macon	Franklin		1828	Chap. 50
Madison	Marshall		Jan. 27, 1851	Chap. 36
Martin	Williamston		Mar. 2, 1774	Chap. 32
McDowell	Marion		Dec. 19, 1842	Chap. 10
Mecklenburg	Charlotte	Sess.	Nov. 3, 1762	Chap. 12
Mitchell	Bakersville		Feb. 16, 1861	Chap. 8
Montgomery	Troy		Apr. 14, 1778	Chap. 21
Moore	Carthage		Apr. 18, 1784	Chap. 76
Nash	Nashville		Nov. 15, 1777	Chap. 30
New Hanover	Wilmington		Nov. 27, 1729	Chap. 10
Northampton	Jackson		1741	Chap. 1
Onslow	Jacksonville	Sess.	1734	Chap. 8
Orange	Hillsboro	Sess.	Mar. 31, 1752	Chap. 6
Pamlico	Bayboro		Feb. 8, 1872	Chap. 132
Pasquotank	Elizabeth City		1670	
Pender	Burgaw		Feb. 16, 1875	Chap. 91
Perquimans	Hertford		1670	
Person	Roxboro	Sess.	Dec. 5, 1791	Chap. 53
Pitt	Greenville	Sess.	Apr. 24, 1760	Chap. 3
Polk	Columbus		Jan. 18, 1847	Chap. 26
Randolph	Asheboro	Sess.	Apr. 14, 1778	Chap. 22
Richmond	Rockingham	Sess.	Oct. 18, 1779	Chap. 16
Robeson	Lumberton	Sess.	Nov. 18, 1786	Chap. 40
Rockingham	Wentworth	Sess.	Nov. 19, 1785	Chap. 23
Rowan	Salisbury	Sess.	Mar. 27, 1753	Chap. 7
Rutherford	Rutherfordton	Sess.	Apr. 14, 1779	Chap. 23

County	County Seat		Created	Statute
Sampson	Clinton	Sess.	Apr. 18, 1784	Chap. 75
Scotland	Laurinburg		Feb. 20, 1899	Chap. 127
Stanly	Albemarle		Jan. 11, 1841	Chap. 13
Stokes	Danbury	Sess.	Nov. 2, 1789	Chap. 14
Surry	Dobson	Sess.	Dec. 5, 1770	Chap. 42
Swain	Bryson City		Feb. 24, 1871	Chap. 94
Transylvania	Brevard		Feb. 15, 1861	Chap. 10
Tyrrell	Columbia	Sess.	Nov. 27, 1729	Chap. 4
Union	Monroe		Dec. 19, 1842	Chap. 12
Vance	Henderson		Mar. 5, 1881	Chap. 113
Wake	Raleigh	Sess.	Dec. 5, 1770	Chap. 22
Warren	Warrenton		Apr. 14, 1779	Chap. 19
Washington	Plymouth	Sess.	Nov. 15, 1799	Chap. 36
Watauga	Boone		Jan. 27, 1849	Chap. 25
Wayne	Goldsboro	Sess.	Oct. 18, 1779	Chap. 17
Wilkes	Wilkesboro	Sess.	Nov. 15, 1777	Chap. 32
Wilson	Wilson		Feb. 13, 1855	Chap. 12
Yadkin	Yadkinville		Dec. 28, 1850	Chap. 40
Yancey	Burnsville		1833	Chap. 83

1 Formerly Pamptecough County, changed to Beaufort County, 1712.

2 Formerly Archdale County, changed to Craven County, 1712.

3 Formerly Wickham County, changed to Hyde County, 1712.

NORTH DAKOTA (53 counties) 39th state.
Organized as territory Mar. 2, 1861.
Admitted as state Nov. 2, 1889.

County	County Seat	Created	Statute
Adams	Hettinger	Mar. 13, 1885	Unnumb.
Barnes	Valley City	Jan. 14, 1875	Chap. 30
Benson	Minnewaukan	Mar. 9, 1883	Chap. 12
Billings	Medora	Feb. 10, 1879	Chap. 11
Bottineau	Bottineau	Jan. 4, 1873	Chap. 18
Bowman	Bowman	Mar. 8, 1883	Chap. 38
Burke	Bowbells	July 6, 1910	
Burleigh	Bismarck	Jan. 4, 1873	Chap. 18
Cass	Fargo	Jan. 4, 1873	Chap. 20
Cavalier	Langdon	Jan. 4, 1873	Chap. 18
Dickey	Ellendale	Mar. 5, 1881	Chap. 40
Divide	Crosby	Dec. 9, 1910	
Dunn	Manning	Mar. 9, 1883	Chap. 39
Eddy	New Rockford	Mar. 9, 1885	Chap. 15
Emmons	Linton	Feb. 10, 1879	Chap. 11

County	County Seat	Created	Statute
Foster	Carrington	Jan. 4, 1873	Chap. 18
Golden Valley	Beach	Nov. 19, 1912	
Grand Forks	Grand Forks	Jan. 4, 1873	Chap. 20
Grant	Carson	Nov. 25, 1916	Unnumb.
Griggs	Cooperstown	Feb. 18, 1881	Chap. 41
Hettinger	Mott	Mar. 9, 1883	Chap. 39
Kidder	Steele	Jan. 4, 1873	Chap. 18
La Moure	La Moure	Jan. 4, 1873	Chap. 20
Logan	Napoleon	Jan. 4, 1873	Chap. 18
McHenry	Towner	Jan. 4, 1873	Chap. 18
McIntosh	Ashley	Mar. 9, 1883	Chap. 26
McKenzie	Watford City	Mar. 9, 1883	Chap. 39
McLean	Washburn	Mar. 8, 1883	Chap. 25
Mercer	Stanton	Jan. 14, 1875	Chap. 30
Morton	Mandan	Jan. 8, 1873	Chap. 19
Mountrail	Stanley	Jan. 4, 1873	Chap. 18
Nelson	Lakota	Mar. 9, 1883	Chap. 27
Oliver	Center	Mar. 12, 1885	Chap. 31
Pembina	Cavalier	Jan. 9, 1867	Chap. 15
Pierce	Rugby	Mar. 11, 1887	Chap. 180
Ramsey	Devils Lake	Jan. 4, 1873	Chap. 18
Ransom	Lisbon	Jan. 4, 1873	Chap. 18
Renville	Mohall	Jan. 4, 1873	Chap. 18
Richland	Wahpeton	Jan. 4, 1873	Chap. 20
Rolette	Rolla	Jan. 4, 1873	Chap. 18
Sargent	Forman	Mar. 3, 1883	Chap. 32
Sheridan	McClusky	Jan. 4, 1873	Chap. 18
Sioux	Fort Yates	Jan. 14, 1915	Chap. 18
Slope	Amidon	Jan. 14, 1915	
Stark	Dickinson	Feb. 10, 1879	Chap. 11
Steele	Finley	Mar. 8, 1883	Chap. 36
Stutsman	Jamestown	Jan. 4, 1873	Chap. 20
Towner	Cando	Mar. 8, 1883	Chap. 37
Traill	Hillsboro	Jan. 12, 1875	Chap. 32
Walsh	Grafton	Feb. 18, 1881	Chap. 51
Ward	Minot	Apr. 14, 1885	Chap. 42
Wells* 1	Fessenden	Jan. 4, 1873	Chap. 18
Williams	Williston	Jan. 8, 1873	Chap. 19

1 Formerly Gingras County, changed to Wells County, Feb. 26, 1881, chap. 53.

OHIO (88 counties) 17th state.
Organized as territory July 13, 1787.
Admitted as state February 19, 1803.

County	County Seat	Created	Statute
Adams	West Union	July 10, 1797	Procl.
Allen	Lima	Feb. 12, 1820	Chap. 37
Ashland	Ashland	Feb. 24, 1846	Unnumb.
Ashtabula	Jefferson	Feb. 10, 1807	Chap. 1
Athens	Athens	Feb. 20, 1805	Chap. 68
Auglaize	Wapakoneta	Feb. 14, 1848	Unnumb.
Belmont	St. Clairsville	Sept. 7, 1801	Procl.
Brown	Georgetown	Dec. 27, 1817	Chap. 12
Butler	Hamilton	Mar. 24, 1803	Chap. 4
Carroll	Carrollton	Dec. 25, 1832	Unnumb.
Champaign	Urbana	Feb. 20, 1805	Chap. 69
Clark	Springfield	Dec. 26, 1817	Chap. 14
Clermont	Batavia	Dec. 6, 1800	Procl.
Clinton	Wilmington	Feb. 19, 1810	Chap. 63
Columbiana	Lisbon	Mar. 25, 1803	Chap. 6
Coshocton	Coshocton	Jan. 31, 1810	Chap. 26
Crawford	Bucyrus	Feb. 12, 1820	Chap. 37
Cuyahoga	Cleveland	Feb. 10, 1808	Chap. 1
Darke	Greenville	Jan. 3, 1809	Chap. 6
Defiance	Defiance	Mar. 4, 1845	Unnumb.
Delaware	Delaware	Feb. 10, 1808	Chap. 10
Erie	Sandusky	Mar. 15, 1838	Unnumb.
Fairfield	Lancaster	Dec. 9, 1800	Procl.
Fayette	Washington C. H.	Feb. 19, 1810	Chap. 39
Franklin	Columbus	Mar. 30, 1803	Chap. 11
Fulton	Wauseon	Feb. 28, 1850	Unnumb.
Gallia	Gallipolis	Mar. 25, 1803	Chap. 8
Geauga	Chardon	Dec. 31, 1805	Unnumb.
Greene	Xenia	Mar. 24, 1803	Chap. 4
Guernsey	Cambridge	Jan. 31, 1810	Chap. 20
Hamilton	Cincinnati	Jan. 2, 1790	Procl.
Hancock	Findlay	Feb. 12, 1820	Chap. 37
Hardin	Kenton	Feb. 12, 1820	Chap. 37
Harrison	Cadiz	Jan. 2, 1813	Chap. 5
Henry	Napoleon	Feb. 12, 1820	Chap. 37
Highland	Hillsboro	Feb. 18, 1805	Chap. 60
Hocking	Logan	Jan. 3, 1818	Chap. 24
Holmes	Millersburg	Jan. 20, 1824	Chap. 36
Huron	Norwalk	Feb. 7, 1809	Chap. 48
Jackson	Jackson	Jan. 12, 1816	Chap. 25
Jefferson	Steubenville	July 27, 1797	Procl.
Knox	Mt. Vernon	Jan. 30, 1808	Chap. 8
Lake	Painesville	Mar. 6, 1840	Unnumb.
Lawrence	Ironton	Dec. 21, 1815	Chap. 8
Licking	Newark	Jan. 30, 1808	Chap. 8
Logan	Bellefontaine	Dec. 30, 1817	Chap. 20

County	County Seat	Created	Statute
Lorain	Elyria	Dec. 26, 1822	Chap. 5
Lucas	Toledo	June 20, 1835	Unnumb.
Madison	London	Feb. 16, 1810	Chap. 67
Mahoning	Youngstown	Feb. 16, 1846	Unnumb.
Marion	Marion	Feb. 12, 1820	Chap. 37
Medina	Medina	Feb. 18, 1812	Chap. 46
Meigs	Pomeroy	Jan. 21, 1819	Chap. 25
Mercer	Celina	Feb. 12, 1820	Chap. 37
Miami	Troy	Jan. 16, 1807	Chap. 32
Monroe	Woodsfield	Jan. 29, 1813	Chap. 25
Montgomery	Dayton	Mar. 24, 1803	Chap. 4
Morgan	McConnelsville	Dec. 29, 1817	Chap. 18
Morrow	Mt. Gilead	Feb. 24, 1848	Unnumb.
Muskingum	Zanesville	Jan. 7, 1804	Chap. 22
Noble	Caldwell	Mar. 11, 1851	Unnumb.
Ottawa	Port Clinton	Mar. 6, 1840	Unnumb.
Paulding	Paulding	Feb. 12, 1820	Chap. 37
Perry	New Lexington	Dec. 26, 1817	Chap. 11
Pickaway	Circleville	Jan. 12, 1810	Chap. 13
Pike	Waverly	Jan. 4, 1815	Chap. 16
Portage	Ravenna	Feb. 10, 1807	Chap. 1
Preble	Eaton	Feb. 15, 1808	Chap. 51
Putnam	Ottawa	Feb. 12, 1820	Chap. 37
Richland	Mansfield	Jan. 30, 1808	Chap. 8
Ross	Chillicothe	Aug. 20, 1798	Procl.
Sandusky	Fremont	Feb. 12, 1820	Chap. 37
Scioto	Portsmouth	Mar. 24, 1803	Chap. 3
Seneca	Tiffin	Feb. 12, 1820	Chap. 37
Shelby	Sidney	Jan. 7, 1819	Chap. 12
Stark	Canton	Feb. 13, 1808	Chap. 46
Summit	Akron	Mar. 3, 1840	Unnumb.
Trumbull	Warren	July 10, 1800	Procl.
Tuscarawas	New Philadelphia	Feb. 13, 1808	Chap. 50
Union	Marysville	Jan. 10, 1820	Chap. 16
Van Wert	Van Wert	Feb. 12, 1820	Chap. 37
Vinton	McArthur	Mar. 23, 1850	Unnumb.
Warren	Lebanon	Mar. 24, 1803	Chap. 4
Washington	Marietta	July 27, 1788	Procl.
Wayne	Wooster	Aug. 15, 1786	Procl.
Williams	Bryan	Feb. 12, 1820	Chap. 37
Wood	Bowling Green	Feb. 12, 1820	Chap. 37
Wyandot	Upper Sandusky	Feb. 3, 1845	Unnumb.

OKLAHOMA (77 counties) 46th state.
Organized as territory May 2, 1890;
Admitted as state November 16, 1907.

County	County Seat	Created	Statute
Adair	Stilwell	July 16, 1907	Const.
Alfalfa	Cherokee	July 16, 1907	Const.
Atoka	Atoka	July 16, 1907	Const.
Beaver	Beaver	July 16, 1907	Const.
Beckham	Sayre	July 16, 1907	Const.
Blaine	Watonga	July 16, 1907	Const.
Bryan	Durant	July 16, 1907	Const.
Caddo	Anadarko	July 16, 1907	Const.
Canadian	El Reno	July 16, 1907	Const.
Carter	Ardmore	July 16, 1907	Const.
Cherokee	Tahlequah	July 16, 1907	Const.
Choctaw	Hugo	July 16, 1907	Const.
Cimarron	Boise City	July 16, 1907	Const.
Cleveland	Norman	July 16, 1907	Const.
Coal	Coalgate	July 16, 1907	Const.
Comanche	Lawton	July 16, 1907	Const.
Cotton	Walters	Aug. 27, 1912	Procl.
Craig	Vinita	July 16, 1907	Const.
Creek	Sapulpa	July 16, 1907	Const.
Custer	Arapaho	July 16, 1907	Const.
Delaware	Jay	July 16, 1907	Const.
Dewey	Taloga	July 16, 1907	Const.
Ellis	Arnett	July 16, 1907	Const.
Garfield	Enid	July 16, 1907	Const.
Garvin	Pauls Valley	July 16, 1907	Const.
Grady	Chickasha	July 16, 1907	Const.
Grant	Medford	July 16, 1907	Const.
Greer	Mangum	July 16, 1907	Const.
Harmon	Hollis	June 2, 1909	Procl.
Harper	Buffalo	July 16, 1907	Const.
Haskell	Stigler	July 16, 1907	Const.
Hughes	Holdenville	July 16, 1907	Const.
Jackson	Altus	July 16, 1907	Const.
Jefferson	Waurika	July 16, 1907	Const.
Johnston	Tishomingo	July 16, 1907	Const.
Kay	Newkirk	July 16, 1907	Const.
Kingfisher	Kingfisher	July 16, 1907	Const.
Kiowa	Hobart	July 16, 1907	Const.
Latimer	Wilburton	July 16, 1907	Const.
Le Flore	Poteau	July 16, 1907	Const.
Lincoln	Chandler	July 16, 1907	Const.
Logan	Guthrie	July 16, 1907	Const.

County	County Seat	Created	Statute
Love	Marietta	July 16, 1907	Const.
Major	Fairview	July 16, 1907	Const.
Marshall	Madill	July 16, 1907	Const.
Mayes	Pryor	July 16, 1907	Const.
McClain	Purcell	July 16, 1907	Const.
McCurtain	Idabel	July 16, 1907	Const.
McIntosh	Eufaula	July 16, 1907	Const.
Murray	Sulphur	July 16, 1907	Const.
Muskogee	Muskogee	July 16, 1907	Const.
Noble	Perry	July 16, 1907	Const.
Nowata	Nowata	July 16, 1907	Const.
Okfuskee	Okemah	July 16, 1907	Const.
Oklahoma	Oklahoma City	July 16, 1907	Const.
Okmulgee	Okmulgee	July 16, 1907	Const.
Osage	Pawhuska	July 16, 1907	Const.
Ottawa	Miami	July 16, 1907	Const.
Pawnee	Pawnee	July 16, 1907	Const.
Payne	Stillwater	July 16, 1907	Const.
Pittsburg	McAlester	July 16, 1907	Const.
Pontotoc	Ada	July 16, 1907	Const.
Pottawatomie	Shawnee	July 16, 1907	Const.
Pushmataha	Antlers	July 16, 1907	Const.
Roger Mills	Cheyenne	July 16, 1907	Const.
Rogers	Claremore	July 16, 1907	Const.
Seminole	Wewoka	July 16, 1907	Const.
Sequoyah	Sallisaw	July 16, 1907	Const.
Stephens	Duncan	July 16, 1907	Const.
Texas	Guymon	July 16, 1907	Const.
Tillman	Frederick	July 16, 1907	Const.
Tulsa	Tulsa	July 16, 1907	Const.
Wagoner	Wagoner	July 16, 1907	Const.
Washington	Bartlesville	July 16, 1907	Const.
Washita	Cordell	July 16, 1907	Const.
Woods	Alva	July 16, 1907	Const.
Woodward	Woodward	July 16, 1907	Const.

OREGON (36 counties) 33rd state.
Organized as territory August 14, 1848.
Admitted as state February 14, 1859.

Baker	Baker	Sept. 22, 1862	Unnumb.
Benton	Corvallis	Dec. 23, 1847	Unnumb.
Clackamas	Oregon City	July 5, 1843	Unnumb.
Clatsop	Astoria	June 22, 1844	Unnumb.
Columbia	Saint Helens	Jan. 16, 1854	Unnumb.

County	County Seat	Created	Statute
Coos	Coquille	Dec. 22, 1853	Unnumb.
Crook	Prineville	Oct. 24, 1882	Unnumb.
Curry	Gold Beach	Dec. 18, 1855	Unnumb.
Deschutes	Bend	Dec. 13, 1916	Procl.
Douglas	Roseburg	Jan. 7, 1852	Unnumb.
Gilliam	Condon	Feb. 25, 1885	Unnumb.
Grant	Canyon City	Oct. 14, 1864	Unnumb.
Harney	Burns	Feb. 25, 1889	Unnumb.
Hood River	Hood River	June 23, 1908	Procl.
Jackson	Medford	Jan. 12, 1852	Unnumb.
Jefferson	Madras	Dec. 12, 1914	Procl.
Josephine	Grants Pass	Jan. 22, 1856	Unnumb.
Klamath	Klamath Falls	Oct. 17, 1882	Unnumb.
Lake	Lakeview	Oct. 24, 1874	Unnumb.
Lane	Eugene	Jan. 28, 1851	Unnumb.
Lincoln	Toledo	Feb. 20, 1893	S. B. 119
Linn	Albany	Dec. 28, 1847	Unnumb.
Malheur	Vale	Feb. 17, 1887	Unnumb.
Marion* 1	Salem	July 5, 1843	Unnumb.
Morrow	Heppner	Feb. 16, 1885	Unnumb.
Multnomah	Portland	Dec. 22, 1854	Unnumb.
Polk	Dallas	Dec. 22, 1845	Unnumb.
Sherman	Moro	Feb. 25, 1889	Unnumb.
Tillamook	Tillamook	Dec. 15, 1853	Unnumb.
Umatilla	Pendleton	Sept. 27, 1862	Unnumb.
Union	La Grande	Oct. 14, 1864	Unnumb.
Wallowa	Enterprise	Feb. 11, 1887	Unnumb.
Wasco	The Dalles	Jan. 11, 1854	Unnumb.
Washington* 2	Hillsboro	July 5, 1843	Unnumb.
Wheeler	Fossil	Feb. 17, 1899	H. B. 153
Yamhill	McMinnville	July 5, 1843	Unnumb.

1 Formerly Champoick County, changed to Marion County, Sept. 3, 1849, unnumbered.

2 Formerly Twality (or Falatine) County, changed to Washington County, Sept. 3, 1849, unnumbered,

(On Dec. 22, 1845 "districts" were renamed "counties.")

PENNSYLVANIA (67 counties) 2nd state.
Admitted as state December 12, 1787.

County	County Seat	Created	Statute
Adams	Gettysburg	Jan. 22, 1800	Chap. 231
Allegheny	Pittsburgh	Sept. 24, 1788	Chap. 408
Armstrong	Kittanning	Mar. 12, 1800	Chap. 264
Beaver	Beaver	Mar. 12, 1800	Chap. 264

County	County Seat	Created	Statute
Bedford	Bedford	Mar. 9, 1771	Unnumb.
Berks	Reading	Sess. Oct. 14, 1751	Unnumb.
Blair	Hollidaysburg	Feb. 26, 1846	Act 55
Bradford* 1	Towanda	Feb. 21, 1810	Chap. 30
Bucks	Doylestown	Mar. 10, 1682	Unnumb.
Butler	Butler	Mar. 12, 1800	Chap. 264
Cambria	Ebensburg	Mar. 26, 1804	Act 78
Cameron	Emporium	Mar. 29, 1860	Act 598
Carbon	Mauch Chunk	Mar. 13, 1843	Act 141
Centre	Bellefonte	Feb. 13, 1800	Chap. 237
Chester	West Chester	Mar. 10, 1682	Unnumb.
Clarion	Clarion	Mar. 11, 1839	Act 27
Clearfield	Clearfield	Mar. 26, 1804	Act 78
Clinton	Lock Haven	June 21, 1839	Act 145
Columbia	Bloomsburg	Mar. 22, 1813	Act 109
Crawford	Meadville	Mar. 12, 1800	Chap. 264
Cumberland	Carlisle	Jan. 27, 1750	Chap. 1
Dauphin	Harrisburg	Mar. 4, 1785	Chap. 182
Delaware	Media	Sept. 26, 1789	Chap. 492
Elk	Ridgway	Apr. 18, 1843	Act 150
Erie	Erie	Mar. 12, 1800	Chap. 264
Fayette	Uniontown	Sept. 26, 1783	Chap. 155
Forest	Tionesta	Apr. 11, 1848	Res. 9
Franklin	Chambersburg	Sept. 9, 1784	Chap. 153
Fulton	McConnellsburg	Apr. 19, 1850	Act 495
Greene	Waynesburg	Feb. 9, 1796	Chap. 4
Huntingdon	Huntingdon	Sept. 20, 1787	Chap. 359
Indiana	Indiana	Mar. 30, 1803	Act 161
Jefferson	Brookville	Mar. 26, 1804	Act 78
Juniata	Mifflintown	Mar. 2, 1831	Act 67
Lackawanna	Scranton	Aug. 21, 1878	Procl.
Lancaster	Lancaster	Sess. Oct. 14, 1728	Chap. 299
Lawrence	New Castle	Mar. 20, 1849	Act 366
Lebanon	Lebanon	Feb. 16, 1813	Act 52
Lehigh	Allentown	Mar. 6, 1812	Act 49
Luzerne	Wilkes-Barre	Sept. 25, 1786	Chap. 291
Lycoming	Williamsport	Apr. 13, 1795	Chap. 314
McKean	Smethport	Mar. 26, 1804	Chap. 78
Mercer	Mercer	Mar. 12, 1800	Chap. 264
Mifflin	Lewistown	Sept. 19, 1789	Chap. 485
Monroe	Stroudsburg	Apr. 1, 1836	Act 144
Montgomery	Norristown	Sept. 10, 1784	Chap. 154
Montour	Danville	May 3, 1850	Act 387
Northampton	Easton	Sess. Oct. 14, 1751	Unnumb.
Northumberland	Sunbury	Mar. 21, 1772	Unnumb.
Perry	New Bloomfield	Mar. 22, 1820	Act 68

County	County Seat	Created	Statute
Philadelphia	Philadelphia	Mar. 10, 1682	Unnumb.
Pike	Milford	Mar. 26, 1814	Act 109
Potter	Coudersport	Mar. 26, 1804	Act 78
Schuylkill	Pottsville	Mar. 1, 1811	Act 54
Snyder	Middleburg	Mar. 2, 1855	Act 555
Somerset	Somerset	Apr. 17, 1795	Chap. 331
Sullivan	Laporte	Mar. 15, 1847	Act 365
Susquehanna	Montrose	Feb. 21, 1810	Chap. 30
Tioga	Wellsboro	Mar. 26, 1804	Act 78
Union	Lewisburg	Mar. 22, 1813	Act 110
Venango	Franklin	Mar. 12, 1800	Chap. 264
Warren	Warren	Mar. 12, 1800	Chap. 264
Washington	Washington	Mar. 28, 1781	Chap. 189
Wayne	Honesdale	Mar. 21, 1798	Chap. 120
Westmoreland	Greensburg	Feb. 26, 1773	Chap. 8
Wyoming	Tunkhannock	Apr. 4, 1842	Act 79
York	York	Sess. Oct. 14, 1748	Unnumb.

1 Formerly Ontario County, changed to Bradford County, Mar. 24, 1812, chap. 109.

RHODE ISLAND (5 counties) 13th state.
Admitted as state May 29, 1790

County	County Seat	Created
Bristol	Bristol	Feb. 17, 1746-7
Kent	East Greenwich	June 11, 1750
Newport* 1	Newport	June 22, 1703
Providence* 2	Providence	June 22, 1703
Washington* 3	West Kingston	June 3, 1729

1 Formerly Rhode Island County, changed to Newport County, June 16, 1729.
2 Formerly Providence Plantations, changed to Providence County, June 16, 1729.
3 Formerly King's County, changed to Washington County, Oct. 29, 1781.

SOUTH CAROLINA (46 counties) 8th state.
Admitted as state May 23, 1788.

County	County Seat	Created	Statute
Abbeville	Abbeville	Mar. 12, 1785	Unnumb.
Aiken	Aiken	Mar. 10, 1871	Act 420
Allendale	Allendale	Feb. 6, 1919	Act 6
Anderson	Anderson	Dec. 20, 1826	Act 9

County	County Seat	Created	Statute
Bamberg	Bamberg	Feb. 25, 1897	Act 344
Barnwell	Barnwell	1798	
Beaufort	Beaufort	Mar. 12, 1785	Unnumb.
Berkeley	Monck's Corner	Jan. 31, 1882	Act 527
Calhoun	St. Matthews	Feb. 14, 1908	Act 567
Charleston	Charleston	Mar. 12, 1785	Unnumb.
Cherokee	Gaffney	Feb. 25, 1897	Act 345
Chester	Chester	Mar. 12, 1785	Unnumb.
Chesterfield	Chesterfield	Mar. 12, 1785	Unnumb.
Clarendon	Manning	Mar. 12, 1785	Unnumb.
Colleton	Walterboro	Mar. 12, 1785	Unnumb.
Darlington	Darlington	Mar. 12, 1785	Unnumb.
Dillon	Dillon	Feb. 5, 1910	Act 436
Dorchester	St. George	Feb. 25, 1897	Act 346
Edgefield	Edgefield	Mar. 12, 1785	Unnumb.
Fairfield	Winnsboro	Mar. 12, 1785	Unnumb.
Florence	Florence	Dec. 22, 1888	Act 99
Georgetown	Georgetown		
Greenville	Greenville	Mar. 22, 1786	Unnumb.
Greenwood	Greenwood	Mar. 2, 1897	Act 347
Hampton	Hampton	Feb. 18, 1878	Act 353
Horry	Conway	Dec. 19, 1801	Unnumb.
Jasper	Ridgeland	Jan. 30, 1912	Act 459
Kershaw	Camden	Feb. 19, 1791	
Lancaster	Lancaster	Mar. 12, 1785	Unnumb.
Laurens	Laurens	Mar. 12, 1785	Unnumb.
Lee	Bishopville	Feb. 25, 1902	Act 651
Lexington	Lexington	Mar. 12, 1785	Unnumb.
Marion	Marion	Mar. 12, 1785	Unnumb.
Marlboro	Bennettsville	Mar. 12, 1785	Unnumb.
McCormick	McCormick	Feb. 19, 1916	Act 398
Newberry	Newberry	Mar. 12, 1785	Unnumb.
Oconee	Walhalla	Jan. 29, 1768	Ordinance of the Convention
Orangeburg	Orangeburg	Mar. 12, 1785	Unnumb.
Pickens	Pickens	Dec. 20, 1826	Act 9
Richland	Columbia	Mar. 12, 1785	Unnumb.
Saluda	Saluda	Feb. 25, 1896	Act 118
Spartanburg	Spartanburg	Mar. 12, 1785	Unnumb.
Sumter	Sumter	1785	Unnumb.
Union	Union	Mar. 12, 1785	Unnumb.
Williamsburg	Kingstree	Mar. 12, 1785	Unnumb.
York	York	Mar. 12, 1785	Unnumb.

(The constitution of 1868 changed "district" to "county."

SOUTH DAKOTA (67 counties) 40th state.
Organized as territory March 2, 1861.
Admitted as state November 2, 1889.

County	County Seat	Created	Statute
Aurora	Plankinton	Feb. 22, 1879	Chap. 12
Beadle	Huron	Feb. 22, 1879	Chap. 12
Bennett	Martin	Mar. 9, 1909	Chap. 280
Bon Homme	Tyndall	Apr. 5, 1862	Chap. 12
Brookings	Brookings	Apr. 5, 1862	Chap. 16
Brown	Aberdeen	Feb. 22, 1879	Chap. 12
Brule	Chamberlain	Jan. 14, 1875	Chap. 31
Buffalo	Gann Valley	Jan. 8, 1873	Chap. 16
Butte	Belle Fourche	Mar. 2, 1883	Chap. 15
Campbell	Mound City	Jan. 8, 1873	Chap. 16
Charles Mix	Lake Andes	May 8, 1862	Chap. 18
Clark	Clark	Jan. 8, 1873	Chap. 16
Clay	Vermillion	Apr. 10, 1862	Chap. 13
Codington	Watertown	1877	
Corson	McIntosh	Mar. 2, 1909	Chap. 133
Custer	Custer	Jan. 11, 1875	Chap. 29
Davison	Mitchell	Jan. 8, 1873	Chap. 16
Day	Webster	Feb. 22, 1879	Chap. 12
Deuel	Clear Lake	Apr. 5, 1862	Chap. 16
Dewey* 1	Timber Lake	Jan. 8, 1873	Chap. 19
Douglas	Armour	Jan. 8, 1873	Chap. 16
Edmunds	Ipswich	Jan. 8, 1873	Chap. 16
Fall River	Hot Springs	Mar. 6, 1883	Chap. 18
Faulk	Faulkton	Jan. 8, 1873	Chap. 16
Grant	Milbank	Jan. 8, 1873	Chap. 16
Gregory	Burke	May 8, 1862	Chap. 18
Haakon	Philip	1914	
Hamlin	Hayti	Jan. 8, 1873	Chap. 16
Hand	Miller	Jan. 8, 1873	Chap. 16
Hanson	Alexandria	Jan. 13, 1871	Chap. 10
Harding	Buffalo	Feb. 26, 1909	Chap. 100
Hughes	Pierre	Jan. 8, 1873	Chap. 16
Hutchinson	Olivet	May 8, 1862	Chap. 15
Hyde	Highmore	Jan. 8, 1873	Chap. 16
Jackson	Kadoka	1914	
Jerauld	Wessington Springs	Mar. 9, 1883	Chap. 23
Jones	Murdo	1916	
Kingsbury	De Smet	Jan. 8, 1873	Chap. 16
Lake	Madison	Jan. 8, 1873	Chap. 16
Lawrence	Deadwood	Jan. 11, 1875	Chap. 29
Lincoln	Canton	Apr. 5, 1862	Chap. 16
Lyman	Kennebec	Jan. 8, 1873	Chap. 19

County	County Seat	Created	Statute
Marshall	Britton	Mar. 10, 1885	Chap. 12
McCook	Salem	Jan. 8, 1873	Chap. 16
McPherson	Leola	Jan. 8, 1873	Chap. 16
Meade	Sturgis	Feb. 7, 1889	Chap. 57
Mellette	White River	Mar. 9, 1909	Chap. 280
Miner	Howard	Jan. 8, 1873	Chap. 16
Minnehaha	Sioux Falls	Apr. 5, 1862	Chap. 16
Moody	Flandreau	Jan. 8, 1873	Chap. 16
Pennington	Rapid City	Jan. 11, 1875	Chap. 29
Perkins	Bison	Feb. 26, 1909	S. B. 100
Potter	Gettysburg	Jan. 14, 1875	Chap. 30
Roberts	Sisseton	Mar. 8, 1883	Chap. 30
Sanborn	Woonsocket	Mar. 9, 1883	Chap. 31
Shannon	(unorganized)	Jan. 11, 1875	Chap. 29
Spink	Redfield	Jan. 8, 1873	Chap. 16
Stanley	Fort Pierre	Jan. 8, 1873	Chap. 19
Sully	Onida	Jan. 8, 1873	Chap. 16
Todd	(unorganized)	Mar. 9, 1909	Chap. 280
Tripp	Winner	Jan. 8, 1873	Chap. 19
Turner	Parker	Jan. 13, 1871	Chap. 10
Union* 2	Elk Point	Apr. 10, 1862	Chap. 14
Walworth	Selby	Jan. 8, 1873	Chap. 16
Washabaugh	(unorganized)	Mar. 9, 1883	Chap. 40
Yankton	Yankton	Apr. 10, 1862	Chap. 19
Ziebach	Dupree	Feb. 1, 1911	Chap. 107

1 Formerly Rusk County, changed to Dewey County, Mar. 9, 1883, chap. 17.

2 Formerly Cole County, changed to Union County, Jan. 7, 1864, chap. 14.

TENNESSEE (95 counties) 16th state.
Organized as territory May 26, 1790.
Admitted as state June 1, 1796.

County	County Seat	Created	Statute
Anderson	Clinton	Nov. 6, 1801	Chap. 45
Bedford	Shelbyville	Dec. 3, 1807	Chap. 37
Benton	Camden	Dec. 19, 1835	Chap. 30
Bledsoe	Pikeville	Nov. 30, 1807	Chap. 9
Blount	Maryville	July 11, 1795	Chap. 6
Bradley	Cleveland	Feb. 10, 1836	Chap. 32
Campbell	Jacksboro	Sept. 11, 1806	Chap. 21
Cannon	Woodbury	Jan. 31, 1836	Chap. 33
Carroll	Huntingdon	Nov. 7, 1821	Chap. 32
Carter	Elizabethton	Apr. 9, 1796	Chap. 31

County	County Seat	Created	Statute
Cheatham	Ashland City	Feb. 28, 1856	Chap. 122
Chester	Henderson	Mar. 4, 1879	Chap. 42
Claiborne	Tazewell	Oct. 29, 1801	Chap. 46
Clay	Celina	June 24, 1870	Chap. 29
Cocke	Newport	Oct. 9, 1797	Chap. 8
Coffee	Manchester	Jan. 8, 1836	Chap. 36
Crockett	Alamo	Dec. 20, 1845	Chap. 25
Cumberland	Crossville	Nov. 16, 1855	Chap. 6
Davidson	Nashville	Sess. Apr. 18, 1783	Chap. 52
Decatur	Decaturville	Nov. 1845	Chap. 7
De Kalb	Smithville	Dec. 11, 1837	
Dickson	Charlotte	Oct. 25, 1803	Chap. 66
Dyer	Dyersburg	Oct. 16, 1823	Chap. 108
Fayette	Somerville	Sept. 29, 1824	Chap. 36
Fentress	Jamestown	Nov. 28, 1823	Chap. 302
Franklin	Winchester	Dec. 3, 1807	Chap. 72
Gibson	Trenton and Humboldt	Oct. 21, 1823	Chap. 111
Giles	Pulaski	Nov. 14, 1809	Chap. 55
Grainger	Rutledge	Apr. 22, 1796	Chap. 28
Greene	Greeneville	Sess. Apr. 18, 1783	Chap. 51
Grundy	Altamont	Jan. 29, 1844	Chap. 204
Hamblen	Morristown	June 8, 1870	Chap. 6
Hamilton	Chattanooga	Oct. 25, 1819	Chap. 113
Hancock	Sneedville	Jan. 7, 1844	Chap. 71
Hardeman	Bolivar	Oct. 16, 1823	Chap. 108
Hardin	Savannah	Nov. 13, 1819	Chap. 6
Hawkins	Rogersville	Sess. Nov. 18, 1786	Chap. 34
Haywood	Brownsville	Nov. 3, 1823	Chap. 145
Henderson	Lexington	Nov. 7, 1821	Chap. 32
Henry	Paris	Nov. 7, 1821	Chap. 32
Hickman	Centerville	Dec. 3, 1807	Chap. 44
Houston	Erin	Jan. 23, 1871	Chap. 46
Humphreys	Waverly	Oct. 19, 1809	Chap. 31
Jackson	Gainesboro	Nov. 6, 1801	Chap. 48
Jefferson	Dandridge	June 11, 1792	Unnumb.
Johnson	Mountain City	Jan. 2, 1836	Chap. 31
Knox	Knoxville	June 11, 1792	Unnumb.
Lake	Tiptonville	June 24, 1870	Chap. 30
Lauderdale	Ripley	Nov. 24, 1835	Chap. 28
Lawrence	Lawrenceburg	Oct. 21, 1817	Chap. 42
Lewis	Hohenwald	Dec. 21, 1843	Chap. 38
Lincoln	Fayetteville	Nov. 14, 1809	Chap. 48
Loudon* 1	Loudon	June 2, 1870	Chap. 2
Macon	Lafayette	Jan. 18, 1842	Chap. 45
Madison	Jackson	Nov. 7, 1821	Chap. 32

County	County Seat		Created	Statute
Marion	Jasper		Nov. 20, 1817	Chap. 109
Marshall	Lewisburg		Feb. 20, 1836	Chap. 35
Maury	Columbia		Nov. 16, 1807	Chap. 94
McMinn	Athens		Nov. 13, 1819	Chap. 7
McNairy	Selmer		Oct. 8, 1823	Chap. 96
Meigs	Decatur		Jan. 20, 1836	Chap. 34
Monroe	Madisonville		Nov. 13, 1819	Chap. 7
Montgomery	Clarksville		Apr. 9, 1796	Chap. 30
Moore	Lynchburg		Dec. 14, 1871	Chap. 96
Morgan	Wartburg		Oct. 15, 1817	Chap. 38
Obion	Union City		Oct. 24, 1823	Chap. 114
Overton	Livingston		Sept. 11, 1806	Chap. 27
Perry	Linden		Nov. 14, 1821	Chap. 202
Pickett	Byrdstown		Feb. 27, 1879	Chap. 34
Polk	Benton		Nov. 28, 1839	Chap. 10
Putnam	Cookeville		Feb. 2, 1842	Chap. 169
Rhea	Dayton		Nov. 30, 1807	Chap. 9
Roane	Kingston		Nov. 6, 1801	Chap. 45
Robertson	Springfield		Apr. 9, 1796	Chap. 30
Rutherford	Murfreesboro		Oct. 25, 1803	Chap. 70
Scott	Huntsville		Dec. 17, 1849	Chap. 45
Sequatchie	Dunlap		Dec. 9, 1857	Chap. 11
Sevier	Sevierville		Sept. 27, 1794	Chap. 11
Shelby	Memphis		Nov. 24, 1819	Chap. 218
Smith	Carthage		Oct. 26, 1799	Chap. 2
Stewart	Dover		Nov. 1, 1803	Chap. 68
Sullivan	Blountville	Sess.	Oct. 18, 1779	Chap. 29
Sumner	Gallatin	Sess.	Nov. 18, 1786	Chap. 32
Tipton	Covington		Oct. 29, 1823	Chap. 126
Trousdale	Hartsville		June 21, 1870	Chap. 27
Unicoi	Erwin		Mar. 23, 1875	Chap. 68
Union* 2	Maynardville		Oct. 9, 1797	Chap. 8
Van Buren	Spencer		Jan. 3, 1840	Chap. 59
Warren	McMinnville		Nov. 26, 1807	Chap. 28
Washington	Jonesboro and JohnsonCity	Sess	Nov. 15, 1777	Chap. 31
Wayne	Waynesboro		Nov. 24, 1817	Chap. 175
Weakley	Dresden		Oct. 21, 1823	Chap. 112
White	Sparta		Sept. 11, 1806	Chap. 36
Williamson	Franklin		Oct. 26, 1799	Chap. 2
Wilson	Lebanon		Oct. 26, 1799	Chap. 2

1 Formerly Christiana County, changed to Loudon County, July 7, 1870, chap. 77.

2 Formerly Cocke County, changed to Union County, Jan. 28, 1846, chap. 123.

TEXAS (254 counties) 28th state.
Admitted as state December 29, 1845.

County	County Seat	Created	Statute
Anderson	Palestine	Mar. 24, 1846	Unnumb.
Andrews	Andrews	Aug. 21, 1876	Chap. 144
Angelina	Lufkin	Apr. 22, 1846	Unnumb.
Arsansas	Rockport	Sept. 18, 1871	Chap. 1
Archer	Archer City	Jan. 22, 1858	Chap. 55
Armstrong	Claude	Aug. 21, 1876	Chap. 144
Atascosa	Jourdanville	Jan. 25, 1856	Chap. 33
Austin	Belleville	Mar. 17, 1836	Const.
Bailey	Muleshoe	Aug. 21, 1876	Chap. 144
Bandera	Bandera	Jan. 26, 1856	Chap. 42
Bastrop	Bastrop	Mar. 17, 1836	Const.
Baylor	Seymour	Feb. 1, 1858	Chap. 75
Bee	Beeville	Dec. 8, 1857	Chap. 14
Bell	Belton	Jan. 22, 1850	Chap. 55
Bexar	San Antonio	Mar. 17, 1836	Const.
Blanco	Johnson City	Feb. 12, 1858	Chap. 130
Borden	Gail	Aug. 21, 1876	Chap. 144
Bosque	Meridian	Feb. 4, 1854	Chap. 38
Bowie	Boston	Dec. 17, 1840	Unnumb.
Brazoria	Angleton	Mar. 17, 1836	Const.
Brazos* 1	Bryan	Jan. 30, 1841	Unnumb.
Brewster	Alpine	Feb. 2, 1887	Chap. 4
Briscoe	Silverton	Aug. 21, 1876	Chap. 144
Brooks	Falfurrias	Mar. 11, 1911	Chap. 39
Brown	Brownwood	Aug. 27, 1856	Chap. 139
Burleson	Caldwell	Jan. 15, 1842	Unnumb.
Burnet	Burnet	Feb. 5, 1852	Chap. 60
Caldwell	Lockhart	Mar. 6, 1848	Chap. 65
Calhoun	Port Lavaca	Apr. 4, 1846	Unnumb.
Callahan	Baird	Feb. 1, 1858	Chap. 75
Cameron	Brownsville	Feb. 12, 1848	Chap. 35
Camp	Pittsburg	Apr. 6, 1874	Chap. 55
Carson	Panhandle	Aug. 21, 1876	Chap. 144
Cass* 2	Linden	Apr. 25, 1846	Unnumb.
Castro	Dimmitt	Aug. 21, 1876	Chap. 144
Chambers	Anahuac	Feb. 12, 1858	Chap. 125
Cherokee	Rusk	Apr. 11, 1846	Unnumb.
Childress	Childress	Aug. 21, 1876	Chap. 144
Clay	Henrietta	Dec. 24, 1857	Chap. 34
Cochran	Morton	Aug. 21, 1876	Chap. 144
Coke	Robert Lee	Mar. 13, 1889	Chap. 77
Coleman	Coleman	Feb. 1, 1858	Chap. 75
Colin	McKinney	Apr. 3, 1846	Chap. 144

County	County Seat	Created	Statute
Collingsworth	Wellington	Aug. 21, 1876	Chap. 144
Colorado	Columbus	Mar. 17, 1836	Const.
Comal	New Braunfels	Mar. 24, 1846	Unnumb.
Comanche	Comanche	Jan. 25, 1856	Chap. 35
Concho	Paint Rock	Feb. 1, 1858	Chap. 75
Cooke	Gainesville	Mar. 20, 1848	Chap. 130
Coryell	Gatesville	Feb. 4, 1854	Chap. 36
Cottle	Paducah	Aug. 21, 1876	Chap. 144
Crane	Crane	Feb. 26, 1887	Chap. 12
Crockett	Ozona	Jan. 22, 1875	Chap. 2
Crosby	Crosbyton	Aug. 21, 1876	Chap. 144
Culberson	Van Horn	Mar. 10, 1911	Chap. 38
Dallam	Dalhart	Aug. 21, 1876	Chap. 144
Dallas	Dallas	Mar. 30, 1846	Unnumb.
Dawson	Lamesa	Feb. 1, 1858	Chap. 75
Deaf Smith	Hereford	Aug. 21, 1876	Chap. 144
Delta	Cooper	July 29, 1870	Chap. 30
Denton	Denton	Apr. 11, 1846	Unnumb.
De Witt	Cuero	Mar. 24, 1846	Unnumb.
Dickens	Dickens	Aug. 21, 1876	Chap. 144
Dimmit	Carrizo Springs	Feb. 1, 1858	Chap. 75
Donley	Clarendon	Aug. 21, 1876	Chap. 144
Duval	San Diego	Feb. 1, 1858	Chap. 75
Eastland	Eastland	Feb. 1, 1858	Chap. 75
Ector	Odessa	Feb. 26, 1887	Chap. 12
Edwards	Rocksprings	Feb. 1, 1858	Chap. 75
Ellis	Waxahachie	Dec. 20, 1849	Chap. 18
El Paso	El Paso	Jan. 3, 1850	Chap. 29
Erath	Stephenville	Jan. 25, 1856	Chap. 34
Falls	Marlin	Jan. 28, 1850	Chap. 80
Fannin	Bonham	Dec. 14, 1837	Unnumb.
Fayette	La Grange	Dec. 14, 1837	Unnumb.
Fisher	Roby	Aug. 21, 1876	Chap. 144
Floyd	Floydada	Aug. 21, 1876	Chap. 144
Foard	Crowell	Mar. 3, 1891	Chap. 15
Fort Bend	Richmond	Dec. 29, 1837	Unnumb.
Franklin	Mount Vernon	Mar. 6, 1875	Chap. 81
Freestone	Fairfield	Sept. 6, 1850	Chap. 39
Frio	Pearsall	Feb. 1, 1858	Chap. 75
Gaines	Seminole	Aug. 21, 1876	Chap. 144
Galveston	Galveston	May 15, 1838	Unnumb.
Garza	Post	Aug. 21, 1876	Chap. 144
Gillespie	Fredericksburg	Feb. 23, 1848	Chap. 47
Glasscock	Garden City	Apr. 4, 1887	Chap. 143
Goliad	Goliad	Mar. 17, 1836	Const.
Gonzales	Gonzales	Mar. 17, 1836	Const.

County	County Seat	Created	Statute
Gray	Pampa	Aug. 21, 1876	Chap. 144
Grayson	Sherman	Mar. 17, 1846	Unnumb.
Gregg	Longview	Apr. 12, 1873	Chap. 27
Grimes	Anderson	Apr. 6, 1846	Unnumb.
Guadalupe	Seguin	Mar. 30, 1846	Unnumb.
Hale	Plainview	Aug. 21, 1876	Chap. 144
Hall	Memphis	Aug. 21, 1876	Chap. 144
Hamilton	Hamilton	Feb. 2, 1842	Unnumb.
Hansford	Spearman	Aug. 21, 1876	Chap. 144
Hardeman	Quanah	Feb. 1, 1858	Chap. 75
Hardin	Kountze	Jan. 22, 1858	Chap. 55
Harris* 3	Houston	Mar. 17, 1836	Const.
Harrison	Marshall	Jan. 28, 1839	Unnumb.
Hartley	Channing	Aug. 21, 1876	Chap. 144
Haskell	Haskell	Feb. 1, 1858	Chap. 75
Hays	San Marcos	Mar. 1, 1848	Chap. 57
Hemphill	Canadian	Aug. 21, 1876	Chap. 144
Henderson	Athens	Apr. 27, 1846	Unnumb.
Hidalgo	Edinburg	Jan. 24, 1852	Chap. 42
Hill	Hillsboro	Feb. 7, 1853	Chap. 26
Hockley	Levelland	Aug. 21, 1876	Chap. 144
Hood	Granbury	Nov. 3, 1865	Chap. 85
Hopkins	Sulphur Springs	Mar. 25, 1846	Unnumb.
Houston	Crockett	June 12, 1837	Unnumb.
Howard	Big Spring	Aug. 21, 1876	Chap. 144
Hudspeth	Sierra Blanca	Feb. 16, 1917	Chap. 25
Hunt	Greenville	Apr. 11, 1846	Unnumb.
Hutchinson	Stinnett	Aug. 21, 1876	Chap. 144
Irion	Mertzon	Mar. 7, 1889	Chap. 87
Jack	Jacksboro	Aug. 27, 1856	Chap. 135
Jackson	Edna	Mar. 17, 1836	Const.
Jasper	Jasper	Mar. 17, 1836	Const.
Jeff Davis	Fort Davis	Mar. 15, 1887	Chap. 38
Jefferson	Beaumont	Mar. 17, 1836	Const.
Jim Hogg	Hebbronville	Mar. 31, 1913	Chap. 73
Jim Wells	Alice	Mar. 25, 1911	Chap. 140
Johnson	Cleburne	Feb. 13, 1854	Chap. 76
Jones	Anson	Feb. 1, 1858	Chap. 75
Karnes	Karnes City	Feb. 4, 1854	Chap. 35
Kaufman	Kaufman	Feb. 26, 1848	Chap. 52
Kendall	Boerne	Jan. 10, 1862	Chap. 38
Kenedy	Sarita	Apr. 2, 1921	Chap. 104
Kent	Clairemont	Aug. 21, 1876	Chap. 144
Kerr	Kerrville	Jan. 26, 1856	Chap. 40
Kimble	Junction	Jan. 22, 1858	Chap. 55
King	Guthrie	Aug. 21, 1876	Chap. 144

County	County Seat	Created	Statute
Kinney	Brackettville	Jan. 28, 1850	Chap. 81
Kleberg	Kingsville	Feb. 27, 1913	Chap. 10
Knox	Benjamin	Feb. 1, 1858	Chap. 75
Lamar	Paris	Dec. 17, 1840	Unnumb.
Lamb	Olton	Aug. 21, 1876	Chap. 144
Lampasas	Lampasas	Feb. 1, 1856	Chap. 44
La Salle	Cotulla	Feb. 1, 1858	Chap. 75
Lavaca	Hallettsville	Apr. 6, 1846	Unnumb.
Lee	Giddings	Apr. 14, 1874	Chap. 75
Leon	Centerville	Mar. 17, 1846	Unnumb.
Liberty	Liberty	Mar. 17, 1836	Const.
Limestone	Groesbeck	Apr. 11, 1846	Unnumb.
Lipscomb	Lipscomb	Aug. 21, 1876	Chap. 144
Live Oak	George West	Feb. 2, 1856	Chap. 59
Llano	Llano	Feb. 1, 1856	Chap. 48
Loving	Mentone	Feb. 26, 1887	Chap. 12
Lubbock	Lubbock	Aug. 21, 1876	Chap. 144
Lynn	Tahoka	Aug. 21, 1876	Chap. 144
Madison	Madisonville	Feb. 2, 1842	Unnumb.
Marion	Jefferson	Feb. 8, 1860	Chap. 48
Martin	Stanton	Aug. 21, 1876	Chap. 144
Mason	Mason	Jan. 22, 1858	Chap. 55
Matagorda	Bay City	Mar. 17, 1836	Const.
Maverick	Eagle Pass	Feb. 2, 1856	Chap. 69
McCulloch	Brady	Aug. 27, 1856	Chap. 141
McLennan	Waco	Jan. 22, 1850	Chap. 54
McMullen	Tilden	Feb. 1, 1858	Chap. 75
Medina	Hondo	Feb. 12, 1848	Chap. 36
Menard	Menard	Jan. 22, 1858	Chap. 55
Midland	Midland	Mar. 4, 1885	Chap. 23
Milam	Cameron	Mar. 17, 1836	Const.
Mills	Goldthwaite	Mar. 15, 1887	Chap. 37
Mitchell	Colorado City	Aug. 21, 1876	Chap. 144
Montague	Montague	Dec. 24, 1857	Chap. 33
Montgomery	Conroe	Dec. 14, 1837	Unnumb.
Moore	Dumas	Aug. 21, 1876	Chap. 144
Morris	Daingerfield	Mar. 6, 1875	Chap. 82
Motley	Matador	Aug. 21, 1876	Chap. 144
Nacogdoches	Nacogdoches	Mar. 17, 1836	Const.
Navarro	Corsicana	Apr. 25, 1846	Unnumb.
Newton	Newton	Apr. 22, 1846	Unnumb.
Nolan	Sweetwater	Aug. 21, 1876	Chap. 144
Nueces	Corpus Christi	Apr. 18, 1846	Unnumb.
Ochiltree	Perryton	Aug. 21, 1876	Chap. 144
Oldham	Vega	Aug. 21, 1876	Chap. 144
Orange	Orange	Feb. 5, 1852	Chap. 59

County	County Seat	Created	Statute
Palo Pinto	Palo Pinto	Aug. 27, 1856	Chap. 138
Panola	Carthage	Mar. 30, 1846	Unnumb.
Parker	Weatherford	Dec. 12, 1855	Chap. 1
Parmer	Farwell	Aug. 21, 1876	Chap. 144
Pecos	Fort Stockton	May 3, 1871	Chap. 70
Polk	Livingston	Mar. 30, 1846	Unnumb.
Potter	Amarillo	Aug. 21, 1876	Chap. 144
Presidio	Maria	Jan. 3, 1850	Chap. 29
Rains	Emory	June 9, 1870	Chap. 3
Randall	Canyon	Aug. 21, 1876	Chap. 144
Reagan	Big Lake	Mar. 7, 1903	Chap. 32
Real	Leakey	Apr. 3, 1913	Chap. 133
Red River	Clarksville	Mar. 7, 1836	Const.
Reeves	Pecos	Apr. 14, 1883	Chap. 103
Refugio	Refugio	Mar. 17, 1836	Const.
Roberts	Miami	Aug. 21, 1876	Chap. 144
Robertson	Franklin	Dec. 14, 1837	Unnumb.
Rockwall	Rockwall	Mar. 1, 1873	Chap. 7
Runnels	Ballinger	Feb. 1, 1858	Chap. 75
Rusk	Henderson	Jan. 16, 1843	Unnumb.
Sabine	Hemphill	Mar. 17, 1936	Const.
San Augustine	San Augustine	Mar. 17, 1836	Const.
San Jacinto	Coldspring	Aug. 13, 1870	Chap. 59
San Patricio	Sinton	Mar. 17, 1836	Const.
San Saba	San Saba	Feb. 1, 1856	Chap. 49
Schleicher	Eldorado	Apr. 1, 1887	Chap. 103
Scurry	Snyder	Aug. 21, 1876	Chap. 144
Shackelford	Albany	Feb. 1, 1858	Chap. 75
Shelby	Center	Mar. 17, 1836	Const.
Sherman	Stratford	Aug. 21, 1876	Chap. 144
Smith	Tyler	Apr. 11, 1846	Unnumb.
Somervell	Glen Rose	Mar. 13, 1875	Chap. 83
Starr	Rio Grande City	Feb. 10, 1848	Chap. 31
Stephens* 4	Breckenridge	Jan. 22, 1858	Chap. 55
Sterling	Sterling City	Mar. 4, 1891	Chap. 16
Stonewall	Aspermont	Aug. 21, 1876	Chap. 144
Sutton	Sonora	Apr. 1, 1887	Chap. 103
Swisher	Tulia	Aug. 21, 1876	Chap. 144
Tarrant	Fort Worth	Dec. 20, 1849	Chap. 17
Taylor	Abilene	Feb. 1, 1858	Chap. 75
Terrell	Sanderson	Apr. 8, 1905	Chap. 70
Terry	Brownfield	Aug. 21, 1876	Chap. 144
Throckmorton	Throckmorton	Jan. 13, 1858	Chap. 30
Titus	Mt. Pleasant	May 11, 1846	Unnumb.
Tom Green	San Angelo	Mar. 13, 1874	Chap. 26
Travis	Austin	Jan. 25, 1840	Unnumb.

County	County Seat	Created	Statute
Trinity	Groveton	Feb. 11, 1850	Chap. 160
Tyler	Woodville	Apr. 3, 1846	Unnumb.
Upshur	Gilmer	Apr. 27, 1846	Unnumb.
Upton	Rankin	Feb. 26, 1887	Chap. 12
Uvalde	Uvalde	Feb. 8, 1850	Chap. 112
Val Verde	Del Rio	Feb. 20, 1885	Chap. 50
Van Zandt	Canton	Mar. 20, 1848	Chap. 119
Victoria	Victoria	Mar. 17, 1836	Const.
Walker	Huntsville	Apr. 6, 1846	Unnumb.
Waller	Hempstead	Apr. 28, 1873	Chap. 38
Ward	Monahans	Feb. 26, 1887	Chap. 12
Washington	Brenham	Mar. 17, 1836	Const.
Webb	Laredo	Jan. 28, 1848	Chap. 32
Wharton	Wharton	Apr. 3, 1846	Unnumb.
Wheeler	Wheeler	Aug. 21, 1876	Chap. 144
Wichita	Wichita Falls	Feb. 1, 1858	Chap. 75
Wilbarger	Vernon	Feb. 1, 1858	Chap. 75
Willacy	Raymondville	Mar. 11, 1911	Chap. 48
Williamson	Georgetown	Mar. 13, 1848	Chap. 78
Wilson	Floresville	Feb. 13, 1860	Chap. 76
Winkler	Kermit	Feb. 26, 1887	Chap. 12
Wise	Decatur	Jan. 23, 1856	Chap. 31
Wood	Quitman	Feb. 5, 1850	Chap. 98
Yoakum	Plains	Aug. 21, 1876	Chap. 144
Young	Graham	Feb. 2, 1856	Chap. 71
Zapata	Zapata	Jan. 22, 1858	Chap. 55
Zavala	Crystal City	Feb. 1, 1858	Chap. 75

1 Formerly Navasoto County, changed to Brazos County, Jan. 28, 1842, unnumbered.

2 Formerly Cass County, changed to Davis County, Dec. 17, 1861, chap. 14; changed to Cass County, May 16, 1871, chap. 95.

3 Formerly Harrisburg County, changed to Harris County, Dec. 28, 1839 by joint resolution.

4 Formerly Buchanan County, changed to Stephens County, Dec. 17, 1861, chap. 14.

UTAH (29 counties) 45th state.
Organized as territory September 9, 1850.
Admitted as state January 4, 1896.

County	County Seat	Created	Statute
Beaver	Beaver	Jan. 5, 1856	Unnumb.
Box Elder	Brigham City	Jan. 5, 1856	Unnumb.
Cache	Logan	Jan. 5, 1856	Unnumb.

County	County Seat	Created	Statute
Carbon	Price	Mar. 8, 1894	Chap. 58
Daggett	Manila	Mar. 4, 1919	Chap. 43
Davis	Farmington	Mar. 3, 1852	Unnumb.
Duchesne	Duchesne	Mar. 7, 1913	Chap. 28
Emery	Castle Dale	Feb. 12, 1880	Chap. 4
Garfield	Panguitch	Mar. 9, 1882	Chap. 52
Grand	Moab	Mar. 13, 1890	Chap. 60
Iron* 1	Parowan	Jan. 31, 1850	Unnumb.
Juab	Nephi	Mar. 3, 1852	Unnumb.
Kane	Kanab	Jan. 16, 1864	Unnumb.
Millard	Fillmore	Oct. 4, 1851	Chap. 38
Morgan	Morgan	Jan. 17, 1862	Unnumb.
Piute	Junction	Jan. 16, 1865	Unnumb.
Rich* 2	Randolph	Jan. 16, 1864	Unnumb.
Salt Lake* 3	Salt Lake City	Mar. 3, 1852	Unnumb.
San Juan	Monticello	Feb. 17, 1880	Chap. 9
Sanpete	Manti	Mar. 3, 1852	Unnumb.
Sevier	Richfield	Jan. 16, 1865	Unnumb.
Summit	Coalville	Jan. 13, 1854	Chap. 63
Tooele	Tooele	Mar. 3, 1852	Unnumb.
Uintah	Vernal	Feb. 18, 1880	Chap. 10
Utah	Provo	Mar. 3, 1852	Unnumb.
Wasatch	Heber City	Jan. 17, 1862	Unnumb.
Washington	St. George	Mar. 3, 1852	Unnumb.
Wayne	Loa	Mar. 10, 1892	Chap. 71
Weber	Ogden	Mar. 3, 1852	Unnumb.

1 Formerly Little Salt Lake County, changed to Iron County, Dec. 3, 1850.

2 Formerly Richland County, changed to Rich County, Jan. 29, 1868, chap. 2.

3 Formerly Great Salt Lake County, changed to Salt Lake County, Jan. 29, 1868, chap. 3.

VERMONT (14 counties) 14th state.
Admitted as state March 4, 1791.

Addison	Middlebury	Oct. 18, 1785	Unnumb.
Bennington	Bennington and Manchester Sess.	Feb. 11, 1779	Unnumb.
Caledonia	St. Johnsbury	Nov. 5, 1792	Unnumb.
Chittenden	Burlington	Oct. 22, 1787	Unnumb.
Essex	Guildhall	Nov. 5, 1792	Unnumb.
Franklin	St. Albans	Nov. 5, 1792	Unnumb.
Grand Isle	North Hero	Nov. 9, 1802	Chap. 84

County	County Seat	Created	Statute
Lamoille	Hyde Park	Oct. 26, 1835	Act 41
Orange	Chelsea	Feb. 22, 1781	Unnumb.
Orleans	Newport City	Nov. 5, 1792	Unnumb.
Rutland	Rutland City	Feb. 22, 1781	Unnumb.
Washington* 1	Montpelier	Nov. 1, 1810	Chap. 74
Windham	Newfane	Feb. 22, 1781	Unnumb.
Windsor	Woodstock	Feb. 22, 1781	Unnumb.

1 Formerly Jefferson County, changed to Washington County, Nov. 8, 1814, chap. 79.

VIRGINIA (96 counties) 10th state.
Admitted as state June 25, 1778.

County	County Seat	Created	Statute
Accomac	Accomac	1634	
Albemarle	Charlottesville	Sess. May 6, 1744	Chap. 31
Alleghany	Covington	Jan. 5, 1822	Chap. 28
Amelia	Amelia	Sess. Feb. 1, 1734	Chap. 31
Amherst	Amherst	Sess. Sept. 14, 1758	Chap. 20
Appomattox	Appomattox	Feb. 8, 1845	Chap. 41
Arlington* 1	Arlington	Mar. 13, 1847	Chap. 53
Augusta	Staunton	Sess. Aug. 1, 1738	Chap. 21
Bath	Warm Springs	Dec. 14, 1790	Chap. 43
Bedford	Bedford	Sess. Feb. 27, 1752	Chap. 16
Bland	Bland	Mar. 30, 1861	Chap. 23
Botetourt	Fincastle	Sess. Nov. 7, 1769	Chap. 40
Brunswick	Lawrenceville	Sess. Nov. 2, 1720	Act 1
Buchanan	Grundy	Feb. 13, 1858	Chap. 156
Buckingham	Buckingham	Sess. Sept. 14, 1758	Chap. 20
Campbell	Rustburg	Sess. Nov. 5, 1781	Chap. 7
Caroline	Bowling Green	Sess. Feb. 1, 1727	Chap. 17
Carroll	Hillsville	Jan. 17, 1842	Chap. 58
Charles City	Charles City	1634	
Charlotte	Charlotte Court	Sess. May 26, 1764	Chap. 4
Chesterfield	Chesterfield	May 1, 1749	
Clarke	Berryville	Mar. 8, 1836	Chap. 19
Craig	New Castle	Mar. 21, 1851	Chap. 25
Culpeper	Culpeper	Mar. 23, 1748	
Cumberland	Cumberland	Mar. 23, 1855	
Dickenson	Clintwood	Mar. 3, 1880	Chap. 140
Dinwiddie	Dinwiddie	Sess. Feb. 27, 1752	Chap. 19
Essex	Tappahannock	Sess. Apr. 16, 1692	Act 5

County	County Seat	Created	Statute
Fairfax	Fairfax	Sess. May 6, 1742	Chap. 27
Fauquier	Warrenton	Sess. Sept. 14, 1758	Chap. 27
Floyd	Floyd	Jan. 15, 1831	Chap. 72
Fluvanna	Palmyra	Sess. May 5, 1777	Chap. 25
Franklin	Rockymount	Sess. Oct. 17, 1785	Chap. 25
Frederick	Winchester	Sess. Aug. 1, 1738	Chap. 21
Giles	Pearlsburg	Jan. 16, 1806	Chap. 53
Gloucester	Gloucester	1651	
Goochland	Goochland	Feb. 1, 1727	Chap. 18
Grayson	Independence	Nov. 7, 1792	Chap. 51
Greene	Standardsville	Jan. 24, 1838	Chap. 59
Greensville	Emporia	Sess. Oct. 16, 1780	Chap. 17
Halifax	Halifax	Sess. Feb. 27, 1752	Chap. 18
Hanover	Hanover	Sess. Nov. 2, 1720	Chap. 15
Henrico	Richmond	1634	
Henry	Martinsville	Sess. Oct. 7, 1776	Chap. 38
Highland	Monterey	Mar. 19, 1847	Chap. 56
Isle of Wight	Isle of Wight	1634	
James City	Williamsburg	1634	
King and Queen	King and Queen	Sess. Apr. 16, 1691	Act 19
King George	King George	Nov. 2, 1720	Chap. 14
King William	King William	Sess. Dec. 5, 1700	Act 4
Lancaster	Lancaster	1652	
Lee	Jonesville	Oct. 25, 1792	Chap. 49
Loudoun	Leesburg	Sess. Mar. 25, 1757	Chap. 22
Louisa	Louisa	Sess. May 6, 1742	Chap. 28
Lunenburg	Lunenburg	Sess. May 6, 1745	Chap. 22
Madison	Madison	Sess. Dec. 4, 1792	Chap. 50
Mathews	Mathews	Dec. 16, 1790	Chap. 41
Mecklenburg	Boydton	Sess. May 26, 1764	Chap. 4
Middlesex	Saluda	Sept. 21, 1674	Act 1
Montgomery	Christiansburg	Sess. Oct. 7, 1776	Chap. 44
Nansemond	Suffolk	1637	
Nelson	Lovingston	Dec. 25, 1807	Chap. 26
New Kent	New Kent	Nov. 20, 1654	
Northampton	Eastville	1634	
Northumberland	Heathsville	Sess. Oct. 12, 1648	Act 1
Nottoway	Nottoway	Dec. 22, 1788	Chap. 64
Orange	Orange	Sess. Feb. 1, 1734	Chap. 24
Page	Luray	Mar. 30, 1831	Chap. 74
Patrick	Stuart	Nov. 26, 1790	Chap. 40
Pittsylvania	Chatham	Sess. Nov. 6, 1766	Chap. 16
Powhatan	Powhatan	Sess. May 5, 1777	Chap. 24
Prince Edward	Farmville	Sess. Feb. 27, 1752	Chap. 15

County	County Seat	Created	Statute
Prince George	Prince George	Sess. Dec. 5, 1700	Chap. 2
Prince William	Manassas	Sess. Feb. 1, 1727	Chap. 17
Pulaski	Pulaski	Mar. 30, 1839	Chap. 50
Rappahannock	Washington	Feb. 8, 1833	Chap. 73
Richmond	Warsaw	Apr. 16, 1692	Act 5
Roanoke	Salem	Mar. 30, 1838	Chap. 60
Rockbridge	Lexington	Oct. 20, 1777	Chap. 18
Rockingham	Harrisonburg	Oct. 20, 1777	Chap. 18
Russell	Lebanon	Sess. Oct. 17, 1785	Chap. 46
Scott	Gate City	Nov. 24, 1814	Chap. 38
Shenandoah* 2	Woodstock	Mar. 24, 1772	Chap. 43
Smyth	Marion	Feb. 23, 1832	Chap. 67
Southampton	Courtland	Apr. 30, 1749	
Spotsylvania	Spotsylvania	Nov. 2, 1720	Chap. 1
Stafford	Stafford	Sess. June 5, 1666	
Surry	Surry	1652	
Sussex	Sussex	Feb. 27, 1752	Chap. 17
Tazewell	Taxewell	Dec. 17, 1799	Chap. 27
Warren	Front Royal	Mar. 9, 1836	Chap. 20
Washington	Abingdon	Sess. Oct. 7, 1776	Chap. 44
Westmoreland	Montross	Sess. July 5, 1653	Unnumb.
Wise	Wise	Feb. 16, 1856	Chap. 107
Wythe	Wytheville	Dec. 1, 1789	Chap. 56
York	Yorktown	1634	

1 Formerly Alexandria County, changed to Arlington County, Mar. 16, 1920.

2 Formerly Dunmore County, changed to Shenandoah County, Oct. 20, 1777 sess., eff. Feb. 1, 1778.

Prior to 1642, Nansemond County was Upper Norfolk County; Northampton County was Accawmack County; Isle of Wight County was Warrosquyoacke County; and York County was Charles River County.

WASHINGTON (39 counties) 42nd state.
Organized as territory March 2, 1853.
Admitted as state November 11, 1889.

County	County Seat	Created	Statute
Adams	Ritzville	Nov. 28, 1883	Unnumb.
Asotin	Asotin	Oct. 27, 1883	Unnumb.
Benton	Prosser	Mar. 8, 1905	Chap. 89
Chelan	Wenatchee	Mar. 13, 1899	Chap. 95
Clallam	Port Angeles	Apr. 26, 1854	Unnumb.
Clark* 1	Vancouver	June 27, 1844	Unnumb.

County	County Seat	Created	Statute
Columbia	Dayton	Nov. 11, 1875	Unnumb.
Cowlitz	Kelso	Apr. 21, 1854	Unnumb.
Douglas	Waterville	Nov. 28, 1883	Unnumb.
Ferry	Republic	Feb. 18, 1899	Chap. 18
Franklin	Pasco	Nov. 28, 1883	Unnumb.
Garfield	Pomeroy	Nov. 29, 1881	Unnumb.
Grant	Ephrata	Feb. 24, 1909	Chap. 17
Grays Harbor* 2	Montesano	Apr. 14, 1854	Unnumb.
Island	Coupeville	Jan. 6, 1853	Unnumb.
Jefferson	Port Townsend	Dec. 22, 1852	Unnumb.
King	Seattle	Dec. 22, 1852	Unnumb.
Kitsap* 3	Port Orchard	Jan. 16, 1857	Unnumb.
Kittitas	Ellensburg	Nov. 24, 1883	Unnumb.
Klickitat	Goldendale	Dec. 20, 1859	Unnumb.
Lewis	Chehalis	Dec. 21, 1845	Unnumb.
Lincoln	Davenport	Nov. 24, 1883	Unnumb.
Mason* 4	Shelton	Mar. 13, 1854	Unnumb.
Okanogan	Okanogan	Feb. 2, 1888	Chap. 35
Pacific	South Bend	Feb. 4, 1851	Unnumb.
Pend Oreille	Newport	Mar. 1, 1911	Chap. 28
Pierce	Tacoma	Dec. 22, 1852	Unnumb.
San Juan	Friday Harbor	Oct. 31, 1873	Unnumb.
Skagit	Mount Vernon	Nov. 28, 1883	Unnumb.
Skamania	Stevenson	Mar. 9, 1854	Unnumb.
Snohomish	Everett	Jan. 14, 1861	Unnumb.
Spokane	Spokane	Jan. 29, 1858	Unnumb.
Stevens	Colville	Jan. 20, 1863	Unnumb.
Thurston	Olympia	Jan. 12, 1852	Unnumb.
Wahkiakum	Cathlamet	Apr. 24, 1854	Unnumb.
Walla Walla	Walla Walla	Apr. 25, 1854	Unnumb.
Whatcom	Bellingham	Mar. 9, 1854	Unnumb.
Whitman	Colfax	Nov. 29, 1871	Unnumb.
Yakima	Yakima	Jan. 21, 1865	Unnumb.

1 Formerly Vancouver County, changed to Clark County, Sept. 3, 1849, unnumbered.

2 Formerly Chehalis County, changed to Grays Harbor County, Mar. 15, 1915, chap. 77.

3 Formerly Slaughter County, changed to Kitsap County, July 13, 1857.

4 Formerly Sawamish County, changed to Mason County, Jan. 8, 1864, unnumbered.

WEST VIRGINIA (55 counties) 35th state
Admitted as state June 20, 1863.

County	County Seat		Created	Statute
Barbour	Philippi		Mar. 3, 1843	Chap. 53
Berkeley	Martinsburg		Feb. 10, 1772	Chap. 43
Boone	Madison		Mar. 11, 1847	Chap. 55
Braxton	Sutton		Jan. 15, 1836	Chap. 18
Brooke	Wellsburg		Nov. 30, 1796	Chap. 58
Cabell	Huntington		Jan. 2, 1809	Chap. 45
Calhoun	Grantsville		Mar. 5, 1856	Chap. 108
Clay	Clay		Mar. 29, 1858	Chap. 158
Doddridge	West Union		Feb. 4, 1845	Chap. 42
Fayette	Fayetteville		Feb. 28, 1831	Chap. 70
Gilmer	Glenville		Feb. 3, 1845	Chap. 43
Grant	Petersburg		Feb. 14, 1866	Chap. 29
Greenbrier	Lewisburg		Oct. 20, 1777	Chap. 18
Hampshire	Romney	Sess.	Feb. 27, 1752	Chap. 14
Hancock	New Cumberland		Jan. 15, 1848	Chap. 58
Hardy	Moorefield	Sess.	Oct. 17, 1785	Chap. 35
Harrison	Clarksburg	Sess.	May 3, 1784	Chap. 6
Jackson	Ripley		Mar. 1, 1831	Chap. 73
Jefferson	Charles Town		Jan. 8, 1801	Chap. 31
Kanawha	Charleston		Nov. 14, 1788	Chap. 14
Lewis	Weston		Dec. 18, 1816	Chap. 85
Lincoln	Hamlin		Feb. 23, 1867	Chap. 61
Logan	Logan		Jan. 12, 1824	Unnumb.
Marion	Fairmont		Jan. 14, 1842	Chap. 59
Marshall	Moundsville		Mar. 12, 1835	Chap. 57
Mason	Point Pleasant		Jan. 2, 1804	Chap. 102
McDowell	Welch		Feb. 20, 1858	Chap. 155
Mercer	Princeton		Mar. 17, 1837	Chap. 53
Mineral	Keyser		Feb. 1, 1866	Chap. 7
Mingo	Williamson		Jan. 30, 1895	Chap. 68
Monongalia	Morgantown		Oct. 7, 1776	Unnumb.
Monroe	Union		Jan. 14, 1799	Chap. 41
Morgan	Berkeley Springs		Feb. 9, 1820	Chap. 34
Nicholas	Summersville		Jan. 30, 1818	Chap. 33
Ohio	Wheeling		Oct. 7, 1776	Unnumb.
Pendleton	Franklin		Dec. 4, 1787	Chap. 94
Pleasants	St. Marys		Mar. 29, 1851	Chap. 27
Pocahontas	Marlinton		Dec. 21, 1821	Chap. 27
Preston	Kingwood		Jan. 19, 1818	Chap. 32
Putnam	Winfield		Mar. 11, 1848	Chap. 59
Raleigh	Beckley		Jan. 23, 1850	Chap. 24
Randolph	Elkins	Sess.	Oct. 16, 1786	Chap. 101
Ritchie	Harrisville		Feb. 18, 1843	Chap. 52

County	County Seat	Created	Statute
Roane	Spencer	Mar. 11, 1856	Chap. 109
Summers	Hinton	Feb. 27, 1871	Chap. 134
Taylor	Grafton	Jan. 19, 1844	Chap. 44
Tucker	Parsons	Mar. 7, 1856	Chap. 110
Tyler	Middlebourne	Dec. 6, 1814	Chap. 40
Upshur	Buckhannon	Mar. 26, 1851	Chap. 26
Wayne	Wayne	Jan. 18, 1842	Chap. 60
Webster	Webster Springs	Jan. 10, 1860	Chap. 47
Wetzel	New Martinsville	Jan. 10, 1846	Chap. 65
Wirt	Elizabeth	Jan. 19, 1848	Chap. 60
Wood	Parkersburg	Dec. 21, 1798	Chap. 43
Wyoming	Pineville	Jan. 26, 1850	Chap. 25

WISCONSIN (71 counties) 30th state.
Organized as territory April 20, 1836, eff. July 3, 1836.
Admitted as state May 29, 1848.

County	County Seat	Created	Statute
Adams	Friendship	Mar. 11, 1848	Unnumb.
Ashland	Ashland	Mar. 27, 1860	Chap. 211
Barron* 1	Barron	Mar. 19, 1859	Chap. 191
Bayfield* 2	Washburn	Feb. 19, 1845	
Brown	Green Bay	Oct. 26, 1818	Procl.
Buffalo	Alma	July 6, 1853	Chap. 100
Burnett	Grantsburg	Mar. 31, 1856	Chap. 94
Calumet**	Chilton	Dec. 7, 1836	Chap. 28
Chippewa	Chippewa Falls	Feb. 3, 1845	Unnumb.
Clark	Neillsville	July 6, 1853	Chap. 100
Columbia	Portage	Feb. 3, 1846	Unnumb.
Crawford	Prairie du Chien	Oct. 26, 1818	Procl.
Dane	Madison	Dec. 7, 1836	Chap. 28
Dodge	Juneau	Dec. 7, 1836	Chap. 28
Door	Sturgeon Bay	Feb. 11, 1851	Chap. 56
Douglas	Superior	Feb. 9, 1854	Chap. 10
Dunn	Menomonie	Feb. 3, 1854	Chap. 7
Eau Clair	Fairchild	Oct. 6, 1856	Chap. 114
Florence	Florence	Mar. 18, 1882	Chap. 165
Fond du Lac	Fond du Lac	Dec. 7, 1836	Chap. 28
Forest	Crandon	Apr. 11, 1885	Chap. 436
Grant	Lancaster	Dec. 8, 1836	Chap. 31
Green	Monroe	Dec. 8, 1836	Chap. 31
Green Lake	Green Lake	Mar. 5, 1858	Chap. 17
Iowa	Dodgeville	Oct. 9, 1829	Unnumb.
Iron	Hurley	Mar. 1, 1893	Chap. 8
Jackson	Black River Falls	Feb. 11, 1853	Chap. 8
Jefferson	Jefferson	Dec. 7, 1836	Chap. 28

County	County Seat	Created	Statute
Juneau	Mauston	Oct. 13, 1856	Chap. 130
Kenosha	Kenosha	Jan. 30, 1850	Chap. 39
Kewaunee	Kewaunee	Apr. 16, 1852	Chap. 363
La Crosse	La Crosse	Mar. 1, 1851	Chap. 131
Lafayette	Darlington	Jan. 31, 1846	Unnumb.
Langlade* 3	Antigo	Feb. 27, 1879	Chap. 114
Lincoln	Merrill	Mar. 4, 1874	Chap. 128
Manitowoc	Manitowoc	Dec. 7, 1836	Chap. 28
Marathon	Wausau	Feb. 9, 1850	Chap. 226
Marinette	Marinette	Feb. 27, 1879	Chap. 114
Marquette	Montello	Dec. 7, 1836	Chap. 28
Milwaukee	Milwaukee	Sept. 6, 1834	Unnumb.
Monroe	Sparta	Mar. 21, 1854	Chap. 35
Oconto	Oconto	Feb. 6, 1851	Chap. 44
Oneida	Rhinelander	Apr. 11, 1885	Chap. 411
Outagamie	Appleton	Feb. 17, 1851	Chap. 83
Ozaukee	Port Washington	Mar. 7, 1853	Chap. 21
Pepin	Durand	Feb. 25, 1858	Chap. 15
Pierce	Ellsworth	Mar. 14, 1853	Chap. 31
Polk	Balsam Lake	Mar. 14, 1853	Chap. 31
Portage	Stevens Point	Dec. 7, 1836	Chap. 28
Price	Phillips	Feb. 26, 1879	Chap. 103
Racine	Racine	Dec. 7, 1836	Chap. 28
Richland	Richland Center	Feb. 18, 1842	Unnumb.
Rock	Janesville	Dec. 7, 1836	Chap. 28
Rusk* 4	Ladysmith	May 15, 1901	Chap. 469
St. Croix	Hudson	Jan. 9, 1840	Chap. 20
Sauk	Baraboo	Jan. 11, 1840	Chap. 23
Sawyer	Hayward	Mar. 10, 1883	Chap. 47
Shawano	Shawano	Feb. 16, 1853	Chap. 9
Sheboygan	Sheboygan	Dec. 7, 1836	Chap. 28
Taylor	Medford	Mar. 4, 1875	Chap. 178
Trempealeau	Whitehall	Jan. 27, 1854	Chap. 2
Vernon* 5	Viroqua	Mar. 1, 1851	Chap. 131
Vilas	Eagle River	Apr. 12, 1893	Chap. 150
Walworth	Elkhorn	Dec. 7, 1836	Chap. 28
Washburn	Shell Lake	Mar. 27, 1883	Chap. 172
Washington	West Bend	Dec. 7, 1836	Chap. 28
Waukesha	Waukesha	Jan. 31, 1846	Unnumb.
Waupaca	Waupaca	Feb. 17, 1851	Chap. 78
Waushara	Wautoma	Feb. 15, 1851	Chap. 77
Winnebago	Oshkosh	Jan. 6, 1840	Chap. 12
Wood	Wisconsin Rapids	Mar. 29, 1856	Chap. 54

1 Formerly Dallas County, changed to Barron County, Mar. 4, 1869, chap. 75.

2 Formerly La Pointe County, changed to Bayfield County, Apr. 12, 1866, chap. 146.
3 Formerly New County, changed to Langlade County, Feb. 19, 1880, chap. 19.
4 Formerly Gates County, changed to Rusk County, June 19, 1905, chap. 463.
5 Formerly Bad Axe County, changed to Vernon County, Mar. 22, 1862, chap. 137.
**(Calumet repealed Aug. 13, 1840, re-established Feb. 18, 1842, eff. Apr. 1, 1842)

WYOMING (23 counties) 44th state.
Organized as territory July 25, 1868.
Admitted as state July 10, 1890.

County	County Seat	Created	Statute
Albany	Laramie	Dec. 16, 1868	Chap. 28
Big Horn	Basin	Mar. 12, 1890	Chap. 48
Campbell	Gillette	Feb. 13, 1911	Chap. 14
Carbon	Rawlins	Dec. 16, 1868	Chap. 35
Converse	Douglas	Mar. 9, 1888	Chap. 90
Crook	Sundance	Dec. 8, 1875	Unnumb.
Fremont	Lander	Mar. 5, 1884	Chap. 46
Goshen	Torrington	Feb. 9, 1911	Chap. 10
Hot Springs	Thermopolis	Feb. 9, 1911	Chap. 9
Johnson* 1	Buffalo	Dec. 8, 1875	Unnumb.
Laramie	Cheyenne	Jan. 9, 1867	Chap. 14
Lincoln	Kemmerer	Feb. 20, 1911	Chap. 67
Natrona	Casper	Mar. 9, 1888	Chap. 90
Niobrara	Lusk	Feb. 14, 1911	Chap. 20
Park	Cody	Feb. 15, 1909	Chap. 19
Platte	Wheatland	Feb. 9, 1911	Chap. 7
Sheridan	Sheridan	Mar. 9, 1888	Chap. 90
Submette	Pinedale	Feb. 15, 1921	Chap. 52
Sweetwater* 2	Green River	Dec. 27, 1867	Chap. 7
Teton	Jackson	Feb. 15, 1921	Chap. 53
Uinta	Evanston	Dec. 1, 1869	Chap. 34
Washakie	Worland	Feb. 9, 1911	Chap. 8
Weston	Newcastle	Mar. 12, 1890	Chap. 47

1 Formerly Pease County, changed to Johnson County, Dec. 13, 1879, chap. 31.
2 Formerly Carter County, changed to Sweetwater County, Dec. 13, 1869, chap. 35.

Part IV

COUNTIES LISTED BY DATE

All dates are those of the English calendar of the date used.

There are no exact dates when much of the early legislation was passed. In most cases, the only date known is that of the session in which the law was enacted. The date given is the opening date of the session. Acts or chapters refer to the section of the laws published in annual reports. Former names of the counties are in parentheses.

Year	Date	County
1634		Charles City, Va.
		Henrico, Va.
		Isle of Wight, Va. (Warrosquyoake, Va.)
		James City, Va.
		Northampton, Va.
		York, Va.
1637		St. Mary's, Md.
1642		
	Dec. 16	Kent, Md.
1643		
	May 10	Essex, Mass.
		Middlesex, Mass.
		Suffolk, Mass.
1645		
	Mar. Sess.	Nansemond, Va. (Act 25) (Upper Norfolk, Va.)
1648		
	Oct. 12 Sess.	Northumberland, Va. (Act 1)
1650		
	Apr. 9 Sess.	Anne Arundel, Md. (Chap. 7)
1651		Gloucester, Va.
1652		Lancaster, Va.
		Surry, Va.
	Nov. 20	York, Me.
1653		
	July 5 Sess.	Westmoreland, Va.

1654		Calvert, Md.
	Nov. 20 Sess.	New Kent, Va.
	Mar. 20	Washington, R. I. (Narragansett, R. I.)
1658		Charles, Md.
1659		Baltimore, Md.
1661		
	Feb. 18	Talbot, Md.
1662		
	May 7	Hampshire, Mass.
1663		Accomack, Va.
1666		
	May 10 Sess.	Fairfield, Conn.
	May 10 Sess.	Hartford, Conn.
	May 10 Sess.	New Haven, Conn.
	May 10 Sess.	New London, Conn.
	Aug. 22 Procl.	Somerset, Md.
	June 5 Sess.	Stafford, Va.
1668		Dorchester, Md.
1670		Chowan, N. C.
		Currituck, N. C.
		Pasquotank, N. C.
		Perquimans, N. C.
1673		New Castle, Del.
1674		Cecil, Md.
	Sept. 21 Sess.	Middlesex, Va. (Act 1)
1682	Mar. 10	Bucks, Pa.
	Mar. 10	Chester, Pa.
		Kent, Del. (St. Jones, Del.)
	Mar. 10	Philadelphia, Pa.
		Sussex, Del. (Deale, Del.)
1683		
	Mar. 1	Bergen, N. J. (Unnumb.)
	Mar. 1	Essex, N. J. (Unnumb.)
	Mar. 1	Middlesex, N. J. (Unnumb.)
	Mar. 1	Monmouth, N. J. (Unnumb.)
	Nov. 1	Albany, N. Y. (Chap. 4)
	Nov. 1	Dutchess, N. Y. (Chap. 4)
	Nov. 1	Kings, N. Y. (Chap. 4)
	Nov. 1	New York, N. Y. (Chap. 4)
	Nov. 1	Orange, N. Y. (Chap. 4)
	Nov. 1	Queens, N. Y. (Chap. 4)
	Nov. 1	Richmond, N. Y. (Chap. 4)
	Nov. 1	Suffolk, N. Y. (Chap. 4)
	Nov. 1	Ulster, N. Y. (Chap. 4)
	Nov. 1	Westchester, N. Y. (Chap. 4)
1685		
	June 2	Barnstable, Mass.

1685	cont.	
	June 2	Bristol, Mass.
	June 2	Plymouth, Mass.
1686		
	May 28	Gloucester, N. J. (Unnumb.)
1688		
	May	Somerset, N. J. (Unnumb.)
1691		
	Apr. 16 Sess.	King and Queen, Va. (Act 19)
1692		
	Nov. 12	Cape May, N. J. (Unnumb.)
	Apr. 16, Sess.	Essex, Va. (Act 5)
	Apr. 16 Sess.	Richmond, Va. (Act 5)
1694	May 17	Burlington, N. J. (Unnumb.)
	May 17	Salem, N. J. (Unnumb.)
1695		
	May 20	Prince George's, Md.
	June 22	Dukes, Mass. (Chap. 7)
	June 22	Nantucket, Mass. (Chap. 7)
1700		
	Dec. 5 Sess.	King William, Va. (Chap. 4)
	Dec. 5 Sess.	Prince George, Va. (Chap. 2)
1703		
	June 22	Newport, R. I. (Rhode Island, R. I.)
	June 22	Providence, R. I. (Providence Plantations, R. I.)
1705		
	Dec. 3	Beaufort, N. C. (Pamptecough, N. C.)
	Dec. 3	Hyde, N. C. (Wickham, N. C.)
	Dec. 3	Craven, N. C. (Archdale, N. C.)
1706		
	Apr. 18	Queen Annes, Md. (Chap. 3)
1714		
	Mar. 13	Hunterdon, N. J. (Unnumb.)
1720		
	Nov. 2 Sess.	Brunswick, Va. (Chap. 1)
	Nov. 2 Sess.	Hanover, Va. (Chap. 15)
	Nov. 2 Sess.	King George, Va. (Chap. 14)
	Nov. 2 Sess.	Spotsylvania, Va. (Chap. 1)
1722		
	Oct. 2 Sess.	Bertie, N. C. (Chap. 5)
		Carteret, N. C.
1726		
	May 12 Sess.	Windham, Conn.
1727		
	Feb. 1 Sess.	Caroline, Va. (Chap. 17)

1727 cont.		
	Feb. 1 Sess.	Goochland, Va. (Chap. 18)
	Oct. 14 Sess.	Lancaster, Pa. (Chap. 299)
	Feb. 1 Sess.	Prince William, Va. (Chap. 17)
1729		
	July	New Hanover, N. C. (Chap. 10)
	Nov. 27	Tyrrell, N. C. (Chap. 4)
	June 3	Washington, R. I.
1731		
	Apr. 5	Worcester, Mass. (Chap. 13)
1734		
	Feb. 1 Sess.	Amelia, Va. (Chap. 31)
		Bladen, N. C. (Chap. 8)
		Onslow, N. C. (Chap. 8)
	Feb. 1 Sess.	Orange, Va. (Chap. 24)
1735		Edgecombe (Province) N. C.
1738		
	Aug. 1 Sess.	Augusta, Va. (Chap. 21)
	Aug. 1 Sess.	Frederick, Va. (Chap. 21)
1739		
	Mar. 15	Morris, N. J. (Chap. 63)
1741		Northampton, N. C. (Chap. 1)
1742		
	May 6 Sess.	Fairfax, Va. (Chap. 27)
	May 6 Sess.	Louisa, Va. (Chap. 28)
	Oct. 29	Worcester, Md. (Chap. 19)
1744		
	May 6 Sess.	Albemarle, Va. (Chap. 31)
1745		
	May 6 Sess.	Lunenburg, Va. (Chap. 22)
1746		
	June 28 Sess.	Granville, N. C. (Chap. 3)
	June 28 Sess.	Johnston, N. C. (Chap. 2)
1747		
	Feb. 17	Bristol, R. I.
1748		
	Jan. 19	Cumberland, N. J. (Chap. 92)
	Mar. 23	Culpeper, Va.
	June 10	Frederick, Md. (Chap. 15)
	Oct. 14 Sess.	York, Pa. (Unnumb.)
1749		
	Mar. 17 Sess.	Anson, N. C. (Chap. 2)
	Apr. 30	Southampton, Va.
	May 1	Chesterfield, Va.
	Mar. 17 Sess.	Duplin, N. C. (Chap. 1)
1750		
	Jan. 27	Cumberland, Pa.
	June 11	Kent, R. I.

1751		
	Oct. 14 Sess.	Berks, Pa. (Unnumb.)
	Oct. 14 Sess.	Litchfield, Conn.
	Oct. 14 Sess.	Northampton, Pa.
1752		
	Feb. 27 Sess.	Bedford, Va. (Chap. 16)
	Feb. 27 Sess.	Dinwiddie, Va. (Chap. 19)
	Feb. 27 Sess.	Halifax, Va. (Chap. 18)
	Feb. 27 Sess.	Hampshire, W. Va. (Chap. 14)
	Mar. 31 Sess.	Orange, N. C. (Chap. 6)
	Feb. 27 Sess.	Prince Edward, Va. (Chap. 15)
	Feb. 27 Sess.	Sussex, Va. (Chap. 17)
1753		
	Mar. 27 Sess.	Rowan, N. C. (Chap. 7)
	May 16 Sess.	Sussex, N. J. (Unnumb.)
1754		
	Feb. 19 Sess.	Cumberland, N. C. (Chap. 8)
1757		
	Mar. 25 Sess.	Loudoun, Va. (Chap. 22)
1758		
	Sept. 14 Sess.	Fauquier, Va. (Chap. 27)
	Dec. 12 7th Sess.	1754. Halifax, N. C. (Chap. 13)
1759		
	Dec. 12 9th Sess.	1754. Hertford, N. C. (Chap. 4)
1760		
	May 28 Sess.	1760 Berkshire, Mass. (Chap. 4)
	May 28	Cumberland, Me. sess. (Chap. 2)
	May 28	Lincoln, Me. sess. (Chap. 2)
	Apr. 24 4th Sess.	1760. Pitt, N. C. (Chap. 3)
1761		
	Sept. 14 7th Sess.	1758 Amherst, Va. (Chap. 20)
	Sept. 14 7th Sess.	1758 Buckingham, Va. (Chap. 20)
1762		
	Nov. 3 Sess.	Mecklenburg, N. C. (Chap. 12)
1764		
	May 26 Sess.	Brunswick, N. C. (Chap. 14)
	Jan. 30 Sess.	Charlotte, Va. (Chap. 4)
	May 26 Sess.	Mecklenburg, Va. (Chap. 4)
1766		
	Nov. 6	Pittsylvania, Va. (Chap. 16)
1768		
	Jan. 29 (Ordnance)	Oconee, S. C.
1769		
	Nov. 7 Sess.	Botetourt, Va. (Chap. 40)
	Apr. 29	Cheshire, N. H. *
	Apr. 29	Grafton, N. H. *
	Apr. 29	Hillsborough, N. H. *
	Apr. 29	Rockingham, N. H. *

(*)not confirmed by the king until Mar. 19, 1771.

1769 cont.

Apr. 29	Strafford, N. H. *

(*)not confirmed by the king until Mar. 19, 1771.

1770

Dec. 5 Sess.	Chatham, N. C. (Chap. 27)
Dec. 5 Sess.	Guilford, N. C. (Chap. 24)
Dec. 5 Sess.	Surry, N. C. (Chap. 42)
Dec. 5 Sess.	Wake, N. C. (Chap. 22)

1771

Mar. 9	Bedford, Pa. (Unnumb.)

1772

Feb. 10 Sess.	Berkeley, W. Va. (Chap. 43)
Mar. 12	Montgomery, N. Y. (Chap. 613) (Tryon, N. Y.)
Mar. 21	Northumberland, Pa. (Unnumb.)
Mar. 24	Shenandoah, Va. (Chap. 43) (Dunmore, Va.)
Mar. 12	Washington, N. Y. (Chap. 613) (Charlotte, N. Y.)

1773

Nov. 16 Sess.	Caroline, Md. (Chap. 10)
Feb. 26	Westmoreland, Pa. (Chap. 8)

1774

Mar. 2	Martin, N. C. (Chap. 32)
Mar. 2	Harford, Md. (Chap. 6)

1776

Oct. 7 Sess.	Henry, Va. (Chap. 38)
Oct. 7 Sess.	Monongalia, W. Va. (Unnumb.)
Sept. 6 (Res. of Convention)	Montgomery, Md.
Oct. 7 Sess.	Montgomery, Va. (Chap. 44)
Oct. 7 Sess.	Ohio, W. Va. (Unnumb.)
Sept. 6 (Res. of Convention)	Washington, Md.
Oct. 7 Sess.	Washington, Va. (Chap. 44)

1777

Feb. 5	Burke, Ga. (Const.)
Apr. 8	Burke, N. C. (Chap. 19)
Feb. 5	Camden, Ga. (Const.)
Apr. 8	Camden, N. C. (Chap. 18)
Apr. 8	Caswell, N. C. (Chap. 17)
Feb. 5	Chatham, Ga. (Const.)
Feb. 5	Effingham, Ga. (Const.)
May 5 Sess.	Fluvanna, Va. (Chap. 25)
Feb. 5	Glynn, Ga. (Const.)
Oct. 20 Sess.	Greenbrier, W. Va. (Unnumb.)
Feb. 5	Liberty, Ga. (Const.)
Nov. 15	Nash, N. C. (Chap. 30)

1777 cont.

May 5 Sess.	Powhatan, Va. (Chap. 24)
Feb. 5	Richmond, Ga. (Const.)
Oct. 20 Sess.	Rockbridge, Va. (Chap. 18)
Oct. 20 Sess.	Rockingham, Va. (Chap. 18)
Nov. 15 Sess.	Washington, Tenn. (Chap. 31)
Feb. 5	Wilkes, Ga. (Const.)
Nov. 15 Sess.	Wilkes, N. C. (Chap. 32)

1778

Apr. 14 3rd Sess.	Franklin, N. C. (Chap. 19)
Apr. 14 3rd Sess.	Gates, N. C. (Chap. 20)
Apr. 14 3rd Sess.	Jones, N. C. (Chap. 18)
Apr. 14 3rd Sess.	Lincoln, N. C. (Chap. 23)
Apr. 14 3rd Sess.	Montgomery, N. C. (Chap. 21)
Apr. 14 Sess.	Randolph, N. C. (Chap. 22)

1779

Feb. 11 Sess.	Bennington, Vt. (Unnumb.)
Oct. 18 2nd Sess.	Richmond, N. C. (Chap. 16)
Apr. 14 3rd Sess.	Rutherford, N. C. (Chap. 23)
Oct. Sess.	Sullivan, Tenn. (Chap. 29)
Apr. 14 3rd Sess.	Warren, N. C. (Chap. 19)
Oct. 18 2nd Sess.	Wayne, N. C. (Chap. 17)

1780

Oct. 16 Sess.	Campbell, Va. (Chap. 7)
May 1 Sess.	Jefferson, Ky. (Unnumb.)
Oct. 16 Sess.	Greensville, Va. (Unnumb.)
May 1 Sess.	Jefferson, Ky. (Unnumb.)
May 1 Sess.	Lincoln, Ky. (Unnumb.)

1781

Feb. 22	Orange, Vt. (Unnumb.)
Feb. 22	Rutland, Vt. (Unnumb.)
Mar. 28	Washington, Pa. (Chap. 189)
Feb. 22	Windham, Vt. (Unnumb.)
Feb. 22	Windsor, Vt. (Unnumb.)

1783

Apr. 18 Sess.	Davidson, Tenn. (Chap. 52)
Sept. 26	Fayette, Pa. (Chap. 155)
Apr. 18 Sess.	Greene, Tenn. (Chap. 51)

1784

Feb. 25	Franklin, Ga. (Unnumb.)
Sept. 9	Franklin, Pa. (Chap. 153)
May 3 Sess.	Harrison, W. Va. (Chap. 6)
Sept. 10	Montgomery, Pa. (Chap. 154)
Apr. 18 Sess.	Moore, N. C. (Chap. 76)
Oct. 18 Sess.	Nelson, Ky. (Chap. 62)
Apr. 18 Sess.	Sampson, N. C. (Chap. 75)
Feb. 25	Washington, Ga. (Unnumb.)

1785		
	Mar. 12	Abbeville, S. C. (Unnumb.)
	Oct. 18	Addison, Vt. (Unnumb.)
	Mar. 12	Beaufort, S. C. (Unnumb.)
	Oct. 17 Sess.	Bourbon, Ky. (Chap. 37)
	Mar. 12	Charleston, S. C. (Unnumb.)
	Mar. 12	Chester, S. C. (Unnumb.)
	Mar. 12	Chesterfield, S. C. (Unnumb.)
	Mar. 12	Clarendon, S. C. (Unnumb.)
	Mar. 12	Colleton, S. C. (Unnumb.)
	Mar. 12	Darlington, S. C. (Unnumb.)
	Mar. 4	Dauphin, Pa. (Chap. 182)
	Mar. 12	Edgefield, S. C. (Unnumb.)
	Mar. 12	Fairfield, S. C. (Unnumb.)
	Oct. 17 Sess.	Franklin, Va. (Chap. 25)
	Oct. 17 Sess.	Hardy, W. Va. (Chap. 35)
	Mar. 12	Lancaster, S. C. (Unnumb.)
	Mar. 12	Laurens, S. C. (Unnumb.)
	Mar. 12	Lexington, S. C. (Unnumb.)
	Oct. 17 Sess.	Madison, Ky. (Chap. 54)
	Mar. 12	Marion, S. C. (Unnumb.)
	Mar. 12	Marlboro, S. C. (Unnumb.)
	Oct. 17 Sess.	Mercer, Ky. (Chap. 44)
	May 2 Sess.	Middlesex, Conn. (Unnumb.)
	Mar. 12	Newberry, S. C. (Unnumb.)
	Mar. 12	Orangeburg, S. C. (Unnumb.)
	Mar. 12	Richland, S. C. (Unnumb.)
	Nov. 19 Sess.	Rockingham, N. C. (Chap. 23)
	Oct. 17 Sess.	Russell, Va. (Chap. 46)
	Mar. 12	Spartanburg, S. C. (Unnumb.) Sumter, S. C.
	Oct. 13 Sess.	Tolland, Conn. (Unnumb.)
	Mar. 12	Union, S. C. (Unnumb.)
	Mar. 12	Williamsburg, S. C. (Unnumb.)
	Mar. 12	York, S. C. (Unnumb.)
1786		
	Apr. 4	Columbia, N. Y. (Chap. 28)
	Feb. 3	Greene, Ga. (Unnumb.)
	Mar. 22	Greenville, S. C. (Unnumb.)
	Nov. 18 Sess.	Hawkins, Tenn. (Chap. 34)
	Sept. 25	Luzerne, Pa. (Chap. 291)
	Oct. 16 Sess.	Randolph, W. Va. (Chap. 101)
	Nov. 18 Sess.	Robeson, N. C. (Chap. 40)
	Nov. 18 Sess.	Sumner, Tenn. (Chap. 32)
1787		
	Oct. 22	Chittenden, Vt. (Unnumb.)
	Sept. 20	Huntingdon, Pa. (Chap. 359)
	Dec. 4	Pendleton, W. Va. (Chap. 94)

Year	Date	County
1788		
	Sept. 24	Allegheny, Pa. (Chap. 408)
	Mar. 7	Clinton, N. Y. (Chap. 63)
	Nov. 3 Sess.	Iredell, N. C. (Chap. 36)
	Nov. 14	Kanawha, W. Va. (Chap. 14)
	Nov. 5	Mason, Ky. (Chap. 4)
	Dec. 22	Nottoway, Va. (Chap. 64)
	July 27	Washington, Ohio (Procl.)
	Nov. 12	Woodford, Ky. (Chap. 10)
1789		
	Dec. 25	Allegany, Md. (Chap. 29)
	Sept. 26	Delaware, Pa. (Chap. 492)
	June 25	Hancock, Me. (Chap. 25)
	Sept. 19	Mifflin, Pa. (Chap. 485)
	Jan. 27	Ontario, N. Y. (Chap. 11)
	Nov. 2 Sess.	Stokes, N. C. (Chap. 14)
	June 25	Washington, Me. (Chap. 25)
	Dec. 1	Wythe, Va. (Chap. 56)
1790		
	Dec. 14	Bath, Va. (Chap. 43)
	Dec. 10	Columbia, Ga. (Unnumb.)
	Dec. 10	Elbert, Ga. (Unnumb.)
	Jan. 2	Hamilton, Ohio (Procl.)
	June 20	Knox, Ind. (Procl.)
	Dec. 16	Mathews, Va. (Chap. 41)
	Nov. 26	Patrick, Va. (Chap. 40)
	Apr. 27	St. Clair, Ill. (Procl.)
1791		
	Dec. 5 Sess.	Buncombe, N. C. (Chap. 52)
	Feb. 16	Herkimer, N. Y. (Chap. 10)
	Dec. 5 Sess.	Lenoir, N. C. (Chap. 47)
	Feb. 16	Otsego, N. Y. (Chap. 10)
	Dec. 5 Sess.	Person, N. C. (Chap. 53)
	Feb. 7	Rensselaer, N. Y. (Chap. 4)
	Feb. 7	Saratoga, N. Y. (Chap. 4)
	Feb. 16	Tioga, N. Y. (Chap. 10)
1792		
	Nov. 15 Sess.	Cabarrus, N. C. (Chap. 21)
	Nov. 5	Caledonia, Vt. (Unnumb.)
	Dec. 6	Clark, Ky. (Chap. 16)
	Nov. 5	Essex, Vt. (Unnumb.)
	Nov. 5	Franklin, Vt. (Unnumb.)
	Nov. 7	Grayson, Va. (Chap. 51)
	Dec. 20	Green, Ky. (Chap. 44)
	Dec. 15	Hardin, Ky. (Chap. 17)
	June 11	Jefferson, Tenn. (Unnumb.)
	June 11	Knox, Tenn. (Unnumb.)
	Oct. 25	Lee, Va. (Chap. 49)

1792 cont.	
June 28	Logan, Ky. (Chap. 12)
Dec. 4	Madison, Va. (Chap. 50)
Nov. 5	Orleans, Vt. (Unnumb.)
June 22	Scott, Ky. (Chap. 3)
June 23	Shelby, Ky. (Chap. 9)
June 22	Washington, Ky. (Chap. 2)
1793	
Dec. 19	Bryan, Ga. (Unnumb.)
Dec. 17	Hancock, Ga. (Unnumb.)
Dec. 21	Harrison, Ky. (Chap. 24)
Dec. 19	McIntosh, Ga. (Unnumb.)
Dec. 19	Montgomery, Ga. (Unnumb.)
Mar. 26	Norfolk, Mass. (Chap. 43)
Dec. 19	Oglethorpe, Ga. (Unnumb.)
Dec. 14	Screven, Ga. (Unnumb.)
Dec. 19	Warren, Ga. (Unnumb.)
1794	
Dec. 17	Campbell, Ky. (Chap. 19)
Dec. 7	Franklin, Ky. (Chap. 13)
Mar. 5	Onondaga, N. Y. (Chap. 18)
Sept. 27	Sevier, Tenn. (Chap. 11)
1795	
July 11	Blount, Tenn. (Chap. 6)
Apr. 13	Lycoming, Pa. (Chap. 314)
Oct. 5	Randolph, Ill. (Procl.)
Apr. 6	Schoharie, N. Y. (Chap. 42)
Apr. 17	Somerset, Pa. (Chap. 331)
1796	
Dec. 14	Bracken, Ky. (Unnumb.)
Nov. 30	Brooke, W. Va. (Chap. 58)
Dec. 13	Bullitt, Ky. (Unnumb.)
Feb. 8	Bulloch, Ga. (Unnumb.)
Apr. 9	Carter, Tenn. (Chap. 31)
Dec. 13	Christian, Ky. (Unnumb.)
Dec. 17	Garrard, Ky. (Unnumb.)
Apr. 22	Grainger, Tenn. (Chap. 28)
Feb. 9	Greene, Pa. (Chap. 4)
Feb. 11	Jackson, Ga. (Unnumb.)
Feb. 20	Jefferson, Ga. (Unnumb.)
Feb. 20	Lincoln, Ga. (Unnumb.)
Dec. 14	Montgomery, Ky. (Unnumb.)
Apr. 9	Montgomery, Tenn. (Chap. 30)
Apr. 9	Robertson, Tenn. (Chap. 30)
Mar. 18	Steuben, N. Y. (Chap. 29)
Dec. 14	Warren, Ky. (Unnumb.)
Aug. 15	Wayne, Ohio (Procl.)

Date	County
1797	
July 10	Adams, Ohio (Procl.)
Oct. 9	Cocke, Tenn. (Chap. 8)
Mar. 10	Delaware, N. Y. (Chap. 33)
July 27	Jefferson, Ohio (Procl.)
Oct. 9	Union, Tenn. (Chap. 8)
	(Cocke, Tenn.)
1798	Barnwell, S. C.
Dec. 20	Barren, Ky. (Chap. 43)
Dec. 13	Boone, Ky. (Chap. 4)
Mar. 15	Chenango, N. Y. (Chap. 31)
Dec. 14	Cumberland, Ky. (Chap. 54)
Feb. 10	Fleming, Ky. (Chap. 32)
Dec. 14	Gallatin, Ky. (Chap. 58)
	Georgetown, S. C.
Dec. 21	Henderson, Ky. (Chap. 57)
Dec. 14	Henry, Ky. (Chap. 49)
Dec. 19	Jessamine, Ky. (Chap. 62)
	Kershaw, S. C.
Dec. 13	Livingston, Ky. (Chap. 61)
Dec. 14	Muhlenberg, Ky. (Chap. 65)
Dec. 17	Ohio, Ky. (Chap. 73)
Mar. 15	Oneida, N. Y. (Chap. 31)
Dec. 13	Pendleton, Ky. (Chap. 47)
Dec. 10	Pulaski, Ky. (Chap. 1)
Feb. 23	Rockland, N. Y. (Chap. 16)
Aug. 20	Ross, Ohio (Procl.)
Mar. 21	Wayne, Pa. (Chap. 120)
Dec. 21	Wood, W. Va. (Chap. 43)
1799	
Apr. 2	Adams, Miss. (Procl.)
Nov. 18 Sess.	Ashe, N. C. (Chap. 36)
Dec. 9	Breckinridge, Ky. (Chap. 72)
Mar. 8	Cayuga, N. Y. (Chap. 26)
Mar. 1	Essex, N. Y. (Chap. 24)
Dec. 13	Floyd, Ky. (Chap. 73)
Nov. 18 Sess.	Greene, N. C. (Chap. 39)
Apr. 2	Jefferson, Miss. (Procl.)
	(Pickering)
Feb. 20	Kennebec, Me. (Chap. 23)
Dec. 19	Knox, Ky. (Chap. 74)
Jan. 14	Monroe, W. Va. (Chap. 41)
Dec. 18	Nicholas, Ky. (Chap. 11)
Oct. 26	Smith, Tenn. (Chap. 2)
Dec. 17 Sess.	Tazewell, Va. (Chap. 27)
Nov. 15 Sess.	Washington, N. C. (Chap. 31)
Oct. 26	Williamson, Tenn. (Chap. 2)
Oct. 26	Wilson, Tenn. (Chap. 2)

1800		
	Jan. 22	Adams, Pa. (Chap. 231)
	Mar. 12	Armstrong, Pa. (Chap. 264)
	Mar. 12	Beaver, Pa. (Chap. 264)
	Mar. 12	Butler, Pa. (Chap. 264)
	Feb. 13	Centre, Pa. (Chap. 237)
	Dec. 6	Clermont, Ohio (Procl.)
	Mar. 12	Crawford, Pa. (Chap. 264)
	Mar. 12	Erie, Pa. (Chap. 264)
	Dec. 9	Fairfield, Ohio (Procl.)
	Mar. 25	Greene, N. Y. (Chap. 59)
	Mar. 12	Mercer, Pa. (Chap. 264)
	July 10	Trumbull, Ohio (Procl.)
	Mar. 12	Venango, Pa. (Chap. 264)
	Mar. 12	Warren, Pa. (Chap. 264)
	June 4	Washington, Ala. (Procl.)
	Dec. 18	Wayne, Ky. (Chap. 46)
1801		
	Dec. 11	Adair, Ky. (Chap. 43)
	Nov. 6	Anderson, Tenn. (Chap. 45)
	Sept. 7	Belmont, Ohio (Procl.)
	Oct. 29	Claiborne, Tenn. (Chap. 46)
	Feb. 3	Clark, Ind. (Procl.)
	Dec. 5	Clarke, Ga. (Unnumb.)
	Dec. 19	Horry, S. C. (Unnumb.)
	Nov. 6	Jackson, Tenn. (Chap. 48)
	Jan. 8	Jefferson, W. Va. (Chap. 31)
	Nov. 6	Roane, Tenn. (Chap. 45)
	Dec. 5	Tattnall, Ga. (Unnumb.)
1802		
	Jan. 27	Claiborne, Miss. (Unnumb.)
	Mar. 30	Genesee, N. Y. (Chap. 64)
	Nov. 9	Grand Isle, Vt. (Chap. 84)
	Mar. 3	St. Lawrence, N. Y. (Chap. 16)
	Jan. 30	Wilkinson, Miss. (Unnumb.)
1803		
	May 11	Baldwin, Ga. (Unnumb.)
	Mar. 24	Butler, Ohio (Chap. 4)
	Mar. 25	Columbiana, Ohio (Chap. 6)
	Dec. 24	Coos, N. H. (Unnumb.)
	Mar. 7	Dearborn, Ind. (Procl.)
	Oct. 25	Dickson, Tenn. (Chap. 66)
	Mar. 30	Franklin, Ohio (Chap. 11)
	Mar. 25	Gallia, Ohio (Chap. 8)
	Mar. 24	Greene, Ohio (Chap. 4)
	Dec. 12	Greenup, Ky. (Chap. 76)
	Mar. 30	Indiana, Pa. (Act 161)
	Mar. 24	Montgomery, Ohio (Chap. 4)

1803 cont.		
	Oct. 25	Rutherford, Tenn. (Chap. 70)
	Mar. 24	Scioto, Ohio (Chap. 3)
	Nov. 1	Stewart, Tenn. (Chap. 68)
	Mar. 24	Warren, Ohio (Chap. 4)
	May 11	Wayne, Ga. (Unnumb.)
	May 11	Wilkinson, Ga. (Unnumb.)
1804		
	Mar. 26	Cambria, Pa. (Act 78)
	Mar. 26	Clearfield, Pa. (Act 78)
	Mar. 26	Jefferson, Pa. (Act 78)
	Jan. 2	Mason, W. Va. (Chap. 102)
	Mar. 26	McKean, Pa. (Act 78)
	Jan. 7	Muskingum, Ohio (Chap. 22)
	Mar. 26	Potter, Pa. (Act 78)
	Mar. 24	Seneca, N. Y. (Chap. 331)
	Mar. 26	Tioga, Pa. (Act 78)
1805		
	Apr. 10	Acadia, La. (Chap. 25)
	Feb. 20	Athens, Ohio (Chap. 68)
	Feb. 20	Champaign, Ohio (Chap. 69)
	Apr. 10	Concordia, La. (Chap. 25)
	Dec. 31	Geauga, Ohio (Unnumb.)
	Feb. 18	Highland, Ohio (Chap. 60)
	Apr. 10	Iberville, La. (Chap. 25)
	Mar. 28	Jefferson, N. Y. (Chap. 51)
	Apr. 10	Lafourche, La. (Chap. 25)
	Mar. 28	Lewis, N. Y. (Chap. 51)
	Apr. 10	Natchitochas, La. (Chap. 25)
	Apr. 10	Orleans, La. (Chap. 25)
	Mar. 4	Oxford, Me. (Chap. 24)
	Apr. 10	Pointe Coupee, La. (Chap. 25)
	Apr. 10	Ouachita, La. (Chap. 25)
1806		
	Apr. 7	Allegany, N. Y. (Chap. 162)
	Mar. 28	Broome, N. Y. (Chap. 89)
	Sept. 11	Campbell, Tenn. (Chap. 21)
	Nov. 14	Casey, Ky. (Unnumb.)
	Dec. 2	Clay, Ky. (Unnumb.)
	Jan. 16	Giles, Va. (Chap. 53)
	Dec. 9	Hopkins, Ky. (Unnumb.)
	Dec. 3	Lewis, Ky. (Unnumb.)
	Mar. 21	Madison, N. Y. (Chap. 70)
	Sept. 11	Overton, Tenn. (Chap. 27)
	Sept. 11	White, Tenn. (Chap. 36)
1807		
	Mar. 31	Ascension, La. (Chap. 1)
	Feb. 10	Ashtabula, Ohio (Chap. 1)

1807 cont.

Mar. 31	Assumption, La. (Chap. 1)
Mar. 31	Avoyelles, La. (Chap. 1)
Dec. 3	Bedford, Tenn. (Chap. 37)
Nov. 30	Bledsoe, Tenn. (Chap. 9)
Feb. 10	Cuyahoga, Ohio (Chap. 1)
Dec. 3	Franklin, Tenn. (Chap. 72)
Dec. 3	Hickman, Tenn. (Chap. 44)
Dec. 10	Jasper, Ga. (Unnumb.) (Randolph, Ga.)
Dec. 10	Jones, Ga. (Unnumb.)
Dec. 10	Laurens, Ga. (Unnumb.)
Nov. 16	Maury, Tenn. (Chap. 94)
Jan. 16	Miami, Ohio (Chap. 32)
Dec. 10	Morgan, Ga. (Unnumb.)
Dec. 25	Nelson, Va. (Chap. 26)
Mar. 31	Plaquemines, La. (Chap. 1)
Feb. 10	Portage, Ohio (Chap. 1)
Dec. 10	Putnam, Ga. (Unnumb.)
Mar. 31	Rapides, La. (Chap. 1)
Nov. 30	Rhea, Tenn. (Chap. 9)
Mar. 31	St. Bernard, La. (Chap. 1)
Mar. 31	St. Charles, La. (Chap. 1)
Mar. 31	St. James, La. (Chap. 1)
Mar. 31	St. John the Baptist, La. (Chap. 1)
Mar. 31	St. Landry, La. (Chap. 1)
Mar. 31	St. Martin, La. (Chap. 1)
Dec. 10	Telfair, Ga. (Unnumb.)
Nov. 26	Warren, Tenn. (Chap. 28)
Mar. 31	West Baton Rouge, La. (Chap. 1)

1808

Mar. 23	Catahoula, La. (Chap. 9)
Mar. 11	Cattaragus, N. Y. (Chap. 60)
Mar. 11	Chautauqua, N. Y. (Chap. 60)
Dec. 15	Columbus, N. C. (Chap. 1)
Apr. 8	Cortland, N. Y. (Chap. 194)
Feb. 10	Delaware, Ohio (Chap. 10)
Jan. 27	Estill, Ky. (Chap. 38)
Mar. 11	Franklin, N. Y. (Chap. 43)
Oct. 11	Harrison, Ind. (Chap. 1)
Dec. 15	Haywood, N. C. (Chap. 1)
Jan. 30	Knox, Ohio (Chap. 8)
Jan. 30	Licking, Ohio (Chap. 8)
Dec. 13	Madison, Ala. (Procl.)
Mar. 11	Niagara, N. Y. (Chap. 60)
Feb. 15	Preble, Ohio (Chap. 51)
Dec. 13	Pulaski, Ga. (Unnumb.)
Jan. 30	Richland, Ohio (Chap. 8)

Year	Date	County
1808 cont.		
	Feb. 13	Stark, Ohio (Chap. 46)
	Feb. 13	Tuscarawas, Ohio (Chap. 50)
1809		
	Feb. 24	Amite, Miss. (Unnumb.)
	Dec. 21	Baldwin, Ala. (Unnumb.)
	Jan. 2	Cabell, W. Va. (Chap. 45)
	Jan. 31	Caldwell, Ky. (Chap. 33)
	Jan. 3	Darke, Ohio (Chap. 6)
	Dec. 21	Franklin, Miss. (Unnumb.)
	Nov. 14	Giles, Tenn. (Chap. 55)
	Oct. 19	Humphreys, Tenn. (Chap. 31)
	Feb. 7	Huron, Ohio (Chap. 48)
	Nov. 14	Lincoln, Tenn. (Chap. 48)
	Mar. 7	Schenectady, N. Y. (Chap. 65)
	Mar. 1	Somerset, Me. (Chap. 62)
	Mar. 27	Sullivan, N. Y. (Chap. 126)
	Dec. 14	Twiggs, Ga. (Unnumb.)
	Dec. 22	Warren, Miss. (Unnumb.)
	Dec. 21	Wayne, Miss. (Unnumb.)
1810		
	Feb. 21	Bradford, Pa. (Chap. 30) (Ontario, Pa.)
	Jan. 18	Butler, Ky. (Chap. 119)
	Feb. 19	Clinton, Ohio (Chap. 63)
	Jan. 31	Coshocton, Ohio (Chap. 26)
	Dec. 22	East Baton Rouge, La. (Dates vary)
	Feb. 19	Fayette, Ohio (Chap. 39)
	Nov. 27	Franklin, Ind. (Chap. 6)
	Jan. 25	Grayson, Ky. (Chap. 133)
	Jan. 31	Guernsey, Ohio (Chap. 20)
	Nov. 23	Jefferson, Ind. (Chap. 2)
	Feb. 16	Madison, Ohio (Chap. 67)
	Jan. 12	Pickaway, Ohio (Chap. 13)
	Jan. 8	Rockcastle, Ky. (Chap. 102)
	Oct. 27	St. Helena, La. (Dates vary)
	Oct. 27	St. Tammany, La. (Dates vary)
	Feb. 21	Susquehana, Pa. (Chap. 30)
	Nov. 1	Washington, Vt. (Chap. 74) (Jefferson, Vt.)
	Nov. 27	Wayne, Ind. (Chap. 6)
1811		
	Jan. 15	Bath, Ky. (Chap. 221)
	Dec. 2	Franklin, Mass. (Chap. 61)
	Dec. 9	Greene, Miss. (Unnumb.)
	Dec. 5	Madison, Ga. (Unnumb.)
	Dec. 9	Marion, Miss. (Unnumb.)
	Apr. 17	St. Mary, La. (Chap. 24)

1811 cont.		
	Mar. 1	Schuylkill, Pa. (Act 54)
	Jan. 15	Union, Ky. (Chap. 220)
1812		
	Oct. 1	Cape Girardeau, Mo. (Procl.)
	Dec. 10	Clarke, Ala. (Unnumb.)
	Dec. 10	Clarke, Miss. (Unnumb.)
	Dec. 10	Emanuel, Ga. (Unnumb.)
	Sept. 14	Gallatin, Ill. (Procl.)
	Feb. 25	Hampden, Mass. (Chap. 137)
	Dec. 18	Hancock, Miss. (Unnumb.)
	Dec. 18	Jackson, Miss. (Unnumb.)
	Sept. 14	Johnson, Ill. (Procl.)
	Mar. 6	Lehigh, Pa. (Act 49)
	Sept. 14	Madison, Ill. (Procl.)
	Feb. 18	Medina, Ohio (Chap. 46)
	Aug. 1	Mobile, Ala. (Procl.)
	Oct. 1	New Madrid, Mo. (Procl.)
	June 12	Putnam, N. Y. (Chap. 143)
	Oct. 1	St. Charles, Mo. (Procl.)
	Oct. 1	Ste. Genevieve, Mo. (Procl.)
	Oct. 1	St. Louis, Mo. (Procl.)
1813		
	Dec. 31	Arkansas, Ark. (Unnumb.)
	Mar. 22	Columbia, Pa. (Act 109)
	Mar. 9	Gibson, Ind. (Chap. 23)
	Jan. 2	Harrison, Ohio (Chap. 5)
	Feb. 16	Lebanon, Pa. (Act 52)
	Jan. 29	Monroe, Ohio (Chap. 25)
	Mar. 22	Union, Pa. (Act 110)
	Mar. 12	Warren, N. Y. (Chap. 50)
	Mar. 9	Warrick, Ind. (Chap. 23)
	Dec. 21	Washington, Ind. (Chap. 10)
	Aug. 21	Washington, Mo. (Unnumb.)
1814		
	Nov. 28	Edwards, Ill. (Unnumb.)
	Dec. 22	Lawrence, Miss. (Unnumb.)
	Sept. 7	Perry, Ind. (Chap. 7)
	Mar. 26	Pike, Pa. (Act 109)
	Sept. 7	Posey, Ind. (Chap. 7)
	Nov. 24	Scott, Va. (Chap. 38)
	Sept. 7	Switzerland, Ind. (Chap. 9)
	Dec. 6	Tyler, W. Va. (Chap. 40)
1815		
	Jan. 11	Allen, Ky. (Chap. 188)
	Jan. 14	Daviess, Ky. (Chap. 190)
	Dec. 18	Jackson, Ind. (Chap. 1)
	Jan. 15	Lawrence, Ark. (Unnumb.)

1815 cont.

Dec. 21	Lawrence, Ohio (Chap. 8)
June 29	Monroe, Ala. (Procl.)
Dec. 26	Orange, Ind. (Chap. 12)
Dec. 9	Pike, Miss. (Unnumb.)
Jan. 4	Pike, Ohio (Chap. 16)
Nov. 21	Wayne, Mich. (Procl.)
Dec. 9	White, Ill. (Unnumb.)

1816

Dec. 31	Crawford, Ill. (Unnumb.)
Dec. 24	Daviess, Ind. (Chap. 63)
Apr. 12	Hamilton, N. Y. (Chap. 120)
Jan. 13	Howard, Mo. (Unnumb.)
Jan. 10	Jackson, Ill. (Unnumb.)
Jan. 12	Jackson, Ohio (Chap. 25)
Dec. 27	Jennings, Ind. (Chap. 45)
Dec. 18	Lewis, W. Va. (Chap. 85)
Jan. 6	Monroe, Ill. (Unnumb.)
Dec. 6	Montgomery, Ala. (Chap. 8)
Mar. 1	Oswego, N. Y. (Chap. 22)
Feb. 15	Penobscot, Me. (Chap. 121)
Dec. 21	Pike, Ind. (Chap. 51)
Jan. 10	Pope, Ill. (Unnumb.)
Dec. 27	Ripley, Ind. (Chap. 45)
Dec. 30	Sullivan, Ind. (Chap. 49)

1817

Jan. 4	Bond, Ill. (Unnumb.)
Dec. 27	Brown, Ohio (Chap. 12)
Dec. 26	Clark, Ohio (Chap. 14)
Dec. 20	Du Bois, Ind. (Chap. 7)
Oct. 21	Lawrence, Tenn. (Chap. 42)
Dec. 30	Logan, Ohio (Chap. 20)
Nov. 20	Marion, Tenn. (Chap. 109)
July 14	Monroe, Mich. (Procl.)
Dec. 29	Morgan, Ohio (Chap. 18)
Oct. 15	Morgan, Tenn. (Chap. 38)
Dec. 26	Perry, Ohio (Chap. 11)
Apr. 7	Tompkins, N. Y. (Chap. 189)
Nov. 24	Wayne, Tenn. (Chap. 175)

1818

Dec. 15	Appling, Ga. (Unnumb.)
Nov. 21	Autauga, Ala. (Unnumb.)
Feb. 7	Bibb, Ala. (Unnumb.) (Cahaba, Ala.)
Feb. 6	Blount, Ala. (Unnumb.)
Oct. 26	Brown, Wis. (Procl.)
Dec. 15	Clark, Ark. (Unnumb.)
Feb. 13	Conecuh, Ala. (Unnumb.)

1818 cont.

Dec. 17	Cooper, Mo. (Unnumb.)
Jan. 29	Crawford, Ind. (Chap. 11)
Oct. 26	Crawford, Wis. (Procl.)
Feb. 9	Dallas, Ala. (Unnumb.)
Dec. 15	Early, Ga. (Unnumb.)
Dec. 28	Fayette, Ind. (Chap. 28)
Feb. 6	Franklin, Ala. (Unnumb.)
Jan. 2	Franklin, Ill. (Unnumb.)
Dec. 11	Franklin, Mo. (Unnumb.)
Dec. 15	Gwinnett, Ga. (Unnumb.)
Dec. 15	Habersham, Ga. (Unnumb.)
Dec. 15	Hall, Ga. (Unnumb.)
Dec. 15	Hempstead, Ark. (Unnumb.)
Jan. 3	Hocking, Ohio (Chap. 24)
Dec. 15	Irwin, Ga. (Unnumb.)
Dec. 8	Jefferson, Mo. (Unnumb.)
Feb. 6	Lauderdale, Ala. (Unnumb.)
Feb. 6	Lawrence, Ala. (Unnumb.)
Jan. 7	Lawrence, Ind. (Chap. 5)
Feb. 6	Limestone, Ala. (Unnumb.)
Dec. 14	Lincoln, Mo. (Unnumb.)
Oct. 26	Mackinac, Mich. (Procl.) (Michilimackinac, Mich.)
Jan. 15	Macomb, Mich. (Jan. 15)
Dec. 14	Madison, Mo. (Unnumb.)
Feb. 13	Marion, Ala. (Unnumb.)
Feb. 6	Marengo, Ala. (Unnumb.)
Jan. 14	Monroe, Ind. (Chap. 6)
Dec. 14	Montgomery, Mo. (Unnumb.)
Feb. 6	Morgan, Ala. (Unnumb.) (Cotaco, Ala.)
Jan. 30	Nicholas, W. Va. (Chap. 33)
Dec. 21	Owen, Ind. (Chap. 26)
Dec. 14	Pike, Mo. (Unnumb.)
Jan. 19	Preston, W. Va. (Chap. 32)
Dec. 15	Pulaski, Ark. (Unnumb.)
Jan. 10	Randolph, Ind. (Chap. 8)
Nov. 20	St. Clair, Ala. (Unnumb.)
Feb. 7	Shelby, Ala. (Unnumb.)
Jan. 10	Spencer, Ind. (Chap. 9)
Feb. 6	Tuscaloosa, Ala. (Unnumb.)
Jan. 2	Union, Ill. (Unnumb.)
Jan. 7	Vanderburgh, Ind. (Chap. 10)
Jan. 21	Vigo, Ind. (Chap. 14)
Dec. 15	Walton, Ga. (Unnumb.)
Jan. 2	Washington, Ill. (Unnumb.)
Dec. 11	Wayne, Mo. (Unnumb.)

1818 cont.

Jan. 17	Whitley, Ky. (Chap. 183)

1819

Mar. 4	Alexander, Ill. (Unnumb.)
Dec. 13	Butler, Ala. (Unnumb.)
Mar. 22	Clark, Ill. (Unnumb.)
Feb. 5	Covington, Miss. (Unnumb.)
Jan. 2	Floyd, Ind. (Chap. 27)
Dec. 13	Greene, Ala. (Unnumb.)
Oct. 25	Hamilton, Tenn. (Chap. 113)
Nov. 13	Hardin, Tenn. (Chap. 6)
Jan. 28	Harlan, Ky. (Chap. 341)
Jan. 28	Hart, Ky. (Chap. 352)
Dec. 13	Henry, Ala. (Unnumb.)
Dec. 13	Jackson, Ala. (Unnumb.)
Dec. 13	Jefferson, Ala. (Unnumb.)
Mar. 26	Jefferson, Ill. (Unnumb.)
Nov. 13	McMinn, Tenn. (Chap. 7)
Jan. 21	Meigs, Ohio (Chap. 25)
Nov. 13	Monroe, Tenn. (Chap. 7)
Jan. 12	Oakland, Mich. (Procl.)
Feb. 6	Owen, Ky. (Chap. 387)
Dec. 13	Perry, Ala. (Unnumb.)
Dec. 21	Rabun, Ga. (Unnumb.)
Jan. 7	Shelby, Ohio (Chap. 12)
Nov. 24	Shelby, Tenn. (Chap. 218)
Jan. 28	Simpson, Ky. (Chap. 342)
Dec. 30	Todd, Ky. (Chap. 460)
Mar. 6	Washington, La. (Unnumb.)
Mar. 26	Wayne, Ill. (Unnumb.)
Dec. 13	Wilcox, Ala. (Unnumb.)

1820

Feb. 12	Allen, Ohio (Chap. 37)
Nov. 16	Boone, Mo. (Chap. 14)
Nov. 25	Callaway, Mo. (Chap. 29)
Nov. 16	Chariton, Mo. (Chap. 14)
Nov. 16	Cole, Mo. (Chap. 16)
Oct. 18	Crawford, Ark. (Unnumb.)
Feb. 12	Crawford, Ohio (Chap. 37)
Nov. 25	Gasconade, Mo. (Chap. 28)
Feb. 12	Grant, Ky. (Chap. 561)
Feb. 12	Hancock, Ohio (Chap. 37)
Feb. 12	Hardin, Ohio (Chap. 37)
Feb. 12	Henry, Ohio (Chap. 37)
Oct. 23	Independence, Ark. (Unnumb.)
Nov. 16	Lafayette, Mo. (Chap. 10) (Lillard, Mo.)
Feb. 12	Marion, Ohio (Chap. 37)

1820 cont.

Jan. 17	Martin, Ind. (Chap. 31)
Feb. 12	Mercer, Ohio (Chap. 37)
Apr. 1	Miller, Ark. (Unnumb.)
Jan. 19	Monroe, Ky. (Chap. 474)
Feb. 9	Morgan, W. Va. (Chap. 34)
Feb. 12	Paulding, Ohio (Chap. 37)
Nov. 2	Perry, Ky. (Chap. 9)
Feb. 3	Perry, Miss. (Chap. 18)
Nov. 16	Perry, Mo. (Chap. 15)
Mar. 22	Perry, Pa. (Act 68)
May 1	Phillips, Ark. (Unnumb.)
Dec. 19	Pickens, Ala. (Chap. 26)
Feb. 12	Putnam, Ohio (Chap. 37)
Nov. 16	Ralls, Mo. (Chap. 12)
Nov. 16	Ray, Mo. (Chap. 14)
Mar. 28	St. Clair, Mich. (Procl.)
Nov. 25	Saline, Mo. (Chap. 27)
Feb. 12	Sandusky, Ohio (Chap. 37)
Jan. 12	Scott, Ind. (Chap. 30)
Feb. 12	Seneca, Ohio (Chap. 37)
Jan. 27	Trigg, Ky. (Chap. 489)
Jan. 10	Union, Ohio (Chap. 16)
Feb. 12	Van Wert, Ohio (Chap. 37)
Feb. 12	Williams, Ohio (Chap. 37)
Feb. 12	Wood, Ohio (Chap. 37)

1821

Jan. 8	Bartholomew, Ind. (Chap. 31)
Dec. 19	Calloway, Ky. (Chap. 112)
Nov. 7	Carroll, Tenn. (Chap. 32)
Dec. 7	Covington, Ala. (Unnumb.) (Jones, Ala.) (Covington, Ala.)
Dec. 21	Decatur, Ind. (Chap. 33)
May 15	Dooly, Ga. (Unnumb.)
Apr. 2	Erie, N. Y. (Chap. 228)
May 15	Fayette, Ga. (Unnumb.)
Feb. 14	Fayette, Ill. (Unnumb.)
Dec. 19	Graves, Ky. (Chap. 112)
Jan. 5	Greene, Ind. (Chap. 49)
Jan. 20	Greene, Ill. (Unnumb.)
Feb. 8	Hamilton, Ill. (Unnumb.)
Nov. 7	Henderson, Tenn. (Chap. 32)
May 15	Henry, Ga. (Unnumb.)
Dec. 31	Henry, Ind. (Chap. 60)
Nov. 7	Henry, Tenn. (Chap. 32)
Dec. 19	Hickman, Ky. (Chap. 112)
Feb. 12	Hinds, Miss. (Chap. 70)

1821 cont.

May 15	Houston, Ga. (Unnumb.)
Jan. 16	Lawrence, Ill. (Unnumb.)
Dec. 14	Lawrence, Ky. (Chap. 274)
Feb. 23	Livingston, N. Y. (Chap. 58)
Nov. 7	Madison, Tenn. (Chap. 32)
May 15	Monroe, Ga. (Unnumb.)
Feb. 9	Monroe, Miss. (Chap. 30)
Feb. 23	Monroe, N. Y. (Chap. 57)
Feb. 12	Montgomery, Ill. (Unnumb.)
Dec. 24	Newton, Ga. (Unnumb.)
Jan. 9	Parke, Ind. (Chap. 24)
Nov. 14	Perry, Tenn. (Chap. 202)
Dec. 17	Pike, Ala. (Chap. 32)
Jan. 31	Pike, Ill. (Unnumb.)
Dec. 19	Pike, Ky. (Chap. 297)
Dec. 21	Pocahontas, W. Va. (Chap. 27)
Dec. 31	Putnam, Ind. (Chap. 36)
Dec. 31	Rush, Ind. (Chap. 35)
Dec. 19	St. Francois, Mo. (Chap. 26)
Jan. 30	Sangamon, Ill. (Unnumb.)
Dec. 28	Scott, Mo. (Chap. 28)
Dec. 31	Shelby, Ind. (Chap. 31)
Jan. 5	Union, Ind. (Chap. 58)

1822

Jan. 5	Alleghany, Va. (Chap. 28)
Dec. 9	Bibb, Ga. (Unnumb.)
Jan. 2	Clay, Mo. (Chap. 39)
Dec. 9	Crawford, Ga. (Unnumb.)
Dec. 9	Davidson, N. C. (Chap. 47)
Dec. 9	De Kalb, Ga. (Unnumb.)
Aug. 12	Duval, Fla. (Unnumb.)
Aug. 12	Escambia, Fla. (Unnumb.)
Aug. 12	Jackson, Fla. (Unnumb.)
Dec. 31	Johnson, Ind. (Chap. 15)
Sept. 10	Lapeer, Mich. (Unnumb.)
Sept. 10	Lenawee, Mich. (Unnumb.)
Dec. 26	Lorain, Ohio (Chap. 5)
Dec. 14	Marion, Mo. (Chap. 38)
Dec. 21	Montgomery, Ind. (Chap. 6)
Dec. 31	Morgan, Ind. (Chap. 24)
Dec. 7	Morgan, Ky. (Chap. 460)
Dec. 9	Pike, Ga. (Unnumb.)
Sept. 10	Saginaw, Mich. (Unnumb.)
Aug. 12	St. Johns, Fla. (Unnumb.)
Sept. 10	Sanilac, Mich. (Unnumb.)
Sept. 10	Shiawassee, Mich. (Unnumb.)

1822 cont.		
	Mar. 22	Terrebonne, La. (Unnumb.)
	Sept. 10	Wastenaw, Mich. (Unnumb.)
1823		
	Dec. 17	Allen, Ind. (Chap. 18)
	Oct. 25	Chicot, Ark. (Unnumb.)
	Jan. 21	Copiah, Miss. (Chap. 49)
	Dec. 8	Decatur, Ga. (Unnumb.)
	Oct. 16	Dyer, Tenn. (Chap. 108)
	Jan. 3	Edgar, Ill. (Unnumb.)
	Nov. 28	Fentress, Tenn. (Chap. 302)
	Jan. 28	Fulton, Ill. (Unnumb.)
	June 24	Gadsden, Fla. (Unnumb.)
	Oct. 21	Gibson, Tenn. (Chap. 111)
	Jan. 8	Hamilton, Ind. (Chap. 52)
	Oct. 16	Hardemann, Tenn. (Chap. 108)
	Nov. 3	Haywood, Tenn. (Chap. 145)
	Jan. 17	Lafayette, La. (Unnumb.)
	Jan. 4	Madison, Ind. (Chap. 50)
	Jan. 24	Marion, Ill. (Unnumb.)
	Oct. 8	McNairy, Tenn. (Chap. 96)
	Dec. 17	Meade, Ky. (Chap. 609)
	July 1	Merrimack, N. H. (Chap. 40)
	July 3	Monroe, Fla. (Unnumb.)
	Jan. 31	Morgan, Ill. (Unnumb.)
	Oct. 24	Obion, Tenn. (Chap. 114)
	Dec. 15	Oldham, Ky. (Chap. 620)
	Oct. 29	Tipton, Tenn. (Chap. 126)
	Dec. 26	Walker, Ala. (Unnumb.)
	Apr. 11	Wayne, N. Y. (Chap. 138)
	Oct. 21	Weakley, Tenn. (Chap. 112)
	Feb. 5	Yates, N. Y. (Chap. 30)
	Jan. 21	Yazoo, Miss. (Chap. 49)
1824		
	Dec. 29	Alachua, Fla. (Unnumb.)
	Dec. 23	Clay, Ill. (Unnumb.)
	Dec. 27	Clinton, Ill. (Unnumb.)
	Dec. 22	Dale, Ala. (Unnumb.)
	Feb. 17	East Feliciana Parish (Unnumb.)
	Dec. 20	Fayette, Ala. (Unnumb.)
	Dec. 20	Hendricks, Ind. (Chap. 19)
	Sept. 29	Fayette, Tenn. (Chap. 36)
	Jan. 20	Holmes, Ohio (Chap. 36)
	Dec. 29	Leon, Fla. (Unnumb.)
	Jan. 12	Logan, W. Va. (Unnumb.)
	Dec. 17	McCracken, Ky. (Chap. 48)
	Dec. 29	Nassau, Fla. (Unnumb.)
	Dec. 29	Orange, Fla. (Unnumb.) (Mosquito, Fla.)

1824 cont.

Nov. 12	Orleans, N. Y. (Chap. 266)
Jan. 23	Simpson, Miss. (Unnumb.)
Jan. 7	Spencer, Ky. (Chap. 708)
Dec. 15	Upson, Ga. (Unnumb.)
Jan. 2	Vermillion, Ind. (Chap. 20)
Dec. 27	Wabash, Ill. (Unnumb.)
Dec. 29	Walton, Fla. (Unnumb.)
Dec. 15	Ware, Ga. (Unnumb.)
Nov. 20	Warren, N. J. (Unnumb.)
Feb. 17	West Feliciana, La. (Unnumb.)

1825

Jan. 13	Adams, Ill. (Unnumb.)
Dec. 12	Baker, Ga. (Unnumb.)
Dec. 24	Butts, Ga. (Unnumb.)
Jan. 10	Calhoun, Ill. (Unnumb.)
Feb. 12	Clay, Ind. (Chap. 15)
Oct. 20	Conway, Ark. (Unnumb.)
Oct. 22	Crittenden, Ark. (Unnumb.)
Jan. 12	Edmonson, Ky. (Chap. 204)
Dec. 30	Fountain, Ind. (Chap. 9)
Jan. 13	Hancock, Ill. (Unnumb.)
Jan. 13	Henry, Ill. (Unnumb.)
Oct. 27	Izard, Ark. (Unnumb.)
Feb. 11	Jefferson, La. (Unnumb.)
Jan. 13	Knox, Ill. (Unnumb.)
Dec. 12	Laurel, Ky. (Chap. 29)
Dec. 23	Lowndes, Ga. (Unnumb.)
Jan. 13	Mercer, Ill. (Unnumb.)
Jan. 13	Peoria, Ill. (Unnumb.)
Jan. 13	Putnam, Ill. (Unnumb.)
Dec. 14	Russell, Ky. (Chap. 39)
Jan. 13	Schuyler, Ill. (Unnumb.)
Dec. 24	Taliaferro, Ga. (Unnumb.)
Dec. 23	Thomas, Ga. (Unnumb.)
Jan. 13	Warren, Ill. (Unnumb.)
Dec. 9	Washington, Fla. (Unnumb.)

1826

Dec. 20	Anderson, S. C. (Chap. 9)
Dec. 11	Carroll, Ga. (Unnumb.)
Dec. 22	Chippewa, Mich. (Unnumb.)
Dec. 11	Coweta, Ga. (Unnumb.)
Dec. 15	Jackson, Mo. (Chap. 20)
Jan. 24	Jones, Miss. (Chap. 47)
Dec. 11	Lee, Ga. (Unnumb.)
Jan. 25	McDonough, Ill. (Unnumb.)
Dec. 11	Muscogee, Ga. (Unnumb.)
Dec. 20	Pickens, S. C. (Chap. 9)

1826 cont.		
	Jan. 20	Tippecanoe, Ind. (Chap. 10)
	Dec. 11	Troup, Ga. (Unnumb.)
	Jan. 18	Vermilion, Ill. (Unnumb.)
1827		
	Jan. 16	Anderson, Ky. (Chap. 35)
	Jan. 26	Delaware, Ind. (Chap. 10)
	Dec. 26	Hamilton, Fla. (Unnumb.)
	Jan. 26	Hancock, Ind. (Chap. 91)
	Dec. 24	Harris, Ga. (Unnumb.)
	Jan. 6	Jefferson, Fla. (Unnumb.)
	Feb. 17	Jo Daviess, Ill. (Unnumb.)
	Oct. 15	Lafayette, Ark. (Unnumb.)
	Dec. 26	Madison, Fla. (Unnumb.)
	Dec. 24	Marion, Ga. (Unnumb.)
	Dec. 24	Meriwether, Ga. (Unnumb.)
	Jan. 29	Perry, Ill. (Unnumb.)
	Oct. 13	St. Francis, Ark. (Unnumb.)
	Jan. 23	Shelby, Ill. (Unnumb.)
	July 5	Sullivan, N. H. (Chap. 48)
	Dec. 14	Talbot, Ga. (Unnumb.)
	Jan. 31	Tazewell, Ill. (Unnumb.)
	Feb. 7	Waldo, Me. (Chap. 354)
	Jan. 19	Warren, Ind. (Chap. 11)
	Jan. 29	Washington, Miss. (Chap. 80)
1828		
	Jan. 7	Carroll, Ind. (Chap. 16)
	Dec. 18	Cass, Ind. (Chap. 19)
	Mar. 13	Claiborne, La. (Act 42)
		Macon, N. C. (Chap. 50)
	Jan. 29	Madison, Miss. (Chap. 14)
	Dec. 20	Randolph, Ga. (Unnumb.)
	Feb. 4	Rankin, Miss. (Chap. 93)
	Oct. 17	Sevier, Ark. (Unnumb.)
	Oct. 17	Washington, Ark. (Unnumb.)
1829		
	Oct. 29	Barry, Mich. (Unnumb.)
	Oct. 29	Berrien, Mich. (Unnumb.)
	Oct. 29	Branch, Mich. (Unnumb.)
	Oct. 29	Calhoun, Mich. (Unnumb.)
	Oct. 29	Cass, Mich. (Unnumb.)
	Jan. 23	Crawford, Mo. (Chap. 19)
	Oct. 29	Eaton, Mich. (Unnumb.)
	Jan. 3	Hancock, Ky. (Chap. 32)
	Oct. 29	Hillsdale, Mich. (Unnumb.)
	Nov. 2	Hot Spring, Ark. (Unnumb.)
	Oct. 29	Ingham, Mich. (Unnumb.)
	Oct. 9	Iowa, Wis. (Unnumb.)

1829 cont.

Nov. 5	Jackson, Ark. (Unnumb.)
Oct. 29	Jackson, Mich. (Unnumb.)
Nov. 2	Jefferson, Ark. (Unnumb.)
Oct. 29	Kalamazoo, Mich. (Unnumb.)
Jan. 19	Macon, Ill. (Unnumb.)
Jan. 17	Macoupin, Ill. (Unnumb.)
Nov. 2	Monroe, Ark. (Unnumb.)
Nov. 2	Pope, Ark. (Unnumb.)
Jan. 22	Randolph, Mo. (Chap. 29)
Oct. 29	St. Joseph, Mich. (Unnumb.)
Nov. 2	Union, Ark. (Unnumb.)
Oct. 29	Van Buren, Mich. (Unnumb.)

1830

Jan. 29	Boone, Ind. (Chap. 24)
Jan. 29	Clinton, Ind. (Chap. 25)
Dec. 25	Coles, Ill. (Unnumb.)
Jan. 29	Elkhart, Ind. (Chap. 23)
Dec. 22	Heard, Ga. (Unnumb.)
Jan. 20	Lowndes, Ala. (Unnumb.)
Jan. 30	Lowndes, Miss. (Chap. 14)
Dec. 25	McLean, Ill. (Unnumb.)
Jan. 29	St. Joseph, Ind. (Chap. 23)
Dec. 23	Stewart, Ga. (Unnumb.)

1831

Mar. 2	Allegan, Mich. (Unnumb.)
Mar. 2	Arenac, Mich. (Unnumb.)
Jan. 12	Audrain, Mo. (Chap. 13)
Dec. 26	Cherokee, Ga. (Unnumb.)
Mar. 2	Clinton, Mich. (Unnumb.)
Jan. 15	Cook, Ill. (Unnumb.)
Feb. 15	Effingham, Ill. (Unnumb.)
Feb. 28	Fayette, W. Va. (Chap. 70)
Jan. 15	Floyd, Va. (Chap. 72)
Mar. 2	Gladwin, Mich. (Unnumb.)
Feb. 10	Grant, Ind. (Chap. 12)
Mar. 2	Gratiot, Mich. (Unnumb.)
Mar. 2	Ionia, Mich. (Unnumb.)
Mar. 2	Isabella, Mich. (Unnumb.)
Mar. 1	Jackson, W. Va. (Chap. 73)
Feb. 15	Jasper, Ill. (Unnumb.)
Mar. 2	Juniata, Pa. (Act 67)
Mar. 2	Kent, Mich. (Unnumb.)
Jan. 15	La Salle, Ill. (Unnumb.)
Mar. 2	Midland, Mich. (Unnumb.)
Jan. 6	Monroe, Mo. (Chap. 15)
Mar. 2	Montcalm, Mich. (Unnumb.)
Mar. 2	Oceana, Mich. (Unnumb.)

1831 cont.

Mar. 2	Ottawa, Mich. (Unnumb.)
Mar. 30	Page, Va. (Chap. 74)
Feb. 9	Rock Island, Ill. (Unnumb.)
Dec. 26	Sumter, Ga. (Unnumb.)

1832

Dec. 18	Barbour, Ala. (Act 11)
Dec. 3	Bartow, Ga. (Unnumb.) (Cass, Ga.)
Dec. 18	Calhoun, Ala. (Act 11) (Benton, Ala.)
Dec. 25	Carroll, Ohio (Unnumb.)
Dec. 18	Chambers, Ala. (Act 11)
Dec. 3	Cobb, Ga. (Unnumb.)
Feb. 4	Columbia, Fla. (Chap. 25)
Dec. 18	Coosa, Ala. (Act 11)
Dec. 3	Floyd, Ga. (Unnumb.)
Dec. 3	Forsyth, Ga. (Unnumb.)
Feb. 8	Franklin, Fla. (Chap. 42)
Dec. 3	Gilmer, Ga. (Unnumb.)
Feb. 2	Huntington, Ind. (Chap. 119)
Feb. 2	La Grange, Ind. (Chap. 117)
Jan. 9	La Porte, Ind. (Chap. 2)
Feb. 10	Livingston, La. (Unnumb.)
Dec. 3	Lumpkin, Ga. (Unnumb.)
Dec. 18	Macon, Ala. (Act 11)
Feb. 2	Miami, Ind. (Chap. 119)
Dec. 3	Murray, Ga. (Unnumb.)
Dec. 3	Paulding, Ga. (Unnumb.)
Dec. 18	Randolph, Ala. (Act 11)
Dec. 18	Russell, Ala. (Act 11)
Feb. 23	Smyth, Va. (Act 67)
Dec. 18	Sumter, Ala. (Act 11)
Dec. 18	Talladega, Ala. (Act 11)
Dec. 18	Tallapoosa, Ala. (Act 11)
Dec. 3	Union, Ga. (Unnumb.)
Feb. 2	Wabash, Ind. (Chap. 119)

1833

Dec. 23	Attala, Miss. (Unnumb.)
Nov. 1	Carroll, Ark. (Unnumb.)
Dec. 23	Carroll, Miss. (Unnumb.)
Jan. 2	Carroll, Mo. (Chap. 24)
Feb. 20	Champaign, Ill. (Unnumb.)
Dec. 23	Choctaw, Miss. (Unnumb.)
Dec. 23	Clarke, Miss. (Unnumb.)
Jan. 2	Clinton, Mo. (Chap. 25)
Nov. 5	Greene, Ark. (Unnumb.)
Jan. 2	Greene, Mo. (Chap. 26)

1833 cont.

Feb. 19	Holmes, Miss. (Chap. 78)
Feb. 26	Iroquois, Ill. (Unnumb.)
Dec. 23	Jasper, Miss. (Unnumb.)
Nov. 16	Johnson, Ark. (Unnumb.)
Dec. 23	Kemper, Miss. (Unnumb.)
Dec. 23	Lauderdale, Miss. (Unnumb.)
Dec. 23	Leake, Miss. (Unnumb.)
Jan. 2	Lewis, Mo. (Chap. 28)
Mar. 21	Livingston, Mich. (Unnumb.)
Nov. 1	Mississippi, Ark. (Unnumb.)
Jan. 5	Morgan, Mo. (Chap. 29)
Dec. 23	Neshoba, Miss. (Unnumb.)
Dec. 23	Noxubee, Miss. (Unnumb.)
Dec. 23	Oktibbeha, Miss. (Unnumb.)
Jan. 26	Pettis, Mo. (Chap. 30)
Nov. 1	Pike, Ark. (Unnumb.)
Jan. 19	Pulaski, Mo. (Chap. 31)
Feb. 8	Rappahannock, Va. (Chap. 73)
Jan. 5	Ripley, Mo. (Chap. 32)
Nov. 5	Scott, Ark. (Unnumb.)
Dec. 23	Scott, Miss. (Unnumb.)
Dec. 23	Smith, Miss. (Chap. 5)
Dec. 23	Tallahatchie, Miss. (Unnumb.)
Nov. 11	Van Buren, Ark. (Unnumb.)
Dec. 18	Walker, Ga. (Unnumb.)
Jan. 5	Warren, Mo. (Chap. 95)
Dec. 23	Winston, Miss. (Unnumb.)
Dec. 23	Yalobusha, Miss. (Unnumb.)
	Yancey, N. C. (Chap. 83)

1834

Sept. 6	Des Moines, Iowa (Unnumb.)
Sept. 6	Dubuque, Iowa (Unnumb.)
Dec. 13	Henry, Mo. (Unnumb.) (Rives, Mo.)
Jan. 25	Hillsborough, Fla. (Chap. 764)
Dec. 13	Johnson, Mo. (Unnumb.)
Jan. 25	Marion, Ky. (Chap. 285)
Sept. 6	Milwaukee, Wis. (Unnumb.)
Feb. 1	White, Ind. (Chap. 30)

1835

Feb. 7	Adams, Ind. (Chap. 25)
Jan. 5	Barry, Mo. (Unnumb.)
Jan. 3	Benton, Mo. (Unnumb.)
Dec. 19	Benton, Tenn. (Chap. 30)
Mar. 3	Cass, Mo. (Unnumb.) (Van Buren, Mo.)
Feb. 7	De Kalb, Ind. (Chap. 25)

1835 cont.	
Feb. 7	Fulton, Ind. (Chap. 25)
Mar. 28	Genesee, Mich. (Unnumb.)
Feb. 7	Jasper, Ind. (Chap. 25)
Feb. 7	Jay, Ind. (Chap. 25)
Feb. 7	Kosciusko, Ind. (Chap. 25)
Oct. 26	Lamoille, Vt. (Act 41)
Nov. 24	Lauderdale, Tenn. (Chap. 28)
June 20	Lucas, Ohio (Unnumb.)
Nov. 3	Marion, Ark. (Unnumb.) (Searcy, Ark.)
Feb. 7	Marshall, Ind. (Chap. 25)
Mar. 12	Marshall, W. Va. (Chap. 57)
Feb. 7	Newton, Ind. (Chap. 25)
Feb. 7	Noble, Ind. (Chap. 24)
Jan. 5	Polk, Mo. (Unnumb.)
Feb. 7	Porter, Ind. (Chap. 25)
Feb. 7	Pulaski, Ind. (Chap. 25)
Oct. 29	Randolph, Ark. (Unnumb.)
Nov. 2	Saline, Ark. (Unnumb.)
Nov. 3	Searcy, Ark. (Unnumb.)
Jan. 2	Shelby, Mo. (Unnumb.)
Feb. 7	Starke, Ind. (Chap. 25)
Feb. 7	Steuben, Ind. (Chap. 25)
Jan. 2	Stoddard, Mo. (Unnumb.)
Feb. 7	Wells, Ind. (Chap. 25)
Oct. 23	White, Ark. (Unnumb.)
Feb. 7	Whitley, Ind. (Chap. 25)
1836	
Mar. 17	Austin, Tex. (Const.)
Mar. 17	Bastrop, Tex. (Const.)
Sept. 30	Benton, Ark. (Unnumb.)
Mar. 17	Bexar, Tex. (Const.)
Feb. 9	Bolivar, Miss. (Unnumb.)
Feb. 10	Bradley, Tenn. (Chap. 32)
Jan. 15	Braxton, W. Va. (Chap. 18)
Mar. 17	Brazoria, Tex. (Const.)
Feb. 4	Brown, Ind. (Chap. 19)
Dec. 29	Caldwell, Mo. (Unnumb.)
Dec. 7	Calumet, Wis. (Act 28)
Jan. 31	Cannon, Tenn. (Chap. 33)
Mar. 29	Chemung, N. Y. (Chap. 77)
Jan. 9	Cherokee, Ala. (Chap. 179)
Feb. 9	Chickasaw, Miss. (Unnumb.)
Dec. 16	Clark, Mo. (Unnumb.)
Mar. 8	Clarke, Va. (Chap. 19)
Feb. 20	Clinton, Ky. (Chap. 245)
Feb. 9	Coahoma, Miss. (Unnumb.)

1836 cont.

Jan. 8	Coffee, Tenn. (Chap. 36)
Mar. 17	Colorado, Tex. (Const.)
Feb. 4	Dade, Fla. (Chap. 937)
Dec. 7	Dane, Wis. (Act 28)
Dec. 20	Davie, N. C. (Chap. 4)
Dec. 29	Daviess, Mo. (Unnumb.)
Jan. 9	De Kalb, Ala. (Chap. 179)
Feb. 9	De Soto, Miss. (Unnumb.)
Dec. 7	Dodge, Wis. (Act 28)
Dec. 7	Fond du Lac, Wis. (Act 28)
Mar. 17	Goliad, Tex. (Const.)
Mar. 17	Gonzales, Tex. (Const.)
Dec. 8	Grant, Wis. (Act 31)
Dec. 8	Green, Wis. (Act 31)
Mar. 17	Harris, Tex. (Const.) (Harrisburg, Tex.)
Dec. 7	Henry, Iowa (Act 21)
Feb. 9	Itawamba, Miss. (Unnumb.)
Mar. 17	Jackson, Tex. (Const.)
Mar. 17	Jasper, Tex. (Const.)
Mar. 17	Jefferson, Tex. (Const.)
Dec. 7	Jefferson, Wis. (Act 28)
Jan. 2	Johnson, Tenn. (Chap. 31)
Jan. 16	Kane, Ill. (Unnumb.)
Feb. 9	Lafayette, Miss. (Unnumb.)
Jan. 28	Lake, Ind. (Chap. 18)
Dec. 7	Lee, Iowa (Act 21)
Mar. 17	Liberty, Tex. (Const.)
Dec. 7	Louisa, Iowa (Act 21)
Sept. 30	Madison, Ark. (Unnumb.)
Dec. 7	Manitowoc, Wis. (Act 28)
Dec. 7	Marquette, Wis. (Act 28)
Jan. 9	Marshall, Ala. (Act 47)
Feb. 9	Marshall, Miss. (Unnumb.)
Feb. 20	Marshall, Tenn. (Chap. 35)
Mar. 17	Matagorda, Tex. (Const.)
Jan. 16	McHenry, Ill. (Unnumb.)
Jan. 20	Meigs, Tenn. (Chap. 34)
Mar. 17	Milam, Tex. (Const.)
Apr. 1	Monroe, Pa. (Act 144)
Dec. 7	Muscatine, Iowa (Act 21)
Mar. 17	Nacogdoches, Tex. (Const.)
Feb. 25	Newton, Miss. (Unnumb.)
Jan. 16	Ogle, Ill. (Unnumb.)
Feb. 9	Panola, Miss. (Unnumb.)
Feb. 9	Pontotoc, Miss. (Unnumb.)
Dec. 7	Portage, Wis. (Act 28)

1836 cont.

Dec. 7	Racine, Wis. (Chap. 28)
Mar. 17	Red River, Tex. (Const.)
Mar. 17	Refugio, Tex. (Const.)
Dec. 7	Rock, Wis. (Act 28)
Mar. 17	Sabine, Tex. (Const.)
Mar. 17	San Augustine, Tex. (Const.)
Mar. 17	San Patricio, Tex. (Const.)
Dec. 7	Sheboygan, Wis. (Act 28)
Mar. 17	Shelby, Tex. (Const.)
Feb. 9	Tippah, Miss. (Unnumb.)
Feb. 9	Tishomingo, Miss. (Unnumb.)
Feb. 9	Tunica, Miss. (Unnumb.)
Dec. 7	Van Buren, Iowa (Act 21)
Mar. 17	Victoria, Tex. (Const.)
Dec. 7	Walworth, Wis. (Chap. 28)
Mar. 9	Warren, Va. (Chap. 20)
Mar. 17	Washington, Tex. (Const.)
Dec. 7	Washington, Wis. (Act 28)
Jan. 16	Whiteside, Ill. (Unnumb.)
Jan. 12	Will, Ill. (Unnumb.)
Jan. 16	Winnebago, Ill. (Unnumb.)

1837

Feb. 7	Atlantic, N. J. (Unnumb.)
Dec. 21	Benton, Iowa (Act 6)
Mar. 4	Boone, Ill. (Unnumb.)
Dec. 21	Buchanan, Iowa (Act 6)
Feb. 28	Bureau, Ill. (Unnumb.)
Jan. 19	Carroll, Md. (Chap. 19)
Mar. 3	Cass, Ill. (Unnumb.)
Dec. 21	Cedar, Iowa (Act 6)
Dec. 21	Clayton, Iowa (Act 6)
Dec. 21	Clinton, Iowa (Act 6)
Dec. 25	Dade, Ga. (Unnumb.)
Mar. 4	De Kalb, Ill. (Unnumb.)
Dec. 11	De Kalb, Tenn.
Dec. 21	Delaware, Iowa (Act 6)
Dec. 14	Fannin, Tex. (Unnumb.)
Dec. 21	Fayette, Iowa (Act 6)
Dec. 14	Fayette, Tex. (Unnumb.)
Dec. 29	Fort Bend, Tex. (Unnumb.)
Dec. 19	Franklin, Ark. (Unnumb.)
June 12	Houston, Tex. (Unnumb.)
Dec. 21	Jackson, Iowa (Act 6)
Dec. 21	Johnson, Iowa (Act 6)
Dec. 21	Jones, Iowa (Act 6)
Dec. 21	Keokuk, Iowa (Act 6)
Dec. 21	Linn, Iowa (Act 6)

1837 cont.

Jan. 6	Linn, Mo. (Unnumb.)
Feb. 27	Livingston, Ill. (Unnumb.)
Jan. 6	Livingston, Mo. (Unnumb.)
Dec. 14	Macon, Ga. (Unnumb.)
Jan. 6	Macon, Mo. (Unnumb.)
Mar. 17	Mercer, W. Va. (Chap. 53)
Feb. 6	Miller, Mo. (Unnumb.)
Dec. 14	Montgomery, Tex. (Unnumb.)
Feb. 7	Passaic, N. J. (Unnumb.)
Dec. 14	Robertson, Tex. (Unnumb.)
Dec. 21	Scott, Iowa (Act 6)
Mar. 4	Stephenson, Ill. (Unnumb.)
Jan. 6	Taney, Mo. (Unnumb.)
Feb. 9	Trimble, Ky. (Chap. 248)
Jan. 16	Washington, Iowa (Slaughter, Iowa)

1838

Feb. 15	Blackford, Ind. (Chap. 97)
Dec. 31	Buchanan, Mo. (Unnumb.)
Jan. 18	Caddo, La. (Unnumb.)
Mar. 6	Caldwell, La. (Act 48)
Jan. 26	Calhoun, Fla. (Act 8)
Feb. 9	Carroll, Ky. (Chap. 773)
Feb. 9	Carter, Ky. (Chap. 760)
Dec. 28	Chattooga, Ga. (Unnumb.)
Dec. 12	Desha, Ark. (Unnumb.)
Mar. 15	Erie, Ohio (Unnumb.)
Mar. 20	Franklin, Me. (Chap. 328)
Apr. 18	Fulton, N. Y. (Chap. 332)
May 15	Galveston, Tex. (Unnumb.)
Jan. 24	Greene, Va. (Chap. 59)
Dec. 15	Henderson, N. C. (Chap. 12)
Jan. 19	Madison, La. (Unnumb.)
Feb. 22	Mercer, N. J. (Unnumb.)
Dec. 30	Newton, Mo. (Unnumb.)
Mar. 23	Piscataquis, Me. (Chap. 355)
Dec. 31	Platte, Mo. (Unnumb.)
Feb. 28	Poinsett, Ark. (Unnumb.)
Mar. 30	Roanoke, Va. (Chap. 60)

1839

Mar. 16	Aroostook, Me. (Chap. 395)
Feb. 18	Breathitt, Ky. (Chap. 1192)
Feb. 1	Brown, Ill. (Unnumb.)
Feb. 22	Carroll, Ill. (Unnumb.)
Jan. 4	Cherokee, N. C. (Chap. 10)
Feb. 15	Christian, Ill. (Unnumb.) (Dane, Ill.)

1839 cont.

Mar. 11	Clarion, Pa. (Act 27)
June 21	Clinton, Pa. (Act 145)
Mar. 1	De Witt, Ill. (Unnumb.)
Feb. 9	Du Page, Ill. (Unnumb.)
Mar. 2	Hardin, Ill. (Unnumb.)
Jan. 28	Harrison, Tex. (Unnumb.)
Jan. 21	Jefferson, Iowa (Unnumb.)
Feb. 28	Jersey, Ill. (Unnumb.)
Mar. 1	Lake, Ill. (Unnumb.)
Feb. 27	Lee, Ill. (Unnumb.)
Feb. 15	Logan, Ill. (Unnumb.)
Jan. 19	Marshall, Ill. (Unnumb.)
Feb. 15	Menard, Ill. (Unnumb.)
Nov. 28	Polk, Tenn. (Chap. 10)
Mar. 30	Pulaski, Va. (Chap. 50)
Feb. 16	Scott, Ill. (Unnumb.)
Mar. 2	Stark, Ill. (Unnumb.)
Mar. 13	Union, La. (Act 22)
Feb. 28	Williamson, Ill. (Unnumb.)

1840

Apr. 1	Alcona, Mich. (Act 119) (Newaygo, Mich.)
Apr. 1	Alpena, Mich. (Act 119) (Anamickee, Mich.)
Apr. 1	Antrim, Mich. (Act 119) (Meegisee, Mich.)
Dec. 22	Belknap, N. H. (Chap. 539)
Feb. 18	Benton, Ind. (Chap. 40)
Dec. 17	Bowie, Tex. (Unnumb.)
Dec. 18	Bradley, Ark. (Unnumb.)
Mar. 24	Calcasieu, La. (Act 72)
Dec. 22	Carroll, N. H. (Chap. 539)
Apr. 1	Charlevoix, Mich. (Act 119) (Reshkauko, Mich.)
Apr. 1	Cheboygan, Mich. (Act 119)
Apr. 1	Clare, Mich. (Act 119) (Kaykakee, Mich.)
Apr. 1	Crawford, Mich. (Act 119) (Shawano, Mich.)
Apr. 1	Emmet, Mich. (Act 119) (Tonedagana, Mich.)
Apr. 1	Grand Traverse, Mich. (Act 119) (Omeena, Mich.)
Feb. 22	Hudson, N. J. (Unnumb.)
Apr. 1	Huron, Mich. (Act 119)
Apr. 1	Iosco, Mich. (Act 119) (Kanotin, Mich.)

1840 cont.

Apr. 1	Kalkaska, Mich. (Act 119) (Wabassee, Mich.)
Jan. 29	Kenton, Ky. (Chap. 175)
Apr. 1	Lake, Mich. (Act 119) (Aishcum, Mich.)
Mar. 6	Lake, Ohio (Unnumb.)
Dec. 17	Lamar, Tex. (Unnumb.)
Apr. 1	Leelanau, Mich. (Act 119)
Apr. 1	Manistee, Mich. (Act 119)
Apr. 1	Mason, Mich. (Act 119) (Notipekago, Mich.)
Apr. 1	Mecosta, Mich. (Act 119)
Apr. 1	Missaukee, Mich. (Act 119)
Apr. 1	Montmorency, Mich. (Act 119) (Cheonoquet, Mich.)
Apr. 1	Newaygo, Mich. (Act 119)
Apr. 1	Ogemaw, Mich. (Act 119)
Apr. 1	Osceola, Mich. (Act 119) (Unwattin, Mich.)
Apr. 1	Oscoda, Mich. (Act 119)
Apr. 1	Otsego, Mich. (Act 119) (Okkuddo, Mich.)
Mar. 6	Ottawa, Ohio (Unnumb.)
Dec. 18	Perry, Ark. (Unnumb.)
Apr. 1	Presque Isle, Mich. (Act 119)
Apr. 1	Roscommon, Mich. (Act 119) (Mikenauk, Mich.)
Jan. 9	St. Croix, Wis. (Chap. 20)
Jan. 11	Sauk, Wis. (Chap. 23)
Mar. 3	Summit, Ohio (Unnumb.)
Jan. 25	Travis, Tex. (Unnumb.)
Apr. 1	Tuscola, Mich. (Act 119)
Jan. 3	Van Buren, Tenn. (Chap. 59)
Apr. 1	Wexford, Mich. (Act 119) (Kautawaubet, Mich.)
Jan. 6	Winnebago, Wis. (Chap. 12)
Dec. 5	Yell, Ark. (Unnumb.)

1841

Jan. 29	Adair, Mo. (Unnumb.)
Jan. 29	Andrew, Mo. (Unnumb.)
Jan. 29	Bates, Mo. (Unnumb.)
Jan. 30	Brazos, Tex. (Unnumb.) (Navasoto, Tex.)
Jan. 11	Caldwell, N. C. (Chap. 11)
Jan. 29	Camden, Mo. (Unnumb.) (Kinderhook, Mo.)
Jan. 11	Cleveland, N. C. (Chap. 9)

1841 cont.

Dec. 29	Coffee, Ala. (Act 190)
Jan. 29	Dade, Mo. (Unnumb.)
Jan. 29	Dallas, Mo. (Unnumb.) (Niangua, Mo.)
Feb. 12	Gentry, Mo. (Unnumb.)
Feb. 17	Grundy, Ill. (Unnumb.)
Jan. 29	Grundy, Mo. (Unnumb.)
Feb. 5	Harrison, Miss. (Chap. 35)
Jan. 20	Henderson, Ill. (Unnumb.)
Jan. 29	Holt, Mo. (Unnumb.) (Nodaway, Mo.)
Jan. 29	Jasper, Mo. (Unnumb.)
Feb. 19	Kendall, Ill. (Unnumb.)
Jan. 20	Mason, Ill. (Unnumb.)
Jan. 29	Nodaway, Mo. (Unnumb.)
Jan. 29	Osage, Mo. (Unnumb.)
Jan. 29	Ozark, Mo. (Unnumb.) (Decatur, Mo.)
Jan. 27	Piatt, Ill. (Unnumb.)
Feb. 24	Richland, Ill. (Unnumb.)
Jan. 29	St. Clair, Mo. (Unnumb.)
Jan. 29	Scotland, Mo. (Unnumb.)
Jan. 29	Shannon, Mo. (Unnumb.)
Jan. 11	Stanly, N. C. (Chap. 13)
Feb. 27	Woodford, Ill. (Unnumb.)
Jan. 29	Wright, Mo. (Unnumb.)
May 19	Wyoming, N. Y. (Chap. 196)

1842

Feb. 15	Ballard, Ky. (Chap. 188)
Feb. 15	Boyle, Ky. (Chap. 189)
Jan. 15	Burleson, Tex. (Unnumb.)
Jan. 17	Carroll, Va. (Chap. 58)
Dec. 12	Catawba, N. C. (Chap. 8)
Jan. 26	Crittenden, Ky. (Chap. 97)
Dec. 21	Fulton, Ark. (Unnumb.)
Feb. 2	Hamilton, Tex. (Unnumb.)
Mar. 3	Letcher, Ky. (Chap. 394)
Jan. 18	Macon, Tenn. (Chap. 45)
Feb. 2	Madison, Tex. (Unnumb.)
Jan. 14	Marion, W. Va. (Chap. 59)
Feb. 12	Marshall, Ky. (Chap. 180)
Dec. 19	McDowell, N. C. (Chap. 10)
Dec. 9	Montgomery, Ark. (Unnumb.)
Dec. 14	Newton, Ark. (Unnumb.)
Nov. 29	Ouachita, Ark. (Unnumb.)
Feb. 2	Putnam, Tenn. (Chap. 169)
Feb. 18	Richland, Wis. (Unnumb.)

1842 cont.	
Feb. 18	Santa Rosa, Fla. (Unnumb.)
Dec. 19	Union, N. C. (Chap. 12)
Jan. 18	Wayne, W. Va. (Chap. 60)
Apr. 4	Wyoming, Pa. (Act 79)
1843	
Feb. 23	Atchison, Mo. (Unnumb.) (Allen, Mo.)
Feb. 17	Appanoose, Iowa (Chap. 34)
Mar. 3	Barbour, W. Va. (Chap. 53)
Feb. 17	Black Hawk, Iowa (Chap. 34)
Feb. 24	Bossier, La. (Act 33)
Mar. 13	Carbon, Pa. (Act 141)
July 5	Clackamas, Ore. (Unnumb.)
Mar. 2	Cumberland, Ill. (Unnumb.)
Feb. 17	Davis, Iowa (Chap. 34)
Mar. 9	Delta, Mich. (Act 89)
Apr. 1	De Sota, La. (Act 88)
Apr. 18	Elk, Pa. (Act 150)
Mar. 1	Franklin, La. (Act 41)
Feb. 24	Hernando, Fla. (Chap. 51) (Benton, Fla.)
Feb. 17	Iowa, Iowa (Chap. 34)
Feb. 24	Johnson, Ky. (Chap. 167)
Mar. 4	Larue, Ky. (Chap. 210)
Dec. 21	Lewis, Tenn. (Chap. 38)
Feb. 17	Mahaska, Iowa (Chap. 34)
July 5	Marion, Ore. (Unnumb.)
Mar. 9	Marquette, Mich. (Act 89)
Feb. 8	Massac, Ill. (Unnumb.)
Feb. 17	Monroe, Iowa (Chap. 34) (Kishkekosh, Iowa)
Feb. 16	Moultrie, Ill. (Unnumb.)
Mar. 9	Ontonagon, Mich. (Act 89)
Jan. 23	Owsley, Ky. (Chap. 43)
Feb. 17	Poweshiek, Iowa (Chap. 34)
Mar. 3	Pulaski, Ill. (Unnumb.)
Feb. 22	Putnam, Mo. (Unnumb.)
Feb. 18	Ritchie, W. Va. (Chap. 52)
Jan. 16	Rusk, Tex. (Unnumb.)
Mar. 7	Sabine, La. (Act 46)
Mar. 9	Schoolcraft, Mich. (Chap. 89)
Feb. 17	Tama, Iowa (Chap. 34)
Mar. 17	Tensas, La. (Act 61)
Feb. 17	Texas, Mo. (Unnumb.) (Ashley, Mo.)
Mar. 11	Wakulla, Fla. (Act 25)
Feb. 17	Wapello, Iowa (Chap. 34)

1843 cont.		
	July 5	Washington, Ore. (Unnumb.) (Twality, Ore.)
	July 5	Yamhill, Ore. (Unnumb.)
1844		
	Mar. 14	Brevard, Fla. (Unnumb.) (St. Lucie, Fla.)
	Mar. 13	Camden, N. J. (Unnumb.)
	June 27	Clark, Wash. (Unnumb.) (Vancouver, Wash.)
	June 22	Clatsop, Ore.
	Jan. 29	Grundy, Tenn. (Chap. 204)
	Jan. 7	Hancock, Tenn. (Chap. 71)
	Jan. 15	Howard, Ind. (Chap. 3) (Richardville, Ind.)
	Jan. 23	Issaquena, Miss. (Chap. 47)
	Feb. 15	Madison, Iowa (Chap. 124)
	Mar. 14	Marion, Fla. (Unnumb.)
	Mar. 25	Morehouse, La. (Act 118)
	Feb. 15	Sunflower, Miss. (Act 49)
	Jan. 19	Taylor, W. Va. (Chap. 44)
	Jan. 4	Ohio, Ind. (Chap. 2)
	Nov. 30	Polk, Ark. (Unnumb.)
	Jan. 15	Tipton, Ind. (Chap. 3)
	Mar. 25	Vermilion, La. (Act 81)
1845		
	Feb. 8	Appomattox, Va. (Chap. 41)
	Feb. 19	Bayfield, Wis. (Unnumb.) (La Pointe, Wis.)
	Feb. 14	Cedar, Mo. (Unnumb.)
	Feb. 3	Chippewa, Wis. (Unnumb.)
	Dec. 20	Crockett, Tenn. (Chap. 25)
	Jan. 1	Dallas, Ark. (Unnumb.)
	Nov.	Decatur, Tenn. (Chap. 7)
	Mar. 4	Defiance, Ohio (Unnumb.)
	Feb. 25	De Kalb, Mo. (Unnumb.)
	Feb. 4	Doddridge, W. Va. (Chap. 42)
	Feb. 14	Dunklin, Mo. (Unnumb.)
	Jan. 15	Fulton, Ky. (Chap. 44)
	Feb. 3	Gilmer, W. Va. (Chap. 43)
	Feb. 14	Harrison, Mo. (Unnumb.)
	Feb. 14	Hickory, Mo. (Unnumb.)
	Mar. 19	Houghton, Mich. (Act 48)
	Feb. 27	Jackson, La. (Act 38)
	Feb. 14	Knox, Mo. (Unnumb.)
	Feb. 14	Lawrence, Mo. (Unnumb.)
	Mar. 10	Levy, Fla. (Chap. 30)
	Dec. 21	Lewis, Wash. (Unnumb.)

1845 cont.

June 10	Marion, Iowa (Chap. 57)
Feb. 14	Mercer, Mo. (Unnumb.)
Feb. 14	Mississippi, Mo. (Unnumb.)
Feb. 14	Moniteau, Mo. (Unnumb.)
Feb. 14	Oregon, Mo. (Unnumb.)
Dec. 22	Polk, Ore. (Unnumb.)
Feb. 25	Reynolds, Mo. (Unnumb.)
Feb. 14	Schuyler, Mo. (Unnumb.)
Feb. 14	Sullivan, Mo. (Unnumb.)
Feb. 3	Wyandot, Ohio (Unnumb.)

1846

Mar. 24	Anderson, Tex. (Unnumb.)
Apr. 22	Angelina, Tex. (Unnumb.)
Feb. 24	Ashland, Ohio (Unnumb.)
Feb. 26	Blair, Pa. (Act 55)
Jan. 13	Boone, Iowa (Chap. 82)
Apr. 4	Calhoun, Tex. (Unnumb.)
Apr. 25	Cass, Tex. (Unnumb.) (Davis, Tex.)
Apr. 11	Cherokee, Tex. (Unnumb.)
Jan. 13	Clarke, Iowa (Chap. 82)
Apr. 3	Collin, Tex. (Unnumb.)
Feb. 3	Columbia, Wis. (Unnumb.)
Mar. 24	Comal, Tex. (Unnumb.)
Jan. 13	Dallas, Iowa (Chap. 82)
Mar. 30	Dallas, Tex. (Unnumb.)
Jan. 13	Decatur, Iowa (Chap. 82)
Apr. 11	Denton, Tex. (Unnumb.)
Mar. 24	De Witt, Tex. (Unnumb.)
Nov. 26	Drew, Ark. (Unnumb.)
Dec. 21	Gaston, N. C. (Chap. 24)
Mar. 17	Grayson, Tex. (Unnumb.)
Apr. 6	Grimes, Tex. (Unnumb.)
Mar. 30	Guadalupe, Tex. (Unnumb.)
Apr. 27	Henderson, Tex. (Unnumb.)
Mar. 25	Hopkins, Tex. (Unnumb.)
Apr. 11	Hunt, Tex. (Unnumb.)
Jan. 13	Jasper, Iowa (Chap. 82)
Jan. 31	Lafayette, Wis. (Unnumb.)
Apr. 6	Lavaca, Tex. (Unnumb.)
Mar. 17	Leon, Tex. (Unnumb.)
Apr. 11	Limestone, Tex. (Unnumb.)
Jan. 13	Lucas, Iowa (Chap. 82)
Feb. 16	Mahoning, Ohio (Unnumb.)
Jan. 13	Marshall, Iowa (Chap. 82)
Apr. 25	Navarro, Tex. (Unnumb.)
Apr. 22	Newton, Tex. (Unnumb.)

1846 cont.

Date	County
Apr. 18	Nueces, Tex. (Unnumb.)
Mar. 30	Panola, Tex. (Unnumb.)
Jan. 17	Polk, Iowa (Chap. 101)
Mar. 30	Polk, Tex. (Unnumb.)
Nov. 25	Prairie, Ark. (Unnumb.)
Apr. 11	Smith, Tex. (Unnumb.)
Jan. 13	Story, Iowa (Chap. 82)
May 11	Titus, Tex. (Unnumb.)
Apr. 3	Tyler, Tex. (Unnumb.)
Apr. 27	Upshur, Tex. (Unnumb.)
Apr. 6	Walker, Tex. (Unnumb.)
Jan. 13	Warren, Iowa (Chap. 82)
Jan. 31	Waukesha, Wis. (Unnumb.)
Jan. 13	Wayne, Iowa (Chap. 82)
Jan. 10	Wetzel, W. Va. (Chap. 65)
Apr. 3	Wharton, Tex. (Unnumb.)

1847

Date	County
Jan. 15	Alexander, N. C. (Chap. 22)
Feb. 20	Allamakee, Iowa (Chap. 66)
Mar. 13	Arlington, Va. (Chap. 53) (Alexandria, Va.)
Dec. 23	Benton, Ore. (Unnumb.)
Mar. 11	Boone, W. Va. (Chap. 55)
Dec. 29	Choctaw, Ala. (Act 213)
Feb. 24	Fremont, Iowa (Chap. 83)
Mar. 19	Highland, Va. (Chap. 56)
Dec. 28	Linn, Ore. (Unnumb.)
Feb. 24	Page, Iowa (Chap. 83)
Jan. 18	Polk, N. C. (Chap. 26)
Feb. 24	Pottawattamie, Iowa (Chap. 84)
Feb. 24	Ringgold, Iowa (Chap. 83)
Feb. 25	Saline, Ill. (Unnumb.)
Mar. 15	Sullivan, Pa. (Act 365)
Feb. 24	Taylor, Iowa (Chap. 83)
Feb. 20	Winnebago, Iowa (Chap. 66)
Feb. 20	Winneshiek, Iowa (Chap. 66)

1848

Date	County
Mar. 11	Adams, Wis. (Unnumb.)
Nov. 30	Ashley, Ark. (Unnumb.)
Feb. 14	Auglaize, Ohio (Unnumb.)
Mar. 14	Bienville, La. (Act 183)
Mar. 6	Caldwell, Tex. (Chap. 65)
Feb. 12	Cameron, Tex. (Chap. 35)
Mar. 20	Cooke, Tex. (Chap. 130)
Apr. 11	Forest, Pa. (Res. 9)
Feb. 23	Gillespie, Tex. (Chap. 47)
Jan. 15	Hancock, W. Va. (Chap. 58)

1848 cont.	
Mar. 1	Hays, Tex. (Chap. 57)
Jan. 8	Holmes, Fla. (Chap. 176)
Feb. 26	Kaufman, Tex. (Chap. 52)
Feb. 12	Medina, Tex. (Chap. 36)
Feb. 24	Morrow, Ohio (Unnumb.)
Mar. 11	Putnam, W. Va. (Chap. 59)
Mar. 16	Red River, La. (Act 219)
Feb. 10	Starr, Tex. (Chap. 31)
Jan. 13	Taylor, Ky. (Chap. 26)
Mar. 20	Van Zandt, Tex. (Chap. 119)
Jan. 28	Webb, Tex. (Chap. 32)
Mar. 13	Williamson, Tex. (Chap. 78)
Jan. 19	Wirt, W. Va. (Chap. 60)
1849	
Jan. 29	Alamance, N. C. (Chap. 14)
Oct. 27	Benton, Minn. (Chap. 5)
Feb. 27	Butler, Mo. (Unnumb.)
Oct. 27	Dakota, Minn. (Chap. 5)
Dec. 20	Ellis, Tex. (Chap. 18)
Jan. 16	Forsyth, N. C. (Chap. 23)
Oct. 27	Itasca, Minn. (Chap. 5)
Feb. 24	Laclede, Mo. (Unnumb.)
Mar. 20	Lawrence, Pa. (Act 366)
Mar. 3	McDonald, Mo. (Unnumb.)
Jan. 13	Putnam, Fla. (Chap. 280)
Oct. 27	Ramsey, Minn. (Chap. 5)
Dec. 17	Scott, Tenn. (Chap. 45)
Dec. 20	Tarrant, Tex. (Chap. 17)
Oct. 27	Wabasha, Minn. (Chap. 5)
Oct. 27	Washington, Minn. (Chap. 5)
Jan. 27	Watauga, N. C. (Chap. 25)
1850	
Jan. 22	Bell, Tex. (Chap. 55)
Feb. 18	Butte, Calif. (Chap. 15)
Feb. 18	Calaveras, Calif. (Chap. 15)
Dec. 6	Calhoun, Ark. (Unnumb.)
Feb. 14	Clinch, Ga. (Unnumb.)
Feb. 18	Colusa, Calif. (Chap. 15)
Feb. 18	Contra Costa, Calif. (Chap. 15)
Feb. 18	El Dorado, Calif. (Chap. 15)
Jan. 3	El Paso, Tex. (Chap. 29)
Jan. 28	Falls, Tex. (Chap. 80)
Sept. 6	Freestone, Tex. (Chap. 39)
Feb. 28	Fulton, Ohio (Unnumb.)
Apr. 19	Fulton, Pa. (Act 495)
Feb. 13	Gordon, Ga. (Unnumb.)
Jan. 31	Iron, Utah (Unnumb.) (Little Salt Lake, Utah)

1850 cont.

Jan. 30	Kenosha, Wis. (Chap. 39)
Jan. 28	Kinney, Tex. (Chap. 81)
Feb. 18	Los Angeles, Calif. (Chap. 15)
Feb. 9	Marathon, Wis. (Chap. 226)
Feb. 18	Marin, Calif. (Chap. 15)
Feb. 18	Mariposa, Calif. (Chap. 15)
Jan. 22	McLennan (Chap. 54)
Feb. 18	Mendocino, Calif. (Chap. 15)
Feb. 18	Monterey, Calif. (Chap. 15)
May 3	Montour, Pa. (Act 387)
Feb. 18	Napa, Calif. (Chap. 15)
Feb. 15	Ocean, N. J. (Unnumb.)
Jan. 3	Presidio, Tex. (Chap. 29)
Jan. 23	Raleigh, W. Va. (Chap. 24)
Feb. 18	Sacramento, Calif. (Chap. 15)
Feb. 18	San Diego, Calif. (Chap. 15)
Feb. 18	San Francisco, Calif. (Chap. 15)
Feb. 18	San Joaquin, Calif. (Chap. 15)
Feb. 18	San Luis Obispo, Calif. (Chap. 15)
Feb. 18	Santa Barbara, Calif. (Chap. 15)
Feb. 18	Santa Clara, Calif. (Chap. 15)
Feb. 18	Santa Cruz, Calif. (Chap. 15) (Branciforte, Calif.)
Feb. 18	Shasta, Calif. (Chap. 15)
Feb. 18	Solano, Calif. (Chap. 15)
Feb. 18	Sonoma, Calif. (Chap. 15)
Feb. 18	Sutter, Calif. (Chap. 15)
Feb. 18	Trinity, Calif. (Chap. 15)
Feb. 11	Trinity, Tex. (Chap. 160)
Feb. 18	Tuolumne, Calif. (Chap. 15)
Feb. 8	Uvalde, Tex. (Chap. 112)
Mar. 23	Vinton, Ohio (Unnumb.)
Feb. 12	Winston, Ala. (Act 58) (Hancock, Ala.)
Feb. 5	Wood, Tex. (Chap. 98)
Jan. 26	Wyoming, W. Va. (Chap. 25)
Dec. 28	Yadkin, N. C. (Chap. 40)
Feb. 18	Yolo, Calif. (Chap. 15)
Feb. 18	Yuba, Calif. (Chap. 15)

1851

Jan. 15	Adair, Iowa (Chap. 9)
Jan. 15	Adams, Iowa (Chap. 9)
Jan. 15	Audubon, Iowa (Chap. 9)
Mar. 1	Bollinger, Mo. (Unnumb.)
Jan. 15	Bremer, Iowa (Chap. 9)
Jan. 15	Buena Vista, Iowa (Chap. 9)
Jan. 15	Butler, Iowa (Chap. 9)

1851 cont.

Jan. 15	Calhoun, Iowa (Chap. 9) (Fox, Iowa)
Jan. 15	Carroll, Iowa (Chap. 9)
Jan. 15	Cass, Iowa (Chap. 9)
Mar. 31	Cass, Minn. (Unnumb.)
Jan. 15	Cerro Gordo, Iowa (Chap. 9)
Jan. 15	Cherokee, Iowa (Chap. 9)
Jan. 15	Chickasaw, Iowa (Chap. 9)
Mar. 31	Chisago, Minn. (Unnumb.)
Jan. 15	Clay, Iowa (Chap. 9)
Mar. 21	Craig, Va. (Chap. 25)
Jan. 15	Crawford, Iowa (Chap. 9)
Feb. 10	Dent, Mo. (Unnumb.)
Jan. 15	Dickinson, Iowa (Chap. 9)
Feb. 11	Door, Wis. (Chap. 56)
Jan. 15	Emmet, Iowa (Chap. 9)
Jan. 15	Floyd, Iowa (Chap. 9)
Jan. 15	Franklin, Iowa (Chap. 9)
Jan. 15	Greene, Iowa (Chap. 9)
Jan. 15	Grundy, Iowa (Chap. 9)
Jan. 15	Guthrie, Iowa (Chap. 9)
Jan. 15	Hancock, Iowa (Chap. 9)
Jan. 15	Hardin, Iowa (Chap. 9)
Jan. 15	Harrison, Iowa (Chap. 9)
Jan. 15	Howard, Iowa (Chap. 9)
May 13	Howard, Md. (Const.)
Jan. 15	Humboldt, Iowa (Chap. 9)
Jan. 15	Ida, Iowa (Chap. 9)
Jan. 29	Jackson, N. C. (Chap. 38)
Jan. 15	Kossuth, Iowa (Chap. 9)
May 1	La Crosse, Wis. (Chap. 131)
Jan. 28	Lane, Ore. (Unnumb.)
Jan. 15	Lyon, Iowa (Chap. 9)
Jan. 27	Madison, N. C. (Chap. 36)
Oct. 4	Millard, Utah (Chap. 38)
Jan. 15	Mills, Iowa (Chap. 9)
Jan. 15	Mitchell, Iowa (Chap. 9)
Jan. 15	Monona, Iowa (Chap. 9)
Jan. 15	Montgomery, Iowa (Chap. 9)
Apr. 25	Nevada, Calif. (Chap. 14)
Mar. 11	Noble, Ohio (Unnumb.)
Jan. 15	O'Brien, Iowa (Chap. 9)
Feb. 6	Oconto, Wis. (Chap. 44)
Jan. 15	Osceola, Iowa (Chap. 9)
Feb. 17	Outagamie, Wis. (Chap. 83)
Feb. 4	Pacific, Wash. (Unnumb.)
Jan. 15	Palo Alto, Iowa (Chap. 9)

1851 cont.

Jan. 15 Pottawattomie, Iowa (Chap. 9)
Feb. 19 Pemiscot, Mo. (Unnumb.)
Apr. 25 Placer, Calif. (Chap. 14)
Mar. 29 Pleasants, W. Va. (Chap. 27)
Jan. 15 Plymouth, Iowa (Chap. 9)
Jan. 15 Pocahontas, Iowa (Chap. 9)
Dec. 20 Polk, Ga. (Act 26)
Jan. 15 Sac, Iowa (Chap. 9)
Jan. 6 Sebastian, Ark. (Unnumb.)
Jan. 15 Shelby, Iowa (Chap. 9)
Jan. 15 Sioux, Iowa (Chap. 9)
Dec. 20 Spalding, Ga. (Act 28)
Feb. 10 Stone, Mo. (Unnumb.)
Jan. 15 Union, Iowa (Chap. 9)
Mar. 26 Upshur, W. Va. (Chap. 26)
Feb. 17 Vernon, Mo. (Unnumb.)
Mar. 1 Vernon, Wis. (Chap. 131)
(Bad Axe, Wis.)
Feb. 17 Waupaca, Wis. (Chap. 78)
Feb. 15 Waushara, Wis. (Chap. 77)
Jan. 15 Webster, Iowa (Chap. 9)
(Risley, Iowa)
Dec. 30 Whitfield, Ga. (Act 27)
Jan. 15 Woodbury, Iowa (Chap. 9)
(Wahkaw)
Jan. 15 Worth, Iowa (Chap. 9)
Jan. 15 Wright, Iowa (Chap. 9)

1852

Jan. 9 Bernalillo, N. M. (Unnumb.)
Feb. 5 Burnet, Tex. (Chap. 60)
Mar. 8 Calhoun, Miss. (Chap. 15)
Dec. 17 Columbia, Ark. (Unnumb.)
Mar. 3 Davis, Utah (Unnumb.)
Jan. 9 Dona Ana, N. M. (Unnumb.)
Jan. 7 Douglas, Ore. (Unnumb.)
Mar. 6 Hennepin, Minn. (Chap. 32)
Jan. 24 Hidalgo, Tex. (Chap. 42)
Jan. 12 Jackson, Ore. (Unnumb.)
Dec. 22 Jefferson, Wash. (Unnumb.)
Mar. 3 Juab, Utah (Unnumb.)
Apr. 16 Kewaunee, Wis. (Chap. 363)
Dec. 22 King, Wash. (Unnumb.)
Feb. 5 Orange, Tex. (Chap. 59)
Dec. 22 Pierce, Wash. (Unnumb.)
Jan. 7 Powell, Ky. (Chap. 325)
Mar. 11 Richland, La. (Act 149)
Jan. 9 Rio Arriba, N. M. (Unnumb.)

1852 cont.

Mar. 3	Salt Lake, Utah (Unnumb.) (Great Salt Lake, Utah)
Jan. 9	San Miguel, N. M. (Unnumb.)
Mar. 3	Sanpete, Utah (Unnumb.)
Jan. 9	Santa Fe, N. M. (Unnumb.)
Apr. 16	Sierra, Calif. (Chap. 145)
Mar. 22	Siskiyou, Calif. (Chap. 146)
Jan. 9	Socorro, N. M. (Unnumb.)
Jan. 9	Taos, N. M. (Unnumb.)
Jan. 15	Taylor, Ga. (Act 29)
Jan. 12	Thurston, Wash. (Unnumb.)
Mar. 3	Tooele, Utah (Unnumb.)
Apr. 20	Tulare, Calif. (Chap. 153)
Mar. 3	Utah, Utah (Unnumb.)
Jan. 9	Valencia, N. M. (Unnumb.)
Mar. 3	Washington, Utah (Unnumb.)
Mar. 3	Weber, Utah (Unnumb.)
Feb. 24	Winn, La. (Act 85)

1853

Mar. 25	Alameda, Calif. (Chap. 41)
Mar. 5	Blue Earth, Minn. (Chap. 11)
July 6	Buffalo, Wis. (Chap. 100)
Dec. 5	Catoosa, Ga. (Act 218)
July 6	Clark, Wis. (Chap. 100)
Dec. 22	Coos, Ore. (Unnumb.)
Dec. 15	Dougherty, Ga. (Act 223)
Mar. 5	Fillmore, Minn. (Chap. 11)
Dec. 20	Fulton, Ga. (Act 225)
Mar. 5	Goodhue, Minn. (Chap. 11)
Dec. 7	Hart, Ga. (Act 226)
Feb. 7	Hill, Tex. (Chap. 26)
May 12	Humboldt, Calif. (Chap. 114)
Jan. 6	Island, Wash. (Unnumb.)
Feb. 11	Jackson, Wis. (Chap. 8)
Feb. 11	Kankakee, Ill. (Unnumb.)
Mar. 5	Le Seuer, Minn. (Chap. 11)
Mar. 5	Nicollet, Minn. (Chap. 11)
Mar. 7	Ozaukee, Wis. (Chap. 21)
Dec. 5	Pickens, Ga. (Act 228)
Mar. 14	Pierce, Wis. (Chap. 31)
Mar. 14	Polk, Wis. (Chap. 31)
Mar. 5	Rice, Minn. (Chap. 11)
Apr. 26	San Bernardino, Calif. (Chap. 78)
Mar. 5	Scott, Minn. (Chap. 11)
Feb. 16	Shawano, Wis. (Chap. 9)
Mar. 5	Sibley, Minn. (Chap. 11)
Jan. 8	Sumter, Fla. (Chap. 548)

1853 cont.	
Dec. 15	Tillamook, Ore. (Unnumb.)
Dec. 16	Webster, Ga. (Act 227) (Kinchafoonee)
Dec. 20	Worth, Ga. (Act 229)
1854	
May 11	Amador, Calif. (Chap. 42)
Mar. 18	Androscoggin, Me. (Chap. 60)
Feb. 4	Bosque, Tex. (Chap. 38)
Nov. 23	Burt, Neb. (Procl.)
Feb. 20	Calhoun, Ga. (Act 217)
Nov. 23	Cass, Neb. (Procl.)
Feb. 18	Charlton, Ga. (Act 220)
Feb. 13	Chattahoochee, Ga. (Act 219)
Apr. 26	Clallam, Wash. (Unnumb.)
Feb. 16	Clay, Ga. (Act 221)
Feb. 9	Coffee, Ga. (Act 222)
Jan. 16	Columbia, Ore. (Unnumb.)
Feb. 4	Coryell, Tex. (Chap. 36)
Apr. 21	Cowlitz, Wash. (Unnumb.)
Nov. 23	Dodge, Neb. (Procl.)
Nov. 23	Douglas, Neb. (Procl.)
Feb. 9	Douglas, Wis. (Chap. 10)
Feb. 3	Dunn, Wis. (Chap. 7)
Jan. 21	Fannin, Ga. (Act 224)
Apr. 14	Grays Harbor, Wash. (Unnumb.) (Chehalis, Wash.)
Feb. 23	Houston, Minn. (Chap. 29)
Feb. 13	Johnson, Tex. (Chap. 76)
Feb. 4	Karnes, Tex. (Chap. 35)
Jan. 14	Lyon, Ky. (Chap. 32)
Mar. 13	Mason, Wash. (Unnumb.) (Sawamish, Wash.)
Feb. 6	McLean, Ky. (Chap. 125)
Mar. 21	Monroe, Wis. (Chap. 35)
Dec. 22	Multnomah, Ore. (Unnumb.)
Nov. 23	Nemaha, Neb. (Procl.) (Forney, Neb.)
Nov. 23	Otoe, Neb. (Procl.) (Pierce, Neb.)
Mar. 18	Plumas, Calif. (Chap. 1)
Nov. 23	Richardson, Neb. (Procl.)
Apr. 4	Sagadahoc, Me. (Chap. 70)
Apr. 17	Schuyler, N.Y. (Chap. 386)
Mar. 9	Skamania, Wash. (Unnumb.)
Apr. 1	Stanislaus, Calif. (Chap. 81)
Jan. 13	Summit, Utah (Chap. 63)
Jan. 27	Trempealeau, Wis. (Chap. 2)

1854 cont.

Dec. 29	Volusia, Fla. (Chap. 624)
Apr. 24	Wahkiakum, Wash. (Unnumb.)
Apr. 25	Walla Walla, Wash. (Unnumb.)
Jan. 11	Wasco, Ore. (Unnumb.)
Nov. 23	Washington, Neb. (Procl.)
Mar. 9	Whatcom, Wash. (Unnumb.)
Feb. 23	Winona, Minn. (Chap. 29)

1855

Aug. 30	Allen, Kan. (Chap. 30)
Aug. 30	Anderson, Kan. (Chap. 30)
Aug. 30	Atchison, Kan. (Chap. 30)
Dec. 12	Barton, Mo. (Unnumb.)
Aug. 30	Bourbon, Kan. (Chap. 30)
Aug. 30	Brown, Kan. (Chap. 30)
Feb. 20	Brown, Minn. (Chap. 6)
Mar. 14	Buffalo, Neb. (Unnumb.)
Aug. 30	Butler, Kan. (Chap. 30)
Feb. 22	Carver, Minn. (Chap. 6)
Aug. 30	Cherokee, Kan. (Chap. 30) (McGee, Kan.)
Mar. 7	Clay, Neb. (Unnumb.)
Aug. 30	Coffey, Kan. (Chap. 30)
Nov. 16	Cumberland, Tenn. (Chap. 6)
Mar. 16	Cuming, Neb. (Unnumb.)
Dec. 18	Curry, Ore. (Unnumb.)
Mar. 7	Dakota, Neb. (Unnumb.)
Feb. 20	Dodge, Minn. (Chap. 6)
Aug. 30	Doniphan, Kan. (Chap. 30)
Aug. 30	Douglas, Kan. (Chap. 30)
Feb. 20	Faribault, Minn. (Chap. 6)
Aug. 30	Franklin, Kan. (Chap. 30)
Feb. 20	Freeborn, Minn. (Chap. 6)
Mar. 16	Gage, Neb. (Unnumb.)
Aug. 30	Geary, Kan. (Chap. 30) (Davis, Kan.)
Aug. 30	Greenwood, Kan. (Chap. 30)
Feb. 7	Harnett, N.C. (Chap. 8)
Aug. 30	Jackson, Kan. (Chap. 30) (Calhoun, Kan.)
Aug. 30	Jefferson, Kan. (Chap. 30)
Aug. 30	Johnson, Kan. (Chap. 30)
Mar. 2	Johnson, Neb. (Unnumb.)
Mar. 6	Lancaster, Neb. (Unnumb.)
Aug. 30	Leavenworth, Kan. (Chap. 30)
Dec. 15	Liberty, Fla. (Chap. 771)
Aug. 30	Linn, Kan. (Chap. 30)
Mar. 6	Loup, Neb. (Unnumb.)

1855 cont.

Jan. 9	Manatee, Fla. (Chap. 628)
Mar. 2	Maries, Mo. (Unnumb.)
n. d.	Marion, Kan. (Chap. 33)
Aug. 30	Marshall, Kan. (Chap. 30)
Apr. 19	Merced, Calif. (Chap. 104)
Aug. 30	Miami, Kan. (Chap. 30)
	(Lykins, Kan.)
Aug. 30	Morris, Kan. (Chap. 30)
	(Wise, Kan.)
Feb. 20	Mower, Minn. (Chap. 6)
Aug. 30	Nemaha, Kan. (Chap. 30)
Aug. 30	Neosho, Kan. (Chap. 30)
	(Dorn, Kan.)
Feb. 20	Olmstead, Minn. (Chap. 6)
Aug. 30	Osage, Kan. (Chap. 30)
	(Weller, Kan.)
Dec. 12	Parker, Tex. (Chap. 1)
Mar. 6	Pawnee, Neb. (Unnumb.)
Feb. 20	Renville, Minn. (Chap. 6)
Aug. 30	Riley, Kan. (Chap. 30)
Mar. 6	Saline, Neb. (Unnumb.)
	(Sarpy, Neb.)
Feb. 20	St. Louis, Minn. (Chap. 6)
	(Superior, Minn.)
Aug. 30	Seward, Kan. (Chap. 30)
	(Godfroy, Kan.)
Mar. 6	Seward, Neb. (Chap. 30)
	(Greene, Neb.)
Aug. 30	Shawnee, Kan. (Chap. 30)
Mar. 2	Snyder, Pa. (Act 555)
Mar. 6	Stanton, Neb. (Unnumb.)
	(Izard, Neb.)
Feb. 20	Stearns, Minn. (Chap. 6)
Feb. 20	Steele, Minn. (Chap. 6)
Feb. 20	Todd, Minn. (Chap. 6)
Aug. 30	Wabaunsee, Kan. (Chap. 30)
	(Richardson, Kan.)
n. d.	Washington, Kan. (Chap. 33)
Mar. 3	Webster, Mo. (Unnumb.)
Aug. 30	Wilson, Kan. (Chap. 30)
Feb. 13	Wilson, N. C. (Chap. 12)
Aug. 30	Woodson, Kan. (Chap. 30)
Feb. 20	Wright, Minn. (Chap. 6)
Mar 13	York, Neb. (Unnumb.)

1856

Jan. 25	Atascosa, Tex. (Chap. 33)
Jan. 26	Bandera, Tex. (Chap. 42)

1856 cont.

Jan. 5	Beaver, Utah (Unnumb.)
Feb. 25	Berrien, Ga. (Act 48)
Jan. 5	Box Elder, Utah (Unnumb.)
Aug. 27	Brown, Tex. (Chap. 139)
Mar. 31	Burnett, Wis. (Chap. 94)
Jan. 26	Butler, Neb. (Unnumb.)
Jan. 5	Cache, Utah (Unnumb.)
Mar. 5	Calhoun, W. Va. (Chap. 108)
Feb. 28	Cheatham, Tenn. (Chap. 122)
Feb. 25	Colquitt, Ga. (Act 46)
Jan. 25	Comanche, Tex. (Chap. 35)
Jan. 26	Dixon, Neb. (Unnumb.)
Oct. 6	Eau Clair, Wis. (Chap. 114)
Jan. 25	Erath, Tex. (Chap. 34)
Jan. 26	Fillmore, Neb. (Unnumb.)
Apr. 19	Fresno, Calif. (Chap. 127)
Dec. 22	Hamilton, Iowa (Chap. 15)
Jan. 26	Haralson, Ga. (Act 47)
Aug. 27	Jack, Tex. (Chap. 135)
Jan. 26	Jefferson, Neb. (Unnumb.) (Jones, Neb.)
Jan. 22	Josephine, Ore. (Unnumb.)
Oct. 13	Juneau, Wis. (Chap. 130)
Jan. 26	Kerr, Tex. (Chap. 40)
Dec. 23	Lafayette, Fla. (Chap. 806)
Mar. 1	Lake, Minn. (Chap. 35)
Feb. 1	Lampasas, Tex. (Chap. 44)
Feb. 2	Live Oak, Tex. (Chap. 59)
Feb. 1	Liano, Tex. (Chap. 48)
Jan. 26	Madison, Neb. (Unnumb.)
Feb. 2	Maverick, Tex. (Chap. 69)
Aug. 27	McCulloch, Tex. (Chap. 141)
Mar. 1	McLeod, Minn. (Chap. 26)
Feb. 23	Meeker, Minn. (Chap. 68)
Feb. 26	Miller, Ga. (Act 49)
Feb. 25	Morrison, Minn. (Chap. 38)
Aug. 27	Palo Pinto, Tex. (Chap. 138)
Jan. 26	Pierce, Neb. (Unnumb.) (Otoe, Neb.)
Mar. 1	Pine, Minn. (Chap. 36)
Jan. 26	Platte, Neb. (Unnumb.)
Jan. 26	Polk, Neb. (Unnumb.)
Mar. 11	Roane, W. Va. (Chap. 109)
Mar. 15	Rowan, Ky.
Feb. 1	San Saba, Tex. (Chap. 49)
Apr. 19	San Mateo, Calif. (Chap. 125)
Jan. 26	Saunders, Neb. (Unnumb.) (Calhoun, Neb.)

1856 cont.

Feb. 25	Sherburne, Minn. (Chap. 38)
Dec. 23	Taylor, Fla. (Chap. 806)
Apr. 9	Tehama, Calif. (Chap. 100)
Feb. 16	Terrell, Ga. (Act 50)
Jan. 26	Thayer, Neb. (Unnumb.) (Jefferson, Neb.)
Mar. 6	Towns, Ga. (Act 51)
Mar. 7	Tucker, W. Va. (Chap. 110)
Jan. 23	Wise, Tex. (Chap. 31)
Feb. 16	Wise, Va. (Chap. 107)
Mar. 29	Wood, Wis. (Chap. 54)
Feb. 2	Young, Tex. (Chap. 71)

1857

May 23	Aitkin, Minn. (Chap. 5)
May 23	Anoka, Minn. (Chap. 64)
Feb. 17	Bay, Mich. (Act 171)
Dec. 8	Bee, Tex. (Chap. 14)
May 23	Carlton, Minn. (Chap. 5)
Feb. 12	Cedar, Neb. (Unnumb.)
Feb. 20	Clay, Kan. (Unnumb.)
Dec. 24	Clay, Tex. (Chap. 34)
May 23	Cottonwood, Minn. (Chap. 14)
May 23	Crow Wing, Minn. (Chap. 5)
Dec. 3	Dawson, Ga. (Act 19)
Mar. 2	Del Norte, Calif. (Chap. 52)
Feb. 20	Dickinson, Kan. (Unnumb.)
Oct. 29	Douglas, Mo. (Unnumb.)
Dec. 19	Glascock, Ga. (Act 20)
Mar. 2	Howell, Mo. (Unnumb.)
Feb. 17	Iron, Mo. (Unnumb.)
Feb. 13	Isanti, Minn. (Chap. 70)
May 23	Jackson, Minn. (Chap. 14)
Jan. 16	Kitsap, Wash. (Unnumb.) (Slaughter, Wash.)
Feb. 10	Knox, Neb. (Unnumb.)
Mar. 23	Lincoln, Minn.
Feb. 17	Lyon, Kan. (Unnumb.) (Breckenridge, Kan.)
May 23	Mahnomen, Minn. (Procl.)
May 23	Martin, Minn. (Chap. 14)
May 23	Mille Lacs, Minn. (Chap. 5)
Dec. 21	Mitchell, Ga. (Act 22)
Dec. 24	Montague, Tex. (Chap. 33)
May 23	Murray, Minn. (Chap. 14)
May 23	Nobles, Minn. (Chap. 14)
Nov. 13	Phelps, Mo. (Unnumb.)
Dec. 18	Pierce, Ga. (Act 23)

1857 cont.

May 23	Pipestone, Minn. (Chap. 14)
Feb. 20	Pottawatomie, Kan. (Unnumb.)
May 23	Rock, Minn. (Chap. 14)
Feb. 7	Sarpy, Neb. (Unnumb.)
Dec. 22	Schley, Ga. (Act 24)
Dec. 9	Sequatchie, Tenn. (Chap. 11)
Mar. 19	Union, N. J. (Chap. 82)
Feb. 27	Waseca, Minn. (Chap. 57)
Dec. 22	White, Ga. (Act 25)
Dec. 22	Wilcox, Ga. (Act 26)

1858

Jan. 22	Archer, Tex. (Chap. 55)
Dec. 11	Banks, Ga. (Act 19)
Feb. 1	Baylor, Tex. (Chap. 75)
Mar. 18	Becker, Minn. (Chap. 34)
Feb. 12	Blanco, Tex. (Chap. 130)
Dec. 21	Bradford, Fla. (Chap. 895) (New River, Fla.)
Dec. 11	Brooks, Ga. (Act 21)
Feb. 13	Buchanan, Va. (Chap. 156)
Feb. 1	Callahan, Tex. (Chap. 75)
Feb. 12	Chambers, Tex. (Chap. 125)
Dec. 31	Clay, Fla. (Chap. 866)
Mar. 18	Clay, Minn. (Chap. 34) (Breckinridge, Minn.)
Mar. 29	Clay, W. Va. (Chap. 158)
Nov. 30	Clayton, Ga. (Act 17)
Feb. 1	Coleman, Tex. (Chap. 75)
Feb. 1	Concho, Tex. (Chap. 75)
Feb. 1	Dawson, Tex. (Chap. 75)
Feb. 1	Dimmit, Tex. (Chap. 75)
Mar. 8	Douglas, Minn. (Chap. 74)
Feb. 1	Du Val, Tex. (Chap. 75)
Feb. 1	Eastland, Tex. (Chap. 75)
Dec. 13	Echols, Ga. (Act 22)
Feb. 1	Edwards, Tex. (Chap. 75)
Feb. 1	Frio, Tex. (Chap. 75)
Mar. 5	Green Lake, Wis. (Chap. 17)
Nov. 4	Hall, Neb. (Unnumb.)
Feb. 1	Hardemann, Tex. (Chap. 75)
Jan. 22	Hardin, Tex. (Chap. 55)
Feb. 1	Haskell, Tex. (Chap. 75)
Feb. 2	Jackson, Ky. (Chap. 167)
Dec. 11	Johnson, Ga. (Act 20)
Feb. 1	Jones, Tex. (Chap. 75)
Mar. 13	Kanabec, Minn. (Chap. 56)
Mar. 20	Kandiyohi, Minn. (Chap. 65)

1858 cont.

Jan. 22	Kimble, Tex. (Chap. 55)
Feb. 1	Knox, Tex. (Chap. 75)
Feb. 1	La Salle, Tex. (Chap. 75)
Jan. 22	Mason, Tex. (Chap. 55)
Feb. 20	McDowell, W. Va. (Chap. 155)
Feb. 1	McMullen, Tex. (Chap. 75)
Jan. 22	Menard, Tex. (Chap. 55)
Nov. 4	Merrick, Neb. (Unnumb.)
Mar. 18	Otter Tail, Minn. (Chap. 34)
Feb. 25	Pepin, Wis. (Chap. 15)
July 20	Polk, Minn. (Chap. 67)
Dec. 10	Quitman, Ga. (Act 18)
Feb. 1	Runnels, Tex. (Chap. 75)
Feb. 1	Shackelford, Tex. (Chap. 75)
Jan. 29	Spokane, Wash. (Unnumb.)
Jan. 22	Stephens, Tex. (Chap. 55) (Buchanan, Tex.)
Dec. 21	Suwanee, Fla. (Chap. 895)
Feb. 1	Taylor, Tex. (Chap. 75)
Jan. 13	Throckmorton, Tex. (Chap. 30)
June 11	Wadena, Minn. (Chap. 179)
Feb. 1	Wichita, Tex. (Chap. 75)
Feb. 1	Wilbarger, Tex. (Chap. 75)
Mar. 18	Wilkin, Minn. (Chap. 64) (Andy Johnson, Minn.) (Toombs, Minn.)
Jan. 22	Zapata, Tex. (Chap. 55)
Feb. 1	Zavala, Tex. (Chap. 75)
1859	Alleghany, N. C. (Chap. 3)
Mar. 19	Barron, Wis. (Chap. 191) (Dallas, Wis.)
Mar. 10	Carter, Mo. (Unnumb.)
Feb. 11	Chase, Kan. (Chap. 46)
Mar. 8	Christian, Mo. (Unnumb.)
Feb. 19	Craighead, Ark. (Act 171)
Feb. 8	Douglas, Ill. (Unnumb.)
Feb. 17	Ford, Ill. (Unnumb.)
Dec. 20	Klickitat, Wash. (Unnumb.)
Feb. 4	Muskegon, Mich. (Act 55)
Jan. 29	Wyandotte, Kan. (Chap. 47)
Mar. 27	Ashland, Wis. (Chap. 211)
Feb. 16	Boyd, Ky. (Chap. 288)
1860	
Mar. 29	Cameron, Pa. (Act 598)
Feb. 27	Cloud, Kan. (Chap. 43) (Shirley, Kan.)
Jan. 11	Dawson, Neb. (Unnumb.)

1860 cont.

Jan. 13	Holt, Neb. (Unnumb.) (West, Neb.)
Jan. 10	Kearney, Neb. (Unnumb.)
Mar. 9	Knox, Me. (Chap. 146)
Jan. 7	Lincoln, Neb. (Unnumb.) (Shorter, Neb.)
Feb. 22	Magoffin, Ky. (Chap. 437)
Feb. 8	Marion, Tex. (Chap. 48)
Feb. 1	Metcalfe, Ky. (Chap. 104)
Feb. 1	Mora, N. M. (Unnumb.)
Jan. 13	Nuckolls, Neb. (Unnumb.)
Feb. 27	Ottawa, Kan. (Chap. 43)
Feb. 27	Republic, Kan. (Chap. 43)
Feb. 15	Saline, Kan. (Chap. 44)
Feb. 25	Watonwan, Minn. (Chap. 13)
Feb. 29	Webster, Ky. (Chap. 822)
Jan. 10	Webster, W. Va. (Chap. 47)
Feb. 13	Wilson, Tex. (Chap. 76)
Mar. 5	Wolfe, Ky. (Chap. 1326)

1861

Nov. 1	Arapahoe, Colo. (Unnumb.)
Feb. 8	Baker, Fla. (Chap. 1, 185)
Mar. 30	Bland, Va. (Chap. 23)
Nov. 1	Boulder, Colo. (Unnumb.)
Nov. 1	Chaffee, Colo. (Unnumb.) (Lake, Colo.)
Nov. 25	Churchill, Nev. (Chap. 24)
Feb. 20	Clay, N. C. (Chap. 6)
Nov. 1	Clear Creek, Colo. (Unnumb.)
Nov. 1	Conejos, Colo. (Unnumb.) (Guadalupe, Colo.)
Nov. 1	Costilla, Colo. (Unnumb.)
Nov. 1	Douglas, Colo. (Unnumb.)
Nov. 25	Douglas, Nev. (Chap. 24)
Nov. 1	El Paso, Colo. (Unnumb.)
Nov. 25	Esmeralda, Nev. (Chap. 24)
Nov. 1	Fremont, Colo. (Unnumb.)
Nov. 1	Gilpin, Colo. (Unnumb.)
Nov. 1	Huerfano, Colo. (Unnumb.)
Nov. 25	Humboldt, Nev. (Chap. 24)
Nov. 1	Jefferson, Colo. (Unnumb.)
Mar. 11	Keweenaw, Mich. (Chap. 118)
May 20	Lake, Calif. (Chap. 498)
Nov. 1	Lake, Colo. (Unnumb.) (Carbonate, Colo.)
Nov. 1	Larimer, Colo. (Unnumb.)
Nov. 25	Lyon, Nev. (Chap. 24)

1861 cont.

Mar. 15	Menominee, Mich. (Chap. 213) (Bleeker, Mich.)
Feb. 16	Mitchell, N. C. (Chap. 8)
Apr. 24	Mono, Calif. (Chap. 233)
Nov. 1	Park, Colo. (Unnumb.)
Feb. 8	Polk, Fla. (Chap. 1, 201)
Nov. 1	Pueblo, Colo. (Unnumb.)
Nov. 1	San Miguel, Colo. (Unnumb.) (Ouray, Colo.)
Jan. 14	Snohomish, Wash. (Unnumb.)
Nov. 25	Storey, Nev. (Chap. 24)
Nov. 1	Summit, Colo. (Unnumb.)
Feb. 15	Transylvania, N. C. (Chap. 10)
Nov. 25	Washoe, Nev. (Chap. 24)
Nov. 1	Weld, Colo. (Unnumb.)
Feb. 8	Worth, Mo. (Unnumb.)

1862

Sept. 22	Baker, Oreg. (Unnumb.)
Feb. 20	Big Stone, Minn. (Chap. 22)
Apr. 5	Bon Homme, S. D. (Chap. 12)
Apr. 5	Brookings, S. D. (Chap. 16)
May 8	Charles Mix, S. D. (Chap. 18)
Feb. 20	Chippewa, Minn. (Chap. 22)
Apr. 10	Clay, S. D. (Chap. 13)
Nov. 15	Cross, Ark. (Unnumb.)
Apr. 5	Deuel, S. D. (Chap. 16) (Grant, S. D.)
May 8	Gregory, S. D. (Chap. 18)
May 8	Hutchinson, S. D. (Chap. 15)
Jan. 10	Kendall, Tex. (Chap. 38)
Apr. 24	Kittson, Minn. (Chap. 17) (Pembina, Minn.)
Dec. 19	Lander, Nev. (Chap. 58)
Apr. 5	Lincoln, S. D. (Chap. 16)
Apr. 5	Minnehaha, S. D. (Chap. 16)
Jan. 17	Morgan, Utah (Unnumb.)
Feb. 20	Pope, Minn. (Chap. 22)
Feb. 6	Redwood, Minn. (Chap. 21)
Feb. 20	Stevens, Minn. (Chap. 22)
Feb. 20	Traverse, Minn. (Chap. 22)
Sept. 27	Umatilla, Ore. (Unnumb.)
Apr. 10	Union, S. D. (Chap. 14) (Cole, S. D.)
Jan. 17	Wasatch, Utah (Unnumb.)
Nov. 26	Woodruff, Ark. (Unnumb.)
Apr. 10	Yankton, S. D. (Chap. 19)

1863		
	Feb. 27	Benzie, Mich. (Act 48)
	Dec. 31	Owyhee, Idaho (Unnumb.)
	Jan. 20	Stevens, Wash. (Unnumb.)
1864		
	Dec. 22	Ada, Idaho (Chap. 29)
	Mar. 16	Alpine, Calif. (Chap. 180)
	Feb. 4	Boise, Idaho (Unnumb.)
	Oct. 14	Grant, Ore. (Unnumb.)
	Feb. 4	Idaho, Idaho (Unnumb.)
	Jan. 16	Kane, Utah (Unnumb.)
	Dec. 22	Kootenai, Idaho (Chap. 30)
	Apr. 1	Lassen, Calif. (Chap. 261)
	Dec. 22	Latah, Idaho (Chap. 30)
	Dec. 21	Mohave, Ariz. (Unnumb.)
	Feb. 4	Nez Perce, Idaho (Unnumb.)
	Feb. 16	Nye, Nev. (Chap. 102)
	Jan. 22	Oneida, Idaho (Unnumb.)
	Dec. 15	Pima, Ariz. (Unnumb.)
	Jan. 16	Rich, Utah (Unnumb.) (Richland, Utah)
	Feb. 4	Shoshone, Idaho (Unnumb.)
	Oct 14	Union, Ore. (Unnumb.)
	Dec. 21	Yavapai, Ariz. (Unnumb.)
	Dec. 21	Yuma, Ariz. (Unnumb.)
1865		
	Feb. 2	Beaverhead, Mont. (Unnumb.)
	Feb. 2	Chouteau, Mont. (Unnumb.)
	Feb. 2	Custer, Mont. (Unnumb.) (Big Horn)
	Feb. 2	Deer Lodge, Mont. (Unnumb.)
	Feb. 2	Gallatin, Mont. (Unnumb.)
	Nov. 3	Hood, Tex. (Chap. 85)
	Feb. 2	Jefferson, Mont. (Unnumb.)
	Feb. 2	Lewis and Clark, Mont. (Unnumb.) (Edgerton, Mont.)
	Feb. 2	Madison, Mont. (Unnumb.)
	Feb. 2	Missoula, Mont. (Unnumb.)
	Jan. 16	Piute, Utah (Unnumb.)
	Jan. 16	Sevier, Utah (Unnumb.)
	Jan. 21	Yakima, Wash. (Unnumb.)
1866		
	Feb. 28	Beltrami, Minn. (Chap. 46)
	Dec. 5	Bullock, Ala. (Act 84)
	Dec. 7	Clay, Ala. (Act 110)
	Dec. 6	Cleburne, Ala. (Act 89)
	Nov. 24	Crenshaw, Ala. (Act 39)
	Feb. 15	Elmore, Ala. (Act 312)

1866 cont.	
Dec. 7	Etowah, Ala. (Act 92) (Baine, Ala.)
Feb. 14	Grant, W. Va. (Chap. 29)
Mar. 22	Inyo, Calif. (Chap. 316)
Apr. 2	Kern, Calif. (Chap. 569)
Feb. 9	Las Animas, Colo. (Unnumb.)
Dec. 5	Lee, Ala. (Act 61)
Oct. 26	Lee, Miss. (Chap. 20)
Mar. 1	Lincoln, Minn. (Chap. 45)
Feb. 26	Lincoln, Nev. (Chap. 48)
Feb. 1	Mineral, W. Va. (Chap. 7)
Dec. 29	Saguache, Colo. (Unnumb.)
1867	
Feb. 16	Adams, Neb. (Unnumb.)
Feb. 28	Bell, Ky. (Chap. 1553)
Feb. 26	Barton, Kan. (Chap. 33)
Feb. 6	Colbert, Ala. (Act 321)
Feb. 26	Comanche, Kan. (Chap. 33)
Feb. 26	Cowley, Kan. (Chap. 33)
Feb. 13	Crawford, Kan. (Chap. 32)
Feb. 26	Ellis, Kan. (Chap. 33)
Feb. 26	Ellsworth, Kan. (Chap. 33)
Feb. 26	Ford, Kan. (Chap. 33)
Feb. 16	Franklin, Neb. (Unnumb.)
Feb. 26	Graham, Kan. (Chap. 33)
Jan. 30	Hale, Ala. (Act 418)
Feb. 16	Hamilton, Neb. (Unnumb.)
Feb. 26	Harper, Kan. (Chap. 33)
Feb. 26	Jewell, Kan. (Chap. 33)
Feb. 7	Labette, Kan. (Chap. 29)
Feb. 4	Lamar, Ala. (Chap. 298) (Jones, Ala.)
Jan. 9	Laramie, Wyo. (Chap. 14)
Feb. 26	Lincoln, Kan. (Chap. 33)
Feb. 23	Lincoln, W. Va. (Chap. 61)
Mar. 5	Little River, Ark. (Act 104)
Feb. 26	McPherson, Kan. (Chap. 33)
Nov. 16	Meagher, Mont. (Unnumb.)
Feb. 26	Mitchell, Kan. (Chap. 33)
Feb. 26	Montgomery, Kan. (Chap. 33)
Feb. 26	Ness, Kan. (Chap. 33)
Feb. 26	Norton, Kan. (Chap. 33) (Billings, Kan.)
Feb. 26	Osborne, Kan. (Chap. 33)
Feb. 26	Pawnee, Kan. (Chap. 33)
Jan. 9	Pembina, N. D. (Chap. 15)
Feb. 26	Phillips, Kan. (Chap. 33)

1867 cont.

Feb. 26	Pratt, Kan. (Chap. 33)
Feb. 26	Reno, Kan. (Chap. 33)
Feb. 26	Rice, Kan. (Chap. 33)
Feb. 11	Robertson, Ky. (Chap. 1317)
Feb. 26	Rooks, Kan. (Chap. 33)
Feb. 26	Rush, Kan. (Chap. 33)
Feb. 26	Russell, Kan. (Chap. 33)
Feb. 26	Sedgwick, Kan. (Chap. 33)
Feb. 26	Smith, Kan. (Chap. 33)
Feb. 26	Stafford, Kan. (Chap. 33)
Feb. 26	Sumner, Kan. (Chap. 33)
Dec. 27	Sweetwater, Wyo. (Chap. 7) (Carter, Wyo.)
Feb. 26	Trego, Kan. (Chap. 33)
Feb. 16	Webster, Neb. (Unnumb.)
Aug. 17	Wicomico, Md. (Const.)

1868

Dec. 16	Albany, Wyo. (Chap. 28)
Dec. 16	Carbon, Wyo. (Chap. 35)
Dec. 30	Chilton, Ala. (Act 142) (Baker, Ala.)
Dec. 10	Escambia, Ala. (Act 34)
Dec. 26	Geneva, Ala. (Act 110)
Mar. 2	Gove, Kan. (Chap. 14)
Mar. 6	Grant, Minn. (Chap. 109)
Jan. 30	Grant, N. M. (Chap. 20)
Oct. 30	Iberia, La. (Act 208)
Mar. 6	Lyon, Minn. (Chap. 112)
July 18	Sharp, Ark. (Act 42)
Mar. 2	Wallace, Kan. (Chap. 14)

1869

Apr. 9	Boone, Ark. (Act 70)
Feb. 15	Colfax, Neb. (Unnumb.)
Jan. 25	Colfax, N. M. (Chap. 24)
Jan. 15	Dawson, Mont. (Unnumb.)
Mar. 5	Elko, Nev. (Chap. 94)
Jan. 26	Elliott, Ky. (Chap. 1297)
Feb. 4	Grant, Ark. (Act 15)
Mar. 4	Grant, La. (Act 82)
Jan. 9	Lemhi, Idaho (Chap. 19)
Jan. 16	Lincoln, N. M. (Chap. 8)
Mar. 10	Menifee, Ky. (Chap. 1872)
Mar. 6	Tangipahoa, La. (Act 85)
Dec. 1	Uinta, Wyo. (Chap. 34)
Mar. 2	White Pine, Nev. (Chap. 60)

1870

Apr. 15	Alcorn, Miss. (Chap. 51)

1870 cont.

Feb. 11	Bent, Colo. (Unnumb.)
July 21	Benton, Miss. (Chap. 50)
Mar. 15	Cameron, La. (Act 102)
Dec. 17	Cheyenne, Neb.
June 24	Clay, Tenn. (Chap. 29)
Feb. 3	Dare, N. C. (Chap. 36)
July 29	Delta, Tex. (Chap. 30)
Oct. 26	Dodge, Ga. (Act 7)
Oct. 17	Douglas, Ga. (Act 5)
May 9	Grenada, Miss. (Chap. 240)
June 8	Hamblen, Tenn. (Chap. 6)
June 24	Lake, Tenn. (Chap. 30)
Jan. 29	Lee, Ky. (Chap. 202)
Apr. 7	Lincoln, Miss. (Chap. 55)
June 2	Loudon, Tenn. (Chap. 2) (Christiana, Tenn.)
Mar. 10	Martin, Ky. (Chap. 554)
Oct. 18	McDuffie, Ga. (Act 8)
Apr. 15	Prentiss, Miss. (Chap. 51)
June 9	Rains, Tex. (Chap. 3)
Oct. 18	Rockdale, Ga. (Act 6)
Aug. 13	San Jacinto, Tex. (Chap. 59)
Feb. 18	Swift, Minn. (Chap. 90)
June 21	Trousdale, Tenn. (Chap. 27)
July 7	Union, Miss. (Chap. 54)

1871

Mar. 10	Aiken, S. C. (Act 420)
Mar. 1	Antelope, Neb. (Unnumb.)
Sept. 18	Aransas, Tex. (Chap. 1)
Mar. 1	Boone, Neb. (Unnumb.)
May 12	Clay, Miss. (Chap. 430) (Colfax, Miss.)
Mar. 1	Greeley, Neb. (Unnumb.)
Jan. 13	Hanson, S. D. (Chap. 10)
June 3	Harlan, Neb. (Unnumb.)
Jan. 23	Houston, Tenn. (Chap. 46)
Mar. 1	Howard, Neb. (Unnumb.)
Mar. 6	Lac Qui Parle, Minn. (Chap. 100)
Mar. 15	Leflore, Miss. (Chap. 238)
Mar. 28	Lincoln, Ark. (Act 68)
Mar. 22	Logan, Ark. (Act 25) (Sarber, Ark.)
Feb. 14	Maricopa, Ariz. (Unnumb.)
May 13	Montgomery, Miss. (Chap. 241)
Dec. 14	Moore, Tenn. (Chap. 96)
Mar. 20	Nevada, Ark. (Act 20)
May 3	Pecos, Tex. (Chap. 70)

1871 cont.

Mar. 1	Sherman, Neb. (Unnumb.)
Feb. 27	Summers, W. Va. (Chap. 134)
Feb. 24	Swain, N. C. (Chap. 94)
Jan. 13	Turner, S. D. (Chap. 10)
Mar. 1	Valley, Neb. (Unnumb.)
Mar. 30	Vernon, La. (Act 71)
Mar. 4	Wayne, Neb. (Unnumb.)
Feb. 27	Webster, La. (Act 26)
Nov. 29	Whitman, Wash. (Unnumb.)
Mar. 6	Yellow Medicine, Minn. (Chap. 98)

1872

Jan. 17	Frontier, Neb. (Unnumb.)
Apr. 1	Garrett, Md. (Chap. 212)
Jan. 30	Graham, N. C. (Chap. 77)
Feb. 29	Harvey, Kan. (Chap. 97)
Feb. 29	Kingman, Kan. (Chap. 97)
Feb. 8	Pamlico, N. C. (Chap. 132)
Mar. 22	Ventura, Calif. (Chap. 151)

1873

Mar. 3	Barber, Kan.
Mar. 24	Baxter, Ark. (Act 26)
Jan. 4	Bottineau, N. D. (Chap. 18)
Jan. 8	Buffalo, S. D. (Chap. 16)
Jan. 4	Burleigh, N. D. (Chap. 18)
Jan. 8	Campbell, S. D. (Chap. 16)
Jan. 4	Cass, N. D. (Chap. 20)
Jan. 4	Cavalier, N. D. (Chap. 18)
Feb. 27	Chase, Neb. (Unnumb.)
Mar. 6	Cheyenne, Kan. (Chap. 72)
Jan. 8	Clark, S. D. (Chap. 16)
Mar. 24	Clay, Ark. (Chap. 27) (Clayton, Ark.)
Apr. 17	Cleveland, Ark. (Act 58) (Dorsey, Ark.)
Jan. 8	Davison, S. D. (Chap. 16)
Mar. 6	Decatur, Kan. (Chap. 72)
Jan. 8	Dewey, S. D. (Chap. 19) (Rusk, S. D.)
Jan. 8	Douglas, S. D. (Chap. 16)
Feb. 27	Dundy, Neb. (Unnumb.)
Jan. 8	Edmunds, S. D. (Chap. 16)
Mar. 1	Eureka, Nev. (Chap. 46)
Jan. 8	Faulk, S. D. (Chap. 11)
Apr. 12	Faulkner, Ark. (Act 44)
Mar. 6	Finney, Kan. (Chap. 72)
Jan. 4	Foster, N. D. (Chap. 18)
Feb. 27	Furnas, Neb. (Unnumb.)

1873 cont.

Apr. 5	Garland, Ark. (Act 34)
Nov. 26	Gosper, Neb.
Jan. 4	Grand Forks, N. D. (Chap. 20)
Mar. 6	Grant, Kan. (Chap. 72)
Jan. 8	Grant, S. D. (Chap. 16)
Mar. 6	Greeley, Kan. (Chap. 72)
Apr. 12	Gregg, Tex. (Chap. 27)
Mar. 6	Hamilton, Kan. (Chap. 72)
Jan. 8	Hamlin, S. D. (Chap. 16)
Jan. 8	Hand, S. D. (Chap. 16)
Feb. 27	Hitchcock, Neb. (Unnumb.)
Mar. 6	Hodgeman, Kan. (Chap. 72)
Apr. 17	Howard, Ark. (Act 57)
Jan. 8	Hughes, S. D. (Chap. 16)
Jan. 8	Hyde, S. D. (Chap. 16)
Mar. 6	Kearny, Kan. (Chap. 72)
Feb. 27	Keith, Neb. (Unnumb.)
Jan. 4	Kidder, N. D. (Chap. 18)
Jan. 8	Kingsbury, S. D. (Chap. 16)
Jan. 8	Lake, S. D. (Chap. 16)
Mar. 6	Lane, Kan. (Chap. 72)
Jan. 4	La Moure, N. D. (Chap. 20)
Apr. 17	Lee, Ark. (Act 60)
Feb. 27	Lincoln, La. (Act 32)
Jan. 4	Logan, N. D. (Chap. 18)
Apr. 16	Lonoke, Ark. (Act 47)
Jan. 8	Lyman, S. D. (Chap. 19)
Jan. 8	McCook, S. D. (Chap. 16)
Jan. 4	McHenry, N. D. (Chap. 18)
Jan. 8	McPherson, S. D. (Chap. 16)
Jan. 8	Miner, S. D. (Chap. 16)
Jan. 8	Moody, S. D. (Chap. 16)
Jan. 8	Morton, N. D. (Chap. 19)
Jan. 4	Mountrail, N. D. (Chap. 18)
Feb. 11	Phelps, Neb. (Unnumb.)
Jan. 4	Ramsey, N. D. (Chap. 18)
Jan. 4	Ransom, N. D. (Chap. 18)
Mar. 6	Rawlins, Kan. (Chap. 72)
Feb. 27	Red Willow, Neb. (Unnumb.)
Jan. 4	Renville, N. D. (Chap. 18)
Jan. 4	Richland, N. D. (Chap. 20)
Mar. 1	Rockwall, Tex. (Chap. 7)
Jan. 4	Rolette, N. D. (Chap. 18)
Oct. 31	San Juan, Wash. (Unnumb.)
Mar. 6	Scott, Kan. (Chap. 72)
Mar. 6	Sheridan, Kan. (Chap. 72)
Jan. 4	Sheridan, N. D. (Chap. 18)

1873 cont.

Mar. 6	Sherman, Kan. (Chap. 72)
Jan. 8	Spink, S. D. (Chap. 16)
Jan. 8	Stanley, S. D. (Chap. 19)
Mar. 6	Stanton, Kan. (Chap. 72)
Mar. 6	Stevens, Kan. (Chap. 72)
Apr. 21	Stone, Ark. (Act 74)
Jan. 4	Stutsman, N. D. (Chap. 20)
Jan. 8	Sully, S. D. (Chap. 16)
Apr. 15	Tate, Miss. (Chap. 1)
Mar. 6	Thomas, Kan. (Chap. 72)
Jan. 8	Tripp, S. D. (Chap. 19)
Apr. 28	Waller, Tex. (Chap. 38)
Jan. 8	Walworth, S. D. (Chap. 16)
Jan. 4	Wells, N. D. (Chap. 18) (Gingras, N. D.)
Mar. 6	Wichita, Kan. (Chap. 72)
Jan. 8	Williams, N. D. (Chap. 19)

1874

Apr. 6	Camp, Tex. (Chap. 55)
Mar. 9	Cook, Minn. (Chap. 100)
Mar. 7	Edwards, Kan. (Chap. 59)
Feb. 2	Elbert, Colo. (Unnumb.)
Feb. 2	Grand, Colo. (Unnumb.)
Feb. 10	Hinsdale, Colo. (Unnumb.)
Feb. 10	La Plata, Colo. (Unnumb.)
Oct. 24	Lake, Ore. (Unnumb.)
Apr. 14	Lee, Tex. (Chap. 75)
Mar. 4	Lincoln, Wis. (Chap. 128)
Feb. 13	Meagher, Mont.
Feb. 17	Modoc, Calif. (Chap. 107)
Feb. 10	Rio Grande, Colo. (Unnumb.)
Feb. 12	San Benito, Calif. (Chap. 87)
Mar. 13	Tom Green, Tex. (Chap. 26)
Apr. 6	Webster, Miss. (Chap. 112) (Sumner, Miss.)

1875

Feb. 19	Baraga, Mich. (Chap. 14)
Jan. 14	Barnes, N. D. (Chap. 30)
Jan. 5	Bear Lake, Idaho (Unnumb.)
Jan. 14	Brule, S. D. (Chap. 31)
Mar. 3	Chautauqua, Kan. (Chap. 106)
Nov. 11	Columbia, Wash. (Unnumb.)
Jan. 22	Crockett, Tex. (Chap. 2)
Dec. 8	Crook, Wyo. (Unnumb.)
Jan. 11	Custer, S. D. (Chap. 29)
Mar. 3	Elk, Kan. (Chap. 106)
Mar. 6	Franklin, Tex. (Chap. 81)

1875 cont.

Dec. 8	Johnson, Wyo. (Unnumb.) Pease, Wyo.)
Jan. 11	Lawrence, S. D. (Chap. 29)
Jan. 14	Mercer, N. D. (Chap. 30)
Mar. 6	Morris, Tex. (Chap. 82)
Feb. 25	Oconee, Ga. (Chap. 123)
Feb. 16	Pender, N. C. (Chap. 91)
Jan. 11	Pennington, S. D. (Chap. 29)
Feb. 1	Pinal, Ariz. (Unnumb.)
Jan. 14	Potter, S. D. (Chap. 30)
Jan. 11	Shannon, S. D. (Chap. 29)
Mar. 13	Somervell, Tex. (Act 83)
Mar. 4	Taylor, Wis. (Chap. 178)
Jan. 12	Traill, N. D. (Chap. 32)
Mar. 23	Unicoi, Tenn. (Chap. 68)

1876

Aug. 21	Andrews, Tex. (Chap. 144)
Aug. 21	Armstrong, Tex. (Chap. 144)
Aug. 21	Bailey, Tex. (Chap. 144)
Aug. 21	Borden, Tex. (Chap. 144)
Aug. 21	Briscoe, Tex. (Chap. 144)
Aug. 21	Carson, Tex. (Chap. 144)
Aug. 21	Castro, Tex. (Chap. 144)
Aug. 21	Childress, Tex. (Chap. 144)
Aug. 21	Cochran, Tex. (Chap. 144)
Aug. 21	Collingsworth, Tex. (Chap. 144)
Aug. 21	Cottle, Tex. (Chap. 144)
Aug. 21	Crosby, Tex. (Chap. 144)
Aug. 21	Dallam, Tex. (Chap. 144)
Aug. 21	Deaf Smith, Tex. (Chap. 144)
Aug. 21	Dickens, Tex. (Chap. 144)
Aug. 21	Donley, Tex. (Chap. 144)
Aug. 21	Fisher, Tex. (Chap. 144)
Aug. 21	Floyd, Tex. (Chap. 144)
Aug. 21	Gaines, Tex. (Chap. 144)
Aug. 21	Garza, Tex. (Chap. 144)
Aug. 21	Gray, Tex. (Chap. 144)
Aug. 21	Hale, Tex. (Chap. 144)
Aug. 21	Hall, Tex. (Chap. 144)
Aug. 21	Hansford, Tex. (Chap. 144)
Aug. 21	Hartley, Tex. (Chap. 144)
Aug. 21	Hemphill, Tex. (Chap. 144)
Aug. 21	Hockley, Tex. (Chap. 144)
Aug. 21	Howard, Tex. (Chap. 144)
Aug. 21	Hutchinson, Tex. (Chap. 144)
Aug. 21	Kent, Tex. (Chap. 144)
Aug. 21	King, Tex. (Chap. 144)

1876 cont.		
	Aug. 21	Lamb, Tex. (Chap. 144)
	Aug. 21	Lipscomb, Tex. (Chap. 144)
	Aug. 21	Lubbock, Tex. (Chap. 144)
	Aug. 21	Lynn, Tex. (Chap. 144)
	Aug. 21	Martin, Tex. (Chap. 144)
	Aug. 21	Mitchell, Tex. (Chap. 144)
	Aug. 21	Moore, Tex. (Chap. 144)
	Aug. 21	Motley, Tex. (Chap. 144)
	Aug. 21	Nolan, Tex. (Chap. 144)
	Aug. 21	Ochiltree, Tex. (Chap. 144)
	Aug. 21	Oldham, Tex. (Chap. 144)
	Aug. 21	Parmer, Tex. (Chap. 144)
	Aug. 21	Potter, Tex. (Chap. 144)
	Aug. 21	Randall, Tex. (Chap. 144)
	Aug. 21	Roberts, Tex. (Chap. 144)
	Jan. 31	San Juan, Colo. (Unnumb.)
	Aug. 21	Scurry, Tex. (Chap. 144)
	Mar. 29	Sharkey, Miss. (Chap. 63)
	Aug. 21	Sherman, Tex. (Chap. 144)
	Aug. 21	Stonewall, Tex. (Chap. 144)
	Aug. 21	Swisher, Tex. (Chap. 144)
	Aug. 21	Terry, Tex. (Chap. 144)
	Aug. 21	Wheeler, Tex. (Chap. 144)
	Aug. 21	Yoakum, Tex. (Chap. 144)
1877		Codington, S. D.
	Jan. 24	Cullman, Ala. (Act 56)
	Mar. 9	Custer, Colo. (Chap. 400)
	Feb. 17	Custer, Neb. (Unnumb.)
	Mar. 28	East Carroll, La. (Act 24)
	Mar. 9	Gunnison, Colo. (Chap. 411)
	Feb. 19	Hayes, Neb. (Unnumb.)
	Jan. 18	Ouray, Colo. (Unnumb.)
	Feb. 1	Quitman, Miss. (Chap. 35)
	Jan. 29	Routt, Colo. (Chap. 393)
	Feb. 19	Sioux, Neb. (Unnumb.)
	Mar. 28	West Carroll, La. (Act 24)
	Feb. 17	Wheeler, Neb. (Unnumb.)
1878		
	Feb. 18	Hampton, S. C. (Act 353)
	Aug. 21	Lackawanna, Pa. (Procl.)
	Mar. 29	Leslie, Ky. (Chap. 666)
1879		
	Feb. 14	Apache, Ariz. (Act 58)
	Feb. 22	Aurora, S. D. (Chap. 12)
	Feb. 22	Beadle, S. D. (Chap. 12)
	Feb. 10	Billings, N. D. (Chap. 11)
	Feb. 22	Brown, S. D. (Chap. 12)

1879 cont.

Feb. 20	Cassia, Idaho (Unnumb.)
Mar. 4	Chester, Tenn. (Chap. 42)
Feb. 22	Day, S. D. (Chap. 12)
Feb. 10	Emmons, N. D. (Chap. 11)
Feb. 27	Langlade, Wis. (Chap. 114) (New, Wis.)
Feb. 27	Marinette, Wis. (Chap. 114)
Feb. 25	Marshall, Minn. (Chap. 10)
Feb. 13	Nance, Neb. (Unnumb.)
Feb. 27	Pickett, Tenn. (Chap. 34)
Feb. 26	Price, Wis. (Chap. 103)
Feb. 10	Stark, N. D. (Chap. 11)
Feb. 20	Washington, Idaho (Unnumb.)

1880

Mar. 3	Dickenson, Va. (Chap. 140)
Feb. 12	Emery, Utah (Chap. 4)
Feb. 17	San Juan, Utah (Chap. 9)
Feb. 18	Uintah, Utah (Chap. 10)

1881

Feb. 1	Cochise, Ariz. (Act 7)
Jan. 8	Custer, Idaho (Unnumb.)
Mar. 5	Dickey, N. D. (Chap. 40)
Feb. 19	Dolores, Colo. (Unnumb.)
Feb. 28	Durham, N. C. (Chap. 138)
Nov. 29	Garfield, Wash. (Unnumb.)
Feb. 8	Gila, Ariz. (Act 17)
Feb. 18	Griggs, N. D. (Chap. 41)
Mar. 10	Graham, Ariz. (Act 87)
Mar. 4	Logan, Kan. (Chap. 48) (St. John, Kan.)
Feb. 17	Norman, Minn. (Chap. 92)
Feb. 23	Pitkin, Colo. (Unnumb.)
Feb. 16	Silver Bow, Mont. (Unnumb.)
Mar. 5	Vance, N. C. (Chap. 113)
Feb. 18	Walsh, N. D. (Chap. 51)

1882

Jan. 31	Berkeley, S. C. (Act 527)
Oct. 24	Crook, Ore. (Unnumb.)
Mar. 18	Florence, Wis. (Chap. 165)
Mar. 9	Garfield, Utah (Chap. 52)
Oct. 17	Klamath, Ore. (Unnumb.)

1883

Nov. 28	Adams, Wash. (Unnumb.)
Oct. 27	Asotin, Wash. (Unnumb.)
Mar. 9	Benson, N. D. (Chap. 12)
Mar. 8	Bowman, N. D. (Chap. 38)
Feb. 19	Brown, Neb. (Chap. 31)

1883 cont.		
	Mar. 2	Butte, S. D. (Chap. 15)
	Feb. 23	Cherry, Neb. (Chap. 32)
	Feb. 20	Cleburne, Ark. (Act 24)
	Feb. 11	Delta, Colo. (Unnumb.)
	Nov. 28	Douglas, Wash. (Unnumb.)
	Mar. 9	Dunn, N. D. (Chap. 39)
	Feb. 11	Eagle, Colo. (Unnumb.)
	Mar. 6	Fall River, S. D. (Chap. 18)
	Nov. 28	Franklin, Wash. (Unnumb.)
	Feb. 10	Garfield, Colo. (Unnumb.)
	Mar. 9	Hettinger, N. D. (Chap. 39)
	Feb. 26	Hubbard, Minn. (Chap. 78)
	Mar. 9	Jerauld, S. D. (Chap. 23)
	Nov. 24	Kittitas, Wash. (Unnumb.)
	Nov. 24	Lincoln, Wash. (Unnumb.)
	Mar. 9	McIntosh, N. D. (Chap. 26)
	Mar. 9	McKenzie, N. D. (Chap. 39)
	Mar. 8	McLean, N. D. (Chap. 25)
	Feb. 14	Mesa, Colo. (Unnumb.)
	Feb. 11	Montrose, Colo. (Unnumb.)
	Feb. 27	Nelson, N. D. (Chap. 28)
	Apr. 14	Reeves, Tex. (Chap. 103)
	Mar. 8	Roberts, S. D. (Chap. 30)
	Mar. 9	Sanborn, S. D. (Chap. 31)
	Mar. 3	Sargent, N. D. (Chap. 32)
	Mar. 10	Sawyer, Wis. (Chap. 47)
	Nov. 28	Skagit, Wash. (Unnumb.)
	Mar, 8	Steele, N. D. (Chap. 36)
	Mar. 8	Towner, N. D. (Chap. 37)
	Mar. 9	Washabaugh, S. D. (Chap. 40)
	Mar. 27	Washburn, Wis. (Chap. 172)
	Feb. 26	Yellowstone, Mont. (Unnumb.)
1884		
	Mar. 5	Fremont, Wyo. (Chap. 46)
	Nov. 8	Garfield, Neb. (Procl.) (Keya Paha, Neb.)
	May 5	Knott, Ky.
	Apr. 3	Sierra, N. M. (Chap. 59)
1885		
	Mar. 13	Adams, N. D. (Unnumb.)
	Mar. 17	Alger, Mich. (Act 23)
	Apr. 14	Archuleta, Colo. (S. B. 144)
	Jan. 13	Bingham, Idaho (Unnumb.)
	Mar. 5	Blaine, Neb. (Chap. 31)
	Mar. 7	Clark, Kan. (Chap. 71)
	Feb. 19	Dawes, Neb. (Chap. 32)
	Mar. 9	Eddy, N. D. (Chap. 15)

1885 cont.		
	Mar. 12	Fergus, Mont. (Unnumb.)
	Apr. 11	Forest, Wis. (Chap. 436)
	Feb. 25	Gilliam, Ore. (Unnumb.)
	Apr. 3	Iron, Mich. (Act 35)
	Feb. 24	Logan, Neb. (Chap. 33)
	Mar. 10	Marshall, S. D. (Chap. 12)
	Mar. 7	Meade, Kan. (Chap. 71)
	Mar. 4	Midland, Tex. (Chap. 23)
	Feb. 16	Morrow, Ore. (Unnumb.)
	Mar. 12	Oliver, N. D. (Chap. 31)
	Apr. 11	Oneida, Wis. (Chap. 411)
	Feb. 25	Sheridan, Neb. (Chap. 34)
	Feb. 20	Val Verde, Tex. (Chap. 50)
	Apr. 14	Ward, N D. (Chap. 42)
	Nov. 2	Box Butte, Neb.
1886		
	Apr. 3	Carlisle, Ky. (Chap. 495)
	Feb. 10	Kiowa, Kan. (Chap. 35)
	Feb. 18	Morton, Kan. (Chap. 37)
1887		
	Mar. 31	Arthur, Neb. (Chap. 21)
	Feb. 2	Brewster, Tex. (Chap. 4)
	Sept. 12	Cascade, Mont. (Unnumb.)
	June 2	Citrus, Fla. (Chap. 3772)
	Feb. 26	Crane, Tex. (Chap. 12)
	May 19	De Soto, Fla. (Chap. 3770)
	Feb. 26	Ector, Tex. (Chap. 12)
	Apr. 4	Glasscock, Tex. (Chap. 143)
	Feb. 7	Gogebic, Mich. (Act 337)
	Mar. 31	Grant, Neb. (Chap. 22)
	Mar. 5	Gray, Kan. (Chap. 81)
	Mar. 5	Haskell, Kan. (Chap. 81)
	Mar. 15	Jeff Davis, Tex. (Chap. 38)
	May 27	Lake, Fla. (Chap. 3771)
	May 13	Lee, Fla. (Chap. 3769)
	Feb. 25	Logan, Colo. (S. B. 72)
	Feb. 26	Loving, Tex. (Chap. 12)
	Mar. 1	Luce, Mich. (Act 363)
	Feb. 17	Malheur, Ore. (Unnumb.)
	Mar. 31	McPherson, Neb. (Chap. 23)
	Mar. 15	Mills, Tex. (Chap. 37)
	May 12	Osceola, Fla. (Chap. 3768)
	Feb. 23	Park, Mont. (Unnumb.)
	June 2	Pasco, Fla. (Chap. 3772)
		(Perkins, Neb.)
	Mar. 11	Pierce, N. D. (Chap. 180)
	Feb. 24	San Juan, N. M. (Chap. 13)
	Apr. 1	Schleicher, Tex. (Chap. 103)

1887 cont.		
	Apr. 1	Sutton, Tex. (Chap. 103)
	Mar. 31	Thomas, Neb. (Chap. 24)
	Feb. 26	Upton, Tex. (Chap. 12)
	Feb. 11	Wallowa, Ore. (Unnumb.)
	Feb. 26	Ward, Tex. (Chap. 12)
	Feb. 9	Washington, Colo. (H. B. 51)
	Feb. 26	Winkler, Tex. (Chap. 12)
1888		Banner, Neb.
	Mar. 9	Converse, Wyo. (Chap. 90)
		(Deuel, Neb.)
	Dec. 22	Florence, S. C. (Act 99)
		Kimball, Neb.
	Mar. 9	Natrona, Wyo. (Chap. 90)
	Feb. 2	Okanogan, Wash. (Chap. 35)
		Rock, Neb.
		Scotts Bluff, Neb.
	Mar. 9	Sheridan, Wyo. (Chap. 90)
1889		
	Apr. 16	Baca, Colo. (S. B. 37)
	Feb. 25	Chaves, N. M. (Chap. 87)
	Mar. 25	Cheyenne, Colo. (S. B. 116)
	Mar. 13	Coke, Tex. (Chap. 77)
	Feb. 25	Eddy, N M. (Chap. 87)
	Feb. 7	Elmore, Idaho (Unnumb.)
	Feb. 25	Harney, Ore. (Unnumb.)
	Mar. 29	Hooker, Neb. (Chap. 1)
	Mar. 7	Irion, Tex. (Chap. 87)
	Apr. 11	Kiowa, Colo. (H. B. 337)
	Apr. 11	Kit Carson, Colo. (S. B. 48)
	Apr. 11	Lincoln, Colo. (S. B. 106)
	Feb. 7	Meade, S. D. (Chap. 57)
	Apr. 16	Montezuma, Colo. (H. B. 220)
	Feb. 19	Morgan, Colo. (S. B. 40)
	Mar. 11	Orange, Calif. (Chap. 110)
	Mar. 25	Otero, Colo. (S. B. 34)
	Mar. 27	Phillips, Colo. (H. B. 127)
	Apr. 11	Prowers, Colo. (S. B. 35)
	Mar. 25	Rio Blanco, Colo. (H. B. 107)
	Apr. 9	Sedgwick, Colo. (H. B. 148)
	Feb. 25	Sherman, Ore. (Unnumb.)
	Mar. 28	Thurston, Neb. (Chap. 3)
	Mar. 15	Yuma, Colo. (H. B. 90)
1890		
	Mar. 12	Big Horn, Wyo. (Chap. 48)
	Mar. 13	Grand, Utah (Chap. 60)
	Feb. 22	Pearl River, Miss. (Chap. 76)
	Mar. 12	Weston, Wyo. (Chap. 47)

1891

Mar. 20	Boyd, Neb. (Chap. 20)
Mar. 7	Canyon, Idaho (Unnumb.)
Feb. 19	Coconino, Ariz. (Act 14)
May 21	Dickinson, Mich. (Act 89)
Mar. 3	Foard, Tex. (Chap. 15)
Mar. 11	Glenn, Calif. (Chap. 94)
Feb. 26	Guadalupe, N. M. (Chap. 88)
Mar. 4	Sterling, Tex. (Chap. 16)

1892

Mar. 10	Wayne, Utah (Chap. 71)

1893

Mar. 6	Bannock, Idaho (Unnumb.)
Feb. 6	Flathead, Mont. (Unnumb.)
Mar. 4	Fremont, Idaho (Unnumb.)
Mar. 2	Granite, Mont. (Unnumb.)
Mar. 1	Iron, Wis. (Chap. 8)
Mar. 22	Kings, Calif. (Chap. 150)
Feb. 20	Lincoln, Ore. (S. B. 119)
Mar. 11	Madera, Calif. (Chap. 143)
Mar. 27	Mineral, Colo. (S. B. 57)
Feb. 16	Ravalli, Mont. (Unnumb.)
Mar. 11	Riverside, Calif. (Chap. 142)
Feb. 7	Teton, Mont. (Unnumb.)
Feb. 23	Union, N. M. (Chap. 49)
Feb. 6	Valley, Mont. (Unnumb.)
Apr. 12	Vilas, Wis. (Chap. 150)

1894

Mar. 8	Carbon, Utah (Chap. 58)
Dec. 31	Roseau, Minn. (Procl.)

1895

Mar. 5	Blaine, Idaho (S. B. 31)
Mar. 4	Carbon, Mont. (H. B. 9)
Mar. 18	Lincoln, Idaho (S. B. 83)
Jan. 30	Mingo, W. Va. (Chap. 68)
Mar. 21	Navajo, Ariz. (Act 60)
Mar. 5	Sweet Grass, Mont. (H. B. 17)

1896

Dec. 24	Red Lake, Minn. (Procl.)
Feb. 25	Saluda, S. C. (Act 118)

1897

Feb. 25	Bamberg, S. C. (Act 344)
Feb. 9	Broadwater, Mont. (H. B. 24)
Feb. 25	Cherokee, S. C. (Act 345)
Feb. 25	Dorchester, S. C. (Act 346)
Mar. 2	Greenwood, S. C. (Act 347)

1898

Apr. 27	Nassau, N. Y. (Chap. 588)

1899		
	Mar. 13	Chelan, Wash. (Chap. 95)
	Feb. 18	Ferry, Wash. (Chap. 18)
	Feb. 23	McKinley, N. M. (Chap. 19)
	Jan. 30	Otero, N. M. (Chap. 3)
	Mar. 15	Santa Cruz, Ariz. (Act 44)
	Feb. 20	Scotland, N. C. (Chap. 127)
	Mar. 23	Teller, Colo. (S. B. 52)
	Feb. 17	Wheeler, Ore. (H. B. 153)
1901		
	Apr. 15	Adams, Colo. (Chap. 57)
	Mar. 18	Denver, Colo. (Chap. 46)
	Mar. 16	Luna, N. M. (Chap. 38)
	Jan. 31	Powell, Mont. (S. B. 3)
	Feb. 11	Rosebud, Mont. (S. B. 21)
	May 15	Rusk, Wis. (Chap. 469) (Gates, Wis.)
1902		
	Dec. 20	Clearwater, Minn. (Procl.)
	Feb. 25	Lee, S. C. (Act 651)
1903		
	Feb. 9	Houston, Ala. (Act 27)
	Feb. 28	Quay, N. M. (Chap. 8)
	Mar. 7	Reagan, Tex. (Chap. 32)
	Feb. 28	Roosevelt, N. M. (Chap. 7)
	Mar. 10	Sandoval, N. M. (Chap. 27)
	Mar. 16	Torrance, N. M. (Chap. 70)
1904		
	Feb. 19	Lamar, Miss. (Chap. 102)
1905		
	Mar. 8	Benton, Wash. (Chap. 89)
	Aug. 17	Crisp. Ga. (Act 19)
	Aug. 17	Grady, Ga. (Act 31)
	Aug. 18	Jeff Davis, Ga. (Act 157)
	Aug. 17	Jenkins, Ga. (Act 142)
	May 24	St. Lucie, Fla. (Chap. 5567)
	Feb. 7	Sanders, Mont. (Chap. 9)
	Aug. 18	Stephens, Ga. (Act 215)
	Apr. 8	Terrell, Ga. (Chap. 70)
	Aug. 17	Tift, Ga. (Act 3)
	Aug. 18	Toombs, Ga. (Act 232)
	Aug. 18	Turner, Ga. (Act 75)
1906		
	July 31	Ben Hill, Ga. (Act 372)
	Apr. 19	Forrest, Miss. (Chap. 165)
	Mar. 31	Jefferson Davis, Miss. (Chap. 166)
	Dec. 19	Koochiching, Minn. (Procl.)
	Dec. 27	Mahnomen, Minn. (Procl.)

1907

July 16	Adair, Okla. (Const.)
July 16	Alfalfa, Okla. (Const.)
July 16	Atoka, Okla. (Const.)
July 16	Beaver, Okla. (Const.)
July 16	Beckham, Okla. (Const.)
July 16	Blaine, Okla. (Const.)
Feb. 21	Bonner, Idaho (H. B. 43)
July 16	Bryan, Okla. (Const.)
July 16	Caddo, Okla. (Const.)
July 16	Canadian, Okla. (Const.)
July 16	Carter, Okla. (Const.)
July 16	Cherokee, Okla. (Const.)
July 16	Choctaw, Okla. (Const.)
July 16	Cimarron, Okla. (Const.)
July 16	Cleveland, Okla. (Const.)
July 16	Coal, Okla. (Const.)
July 16	Comanche, Okla. (Const.)
July 16	Craig, Okla. (Const.)
July 16	Creek, Okla. (Const.)
July 16	Custer, Okla. (Const.)
July 16	Delaware, Okla. (Const.)
July 16	Dewey, Okla. (Const.)
July 16	Ellis, Okla. (Const.)
July 16	Garfield, Okla. (Const.)
July 16	Garvin, Okla. (Const.)
July 16	Grady, Okla. (Const.)
July 16	Grant, Okla. (Const.)
July 16	Greer, Okla. (Const.)
July 16	Harper, Okla. (Const.)
July 16	Haskell, Okla. (Const.)
July 16	Hughes, Okla. (Const.)
Aug. 6	Imperial, Calif. (Unnumb.)
July 16	Jackson, Okla. (Const.)
July 16	Jefferson, Okla. (Const.)
July 16	Johnston, Okla. (Const.)
July 16	Kay, Okla. (Const.)
July 16	Kingfisher, Okla. (Const.)
July 16	Kiowa, Okla. (Const.)
July 16	Latimer, Okla. (Const.)
Mar. 6	Lee, N. C. (Chap. 624)
July 16	Leflore, Okla. (Const.)
July 16	Lincoln, Okla. (Const.)
July 16	Logan, Okla. (Const.)
July 16	Love, Okla. (Const.)
July 16	Major, Okla. (Const.)
July 16	Marshall, Okla. (Const.)
July 16	Mayes, Okla. (Const.)

1907 cont.

July 16	McClain, Okla. (Const.)
July 16	McCurtain, Okla. (Const.)
July 16	McIntosh, Okla. (Const.)
July 16	Murray, Okla. (Const.)
July 16	Muskogee, Okla. (Const.)
July 16	Noble, Okla. (Const.)
July 16	Nowata, Okla. (Const.)
July 16	Okfuskee, Okla. (Const.
July 16	Oklahoma, Okla. (Const.)
July 16	Okmulgee, Okla. (Const.)
July 16	Osage, Okla. (Const.)
July 16	Ottawa, Okla. (Const.)
July 16	Pawnee, Okla. (Const.)
July 16	Payne, Okla. (Const.)
July 16	Pittsburgh, Okla. (Const.)
July 16	Pontotoc, Okla. (Const.)
July 16	Pottawatomie, Okla. (Const.)
July 16	Pushmataha, Okla. (Const.)
July 16	Roger Mills, Okla. (Const.)
July 16	Rogers, Okla. (Const.)
July 16	Seminole, Okla. (Const.)
July 16	Sequoyah, Okla. (Const.)
July 16	Stephens, Okla. (Const.)
July 16	Texas, Okla. (Const.)
July 16	Tillman, Okla. (Const.)
July 16	Tulsa, Okla. (Const.)
Feb. 21	Twin Falls, Idaho (H. B. 48)
July 16	Wagoner, Okla. (Const.)
July 16	Washington, Okla. (Const.)
July 16	Washita, Okla. (Const.)
July 16	Woods, Okla. (Const.)
July 16	Woodward, Okla. (Const.)

1908

Feb. 14	Calhoun, S. C. (Act 567)
	Forrest, Miss.
June 23	Hood River, Ore. (Procl.)
July 3	La Salle, La. (Act 177)
	Morrill, Neb.

1909

Mar. 9	Bennett, S. D. (Chap. 280)
Feb. 5	Clark, Nev. (Chap. 11)
Mar. 2	Corson, S. D. (Chap. 133)
Feb. 25	Curry, N. M. (Chap. 6)
Nov. 2	Garden, Neb. (Election)
Feb. 24	Grant, Wash. (Chap. 17)
Mar. 10	Greenlee, Ariz. (Chap. 21)
Feb. 26	Harding, S. D. (S. B. 100)

1909 cont.

June 2	Harmon, Okla. (Procl.)
May 5	Jackson, Colo. (Chap. 179)
Mar. 9	Lincoln, Mont. (Chap. 133)
Mar. 9	Mellette, S. D. (Chap. 280)
Apr. 30	Palm Beach, Fla. (Chap. 5970)
Feb. 15	Park, Wyo. (Chap. 19)
Feb. 26	Perkins, S. D. (S. B. 100)
Mar. 9	Todd, S. D. (Chap. 280)

1910

July 6	Burke, N. D.
Feb. 5	Dillon, S. C. (Act 436)
Dec. 9	Divide, N. D.
June 15	Evangeline, La. (Act 15)
Mar. 16	George, Miss. (Chap. 248)
Nov. 23	Pennington, Minn. (Procl.)
Mar. 16	Walthall, Miss. (Chap. 321)

1911

Mar. 3	Adams, Idaho (Chap. 31)
Feb. 23	Avery, N. C. (Chap. 33)
Feb. 7	Bonneville, Idaho (Chap. 5)
Mar. 22	Brooks, Tex. (Chap. 39)
Feb. 13	Campbell, Wyo. (Chap. 14)
Feb. 27	Clearwater, Idaho (Chap. 24)
May 29	Crowley, Colo. (Chap. 111)
Mar. 10	Culberson, Tex. (Chap. 38)
Feb. 9	Goshen, Wyo. (Chap. 10)
Feb. 17	Hoke, N. C. (Chap. 24)
Feb. 9	Hot Springs, Wyo. (Chap. 9)
Mar. 25	Jim Wells, Tex. (Chap. 140)
Mar. 3	Lewis, Idaho (Chap. 37)
Feb. 20	Lincoln, Wyo. (Chap. 67)
Feb. 10	Mineral, Nev. (Chap. 13)
Feb. 27	Moffat, Colo. (Chap. 173)
Feb. 11	Musselshell, Mont. (Chap. 25)
Feb. 14	Niobrara, Wyo. (Chap. 20)
Mar. 1	Pend Oreille, Wash. (Chap. 28)
May 23	Pinellas, Fla. (Chap. 6247)
Feb. 9	Platte, Wyo. (Chap. 7)
Feb. 9	Washakie, Wyo. (Chap. 8)
Mar. 11	Willacy, Tex. (Chap. 48)
Feb. 1	Ziebach, S. D. (Chap. 107)

1912

June 12	Allen, La. (Act 6)
June 12	Beauregard, La. (Act 8)
Feb. 29	Blaine, Mont. (P and E)
July 30	Bleckley, Ga. (Act 355)
Apr. 19	Bronx, N. Y. (Chap. 548)

Year	Date	County
1912 cont.		
	Aug. 22	Cotton, Okla. (Procl.)
	Nov. 19	Golden Valley, N. D.
	Feb. 28	Hill, Mont. (P and E)
	Jan. 30	Jasper, S. C. (Act 459)
	June 12	Jefferson Davis, La. (Act 7)
	Mar. 12	McCreary, Ky. (Chap. 46)
	Aug. 14	Wheeler, Ga. (Act 449)
1913		
	Mar. 8	Alamosa, Colo. (Chap. 6)
	Apr. 24	Bay, Fla. (Chap. 6505)
	Jan. 13	Big Horn, Mont. (P and E)
	Mar. 7	Duchesne, Utah (Chap. 28)
	Dec. 9	Fallon, Mont. (P and E)
	Jan. 30	Franklin, Idaho (Chap. 5)
	Jan. 28	Gooding, Idaho (Chap. 4)
	Feb. 18	Jefferson, Idaho (Chap. 25)
	Mar. 31	Jim Hogg, Tex. (Chap. 73)
	Feb. 27	Kleberg, Tex. (Chap. 10)
	Feb. 18	Madison, Idaho (Chap. 26)
	Jan. 28	Minidoka, Idaho (Chap. 3)
	Jan. 30	Power, Idaho (Chap. 6)
	Apr. 3	Real, Tex. (Chap. 133)
	Apr. 25	Seminole, Fla. (Chap. 6511)
	Mar. 24	Sheridan, Mont. (P and E)
	Mar. 24	Stillwater, Mont. (P and E)
1914		
	July 27	Bacon, Ga. (Act 298)
	July 7	Barrow, Ga. (Act 278)
	July 17	Candler, Ga. (Act 282)
	Aug. 11	Evans, Ga. (Act 371)
		Haakon, S. D.
		Jackson, S. D.
	Dec. 12	Jefferson, Ore. (Procl.)
	Aug. 7	Mineral, Mont. (P and E)
	May 27	Richland, Mont. (P and E)
	Sept. 3	Sioux, N. D. (Chap. 18)
	May 7	Toole, Mont. (P and E)
	Aug. 17	Wibaux, Mont. (P and E)
1915		
	Jan. 23	Benewah, Idaho (Chap. 4)
	Jan. 23	Boundary, Idaho (Chap. 7)
	Apr. 30	Broward, Fla. (Chap. 6934)
	Mar. 19	Gem, Idaho (Chap. 165)
	June 3	Okaloosa, Fla. (Chap. 6937)
	Feb. 5	Phillips, Mont. (P and E)
	Feb. 5	Prairie, Mont. (P and E)
	Jan. 14	Slope, N. D.

1915 cont.	
Jan. 26	Teton, Idaho (Chap. 8)
1916	
Dec. 13	Deschutes, Ore. (Procl.)
Nov. 25	Grant, N. D. (Unnumb.)
	Jones, S. D.
Feb. 19	McCormick, S. C. (Act 398)
Apr. 3	Stone, Miss. (Chap. 527)
1917	
Aug. 15	Atkinson, Ga. (Act 180)
Feb. 6	Butte, Idaho (Chap. 98)
Feb. 6	Camas, Idaho (Chap. 97)
Feb. 22	Carter, Mont. (Chap. 56)
Feb. 28	De Baca, N. M. (Chap. 11)
Apr. 28	Flagler, Fla. (Chap. 7379)
Feb. 16	Hudspeth, Tex. (Chap. 25)
Mar. 7	Lea, N. M. (Chap. 23)
May 8	Okeechobee, Fla. (Chap. 7401)
Feb. 28	Payette, Idaho (Chap. 11)
Aug. 21	Treutlen, Ga. (Act 250)
Feb. 26	Valley, Idaho (Chap. 99)
Feb. 22	Wheatland, Mont. (Chap. 55)
1918	
July 30	Cook, Ga. (Act 292)
Mar. 28	Humphreys, Miss. (Chap. 348)
1919	
Feb. 6	Allendale, S. C. (Act 6)
Feb. 11	Caribou, Idaho (Chap. 5)
Feb. 1	Clark, Idaho (Chap. 3)
Mar. 4	Daggett, Utah (Chap. 43)
Feb. 7	Garfield, Mont. (Chap. 4)
Feb. 17	Glacier, Mont. (Chap. 21)
Feb. 25	Hidalgo, N. M. (Chap. 11)
Feb. 8	Jerome, Idaho (Chap. 4)
Aug. 11	Lanier, Ga. (Act 78)
Feb. 20	McCone, Mont. (Chap. 33)
Mar. 18	Pershing, Nev. (Chap. 62)
Feb. 17	Pondera, Mont. (Chap. 22)
Mar. 7	Powder River, Mont. (Chap. 141)
Feb. 18	Roosevelt, Mont. (Chap. 23)
Feb. 7	Treasure, Mont. (Chap. 5)
1920	
Aug. 14	Brantley, Ga. (Act 626)
Aug. 30	Daniels, Mont. (P and E)
Oct. 4	Golden Valley, Mont, (P and E)
Dec. 10	Judith Basin, Mont. (P and E)
Aug. 17	Lamar, Ga. (Act 738)
Feb. 11	Liberty, Mont. (P and E)

1920 cont.		
	Aug. 14	Long, Ga. (Act 814)
	July 8	Seminole, Ga. (Act 319)
1921		
	Feb. 25	Catron, N. M. (Chap. 28)
	Apr. 23	Charlotte, Fla. (Chap. 8513)
	Apr. 25	Dixie, Fla. (Chap. 8514)
	Apr. 23	Glades, Fla. (Chap. 8513)
	Apr. 23	Hardee, Fla. (Chap. 8513)
	Mar. 4	Harding, N. M. (Chap. 48)
	Apr. 23	Highlands, Fla. (Chap. 8513)
	Apr. 2	Kenedy, Tex. (Chap. 104)
	May 14	Sarasota, Fla. (Chap. 8515)
	Feb. 15	Sublette, Wyo. (Chap. 52)
	Feb. 15	Teton, Wyo. (Chap. 53)
	May 20	Union, Fla. (Chap. 8516)
1922		
	Nov. 28	Lake of the Woods, Minn. (Procl.)
1923		
	May 8	Collier, Fla. (Chap. 9362)
	May 11	Hendry, Fla. (Chap. 9360)
	May 11	Lake, Mont. (Procl.)
1924		
	July 18	Peach, Ga. (Act 274)
	Nov. 24	Petroleum, Mont. (Procl.)
1925		
	Dec. 4	Gilchrist, Fla. (Chap. 11, 371)
	June 6	Gulf, Fla. (Chap. 10, 132)
	May 30	Indian River, Fla. (Chap. 10, 148)
	May 30	Martin, Fla. (Chap. 10, 180)
1949		
	Mar. 16	Los Alamos, N. M. (Chap. 134)

Part V

COUNTIES WHOSE NAMES HAVE CHANGED

The present name of many counties have been changed from the names under which the counties were originally created.

The following tabulation shows the present name of the county and the date and statute under which it was created, followed by the old name of the county and the date and statate when it was created.

Alcona, Mich. (Mar. 8, 1843, act 67); Neewaygo (Apr. 1, 1840, act 119)
Alpena, Mich. (Mar. 8, 1843, act 67); Anamickee (Apr. 1, 1840, act 119)
Antrim, Mich. (Mar. 8, 1843, act 67); Meegisee (Apr. 1, 1840, act 119)
Arlington, Va. (Mar. 16, 1920, chap. 241); Alexandria (Mar. 13, 1847, chap. 53)
Atchison, Mo. (Feb. 14, 1845, unnumbered); Allen (Feb. 23, 1843, unnumbered)

Barron, Wis. (Mar. 4, 1869, chap. 75); Dallas (Mar. 19, 1859, chap. 191)
Bartow, Ga. (Dec. 6, 1861, act 97); Cass (Dec. 3, 1832, unnumbered)
Bayfield, Wis. (Apr. 12, 1866, chap. 146); La Pointe (Feb. 19, 1845 unnumbered)
Beaufort, N. C. (1712); Pamptecough (1705)
Bibb, Ala. (Dec. 4, 1820, act 24); Cahaba (Feb. 7, 1818, unnumbered)
Bradford, Fla. (Dec. 6, 1861, chap. 1, 300); New River (Dec. 21, 1858, chap. 895)
Bradford, Pa. (Mar. 24, 1812, chap. 109); Ontario (Feb. 21, 1810, chap. 30)
Brazos, Texas (Jan. 28, 1842, unnumbered); Navasoto (Jan. 30, 1841, unnumbered)
Brevard, Fla. (Jan. 6, 1855, chap. 651); St. Lucie (Mar. 14, 1844, unnumbered)

Calhoun, Ala. (Jan. 29, 1858, act 306); Benton (Dec. 18, 1832, act 11)
Calhoun, Iowa (Jan. 12, 1853, chap. 12); Fox (Jan. 15, 1851, chap. 9)
Camden, Mo. (Feb. 23, 1843, unnumbered); Kinderhook (Jan. 29, 1841, unnumbered.)
Cass, Mo. (Feb. 19, 1849, unnumbered); Van Buren (Mar. 3, 1835 unnumbered)
Cass, Tex. (May 16, 1871, chap. 95); Davis (Dec. 17, 1861, chap. 14); Cass (Apr. 25, 1846, unnumbered)
Chaffee, Colo. (Feb. 10, 1879, unnumbered); Lake (Nov. 1, 1861, unnumbered)
Charlevoix, Mich. (Mar. 8, 1843, act 67); Reshkauko (Apr. 1, 1840, act 119)
Cherokee, Kan. (Feb. 18, 1860, chap. 30); McGee (Aug. 30, 1855, chap. 30)
Chilton, Ala. (Dec. 17, 1874, act 72); Baker (Dec. 30, 1868, act 142)
Christian, Ill. (Feb. 1, 1840, unnumbered); Dane (Feb. 15, 1839, unnumbered)
Clare, Mich. (Mar. 8, 1843, act 67); Kaykakee (Apr. 1, 1840, act 119)
Clark, Wash. (Sept. 3, 1849, unnumbered); Vancouver (June 27, 1844, unnumbered)
Clay, Ark. (Dec. 6, 1875, act 42); Clayton (Mar. 24, 1873, act 27)
Clay, Minn. (Mar. 6, 1862, chap. 33); Breckinridge (Mar. 18, 1858, chap. 34)
Clay, Miss. (Apr. 10, 1876, chap. 103); Colfax (May 12, 1871, chap. 430)
Cleveland, Ark. (Mar. 5, 1885; act 38); Dorsey (Apr. 17, 1873, act 58)
Cloud, Kan. (Feb. 26, 1867, chap. 40); Shirley (Feb. 27, 1860, chap. 43)
Conejos, Colo. (Nov. 7, 1861, unnumbered); Guadalupe (Nov. 1, 1861, unnumbered)
Covington, Ala. (Oct. 10, 1868, act 39); Jones (Aug. 6, 1868, unnumbered); Covington (Dec. 7, 1821, unnumbered)
Craven, N. C. (1712); Archdale (Dec. 3, 1705)
Crawford, Mich. (Mar. 8, 1843, act 67); Shawano (Apr. 1, 1840, act 119)
Custer, Mont. (Feb. 16, 1877, unnumbered); Big Horn (Feb. 2, 1865, unnumbered)

Dallas, Mo. (Dec. 16, 1844, unnumbered); Niangua (Jan. 29, 1841, unnumbered)
Dewey, S. D. (Mar. 9, 1883, chap. 17); Rusk (Jan. 8, 1873, chap. 19)

Emmet, Mich. (Mar. 8, 1843, act 67); Tonedagana (Apr. 1, 1840, act 119)
Etowah, Ala. (Dec. 1, 1868, act 20); Baine (Dec. 7, 1866, act 92)

Finney, Kan. (Feb. 21, 1883, chap. 71); Sequoyah (Mar. 6, 1873, chap. 72)

Geary, Kan. (Feb. 28, 1889, chap. 132); Davis (Aug. 30, 1855, chap. 30)
Grays Harbor, Wash. (Mar. 15, 1915, chap. 77); Chehalis (Apr. 14, 1854, unnumbered)

Harris, Tex. (Dec. 28, 1839, joint resolution); Harrisburg (Mar. 17, 1836 Tex. const.)
Henry, Mo. (Feb. 15, 1841, unnumbered); Rives (Dec. 13, 1834, unnumbered)
Hernando, Fla. (Dec. 24, 1850, chap. 415); Benton (Mar. 6, 1844); Hernando (Feb. 24, 1843, chap. 51)
Holt, Mo. (Feb. 15, 1841, unnumbered); Nodaway (Jan. 29, 1841, unnumbered)
Holt, Neb. (Jan. 9, 1862, unnumbered); West (Jan. 13, 1860, unnumbered)
Howard, Ind. (Dec. 28, 1846, chap. 168); Richardville (Jan. 15, 1844, chap. 3)
Hyde, N. C. (1712); Wickham (Dec. 3, 1705)

Iosco, Mich. (Mar. 8, 1843, act 67); Kanotin (Apr. 1, 1840, act 119)
Iron, Utah (Dec. 3, 1850, unnumbered); Little Salt Lake County, (Jan. 31, 1850)
Isle of Wight, Va. (1637); Warrosquoyoake (1634).

Jackson, Kan. (Feb. 11, 1859, chap. 99); Calhoun (Aug. 30, 1855, chap. 30)
Jasper, Ga. (Dec. 10, 1812, unnumbered); Randolph (Dec. 10, 1807, unnumbered)
Jefferson, Miss. (Jan. 11, 1802, unnumbered); Pickering (Apr. 2, 1799)
Jefferson, Neb. (Oct. 23, 1865); Jones (Jan. 26, 1856, unnumbered)
Johnson, Wyo. (Dec. 13, 1879, chap. 31); Pease (Dec. 8, 1875, unnumbered)

Kalkaska, Mich. (Mar. 8, 1843, act 67); Wabasee (Apr. 1, 1840, act 119)
Kent, Del. (1683); St. Jones (1682)

Kitsap, Wash. (July 13, 1857, unnumbered); Slaughter (Jan. 16, 1857, unnumbered)

Knox, Neb. (Feb. 21, 1873); L'eau Qui Court, (Feb. 10, 1857, unnumbered)

Lafayette, Mo. (Feb. 16, 1825, chap. 1); Lillard (Nov. 16, 1820, chap. 10)

Lake, Colo. (Feb. 10, 1879, unnumbered); Carbonate (Nov. 1, 1861, unnumbered)

Lake, Mich. (Mar. 8, 1843, act 67); Aishcum (Apr. 1, 1840, act 119)

Lamar, Ala. (Feb. 8, 1877, act 205); Sanford (Oct. 8, 1868, act 13); Jones (Feb. 4, 1867, act 298)

Langlade, Wis. (Feb. 19, 1880, chap. 19); New (Feb. 27, 1879, chap. 114)

Lewis and Clark, Mont. (Dec. 20, 1867, unnumbered; eff. Mar. 1, 1868); Edgerton (Feb. 2, 1865, unnumbered)

Lincoln, Minn. ; Rock (Mar. 23, 1857, chap. 14)

Lincoln, Neb. (Dec. 11, 1861, unnumbered); Shorter (Jan. 7, 1860, unnumbered)

Logan, Ark. (Dec. 14, 1875, act 62); Sarber (Mar. 22, 1871, act 25)

Logan, Kan. (Feb. 24, 1887, chap. 173); St. John (Mar. 4, 1881, chap. 48)

Loudon, Tenn. (July 7, 1870, chap. 77); Christiana (June 2, 1870, chap. 2)

Lyon, Iowa (Sept. 11, 1862, chap. 23). Buncombe (Jan. 15, 1851, chap. 9)

Lyon, Kan. (Feb. 5, 1862, chap. 61); Breckenridge (Feb. 17, 1857, unnumbered)

Mackinac, Mich. (Mar. 9, 1843, chap. 89); Michilimackinac (Oct. 26, 1818, procl.)

Marion, Ark. (Sept. 29, 1836, unnumbered); Searcy (Nov. 3, 1835, unnumbered)

Marion, Ore. (Sept. 3, 1849, unnumbered); Champoick (July 5, 1843, unnumbered)

Mason, Mich. (Mar. 8, 1843, act 67); Notipekago (Apr. 1, 1840, act 119)

Mason, Wash. (Jan. 8, 1864, unnumbered); Sawamish (Mar. 13, 1854)

Menominee, Mich. (Mar. 19, 1863, act 163); Bleeker (Mar. 15, 1861, act 213)

Miami, Kan. (June 3, 1861, chap. 18); Lykins (Aug. 30, 1855, chap. 30)

Monroe, Iowa (Jan. 19, 1846); Kishkekosh (Feb. 17, 1843, chap. 34)

Montgomery, N. Y. (Apr. 2, 1784, chap. 17); Tryon (Mar. 12, 1772, chap. 613)

Montmorency, Mich. (Mar. 8, 1843, act 67); Chednoquet (Apr. 1, 1840, act 119)

Morgan, Ala. (June 14, 1821, unnumbered); Cotaco (Feb. 6, 1818, unnumbered)

Morris, Kan. (Feb. 11, 1859, chap. 60); Wise (Aug. 30, 1855, chap. 30)

Nansemond, Va. (1645); Upper Norfolk 1637

Nemaha, Neb. (Nov. 23, 1854 procl.); Forney

Neosho, Kan. (June 3, 1861, chap. 18); Dorn (Aug. 30, 1855, chap. 30)

Newport, R. I. (June 16, 1729); Rhode Island (June 22, 1703)

Northampton, Va. (1642); Accawmack (1634)

Norton, Kan. (Feb. 19, 1874, chap. 55); Billings (Mar. 6, 1873, chap. 72); Norton (Feb. 26, 1867).

Orange, Fla. (Jan. 30, 1845, chap. 31); Mosquito (Dec. 29, 1824, unnumbered)

Osage, Kan. (Feb. 11, 1859, chap. 100); Weller (1855, chap. 30)

Osceola, Mich. (Mar. 8, 1843, act 67); Unwattin (Apr. 1, 1840, act 119)

Otoe, Neb.; Pierce

Otsego, Mich. (Mar. 8, 1843, act 67); Okkuddo (Apr. 1, 1840, act 119)

Ouray, Colo. (Mar. 2, 1883, unnumbered); Uncompahgre (Feb. 27, 1883, unnumbered)

Ozark, Mo. (Mar. 24, 1845, unnumbered); Decatur (Feb. 22, 1843, unnumbered); Ozark (Jan. 29, 1841, unnumbered)

Pierce, Neb.; Otoe

Providence, R. I. (June 16, 1729); Providence Plantations (June 22, 1703)

Rich, Utah (Jan. 29, 1868, chap. 2); Richland (Jan. 16, 1864, unnumbered)

Roscommon, Mich. (Mar. 8, 1843, act 67); Mikenauk (Apr. 1, 1840, act 119)

Rusk, Wis. (June 19, 1905, chap. 463); Gates (May 15, 1901, chap. 469)

St. Louis, Minn. (Mar. 3, 1855, chap. 22); Superior (Feb. 20, 1855, chap. 6)

Salt Lake, Utah (Jan. 29, 1868, chap. 3); Great Salt Lake (Mar. 3, 1852, unnumbered)

San Miguel, Colo. (Mar. 2, 1883, unnumbered); Ouray (Nov. 1, 1861, unnumbered)
Santa Cruz, Calif. (Apr. 5, 1850, chap. 61); Branciforte (Feb. 18, 1850, chap. 15)
Saunders, Neb. (Jan. 8, 1862, unnumbered); Calhoun (Jan. 26, 1856, unnumbered)
Seward, Kan. (June 3, 1861, chap. 18); Godfroy (Aug. 30, 1855, chap. 30)
Seward, Neb. (Jan. 3, 1862, unnumbered); Greene (Mar. 6, 1855, unnumbered)
Shenandoah, Va. (Mar. 24, 1777, chap. 43); Dunmore (Feb. 10, 1772 sess. chap. 43)
Stanton, Neb. ; Izard (Mar. 6, 1855, unnumbered)
Stephens, Tex. (Dec. 17, 1861, chap. 4); Buchanan (Jan. 22, 1858, chap. 55)
Sussex, Del. (1683); Deal (1682)
Sweetwater, Wyo. (Dec. 13, 1869, chap. 35); Carter (Dec. 27, 1867, chap. 35)

Texas, Mo. (Feb. 14, 1845, unnumbered); Ashley (Feb. 17, 1843, unnumbered)
Thayer, Neb. (Oct. 30, 1871); Jefferson (Jan. 26, 1856, unnumbered)

Union, S. D. (Jan. 7, 1864, chap. 14); Cole (Apr. 10, 1862, chap. 14)
Union, Tenn. (Jan. 28, 1846, chap. 123); Cocke (Oct. 9, 1797, chap. 8)

Vernon, Wis. (Mar. 22, 1862, chap. 137); Bad Axe (Mar. 1, 1851, chap. 131)

Wabaunsee, Kan. (Feb. 11, 1859, chap. 49); Richardson (Aug. 30, 1855, chap. 30)
Washington, Iowa (Jan. 25, 1839, unnumbered); Slaughter (Jan. 16, 1837)
Washington, N. Y. (Apr. 2, 1784, chap. 17); Charlotte (Mar. 12, 1772, chap. 613)
Washington, Ore. (Sept. 3, 1849, unnumbered); Twality (July 5, 1843)
Washington, R. I. (Oct. 29, 1781); King's (June 16, 1729)
Washington, Vt. (Nov. 8, 1814, chap. 79); Jefferson (Nov. 1, 1810, chap. 74)
Webster, Ga. (Feb. 21, 1856, act 367); Kinchafoonee (Dec. 16, 1853, act 227)
Webster, Iowa (Jan. 12, 1853, chap. 12); Risley (Jan. 15, 1851, chap. 9)

Webster, Miss. (Jan. 30, 1882, chap. 132); Sumner (Apr. 6, 1874, chap. 112)
Wells, N D. (Feb. 26, 1881, chap. 53); Gingras (Jan. 4, 1873, chap. 18)
Wexford, Mich. (Mar. 8, 1843, act 67); Kautawaubet (Apr. 1, 1840, act 119)
Wilkin, Minn. (Mar. 6, 1868, chap. 115); Andy Johnson (Mar. 8, 1862, chap. 25)
Winston, Ala. (Jan. 22, 1858, act 322); Hancock (Feb. 12, 1850, act 58)
Woodbury, Iowa (Jan. 12, 1853, chap. 12); Wahkaw (Jan. 15, 1851, chap. 9)

York, Va. (1642); Charles River (1634)

PART VI

COUNTY SEATS

(The name of the county is enclosed in parentheses.)

Abbeville, Ala. (Henry)
Abbeville, Ga. (Wilcox)
Abbeville, La. (Vermilion)
Abbeville, S. C. (Abbeville)
Aberdeen, Miss. (Monroe)
Aberdeen, S. D. (Brown)
Abilene, Kan. (Dickinson)
Abilene, Tex. (Taylor)
Abingdon, Va. (Washington)
Accomac, Va. (Accomack)
Ackerman, Miss. (Choctaw)
Ada, Minn. (Norman)
Ada, Okla. (Pontotoc)
Adel, Ga. (Cook)
Adel, Iowa (Dallas)
Adrian, Mich. (Lenawee)
Aiken, S. C. (Aiken)
Ainsworth, Neb. (Brown)
Aitkin, Minn. (Aitkin)
Akron, Colo. (Washington)
Akron, Ohio (Summit)
Alamo, Ga. (Wheeler)
Alamo, Tenn. (Crockett)
Alamogordo, N. M. (Otero)
Alamosa, Colo. (Alamosa)
Albany, Ga. (Dougherty)
Albany, Ky. (Clinton)
Albany, Mo. (Gentry)
Albany, N. Y. (Albany)
Albany, Ore. (Linn)
Albany, Tex. (Shackelford)
Albemarle, N. C. (Stanly)
Albert Lea, Minn. (Freeborn)
Albia, Iowa (Monroe)
Albion, Ill. (Edwards)
Albion, Ind. (Noble)
Albion, Neb. (Boone)
Albion, N. Y. (Orleans)
Albuquerque, N. M. (Bernalillo)
Aledo, Ill. (Mercer)
Alexandria, Ky. (Campbell)
Alexandria, La. (Rapides)
Alexandria, Minn. (Douglas)
Alexandria, S. D. (Hanson)
Alfred, Me. (York)
Algona, Iowa (Kossuth)
Alice, Tex. (Jim Wells)
Allegan, Mich. (Allegan)
Allendale, S. C. (Allendale)
Allentown, Pa. (Lehigh)
Alliance, Neb. (Box Butte)
Allison, Iowa (Butler)
Alma, Ga. (Bacon)
Alma, Kan. (Wabaunsee)
Alma, Neb. (Harlan)
Alma, Wis. (Buffalo)
Alpena, Mich. (Alpena)
Alpine, Tex. (Brewster)
Altamont, Tenn. (Grundy)
Alton, Mo. (Oregon)
Alturas, Calif. (Modoc)
Altus, Okla. (Jackson)
Alva, Okla. (Woods)
Amarillo, Tex. (Potter)
Amelia, Va. (Amelia)
American Falls, Idaho (Power)
Americus, Ga. (Sumter)
Amherst, Va. (Amherst)
Amidon, N. D. (Slope)
Amite, La. (Tangipahoa)

Anaconda, Mont. (Deer Lodge)
Anadarko, Okla. (Caddo)
Anahuac, Tex. (Chambers)
Anamosa, Iowa (Jones)
Andalusia, Ala. (Covington)
Anderson, Ind. (Madison)
Anderson, S. C. (Anderson)
Anderson, Tex. (Andrews)
Angleton, Tex. (Brazoria)
Angola, Ind. (Steuben)
Ann Arbor, Mich. (Wastenaw)
Annapolis, Md. (Anne Arundel)
Anniston, Ala. (Calhoun)
Anoka, Minn. (Anoka)
Arnett, Okla. (Ellis)
Anson, Tex. (Jones)
Anthony, Kan. (Harper)
Antigo, Wis. (Langlade)
Antlers, Okla. (Pushmataha)
Apalachicola, Fla. (Franklin)
Appleton, Wis. (Outagamie)
Appling, Ga. (Columbia)
Appomattox, Va. (Appomattox)
Arapaho, Okla. (Custer)
Arcadia, Fla. (De Soto)
Arcadia, La. (Bienville)
Archer City, Tex. (Archer)
Arco, Idaho (Butte)
Ardmore, Okla. (Carter)
Arkadelphia, Ark. (Clark)
Arkansas City, Ark. (Desha)
Arlington, Va. (Arlington)
Armour, S. D. (Douglas)
Arthur, Neb. (Arthur)
Ashburn, Ga. (Turner)
Ashdown, Ark. (Little River)
Asheboro, N. C. (Randolph)
Asheville, N. C. (Buncombe)
Ashland, Ala. (Clay)
Ashland, Kan. (Clark)
Ashland, Miss. (Benton)
Ashland, Ohio (Ashland)
Ashland, Tenn. (Cheatham)
Ashland, Wis. (Ashland)
Ashley, N D. (McIntosh)
Asotin, Wash. (Asotin)
Aspen, Colo. (Pitkin)
Aspermont, Tex. (Stonewall)

Astoria, Ore. (Clatsop)
Atchison, Kan. (Atchison)
Athens, Ala. (Limestone)
Athens, Ga. (Clarke)
Athens, Ohio (Athens)
Athens, Tenn. (McMinn)
Athens, Tex. (Henderson)
Atlanta, Ga. (Fulton)
Atlanta, Mich. (Montmorency)
Atlantic, Iowa (Cass)
Atoka, Okla. (Atoka)
Atwood, Kan. (Rawlins)
Auburn, Calif. (Pacer)
Auburn, Ind. (De Kalb)
Auburn, Me. (Androscoggin)
Auburn, Nebr. (Nemaha)
Auburn, N. Y. (Cayuga)
Audubon, Iowa (Audubon)
Augusta, Ark. (Woodruff)
Augusta, Ga. (Richmond)
Augusta, Me. (Kennebec)
Aurora, Neb. (Hamilton)
Austin, Minn. (Mower)
Austin, Nev. (Lander)
Austin, Tex. (Travis)
Ava, Mo. (Douglas)
Aztec, N. M. (San Juan)

Bad Axe, Mich. (Huron)
Bagley, Minn. (Clearwater)
Bainbridge, Ga. (Decatur)
Baird, Tex. (Callahan)
Baker, Mont. (Fallon)
Baker, Ore. (Baker)
Bakersfield, Calif. (Kern)
Bakersville, N. C. (Mitchell)
Baldwin, Mich. (Lake)
Ballinger, Tex. (Runnels)
Ballston Spa, N. Y. (Saratoga)
Balsam Lake, Wis. (Polk)
Bamberg, S. C. (Bamberg)
Bandera, Tex. (Bandera)
Bangor, Me. (Penobscot)
Baraboo, Wis. (Sauk)
Barbourville, Ky. (Knox)
Bardstown, Ky. (Nelson)
Bardswell, Ky. (Carlisle)

Barnesville, Ga. (Lamar)
Barnstable, Mass. (Barnstable)
Barnwell, S. C. (Barnwell)
Barron, Wis. (Barron)
Bartlesville, Okla. (Washington)
Bartlett, Neb. (Wheeler)
Bartow, Fla. (Polk)
Basin, Wyo. (Big Horn)
Bassett, Neb. (Rock)
Bastrop, La. (Morehouse)
Bastrop, Tex. (Bastrop)
Batavia, N. Y. (Genesee)
Batavia, Ohio (Clermont)
Batesville, Ark. (Independence)
Batesville, Miss. (Panola)
Bath, Me. (Sagadahoc)
Bath, N. Y. (Steuben)
Baton Rouge, La. (East Baton Rouge)
Baudette, Minn. (Lake of the Woods)
Baxley, Ga. (Appling)
Bay City, Mich. (Bay)
Bay City, Tex. (Matagorda)
Bay Minette, Ala. (Baldwin)
Bay St. Louis, Miss. (Hancock)
Bay Springs, Miss. (Jasper)
Bayboro, N. C. (Pamlico)
Beach, N. D. (Golden Valley)
Beatrice, Neb. (Gage)
Beattyville, Ky. (Lee)
Beaufort, N. C. (Carteret)
Beaufort, S. C. (Beaufort)
Beaumont, Tex. (Jefferson)
Beaver, Okla. (Beaver)
Beaver, Pa. (Beaver)
Beaver, Utah (Beaver)
Beaver City, Neb. (Furnas)
Beckley, W. Va. (Raleigh)
Bedford, Ind. (Lawrence)
Bedford, Iowa (Taylor)
Bedford, Ky. (Trimble)
Bedford, Pa. (Bedford)
Bedford, Va. (Bedford)
Beeville, Tex. (Bee)
Bel Air, Md. (Hartford)
Belfast, Me. (Waldo)
Bellaire, Mich. (Antrim)
Bellefontaine, Ohio (Logan)
Bellefonte, Pa. (Centre)
Belle Fourche, S. D. (Butte)
Belleville, Ill. (St. Clair)
Belleville, Kan. (Republic)
Belleville, Tex. (Austin)
Bellingham, Wash. (Whatcom)
Belmont, N. Y. (Allegany)
Beloit, Kan. (Mitchell)
Belton, Tex. (Bell)
Belvidere, Ill. (Boone)
Belvidere, N. J. (Warren)
Belzoni, Miss. (Humphreys)
Bemidji, Minn. (Beltrami)
Bend, Ore. (Deschutes)
Benjamin, Tex. (Knox)
Benkelman, Neb. (Dundy)
Bennettsville, S. C. (Marlboro)
Bennington, Vt. (Bennington)
Benson, Minn. (Swift)
Benton, Ark. (Saline)
Benton, Ill. (Franklin)
Benton, Ky. (Marshall)
Benton, La. (Bossier)
Benton, Mo. (Scott)
Benton, Tenn. (Polk)
Bentonville, Ark. (Benton)
Berkeley Springs, W. Va. (Morgan)
Bernalillo, N. M. (Sandoval)
Berryville, Ark. (Carroll)
Berryville, Va. (Clarke)
Bessemer, Mich. (Gogebic)
Bethany, Mo. (Harrison)
Beulah, Mich. (Benzie)
Big Lake, Tex. (Reagan)
Big Rapids, Mich. (Mecosta)
Big Spring, Tex. (Howard)
Bigtimber, Mont. (Sweet Grass)
Billings, Mont. (Yellowstone)
Binghamton, N. Y. (Broome)
Birmingham, Ala. (Jefferson)
Bisbee, Ariz. (Cochise)
Bishopville, S. C. (Lee)
Bismarck, N. D. (Burleigh)
Bison, S. D. (Perkins)

Blackfoot, Idaho (Bingham)
Black River Falls, Wis. (Jackson)
Blackshear, Ga. (Pierce)
Blair, Neb. (Washington)
Blairsville, Ga. (Union)
Blakely, Ga. (Early)
Bland, Va. (Bland)
Bloomfield, Ind. (Greene)
Bloomfield, Iowa (Davis)
Bloomfield, Mo. (Stoddard)
Bloomington, Ill. (McLean)
Bloomington, Ind. (Monroe)
Bloomsburg, Pa. (Columbia)
Blountstown, Fla. (Calhoun)
Blountville, Tenn. (Sullivan)
Blue Earth, Minn. (Faribault)
Blue Ridge, Ga. (Fannin)
Bluffton, Ind. (Wells)
Blythesville, Ark. (Mississipi)
Boerne, Tex. (Kendall)
Boise, Idaho (Ada)
Bolivar, Mo. (Polk)
Bolivar, Tenn. (Hardeman)
Bonham, Tex. (Fannin)
Bonifay, Fla. (Holmes)
Bonners Ferry, Idaho (Boundary)
Boone, Iowa (Boone)
Boone, N. C. (Watauga)
Booneville, Ark. (Logan)
Booneville, Ky. (Owsley)
Booneville, Miss. (Prentiss)
Boonville, Ind. (Warrick)
Boonville, Mo. (Cooper)
Boston, Mass. (Suffolk)
Boston, Tex. (Bowie)
Bottineau, N. D. (Bottineau)
Boulder, Colo. (Boulder)
Boulder, Mont. (Jefferson)
Bowbells, N. D. (Burke)
Bowling Green, Ky. (Warren)
Bowling Green, Mo. (Pike)
Bowling Green, Ohio (Wood)
Bowling Green, Va. (Caroline)
Bowman, N. D. (Bowman)
Boydton, Va. (Mecklenburg)
Bozeman, Mont. (Gallatin)
Brackettville, Tex. (Kinney)
Bradenton, Fla. (Manatee)
Brady, Tex. (McCulloch)
Brainerd, Minn. (Crow Wing)
Brandenburg, Ky. (Meade)
Brandon, Miss. (Rankin)
Brazil, Ind. (Clay)
Breckenridge, Colo. (Summit)
Breckenridge, Minn. (Wilkin)
Breckenridge, Tex. (Stephens)
Brenham, Tex. (Washington)
Brevard, N. C. (Transylvania)
Brewster, Neb. (Blaine)
Brewton, Ala. (Escambia)
Bridgeport, Calif. (Mono)
Bridgeport, Conn. (Fairfield)
Bridgeport, Neb. (Morrill)
Bridgeton, N. J. (Cumberland)
Brigham City, Utah (Box Elder)
Brighton, Colo. (Adams)
Bristol, Fla. (Liberty)
Bristol, R. I. (Bristol)
Britton, S. D. (Marshall)
Broadus, Mont. (Powder River)
Broken Bow, Neb. (Custer)
Bronson, Fla. (Levy)
Bronx, N. Y. (Bronx, N.Y.C.)
Brookhaven, Miss. (Lincoln)
Brookings, S. D. (Brookings)
Brooklyn, N. Y. (Kings)
Brooksville, Fla. (Hernando)
Brooksville, Ky. (Bracken)
Brooksville, Pa. (Jefferson)
Brookville, Ind. (Franklin)
Brownsfield, Tex. (Terry)
Brownstown, Ind. (Jackson)
Brownsville, Ky. (Edmonson)
Brownsville, Tenn. (Haywood)
Brownsville, Tex. (Brownsville)
Brownwood, Tex. (Brown)
Brunswick, Ga. (Glynn)
Bryan, Ohio (Williams)
Bryan, Tex. (Brazos)
Bryson City, N. C. (Swain)
Buchanan, Ga. (Haralson)
Buckhannon, W. Va. (Upshur)
Buckingham, Va. (Buckingham)

Bucyrus, Ohio (Crawford)
Buena Vista, Ga. (Marion)
Buffalo, Minn. (Wright)
Buffalo, Mo. (Dallas)
Buffalo, N. Y. (Erie)
Buffalo, Okla. (Harper)
Buffalo, S. D. (Harding)
Buffalo, Wyo. (Johnson)
Bunnell, Fla. (Flagler)
Burgaw, N. C. (Pender)
Burke, S. D. (Gregory)
Burkesville, Ky. (Cumberland)
Burley, Idaho (Cassia)
Burlington, Colo. (Kit Carson)
Burlington, Iowa (Des Moines)
Burlington, Kan. (Coffey)
Burlington, Ky. (Boone)
Burlington, Vt. (Chittenden)
Burnet, Tex. (Burnet)
Burns, Ore. (Harney)
Burnsville, N. C. (Yancey)
Burwell, Neb. (Garfield)
Bushnell, Fla. (Sumter)
Butler, Ala. (Choctaw)
Butler, Ga. (Taylor)
Butler, Mo. (Bates)
Butler, Pa. (Butler)
Butte, Mont. (Silver Bow)
Butte, Neb. (Boyd)
Byrdstown, Tenn. (Pickett)

Cadillac, Mich. (Wexford)
Cadiz, Ky. (Trigg)
Cadiz, Ohio (Harrison)
Cairo, Ga. (Grady)
Cairo, Ill. (Alexander)
Caldwell, Idaho (Canyon)
Caldwell, Ohio (Noble)
Caldwell, Tex. (Burleson)
Caledonia, Minn. (Houston)
Calhoun, Ga. (Gordon)
Calhoun, Ky. (McLean)
California, Mo. (Moniteau)
Cambridge, Ill. (Henry)
Cambridge, Md. (Dorchester)
Cambridge, Mass. (Middlesex)
Cambridge, Minn. (Isanti)
Cambridge, Ohio (Guernsey)
Camden, Ala. (Wilcox)
Camden, Ark. (Ouachita)
Camden, N. J. (Camden)
Camden, N. C. (Camden)
Camden, S. C. (Kershaw)
Camden, Tenn. (Benton)
Camdenton, Mo. (Camden)
Cameron, La. (Cameron)
Cameron, Tex. (Milam)
Camilla, Ga. (Mitchell)
Campbellsville, Ky. (Taylor)
Campton, Ky. (Wolfe)
Canadian, Tex. (Hemphill)
Canadaigua, N. Y. (Ontario)
Cando, N. D. (Towner)
Cannelton, Ind. (Perry)
Canon City, Colo. (Fremont)
Canton, Ga. (Cherokee)
Canton, Miss. (Madison)
Canton, N. Y. (St. Lawrence)
Canton, Ohio (Stark)
Canton, S. D. (Lincoln)
Canton, Tex. (Van Zandt)
Canyon, Tex. (Randall)
Canyon City, Ore. (Grant)
Cape May Court House, N. J. (Cape May)
Carlinville, Ill. (Macoupin)
Carlisle, Ky. (Nicholas)
Carlisle, Pa. (Cumberland)
Carlsbad, N. M. (Eddy)
Carlton, Minn. (Carlton)
Carlyle, Ill. (Clinton)
Carmel, N. Y. (Putnam)
Carmi, Ill. (White)
Carnesville, Ga. (Franklin)
Caro, Mich. (Tuscola)
Carrington, N. D. (Foster)
Carrizo Springs, Tex. Dimmit)
Carrizozo, N. M. (Lincoln)
Carroll, Iowa (Carroll)
Carrollton, Ala. (Pickens)
Carrollton, Ga. (Carroll)
Carrollton, Ill. (Greene)
Carrollton, Ky. (Carroll)
Carrollton, Miss. (Carroll)

Carrollton, Mo. (Carroll)
Carrollton, Ohio (Carroll)
Carson, N. D. (Grant)
Cartersville, Ga. (Bartow)
Carthage, Ill. (Hancock)
Carthage, Miss. (Leake)
Carthage, Mo. (Jasper)
Carthage, N. C. (Moore)
Carthage, Tenn. (Smith)
Carthage, Tex. (Panola)
Caruthersville, Mo. (Pemiscot)
Cascade, Idaho (Valley)
Casper, Wyo. (Natrona)
Cassopolis, Mich. (Cass)
Cassville, Mo. (Barry)
Castle Dale, Utah (Emery)
Castle Rock, Colo. (Douglas)
Cathlamet, Wash. (Wahkiakum)
Catlettsburg, Ky. (Boyd)
Catskill, N. Y. (Greene)
Cavalier, N. D. (Pembina)
Cedar Rapids, Iowa (Linn)
Cedartown, Ga. (Polk)
Celina, Ohio (Mercer)
Celina, Tenn. (Clay)
Center, Neb. (Knox)
Center, N. D. (Oliver)
Center, Tex. (Shelby)
Center City, Minn. (Chisago)
Centerville, Ala. (Bibb)
Centerville, Iowa (Appanoose)
Centerville, Mo. (Reynolds)
Centerville, Tenn. (Hickman)
Centerville, Tex. (Leon)
Central City, Colo. (Gilpin)
Central City, Neb. (Merrick)
Centre, Ala. (Cherokee)
Centreville, Md. (Queen Anne's)
Centreville, Mich. (St. Joseph)
Chadron, Neb. (Dawes)
Challis, Idaho (Custer)
Chalmette, La. (St. Bernard)
Chamberlain, S. D. (Brule)
Chambersburg, Pa. (Franklin)
Chandler, Okla. (Lincoln)
Channing, Tex. (Hartley)
Chappell, Neb. (Deuel)
Chardon, Ohio (Geauga)
Charles City, Iowa (Floyd)
Charles City, Va. (Charles City)
Charleston, Ark. (Franklin)
Charleston, Ill. (Coles)
Charleston, Miss. (Tallahatchie)
Charleston, Mo. (Mississippi)
Charleston, S. C. (Charleston)
Charleston, W. Va. (Kanawha)
Charles Town, W. Va. (Jefferson)
Charlevoix, Mich. (Charlevoix)
Charlton, Iowa (Lucas)
Charlotte, Mich. (Eaton)
Charlotte, N. C. (Mecklenburg)
Charlotte, Tenn. (Dickson)
Charlotte Court, Va. (Charlotte)
Charlottesville, Va. (Albemarle)
Chaska, Minn. (Carver)
Chatham, Va. (Pittsylvania)
Chatom, Ala. (Washington)
Chatsworth, Ga. (Murray)
Chattanooga, Tenn. (Hamilton)
Cheboygan, Mich. (Cheboygan)
Chehalis, Wash. (Lewis)
Chelsea, Vt. (Orange)
Cherokee, Iowa (Cherokee)
Cherokee, Okla. (Cherokee)
Chester, Ill. (Randolph)
Chester, Mont. (Liberty)
Chester, S. C. (Chester)
Chesterfield, S. C. (Chesterfield)
Chesterfield, Va. (Chesterfield)
Chestertown, Md. (Kent)
Cheyenne, Okla. (Roger Mills)
Cheyenne, Wyo. (Laramie)
Cheyenne Wells, Colo. (Cheyenne)
Chicago, Ill. (Cook)
Chickasha, Okla. (Grady)
Childress, Tex. (Childress)
Chillicothe, Mo. (Livingston)
Chillicothe, Ohio (Ross)
Chilton, Wis. (Calumet)

Chinook, Mont. (Blaine)
Chipley, Fla. (Washington)
Chippewa Falls, Wis. (Chippewa)
Choteau, Mont. (Teton)
Christiansburg, Va. (Montgomery)
Cimarron, Kan. (Gray)
Cincinnati, Ohio (Hamilton)
Circle, Mont. (McCone)
Circleville, Ohio (Pickaway)
Clairemont, Tex. (Kent)
Clanton, Ala. (Chilton)
Claremore, Okla. (Rogers)
Clarendon, Ark. (Monroe)
Clarendon, Tex. (Donley)
Clarinda, Iowa (Page)
Clarion, Iowa (Wright)
Clarion, Pa. (Clarion)
Clark, S. D. (Clark)
Clarkesville, Ga. (Habersham)
Clarksburg, W. Va. (Harrison)
Clarksdale, Miss. (Coahoma)
Clarksville, Ark. (Johnson)
Clarksville, Tenn. (Montgomery)
Clarksville, Tex. (Red River)
Claude, Tex. (Armstrong)
Claxton, Ga. (Evans)
Clay, W. Va. (Clay)
Clay Center, Kan. (Clay)
Clay Center, Neb. (Clay)
Clayton, Ala. (Barbour)
Clayton, Ga. (Rabun)
Clayton, Mo. (St. Louis)
Clayton, N. M. (Union)
Clear Lake, S. D. (Deuel)
Clearfield, Pa. (Clearfield)
Clearwater, Fla. (Pinellas)
Cleburne, Tex. (Johnson)
Cleveland, Ga. (White)
Cleveland, Miss. (Bolivar)
Cleveland, Ohio (Cuyahoga)
Cleveland, Tenn. (Bradley)
Clifton, Ariz. (Greenlee)
Clinton, Ark. (Van Buren)
Clinton, Ill. (De Witt)
Clinton, Iowa (Clinton)
Clinton, Ky. (Hickman)
Clinton, La. (East Feliciana)
Clinton, Mo. (Henry)
Clinton, N. C. (Sampson)
Clinton, Tenn. (Anderson)
Clintwood, Va. (Dickenson)
Clovis, N. M. (Curry)
Coalgate, Okla. (Coal)
Coalville, Utah (Summit)
Cochran, Ga. (Bleckley)
Cody, Wyo. (Park)
Coeur d'Alene, Idaho (Kootenai)
Coffeyville, Miss. (Yalobusha)
Colby, Kan. (Thomas)
Coldspring, Tex. (San Jacinto)
Coldwater, Kan. (Comanche)
Coldwater, Mich. (Branch)
Coleman, Tex. (Coleman)
Colfax, La. (Grant)
Colfax, Wash. (Whitman)
Collins, Miss. (Covington)
Colorado City, Tex. (Mitchell)
Colorado Springs, Colo. (El Paso)
Colquitt, Ga. (Miller)
Columbia, Ky. (Adair)
Columbia, La. (Caldwell)
Columbia, Miss. (Marion)
Columbia, Mo. (Boone)
Columbia, N. C. (Tyrrell)
Columbia, S. C. (Richland)
Columbia, Tenn. (Maury)
Columbia City, Ind. (Whitley)
Columbiana, Ala. (Shelby)
Columbus, Ga. (Muscogee)
Columbus, Ind. (Bartholomew)
Columbus, Kan. (Cherokee)
Columbus, Miss. (Lownden)
Columbus, Mont. (Stillwater)
Columbus, Neb. (Platte)
Columbus, N. C. (Polk)
Columbus, Ohio (Franklin)
Columbus, Tex. (Colorado)
Colusa, Calif. (Colusa)
Colville, Wash. (Stevens)
Comanche, Tex. (Comanche)
Concord, N. H. (Merrimack)

Concord, N. C. (Cabarrus)
Concordia, Kan. (Cloud)
Condon, Ore. (Gilliam)
Conejos, Colo. (Conejos)
Connersville, Ind. (Fayette)
Conrad, Mont. (Pondera)
Conroe, Tex. (Montgomery)
Convent, La. (St. James)
Conway, Ark. (Faulkner)
Conway, S. C. (Horry)
Conyers, Ga. (Rockdale)
Cookeville, Tenn. (Putnam)
Cooper, Tex. (Delta)
Cooperstown, N. Y. (Otsego)
Cooperstown, N. D. (Griggs)
Coquille, Ore. (Coos)
Cordele, Ga. (Crisp)
Cordell, Okla. (Washita)
Corning, Ark. (Clay)
Corning, Iowa (Adams)
Corinth, Miss. (Alcorn)
Corpus Christi, Tex. (Nueces)
Corsicana, Tex. (Navarro)
Cortez, Colo. (Montezuma)
Cortland, N. Y. (Cortland)
Corunna, Mich. (Shiawassee)
Corvallis, Ore. (Benton)
Corydon, Ind. (Harrison)
Corydon, Iowa (Wayne)
Coshocton, Ohio (Coshocton)
Cottonwood Falls, Kan. (Chase)
Cotulla, Tex. (La Salle)
Coudersport, Pa. (Potter)
Council, Idaho (Adams)
Council Bluffs, Iowa (Pottawatamie)
Council Grove, Kan. (Morris)
Coupeville, Wash. (Island)
Courtland, Va. (Southampton)
Coushatta, La. (Red River)
Covington, Ga. (Newton)
Covington, Ind. (Fountain)
Covington, Ky. (Kenton)
Covington, La. (St. Tammany)
Covington, Tenn. (Tipton)
Covington, Va. (Alleghany)
Craig, Colo. (Moffat)
Crandon, Wis. (Forest)
Crane, Tex. (Crane)
Crawfordsville, Ind. (Montgomery)
Crawfordville, Fla. (Wakulla)
Crawfordville, Ga. (Taliaferro)
Creede, Colo. (Mineral)
Crescent City, Calif. (Del Norte)
Cresco, Iowa (Howard)
Creston, Iowa (Union)
Crestview, Fla. (Okaloosa)
Cripple Creek, Colo. (Teller)
Crockett, Tex. (Houston)
Crookston, Minn. (Polk)
Crosby, N. D. (Divide)
Crosbyton, Tex. (Crosby)
Cross City, Fla. (Dixie)
Crossville, Tenn. (Cumberland)
Crowell, Tex. (Foard)
Crowley, La. (Acadia)
Crown Point, Ind. (Lake)
Crystal City, Tex. (Zavala)
Crystal Falls, Mich. (Iron)
Cuero, Tex. (De Witt)
Cullman, Ala. (Cullman)
Culpeper, Va. (Culpeper)
Cumberland, Md. (Allegany)
Cumberland, Va. (Cumberland)
Cumming, Ga. (Forsyth)
Currituck, N. C. (Currituck)
Cusseta, Ga. (Chattahoochee)
Custer, S. D. (Custer)
Cut Bank, Mont. (Glacier)
Cuthbert, Ga. (Randolph)
Cynthiana, Ky. (Harrison)

Dade City, Fla. (Pasco)
Dadeville, Ala. (Tallapoosa)
Dahlonega, Ga. (Lumpkin)
Daingerfield, Tex. (Morris)
Dakota City, Iowa (Humboldt)
Dakota City, Neb. (Dakota)
Dalhart, Tex. (Dallam)
Dallas, Ga. (Paulding)
Dallas, Ore. (Polk)

Dallas, Tex. (Dallas)
Dalles, Ore. (Wasco)
Dalton, Ga. (Whitefield)
Danbury, N. C. (Stokes)
Dandridge, Tenn. (Jefferson)
Danielsville, Ga. (Madison)
Danville, Ark. (Yell)
Danville, Ill. (Vermilion)
Danville, Ind. (Hendricks)
Danville, Ky. (Boyle)
Danville, Pa. (Montour)
Dardanelle, Ark. (Yell)
Darien, Ga. (McIntosh)
Darlington, S. C. (Darlington)
Darlington, Wis. (Lafayette)
Davenport, Iowa (Scott)
Davenport, Wash. (Lincoln)
David City, Neb. (Butler)
Dawson, Ga. (Terrell)
Dawsonville, Ga. (Dawson)
Dayton, Ohio (Montgomery)
Dayton, Tenn. (Rhea0
Dayton, Wash. (Columbia)
Deadwood, S. D. (Lawrence)
Decatur, Ala. (Morgan)
Decatur, Ga. (De Kalb)
Decatur, Ill. (Macon)
Decatur, Ind. (Adams)
Decatur, Miss. (Newton)
Decatur, Tenn. (Meigs)
Decatur, Tex. (Wise)
Decaturville, Tenn. (Decatur)
Decorah, Iowa (Winneshiek)
Dedham, Mass. (Norfolk)
Deer Lodge, Mont. (Powell)
Defiance, Ohio (Defiance)
De Funiak Springs, Fla. (Walton)
De Kalb, Miss. (Kemper)
De Land, Fla. (Volusia)
Delaware, Ohio (Delaware)
Delhi, N. Y. (Delaware)
Del Norte, Colo. (Rio Grande)
Delphi, Ind. (Carroll)
Del Rio, Tex. (Val Verde)
Delta, Colo. (Delta)
Deming, N. M. (Luna)
Denison, Iowa (Crawford)
Denton, Md. (Caroline)
Denton, Tex. (Denton)
Denver, Colo. (Denver)
De Queen, Ark. (Sevier)
De Ridder, La. (Beauregard)
De Valls Bluff, Ark. (Prairie)
Des Arc, Ark. (Prairie)
Des Moines, Iowa (Polk)
De Smet, S. D. (Kingsbury)
Detroit, Mich. (Wayne)
Detroit Lakes, Minn. (Becker)
Devils Lake, N. D. (Ramsey)
De Witt, Ark. (Arkansas)
Dickens, Tex. (Dickens)
Dickinson, N. D. (Stark)
Dighton, Kan. (Lane)
Dillon, Mont. (Beaverhead)
Dillon, S. C. (Dillon)
Dimmitt, Tex. (Castro)
Dinwiddie, Va. (Dinwiddie)
Dixon, Ill. (Lee)
Dixon, Ky. (Webster)
Dobson, N. C. (Surry)
Dodge City, Kan. (Ford)
Dodgeville, Wis. (Iowa)
Donaldsonville, Ga. (Seminole)
Donaldsonville, La. (Ascension)
Doniphan, Mo. (Ripley)
Dothan, Ala. (Houston)
Double Springs, Ala. (Winston)
Douglas, Ga. (Coffee)
Douglas, Wyo. (Converse)
Douglasville, Ga. (Douglas)
Dover, Del. (Kent)
Dover-Foxcroft, Me. (Piscataquis)
Dover, N. H. (Strafford)
Dover, Tenn. (Steward)
Downieville, Calif. (Sierra)
Doylestown, Pa. (Bucks)
Dresden, Tenn. (Weakley)
Driggs, Idaho (Teton)
Dublin, Ga. (Laurens)
Dubois, Idaho (Clark)
Dubuque, Iowa (Dubuque)
Duchesne, Utah (Duchesne)
Duluth, Minn. (St. Louis)

Dumas, Tex. (Moore)
Duncan, Okla. (Stephens)
Dunlap, Tenn. (Sequatchie)
Dupree, S. D. (Ziebach)
Durand, Wis. (Pepin)
Durango, Colo. (La Plata)
Durant, Okla. (Bryan)
Durham, N. C. (Durham)
Dyersburg, Tenn. (Dyer)

Eads, Colo. (Kiowa)
Eagle, Colo. (Eagle)
Eagle Pass, Tex. (Maverick)
Eagle River, Mich. (Keweenah)
Eagle River, Wis. (Vilas)
East Greenwich, R. I. (Kent)
Eastland, Tex. (Eastland)
Eastman, Ga. (Dodge)
Easton, Md. (Talbot)
Easton, Pa. (Northampton)
Eastville, Va. (Northampton)
Eaton, Ohio (Preble)
Eatonton, Ga. (Putnam)
Ebensburg, Pa. (Cambria)
Eddyville, Ky. (Lyon)
Edenton, N. C. (Chowan)
Edgard, La. (St. John The Baptist)
Edgartown, Mass. (Dukes)
Edgefield, S. C. (Edgefield)
Edina, Mo. (Knox)
Edinburg, Tex. (Hidalgo)
Edmonton, Ky. (Metcalfe)
Edna, Tex. (Jackson)
Edwardsville, Ill. (Madison)
Effingham, Ill. (Effingham)
Ekalaka, Mont. (Carter)
Elba, Ala. (Coffee)
Elberton, Ga. (Elbert)
Elbow Lake, Minn. (Grant)
El Centro, Calif. (Imperial)
El Dorado, Ark. (Union)
El Dorado, Kan. (Butler)
Eldorado, Iowa (Hardin)
Eldorado, Tex. (Schleicher)
Elizabeth, N. J (Union)
Elizabeth, W. Va. (Wirt)
Elizabeth City, N. C. (Pasquotank)
Elizabethton, Tenn. (Carter)
Elizabethtown, Ill. (Hardin)
Elizabethtown, N. Y. (Essex)
Elizabethtown, N. C. (Bladen)
Elkader, Iowa (Clayton)
Elkhorn, Wis. (Walworth)
Elkins, W. Va. (Randolph)
Elk Point, S. D. (Union)
Elk River, Minn. (Sherburne)
Elko, Nev. (Elko)
Elkton, Ky. (Todd)
Elkton, Md. (Cecil)
Ellaville, Ga. (Schley)
Ellendale, N. D. (Dickey)
Ellensburg, Wash. (Kittitas)
Ellicott City, Md. (Howard)
Ellijay, Ga. (Gilmer)
Ellisville, Miss. (Jones)
Ellsworth, Kan. (Ellsworth)
Ellsworth, Me. (Hancock)
Ellsworth, Wis. (Pierce)
Elmira, N. Y. (Chemung)
El Paso, Tex. (El Paso)
El Reno, Okla. (Canadian)
Elwood, Neb. (Gosper)
Ely, Nev. (White Pine)
Elyria, Ohio (Lorain)
Emmetsburg, Iowa (Palo Alto)
Emmett, Idaho (Gem)
Eminence, Mo. (Shannon)
Emory, Tex. (Rains)
Emporia, Kan. (Lyon)
Emporia, Va. (Greensville)
Emporium, Pa. (Cameron)
English, Ind. (Crawford)
Enid, Okla. (Garfield)
Enterprise, Ala. (Coffee)
Enterprise, Ore. (Wallowa)
Ephrata, Wash. (Grant)
Erie, Kan. (Neosho)
Erie, Pa. (Erie)
Erin, Tenn. (Houston)
Erwin, Tenn. (Unicoi)
Escanaba, Mich. (Delta)
Estancia, N. M. (Torrence)

Estherville, Iowa (Emmet)
Eufaula, Ala. (Barbour)
Eufaula, Okla. (McIntosh)
Eugene, Ore. (Lane)
Eureka, Ark. (Carroll)
Eureka, Calif. (Humboldt)
Eureka, Ill. (Woodford)
Eureka, Kan. (Greenwood)
Eureka, Nev. (Eureka)
Eureka Springs, Ark. (Carroll)
Eutaw, Ala. (Greene)
Evanston, Wyo. (Uinta)
Evansville, Ind. (Vanderburgh)
Evening Shade, Ark. (Sharp)
Everett, Wash. (Snohomish)
Everglades, Fla. (Collier)
Evergreen, Ala. (Conecuh)
Exeter, N. H. (Rockingham)

Fairbury, Neb. (Jefferson)
Fairchild, Wis. (Eau Clair)
Fairfax, Va. (Fairfax)
Fairfield, Calif. (Solano)
Fairfield, Idaho (Camas)
Fairfield, Ill. (Wayne)
Fairfield, Iowa (Jefferson)
Fairfield, Tex. (Freestone)
Fairmont, Minn. (Martin)
Fairmont, W. Va. (Marion)
Fairplay, Colo. (Park)
Fairview, Okla. (Major)
Falfurrias, Tex. (Brooks)
Fall River, Mass. (Bristol)
Fallon, Nev. (Churchill)
Falls City, Neb. (Richardson)
Falmouth, Ky. (Pendleton)
Fargo, N. D. (Cass)
Faribault, Minn. (Rice)
Farmerville, La. (Union)
Farmington, Me. (Franklin)
Farmington, Mo. (St. Francois)
Farmington, Utah (Davis)
Farmville, Va. (Prince Edward)
Farwell, Tex. (Farmer)
Faulkton, S. D. (Faulk)
Fayette, Ala. (Fayette)
Fayette, Miss. (Jefferson)
Fayette, Mo. (Howard)
Fayetteville, Ark. (Washington)
Fayetteville, Ga. (Fayette)
Fayetteville, N. C. (Cumberland)
Fayetteville, Tenn. (Lincoln)
Fayetteville, W. Va. (Fayette)
Fergus Falls, Minn. (Otter Tail)
Fernandina, Fla. (Nassau)
Fessenden, N. D. (Wells)
Fillmore, Utah (Millard)
Fincastle, Va. (Botetourt)
Findlay, Ohio (Hancock)
Finley, N. D. (Steele)
Fitchburg, Mass. (Worcester)
Fitzgerald, Ga. (Ben Hill)
Flagstaff, Ariz. (Coconino)
Flandreau, S. D. (Moody)
Flemingsburg, Ky. (Fleming)
Flemington, N. J. (Hunterdon)
Flint, Mich. (Genesee)
Florence, Ala. (Lauderdale)
Florence, Ariz. (Pindal)
Florence, S. C. (Florence)
Florence, Wis. (Florence)
Floresville, Tex. (Wilson)
Floyd, Va. (Floyd)
Floydada, Tex. (Floyd)
Foley, Minn. (Benton)
Folkston, Ga. (Charlton)
Fond Du Lac, Wis. (Fond Du Lac)
Fonda, N. Y. (Montgomery)
Fordyce, Ark. (Dallas)
Forest, Miss. (Scott)
Forest City, Iowa (Winnebago)
Forman, N. D. (Sargent)
Forrest City, Ark. (St. Francis)
Forsyth, Ga. (Monroe)
Forsyth, Mo. (Taney)
Forsyth, Mont. (Rosebud)
Fort Benton, Mont. (Chouteau)
Fort Collins, Colo. (Larimer)
Fort Davis, Tex. (Jeff Davis)
Fort Dodge, Iowa (Webster)
Fort Gaines, Ga. (Clay)

Fort Lauderdale, Fla. (Broward)
Fort Madison, Iowa (Lee)
Fort Morgan, Colo. (Morgan)
Fort Myers, Fla. (Lee)
Fort Payne, Ala. (De Kalb)
Fort Pierce, Fla. (St. Lucie)
Fort Pierre, S. D. (Stanley)
Fort Scott, Kan. (Bourbon)
Fort Smith, Ark. (Sebastian)
Fort Stockton, Tex. (Pecos)
Fort Sumner, N. M. (De Baca)
Fort Valley, Ga. (Peach)
Fort Wayne, Ind. (Allen)
Fort Worth, Tex. (Tarrant)
Fort Yates, N. D. (Sioux)
Fossil, Ore. (Wheeler)
Fowler, Ind. (Benton)
Frankfort, Ind. (Clinton)
Frankfort, Ky. (Franklin)
Franklin, Ga. (Heard)
Franklin, Ind. (Johnson)
Franklin, Ky. (Franklin)
Franklin, La. (St. Mary)
Franklin, Neb. (Franklin)
Franklin, N. C. (Macon)
Franklin, Pa. (Venango)
Franklin, Tenn. (Williamson)
Franklin, Tex. (Robertson)
Franklin, W. Va. (Pendleton)
Franklinton, La. (Washington)
Frederick, Md. (Frederick)
Frederick, Okla. (Tillman)
Fredericksburg, Tex. (Gillespie)
Fredericktown, Mo. (Madison)
Fredonia, Kan. (Wilson)
Freehold, N. J. (Monmouth)
Fremont, Neb. (Dodge)
Fremont, Ohio (Sandusky)
Freeport, Ill. (Stephenson)
Frenchburg, Ky. (Menifee)
Fresno, Calif. (Fresno)
Friday Harbor, Wash. (San Juan)
Friendship. Wis. (Adams)
Front Royal, Va. (Warren)
Fullerton, Neb. (Nance)
Fulton, Miss. (Itawamba)
Fulton, Mo. (Callaway)

Gadsden, Ala. (Etowah)
Gaffney, S. C. (Cherokee)
Gail, Tex. (Borden)
Gainesboro, Tenn. (Jackson)
Gainesville, Fla. (Alachua)
Gainesville, Ga. (Hall)
Gainesville, Mo. (Ozark)
Gainesville, Tex. (Cooke)
Galena, Ill. (Jo Daviess)
Galena, Mo. (Stone)
Galesburg, Ill. (Knox)
Gallatin, Mo. (Daviess)
Gallatin, Tenn. (Sumner)
Gallipolis, Ohio (Gallia)
Gallup, N. M. (McKinley)
Galveston, Tex. (Galveston)
Gann Valley, S. D. (Buffalo)
Garden City, Kan. (Finney)
Garden City, Tex. (Glasscock)
Garner, Iowa (Hancock)
Garnett, Kan. (Anderson)
Gastonia, N. C. (Gaston)
Gate City, Va. (Scott)
Gatesville, N. C. (Gates)
Gatesville, Tex. (Coryell)
Gaylord, Mich. (Otsego)
Gaylord, Minn. (Sibley)
Geneseo, N. Y. (Livingston)
Geneva, Ala. (Geneva)
Geneva, Ill. (Kane)
Geneva, Neb. (Fillmore)
Genevieve, Mo. (Ste. Genevieve)
Georgetown, Colo. (Clear Creek)
Georgetown, Del. (Sussex)
Georgetown, Ga. (Quitman)
Georgetown, Ky. (Scott)
Georgetown, Ohio (Brown)
Georgetown, S. C. (Georgetown)
Georgetown, Tex. (Williamson)
George West, Tex. (Live Oak)
Gering, Neb. (Scotts Bluff)
Gettysburg, Pa. (Adams)

Gettysburg, S. D. (Potter)
Gibson, Ga. (Glascock)
Giddings, Tex. (Lee)
Gillette, Wyo. (Campbell)
Gilmer, Tex. (Upshur)
Girard, Kan. (Crawford)
Gladwin, Mich. (Gladwin)
Glasgow, Ky. (Barren)
Glasgow, Mont. (Valley)
Glenroe, Minn. (McLeon)
Glendive, Mont. (Dawson)
Glen Rose, Tex. (Somervell)
Glenville, W. Va. (Gilmer)
Glenwood, Iowa (Mills)
Glenwood, Minn. (Pope)
Glenwood Springs, Colo. (Garfield)
Globe, Ariz. (Gila)
Gloucester, Va. (Gloucester)
Golconda, Ill. (Pope)
Gold Beach, Ore. (Curry)
Golden, Colo. (Jefferson)
Goldendale, Wash. (Klickitat)
Goldfield, Nev. (Esmeralda)
Goldsboro, N. C. (Wayne)
Goldthwaithe, Tex. (Mills)
Goliad, Tex. (Goliad)
Gonzales, Tex. (Gonzalez)
Goochland, Va. (Goochland)
Gooding, Idaho (Gooding)
Goodland, Kan. (Sherman)
Goshen, Ind. (Elkhart)
Goshen, N. Y. (Orange)
Gove, Kan. (Gove)
Grafton, N. D. (Walsh)
Grafton, W. Va. (Taylor)
Graham, N. C. (Alamance)
Graham, Tex. (Young)
Granbury, Tex. (Hood)
Grand Forks, N. D. (Grand Forks)
Grand Haven, Mich. (Ottawa)
Grand Island, Neb. (Hall)
Grand Junction, Colo. (Mesa)
Grand Marais, Minn. (Cook)
Grand Rapids, Mich. (Kent)
Grand Rapids, Minn. (Itasca)
Grangeville, Idaho (Idaho)
Granite Falls, Minn. (Yellow Medicine)
Grant, Neb. (Perkins)
Grant City, Mo. (Worth)
Grantsburg, Wis. (Burnett)
Grants Pass, Ore. (Josephine)
Grantsville, W. Va. (Calhoun)
Gray, Ga. (Jones)
Grayling, Mich. (Crawford)
Grayson, Ky. (Carter)
Great Bend, Kan. (Barton)
Great Falls, Mont. (Cascade)
Greeley, Colo. (Weld)
Greeley, Neb. (Greeley)
Green Bay, Wis. (Brown)
Greencastle, Ind. (Putnam)
Green Cove Springs, Fla. (Clay)
Greeneville, Tenn. (Greene)
Greenfield, Ind. (Hancock)
Greenfield, Iowa (Adair)
Greenfield, Mass. (Franklin)
Greenfield, Mo. (Dade)
Green Lake, Wis.(Green Lake)
Green River, Wyo. (Sweetwater)
Greensboro, Ala. (Hale)
Greensboro, Ga. (Greene)
Greensboro, N. C. (Guilford)
Greensburg, Ind. (Decatur)
Greensburg, Kan. (Kiowa)
Greensburg, La. (St. Helena)
Greensburg, Ky. (Green)
Greensburg, Pa. (Westmoreland)
Greenup, Ky. (Greenup)
Greenville, Ala. (Butler)
Greenville, Ga. (Meriwether)
Greenville, Ill. (Bond)
Greenville, Ky. (Muhlenberg)
Greenville, Miss. (Washington)
Greenville, Mo. (Wayne)
Greenville, N. C. (Pitt)
Greenville, Ohio (Darke)
Greenville, S. C. (Greenville)
Greenville, Tex. (Hunt)
Greenwood, Ark. (Sebastian)

Greenwood, Miss. (Leflore)
Greenwood, S. C. (Greenwood)
Grenada, Miss. (Grenada)
Gretna, La. (Jefferson)
Griffin, Ga. (Spalding)
Groesbeck, Tex. (Limestone)
Grove, Okla. (Delaware)
Grove Hill, Ala. (Clarke)
Groveton, Tex. (Trinity)
Grundy, Va. (Buchanan)
Grundy Center, Iowa (Grundy)
Guildhall, Vt. (Essex)
Gulfport, Miss. (Harrison)
Gunnison, Colo. (Gunnison)
Guntersville, Ala. (Marshall)
Guthrie, Okla. (Logan)
Guthrie, Tex. (King)
Guthrie Center, Iowa (Guthrie)
Guymon, Okla. (Texas)

Hackensack, N. J. (Bergen)
Hagerstown, Md. (Washington)
Hahnville, La. (St. Charles)
Hailey, Idaho (Blaine)
Halifax, N. C. (Halifax)
Halifax, Va. (Halifax)
Hallettsville, Tex. (Lavaca)
Hallock, Minn. (Kittson)
Hamburg, Ark. (Ashley)
Hamilton, Ala. (Marion)
Hamilton, Ga. (Harris)
Hamilton, Mont. (Ravalli)
Hamilton, Ohio (Butler)
Hamilton, Tex. (Hamilton)
Hamlin, W. Va. (Lincoln)
Hampton, Ark. (Calhoun)
Hampton, Iowa (Franklin)
Hampton, S. C. (Hampton)
Hanford, Calif. (Kings)
Hanover, Va. (Hanover)
Hardin, Ill. (Calhoun)
Hardin, Mont. (Big Horn)
Hardinsburg, Ky. (Breckenridge)
Hardy, Ark. (Sharp)
Harlan, Iowa (Shelby)
Harlan, Ky. (Harlan)
Harlowton, Mont. (Wheatland)
Harrisburg, Ark. (Poinsett)
Harrisburg, Ill. (Saline)
Harrisburg, Neb. (Banner)
Harrisburg, Pa. (Dauphin)
Harrison, Ark. (Boone)
Harrison, Mich. (Clare)
Harrison, Neb. (Sioux)
Harrisonburg, La. (Catahoula)
Harrisonburg, Va. (Rockingham)
Harrisonville, Mo. (Cass)
Harrisville, Mich. (Alcona)
Harrisville, W. Va. (Ritchie)
Harrodsburg, Ky. (Mercer)
Hart, Mich. (Oceana)
Hartford, Conn. (Hartford)
Hartford, Ky. (Ohio)
Hartford City, Ind. (Blackford)
Hartington, Neb. (Cedar)
Hartsville, Tenn. (Trousdale)
Hartville, Mo. (Wright)
Hartwell, Ga. (Hart)
Haskell, Tex. (Haskell)
Hastings, Mich. (Barry)
Hastings, Minn. (Dakota)
Hastings, Neb. (Adams)
Hattiesburg, Miss. (Forrest)
Havana, Ill. (Mason)
Havre, Mont. (Hill)
Hawesville, Ky. (Hancock)
Hawkinsville, Ga. (Pulaski)
Hawthorne, Nev. (Mineral)
Hayes Center, Neb. (Hayes)
Hayesville, N. C. (Clay)
Hayneville, Ala. (Lowndes)
Hays, Kan. (Ellis)
Hayti, S. D. (Hamlin)
Hayward, Wis. (Sawyer)
Hazard, Ky. (Perry)
Hazlehurst, Ga. (Jeff Davis)
Hazlehurst, Miss. (Copiah)
Heathsville, Va. (Northumberland)
Heber City, Utah (Wasatch)
Heber Springs, Ark. (Cleburne)
Hebbronville, Tex. (Jim Hogg)
Hebron, Neb. (Thayer)
Heflin, Ala. (Cleburne)

Helena, Ark. (Phillips)
Helena, Mont. (Lewis and Clark)
Hemphill, Tex. (Sabine)
Hempstead, Tex. (Waller)
Henderson, Ky. (Henderson)
Henderson, N. C. (Vance)
Henderson, Tenn. (Chester)
Henderson, Tex. (Rusk)
Hendersonville, N. C. (Henderson)
Hennepin, Ill. (Putnam)
Henrietta, Tex. (Clay)
Heppner, Ore. (Morrow)
Hereford, Tex. (Deaf Smith)
Herkimer, N. Y. (Herkimer)
Hermann, Mo. (Gasconade)
Hermitage, Mo. (Hickory)
Hernando, Miss. (De Soto)
Hertford, N. C. (Perquimans)
Hettinger, N. D. (Adams)
Hiawassee, Ga. (Towns)
Hiawatha, Kan. (Brown)
Hickman, Ky. (Fulton)
Highmore, S. D. (Hyde)
Hill City, Kan. (Graham)
Hillsboro, Ill. (Montgomery)
Hillsboro, Mo. (Jefferson)
Hillsboro, N. C. (Orange)
Hillsboro, N. D. (Traill)
Hillsboro, Ohio (Highland)
Hillsboro, Ore. (Washington)
Hillsboro, Tex. (Hill)
Hillsdale, Mich. (Hillsdale)
Hillsville, Va. (Carroll)
Hindman, Ky. (Knott)
Hinesville, Ga. (Liberty)
Hinton, W. Va. (Summers)
Hobart, Okla. (Kiowa)
Hodgenville, Ky. (Larue)
Hohenwald, Tenn. (Lewis)
Holbrook, Ariz. (Navajo)
Holdenville, Okla. (Hughes)
Holdrege, Neb. (Phelpa)
Hollidaysburg, Pa. (Blair)
Hollis, Okla. (Harmon)
Hollister, Calif. (San Benito)
Holly Springs, Miss. (Marshall)
Holton, Kan. (Jackson)
Holyoke, Colo. (Phillips)
Homer, Ga. (Banks)
Homer, La. (Claiborne)
Homerville, Ga. (Clinch)
Hondo, Tex. (Medina)
Honesdale, Pa. (Wayne)
Hood River, Ore. (Hood River)
Hope, Ark. (Hempstead)
Hopkinsville, Ky. (Christian)
Hot Springs, Ark. (Garland)
Hot Springs, S. D. (Fall River)
Hot Sulphur Springs, Colo. (Grand)
Houghton, Mich. (Houghton)
Houlton, Me. (Aroostook)
Houma, La. (Terrebonne)
Houston, Miss. (Chickasaw)
Houston, Mo. (Texas)
Houston, Tex. (Harris)
Howard, Kan. (Elk)
Howard, S. D. (Miner)
Howell, Mich. (Livingston)
Hoxie, Kan. (Sheridan)
Hudson, N. Y. (Columbia)
Hudson, Wis. (St. Croix)
Hudson Falls, N. Y. (Washington)
Hugo, Colo. (Lincoln)
Hugo, Okla. (Choctaw)
Hugoton, Kan. (Stevens)
Humboldt, Tenn. (Gibson)
Huntingdon, Pa. (Huntingdon)
Huntingdon, Tenn. (Carroll)
Huntington, Ind. (Huntington)
Huntington, W. Va. (Cabell)
Huntsville, Ala. (Madison)
Huntsville, Ark. (Madison)
Huntsville, Mo. (Randolph)
Huntsville, Tenn. (Scott)
Huntsville, Tex. (Walker)
Hugoton, Kan. (Stevens)
Hurley, Wis. (Iron)
Huron, S. D. (Beadle)
Hutchinson, Kan. (Reno)
Hyannis, Neb. (Grant)
Hyde Park, Vt. (Lamoille)

Hyden, Ky. (Leslie)
Hysham, Mont. (Treasure)

Idabel, Okla. (McCurtain)
Ida Grove, Iowa (Ida)
Idaho City, Idaho (Boise)
Idaho Falls, Idaho (Bonneville)
Imperial, Neb. (Chase)
Independence, Calif. (Inyo)
Independence, Iowa (Buchanan)
Independence, Kan. (Montgomery)
Independence, Ky. (Kenton)
Independence, Mo. (Jackson)
Independence, Va. (Grayson)
Indiana, Pa. (Indiana)
Indianola, Iowa (Warren)
Indianola, Miss. (Sunflower)
Inez, Ky. (Martin)
International Falls, Minn. (Koochiching)
Inverness, Fla. (Citrus)
Iola, Kan. (Allen)
Ionia, Mich. (Ionia)
Iowa City, Iowa (Johnson)
Ipswich, S. D. (Edmunds)
Iron Mountain, Mich. (Dickinson)
Ironton, Mo. (Iron)
Ironton, Ohio (Lawrence)
Irvine, Ky. (Estill)
Irwinton, Ga. (Wilkinson)
Isle of Wight, Va. (Isle of Wight)
Ithaca, Mich. (Gratiot)
Ithaca, N. Y. (Tompkins)
Iuka, Miss. (Tishomingo)
Ivanhoe, Minn. (Lincoln)

Jacksboro, Tenn. (Campbell)
Jacksboro, Tex. (Jack)
Jackson, Calif. (Amador)
Jackson, Ga. (Butts)
Jackson, Ky. (Breathitt)
Jackson, Mich. (Jackson)
Jackson, Minn. (Jackson)
Jackson, Miss. (Hinds)
Jackson, Mo. (Cape Girardeau)
Jackson, N. C. (Northampton)
Jackson, Ohio (Jackson)
Jackson, Tenn. (Madison)
Jackson, Wyo. (Teton)
Jacksonville, Fla. (Duval)
Jacksonville, Ill. (Morgan)
Jacksonville, N. C. (Onslow)
Jamaica, N. Y. (Queens, NYC)
Jamestown, Ky. (Russell)
Jamestown, N. D. (Stutsman)
Jamestown, Tenn. (Fentress)
Janesville, Wis. (Rock)
Jasper, Ala. (Walker)
Jasper, Ark. (Newton)
Jasper, Fla. (Hamilton)
Jasper, Ga. (Pickens)
Jasper, Ind. (Du Bois)
Jasper, Tenn. (Marion)
Jasper, Tex. (Jasper)
Jay, Okla. (Delaware)
Jefferson, Ga. (Jackson)
Jefferson, Iowa (Greene)
Jefferson, N. C. (Ashe)
Jefferson, Ohio (Ashtabula)
Jefferson, Tex. (Marion)
Jefferson, Wis. (Jefferson)
Jefferson City, Mo. (Cole)
Jeffersonville, Ga. (Twiggs)
Jeffersonville, Ind. (Clark)
Jena, La. (Lasalle)
Jennings, La. (Jefferson Davis)
Jerome, Idaho (Jerome)
Jersey City, N. J. (Hudson)
Jerseyville, Ill. (Jersey)
Jesup, Ga. (Wayne)
Jetmore, Kan. (Hodgeman)
Johnson, Kan. (Stanton)
Johnson City, Tenn. (Washington)
Johnson City, Tex. (Blanco)
Johnstown, N. Y. (Fulton)
Joliet, Ill. (Will)
Jonesboro, Ark. (Craighead)
Jonesboro, Ga. (Clayton)
Jonesboro, Ill. (Union)

Jonesboro, La. (Jackson)
Jonesboro, Tenn. (Washington)
Jonesville, Va. (Lee)
Jordan, Mont. (Garfield)
Jourdanton, Tex. (Atascosa)
Julesburg, Colo. (Sedgwick)
Junction, Tex. (Kimble)
Junction, Utah (Piute)
Junction City, Kan. (Geary)
Juneau, Wis. (Dodge)

Kadoka, S. D. (Jackson)
Kahoka, Mo. (Clark)
Kalamazoo, Mich. (Kalamazoo)
Kalispell, Mont. (Flathead)
Kalkaska, Mich. (Kalkaska)
Kanab, Utah (Kane)
Kankakee, Ill. (Kankakee)
Kansas City, Kan. (Wyandotte)
Karnes City, Tex. (Karnes)
Kaufman, Tex. (Kaufman)
Kearney, Neb. (Buffalo)
Keene, N. H. (Cheshire)
Kelso, Wash. (Cowlitz)
Kemmerer, Wyo. (Lincoln)
Kenansville, N. C. (Duplin)
Kennebec, S. D. (Lyman)
Kennett, Mo. (Dunklin)
Kenosha, Wis. (Kenosha)
Kentland, Ind. (Newton)
Kenton, Ohio (Hardin)
Kenton, Okla. (Cimarron)
Keokuk, Iowa (Lee)
Keosauqua, Iowa (Van Buren)
Kermit, Tex. (Winkler)
Kerrville, Tex. (Kerr)
Keshena, Wis. (Menominee)
Kewaunee, Wis. (Kewaunee)
Keyser, W. Va. (Mineral)
Keytesville, Mo. (Chariton)
Key West, Fla. (Monroe)
Kimball, Neb. (Kimball)
King and Queen, Va. (King and Queen)
Kingfisher, Okla. (Kingfisher)
King George, Va. (King George)
Kingman, Ariz. (Mohave)
Kingman, Kan. (Kingman)
King William, Va. (King William)
Kingston, Mo. (Caldwell)
Kingston, N. Y. (Ulster)
Kingston, Tenn. (Roane)
Kingstree, S. C. (Williamsburg)
Kingsville, Tex. (Kleberg)
Kingwood, W. Va. (Preston)
Kinsley, Kan. (Edwards)
Kinston, N. C. (Lenoir)
Kiowa, Colo. (Elbert)
Kirksville, Mo. (Adair)
Kissimmee, Fla. (Osceola)
Kittanning, Pa. (Armstrong)
Klamath Falls, Ore. (Klamath)
Knox, Ind. (Starke)
Knoxville, Ga. (Crawford)
Knoxville, Iowa (Marion)
Knoxville, Tenn. (Knoxville)
Kokomo, Ind. (Howard)
Kosciusko, Miss. (Attala)
Kountze, Tex. (Hardin)

L'Anse, Mich. (Baraga)
La Belle, Fla. (Hendry)
Lacon, Ill. (Marshall)
Laconia, N. H. (Belknap)
La Crosse, Kan. (Rush)
La Crosse, Wis. (La Crosse)
Ladysmith, Wis. (Rusk)
Lafayette, Ala. (Chambers)
Lafayette, Ga. (Walker)
Lafayette, Ind. (Tippecanoe)
Lafayette, La. (Lafayette)
Lafayette, Tenn. (Macon)
La Grande, Ore. (Union)
La Grange, Ga. (Troup)
La Grange, Ind. (La Grange)
La Grange, Ky. (Oldham)
La Grange, Tex. (Fayette)
La Junta, Colo. (Otero)
La Moure, N. D. (La Moure)
La Plata, Md. (Charles)
La Porte, Ind. (La Porte)
Lake Andes, S. D. (Charles Mix)

Lake Butler, Fla. (Union)
Lake Charles, La. (Calcasieu)
Lake City, Ark. (Craighead)
Lake City, Colo. (Hinsdale)
Lake City, Fla. (Columbia)
Lake City, Mich. (Missaukee)
Lake George, N. Y. (Warren)
Lake Pleasant, N. Y. (Hamilton)
Lake Providence, La. (East Carroll)
Lake Village, Ark. (Lake Village)
Lakeland, Ga. (Lanier)
Lakeport, Calif. (Lake)
Lakeview, Ore. (Lake)
Lakin, Kan. (Kearny)
Lakota, N. D. (Nelson)
Lamar, Colo. (Prowers)
Lamar, Mo. (Barton)
Lamesa, Tex. (Dawson)
Lampasas, Tex. (Lampasas)
Lancaster, Ky. (Garrard)
Lancaster, Mo. (Schuyler)
Lancaster, N. H. (Coos)
Lancaster, Ohio (Fairfield)
Lancaster, Pa. (Lancaster)
Lancaster, S. C. (Lancaster)
Lancaster, Va. (Lancaster)
Lancaster, Wis. (Grant)
Lander, Wyo. (Fremont)
Langdon, N. D. (Cavalier)
Lapeer, Mich. (Lapeer)
Laporte, Pa. (Sullivan)
Laramie, Wyo. (Albany)
Laredo, Tex. (Webb)
Larned, Kan. (Pawnee)
Las Animas, Colo. (Bent)
Las Cruces, N. M. (Dona Ana)
Las Vegas, Nev. (Clark)
Las Vegas, N. M. (San Miguel)
Laurel, Miss. (Jones)
Laurens, S. C. (Laurens)
Laurinsburg, N. C. (Scotland)
Lawrence, Kan. (Douglas)
Lawrence, Mass. (Essex)
Lawrenceburg, Ind. (Dearborn)
Lawrenceburg, Ky. (Anderson)
Lawrenceburg, Tenn. (Lawrence)
Lawrenceville, Ga. (Gwinnett)
Lawrenceville, Ill. (Lawrence)
Lawrenceville, Va. (Brunswick)
Lawton, Okla. (Comanche)
Leadville, Colo. (Lake)
Leakesville, Miss. (Greene)
Leakey, Tex. (Real)
Leavenworth, Kan. (Leavenworth)
Lebanon, Ind. (Boone)
Lebanon, Ky. (Marion)
Lebanon, Mo. (Lebanon)
Lebanon, Ohio (Warren)
Lebanon, Pa. (Lebanon)
Lebanon, Tenn. (Wilson)
Lebanon, Va. (Russell)
Le Center, Minn. (Le Sueur)
Leesburg, Ga. (Lee)
Leesburg, Va. (Loudoun)
Leesville, La. (Vernon)
Leitchfield, Ky. (Grayson)
Leland, Mich. (Leelanau)
Le Mars, Iowa (Plymouth)
Lenoir, N. C. (Caldwell)
Leola, S. D. (McPherson)
Leon, Iowa (Decatur)
Leonardtown, Md. (St. Mary's)
Leoti, Kan. (Wichita)
Levelland, Tex. (Hockley)
Lewisburg, Pa. (Union)
Lewisburg, Tenn. (Marshall)
Lewisburg, W. Va. (Greenbrier)
Lewiston, Idaho (Nez Perce)
Lewistown, Ill. (Fulton)
Lewistown, Mont. (Fergus)
Lewistown, Pa. (Mifflin)
Lewisville, Ark. (Lafayette)
Lexington, Ga. (Oglethorpe)
Lexington, Ky. (Fayette)
Lexington, Miss. (Holmes)
Lexington, Mo. (Lafayette)
Lexington, Neb. (Sawson)
Lexington, N. C. (Davidson)
Lexington, S. C. (Lexington)
Lexington, Tenn. (Henderson)
Lexington, Va. (Rockbridge)

Libby, Mont. (Lincoln)
Liberal, Kan. (Seward)
Liberty, Ind. (Union)
Liberty, Ky. (Casey)
Liberty, Miss. (Amite)
Liberty, Mo. (Clay)
Liberty, Tex. (Liberty)
Lillington, N. C. (Harnett)
Lima, Ohio (Allen)
Lincoln, Ill. (Logan)
Lincoln, Kan. (Lincoln)
Lincoln, Neb. (Lancaster)
Lincolnton, Ga. (Lincoln)
Linden, Ala. (Marengo)
Linden, Tenn. (Perry)
Linden, Tex. (Cass)
Linn, Mo. (Osage)
Linneus, Mo. (Linn)
Linton, N. D. (Emmons)
Lipscomb, Tex. (Lipscomb)
Lisbon, N. D. (Ransom)
Lisbon, Ohio (Columbiana)
Litchfield, Conn. (Litchfield)
Litchfield, Minn. (Meeker)
Little Falls, Minn. (Morrison)
Little Rock, Ark. (Pulaski)
Littleton, Colo. (Araphoe)
Little Valley, N. Y. (Cattaraugus)
Live Oak, Fla. (Suwanee)
Livingston, Ala. (Sumter)
Livingston, La. (Livingston)
Livingston, Mont. (Park)
Livingston, Tenn. (Overton)
Livingston, Tex. (Polk)
Llano, Tex. (Llano)
Loa, Utah (Wayne)
Lockhart, Tex. (Caldwell)
Lock Haven, Pa. (Clinton)
Lockport, N. Y. (Niagara)
Logan, Iowa (Harrison)
Logan, Ohio (Hocking)
Logan, Utah (Cache)
Logan, W. Va. (Logan)
Logansport, Ind. (Cass)
London, Ky. (Laurel)
London, Ohio (Madison)
Long Prairie, Minn. (Todd)
Longview, Tex. (Gregg)
Lonoke, Ark. (Lonoke)
Lordsburg, N. M. (Hidalgo)
Los Alamos, N.M. (Los Alamos)
Los Angeles, Calif. (Los Angeles)
Los Lunas, N. M. (Valencia)
Loudon, Tenn. (Loudon)
Louisa, Ky. (Lawrence)
Louisa, Va. (Louisa)
Louisburg, N. C. (Franklin)
Louisville, Ga. (Jefferson)
Louisville, Ill. (Clay)
Louisville, Ky. (Jefferson)
Louisville, Miss. (Winston)
Loup City, Neb. (Sherman)
Lovelock, Nev. (Pershing)
Lovingston, Va. (Nelson)
Lovington, N. M. (Lea)
Lowell, Mass. (Middlesex)
Lowville, N. Y. (Lewis)
Lubbock, Tex. (Lubbock)
Lucedale, Miss. (George)
Ludington, Mich. (Mason)
Ludowici, Ga. (Long)
Lufkin, Tex. (Angelina)
Lumberton, N. C. (Robeson)
Lumpkin, Ga. (Stewart)
Lunenburg, Va. (Lunenburg)
Luray, Va. (Page)
Lusk, Wyo. (Niobrara)
Luverne, Ala. (Crenshaw)
Luverne, Minn. (Rock)
Lynchburg, Tenn. (Moore)
Lyndon, Kan. (Osage)
Lyons, Ga. (Toombs)
Lyons, Kan. (Rice)
Lyons, N. Y. (Wayne)

Mc Alester, Okla. (Pittsburg)
Mc Arthur, Ohio (Vinton)
Macclenny, Fla. (Baker)
Mc Clusky, N. D. (Sheridan)
Mc Connellsburg, Pa. (Fulton)
Mc Connelsville, Ohio (Morgan)
Mc Cook, Neb. (Red Willow)

Mc Cormick, S. C. (McCormick)
Mc Donough, Ga. (Henry)
Mc Intosh, S. D. (Corson)
Mc Kee, Ky. (Jackson)
Mc Kinney, Tex. (Collin)
Mc Leansboro, Ill. (Hamilton)
Mc Minnville, Ore. (Yamhill)
Mc Minnville, Tenn. (Warren)
Mc Pherson, Kan. (Mc Pherson)
Mc Rae, Ga. (Telfair)
Machais, Me. (Washington)
Macomb, Ill. (Mc Donough)
Macon, Ga. (Bibb)
Macon, Miss. (Noxubee)
Macon, Mo. (Macon)
Madera, Calif. (Madera)
Madill, Okla. (Marshall)
Madison, Fla. (Madison)
Madison, Ga. (Morgan)
Madison, Ind. (Jefferson)
Madison, Minn. (Lac Qui Parle)
Madison, Neb. (Madison)
Madison, S. D. (Lake)
Madison, Va. (Madison)
Madison, W. Va. (Boone)
Madison, Wis. (Dane)
Madisonville, Ky. (Hopkins)
Madisonville, Tenn. (Monroe)
Madisonville, Tex. (Madison)
Madras, Ore. (Jefferson)
Magnolia, Ark. (Columbia)
Magnolia, Miss. (Pike)
Mahnomen, Minn. (Mahnomen)
Malad City, Idaho (Oneida)
Malone, N. Y. (Franklin)
Malta, Mont. (Phillips)
Malvern, Ark. (Hot Spring)
Manassas, Va. (Prince William)
Manchester, Iowa (Delaware)
Manchester, Ky. (Clay)
Manchester, N. H. (Hillsborough)
Manchester, Tenn. (Coffee)
Manchester, Vt. (Bennington)
Mandan, N. D. (Morton)
Manhattan, Kan. (Riley)
Mangum, Okla. (Greer)
Manila, Utah (Daggett)
Manistee, Mich. (Manistee)
Manistique, Mich. (Schoolcraft)
Manitowoc, Wis. (Manitowoc)
Mankato, Kan. (Jewell)
Mankato, Minn. (Blue Earth)
Mansfield, Ohio (Richland)
Manteo, N. C. (Dare)
Manti, Utah (Sanpete)
Mantorville, Minn. (Dodge)
Maquoketa, Iowa (Jackson)
Manning, N. D. (Dunn)
Manning, S. C. (Clarendon)
Mansfield, La. (Desoto)
Many, La. (Sabine)
Marble Hill, Mo. (Bollinger)
Marengo, Iowa (Iowa)
Maria, Tex. (Presidio)
Marianna, Ark. (Lee)
Marianna, Fla. (Jackson)
Marietta, Ga. (Cobb)
Marietta, Ohio (Washington)
Marietta, Okla. (Love)
Marinette, Wis. (Marinette)
Marion, Ala. (Perry)
Marion, Ark. (Crittenden)
Marion, Ill. (Williamson)
Marion, Ind. (Grant)
Marion, Kan. (Marion)
Marion, Ky. (Crittendon)
Marion, N. C. (Mc Dowell)
Marion, Ohio (Marion)
Marion, S. C. (Marion)
Marion, Va. (Smyth)
Mariposa, Calif. (Mariposa)
Markleeville, Calif. (Alpine)
Marks, Miss. (Quitman)
Marksville, La. (Avoyelles)
Marlin, Tex. (Falls)
Marlinton, W. Va. (Pocahontas)
Marquette, Mich. (Marquette)
Marshall, Ark. (Searcy)
Marshall, Ill. (Clark)
Marshall, Mich. (Calhoun)
Marshall, Minn. (Lyon)
Marshall, Mo. (Saline)
Marshall, N. C. (Madison)

Marshall, Tex. (Harrison)
Marshalltown, Iowa (Marshall)
Marshfield, Mo. (Webster)
Martin, S. D. (Bennett)
Martinez, Calif. (Contra Costa)
Martinsburg, W. Va. (Berkeley)
Martinsville, Ind. (Morgan)
Martinsville, Va. (Henry)
Marysville, Calif. (Yuba)
Marysville, Kan. (Marshall)
Marysville, Mo. (Nodaway)
Marysville, Ohio (Union)
Maryville, Tenn. (Blount)
Mason, Mich. (Ingham)
Mason, Tex. (Mason)
Mason City, Iowa (Cerro Gordo)
Matador, Tex. (Motley)
Mathews, Va. (Mathews)
Mauch Chunk, Pa. (Carbon)
Mauston, Wis. (Juneau)
Mayersville, Miss. (Issaquena)
Mayfield, Ky. (Graves)
Maynardville, Tenn. (Union)
Mayo, Fla. (Lafayette)
Mays Landing, N. J. (Atlantic)
Maysville, Ky. (Mason)
Maysville, Mo. (De Kalb)
Mayville, N. Y. (Chautauqua)
Meade, Kan. (Meade)
Meadville, Miss. (Franklin)
Meadville, Pa. (Crawford)
Medford, Okla. (Grant)
Medford, Ore. (Jackson)
Medford, Wis. (Taylor)
Media, Pa. (Delaware)
Medicine Lodge, Kan. (Barber)
Medina, Ohio (Medina)
Medora, N. D. (Billings)
Meeker, Colo. (Rio Blanco)
Melbourne, Ark. (Izard)
Memphis, Mo. (Scotland)
Memphis, Tenn. (Shelby)
Memphis, Tex. (Hall)
Mena, Ark. (Polk)
Menard, Tex. (Menard)
Mendenhall, Miss. (Simpson)
Menominee, Mich. (Menominee)
Menomonie, Wis. (Dunn)
Mentone, Tex. (Lovin)
Merced, Calif. (Merced)
Mercer, Pa. (Mercer)
Meridian, Miss. (Lauderdale)
Meridian, Tex. (Bosque)
Merrill, Wis. (Lincoln)
Mertzon, Tex. (Irion)
Metropolis, Ill. (Massac)
Metter, Ga. (Candler)
Mexico, Mo. (Audrain)
Miami, Fla. (Dade)
Miami, Okla. (Ottawa)
Miami, Tex. (Miami)
Middlebourne, W. Va. (Tyler)
Middleburg, Pa. (Snyder)
Middlebury, Vt. (Addison)
Middletown, Conn. (Middletown)
Midland, Mich. (Midland)
Midland, Tex. (Midland)
Mifflintown, Pa. (Juniata)
Milaca, Minn. (Mille Lacs)
Milan, Mo. (Sullivan)
Milbank, S. D. (Grant)
Miles City, Mont. (Custer)
Milford, Pa. (Pike)
Milledgeville, Ga. (Baldwin)
Millen, Ga. (Jenkins)
Miller, S. D. (Hand)
Millersburg, Ohio (Holmes)
Milton, Fla. (Santa Rosa)
Milwaukee, Wis. (Milwaukee)
Minden, La. (Webster)
Minden, Neb. (Kearney)
Minden, Nev. (Minden)
Mineola, N. Y. (Nassau)
Minneapolis, Kan. (Ottawa)
Minneapolis, Minn. (Hennepin)
Minnewaukan, N. D. (Benson)
Minot, N. D. (Ward)
Mio, Mich. (Oscoda)
Missoula, Mont. (Missoula)
Mitchell, S. D. (Davison)
Moab, Utah (Grand)
Mobile, Ala. (Mobile)
Mocksville, N. C. (Davie)
Modesto, Calif. (Stanislaus)

Mohall, N. D. (Renville)
Monahans, Tex. (Ward)
Monck's Corner, S. C. (Berkeley)
Monmouth, Ill. (Warren)
Monroe, Ga. (Walton)
Monroe, La. (Ouachita)
Monroe, Mich. (Monroe)
Monroe, N. C. (Union)
Monroe, Wis. (Green)
Monroeville, Ala. (Monroe)
Montague, Tex. (Montague)
Montello, Wis. (Marquette)
Monterey, Va. (Highland)
Montesano, Wash. (Grays Harbor)
Montevideo, Minn. (Chippewa)
Montezuma, Iowa (Poweshiek)
Montgomery, Ala. (Montgomery)
Montgomery City, Mo. (Montgomery)
Monticello, Ark. (Drew)
Monticello, Fla. (Jefferson)
Monticello, Ga. (Jasper)
Monticello, Ill. (Piatt)
Monticello, Ind. (White)
Monticello, Ky. (Wayne)
Monticello, Miss. (Lawrence)
Monticello, Mo. (Lewis)
Monticello, N. Y. (Sullivan)
Monticello, Utah (San Juan)
Montpelier, Vt. (Washington)
Montrose, Colo. (Montrose)
Montrose, Pa. (Susquehanna)
Montross, Va. (Westmoreland)
Moorefield, W. Va. (Hardy)
Moore Haven, Fla. (Glades)
Moorhead, Minn. (Clay)
Mora, Minn. (Kanabec)
Mora, N. M. (Mora)
Morehead, Ky. (Rowan)
Morgan, Ga. (Calhoun)
Morgan, Utah (Morgan)
Morganfield, Ky. (Union)
Morganton, N. C. (Burke)
Morgantown, Ky. (Butler)
Morgantown, W. Va. (Monongalia)
Moro, Ore, (Sherman)
Morrilton, Ark. (Conway)
Morris, Ill. (Grundy)
Morris, Minn. (Stevens)
Morrison, Ill. (Whiteside)
Morristown, N. J. (Morris)
Morristown, Tenn. (Hamblen)
Morton, Tex. (Cochran)
Moscow, Idaho (Latah)
Mosquero, N. M. (Harding)
Mott, N. D. (Hettinger)
Moulton, Ala. (Lawrence)
Moultrie, Ga. (Colquitt)
Mound City, Ill. (Pulaski)
Mound City, Kan. (Linn)
Mound City, S. D. (Campbell)
Moundsville, W. Va. (Marshall)
Mount Ayr, Iowa (Ringgold)
Mount Carmel, Ill. (Wabash)
Mount Carroll, Ill. (Carroll)
Mount Clemens, Mich. (Macomb)
Mount Gilead, Ohio (Morrow)
Mount Holly, N. J. (Burlington)
Mount Ida, Ark. (Montgomery)
Mount Olivet, Ky. (Robertson)
Mount Pleasant, Iowa (Henry)
Mount Pleasant, Mich. (Isabella)
Mount Pleasant, Tex. (Titus)
Mount Sterling, Ill. (Brown)
Mount Sterling, Ky. (Montgomery)
Mount Vernon, Ga. (Montgomery)
Mount Vernon, Ill. (Jefferson)
Mount Vernon, Ind. (Posey)
Mount Vernon, Ky. (Rockcastle)
Mount Vernon, Mo. (Lawrence)
Mount Vernon, Ohio (Knox)
Mount Vernon, Tex. (Franklin)
Mount Vernon, Wash. (Skagit)
Mountain City, Tenn. (Johnson)
Mountain Home, Ark. (Baxter)
Mountain Home, Idaho (Elmore)
Mountain View, Ark. (Stone)
Muleshoe, Tex. (Bailey)
Mullen, Neb. (Hooker)

Muncie, Ind. (Delaware)
Munfordville, Ky. (Hart)
Munising, Mich. (Alger)
Murdo, S. D. (Jones)
Murfreesboro, Ark. (Pike)
Murfreesboro, Tenn. (Rutherford)
Murphy, Idaho (Owyhee)
Murphy, N. C. (Cherokee)
Murphysboro, Ill. (Jackson)
Murray, Ky. (Calloway)
Muscatine, Iowa (Muscatine)
Muskegon, Mich. (Muskegon)
Muskogee, Okla. (Muskogee)

Nacogdoches, Tex. (Nacogdoches)
Nahunta, Ga. (Brantley)
Nantucket, Mass. (Nantucket)
Napa, Calif. (Napa)
Napoleon, N. D. (Logan)
Napoleon, Ohio (Henry)
Napoleonville, La. (Assumption)
Nashua, N. H. (Hillsborough)
Nashville, Ark. (Howard)
Nashville, Ga. (Berrien)
Nashville, Ill. (Washington)
Nashville, Ind. (Brown)
Nashville, N. C. (Nash)
Nashville, Tenn. (Davidson)
Natchez, Miss. (Adams)
Natchitoches, La. (Natchitoches)
Nebraska City, Neb. (Otoe)
Neillsville, Wis. (Clark)
Neligh, Neb. (Antelope)
Nelson, Neb. (Nuckolls)
Neosho, Mo. (Newton)
Nephi, Utah (Juab)
Ness City, Kan. (Ness)
Nevada, Iowa (Story)
Nevada, Mo. (Vernon)
Nevada City, Calif. (Nevada)
New Albany, Ind. (Floyd)
New Albany, Miss. (Miss)
Newark, N. J. (Essex)
Newark, Ohio (Licking)
New Augusta, Miss. (Perry)
New Bedford, Mass. (Bristol)
New Bern, N. C. (Craven)
Newberry, Mich. (Luce)
Newberry, S. C. (Newberry)
New Bloomfield, Pa. (Perry)
New Braunfels, Tex. (Comal)
New Brunswick, N. J. (Middlesex)
Newburyport, Mass. (Essex)
New Castle, Ind. (Henry)
New Castle, Ky. (Henry)
New Castle, Pa. (Lawrence)
New Castle, Va. (Craig)
Newcastle, Wyo. (Weston)
New City, N. Y. (Rockland)
New Cumberland, W. Va. (Hancock)
Newfane, Vt. (Windham)
New Hampton, Iowa (Chickawaw)
New Haven, Conn. (New Haven)
New Iberia, La. (Iberia)
New Kent, Va. (New Kent)
Newkirk, Okla. (Kay)
Newland, N. C. (Avery)
New Lexington, Ohio (Perry)
New London, Conn. (New London)
New London, Mo. (Ralls)
New Madrid, Mo. (New Madrid)
New Martinsville, W. Va. (Wetzel)
Newnan, Ga. (Coweta)
New Orleans, La. (Orleans)
New Philadelphia, Ohio (Tuscarawas)
Newport, Ark. (Jackson)
Newport, Ind. (Vermillion)
Newport, Ky. (Campbell)
Newport, N. H. (Sullivan)
Newport, R. I. (Newport)
Newport, Tenn. (Cocke)
Newport, Wash. (Pend Oreille)
Newport City, Vt. (Orleans)
New Roads, La. (Pointe Coupee)
New Rockford, N. D. (Eddy)

Newton, Ga. (Baker)
Newton, Ill. (Jasper)
Newton, Iowa (Jasper)
Newton, Kan. (Harvey)
Newton, N. J. (Sussex)
Newton, N. C. (Catawba)
Newton, Tex. (Newton)
New Ulm, Minn. (Brown)
New York City, N. Y. (New York)
Nezperce, Idaho (Lewis)
Nicholasville, Ky. (Jessamine)
Noblesville, Ind. (Hamilton)
Nogales, Ariz. (Santa Cruz)
Norman, Okla. (Cleveland)
Norristown, Pa. (Montgomery)
Northampton, Mass. (Hampshire)
North Hero, Vt. (Grand Isle)
North Platte, Neb. (Lincoln)
Northwood, Iowa (Worth)
Norton, Kan. (Norton)
Norwalk, Ohio (Huron)
Norwich, Conn. (New London)
Norwich, N. Y. (Chenango)
Nottoway, Va. (Nottoway)
Nowata, Okla. (Nowata)

Oak Grove, La. (West Carroll)
Oakland, Calif. (Alameda)
Oakland, Md. (Garrett)
Oberlin, Kan. (Decatur)
Oberlin, La. (Allen)
Ocala, Fla. (Marion)
Ocilla, Ga. (Irwin)
Oconto, Wis. (Oconto)
Odessa, Tex. (Ector)
Ogallala, Neb. (Keith)
Ogden, Utah (Weber)
Oglethorpe, Ga. (Macon)
Okanogan, Wash. (Okanogan)
Okeechobee, Fla. (Okeechobee)
Okemah, Okla. (Okfuskee)
Oklahoma City, Okla. (Oklahoma)
Okmulgee, Okla. (Okmulgee)
Okolona, Miss. (Chickasaw)
Olathe, Kan. (Johnson)
Olivet, S. D. (Hutchinson)
Olivia, Minn. (Renville)
Olney, Ill. (Richland)
Olton, Tex. (Lamb)
Olympia, Wash. (Thurston)
Omaha, Neb. (Douglas)
Onawa, Iowa (Monona)
O'Neill, Neb. (Holt)
Oneonta, Ala. (Blount)
Onida, S. D. (Sully)
Ontonagon, Mich. (Ontonagon)
Opelika, Ala. (Lee)
Opelousas, La. (St. Landry)
Oquawka, Ill. (Henderson)
Orange, Tex. (Orange)
Orange, Va. (Orange)
Orange City, Iowa (Sioux)
Orangeburg, S. C. (Orangeburg)
Ord, Neb. (Valley)
Ordway, Colo. (Crowley)
Oregon, Ill. (Ogle)
Oregon, Mo. (Holt)
Oregon City, Ore. (Clackamas)
Orlando, Fla. (Orange)
Orofino, Idaho (Clearwater)
Oroville, Calif. (Butte)
Ortonville, Minn. (Big Stone)
Osage, Iowa (Mitchell)
Osborne, Kan. (Osborne)
Osceola, Ark. (Mississippi)
Osceola, Iowa (Clarke)
Osceola, Mo. (St. Clair)
Osceola, Neb. (Polk)
Oshkosh, Neb. (Garden)
Oshkosh, Wis. (Winnebago)
Oskaloosa, Iowa (Mahaska)
Oskaloosa, Kan. (Jefferson)
Ossipee, N. H. (Carroll)
Oswego, Kan. (Labette)
Oswego, N. Y. (Oswego)
Ottawa, Ill. (La Salle)
Ottawa, Kan. (Franklin)
Ottawa, Ohio (Putnam)
Ottumwa, Iowa (Wapello)
Ouray, Colo. (Ouray)
Ovid, N. Y. (Seneca)
Owatonna, Minn. (Steele)

Owego, N. Y. (Tioga)
Owensboro, Ky. (Daviess)
Owenton, Ky. (Owen)
Owingsville, Ky. (Bath)
Oxford, Miss. (Lafayette)
Oxford, N. C. (Granville)
Ozark, Ala. (Dale)
Ozark, Ark. (Franklin)
Ozark, Mo. (Christian)
Ozona, Tex. (Crockett)

Paducah, Ky. (Mc Cracken)
Paducah, Tex. (Cottle)
Pagosa Springs, Colo. (Archuleta)
Painesville, Ohio (Lake)
Paint Rock, Tex. (Concho)
Paintsville, Ky. (Johnson)
Palatka, Fla. (Putnam)
Palestine, Tex. (Anderson)
Palmyra, Mo. (Marion)
Palmyra, Va. (Fluvanna)
Palo Pinto, Tex. (Palo Pinto)
Pampa, Tex. (Gray)
Panama City, Fla. (Bay)
Panguitch, Utah (Garfield)
Panhandle, Tex. (Carson)
Paoli, Ind. (Orange)
Paola, Kan. (Miami)
Papillion, Neb. (Sarpy)
Paragould, Ark. (Greene)
Paris, Ark. (Logan)
Paris, Idaho (Bear Lake)
Paris, Ill. (Edgar)
Paris, Ky. (Bourbon)
Paris, Mo. (Monroe)
Paris, Tenn. (Henry)
Paris, Tex. (Lamar)
Park Rapids, Minn. (Hubbard)
Parker, S. D. (Turner)
Parkersburg, W. Va. (Wood)
Parowan, Utah (Iron)
Parsons, W. Va. (Tucker)
Pascagoula, Miss. (Jackson)
Pasco, Wash. (Franklin)
Paterson, N. J. (Passaic)
Paulding, Miss. (Jasper)
Paulding, Ohio (Paulding)
Pauls Valley, Okla. (Garvin)
Paw Paw, Mich. (Van Buren)
Pawhuska, Okla. (Osage)
Pawnee, Okla. (Pawnee)
Pawnee City, Neb. (Pawnee)
Paxton, Ill. (Ford)
Payette, Idaho (Payette)
Pearlsburg, Va. (Giles)
Pearsall, Tex. (Frio)
Pearson, Ga. (Atkinson)
Pecos, Tex. (Reeves)
Pekin, Ill. (Tazewell)
Pell City, Ala. (Saint Clair)
Pembroke, Ga. (Bryan)
Pender, Neb. (Thurston)
Pendleton, Ore. (Umatilla)
Penn Yann, N. Y. (Yates)
Pensacola, Fla. (Escambia)
Peoria, Ill. (Peoria)
Perry, Fla. (Taylor)
Perry, Ga. (Houston)
Perry, Okla. (Noble)
Perryton, Tex. (Ochiltree)
Perryville, Ark. (Perry)
Perryville, Mo. (Perry)
Peru, Ind. (Miami)
Petersburg, Ill. (Menard)
Petersburg, Ind. (Pike)
Petersburg, W. Va. (Grant)
Petoskey, Mich. (Emmet)
Phenix City, Ala. (Russell)
Philadelphia, Miss. (Neshoba)
Philadelphia, Pa. (Philadelphia)
Philip, S. D. (Haakon)
Philipsburg, Mont. (Granite)
Philippi, W. Va. (Barbour)
Phillips, Wis. (Price)
Phillipsburg, Kan. (Phillips)
Phoenix, Ariz. (Maricopa)
Pickens, S. C. (Pickens)
Pierce, Neb. (Pierce)
Pierre, S. D. (Hughes)
Piggott, Ark. (Clay)
Pikeville, Ky. (Pike)
Pikeville, Tenn. (Bledsoe)
Pinckneyville, Ill. (Perry)

Pine Bluff, Ark. (Jefferson)
Pine City, Minn. (Pine)
Pinedale, Wyo. (Sublette)
Pineville, Ky. (Bell)
Pineville, Mo. (Mc Donald)
Pineville, W. Va. (Wyoming)
Pioche, Nev. (Lincoln)
Pipestone, Minn. (Pipestone)
Pittsboro, Miss. (Calhoun)
Pittsboro, N. C. (Chatham)
Pittsburg, Tex. (Camp)
Pittsburgh, Pa. (Allegheny)
Pittsfield, Ill. (Pike)
Pittsfield, Mass. (Berkshire)
Placerville, Calif. (El Dorado)
Plains, Tex. (Yoakum)
Plainview, Tex. (Hale)
Plankinton, S. D. (Aurora)
Plaquemine, La. (Iberville)
Platte City, Mo. (Platte)
Plattsburg, Mo. (Clinton)
Plattsburg, N. Y. (Clinton)
Plattsmouth, Neb. (Cass)
Plentywood, Mont. (Sheridan)
Plymouth, Ind. (Marshall)
Plymouth, Mass. (Plymouth)
Plymouth, N. C. (Washington)
Pocahontas, Ark. (Randolph)
Pocahontas, Iowa (Pocahontas)
Pocatello, Idaho (Bannock)
Point Pleasant, W. Va. (Mason)
Pointe-a-la-Hache, La. (Plaquemines)
Polson, Mont. (Lake)
Pomeroy, Ohio (Meigs)
Pomeroy, Wash. (Garfield)
Ponca, Neb. (Dixon)
Pond Creek, Okla. (Brant)
Pontiac, Ill. (Livingston)
Pontiac, Mich. (Oakland)
Pontotoc, Miss. (Pontotoc)
Poplar Bluff, Mo. (Butler)
Poplarville, Miss. (Pearl River)
Port Allen, La. (West Baton Rouge)
Port Angeles, Wash. (Clallam)
Port Clinton, Ohio (Ottawa)
Port Gibson, Miss. (Claiborne)
Port Huron, Mich. (St. Clair)
Port Lavaca, Tex. (Calhoun)
Port Orchard, Wash. (Kitsap)
Port Townsend, Wash. (Jefferson)
Port Washington, Wis. (Ozaukee)
Portage, Wis. (Columbia)
Portales, N. M. (Roosevelt)
Portland, Ind. (Jay)
Portland, Me. (Cumberland)
Portland, Ore. (Multnomah)
Portsmouth, Ohio (Scioto)
Portsmouth, Va. (Norfolk)
Post, Tex. (Garza)
Poteau, Okla. (Le Flore)
Potosi, Mo. (Washington)
Pottsville, Pa. (Schuylkill)
Poughkeepsie, N. Y. (Dutchess)
Powhatan, Ark. (Lawrence)
Powhatan, Va. (Powhatan)
Prairie du Chien, Wis. (Crawford)
Pratt, Kan. (Pratt)
Prattville, Ala. (Autauga)
Prentiss, Miss. (Jefferson Davis)
Prescott, Ariz. (Yavapai)
Prescott, Ark. (Nevada)
Preston, Ga. (Webster)
Preston, Idaho (Franklin)
Preston, Minn. (Fillmore)
Prestonburg, Ky. (Floyd)
Price, Utah (Carbon)
Primghar, Iowa (O'Brien)
Prince Frederick, Md. (Calvert)
Prince George, Va. (Prince George)
Princess Anne, Md. (Somerset)
Princess Anne, Va. (Princess Anne)
Princeton, Ill. (Bureau)
Princeton, Ind. (Gibson)
Princeton, Ky. (Caldwell)
Princeton, Mo. (Mercer)
Princeton, W. Va. (Mercer)

Prineville, Ore. (Crook)
Prosser, Wash. (Benton)
Providence, R. I. (Providence)
Provo, Utah (Utah)
Pryor, Okla. (Mayes)
Pueblo, Colo. (Pueblo)
Pulaski, Tenn. (Giles)
Pulaski, Va. (Pulaski)
Punta Gorda, Fla. (Charlotte)
Purcell, Okla. (Mc Clain)
Purvis, Miss. (Lamar)
Putnam, Conn. (Windham)

Quanah, Tex. (Hardeman)
Quincy, Calif. (Plumas)
Quincy, Fla. (Gadsden)
Quincy, Ill. (Adams)
Quitman, Ga. (Brooks)
Quitman, Miss. (Clarke)
Quitman, Tex. (Wood)

Racine, Wis. (Racine)
Raeford, N. C. (Hoke)
Raleigh, Miss. (Smith)
Raleigh, N. C. (Wake)
Randolph, Utah (Rich)
Rankin, Tex. (Upton)
Rapid City, S. D. (Pennington)
Raton, N. M. (Colfax)
Ravenna, Ohio (Portage)
Rawlins, Wyo. (Carbon)
Raymond, Miss. (Hinds)
Raymondville, Tex. (Willacy)
Rayville, La. (Richland)
Reading, Pa. (Berks)
Red Bluff, Calif. (Tehama)
Red Cloud, Neb. (Webster)
Red Lake Falls, Minn. (Red Lake)
Red Lodge, Mont. (Carbon)
Red Oak, Iowa (Montgomery)
Red Wing, Minn. (Goodhue)
Redding, Calif. (Shasta)
Redfield, S. D. (Spink)
Redwood City, Calif. (San Mateo)
Redwood Falls, Minn. (Redwood)
Reed City, Mich. (Osceola)
Refugio, Tex. (Refugio)
Reidsville, Ga. (Tattall)
Reno, Nev. (Washoe)
Rensselaer, Ind. (Jasper)
Republic, Wash. (Ferry)
Reserve, N. M. (Catron)
Rexburg, Idaho (Madison)
Rhinelander, Wis. (Oneida)
Richfield, Kan. (Morton)
Richfield, Utah (Sevier)
Richland, Wis. (Richland Center)
Richmond, Ind. (Wayne)
Richmond, Ky. (Madison)
Richmond, Mo. (Ray)
Richmond, Tex. (Fort Bend)
Richmond, Va. (Henrico)
Rico, Colo. (Dolores)
Ridgeland, S. C. (Jasper)
Ridgway, Pa. (Elk)
Rigby, Idaho (Jefferson)
Ringgold, Ga. (Catoosa)
Rio Grande City, Tex. (Starr)
Ripley, Miss. (Tippah)
Ripley, Tenn. (Lauderdale)
Ripley, W. Va. (Jackson)
Rising Sun, Ind. (Ohio)
Rison, Ark. (Cleveland)
Ritzville, Wash. (Adams)
Riverhead, N. Y. (Suffolk)
Riverside, Calif. (Riverside)
Robert Lee, Tex. (Coke)
Robbinsville, N. C. (Graham)
Robinson, Ill. (Crawford)
Roby, Tex. (Fisher)
Rochester, Ind. (Fulton)
Rochester, Minn. (Olmsted)
Rochester, N. Y. (Monroe)
Rock Island, Ill. (Rock Island)
Rock Port, Mo. (Atchison)
Rock Rapids, Iowa (Lyon)
Rockford, Ala. (Coosa)
Rockford, Ill. (Winnebago)
Rockingham, N. C. (Richmond)
Rockland, Me. (Knox)

Rockport, Ind. (Spencer)
Rockport, Tex. (Aransas)
Rocksprings, Tex. (Edwards)
Rockville, Ind. (Parks)
Rockville, Md. (Montgomery)
Rockwall, Tex. (Rockwall)
Rockwell City, Iowa (Calhoun)
Rockymount, Va. (Franklin)
Rogers City, Mich. (Presque Isle)
Rogersville, Tenn. (Hawkins)
Rolla, Mo. (Phelps)
Rolla, N. D. (Rolette)
Rolling Fork, Miss. (Sharkey)
Rome, Ga. (Floyd)
Rome, N. Y. (Oneida)
Romney, W. Va. (Hampshire)
Roscommon, Mich. (Roscommon)
Roseau, Minn. (Roseau)
Roseburg, Ore. (Douglas)
Rosedale, Miss. (Bolivar)
Roswell, N. M. (Chaves)
Roundup, Mont. (Musselshell)
Roxboro, N. C. (Person)
Rugby, N. D. (Pierce)
Rupert, Idaho (Minidoka)
Rushville, Ill. (Schuyler)
Rushville, Ind. (Rush)
Rushville, Neb. (Sheridan)
Rusk, Tex. (Cherokee)
Russell, Kan. (Russell)
Russell Springs, Kan. (Logan)
Russellville, Ala. (Franklin)
Russellville, Ark. (Pope)
Russelville, Ky. (Logan)
Rustberg, Va. (Campbell)
Ruston, La. (Lincoln)
Rutherfordton, N. C. (Rutherford)
Rutland City, Vt. (Rutland)
Rutledge, Tenn. (Grainger)
Ryan, Okla. (Jefferson)
Ryegate, Mont. (Golden Valley)

Sac City, Iowa (Sac)
Sacramento, Calif. (Sacramento)
Safford, Ariz. (Graham)
Saginaw, Mich. (Saginaw)
Saguache, Colo. (Saguache)
St. Albans, Vt. (Franklin)
St. Anthony, Idaho (Fremont)
St. Augustine, Fla. (St. Johns)
St. Charles, Mo. (St. Charles)
St. Clairsville, Ohio (Belmont)
St. Cloud, Minn. (Stearns)
St. Francis, Kan. (Cheyenne)
St. Francisville, La. (West Feliciana)
St. George, S. C. (Dorchester)
St. George, Utah (Washington)
St. Helens, Ore. (Columbia)
St. Ignace, Mich. (Mackinac)
St. James, Minn. (Watonwan)
St. John, Kan. (Stafford)
St. Johns, Ariz. (Apache)
St. Johns, Mich. (Clinton)
St. Johnsbury, Vt. (Caledonia)
St. Joseph, La. (Tensas)
St. Joseph, Mich. (Berrien)
St. Joseph, Mo. (Buchanan)
St. Maries, Idaho (Benewah)
St. Martinsville, La. (St. Martin)
St. Marys, W. Va. (Pleasants)
St. Matthews, S. C. (Calhoun)
St. Paul, Minn. (Ramsey)
St. Paul, Neb. (Howard)
St. Peter, Minn. (Nicollet)
Salem, Ark. (Fulton)
Salem, Ill. (Marion)
Salem, Ind. (Washington)
Salem, Mass. (Essex)
Salem, Mo. (Dent)
Salem, N. J. (Salem)
Salem, Ore. (Marion)
Salem, S. D. (Mc Cook)
Salem, Va. (Roanoke)
Salida, Colo. (Chaffee)
Salina, Kan. (Saline)
Salinas, Calif. (Monterey)
Salisbury, Md. (Wicomico)
Salisbury, N. C. (Rowan)
Sallisaw, Okla. (Sequoyah)

Salmon, Idaho (Lemhi)
Salt Lake City, Utah (Salt Lake)
Saluda, S. C. (Saluda)
Saluda, Va. (Middlesex)
Salyersville, Ky. (Magoffin)
San Andreas, Calif. (Calaveras)
San Angelo, Tex. (Tom Green)
San Antonio, Tex. (Bexar)
San Augustine, Tex. (San Augustine)
San Bernardino, Calif. (San Bernardino)
San Diego, Calif. (San Diego)
San Diego, Tex. (Duval)
San Francisco, Calif. (San Francisco)
San Jose, Calif. (Santa Clara)
San Luis, Colo. (Costilla)
San Luis Obispo, Calif. (San Luis Obispo)
San Marcos, Tex. (Hays)
San Rafael, Calif. (Marin)
San Saba, Tex. (San Saba)
Sanderson, Tex. (Terrell)
Sandersville, Ga. (Washington)
Sandpoint, Idaho (Bonner)
Sandusky, Mich. (Sanilac)
Sandusky, Ohio (Erie)
Sandy Hook, Ky. (Elliott)
Sanford, Fla. (Seminole)
Sanford, N. C. (Lee)
Santa Ana, Calif. (Orange)
Santa Barbara, Calif. (Santa Barbara)
Santa Cruz, Calif. (Santa Cruz)
Santa Fe, N. M. (Santa Fe)
Santa Rosa, Calif. (Sonoma)
Santa Rosa, N. M. (Guadalupe)
Sapulpa, Okla. (Creek)
Sarasota, Fla. (Sarasota)
Sardis, Miss. (Panola)
Sarita, Tex. (Kenedy)
Sault Ste Marie, Mich. (Chippewa)
Savannah, Ga. (Chatham)
Savannah, Mo. (Andrew)
Savannah, Tenn. (Hardin)
Sayre, Okla. (Beckham)
Schenectady, N. Y. (Schenectady)
Schoharie, N. Y. (Schoharie)
Schuyler, Neb. (Colfax)
Scobey, Mont. (Daniels)
Scott City, Kan. (Scott)
Scottsboro, Ala. (Jackson)
Scottsburg, Ind. (Scott)
Scottsville, Ky. (Allen)
Scranton, Pa. (Lackawanna)
Searcy, Ark. (White)
Seattle, Wash. (King)
Sebring, Fla. (Highlands)
Sedalia, Mo. (Pettis)
Sedan, Kan. (Chautauqua)
Seguin, Tex. (Guadalupe)
Selby, S. D. (Walworth)
Selma, Ala. (Dallas)
Selmer, Tenn. (Mc Nairy)
Seminole, Tex. (Gaines)
Senatobia, Miss. (Tate)
Seneca, Kan. (Nemaha)
Sevierville, Tenn. (Sevier)
Seward, Neb. (Seward)
Seymour, Tex. (Baylor)
Shakopee, Minn. (Scott)
Sharon Springs, Kan. (Wallace)
Shawano, Wis. (Shawano)
Shawnee, Okla. (Pottawattamie)
Shawneetown, Ill. (Gallatin)
Sheboygan, Wis. (Sheboygan)
Shelby, Mont. (Toole)
Shelby, N. C. (Cleveland)
Shelbyville, Ill. (Shelby)
Shelbyville, Ind. (Shelby)
Shelbyville, Ky. (Shelby)
Shelbyville, Mo. (Shelby)
Shelbyville, Tenn. (Bedford)
Shell Lake, Wis. (Washburn)
Shelton, Wash. (Mason)
Shepherdsville, Ky. (Bullitt)
Sheridan, Ark. (Grant)
Sheridan, Wyo. (Sheridan)
Sherman, Tex. (Grayson)
Shoals, Ind. (Martin)
Shoshone, Idaho (Lincoln)

Shreveport, La. (Caddo)
Sibley, Iowa (Osceola)
Sidney, Iowa (Fremont)
Sidney, Mont. (Richland)
Sidney, Neb. (Cheyenne)
Sidney, Ohio (Shelby)
Sierra Blanca, Tex. (Hudspeth)
Sigourney, Iowa (Keokuk)
Silver City, N. M. (Grant)
Silverton, Colo. (San Juan)
Silverton, Tex. (Briscoe)
Sinton, Tex. (San Patricio)
Sioux City, Iowa (Woodbury)
Sioux Falls, S. D. (Minnehaha)
Sisseton, S. D. (Roberts)
Skowhegan, Me. (Somerset)
Slayton, Minn. (Murray)
Smethport, Pa. (Mc Kean)
Smith Center, Kan. (Smith)
Smithfield, N. C. (Johnston)
Smithland, Ky. (Livingston)
Smithville, Tenn. (De Kalb)
Sneedville, Tenn. (Hancock)
Snow Hill, Md. (Worcester)
Snow Hill, N. C. (Greene)
Snyder, Tex. (Scurry)
Socorro, N. M. (Socorro)
Soda Springs, Idaho (Caribou)
Somerset, Ky. (Pulaski)
Somerset, Pa. (Somerset)
Somerville, N. J. (Somerset)
Somerville, Tenn. (Fayette)
Sonora, Calif. (Tuolumne)
Sonora, Tex. (Sutton)
Soperton, Ga. (Treutlen)
South Bend, Ind. (St. Joseph)
South Bend, Wash. (Pacific)
South Paris, Me. (Oxford)
Southport, N. C. (Brunswick)
Sparta, Ga. (Hancock)
Sparta, N. C. (Alleghany)
Sparta, Tenn. (White)
Sparta, Wis. (Monroe)
Spartanburg, S. C. (Spartanburg)
Spearman, Tex. (Hansford)
Spencer, Ind. (Owen)
Spencer, Iowa (Clay)
Spencer, Tenn. (Van Buren)
Spencer, W. Va. (Roane)
Spirit Lake, Iowa (Dickinson)
Spokane, Wash. (Spokane)
Spotsylvania, Va. (Spotsylvania)
Springfield, Colo. (Baca)
Springfield, Ga. (Effingham)
Springfield, Ill. (Sangamon)
Springfield, Ky. (Washington)
Springfield, Mass. (Hampden)
Springfield, Mo. (Greene)
Springfield, Ohio (Clark)
Springfield, Tenn. (Robertson)
Springview, Neb. (Keya Paha)
Stafford, Va. (Stafford)
Standardsville, Va. (Greene)
Standish, Mich. (Arenac)
Stanford, Ky. (Lincoln)
Stanford, Mont. (Judith Basin)
Stanley, N. D. (Mountrail)
Stanton, Ky. (Powell)
Stanton, Mich. (Montcalm)
Stanton, Neb. (Stanton)
Stanton, N. D. (Mercer)
Stanton, Tex. (Martin)
Stapleton, Neb. (Logan)
Star City, Ark. (Lincoln)
Starke, Fla. (Bradford)
Starkville, Miss. (Oktibbeha)
Staten Island, N. Y. (Richmond)
Statenville, Ga. (Echols)
Statesboro, Ga. (Bulloch)
Statesville, N. C. (Iredell)
Staunton, Va. (Augusta)
Steamboat Springs, Colo. (Routt)
Steele, N. D. (Kidder)
Steelville, Mo. (Crawford)
Stephenville, Tex. (Erath)
Sterling, Colo. (Logan)
Sterling City, Tex. (Sterling)
Steubenville, Ohio (Jefferson)
Stevens Point, Wis. (Portage)
Stevenson, Wash. (Skamania)

Stigler, Okla, (Haskell)
Stillwater, Minn. (Washington)
Stillwater, Okla. (Payne)
Stilwell, Okla. (Adair)
Stinnett, Tex. (Hutchinson)
Stockton, Calif. (San Joaquin)
Stockton, Kan. (Rooks)
Stockton, Mo. (Cedar)
Stockville, Neb. (Frontier)
Storm Lake, Iowa (Buena Vista)
Stratford, Tex. (Sherman)
Stroudsburg, Pa. (Monroe)
Stuart, Fla. (Martin)
Stuart, Va. (Patrick)
Sturgeon Bay, Wis. (Door)
Sturgis, S. D. (Meade)
Sublette, Kan. (Haskell)
Suffolk, Va. (Nansemond)
Sullivan, Ill. (Moultrie)
Sullivan, Ind. (Sullivan)
Sulphur, Okla. (Murray)
Sulphur Springs, Tex. (Hopkins)
Summerville, Ga. (Chattooga)
Summersville, W. Va. (Nicholas)
Sumner, Miss. (Tallahatchie)
Sumter, S. C. (Sumter)
Sunbury, Pa. (Northumberland)
Sundance, Wyo. (Crook)
Superior, Mont. (Mineral)
Superior, Wis. (Douglas)
Surry, Va. (Surry)
Susanville, Calif. (Lassen)
Sussex, Va. (Sussex)
Sutton, W. Va. (Braxton)
Swainsboro, Ga. (Emanuel)
Swan Quarter, N. C. (Hyde)
Sweetwater, Tex. (Nolan)
Sycamore, Ill. (De Kalb)
Sylva, N. C. (Jackson)
Sylvania, Ga. (Screven)
Sylvester, Ga. (Worth)
Syracuse, Kan. (Hamilton)
Syracuse, N. Y. (Onondaga)
Tacoma, Wash. (Pierce)
Tahlequah, Okla. (Cherokee)
Tahoka, Tex. (Lynn)
Talbotton, Ga. (Talbot)
Talladega, Ala. (Talladega)
Tallahassee, Fla. (Leon)
Tallulah, Fla. (Madison)
Taloga, Okla. (Dewey)
Tampa, Fla. (Hillsborough)
Taos, N. M. (Taos)
Tappahannock, Va. (Essex)
Tarboro, N. C. (Edgecombe)
Tavares, Fla. (Lake)
Tawas City, Mich.
Taylor, Neb. (Loup)
Taylorville, Ill. (Christian)
Taylorsville, Ky. (Spencer)
Taylorsville, N. C. (Alexander)
Tazewell, Tenn. (Claiborne)
Tazewell, Va. (Tazewell)
Tecumseh, Neb. (Johnson)
Tekamah, Neb. (Burt)
Telluride, Colo. (San Miguel)
Terre Haute, Ind. (Vigo)
Terry, Mont. (Prairie)
Texarkana, Ark. (Miller)
Thedford, Neb. (Thomas)
Thermopolis, Wyo. (Hot Springs)
Thibodaux, La. (Lafourche)
Thief River Falls, Minn. (Pennington)
Thomaston, Ga. (Upson)
Thomasville, Ga. (Thomas)
Thompson Falls, Mont. (Sanders)
Thomson, Ga. (Mc Duffie)
Throckmorton, Tex. (Throckmorton)
Tierra Amarilla, N. M. (Rio Arriba)
Tiffin, Ohio (Seneca)
Tifton, Ga. (Tift)
Tilden, Tex. (Mc Mullen)
Tillamook, Ore. (Tillamook)
Timber Lake, S. D. (Dewey)
Tionesta, Pa. (Forest)
Tipton, Ind. (Tipton)

Tipton, Iowa (Cedar)
Tiptonville, Tenn. (Lake)
Tishomingo, Okla. (Johnston)
Titusville, Fla. (Brevard)
Toccoa, Ga. (Stephens)
Toledo, Ill. (Cumberland)
Toledo, Iowa (Tama)
Toledo, Ohio (Lucas)
Toledo, Ore. (Lincoln)
Tolland, Conn. (Tolland)
Tompkinsville, Ky. (Monroe)
Toms River, N. J. (Ocean)
Tonopah, Nev. (Nye)
Tooele, Utah (Tooele)
Topeka, Kan. (Shawnee)
Torrington, Wyo. (Goshen)
Toulon, Ill. (Stark)
Towanda, Pa. (Bradford)
Towner, N. D. (McHenry)
Townsend, Mont. (Broadwater)
Towson, Md. (Baltimore)
Traverse City, Mich. (Grand Traverse)
Trenton, Fla. (Gilchrist)
Trenton, Ga. (Dade)
Trenton, Mo. (Grunda)
Trenton, Neb. (Hitchcock)
Trenton, N. J. (Mercer)
Trenton, N. C. (Jones)
Trenton, Tenn. (Gibson)
Tribune, Kan. (Greeley)
Trinidad, Colo. (Las Animos)
Troy, Ala. (Pike)
Troy, Kan. (Doniphan)
Troy, Mo. (Lincoln)
Troy, N. Y. (Rensselaer)
Troy, N. C. (Montgomery)
Troy, Ohio (Miami)
Truth or Consequences, N. M. (Sierra)
Tryon, Neb. (Mc Pherson)
Tucson, Ariz. (Pima)
Tucumcari, N. M. (Quay)
Tulia, Tex. (Swisher)
Tulsa, Okla. (Tulsa)
Tunica, Miss. (Tunica)
Tunkhannock, Pa. (Wyoming)
Tupelo, Miss. (Lee)
Tuscaloosa, Ala. (Tuscaloosa)
Tuscola, Ill. (Douglas)
Tuscumbia, Ala. (Colbert)
Tuscumbia, Mo. (Miller)
Tuskegee, Ala. (Macon)
Twin Falls, Idaho (Twin Falls)
Two Harbors, Minn. (Lake)
Tyler, Tex. (Smith)
Tylertown, Miss. (Walthall)
Tyndall, S. D. (Bon Homme)

Ukiah, Calif. (Mendocino)
Ulysses, Kan. (Grant)
Union, Mo. (Franklin)
Union, S. C. (Union)
Union, W. Va. (Monroe)
Union City, Tenn. (Obion)
Union Springs, Ala. (Bullock)
Uniontown, Pa. (Fayette)
Unionville, Mo. (Putnam)
Upper Marlboro, Md. (Prince George's)
Upper Sandusky, Ohio (Wyandot)
Urbana, Ill. (Champaign)
Urbana, Ohio (Champaign)
Utica, N. Y. (Oneida)
Uvalde, Tex. (Uvalde)

Vaiden, Miss. (Carroll)
Valdosta, Ga. (Lowndes)
Vale, Ore. (Malheur)
Valentine, Neb. (Cherry)
Valley City, N. D. (Barnes)
Valparaiso, Ind. (Porter)
Van Buren, Ark. (Crawford)
Van Buren, Mo. (Carter)
Van Buren, Tenn. (Culbertson)
Van Wert, Ohio (Van Wert)
Vanceburg, Ky. (Lewis)
Vancouver, Wash. (Clark)
Vandalia, Ill. (Fayette)
Vega, Tex. (Oldham)
Ventura, Calif. (Ventura)
Vermillion, S. D. (Clay)

Vernal, Utah (Uintah)
Vernon, Ala. (Lamar)
Vernon, Ind. (Jennings)
Vernon, Tex. (Wilbarger)
Vero Beach, Fla. (Indian River)
Versailles, Ind. (Ripley)
Versailles, Ky. (Woodford)
Versailles, Mo. (Morgan)
Vevay, Ind. (Switzerland)
Vicksburg, Miss. (Warren)
Victoria, Tex. (Victoria)
Vidalia, La. (Concordia)
Vienna, Ga. (Dooly)
Vienna, Ill. (Johnson)
Vienna, Mo. (Maries)
Ville Platte, La. (Evangeline)
Vincennes, Ind. (Knox)
Vinita, Okla. (Craig)
Vinton, Iowa (Benton)
Virginia, Ill. (Cass)
Virginia City, Mont. (Madison)
Virginia City, Nev. (Storey)
Viroqua, Wis. (Vernon)
Visalia, Calif. (Tulare)

Wabash, Ind. (Wabash)
Wabasha, Minn. (Wabasha)
Waco, Tex. (Mc Lennan)
Wadena, Minn. (Wadena)
Wadesboro, N. C. (Anson)
Wagoner, Okla. (Wagoner)
Wahoo, Neb. (Saunders)
Wahpeton, N. D. (Richland)
Wakeeney, Kan. (Trego)
Walden, Colo. (Jackson)
Waldron, Ark. (Scott)
Walhalla, S. C. (Oconee)
Walker, Minn. (Cass)
Walla Walla, Wash. (Walla Walla)
Wallace, Idaho (Shoshone)
Walnut Ridge, Ark. (Lawrence)
Walsenburg, Colo. (Huerfano)
Walterboro, S. C. (Colleton)
Walters, Okla. (Cotton)
Walthall, Miss. (Webster)
Wampsville, N. Y. (Madison)
Wapakoneta, Ohio (Auglaize)
Wapello, Iowa (Louisa)
Warm Springs, Va. (Bath)
Warren, Ark. (Bradley)
Warren, Minn. (Marshall)
Warren, Ohio (Trumbull)
Warren, Pa. (Warren)
Warrensburg, Mo. (Johnson)
Warrenton, Ga. (Warren)
Warrenton, Mo. (Warren)
Warrenton, N. C. (Warren)
Warrenton, Va. (Faquier)
Warsaw, Ind. (Kosciusko)
Warsaw, Ky. (Gallatin)
Warsaw, Mo. (Benton)
Warsaw, N. Y. (Wyoming)
Warsaw, Va. (Richmond)
Wartburg, Tenn. (Morgan)
Waseca, Minn. (Waseca)
Washburn, N. D. (Mc Lean)
Washburn, Wis. (Bayfield)
Washington, Ga. (Wilkes)
Washington, Ind. (Daviess)
Washington, Iowa (Washington)
Washington, Kan. (Washington)
Washington, N. C. (Beaufort)
Washington, Pa. (Washington)
Washington, Va. (Rappahannock)
Washington Court House, Ohio (Fayette)
Water Valley, Miss. (Yalobusha)
Waterloo, Ill. (Monroe)
Waterloo, Iowa (Black Hawk)
Waterloo, N. Y. (Seneca)
Watertown, N. Y. (Jefferson)
Watertown, S. D. (Codington)
Waterville, Wash. (Douglas)
Watford City, N. D. (Mc Kenzie)
Watkins Glen, N. Y. (Schuyler)
Watkinsville, Ga. (Oconee)
Watonga, Okla. (Blaine)
Watseka, Ill. (Iroquois)
Wauchula, Fla. (Hardee)

Waukegan, Ill. (Lake)
Waukesha, Wis. (Waukesha)
Waukon, Iowa (Allamakee)
Waupaca, Wis. (Waupaca)
Waurika, Okla. (Jefferson)
Wausau, Wis. (Marathon)
Wauseon, Ohio (Fulton)
Wautoma, Wis. (Waushara)
Waverly, Iowa (Bremer)
Waverly, Ohio (Pike)
Waverly, Tenn. (Humphreys)
Waxahachie, Tex. (Ellis)
Waycross, Ga. (Warr)
Wayne, Neb. (Wayne)
Wayne, W. Va. (Wayne)
Waynesboro, Ga. (Burke)
Waynesboro, Miss. (Wayne)
Waynesboro, Tenn. (Wayne)
Waynesburg, Pa. (Greene)
Waynesville, Mo. (Pulaski)
Waynesville, N. C. (Haywood)
Weatherford, Tex. (Parker)
Weaverville, Calif. (Trinity)
Webster, S. D. (Day)
Webster City, Iowa (Hamilton)
Webster Springs, W. Va. (Webster)
Wedowee, Ala. (Randolph)
Weiser, Idaho (Washington)
Welch, W. Va. (Mc Dowell)
Wellington, Kan. (Sumner)
Wellington, Tex. (Collingsworth)
Wellsboro, Pa. (Tioga)
Wellsburg, W. Va. (Brooke)
Wenatchee, Wash. (Chelan)
Wentworth, N. C. (Rockingham)
Wessington Springs, S. D. (Jerauld)
West Bend, Wis. (Washington)
West Branch, Mich. (Ogemaw)
West Chester, Pa. (Chester)
West Kingston, R. I. (Washinton)
West Liberty, Ky. (Morgan)
West Palm Beach, Fla. (Palm Beach)
West Plains, Mo. (Howell)
West Point, Miss. (Clay)
West Union, Iowa (Fayette)
West Union, Ohio (Adams)
West Union, W. Va. (Doddridge)
Westcliffe, Colo. (Custer)
Westminster, Md. (Carroll)
Westmoreland, Kan. (Pottawatomie)
Weston, W. Va. (Lewis)
Westpoint, Neb. (Cuming)
Wetumpka, Ala. (Elmore)
Wewahitchka, Fla. (Gulf)
Wewoka, Okla. (Seminole)
Wharton, Tex. (Wharton)
Wheatland, Wyo. (Platte)
Wheaton, Ill. (Du Page)
Wheaton, Minn. (Traverse)
Wheeler, Tex. (Wheeler)
Wheeling, W. Va. (Ohio)
White Cloud, Mich. (Newaygo)
White Plains, N. Y. (Westchester)
White River, S. D. (Mellette)
White Sulphur Springs, Mont. (Meagher)
Whitehall, Wis. (Trempealeau)
Whitesburg, Ky. (Letcher)
Whiteville, N. C. (Columbus)
Whitley City, Ky. (Mc Creary)
Wibaux, Mont. (Wibaux)
Wichita, Kan. (Sedgwick)
Wichita Falls, Tex. (Wichita)
Wickliffe, Ky. (Ballard)
Wiggins, Miss. (Stone)
Wilber, Neb. (Saline)
Wilburton, Okla. (Latimer)
Wilkes-Barre, Pa. (Luzerne)
Wilkesboro, N. C. (Wilkes)
Williamsburg, Ky. (Whitley)
Williamsburg, Va. (James City)
Williamson, W. Va. (Mingo)
Williamsport, Ind. (Warren)
Williamsport, Pa. (Lycoming)
Williamston, N. C. (Martin)
Williamstown, Ky. (Grant)

Willimantic, Conn. (Windham)
Williston, N. D. (Williams)
Willmar, Minn. (Kandiyohi)
Willows, Calif. (Glenn)
Wilmington, Del. (New Castle)
Wilmington, N. C. (New Hanover)
Wilmington, Ohio (Clinton)
Wilson, N. C. (Wilson)
Winamac, Ind. (Pulaski)
Winchester, Ill. (Scott)
Winchester, Ind. (Randolph)
Winchester, Ky. (Clark)
Winchester, Tenn. (Franklin)
Winchester, Va. (Frederick)
Winder, Ga. (Barrow)
Windom, Minn. (Cottonwood)
Windsor, N. C. (Bertie)
Winfield, Kan. (Cowley)
Winfield, La. (Winn)
Winfield, W. Va. (Putnam)
Winnemucca, Nev. (Humboldt)
Winner, S. D. (Tripp)
Winnett, Mont. (Petroleum)
Winnsboro, La. (Franklin)
Winnsboro, S. C. (Fairfield)
Winona, Minn. (Winona)
Winona, Miss. (Montgomery)
Winston-Salem, N. C. (Forsyth)
Winterset, Iowa (Madison)
Winton, N. C. (Hertford)
Wiscasset, Me. (Lincoln)
Wisconsin Rapids, Wis. (Wood)
Wise, Va. (Wise)
Wolf Point, Mont. (Roosevelt)
Woodbine, Ga. (Camden)
Woodbury, N. J. (Gloucester)
Woodbury, Tenn. (Cannon)
Woodland, Calif. (Yolo)
Woodsfield, Ohio (Monroe)
Woodstock, Ill. (Mc Henry)
Woodstock, Vt. (Windsor)
Woodstock, Va. (Shenandoah)
Woodsville, N. H. (Grafton)
Woodville, Miss. (Wilkinson)
Woodville, Tex. (Tyler)
Woodward, Okla. (Woodward)
Woonsocket, S. D. (Sanborn)
Wooster, Ohio (Wayne)
Worcester, Mass. (Worcester)
Worland, Wyo. (Washakie)
Worthington, Minn. (Nobles)
Wray, Colo. (Yuma)
Wrightsville, Ga. (Johnson)
Wynne, Ark. (Cross)
Wytheville, Va. (Wythe)

Xenia, Ohio (Greene)

Yadkinville, N. C. (Yadkin)
Yakima, Wash. (Yakima)
Yanceyville, N. C. (Caswell)
Yankton, S. D. (Yankton)
Yates Center, Kan. (Woodson)
Yazoo City, Miss. (Yazoo)
Yellville, Ark. (Marion)
Yerington, Nev. (Lyon)
York, Neb. (York)
York, Pa. (York)
York, S. C. (York)
Yorktown, Va. (York)
Yorkville, Ill. (Kendall)
Youngstown, Ohio (Mahoning)
Yreka, Calif. (Siskiyou)
Yuba City, Calif. (Sutter)
Yuma, Ariz. (Yuma)

Zanesville, Ohio (Muskingum)
Zapata, Tex. (Zapata)
Zebulon, Ga. (Pike)

PART VII

PERSONS FOR WHOM COUNTIES HAVE BEEN NAMED

The following list shows the persons for whom 2,137 counties have been named. Many counties have been named for the same person. The name of the county is the same as the person's family name except in the cases where the deviation is shown in parenthesis.

Adair, John
Adams, Alva
Adams, John
Adams, John Quincy
Adams, John Quincy (Pres.)
Addison, Joseph
Aiken, William
Aitken, William Alexander
Albany, Duke of
Albemarle, Earl of
Alcorn, James Lusk
Alexander, William Julius
Alexander, William M.
Alger, Russell Alexander
Allen, Ethan
Allen, Henry Watkins
Allen, John
Allen, Paul H.
Allen, William
Amador, Jose Maria
Amelia
Amherst, Jeffrey
Ana (Dona Ana)
Anderson, Joseph
Anderson, Joseph C.
Anderson, Kenneth Lewis
Anderson, Richard Clough
Anderson, Robert
Andrews, Richard
Anne (Princess Anne)
Anne (Queen Anne)
Anson, George
Appanoose
Appling, Daniel
Aranzazu
Archer, Dr. Branch Tanner
Archuleta, Antonio D.
Armstrong, John
Arthur, Chester Alan
Arundel, Anne (Anne Arundel)
Ashe, Samuel
Ashley, Chester
Atchison, David Rice
Atkinson, William Yates
Atoka
Attala
Audrain, James H.
Audubon, John James
Augusta
Augustus, William (Cumberland)
Aurora
Austin, Stephen Fuller
Avery, Waitstill

Baca, Ezequiel Cabeza de
Bacon, Augustus Octavius
Bailey, Peter James

Baker, Edward Dickinson
Baker, James McNair
Baker, John
Baldwin, Abraham
Ballard, Bland W.
Baltimore, Lord
Baltimore, Cecil (Cecil)
Banks, Richard
Baraga, Frederic
Barber, Thomas W.
Barbour, James
Barbour, Philip Pendleton
Barnes, A. H.
Barron, Henry D.
Barrow, David Crenshaw
Barry, William Taylor
Bartholomew, Joseph
Barton, Clara
Barton, David
Bartow, Francis
Bastrop, Baron de
Bates, Frederick
Baxter, Elisha
Bayfield, Henry W.
Baylor, Henry Weidner
Beadle, William Henry Harrison
Beaufort, Duke of
Beauregard, Pierre Gustave Toutant
Becker, George Loomis
Beckham, John Crepps Wickliffe
Bedford, Duke of
Bedford, Thomas
Bee, Barnard E.
Belknap, Jeremy
Bell, Joshua Fry
Bell, Peter Hansborough
Beltrami, Giacomo Constantino
Benewah
Bennett, Granville G.
Bennett, John E.
Benson, B. W.
Bent, William
Benton, Samuel
Benton, Thomas Hart
Berkeley, John
Berkeley, Norborne
Berkeley, Norborne (Botetourt)
Berkeley, William
Berrien, John MacPherson
Bertie, Henry
Bertie, James
Bexar, Duke of
Bienville, Sieur de
Bibb, William Wyatt
Billings, Frederick
Bingham, Henry Harrison
Blackford, Isaac Newton
Black Hawk
Bladen, Martin
Blaine, James Gillespie
Blair, John
Bland, Richard
Bleckley, Logan Edwin
Bledsoe, Abraham
Bledsoe, Anthony
Blount, William
Bolivar, Simon
Bollinger, George F.
Bond, Shadrach
Bonner, Edwin L.
Bonneville, Benjamin Louis Eulalie de
Boone, Daniel
Boone, Nathan
Borden, Gail
Bossier, John Baptiste
Bossier, Pierre Evariste John Baptiste
Botetourt, Lord
Bottineau, Pierre
Bowie, James
Bowman, E. M.
Boyd, James E.
Boyd, Linn
Boyle, John
Bracken, William
Bradford, Richard
Bradford, William
Bradley, Edward
Bradley, William L.
Branch, John
Brantley, Benjamin D.
Braxton, Carter
Breathitt, John
Breckinridge, John

Castillo, Bernal de (Bernalillo)
Castro, Henry
Caswell, Richard
Catherine of Braganza
Catherine (Queens)
Catron, Thomas Benton
Cavalier, Charles
Chaffee, Jerome Bunty
Chambers, Henry
Chambers, Thomas Jefferson
Charles I, King
Charles II, King
Charles II, King (Kings Co.)
Charlevoix, Pierre Francois Xavier de
Charlotte
Charlton, Robert Milledge
Chase, Champion S.
Chase, Salmon Portland
Chatham, Earl of
Chaves, Mariano
Cheatham, Benjamin F.
Cheatham, Edwin S.
Cheatham, Nathaniel
Cherry, Samuel A.
Chester, Robert I.
Chesterfield, Earl of
Chevalier, Marinette (Marinette)
Childress, George Campbell
Chilton, William Parish
Chittenden, Thomas
Chorette, Joseph (Charitan)
Chouteau, Charles P.
Christian, William
Churchill, Charles C.
Churchill, John (Marlboro)
Claiborne, William Charles Coles
Clarendon, Earl of
Clark, Charles F.
Clark, George Rogers
Clark, Newton
Clark, Sam
Clark, William
Clark, William Andrews
Clark, William (Lewis and Clark)
Clarke, Charles F. (Clark)
Clarke, Elijah
Clarke, James
Clarke, Joshua G.
Clarke, John
Clay, Green
Clay, Henry
Clay, Henry Jr.
Clayton, Augustin Smith
Clayton, John Middleton
Clayton, John Middleton (Clay)
Cleburne, Patrick Ronayne
Cleveland, Benjamin
Cleveland, Grover
Clinch, Duncan Lamont
Clinton De Witt (De Witt)
Clinton, De Witt
Clinton, George
Cloud, William F.
Cobb, Thomas Willis
Cochise
Cochran, Robert
Cocke, William
Codington, G. S. S.
Coffee, John
Coffey, A.
Coke, Richard
Colbert, George
Cole, Stephen
Coleman, Robert M.
Coles, Edward
Colfax, Schuyler
Colleton, John
Collier, Barron Gift
Collingsworth, James T.
Colquitt, Walter Terry
Columbus, Christopher
Converse, A. H.
Conway, Francis Seymour (Hertford)
Conway, Henry
Cook, Daniel Pope
Cook, John
Cook, Michael
Cook, Philip
Cooke, William G. (Cooke)
Cooper, Sarshel
Corson, Dighton

Coryell, James
Cottle, George Washington
Covington, Leonard Wales
Coweta
Cowley, Matthew
Craig, Granville
Craig, Robert
Craighead, Thomas B.
Crane, William Cary
Craven, William
Crawford, Samuel J.
Crawford, William
Crawford, William Harris
Crenshaw, Anderson
Crisp, Charles Frederick
Crittenden, John Jordan
Crittenden, Robert
Crockett, David
Crook, George
Crosby, Stephen
Cross, Edward
Crowley, John H.
Culberson, David Browning
Cullman, John G.
Culpeper, Thomas
Cumberland, Duke of
Cuming, Thomas B.
Curry, George
Curry, George Law
Custer, George Armstrong

Dade, Francis Langhorne
Daggett, Ellsworth
Dale, Sam
Dallam, James Wilmer
Dallas, Alexander James
Dallas, George Mifflin
Dane, Nathan
Daniels, Mansfield A.
Dare, Virginia
Darke, William
Darlington
Davidson, William Lee
Davie, William Richardson
Daviess, Joseph Hamilton
Daviess, Joseph Hamilton (Jo Daviess)
Davis, Andrew J. (Andrew)
Davis, Daniel C.
Davis, Garrett
Davis, Jefferson (Jeff Davis)
Davis, Jefferson (Jefferson Davis)
Davison, Henry C.
Dawes, James William
Dawson, Andrew
Dawson, Jacob
Dawson, Nicholas
Dawson, William Crosby
Day, Merritt H.
Dearborn, Henry
De Baca, Ezequiel Cabeza
Decatur, Stephen
De Kalb, Johann
Delawarr, Baron (Delaware)
De Leon, Martin
De Leon, Ponce
Dent, Lewis
Denton, John B.
Denver, James William
De Puy, Elvira Merrick (Merrick)
Desha, Benjamin
De Soto, Hernando
De Soto, Hernando (Hernando)
Deuel, Jacob S.
Deuell, Henry Porter
Dewey, George
Dewey, William Pitt
De Witt, Clinton
De Witt, Green
Dickens, J.
Dickenson, William J.
Dickey, Alfred
Dickinson, Daniel Stevens
Dickinson, Donald McDonald
Dickson, William
Dillon, J. W.
Dimmit, Philip
Dinwiddie, Robert
Dixon
Doddridge, Philip
Dodge, Augustus Caesar
Dodge, Henry
Dodge, Henry (Henry)

Dodge, William Earle
Doniphan, Alexander William
Donley, Stockton P.
Dooly, John
Dorset, Earl
Dougherty, Charles
Douglas, Stephen Arnold
Drew, Thomas Stevenson
Du Bois, Toussaint
Dubuque, Julien
Duchesne
Dundy, Elmer S.
Dunk, George Montagu(Halifax)
Dunklin, Daniel
Dunn, Charles
Dunn, John P.
Du Page
Durham, Dr. Bartholomew
Duval, Burr H.
Duval, William Pope
Dyer, Robert Henry

Early, Peter
Eastland, William Mosby
Eaton, John Henry
Echols, Robert M.
Ector, Matthew Duncan
Eddy, Charles B.
Eddy, E. B.
Edgar, John
Edgecombe, Richard
Edmonson, John
Edmunds, Newton
Edward (Prince Edward)
Edwards, Hayden
Edwards, Ninian
Edwards, W. C.
Effingham, Edward
Elbert, Samuel
Elbert, Samuel Hitt
Elliott, John Milton
Ellis, Abraham M.
Ellis, George
Ellis, Richard
Ellsworth, Allen
Elmore, Ida
Elmore, John Archer
Emanuel, David
Emery, George W.
Emmet, Robert
Emmons, James A.
Erath, George Bernard
Essex, Earl of
Estill, James
Evangeline
Evans, Clement Anselm

Fairchild, Caribou (Caribou)
Fairfax, Thomas
Fannin, James Walker
Faribault, Jean Baptiste
Faulk, Andrew Jackson
Faulkner, Sanford C.
Fauquier, Francis
Fentress, James
Fergus, John
Ferry, Elisha P.
Fillmore, Millard
Fillmore, Millard (Millard)
Finney, David W.
Fisher, King
Fisher, Samuel Rhoads
Fitz Roy, Augustus Henry (Grafton)
Flagler, Henry Morrison
Fleming, John
Floyd, Charles
Floyd, Dolfin Ward
Floyd, John
Foard, Robert J.
Fontaine, James (Fountain)
Ford, James Hobart
Ford, Thomas
Forrest, Nathan Bedford
Forsyth, Benjamin
Forsyth, John
Franklin, Benjamin
Frederick
Frederick, Louis
Freeborn, William
Fremont, John Charles
Fulton, Robert
Fulton, William Savin
Furnas, Robert Wilkinson

Gadsden, James
Gage, William D.
Gaines, James
Gallatin, Abraham Alfonse
  Albert
Galvez, Bernardo de
Garfield, James Abram
Garland, Augustus Hill
Garrard, James
Garrett, John Work
Garvin, Samuel
Gaston, William
Gates Horation
Geary, John White
Gentry, Richard
George I (Hanover)
George I, King (King
  George)
George, James Zachariah
George III, King
Gibson, John
Gilchrist, Albert Waller
Giles, William Branch
Gillespie, Richard Addison
Gilliam, Cornelius
Gilmer, George Rockingham
Gilmer, Thomas Walker
Gilpin, William
Girardot, Sieur de (Cape
  Girardot)
Gladwin, Henry
George (Prince George)
George (Northampton)
Glascock, Thomas
Glasscock, George W.
Glenn, Hugh J.
Gloucester, Duke of
Glynn, John
Gonzales, Rafael
Gooch, William (Goochland)
Goodhue, James Madison
Gooding, Frank Robert
Gordon, William Washington
Gosper, John J.
Gove, Grenville L.
Grady, Henry Woodfin
Grafton, Duke of
Graham, John L.
Graham, William Alexander
Grainger, Mary
Grant
Grant, Jedediah Morgan
  (Morgan)
Grant, Moses
Grant, Samuel
Grant, Ulysses Simpson
Granville, Earl of
Gratiot, Charles
Graves, Benjamin
Gray, Alfred
Gray, Peter W.
Gray, Robert
Grayson, Peter William
Grayson, William
Greeley, Horace
Green, Thomas (Tom Green)
Greene, Nathanael (Green)
Greene, Nathanael
Greene, Nathanael (Greens-
  ville)
Greenlee, Marc
Greenup, Christopher
Greenwood, Alfred Burton
Greer, John A.
Gregg, John
Gregory, John Shaw
Griggs, Alexander
Grimes, Jesse
Grundy, Felix
Guilford, Earl of
Gunnison, John William
Guthrie, Edwin
Gwinnett, Button

Haakon, King
Habersham, Joseph
Hale, John C.
Hale, Stephen F.
Halifax, Earl of
Hall, Augustus
Hall, Lyman
Hall, Warren D. C.
Hamblen, Hezekiah
Hamilton, Alexander
Hamilton, James

Hamilton, William H.
Hamlin, Hannibal
Hampden, John
Hampton, Wade
Hancock, John
Hancock, Judith
Hand, George H.
Hanover, Duke of
Hansford, John M.
Hanson, Joseph R.
Haralson, Hugh Anderson
Hardee, Cary Augustus
Hardeman, Bailey
Hardeman, Thomas Jones
Hardin, John
Hardin, John J.
Hardin, Joseph
Hardin, William
Harding, J. A.
Harding, Warren Gamaliel
Hardlee, Florence (Florence)
Hardy, Samuel
Harford, Henry
Harlan, Silas
Harlan, Thomas
Harmon, Judson
Harnett, Cornelius
Harney, William Selby
Harper, Marion
Harper, O. G.
Harris, Charles
Harris, John Richardson
Harrison, Albert Galliton
Harrison, Benjamin
Harrison, Jonas
Harrison, William Henry
Hart, Nancy Morgan
Hart, Nathaniel
Hartley, Oliver Cromwell
Hartley, Rufus K.
Harvey, James Madison
Haskell, Charles Nathaniel
Haskell, Charles Ready
Haskell, Dudley Chase
Hastings, Selina (Huntingdon)
Hawkins, Benjamin
Hay, George Henry (Duplin)
Hayes, Rutherford Birchard
Hays, John Coffee
Haywood, John
Heard, Stephen
Hemphill, John
Hempstead, Edward
Henderson, James
Henderson, James Pinckney
Henderson, Leonard
Henderson, Richard
Hendricks, William
Hendry, Francis Asbury
Hennepin, Louis
Henry, Prince
Henry, King (Gloucester)
Henry, Patrick
Henry, Patrick (Patrick)
Herkimer, Nicholas
Hertford, Marquis of
Hettinger
Hickman, Edwin
Hickman, Paschal
Hidalgo, Miguel
Hill, Benjamin Harvey
(Ben Hill)
Hill, George W.
Hill, James Jerome
Hill, Jerome (Jerome)
Hill, Wills
Hillsborough, Earl of
Hinds, Thomas
Hinsdale, George A.
Hitchcock, Phineas Warrener
Hockley, George Washington
Hodgeman, Amos
Hogg, James Stephen
(Jim Hogg)
Hoke, Robert Frederick
Holmes, Andrew Hunter
Holmes, David
Holmes, Thomas J.
Holmes
Holt, David Rice
Holt, Joseph
Hood, Arthur William Acland
Hood, John Bell
Hooker, Joseph

Hopkins, Eldridge
Hopkins, Samuel
Horry, Peter
Houghton, Douglas
Houston, George Smith
Houston, John
Houston, Samuel
Howard, Benjamin
Howard, James
Howard, John Eager
Howard, Oliver Otis
Howard, Tilghman Ashurst
Howard, Volney Erskine
Howell, James
Hubbard, Lucius Frederick
Hudson, Henry
Hudspeth, Claude Benton
Hughes, Alexander
Hughes, William C.
Hulst, Florence (Florence)
Humboldt, Friedrich Heinrich Alexander von
Humphreys, Benjamin Grubb
Humphreys, Parry Wayne
Hunt, Memucan
Hunter, Robert (Hunterdon)
Huntingdon, Countess of
Huntington, Samuel
Hutchinson, Anderson
Hutchinson, John
Hyde, Edward
Hyde, Edward (Clarendon)
Hyde, James

Iberville, Pierre Le Moyne
Ingham, Samuel Delucenna
Iredell, James
Irion, Robert Anderson
Irwin, Jared
Isabella
Itawamba
Izard, George

Jack, Patrick Churchill
Jack, William Houston
Jackson, Andrew (Hickory)
Jackson, Andrew
Jackson, Henry
Jackson, James
Jackson, John R.
Jackson, Thomas Jonathan (Stonewall)
James II, King (Jamestown)
James II, King (Duke of York and Albany)
James II, King (York)
Jasper, William
Jay, John
Jefferson, Thomas
Jenkins, Charles Jones
Jennings, Jonathan
Jerauld, H. A.
Jessamine, Douglas
Jewell, Lewis R.
Johnson, Benjamin
Johnson, Cave
Johnson, E. P.
Johnson, Herschel Vespasian
Johnson, John
Johnson, Middleton Tate
Johnson, Richard Mentor
Johnson, Thomas
Johnston, Douglas H.
Johnston, Gabriel
Jones, Anson
Jones, George Wallace
Jones, James
Jones, John Paul
Jones, Willie
Juneau, Solomon

Kalb, Johann de
Kane, Elisha Kent
Kane, Thomas Leiper
Karnes, Henry Wax
Kaufman, David Spangler
Kearney, Stephen Watts
Kearny, Philip
Keith, M. C.
Kemper, Reuben
Kendall, Amos
Kendall, George Wilkins
Kenedy, Mifflin

Kent, Andrew
Kent, James
Kenton, Simon
Keokuk
Keppel, William Anne (Albemarle)
Kern, Edward
Kerr, James
Kershaw, Joseph
Kidder, Jefferson Parish
Kimball, Thomas Lord
Kimble, George C.
King, William
King, William Rufus de Vane
Kingman, Samuel Austin
Kingsbury, George Washington
Kinney, H. L.
Kitsap
Kittson, Norman Wolfred
Kittson, Norman Wolfred (Norman)
Kleberg, Robert
Knott, James Proctor
Knox, Henry
Kosciusko, Thaddeus
Kossuth, Lajos

Lafayette, Marquis de (Fayette)
Lafayette, Marquis de
Lamar, Lucius Quintus Cincinnatus
Lamar, Mirabeau Buonaparte
Lamb, George A.
La Moure, Judson
Lander, Frederick William
Lane, James Henry
Lane, Joseph
Langlade, Charles
Lanier, Sidney
La Ramie, Jacques
Larimer, William
Larue, John
La Salle, Robert Cavalier de
Lassen Peter
Latimer, J. S.
Lauderdale, James
Laurens, Henry
Laurens, John
Lawrence, James
Lawrence, John
Lea, Joseph C.
Leake, Walter
Leavenworth, Henry
Le Bref, Pepin (Pepin)
Lee, Henry
Lee, Richard Henry
Lee, Robert Edward
Lee
Le Flore, Greenwood
Le Moyne, Jean Baptiste (Bienville)
Lennox, Charles (Richmond)
Lenoir, William
Leon, Martin de
Leon, Ponce de
Leslie, Preston Hopkins
Le Sueur, Pierre Charles
Letcher, Robert Perkins
Levy, David
Lewis, Charles
Lewis, Meriwether
Lewis, Meriwether (Lewis and Clark)
Lewis, Morgan
Liguest, Pierre Laclede
Lincoln, Abraham
Lincoln, Benjamin
Lincoln
Linn, Lewis Field
Lipscomb, Abner S.
Limhi (Lemhi)
Livingston, Edward
Livingston, Robert R.
Logan, Benjamin
Logan, James
Logan, John
Logan, John Alexander
Long, Crawford Williamson
Loudoun, Earl of (Loudon)
Louis, Frederick
Louisa, Queen
Loving, Oliver
Lowndes, William Jones

Lubbock, Thomas S.
Lucas, Robert
Luce, Cyrus Gray
Lumpkin, Wilson
Luna, Solomon
Lunenburg, Duke of Brunswick
Luzerne, Chevalier de la
Lyman, W. P.
Lynn, W.
Lyon, Chittenden
Lyon, Nathaniel

Macon, Alexander
Macon, Nathaniel
Madison, James
Magoffin, Beriah
Mahaska
Major, John C.
Makee, Allan (Allamakee)
Marin
Marion, Francis
Marlborough, Duke of (Marlboro)
Marquette, Jacques
Marshall, Francis J.
Marshall, John
Marshall, William Rainey
Marshall
Marshall, William Rogerson
Martin, Henry
Martin, John Preston
Martin, John P.
Martin, John Wellborn
Martin, Josiah
Martin, Wyly
Mary II (King and Queen)
Mason, Charles H.
Mason, George
Mason, G. T.
Mason, Stevens Thomson
Massey, Louisa
Mathews, Thomas
Maury, Abram
Maverick, Samuel Augustus
Mc Clain, Charles
Mc Cone, George
Mc Cook, Edwin, S.
Mc Cormick, Cyrus Hall
Mc Cracken, Virgil
Mc Creary, James Bennett
Mc Culloch, Benjamin
Mc Curtain, Green
Mc Donald, Alexander
Mc Donough, Thomas
Mc Dowell, James
Mc Dowell, Joseph
Mc Duffie, George
Mc Henry, James
Mc Henry, William
Mc Intosh, E. H.
Mc Intosh, D. N.
Mc Intosh, William
Mc Kean, Thomas
Mc Kenzie, Alexander
Mc Kinley, William
Mc Kinney, Collin (Collin)
Mc Lean, Alney
Mc Lean, John
Mc Lean, John A.
Mc Lennan, Neil
Mc Leod, Martin
Mc Minn, Joseph
Mc Mullen, John
Mc Nairy, John
Mc Pherson, James Birdseye
Meade, George Gordon
Meade, James
Meagher, Thomas Francis
Mecklenburg, Princess of
Mecosta
Medina
Meeker, Bradley B.
Meigs, Return Jonathan
Mellette, Arthur C.
Menard, Michael Branamour
Menard, Pierre
Mendoza, Antonio (Mendocino)
Menifee, Richard Hickman
Mercer, Hugh
Mercer, John Francis
Mercer, William H. H.
Meriwether, David
Metcalfe, Thomas
Mey, Cornelius Jacobsen (Cape May)

Mifflin, Thomas
Milam, Benjamin Rush
Miller, Andrew Jackson
Miller, James
Miller, John
Mills, Frederick D.
Mills, John T.
Mills, Roger Quarles (Roger Mills)
Miner, Ephraim
Miner, Nelson
Missaukee
Mitchell, Asa
Mitchell, Eli
Mitchell, Elisha
Mitchell, Henry
Mitchell, John
Mitchell, William D.
Mix, Charles E.
Mix, Charles H.
Moffat, David Halliday
Monona
Monroe, James
Montague, Daniel
Montcalm, Louis Joseph de Saint Véran
Monterey, Count of
Montezuma
Montgomery, John
Montgomery, Lemuel Purnell
Montgomery, Richard
Montmorency
Mountour
Moody, Gideon Curtis
Moore, Alfred
Moore, Edwin Ward
Moore, William
Morehouse, Abraham
Morgan, Christopher A.
Morgan, Daniel
Morrill, Charles Henry
Morris, Lewis
Morris, Thomas
Morris, W. W.
Morrison, Allan
Morrison, William
Morrow, Jackson L.
Morrow, Jeremiah
Morton, Oliver Hazard Perry Throck
Motier, Marie Jean Paul Roch Yves Gilbert (see Lafayette)
Mottley, Dr. Junius William (Motley)
Moultrie, William
Moyne, Jean Baptiste Le (Bienville)
Mower, John E.
Muhlenberg, John Peter Gabriel
Murray, Thomas W.
Murray, William Henry
Murray, William Henry (Alfalfa)
Murray, William Pitt

Nance, Albinus
Nash, Francis
Navarro, Juan Jose Antonio
Nelson, N. E.
Nelson, Thomas
Neri, Felipe Enrique (Bastrop)
Ness, Noah V.
Newaygo
Newberry
Newton, Isaac
Newton, John
Newton, Thomas Willoughby
Nicholas, George
Nicholas, Wilson Cary
Nicollet, Joseph Nicolas
Noble, James
Noble, Warren P.
Noble, John Willock
Nobles, William H.
Nolan, Philip
Northampton, Earl of
North, Frances (Guilford)
Norton, Orloff
Nuckolls, Stephen Friel
Nye, James Warren

Obion
O'Brien, William Smith
Ochiltree, William Beck
O'Fallon, Benjamin (Fallon)
Ogle, Joseph
Oglethorpe, James Edward
Oldham, William
Oldham, Williamson Simpson
Oliver, Harry S.
Olmsted, David
Onslow, Arthur
Orange, Prince of
Osborn, Vincent B.
Osceola
Otero, Miguel
Otero, Miguel Antonio
Ouray
Overton, John
Owen, Abraham
Owsley, William
Oxford, Earl of

Page, John
Parke, Benjamin
Parker, Isaac
Parmer, Martin
Pasco, Samuel
Paulding, John
Payette, Francis
Payne, David L.
Pender, William Dorsey
Pendleton, Edmund
Pennington, Edmund
Pennington, John L.
Perkins, Charles Elliott
Perkins, Henry
Perry, Oliver Hazard
Pershing, John Joseph
Person, Thomas
Pettis, Spencer
Phelps, John Smith
Phelps, William
Phillips, Benjamin D.
Phillips, R. O.
Phillips, Sylvanus
Phillips, William
Piatt, Benjamin
Pickens, Andrew
Pickett, H. L.
Pierce, Franklin
Pierce, Gilbert Ashville
Pike, Zebulon Montgomery
Pitkin, Frederick Walter
Pitt, William
Pitt, William (Chatham)
Pleasants, James
Pocahontas
Poinsett, Joel Roberts
Polk, James Knox
Polk, William
Pontotoc
Pope, John
Pope, Nathaniel
Porter, David
Posey, Thomas
Potter, James
Potter, Joel
Potter, Robert
Powell, John Wesley
Powell, Lazarus Whitehead
Poweshiek
Powhatan
Pratt, Caleb
Pratt, Charles (Camden)
Preble, Edward
Prentiss, Sergeant Smith
Preston, James Patton
Price, William Thompson
Prowers, John W.
Pulaski, Casimir
Putnam, Israel

Quay, Matthew Stanley
Quitman, John Anthony

Rabun, William
Rains, Emory
Raleigh, Sir Walter
Ralls, Daniel
Ramsey, Alexander
Randall, Horace

Randolph, Edmund Jennings
Randolph, John
Randolph, Peyton
Randolph, Thomas
Rankin, Christopher
Ransom, Thomas Edward Greenfield
Ravalli, Father Anthony
Rawlins, John Aaron
Ray, John
Reagan, John Henninger
Real, Julius
Reeves, George R.
Reno, Jesse Lee
Rensselaer, Kiliaen Van
Renville, Gabriel
Renville, Joseph
Reynolds, Thomas
Rhea, John
Rice, Henry Mower
Rice, Samuel Allen
Rich, Charles Coulson
Rich, M. T.
Richardson, William Alexander
Richards, Franklin R. (Franklin)
Richmond, Duke of
Riggs, Ada (Ada)
Riley, Bennett
Ringgold, Samuel
Ripley, Eleazar Wheelock
Ritchie, Thomas
Roane, Archibald
Roane, Spencer
Roberts, John S.
Roberts, Oran Milo
Roberts, S. G.
Robertson, George
Robertson, James
Robertson, Sterling Clark
Robeson, Thomas
Robinson, Wayne (Wayne)
Rockingham, Marquis of
Rogers, Clement V.
Rolette, Joseph
Rooks, John C.
Rollins, Josephine (Josephine)
Roosevelt, Theodore
Ross, James
Routt, John Long
Rowan, John
Rowan, Matthew
Roy, Augustus Henry Fitz (Grafton)
Runnels, Hardin Richard
Rush, Alexander
Rush, Benjamin
Rusk, Jeremiah McLain
Rusk, Thomas Jefferson
Russell, Avra P.
Russell, Gilbert Christian
Russell, John (Bedford)
Russell, William
Rutherford, Griffith

St. Augustine (San Augustine)
St. Benedict (San Benito)
St. Bernard
St. Bernard (San Bernardino)
St. Charles
St. Clair, Arthur
St. Claire (Santa Clara)
St. Croix
St. Didacus (San Diego)
St. Francis
St. Francis (San Francisco)
St. Genevieve (Ste. Genevieve)
St. Helena
St. Hyacinth (San Jacinto)
St. Joachim (San Joaquin)
St. John (San Juan)
St. John the Baptist
St. Joseph
St. Landry
St. Lawrence
St. Louis
St. Louis (San Luis Obispo)
St. Lucie
St. Martin
St. Mary
St. Matthew (San Mateo)
St. Michael (San Miguel)
St. Patrick (San Patricio)
St. Rose (Santa Rosa)
St. Tammany

Sampson, John
Sanborn, George W.
Sanders, Wilbur Fisk
Sanilac
San Pitch (Sanpete)
Sargent, H. E.
Sarpy, Peter A.
Saunders, Alvin
Sawyer, Philetus
Schleicher, Gustave
Schley, William
Schoolcraft, Henry Rowe
Schuyler, Philip John
Scott, Abram M.
Scott
Scott, Andrew
Scott, Charles
Scott, John
Scott, Winfield
Screven, James
Scurry, Richardson
Searcy, Richard
Sebastian, William King
Sedgwick, John
Sequoyah
Sevier, Ambrose Hundley
Sevier, John
Seward, William Henry
Shackelford, Dr. John
Shannon, George
Shannon, Peter C.
Sharkey, William Lewis
Sharp, Ephraim
Shelby, Isaac
Sherburne, Moses
Sheridan, Philip Henry
Sherman, Sidney
Sherman, William Tecumseh
Sibley, Henry Hastings
Simpson, John
Simpson, Josiah
Smith, Daniel
Smith, David
Smith, Erastus (Deaf Smith)
Smith, James
Smith, J. Nelson
Smyth, Alexander
Snyder, Simon
Solano
Somerset, Earl of
Somerset, Henry (Beaufort)
Somerset, Mary
Somervell, Alexander
Sophia, Charlotte (Mecklenburg)
Soto, Hernando de
Southampton, Earl of
Spalding, Thomas
Spencer, Spear
Spink, Solomon Lewis
Spotswood, Alexander
Stafford, Lewis
Stanislaus
Stanley, David Sloane
Stanly, John
Stanton, Edward McMasters
Stanhope, Philip Dormer (Chesterfield)
Stark, George
Stark, John
Starr, James Harper
Stearns, Charles Thomas
Steele, Franklin
Stephens, Alexander Hamilton
Stephens, John Hall
Stephenson, Benjamin
Sterling, W. S.
Steuben, Friedrich Wilhelm Ludolf Gerhard Augustin von
Stevens, Isaac Ingalls
Stevens, Thaddeus
Stewart, Daniel
Stewart, Duncan
Stoddard, Amos
Stokes, John
Stone, John Marshall
Stone, William
Storey, Edward Farris
Story, Joseph
Strafford, Earl of
Stutsman, Enos
Sublette, William Lewis
Sullivan, Daniel
Sullivan, James

Sullivan, John
Sully, Alfred
Summers, George William
Sumner, Charles
Sumner, Jethro
Sumter, Thomas
Surry, Lord
Sutter, John Augustus
Sutton, John S.
Swain, David Lowrie
Swift, Henry Adoniram
Swisher, James Gibson
Swisher, John G.

Talbot, Matthew
Talbot, Grace
Taliaferro, Benjamin
Taomah (Tama)
Taney, Roger Brooke
Tarrant, Edward H.
Tate, T. S.
Tattnall, Josiah
Taylor, Edward
Taylor, John
Taylor, William R.
Taylor, Zachary
Tazewell, Henry
Tazewell, Littleton Waller
Telfair, Edward
Teller, Henry Moore
Terrell, Alexander Watkins
Terrell, William
Terry, Benjamin Franklin
Thayer, John Milton
Thomas, George Henry
Thomas, Jett
Throckmorton, William Edward
Thurston, John Mellen
Thurston, Samuel Royal
Tift, Nelson
Tillman, Benjamin Ryan
Tippah
Tipton, Jacob
Tipton, John
Tishomingo
Titus, Andrew Jackson
Todd, John
Todd, John Blair Smith
Tompkins, Daniel D.
Tuilla
Toole, Joseph Kemp
Toombs, Robert
Torrance, Francis J.
Towner, O. M.
Towns, George Washington Bonaparte
Traill, Walter
Travis, William Barrett
Trego, Edward P.
Treutlen, John Adam
Trigg, Stephen
Trimble, Robert
Tripp, Bartlett
Troup, George Michael
Trousdale, William
Trumbull, Jonathan
Tucker, Henry St. George
Turner, Henry Gray
Turner, John W.
Tuscaloosa
Twiggs, John
Tyler, John
Tyrrell, John

Ugalde, Juan de (Uvalde)
Upshur, Abel Parker
Upson, Stephen
Upton, John Cunningham

Van Buren, Martin
Van Cortlandt, Pierre (Cortland)
Van Rensselaer, (Rensselaer)
Van Wert, Isaac
Van Zandt, Isaac
Vance, Zebulon Baird
Vanderburgh, Henry
Vernon, Miles
Victoria, Guadalupe
Vigo, Joseph Maria Francesco
Vilas, William Freeman
Vincent, Marshall (Marshall)

Part VIII

INDEPENDENT CITIES

Following is a list of cities that are not included within counties.

Indiana
- Indianapolis

Maryland
- Baltimore

Missouri
- St. Louis

Nevada
- Carson City

Virginia
- Alexandria
- Bedford
- Bristol
- Buena Vista
- Charlottesville
- Chesapeake
- Clifton Forge
- Colonial Heights
- Covington
- Danville
- Emporia
- Fairfax
- Falls Church
- Franklin
- Fredericksburg
- Galax
- Hampton
- Harrisonburg
- Hopewell
- Lexington
- Lynchburg
- Martinsville
- Newport News
- Norfolk
- Norton
- Petersburg
- Portsmouth
- Radford
- Richmond
- Roanoke
- Salem
- South Boston
- Staunton
- Suffolk
- Virginia Beach

Part IX

ALASKA

Alaska has no counties. Instead, there are 29 census divisions called boroughs or reservations. These, with 1970 populations and name derivations, are listed below.

ALEUTIAN ISLANDS (1970 pop. 8, 057) from Aleuts, name of indigenes.

ANCHORAGE (124, 542) developed from fact of the anchorage of ships offshore from construction camp of Alaska Railroad.

ANGOON (503) from Tlingit Indian village formerly named Augoon.

BARROW (2663) for Sir John Barrow.

BETHEL (7, 579) from a Biblical reference, Gen. 35:1.

BRISTOL BAY (3, 485) for Admiral the Earl of Bristol, England.

BRISTOL BAY BOROUGH (1, 147) for the Earl of Bristol.

CORDOVA-McCARTHY (1, 857) from the town Puerto Cordova, named in 1790 by Senor Don Calvador Fidalgo; and, perhaps, a prospector named McCarthy.

FAIRBANKS (45, 864) for Charles Warren Fairbanks (1852-1918), Indiana senator and Theodore Roosevelt's Vice-President.

HAINES (1, 504) for Haines Mission, formerly Willard Mission, founded 1881.

JUNEAU (13, 556) for Joseph Juneau (1826-1899), gold miner.

KENAI-COOK INLET (14, 250) for Kenai Indians, and/or Fort Kenai, a U. S. Military Post; and Captain James Cook (1728-1779), English explorer.

KETCHIKAN (10, 041) from an adaptation of a Tlingit Indian name meaning "eagle wing river."

KOBUK (4, 434) from an Eskimo word for "big river."

KODIAK [sometimes Kadiak] (9, 409) for the indigenous Kodiak brown bear; Eskimo word for island.

KUSKOKWIM (2, 306) from an Eskimo word of unknown origin, alst syllable meaning "river."

MATANUSKA-SUSITNA (6, 509) from "Matanuska," Russian for "copper river people"; and "Susitna," from which name is adapted.

NOME (5, 749) attributed to explorer's 1850-52 map on H. M. S. Herald marked for London royal cartographer "C[ape] Name?" intending the latter's discretion in naming. The "a" mistaken for an "o, " and the "?" for a request for approval, "Nome" was accepted.

OUTER KETCHIKAN (1, 676) see Ketchikan.

PRINCE OF WALES (2, 106) named May 9, 1778 by Capt. James Cook.

SEWARD (2, 336) for William Henry Seward (1801-1872), U. S. Secretary of State 1861-1869, who negotiated Alaska's purchase.

SITKA (6, 109) from a Tlingit Indian name for "by the sea. "

SKAGWAY-YAKUTAT (2, 157) from "Skagway" Tlingit Indian word for "home of the north wind"; and "Yakutat [or, Jacootat], " an Indian name.

SOUTHEAST FAIRBANKS (4, 179) see Fairbanks.

UPPER YUKON (1, 684) see Yukon-Koyukuk.

VALDEZ-CHITINA-WHITTIER (3, 098) for Antonio Valdés y Basan, a Spanish naval officer; "chitina, " an Indian name for "copper river"; and John Greenleaf Whittier (1807-1892), American poet.

WADE-HAMPTON (3, 917) for Frederick Coate Wade (1860-1924), lawyer and junior councilor at 1903 Alaska tribunal; Hampton not known.

WRANGELL-PETERSBURG (4, 913) for Admiral Baron Ferdinand Petrovich von Wrangell (1794-1870) and Peter Buschmann Petersburg, owner of a sawmill and salmon cannery.

YUKON-KOYUKUK (4, 752) from "Yukon, " an Indian word meaning "big river"; and "Koyukuk, " a Russian adaptation of uncertain origin.